The Handbook of Memory Disorders

Second Edition

The Handbook of Memory Disorders

SECOND EDITION

Edited by

Alan D. Baddeley
Department of Experimental Psychology,
University of Bristol, UK

Michael D. Kopelman
University Department of Psychiatry and Psychology,
St Thomas's Hospital, Kings College London, London, UK
and
Barbara A. Wilson
MRC Cognition and Brain Sciences Unit, Cambridge, UK

JOHN WILEY & SONS, LTD

Other Wiley Editorial Offices

John Wiley & Sons, Inc., 111 River Street, Hoboken, NJ 07030, USA

Jossey-Bass, 989 Market Street, San Francisco, CA 94103-1741, USA

Wiley-VCH Verlag GmbH, Boschstr. 12, D-69469 Weinheim, Germany

John Wiley & Sons Australia, Ltd., 33 Park Road, Milton, Queensland 4064, Australia

John Wiley & Sons (Asia) Pte Ltd., 2 Clementi Loop #02-01, Jin Xing Distripark, Singapore 129809

John Wiley & Sons Canada, Ltd., 22 Worcester Road, Etobicoke, Ontario, Canada M9W 1L1

Library of Congress Cataloging-in-Publication Data
The handbook of memory disorders / edited by Alan D. Baddeley, Michael D. Kopelman and
Barbara A. Wilson. (2nd ed.)
    p.   cm.
  Includes bibliographical references and index.
  ISBN 0-471-49819-X (cased)
    1. Memory disorders—Handbooks, manuals, etc.   I. Baddeley, Alan D.   II. Kopelman, Michael D.
III. Wilson, Barbara A.

  RC394.M46H38   2002
  616.8′4—dc21   12788733

British Library Cataloguing in Publication Data

A catalogue record for this book is available from the British Library

ISBN 0-471-49819-X

Typeset in 10/12 pt Times by TechBooks, New Delhi, India
Printed and bound in Great Britain by Antony Rowe Ltd, Chippenham, Wiltshire, UK
This book is printed on acid-free paper responsibly manufactured from sustainable forestry
in which at least two trees are planted for each one used for paper production.

Contents

About the Editors

Alan D. Baddeley, *Department of Experimental Psychology, University of Bristol, 8 Woodland Road, Bristol, BS8 1TN, UK*

Alan Baddeley was Director of the Medical Research Council Applied Psychology Unit in Cambridge, UK for over 20 years. He is now a research Professor of Cognitive Psychology at the University of Bristol. He is a cognitive psychologist with broad interests in the functioning of human memory under both normal conditions and conditions of brain damage and stress.

Michael D. Kopelman, *Neuropsychiatry and Memory Disorders Clinic, St Thomas's Hospital, Lambeth Palace Road, London SE1 7EH, UK*

Michael Kopelman is Professor of Neuropsychiatry in the Guys, King's and St Thomas's School of Medicine, Kings College, London. He holds qualifications in both neuropsychiatry and neuropsychology, and has particular interest and expertise in a wide range of memory disorders, both neurological and psychogenic. He runs a neuropsychiatry and memory disorders clinic at St Thomas's Hospital.

Barbara A. Wilson, *MRC Cognition and Brain Sciences Unit, 15 Chaucer Road, Cambridge CB2 2EF, UK*

Barbara Wilson is a senior scientist at the MRC Cognition and Brain Sciences Unit and is Director of Research at the Oliver Zangwill Centre for Neuropsychological Rehabilitation, Ely, UK. A clinical psychologist with particular interest in both the impact of neuropsychological memory deficits on everyday functioning and improving methods of neurorehabilitation, she was the founding editor of the journal *Neuropsychological Rehabilitation*.

Contributors

Alan D. Baddeley, *Department of Experimental Psychology, University of Bristol, 8 Woodland Road, Bristol BS8 1TN, UK*

Juliana V. Baldo, *Scripps College, 1030 Columbia Avenue, Claremont, CA 91711-394, USA*

James T. Becker, *UPMC Health System, Western Psychiatric Institute and Clinic, Neuropsychology Research Program, Suite 830, 3501 Forbes Avenue, Pittsburgh, PA 15213-3323, USA*

Aaron S. Benjamin, *Rotman Research Institute of the Baycrest Center, Department of Psychology, University of Toronto, 100 St George Street, Toronto, Ontario M5S 3G3, Canada*

Jason Brandt, *Department of Psychiatry and Behavioural Sciences, Johns Hopkins University School of Medicine, 600 North Wolfe Street/Meyer 218, Baltimore, MD 21287-7218, USA*

Giovanni Augusto Carlesimo, *Clinica Neurologia, Università Tor Vergata, Rome, Italy*

Alan D. Castel, *Rotman Research Institute of the Baycrest Center, Department of Psychology, University of Toronto, 100 St George Street, Toronto, Ontario M5S 3G3, Canada*

Linda Clare, *Sub-department of Clinical Health Psychology, University College London, Gower Street, London WC1E 6BT, UK*

Sally G. Cox, *MRC Cognition and Brain Sciences Unit, 15 Chaucer Road, Cambridge CB2 2EF, UK*

Fergus I.M. Craik, *Rotman Research Institute of the Baycrest Center, Department of Psychology, University of Toronto, 100 St George Street, Toronto, Ontario M5S 3G3, Canada*

H. Valerie Curran, *Sub-Department of Clinical Health Psychology, University College London, Gower Street, London WC1E 6BT, UK*

Tim Dalgleish, *MRC Cognition and Brain Sciences Unit, 15 Chaucer Road, Cambridge CB2 2EF, UK*

Antonio R. Damasio, *University of Iowa Hospitals and Clinics, 200 Hawkins Drive, Iowa City, IO 52242, USA*

Sergio Della Sala, *Department of Psychology, University of Aberdeen, Kings College, Aberdeen AB24 2UB, UK*

Chad S. Dodson, *Department of Psychology, Harvard University, 33 Kirkland Street, Cambridge, MA 02138, USA*

Susan E. Gathercole, *Department of Psychology, University of Bristol, 8 Woodland Road, Bristol BS8 1TN, UK*

Asaf Gilboa, *Department of Psychology and Rotman Institute, Baycrest Center for Geriatric Care, 3650 Bathurst Street, North York, Ontario M6A 2E1, Canada*

Elizabeth L. Glisky, *Department of Psychology, University of Arizona, PO Box 210068, Tucson, AZ 85721, USA*

Georg Goldenberg, *Neuropsychologishes Abteilung, Krankenhaus München Bogenhausen, Englschalkingerstrasse 77, D 81925 Münich, Germany*

Kim S. Graham, *MRC Cognition and Brain Sciences Unit, Addenbrooke's Hospital, Elsworth House, Hills Road, Cambridge CB2 2QQ, UK*

Gerri Hanten, *Departments of Physical Medicine and Rehabilitation, Neurosurgery and Psychiatry, and Behavioral Sciences, Baylor College of Medicine, Houston, TX 77030, USA*

Diane B. Howieson, *Dept of Neurology, Oregon Health Sciences University, 3181 SW Sam Jackson Park Road, Portland, OR 97201-3098, USA*

Narinder Kapur, *Wessex Neurological Centre, Southampton General Hospital, Southampton SO16 6YD, UK*

Jill D. Kester, *Rotman Research Institute of the Baycrest Center, Department of Psychology, University of Toronto, 100 St George Street, Toronto, Ontario M5S 3G3, Canada*

Michael D. Kopelman, *University Department of Psychiatry and Psychology, St Thomas's Hospital (King's College London), Lambeth Palace Road, London SE1 7EH, UK*

Harvey S. Levin, *Departments of Physical Medicine and Rehabilitation, Neurosurgery and Psychiatry, and Behavioral Sciences, Baylor College of Medicine, Houston, TX 77030, USA*

Muriel D. Lezak, *Department of Neurology, Oregon Health Sciences University, 3181 SW Sam Jackson Park Road, Portland, OR 97201-3098, USA*

Robert H. Logie, *Department of Psychology, University of Aberdeen, King's College, Aberdeen AB24 2UB, UK*

Joseph R. Manns, *Veteran Affairs Healthcare System, San Diego, and Departments of Psychiatry, Neurosciences and Psychology, University of California, San Diego, CA 92161, USA*

Andrew R. Mayes, *Department of Psychology, Eleanor Rathbone Building, PO Box 147, University of Liverpool, Liverpool L69 7ZA, UK*

Peter McKenna, *Addenbrooke's NHS Trust, Fulbourn Hospital, Cambridge CB1 5EF, UK*

Judith A. Middleton, *Department of Clinical Neuropsychology, Radcliffe Infirmary NHS Trust, Nuffield III, Woodstock Road, Oxford OX2 6HE, UK*

Morris Moscovitch, *Department of Psychology and Rotman Institute, Baycrest Center for Geriatric Care, 3650 Bathurst Street, North York, Ontario M6A 2E1, Canada*

Cynthia A. Munro, *Department of Psychiatry and Behavioural Sciences, Johns Hopkins University School of Medicine, 600 North Wolfe Street/Meyer 218, Baltimore, MD 21287-7218, USA*

Jaap Murre, *Faculteit der Psychologie, Universiteit van Amsterdam, Roetersstraat 15, 1018 WB Amsterdam, The Netherlands*

Margaret O'Connor, *Division of Behavioral Neurology, Beth Israel Deaconess Medical Center, Boston, MA 02130, USA*

Tisha Ornstein, *Department of Psychiatry, University of Cambridge, Addenbrooke's NHS Trust, Hills Road, Cambridge CB2 2QQ, UK*

Amy A. Overman, *UPMC Health System, Western Psychiatric Institute and Clinic, Neuropsychology Research Program, 502 Iroquois Building, 3600 Forbes Avenue, Pittsburgh, PA 15213-3418, USA*

Costanza Papagno, *Dipartimento di Psicologia, Università degli Studi di Milano-Bicocca, Piazza dell' Ateneo Nuovo 1, 20126 Milano, Italy*

Michael D. Rugg, *Institute of Cognitive Neuroscience, University College London, Alexander House, 17 Queen Square, London WC1 3AR, UK*

Daniel L. Schacter, *Department of Psychology, Harvard University, 33 Kirkland Street, Cambridge, MA 02138, USA*

Arthur P. Shimamura, *Department of Experimental Psychology, University of California, Berkeley, CA 94720, USA*

Julie Snowden, *Cerebral Function Unit, Department of Neurology, Greater Manchester Neuroscience Centre, Salford M6 8HD, UK*

Larry R. Squire, *Veteran Affairs Healthcare System, San Diego, and Departments of Psychiatry, Neurosciences and Psychology, University of California, San Diego, CA 92161, USA*

Robyn L. Tate, *Rehabilitation Studies Unit, Department of Medicine, University of Syndey, PO Box 6, Ryde, NSW 1680, Australia*

Christine M. Temple, *Department of Psychology, Developmental Neuropsychology Unit, University of Essex, Wivenhoe Park, Colchester CO4 3SQ, UK*

Daniel Tranel, *Department of Neurology, University of Iowa Hospitals and Clinics, 200 Hawkins Drive, Iowa City, IO 52242, USA*

Giuseppe Vallar, *Dipartimento di Psicologia, Università degli Studi di Milano-Bicocca, Piazza dell' Ateneo Nuovo 1, 20126 Milano, Italy*

Mieke Verfaellie, *Memory Disorders Research Center (151A), Boston VA Health Care System, 150 South Huntington Avenue, Boston, MA 02130, USA*

Stefano Vicari, *Ospedale Pediatrico Bambino Gesù, I.R.C.C.S., Lungomare G. Marconi 36, 1-00058 Santa Marinella, Rome, Italy*

Herbert Weingartner, *National Institute on Drug Abuse, National Institutes of Health, Bethesda, MD 20892-9555, USA*

Barbara A. Wilson, *MRC Cognition and Brain Sciences Unit, Box 58, Addenbrooke's Hospital, Hills Road, Cambridge CB2 2QQ, UK*

Bob Woods, *Dementia Services Development Centre, University of Wales, Normal Site, Holyhead Road, Bangor LL57 2PX, UK*

Preface

Some 7 years ago, the First Edition of the *Handbook of Memory Disorders* was published. As editors, we hoped to summarize the substantial progress that had been made in understanding memory problems and in applying such knowledge to the assessment and treatment of memory-disordered patients. We hoped that the *Handbook* would provide a useful resource for our clinical colleagues and for the training of people entering the area. We approached what we regarded as an outstanding array of potential contributors and were delighted to find that they appeared to share our enthusiasm, producing some outstanding chapters. The resulting *Handbook* seems to have been very successful, not only in its primary aim but also in providing a valuable source for the wide range of people involved in memory research. The field has continued to be extremely active, resulting in a clear need for revision. Furthermore, our publishers were happy to extend the scope of an already substantial volume so as to allow coverage of these new developments.

The new edition differs from the original in a number of important ways. First of all, Fraser Watts, having moved out of the field, has relinquished his editorial role. His place has been taken by Michael Kopelman: our names are listed in alphabetical order, reflecting our joint and equal contributions to this volume. As on the first occasion, virtually every contributor we asked agreed to take part in the project, with those who participated in the first volume all preparing totally new chapters. In terms of content, we have kept most, but not all, of the original topics but have split some into two separate chapters, as in the case of visual and verbal short-term memory deficits, and Alzheimer's disease and subcortical dementia. Probably the most substantial change has been in our treatment of developmental memory disorders, where a single chapter has been replaced by a whole section, comprising an overview of the development of memory in normal children, chapters on specific memory disorders and on general learning disability, and finally a chapter on the assessment and treatment of children with memory problems. This change reflects the substantial growth of research in this area, together with the encouraging tendency for it to establish clear links with both mainstream cognitive psychology and research on memory deficits in adults. Another area that has been extremely active in recent years has been that linking executive deficits, often resulting from frontal lobe damage, to impaired memory performance. This line of development is reflected in chapters on the role of the frontal lobes in memory, on confabulation, and on the neuropsychological basis of false memory. The increased size of the volume has also allowed us to include chapters on developments in closely related areas. One of these includes a discussion of research on animals for the understanding of human memory disorders, while a second reviews the development of computational modelling approaches that are of relevance to the understanding of memory disorders. Finally, perhaps the most pervasive change within the field in recent years has been the great increase in the application of structural and functional imaging techniques to the study of memory and its disorders. A chapter overviewing these is included to supplement the many references to such techniques that occur in the various chapters.

We are happy to offer this new edition as a worthy successor to the first, and would like to thank our contributors for responding so positively to the challenge of reviewing this important and vital field. We would also like to thank Michael Coombs and Lesley Valerio from John Wiley & Sons, Ltd. for encouraging the enterprise and keeping it afloat, and various others who have made it happen, including Dee Roberts, Julia Darling, Claire Hook, Catherine Charlton and Kristen Hindes.

ADB
MDK
BAW

Preface to the First Edition

One of the most striking features of the study of memory in recent years has been the extent to which work on clinical populations of subjects has contributed to the understanding of normal function. This has led to a large number of books and conference papers by and for memory research workers. While this material is beginning to filter through to clinicians and practitioners, the process has so far been a relatively slow one. The primary purpose of the present *Handbook* is to speed up this process by encouraging our colleagues with expertise in specific areas of memory deficit to summarize recent work in a way that will make it accessible to the practising clinician.

The book has four components. It begins with a section containing two brief review chapters concerned with the psychology and neurobiological basis of memory. This is followed by three more specialized sections. The first of these describes a range of different types of memory deficit, the second is concerned with issues of assessment of memory performance, while the third is concerned with the clinical management of memory problems.

We attempted to bring together as strong an international team as we could, and were delighted that our colleagues appeared to share our enthusiasm for the project and, almost without exception, agreed to participate. In editing the book we have learned a great deal, and in the process have become convinced that our research colleagues are likely to find it just as useful as our more clinically orientated colleagues, in providing an up-to-date account of the current state of knowledge in the area of memory disorders, a field that has become so extensive that even the most diligent reader is unlikely to be able to keep fully up to date outside his or her area of particular expertise.

We are grateful to Michael Coombs of John Wiley & Sons for convincing us of the potential value of such an enterprise, and to Mrs Julia Darling, without whose efficient administrative and secretarial help the book would not have been possible. Finally, we would like to thank our contributors for finding time in their busy writing schedules to share their expertise with a wider audience.

The psychology of memory has gained immeasurably from the study of patients; we would like to think that this *Handbook*, by summarizing what has been learned and feeding it back to our clinical colleagues, may represent a small step in the direction of repaying that help.

ADB
BAW
FNW

Theoretical Background

CHAPTER 1

The Psychology of Memory

Alan D. Baddeley

Department of Experimental Psychology, University of Bristol, UK

In editing the first edition of this *Handbook*, we declared the aim of making available the substantial amount of information that had been acquired concerning memory deficits, not only to researchers with a specific interest in the area but also to a wider audience, including particularly clinicians for whom memory deficit is just one of many problems confronting their patients. Rather than requiring each of our authors to provide an account of the concepts underlying their study of memory, it seemed sensible to provide this information in a single chapter. Hence, if you are already familiar with the psychology of memory, or indeed have read the equivalent chapter in the previous edition, then I suggest you stop here. If not, then I will try to provide a brief overview of the concepts and techniques that are most widely used. Although it may not appear to be the case from sampling the literature, there is in fact a great deal of agreement as to what constitutes the psychology of memory, much of it developed through the interaction of the study of normal memory in the laboratory and of its breakdown in brain-damaged patients. A somewhat more detailed account can be found in Parkin & Leng (1993) and Baddeley (1999), while a more extensive overview is given by Baddeley (1997), and within the various chapters comprising the *Handbook of Memory* (Tulving & Craik, 2000).

THE FRACTIONATION OF MEMORY

The concept of human memory as a unitary faculty began to be seriously eroded in the 1960s with the proposal that long-term memory (LTM) and short-term memory (STM) represent separate systems. Among the strongest evidence for this dissociation was the contrast between two types of neuropsychological patient. Patients with the classic amnesic syndrome, typically associated with damage to the temporal lobes and hippocampi, appeared to have a quite general problem in learning and remembering new material, whether verbal or visual (Milner, 1966). They did, however, appear to have normal short-term memory (STM), as measured for example by digit span, the capacity to hear and immediately repeat back a unfamiliar sequence of numbers. Shallice & Warrington (1970) identified an exactly opposite pattern of deficit in patients with damage to the perisylvian region of the left hemisphere. Such patients had a digit span limited to one or two, but apparently normal

The Handbook of Memory Disorders. Edited by A.D. Baddeley, M.D. Kopelman and B.A. Wilson
© 2002 John Wiley & Sons, Ltd.

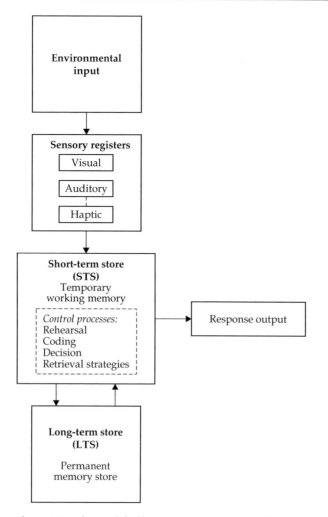

Figure 1.1   The model of human memory proposed by Atkinson & Shiffrin (1968). Reproduced by permission from Atkinson & Shiffrin (1968)

LTM. By the late 1960s, the evidence seemed to be pointing clearly to a two-component memory system. Figure 1.1 shows the representation of such a system from an influential model of the time, that of Atkinson & Shiffrin (1968). Information is assumed to flow from the environment through a series of very brief sensory memories, that are perhaps best regarded as part of the perceptual system, into a limited capacity short-term store. They proposed that the longer an item resides in this store, the greater the probability of its transfer to LTM. Amnesic patients were assumed to have a deficit in the LTM system, and STM patients in the short-term store.

By the early 1970s, it was clear that the model had encountered at least two problems. The first of these concerned the learning assumption. Evidence suggested that merely holding an item in STM did not guarantee learning. Much more important was the processing that the item underwent. This is emphasized in the *levels-of-processing* framework proposed by Craik & Lockhart (1972). They suggested that probability of subsequent recall or recognition was a direct function of the *depth* to which an item was processed. Hence, if the subject merely noted the visual characteristics of a word, for example whether it was in upper or lower case, little learning would follow. Slightly more would be remembered if the word were also processed acoustically by deciding, for example, whether it rhymed with a specified target word. By far the best recall, however, followed semantic processing, in which the subject made a judgement about the meaning of the word, or perhaps related it to a specified sentence, or to his/her own experience.

This levels of processing effect has been replicated many times, and although the specific interpretation proposed is not universally accepted, there is no doubt that a word or experience that is processed in a deep way that elaborates the experience and links it with prior knowledge, is likely to be far better retained than one that receives only cursory analysis. The effect also occurs in the case of patients with memory deficits, making it a potentially useful discovery for those interested in memory rehabilitation, although it is important to remember that cognitive impairment may hinder the processes necessary for such elaboration. Indeed, it was at one point suggested that failure to elaborate might be at the root of the classic amnesic syndrome, although further investigation showed this was not the case (see Baddeley, 1997; and Chapter 16, this volume, for further discussion).

A second problem for the Atkinson & Shiffrin model was presented by the data on STM patients that had initially appeared to support it. Although such patients argued strongly for a dissociation between LTM and STM, the Atkinson & Shiffrin model assumed that STM was necessary, indeed crucial, for long-term learning, and indeed for many other cognitive activities. In fact, STM patients appeared to have normal LTM, and with one or two minor exceptions, such as working out change while shopping, had very few everday cognitive problems.

This issue was tackled by Baddeley & Hitch (1974), who were explicitly concerned with the relationship between STM and LTM. A series of experiments attempted to block STM in normal subjects by requiring them to recite digit sequences while performing other tasks, such as learning, reasoning or comprehending, that were assumed to depend crucially upon STM. Decrement occurred, with the impairment increasing with the length of the digit sequence that was being retained, suggesting that STM and LTM *did* interact. However, the effect was far from dramatic, again calling into question the standard model. Baddeley & Hitch proposed that the concept of a simple unitary STM be replaced by a more complex system which they termed "*working memory*", so as to emphasize its functional importance in cognitive processing. The model they proposed is shown in Figure 1.2.

Working memory is assumed to comprise an attentional controller, the *central executive*, assisted by two subsidiary systems, the *phonological loop* and the *visuospatial sketchpad*. The phonological (or articulatory) loop is assumed to comprise a store that holds memory

Figure 1.2   The Baddeley & Hitch (1974) model of working memory. Reproduced by permission from Baddeley & Hitch (1974)

traces for a couple of seconds, combined with a subvocal rehearsal process. This is capable of maintaining the items in memory using subvocal speech, which can also be used to convert nameable but visually presented stimuli, such as letters or words, into a phonological code. STM patients were assumed to have a deficit in this system, whereas the remainder of working memory was assumed to be spared (Vallar & Baddeley, 1984). Subsequent research, based on STM patients, normal children and adults, and children with specific language impairment, suggest that the phonological loop system may have evolved for the purpose of language acquisition (Baddeley et al., 1998). A more detailed account of this system and its breakdown is given in Chapter 12, this volume.

The visuospatial sketchpad (or scratchpad) is assumed to allow the temporary storage and manipulation of visual and spatial information. Its function can be disrupted by concurrent visuospatial activity and, as in the case of the phonological loop, our understanding has been advanced by the study of neuropsychological patients. More specifically, there appear to be separate visual and spatial components, which may be differentially disrupted. A more detailed account of this system and the relevant neuropsychological evidence is given in Chapter 13, this volume.

The third component of the model, the central executive, was assumed to provide an attentional control system, both for the subsystems of working memory and for other activities. Baddeley (1986) suggested that a good account of it might be provided by the *supervisory attentional system* (SAS) proposed by Norman & Shallice (1986) to account for the attentional control of action. They assume that much activity is controlled by well-learned habits and schemata, guided by environmental cues. Novel actions that needed to respond to unexpected situations, however, depended upon the intervention of the limited-capacity SAS. This was assumed to be capable of overriding habits so as to allow novel actions in response to new challenges. Slips of action, such as driving to the office rather than the supermarket on a Saturday morning, were attributed to the failure of the SAS to override such habits. The problems in action control shown by patients with frontal lobe damage were also attributed to failure of the SAS; hence, perseverative activity might reflect the failure of the SAS to break away from the domination of action by environmental cues (Shallice, 1988).

Both Shallice himself and others have extended their account to include a range of potentially separable executive processes, hence providing an account of the range of differing deficits that may occur in patients with frontal lobe damage (Baddeley, 1996; Duncan, 1996; Shallice & Burgess, 1996). Given the far from straightforward mapping of anatomical location onto cognitive function, Baddeley & Wilson (1988) suggested that the term "frontal lobe syndrome" be replaced by the more functional term, *"dysexecutive syndrome"*. For a recent review of this area, see Roberts et al. (1998) and Stuss & Knight (2002).

The implications of frontal lobe function and executive deficit for the functioning of memory are substantial, since the executive processes they control play a crucial role in the selection of strategy and stimulus processing that has such a crucial influence in effective learning. These issues are discussed in Chapters 15, 16 and 17, this volume.

More recently, a fourth component of WM has been proposed, the *episodic buffer*. This is assumed to provide a multimodal temporary store of limited capacity that is capable of integrating information from the subsidiary systems with that of LTM. It is assumed to be important for the *chunking* of information in STM (Miller, 1956). This is the process whereby we can take advantage of prior knowledge to package information more effectively and hence to enhance storage and retrieval. For example, a sequence of digits that comprised a number of familiar dates, such as 1492 1776 1945, would be easier to recall then the same 12 digits in random order. The episodic buffer is also assumed to play an important role in immediate memory for prose, allowing densely amnesic patients with well-preserved intelligence and/or executive capacities to show apparently normal immediate, although not delayed, recall of a prose passage that would far exceed the capacity of either of the subsidiary systems (Baddeley & Wilson, in press). It seems unlikely that the episodic buffer will reflect a single anatomical location, but it is probable that frontal areas will be crucially involved. For a more detailed account, see Baddeley (2000).

LONG-TERM MEMORY

As in the case of STM, LTM has proved to be profitably fractionable into separate components. Probably the clearest distinction is that between *explicit* (or *declarative*) and *implicit* (or *non-declarative*) memory. Once again, neuropsychological evidence has proved crucial. It has been known for many years that densely amnesic patients are able to learn certain things; e.g. the Swiss psychiatrist Claparède (1911) pricked the hand of a patient while shaking hands one morning, finding that she refused to shake hands the next day but could not recollect why. There was also evidence that such patients might be able to acquire motor skills (Corkin, 1968). Probably the most influential work, however, stemmed from the demonstration by Warrington & Weiskrantz (1968) that densely amnesic patients were capable of showing learning of either words or pictures, given the appropriate test procedure. In their initial studies, patients were shown a word or a line drawing, and subsequently asked to identify a degraded version of the item in question. Both patients and control subjects showed enhanced identification of previously presented items, to a similar degree. This procedure, which is typically termed "*priming*", has since been investigated widely in both normal subjects and across a wide range of neuropsychologically impaired patients (for review, see Schacter, 1994).

   It has subsequently become clear that a relatively wide range of types of learning may be preserved in amnesic patients, ranging from motor skills, through the solution of jigsaw puzzles (Brooks & Baddeley, 1976) to performance on concept formation (Kolodny, 1994) and complex problem-solving tasks (Cohen & Squire, 1980); a review of this evidence is provided by Squire (1992). The initial suggestion, that these may all represent a single type of memory, now seems improbable. What they appear to have in common is that the learning does *not* require the retrieval of the original learning episode, but can be based on implicit memory that may be accessed indirectly through performance, rather than depending on recollection. Anatomically, the various types of implicit memory appear to reflect different parts of the brain, depending upon the structures that are necessary for the relevant processing. While pure amnesic patients typically perform normally across the whole range of implicit measures, other patients may show differential disruption. Hence Huntingdon's disease patients may show problems in motor learning while semantic priming is intact, whereas patients suffering from Alzheimer's disease show the opposite pattern (see Chapters 26 and 27, this volume).

   In contrast to the multifarious nature and anatomical location of implicit memory systems, explicit memory appears to depend crucially on a system linking the hippocampi with the temporal and frontal lobes, the so-called Papez circuit (see Chapter 2, this volume). Tulving (1972) proposed that explicit memory itself can be divided into two separate systems, *episodic* and *semantic* memory, respectively. The term "episodic memory" refers to our capacity to recollect specific incidents from the past, remembering incidental detail that allows us in a sense to relive the event or, as Tulving phrases it, to "travel back in time". We seem to be able to identify an individual event, presumably by using the context provided by the time and place it occurred. This means that we can recollect and respond appropriately to a piece of information, even if it is quite novel and reflects an event that is inconsistent with many years of prior expectation. Learning that someone had died, for example, could immediately change our structuring of the world and our response to a question or need, despite years of experiencing them alive.

Episodic memory can be contrasted with "semantic memory", our generic knowledge of the world; knowing the meaning of the word "salt", for example, or its French equivalent, or its taste. Knowledge of society and the way it functions, and the nature and use of tools are also part of semantic memory, a system that we tend to take for granted, as indeed did psychologists until the late 1960s. At this point, attempts by computer scientists to build machines that could understand text led to the realization of the crucial importance of the capacity of memory to store knowledge. As with other areas of memory, theory has gained substantially from the study of patients with memory deficits in general, and in particular of semantic dementia patients (see Chapter 14, this volume).

While it is generally accepted that both semantic and episodic memory comprise explicit as opposed to implicit memory systems, the relationship between the two remains controversial. One view suggests that semantic memory is simply the accumulation of many episodic memories for which the detailed contextual cue has disappeared, leaving only the generic features (Squire, 1992). Tulving, on the other hand, suggests that they are separate. He regards the actual experience of recollection as providing the crucial hallmark of episodic memory (Tulving, 1989). It is indeed the case that subjects are able to make consistent and reliable judgements about whether they "remember" an item, in the sense of recollecting the experience of encountering it, or simply "know" that it was presented, and that "remember" items are sensitive to variables such as depth of processing, which have been shown to influence episodic LTM, while "know' responses are not (for review, see Gardiner & Java, 1993). If one accepts Tulving's definition, then this raises the further question of whether there are other types of non-episodic but explicit memory.

Once again, neuropsychological evidence is beginning to accumulate on this issue, particularly from the study of developmental amnesia, a rather atypical form of memory deficit that has recently been discovered to occur in children with hippocampal damage (Vargha-Khadem et al., 2002; Baddeley et al., 2001). This is discussed in Chapter 24, this volume, on development of memory. Such evidence, combined with a reanalysis of earlier neuropsychological data, coupled with evidence from animal research and from neuroimaging, makes the link between semantic and episodic memory a particularly lively current area of research (see Baddeley et al., 2002, for a range of recent papers on this topic).

Despite considerable controversy over the details, Figure 1.3 shows what would rather broadly be accepted as reflecting the overall structure of long-term memory. It should be adequate for navigating through the subsequent chapters. If you are unfamiliar with memory research, however, there are one or two other things that you might find useful, which are discussed in the sections below.

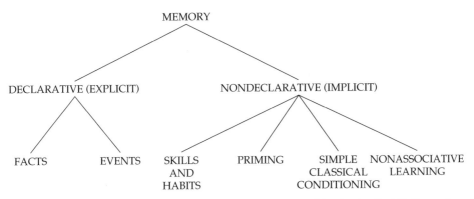

Figure 1.3   The fractionation of long-term memory proposed by Squire (1992). Reproduced by permission from Squire (1992)

STAGES OF MEMORY

It is often useful to separate out three aspects of any memory system: *encoding*, the processes whereby information is registered; *storage*, the maintenance of information over time; and *retrieval*, which refers to the accessing of the information by recognition, recall or implicitly by demonstrating that a relevant task is performed more efficiently as a result of prior experience. Encoding is typically studied by varying the nature of the material and/or the way that it is processed during learning. The effect of levels of processing is a good example of this, where processing the visual characteristics of a word leads to a much poorer subsequent recall or recognition than processing it in terms of meaning.

Storage is measured through forgetting. Somewhat surprisingly, although learning is influenced by a wide range of factors that compromise brain function temporarily or permanently, rate of loss of information from memory appears to be relatively insensitive to either patient type, or encoding procedures (Kopelman, 1985). While there have been suggestions that patients whose amnesia stems from damage to the temporal lobes forget at a different rate from those with hippocampal damage (e.g. Huppert & Piercy, 1979), this has not been borne out by subsequent research (Greene et al. 1996; Kopelman, 1985), although it would certainly be premature to conclude that patients never forget more rapidly (see e.g. Kapur *et al.*, 1997).

Given that information has been stored, if it is to be used then it must be retrieved, directly in the case of explicit memory, or indirectly in the case of implicit memory, to have an impact on subsequent performance. The two principal methods of memory retrieval involve recall, in which case the subject is required to reproduce the stimulus items, or recognition. This requires the subject to say whether a given item was presented or not (yes/no recognition) or to choose the previously presented item from a set of two or more alternatives (forced-choice recognition). Yes/no recognition performance will be influenced by the degree of caution the subject applies. By saying "yes" to everything he/she can, of course, correctly categorize all the targets while not necessarily indicating any memory. Such a subject would of course be discounted, but more subtle differences in the level of caution applied in deciding on whether an item was presented before ("old"), or has just been presented ("new") may also markedly influence performance.

There are a number of procedures for dealing with different degrees of caution among subjects. One is to apply a *guessing correction*, which assumes that the subject guesses on a proportion of the items that are not remembered. On the assumption that the guess is equally likely to be right or wrong, there are likely to be as many items correctly guessed ("hits") as those erroneously classed as "old" ("false alarms"). A guessing correction can then be applied by simply deducting the total number of false alarms from the total hit score. An alternative and slightly more complex way of dealing with the criterion is to utilize *signal detection theory*, which yields two measures, one representing the hypothetical strength of the memory trace, and the other the criterion of degree of caution employed by that subject (Lockhart, 2000). With forced-choice procedures, all subjects are *required always* to choose one item from each set, with the result that degree of caution does not become relevant. In general, recognition is assumed to place a less heavy load on the retrieval processes than recall, where it is necessary not only to discriminate "new" and "old" items but also to produce them.

Probably the simplest recall measure is *free recall*, in which a sequence of items, typically words, is presented, and the subject is required to recall as many as possible in any order he/she wishes. When recall is immediate, the probability of a word being recalled correctly is typically highly dependent on its serial position during presentation, with the first one or two words enjoying a modest advantage (the *primacy effect*), the middle items showing a relatively flat function, and the final words showing the best recall (the *recency effect*). Even though recall is immediate, apart from the recency effect, overall performance in free recall is principally dependent on LTM, with variables such as the imageability, frequency and semantic associability of the words all influencing performance.

A frequent variant of free recall is to use groups of words from the same semantic category; e.g. a 16 item list might have four animals, four flowers, four colours and four professions. Even when they are presented in scrambled order, subjects tend to recall the words in semantic clusters, indicating that they are using meaning as a basis for encoding and retrieval. Such effects become stronger when the same list is repeated for several trials. Indeed, even totally unrelated words will tend to be chunked into clusters that are seen as meaningfully related to the person learning (Tulving and Patkau, 1962). In the case of prose, initial level of recall performance tends to be set in terms of the number of word clusters or chunks, rather than the absolute number of words recalled (Tulving & Patkau, 1962).

The recency effect tends to follow a very different pattern, being insensitive to a wide range of variables that typically enhance LTM, but to be very sensitive to disruption by a brief subsequent delay filled by an activity such as counting (Glanzer, 1972). The recency effect was, and in some models still is, regarded as representing STM. However, recency effects that broadly follow the same principles can occur over periods of minutes or even days or weeks, as for example in the recall of rugby games played, or parking locations over multiple visits to a laboratory (Baddeley & Hitch, 1977; da Costa Pinto & Baddeley, 1991). It is also the case that a concurrent STM task, such as digit span, leaves the recency effect intact, again suggesting the need for a more complex model (Baddeley & Hitch, 1974). One view is that recency represents an implicit priming mechanism which may operate across a range of different stores, some involving STM, others LTM (for discussion of this view, see Baddeley & Hitch, 1993).

A slightly more complex LTM task involves serial recall, whereby the subject is presented with a sequence of items, typically well beyond memory span, and required to recall them in the order of presentation, with testing continuing either for a standard number of trials or until the subject has completely mastered the sequence. The serial position curve in this case tends to be bowed, with maximum errors somewhere just beyond the middle. It was used extensively in the 1940s and 1950s, but is less common now.

A popular method of testing LTM is through *paired associate learning*, whereby the subject is required to link together a number of word pairs (e.g. "cow–tree") and is tested by being presented with the stimulus word "cow" and required to produce the response "tree". This technique forms a part of many clinical memory tests, which may contain pairs that fit together readily, such as "cow–milk", together with more arbitrary pairs, such as "dog–cloud". A particular variant of this of course is involved in learning a new vocabulary word in one's own (e.g. "lateen", a kind of sail), or a second language (e.g. "hausrecker", grasshopper). Finally, more complex and realistic material may be used, as in the recall of prose passages or complex visual scenes. These have the advantage of being closer to the environment in which a patient might typically need to use memory. This leads on to a final topic, namely that of everyday memory.

EVERYDAY MEMORY

For over 100 years there has been a tendency for memory research to be pulled in two somewhat different directions. Ebbinghaus (1885) initially demonstrated that memory can be studied objectively by simplifying the remembering task to that of rapidly repeating back sequences of unfamiliar pseudowords, *nonsense syllables*. On the other hand, a more naturalistic approach to psychology was advocated by Galton (1883) and subsequently developed by Bartlett (1932), who required his subjects to recall complex prose passages, often involving unfamiliar material, such as legends from North American Indian culture. Open conflict between these two approaches surfaced more recently with the claim by Neisser (1978) that none of the interesting aspects of memory were being studied by psychologists, evoking a counter-blast from Banaji & Crowder (1989), who claimed that most studies of everday memory were trivial and uninformative. To some extent the controversy was an artificial one, as unfortunately they often are in contemporary psychology. There is no doubt that investigating the detailed nature of memory and producing precise testable models is most readily pursued within the laboratory, with its degree of experimental control. On the other hand, the everyday world and the clinic provide a fruitful source of problems, and a way of testing the generality of laboratory-based theories. A model that can elegantly predict which of two simple responses the subject will make in the laboratory may be of interest to the modelling enthusiast, but unless it can be generalized to more ambitious and important questions, it is unlikely to advance the study of memory. On the other hand, merely observing complex and intriguing phenomena is equally unlikely to generate constructive scientific theory.

There have been two constructive responses to the real world–laboratory dilemma, one being to attempt to generalize laboratory findings to complex real-world situations, and the other being to identify phenomena in everyday life that are not readily accounted for by current memory models. Examples of the first type include the previously described work studying recency effects in the recall of parking locations or rugby games. The attempt to extend laboratory-based recall studies from lists of unrelated words to the oral tradition of memory for songs and poems is another such example (Rubin, 1995).

A good example of identifying a problem in the world that requires solution is that of *prospective memory*, our capacity to remember to do something at a given time or place. It is typically when we forget to do things that we complain that our memories are terrible. But despite its practical importance, it is far from clear how prospective memory works. It certainly does require memory, since amnesic patients tend to be appallingly bad at it, but young intelligent people are often not particularly good at remembering to do things at the right time either. There is clearly an element of motivation, and almost certainly one of strategy, in successful prospective memory. Elderly people tend to forget fewer appointments than the young, partly because they know their memory is vulnerable and find ways to support it, e.g. by writing things down, or by concentrating on the need to remember and constructing internal reminders. Hence, despite making more prospective memory errors than the young under laboratory conditions, in real life they may often make fewer errors.

For long a neglected topic, prospective memory is now a very active one, with studies based on observational and diary measures now supplemented with a range of laboratory-based methods. There is, I suspect, a danger that the more tractable laboratory tasks may come to dominate this area, suggesting the need for a continued attempt to check their validity outside the laboratory. My current suspicion is that prospective memory represents a type of task that we require our memory system to perform, rather than itself reflecting a single memory system or process. That does not, of course, make it any less important or interesting, but does suggest that we are unlikely to reach any simple unitary theoretical solution to the problems it raises.

One area in which the laboratory-based and everyday approaches to memory appear to work effectively together is in the assessment of memory deficits. Traditional measures of memory have tended to rely on classical laboratory techniques, such as paired associate learning and the recall of complex figures, with measures tailored to patient use and then standardized against normal control subjects. However, patients sometimes complain that their problem is not in learning to associate pairs of words or remember complicated figures, but rather in forgetting appointments and failing to remember people's names, or the way around the hospital. Sunderland et al. (1983) decided to check the validity of such standard laboratory-based memory tests against the incidence of memory errors reported by patients and their carers. They tested a group of head-injured patients and subsequently a group of normal elderly subjects (Sunderland et al., 1983, 1986). They found that head injury and age both led to a clear reduction in performance on the standardized tests, together with an increase in memory complaints. However, there was no reliable association between reports of memory errors by the patients or carers and performance on most of the objective tests, with the only task showing a significant correlation being the recall of a prose passage.

Concerned with this problem herself, Barbara Wilson devised a memory test that attempted to capture the range of problems reported most frequently by her patients, whose memory deficits typically resulted from some form of brain injury, most frequently resulting from head injury or cardiovascular accident. She developed the Rivermead Behavioural Memory Test (RMBT), which comprises 12 subcomponents, testing such features as the capacity to memorize and recall a new name, recognition of previously presented unfamiliar faces, and of pictures of objects, recalling a brief prose passage immediately and after a delay, and the immediate and delayed recall of a simple route. The test also involves measures of orientation in time and place, and some simple tests of prospective memory. The RMBT proved sensitive to memory deficits and, in contrast to more conventional methods, correlated well with frequency of memory lapses, as observed by therapists working with the patients over a period of many hours (Wilson et al., 1989). In a study following up a group of amnesic patients several years later, Wilson (1991) found that level of performance on the test accurately predicted capacity to cope independently, in contrast to more conventional measures, such as the Wechsler Memory Scale–Revised.

The strength of the RBMT and of other tests using a similar philosophy, such as the Behavioural Assessment of the Dysexecutive Syndrome Test (Wilson et al., 1996), typically stems from their attempting to provide sensitive objective measures that simulate the real-world problems typically confronting a patient. They are excellent for predicting how well a patient will cope, but should not be regarded as a substitute for tests that attempt to give a precise estimate of the various types of memory function. Such theoretically driven tests are likely to be crucial in understanding the nature of the patient's problems, and hence in providing advice and help (see Chapter 28 on treatment, this volume). It is typically the case, however, that patients feel more comfortable with material that appears to relate to their practical problems, and this has led to a development of a number of theoretically targeted tests that use naturalistic materials. The Doors and People Test of visual and verbal recall and recognition (Baddeley et al., 1994) and the Autobiographical Memory Inventory (Kopelman et al., 1990) are two examples.

CONCLUSION

The psychology of memory has developed enormously since the days when memory was regarded as a single unitary faculty. The study of patients with memory deficits has played a major role in this development, and seems likely to continue to do so.

REFERENCES

Atkinson, R.C. & Shiffrin, R.M. (1968). Human memory: a proposed system and its control processes. In K.W. Spence (ed.), *The Psychology of Learning and Motivation: Advances in Research and Theory, Vol. 2* (pp. 89–195). New York: Academic Press.

Baddeley, A.D. (1986). *Working Memory*. Oxford: Clarendon Press.

Baddeley, A.D. (1996). Exploring the Central Executive. *Quarterly Journal of Experimental Psychology*, **49A**(1), 5–28.

Baddeley, A.D. (1997). *Human memory: Theory and Practice* (revised edn). Hove: Psychology Press.

Baddeley, A.D. (1999). *Essentials of Human Memory*. Hove: Psychology Press.

Baddeley, A.D. (2000). The episodic buffer: a new component of working memory? *Trends in Cognitive Sciences*, **4**(11), 417–423.

Baddeley, A.D., Aggleton, J.A. & Conway, M.A. (2002). *Episodic Memory*. Oxford: Oxford University Press.

Baddeley, A.D., Emslie, H. & Nimmo-Smith, I. (1994). *Doors and People: A Test of Visual and Verbal Recall and Recognition*. Bury St. Edmunds: Thames Valley Test Company.

Baddeley, A.D., Gathercole, S.E. & Papagno, C. (1998). The phonological loop as a language learning device. *Psychological Review*, **105**(1), 158–173.

Baddeley, A.D. & Hitch, G.J. (1974) Working memory. In G.A. Bower (ed.), *Recent Advances in Learning and Motivation*, Vol. 8 (pp. 47–89). New York: Academic Press.

Baddeley, A.D., & Hitch, G. (1977). Recency re-examined. In S. Dornic (ed.), *Attention and Performance VI* (pp. 647–667). Hillsdale, NJ Erlbaum.

Baddeley, A.D. & Hitch, G.J. (1993). The recency effect: implicit learning with explicit retrieval? *Memory and Cognition*, **21**, 146–155.

Baddeley, A.D., Vargha-Khadem, F. & Mishkin, M. (2001). Preserved recognition in a case of developmental amnesia: implications for the acquisition of semantic memory. *Journal of Cognitive Neuroscience*, **13**(3), 357–369.

Baddeley, A.D., & Wilson, B. (1988). Frontal amnesia and the dysexecutive syndrome. *Brain and Cognition*, **7**, 212–230.

Baddeley, A.D. & Wilson, B.A. (in press). Prose recall and amnesia: implications for the structure of working memory. *Neuropsychologia*.

Banaji, M.R. & Crowder, R.G. (1989). The bankrupcy of everyday memory. *American Psychologist*, **44**, 1185–1193.

Bartlett, F.D. (1932). *Remembering*. Cambridge: Cambridge University Press.

Brooks, D.N. & Baddeley, A.D. (1976). What can amnesic patients learn? *Neuropsychologia*, **14**, 111–122.

Claperède, E. (1911). Recognition et moiité. *Archives de Psychologie*, **11**, 79–90.

Cohen, N.J. & Squire, L.R. (1980). Preserved learning and retention of pattern analyzing skill in amnesia: dissociation of knowing how and knowing what. *Science*, **210**, 207–210.

Corkin, S. (1968). Acquisition of motor skill after bilateral medial temporal lobe excision. *Neuropsychologia*, **6**, 255–265.

Craik, F.I.M. & Lockhart, R.S. (1972). Levels of processing: a framework for memory research. *Journal of Verbal Learning and Verbal Behavior*, **11**, 671–684.

da Costa Pinto, A. & Baddeley, A.D. (1991). Where did you park your car? Analysis of a naturalistic long-term recency effect. *European Journal of Cognitive Psychology*, **3**, 297–313.

Duncan, J. (1996). Attention, intelligence and the frontal lobes. In M. Gazzaniga (ed.), *The Cognitive Neurosciences* (pp. 721–733). Cambridge, MA: MIT Press.

Ebbinghaus, H. (1885). *Über das Gedächtnis*. Leipzig: Dunker.

Galton, F. (1883). *Inquiries into Human Faculty and Its Development* (Everyman edn). London: Dent.

Gardiner, J.M. & Java, R.J. (1993). Recognising and remembering. In A.F. Collins, S.E. Gathercole, M.A. Conway & P.E. Morris (eds), *Theories of Memory* (pp. 163–188). Hove: Erlbaum.

Glanzer, M. (1972). Storage mechanisms in recall. In G.H. Bowers (ed.), *The Psychology of Learning and Motivation: Advances in Research and Theory*, Vol. 5. New York: Academic Press.

Greene J.D.W., Baddeley A.D. & Hodges J.R. (1996). Analysis of the episodic memory deficit in early Alzheimer's disease: evidence from the doors and people test. *Neuropsychologia*, **34**(6), 537–551.

Huppert, F.A. & Piercy, M. (1979). Normal and abnormal forgetting in amnesia: effect of locus of lesion. *Cortex*, **15**, 385–390.

Kapur, N., Millar, J. Colbourn, C. et al. (1997). Very long-term amnesia in association with temporal lobe epilepsy: evidence for multiple-stage consolidation processes. *Brain & Cognition*, **35**, 58–70.

Kolodny, J.A. (1994). Memory processes in classification learning—an investigation of amnesic performance in categorisation of dots, patterns and artistic styles. *Psychological Science*, **5**, 164–169.

Kopelman, M.D. (1985). Rates of forgetting in Alzheimer-type dementia and Korsakoff's syndrome. *Neuropsychologia*, **15**, 527–541.

Kopelman, M., Wilson, B.A. & Baddeley, A. (1990). The autobiographical memory interview. Bury St. Edmunds: Thames Valley Test Company.

Lockhart, R.S. (2000). Methods of memory research. In E. Tulving & F.I.M. Craik (eds), *The Oxford Handbook of Memory* (pp. 45–57). Oxford: Oxford University Press.

Miller, G.A. (1956). The magical number seven, plus or minus two: some limits on our capacity for processing information. *Psychological Review*, **63**, 81–97.

Milner, B. (1966). Amnesia following operation on the temporal lobes. In C.W.M. Whitty & O. L. Zangwill (eds), *Amnesia*. London: Butterworth.

Neisser, U. (1978). Memory: what are the important questions? In M.M. Gruneberg, P.E. Morris & R.N. Sykes (eds), *Practical Aspects of Memory*. London: Academic Press.

Norman, D.A. & Shallice, T. (1986). Attention to action: willed and automatic control of behaviour. In R.J. Davidson, G.E. Schwarts & D. Shapiro (Eds), *Consciousness and Self-regulation. Advances in Research and Theory, Vol. 4* (pp. 1–18). New York: Plenum.

Parkin, A.J. & Leng, N.R.C. (1993). *Neuropsychology of the Amnesic Syndrome*. Hove, UK: Erlbaum.

Roberts, A.C., Robbins, T.W. & Weiskrantz, L. (1998). *The Prefrontal Cortex: Executive and Cognitive Functions*. Oxford: Oxford University Press.

Rubin, D.C. (1995). *Memory in Oral Traditions: The Cognitive Psychology of Epic Ballads and Counting-out Rhymes*. New York: Oxford University Press.

Schacter, D.L. (1994). Priming and multiple memory systems: perceptual mechanisms of implicit memory. In D.L. Schacter & E. Tulving (eds), *Memory Systems*. Cambridge, MA: MIT Press.

Shallice, T. (1988). *From Neuropsychology to Mental Structure*. Cambridge: Cambridge University Press.

Shallice, T. & Burgess, P. (1996). The domain of supervisory processes and temporal organization of behaviour. *Philosophical Transactions of the Royal Society of London Series B—Biological Sciences*, **351**(1346), 1405–1411.

Shallice, T. & Warrington, E.K. (1970). Independent functioning of verbal memory stores: a neuropsychological study. *Quarterly Journal of Experimental Psychology*, **22**, 261–273.

Squire, L.R. (1992). Declarative and non-declarative memory: multiple brain systems supporting learning and memory. *Journal of Cognitive Neuroscience*, **4**, 232–243.

Stuss, D. & Knight, R.T. (2002). *Principles of Frontal Lobe Function*. New York: Oxford University Press.

Sunderland, A., Harris, J.E. & Baddeley, A.D. (1983). Do laboratory tests predict everyday memory? *Journal of Verbal Learning and Verbal Behavior*, **22**, 341–357.

Sunderland, A., Watts, K., Harris, J.E. & Baddeley, A.D. (1986). Subjective memory assessment and test performance in the elderly. *Journal of Gerontology*, **41**, 376–385.

Tulving, E. (1972). Episodic and semantic memory. In E. Tulving & W. Donaldson (Eds), *Organization of Memory* pp. 381–403. New York: Academic Press.

Tulving, E. (1989). Memory: performance, knowledge and experience. *European Journal of Cognitive Psychology*, **1**, 3–26.

Tulving, E. & Craik, F.I.M. (2000). *Handbook of Memory*. Oxford: Oxford University Press.

Tulving, E. & Patkau, J.E. (1962). Concurrent effects of contextual constraint and word frequency on immediate recall and learning of verbal material. *Canadian Journal of Psychology*, **16**, 83–95.

Vallar, G. & Baddeley, A.D. (1984). Fractionation of working memory. Neuropsychological evidence for a phonological short-term store. *Journal of Verbal Learning and Verbal Behaviour*, **23**, 151–161.

Vargha-Khadem, F., Gadian, D. & Mishkin, M. (2002). Dissociations in cognitive memory: the syndrome of developmental amnesia. In A. Baddeley, M. Conway & J. Aggleton (Eds). *Episodic Memory*. Oxford: Oxford University Press (pp. 153–163).

Warrington, E.K. & Weiskrantz, L. (1968). New methods of testing long-term retention with special reference to amnesic patients. *Nature*, **217**, 972–974.

Wechsler, D. (1987). *Wechsler Memory Scale—Revised*. San Antonio, TX: The Psychological Corporation.

Wilson, B.A. (1991). Long-term prognosis of patients with severe memory disorders. *Neuropsychological Rehabilitation*, **1**, 117–134.

Wilson, B.A., Alderman, N., Burgess, P. et al. (1996). Behavioural assessment of the dysexecutive syndrome. Bury St Edmunds: Thames Valley Test Company.

Wilson, B., Cockburn, J., Baddeley, A. & Hiorns, R. (1989). The development and validation of a test battery for detecting and monitoring everyday memory problems. *Journal of Clinical and Experimental Neuropsychology*, **11**, 855–870.

CHAPTER 2

Neurobiological Foundations of Human Memory

Daniel Tranel

and

Antonio R. Damasio

University of Iowa Hospitals and Clinics, Iowa City, IO, USA

Memory refers to knowledge that is stored in the brain, and to the processes of acquiring, consolidating and retrieving such knowledge (see Chapter 1). Memory is, arguably, the most basic and important operation of the brain. Few cognitive processes, including recognition, language, planning, problem-solving, decision-making and creativity, can operate effectively without a contribution from memory. One only needs to see the tragedy of Alzheimer's disease, in which an impairment of memory reduces an individual to a complete dependence on others, to appreciate how critical memory is for nearly every aspect of our lives. And memory is just as pervasive in terms of its neural underpinnings—one could say that virtually the entire brain is devoted to memory, in one way or another.

This chapter is built around the following organizing questions: What are the neurobiological foundations of memory? Which neural structures play a role in memory? How are different structures specialized for different kinds of memory and for different sub-components of memory processes? In addressing these questions, our focus is on *neural systems*, i.e. articulated collections of neuroanatomical units, such as varied cortical regions and subcortical nuclei, each containing myriad neurons operating in concert to perform a psychological function. The investigation of memory has proceeded along different levels in neuroscience, ranging from the systems/cognitive level to cellular and molecular mechanisms. We begin with a brief review of some of the main findings from molecular and cellular studies of memory, although a full review of this topic is outside the scope of this chapter (see Chen & Tonegawa, 1997; Hawkins et al., 1998; Kandel et al., 2000; Martin et al., 2000b; Micheau & Riedel, 1999; Shors & Matzel, 1997).

MOLECULAR AND CELLULAR BASIS OF MEMORY

Learning is generally defined as a relatively permanent change in performance caused by experience. Investigations of memory at the level of molecules and cells have focused on

The Handbook of Memory Disorders. Edited by A.D. Baddeley, M.D. Kopelman and B.A. Wilson
© 2002 John Wiley & Sons, Ltd.

the issue of what events occur in the brain when an organism learns something. Is there some kind of modification in neurons, or in the connections between neurons, that takes place as a result of learning? How is it that two stimuli can be associated with each other? What types of signaling mechanims are used for such processes?

One of the most important early attempts to address these questions came from Donald Hebb, who proposed in 1949 that the co-activation of connected cells would result in a modification such that when a presynaptic cell fires, the probability of a postsynaptic cell firing is increased. In Hebb's words, "When an axon of cell A is near enough to excite cell B or repeatedly or persistently takes part in firing it, some growth or metabolic change takes place in both cells, such that A's efficiency, as one of the cells firing B, is increased" (1949, p. 62). Hebb could not, at the time, specify exactly what was meant by "growths" or "metabolic changes", but the principle served as a very useful starting point and in fact it has become one of most widely cited heuristics for neurobiological investigations of learning and memory.

At the molecular level, some important advances in the understanding of learning and memory have come from the work of Eric Kandel and his colleagues (e.g. Kandel & Schwartz, 1982; Hawkins et al., 1983). Kandel noted that the marine mollusc *Aplysia californica* had a relatively simple nervous system (containing approximately 10 000 neurons, compared to the 10^{12} or so neurons that are present in the human brain). Moreover, the neurons are unusually large and easily identifiable, making *Aplysia* far more amenable to molecular- and cellular-level studies than are vertebrates with infinitely more complex nervous systems.

The work in *Aplysia* was complemented by another set of investigations, which capitalized on genetic manipulations to investigate the molecular and cellular bases of memory. The bulk of the early studies in this domain focused on the organism *Drosophila melanogaster* (a fruit fly), which is easy to culture, is prolific, has a short generation cycle, and makes hundreds of single-gene mutations affecting varied traits, such as enzyme kinetics and neuronal ion channel function. These features allowed many important discoveries regarding the genetic dissection of learning and memory (e.g. Dudai, 1988; Tully, 1991). More recently, investigations have focused on gene targeting and transgenic technologies in mutant mice, to extend the understanding of the genetics of mechanisms that underlie synaptic plasticity and the relationship of these synaptic mechanisms to activity-dependent neural development, learning and megmory (e.g. Chen & Tonegawa, 1997).

Kandel's work provided direct evidence that alterations of synaptic efficacy play a causal role in learning, supporting the principle articulated by Hebb. Specifically, Kandel's group discovered that the behavioral habituation of the gill and siphon withdrawal reflex (a reliable behavioral preparation in *Aplysia*) was mediated by a reduction in transmitter release at a defined synaptic locus (Castellucci & Kandel, 1974; Pinsker et al. 1970). Subsequently, it was shown that habituation was accompanied by alterations in the morphology of electrophysiologically identified synapses (Bailey & Chen, 1983). Modern work has identified some of the signal transduction pathways that subserve plasticity in neuronal systems, and that appear to play pivotal roles in the formation of memories. For example, it has been shown that a learning event induces activation of a variety of kinases with specific time courses; the early phase of memory formation appears to be dependent on the calcium calmodulin-dependent protein kinase II, whereas the transformation of information from short-term to long-term storage may depend on activation of both protein tyrosine kinases and mitogen-activated protein kinases (for review, see Micheau & Riedel, 1999).

A critical discovery concerning the neurobiology of memory came in 1973, when the phenomenon of long-term potentiation (LTP) was first reported (Bliss & Lomo, 1973).

LTP is typically defined as a long-lasting increase in synaptic efficacy following high-frequency stimulation of afferent fibers—in other words, an increase in a postsynaptic cell's excitability that lasts for hours, or even days or weeks, after a related presynaptic cell has been stimulated with a high-frequency volley of pulses (known as a tetanus). As a specific example, when the primary afferents of dentate granule cells in hippocampus are stimulated with a tetanic stimulus, the depolarization potential of the postsynaptic cell is enhanced, and this potentiation lasts for a considerable period of time. Investigation of the mechanisms underlying LTP has been one of the most active areas of research in neuroscience over the past two decades (for reviews, see Martin et al., 2000b; Shors & Matzel, 1997).

LTP was initially discovered in the hippocampus, which was already believed, based on earlier studies in patient H.M. (see below), to serve a crucial role in memory. Along with several other characteristics of LTP, including its rapid induction, persistence, and correlation with natural brain rhythms, this led to wide acceptance of the notion that LTP serves as a basic mechanism for learning in the mammalian brain. This idea received additional support from a series of experiments by Richard Morris and colleagues (e.g. Morris et al. 1990). Previously, most experiments investigating LTP had been done *in vitro*, i.e. in a slice of hippocampal tissue kept alive in a nutrient bath. Morris et al. conducted their experiments in awake, behaving animals. First, it was established that the hippocampus was important for the learning of spatial information, e.g. in order for a rat to learn successfully to swim to a submerged platform through an opaque water solution (known as the "water maze test"), the rat must have an intact hippocampus (e.g. Morris et al., 1982). Then, Morris et al. applied various doses of a substance known as AP5 (or APV), which blocks induction of LTP in slice preparations, to rats performing the water maze test. This application blocked the learning curve at the behavioral level, i.e. rats failed to acquire spatial knowledge about the location of the submerged platform. Furthermore, the relationship was dose-dependent, meaning that the more AP5 reached the hippocampus, the more diminished was the learning curve. Morris et al. also demonstrated that the retardation of the behavioral learning curve in the water maze task was directly congruent with the extent to which LTP was blocked in the hippocampus. In other words, less LTP was correlated with poorer learning, and more LTP was correlated with better learning. These results provided strong behavioral evidence supporting the role of LTP in the cellular basis of learning.

Work on the molecular and cellular bases of memory has led to three general principles. First, the findings suggest that information storage is intrinsic to sensorimotor pathways mediating a particular learned behavior. Second, information storage is an alteration in the efficacy of existing neural pathways. A corollary of this second principle is that overall synaptic throughput can be enhanced by having more presynaptic terminals available to release neurotransmitter. A third principle is that the detection of contiguity in classical conditioning is a biological property of neurons. This property arises out of a capacity for dual activation of adenylate cyclase, by a G-protein, which is believed to represent the unconditioned stimulus in classical conditioning paradigms, and by calcium calmodulin, which is believed to represent the conditioned stimulus. The consequence of the "allosteric" modification of the adenylate cyclase is that its subsequent activation by unconditioned stimuli will result in greater production of cAMP and, in turn, enhanced phosphorylation of presynaptic K^+ channels. Later conditioned stimuli will then cause even greater transmitter release than occurs after presynaptic facilitation on its own.

Another important discovery at the molecular level includes the finding that glutamate is an important neurotransmitter released by hippocampal afferents. It is an excitatory neurotransmitter for most pyramidal neurons, and it binds to three different receptor types on the postsynaptic cell. One of them is known as the NMDA receptor, because it is activated by the glutamate analog, N-methyl-D-aspartate. The NMDA receptor is a protein that has binding sites for both glutamate and glycine, and also has a channel that opens to extracellular ions only when the cell is depolarized from its resting level by about 30 mV or more. This property (i.e. a dual requirement for both receptor-site binding and previous depolarization of the cell) implies that the NMDA receptor may act as a sort of conjunction detector. In other words, the NMDA receptor might be one important cellular mechanism for LTP and associative learning. Convergent evidence comes from molecular studies showing that AP5, which was alluded to earlier, blocks LTP in CA1 pyramidal cells by acting as an antagonist for glutamate, competing for specific receptor sites on the NMDA receptor. Also, blocking activation of the NMDA receptor with gene knockouts blocks LTP in CA1 (Tsien et al., 1996). Finally, there is recent evidence indicating that nitric oxide (NO) is an important retrograde messenger during LTP in hippocampus (e.g. Hawkins et al., 1998). Another molecule that may serve a role as a retrograde messenger is carbon monoxide (CO) (e.g. Zhuo et al., 1993).

A few additional comments regarding research on the molecular and cellular basis of memory are warranted. For one thing, it is important to note that, even with the intense research efforts over the past few decades, many of the ideas in this domain remain open to debate and most of the fundamental mechanisms have yet to be fully clarified. Even the phenomenon of LTP, for example, which is widely accepted as a basic learning mechanism, has been critically evaluated in regard to its role in learning; it has been proposed, for example, that LTP may serve as a neural equivalent to an arousal or attention device in the brain (Shors & Matzel, 1997), rather than as a learning mechanism *per se*. Shors & Matzel note that there is little empirical evidence that directly links LTP to the actual storage of memories, although it is probably true that no better mechanism has yet been postulated. This position is elaborated by Martin et al. (2000b), who note that there are many data supporting the notion that synaptic plasticity is necessary for learning and memory, but very few data that support the notion of sufficiency.

TERMS AND DEFINITIONS

As outlined by Baddeley in Chapter 1, the process of memory formation is generally considered to have three basic steps: (a) acquisition; (b) consolidation; and (c) storage. *Acquisition* refers to the process of bringing information into the brain and into a first-stage memory "buffer", via sensory organs and primary sensory cortices (e.g. visual, auditory, somatosensory). *Consolidation* is the process of rehearsing knowledge and building a robust representation of it in the brain. *Storage* refers to the process of creating a relatively stable "memory trace" or "record" of knowledge in the brain. It is important to note that the brain uses *dynamic* records, rather than static, immutable memory traces. Moreover, such records can be modified to reflect evolving experience. In a general sense, these records can be thought of as sets of neuronal circuit changes which can be reactivated (see section on Theoretical Framework, below).

Conscious remembering is the process of retrieving or reactivating knowledge in such a way that it can become a mental image (as in recall and recognition). Another form of "remembering" involves reactivation of knowledge in such a way that it can be translated into a motor output, as in the movement of limbs or the vocal apparatus, or in autonomic activity. These two forms of remembering have been distinguished both theoretically and empirically

(Squire, 1992): *declarative* memory refers to knowledge such as facts and events that can be brought into consciousness (and inspected in the "mind's eye"), whereas *nondeclarative* memory refers to knowledge that cannot be deliberately brought into consciousness and, instead, is a collection of various motor skills, habits and conditioning.

PARADIGMS

The neurobiology of memory at systems level moved into the center stage of neuropsychology and neuroscience about four decades ago, when the now-famous case of H.M. was first described (Scoville & Milner, 1957). Following a bilateral resection of the mesial temporal lobes that was done to control his seizures, H.M. developed a profound inability to learn new factual (declarative) knowledge (Corkin, 1984; Milner, 1972; Milner et al., 1998). Another important case was the patient known as Boswell (Damasio et al., 1985). Following herpes simplex encephalitis that damaged nearly all of the mesial and anterolateral parts of his temporal lobes, Boswell developed one of the most profound amnesic syndromes that has ever been described. Not only could Boswell not learn any new factual knowledge, but he was also incapable of retrieving factual knowledge from his past. This latter feature distinguishes Boswell from patient H.M., whose retrieval of knowledge acquired prior to the time of his operation was deemed mostly intact.

Careful investigations of H.M. and Boswell, and of other patients with brain damage who have been described over the years, have furnished a wealth of information about the neurobiology of memory. These studies exemplify what is known as the *lesion method*, in which a documented area of brain damage is related to a carefully studied impairment of cognitive function (Damasio & Damasio, 1989, 1997). The lesion method has been used with a variety of patient populations, such as patients with herpes simplex encephalitis, cerebral anoxia/ischemia and Alzheimer's disease (Tranel et al., 2000b), and these investigations have yielded many key discoveries about the neural basis of memory. Recently, findings from lesion studies have been confirmed and expanded by investigations using functional imaging techniques, including *positron emission tomography* (PET) and *functional magnetic resonance imaging* (fMRI). These techniques allow the monitoring of large neuronal populations while subjects engage in various cognitive tasks (for review, see Cabeza & Nyberg, 2000). In PET, regional blood flow is measured by marking the blood with a radioactive tracer (e.g. $H_2{}^{15}O$); fMRI allows the measurement of local changes in the oxygen levels of neural tissue. In this chapter, we review findings derived primarily from work using the lesion method, and incorporate new findings from the functional imaging literature wherever pertinent. For some topics—working memory being a prime example—most of the available evidence has been derived from functional imaging studies.

MEMORY SYSTEMS IN THE HUMAN BRAIN

Hippocampus and Related Structures

Anatomy

The mesial temporal lobe contains a number of structures that are critical for memory, including the hippocampus, the amygdala, the entorhinal and perirhinal cortices, and the

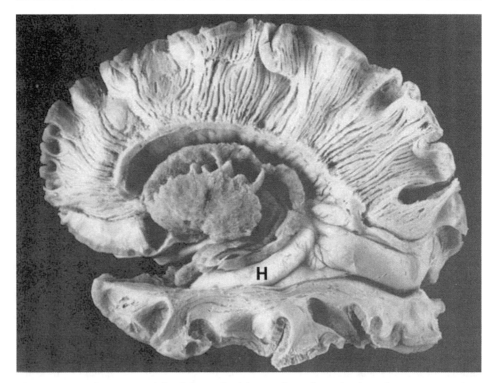

Figure 2.1 A dissection of the left cerebral hemisphere from the lateral aspect, revealing the hippocampus (marked with an **H**) and related structures deep within the temporal lobe (highlighted in white shading). Adapted by permission from Gluhbegovic & Williams (1980)

portion of the parahippocampal gyrus not occupied by the entorhinal cortex (Figures 2.1 and 2.2). Following the recommendations outlined by Zola (1997), the term "*hippocampus*" is used to refer to the cell fields of the hippocampus proper and the dentate gyrus; the term "*hippocampal region*" includes the hippocampus proper, the dentate gyrus, and the subicular region; and the term "*hippocampal formation*" includes the hippocampal region and the entorhinal cortex. This entire set of structures can be referred to conveniently as the "*hippocampal complex*", and collectively it comprises the key component of the mesial temporal lobe memory system.

The different components of this system are highly interconnected by means of recurrent neuroanatomical circuits, e.g. the perirhinal and parahippocampal cortices provide approximately two-thirds of the cortical input to the entorhinal cortex (Insausti et al. 1987; Suzuki & Amaral, 1994), and the entorhinal cortex in turn provides the primary source of cortical projections to the hippocampus and dentate gyrus (Suzuki & Amaral, 1994; Van Hoesen & Pandya, 1975). The higher-order association cortices of the temporal lobe receive signals from the association cortices of all sensory modalities, and also receive feedback projections from the hippocampus. Some of these relationships are diagrammed in Figure 2.3. The diagram illustrates how structures in the hippocampal complex have access to, and influence over, signals from virtually the entire brain. Thus, the hippocampal complex is situated strategically, from a neuroanatomical point of view, to create records

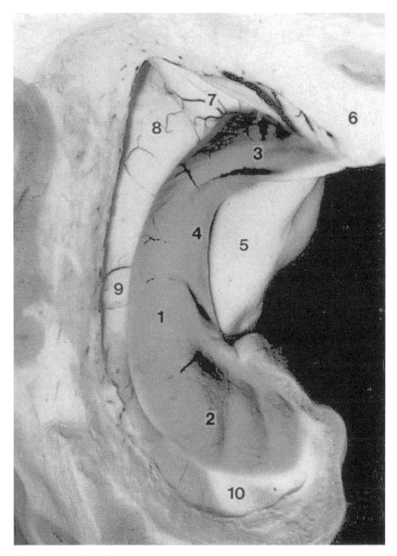

Figure 2.2 The hippocampus (1–4; highlighted in gray overtones) and related structures (5–10). Adapted by permission from Duvernoy (1988)

that bind together various aspects of memory experiences, including visual, auditory and somatosensory information.

As alluded to earlier, the importance of the hippocampal complex for the acquisition of new factual knowledge was discovered several decades ago, when the case of H.M. was initially described, and in a general sense this can be considered the principal function of the hippocampal complex. In short, the hippocampal complex is essential for creating records of interactions between the organism and the world outside, as well as records of thought processes, such as those engaged in planning. However, the precise computational operations performed by the hippocampus remain to be fully clarified (Cohen & Eichenbaum, 1993;

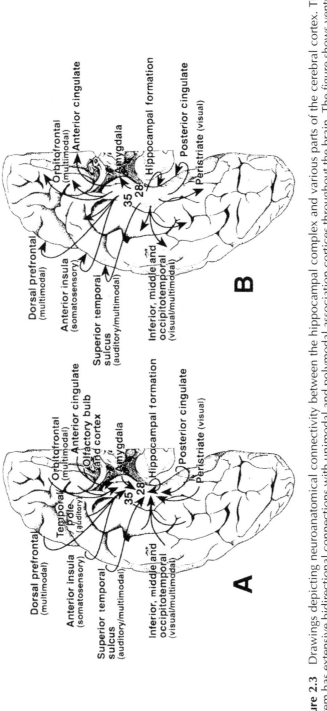

Figure 2.3 Drawings depicting neuroanatomical connectivity between the hippocampal complex and various parts of the cerebral cortex. The system has extensive bidirectional connections with unimodal and polymodal association cortices throughout the brain. The figure shows ventral views of the human brain depicting input (A) and output (B) relationships of the entorhinal (area 28) and perirhinal (area 35) cortices (Van Hoesen, 1982). These areas receive extensive direct or indirect sensory-specific (unimodal) association input (olfactory, auditory, somatosensory and visual), as well as multimodal sensory input from the prefrontal, superior temporal and occipitotemporal regions of the cortex. Limbic system input from the amygdala, hippocampal formation, temporal polar and cingulate areas is another important anatomical feature. In all instances, the input structures receive direct or indirect feedback from areas 28 and 35. The powerful interconnections between the entorhinal/perirhinal cortices and the hippocampal formation assure widespread cortical and hippocampal interactions with a multitude of neural systems

Eichenbaum, et al., 1992; Mishkin, 1978; Squire, 1992), and this remains an area of intense scientific inquiry. It is still unclear, for example, to what extent and in what ways the hippocampal complex participates in processes such as consolidation (McGaugh, 2000) and encoding and retrieval (e.g. Gabrieli et al., 1998).

The case of H.M. also had some other lessons: because H.M. could hold information in mind briefly (e.g. for a few seconds), it was clear that mesial temporal structures were not necessary for "immediate" memory. It was shown, for example, that up to delays of about 40 s, H.M. could perform accurately in a delayed matching to sample paradigm (Sidman et al., 1968). Also, H.M. was able to retrieve at least some information about his past, suggesting that these structures were not the repository of all older memories. These ideas have proved remarkably robust, and many of the general conclusions proposed by Milner and colleagues many years ago (Milner, 1972; Milner et al., 1968) remain correct in their essence. These principles and several related themes are developed in more detail immediately below.

Immediate Memory

Immediate memory refers to a type of memory that has a short duration (a minute or so) and limited capacity (about 7 ± 2 "chunks" of information); it is also known as "primary" or "short-term" memory (see Chapter 1). (There is some new evidence for a kind of memory termed "medium-term" memory, which may have a somewhat larger capacity than short-term memory but still be "disposable"; see Melcher, 2001). The notion that the mesial temporal lobe memory system is not crucial for immediate memory has been demonstrated in compelling fashion in our patient Boswell, whose neuropsychological and neuroanatomical profiles have been published elsewhere (Damasio et al., 1985, 1989; Tranel et al., 2000b). Despite complete bilateral temporal lobe damage and a profound amnesic syndrome that prevents learning of any type of factual knowledge, Boswell has a completely intact immediate memory, which covers about 45 s. That is, Boswell can retain information for up to about 45 s; after that, the information disappears without a trace. If he is prompted to rehearse repeatedly—say, every several seconds or so—he can continue to "hold" information in his immediate memory span, but after enough time passes (and this need only be a minute or so), whatever information he had "in mind" is completely gone; it is not even possible to find evidence of priming, and extensive cuing is of no benefit. We have probed this manifestation repeatedly over the 25 years that we have been studying this patient, and the phenomenon is robust and completely reliable. Coupled with the original observations of this effect in patient H.M. mentioned above (Sidman et al., 1968), these findings provide definitive support for the idea that the hippocampal complex is not involved in immediate memory. In fact, there is a remarkable similiarity between H.M. and Boswell in terms of the time window that appears unaffected by their bilateral hippocampal lesions; both patients can hold information for about 40–45 s, whereafter, without rehearsal, it will vanish.

Retrograde Memory

The idea that the hippocampal complex is not the repository of old memories, and is not crucial for retrieving knowledge that had been acquired and consolidated prior to the onset of brain damage, was advanced initially by Milner and colleagues on the basis of studies of H.M. (Milner, 1972). This idea has been refined over the years, in light of additional evidence, but its essence remains a cornerstone in most published accounts of models of memory (in a careful consideration of the key evidence available to date, Nadel & Moscovitch, 1997, challenged this idea, pointing out that the hippocampus and related structures probably *are* required for recovering remote memories, especially autobiographical ones. Nadel & Moscovitch acknowledged that various types of semantic knowledge retrieval may be relatively independent of hippocampal function). What can be said for sure is that the hippocampal complex is not necessary for permanent memory storage and retrieval of all types of knowledge, since extensive damage to this system does not prevent patients from retrieving old, remote memories of many types, e.g. the hippocampal system appears to have only a temporary role in the formation and maintenance of at least some aspects of declarative memory (Alvarez & Squire, 1994; Squire, 1992; Zola-Morgan & Squire, 1993); permanent memory is established in other brain regions, most likely the neo-cortices (see below). These conclusions are supported by data showing that some patients with bilateral hippocampal damage have a temporally-graded defect in retrograde memory (Rempel-Clower et al., 1997; Victor & Agamanolis, 1990; but see Nadel & Moscovitch, 1997, for alternative interpretations of these data); i.e. there may be a defect for memories acquired close in time to the onset of the brain injury, but the farther back one goes in the autobiography of the patient, the more intact memory will become. Circumscribed hippocampal damage may produce no retrograde amnesia whatsoever (Zola-Morgan et al., 1986). Studies in nonhuman animals have also provided consistent support for this idea, showing in nearly all cases a clear temporal gradient in retrograde amnesia, whereby memory performance steadily improves the farther back in time one goes from surgical removal of mesial temporal structures (for review, see Milner et al., 1998).

Amnesia Severity is Correlated with Extent of Damage to Mesial Temporal Lobe

The importance of mesial temporal lobe structures for factual learning is also supported by the fairly robust relationship between the degree of structural damage in these structures and the extent of memory impairment (e.g. Corkin et al., 1997; Squire & Zola, 1996; see also Bachevalier & Meunier, 1996). Studies in patients with anoxia/ischemia have been particularly informative in this regard (Tranel et al., 2000b). When damage is limited to the hippocampal region, and even to specific subregions within the hippocampus (particularly the CA1 field), the degree of amnesia is relatively mild and circumscribed. Lesions that affect more of the mesial temporal region, e.g. the hippocampus plus entorhinal cortex, produce a more severe memory impairment. And even more extensive damage, that affects structures such as the perirhinal cortex and more of the parahippocampal gyrus in addition to the entorhinal cortex and hippocampal region, tends to produce an even more severe amnesia. This relationship holds for both the human cases and for monkeys with surgically-induced mesial temporal lesions (for review, see Squire & Zola, 1996). In the post mortem studies available to date, it has been shown that the critical region affected by anoxia/ischemia is the CA1 field of the hippocampus (Rempel-Clower et al., 1996; Zola-Morgan et al., 1986). As noted, the extent of neuronal damage in this region tends to be well correlated with the degree of memory impairment, and in cases of relatively limited anoxia/ischemia this may be the only region that shows cell loss.

Material-specific Memory Impairments

Another strong consensus regarding the mesial temporal lobe memory system is that there is a laterality effect, whereby the left-sided system mediates memory for verbal material, and the right-sided system mediates memory for nonverbal material (Milner, 1971). That is, the left- and right-sided hippocampal complexes, although roughly comparable in anatomical terms, have major differences in their functional roles, differences which parallel the typical functional arrangement of the brain, whereby most individuals develop left-hemisphere specialization for language, and right-hemisphere specialization for spatial and nonlinguistic abilities. Thus, unilateral damage to the left hippocampal complex will tend to produce disproportionate impairments in the learning of verbally-coded material (e.g. names, verbal facts), whereas unilateral damage to the right hippocampal complex will tend to produce disproportionate impairments in the learning of nonverbal material, such as faces, geographical routes, melodies and spatial information (e.g. Barrash et al., 2000; Milner, 1971; Tranel, 1991). These patterns are known as "*material-specific memory impairments*", and the basic findings have now been replicated in functional imaging studies (Brewer et al., 1998; Wagner et al., 1998), although there is some indication from the functional imaging literature that mesial temporal lobe activations are left-lateralized for verbal material and bilateral for nonverbal material (Grady et al., 1998). Also, it has been shown that mesial temporal lobe activation is especially pronounced for spatial material (e.g. Maguire et al., 1998), such as route-finding and spatial location, a result that is consistent with recent findings from lesion work (Barrash et al., 2000). There is some evidence that the posterior aspect of the mesial temporal lobe region may be more involved in memory encoding processes, while the anterior aspect is more involved in memory retrieval processes (for reviews, see Gabrieli et al., 1998; Schacter & Wagner, 1999; Wagner et al., 1999); however, this is not a well-established finding, and other conclusions have been reached on the basis of meta-analyses of the available evidence (e.g. Lepage et al., 1998).

Declarative vs. Non-declarative Memory

As noted earlier, the hippocampal complex is crucial for the learning of material that is declarative in nature, i.e. information that can be "declared" and "brought to mind". This includes items such as words, names and faces; in essence, material that comprises the conscious recollection of facts and events, and that is propositional—it can be either true or false. The hippocampal system, however, does not appear to be critical for learning that is of the type known as "nondeclarative". Nondeclarative memory refers to changes in performance that result from experience, but which are not accessible to, or available in, conscious recall. Thus, acquisition of motor skills, habits and certain forms of conditioned responses and priming effects are largely independent of hippocampal function, and can proceed successfully even when the mesial temporal lobes are extensively damaged (exceptions to this general statement have been reported; e.g. Ostergaard, 1999; see also

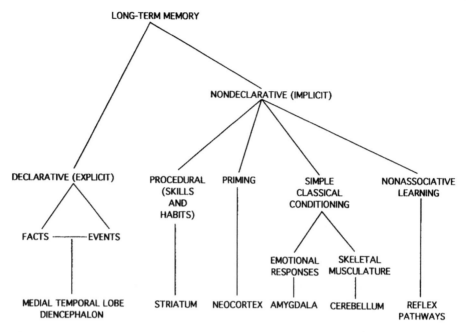

Figure 2.4   The diagram indicates various neural structures thought to be important for different types of declarative and nondeclarative memory. Reproduced by permission from Milner et al. (1998)

Gooding et al., 2000, who noted that word priming does not represent a type of memory function that is spared in amnesia). With regard to the independence of motor skill learning from the hippocampal system, the phenomenon was first reported by Milner (1962) in patient H.M., using a mirror drawing task, and it has been replicated in many other patients with mesial temporal damage and severe amnesia for declarative information (e.g. Cohen & Squire, 1980; Gabrieli et al. 1993; Tranel et al., 1994; Warrington & Weiskrantz, 1968). The independence of nondeclarative memory from the mesial temporal lobe system has also been supported in functional neuroimaging studies (for review, see Gabrieli et al., 1998). The neuroanatomical and behavioral distinctions between declarative and nondeclarative memory are diagrammed in Figure 2.4.

Other Temporal Lobe Structures

Anatomy

Temporal lobe structures outside the mesial temporal region also play important roles in memory, albeit different from the role played by the hippocampus and related mesial temporal structures. These structures include anatomical units in anterior, inferior and lateral portions of the temporal lobes (Figure 2.5), which we refer to collectively as the "nonmesial temporal region". Included are cortices in the temporal pole (Brodmann area 38), the inferotemporal region (Brodmann areas 20/21, 36, part of 37) and the region of transition between the posterior temporal lobe and the inferior occipital lobe (Brodmann area 37).

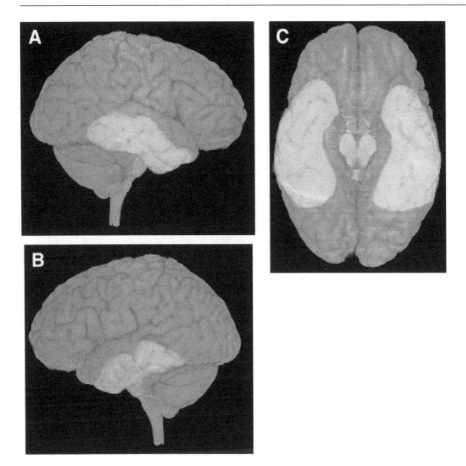

Figure 2.5 Lateral (**A**, left hemisphere; **B**, right hemisphere) and inferior (**C**) views of the cerebral hemispheres of a normal brain (reconstructed in three dimensions from MR data, using Brainvox, as described in Frank et al., 1997). The regions shaded in white, which we refer to collectively as the "nonmesial" temporal region, are of particular importance for retrograde memory

Retrograde Memory

It was noted earlier that mesial temporal lobe structures are probably not the repository of all types of older memories, i.e. information that was acquired at remote points in time, prior to the onset of brain injury (Figure 2.6). In many respects, nonmesial temporal structures can be considered to comprise such a repository, i.e. these structures appear to hold records for knowledge that was learned previously and that has been stored as part of long-term memory, what is commonly known as *retrograde memory*. Evidence from lesion studies has supported this notion, e.g. when nonmesial temporal lobe structures are damaged bilaterally, patients demonstrate severe impairments in retrieval of retrograde memory (e.g. Kapur et al., 1992, 1994; Kopelman, 1993; Markowitsch et al., 1993a, 1993b; O'Connor et al., 1992). When such lesions spare the mesial temporal region, the patients may demonstrate preservation of anterograde memory, thus displaying a pattern that is a sort of cognitive

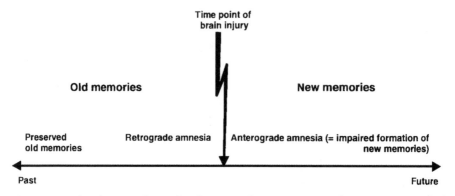

Figure 2.6   The diagram shows the distinction between retrograde memory (so-called "old" memories) and anterograde memory (so-called "new" memories), which is demarcated by the time point of onset of brain injury. Reproduced by permission from Markowitsch (2000)

and neuroanatomical mirror image to that of patient H.M. (e.g. Kapur et al., 1994; for review, see Hodges, 1995). The comparison of cases H.M. and Boswell also supports this notion: as noted earlier, Boswell has, unlike H.M., a severe deficit in retrograde memory, and this deficit has been attributed to Boswell's nonmesial temporal lesions (which H.M. lacks). We hasten to add, though, that this picture is quite complex, and it cannot be claimed that there is a simple isomorphic relationship, whereby the hippocampal system is linked with anterograde memory whilst the nonmesial temporal system is linked with retrograde memory. Infact, in a recent review of the relevant literature, Kopelman (2000) noted that there is very little convincing evidence for "focal" retrograde amnesia.

We recently had an opportunity to conduct a strong test of this notion in a patient who sustained partially "reversible" bilateral temporal lobe lesions (Jones et al., 1998). The patient was a 70 year-old woman with limbic encephalitis. Shortly after the onset of her condition, neuropsychological investigation revealed severe multimodal anterograde and retrograde memory impairments. An [^{18}F] fluorodeoxyglucose (FDG) resting PET scan at this same epoch revealed cortical hypometabolism that was especially pronounced in right anterolateral temporal structures. Two years later, the patient showed marked resolution of her retrograde memory defect, with persistent anterograde memory impairment. A repeat FDG resting PET showed improved metabolism in the anterolateral temporal cortex, but metabolism in both mesial temporal regions had declined markedly. In sum, striking re-covery of retrograde memory, but not anterograde memory, occurred in conjunction with improvement in anterolateral temporal metabolism and despite reduction in mesial tempo-ral metabolism. These findings provide further support for the notion that mesial temporal structures are not the repository of retrograde factual knowledge, and for the idea that antero-lateral temporal lobe structures are critical for the retrieval of retrograde factual knowledge.

The Left- and Right-sided Systems

Lesion studies have generally supported a conventional laterality effect in regard to non-mesial temporal lobe structures, whereby left-sided structures are more important for verbally-coded material, whereas right-sided structures are more important for nonverbal, visuospatial material (e.g. O'Connor et al., 1992; for review, see Markowitsch, 1995). Two HSE cases published recently by our group also support this idea: one patient had a unilateral left anterolateral temporal lesion and impaired retrieval of verbal information (particularly names of concrete entities), with spared retrieval of nonverbal knowledge; a second patient had a unilateral right anterolateral temporal lesion and impaired retrieval of nonverbal knowledge, with relative sparing of retrieval of verbal information (see cases LR488 and FR1465, respectively, in Tranel et al., 2000b).

The weight of the available evidence also points to another asymmetry in the roles played by nonmesial temporal structures in retrograde memory, especially memory for episodic, unique, autobiographical information. Specifically, there is consistent support for the idea that structures on the right are more critical for this type of knowledge than are structures on the left. Moreover, the evidence suggests that right-sided nonmesial temporal structures operate in concert with interconnected right prefrontal cortices to subserve the retrieval of unique, factual memories, especially for autobiographical knowledge. This idea has received impressive support from both lesion and functional imaging studies (Calabrese et al., 1996; Fletcher et al., 1997; Jones et al., 1998; Kroll et al., 1997; Levine et al., 1998; Nyberg et al., 1996; O'Connor et al., 1992; Tranel et al., 2000b). It remains an open question as to what the specific contributions of temporal vs. frontal structures may be—one suggestion is that frontal cortices may play an important role in the "connectedness" or "interrelatedness" of unique memories in space and time, and in the methods of memory search utilized in effortful retrieval, whereas temporal cortices are more important for "holding" specific knowledge of facts and events (Calabrese et al., 1996; Jones et al., 1998; Markowitsch, 1995).

Unique and Nonunique Knowledge

An important principle regarding the organization of memory in nonmesial temporal structures is that there is a gradient of specialization that corresponds to the level of specificity of material, i.e. its uniqueness. In general, this gradient follows a posterior–anterior axis, along which there is an increasing level of specificity associated with more anterior parts of the nonmesial temporal cortices. Specifically, material that is acquired, stored and retrieved at a nonunique level is supported predominantly by structures situated more posteriorly in the nonmesial temporal region, whereas material that is acquired, stored, and retrieved at a unique level is supported predominantly by structures situated more anteriorly in the nonmesial temporal region.

This principle can be illustrated by taking the example of name retrieval. Retrieval of names for nonunique entities, such as animals or tools, is associated with structures in the inferotemporal region (IT), formed primarily by the lateral and inferior aspects of Brodmann areas 20/21, 36, and 37 (see Figure 2.5). These items are normally learned and remembered at nonunique level, or what is known as the "basic object level". Hence, one learns to recognize and to name animals, e.g. "raccoon" or "pig"; normally, there is no requirement to identify a specific example of one individual raccoon or pig. The same applies to the category of tools/utensils: we use and name artifacts such as pencils, hammers and spoons with no demand for recognition of such items as specific, unique exemplars. By contrast, the retrieval of names for unique entities, such as persons or landmarks, is associated with structures in the anteriormost aspect of the nonmesial temporal region, especially the temporal pole (TP; Brodmann area 38). Consider, for example, the category of unique persons: here, there is typically a requirement for recognition and naming at a specific, unique level. Thus, we identify known individuals as unique exemplars, e.g. "Bill Clinton", "Tiger Woods", "Eric Kandel". As another example, we recognize and name many geographical entities at unique level, e.g. "Iowa", "the Sear's Tower", "Old Faithful". In these categories—unique persons and places—it is insufficient to operate at a more superordinate level, e.g. it does not suffice to recognize one's boss as simply "a man" or one's hometown as simply "a mid-western city".

The association of name retrieval with structures in the left IT and TP regions, and the gradient of specialization related to level of uniqueness articulated above, have been supported by lesion studies (Damasio et al., 1996; Tranel et al., 1997a, 1998), and also by studies using electrophysiological (Nobre et al., 1994; Ojemann, 1991) and functional imaging (Damasio et al., 1996; Grabowski et al., submitted; Martin et al., 1995; Raichle et al., 1994; Silveri et al., 1997) techniques. The retrieval of *conceptual* knowledge for concrete entities—i.e. knowledge about what things are, or their meaning, independent of what they are called—has also been associated with neural units in the IT and TP regions and with structures in the vicinity of these regions, especially in the occipitotemporal region. Moreover, there is considerable evidence supporting a certain degree of category-specificity in regard to which neural regions correspond to particular categories of entities. In a lesion study, for example, we demonstrated that the retrieval of concepts for unique persons is associated with right temporal polar structures, the retrieval of concepts for animals is associated with right mesial occipital/ventral temporal structures, as well as the left mesial occipital region, and the retrieval of concepts for tools is associated with structures in the left occipital-temporal-parietal junction (Tranel et al., 1997b). Many of these findings have been reviewed in recent publications (Caramazza, 2000; Forde & Humphreys, 1999; Gainotti et al., 1995; Humphreys & Forde, 2000; Martin et al., 2000a).

Modality-specific Early Sensory Cortices

Each of the cortices related to primary sensory modalities (e.g. visual, auditory, somatosensory) has associated with it a band of adjacent cortex that is termed a *"primary association area"*, and these association cortices appear to play an interesting supportive role in memory. Take, for example, the visual modality. Cortices in the lingual and fusiform gyri, immediately adjacent to primary visual cortex in the inferior mesial occipital lobe, contain important neural units for the processing of color and form, as shown by both lesion (e.g. Rizzo et al., 1993) and functional imaging (e.g. Chao & Martin, 1999; Clark et al., 1997) studies. Moreover, it has been shown that within these sectors, the processing of different components of visual information, e.g. color and motion, can be segregated (e.g. Cavanagh et al., 1998; Heywood et al., 1998; for review, see Tranel, 2001a).

These regions have an intriguing functional design feature. Specifically, it appears that the same association cortices used for the *perception* of information are used for the *recall* of the information, e.g. when that information is retrieved via mental imagery (e.g. Kosslyn, 1994). The basic idea is that when vivid remembering occurs—e.g. when you bring into your "mind's eye" the visual image of a highly familiar face or place, or into your "mind's ear" the auditory image of one of your favorite songs—the same cortices are utilized as are used when you perceive these stimuli from the world outside. This notion is not new (cf. James, 1893) and it has remained somewhat controversial (e.g. Farah, 1988; Goldenberg, 1998).

However, the weight of recent experimental findings points strongly to the correctness of the basic principle, e.g. in an elegant fMRI study by Wheeler et al. (2000) it was shown that the retrieval of vivid visual images activated cortices in the left ventral fusiform region that are associated with the perception of object properties, such as shape, color and texture, and bilateral dorsal regions near the precuneus that are associated with the perception of spatial properties of objects. A similar effect was obtained for the retrieval of vivid auditory images: this task activated regions near the superior temporal gyrus that are known to be involved in the perception of auditory stimuli. Wheeler et al. interpreted their findings as suggesting that the retrieval of vivid visual and auditory information can be associated with a reactivation of some of the same sensory regions that were activated during perception of that information, a conclusion that is consistent with other recent studies of this issue (e.g. D'Esposito et al., 1997; Kreiman et al., 2000a; Kosslyn et al., 1999; Zatorre et al., 1996).

Amygdala

The role of the amygdala in memory has been equivocal. Lesion studies in nonhuman primates yielded conflicting results—some studies reported that that amygdala is critical for normal learning (e.g. Mishkin, 1978), while others indicated that the amygdala does not play a critical role in learning (e.g. Murray & Gaffan, 1994; Zola-Morgan et al., 1989). Studies in humans failed to resolve this issue, as it remained unclear to what extent memory impairments could be reliably and unequivocally associated with amygdala damage (e.g. Nahm et al., 1993; Tranel & Hyman, 1990). While there is considerable circumstantial evidence that the amygdala ought to have a role in memory—e.g. the demonstration of LTP in the amygdala (Clugnet & LeDoux, 1990), its connectivity (Amaral et al., 1992) and its clear role in associative learning in nonhuman animals (e.g. Davis, 2000; Gallagher, 2000)—the literature on human subjects with amygdala damage revealed an impressive *absence* of memory impairments in most of the relevant cases (e.g. Aggleton, 1992). In short, in humans there is a remarkable paucity of convincing evidence that the amygdala plays a key role in learning and memory for conventional declarative types of knowledge.

There is, however, one theme that has received considerable empirical support in recent years, and that helps clarify the role of the amygdala in memory: specifically, the amygdala has an important role in emotional memory. This literature was accumulated first in nonhuman animals, where a large number of studies demonstrated that the amygdala is critically important for the acquisition and expression of emotional memories (Bianchin et al., 1999; Cahill & McGaugh, 1998; McGaugh et al., 1992). Moreover, the amygdala appeared to play a critical role during a narrow and highly specific time window, viz. immediately after acquisition and for a short duration of time thereafter, and these findings have been interpreted as supporting the idea that the amygdala has a specific role in consolidation processes of motivated learning that are influenced by emotional arousal (Cahill & McGaugh, 1998; McGaugh, 2000). Other studies indicated that the amygdala exerts a modulatory effect on secondary structures, including the hippocampus, that are directly involved in memory consolidation (McGaugh et al., 1996; Roozendaal et al., 1999).

Building on this background, recent studies in humans have also begun to yield convergent evidence that the amygdala plays a key role in emotional memory. These studies capitalized on a basic and robust memory effect that had been previously established in experimental psychological studies of normal individuals. Specifically, when subjects are asked to learn various types of material, there is normally a marked enhancement of recognition and recall when the material comprises highly aversive, emotionally arousing stimuli (e.g. Burke et al., 1992), an effect that fits well with naturalistic observations that memory for salient information is often enhanced by emotional arousal (Winograd & Neisser, 1992). In several case studies of subjects with bilateral amygdala damage, it has been shown that these subjects fail to demonstrate this effect of memory enhancement with aversive, highly arousing stimuli, i.e. the subjects do not remember emotionally charged stimuli any better than stimuli that are emotionally neutral (e.g. Adolphs et al., 1997; Cahill et al., 1995; Phelps et al., 1998). Convergent evidence was provided by functional imaging studies, which showed that amygdala activation at the time of stimulus acquisition correlated positively with how well those same stimuli were remembered at a later juncture, but only in those cases where the stimuli were emotionally highly arousing (Cahill et al., 1996; Hamann et al., 1999). In sum, several lines of evidence converge on the conclusion that the amygdala aids in the potentiation of memory traces for emotionally arousing stimuli during their acquisition and consolidation into long-term declarative memory.

The influence of emotion on declarative memory, and the role of the amygdala in this process, have been clarified further in other recent studies, e.g. we showed that emotionally arousing stimuli were remembered better than neutral stimuli, but only after a significant time delay (Adolphs et al., 2000). Specifically, memory performance after a 30 min delay failed to reveal any effect for emotionally arousing stimuli; after a 24 h delay, however, the effect emerged clearly, in that there was clear superiority of memory for emotional stimuli. This finding is intriguing in light of other evidence that has shown that the amygdala is especially active during REM sleep (Maquet et al., 1996), a state that may play a key role in memory consolidation (Stickgold, 1999). Also, there is an emerging picture suggesting that both the left and right amygdala participate substantially in mediating the effect of emotional arousal on memory; however, the specific contributions or mechanisms of each amygdala may differ (Adolphs et al. 2000; Cahill et al., 1996; LaBar & Phelps, 1998; Lane et al., 1997) and bilateral amygdala damage may be required to abolish the effect altogether (Adolphs et al., submitted). Finally, it should be noted that the basic theme in this literature—that the amygdala plays an important role in declarative memory when the material is emotionally charged—is quite consonant with another series of lesion studies demonstrating a key role for the amygdala in the recognition of emotional facial expressions, especially negative ones (Adolphs et al., 1994, 1995, 1996, 1999a; Calder et al., 1996; Young et al., 1996), in recognizing emotional arousal (Adolphs et al., 1999b) and in processing affective and social cues from facial expressions and other visual stimuli (Adolphs & Tranel, 1999; Adolphs et al., 1998; for review, see Adolphs & Tranel, 2000). The notion of an important role for the amygdala in processing emotion—especially unpleasant emotion—has received additional support from functional imaging studies, which have shown that visual (e.g. Breiter et al., 1996; Morris et al., 1998; Whalen et al., 1998), auditory (Phillips et al., 1998), olfactory (Zald & Pardo, 1997), and gustatory (Zald et al., 1998) stimuli all appear to engage the amygdala when signaling unpleasant and arousing emotions.

Frontal Lobes

Traditionally, the frontal lobes have not been considered to contain neuroanatomical systems essential for basic forms of memory, and it is true that many patients with frontal

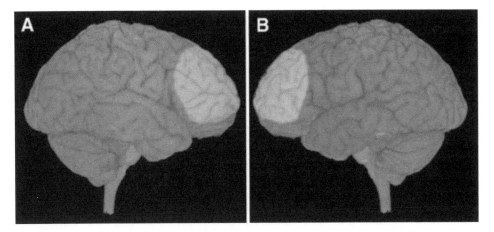

Figure 2.7   Lateral views of the left (**A**) and right (**B**) cerebral hemispheres, showing dorsolateral prefrontal regions (shaded in white) that have been associated with working memory (verbal working memory for left-hemisphere structures; spatial working memory for right-hemisphere structures) and with processes involved in encoding and retrieval

lobe damage are free of conventional memory deficits. Nonetheless, frontal lobe systems clearly play at least a secondary role in various types of memory, via their involvement in processes such as attention, encoding and problem-solving (cf. Shimamura et al., 1991). Also, a rapidly growing body of literature based largely on functional imaging procedures has now demonstrated quite compellingly that certain sectors of the frontal lobes are of primary importance for one particular type of memory, viz. *working memory*. Some of the main conclusions regarding the role of the frontal lobes in memory are reviewed below.

Dorsolateral Prefrontal Region

The dorsolateral prefrontal sector includes the expanse of cortex and attendant white matter on the convexity of the hemispheres in the frontal lobes (Figure 2.7). The dorsolateral prefrontal region plays an important role in working memory. *"Working memory"* refers to the ability to hold a limited amount of information in an active state ("on-line") for a brief period of time, and to manipulate that information (Baddeley, 1992). The amount of information that can be kept active in working memory is generally considered to comprise up to about 10 items, and the duration of working memory covers up to about 1 min of time. Working memory is used to bridge temporal gaps, i.e. to hold representations in a mental workspace long enough, so that we can make appropriate responses to stimulus configurations or contingencies in which some, or even all, of the basic ingredients are no longer extant in perceptual space. Typical everyday examples of working memory include the process of looking up a phone number and holding it "in mind" while you cross the room, pick up the phone, and dial the number; another example is the construction of a geographical "mental map" when you listen to someone give you multistep directions to a particular destination on the other side of town. Working memory is important not only as a basic memory ability (e.g. to bridge temporal gaps) but also as a fundamental building block for higher-order cognitive processes, such as reasoning, decision-making and problem solving (e.g. Jonides, 1995). Conceptually, working memory has at least some overlap with the construct of short-term (or immediate) memory, as both notions emphasize limited storage capacity and a brief duration of processing (see Chapter 1).

Although the articulation of working memory as a psychological construct has been in place for some time (cf. Baddeley, 1986), most of the earlier work regarding the neural substrates of working memory was conducted in nonhuman animals, using the well-known delayed nonmatching (or matching) to sample paradigms (for review, see Goldman-Rakic, 1992, 1995). In these studies, it was shown that dorsolateral prefrontal lesions impaired the ability of the animal to "hold" information for brief periods of time, e.g. for the moment or two during which the animal had to remember which location or which object might be associated with a food reward. Curiously, lesion studies in humans failed to make much of a contribution to this literature, and it is difficult to find compelling examples of human cases who developed profound working memory impairments in connection with dorsolateral prefrontal lesions (for some partial exceptions, see Bechara et al., 1998). In sharp contrast, functional imaging studies have generated a rich and rapidly expanding body of evidence linking working memory to dorsolateral prefrontal structures, e.g. in the recent review by Cabeza & Nyberg (2000) more than 60 such studies were summarized. We summarize here some of the main findings from this literature (for recent reviews, see D'Esposito, 2000; Smith & Jonides, 1998; Smith et al., 1998).

A typical paradigm for the investigation of working memory in functional imaging studies is the "n-back" task, in which subjects must indicate whether or not each item in a continuous stream of items matches an item that occurred one, two or n items back in the series. A specific example of this type of task is illustrated in Figure 2.8, taken from Smith et al. (1996). The investigators presented subjects a continuous stream of single letters, which appeared at random locations around an imaginary circle centered on a fixation cross. Two conditions were utilized: in the verbal memory condition (lower part of Figure 2.8), subjects were asked to decide whether or not each letter matched the letter presented three stimuli previously, i.e. "3-back" (and regardless of location). In the spatial memory condition (top part of Figure 2.8), subjects were asked ot decide whether or not the position of each letter matched the position of the letter presented three stimuli previously, again "3-back" (and regardless of letter identity).

Two main conclusions have emerged from studies of this type. First, in functional imaging studies, performance of working memory tasks consistently activates structures in the dorsolateral prefrontal cortex, including areas Brodmann 6, 44, 9, and 46. Second, there is a fairly consistent laterality effect in many of the studies: the left dorsolateral prefrontal sector is preferentially activated by verbal working memory tasks, while the right dorsolateral prefrontal sector is preferentially activated by spatial working memory tasks, e.g. in the task illustrated in Figure 2.8, Smith et al. (1996) found left-sided dorsolateral prefrontal activation in the verbal condition and right-sided dorsolateral prefrontal activation in the spatial condition. The literature also contains some hints regarding other subdivisions within the dorsolateral sector, e.g. activations in Brodmann areas 9 and 46 seem to occur most consistently with tasks that require manipulation of the contents of working memory (such as the n-back task), whereas tasks requiring simple maintenance or "holding" of information over a short time interval may be more related to areas Brodmann 6 and 44 (e.g. D'Esposito et al., 1998). Smith & Jonides (1998) and Smith et al. (1998) have discussed these and related issues at some length, and have addressed distinctions between, for example, storage and

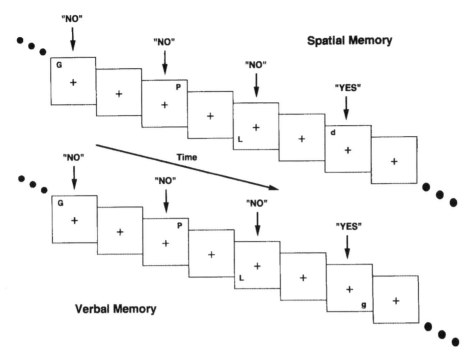

Figure 2.8 The drawing shows a typical working memory task paradigm requiring spatial (top) or verbal (bottom) processing. G, 00; P, 00; d, 00; L, 00; g, 00. Reproduced by permission from Smith et al. (1996)

rehearsal processes, and "executive" functions that are believed to regulate the processing of working memory contents (see also Prabhakaran et al., 2000).

Before leaving the topic of the dorsolateral prefrontal sector and memory, it is worth mentioning one other line of investigation that has received considerable attention in the recent literature (again, primarily from functional imaging studies), specifically, distinctions between episodic and semantic memory, and between the processes of encoding and retrieval. Different sectors of the dorsolateral prefrontal region have been associated with different aspects of these processes. For example, Tulving and colleagues (Nyberg et al., 1996, 1998; Tulving et al., 1994, 1996) have suggested that left prefrontal structures are specialized for the retrieval of general knowledge (semantic memory) and for the encoding of novel aspects of incoming information into episodic memory (specific unique events), and that right prefrontal structures are specialized for episodic memory retrieval and, in particular, for retrieval "attempts" that occur in episodic mode (as when one attempts to remember a specific, unique episode, e.g. "Where did you watch the Super Bowl last year?"). These ideas have been explored at some length in recent functional imaging studies (for review, see Cabeza & Nyberg, 2000) and have received considerable empirical support. As was the case for working memory reviewed above, lesion studies have contributed very little to this literature, perhaps as a consequence of the fact that separating the processes of encoding and retrieval using the lesion method (especially in humans) is very difficult (although this criticism has also been leveled at functional imaging studies; Rugg & Wilding, 2000). In any event, it is interesting to note that prefrontal structures in right dorsolateral sectors (e.g. areas

47, 10) that have been associated with episodic retrieval in functional imaging studies, are highly connected to right anterior temporal structures (e.g. Pandya & Yeterian, 1985) that have been implicated in lesion studies as being important for retrograde, autobiographical, unique-level knowledge, material that is very much akin to episodic memory (see section on Temporal Lobes above).

The dorsolateral prefrontal region has also been associated with the capacities of judging the *recency* and *frequency* of events (e.g. Milner et al., 1991, Smith & Milner, 1988). Conceptually, recency and frequency judgments probably share some features with the notions of working memory and episodic retrieval, which could help explain the common neuroanatomical substrate. For example, consider the following question: "When was the last time you talked to your mother on the telephone?" To arrive at an answer, which may be anywhere from a few minutes ago up to many years ago, you engage in a memory search that requires complex co-activations and associations between retrieval of various interrelated memories, especially episodic ones, and allows you to make a judgment of *recency*. A similar process occurs when one is asked to judge the *frequency* of events, e.g. "How many times was the overnight low temperature below zero last winter?". Laboratory studies have suggested some degree of hemispheric specialization for recency and frequency judgments, with the left dorsolateral prefrontal region being relatively more important for verbally-coded information and the right being relatively more important for visuospatial information, an arrangement that would be in keeping with the gist of the laterality effects associated with working memory, reviewed above. The dorsolateral prefrontal sector has also been linked to other types of "cognitive estimations" that require rough approximations rather than retrieval of rote knowledge, such as ballparking the number of swine that live in Iowa, or the number of folk singers who have recording contracts, or the number of e-mails you received during the past year (Shallice & Evans, 1978; for an exception, see Taylor & O'Carroll, 1995).

Ventromedial Prefrontal Region

The ventromedial prefrontal sector, which comprises the mesial part of the orbital cortices (parts of areas 11 and 12) and the lower mesial sector formed by parts of areas 32 and 10 (Figure 2.9), does not appear to play a significant role in conventional forms of memory, neither does it appear to be involved in working memory. In fact, patients with extensive bilateral damage to ventromedial prefrontal cortices are usually entirely free of conventional memory impairments (i.e. learning and recall are normal) and they have also been shown to have normal working memory (Bechara et al., 1998). However, the ventromedial prefrontal region plays a critical role in behavioral regulation and response selection, which depend in turn on the ability to learn and retrieve certain types of "emotional" information in connection with different types of factual knowledge. This idea, which has been termed the "somatic marker hypothesis" (Damasio, 1994; Damasio et al., 1990), has been investigated in detail with a series of studies in our laboratory (e.g. Bechara et al., 2000; Tranel et al., 2000a). The basic notion is that the ventromedial prefrontal region contains neural units which help link factual knowledge to pertinent emotions and feelings (somatic markers); specifically, learning associations between complex situations and the types of bioregulatory states associated with such situations in prior experience. In a sense, then, the ventromedial prefrontal region performs a memory function: it establishes linkages between

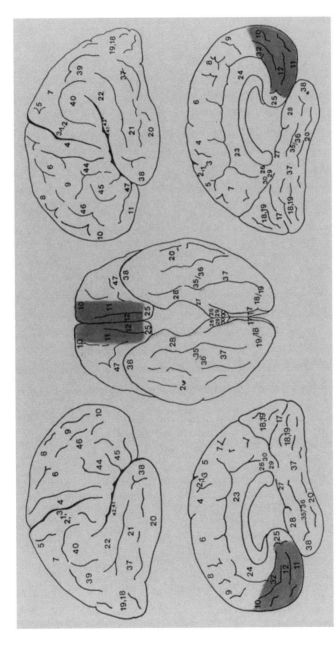

Figure 2.9 Drawings of lateral (upper right) and mesial (lower right) views of the left hemisphere; lateral (upper left) and mesial (lower left) views of the right hemisphere; and inferior view of the brain (center; left hemisphere on the right). The location of the ventromedial prefrontal region is marked in dark shading. The region is comprised by parts of areas 11, 12, 32, and 10, and it is important for higher-order memory processes that are involved in planning and decision-making, especially processes that shape learning of reward and punishment contingencies. Reproduced by permission from Tranel (1994)

dispositions for aspects of various situations (especially complex, socially-oriented ones), and dispositions for the types of emotion that, in the individual's experience, have been associated with those situations.

Our experiments have shown that these linkages are critical for advantageous decision-making and proper behavioral guidance (e.g. Bechara et al., 2000; Damasio et al., 1990; Tranel, 2001b; Tranel et al., 2000a). Damage to the ventromedial prefrontal region produces a pattern of maladaptive social behavior and poor decision-making. Patients with such damage behave as if they have no regard for the future consequences of their behavior; in fact, they may act like psychopaths. Moreover, damage to this region sustained early in life may preclude the development of normal socialization and reward/punishment sensitivity, yielding a lifelong pattern of sociopathic behavior (Anderson et al., 1999, 2001). The idea that the ventromedial prefrontal region has a special type of "memory" function has received support from other studies as well, e.g. Rolls and colleagues have advanced the idea that the orbitofrontal region contains representations of primary reinforcers from different sensory modalities (touch, taste, smell), which help shape learning of reward and punishment contingencies (Francis et al., 1999). Rolls (2000) has suggested that the orbitofrontal cortex is crucial for learning associations between various stimuli and these primary reinforcers, and for controlling and modifying reward- and punishment-related behavior in response to such associations. Relatedly, neurophysiology studies have shown that neurons in the orbitofrontal cortex are especially sensitive to motivational aspects of response outcome expectancies (Hikosaka & Watanabe, 2000; Watanabe, 1998). This is compatible with our idea that the ventromedial prefrontal cortices are important for the integration of cognitive and motivational information for the purposes of goal-directed behavior.

Basal Forebrain

Situated immediately behind the posterior extent of the ventral frontal lobes is a hetero-geneous set of structures that collectively form what is known as the *basal forebrain*. The nucleus accumbens, septum, diagonal band nuclei and substantia innominata are the key components of this region. These basal forebrain nuclei contain many cholinergic neurons which innervate large sectors of the cerebral cortex. Also, a number of important fiber path-ways, including the fornix, stria terminalis, diagonal band of Broca, medial forebrain bundle and ventral amygdalofugal pathway, traverse the basal forebrain *en route* to the cerebral cortex and deliver monoamines to varied cortical regions. Thus, a critical function of the basal forebrain is to provide neurotransmitters such as acetylcholine to the hippocampus and many regions of the cerebral cortex (Everitt & Robbins, 1997; Sarter & Bruno, 1997) and dopamine, norepinephrine, and serotonin to various parts of the cerebral cortex. When deliv-ery of these neurotransmitters is disrupted by basal forebrain damage, memory is frequently impaired. The basal forebrain is very difficult to image with functional imaging approaches such as PET and fMRI; hence, most of what is known about the role of the basal forebrain in memory has been derived from lesion studies (see Tranel et al., 2000b, for review).

The amnesia typical of patients with basal forebrain dysfunction has a number of intrigu-ing features:

1. Patients are able to learn separate modal stimuli, but cannot learn properly the relation-ships and integrations of those stimuli.

2. Relatedly, patients cannot develop a time-tag for the separate stimuli they learn; i.e. they fail to learn the temporal relationship between a particular stimulus and other related information.
3. The patients confabulate freely, and this occurs spontaneously, rather than in response to a need to "fill in" gaps when questioning leads to obvious memory problems.
4. Cuing is helpful in facilitating recall and recognition, for both anterograde and retrograde memories.

We have proposed that the amnesia of basal forebrain patients is, in part, a consequence of dysfunction in mesial temporal lobe structures such as the hippocampus proper, amygdala and parahippocampal gyrus, caused by the basal forebrain lesion. For example, the disruption of delivery of acetylcholine and perhaps other neurotransmitters to the hippocampus and other regions of the cerebral cortex might provide the mechanism whereby patients can continue to learn modal pieces of information, but not the temporal relationships of those items (Tranel et al., 2000b).

In sum, a key role of the basal forebrain is to support neural processes by which temporal and spatial linkages, crucial in the process of acquiring and retrieving knowledge that must be bound together in time and space in order to form accurate "episodes", are developed. The key anatomical correlate in the confabulation typical of basal forebrain patients may be damage to the septal nuclei, diagonal band nuclei, medial parts of the substantia innominata, or nucleus accumbens (see Goldenberg et al., 1999). Projection pathways, such as the precommissural fornix, medial forebrain bundle, diagonal band of Broca and ventroamygdalofugal tract may also be damaged. Most of the basic "memory-making" structures, including the mesial temporal region, the dorsolateral, anterior and nonspecific midline thalamic nuclei, and the dorsolateral prefrontal cortices, are structurally intact in basal forebrain patients, which could explain why the patients can continue to learn modal pieces of information. In sum, the key deficit in basal forebrain amnesia appears to involve a deprivation of cholinergic innervation to the hippocampus and cerebral cortex and, in addition, interruption of cortically-bound projections of such neurotransmitters as norepinephrine, dopamine and serotonin.

Basal Ganglia

The basal ganglia are a set of grey-matter nuclei that include the caudate nucleus, putamen, globus pallidus and subthalamic nucleus. The basal ganglia have been linked to various forms of *nondeclarative* memory, particularly "procedural" types of memory that depend on a motor act for their realization, e.g. riding a bicycle, skating, skiing. One recent proposal is that the basal ganglia have learning and memory functions that derive from their influence on motor and cognitive pattern generators (Graybiel, 1998). In the lesion literature, much of the evidence for this conclusion is indirect, and derives from the well-replicated finding that patients with damage to memory systems in the mesial temporal lobe (the hippocampus and related structures) often show remarkable sparing of nondeclarative memory (as reviewed earlier). Since the basal ganglia are typically intact in such patients, these findings have been interpreted as consistent with the idea that the basal ganglia play a role in nondeclarative memory. More direct evidence has been furnished in studies that demonstrate impairments of the learning and retrieval of nondeclarative forms of memory in patients with basal ganglia dysfunction, such as patients with Parkinson's or Huntington's disease (e.g. Heindel et al., 1989; Koenig et al., 1999). Also, it has been shown that procedural learning is impaired by neostriatal lesions (e.g. Saint-Cyr & Taylor, 1988).

The caudate nucleus, which together with the putamen forms the *striatal* component of the basal ganglia, may be particulary important for a type of nondeclarative memory that has to do with the development of habits and other "nonconscious" response tendencies. The tendencies we develop to respond to certain situations in certain ways, behaviors such as following the same route home each day, or repeatedly seeking out a particular person for moral support and encouragement, are examples of habits and response tendencies that we engage on a fairly automatic basis, with little or no conscious deliberation. It has been shown that damage to the caudate nucleus can impair habit learning in experimental animals (e.g. Packard et al., 1989) and humans (e.g. Knowlton et al., 1996; for review, see White, 1997). Evidence consistent with these findings comes from a study we conducted in patient Boswell, in which we demonstrated that, despite his profound amnesia for declarative knowledge, Boswell could learn to discriminate between individuals who had treated him kindly in the past vs. those who had not, as evidenced by his tendency to approach or to avoid such individuals, even though he had no conscious knowledge of who those individuals were (Tranel & Damasio, 1993). In a detailed empirical study of this phenomenon, we reasoned that Boswell's preserved—albeit non-conscious—ability to learn "good guys" from "bad guys" may rely on intact caudate function (Tranel & Damasio, 1993). This finding is especially interesting in light of new neurophysiological evidence that has suggested that the caudate nucleus plays a role in connecting motivational values to sensory (e.g. visual) stimuli (Kawagoe et al., 1998).

Cerebellum

The cerebellum, along with the basal ganglia, has been shown to participate in various forms of procedural learning and memory (e.g. Glickstein, 1993; Thompson, 1986, 1990). In fact, studies using the eyeblink conditioning paradigm in experimental animals have provided compelling evidence that the cerebellum and related brainstem circuitry contain the essential memory traces that are formed during classical conditioning (e.g. Thompson & Krupa, 1994; Thompson et al., 1998). This effect has also been found in humans, in whom it has been shown that cerebellar lesions abolish delay eyeblink conditioning (Daum et al., 1993), and more recently, functional imaging studies have provided convergent evidence (Gabrieli et al., 1998; Kawashima et al., 1995). The cerebellum is also known to have a role in learning movement coordination (Thach, 1998).

Thalamus

Some structures in the diencephalon also play an important role in memory. In particular, the dorsolateral and anterior nuclei of the thalamus, the mammillary bodies, and two related fiber tracts—the mammillothalamic tract, which connects the mesial hippocampal complex to the anterior nuclei of the thalamus, and the ventroamygdalofugal pathway, which connects the amygdala to the dorsomedial thalamic nuclei—have been linked to memory. In general, these structures appear to support memory capacities in a way that supplements the mesial temporal system (Butters & Stuss, 1989), in particular, by providing important contributions to the acquisition of factual knowledge (declarative memory). In fact, damage to these structures can produce a severe anterograde amnesia that resembles the amnesia associated with mesial temporal damage. Characteristically, there is a major defect in the acquisition of *declarative* knowledge, with sparing of learning of *non-declarative* information. However, more so than with the amnesia associated with mesial temporal lesions, diencephalic amnesia may involve the retrograde compartment as well. The retrograde amnesia tends to have a temporal gradient—retrieval of memories acquired closer in time to the onset of the lesion is more severely affected, while retrieval of more remote memories is better preserved (although there is considerable variability in this pattern across various cases and studies). Severe alcoholism (Butters & Stuss, 1989) and stroke (Graff-Radford et al., 1990) are two frequent causes of damage to the diencephalon. The amnesia that develops after prolonged alcoholism is part of a distinctive condition known as Wernicke–Korsakoff syndrome, which has been extensively studied from both neuroanatomical and neuropsychological perspectives (e.g. Victor et al., 1989).

Anterior parts of the thalamus may make important contributions to the temporal sequencing of memories, i.e. situating memories in correct temporal context. Also, the thalamus appears to have material-specific functions that parallel those of the mesial temporal memory system: left-sided thalamic nuclei are specialized for verbal information and right-sided nuclei are specialized for nonverbal, visuospatial material. The diencephalon gives rise to a number of important neurochemical systems that innervate widespread regions of cerebral cortex. Thus, structures such as the mammillary bodies and certain thalamic nuclei may provide to the cortex important neurotransmitters that are needed for normal memory function. It follows that damage to the diencephalon may disrupt not only important neuroanatomical connections between limbic regions (including the hippocampal complex) and the neocortex, but also memory-related neurochemical influences on the cortex. There is also evidence from a recent case study that damage to the mammillary bodies alone can produce memory impairment (Tanaka et al., 1997).

A THEORETICAL FRAMEWORK

The neurobiological foundations of memory at systems level can be understood in the context of a theoretical framework presented in prior publications (Damasio, 1989a, 1989b; Damasio & Damasio, 1993, 1994). The framework posits an *image space* and a *dispositional space*. The image space is made up of mental images of all sensory types (e.g. visual, auditory, somatosensory). Some of those images constitute the manifest mental contents that we experience consciously, and others remain nonconscious. The dispositional space is that in which dispositions contain the knowledge base and the mechanisms with which (a) images can be constructed from recall, (b) movements can be generated, and (c) the processing of images can be facilitated. The contents of the dispositional space are implicit, i.e. they are nonconscious and exist in latent form. The engagement of dispositions can produce a wide variety of outcomes, e.g. they hold records for an image that was actually perceived on a previous occasion, and they participate in the attempt to reconstruct a similar image from memory. In this view, all of our memory, including that which is inherited from evolution and available at birth and that acquired through learning thereafter, exists in dispositional form (implicitly, covertly, nonconsciously), with the potential to become an explicit image or action. Dispositions, though, are *not* words; they are abstract records of potentialities. Words, which can signify entities, events and relationships, and the rules with which we put words together, also exist as dispositions, and become expressed as images and actions, e.g. as in speech.

The bridge between the notions of mental and dispositional space and the brain is as follows. The areas of cerebral cortex located in and around the cortical arrival points of visual, auditory and other sensory signals (the early sensory cortices), as well as parts of limbic structures and some noncortical structures, support explicit neural patterns. These neural patterns of maps continuously change under the influence of internal and external inputs, and are likely to be the bases for images. Dispositions are held in higher-order cortices, parts of the limbic cortices, and numerous subcortical nuclei (e.g. amygdala, brainstem nuclei). When disposition circuits are activated, they signal to other circuits and cause images or actions to be generated from elsewhere in the brain. The framework proposes that dispositions are held in neuron ensembles called *convergence zones*. To the partition between an image space and a dispositional space, then, corresponds a partition in (a) explicit neural pattern maps, activated in early sensory cortices, in limbic cortices, and in some subcortical nuclei; and in (b) convergence zones, located in higher-order cortices and in some subcortical nuclei.

When we evoke the concept of a concrete entity, we activate sensory and motor patterns in cerebral cortices appropriate to represent pertinent features (e.g. shape, color, sound, motion) of the concept. These patterns are generated from dispositions contained in convergence zones. We assume that on different occasions, different combinations of features might be retrieved at different levels of strength and with different degrees of automaticity, depending on prevailing situational and autobiographical factors. We also believe that the anatomical placement of convergence zones is suited for the most efficient interaction with the cortical regions that contain the relevant dispositions, and with sensory cortices where the dispositions can be reactivated. The placement of convergence zones is due primarily to biological evolution, is transmitted genomically and is secondarily shaped by learning, thus affording considerable individual neuroanatomical and neurophysiological differences.

Convergence zones operate as *intermediary* (or *mediational*) systems for both concept retrieval and word retrieval. To illustrate, consider first an example of concept retrieval: when a stimulus depicting a given tool is shown to a subject and the visual properties of that stimulus are processed, a particular intermediary region becomes active and promotes the explicit sensorimotor representation of knowledge pertaining to that tool, which occurs in the appropriate early sensory cortices and motor structures. The evocation of some part of the potentially large number of such images, over a brief lapse of time and in varied sensorimotor cortices, constitutes the conceptual evocation for the tool. When a concept from another category is evoked, say that of an animal or of a person, different intermediary regions are engaged.

The intermediary systems process *preferentially* certain physical characteristics, features and contexts of entities, and because entities within a given conceptual category tend to share more of those characteristics and features than entities outside of it (Humphreys et al., 1997; Tranel et al., 1997c), lesions at a particular site are more likely to impair the recognition of stimuli from that category, rather than another. This account also explains why certain neural regions are preferentially activated by stimuli from certain conceptual categories in functional imaging studies (for review, see Martin et al., 2000a) and why there might even be category specificity at the single neuron level (Kreiman et al., 2000b).

The same design applies to word retrieval. When a subject is shown a picture of a tool and asked to name it, the processing will activate an appropriate "concept" intermediary region—which will promote concept retrieval as outlined above—and in turn, the concept intermediary region will activate the corresponding "word" intermediary, which will promote the retrieval of lexical knowledge (e.g. the phoneme structures of the appropriate morphemes) required for word production. Thus, word-form production (including retrieval of linguistic knowledge) is dependent on three kinds of neural structures: (a) structures that support conceptual knowledge; (b) structures that support the implementation of word-forms in eventual vocalization (the classical language areas located in the left perisylvian region, including Broca's area); and (c) word intermediary structures, which are partially separable from the other two kinds of structures, and which are engaged by the structures in (a) to trigger and guide the implementation process executed in (b). Word intermediary structures are located outside the classical language-related areas; examples include, for the case of concrete entities, areas in inferotemporal (IT) and temporopolar (TP) cortices. We note that this neural account has a counterpart in some cognitive linguistic models, which include the notion of an intermediary unit (termed "lemma") interposed between "semantics" (conceptual knowledge) and output phonology (e.g. Gordon, 1997; Levelt et al., 1999).

The architecture we propose is *not* constituted by rigid "centers" and "pathways", but rather by flexible neuron ensembles interconnected by flexible bidirectional pathways. The operation of this neural architecture is probability-driven and depends on the circumstances of the organism, e.g. the demands of a given task and the experimental conditions of a given subject. The ensembles and pathways hypothesized to comprise this architecture are seen as "preferred systems" rather than as "single-and-only" systems, i.e. we presume that certain systems support the most efficient, effective and complete version of a certain performance, but we imagine that there are other systems that can support parts of the performance, albeit not necessarily as efficiently.

The available evidence suggests the existence of multiple functional systems operating to hold records of, and support retrieval of, concepts and words. The systems have some separable neuroanatomical components, segregated by both evolutionary and individual learning selections. Nonetheless, some components may be shared or be so anatomically close as to make experimental separation difficult or impossible. So far, the available evidence suggests that there is a preferred system, involving ventral occipitotemporal cortices bilaterally and anterolateral temporal cortices on the right, that excels at supporting conceptual knowledge for concrete entities such as persons and animals. A different preferred system, located at the left temporal-occipital-parietal junction, excels at supporting conceptual knowledge for concrete entities such as tools.

There is also evidence for systems involved in the retrieval of words denoting concrete entities, all of which are located in left hemisphere. In regard to tools, the system is located in the vicinity of the system related to concept retrieval, and whether or not these regions are one and the same, or closely contiguous, is an open question. For persons and animals, the preferred systems for word retrieval include the left temporal polar and anterior inferotemporal regions, respectively. Finally, there is preliminary evidence that there is another preferred system, comprising networks in the dorsal component of temporo-occipital and parietal cortices and the ventrolateral premotor/prefrontal region, that excels at processing concepts of actions and spatial relationships and their corresponding words (Damasio et al., in press; Tranel et al., in press); again, whether there are neuroanatomically separable subparts for concepts and for words remains an open question.

In conclusion, the retrieval of words denoting concrete entities would occur when intermediaries for concepts trigger intermediaries for words, which leads, in turn, to the activation of sensory and motor cortices of the acoustic, kinesthetic and motor patterns necessary to experience the words mentally, and implement them vocally or in written form. Both the concept and the word components of the overall system operate on the basis of intermediaries. Concept intermediaries can activate word intermediaries, and vice versa. Intermediaries also interact bidirectionally with sensory and motor cortices. An auditory sensory pattern can thus engage a word intermediary and, in turn, engage a concept intermediary and link to concept evocation in the appropriate sensory and/or motor cortices.

CONCLUDING COMMENTS

Detailed neuropsychological and neuroanatomical investigations of brain-damaged patients, and more recently, functional imaging studies, have progressively both expanded and refined the roster of cortical and subcortical structures that are critical for learning and memory. As far as declarative knowledge is concerned, the roster includes at cortical level the early association cortices, the higher-order association cortices of the temporal, frontal and occipital regions, and the limbic-related cortices of the temporal lobe (entorhinal cortex, Brodmann area 38, and the posterior parahippocampal gyrus). At subcortical level, the roster includes the hippocampus proper, the amygdala, the basal forebrain nuclei and projection systems, the thalamus and hypothalamus, and neurotransmitter nuclei in the brainstem. Also, the evidence suggests that structures critical for the learning and memory of nondeclarative knowledge include the primary somatomotor cortices, the neostriatum, some thalamic nuclei and the cerebellum. Lesion and functional imaging studies have paved the way for the development of detailed theoretical accounts in which the contents and processes of memory can be related to specific neural systems (e.g. Cohen & Eichenbaum, 1993; Damasio, 1989a, b; Edelman, 1987; Fuster, 1995; Kosslyn & Koenig, 1995; Squire, 1987).

ACKNOWLEDGEMENT

This study was supported by a grant from the National Institute for Neurological Diseases and Stroke (Program Project Grant NS 19632). We thank Dr Ralph Adolphs for generous and patient assistance with the figures and Ellen Steffensmeier for help with the bibliography.

REFERENCES

Adolphs, R., Cahill, L., Schul, R. & Babinsky, R. (1997). Impaired declarative memory for emotional material following bilateral amygdala damage in humans. *Learning and Memory*, **4**, 291–300.
Adolphs, R., Damasio, H., Tranel, D. & Damasio, A.R. (1996). Cortical systems for the recognition of emotion in facial expressions. *Journal of Neuroscience*, **16**, 7678–7687.
Adolphs, R., Denburg, N.L. & Tranel, D. The amygdala's role in long-term declarative memory for gist and detail. *Behavioral Neuroscience* (submitted).
Adolphs, R., Russell, J.A. & Tranel, D. (1999b). A role for the human amygdala in recognizing emotional arousal from unpleasant stimuli. *Psychological Science*, **10**, 167–171.

Adolphs, R. & Tranel, D. (1999). Preferences for visual stimuli following amygdala damage. *Journal of Cognitive Neuroscience*, **11**, 610–616.

Adolphs, R. & Tranel, D. (2000). The amygdala and processing of facial emotional expressions. In J. Aggleton (ed.), *The Amygdala*, 2nd edn. New York: Wiley-Liss (in press).

Adolphs, R., Tranel, D. & Damasio, A.R. (1998). The human amygdala in social judgment. *Nature*, **393**, 470–474.

Adolphs, R., Tranel, D., Damasio, H. & Damasio, A.R. (1994). Impaired recognition of emotion in facial expressions following bilateral damage to the human amygdala. *Nature*, **372**, 669–672.

Adolphs, R., Tranel, D., Damasio, H. & Damasio, A.R. (1995). Fear and the human amygdala. *Journal of Neuroscience*, **15**, 5879–5891.

Adolphs, R., Tranel, D. & Denburg, N. (2000). Impaired emotional declarative memory following unilateral amygdala damage. *Learning and Memory*, **7**, 180–186.

Adolphs, R., Tranel., Hamann, S. *et al.* (1999a). Recognition of facial emotion in nine individuals with bilateral amygdala damage. *Neuropsychologia*, **37**, 1111–1117.

Aggleton, J.P. (1992). The functional effects of amygdala lesions in humans: a comparison with findings from monkeys. In J.P. Aggleton (ed.), *The Amygdala: Neurobiological Aspects of Emotion, Memory, and Mental Dysfunction* (pp. 485–503). New York: Wiley-Liss.

Alvarez, P. & Squire, L.R. (1994). Memory consolidation and the medial temporal lobe: a simple network model. *Proceedings of the National Academy of Sciences*, **91**, 7041–7045.

Amaral, D.G., Price, J.L., Pitkänen, A. & Carmichael, S.T. (1992). Anatomical organization of the primate amygdaloid complex. In J.P. Aggleton (ed.), *The Amygdala: Neurobiological Aspects of Emotion, Memory, and Mental Dysfunction* (pp. 1–66). New York: Wiley-Liss.

Anderson, S.W., Bechara, A., Damasio, H., Tranel, D. & Damasio, A.R. (1999). Impairment of social and moral behavior related to early damage in the human prefrontal cortex. *Nature Neuroscience*, **2**, 1032–1037.

Anderson, S.W., Damasio, H., Tranel, D. & Damasio, A.R. (2001). Severe long-term sequelae of prefrontal cortex damage acquired in early childhood. *Developmental Neuropsychology* (in press).

Bachevalier, J. & Meunier, M. (1996). Cerebral ischemia: are the memory deficits associated with hippocampal cell loss? *Hippocampus*, **6**, 553–560.

Baddeley, A.D. (1986). *Working Memory*. New York: Oxford University Press.

Baddeley, A.D. (1992). Working memory. *Science*, **255**, 566–569.

Bailey, C.H. & Chen, M.C. (1983). Morphological basis of long-term habituation and sensitization in *Aplysia*. *Science*, **220**, 91–93.

Barrash, J., Damasio, H., Adolphs, R. & Tranel, D. (2000). The neuroanatomical correlates of route learning impairment. *Neuropsychologia*, **38**, 820–836.

Bechara, A., Damasio, H., Tranel, D. & Anderson, S.W. (1998). Dissociation of working memory from decision making within the human prefrontal cortex. *Journal of Neuroscience*, **18**, 428–437.

Bechara, A., Tranel, D. & Damasio, H. (2000). Characterization of the decision-making deficit of patients with ventromedial prefrontal cortex lesions. *Brain*, **123**, 2189–2202.

Bianchin, M., Mello e Souza, T., Medina, J.H. & Izquierdo, I. (1999). The amygdala is involved in the modulation of long-term memory, but not in working or short-term memory. *Neurobiology of Learning and Memory*, **71**, 127–131.

Bliss, T.V.P. & Lomo, T. (1973). Long-lasting potentiation of synaptic transmission in the dentate area of the anesthetized rabbit following stimulation of the perforant path. *Journal of Physiology (London)*, **232**, 331–356.

Breiter, H.C., Etcoff, N.L., Whalen, P.J. et al. (1996). Response and habituation of the human amygdala during visual processing of facial expression. *Neuron*, **17**, 875–887.

Brewer, J.B., Zhao, Z., Glover, G.H. & Gabrieli, J.D.E. (1998). Making memories: brain activity that predicts whether visual experiences will be remembered or forgotten. *Science*, **281**, 1185–1187.

Burke, A., Heuter, F. & Reisberg, D. (1992). Remembering emotional events. *Memory and Cognition*, **20**, 277–290.

Butters, N. & Stuss, D.T. (1989). Diencephalic amnesia. In F. Boller & J. Grafman (eds), *Handbook of Neuropsychology*, Vol. 3 (pp. 107–148). Amsterdam: Elsevier.

Cabeza, R. & Nyberg, L. (2000). Imaging cognition II: an empirical review of 275 PET and fMRI studies. *Journal of Cognitive Neuroscience*, **12**, 1–47.

Cahill, L., Babinsky, R., Markowitsch, H.J. & McGaugh, J.L. (1995). The amygdala and emotional memory. *Nature*, **377**, 295–296.

Cahill, L., Haier, R.J., Fallon, J. et al. (1996). Amygdala activity at encoding correlated with long-term, free recall of emotional information. *Proceedings of the National Academy of Sciences of the USA*, **93**, 8016–8021.

Cahill, L. & McGaugh, J.L. (1998). Mechanisms of emotional arousal and lasting declarative memory. *Trends in Neurosciences*, **21**, 294–299.

Calabrese, P., Markowitsch, H.J., Durwen, H.F. et al. (1996). Right temporofrontal cortex as a critical locus for the ecphory of old episodic memories. *Journal of Neurology, Neurosurgery and Psychiatry*, **61**, 304–310.

Calder, A.J., Young, A.W., Rowland, D. et al. (1996). Facial emotion recognition after bilateral amygdala damage: differentially severe impairment of fear. *Cognitive Neuropsychology*, **13**, 699–745.

Caramazza, A. (2000). The organization of conceptual knowledge in the brain. In M.S. Gazzaniga (ed.), *The New Cognitive Neurosciences*, 2nd edn (pp. 1037–1046). Cambridge, MA: MIT Press.

Castellucci, V.F. & Kandel, E.R. (1974). A quantal analysis of the synaptic depression underlying habituation of the gill-withdrawal reflex in *Aplysia*. *Proceedings of the National Academy of Sciences*, **71**, 5004–5008.

Cavanagh, P., Henaff, M.-A., Michel, F. et al. (1998). Complete sparing of high-contrast color input to motion perception in cortical color blindness. *Nature Neuroscience*, **1**, 242–247.

Chao, L.L. & Martin, A. (1999). Cortical regions associated with perceiving, naming, and knowing about colors. *Journal of Cognitive Neuroscience*, **11**, 25–35.

Chen, C. & Tonegawa, S. (1997). Molecular genetic analysis of synaptic plasticity, activity-dependent neural development, learning, and memory in the mammalian brain. *Annual Review of Neuroscience*, **20**, 157–184.

Clark, V.P., Parasuraman, R., Keil, K. et al. (1997). Selective attention to face identity and color studied with fMRI. *Human Brain Mapping*, **5**, 293–297.

Clugnet, M.C. & LeDoux, J.E. (1990). Synaptic plasticity in fear conditioning circuits—induction of LTP in the lateral amygdala by stimulation of the medial geniculate body. *Journal of Neuroscience*, **10**, 2818–2824.

Cohen, N.J. & Eichenbaum, H. (1993). *Memory, Amnesia, and the Hippocampal System*. Cambridge, MA: MIT Press.

Cohen, N.J. & Squire, L.R. (1980). Preserved learning and retention of pattern-analyzing skill in amnesia: dissociation of knowing how and knowing that. *Science*, **110**, 207–210.

Corkin, S. (1984). Lasting consequences of bilateral medial temporal lobectomy: clinical course and experimental findings in HM. *Seminars in Neurology*, **4**, 249–259.

Corkin, S., Amaral, D.G., Johnson, K.A. & Hyman, B.T. (1997). HM's MRI scan shows sparing of the posterior half of the hippocampus and parahippocampal gyrus. *Journal of Neuroscience*, **17**, 3964–3979.

Damasio, A.R. (1989a). Time-locked multiregional retroactivation: a systems-level proposal for the neural substrates of recall and recognition. *Cognition*, **33**, 25–62.

Damasio, A.R. (1989b). The brain binds entities and events by multiregional activation from convergence zones. *Neural Computation*, **1**, 123–132.

Damasio, A.R. (1994). *Descartes' Error: Emotion, Reason and the Human Brain*. New York: Grosset/Putnam.

Damasio, A.R. & Damasio, H. (1993). Cortical systems underlying knowledge retrieval: evidence from human lesion studies. In T.A. Poggio & D.A. Glaser (eds), *Exploring Brain Functions: Models in Neuroscience* (pp. 233–248). New York: Wiley.

Damasio, A.R. & Damasio, H. (1994). Cortical systems for retrieval of concrete knowledge: the convergence zone framework. In C. Koch (ed.), *Large-scale Neuronal Theories of the Brain* (pp. 61–74). Cambridge, MA: MIT Press.

Damasio, A.R., Eslinger, P., Damasio, H., Van Hoesen, G.W. & Cornell, S. (1985). Multimodal amnesic syndrome following bilateral temporal and basal forebrain damage. *Archives of Neurology*, **42**, 252–259.

Damasio, A.R., Tranel, D. & Damasio, H. (1989). Amnesia caused by herpes simplex encephalitis, infarctions in basal forebrain, Alzheimer's disease, and anoxia. In F. Boller, & J. Grafman (eds), *Handbook of Neuropsychology*, Vol. 3 (pp. 149–166). Amsterdam: Elsevier.

Damasio, A.R., Tranel, D. & Damasio, H. (1990). Individuals with sociopathic behavior caused by frontal damage fail to respond autonomically to social stimuli. *Behavioural Brain Research*, **41**, 81–94.

Damasio, H. & Damasio, A.R. (1989). *Lesion Analysis in Neuropsychology*. New York: Oxford University Press.

Damasio, H. & Damasio, A.R. (1997). The lesion method in behavioral neurology and neuropsychology. In Feinberg, T.E. & Farah, M.J. (eds), *Behavioral Neurology and Neuropsychology* (pp. 69–82). New York: McGraw-Hill.

Damasio, H., Grabowski, T.J., Tranel, D., Hichwa, R. & Damasio, A. (1996). A neural basis for lexical retrieval. *Nature*, **380**, 499–505.

Damasio, H., Grabowski, T.J., Tranel, D. et al. (in press). Neural correlates of naming actions and of naming spatial relations. *NeuroImage*.

Daum, I., Schugens, M.M., Ackermann, H. et al. (1993). Classical conditioning after cerebellar lesions in humans. *Behavioral Neuroscience*, **107**, 748–756.

Davis, M. (2000). The role of the amygdala in conditioned and unconditioned fear and anxiety. In J.P. Aggleton (ed.), *The Amygdala: A Functional Analysis* (pp. 213–287). New York: Oxford University Press.

D'Esposito, M. (2000). Functional neuroimaging of working memory. In R. Cabeza & A. Kingstone (eds), *Handbook of Functional Neuroimaging of Cognition*. (pp. 293–327). Cambridge, MA: MIT Press.

D'Esposito, M., Aguirre, G.K., Zarahn, E. et al. (1998). Functional MRI studies of spatial and non-spatial working memory. *Cognitive Brain Research*, **7**, 1–13.

D'Esposito, M., Detre, J.A., Aguirre, G.K. et al. (1997). A functional MRI study of mental image generation. *Neuropsychologia*, **35**, 725–730.

Dudai, Y. (1988). Neurogenetic dissection of learning and short-term memory in *Drosophila*. *Annual Review of Neuroscience*, **11**, 537–563.

Duvernoy, H.M. (1988). *The Human Hippocampus: An Atlas of Applied Anatomy*. Munich: J.F. Bergmann Verlag.

Edelman, G. (1987). *Neural Darwinism*. New York: Basic Books.

Eichenbaum, H., Otto, T. & Cohen, N. (1992). The hippocampus: what does it do? *Behavioral Neural Biology*, **57**, 2–36.

Everitt, B.J. & Robbins, T.W. (1997). Central cholinergic systems and cognition. *Annual Review of Psychology*, **48**, 649–684.

Farah, M.J. (1988). Is visual imagery really visual? Overlooked evidence from neuropsychology. *Psychological Review*, **95**, 307–317.

Fletcher, P.C., Frith, C.D. & Rugg, M.D. (1997). The functional neuroanatomy of episodic memory. *Trends in Neurosciences*, **20**, 213–218.

Forde, E.M.E. & Humphreys, G.W. (1999). Category-specific recognition impairments: a review of important case studies and influential theories. *Aphasiology*, **13**, 169–193.

Francis, S., Rolls, E.T., Bowtell, R. et al. (1999). The representation of pleasant touch in the brain and its relationship with taste and olfactory areas. *NeuroReport*, **10**, 453–459.

Frank, R.J., Damasio, H. & Grabowski, T.J. (1997). Brainvox: an interactive, multimodal, visualization and analysis system for neuroanatomical imaging. *NeuroImage*, **5**, 13–30.

Fuster, J.M. (1995). *Memory in the Cerebral Cortex*. Cambridge, MA: MIT Press.

Gabrieli, J.D.E., Brewer, J.B. & Poldrack, R.A. (1998). Images of medial temporal lobe functions in human learning and memory. *Neurobiology of Learning and Memory*, **70**, 275–283.

Gabrieli, J.D.E., Corkin, S., Mickel, S.F. & Growden, J.H. (1993). Intact acquisition and long-term retention of mirror-tracing skill in Alzheimer's disease and in global amnesia. *Behavioral Neuroscience*, **107**, 899–910.

Gainotti, G., Silveri, M.C., Daniele, A. & Giustolisi, L. (1995). Neuroanatomical correlates of category-specific semantic disorders: a critical survey. *Memory*, **3**, 247–264.

Gallagher, M. (2000). The amygdala and associative learning. In J.P. Aggleton (ed.), *The Amygdala: A Functional Analysis* (pp. 311–329). New York: Oxford University Press.

Glickstein, M. (1993). Cerebellar function in normal movement and in motor learning. In P. Andersen, O. Hvalby, O. Paulsen & B. Hokfelt (eds), *Memory Concepts—1993* (pp. 127–135). Amsterdam: Elsevier.

Gluhbegovic, N. & Williams, T.H. (1980). *The Human Brain: A Photographic Guide*. New York: Harper & Row.

Goldenberg, G. (1998). Is there a common substrate for visual recognition and visual imagery? *Neurocase*, **4**, 141–147.

Goldenberg, G., Schuri, U., Gromminger, O. & Arnold, U. (1999). Basal forebrain amnesia: does the nucleus accumbens contribute to human memory? *Journal of Neurology, Neurosurgery & Psychiatry*, **67**, 163–168.

Goldman-Rakic, P.S. (1992). Working memory and the mind. *Scientific American*, **267**, 111–117.

Goldman-Rakic, P.S. (1995). Architecture of the prefrontal cortex and the central executive. In Grafman, J., Holyoak, K. & Boller, F. (eds), *Structure and Functions of the Human Prefrontal Cortex* (pp. 71–83). New York: New York Academy of Sciences.

Gooding, P.A., Mayes, A.R. & van Eijk, R. (2000). A meta-analysis of indirect memory tests for novel material in organic amnesics. *Neuropsychologia*, **39**, 666–676.

Gordon, B. (1997). Models of naming. In H. Goodglass & A. Wingfield (eds), *Anomia: Neuroanatomical and Cognitive Correlates* (pp. 31–64). New York: Academic Press.

Grabowski, T.J., Damasio, H., Tranel, D. et al. A role for left temporal pole in the retrieval of words for unique entities. *Journal of Neuroscience* (submitted).

Grady, C.L., McIntosh, A.R., Rajah, M.N. & Craik, F.L. (1998). Neural correlates of the episodic encoding of pictures and words. *Proceedings of the National Academy of Sciences of the USA*, **95**, 2703–2708.

Graff-Radford, N.R., Tranel, D., Van Hoesen, G.W. & Brandt, J.P. (1990). Diencephalic amnesia. *Brain*, **113**, 1–25.

Graybiel, A.M. (1998). The basal ganglia and chunking of action repertoires. *Neurobiology of Learning and Memory*, **70**, 119–136.

Hamann, S.B., Ely, T.D., Grafton, S.T. & Kilts, C.D. (1999). Amygdala activity related to enhanced memory for pleasant and aversive stimuli. *Nature Neuroscience*, **2**, 289–293.

Hawkins, R.D., Abrams, T.W., Carew, T.J. & Kandel, E.R. (1983). A cellular mechanism of classical conditioning in *Aplysia*: activity-dependent amplification of presynaptic facilitation. *Science*, **219**, 400–405.

Hawkins, R.D., Son, H. & Arancio, O. (1998). Nitric oxide as a retrograde messenger during long-term potentiation in hippocampus. In R.R. Mize, T.M. Dawson, V.L. Dawson & M.J. Friedlander (eds), *Progress in Brain Research*, Vol. 118 (pp. 155–172). Amsterdam: Elsevier.

Hebb, D.O. (1949). *Organization of Behavior*. New York: Wiley.

Heindel, W.C., Salmon, D.P., Shults, C.W. et al. (1989). Neuropsychological evidence for multiple implicit memory systems: a comparison of Alzheimer's, Huntington's and Parkinson's disease patients. *Journal of Neuroscience*, **9**, 582–587.

Heywood, C.A., Kentridge, R.W. & Cowey, A. (1998). Form and motion from colour in cerebral achromatopsia. *Experimental Brain Research*, **123**, 145–153.

Hodges, J.R. (1995). Retrograde amnesia. In A. Baddeley, B.A. Wilson & F.N. Watts (eds), *Handbook of Memory Disorders* (pp. 81–107). New York: Wiley.

Hikosaka, K. & Watanabe, M. (2000). Delay activity of orbital and lateral prefrontal neurons in the monkey varying with different rewards. *Cerebral Cortex*, **10**, 263–271.

Humphreys, G.W. & Forde, E.M.E. (2000). Hierarchies, similarity and interactivity in object recognition: On the multiplicity of "category-specific" deficits in neuropsychological populations. *Behavioural Brain Sciences* (in press).

Humphreys, G.W., Riddoch, M.J. & Price, C.J. (1997). Top-down processes in object identification: evidence from experimental psychology, neuropsychology and functional anatomy. *Philosophical Transactions of the Royal Society of London* B, **352**, 1275–1282.

Insausti, R., Amaral, D.G. & Cowan, W.M. (1987). The entorhinal cortex of the monkey: II. Cortical afferents. *Journal of Comparative Neurology*, **264**, 356–395.

James, W. (1893). *Principles of Psychology*. New York: Holt.

Jones, R., Grabowski, T.J. & Tranel, D. (1998). The neural basis of retrograde memory: evidence from positron emission tomography for the role of non-mesial temporal lobe structures. *Neurocase*, **4**, 471–479.

Jonides, J. (1995). Working memory and thinking. In E.E. Smith & D. Osherson (eds), *An Invitation to Cognitive Science: Thinking*, Vol. 3 (pp. 215–265). Cambridge, MA: MIT Press.

Kandel, E.R. & Schwartz, J.H. (1982). Molecular biology of learning: modulation of transmitter release. *Science*, **218**, 433–443.

Kandel, E.R., Schwartz, J.H. & Jessell, T.M. (2000). *Principles of Neural Science*, 4th edn. New York: Elsevier.

Kandel, E.R. & Squire, L.R. (2000). Neuroscience: breaking down scientific barriers to the study of brain and mind. *Science*, **290**, 1113–1120.

Kapur, N., Ellison, D., Smith, M.P. et al. (1992). Focal retrograde amnesia following bilateral temporal lobe pathology. *Brain*, **115**, 73–85.

Kapur, N., Ellison, D., Parkin, A.J. et al. (1994). Bilateral temporal lobe pathology with sparing of medial temporal lobe structures: lesion profile and pattern of memory disorder. *Neuropsychologia*, **32**, 23–38.

Kawagoe, R., Takikawa, Y. & Hikosaka, O. (1998). Expectation of reward modulates cognitive signals in the basal ganglia. *Nature Neuroscience*, **1**, 411–416.

Kawashima, R., Roland, P.E. & O'Sullivan, B.T. (1995). Functional anatomy of reaching and visuo-motor learning: a positron emission tomography study. *Cerebral Cortex*, **5**, 111–122.

Knowlton, B.J., Mangels, J.A. & Squire, L.R. (1996). A neostriatal habit learning system in humans. *Science*, **273**, 1399–1402.

Koenig, O., Thomas-Anterion, C. & Laurent, B. (1999). Procedural learning in Parkinson's disease: intact and impaired cognitive components. *Neuropsychologia*, **37**, 1103–1109.

Kopelman, M.D. (1993). The neuropsychology of remote memory. In F. Boller & J. Grafman (eds), *Handbook of Neuropsychology*, Vol. 8. (pp. 215–238). Amsterdam: Elsevier.

Kopelman, M.D. (2000). Focal retrograde amnesia and the attribution of causality: an exceptionally critical review. *Cognitive Neuropsychology*, **17**, 585–621.

Kosslyn, S.M. (1994). *Image and Brain: The Resolution of the Imagery Debate*. Cambridge, MA: MIT Press.

Kosslyn, S.M. & Koenig, O. (1995). *Wet Mind: The New Cognitive Neuroscience*. New York: Free Press.

Kosslyn, S.M., Pascual-Leone, A., Felician, O. et al. (1999). The role of area 17 in visual imagery: convergent evidence from PET and rTMS. *Science*, **284**, 167–170.

Kreiman, G., Koch, C. & Fried, I. (2000a). Imagery neurons in the human brain. *Nature*, **408**, 357–361.

Kreiman, G., Koch, C. & Fried, I. (2000b). Category-specific visual responses of single neurons in the human medial temporal lobe. *Nature Neuroscience*, **3**, 946–953.

Kroll, N.E., Markowitsch, H.J., Knight, R.T. & von Cramon, D.Y. (1997). Retrieval of old memories: the temporofrontal hypothesis. *Brain*, **120**, 1377–1399.

LaBar, K.S. & Phelps, E.A. (1998). Arousal-mediated memory consolidation: role of the medial temporal lobe in humans. *Psychological Science*, **9**, 490–494.

Lane, R.D., Reiman, E.M., Bradley, M.M. et al. (1997). Neuroanatomical correlates of pleasant and unpleasant emotion. *Neuropsychologia*, **35**, 1437–1444.

Lepage, M., Habib, R. & Tulving, E. (1998). Hippocampal PET activations of memory encoding and retrieval: the HIPER model. *Hippocampus*, **8**, 313–322.

Levelt, W.J.M., Roelofs, A. & Meyer, A.S. (1999). A theory of lexical access in speech production. *Behavioral and Brain Sciences*, **22**, 1–75.

Levine, B., Black, S.E., Cabeza, R. et al. (1998). Episodic memory and the self in a case of isolated retrograde amnesia. *Brain*, **121**, 1951–1973.

Maguire, E.A., Frith, C.D., Burgess, N. et al. (1998). Knowing where things are: parahippocampal involvement in encoding object locations in virtual large-scale space. *Journal of Cognitive Neuroscience*, **10**, 61–76.

Maquet, P., Peters, J., Aerts, J. et al. (1996). Functional neuroanatomy of human rapid-eye-movement sleep and dreaming. *Nature*, **383**, 163–166.

Markowitsch, H.J. (1995). Which brain regions are critically involved in the retrieval of old episodic memory? *Brain Research Reviews*, **21**, 117–127.

Markowitsch, H.J. (2000). The anatomical basis of memory. In M.S. Gazzaniga (ed.), *The New Cognitive Neurosciences*, 2nd edn (pp. 781–795). Cambridge, MA: MIT Press.

Markowitsch, H.J., Calabrese, P., Haupts, M. et al. (1993a). Searching for the anatomical basis of retrograde amnesia. *Journal of Clinical and Experimental Neuropsychology*, **15**, 947–967.

Markowitsch, H.J., Calabrese, P., Liess, J. et al. (1993b). Retrograde amnesia after traumatic brain injury of the fronto-temporal cortex. *Journal of Neurology, Neurosurgery and Psychiatry*, **56**, 988–992.

Martin, A., Haxby, J.V., Lalonde, F.M. et al. (1995). Discrete cortical regions associated with knowledge of color and knowledge of action. *Science*, **270**, 102–105.

Martin, A., Ungerleider, L.G. & Haxby, J.V. (2000a). Category specificity and the brain: the sensory/motor model of semantic representations of objects. In M.S. Gazzaniga (ed.), *The New Cognitive Neurosciences*, 2nd edn (pp. 1023–1036). Cambridge, MA: MIT Press.

Martin, S.J., Grimwood, P.D. & Morris, R.G.M. (2000b). Synaptic plasticity and memory: an evaluation of the hypothesis. *Annual Review of Neuroscience*, **23**, 649–711.

McGaugh, J.L. (2000). Memory—a century of consolidation. *Science*, **287**, 248–251.

McGaugh, J.L., Cahill, L. & Roozendaal, B. (1996). Involvement of the amygdala in memory storage: interaction with other brain systems. *Proceedings of the National Academy of Sciences*, **93**, 13508–13514.

McGaugh, J.L., Introini-Collison, I.B., Cahill, L. (1992). Involvement of the amygdala in neuromodulatory influences on memory storage. In J.P. Aggleton (ed.), *The Amygdala: Neurobiological Aspects of Emotion, Memory, and Mental Dysfunction* (pp. 431–451). New York: Wiley-Liss.

Melcher, D. (2001). Persistence of visual memory for scenes. *Nature*, **412**, 401.

Micheau, J. & Riedel, G. (1999). Protein kinases: which one is the memory molecule? *Cellular and Molecular Life Sciences*, **55**, 534–548.

Milner, B. (1962). Les troubles de la mémoire accompagnant les lésions hippocampiques bilatérales. In *Physiologie de l'Hippocampe, Colloques Internationaux*, No. 107 (pp. 257–272). Paris: CNRS.

Milner, B. (1971). Interhemispheric differences in localization of psychological processes in man. *British Journal of Medicine*, **27**, 272–277.

Milner, B. (1972). Disorders of learning and memory after temporal lobe lesions in man. *Clinical Neurosurgery*, **19**, 421–446.

Milner, B., Corkin, S. & Teuber, H.-L. (1968). Further analysis of the hippocampal amnesic syndrome. *Neuropsychologia*, **6**, 215–234.

Milner, B., Corsi, P. & Leonard, G. (1991). Frontal-lobe contribution to recency judgments. *Neuropsychologia*, **29**, 601–618.

Milner, B., Squire, L.R. & Kandel, E.R. (1998). Cognitive neuroscience and the study of memory. *Neuron*, **20**, 445–468.

Mishkin, M. (1978). Memory in monkeys severely impaired by combined but not separate removal of amygdala and hippocampus. *Nature*, **273**, 297–298.

Morris, J.S., Friston, K.J., Buchel, C. et al. (1998). A neuromodulatory role for the human amygdala in processing emotional facial expressions. *Brain*, **121**, 47–57.

Morris, R.G.M., Davis, S. & Butcher, S.P. (1990). Hippocampal synaptic plasticity and NMDA receptors: a role in information storage? *Philosophical Transactions of the Royal Society of London B*, **329**, 187–204.

Morris, R.G.M., Garrud, P., Rawlins, J.N.P. & O'Keefe, J. (1982). Place navigation impaired in rats with hippocampal lesions. *Nature*, **297**, 681–683.

Murray, E.A. & Gaffan, D. (1994). Removal of the amygdala plus subjacent cortex disrupts the retention of both intramodal and crossmodal associative memories in monkeys. *Behavioral Neuroscience*, **108**, 494–500.

Nahm, F.K.D., Tranel, D., Damasio, H. & Damasio, A.R. (1993). Cross-modal associations and the human amygdala. *Neuropsychologia*, **31**, 727–744.

Nadel, L. & Moscovitch, M. (1997). Memory consolidation, retrograde amnesia and the hippocampal complex. *Current Opinion in Neurobiology*, **7**, 217–227.

Nobre, A.C., Allison, T. & McCarthy, G. (1994). Word recognition in the human inferior temporal lobe. *Nature* **372**, 260–263.

Nyberg, L., Cabeza, R. & Tulving, E. (1996). PET studies of encoding and retrieval: the HERA model. *Psychonomic Bulletin Review*, **3**, 135–148.

Nyberg, L., Cabeza, R. & Tulving, E. (1998). Asymmetric frontal activation during episodic memory: what kind of specificity? *Trends in Cognitive Sciences*, **2**, 419–420.

O'Connor, M., Butters, N., Miliotis, P. (1992). The dissociation of anterograde and retrograde amnesia in a patient with herpes encephalitis. *Journal of Clinical and Experimental Neuropsychology*, **14**, 159–178.

Ojemann, G.A. (1991). Cortical organization of language. *Journal of Neuroscience*, **11**, 2281–2287.

Ostergaard, A.L. (1999). Priming deficits in amnesia: now you see them, now you don't. *Journal of the International Neuropsychological Society*, **5**, 175–190.

Packard, M.G., Hirsh, R. & White, N.M. (1989). Differential effects of fornix and caudate nucleus lesions on two radial maze tasks: evidence for multiple memory systems. *Journal of Neuroscience*, **9**, 1465–1472.

Pandya, D.N. & Yeterian, E.H. (1985). Architecture and connections of cortical association areas. In A. Peters & E.G. Jones (eds), *Cerebral Cortex*, **4**, 3–61.

Phelps, E.A., LaBar, K., Anderson, A.K. et al. (1998). Specifying the contributions of the human amygdala to emotional memory: a case study. *Neurocase*, **4**, 527–540.

Phillips, M.L., Young, A.W., Scott, S.K. et al. (1998). Neural responses to facial and vocal expressions of fear and disgust. *Proceedings of the Royal Society of London, Series B*, **265**, 1809–1817.

Pinsker, H., Kupfermann, I., Castellucci, V.F. & Kandel, E.R. (1970). Habituation and dishabituation of the gill-withdrawal reflex in *Aplysia*. *Science*, **167**, 1740–1742.

Prabhakaran, V., Narayanan, K., Zhao, Z. & Gabrieli, J.D. (2000). Integration of diverse information in working memory within the frontal lobe. *Nature Neuroscience*, **3**, 85–90.

Raichle, R.E., Fiez, J.A., Videen, T.O. et al. (1994). Practice-related changes in human brain functional anatomy during nonmotor learning. *Cerebral Cortex*, **4**, 8–26.

Rempel-Clower, N.L., Zola-Morgan, S.M., Squire, L.R. & Amaral, D.G. (1996). Three cases of enduring memory impairment after bilateral damage limited to the hippocampal formation. *Journal of Neuroscience*, **16**, 5233–5255.

Rizzo, M., Smith, V., Pokorny, J. & Damasio, A.R. (1993). Color perception profiles in central achromatopsia. *Neurology*, **43**, 995–1001.

Rolls, E.T. (2000). The orbitofrontal cortex and reward. *Cerebral Cortex*, **10**, 284–294.

Roozendaal, B., Nguyen, B.T., Power, A.E. & McGaugh, J.L. (1999). Basolateral amygdala no-radrenergic influence enables enhancement of memory consolidation induced by hippocampal glucocorticoid receptor activation. *Proceedings of the National Academy of Sciences*, **96**, 11642–11647.

Rugg, M.D. & Wilding, E.L. (2000). Retrieval processing and episodic memory. *Trends in Cognitive Sciences*, **4**, 108–115.

Saint-Cyr, J.A. & Taylor, A.E. (1988). Procedural learning and neostriatal dysfunction in man. *Brain*, **111**, 941–959.

Sarter, M. & Bruno, J.P. (1997). Cognitive functions of cortical acetylcholine: toward a unifying hypothesis. *Brain Research Reviews*, **23**, 28–46.

Schacter, D.L. & Wagner, A.D. (1999). Medial temporal lobe activations in fMRI and PET studies of episodic encoding and retrieval. *Hippocampus*, **9**, 7–24.

Scoville, W.B. & Milner, B. (1957). Loss of recent memory after bilateral hippocampal lesions. *Journal of Neurology, Neurosurgery and Psychiatry*, **20**, 11–21.

Shallice, T. & Evans, M.E. (1978). The involvement of the frontal lobes in cognitive estimation. *Cortex*, **14**, 294–303.

Shimamura, A.P., Janowsky, J.S. & Squire, L.R. (1991). What is the role of frontal lobe damage in memory disorders? In H.S. Levin, H.M. Eisenberg & A.L. Benton (eds), *Frontal Lobe Function and Dysfunction* (pp. 173–195). New York: Oxford University Press.

Shors, T.J. & Matzel, L.D. (1997). Long-term potentiation: what's learning got to do with it? *Behavioral and Brain Sciences*, **20**, 597–655.

Sidman, M., Stoddard, L.T. & Mohr, J.P. (1968). Some additional quantitative observations of immediate memory in a patient with bilateral hippocampal lesions. *Neuropsychologia*, **6**, 245–254.

Silveri, M.C., Gainotti, G., Perani, D. et al. (1997). Naming deficit for non-living items: neuropsychological and PET study. *Neuropsychologia*, **35**, 359–367.

Smith, E.E. & Jonides, J. (1998). Neuroimaging analyses of human working memory. *Proceedings of the National Academy of Sciences USA*, **95**, 12061–12068.

Smith, E.E., Jonides, J. & Koeppe, R.A. (1996). Dissociating verbal and spatial working memory using PET. *Cerebral Cortex*, **6**, 11–20.

Smith, E.E., Jonides, J., Marshuetz, C. & Koeppe, R.A. (1998). Components of verbal working memory: evidence from neuroimaging. *Proceedings of the National Academy of Sciences USA*, **95**, 876–882.

Smith, M.L. & Milner, B. (1988). Estimation of frequency of occurrence of abstract designs after frontal or temporal lobectomy. *Neuropsychologia*, **26**, 297–306.

Squire, L.R. (1987). *Memory and Brain*. New York: Oxford University Press.

Squire, L.R. (1992). Memory and the hippocampus: a synthesis from findings with rats, monkeys and humans. *Psychological Review*, **99**, 195–231.

Squire, L.R. & Zola, S.M. (1996). Ischemic brain damage and memory impairment: a commentary. *Hippocampus*, **6**, 546–552.

Stickgold, R. (1999). Sleep: off-line memory reprocessing. *Trends in Cognitive Sciences*, **2**, 484–492.

Suzuki, W.A. & Amaral, D.G. (1994). Perirhinal and parahippocampal cortices of the macaque monkey: cortical afferents. *Journal of Comparative Neurology*, **350**, 497–533.

Tanaka, Y., Miyazawa, Y., Akaoka, F. & Yamada, T. (1997). Amnesia following damage to the mammillary bodies. *Neurology*, **48**, 160–165.

Taylor, R. & O'Carroll, R. (1995). Cognitive estimation in neurological disorders. *British Journal of Clinical Psychology*, **34**, 223–228.

Thach, W.T. (1998). A role for the cerebellum in learning movement coordination. *Neurobiology of Learning & Memory*, **70**, 177–188.

Thompson, R.F. (1986). The neurobiology of learning and memory. *Science*, **233**, 941–947.

Thompson, R.F. (1990). Neural mechanisms of classical conditioning in mammals. *Philosophical Transactions of the Royal Society of London B*, **329**, 161–170.

Thompson, R.F. & Krupa, D.J. (1994). Organization of memory traces in the mammalian brain. *Annual Review of Neuroscience*, **17**, 519–550.

Thompson, R.F., Thompson, J.K., Kim, J.J. et al. (1998). The nature of reinforcement in cerebellar learning. *Neurobiology of Learning & Memory*, **70**, 150–176.

Tranel, D. (1991). Dissociated verbal and nonverbal retrieval and learning following left anterior temporal damage. *Brain and Cognition*, **15**, 187–200.

Tranel, D. (1994). "Acquired sociopathy": The development of sociopathic behavior following focal brain damage. In D.C. Fowles, P. Sutker & S.H. Goodman (eds), *Progress in Experimental Personality and Psychopathology Research*, Vol. 17 (pp. 285–311). New York: Springer.

Tranel, D. (2001a). Central color processing and its disorders. In F. Boller & J. Grafman (eds), *Handbook of Neuropsychology*, 2nd edn; Volume 4 (M. Behrmann, Section ed.) (pp. 1–14). Amsterdam: Elsevier.

Tranel, D. (2001b). Emotion, decision-making, and the ventromedial prefrontal cortex. In D.T. Stuss & R.T. Knight (eds), *Frontal Lobes 2000*. New York: Oxford University Press (in press).

Tranel, D., Adolphs, R., Damasio, H. & Damasio, A.R. A neural basis for the retrieval of words for actions. *Cognitive Neuropsychology* (in press).

Tranel, D., Bechara, A. & Damasio, A.R. (2000a). Decision making and the somatic marker hypothesis. In M.S. Gazzaniga (ed.), *The New Cognitive Neurosciences* (pp. 1047–1061). Cambridge, MA: MIT Press.

Tranel, D. & Damasio, A. R. (1993). The covert learning of affective valence does not require structures in hippocampal system or amygdala. *Journal of Cognitive Neuroscience*, **5**, 79–88.

Tranel, D., Damasio, A.R., Damasio, H. & Brandt, J.P. (1994). Sensorimotor skill learning in amnesia: additional evidence for the neural basis of nondeclarative memory. *Learning and Memory*, **1**, 165–179.

Tranel, D., Damasio, H. & Damasio, A.R. (1997a). A neural basis for the retrieval of conceptual knowledge. *Neuropsychologia*, **35**, 1319–1327.

Tranel, D., Damasio, H. & Damasio, A.R. (1997b). On the neurology of naming. In H. Goodglass & A. Wingfield (eds), *Anomia: Neuroanatomical and Cognitive Correlates* (pp. 65–90). New York: Academic Press.

Tranel, D., Damasio, H. & Damasio, A.R. (1998). The neural basis of lexical retrieval. In Parks, R.W., Levine, D.S. & Long, D.L. (eds), *Fundamentals of Neural Network Modeling: Neuropsychology and Cognitive Neuroscience* (pp. 271–296). Cambridge, MA: MIT Press.

Tranel, D., Damasio, H. & Damasio, A.R. (2000b). Amnesia caused by herpes simplex encephalitis, infarctions in basal forebrain, and anoxia/ischemia. In F. Boller & J. Grafman (eds), *Handbook of*

Neuropsychology, 2nd edn Volume 2 (L. Cermak, Section ed.) (pp. 85–110). Amsterdam: Elsevier Science.

Tranel, D. & Hyman, B.T. (1990). Neuropsychological correlates of bilateral amygdala damage. *Archives of Neurology*, **47**, 349–355.

Tranel, D., Logan, C.G., Frank, R.J. & Damasio, A.R. (1997c). Explaining category-related effects in the retrieval of conceptual and lexical knowledge for concrete entities: operationalization and analysis of factors. *Neuropsychologia*, **35**, 1329–1339.

Tsien, J.Z., Huerta, P.T. & Tonegawa, S. (1996). The essential role of hippocampal CA1 NMDA receptor-dependent synaptic plasticity in spatial memory. *Cell*, **87**, 1327–1338.

Tully, T. (1991). Genetic dissection of learning and memory in *Drosophila melanogaster*. In J. Madden IV (ed.), *Neurobiology of Learning, Emotion, and Affect* (pp. 29–66). New York: Raven Press.

Tulving, E., Kapur, S., Craik, F.I.M. et al. (1994). Hemispheric encoding/retrieval asymmetry in episodic memory: positron emission tomography findings. *Proceedings of the National Academy of Sciences of the USA*, **91**, 2016–2020.

Tulving, E., Markowitsch, H.J., Craik, F.I.M. et al. (1996). Novelty and familiarity activations in PET studies of memory encoding and retrieval. *Cerebral Cortex*, **6**, 71–79.

Van Hoesen, G.W. (1982). The parahippocampal gyrus. *Trends in Neurosciences*, **5**, 345–350.

Van Hoesen, G.W. & Pandya, D.N. (1975). Some connections of the entorhinal (area 28) and perirhinal (area 35) cortices of the rhesus monkey: I. Temporal lobe afferents. *Brain Research*, **95**, 1–24.

Victor, M., Adams, R.D. & Collins, G.H. (1989). *The Wernicke–Korsakoff syndrome*, 2nd edn. Philadelphia, PA: F.A. Davis.

Victor, M. & Agamanolis, D. (1990). Amnesia due to lesions confined to the hippocampus: a clinical–pathological study. *Journal of Cognitive Neuroscience*, **2**, 246–257.

Wagner, A.D., Koutstaal, W. & Schacter, D.L. (1999). When encoding yields remembering: insights from event-related neuroimaging. *Phil. Trans. R. Soc. Lond.* B, **354**, 1307–1323.

Wagner, A.D., Schacter, D.L., Rotte, M. et al. (1998). Building memories: remembering and forgetting of verbal experiences as predicted by brain activity. *Science*, **281**, 1188–1191.

Warrington, E.K. & Weiskrantz, L. (1968). New method of testing long-term retention with special reference to amnestic patients. *Nature*, **217**, 972–974.

Watanabe, M. (1998). Cognitive and motivational operations in primate prefrontal neurons. *Reviews in the Neurosciences*, **9**, 225–241.

Whalen, P.J., Rauch, S.L., Etcoff, N.L. et al. (1998). Masked presentations of emotional facial expressions modulate amygdala activity without explicit knowledge. *Journal of Neuroscience*, **18**, 411–418.

Wheeler, M.E., Petersen, S.E. & Buckner, R.L. (2000). Memory's echo: vivid remembering reactivates sensory-specific cortex. *Proceedings of the National Academy of Science of the USA*, **97**, 11125–11129.

White, N.M. (1997). Mnemonic functions of the basal ganglia. *Current Opinion in Neurobiology*, **7**, 164–169.

Winograd, E. & Neisser, U. (1992). *Affect and Accuracy in Recall: Studies of "Flashbulb" Memories*. Cambridge, MA: Harvard University Press.

Young, A.W., Hellawell, D.J., Van de Wal, C. & Johnson, M. (1996). Facial expression processing after amygdalotomy. *Neuropsychologia*, **34**, 31–39.

Zald, D.H., Lee, J.T., Fluegel, K.W. & Pardo, J.V. (1998). Aversive gustatory stimulation activates limbic circuits in humans. *Brain*, **121**, 1143–1154.

Zald, D.H. & Pardo, J.V. (1997). Emotion, olfaction, and the human amygdala: amygdala activation during aversive olfactory stimulation. *Proceedings of the National Academy of Sciences of the USA*, **94**, 4119–4124.

Zattore, R.J., Halpern, A.R., Perry, D.W. et al. (1996). Hearing in the mind's ear: a PET investigation of musical imagery and perception. *Journal of Cognitive Neuroscience*, **8**, 29–46.

Zhuo, M., Small, S.A., Kandel, E.R. & Hawkins, R.D. (1993). Nitric oxide and carbon monoxide produce activity-dependent long-term synaptic enhancement in hippocampus. *Science*, **260**, 1946–1950.

Zola, S. (1997). Amnesia: neuroanatomic and clinical aspects. In T.E. Feinberg & M.J. Farah (eds), *Behavioral Neurology and Neuropsychology* (pp. 447–461). New York: McGraw-Hill.

Zola-Morgan, S.M. & Squire, L.R. (1993). Neuroanatomy of memory. *Annual Review of Neuroscience*, **16**, 547–563.

Zola-Morgan, S.M., Squire, L.R. & Amaral, D.G. (1986). Human amnesia and the medial temporal region: enduring memory impairment following a bilateral lesion limited to field CA1 of the hippocampus. *Journal of Neuroscience*, **6**, 2950–2967.

Zola-Morgan, S., Squire, L.R., Amaral, D.G. & Suzuki, W.A. (1989). Lesions of perirhinal and parahippocampal cortex that spare the amygdala and hippocampal formation produce severe memory impairment. *Journal of Neuroscience*, **9**, 4355–4370.

CHAPTER 3

Functional Neuroimaging of Memory

Michael D. Rugg

Institute of Cognitive Neuroscience, University College London, UK

This chapter is concerned with how functional neuroimaging methods have been used to study the functional organization and neural bases of memory, and the practical and conceptual limitations of these methods. Throughout the chapter, "functional neuroimaging" will be used to refer to the non-invasive measurement of brain activity as indexed by changes in haemodynamic variables detected with positron emission tomography (PET) and functional magnetic resonance imaging (fMRI). The chapter focuses primarily on studies published since the late 1990s; more comprehensive reviews of the earlier literature can be found in Fletcher et al. (1997), Desgranges et al. (1998), and Schacter & Buckner (1998).

There are two principal applications of functional neuroimaging to the study of memory. First, functional neuroimaging can be employed to identify the neural substrates of specific memory functions. In this case, the identity of the functions is assumed, and the question addressed is purely an anatomical one. Second, functional neuroimaging can be employed to dissociate different memory functions. This application of neuroimaging is based on the assumption that the neural substrates of cognitive functions, such as memory, are invariant, i.e. the same function has only a single neuroanatomic basis. Under this assumption, if two experimental conditions are associated with qualitatively different patterns of brain activity, it can be assumed that the conditions engaged cognitive operations that were at least partially distinct (Rugg, 1999).

In both of the applications noted above, the rationale for using functional neuroimaging to study memory is closely related to the "lesion–deficit" approach, in which the identity and neural bases of different memory functions are inferred from the effects of localized lesions. Functional neuroimaging complements and extends lesion data in three main ways. First, it permits hypotheses derived from lesion studies to be tested in normal subjects. Second, functional neuroimaging permits investigation of the function of brain regions that are damaged selectively in humans only rarely, e.g. circumscribed lesions to the precuneus are very rare, but evidence from functional neuroimaging strongly suggests a role for this region in memory retrieval (see below).

A third way in which functional neuroimaging goes beyond lesion data is in its capacity to provide information about different stages of memory processing. An enduring problem in

The Handbook of Memory Disorders. Edited by A.D. Baddeley, M.D. Kopelman and B.A. Wilson
© 2002 John Wiley & Sons, Ltd.

the interpretation of neuropsychological findings is in distinguishing the effects of lesions on encoding from those on retrieval, permitting the brain structures necessary for these functions to be independently identified. Functional neuroimaging methods are well suited to addressing this question and, as will be seen in the section on Episodic Memory, below, a large number of studies have investigated the neural correlates of encoding and retrieval in episodic memory.

Together with advantages over the lesion method, functional neuroimaging has a significant disadvantage. Functional neuroimaging data provide information about the neural *correlates* of cognitive operations, but offer no means for determining which of these correlates are *necessary* for the operations to occur. To establish a causal role for, say, the left prefrontal cortex in memory encoding (see below), it is necessary to demonstrate not only that the region is active during encoding, but that disruption of its function leads to an encoding impairment. Although methods exist for the reversible disruption of some brain regions in neurologically intact subjects (e.g. transcranial magnetic stimulation), the lesion–deficit approach remains the most important means of investigating the consequences of focal disruption of brain function. Thus, despite the advantages of functional neuroimaging, evidence from lesion studies will continue to have a central role in understanding the neural bases of cognitive function. Indeed, one consequence of the employment of functional neuroimaging to study memory has been the identification of several regions for which a role in memory had previously been unsuspected, and where converging evidence from lesion studies is now required.

In the following section, the methods of PET and fMRI are described, and issues relating to experimental design and data interpretation discussed briefly. While these issues are not specific to memory research, some appreciation of them is necessary for an informed interpretation of findings from functional neuroimaging studies of memory.

METHODS

As employed in "cognitive activation" studies, PET and fMRI both depend on the fact that there is a close coupling in the normal brain between changes in the activity of a neuronal population and changes in its blood supply, such that an increase in activity is associated with an increase in supply and vice versa (Raichle, 1987). Neither the physiological mechanisms underlying this coupling, nor its functional significance, are fully understood. Nevertheless, the coupling allows methods sensitive to haemodynamic variables to be used to detect differences in local neural activity. In the case of PET, the haemodynamic variable is regional cerebral blood flow (rCBF), indexed by the accumulation over time of a radiotracer introduced into the bloodstream (usually $^{15}O_2$). fMRI detects changes in blood oxygenation, taking advantage of the facts that the blood draining from a neuronal population is more oxygenated when the population is relatively active than when it is less active, and that oxygenated and deoxygenated haemoglobin differ in their magnetic susceptibility and hence the MR signal they return.

The fact that functional neuroimaging methods rely on indirect measures of neural activity leads to two important caveats in data interpretation. First, a change in the activity of a neural population can have a haemodynamic correlate only if it causes a change in metabolic demand, e.g. a change solely in the *timing* of the activity of a pool of neurons may have little or no metabolic consequence, and hence go undetected. Thus, negative findings for a particular brain region in, say, an fMRI study need not mean that neural activity in the area was not sensitive to the experimental manipulation; merely that any change in activity did not have a metabolic correlate on a spatial scale detectable by the fMRI method. The second caveat concerns the interpretation of findings from subject populations in whom cerebrovascular function may be compromised, e.g. stroke patients. In the absence of carefully designed control conditions, it may be impossible to determine whether a difference between a patient and a control group in a task-related haemodynamic measure reflects a difference in neural activity, or merely in its vascular correlates.

Until the mid-1990s, PET was the preeminent method for localizing the neural correlates of cognitive function in normal subjects, and was employed in a substantial number of memory studies. Compared with fMRI, the PET method suffers from a number of disadvantages and PET studies of memory are now relatively rare. Among the more important of PET's disadvantages are its relatively low spatial resolution, and the limited number of observations that can be made on an experimental subject before coming up against radiation dosimetry limits. A further disadvantage stems from the relatively long interval that is needed to acquire PET data (>30 s). This limits the temporal resolution of the method and necessitates the use of blocked experimental designs, where data are accumulated over a succession of trials which together constitute a single experimental condition. Such designs make it very difficult to distinguish between experimental effects that are stimulus-related (i.e. which reflect changes in neural activity associated with processing of individual experimental items) and effects that reflect tonic, "state-related" changes in activity (e.g. due to changes in "task set" or arousal level). A second disadvantage of blocked designs is that they do not allow data associated with different experimental trials to be sorted and analysed *post hoc*. This constraint is especially restrictive when the neural correlates of behavioural variability (e.g. accurate vs. inaccurate recognition judgements) are the focus of experimental interest.

In early fMRI studies experimental designs tended to be rather simple, often comprising alternating blocks of two conditions (e.g. task vs. baseline). Such designs suffer from many of the same disadvantages as those already noted for the blocked designs employed with PET. Even with such simple designs, however, fMRI offers a number of significant advantages over the PET method. These include an unrestricted number of observations per subject, and greater spatial resolution. Furthermore, the speed with which fMRI data can be acquired (typically <3 s for a whole brain volume) means that the length of trial blocks is flexible, and with no need to impose an interval of ~10 min between successive blocks (required in PET studies to allow decay of the radiotracer), different experimental conditions can be administered in a counterbalanced order in the course of a single experimental run.

More important, the speed of fMRI data acquisition makes it possible to obtain data on a trial-wise basis—so-called *"event-related" fMRI* (Josephs et al., 1997; Zarahn et al., 1997). The development of the event-related method has had a major impact on functional neuro-imaging studies of memory. Using this method, it is possible both to dissociate stimulus- and state-related effects (e.g. Donaldson et al., 2001) and to segregate data *post hoc* on the basis of performance. In addition, event-related fMRI provides some information, albeit limited, about the time course of stimulus-elicited neural activity. The maximum temporal resolution that can be achieved has still to be determined, but for whole brain data it seems likely to be around 0.5 s.

Against the advantages of fMRI over PET must be set one major disadvantage. Whereas PET detects activity in all brain regions with roughly equal sensitivity, the sensitivity of fMRI is variable across regions. Intracranial inhomogeneities in the applied magnetic field give rise to "susceptibility artefact", which results in signal "drop-out". Because susceptibility artefact is most marked in the vicinity of air–bone boundaries, basal temporal and ventromedial frontal regions are affected particularly badly. When these regions are of primary interest, PET currently remains the technique of choice.

EXPERIMENTAL STUDIES

The following sections give an overview of findings from functional neuroimaging studies of long-term memory. They focus on two areas—priming and episodic memory—which have attracted much attention in the neuropsychological literature, and in which sufficient studies have been conducted to allow some general conclusions to be drawn. Readers are referred to Chapters 1, 12 and 13 of the present volume for discussion of the voluminous literature on working memory. In discussing findings from studies in these areas, the location of the regions responding to experimental manipulations will be described in broad terms only, by reference to major landmarks and, when appropriate, Brodmann area(s) (BA) as inferred from standard brain atlases (e.g. Talaraich & Tournoux, 1998; Duvernoy, 1999).

Priming

"Priming" refers to facilitation of the identification or production of an experimental item following prior experience with the item. Priming effects are typically studied with "indirect" memory tests, employing instructions which stress "on-line" processing and make no reference to a past study episode. Priming has received considerable attention in the experimental and neuropsychological literature, both because performance on indirect and direct memory tests (when explicit, intentional retrieval of study items is required) can be dissociated in normal subjects (Roediger & McDermott, 1993), and also because amnesic patients show normal or near-normal priming on a range of indirect tests (Moscovitch et al., 1993; but see Ostergaard & Jernigan, 1993). These observations have led many authors to conclude that priming is a form of implicit memory that relies on a memory system distinct from that supporting explicit or "declarative" memory (Tulving & Schacter, 1990).

Several functional neuroimaging studies have investigated the neural correlates of priming with indirect memory tasks similar to those employed in the behavioural research mentioned above. Studies have been conducted using both blocked and, more recently, event-related designs. The earliest such study (Squire et al., 1992) employed PET and examined the neural correlates of word stem completion. In different experimental blocks subjects were scanned while they gave completions to three-letter word stems belonging to either experimentally novel or previously studied words. The key finding was that blocks containing stems belonging to previously studied words were associated with lower activity in the ventral occipitotemporal cortex (BA 19/37) than were blocks containing novel stems (a similar though smaller effect was also observed in a cued recall version of the task where the stems were used as explicit retrieval cues). Subsequent studies have reported such "repetition-suppression effects" in a variety of indirect memory tests, including, in addition to visual word stem completion, auditory stem completion (e.g. Badgaiyan et al., 1999), word fragment completion (Blaxton, 1989), object identification (Buckner et al., 1998b) and semantic decision (Demb et al., 1995). The general finding from these studies was that primed items were associated with lower levels of activity than unprimed items, both in extrastriate regions thought to support perceptual identification, and in other regions, such as left prefrontal cortex, activated by specific combinations of item and task.

Several studies have sought to relate the repetition suppression effects in different regions to distinctions drawn in the behavioural literature between different classes of priming. One such distinction is between perceptual (or "data-driven") priming, held to depend on overlap between study and test processing in "early", modality-specific perceptual operations, and conceptual (conceptually-driven) priming, resulting from processing overlap at the semantic level (Blaxton, 1989). On the basis of its specificity for tasks requiring lexical/semantic processing (Demb et al., 1995; Wagner et al., 1997, 2000), it has been suggested (Schacter & Buckner, 1998) that the suppression effect observed in the left inferior prefrontal cortex is a reflection of conceptual priming, a suggestion consistent with the proposed role of this structure in high-level language processing (Gabrieli et al., 1998). The suggestion gains further support from the finding that word stem repetition was associated with reduction in left prefrontal activity regardless of whether the stems were presented visually or auditorily (Buckner et al., 2000), implying that the left frontal region subserves amodal aspects of word processing. Preliminary evidence of left frontal repetition suppression effects in amnesic patients (Gabrieli et al., 1998; Buckner & Koutstaal, 1998) is also consistent with the view that these effects reflect a form of memory for relatively abstract stimulus features that is distinct from explicit memory.

Evidence linking suppression effects in extrastriate cortex to perceptual priming comes from studies of word stem completion, which found suppression to be present only when study and test items are presented in the same sensory modality (Badgaiyan et al., 1999; Schacter et al., 1999). Along with the reduction in repetition suppression, these studies reported that cross-modal priming was associated with increased activity in the anterior prefrontal cortex. Consistent with the hypothesis that the prefrontal effects reflected the engagement of explicit memory for items repeated across modality (Jacoby et al., 1993), Badgaiyan et al. (2001) reported that divided visual attention during study (a manipulation held selectively to impair explicit memory) abolished the effects.

Further evidence pointing to the perceptual specificity of extrastriate repetition suppression effects comes from an event-related fMRI study of Koutsaal et al. (2001). These authors employed as stimuli pictures of visual objects, and compared the effects of repeating the same stimulus (e.g. the same picture of an umbrella as was first presented) with those of presenting a different exemplar of the same object (picture of a different umbrella). In most of the regions demonstrating suppression effects for repetition of the same stimulus, effects were attenuated for repetition at the exemplar level. Within extrastriate areas, the attenuation was greater in the right than the left hemisphere. This finding led the authors to suggest that, in accord with evidence from behavioural studies (e.g. Marsolek et al., 1992), form-specific priming effects depend primarily on right occipitotemporal regions, the corresponding regions of the left hemisphere supporting priming at a more abstract level of representation.

Findings from the PET studies of word stem completion by Badgaiyan et al. (1999, 2001) are also consistent with the idea that repetition suppression effects in the left ventral extrastriate cortex reflect processing overlap at a relatively abstract level of representation. These authors reported that some of the regions that showed suppression effects on visual word stem completion tasks showed similar effects when the task was presented auditorily, suggesting that this region supports word processing at the supramodal level. It is currently unclear, however, how this suggestion can be reconciled with the finding (noted above) that the same region fails to exhibit repetition suppression when priming is across-modality.

Another distinction that has been drawn in the behavioural literature is between priming for items that are pre-experimentally familiar (e.g. words, pictures of known objects) as opposed to those that are novel (e.g. non-words, nonsense objects). Whereas familiar items have pre-existing memory representations, novel items, especially if their constituent parts are themselves unfamiliar, do not. So to the extent that priming is supported by activation of pre-existing memory representations (Bowers, 2000), priming effects should be greater for familiar than for unfamiliar items. Whereas studies of healthy subjects provide a somewhat mixed picture of whether, and in what circumstances, priming effects for familiar and novel items differ in their magnitude or longevity, Gooding et al. (2000) have argued that priming effects in amnesic patients are reliably greater for familiar than for novel items. According to these authors, priming for novel material is supported at least partially by memory processes that are compromised in amnesia.

Two functional neuroimaging studies in particular are relevant to this issue. Using PET, Schacter et al. (1995) investigated brain activity while subjects made possible/impossible decisions about line drawings of pre-experimentally novel objects. In different blocks, stimuli consisted predominantly of possible or impossible objects presented for the first or the second time. Blocks containing repeated possible objects were associated with greater activity in inferior temporal/fusiform cortex (BA 21/37) than were first presentations (i.e. a "repetition enhancement effect"). Henson et al. (2000a) used event-related fMRI to study short-term repetition effects of faces and symbols, in each case separated according to whether the items were pre-experimentally familiar (e.g. famous vs. unknown faces). Repetition effects in a right fusiform region (the so-called "fusiform face area"; Kanwisher, 2000) showed a crossover interaction, in that suppression was observed for familiar items whereas unfamiliar stimuli were associated with repetition enhancement. Together, the findings from these two studies add weight to the suggestion (Gooding et al., 2000) that the neural bases of repetition effects differ according to an item's pre-experimental familiarity. The relevance of these findings to behavioural priming effects observed with pre-experimental unfamiliar materials remains to be elucidated, however.

Finally, it should be noted that in the majority of priming studies cited above the study–test interval was relatively brief, at most a matter of minutes. In an exception to this pattern, van Turennout et al. (2000) compared the effects of object repetition over study–test periods of 30 s and 3 days, and reported that in the ventral extrastriate cortex repetition elicited suppression effects that barely differed across the two delays. This finding suggests that a single encounter with an item can give rise to long-lasting changes in the cortical regions thought to support object processing, and is consistent with evidence of long-lasting priming effects on behavioural measures of visual object processing (e.g. ~3 months in the picture-naming task of Cave, 1997).

Interpretation of Repetition Suppression Effects

Squire et al. (1992) noted that their finding of a repetition suppression effect suggested a possible neural mechanism for behavioural priming: namely, that primed items require fewer neural resources for their processing than unprimed ones, and therefore are processed with greater efficiency. Wiggs & Martin (1998) drew a direct analogy between the repetition suppression effects observed in functional neuroimaging studies and the effects observed on single neuron firing rates in monkey inferotemporal visual cortex, where the repetition of a visual object is associated with reduction in the activity of some of the neurons activated by the object on its first presentation (Li et al., 1993). Wiggs & Martin proposed that suppression effects in both neuroimaging and single unit data (along with priming effects on behaviour) were a reflection of the development of a "sparser", more selectively tuned stimulus representation, a process involving "drop-out" of neurons coding inessential or non-discriminating stimulus features.

Wiggs & Martin's proposal, and others like it, encounters a number of difficulties. First, it is not clear how the proposal can account for the finding that the repetition of pre-experimentally novel items (analogous to the items employed in single neuron studies with monkeys) can elicit enhanced responses. Second, it is unclear how analogous in other respects the single neuron results in monkeys are to findings from human studies. In particular, it is not presently known whether neuronal repetition suppression effects reported in the monkey reflect priming. Brown and colleagues (e.g. Brown & Xiang, 1988), for example, have argued that these effects are a neural substrate of recognition memory. Furthermore, the neuronal effects onset early (ca. 90–100 ms) and almost certainly reflect modulation of initial perceptual processing. The onset latency of the neuronal activity reflected in human repetition suppression effects is not known for certain. On the basis of findings from a study in which event-related fMRI was combined with magnetoencephalography, however, it has been claimed (Dale et al., 2000) that suppression effects in extrastriate cortex onset relatively late (ca. 300 ms), at about the same time as suppression effects are also seen in prefrontal cortex. If confirmed, this finding would suggest that the extrastriate repetition suppression observed with functional neuroimaging is not a direct correlate of the neuronal effects seen in the monkey. Of course, this conclusion would not mean that repetition suppression as revealed by functional neuroimaging does not underlie repetition effects on behaviour. It would suggest, however, that priming of familiar items involves modification of processes "downstream" of the items' initial perceptual analysis.

Conclusions

PET and fMRI studies employing the kinds of indirect memory tests used to assess behavioural priming effects have led to the identification a robust neural correlate of such effects: repetition suppression. The studies have also had some success in correlating suppression effects in different regions with different forms of priming identified at the behavioural level, although difficulties remain (e.g. see Badgaiyan et al., 2001). Somewhat suprisingly, however, the functional neuroimaging literature on priming contains few attempts to demonstrate rigorously that the effects observed in indirect tests are indeed correlates of implicit memory, rather than reflections of incidental or even intentional explicit memory. Thus, while some studies have contrasted the effects of stimulus repetition in indirect and direct versions of otherwise similar tests (e.g. Squire et al., 1992; Schacter et al., 1996), none has followed the behavioural literature in crossing a task manipulation with variables thought to have dissociative effects on priming and explicit memory (variables such as depth of study processing, divided attention, modality change, etc.). Indeed, relatively few studies employing indirect tests alone have employed variables capable of dissociating implicit and explicit memory of study items (a notable example of such a study being Badgaiyan et al., 2001), researchers often seemingly content to assume that the employment of an indirect test is sufficient to ensure that explicit memory is not engaged (cf. Jacoby & Kelley, 1992; Rugg et al., 1997). Until a significant number of such experiments are performed, the full picture of the neural activity specific to priming, as distinct from activity shared or specifically associated with explicit memory, will not be clear.

Episodic Memory

Episodic memory refers to memory processes supporting the recollection of specific events and the context in which they occurred. It is usually assessed with direct tests, such as recall and recognition, which have in common the requirement intentionally to retrieve information about a specific past processing episode.

Evidence from lesion studies indicates that episodic memory depends upon a network of cortical and subcortical structures, prominent among which are the hippocampus and adjacent medial temporal cortex, and the prefrontal cortex. The effects of lesions to these regions differ. As detailed in Chapters 4, 8 and 9 of the present volume, bilateral damage to the medial temporal lobe causes a severe, generalized impairment in the acquistion of new episodic memories, and a more variable impairment in the recollection of events experienced premorbidly. By contrast, lesions of the prefrontal cortex have only a limited effect on many tests of episodic memory, unless highly elaborate encoding or retrieval strategies are required. The effects of prefrontal lesions are, however, prominent on tests that emphasize the retrieval of contextual features of prior events, such as when and where they occurred (Chapter 17; Stuss et al., 1994).

Encoding

Functional neuroimaging studies of encoding have taken several approaches. A number studies employed designs in which encoding was operationalized as the contrast between two study conditions, known *a priori* to give rise to different levels of performance on direct memory tests. A consistent finding was that the task promoting relatively good memory performance was associated with greater activity in the ventral and dorsal regions of the left inferior frontal gyrus (BAs 44/45/47; for review, see Buckner et al., 1999). Differences in left frontal activity were found, for example, in contrasts between intentional learning vs. reading (Kapur et al., 1996), semantic vs. nonsemantic classification (Kapur et al., 1994; Demb et al., 1995; Wagner et al., 1998b), and full vs. divided attention (Shallice et al., 1994). These and similar findings were taken by Tulving et al. (1994) as evidence for a key role for left prefrontal cortex in episodic encoding. They proposed that engagement of this region occurs whenever semantic information is retrieved about a study item, and thus is available for incorporation into the episodic representation that includes the item.

The bulk of the early encoding studies employed verbal material (for an exception see Haxby et al., 1996), making it difficult to establish whether the left-sided lateralization of the frontal "encoding" effects was specific for verbal material. Findings from later studies, in which nonverbal as well as verbal items were employed, add further weight to the proposal that the prefrontal cortex is engaged during episodic encoding, and indicate that the lateralization of encoding-related prefrontal activity is material-dependent (e.g. Kelley et al., 1998; Wagner et al., 1998a; McDermott et al., 1999). The finding that encoding of non-verbal material, such as unfamiliar faces, activates right prefrontal regions (Kelley et al., 1998) suggests that the role of the prefrontal cortex in encoding goes beyond those aspects of semantic processing held to be supported by the left prefrontal cortex.

Whereas the findings from these early studies consistently point to the involvement of the prefrontal cortex in episodic encoding, findings for the medial temporal lobe have been more variable. Several of the aforementioned studies failed to report any effect at all (e.g. Shallice et al., 1994), whereas others did find effects in the vicinity of the hippocampus (e.g. Kelley et al., 1998). The inconsistency of the findings is perhaps surprising in light of the key role proposed for the hippocampus in episodic memory. The inconsistency may reflect the failure to employ contrasts which sufficiently emphasize encoding-related differences in medial temporal activity, e.g. "shallow", non-semantic encoding tasks may give rise to poor subsequent memory, not because there is a failure to engage hippocampally-mediated encoding operations but because the encoded information is difficult to access in subsequent memory tests.

In this respect, it is noteworthy that it is widely held that a key role for the hippocampus during encoding is in some sense to "bind" together in memory disparate elements of a study episode (e.g. Eichenbaum et al., 1992). According to this view, differential activation of the hippocampus at encoding should be revealed by contrasts that compare conditions that vary the extent to which study items are processed associatively rather than independently. Consistent with this prediction, studies that have contrasted tasks requiring the explicit formation of inter-item associations with tasks emphasizing item-specific processing have reported more activity in the vicinity of the hippocampus during the associative condition (Henke et al., 1997, 1999; Montaldi et al., 1998; the imaging method employed in this latter study was single photon emission tomography, a method similar in some respects to PET but with lower spatial resolution).

Another approach to the investigation of memory encoding has been to contrast a condition in which the same item or items are presented repeatedly with one in which items are trial-unique. Studies adopting this approach (Stern et al., 1996; Gabrieli et al., 1997; Rombouts et al., 1997, 1999; Constable et al., 2000) have consistently reported activation in medial temporal regions in the vicinity of the parahippocampal cortex and hippocampus. These findings suggest that, at least for complex visual material (no study employed exclusively verbal material), the medial temporal lobe is sensitive to relative novelty. To the extent that novel stimuli engage episodic encoding operations more than experimentally familiar items, the findings indicate a role for the medial temporal regions in the support of these operations. An alternative explanation, however, is that the findings reflect repetition suppression effects analogous to those discussed in the section on Priming, above. By this argument, the findings are a reflection of the facilitated processing that accompanies stimulus repetition, rather than processes associated specifically with the encoding of unrepeated items.

More generally, findings from studies that use across-task or across-block contrasts to reveal activity related to memory encoding all suffer from a common difficulty of interpretation. Whereas some of the effects revealed by such contrasts may indeed reflect neural activity responsible for differences in the effectiveness with which information is encoded into memory, other effects may arise because of differences between conditions that have nothing to do with memory-encoding operations.

This problem can be overcome by employing only a single encoding task, and searching for regions where activity correlates with subsequent memory performance. This approach was adopted in several studies (Cahill et al., 1996; Alkire et al., 1998; Fernández et al., 1998, 1999), all of which reported that the amount of medial temporal activity during encoding correlated with subsequent memory performance, either across (Cahill et al., 1996; Alkire et al., 1998) or within (Fernández et al., 1998, 1999) subjects. Because the data in these studies were obtained over blocks of items, the findings are ambiguous with respect to whether the medial temporal activity "predicting" subsequent memory was state- or item-related.

Insight into regions supporting the encoding of individual study items can be obtained by using event-related fMRI. By adapting a procedure employed in event-related potential studies of memory encoding (for reviews, see Rugg, 1995; Wagner et al., 1999), activity elicited by study items can be contrasted according to whether the items are remembered or forgotten in a subsequent memory test, allowing identification of regions in which activity at the time of encoding predicts subsequent memory performance. Regions exhibiting such "subsequent memory effects" are good candidates as ones playing a role in episodic encoding.

This approach has been employed in several studies (with words, Wagner et al., 1998b; Baker et al., 2001; Buckner et al., 2001; Kirchhoff et al., 2000; Otten et al., 2001: with non-verbal material, Brewer et al, 1998; Kirchhoff et al., 2000). In most of the studies employing words, subsequently remembered items elicited greater activity in the inferior prefrontal cortex, especially on the left, than did words that were subsequently forgotten. Subsequent memory effects were also reported in the medial temporal lobe, in parahippocampal cortex in the study of Wagner et al. (1998b), and in the vicinity of the hippocampus proper in Otten et al. (2001). Results from the studies employing nonverbal material were consistent with these findings. Subsequent memory effects in the prefrontal cortex were right-lateralized, while subsequent memory effects in the parahippocampal cortex were observed bilaterally in both studies and in the right hippocampus in Kirchoff et al. (2001).

The event-related findings are broadly consistent with the findings from the blocked experiments discussed earlier. This consistency is highlighted by the study of Otten et al. (2001), when regions exhibiting item-specific subsequent memory effects could be compared directly with the regions demonstrating greater activity for semantic relative to non-semantic study tasks—the contrast at the heart of the original proposal that the left prefrontal cortex plays a key role in episodic encoding (Tulving et al., 1994). Otten et al. (2001) employed two different encoding tasks, requiring judgements about semantic and letter-level features, respectively. The left frontal and anterior hippocampal regions that exhibited subsequent memory effects in the semantic study task were, in the main, a subset of the regions identified by the between-task contrast. These regions seem likely, therefore, to support the processes responsible for conferring the mnemonic advantage on the semantically studied items. Subsequent memory effects were, however, found in only a small fraction of the regions identified by the between-task contrast, emphasizing that such contrasts conflate processes related to encoding with other processes that may have nothing to do with memory. Interestingly, Otten et al. (2001) found that subsequent memory effects for their non-semantic task were located in a subset of the left frontal and hippocampal regions exhibiting subsequent memory effects in the semantic task. They suggested that memory for these items was supported by "incidental" semantic processing, rather than processing engaged specifically by the non-semantic discrimination task.

Interpretation of Findings from Encoding Studies

Prefrontal cortex.   The findings from both blocked and event-related studies suggest that episodic encoding of verbal material depends on processes supported by the left inferior prefrontal cortex, as was originally proposed by Tulving et al. (1994). The prefrontal cortex also appears to play an important role in the encoding of non-verbal material, when a bilateral or right-lateralized pattern of prefrontal activity is observed.

What are the cognitive operations associated with these prefrontal effects? Whereas little can be said at present about the operations engaged by nonverbal material and supported by the right prefrontal regions, there is more evidence about the possible role of the left prefrontal cortex. The overlap between regions activated by "depth of processing" manipulations and those identified by event-related, "subsequent memory" experiments suggests the existence of cognitive operations that are engaged differentially both by semantic vs. nonsemantic processing, and by effective vs. less effective encoding within semantic processing tasks. It has been suggested that the operations supported by the regions of the left inferior prefrontal cortex identified in contrasts between semantic and non-semantic tasks might contribute to "semantic working memory" (Gabrieli et al., 1998)—the temporary storage, manipulation and selection of an item's semantic attributes. According to this hypothesis (see also Buckner & Koutstaal, 1998; Wagner et al., 1998b, 1999), the more a study item engages semantic working memory, the more likely it is that its semantic features will be incorporated into a representation of the study episode and, therefore, the more likely it is that the episode will be accessible in a subsequent memory test (an idea very similar to the original proposal of Tulving et al. 1994). It is easy to see how this hypothesis can encompass the findings from between-task comparisons. Additional assumptions are needed, however, to allow the hypothesis to account for subsequent memory effects. In at least one subsequent memory experiment (Otten et al., 2001), study task performance, as assessed by accuracy and RT, was equivalent for subsequently remembered and forgotten items. Thus, there was no evidence that the two classes of items differentially engaged the cognitive operations supporting the semantic judgment task. It is therefore necessary to assume that the engagement of semantic working memory in such tasks goes beyond what is required to perform the task itself, and it is the extent of this additional processing that is particularly important for memory encoding. This raises the intriguing question of exactly what causes some items to receive "additional" processing? Presumably this is determined by a combination of subject and item variables that is likely to prove difficult to disentangle.

Medial temporal lobe.   Given the strength of the evidence of a key role for the medial temporal lobe in episodic memory, it is unsurprising that studies have found greater medial temporal lobe activity for study items or conditions associated with good, as opposed to poor, subsequent memory. There is, however, considerable variation between studies with regard to the specific medial temporal regions differentially engaged by encoding manipulations. This variability persists even if consideration is restricted to studies of subsequent memory effects, arguably the "purest" way to identify regions where activity correlates specifically with encoding. For example, in two studies that were in many ways similar, subsequent memory effects were observed in the posterior parahippocampal gyrus (extending into the fusiform gyrus) in one case (Wagner et al., 1998b), and in anterior and posterior hippocampus in the other (Otten et al., 2001; see Lepage et al., 1998; Schacter & Wagner, 1998, for further discussion of the possible significance of anterior vs. posterior hippocampal activations). While these and similar findings are consistent with the widely held view that the medial temporal lobe plays an important role in memory encoding, they give little clue as to what roles might be played by the different parts of this region.

Concluding Comments

With few exceptions, encoding studies have focused on tasks requiring semantic analysis of study items, with many studies actually operationalizing encoding in terms of a contrast between semantic and non-semantic study tasks. The emphasis on semantically mediated encoding operations is understandable in light of the large literature, much of it conducted within the "levels of processing" framework (Lockhart, 1992), that highlights the benefit of semantic encoding for subsequent episodic retrieval. However, this emphasis is at the expense of other research, conducted within the "transfer appropriate processing" frame-work (e.g. Morris et al., 1977; Roediger et al., 1989), which indicates that the advantage of semantic relative to non-semantic encoding is diminished if memory is tested with tests that recapitulate the processing engaged during study, e.g. by testing memory for items encoded in a phonological study task with phonological cued recall. It will be of interest to determine whether regions identified as playing a key role in semantically-mediated encoding are the same as those engaged during successful encoding in non-semantic study tasks, especially when memory is assessed with tests that maximize overlap between study and test processing.

Retrieval

To an even greater extent than for encoding, neuroimaging studies of episodic retrieval have focused on memory for pre-experimentally familiar words. While some studies have investigated retrieval using free recall, most have employed memory tests that involve the presentation of cues in some way related to the studied items, as in cued recall and recognition. Whereas an understanding of free recall is undoubtedly important, this test is arguably not ideal for studies that aim to dissociate and characterize the different processes engaged during episodic retrieval. Unlike tests that employ discrete retrieval cues, free recall provides little basis for controlling the frequency and timing of retrieval attempts (although see Fletcher et al., 1998).

One consideration when interpreting findings from functional imaging studies of mem-ory retrieval arises from the argument that few, if any, retrieval tasks are "process pure" (Jacoby & Kelley, 1992). A well-known example of this problem is the influence of ex-plicit memory on indirect memory tests intended to assess implicit memory (cf. section on Priming, above). But as pointed out by Jacoby and his associates, performance on direct memory tests used to assess explicit memory can also be influenced by more than one kind of memory. The most common retrieval task in neuroimaging studies of episodic memory—recognition memory—is a task on which performance is almost certainly determined by multiple processes (e.g. Yonelinas, 1994).

Blocked Retrieval Studies

As in studies of priming and encoding, early PET and fMRI studies of episodic retrieval employed blocked designs. The interpretation of findings from such designs is particularly difficult in the case of retrieval tasks. First, the confounding of state- and item-related effects makes it very difficult to distinguish processing elicited by a specific cue (e.g. a recognition memory test item) from more tonic processes associated with mere engagement in the retrieval task; second, as noted previously, blocked designs do not permit separate assessment of activity associated with different classes of response (e.g. recognition hits vs. misses).

In an attempt to overcome the first of these problems, several studies have varied the ratio of "old" and "new" retrieval cues across different test blocks (e.g. Rugg et al., 1996; Stark & Squire, 2000a), on the assumption that effects that co-vary with the proportion of old items will reflect item-specific consequences of successful retrieval. This approach has two problems. First, even when the assumption is warranted, it is not possible to dissociate state-related activity from item-related activity that is common to old and new items. Second, contrary to the assumption, variation in the old: new ratio may not be sufficient to dissociate item- and state-related correlates of retrieval success; state-related activity might also co-vary with the old: new ratio, e.g. as a consequence of different expectancies induced about the structure of the stimulus sequence. This possibility is highlighted by the findings of Wagner et al. (1998c), who obtained differences in prefrontal activity between two identically structured test blocks, merely by informing subjects that the old: new ratios in each block were different.

Problems of interpretation notwithstanding, findings from blocked studies of retrieval are summarized briefly below, focusing on those regions where retrieval-related activity has been reported most consistently.

Prefrontal cortex.   Activation of the prefrontal cortex has been reported in the majority of functional neuroimaging studies of episodic retrieval (for review, see Fletcher & Henson, 2001). Surprisingly, even when the experimental material was verbal, these retrieval-related effects were often right-lateralized. Thus, right-lateralized prefrontal activation (relative to appropriate control tasks) has been reported for free recall (e.g. Fletcher et al., 1998), word-stem cued recall (e.g. Squire et al., 1992), recall of paired associates (e.g. Shallice et al., 1994) and recognition memory (e.g. Nyberg et al., 1995).

The consistency with which right prefrontal activation has been reported in studies of episodic retrieval contrasts with the diversity of views that have been put forward as to its functional significance (e.g. Nyberg et al., 1995, vs. Rugg et al., 1996). One issue that arose early on concerns whether retrieval-related activity in the right prefrontal cortex is state- or item-related (Fletcher et al., 1997). This issue has proved difficult to settle; as already noted, the findings from blocked studies leave it uncertain whether the right prefrontal activations reflect state-related effects, item-related effects or some mixture of the two.

A second issue is whether right prefrontal activity during retrieval can be dissociated neuroanatomically. It has been suggested, for example, that a distinction should be drawn between the retrieval functions supported by dorsolateral (BA46/9), ventrolateral (BA 47) and anterior (BA10) regions (Fletcher & Henson, 2001; see also Christoff & Gabrieli, 2000). A further anatomical dissociation, in the form of differential lateralization, has been proposed in light of the fact that activation of the right prefrontal cortex is accompanied in many studies by activity in one or more left prefrontal regions. Nolde et al. (1998) suggested that left prefrontal activity reflects the engagement of what they termed "reflective" retrieval processes, contrasting these with the "heuristic" processes supported by the right prefrontal cortex.

Parietal cortex.   Medial and lateral parietal regions have been consistently identified during episodic retrieval, usually including the region known as the precuneus (medial BA7). There is evidence from experiments manipulating the relative proportions of old and new items that activation of the precuneus is associated with successful, as opposed to unsuccessful, retrieval (Kapur et al., 1995; Rugg et al., 1996).

Another parietal region consistently activated during episodic retrieval lies on the lateral surface of the parietal lobe and includes both inferior (BA 39/40) and superior (BA7) regions (e.g. Cabeza et al., 1997). Like the medial parietal region noted above, there is evidence that lateral parietal activation is associated with successful retrieval. Unlike the medial parietal cortex, however, activation of the lateral parietal regions seems to exhibit an element of task specificity, in that it has been found to be more prominent during recognition memory than cued recall (Cabeza et al., 1997; Rugg et al., 1998).

Medial temporal lobe.   Retrieval-related medial temporal lobe activity has been reported in numerous blocked studies (for review, see Lepage et al., 1998; Schacter & Wagner, 1998), albeit with much less consistency than in the case of prefrontal and parietal regions (see Buckner et al., 1995, experiments 2 and 3; Rugg et al., 1996, 1998, for examples of negative findings). Medial temporal activation has been reported both for task-wise contrasts (e.g. Squire et al., 1992) and also in studies where the contrast was within-task and involved manipulation of the old: new ratio (Stark & Squire, 2000a, 2000b; but see also Rugg et al., 1996, 1998). These latter findings are important, as they suggest that the medial temporal regions contribute to, or are at least sensitive to, the outcome of a successful retrieval attempt (although it is important to bear in mind the caveats about interpretation of such studies that were discussed earlier). As noted by Schacter & Wagner (1998), it is difficult to discern any pattern among studies reporting retrieval-related medial temporal effects in the location of the activity (e.g. hippocampal vs. extra-hippocampal; anterior vs. posterior); neither is it easy to see what distinguishes studies reporting positive findings from those failing to find an effect.

Event-related Studies

The majority of event-related studies of episodic retrieval have employed variants of yes/no recognition memory, and have focused on the neural correlates of retrieval success, i.e. patterns of brain activation associated with the retrieval of information from memory (Rugg & Henson, in press).

Processing common to old and new items.   One event-related study assessed activity separately for cues corresponding to studied and unstudied items. In Ranganath et al. (2000)

two test tasks were contrasted. In the "general" task, yes/no recognition judgements were required, whereas in the specific task, subjects judged whether test items were new, or larger or smaller than at study. The intertask contrast showed increased activity from left anterior prefrontal cortex (BA 10) in the more specific task, an effect that was apparent for both old and new test items. This finding is consistent with blocked studies contrasting source and recognition judgements (Henson et al., 1999a; Rugg et al., 1999), and suggests that the left anterior prefrontal cortex supports operations engaged when a retrieval task requires recovery of a high level of perceptual detail. Crucially, the findings of Ranganath et al. (2000) indicate that these operations are not necessarily associated with retrieval success, and may instead reflect differential engagement of pre-retrieval processes.

Retrieval success.   Two early event-related fMRI studies of recognition memory (Buckner et al., 1998a; Schacter et al., 1997) failed to find reliable differences between responses elicited by correctly classified old and new words. Later studies, however, consistently reported differences in activity elicited by old and new items, e.g. Konishi et al. (2000) reported greater activity for old items in inferior and lateral parietal cortex bilaterally, in medial parietal cortex (BA 7/31) and in several prefrontal regions, including bilateral anterior (BA 10) and left ventral/dorsolateral (BA 45/47/46) areas.

Donaldson et al. (2001) investigated both item- and state-related activity during recognition memory. State-related effects, which were identified by interrupting the recognition task by regular "rest" periods, were found in a number of regions, some of which overlapped those exhibiting item-related effects. Because Donaldson et al. did not include a control condition in which words were presented in the context of a task imposing no demands on memory, it is not possible to assess which, if any, of these regions exhibited activity tied specifically to the requirement to engage in recognition memory, rather than to more general aspects of word processing. The same problem of interpretation does not exist for the contrast between responses elicited by old and new words. The findings from this contrast agreed well with those described by Konishi et al. (2000).

Henson et al. (1999b, 2000) employed recognition memory tests in which subjects were required not only to judge whether a word was old or new, but also to provide information about the subjective experience accompanying the judgement. In the first study subjects signalled whether each test word was new, whether it was judged old on the basis of recollection of some aspect of the study episode (a Remember response; Tulving, 1985), or judged old solely on the basis of an acontextual sense of familiarity (a Know response). Relative to new words, Remembered old words elicited enhanced activity in a network similar to that identified by Konishi et al. (2000) and Donaldson et al. (2001). Direct contrasts between the two classes of old items revealed relatively greater activity for Remembered items in the left dorsal anterior prefrontal (BA 8/9), inferior and superior lateral parietal cortex (BA 40/19) and posterior cingulate (BA 24), whereas items assigned a Know judgement elicited relatively more activity in the right dorsolateral prefrontal (BA 46), anterior cingulate (BA 9/32) and dorsal medial parietal (BA 7) regions. These findings were broadly replicated in a similar study by Eldridge et al. (2000), with the important additional finding that "Remembered" words elicited greater activity in the left hippocampus than did either new words or old words given a "Know" judgement.

Henson et al. (1999b) proposed that their finding of greater right dorsolateral frontal activity for Know judgments reflected the role of this region in monitoring the products of a retrieval attempt (Burgess & Shallice, 1996). They tested this proposal (Henson et al., 2000b) with a recognition memory test employing confidence judgements, predicting that nonconfident decisions would be associated with greater right dorsolateral activity than confident decisions. The prediction was borne out; the same region responsive to Know judgements in Henson et al. (1999b) was more active when correctly classified items (whether old or new) were assigned a nonconfident than a confident decision. The study of Henson et al. (2000b) also provided an opportunity to investigate effects related to retrieval success. The findings for the old minus new contrast revealed greater activity in much the same network identified in other studies, as well as a late-onsetting effect (old > new) in the right anterior prefrontal cortex (BA 10).

In two studies event-related activity was investigated in "false memory" paradigms (see Roediger, 1996, and accompanying articles). In McDermott et al. (2000), subjects studied compound words such as "nosebleed" and "skydive". At test, yes/no recognition judgements were made on new words, studied words, and new words formed by recombining the component parts of some of the study words (e.g. nosedive). Recombined items attract considerably more false alarms than do new items formed from unstudied words and, it has been proposed (Jones & Jacoby, 2001), are rejected as old when they elicit recollection of one or both of the original study words, allowing the sense of familiarity engendered by the items to be successfully "opposed". Consistent with this interpretation, relative to new items, correctly rejected recombined words activated many of the same regions as were activated by truly old items. In addition, recombined items elicited greater dorsolateral prefrontal activity than did truly old words.

Cabeza et al. (2001) employed test items consisting of new and old words, along with "related lure" items—new words strongly related semantically to study items. The majority of the related lures were incorrectly classified as old. Relative to the activity elicited by new items, Cabeza et al. reported that a region of the anterior temporal lobe bilaterally, including the hippocampus, was more active for both old and misclassified related lures, a finding they took to reflect the role of this structure in retrieval of relatively abstract episodic information. Other areas showing greater activity for both old and related lure items relative to new words were bilateral dorsolateral prefrontal cortex (BA 46), bilateral inferior parietal cortex (BA 39/40) and the precuneus (BA 7/19/31). Among areas showing relatively greater activity for related lures was a region of orbitofrontal cortex on the right (BA 11).

In the final study to be mentioned in this section, Maratos et al. (2001) required subjects to study words embedded in sentences that varied in their rated emotionality (neutral, negative or positive). At test, the requirement was merely to discriminate between studied and unstudied words, without regard to the studied words' encoding contexts. Relative to new items, recognized studied words gave rise to a pattern of activity very similar to that observed in previous studies. More interestingly, relative to recognized test words from emotionally neutral contexts, words from negative contexts activated the left amygdala and hippocampus, and the right dorsolateral prefrontal cortex. In the analogous comparison, items from positive contexts activated the orbitofrontal cortex. Maratos et al. (2001) attributed these findings to the incidental retrieval of the emotional contexts. They argued that the hippocampal and right dorsolateral effects reflected the fact that emotionally negative contexts were associated with a richer and more salient episodic content than were the neutral and positive contexts.

Functional Significance of Retrieval-related Activity

Prefrontal cortex. The prefrontal region most consistently associated with retrieval success in event-related studies is the anterior prefrontal cortex (BA 10). In marked contrast with the findings from blocked studies, these anterior prefrontal effects were observed more often on the left than on the right. Dorsolateral prefrontal activations (BA 9/46)—both left- and right-sided—were also sometimes detected.

What processes are supported by left prefrontal cortex during episodic retrieval? The finding of Henson et al. (1999b) that the left anterior cortex was more active for recognized items accorded Remember rather than Know judgements, is consistent with a role in the processing of retrieved information with a relatively high level of episodic content. A similar conclusion can be drawn from the finding of McDermott et al. (2000), when left anterior prefrontal cortex was activated both by recognized old items and by correctly rejected related lures (items which, it is assumed, elicited recollection of the study episode). An important question is how to reconcile the proposed role for this region in recollection with the finding of Ranganath et al. (2000), that left anterior prefrontal cortex can also be activated by retrieval cues corresponding to unstudied items, when little or no recollection is possible.

As already noted, the question of whether activation of right anterior prefrontal cortex during episodic retrieval reflects state- or item-related processing has been much debated. According to Tulving and colleagues, the functional role of right prefrontal cortex is to support "retrieval mode", a mental state in which environmental events are treated as retrieval cues, and retrieved episodic memories are experienced "autonoetically" (Tulving, 1983; Wheeler et al., 1997). From this viewpoint, right prefrontal activity should be state- rather than item-related and, critically, should not vary according to whether a retrieval attempt is successful or unsuccessful. An alternative viewpoint (e.g. Rugg et al., 1996) posits that right prefrontal activity is item-related and associated specifically with retrieval success. The findings from event-related studies do not clearly distinguish these two positions; while the findings indicate that there are circumstances under which the right prefrontal cortex exhibits item-related activity, no study has satisfactorily addressed the question of whether this region also demonstrates task-dependent, state-related activity. There is no reason in principle why this issue cannot be resolved using designs that allow concurrent measurement of both classes of activity (cf. Donaldson et al., 2001).

The other prefrontal region activated in some event-related studies is dorsolateral prefrontal cortex. Dorsolateral prefrontal activation seems most likely to be found when task demands exceed those of simple recognition—whether by virtue of the requirement to make an introspective judgement about the recognition decision (Eldridge et al., 2000; Henson et al., 1999b, 2000b), or to discriminate between "true" and "false" recollections (McDermott et al., 2000; Cabeza et al., 2001). As suggested previously (Fletcher et al., 1998; Henson et al., 1999a), these demands may include the engagement of monitoring processes that operate on the products of retrieval.

Parietal cortex. In the majority of studies reviewed, the lateral and medial parietal cortex were found to exhibit greater activity for items eliciting successful rather than unsuccessful retrieval, regardless of the exact form of the retrieval task. In most of the studies, the lateral parietal activations were lateralized to, or more extensive, on the left. The findings are consistent with a number of previous studies in which retrieval success was investigated with blocked designs and, broadly speaking, with two meta-analyses of studies employing such designs (Habib & Lepage, 1999; Lepage et al., 2000). The findings of Henson et al. (1999b) and Eldridge et al. (2000), that left lateral parietal activity was greater for items accorded Remember rather than Know responses, suggest that activity in this region may be a function of the amount of episodic information retrieved in response to the test item.

On the basis of the findings from event-related studies, the functional role of medial parietal cortex in memory would appear to be similar to that proposed for lateral parietal cortex. Activations related to retrieval success were found in both the precuneus (e.g. Konishi et al., 2000) and more ventrally in the posterior cingulate (Henson et al., 1999b). There was little evidence to suggest that activity in these two medial regions could be dissociated from one another, or from activity in lateral cortex, although other studies have demonstrated task-based dissociations between these regions (Rugg et al., 1998; Shallice et al., 1994). A frequently cited role for the medial parietal cortex is in the support of visual imagery (Fletcher et al., 1995). According to this argument, activation of the medial parietal region during successful retrieval reflects the strong demands placed on visual imagery by the representational demands of retrieved episodic information.

Medial temporal lobe. Few event-related studies have reported retrieval-related activation in the hippocampus or adjacent medial temporal cortex. The positive findings that were obtained (Eldridge et al., 2000; Cabeza et al., 2001; Maratos et al., 2001) were for test items likely to have elicited strong episodic recollection and, as such, they are consistent with the proposal that retrieval-related hippocampal activity is associated specifically with this form of memory (Rugg et al., 1997; Schacter et al., 1996). The failure to find hippocampal activation in other studies of recognition memory may to some extent reflect the fact that recognition judgements can be made on the basis of an acontextual sense of familiarity in the absence of the (hippocampally-mediated) retrieval of a study episode (Aggleton & Brown, 1999). This possibility seems unlikely, however, to account fully for the inconsistent findings noted above; two other studies in which contrasts were performed between recollected and new items (Henson et al., 1999b; McDermott et al., 2000) failed to find differential hippocampal activity.

It is unclear why medial temporal activity is not consistently detected during episodic retrieval. One possibility is that the null findings are a consequence of the neural dynamics of the hippocampus, such that retrieval-related neural activity does not always give rise to changes in metabolic demand on a spatial scale large enough to be detected by current methods. Alternatively, the lack of positive findings may be a sign that the contribution of the medial temporal lobe to retrieval is often overshadowed by encoding-related activity. By this argument (e.g. Rugg et al., 1997; Stark & Squire, 2000b), the failure to find differential activity for contrasts between responses to old and new items reflects the fact that medial temporal structures are active both in support of retrieval of old information and the encoding of new information associated with contextually novel items.

Conclusions

Event-related fMRI has allowed the neural correlates of memory retrieval to be dissociated with a level of precision (in the functional, not the anatomical, sense) unavailable to blocked designs. It is important, however, that the method is applied to tasks other than those based around recognition memory. The neural correlates of episodic memory retrieval appear in part to be task-dependent (Allan et al., 2000; Cabeza et al., 1997; Rugg et al., 1998), and hypotheses formulated on the basis of the existing, rather narrow dataset need to be challenged by findings from a much wider range of tasks.

GENERAL CONCLUSIONS

The findings from functional neuroimaging studies stengthen and refine conclusions drawn on the basis of neuropsychological evidence, but go beyond this evidence in a number of significant ways. Findings from studies of indirect and direct tests are consistent with the widely-held view that priming and explicit memory (for familiar items at least) rely on qualitatively different kinds of memory. And evidence of involvement of the hippocampus and adjacent regions of the medial temporal lobe during episodic encoding and retrieval is unsurprising, given the range of other evidence about the importance of these structures for episodic remembering (what is more surprising, perhaps, is the lack of consistency across studies as to the circumstances and location in which medial temporal activation is found).

Of more interest are findings identifying regions not previously recognized as playing an important role in episodic memory. Chief among these is the prefrontal cortex; lesion studies gave little clue that different prefrontal regions might be involved selectively in encoding or retrieval, or that lateralization of memory processing in the prefrontal cortex might be anything other than material-dependent. In the case of other regions—notably, the medial and lateral parietal areas consistently activated during episodic retrieval—it is little exaggeration to say that their involvement in memory was completely unsuspected before the advent of functional neuroimaging.

Thus, the principal contribution of functional neuroimaging to the understanding of human memory has not been in respect of the brain area—the medial temporal lobe—recognized above all others for its contribution to episodic memory. Instead, it has been to identify other regions which, along with the medial temporal lobe, might belong to distributed networks supporting encoding and retrieval operations. Among the many questions arising out of the findings reviewed above, one is paramount—which of the many regions implicated by functional neuroimaging studies support operations that are necessary for, rather than mere correlates of, normal memory function? For the reasons noted at the opening of this chapter, this question is best addressed by investigating the sequelae of focal lesions. It is to be hoped, therefore, that it will motivate the study of a more diverse range of lesion locations than those conventionally investigated in neuropsychological studies of memory.

ACKNOWLEDGEMENT

The author is supported by the Wellcome Trust.

REFERENCES

Allan, K., Dolan, R.J., Fletcher, P.C. & Rugg, M.D. (2000). The role of the anterior right prefrontal cortex in episodic memory retrieval. *Neuroimage*, **11**, 217–227.

Aggleton, J.P. & Brown, M.W. (1999). Episodic memory, amnesia, and the hippocampal–anterior thalamic axis. *Behavioral and Brain Sciences*, **22**, 425–444.

Alkire, M.T., Haier, R.J., Fallon, J.H. & Cahill, L. (1998). Hippocampal, but not amygdala, activity at encoding correlates with long-term, free recall of nonemotional information. *Proceedings of the National Academy of Sciences of the USA*, **95**, 14506–14510.

Badgaiyan, R.D., Schacter, D.L. & Alpert, N.M. (1999). Auditory priming within and across modalities: evidence from positron emission tomography. *Journal of Cognitive Neuroscience*, **11**, 337–348.

Badgaiyan, R.D., Schacter, D.L. & Alpert, N.M. (2001). Priming within and across modalities: exploring the nature of rCBF increases and decreases. *Neuroimage*, **13**, 272–282.

Baker, J.T., Sanders, A.L., Maccotta, L. & Buckner, R.L. (2001). Neural correlates of verbal memory encoding during semantic and structural processing tasks. *NeuroReport*, **12**, 1251–1256.

Blaxton, T.A. (1989) Investigating dissociations among memory measures—support for a transfer-appropriate processing framework. *Journal of Experimental Psychology: Learning, Memory and Cognition*, **15**, 657–668.

Bowers, J.S. (2000). In defense of abstractionist theories of repetition priming and word identification. *Psychonomic Bulletin and Reviews*, **7**, 83–99.

Brewer, J.B., Zhao, Z., Desmond, J.E. et al. (1998). Making memories: brain activity that predicts how well visual experience will be remembered. *Science*, **281**, 1185–1187.

Brown, M.W. & Xiang, J.Z. (1998) Recognition memory: neuronal substrates of the judgement of prior occurrence. *Progress in Neurobiology*, **55**, 149–189.

Buckner, R.L. & Koutstaal, W. (1998). Functional neuroimaging studies of encoding, priming, and explicit memory retrieval. *Proceedings of the National Academy of Sciences of the USA*, **95**, 891–898.

Buckner, R.L., Kelley, W.M. & Petersen, S.E. (1999). Frontal cortex contributes to human memory formation. *Nature Neuroscience*, **2**, 311–314.

Buckner, R.L., Wheeler, M.E. & Sheridan, M. (2001). Encoding processes during retrieval tasks. *Journal of Cognitive Neuroscience*, **13**, 406–415.

Buckner, R.L., Koutstaal, W., Schacter, D.L. & Rosen, B.R. (2000). Functional MRI evidence for a role of frontal and inferior temporal cortex in amodal components of priming. *Brain*, **123**, 620–640.

Buckner, R.L., Petersen, S.E., Ojemann, J.G. et al. (1995). Functional anatomical studies of explicit and implicit memory retrieval. *Journal of Neuroscience*, **15**, 12–29.

Buckner, R.L., Koutstaal, W., Schacter, D.L. et al. (1998a). Functional–anatomic study of episodic retrieval: II selective averaging of event-related fMRI trials to test the retrieval success hypothesis. *Neuroimage*, **7**, 163–175.

Buckner, R.L., Goodman, J., Burock, M. et al. (1998b). Functional–anatomic correlates of object priming in humans revealed by rapid presentation event-related fMRI. *Neuron*, **20**, 285–296.

Burgess, P.W. & Shallice, T. (1996). Confabulation and the control of recollection. *Memory*, **4**, 359–411.

Cabeza, R., Kapur, S., Craik, F.I.M. et al. (1997). Functional neuroanatomy of recall and recognition: a PET study of episodic memory. *Journal of Cognitive Neuroscience*, **9**, 254–265.

Cabeza, R., Rao, S.M., Wagner, A.D. et al. (2001). Can medial temporal lobe regions distinguish true from false? An event-related fMRI study of veridical and illusory recognition memory. *Proceedings of the National Academy of Sciences of the USA*, **10**, 98: 4805–4810.

Cahill, L., Haier, R.J., Fallon, J. et al. (1996). Amygdala activity at encoding correlated with long-term, free recall of emotional information. *Proceedings of the National Academy of Sciences of the USA*, **93**, 8016–8021.

Cave, C.B. (1997). Very long-lasting priming in picture naming. *Psychological Science*, **8**, 322–325.

Christoff, K. & Gabrieli, J.D.E. (2000). The frontopolar cortex and human cognition: evidence for a rostrocaudal hierarchical organization within the human prefrontal cortex. *Psychobiology*, **28**, 168–186.

Constable, R.T., Carpentier, A., Pugh, K. et al. (2000). Investigation of the human hippocampal formation using a randomized event-related paradigm and Z-shimmed functional MRI. *Neuroimage*, **12**, 55–62.

Dale, A.M., Liu, A.K., Fischl, B.R. et al. (2000). Dynamic statistical parametric mapping: combining fMRI and MEG for high-resolution imaging of cortical activity. *Neuron*, **26**, 55–67.

Demb, J.B., Desmond, J.E., Wagner, A.D. et al. (1995). Semantic encoding and retrieval in the left inferior prefrontal cortex: a functional MRI study of task difficulty and process specificity. *Journal of Neuroscience*, **15**, 5870–5878.

Desgranges, B., Baron, J.-C. & Eustache, F. (1998). The functional neuroanatomy of episodic memory: the role of the frontal lobes, the hippocampal formation, and other areas. *Neuroimage*, **8**, 198–213.

Donaldson, D.J., Petersen, S.E., Ollinger, J.M. & Buckner, R.L. (2001). Separating state and item related processing during recognition memory using functional MRI. *Neuroimage*, **13**, 129–142.

Duvernoy, H.M. (1999). *The Human Brain*, 2nd edn. New York: Springer-Verlag.

Eichenbaum, H., Otto, T. & Cohen, N.J. (1992). The hippocampus—what does it do? *Behavioural and Neural Biology*, **57**, 2–36.

Eldridge, L.L., Knowlton, B.J., Furmanski, C.S. et al. (2000). Remembering episodes: a selective role for the hippocampus during retrieval. *Nature Neuroscience*, **3**, 1149–1152.

Fernández, G., Brewer, J.B., Zhao, Z. et al. (1999). Level of sustained entorhinal activity at study correlates with subsequent cued-recall performance: a functional magnetic resonance imaging study with high acquisition rate. *Hippocampus*, **9**, 35–44.

Fernández, G., Weyerts, H., Schrader-Bolsche, M. et al. (1998). Successful verbal encoding into episodic memory engages the posterior hippocampus: a parametrically analyzed functional magnetic resonance study. *Journal of Neuroscience*, **18**, 1841–1847.

Fletcher, P.C. & Henson, R.N.A. (2001). Prefrontal cortex and human memory—insights from functional neuroimaging. *Brain*, **124**, 849–881.

Fletcher, P.C., Frith, C.D. & Rugg, M.D. (1997). The functional neuroanatomy of episodic memory. *Trends in Neuroscience*, **20**, 213–218.

Fletcher, P.C., Shallice, T., Frith, C.D. et al. (1998). The functional roles of the prefrontal cortex in episodic memory: II. Retrieval. *Brain*, **121**, 1249–1256.

Fletcher, P., Frith, C.D., Baker, S. et al. (1995). The mind's eye—activation of the precuneus in memory related imagery. *Neuroimage*, **2**, 196–200.

Gabrieli, J.D.E., Brewer, J.B., Desmond, J.E. & Glover, G.H. (1997). Separate neural bases of two fundamental memory processes in the human medial temporal lobe. *Science*, **276**, 264–266.

Gabrieli, J.D.E., Poldrack, R.A. & Desmond, J.E. (1998). The role of left prefrontal cortex in language and memory. *Proceedings of the National Academy of Sciences of the USA*, **95**, 906–913.

Gooding, P.A., Mayes, A.R. & van Eijk, R.A. (2000). Meta-analysis of indirect memory tests for novel material in organic amnesics. *Neuropsychologia*, **38**, 666–676.

Habib, R. & Lepage, M. (1999). Novelty assessment in the brain. In E. Tulving (ed.), Memory, *Consciousness and the Brain* (pp. 265–277). London: Psychology Press.

Haxby, J.V., Ungerleider, L.G., Horwitz, B. et al. (1996). Face encoding and recognition in the human brain. *Proceedings of the National Academy of Sciences of the USA*, **93**, 922–927.

Henke, K., Buck, A., Weber, B. & Wieser, H.G. (1997). Human hippocampus establishes associations in memory. *Hippocampus*, **7**, 249–256.

Henke, K., Weber, B., Kneifel, S. et al. (1999). Human hippocampus associates information in memory. *Proceedings of the National Academy of Sciences of the USA*, **96**, 5884–5889.

Henson, R., Shallice, T. & Dolan, R. 2000a. Neuroimaging evidence for dissociable forms of repetition priming. *Science*, **287**, 1269–1272.

Henson, R.N., Shallice, T. & Dolan, R.J. (1999a). Right prefrontal cortex and episodic memory retrieval: a functional MRI test of the monitoring hypothesis. *Brain*, **122**, 1367–1381.

Henson, R.N.A., Rugg, M.D., Shallice, T. et al. (1999b). Recollection and familiarity in recognition memory: an event-related fMRI study. *Journal of Neuroscience*, **19**, 3962–3972.

Henson, R.N.A., Rugg, M.D., Shallice, T. & Dolan, R.J. (2000b). Confidence in recognition memory for words: dissociating right prefrontal roles in episodic retrieval. *Journal of Cognitive Neuroscience*, **12**, 913–923.

Jacoby, L.L., Toth, J.P. & Yonelinas, A.P. (1993). Separating conscious and unconscious influences of memory: measuring recollection. *Journal of Experimental Psychology: General*, **122**, 139–154.

Jacoby, L.L. & Kelley, C. (1992). Unconscious influences of memory: dissociations and automaticity. In A.D. Milner & M.D. Rugg (eds), *The Neuropsychology of Consciousness* (pp. 201–233). London: Academic Press.

Jones, T.C. & Jacoby, L.L. (2001). Feature and conjunction errors in recognition memory: evidence for dual-process theory. *Journal of Memory and Language*, **45**, 82–102.

Josephs, O., Turner, R. & Friston, K.J. (1997). Event-related fMRI. *Human Brain Mapping*, **5**, 243–248.

Kanwisher, N. (2000). Domain specificity in face perception. *Nature Neuroscience*, **3**, 759–763.

Kapur, S., Craik, F., Brown, G.M. et al. (1995). Functional role of the prefrontal cortex in memory retrieval: a PET study. *NeuroReport*, **6**, 1880–1884.

Kapur, S., Craik, F.I.M., Tulving, E. et al. (1994). Neuroanatomical correlates of encoding in episodic memory: levels of processing effect. *Proceedings of the National Academy of Sciences of the USA*, **91**, 2008–2011.

Kapur, S., Tulving, E., Cabeza. R. et al. (1996). Neural correlates of intentional learning of verbal materials: a PET study in humans. *Cognitive Brain Research*, **4**, 243–249.

Kelley, W., Miezin, F., McDermott. K. et al. (1998). Hemispheric specialization in human dorsal frontal cortex and medial temporal lobe for verbal and nonverbal memory encoding. *Neuron*, **20**, 927–936.

Kirchhoff, B.A., Wagner, A.D. et al. (2000). Prefrontal–temporal circuitry for episodic encoding and subsequent memory. *Journal of Neuroscience*, **20**, 6173–6180.

Konishi, S., Wheeler, M., Donaldson, D.I. & Buckner, R. (2000). Neural correlates of episodic retrieval success. *Neuroimage*, **12**, 276–286.

Koutstaal, W., Wagner, A.D., Rotte, M. et al. (2001). Perceptual specificity in visual object priming: functional magnetic resonance imaging evidence for a laterality difference in fusiform cortex. *Neuropsychologia*, **39**, 184–199.

Lepage, M., Habib, R. & Tulving, E. (1998). Hippocampal PET activations of memory encoding and retrieval: the HIPER model. *Hippocampus*, **8**, 313–322.

Lepage, M., Ghaffar, O., Nyberg, L. & Tulving, E. (2000). Prefrontal cortex and episodic memory retrieval mode. *Proceedings of the National Academy of Sciences of the USA* **97**, 506–511.

Li, L., Miller, E.K. & Desimone, R. (1993). The representation of stimulus familiarity in anterior inferior temporal cortex. *Journal of Neurophysiology*, **69**, 1918–1929.

Lockhart, R.S. (1992). Levels of processing. In L.R. Squire (ed.), *Encyclopedia of Learning and Memory* (pp. 106–108). New York: Macmillan.

McDermott, K.B., Buckner, R.L., Petersen, S.E. et al. (1999). Set- and code-specific activation in frontal cortex: an fMRI study of encoding and retrieval of faces and words. *Journal of Cognitive Neuroscience*, **11**, 631–640.

McDermott, K.B., Jones, T.C., Petersen, S.E. et al. (2000). Retrieval success is accompanied by enhanced activation in anterior prefrontal cortex during recognition memory: an event-related fMRI study. *Journal of Cognitive Neuroscience*, **12**, 965–976.

Maratos, E.J., Dolan, R.J., Morris, J.S. et al. (2001). Neural activity associated with episodic memory for emotional context. *Neuropsychologia*, **39**, 910–920.

Marsolek, C.J., Kosslyn, S.M. & Squire, L.R. (1992). Form-specific visual priming in the right cerebral hemisphere. *Journal of Experimental Psychology: Learning, Memory and Cognition*, **18**, 492–508.

Morris, C.D., Bransford, J.D. & Franks, J.J. (1977). Levels of processing versus transfer appropriate processing. *Journal of Verbal Learning and Verbal Behavior*, **16**, 519–533.

Montaldi, D., Mayes, A.R., Barnes, A. et al. (1998). Associative encoding of pictures activates the medial temporal lobes. *Human Brain Mapping*, **6**, 85–104.

Moscovitch, M., Vriezen, E. & Goshen-Gottstein, Y. (1993). Implicit tests of memory in patients with focal lesions or degenerative brain disorders. In F. Boller & J. Grafman (eds), *Handbook of Neuropsychology*, Vol. 8 (pp. 133–173). Amsterdam: Elsevier.

Nolde, S.F., Johnson, M.K. & Raye, C.L. (1998). The role of prefrontal cortex during tests of episodic memory. *Trends in Cognitive Sciences*, **2**, 399–406.

Nyberg, L., Tulving, E., Habib, R. et al. (1995). Functional brain maps of retrieval mode and recovery of episodic information. *Neuroreport*, **7**, 249–252.

Ostergaard, A.L. & Jernigan, T.L. (1993). Are word priming and explicit memory mediated by different brain structures? In P. Graf & M.E.J. Masson (eds), *Implicit Memory: New Directions in Cognition, Development, and Neuropsychology* (pp. 327–349). Hillsdale, NJ: Erlbaum.

Otten, L.J., Henson, R.N.A. & Rugg, M.D. (2001). Depth of processing effects on neural correlates of memory encoding: relationship between findings from across- and within-task comparisons. *Brain*, **124**, 399–412.

Raichle, M.E. (1987). Circulatory and metabolic correlates of brain function in normal humans. In F. Plum & V. Mountcastle (eds), *Handbook of Physiology: the Nervous System*, Vol. 5 (pp. 643–674). Baltimore, MD: American Physiological Society.

Ranganath, C., Johnson, M.K., D'Esposito, M.D. et al. (2000). Left anterior prefrontal activation increases with demands to recall specific perceptual information. *Journal of Neuroscience*, **20**, RC108.

Roediger, H.L. & McDermott, K.B. (1993). Implicit memory in normal human subjects. In F. Boller & J. Grafman (eds), *Handbook of Neuropsychology*, Vol. 8 (pp. 63–131). Amsterdam: Elsevier.

Roediger, H.L., Weldon, M.S. & Challis, B.H. (1989). Explaining dissociations between implicit and explicit measures of retention: a processing account. In H.L. Roediger, & F.I.M. Craik (eds), *Varieties of Memory and Consciousness* (pp. 3–41). Hillsdale, NJ: Erlbaum.

Rombouts, S.A., Machielsen, W.C., Witter, M.P. et al. (1997). Visual association encoding activates the medial temporal lobe: a functional magnetic resonance imaging study. *Hippocampus*, **7**, 594–601.

Rombouts, S.A., Scheltens, P., Machielson, W.C. et al. (1999). Parametric fMRI analysis of visual encoding in the human medial temporal lobe. *Hippocampus*, **9**, 637–643.

Rugg, M.D. (1995). ERP studies of memory. In M.D. Rugg & M.G.H. Coles (eds), *Electrophysiology of Mind: Event-Related Brain Potentials and Cognition* (pp. 789–802). Oxford: Oxford University Press.

Rugg, M.D. (1999). Functional neuroimaging in cognitive neuroscience. In P. Hagoort & C. Brown (eds), *Neurocognition of Language* (pp. 15–36). Oxford: Oxford University Press.

Rugg, M.D. & Henson, R.N.A. (in press). Episodic memory retrieval: an event-related functional neuroimaging perspective. In A.E. Parker, E.L.Wilding & T. Bussey, (eds), *The Cognitive Neuroscience of Memory Encoding and Retrieval*. Hove: Psychology Press.

Rugg, M.D., Fletcher, P.C., Chua, P.M.-L. & Dolan, R.J. (1999). The role of the prefrontal cortex in recognition memory and memory for source: an fMRI study. *Neuroimage*, **10**, 520–529.

Rugg, M.D., Fletcher, P.C., Frith, C.D. et al. (1996). Differential activation of the prefrontal cortex in successful and unsuccessful memory retrieval. *Brain*, **119**, 2073–2083.

Rugg, M.D., Fletcher, P.C., Frith, C.D. et al. (1997). Brain regions supporting intentional and incidental memory: a PET study. *NeuroReport*, **8**, 1283–1287.

Rugg, M.D., Fletcher, P.C., Allan, K. et al. (1998). Neural correlates of memory retrieval during recognition memory and cued recall. *Neuroimage*, **8**, 262–273.

Schacter, D.L. & Wagner, A.D. (1998). Medial temporal lobe activations in fMRI and PET studies of episodic encoding and retrieval. *Hippocampus*, **9**, 7–24.

Schacter, D.L. & Buckner, R.L. (1998). Priming and the brain. *Neuron*, **20**, 185–195.

Schacter, D.L., Badgaiyan, R.D. & Alpert, N.M. (1999). Visual word stem completion priming within and across modalities: a PET study. *NeuroReport*. **10**, 2061–2065.

Schacter, D.L., Alpert, N.M., Savage, C.R. et al. (1996). Conscious recollection and the human hippocampal formation: evidence from positron emission tomography. *Proceedings of the National Academy of Science of the USA*, **93**, 321–325.

Schacter, D.L., Buckner, R.L., Koutstaal, W. et al. (1997). Late onset of anterior prefrontal activity during retrieval of veridical and illusory memories: a single trial fMRI study. *Neuroimage*, **6**, 259–269.

Schacter, D.L., Reiman, E., Uecker, A. et al. (1995). Brain regions associated with retrieval of structurally coherent visual information. *Nature*, **376**, 587–90.

Shallice, T., Fletcher, P., Frith, C.D. et al. (1994). Brain regions associated with acquisition and retrieval of verbal episodic memory. *Nature*, **368**, 633–635.

Squire, L.R., Ojemann, J.G., Miezin, F.M. et al. (1992). Activation of the hippocampus in normal humans: a functional anatomical study of memory. *Proceedings of the National Academy of Science of the USA*, **89**, 1837–1841.

Stark, C.E. & Squire, L.R. (2000a). fMRI activity in the medial temporal lobe during recognition memory as a function of study–test interval. *Hippocampus*, **10**, 329–337.

Stark, C.E. & Squire, L.R. (2000b). Functional magnetic resonance imaging (fMRI) activity in the hippocampal region during recognition memory. *Journal of Neuroscience*, **20**, 7776–7781.

Stern, C.E., Corkin, S., Gonzalez, R.G. et al. (1996). The hippocampal formation participates in novel picture encoding: evidence from functional magnetic resonance imaging. *Proceedings of the National Academy of Science of the USA*, **93**, 8660–8665.

Stuss, D.T., Eskes, G.A. & Foster, J.K. (1994). Experimental neuropsychological studies of frontal lobe functions. In J.C. Boller & J. Grafman (eds), *Handbook of Neuropsychology*, Vol. 9 (pp. 149–183). Amsterdam: Elsevier.

Talairach, J. & Tournoux, P. (1998). *Co-planar Stereotaxic Atlas of the Human Brain*. Stuttgart: Thieme Verlag.

Tulving, E. (1983). *Elements of Episodic Memory*. Oxford: Oxford University Press.

Tulving, E. (1985). Memory and consciousness. *Canadian Psychologist*, **26**, 1–12.

Tulving, E. & Schacter, D.L. (1990). Priming and human memory systems. *Science*, **247**, 301–306.

Tulving, E., Kapur, S., Craik, F.I.M. et al. (1994). Hemispheric encoding/retrieval asymmetry in episodic memory: positron emission tomography findings. *Proceedings of the National Academy of Science of the USA*, **91**, 2016–2020.

van Turennout, M., Ellmore, T. & Martin, A. (2000). Long-lasting cortical plasticity in the object naming system. *Nature Neuroscience*, **3**, 1329–1334.

Wagner, A.D., Koutstaal, W. & Schacter, D.L. (1999). When encoding yields remembering: insights from event-related neuroimaging. *Philosophical Transactions of the Royal Society of London B: Biological Sciences*, **354**, 1307–1324.

Wagner, A.D., Desmond, J.E., Glover, G.H. & Gabrieli, J.D. (1998c). Prefrontal cortex and recognition memory. Functional MRI evidence for context-dependent retrieval processes. *Brain*, **121**, 1985–2002.

Wagner, A.D., Desmond, J.E., Demb, J.B. et al. (1997). Semantic repetition priming for verbal and pictorial knowledge: a functional MRI study of left inferior prefrontal cortex. *Journal of Cognitive Neuroscience*, **9**, 714–726.

Wagner, A.D., Koutstaal, W., Maril, A. et al. (2000). Task-specific repetition priming in left inferior prefrontal cortex. *Cerebral Cortex*. **10**, 1176–1184.

Wagner, A.D., Poldrack, R.A., Eldridge, L.L. et al. (1998a). Material-specific lateralization of prefrontal activation during episodic encoding and retrieval. *NeuroReport*, **9**, 3711–3717.

Wagner, A.D., Schacter, D.L., Rotte, M. et al. (1998b). Building memories: remembering and forgetting of verbal experiences as predicted by brain activity. *Science*, **21**, 188–191.

Wiggs, C.L. & Martin, A. (1998). Properties and mechanisms of perceptual priming. *Current Opinion in Neurobiology*, **8**, 227–233.

Wheeler, M.A., Stuss, D.T. & Tulving, E. (1997). Toward a theory of episodic memory: the frontal lobes and autonoetic consciousness. *Psychological Bulletin*, **121**, 331–354.

Yonelinas, A.P. (1994). Receiver-operating characteristics in recognition memory: evidence for a dual-process model. *Journal of Experimental Psychology: Learning, Memory and Cognition*, **20**, 1341–1354.

Zarahn, E., Aguirre, G.K. & D'Esposito, M. (1997). A trial-based experimental design for fMRI. *Neuroimage*, **5**, 179–197.

CHAPTER 4

The Medial Temporal Lobe and Memory for Facts and Events

Joseph R. Manns

and

Larry R. Squire

Veteran Affairs Healthcare System and University of California, San Diego, CA, USA

The hippocampus, together with anatomically related structures in the medial temporal lobe and diencephalon, supports the capacity for conscious recollection. This capacity, termed declarative memory, can be contrasted with a collection of nonconscious (nondeclarative) memory abilities that are expressed through performance rather than recollection and that are supported by structures outside the medial temporal lobe. The distinction between declarative and nondeclarative memory is based on studies of humans, monkeys, and rodents (Eichenbaum & Cohen, 2001; Gabrieli, 1998; Schacter & Tulving, 1994; Squire, 1992). More recently, attention has been directed towards the question of how the different anatomical components of the medial temporal lobe memory system contribute to declarative memory. The medial temporal lobe memory system is composed of the hippocampal region (CA fields, dentate gyrus, and the subicular complex) and the adjacent perirhinal, entorhinal, and parahippocampal cortices (Squire & Zola-Morgan, 1991).

The purpose of this chapter is to consider to what extent separate functions can be ascribed to the hippocampal region and the adjacent cortices. The discussion draws on studies of both experimental animals and humans. Because anatomical information is critical, the human studies draw especially on those cases for which radiological information (from structural magnetic resonance imaging) or neurohistological information is available.

Recent discussions of the function of medial temporal lobe structures make prominent mention of the distinction between episodic and semantic memory (Cermak, 1984; Kinsbourne & Wood, 1975; Schacter & Tulving, 1982; Tulving, 1991), and this distinction can serve as a useful framework for the data reviewed here. Episodic and semantic memory are two different forms of declarative memory (Tulving, 1983). "Episodic memory" refers

The Handbook of Memory Disorders. Edited by A.D. Baddeley, M.D. Kopelman and B.A. Wilson
© 2002 John Wiley & Sons, Ltd.

to memory for specific events, including memory for when and where events occurred. "Semantic memory" refers to memory for facts, including general knowledge about the world.

At least three distinct ideas have been discussed concerning the medial temporal lobe and episodic and semantic memory. One idea is that episodic memory depends on the integrity of the medial temporal lobe but that semantic memory can be acquired independently of the medial temporal lobe (Tulving, 1991). A second idea is that the hippocampus has a privileged, perhaps even exclusive, role in episodic memory and that semantic memory depends on medial temporal lobe structures adjacent to the hippocampus, such as the perirhinal cortex (Aggleton & Brown, 1999; Nadel et al., 2000; Vargha-Khadem et al., 1997). Still a third idea is that the hippocampus (and other medial temporal lobe structures) contribute similarly to episodic and semantic memory (Squire & Zola, 1998; Verfaellie et al., 1995).

Another distinction, related to episodic and semantic memory, focuses on the idea that recognition is composed of two processes: remembering (a recollective process akin to episodic memory) and familiarity discrimination (akin to semantic memory) (Mandler, 1980). In parallel with the second of the three ideas outlined above, it has been suggested that remembering might depend more on the hippocampus and that the ability to make familiarity discriminations might depend more on adjacent cortex (Brown & Aggleton, 2001).

ANIMAL STUDIES

In nonhuman animals, bilateral medial temporal lobe lesions, as well as lesions restricted to the hippocampal region (the CA fields of the hippocampus, dentate gyrus, and subicular complex), cause anterograde amnesia. This impairment has been demonstrated by a wide range of memory tasks, including tasks of recognition memory, such as trial-unique delayed nonmatching to sample and the visual-paired comparison task. Such lesions also cause retrograde amnesia, that is, loss of memory for information acquired before the lesion. In the present context, the interesting questions with respect to both anterograde and retrograde amnesia are whether the effects of medial temporal lobe lesions can be understood in terms of the distinction between episodic and semantic memory, and how the effects of restricted hippocampal lesions compare to the effects of lesions to adjacent cortex.

Anterograde Amnesia

One of the most widely used tasks for assessing declarative memory in monkeys is the delayed nonmatching to sample (DNMS) task of recognition memory (Gaffan, 1974; Mishkin & Delacour, 1975). In the DNMS task, a sample object is first presented to the animal, and then after a delay the original object is presented together with a new object. Different objects are used for each trial, and the animal is rewarded for selecting the new object. Monkeys with selective bilateral damage to the hippocampal region produced by ischemia (Zola-Morgan et al., 1992), radio-frequency (Alvarez et al., 1995) or ibotenic acid (Beason-Held et al., 1999; Zola et al., 2000; but see Murray & Mishkin, 1998) are impaired on this task (Zola & Squire, 2001). Lesions of the perirhinal cortex also impair DNMS performance (Buffalo et al., 1999; Meunier et al., 1993), and large lesions of the adjacent cortex (perirhinal plus parahippocampal cortex) that substantially disconnect the neocortex from the hippocampal region impair DNMS performance more severely than restricted hippocampal lesions (Suzuki et al., 1993; Zola-Morgan et al., 1989, 1994). This finding suggests that the hippocampal region is not uniquely important for this recognition memory task and that the adjacent cortex also supports performance.

The DNMS task has also been adapted for the rat (Mumby et al., 1990). Although the effects of bilateral damage to the hippocampal region have been mixed (see Brown & Aggleton, 2001), the data suggest that an impairment of recognition memory is found when the lesions are sufficiently large and when the delay interval is sufficiently long (> 30 s) (for discussion of DNMS and related tasks, see Clark et al., 2001; Dudchenko et al., 2000). In addition, as in the monkey, damage to the perirhinal cortex exacerbates the deficit in DNMS associated with more restricted damage (in this case, fornix section; Wiig & Bilkey, 1995).

On the one hand, the DNMS task appears to assess episodic-like memory. That is, the task requires that animals retrieve information from a single event (the sample object). On the other hand, the task can be solved in the absence of a specific recollection of the sample presentation. For example, the sample object could be recognized as familiar (and the novel as unfamiliar) without specifically recollecting the learning event. That is, the choice of the novel object could be guided by a simple judgment of relative familiarity. Indeed, it is difficult to prove that animals can recollect the past by episodic remembering (i.e. by mental time travel; for a recent report of episodic-like memory in birds, see Clayton & Dickinson, 1998). It has been suggested that animals can make judgments only about the factual information at hand, and that the capacity for episodic memory is uniquely human (Tulving, 1993).

While a good deal of the work on declarative memory in experimental animals has depended on the DNMS task, other tasks have also been used. In work with monkeys, the visual paired-comparison (VPC) task measures how much time an animal spends looking at a new picture and a recently presented (now familiar) picture when the two pictures are presented together (Bachevalier, 1990). Normal animals prefer to look at the new picture, and this spontaneous preference for novelty indicates that the familiar picture has been recognized.

Monkeys with selective damage to the hippocampal region performed normally when the delay between the first and second presentation of pictures was only 1 s but were impaired at delays of 10 s, 1 min and 10 min (Zola et al., 2000). A rodent version of the VPC task has also been developed that measures the time an animal spends exploring a novel object when the novel object is placed in an arena together with a recently presented (familiar) object (Ennaceur & Delacour, 1988). Rats with radio-frequency or ibotenic acid lesions of the hippocampal region performed normally when the delay between the first and second presentation of objects was short (10 s), but they performed poorly when the delay was extended (Clark et al., 2000). Similar findings have been reported for rats with ischemic damage to the CA1 region of the hippocampus (Wood & Phillips, 1991), rats with intrahippocampal infusions of APV (Baker & Kim, 2002), and for mice lacking the NMDAR-1 subunit in the CA1 region (Rampon et al., 2000). Because the VPC task depends on spontaneous reactions to novelty, it would appear to be a task that could be performed without relying on recollection of previous events. If so, then the finding that restricted hippocampal lesions impair performance on the VPC task could be understood by supposing that the hippocampus ordinarily contributes to simple judgments of familiarity. However these tasks are performed, the available data from recognition memory tasks provide no evidence for a separate or privileged role of the hippocampus relative to adjacent cortical structures.

Performance on certain other tasks, including tasks of associative transitivity (Bunsey & Eichenbaum, 1996), transitive inference (Dusek & Eichenbaum, 1997) and transverse patterning (Dusek & Eichenbaum, 1998) was severely impaired by selective hippocampal lesions. Because the impairment was so severe (performance was at chance), these findings suggest that the hippocampus may be especially important for tasks like these, i.e. tasks thought to emphasize the processing of relationships among stimuli and that result in their representation as declarative memory (Eichenbaum & Cohen, 2001). At the same time, lesions of adjacent cortex also produced severe, virtually maximal deficits (Dusek & Eichenbaum, 1997). Accordingly, it is difficult to know whether the cortical lesions are disrupting an essential contribution of the cortex itself, or whether they are simply disconnecting the hippocampus from neocortex.

Retrograde Amnesia

Bilateral lesions of the hippocampal region can impair memory when training occurs a few days before surgery but spare memory when training occurs remote to surgery (temporally-graded retrograde amnesia). A recent review of retrograde amnesia in experimental animals (Squire et al., 2001) identified 13 studies in which equivalent training was given at two or more times before bilateral damage to the fornix, the hippocampal region or the entorhinal cortex. Eleven of these studies found temporally-graded retrograde amnesia.

Some of the tasks that have been used in studies of retrograde amnesia appear to be tests of semantic memory more than of episodic memory. For example, consider trace eyeblink conditioning. Trace eyeblink conditioning requires that an animal respond appropriately to a conditioned stimulus and does not depend on memory of a particular past event in any obvious way. In the rabbit, hippocampal lesions abolished 1 day-old trace eyeblink conditioning but did not affect 28 day-old trace eyeblink conditioning (Kim et al., 1995). This result, among others from the 13 studies mentioned above, suggests that the hippocampus is important for recently acquired semantic memory.

Similar retrograde effects (on what seem best understood as tasks of semantic memory) have been found following lesions of adjacent cortex (see Squire et al., 2001). The available data suggest that retrograde amnesia is more severe and more extensive after large medial temporal lobe lesions than what is observed following restricted hippocampal lesions. Thus, it appears that the hippocampal region is not uniquely involved in recovering past (premorbid) memories and that the adjacent cortex is also important.

HUMAN STUDIES

This section considers studies of recognition memory, fact learning, and remote memory in amnesic patients with medial temporal lobe lesions. The first two topics concern the nature of anterograde amnesia, and the third topic concerns the nature of retrograde amnesia. In the case of recognition memory, the question of interest is whether hippocampal lesions impair or spare recognition performance, and if so, whether the processes of recollection and familiarity are differentially affected. In the case of fact learning, the question of interest is whether fact learning is impaired or spared in amnesic patients with restricted hippocampal damage. In the case of remote memory, the question of interest is whether recall of past events after restricted hippocampal damage, or more extensive medial temporal lobe damage, is as detailed and full of content as in intact individuals. As one examines the more autobiographical and episodic-like aspects of remote recollections, can one find evidence of impaired performance after restricted hippocampal lesions, or after more extensive damage?

Anterograde Studies

In humans, as with experimental animals, bilateral damage restricted to the hippocampal region (CA fields, dentate gyrus, and subicular complex) impairs performance on standard tasks of recognition memory (Manns & Squire, 1999; Reed & Squire, 1997). In one study (Manns & Squire, 1999), damage limited to the hippocampal region impaired performance on verbal and visual four-choice recognition memory tasks (the Doors and People Test). Some effort has been directed toward isolating different aspects of recognition memory. Tulving (1985) introduced the distinction between "remembering" and "knowing" to reflect the operation of episodic and semantic memory, respectively. When a recently presented item evokes a recollection of the learning episode itself, one is said to "remember". By contrast, when a recently presented item is experienced simply as familiar without evoking source knowledge about the item, one is said to experience "knowing". In studies of recognition memory that ask for judgments of remembering and knowing, amnesic patients were found to be impaired at both remembering and knowing (Knowlton & Squire, 1995; Yonelinas et al., 1998). Further, in one study (Knowlton & Squire, 1995), the five patients whose damage appeared to be limited to the hippocampal formation were impaired on both measures ($p < 0.05$) (Figure 4.1).

In a study of normal volunteers using functional magnetic resonance imaging (fMRI), more hippocampal activation occurred when retrieval was associated with remembering than when retrieval was associated only with knowing (Eldridge et al., 2000; for a related report, see Maguire & Mummery, 1999). This difference could reflect a qualitative distinction between episodic and semantic remembering, or perhaps the fact that remembering evoked more information content than did knowing. In another fMRI study, robust activation occurred in the hippocampal region during recognition memory testing (Stark & Squire, 2000). Hippocampal activation was observed even when activity associated with all the study items was compared to activity associated with all the foil items, regardless of remembering or knowing.

Another study of recognition memory involved the case known as Jon, who developed amnesia perinatally and appears to have damage restricted to the hippocampal region. Jon performed as well as young adults on many recognition memory tests (Baddeley et al., 2001), including the recognition portions of the Doors and People Test that are failed by patients with adult-onset amnesia (Manns & Squire, 1999). Interestingly, Jon was described as being unable to learn the distinction between remembering and knowing, and it was suggested that he may specifically lack the capacity to recollect the contextual detail of recent events sufficiently well to experience remembering. Thus, it was suggested that, for Jon, restricted damage to the hippocampal region has resulted in a selective loss of episodic memory (Vargha-Kadhem et al., 1997).

The authors considered two ways to understand these findings (Baddeley et al., 2001). First, Jon's restricted hippocampal damage may have spared recognition memory, at least the component of recognition memory that is based more on familiarity and less on recollection.

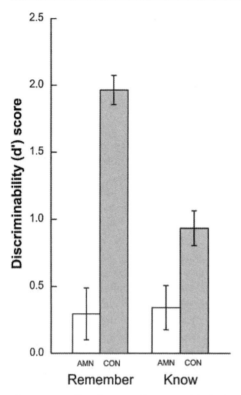

Figure 4.1   The d′ scores for items labeled "remember" or "know" for five amnesic patients (AMN; A.B., J.L., L.J., P.H., and W.H.) and 12 controls (CON). Participants were tested 10 min after the study phase. Brackets show SEM. Adapted from Knowlton & Squire (1995)

If so, then it becomes important to understand why other patients with restricted hippocampal damage are typically impaired on both the episodic and semantic aspects of recognition memory. Might Jon's lesion differ in size or location from the lesions in other amnesic study patients? Might Jon's pattern of performance reflect a rather mild memory impairment relative to the amnesic patients typically available for study? A second possibility is that Jon's pattern of performance might be based on the developmental nature of his deficit, and therefore on the possibility of functional reorganization in the infant brain, as well as the acquisition during childhood of alternative learning strategies. More tests with additional adult-onset patients will be useful in order to sample across as wide as possible a range of severity of memory impairment. (For reports of relatively spared recognition memory in a mildly impaired patient [Y.R.] with hippocampal damage, see Mayes et al., 2002; Holdstock et al., 2002.)

   Another approach to asking about episodic and semantic memory in amnesic patients is to consider their capacity for the acquisition of new factual knowledge. In one study (Hamann & Squire, 1995), two patients with damage thought to be limited to the hippocampal region were impaired at learning novel three-word sentences (e.g. "Dentist cured hiccup") despite extended training across four weeks (Figure 4.2). Patients and controls were trained in weekly sessions (two trials for each of the 20 sentences per session). The first two words of the sentence were presented, and participants were asked to complete the

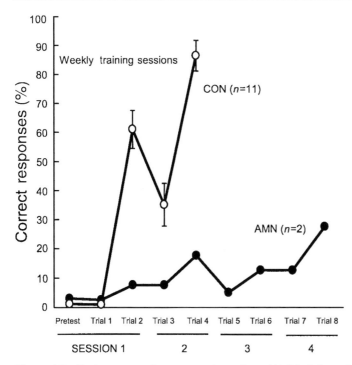

Figure 4.2 Performance of two amnesic patients (AMN; A.B. and L.J.) and 11 controls on a pretest of 40 two-word sentence frames and in weekly sessions in which 20 of the sentence frames from the pretest were trained using a study-test procedure. Brackets show SEM. Adapted from Hamann & Squire (1995)

sentence with the appropriate word. Inasmuch as the testing made no reference to the study episodes, and training occurred on several sessions across several weeks, it seems unlikely that participants relied much on specific, episodic memories from the training sessions. Accordingly, the data suggest that acquisition of semantic memory is to some extent dependent on the hippocampal region. At the same time, it is difficult to rule out the possibility that controls were advantaged by being able to retrieve the training episodes themselves, and that the difficulty experienced by the patients was due to impaired episodic memory more than to impaired semantic memory.

A different way to assess the ability of amnesic patients to learn new facts is to ask to what extent amnesic patients acquire knowledge about the world after they become amnesic. Figure 4.3 shows data for two patients with damage thought to be limited to the hippocampal region (A.B. and L.J.), who became amnesic in 1976 and 1988, respectively (Reed & Squire, 1998). Across eight different tests of information that could only have been acquired after the onset of amnesia, the patients were impaired relative to the controls (72% correct vs. 87% correct; $t[9] = 2.28$, $p < 0.05$). Yet it is also true that the patients were able to acquire a considerable amount of information. Similar findings, i.e. a residual albeit impaired capacity for learning new facts, have been reported by others (Kitchener et al., 1998; Verfaellie et al. 2000).

A final example of human learning that appears to provide a test of semantic memory capacity is trace eyeblink classical conditioning. As described earlier in this chapter, trace eyeblink conditioning simply requires a response to a conditioned stimulus (CS) and does

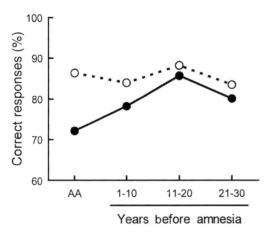

Figure 4.3 Performance for two amnesic patients (A.B. and L.J.; closed circles) and nine controls (open circles) on eight tests of fact knowledge. The scores are group means based on each subject's median score for the eight tests. AA, anterograde amnesia. From Reed & Squire (1998)

not depend on event memory. In the case of human studies, the finding of interest is that trace eyeblink conditioning (but not delay eyeblink conditioning) is impaired in patients with restricted damage limited to the hippocampal region (Clark & Squire, 1998, 2000). In addition, successful trace eyeblink conditioning requires that subjects become aware of the stimulus contingencies, i.e. that the CS precedes the US (Clark & Squire, 1998; Manns, Clark, & Squire, 2000). If trace conditioning is a form of semantic learning, then these findings support the idea that the hippocampal region is important for semantic memory.

While the data indicate that semantic learning is impaired in amnesic patients, it is difficult to decide whether their capacity for semantic learning is impaired in proportion to their impaired capacity for episodic learning, or whether semantic learning is partially and disproportionately spared. The memory impairment associated with restricted hippocampal damage is relatively mild, at least in comparison to what is found after larger lesions of the medial temporal lobe (Stefanacci et al., 2000), and patients like A.B. and L.J. are capable of a considerable amount of learning about both facts and events (Reed & Squire, 1998). The question of interest is whether their capacity for fact learning (semantic memory) exceeds what would be expected, given their capacity for event learning (episodic memory) (for further discussion of this issue in the context of both adult-onset and developmental amnesia, see Squire & Zola, 1998). Studies designed to compare the ability to learn facts and the ability, for example, to acquire source memory about when and where the facts were learned should be especially illuminating. On the basis of the data currently available, there appears to be little positive evidence for the idea that episodic and semantic learning are affected differently in adult-onset amnesia.

Retrograde Amnesia

Loss of premorbid memory (retrograde amnesia) following damage to the medial temporal lobe has been documented extensively, and has also been discussed in the context of the distinction between episodic and semantic memory. However, a difficulty arises in the case of past memory, especially remote autobiographical memory, because it is not easy to agree as to when an individual is engaged in episodic retrieval of specific events and when an individual is drawing on a well-rehearsed base of semantic knowledge. This point was developed in some detail by Cermak (1984). Consequently, caution is merited when trying to interpret the facts of retrograde amnesia in terms of episodic and semantic memory. Regardless of uncertainties about definition, it remains important to assess the quantitative and qualitative features of remote memory for facts and events in amnesic patients. Is remote memory intact? Or is there some aspect of remote remembering that is lost after medial temporal lobe lesions or restricted hippocampal lesions? The question of interest, then, is how the capacity of amnesic patients to recollect past facts and events compares with the capacity of intact individuals and how this capacity relates to neuroanatomy.

With respect to the recall of facts, patients with histologically-confirmed lesions limited to the hippocampal formation (patients L.M. and W.H.; Rempel-Clower et al., 1996) were found to be impaired at recalling news events and other factual information that occurred a decade or more before the onset of their amnesia (Beatty et al., 1987, 1988; Rempel-Clower et al., 1996; Squire et al., 1989). Information about more remote facts was intact. It seems unlikely that normal individuals could consistently evoke the learning episode when recollecting 10 year-old facts; and if individuals do not remember the learning episode, then such recollections must be based on semantic memory. Accordingly, these findings suggest that the hippocampal formation is important for retrieval of recently acquired semantic memory (for additional evidence, see Schmidtke & Vollmer, 1997; Verfaellie et al., 1995).

Larger lesions of the medial temporal lobe also spare remote memory for factual knowledge. E.P. became amnesic in 1992 at the age of 70, after an episode of herpes simplex encephalitis. He has extensive, virtually complete bilateral damage to the hippocampus, amygdala, entorhinal cortex and perirhinal cortex, as well as damage to the anterior parahippocampal cortex and anterior fusiform gyrus (Stefanacci et al., 2000). E.P. grew up in the Hayward-Castro Valley area of California during the 1930s and 1940s, moved away at the age of 28, and has returned only occasionally. E.P. was age-matched to five controls who attended his high school, lived in the area about as long as he did, and also moved away at about the age that he did. All six individuals were given four tests of topographical memory to assess their spatial knowledge of the region where they grew up (Teng & Squire, 1999). They were asked to describe how they would navigate from their homes to different locations in the area (familiar navigation), between different locations in the area (novel navigation), and between these same locations when a main street was blocked off (alternative routes). They were also asked to imagine themselves in particular locations and facing particular directions and then to point towards specific landmarks (pointing to landmarks). E.P. performed well on all four tests (Figure 4.4). In contrast to E.P.'s superb navigational knowledge about where he grew up, he has no knowledge of his current neighborhood, where he has lived since 1993 (after he became amnesic).

These findings indicate that factual (semantic) knowledge about the remote past is independent of medial temporal lobe structures. It is also interesting that the cognitive abilities that permit E.P. to reconstruct the layout of the neighborhood that he lived in 50 years ago does not permit him to acquire similar knowledge about his current neighborhood. The ability to acquire this new knowledge depends on the medial temporal lobe.

A different amnesic patient (K.C.) was able, like E.P., to answer questions about the spatial layout of the neighborhood in which he grew up, and succeeded altogether at six

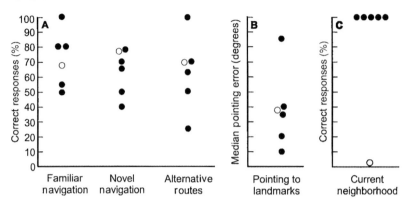

Figure 4.4 Performance on four tasks of topographical memory for patient E.P. (open circles) and five control subjects (closed circles). (**A**) Percentage correct score on three navigation tasks within the neighborhood where participants grew up. The tasks required recalling either familiar routes, novel routes, or alternative routes (when the most direct route was blocked). (**B**) Median error in degrees on a task in which participants pointed to particular locations while imagining themselves oriented at other locations. (**C**) Percentage correct score on a navigation task of participants' current neighborhood. Adapted from Teng & Squire (1999)

tests of remote spatial memory (Rosenbaum et al., 2000). However, K.C. was impaired at recognizing pictures of houses and other landmarks in his neighborhood and at locating cities on maps of Canada and the province of Ontario where he lived. This pattern of performance is difficult to interpret in the context of medial temporal lobe function because K.C.'s amnesia is the result of a closed-head injury. Magnetic resonance imaging indicates that the injury damaged not just the left medial temporal lobe and a small portion of the right medial temporal lobe but also did substantial damage to the left frontal, left parietal, left retrosplenial and left occipital corticies. A smaller lesion is also present in the right parietal cortex. Accordingly, it is unclear what aspects of K.C.'s impaired performance are attributable to medial temporal lobe pathology. In summary, patients with histologically-confirmed lesions limited to the hippocampal formation (L.M. and W.H.), and a patient with a radiologically-confirmed lesion limited largely to the medial temporal lobe (E.P.), have good access to factual knowledge from their early life.

The ability of amnesic patients to retrieve autobiographical (episodic) memories from their past has also been studied at some length. It has been useful to ask whether amnesic patients can produce autobiographical recollections and to consider how their recollections compare to those produced by normal individuals. The matter is of interest because of early suggestions that amnesic patients may not be capable of true autobiographical remembering (Cermak, 1984; Kinsbourne & Wood, 1975), and because patient K.C. reportedly cannot produce specific event-based recollections (Tulving et al., 1988). More recently, this idea has been applied to medial temporal lobe amnesia, and it has been suggested that the remote autobiographical memories produced by patients with medial temporal lobe damage lack the detail found in the recollections of normal individuals (Nadel & Moscovitch, 1997; Nadel et al., 2000).

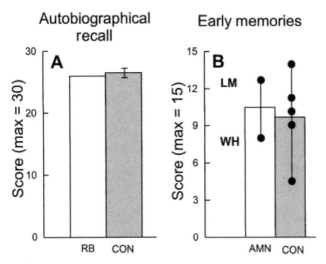

Figure 4.5 (**A**) Total score for patient R.B. and six controls (CON) on 10 autobiographical recollections when each recollection was scored on a 0–3 scale for content. From Zola-Morgan et al., 1986). (**B**) Total scores for patients L.M. and W.H. and five controls (CON) on five autobiographical recollections from childhood and adolescence when each recollection was scored on a 0–3 scale for content. From MacKinnon & Squire (1989)

These issues have been investigated in patients whose lesions were subsequently identified in the course of a detailed neurohistological examination. Patient R.B. became amnesic in 1978, at the age of 52, as the result of an ischemic event that occurred as a complication of open heart surgery (Zola-Morgan et al., 1986). After his death in 1983, a circumscribed bilateral lesion was found in the CA1 region of the hippocampus. Minor pathology was found elsewhere (left globus pallidus, right postcentral gyrus, left internal capsule, patchy loss of cerebellar Purkinje cells), but the only damage that could be reasonably associated with the memory impairment was in the hippocampus. R.B. was given the Crovitz word-probe test, which involves presenting single words (e.g. "bird", "ticket", "window") as cues and asking for an autobiographical recollection of a specific event from any period in the past that involves the cue word (Crovitz & Schiffman, 1974). R.B. produced well-formed episodic memories, and his score was as good as the average score obtained by six controls (Figure 5A). Each of 10 recollections was scored on a 0–3 scale, and a score of 3 was assigned when the recollection involved a specific, detailed memory of an episode. Thus, despite a lesion that would be expected to markedly disrupt the function of the hippocampus, R.B. could recollect autobiographical episodes as well as normal individuals.

Two other patients, L.M. and W.H., became amnesic at the age of 54 and 63, respectively. They were subsequently found to have bilateral lesions involving all the cell fields of the hippocampus (Rempel-Clower et al., 1996). There was also extensive loss of cells in the dentate gyrus and some cell loss in the entorhinal cortex. In addition, W.H. had extensive, patchy cell loss in the subiculum. The only damage detected outside the hippocampal formation was in the medial septum, right lateral occipitotemporal cortex and left medial temporal sulcus (patient L.M.) and in the pons and striatum (patient W.H.). Both patients also had patchy loss of cerebellar Purkinje cells, as frequently seen in cases of ischemia and anoxia.

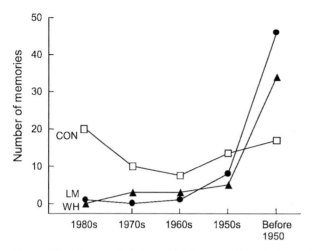

Figure 4.6 Time periods from which two patients (L.M. and W.H.) and five controls drew autobiographical memories in response to 75 single-word cues. L.M. and W.H. became amnesic in 1984 and 1986, respectively. From Rempel-Clower et al. (1996)

These two patients were given a number of tests of autobiographical remembering (MacKinnon & Squire, 1989). Although both patients had difficulty producing recollections from their recent past, when the questions concerned their childhood and adolescence, they performed well. For example, one test asked structured questions about common events likely to have been experienced by most persons, e.g. "Tell me as much as you can about: your most embarrassing moment in high school; the day you first got your driver's license; the day you learned to ride a bike". Although only five questions were asked of each participant, L.M., W.H. and the controls performed similarly. Figure 4.5B shows their performance when each recollection was scored on a 0–3 scale.

In another test, 75 single-word cues were given (Crovitz & Schiffman, 1974), and participants attempted to recollect a specific episode from their lives that involved each word. Control subjects, like typical middle-aged individuals (McCormick, 1979), drew their memories predominantly from the recent past and from the remote past, and less often from the middle of their lives (Figure 4.6). L.M. and W.H. differed strikingly from the controls with respect to the temporal distribution of their recollections. Specifically, they drew most of their recollections from before 1950 and produced very few recollections from the period after 1960. In 1960, L.M. was 30 years old, and W.H. was 37 years old. In summary, these findings for L.M. and W.H. suggest that autobiographical recall of remote episodes is spared in the presence of moderately severe amnesia and bilateral damage to the hippocampal formation.

Although these findings are consistent with the idea that remote episodic remembering is intact after damage to the hippocampal formation, it remains possible that more sensitive tests or more sensitive scoring methods will reveal some abnormality. The importance of these issues was underscored recently by a report in which five memory-impaired patients attempted to produce two autobiographical recollections from each of five periods of life (Moscovitch et al., 2000). The recollections were found to be abnormal when they were scored for the total number of details that were recounted as part of each recollection. These findings are not relevant in any clear way to the facts of medial temporal lobe amnesia. The five patients included patient K.C., a basal forebrain patient, a diencephalic patient, an Alzheimer's disease patient, and a post-encephalitic patient. Unfortunately, no other anatomical information was provided. Nevertheless, the study raises an important methodological point about the assessment of autobiographical recollections, namely, that scoring the number of details may provide a better measure of remote memory capacity than a simple 0–3 scale.

To consider this issue further, two amnesic patients (A.B. and L.J.) were given 24 single-word cues and asked to recollect a specific episode from their first one-third of life before the onset of their amnesia (Bayley & Squire, 2001). L.J., aged 60 at the time of the test, has a radiologically confirmed bilateral lesion confined to the hippocampal region (Reed & Squire, 1998). A.B., aged 59 at test, is presumed to have hippocampal damage because of his etiology (cardiac arrest), but this cannot be confirmed because he is ineligible for magnetic resonance imaging. Overall, the two patients provided well-formed episodic memories (score = 3.0 on a 0–3 scale) in response to 83.4% of the cue words (for controls, 94.8% of the cue words). The number of unique details per 3.0 point memory was 29.1 for L.J. and 29.9 for A.B. (control mean = 27.8, range = 21.1–35.0). In addition, the amnesic patients tended to repeat details during the testing session, presumably due to their anterograde amnesia (patients = 4.0 repeats; controls = 0.9 repeats). These results suggest, in keeping with what has been found with less thorough scoring methods, that the hippocampal formation is not required to produce detailed episodic memories from early life.

Continuing study of patient E.P. indicates that he also has considerable capacity for detailed autobiographical remembering from early life (Bayley & Squire, 2001; Reed & Squire, 1998). Thus, E.P. provided well-formed memories (score = 3.0) for 18 of 24 cue words (75%), and provided 22.7 unique details for each of these memories (Bayley & Squire, 2001). Because E.P.'s lesion extends laterally beyond the medial temporal lobe to involve the fusiform gyrus, it is difficult to know whether his slightly reduced performance is a consequence of medial temporal lobe damage. In any case, E.P. is capable of much more autobiographical remembering than patient K.C. (Tulving et al., 1988) and also much more than patient G.T., who has large temporal lobe lesions that involve the full lateral extent of the anterotemporal cortex (Reed & Squire, 1998).

It is also of interest that E.P. has mildly impoverished knowledge about living and nonliving things (Stefanacci et al., 2000; their Figure 11). For example, when asked to point to a drawing of a seal among seven other drawings of animals that live in the water, E.P. pointed to a seahorse. Overall on this test, he pointed correctly to 43 out of 48 items (control range = 47–48). On another test, E.P. performed just below the control range when asked eight yes/no questions about each of 24 different items. For example, he answered affirmatively when asked if a rhinoceros has antlers. Overall on this test, he was correct on all eight questions for six of the 24 items (control range = 8–18), and provided 162 out of 192 correct answers (control range = 162–181). Thus, E.P.'s autobiographical remembering occurs in the context of a mild impairment for some aspects of semantic knowledge (the names of objects and their properties). There is no suggestion in the data available to date that E.P.'s temporal lobe damage has affected his episodic memory more than his semantic memory.

CONCLUSION

Findings from experimental animals and amnesic patients with damage to the hippocampus and related structures have illuminated the contribution of the medial temporal lobe to memory for facts and events. First, patients with damage to the hippocampal region were impaired relative to controls on a recognition test, regardless of whether the test words were associated with "remembering" or "knowing" (Figure 4.1). Remembering and knowing have been linked to episodic and semantic memory, respectively. Thus, the hippocampal region appears to be important for memory, even in the absence of episodic remembering. Second, patients with damage to the hippocampal region were impaired at learning novel three-word sentences, despite extended training (Figure 4.2), indicating that the hippocampal region is important in the learning of fact-like material. Third, patients with damage to the hippocampal region acquired less knowledge about the world after the onset of amnesia than controls did during the same time period (Figure 4.3). This finding shows directly that the hippocampal region normally contributes to the acquisition of semantic memory. Fourth, a profoundly amnesic patient (E.P.) with extensive and nearly complete damage to the medial temporal lobe had intact remote topographical memory of his childhood neighborhood (Figure 4.4) and a considerable capacity for autobiographical remembering. This finding shows that the medial temporal lobe is not essential for aspects of remote factual memory and that detailed recall of remote events is possible despite large medial temporal lobe lesions. Fifth, a patient with histologically-confirmed damage restricted to the CA1 field of the hippocampus (R.B.) exhibited normal autobiographical recall (Figure 4.5A), and two patients with histologically-confirmed damage to the hippocampal region and entorhinal cortex (L.M. and W.H.) exhibited normal autobiographical memory from early life (Figure 4.5B and Figure 4.6). This result shows that the hippocampus and the entorhinal cortex are not necessary for the recall of either remote factual knowledge or remote autobiographical events. In contrast, these structures are important for recalling more recent factual knowledge (Squire et al., 1989; and Figure 4.3) and more recent autobiographical events (Figure 4.6).

The available data suggest that the hippocampus and related structures in the medial temporal lobe are needed for acquiring and, for a limited time after learning, retrieving memory for facts as well as memory for specific events. If the distinction between facts and events (semantic and episodic memory) does not illuminate the function of the medial temporal lobe or its anatomical components, it nevertheless seems likely that the different components of the medial temporal lobe do make different and specialized contributions to declarative memory. For example, the available data suggest that the parahippocampal cortex contributes especially to spatial memory, and the perirhinal cortex contributes especially to visual memory (Suzuki & Amaral, 1994; Zola & Squire, 2000). The hippocampus lies at the end of the processing hierarchy of the medial temporal lobe and is in a position to extend and combine the processing accomplished by structures that lie earlier in the hierarchy (Figure 4.7). It has been suggested that the hippocampus is especially well suited for one-trial learning and for rapidly forming conjunctions between arbitrarily different stimuli (for discussion, see Eichenbaum & Cohen, 2001; Squire, 1992). If so, it is possible that adjacent cortex might contribute more to other kinds of tasks (e.g. when learning is less explicitly associative or when learning is gradual).

It is of interest that in the rat lesions of hippocampus plus subiculum and lesions of perirhinal, entorhinal, and postrhinal cortices produced similarly severe impairments on

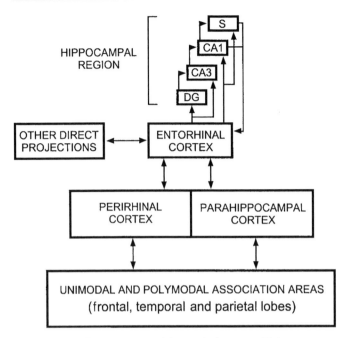

Figure 4.7 Schematic view of the medial temporal lobe memory system. The entorhinal cortex is a major source of projections to the hippocampal region, which includes the dentate gyrus (DG), the cell fields of the hippocampus (CA3, CA1), and the subicular complex (S). Nearly two-thirds of the cortical input to entorhinal cortex originates in the adjacent perirhinal and parahippocampal cortices, which in turn receive projections from unimodal and polymodal areas in the frontal, temporal and parietal lobes. The entorhinal cortex also receives other direct inputs from orbital frontal cortex, insular cortex and superior temporal gyrus. All these projections are reciprocal

the socially acquired food preference task (Alvarez et al., 2001). Both groups of animals performed above chance. If one assumes that the cortical lesion has fully disconnected the hippocampus from the neocortex, then this finding suggests that, in the case of this one-trial associative learning task, the adjacent cortex may not contribute much beyond what is contributed by the hippocampus itself. This result can be contrasted with delayed nonmatching to sample, where the effects of restricted hippocampal damage are exacerbated by damage to adjacent cortex (Zola-Morgan et al., 1994). A particularly interesting example comes from a task of paired-associate learning, which is acquired gradually by monkeys in more than 8000 trials (Murray et al., 1993). Following damage to perirhinal and entorhinal cortex, postoperative performance was much more severely impaired than after damage to the hippocampus and the immediately adjacent cortex (posterior entorhinal cortex and parahippocampal cortex). This finding suggests, in the case of the paired-associate task, that the perirhinal cortex may contribute more to performance than the hippocampus.

Further systematic work on this issue should be informative. The effects of separate and combined lesions can be studied within the same species and the same tasks with an eye towards revealing qualitative, distinct effects of hippocampal lesions and lesions of perirhinal or entorhinal cortices. It remains possible that there is no simple division of labor between these regions, and that differences in function may be better understood as matters of degree that apply in a graded way across the hippocampus and adjacent cortex. If so, distinctive contributions of different structures may be difficult to reveal by behavioral measures.

ACKNOWLEDGEMENT

Supported by the Medical Research Service of the Department of Veterans Affairs, NIMH Grant 24600, NARSAD Grant 9098, and the Metropolitan Life Foundation.

REFERENCES

Aggleton, J.P. & Brown, M.W. (1999). Episodic memory, amnesia, and the hippocampal–anterior thalamic axis. *Behavioral and Brain Sciences*, **22**, 425–489.

Alvarez, P., Lipton, P.A., Melrose, R. & Eichenbaum, H. (2001). Differential effects of damage within the hippocampal region on memory for a natural, nonspatial odor–odor association. *Learning and Memory*, **8**, 79–86.

Alvarez, P., Zola-Morgan, S. & Squire, L.R. (1995). Damage limited to the hippocampal region produces long-lasting memory impairment in monkeys. *Journal of Neuroscience*, **15**, 3796–3807.

Bachevalier, J. (1990). Ontogenetic development of habit and memory formation in primates. *Annals of the New York Academy of Sciences*, **608**, 457–474.

Baddeley, A., Vargha-Khadem, F. & Mishkin, M. (2001). Preserved recognition in a case of developmental amnesia; Implications for the acquisition of semantic memory. *Journal of Cognitive Neuroscience*, **13**, 357–369.

Baker K.B. & Kim, J.J. (2002). Effects of stress and hippocampal NMDA receptor antagonism on recognition memory in rats. *Learning and Memory*, **9**, 58–68.

Bayley, P. & Squire, L. (2001). Detailed recall of remote autobiographical memories in amnesia. *Society for Neuroscience Abstracts*, **27**, 347.7.

Beason-Held, L.L., Rosene, D.L., Killiany, R.J. & Moss, M.B. (1999). Hippocampal formation lesions produce memory impairment in the rhesus monkey. *Hippocampus*, **9**, 562–574.

Beatty, W.W., Salmon, D.P., Bernstein, N. & Butters, N. (1987). Remote memories in a patient with amnesia due to hypoxia. *Psychological Medicine*, **17**, 657–665.

Beatty, W.W., Salmon, D.P., Butters, N. et al. (1988). Retrograde amnesia in patients with Alzheimer's disease or Huntington's disease. *Neurobiology of Aging*, **9**, 181–186.

Brown, M.W. & Aggleton, J.P. (2001). Recognition memory: what are the roles of the perirhinal cortex and hippocampus? *Nature Reviews Neuroscience*, **2**, 51–61.

Buffalo, E.A., Ramus, S.J., Clark, R.E. et al. (1999). Dissociation between the effects of damage to perirhinal cortex and area TE. *Learning and Memory*, **6**, 572–599.

Bunsey, M. & Eichenbaum, H. (1996). Conservation of hippocampal memory function in rats and humans. *Nature*, **379**, 255–257.

Cermak, L.S. (1984). The episodic-semantic distinction in amnesia. In L. Squire & N. Butters (eds), *Neuropsychology of Memory*. New York: Guilford.

Clark, R.E. & Squire, L.R. (2000). Awareness and the conditioned eyeblink response. In D.S. Woodruff-Pak & J.E. Steinmetz (eds), *Eyeblink Classical Conditioning: Human*. Nowell, MA: Kluwer Academic.

Clark, R.E. & Squire, L.R. (1998). Classical conditioning and brain systems: A key role for awareness. *Science*, **280**, 77–81.

Clark, R.E., West, A.N., Zola, S.M. & Squire, L.R. (2001). Rats with lesions of the hippocampus are impaired on the delayed nonmatching-to-sample task. *Hippocampus*, **11**, 176–186.

Clark, R.E., Zola, S.M. & Squire, L.R. (2000). Impaired recognition memory in rats after damage to the hippocampus. *Journal of Neuroscience*, **20**, 8853–8860.

Clayton, N.S. & Dickinson, A. (1998). Episodic-like memory during cache recovery by scrub jays. *Nature*, **395**, 272–274.

Crovitz, H.F. & Schiffman, H. (1974). Frequency of episodic memories as a function of their age. *Bulletin of the Psychonomic Society*, **4**, 517–518.

Dudchenko, P.A., Wood, E.R. & Eichenbaum, H. (2000). Neurotoxic hippocampal lesions have no effect on odor span and little effect on odor recognition memory but produce significant impairments on spatial span, recognition, and alternation. *Journal of Neuroscience*, **20**, 2964–2977.

Dusek, J.A. & Eichenbaum, H. (1997). The hippocampus and memory for orderly stimulus relations. *Proceedings of the National Academy of Science of the USA*, **94**, 7109–7114.

Dusek, J.A. & Eichenbaum, H. (1998). The hippocampus and transverse patterning guided by olfactory cues. *Behavioral Neuroscience*, **112**, 762–771.

Eichenbaum, H. & Cohen, N.J. (2001). *From Conditioning to Conscious Recollection: Memory Systems of the Brain*. Oxford: Oxford University Press.

Eldridge, L.L., Knowlton, B.J., Furmanski, C.S. et al. (2000). Remembering episodes: a selective role for the hippocampus during retrieval. *Nature Neuroscience*, **3**, 1149–1152.

Ennaceur, A. & Delacour, J. (1988). A new one-trial test for neurobiological studies of memory in rats: 1. Behavioural data. *Behavioral Brain Research*, **31**, 47–59.

Gabrieli, J.D.E. (1998). Cognitive neuroscience of human memory. *Annual Review of Psychology*, **49**, 87–115.

Gaffan, D. (1974). Recognition impaired and association intact in the memory of monkeys after transaction of the fornix. *Journal of Comparative Physiological Psychology*, **86**, 1100–1109.

Hamann, S.B. & Squire, L.R. (1995). On the acquisition of new declarative knowledge in amnesia. *Behavioral Neuroscience*, **109**, 1027–1044.

Holdstock, J.S., Mayes, A.R., Roberts, N. et al. (2002). Under what conditions is recognition spared relative to recall after selective hippocampal damage in humans? *Hippocampus*, **12**, 341–351.

Kim, J.J., Clark, R.E. & Thompson, R.F. (1995). Hippocampectomy impairs the memory of recently, but not remotely, acquired trace eyeblink conditioned responses. *Behavioral Neuroscience*, **109**, 195–203.

Kinsbourne, M. & Wood, F. (1975). Short-term memory processes and the amnesic syndrome. In D. Deutsch & J.A. Deutsch (eds), *Short-term Memory*. San Diego, CA: Academic Press.

Kitchener, E.G., Hodges, J.R. & McCarthy, R. (1998). Acquisition of post-morbid vocabulary and semantic facts in the absence of episodic memory. *Brain*, **121**, 1313–1327.

Knowlton, B.J. & Squire, L.R. (1995). Remembering and knowing: two different expressions of declarative memory. *Journal of Experimental Psychology: Learning, Memory and Cognition*, **21**, 699–710.

MacKinnon, D. & Squire, L.R. (1989). Autobiographical memory in amnesia. *Psychobiology*, **17**, 247–256.

Maguire, E.A. & Mummery, C.J. (1999). Differential modulation of a common memory retrieval network revealed by positron emission tomography. *Hippocampus*, **9**, 54–61.

Mandler, G. (1980). Recognizing: the judgment of previous occurrence. *Psychological Review*, **87**, 252–271.

Manns, J.R., Clark, R.E. & Squire, L.R. (2000). Awareness predicts the magnitude of single-cue trace eyeblink conditioning. *Hippocampus*, **10**, 181–186.

Manns, J.R. & Squire, L.R. (1999). Impaired recognition memory on the Doors and People Test after damage limited to the hippocampal region. *Hippocampus*, **9**, 495–499.

Mayes, A.R., Holdstock, J.S., Isaac, C.L. et al. (2002). Relative sparing of item recognition memory in a patient with adult-onset damage limited to the hippocampus. *Hippocampus*, **12**, 325–340.

McCormick, P.D. (1979). Autobiographical memory in the aged. *Canadian Journal of Psychology*, **33**, 118–124.

Meunier, M., Bachevalier, J., Mishkin, M. & Murray, E.A. (1993). Effects on visual recognition of combined and separate ablations of the entorhinal and perirhinal cortex in rhesus monkeys. *Journal of Neuroscience*, **13**, 5418–5432.

Mishkin, M. & Delacour, J. (1975). An analysis of short-term visual memory in the monkey. *Journal of Experimental Psychology: Animal Behavior Processes*, **1**, 326–334.

Moscovitch, M., Yaschyshyn, T., Ziegler, M. & Nadel, L. (2000). Remote episodic memory: was Endel Tulving right all along? In E. Tulving (ed.), *Memory, Consciousness, and the Brain: The Tallinn Conference*. Philadelphia, PA: Psychology Press.

Mumby, D.G., Pinel, J.P.J. & Wood, E.R. (1990). Nonrecurring-items delayed nonmatching-to-sample in rats: a new paradigm for testing nonspatial working memory. *Psychobiology*, **18**, 321–326.

Murray, E.A., Gaffan, D. & Mishkin, M. (1993). Neural substrates of visual stimulus–stimulus association in rhesus monkeys. *Journal of Neuroscience*, **13**, 4549–4561.

Murray, E.A. & Mishkin, M. (1998). Object recognition and location memory in monkeys with excitotoxic lesions of the amygdala and hippocampus. *Journal of Neuroscience*, **18**, 6568–6582.

Nadel, L. & Moscovitch, M. (1997). Memory consolidation, retrograde amnesia and the hippocampal complex. *Current Opinion in Neurobiology*, **7**, 217–227.

Nadel, L., Samsonovich, A., Ryan, L. & Moscovitch, M. (2000). Multiple trace theory of human memory: computational, neuroimaging, and neuropsychological results. *Hippocampus*, **10**, 352–368.

Rampon, C., Tang, Y.P., Goodhouse, J. et al. (2000). Enrichment induces structural changes and recovery from nonspatial memory deficits in CA1 NMDAR1-knockout mice. *Nature Neuroscience*, **3**, 238–244.

Reed, J.M. & Squire, L.R. (1998). Retrograde amnesia for facts and events: findings from four new cases. *Journal of Neuroscience*, **18**, 3943–3954.

Reed, J.M. & Squire, L.R. (1997). Impaired recognition memory in patients with lesions limited to the hippocampal formation. *Behavioral Neuroscience*, **111**, 667–675.

Rempel-Clower, N., Zola, S.M., Squire, L.R. & Amaral, D.G. (1996). Three cases of enduring memory impairment following bilateral damage limited to the hippocampal formation. *Journal of Neuroscience*, **16**, 5233–5255.

Rosenbaum, R.S., Priselac, S., Kohler, S. et al. (2000). Remote spatial memory in an amnesic person with extensive bilateral hippocampal lesions. *Nature Neuroscience*, **3**, 1044–1048.

Schacter, D. & Tulving, E. (1994). *Memory Systems 1994*. Cambridge, MA: MIT Press.

Schacter, D.L. & Tulving, E. (1982). Memory, amnesia, and the episodic/semantic distinction. In N.E. Spear & R.L. Isaacson (eds), *The Expression of Knowledge*. New York: Plenum.

Schmidtke, K. & Vollmer, H. (1997). Retrograde amnesia: a study of its relation to anterograde amnesia and semantic memory deficits. *Neuropsychologia*, **35**, 505–518.

Squire, L.R. (1992). Memory and the hippocampus: a synthesis from findings with rats, monkeys, and humans. *Psychological Review*, **99**, 195–231.

Squire, L.R., Clark, R.E. & Knowlton, B.J. (2001). Retrograde amnesia. *Hippocampus*, **11**, 50–55.

Squire, L.R., Haist, F., & Shimamura, A.P. (1989). The neurology of memory: quantitative assessment of retrograde amnesia in two groups of amnesic patients. *Journal of Neuroscience*, **9**, 828–839.

Squire, L.R. & Zola-Morgan, S. (1991). The medial temporal lobe memory system. *Science*, **253**, 1380–1386.

Squire, L.R. & Zola, S.M. (1998). Episodic memory, semantic memory, and amnesia. *Hippocampus*, **8**, 205–211.

Stark, C.E.L. & Squire, L.R. (2000). fMRI activity in the medial temporal lobe during recognition memory as a function of study–test interval. *Hippocampus*, **10**, 329–337.

Stefanacci, L., Buffalo, E.A., Schmolck, H. & Squire, L.R. (2000). Profound amnesia following damage to the medial temporal lobe: a neuroanatomical and neuropsychological profile of patient E.P. *Journal of Neuroscience*, **20**, 7024–7036.

Suzuki, W.A. & Amaral, D.G. (1994). Topographic organization of the reciprocal connections between the monkey entorhinal cortex and the perirhinal and parahippocampal cortices. *Journal of Neuroscience*, **14**, 1856–1877.

Suzuki, W.A., Zda-Morgan, S., Squire, L.R. & Amaral, D.G. (1993). Lesions of the perirhinal and parahippocampal cortices in the monkey produce long-lasting memory impairment in the visual and tactual modalities. *Journal of Neuroscience*, **13**, 2430–2451.

Teng, E. & Squire, L.R. (1999). Memory for places learned long ago is intact after hippocampal damage. *Nature*, **400**, 675–677.

Tulving, E. (1983). *Elements of Episodic Memory*. Oxford: Oxford University Press.

Tulving, E. (1985). Memory and consciousness. *Canadian Psychologist*, **26**, 1–12.

Tulving, E. (1991). Concepts in human memory. In L.R. Squire, N.M. Weinberger, G. Lynch & J.L. McGaugh (eds), *Memory: Organization and Locus of Change*. New York: Oxford University Press.

Tulving, E. (1993). Human memory. In P. Anderson, O. Hvalby, O. Paulsen & B. Hokfelt (eds), *Memory Concepts—1993*. Amsterdam: Elsevier Science.

Tulving, E., Schacter, D.L., McLachland, D. & Moscovitch, M. (1988). Priming of semantic autobiographical knowledge: a case study of retrograde amnesia. *Brain and Cognition*, **8**, 3–20.

Vargha-Khadem, F., Gadian, D.G., Watkins, K.E. et al. (1997). Differential effects of early hippocampal pathology on episodic and semantic memory. *Science*, **277**, 376–380.

Verfaellie, M., Koseff, P. & Alexander, M.P. (2000). Acquisition of novel semantic information in amnesia: effects of lesion location. *Neuropsychologia*, **38**, 484–492.

Verfaellie, M., Reiss, L. & Roth, H.L. (1995). Knowledge of New English vocabulary in amnesia: an examination of premorbidly acquired semantic memory. *Journal of the International Neuropsychological Society*, **1**, 443–453.

Wiig, K.A. & Bilkey, D.K. (1995). Lesions of rat perirhinal cortex exacerbate the memory deficit observed following damage to the fimbria-fornix. *Behavioral Neuroscience*, **109**, 620–630.

Wood, E.R. & Phillips, A.G. (1991). Deficits on a one trial object recognition task by rats with hippocampal CA1 lesions produced by cerebral ischemia. *Neuroscience Research Communications*, **9**, 177–182.

Yonelinas, A.P., Kroll, N.E.A., Dobbins, I. et al. (1998). Recollection and familiarity deficits in amnesia: convergence of remember–know, process dissociation, and receiver operating characteristic data. *Neuropsychology*, **12**, 323–339.

Zola-Morgan, S., Squire, L.R. & Amaral, D.G. (1986). Human amnesia and the medial temporal region: enduring memory impairment following a bilateral lesion limited to field CA1 of the hippocampus. *Journal of Neuroscience*, **6**, 2950–2967.

Zola-Morgan, S., Squire, L.R. & Amaral, D.G. (1989). Lesions of the hippocampal formation but not lesions of the fornix or the mammillary nuclei produce long-lasting memory impairment in monkeys. *Journal of Neuroscience*, **9**, 898–913.

Zola-Morgan, S., Squire, L.R. & Ramus, S.J. (1994). Severity of memory impairment in monkeys as a function of locus and extent of damage within the medial temporal lobe memory system. *Hippocampus*, **4**, 483–495.

Zola-Morgan, S., Squire, L.R., Rempel, N.L. et al. (1992). Enduring memory impairment in monkeys after ischemic damage to the hippocampus. *Journal of Neuroscience*, **12**, 1582–2596.

Zola, S.M. & Squire, L. (2000). The medial temporal lobe and the hippocampus. In E. Tulving & F.I.M. Craik (eds), *Oxford Handbook of Memory*. New York: Oxford University Press.

Zola, S.M. & Squire, L.R. (2001). Relationship between magnitude of damage to the hippocampus and impaired recognition memory in monkeys. *Hippocampus*, **11**, 92–98.

Zola, S.M., Squire, L.R., Teng, E. et al. (2000). Impaired recognition memory in monkeys after damage limited to the hippocampal region. *Journal of Neuroscience*, **20**, 451–463.

CHAPTER 5

Connectionist Models of Memory Disorders

Jaap Murre

University of Amsterdam, The Netherlands

WHY MODEL?

There are many good reasons to construct models. In the field of memory disorders data are complex, fragmentary, multidisciplinary and based on few observations. This implies that precise quantitative fits are either impossible or of limited use. Nonetheless, models can still play an important role in the organization of the data and in the ongoing debates about what are the essential issues in the field. Perhaps it is instructive to compare its role to that of the maps made in the early fifteenth century. In those days, sailors and explorers discovered many new coasts, seas and rivers. A great variety of data were available to aid in navigation but, much as in neuropsychology, they were often anecdotal, incomplete, distorted, unreliable or of unknown reliability, and they were formulated in many different formats. Maps brought these data together in a systematic way, with the result that long voyages by ship became increasingly less dependent on the intuition and experience of individual sailors.

In a given field, one can often observe that model construction passes through a series of development stages. In the initial construction stage modellers are forced to select the essential data that should be addressed. This stage also unveils any hidden assumptions and "white spaces" in existing theories. In the field of memory disorders, use of certain terms and metaphors, such as "activation", "consolidation", "arousal", "loop", "store" and "index", for example, often leads us to believe that we have a pretty good idea of what these structures and processes are. When we start to build a model, however, they often prove inadequate and more detailed descriptions need to be developed. But when this additional work has been done, even rather coarse models are already able to provide important proofs of existence of the type, "X can indeed work this way". Here, X could stand for prevalent terms such as "consolidation", "transfer" (of memory), "shrinkage" (of retrograde amnesia) and many other terms. Providing even a single detailed implementation of their underlying mechanisms may be sufficient to show that a proposed mechanism can *in principle* account for the observed phenomenon.

The Handbook of Memory Disorders. Edited by A.D. Baddeley, M.D. Kopelman and B.A. Wilson
© 2002 John Wiley & Sons, Ltd.

When a model has been tested against a large body of data, it typically provides us with a concise description of these data. We could call this the descriptive stage of modelling. Even if the model that has reached this stage is later shown to be wrong, it will often continue to serve an important purpose. Thus, Einstein's Theory of Relativity shows that Newtonian mechanics are wrong, but because the latter provide a concise and good-enough description of how physical bodies move and interact, the theory remains in use and has a great number of theoretical and practical applications, such as in the construction of bridges.

In the final stage, we arrive at the role traditionally assigned to models, namely precise quantitative prediction of new and unexpected phenomena. Mature models, fuelled by high quality data, should be able to guide research with such predictions. But even in the organizing stage of modelling we are often already able to derive interesting predictions, albeit of a more qualitative nature.

In order to formulate a model, one needs a language in which to express it. Many styles of formulating models exist in psychology, but most can be classified as either computational or mathematical. The distinction is not strict, in the sense that a computational model is nearly always formulated with mathematical equations. The main difference is that a mathematical model aims to derive the behaviour of the model analytically, by proposing theorems and deriving proofs for them, whereas a computational model's behaviour is evaluated mainly with computer simulations. Because mathematical models yield exact results, they are generally to be preferred. Unfortunately, many interesting models in neuropsychology are too difficult to be evaluated mathematically and we must take recourse to computer simulation.

In the following sections we will discuss several computational models of amnesia and related memory disorders. Most of the recent models are formulated and implemented as connectionist models. For those readers unfamiliar with connectionism, I precede the discussion of the models with a very brief introduction to connectionism.

A VERY BRIEF INTRODUCTION TO CONNECTIONISM

Connectionism (also called *neural networks*) is a modelling formalism based on the metaphor of networks of interconnected neurons that exchange simple signals, called *activations*, over the connections. Of particular importance is the learning capacity of many connectionist models, which makes them particularly suitable for modelling human memory. Learning is achieved by adjusting the efficiency (i.e. strength or *weight*) of each connection in such a way that the behaviour of the network is slowly moulded into some type of desired or target behaviour. This target behaviour may be provided by the modeller in the form of teaching or target signals. This is called error-correcting learning. Sometimes, neural networks are able to extract regularities from the stimuli to which they are exposed without being told what to aim for. They typically achieve this regularity learning by creating and updating internal category structures.

Figure 5.1 shows an artificial neuron or *node*. On its input side it receives input activations, which are weighed by the weight of the connection over which they arrive. Thus, if an activation signal of 0.5 arrives and if the weight is -1.8, the weighed signal is -0.9. All weighed inputs to a node are added and form its *net input*. A node is able to transform its net input into a new output signal (activation). An example of such an activation rule is: send a 1 if the net input is greater than 0 and a 0 otherwise.

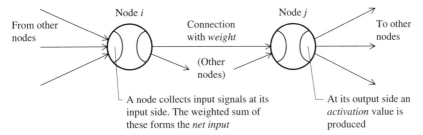

Figure 5.1 Two artificial nodes with connections. Node *i* sends an activation value a_i to node *j*, where it will contribute towards its net input. Connections have weights, e.g. if the weight on the connection *w* is 1.3 and if a_i is 0.6 then the contribution towards the net input of node *j* is 1.3 times 0.6, which is 0.78

There are two important approaches to learning that are relevant for models of memory and amnesia: error-correcting learning and Hebbian learning, which will be briefly introduced in the following two sections.

Error-correcting Learning: Perceptron and Backpropagation

The most popular learning algorithm for neural networks is *backpropagation*. Among many other applications it forms the basis of the prominent model of amnesia by McClelland et al. (1995), discussed below. Backpropagation is a form of error-correcting learning: for every input pattern, a target output pattern is presented, which the network must learn to produce on the basis of the input, e.g. Sejnowski & Rosenberg (1987) trained a network to pronounce text by presenting it with texts (on the input side) and a target phonetic transcription (on the output side). The backpropagation network was powerful enough to learn the task and when enough samples had been presented, it was able to generalize its behaviour and pronounced texts it had not encountered before.

Backpropagation has been re-invented several times but it was not until the publication by Rumelhart et al. (1986) that it received the enormous popularity it has enjoyed over the past 15 years. The underlying learning mechanism of backpropagation is based on a learning rule pioneered by Frank Rosenblatt in the late 1950s—the perceptron learning rule (Rosenblatt, 1958, 1962). The perceptron is limited to input and output values of 0 and 1 (i.e. no graded values are allowed). Given a certain input pattern, *P*, for each output node, a target signal (also 0 or 1) must be available. The network must learn to produce these target signals, given the input pattern *P*. An output node's activation becomes 1 if its net input is higher than 0, and becomes 0 otherwise.

The perceptron learning rule is straightforward:

- If the output is already equal to the output target, the weight is left unchanged (in this case the correct response is present).
- Otherwise, if the spontaneous activation is lower than the target activation, the weights to the output node are clearly too low. Therefore, they are increased by some small amount. If the spontaneous activation is higher than target, the weights are decreased by a small amount.
- Never change weights from input nodes with activation value 0, as they do not contribute the spontaneous output and are therefore better left undisturbed.

When a training pattern (input–target pair) is presented, the learning rule is applied to all weights in the network. An entire training set, consisting of many patterns, is usually presented several times until the total error (measured over all patterns and all nodes) decreases no further.

The perceptron is a two-layer network. It has no middle layers (called *hidden* layers) and so it cannot do any internal processing. This is a severe limitation, because Minsky & Papert (1969) proved that two-layer networks are not able to represent certain important logical relationships between input and output. They showed that there are many interesting pattern sets for which there exist no weight values that allow a network to produce an error-free output for every input pattern. Nonetheless, if a solution does exist, the perceptron learning rule is guaranteed to find it (Rosenblatt, 1958). Although limited in processing capacity, the perceptron already possesses many characteristics that are psychologically plausible, e.g. it has *content addressable memory* (finding the correct output on the basis of an incomplete or distorted input pattern) and *graceful degradation* (gradual decline in performance, rather than a sudden drop with progressive lesioning of the weights).

The backpropagation algorithm by Rumelhart et al. (1986) remedied the shortcomings of the perceptron algorithm because: (a) it can be used in networks with one or more hidden layers; and (b) it can be used with networks that have graded inputs and outputs that lay, for example, between 0 and 1. Already in 1960, Widrow & Hoff (1960) had published a learning rule that could be used with one type of graded activation rules: the delta-rule. The backpropagation rule can be seen as a generalization of this learning rule and is, therefore, often called the *generalized delta rule*. It is also known as the *multi layer perceptron*.

The backpropagation learning rule is very similar to the perceptron rule when applied to the weights connected to the output units. For these units a target signal is available that can be used immediately to derive an error value to update the weights. For connections to hidden units, however, an error signal is not provided. In this case, a local error signal is derived artificially by using the error values of the nodes *to* which the hidden unit connects. The error values, thus, flow *backward* through the connections: from the output nodes to the hidden nodes, hence the name of the algorithm. When the error values are backpropagated, they are also weighed by the connections. Once error values are available in all output and hidden nodes, they are used as in the perceptron rule, except that we are now using graded activation values (e.g. real values between 0 and 1). Also, there is usually an added term in the learning rule that affects the learning rate for target activation values near the extreme values. This added term slows down the algorithm but is included because it can be shown mathematically that its addition ensures that the total error (summed over all patterns and all output nodes) will never increase during learning.

Backpropagation will not always find an optimal solution in the form of a set of weights that maximizes the performance but it will typically deliver at least a "good" solution. For many interesting learning problems, it can be proved that is not feasible to find the globally optimal solution within a reasonable amount of time, so for these problems we must make do with a suboptimal solution.

Standard backpropagation works with feedforward networks only. This means that higher layers cannot be connected to lower layers (i.e. those closer to the input). This limits their use to input–output associations and makes it hard to apply them to time-varying signals, because in such cases the system must retain an internal state that reflects the history of the signal thus far. Generalizations of the backpropagation learning algorithm to networks with recurrent connections are already presented in Rumelhart et al., (1986a). A simplified version of this rather complicated algorithm is the Simple Recurrent Network (Elman, 1990), which is also able to learn small grammars. Unfortunately, the suitability of the Simple Recurrent Network as a psychological model of grammar acquisition is very limited (Sharkey et al., 2000).

Despite its wide use in psychological models, backpropagation produces implausible forgetting behaviour. Ratcliff (1990) showed that when a network was trained with extremely simple, non-overlapping patterns (of the type 00001000), learning of a single additional pattern caused forgetting of all other patterns the network had acquired earlier. McCloskey & Cohen (1989) had similar experiences and coined the term "catastrophic interference". Such severe interference does occur in human subjects, but only when a stimulus must first be associated with one response (e.g. "Chair–five") and then with another (e.g. "Chair–two"). Because the stimuli are the same, learning of the second response causes forgetting of the first response. There are also cases where backpropagation forgets too little compared to human subjects (cf. Osgood, 1949), for which Murre (1995) has coined the term "*hypertransfer*".

There are various ways to make the memory behaviour of backpropagation more plausible. The most straightforward solution is to limit the number of hidden nodes that can fire in a representation. Thus, instead of having a fully distributed representation with roughly half the nodes being active, we would have only a few per cent firing. Such a semi-distributed (French, 1992; Murre, 1992) or localized approach (Page, 2000) is biologically plausible while still reducing the retroactive interference to psychologically acceptable levels. Another approach is to use interleaved learning with *random rehearsal* (Murre, 1992, 140ff.): when new patterns are being learned, a random selection of old patterns is relearned as well. McClelland et al. (1995) use this approach in their model of retrograde amnesia discussed below.

Hebbian Learning

Another type of learning is associative in nature and finds its roots in the work of Hebb (1949). Hebbian learning can be summarized as "neurons that fire together, wire together". Early uses in connectionist models were by Steinbuch (1961) and Willshaw et al. (1969). A great many variants and applications of the Hebb rule have since been published. Its biological plausibility was first demonstrated directly by Bliss & Lomo (1973) in the form of long-term potentiation in the hippocampus. Hebbian learning plays an important role in many psychological models of learning and memory (McClelland & Rumelhart, 1986; Rumelhart & McClelland, 1986). Three of the models of amnesia discussed below are based on a form of Hebbian learning.

When the Hebb rule is used with a two-layer network, an input pattern is typically associated directly with an output pattern. Weights between activated input nodes and output nodes are increased. Some variants of this rule decrease the weight if the input node is inactive and the output node is active. As with error-correcting learning, such Hebbian networks show content addressable memory and graceful degradation. Hebbian learning is also used frequently in combination with Hopfield networks (Hopfield, 1982). These networks have full, recurrent connectivity, where every node is connected to every other node with symmetrical connections (self-connections are not allowed). These networks have more processing capacity and can even be used to solve complicated optimization problems in econometrics.

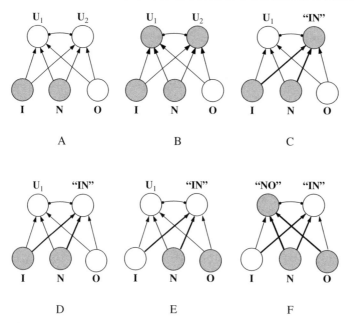

Figure 5.2 Schematic overview of competitive learning. The connections with circles at the end indicate inhibitory connections, arrow-heads indicate excitatory connections. (A) Letters "i" and "n" of the word "in", have been presented. (B) Uncommitted representation nodes U_1 and U_2 are competing. Assume that the weights are initially equally strong with small random variations. (C) Node U_2 has won the competition process, because its connections happened to be a little bit stronger. After resolution of the competition process, the connections from letter nodes I and N to node U_2 are being strengthened (Hebbian learning), while the connection from O to U_2 is being weakened (anti-Hebbian learning). (D) When the word "in" is presented again, the "in"-node would very rapidly become activated. (E) When the word "no" is presented, however, the other node will become activated. (F) Hebbian learning further establishes the previously uncommitted node U_1 as the "no"-node

The Hebb rule also forms the basis of a class of learning algorithms called "competitive learning" (Rumelhart & Zipser, 1985), many variants of which have been developed (e.g. Grossberg, 1976). A key ingredient in nearly all of these algorithms is a form of competition between the nodes: only one node (or a few nodes) can be active in a layer. The node with the highest net input wins the competition. The principle of competitive learning is illustrated in Figure 5.2. A similar network was used for the amnesia model by Alvarez & Squire (1994), discussed below. The network has three input nodes, which only serve to hold the input pattern. In this case the input nodes represent the letters "i", "n" and "o", so that the words "in" and "no" can be formed. The network also has two uncommitted representation nodes, U_1 and U_2. Initially, these do not represent any specific pattern. One of the main goals of a competitive learning procedure is to have these nodes represent specific input patterns or categories of related input patterns. Crucial in this learning process is that U_1 and U_2 inhibit each other strongly, so that only one node can remain active. This is known as "*winner-take-all competition*" (WTA competition). Figure 5.2 shows how first the word "in" is learned, and then the word "no".

Learning proceeds in two stages: First, a process of competition among the representation nodes takes place, as a result of which a single "winning" node remains activated (in this case node U_2). Second, the connections to this node are adjusted using Hebbian learning. As a result of the learning procedure, the input pattern "in" will now always activate this node, so that U_2 has become the *"in"-node*. Pattern "no" activates the other uncommitted node U_1, which after subsequent learning becomes the *"no"-node*. In this way, we could produce a word recognizer that learns in an unsupervized manner: simply by presenting many words to the system, it will develop "word-recognition nodes" (Murre, 1992; Murre et al., 1992).

The value of unsupervised learning lies in the fact that it is possible to discover regularities in the input patterns and to form categories or other higher-level units in an autonomous fashion. It is very likely that such processes play a crucial role in the acquisition of cognitive skills and the formation of semantic categories. Networks such as shown in Figure 5.2 can serve as *modules* or building blocks in larger networks, e.g. we could have lower-level modules that recognize letters on the basis of handwritten patterns. On top of the letter modules we could then position one or more word modules. It would suffice to provide such a model with enough handwritten words to allow it to discover both letter-units and word-units. If it were trained with Russian input patterns, it would develop nodes recognizing Cyrillic letters and Russian words. The outcome of the learning process is, thus, strongly determined by the input patterns.

The modular architecture of such a model facilitates learning certain types of material and impedes the learning of others. When different networks are generated in a process of simulated evolution, certain types of modular architectures are selected as "highly fit", in that they are particularly efficient at solving a given learning task (e.g. learning to recognize handwritten digits on the basis of examples; Happel & Murre, 1994). Such processes could provide us with pointers to how inborn or "native" knowledge interacts with patterns encountered in the world around us. An efficient modular architecture, which is "innate", will lead to very rapid discovery of the crucial units of processing, such as letters and words.

Several computational models of amnesia introduce some level of modularity to shape the learning process and the formation of long-term memory. Unfortunately, at this point our knowledge of the neuroanatomy of memory is very incomplete, which forces modellers to use a global approach with only a few modules or systems. Before discussing some models in more detail, we will first review some of the neuroanatomical considerations that are pertinent to most computational models of memory disorders.

GLOBAL ANATOMY OF LONG-TERM MEMORY

Currently, most models of memory disorders are still based on extreme simplifications of the neuroanatomy, typically focusing on the hippocampus and adjacent temporal lobe structures (e.g. entorhinal and perirhinal cortices, parahippoampal gyrus, etc.). Figure 5.3a gives a partial view of the neuroanatomical hierarchy derived by Felleman & Van Essen (1991), who position the hippocampus at the top of the neuroanatomical hierarchy of interconnected brain areas, with the sensory and motor organs at the bottom. Squire (1992) and Squire & Zola-Morgan (1991) give a similar hierarchy (see Figure 5.3b).

Most computational models of amnesia assume this basic neuroanatomical framework and subscribe to the view that the neocortex and hippocampus play different roles in

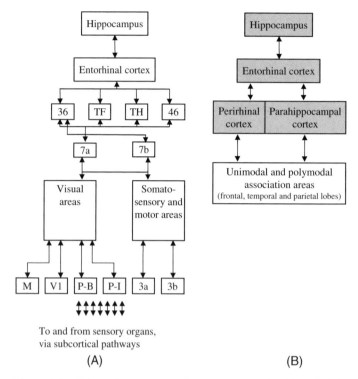

Figure 5.3 Schematic overview of neuroanatomy. (A) How the hippocampus is located at the top of the neuroanatomical hierarchy; illustration by Felleman & Van Essen (1990). Shown is a small part of a combination of the maps of the visual and somatosensory areas. (B) Similar hierarchy according to Squire (1992; Squire & Zola-Morgan, 1991), but simplified even further

long-term memory storage. They also tend to assume a process of long-term memory consolidation. While initially the retrieval of a recently experienced event is reliant upon the hippocampal system, repeated reinstatement of the hippocampal–neocortical ensemble over time results in the formation of a more permanent—hippocampally-independent—memory representation in the neocortex. We will discuss some of the evidence and counter-evidence for a long-term consolidation process in more detail below.

Why the brain might employ two different systems for the storage of memory remains an unanswered question. We have argued that the neocortex does not have sufficient connectivity to rapidly link activated areas in the short time that an individual experiences an event (Murre & Sturdy, 1995). This scarcity of cortical connections makes it highly unlikely that neural connections will be in place when two brain sites must be associated in order to support a new memory representation. We have developed a computational model of long-term neural linking in the cerebral cortex, based on the idea that many intermediate neurons must be recruited to connect two faraway neural areas (Murre & Raffone, submitted). This process is slow and accumulative and cannot normally take place in a single learning trial.

McClelland et al. (1995) have put forward an alternative hypothesis for the different roles of hippocampus and cortex. In their view, memory consolidation helps prevent catastrophic interference in sequential learning. Their hypothesis finds support in computer simulations, in which newly acquired knowledge must be integrated into the existing knowledge database. They use a backpropagation network and contrast *focused learning*, where semantic memory can rapidly learn new facts, with *interleaved learning*, where learning of new facts (temporarily stored in a "hippocampus") is interleaved with additional learning of already learned facts. As was discussed above, focused learning will lead to catastrophic interference, causing overwriting of old facts by newly learned facts, e.g. McClelland et al. (1995) show that learning about "penguin" might lead to the forgetting of "robin" and other birds. They also show that interleaved learning does not suffer from this problem. It is not clear what the memory behaviour of their model would be if it were based on some modified form of backpropagation that remedies the catastrophic interference (e.g. see French, 1999). But even if catastrophic interference were not a problem, it is likely that a network's generalization behaviour could still be improved by using a form of slow, interleaved learning (Grossberg, 1976).

The two hypotheses put forward are both plausible in the sense that it may make sense from both a neuroanatomical and a functional point of view for the human brain to have evolved a learning system with different roles for the hippocampus and neocortex. Damage to different parts of this system causes characteristic forms of amnesia. Next, we will review how various connectionist models of amnesia explain these characteristics.

MODELS OF AMNESIA

Retrograde Amnesia

Since the 1950s, many models have been published that address aspects of the formation of long-term memory, hippocampus–cortex interaction, and retrograde amnesia (e.g. Milner, 1957, 1989; Mishkin, 1982; O'Keefe & Nadel, 1978; Rolls, 1990; Squire & Zola-Morgan, 1991; Squire et al., 1984; Teyler & DiScenna, 1986; Treves & Rolls, 1994; Wickelgren, 1979, 1987). The four connectionist models discussed in this section have their roots in these earlier models. Through their implementation, they provide existence proofs, demonstrating that many of the earlier, mostly verbally stated ideas are indeed viable. We will in turn review the models by Alvarez & Squire (1994), McClelland et al. (1995), Murre (1996, 1997), and Nadel & Moscovitch (1997).

Alvarez & Squire

Alvarez & Squire (1994; see also Squire & Alvarez, 1995) present a connectionist model of an earlier, non-computational, model of long-term memory and amnesia by Squire and co-workers (e.g. Squire, 1992; Squire et al., 1984; Squire & Zola-Morgan, 1991). The model's global anatomy is shown in Figure 3b and its connectionist implementation in Figure 5.4. In the neural network, the medial temporal lobe system is represented by four artificial neurons. Similar modules of four neurons make up two "cortical areas". In each of these modules, only one neuron can remain activated. An assumption in this model is that connections to and from the medial temporal lobe system have a 50-fold-higher learning rate than the corticocortical connections. A similar assumption is made in the models by McClelland et al. (1995) and Murre (1996, 1997), both discussed below.

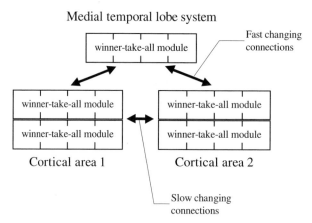

Figure 5.4 Connectionist model of retrograde amnesia according to Alvarez & Squire (1994)

Simulations with the model showed an initial steep forgetting curve due to fast decay of the "medial temporal lobe" connections. Connections within the "cortex" had a slower decay rate. Following learning of a pattern, the system received intermittent consolidation trials, during which one of the learned patterns was reactivated and relearned. As this process progressed, the patterns gained a stronger "cortical" base, while the "corticocortical" connections increased in strength. As a result, the forgetting curve also becomes less steep because in the later stages, memory is more dependent on the "corticocortical" connections and these have a slower decay. Recall was tested by presenting half of a pattern and assessing how well the other half was recalled.

When the "medial temporal lobe system" was lesioned immediately after training, performance was near chance because the system was still fully dependent on the "medial temporal lobe" connections. After sufficient consolidation, lesioning showed no effect on performance, because pattern recall had become fully independent of the "medial temporal lobe system". The simulations, thus, showed a clear "Ribot gradient", with a high loss of recent memories and little loss of remote memories.

McClelland et al.

Like many other models of long-term memory and amnesia, McClelland et al. (1995) suggest that during initial learning, a copy of the cortical representation is first stored in the hippocampus. This "summary sketch" must be sufficient to retrieve the whole of the neocortical trace. As discussed above, McClelland et al. (1995) stress the importance of the hippocampus in temporarily holding a memory representation so that it can be transferred to the neocortex in a process of interleaved learning. This means that learning of a new memory representation by the neocortex is interleaved with relearning of existing ones. Interleaved learning may counteract any "catastrophic interference" with existing representations, which they feel might occur when a new representation is stored directly to the neocortex.

Like Alvarez & Squire's model, McClelland et al. (1995) report simulations with curves before and after disabling the "hippocampus" and show that the "lesions" result in a Ribot effect: recent memories are harder to retrieve than older memories. The unlesioned model shows normal forgetting over time. They fitted their backpropagation-based simulations to experimental data by Squire and Zola-Morgan (1991), who obtained evidence for memory consolidation in monkeys over a period of about 10 weeks.

The "neocortex" of the model by McClelland et al. is a three-layer backpropagation network. The "hippocampus" is not implemented as a neural network, but patterns are simply stored until they are selected (randomly) for interleaved learning. At each time step, some patterns are lost from the hippocampal store. It depends on the amount of training a pattern has had (during interleaved learning), whether loss from the hippocampal store will mean that the pattern can be recalled from the backpropagation network alone.

Murre's TraceLink

A schematic drawing of the TraceLink model (Murre, 1994, 1996, 1997; Murre & Meeter, submitted) is shown in Figure 5.5. Its three main components are: (a) a trace system; (b) a link system; and (c) a modulatory system. The role of the trace system is analogous to that of the "neocortex" in the models discussed above, and the role of link system to that of the "medial temporal lobe" or "hippocampus". The neurons in TraceLink fire stochastically: they have a higher probability of firing (i.e. signalling a '1') when they receive a higher net input.

Each node in the trace system is connected to other trace nodes and to and from a random subset of the nodes in the link system. As in the model by Alvarez & Squire (1994), the learning rate in the trace system is lower than that of the link system. The link system's function is to interconnect trace nodes without direct "corticocortical" connections. In addition, link nodes are also interconnected within the link system (i.e. there are link–link connections).

The modulatory system includes certain basal forebrain nuclei, especially the nucleus basalis with its cholinergic inputs, to the hippocampus via the fornix (see also Hasselmo, 1995, 1999) and several areas that have a more indirect, controlling function. The role of the system is to trigger increased plasticity in the link system, so that it can rapidly record a new episodic representation. It may be activated directly through central states, such as arousal and attention, and through stimulus-specific factors, such as novelty and biological relevance (i.e. emotional stimuli involving danger, food, sex, shelter, etc.). During

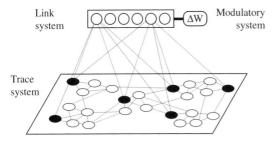

Figure 5.5 Overview of the TraceLink model of Murre (1994, 1996, 1997, Murre & Meeter, submitted). See text for an explanation

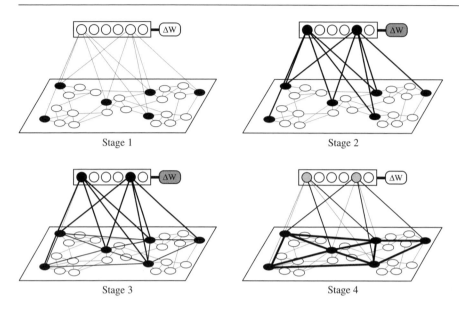

Figure 5.6 Normal episodic learning in Murre's TraceLink model. See text for an explanation

normal acquisition of a memory representation, it passes through roughly four stages (see Figure 5.6):

- *Stage 1*. Sensory, motor and other information, comprising the episode-to-be-remembered, activate a number of nodes in the trace system (filled circles).
- *Stage 2*. Via the trace system a set of link nodes is activated, possibly within less than a second. If the episode is sufficiently novel or interesting, the modulatory system will be activated. This will allow strengthening of connections between activated link nodes and trace nodes (shown by the thickening of the connections). In TraceLink, modification of connection strengths follows a Hebbian rule (Hebb, 1949; also see discussion above).
- *Stage 3*. This stage represents the initial consolidation process. Repeated activation takes place, leading to the gradual formation of trace–trace connections. These are initially weak, but grow in strength with each consolidation episode. The repeated reactivation of already learned representations is a random process that is initiated by randomly activating a number of nodes in the link system. Consolidation occurs by further strengthening of the trace–trace connections (trace–link connections are not strengthened further at this time; this follows the model of cholinergic processes in the hippocampus by Hasselmo, 1995, 1999)
- *Stage 4*. In the final stage of consolidation, trace–trace connections have become very strong and retrieval has become independent of the link system. In both the link and trace system, the learning of new memory representations will result in the gradual overwriting of older representations (i.e. forgetting). This interference process is more evident in the link system compared to the trace system, however, because the link system has a lower capacity and higher plasticity.

The four stages portray a process whereby memory representations are slowly being stored by the trace system, while there are gradually overwritten in the link system. This (apparent) movement from link system to trace system is the basis for explaining retrograde amnesia, which is analogous to that of the models by Alvarez & Squire and McClelland et al. By inactivating the link nodes (i.e. modelling a hippocampal lesion), all memory representations at stage 2 are lost. Stage 3 representations may be preserved, if they have received sufficient consolidation, and stage 4 representations will always be intact. Lesioning of the link system, therefore, results in a characteristic Ribot gradient. More details on the explanation of amnesia by the TraceLink model can be found in Murre & Meeter (submitted), in which 10 new simulations of different aspects of amnesia are presented.

Nadel & Moscovitch's Multiple Trace Theory of Memory Consolidation

Nadel & Moscovitch (1997; Moscovitch & Nadel, 1999) do not agree with the general approach followed by the three models discussed above. To a large extent, they propose the opposite view, arguing that the hippocampus remains crucial for the successful retrieval of a memory representation, even if it is 25–40 years old. Some of this evidence is based on the observation that many patients with bilateral hippocampal atrophy show memory deficits of this length.

The initial storage of an episode in the model by Nadel & Moscovitch's (1997) model is very similar to that of Alvarez & Squire (1994), McClelland et al. (1995), and Murre (1996, 1997). They summarize the general approach taken by the latter models under the heading of the "standard model", in which the hippocampus acts as an intermediate system that binds together disparate elements of a neocortical memory trace. Unlike this "standard model", however, repeated reactivation of memories in the multiple trace model creates recoded traces of the experience within the *hippocampal complex* and not in the neocortex. This form of consolidation is, thus, largely opposite to what happens in the models above, where additional traces are created (or connections strengthened) primarily in the *neocortex*.

As a consequence of this hippocampal consolidation, an older memory representation will have many more traces in the hippocampus (copies or replicas of the original representation), compared to a new memory representation, which will have only a few. An older memory is thus much less vulnerable to partial damage of the hippocampus, as there is always a high probability that some replicas of a memory representation will survive a lesion (it is assumed that any given replica suffices to retrieve an entire episode). The multiple trace theory, therefore, also predicts Ribot gradients, but only in cases of partial damage to the hippocampus. With full bilateral lesions, all traces are lost—even of the very old memories—and the model predicts a flat gradient.

In a recent paper, Nadel et al. (2000) report a connectionist version of their multiple trace model, which is somewhat similar to the TraceLink model above. The network is trained with interleaved trace replication periods between presentation of new patterns (cf. consolidation periods in the models above). A crucial difference is that trace replication takes place in the "hippocampus" only, whereas in TraceLink, for example, consolidation takes place in the trace system ("neocortex") only. The simulations by Nadel et al. (2000) show that partial lesions of the "hippocampus" give plausible Ribot curves, whereas a complete lesion leads to a flat gradient. In the latter case, both early and remote memories are lost due a continuing dependence on the "hippocampus" being intact. The paper by

Nadel et al. (2000) also includes an analytical implementation of the theory, which we shall not discuss here.

Long-term Memory Consolidation

Three of the computational models discussed above, namely those by Alvarez & Squire (1994), McClelland et al. (1995) and Murre (1996, 1997), assume that some type of consolidation process takes place. The nature of this process to date remains very much a mystery. A similar criticism may apply to the multiple trace theory by Nadel & Moscovitch (1997), who still need some type of trace replication process that may be similar to the consolidation processes assumed in the other three models. Many theorists have proposed that consolidation takes place during sleep, and recent evidence for this makes the case for it quite strong (Sejnowski & Destexhe, 2000).

In 1983, Crick & Mitchison (1983) and Hopfield et al. (1983) advanced a particularly interesting idea about the contribution of sleep to memory consolidation. They proposed that during REM sleep, memory representations are evoked randomly and *unlearned*. The reasoning was that randomly cued memories would tend to consist of bizarre and unwanted mixtures of intact memories. By unlearning these bizarre associations, the original memories would be "cleaned up". Despite its intuitive appeal and a promising initial simulation (Hopfield et al., 1983), further implementations have remained unsuccessful and little empirical evidence has been uncovered for this hypothesis (Blagrove, 1991).

It is interesting to note that the unlearning hypothesis is largely opposite to the approach taken by Alvarez & Squire (1994), McClelland et al. (1995), Murre (1996, 1997) and Murre & Meeter (submitted). So, it is fair to ask what the evidence is for the consolidation hypothesis, which assumes re-activation and additional cortical strengthening during sleep. Unfortunately, despite many decades of interest in the relationship between sleep and memory (Jenkins & Dallenback, 1924), the evidence for the sleep-consolidation hypothesis remains circumstantial and the critical experiment still has to be carried out.

A direct test of the hippocampal consolidation hypothesis in episodic memory could be based on deactivating the hippocampus in experimental animals during sleep only, so that consolidation would be prevented. Absence of consolidation could be tested by allowing different animals varying amounts of consolidation time, after which the hippocampus would be lesioned. Normally, this produces Ribot gradients (e.g. Kim & Fanselow, 1992), but in the blocked-consolidation case we would expect a flat gradient for the hippocampal group, since no "transfer" to the cortex would have taken place. To obtain a reliable Ribot gradient, it would be necessary to run the experiment for as long as 2–3 weeks, while the animals would be allowed to behave freely during the non-sleep periods. The length of time of the experiment, the need for repeated and rapid deactivation and reactivation of the hippocampus, the inaccessibility of this neuroanatomical structure, and the necessity to work with freely behaving animals make this a particularly difficult experiment, but in principle it could be done.

The strongest circumstantial evidence to date for the sleep-consolidation hypothesis in episodic memory comes from the studies by Wilson & McNaughton (1994), who showed that hippocampal representations of new episodes of spatial exploration in rats are reactivated during subsequent slow-wave sleep. In birds, it has recently been observed that neural activity patterns during sleep match those during sensorimotor activity recorded early during daytime singing (Dave & Margoliash, 2000). Other evidence for consolidation during sleep has recently been obtained by Stickgold et al. (2000), who showed that performance on a visual discrimination task gives maximal improvements 48–96 h after initial training, without intervening practice. An experimental group was deprived of one night of sleep following the practice trials, and they were then allowed two full nights of recovery sleep. Yet, they did not show significant improvement. This experiment in particular clearly illustrates that sleep may play a pivotal role in long-term consolidation. It also makes clear that hippocampus-to-cortex consolidation is not the only type of consolidation occurring in the brain. Many types of procedural learning occur at roughly the same rate in densely amnesic patients with full hippocampal lesions. It therefore seems reasonable to assume that this type of learning involves some kind of extrahippocampal consolidation process.

In addition to consolidation during sleep, there are also other ways in which cortical memories could be strengthened. One obvious manner is as a side effect of consciously and explicitly remembering of episodes (e.g. during retelling of experiences in conversation). Depending on the assumptions of the model, this might strengthen primarily the hippocampal base, the neocortical base, or both. Nadel & Moscovitch (1997) seem to be thinking of this type of remembering as the main cause of their trace replication process. Since the remembering always occurs in a different context, it is likely that a new hippocampal trace is added to the hippocampus that differs slightly from the earlier traces. Notice that this mechanism is not incompatible with the sleep-consolidation hypothesis, and models such as TraceLink could easily incorporate it as well.

An earlier and non-neuroanatomical version of the explicit-consolidation hypothesis has been called the "knitting hypothesis" (A.D. Baddeley, personal communication, 1993). Memory recall is nearly always based on the availability of certain cues. The "knitting hypothesis" postulates that as part of any mental context, a large number of possible retrieval cues are available. A subset of these will be effective in retrieving a given episode from memory. With time (and intervening events) the mental context or set of available cues changes gradually. If an episode is not rehearsed, this means that fewer cues will be available for retrieval. After more time has passed, very few cues may be available to retrieve an episode (see also Mensink & Raaijmakers, 1988). Such forgetting can be prevented by rehearsing an episode, whereby either new cues are added to the current mental context or the memory representation is attached to new context cues. By repeatedly rehearsing the episode it becomes "knitted" into the current context. The prominence of recent memories is thus explained by the overlap between the current context and the context at the time of learning, which is greater for recent memories than for older memories.

The "knitting hypothesis" can also explain Ribot gradients. Older memories that have not been forgotten will have been better rehearsed than more recent memories. They have become very strong in the sense that they have been "knitted" into many different contexts. Most of these contexts will be old and will not resemble the current context very much. It is therefore not necessary that these strong, old memories are also very easily retrieved. In case of trauma, the knitting hypothesis assumes that a random mental context is installed that replaces the current one. As a consequence, nearly all recent memories become irretrievable, while certain old memories may surface randomly. These old memories may reinstate a mixture of old contexts. Old, "well-knitted" memories have a much higher chance of overlap with an (old) random context because they have many more context cues. The trauma thus causes the disappearance of most recent memories and a much smaller fraction of old memories.

A possible variant of the explicit-consolidation hypothesis is the implicit-consolidation hypothesis. It has long been observed that presentation of certain words, such as "cup", may prime semantically related words, such as "tea" or "coffee". It is possible that similar priming occurs in autobiographical memory, so that, for example, seeing a news item on television about Paris primes the episodic memory of a short holiday spent there once. This holiday need not become conscious to enjoy a certain amount of strengthening because of this priming.

In summary, there are different candidate mechanisms for long-term consolidation. These mechanisms are not mutually exclusive and very little is known about their relative contribution to long-term memory. It seems worthwhile, therefore, to direct more research efforts to this topic.

Anterograde Amnesia

The models discussed so far concentrate on explaining retrograde amnesia, in particular the Ribot gradient. There are only a few computational models that target the neuropsychology of anterograde amnesia specifically. An example is the ELAN model by Phaf (1994). It models experimental data on implicit memory, which is preserved in anterograde amnesia. The ELAN model is built from CALM modules, a basic building block for neural networks that is able to categorize incoming stimuli and to learn new categories (Murre et al., 1992; Murre, 1992). A CALM module contains an "arousal system" that regulates the learning rate, based on the perceived novelty of the stimulus. The ELAN model is able to simulate free recall and stem completion experiments, including effects of word frequency. After lesioning the arousal system, free recall is strongly impaired but performance on the stem completion task is unaffected. This mimics the behaviour of patients with anterograde amnesia. The ELAN model does not address retrograde amnesia.

Gluck & Meyers (1993, 2001) present a well-tested computational model of anterograde amnesia. The model is based on a backpropagation network and focuses mainly on procedural learning tasks. They assume that the hippocampus controls a "compression mechanism" that is always operative, including during procedural learning. This mechanism constantly extracts the invariant aspects of the world around us, so that only a compact representation needs to be retained in the brain. Whereas procedural learning itself can still occur in the absence of the hippocampus, many aspects of the learning behaviour become abnormal, e.g. interaction with the experimental context, which may disappear in certain experiments.

Whereas all of the four models of retrograde amnesia discussed above can simulate the Ribot gradient and certain other data, they do not all aim to predict the details of anterograde amnesia. The model by Nadel & Moscovitch (1997) currently does not address anterograde amnesia. The models by Alvarez & Squire (1994) and McClelland et al. (1995) predict essentially a near-perfect correlation between anterograde and retrograde amnesia. The reason for this is that they assume that anterograde amnesia is caused by a failing or lesioned hippocampus (or medial temporal lobe system).

Although the data do not suffice to settle this issue at present, our reading of the literature is that the degree of hippocampal pathology predicts the severity of both retrograde and anterograde amnesia, which are, therefore, strongly intercorrelated. The degree of anterograde amnesia, however, is by no means a perfect predictor of retrograde amnesia. In populations of patients with Alzheimer's and Korsakoff's disease (Kopelman, 1989, 1991;

Schmidtke & Vollmer, 1997; Shimamura & Squire, 1986), correlations range from 0.30 to 0.60: in populations of patients with closed-head injuries, they tend to be higher (Russel & Nathan, 1946), but not in excess of 0.70. Cases of strong anterograde amnesia and nearly absent retrograde amnesia have been reported as well (e.g. Hodges & Carpenter, 1991). In addition to the clinical data, it has been observed that cholinergic blockade gives rise to severe anterograde amnesia with virtually no retrograde amnesia, (Kopelman, 1986). Following Meudell (1992) and Kopelman (1989), we conclude a partial independence of anterograde and retrograde amnesia, with retrograde amnesia being a better predictor of anterograde amnesia than the other way around.

The TraceLink model (Murre, 1996, 1997; Murre & Meeter, submitted) addresses these correlations by assuming the existence of a modulatory system. This system, involving among others certain basal forebrain nuclei, controls the storage of new episodes in the hippocampus. It can be selectively impaired so that the degree of anterograde amnesia is not a reliable indicator of the extent of retrograde amnesia.

MODELS OF MEMORY DISORDERS IN DEMENTIA

Alzheimer's Dementia

A few models have specially addressed the issue of the progressive development of memory disorders in Alzheimer's disease. One example is the model by Ruppin & Reggia (1995; see also Carrie, 1993), who model memory performance during progressive Alzheimer's disease, using a model of the cortex in which synapses are gradually lost. At the same time a mechanism of synaptic compensation (Bertoni-Freddari et al., 1990; DeKosky & Scheff, 1990) causes the remaining synapses to increase their strengths (effectiveness), thus counteracting general loss of input excitation. In contrast to an earlier model by Carrie (1993), which showed a flat Ribot gradient, the model by Ruppin & Reggia (1995) is able to produce Ribot gradients, because remote memories benefit more from the synaptic compensation process than recent memories. This work constitutes an important contribution in that it presents and investigates yet another possible factor that may underlie Ribot gradients: synaptic compensation. The model by Ruppin & Reggia (1995) is not able to explain Ribot gradients extending before the onset of the disease.

Semantic Dementia

Semantic dementia is a recently documented syndrome that appears as almost a mirror image of amnesia, showing a progressive loss of verbal and non-verbal semantic memory (i.e. knowledge about the meanings of words, objects, facts and concepts), but with preserved episodic memory (i.e. no anterograde amnesia). It is associated with non-Alzheimer degenerative pathology of the inferolateral temporal neocortex, with relative sparing (at least in the early stages) of the hippocampal complex.

Murre et al. (2001) review the literature on semantic dementia and argue that it may have important implications for models of long-term memory. They also discuss how various computational models of amnesia can be applied to semantic dementia. No simulations have been published to date, although Murre (1996, 1997) derives predictions about semantic dementia from the TraceLink model, such as the "inverse Ribot gradient"—a loss of distant memories with relative preservation of more recently experienced memories. This prediction was based on the idea that the neocortical basis is severely deteriorated in semantic dementia but the link system is still intact. This would allow memories to enter stages 1 and 2 but would prevent them passing to stages 3 and 4 (see Figure 5.6). The lack of consolidation would cause them to be overwritten relatively rapidly in the high-decay link system.

The predicted effect was subsequently observed by Graham & Hodges (1997; see also Snowden et al., 1996). In the patients studied by Graham & Hodges (1997), recent memories could be retrieved up to about 3 years, after which they were rapidly lost. It seems that these data are problematic for Nadel & Moscovitch's (1997) multiple trace theory (Graham, 1999). If the hippocampus is preserved, which appears to be the case with semantic dementia, all memories should be easily retrieved. In other words, there should be no memory problem whatsoever in semantic dementia. This is clearly is not the case. Moscovitch & Nadel (1999), however, argue that all memories are depressed to some extent because of the continuing loss of semantic building blocks. According to their view, the inverse Ribot gradient found by Graham & Hodges (1997) is nothing more than a severely depressed "normal" forgetting gradient, and this is caused by a progressive degeneration of neocortical retrieval cues. The fact that remote memories are more severely affected is explained by arguing that memories that spared in semantic dementia are more perceptual in nature.

CONCLUSION

Models are playing an increasingly important role in the field of memory disorders. This is particularly evident from the vivid debates in the recent literature, where models are primarily used to prove that proposed mechanisms indeed work as claimed (e.g. Nadel et al., 2000). It is also clear, however, that the current generation of connectionist models has not yet left the initial stage of modelling.

One impediment that we can foresee in the further development of models is the lack of high-quality quantitative data, a problem that is prominent in the entire field of neuropsychology. In the years to come it is therefore likely that modellers will have to limit themselves to qualitative models. In most tests of retrograde amnesia, for example, questions for remote time periods are made easier than for recent time periods. This makes it very difficult to fit forgetting curves to these data. There are additional reasons why these data are not very suitable for quantitative modelling, e.g. a large number of the standard tests have only three or four time periods and these periods are often not sharply defined (e.g. "early adulthood"). Furthermore, the published data are typically based on very small numbers of five to ten patients.

Whereas the lack of high-quality data poses a limit on one form of modelling, it is likely that our rapidly increasing knowledge of the neurobiology of memory will allow models of amnesia and other disorders to become more neurobiologically informed (Sejnowski & Destexhe, 2000). Connectionist modelling is an excellent method of integrating the various sources of knowledge from neurobiology and neuropsychology and—like maps—may eventually be useful for both the theorist and the practitioner.

REFERENCES

Alvarez, R. & Squire, L.R. (1994). Memory consolidation and the medial temporal lobe: a simple network model. *Proceedings of the National Academy of Sciences of the USA*, **91**, 7041–7045.

Bertoni-Freddari, C., Fattoretti, P., Casoli T. et al. (1990). Morphological adaptive response of the synaptic junctional zones in the human dentate gyrus during aging and Alzheimer's disease. *Brain Research*, **517**, 69–75.

Blagrove, M. (1991). A critical review of neural net theories of dream sleep. *Journal of Intelligent Systems*, **1**, 227–257.

Bliss, T.V.P. & Lomo, T. (1973). Long-lasting potentiation of synaptic transmission in the dentate area of the anaesthetized rabbit following stimulation of the perforant path. *Journal of Physiology (London)*, **232**, 331–356.

Carrie, J.R. (1993). Evaluation of a neural network model of amnesia in diffuse cerebral atrophy. *British Journal of Psychiatry*, **163**, 217–222.

Crick, F. & Mitchison, G. (1983). The function of dream sleep. *Nature*, **304**, 111–114.

Dave, S.A. & D. Margoliash (2000). Song replay during sleep and computational rules for sensorimotor vocal learning. *Science*, **290**, 812–816.

DeKosky, S.T. & Scheff, S.W. (1990). Synapse loss in frontal cortex biopsies in Alzheimer's disease: correlation with cognitive severity. *Annals of Neurology*, **27**, 457–464.

Elman, O. (1990). Finding structure in time. *Cognitive Science*, **14**, 179–211.

Felleman, D.J. & Van Essen, D.C. (1991). Distributed hierarchical processing in the primate cerebral cortex. *Cerebral Cortex*, **1**, 1–47.

French, R.M. (1992). Semi-distributed representations and catastrophic forgetting in connectionist networks. *Connection Science*, **4**, 365–377.

French, R.M. (1999). Catastrophic forgetting in connectionist networks. *Trends in Cognitive Sciences*, **3**, 128–135.

Gluck, M.A. & Meyers, C.E. (2001). *Gateway to Memory: An Introduction to Neural Network Modeling of the Hippocampus and Learning*. Cambridge, MA: MIT Press.

Gluck, M.A. & Meyers, C.E. (1993). Hippocampal mediation of stimulus representation: a computational theory. *Hippocampus*, **3**, 491–516.

Graham, K.S. & Hodges, J.R. (1997). Differentiating the roles of the hippocampal complex and the neocortex in long-term memory storage: evidence from the study of semantic dementia and Alzheimer's disease. *Neuropsychology*, **11**, 77–89.

Graham, K.S. (1999). Semantic dementia: a challenge to the Multiple Trace Theory of memory consolidation? *Trends in Cognitive Sciences*, **3**, 85–87.

Graham, K.S., Murre, J.M.J. & Hodges, J.R. (1999). Episodic memory in semantic dementia: a computational approach based on the Trace Link model. In J. Reggia, e. Ruppin & D. Glanzman (eds), *Neutal Modelling in Brain Disorders*. Progress in Brain Research, Vol. 121. Amsterdam: Elsevier.

Grossberg, S. (1976). Adaptive pattern classification and universal recoding, II: Feedback, expectation, olfaction, and illusions. *Biological Cybernetics*, **23**, 187–202.

Happel, B.L.M., & Murre, J.M.J. (1994). The design and evolution of modular neural network architectures. *Neural Networks*, **7**, 985–1004.

Hasselmo, M.E. (1995). Neuromodulation and cortical function: modeling the physiological basis of behavior. *Behavioral Brain Research*, **67**, 1–27.

Hasselmo, M.E. (1999). Neuromodulation and the hippocampus: memory function and dysfunction in a network simulation. In J.A. Reggia, E. Ruppin and D. Glanzman (eds), *Disorders of Brain, Behavior and Cognition: The Neurocomputational Perspective* (pp. 3–18). Amsterdam: Elsevier.

Hebb, D.O. (1949). *The Organization of Behavior*. New York: Wiley.

Hodges, J.R. & Carpenter, K. (1991). Anterograde amnesia with fornix damage following removal of IIIrd ventricle colloid cyst. *Journal of Neurology, Neurosurgery, and Psychiatry*, **54**, 633–638.

Hopfield, J.J., Feinstein, D.I. & Palmer, R.G. (1983). "Unlearning" has a stabilizing effect in collective memories. *Nature*, **304**, 158–159.

Hopfield, J.J. (1982). Neural networks and physical systems with emergent collective computational abilities. *Proceedings of the National Academy of Sciences of the USA*, **79**, 2554–2558.

Jenkins, J.G. & Dallenbach, K.M. (1924). Obliviscence during sleep and waking. *American Journal of Psychology*, **35**, 605–612.

Kim, J.J. & Fanselow, M.S. (1992). Modality-specific retrograde amnesia for fear. *Science*, **256**, 675–677.

Kopelman, M.D. (1986). The cholinergic neurotransmitter system in human memory and dementia: a review. *Quarterly Journal of Experimental Psychology*, **38A**, 535–573.

Kopelman, M.D. (1989). Remote and autobiographical memory, temporal context memory, and frontal atrophy in Korsakoff and Alzheimer patients. *Neuropsychologia*, **27**, 437–460.

Kopelman, M.D. (1991). Frontal dysfunction and memory deficits in the alcoholic Korsakoff syndrome and Alzheimer-type dementia. *Brain*, **114**, 117–137.

McClelland, J.L. & Rumelhart, D.E. (eds)(1986). *Parallel Distributed Processing. Explorations in the Microstructure of Cognition, Vol. 2: Psychological and Biological Models*. Cambridge, MA: MIT Press.

McClelland, J.L., McNaughton, B.L. & O'Reilly, R.C. (1995). Why there are complementary learning systems in the hippocampus and neocortex: insights from the successes and failures of connectionist models of learning and memory. *Psychological Review*, **102**, 419–457.

McCloskey, M. & Cohen, N.J. (1989). Catastrophic interference in connectionist networks: the sequential learning problem. In G.H. Bower (ed.), *The Psychology of Learning and Motivation* (pp. 109–164). New York: Academic Press.

Mensink, G.J. & Raaijmakers, J.G.W. (1988). A model for interference and forgetting. *Psychological Review*, **95**, 434–455.

Meudell, P.R. (1992). Irrelevant, incidental and core features in the retrograde amneisa associated with Korsakoff's psychosis: a review. *Behavioural Neurology*, **5**, 67–74.

Milner, P.M. (1957). The cell assembly: Mark II. *Psychological Review*, 64, 242–252.

Milner, P.M. (1989). A cell assembly theory of hippocampal amnesia. *Neuropsychologia*, **6**, 215–234.

Minsky, M.L. & Papert, S.A. (1969). *Perceptrons*. Cambridge, MA: MIT Press.

Mishkin, M. (1982). A memory system in the monkey. *Philosophical Transactions of the Royal Society B*, **298**, 85–95.

Moscovitch, M. & Nadel, L. (1999). Multiple-trace theory and semantic dementia: response to K.S. Graham (1999). *Trends in Cognitive Sciences*, **3**, 87–89.

Murre, J.M.J. (1992). *Categorization and Learning in Modular Neural Networks*. Hemel Hempstead: Harvester Wheatsheaf; and Hillsdale, NJ: Erlbaum.

Murre, J.M.J. (1994). A model for categorization and recognition in amnesic patients. In M. Gazzaniga (ed.), *Proceedings of the Cognitive Neuroscience Meeting 1994* (p. 38), San Francisco, CA.

Murre, J.M.J. (1995). Transfer of learning in back-propagation and in related neural network models. In J.P. Levy, D. Bairaktaris, J.A. Bullinaria & P. Cairns (eds), *Connectionist Models of Memory and Language* (pp. 73–94). London: UCL Press.

Murre, J.M.J. (1996). TraceLink: a model of amnesia and consolidation of memory. *Hippocampus*, **6**, 675–684.

Murre, J.M.J. (1997). Implicit and explicit memory in amnesia: some explanations and predictions by the TraceLink Model. *Memory*, **5**, 213–232.

Murre, J.M.J., Graham, K.S. & Hodges, J.R. (2001). Semantic dementia: relevance to connectionist models of long-term memory. *Brain*, **124**, 647–675.

Murre, J.M.J. & Meeter, M. (submitted). *TraceLink: A Connectionist Model of Consolidation and Amnesia*.

Murre, J.M.J., Phaf, R.H. & Wolters, G. (1992). CALM: categorizing and learning module. *Neural Networks*, **5**, 55–82.

Murre, J.M.J. & Raffone, A. (submitted). *Long-range Synaptic Self-organization in Cortical Networks*.

Murre, J.M.J. & Sturdy, D.P.F. (1995). The mesostructure of the brain: analyses of quantitative neuroanatomy. *Biological Cybernetics*, **73**, 529–545.

Nadel L. & Moscovitch, M. (1997). Memory consolidation, retrograde amnesia and the hippocampal complex. *Current Opinion in Neurobiology*, **7**, 217–227.

Nadel, L., Samsonovich, A., Ryan, L. & Moscovitch, M. (2000). Multiple trace theory of human memory: computational, neuroimaging, and neuropsychological results. *Hippocampus*, **10**, 352–368.

O'Keefe, J. & Nadel, L. (1978). *The Hippocampus as a Cognitive Map*. Oxford: Clarendon.

Osgood, C.E. (1949). The similarity paradox in human learning: a resolution. *Psychological Review*, **56**, 132–143.

Page, M. (2000). Connectionist modelling in psychology: a localist manifesto. *Behavioral and Brain Sciences*, **23**, 443–512.

Phaf, R.H. (1994). *Learning in Natural and Connectionist Systems: Experiments and a Model*. Dordrecht: Kluwer Academic.

Rolls, E.T. (1990). Functions of neuronal networks in the hippocampus and of backprojections in the cerebral cortex in memory. In J.L. McGaugh, N.M. Weinberger & G. Lynch (eds), *Brain Organization and Memory: Cells, Systems, and Circuits*. Oxford: Oxford University Press, 184–210.

Rosenblatt, F. (1958). The perceptron: a probabilistic model for information storage and organization in the brain. *Psychological Review*, **65**, 386–408.

Rosenblatt, F. (1962). *Principles of Neurodynamics*. Washington, DC: Spartan.

Rumelhart, D.E., Hinton, G.E. & Williams, R.J. (1986). Learning internal representations by error propagation. In D.E. Rumelhart, & J.L. McClelland (eds), *Parallel Distributed Processing. Explorations in the Microstructure of Cognition, Vol. 1: Foundations*. Cambridge, MA: MIT Press.

Rumelhart, D.E. & McClelland, J.L. (eds)(1986). *Parallel Distributed Processing. Explorations in the Microstructure of Cognition. Vol. 1: Foundations*. Cambridge, MA: MIT Press.

Rumelhart, D.E. & Zipser, D. (1985). Feature discovery by competitive learning. *Cognitive Science*, **9**, 75–112.

Ruppin, D. & Reggia, J.A. (1995). A neural model of memory impairment in diffuse cerebral atrophy. *British Journal of Psychiatry*, **166**, 19–28.

Russel, W.R. & Nathan, P.W. (1946). Traumatic amnesia. *Brain*, 69, 280–300.

Schmidtke, K. & Vollmer, H. (1997). Retrograde amnesia: a study of its relation to anterograde amnesia and semantic memory deficits. *Neuropsychologia*, **35**, 505–518.

Sejnowski, T.J. & Destexhe, A. (2000). Why do we sleep? *Brain Research* (in press).

Sejnowski, T.J. & C.R. Rosenberg (1987). Parallel networks that learn to pronounce English text. *Complex Systems*, **1**, 145–168.

Sharkey, N., Sharkey, A. & Jackson, S. (2000). Are SRNs sufficient for modelling language acquisition? In P. Broeder & J.M.J. Murre (eds), *Models of Language Acquisition: Inductive and Deductive Approaches* (pp. 33–54). Oxford: Oxford University Press.

Shimamura, A.P. & Squire, L.R. (1986). Korsakoff's syndrome: a study of the relation between anterograde amnesia and remote memory impairment. *Behavioral Neuroscience*, **100**, 165–170.

Snowden, J.S., Griffiths, H.L. & Neary, D. (1996). Semantic–episodic memory interactions in semantic dementia: implications for retrograde memory function. *Cognitive Neuropsychology*, **13**, 1101–1137.

Squire, L.R. (1992). Memory and the hippocampus: a synthesis from findings with rats, monkeys, and humans. *Psychological Review*, **99**, 195–231.

Squire, L.R. & Alvarez, P. (1995). Retrograde amnesia and memory consolidation: a neurobiological perspective. *Current Opinion in Neurobiology*, **5**, 169–175.

Squire, L.R., Cohen, N.J. & Nadel, L. (1984). The medial temporal region and memory consolidation: a new hypothesis. In H. Weingarter & E. Parker (eds), *Memory Consolidation* (pp. 185–210). Hillsdale, NJ: Erlbaum.

Squire, L.R. & Zola-Morgan, S. (1991). The medial temporal lobe memory system. *Science*, **253**, 1380–1386.

Steinbuch, K. (1961). Die Lernmatrix. *Kybernetik*, **1**, 36–45.

Stickgold, R., James, L. & Hobson, J.A. (2000). Visual discrimination learning requires sleep after training. *Nature Neuroscience*, **3**, 1237–1238.

Teyler, T.J. & DiScenna, P. (1986). The hippocampal memory indexing theory. *Behavioral Neuroscience*, **100**, 147–154.

Treves, A. & Rolls, E.T. (1994). Computational analysis of the role of the hippocampus in memory. *Hippocampus*, **4**, 374–391.

Wickelgren, W.A. (1979). Chunking and consolidation: a theoretical synthesis of semantic networks, configuring in conditioning, S-R versus cognitive learning, normal forgetting, the amnesic syndrome, and the hippocampal arousal system. *Psychological Review*, **86**, 44–60.

Wickelgren, W.A. (1987). Site fragility theory of chunking and consolidation in a distributed asso-
    ciative memory. In N.W. Milgram, C.M. MacLeod & T.C. Petit (eds), *Neuroplasticity, Learning,
    and Memory* (pp. 301–325). New York: Alan R. Liss.
Widrow, B. & Hoff, M.E. (1960). Adaptive switching circuits. *1960 IRE WESCON Convention Record,*
    Part 4, 96–104.
Willshaw, D.J., Buneman, O.P. & Longuet-Higgins, H.C. (1969). Non-holographic associative mem-
    ory. *Nature*, **222**, 960–962.
Wilson, M.A. & MeNaughton, B.L. (1994). Reachvation of hippocampal enseuable memories during
    sleep. *Science*, **265**, 676–679.

CHAPTER 6

Psychopharmacology of Human Memory

H. Valerie Curran

Clinical Health Psychology, University College London, UK

and

Herbert Weingartner

National Institutes of Health, Bethesda, MD, USA

Psychopharmacology—the study of the psychological effects of substances which act on the brain—became a discipline about 50 years ago. However, interest in the effects of psychoactive drugs on memory can be traced further back. For example, in 1909 the *Psychological Review* published a study by E.E. Jones of "introspections obtained on three occasions when chloroform was administered to the author", who notes the "complete disappearance of memory accompanied his fading consciousness". From this era of introspection, sporadic drug studies of memory dedicatedly followed the psychological fashions of the day. Thus in the 1930s, J.R. Jones (1933) found no effect of aspirin on the rate of learning nonsense syllables and Cattell (1930) reported that 10 g alcohol improved intelligence but impaired associative memory. Later, in the 1950s, a series of studies by Hannah Steinberg and colleagues documented how nitrous oxide induced temporary amnesia via "retarding the formation of associations" (Steinberg & Summerfield, 1957). Later, drug effects were studied within the framework of models of information processing (e.g. Berry et al., 1965) and, with the emergence of the cognitive era in the 1970s, studies by Ghoneim, Mewaldt and colleagues showed how the effects of drugs supported the distinction between short- and long-term memory (e.g. Ghoneim & Mewaldt, 1975). In the decades since then, psychopharmacological studies have been conducted within various theoretical constructs of memory processes, functions or systems. Although much early work was simply descriptive, much current research on how drugs impact of memory are model-driven. This research has also capitalized on the surge of developments in cognitive neuroscience beyond those concerned with memory *per se*.

A range of drugs affects memory, often impairing some aspects of memory whilst sparing other aspects. So, like people with brain damage, people given a centrally acting drug may display normal performance on some memory tasks and yet severe impairments on others. Drugs can therefore allow dissociations to be drawn between different aspects of memory

The Handbook of Memory Disorders. Edited by A.D. Baddeley, M.D. Kopelman and B.A. Wilson
© 2002 John Wiley & Sons, Ltd.

and, in this way, compliment research with brain-damaged people or research showing developmental or functional dissociations (cf. Nyberg & Tulving, 1996). Clearly, memory does not happen in a vacuum and much psychopharmacological research also examines other cognitive functions that may be spared or impaired by drugs, particularly those functions which influence memory.

Psychoactive drugs also provide tools for exploring the neurochemical bases of memory and memory disorders. Drugs known to affect the release of a particular neurotransmitter can be used to explore what functional role(s) that neurotransmitter plays in memory. Although linking the behavioural changes induced by a drug with neurobiological mechanisms is often problematic, ultimately such studies may elucidate the neurochemical correlates of memory and may help in the development of drug treatments for cognitive disorders.

Much current clinical research on drugs and memory is focused on drugs for the treatment of cognitive disorders. However, it is important to remember that drugs can sometimes be *causes* of cognitive disorders. For example, it has been estimated that about 10% of older patients attending memory clinics display cognitive impairments that are drug-induced rather than organic (e.g. Starr & Whalley, 1994; Gray et al., 1999). These patients may have memory problems and/or confusional states similar to those seen in organic dementia. This drug-related "pseudo-dementia" is particularly a problem for people who take several different medications. Physical changes with age mean that older people metabolize drugs less efficiently than younger people and so drugs have more marked and prolonged effects in the elderly. However, unlike organic states, these problems generally respond favourably to drug reduction regimes. Prescribed drugs most often associated with memory impairment include the benzodiazepine sleeping pills and tranquillizers (e.g. triazolam, alprazolam) and drugs with anticholinergic properties (e.g. tricylic antidepressants, several types of neuroleptics). Drug-related memory impairments may also be associated with drugs used non-medically, such as alcohol and a wide range of illicit substances. An awareness of the potential cognitive effects of a patient's medication is useful when carrying out neuropsychological assessments, e.g. a person with organic brain damage who feels anxious before an assessment may calm his/her nerves by taking a benzodiazepine and adversely affect his/her subsequent performance. Such problems can be reduced by timing assessments outside the peak effects of the particular drug taken.

In this chapter, we begin by briefly outlining some key issues in studying and interpreting drug effects before discussing the drugs most intensively studied in terms of memory—anticholinergic drugs and the benzodiazepines. Subsequent sections provide briefer overviews of drugs acting on glutamate and those acting on monamine systems. We then address the issue of how specific are the effects of drugs on memory. The final section highlights some issues for the development of drugs that aim to alleviate cognitive dysfunction, especially the so-called "antidementia" drugs. As we shall see, issues of specificity apply as much to putative memory-enhancing drugs as to memory-inhibiting drugs. Although different subsections focus on different drugs and their major neurotransmitter action, it should be emphasized that neurobiological systems interact in complex ways, so that alterations in release of one neurotransmitter will also affect the release of others. In describing the effects of drugs, we use the language of Tulving's memory systems (Tulving, 1985; Tulving & Schacter, 1990), which encompasses many current findings of differential drug effects.

RESEARCHING DRUG-INDUCED AMNESIA

Studies of drug-induced amnesia have certain methodological advantages over studies of amnesia in brain-damaged patients. Drugs can be used to induce a temporary, reversible amnesia. The degree of amnesia can be manipulated by using different doses, and placebo conditions mean that each participant can act as his/her own control. Drugs can be given at different points in remembering, e.g. during encoding or at retrieval. Further, in studies of brain damage, the effects of lesions in different brain areas necessarily involve comparisons between different patients; in psychopharmacological studies, the effects of several different drugs can be examined in the same person. In many cases, there are drugs with varying agonist and antagonist properties, so the researcher has a chemical toolkit for probing cognitive functions. Characteristics of the volunteers, such as age, psychopathology or organic state, can also be varied.

At the same as having these advantages, psychopharmacological studies have some unique problems. Central among these is the issue of *specificity* at both the neurobiological and psychological level. At the neurobiological level, it is sometimes found that drugs with different pharmacological actions produce remarkably similar effects on human memory. This makes it hard to link specific drug actions with specific memory effects. There are at least 50 different neurotransmitters in the brain and these act and interact to provide complex chemical communication codes for the brain's 100 billion or so neurons. Our knowledge and the content of this chapter is restricted to just a few of these neurotransmitters and, even for those, it is glaringly incomplete. The drugs currently available have diffuse effects on the central nervous system and changes in one neurotransmitter system will have effects on others. Defining the mechanisms of drug-induced changes in memory at a neurobiological level thus remains an enormous challenge.

In terms of psychological specificity, no drug currently exists that *only* affects memory. Many drugs affect arousal and many alter aspects of attentional and executive functions. Performance changes on a memory task following a drug may reflect alterations in memory, arousal or attentional processes or a combination of effects. It is important, therefore, to delineate specific memory effects of a drug as distinct from indirect effects due to changes in non-memory functions.

Anticholinergic Drugs and Benzodiazepines

Interest in the cholinergic system originally stemmed from observations of reduced cholinergic markers in post-mortem brains of people who had had Alzheimer's disease (AD), and by demonstrations that this reduction correlated with the degree of cognitive impairment and with cortical pathology (Perry et al., 1978). Around the same time, Drachman & Leavitt (1974) had shown that a drug that antagonizes or "blocks" the action of acetylcholine could induce profound memory impairments in healthy young people. Together, this work led to the cholinergic hypothesis of AD (Bartus et al., 1982) and proposals that cholinergic blocking drugs could be pharmacological "models" of AD (Weingartner, 1985). Although several neurotransmitters are affected in AD (Curran & Kopelman, 1996), cholinergic depletion remains the most clearly documented neurochemical loss, and all drug treatments currently available for AD (e.g. tacrine, donepezil) are designed to ameliorate or moderate this cholinergic deficit. Scopolamine (SP; also known as hyoscine) is the most widely researched cholinergic antagonist. Its effects can be attenuated or reversed by giving a cholinergic agonist like physostigmine or arecholine. Scopolamine selectively blocks muscarinic cholinergic receptors and, at high doses, also blocks nicotinic cholinergic receptors.

Interest in the effects of benzodiazepines (BDZs) on memory initially stemmed from clinical considerations in anesthesiology (cf. Ghoneim & Mewaldt, 1990). Anaesthetists value drugs that ensure a sufficient period and depth of anterograde amnesia, so that even if a patient regained consciousness during an operation, he/she would not remember doing so. In this respect, BDZs proved to be ideal drugs. BDZs such as diazepam (trade name Valium), alprazolam (Xanax), lorazepam (Ativan) and 30 or more similar compounds all act via specific benzodiazepine receptors to facilitate the transmission of GABA (γ-aminobutyric acid), the major inhibitory neurotransmitter in the brain. BDZs act as agonists at the $GABA_A$–BDZ receptor (the single term BDZ used here refers to these full agonists). The BDZ receptor can be blocked by a BDZ antagonist, such as flumazenil. Compounds also exist which have *opposite* effects to BDZs at the same receptor, e.g. β-carbolines act as inverse agonists to *inhibit* the transmission of GABA. Several other compounds act as partial agonists, binding to the receptor but producing less effect than full agonists. BDZ receptors are found throughout the brain, but highest concentrations are in areas of known importance for memory functions: the cerebral cortex, limbic system and cerebellar cortex.

Despite their differing pharmacological actions, SP and BDZs produce remarkably similar effects on memory. Performance on brief "span" tasks (e.g. digit span, block span) is unaffected but performance on more complex tasks, where information is manipulated whilst it is retained, can be impaired (Rusted & Warburton, 1988). On the whole, the evidence points to a reduction in speed with which information is processed, rather than qualitative effects on working memory. For example, response times are usually much more affected than error rates (Rusted, 1994).

The most marked and robust effects of benzodiazepines and scopolamine are on tasks that tap episodic memory (Kopelman & Corn, 1988; Ghoneim & Mewaldt, 1990; Curran, 1991, 2000a). These impairments are consistently dose-related. Information presented *after* the drug is administered is poorly remembered. No study has found retrograde impairments of memory—information studied *before* the drug is administered is retrieved intact. BDZs and SP therefore impede the acquisition of new information. Once learning has been accomplished, the rate of forgetting is normal (Brown et al., 1983; Kopelman & Corn, 1988) and there is no increased susceptibility to interference when initial acquisition levels on drug and placebo are matched (Gorissen et al., 1998). Studies of metamemory with volunteers administered a BDZ suggest that people are not aware of having memory deficits (Bacon et al., 1998).

The degree and duration of anterograde amnesia depends on several factors besides the particular drug and its dose. Each drug has its own time curve of absorption and elimination, over which effects on memory will vary. For example, following one oral dose of the BDZ lorazepam, peak memory impairments occur from 1.5 to 5 h, after which effects slowly subside. If the same drug is administered intravenously it will have a more rapid onset of effect, and so the route of administration is important. The time after drug administration at which information is presented and retrieval is required is also critical, e.g. immediate recall is less impaired than recall tested several minutes or more after study, a similar pattern to that seen in amnesic people (Baddeley, 2000).

The degree of amnesia observed also depends on the characteristics of the people tested. As would be predicted from the hypothesis that both normal and abnormal aging is associated with cholinergic depletion, older healthy adults and Alzheimer patients show SP-induced memory impairments at lower doses of the drug than those needed to induce impairments in younger people (Sunderland et al., 1986; Molchan et al., 1992). Further, the effects of a single dose differ in those who have taken the drug before, compared with those who are drug-naïve. The brain adapts to repeated administration of a drug, so that, for example, 1 mg alprazolam will produce marked anterograde amnesia in someone who has never taken it before, but less impairment in a patient who takes the drug daily for an anxiety disorder.

There is general agreement that these drugs impair acquisition (encoding/consolidation) of new information and not retrieval. Retrieval of material learned before a drug is ingested is not impaired and, interestingly, can be improved when retrieval takes place on drug. One explanation of this retrograde facilitation could be that poor memory for material studied post-drug reduces interference on retrieval of material studied pre-drug. However, studies have shown that retrograde facilitation following ingestion of the benzodiazepine triazolam can occur without any suppression of post-drug learning (Weingartner et al., 1995a). Another possible explanation relates to inhibitory processes. In a non-drug state, the retrieval of stipulated information can inhibit the retrieval of similar information (e.g. Anderson et al., 2000). This effect is seen in placebo subjects asked to recall a word list studied post-drug and then one studied before drug. However, subjects given benzodiazepines do not show this pattern, and so it is conceivable that the drug may facilitate performance by disinhibiting retrieval processes. This disinhibition may mean increased reliance on automatic rather than controlled processing, as suggested by Fillmore et al. (1999), who showed, using the process dissociation procedure, that alcohol given *after* study increased reliance on automatic rather than controlled processing in memory. BDZs, which share a GABAergic action with alcohol, may have a similar effect. Retrograde facilitation is the opposite of notions of "state-dependent retrieval", where performance is meant to be facilitated when encoding and retrieval taking place in the same drug state. State-dependent effects are quantitatively small and, as argued elsewhere (Curran, 2000a), do not explain the marked effects of drugs like BDZs or SP on acquisition.

What is the mechanism underpinning the anterograde amnesic effects of these drugs? One suggestion is that drugs impair the encoding of contextual information (Brown & Brown, 1990; Curran et al., 1993). The recall of word lists following a BDZ often shows increased intrusion errors that are semantic or phonemic associates of studied words, without subjects being aware of such errors (e.g. Bacon et al., 1998). Such errors have been widely assessed in the context of the false recognition paradigm (Roediger & McDermott, 1995). In this paradigm, subjects study several series of semantically related word lists (e.g. candy, bitter, sugar . . .) and are then given a recognition task in which a non-presented associate of studied words (e.g. sweet) is presented alongside other lures. Using this paradigm, Minzer & Griffiths (2000, 2001) showed that SP and the BDZ triazolam decreased false as well as true recognition rates relative to placebo. This is similar to the pattern seen when comparing amnesic people with controls (e.g. Schacter et al., 1998). However, a low dose of alcohol induced a pattern more similar to that seen in older adults, whereby false recognition rates were slightly increased (Milani & Curran, 2000).

False recognition is one example of what Schacter (1999) terms "misattribution" errors. Another example of misattribution is seen when people may remember a studied item but not where or when they had studied it. These types of source errors are also increased by BDZs and SP, e.g. Weingartner et al. (1998) found that the BDZ triazolam (0.375 mg) impaired healthy participants' ability to differentiate between memories for category exemplars which they had generated themselves at study, as opposed to those generated by the experimenter. Using a similar task, Mintzer & Griffiths (1999) assessed the effects of three doses each of the BDZ triazolam (0.125, 0.25, 0.5 mg) and a related GABA-ergic sleeping pill, zolpidem (5, 10, 20 mg) on memory for target words and for their source. Both drugs produced dose-related impairments in memory for target words; however, only the highest doses of each impaired memory for source. This suggests that impaired memory for contextual information does not account for the episodic memory impairments induced by lower doses of BDZs and related drugs.

A criticism of many pharmacological studies is their "diagnostic" assumptions about cognitive tasks. Often studies have used verbal learning tasks to "assess" episodic memory, implicitly assuming a one-to-one relationship between a task and the episodic memory system. Clearly, many verbal learning tasks are only minimally episodic in nature and performance will depend on other memory systems, including working memory and se-mantic memory. In Tulving's theory, the essence of episodic memory is to enable "mental time travel"—the capacity to remember in the sense of re-experiencing events in subjective time (Wheeler et al., 1997). One way of evaluating episodic memory is therefore to tap into people's subjective awareness which accompanies retrieval of a memory. Experiential approaches using the remember–know paradigm (Tulving, 1985) are based on a distinc-tion between "remembering," in the sense of re-experiencing as a participant in an event and "knowing," in the sense of a personally detached observer of an event. "Remember" responses are reduced by BDZs and by alcohol, but "know" responses are not decreased (Curran et al., 1993; Bishop & Curran, 1995; Curran & Hilderbrandt, 1999). These find-ings, along with those of Mintzer & Griffiths (2000) using the remember–know procedure, suggest that BDZs and SP impair people's ability to mentally re-experience in subjective time (episodic memory) but leave semantic memory (reflected by "knowing") intact.

Semantic memory has received relatively limited attention from psychopharmacology. Although some studies have assessed retrieval efficiency, acquisition of new semantic knowledge has been largely ignored. On the whole, these drugs do not appear to impede people's ability to *retrieve* items of general knowledge or other well-established memories, e.g. the performance of healthy young subjects is generally intact on tasks like verbal fluency (e.g. Curran et al., 1991; Knopman, 1991). Very high doses and/or intravenous administra-tion of SP can produce performance deficits on verbal fluency, but these doses also induce significant sedation (Drachman & Leavitt, 1974). Molchan et al. (1992) and Sunderland et al. (1986, 1997) showed that fluency impairments in older volunteers were evident with an intravenous dose of SP (0.5 mg). Bishop et al. (1996) used a sentence verification task that requires speeded retrieval from semantic memory, and found that a higher dose of SP (0.6 mg s.c.) increased both response times and errors compared with a lower dose (0.3 mg s.c.). Further, following BDZs, conceptual priming in category generation tasks is intact, even though subjects' explicit recall of studied category exemplars shows marked impair-ment (Bishop & Curran, 1998). Taken as a whole, these findings therefore provide evidence that episodic and semantic memory can be dissociated pharmacologically.

The contents of episodic and semantic memory are directly accessible to consciousness— we can bring to mind both personal experiences and impersonal facts. In contrast, procedural memory is expressed indirectly through skilled performance. Procedural memory is largely resistant to BDZ- or SP-induced impairments (e.g. Nissen et al., 1987; Bishop et al., 1996).

Procedural learning tasks, such as pursuit rotor, reading mirror-reversed words or serial reaction time tasks, show very similar effects of both BDZs and SP, with learning the curves for the drug generally being parallel to those for placebo (cf. Ghoneim & Mewaldt, 1990).

Another indirect test of memory includes what is usually termed priming: the general facilitation of a response from having recently been exposed to a stimulus. As already noted, there is some evidence that conceptual priming is intact following BDZs. Perceptual priming studies have produced an intriguing finding, that one particular BDZ (lorazepam), but not others, produces impairments on tasks tapping perceptual priming, such as wordstem, word fragment or picture completion (e.g. Brown et al., 1989; Knopman, 1991; Danion et al., 1992; Curran & Gorenstein, 1993; Vidailhet et al., 1996; Bishop & Curran, 1995; Bishop et al., 1996). Task purity criticisms can be applied to some earlier studies on the grounds that explicit impairments contaminated performance on the "implicit" task. However, these could not explain findings of several studies that compared lorazepam with another drug (a different BDZ or SP) and found that, although each drug produced the same impairment on an explicit task, only lorazepam impaired perceptual priming (e.g. Sellal et al., 1992; Bishop et al., 1996). The lorazepam-induced impairment of priming is attenuated by co-administration of the BDZ antagonist, flumazenil (Bishop & Curran, 1995). That one BDZ and not others suppresses priming supports a distinction between a system mediating perceptual priming (such as Tulving & Schacter's perceptual representational system) and other memory systems. The mechanism of this apparently unique effect of lorazepam is not yet known. One could speculate that there is a second population of BDZ receptors, perhaps concentrated in posterior cortical areas, to which lorazepam binds but not other BDZs. Subtypes of BDZ receptors have now been identified by microbiological studies, but their possible functional significance is not yet known.

Differential effects of drugs on explicit memory and priming mean that drugs may provide useful tools in studies of consciousness and memory. Some of this work has focused on whether anaesthetized people can remember anything that occurred whilst they were unconscious (for review, see Andrade, 1996). However, drugs may alter aspects of consciousness without obliterating it entirely. Recently, Perry et al. (1999) have speculated that acetylcholine may be a neurotransmitter correlate of "consciousness". On the basis of pathological, pharmacological and electrophysiological evidence, they suggest that the action of acetylcholine in the cortex and thalamus is essential for the normal experience of consciousness. At very high doses, scopolamine can produce hallucinations, which most would interpret as "changes in consciousness". However, drugs acting on other neurotransmitters can also have this effect (e.g. serotonergic/dopaminergic compounds such as LSD) and other clinical disorders involving hallucinations, such as schizophrenia, are thought to involve dopaminergic and glutamatergic more than cholinergic systems. It seems more likely that multiple neurotransmitters contribute to consciousness.

Glutamate, NMDA Blockers and Memory

The excitatory amino acids, notably glutamate and aspartate, are the most prevalent excitatory neurotransmitters in the brain and play an important role in cortico–cortical and cortical–subcortical interactions (Cotman & Monaghan, 1987). Extensive research with animals has implicated the importance of glutamate, and especially the glutamatergic n-methyl-D-aspartate (NMDA) receptor, in memory. Much of this research concerns long-term potentiation (LTP), an enduring form of synaptic plasticity that was initially identified in the hippocampus and more recently in the amygdala. LTP has been proposed as a mediator of learning and memory (for review see Malenka and Nicholl, 1999) although it is not yet clear how LTP at the synaptic level relates to memory at a behavioural level. Drugs that block the NMDA receptor (e.g. ketamine) inhibit the induction of LTP in the hippocampus (Harris et al., 1984) and there is considerable evidence that LTP is mediated by the NMDA receptor (e.g. Muller et al., 1988; Zhang & Levy, 1992; Maren, 1999).

In the human brain, NMDA receptors are densely localized in the cerebral cortex and the hippocampus. The NMDA receptor antagonist, ketamine, produces robust impairments on tests of frontal cortical function, such as the Wisconsin Card Sorting Task, and verbal fluency (Krystal et al., 1994; Malhotra et al., 1996). Ketamine also induces marked impairment of episodic memory (e.g. Adler et al., 1998; Newcomer et al., 1999). Like BDZs and scopolamine, a single dose of ketamine disrupts acquisition of new information but not its retrieval. Although ketamine is used clinically as an anaesthetic (especially in veterinary medicine) it is also a street drug, taken for its mood- and consciousness-altering properties. Research with ketamine abusers has shown that the drug acutely impairs not only episodic memory but also retrieval from semantic memory, on tasks such as sentence verification (Curran & Morgan, 2000). Indeed, impairment of both episodic and semantic memory is seen in a recent study, showing that a single dose of ketamine produces similar impairments on both "remembering" and "knowing" states of subjective awareness in recognition (Hetem et al., 2000). Further, frequent use of ketamine (2–4 times/week) produces effects on both episodic memory and verbal fluency which persist days beyond the ingestion of a single dose (Curran & Monaghan, 2001), and may reflect neurotoxicity.

Interest in NMDA antagonists has been stimulated by the hypothesis that excitotoxicity may be a neuropathological mechanism, which could explain various degenerative disorders. The basic idea is that normal excitatory neurotransmission is disturbed by some process that triggers excessive glutamate activity (Stahl, 1996). This in turn causes excessive calcium release into the neuron, which eventually kills the neuron. Theoretically, drugs that block the NMDA receptor should protect the neuron against excitotoxicity, and may therefore help stop the progression of neurodegeneration. However, NMDA blockers such as ketamine produce not only anterograde amnesia but also dissociative and psychotic-like symptoms, and therefore would not be suitable medications. These properties of ketamine suggest that the drug may model some aspects of schizophrenia (e.g. Krystal et al., 1994).

Monoamines, Monaminergic Drugs and Memory

Monoamines include the catecholamines (dopamine, noradrenaline, adrenaline) and the indolamine, serotonin (also termed 5-hydroxytriptamine or 5-HT). Compared to research on drugs like scopolamine or BDZs, there is little research on the memory effects of monoaminergic drugs.

Dopaminergic compounds exert their most consistent effect on executive functions. In a thoughtful review of functional imaging, electrophysiological and psychopharmacological studies of attention and arousal, Coull (1998) argues that cholinergic and noradrenergic systems are involved in "low-level" aspects of attention (e.g. attention orientating) whereas the dopaminergic system is associated with more executive aspects of attention, such as attentional set-shifting or working memory. Thus, dopamine antagonists impair performance on frontal tests like the Tower of London test (e.g. Danion et al., 1992) or attentional set switching (e.g. Vitiello et al., 1997). There is evidence that the effects of catecholamines vary according to an individual's level of functioning. For example, the dopamine agonist, bromocriptine, improved performance on a working memory task only of people who had lower initial levels of performance (Kimberg et al., 1997). Similarly, methylphenidate (an indirect catecholamine agonist, widely prescribed for attention deficit hyperactivity disorder) improved working memory only in individuals who had lower baseline performance (e.g. Mehta et al., 2000). The variable cognitive response of healthy subjects to amphetamine may well reflect similar individual differences in baseline performance.

Our memory for personally experienced emotional events tends to be particularly durable and vivid. The neurobiological basis of enhanced memory for emotional as opposed to neutral information has been explored in a series of studies by Cahill, McGaugh and colleagues (cf. McGaugh et al., 2000). They showed that drugs affecting adrenergic systems modulate emotional memory. Thus, the β-adrenergic antagonist propanolol impairs healthy people's recall of emotionally arousing (but not neutral) elements of a story (Cahill et al., 1994), whereas stimulation of noradrenaline (with yohimbine) produces some enhancement of memory for emotional elements of the same story (O'Carroll et al., 1999a). Using the same task with two patients who had bilateral damage to the amygdala, they found a similar pattern of memory for the emotional and neutral story elements. Together with evidence that noradrenaline is released in the rat amygdala in response to learning to avoid an aversive stimulus, Cahill et al. suggest that their findings imply that adrenergic function in the amygdala mediates memory for emotional material (McGaugh et al., 2000). However, it should be noted that β-blockers do not consistently produce a selective impairment of emotional memory (O'Carroll et al., 1999b) and that BDZs impair memory equally for both neutral and emotional elements of the Cahill et al. story (Curran & Zangara, in preparation).

Serotonin has been implicated in learning, with some studies showing that rapid depletion of brain tryptophan (the amino acid precursor to serotonin) produces impaired learning and memory (Park et al., 1994; Riedel et al., 1999). However, studies have not produced a consistent pattern of results. Subtle impairments of episodic memory in people using the illicit drug ecstasy (methylenedioxymethamphetamine) have been linked to serotonergic dysfunction (Morgan, 2000), although there are significant methodological problems with many studies of illicit users of this drug (Curran, 2000b). Serotonin is thought to mediate mood, and some apparent cognitive effects of drugs like ecstasy may be by-products of depressed mood.

Specificity of Drug Effects on Memory

Neurobiological Specificity

As will be evident from the discussion of SP and BDZs, drugs that are pharmacologically distinct can produce remarkably similar effects on human memory. Indeed, the few attempts to distinguish the memory effects of scopolamine and BDZs by directly comparing these drugs have had limited success (e.g. Frith et al., 1984; Curran et al., 1991). This similarity may reflect a common neurochemical action. Acetylcholine interacts with other neurotransmitters and especially with the amino acids, GABA and glutamate, which control basal forebrain cholinergic neurons (Perry et al., 1999; Sarter & Bruno, 2000). In research with rats, injection of a benzodiazepine into the medial septum *reduces* acetycholine release in the hippocampus by 50%; injecting a benzodiazepine antagonist (flumazenil) *increases* acetylcholine release in the hippocampus by 95% (Imperato et al., 1994).

With humans, relevant research is seen in studies that have used *cross-reversal designs*, attempting to attenuate the effects of benzodiazepine with a cholinergic agonist or the effects of scopolamine with a benzodiazepine antagonist. On the whole, the few studies to date provide little evidence of cross-reversal of either drugs' memory effects (e.g. Ghoneim & Mewaldt, 1977; Preston et al., 1989), indicating that the neurochemical bases of their memory effects are dissociable. Interpretation of these studies is not clear cut, as a critical factor is the relative doses of agonist and antagonist.

Psychological Specificity

Benzodiazepines, scopolamine and ketamine all produce dose-related reductions in arousal and this may contribute to performance decrements on tasks tapping memory and other cognitive functions. This issue of "sedation vs. amnesia" has been particularly debated within the benzodiazepine literature. However, based on four main lines of evidence, there now seems an emerging consensus that the amnestic effects of BDZs are not simply secondary to their sedative effects. First, studies have shown that doses of a benzodiazepine antagonist (flumazenil) which reverse sedative and attentional effects do not reverse amnestic effects (Curran & Birch, 1991; Hommer et al., 1993). Second, studies of repeated dosing show that tolerance to sedative and attentional effects develops before tolerance to memory impairments (e.g. Ghoneim et al., 1981; Curran et al., 1994). Third, there appear to be differential dose–response effects on measures of sedation and memory (Weingartner et al., 1995b). Fourth, a drug like an antihistamine can produce the same sedative effects as scopolamine and a benzodiazepine without producing any impairments of explicit memory (Curran et al., 1998). Taken as a whole, then, research suggests that the sedative and amnestic effects of SP and BDZs can be relatively independent of each other.

The attentional effects of BDZs are inconsistent and much less robust than their effects on memory. To examine the effects of attentional load on the memory effects of BDZs, Gorissen & Ehling (1998) gave participants dual tasks, whereby they performed a visual discrimination task of varying levels of complexity concurrently with a paired-associate learning task. The BDZ diazepam (15 mg) impaired subsequent recall of paired associates, but the level of impairment did not interact with the level of complexity of the visual discrimination task. Although dividing attention did reduce people's memory performance, it was no more disruptive to those given diazepam than to those given placebo. This would suggest that reduced attentional resources cannot account for the amnestic effects of BDZs.

The effects of BDZs on executive type tasks have been particularly inconsistent and warrant further research, e.g. Coull et al. (1995) report a significant impairment following 10 mg diazepam on the Tower of London task, whereas Gorissen et al. (1998) found no effect of a larger dose of diazepam (15 mg) on this task, and Danion et al. (1992) report no effect of the BDZ lorazepam (2.5 mg) on a similar task (Tower of Toronto).

In the scopolamine literature, the specificity debate has focused more on the attentional effects of the drug. Lawrence & Sahakian (1995) suggest that impairment of attentional function may be the main locus of scopolamine's effect on cognition. Rusted (1994) points out that impairment of a supposedly unitary or "all-purpose" central executive mechanism cannot encompass the range of observed effects of SP on attention and memory. She argues that impairment of a single resource system would mean that memory and attentional impairments should occur together, and studies do not show a consistent pattern of correspondence, e.g. several studies have reported that scopolamine can produce amnestic effects at doses that do not impair performance on tests of attention or vigilance (Sunderland et al., 1986; Kopelman & Corn, 1988). Studies of the relation between the sedative and amnesic effects of SP generally suggest that sedation may contribute to performance impairments on tasks, but does not account for amnesia (e.g. Kopelman & Corn, 1988; Curran et al., 1991). Further, co-administration of a stimulant drug (dextroamphetamine), which increases arousal, does not attenuate or reverse the amnesic effect of SP (Martinez et al., 1997).

Terms like "attention", "executive function" and "arousal" are umbrella concepts that cover a range of differing systems, processes or functions. There may be separate mechanisms responsible for different aspects of attention and arousal, and these may be moderated by different neurobiological substrates. Given the very widespread innervation of the cortex by basal forebrain cholinergic neurons, it seems likely that the cholinergic system subserves multiple cognitive operations. For example, based largely on evidence from animal studies, Sarter & Bruno (1997) argue that cortical cholinergic inputs mediate the detection and selection of stimuli for extended processing and the allocation of resources required to do this. Another view is put forward by Everitt & Robbins (1997), who argue that basal forebrain cholinergic projections probably subserve a common electrophysiological function of boosting signal-to-noise ratios in cortical areas. However, they propose that this has differing *psychological* effects, depending on the neural network operations within the various cortical domains.

What is clear is that the diffuse pharmacological and psychological effects of drugs like BDZs, scopolamine or ketamine restrict the degree to which they "model" organic dysfunction. Although scopolamine was seen as a model of AD, the drug's effects only partially parallel the anterograde memory deficits observed in AD. The drug does not mimic the extensive retrograde memory loss or the range of working memory impairments seen in AD. This is not surprising, given the multiple pathology in AD. In an effort to model the multiple neurotransmitter deficits in AD, Sunderland, Weingartner and others have combined drugs that act as cholinergic blockers with drugs that act on other neurotransmitters (Sunderland et al., 1997). For instance, Vitiello et al. (1997) assessed the effects of a dopaminergic antagonist (haloperidol) and a serotonergic antagonist (metergoline), both alone and combined with scopolamine. Scopolamine alone produced the standard impairment on tasks tapping episodic but not semantic memory; haloperidol alone selectively impaired the ability of participants to switch cognitive sets, and metergoline produced no cognitive impairments. The combination of drugs in any pair neither antagonized nor significantly attenuated these cognitive effects, suggesting that cholinergic effects on memory are distinct from dopaminergic effects on executive functions.

PHARMACOLOGICAL TREATMENTS OF IMPAIRED MEMORY FUNCTION

In terms of strategies for enhancing memory, the largest effort has been directed towards the development of treatments for AD. The different pathological manifestations in AD include cortical and subcortical β-amyloidosis (which results in plaque formation), abnormal tau (which results in the development of tangles and dystrophic dendrites), neuronal and synaptic loss and various neurotransmitter deficits. Although cholinergic deficits do not account for the spectrum of cognitive symptoms in AD, currently available treatments are designed to ameliorate cholinergic deficits. The main strategy for doing this has been to inhibit the enzyme acetlycholinesterase (AChE). AChE inhibitors (e.g. tacrine, donepezil hydrochloride, rivastigmine) prevent the hydrolysis of synaptically released acetylcholine and therefore increase the efficiency of cholinergic transmission.

AChE inhibitors have modest effects of slowing down the rate of cognitive deterioration over time in some patients with mild to moderate AD. Side effects can be problematic, and only a proportion of patients will show cognitive improvement with treatment (see Knopman, 1995). There is substantial clinical heterogeneity in patients meeting the diagnostic criteria for AD (Cummings, 2000) and various "sub-types" of AD have been suggested on the bases of neuropathological and/or cognitive variations (e.g. Richards, 1997). The pattern of progression of pathology in AD is also very different from one patient to another. It is possible that different clinical subgroups will show a different response to different pharmacological treatments. As we have argued in a previous edition of this volume, it is important that studies characterize each patient's symptoms very carefully, so as to allow an evaluation of not just "group" effects but also an analysis of which patient characteristics predict response to treatment (Lombardi & Weingartner, 1995).

Specificity of drug effects is an issue with cognitive-enhancing drugs in a parallel way to debates on the specificity of cognitive impairing drugs. It is not clear to what extent antidementia drugs produce any specific improvement in memory functions. Sahakian et al. (1993) showed that tacrine improved choice reaction time and improved performance on a task in which patients learnt to follow a simple rule and then reverse this rule. However, it had no effect compared with placebo on any memory task, leading Sahakian et al. to argue that tacrine improved attentional functions. Cholinergic agonists such as nicotine increase the effect of ACh, either directly or by sensitizing the receptor site. There is evidence that AD is associated with a reduced number of nicotinic cholinergic receptors, and that tacrine increases the number of nicotinic cholinergic receptors in AD patients (Nordberg et al., 1992). Subcutaneous nicotine has been shown to improve AD patients' performance on rapid information processing and psychomotor speed tasks, but had no effect on memory performance (cf. Lawrence & Sahakian, 1995). This again suggests that tacrine and the cholinergic system are involved in attentional/information processing rather than memory.

Evidence from animal studies has implicated depletion of nerve growth factor (NGF) as a possible mediator of cholinergic depletion in AD (when NGF is given to animals, cholinergic function is increased). Other approaches have shown some promise in AD, such as oestrogen therapy in post-menopausal women and vitamin E. A range of non-cholinergic techniques are currently being explored, including vasodilators like Hydergine, the so-called "nootropics" (putative cognitive enhancers such as piracetam) and a range of other compounds (e.g. neuropeptides, opiate antagonists, BDZ inverse agonists, and herbal preparations such as *Ginko biloba* and ginseng). There are also neurotropic agents, such as oligonucleotides, which are intended to modify biosynthetic pathways involved in the generation of AD pathology. Whether any of these agents have the potential to improve cognitive function in AD is not yet known.

There is a wide range of other disorders in which memory is impaired, including Parkinson's disease, Wernicke–Korsakoff syndrome, vascular accidents such as repeated aneurysms and stroke, closed head injury, herpes simplex encephalitis, surgery involving medial temporal and diencephalic structures and so on. Within each disorder, the symptoms, including memory deficits, vary considerably from one patient to another.

In the case of some disorders, the underlying pathology suggests that pharmacological intervention may be helpful—memory deficits stemming from neurochemical imbalances are likely to be ameliorated, if not reversed, by a drug therapy that corrects that imbalance. There may also be role for a drug therapy in other cases where one might improve symptoms rather than correct any hypothesized imbalance, e.g. two studies of patients with traumatic brain injury have reported that the dopamine agonist, bromocriptine, improves performance on executive tests such as verbal fluency and WCST (Powell et al., 1996; McDowell et al., 1998). Bromocriptine may act to enhance motivation via dopamine "reward" systems.

SOME PROSPECTS FOR FUTURE RESEARCH

Much of this chapter has illustrated how different classes of drugs might alter cognitive functioning in general and memory in particular. One of the subthemes developed concerns the specificity of the observed cognitive effects. Clearly, it is difficult to define the cognitive pathway through which some aspect of memory is altered by a drug. This fuzzy picture is complicated further because the drugs known to alter cognitive functions have a broad spectrum of effects in the CNS. Most affect multiple brain sites—types of receptors and brain regions as well multiple neurotransmitter systems. More specific drugs are being produced, which will help in teasing apart the neurochemistry of memory. The use of radiolabelled drugs in imaging studies allows delineation of receptors in the living brain, and provides a means of assessing abnormalities in receptor populations in neurological and psychiatric disorders. A drug and placebo can be administered during functional imaging and this allows drug-induced changes in activation to be monitored during encoding or retrieval (cf. Fletcher et al., 1996). Researchers are also beginning to use computational approaches to simulate the effects of drugs on human memory (e.g. Hasselmo & Wyble, 1997). Future research in the field will doubtless become far broader in the scope of cognitive functions under study. It will build on developments throughout neuroscience, e.g. in our understanding of the interaction of cognition and emotion, or of the cognitive operations associated with prefrontal brain regions, or the operations that reflect the interaction of prefrontal regions with reward systems in the brain.

This chapter has presented a top-down perspective on drugs and memory. That is, we discuss the psychopharmacology of memory from its integrated endpoint—what a human can tell us about past experiences. In focusing upon human memory, we have not covered the extensive literature on animal cognition or the virtual explosion of memory research at the molecular and cellular levels. There is still a long way to go in intergrating such basic science research into our thinking about how drugs might alter human memory. We have relatively weak animal models of phenomena such as cognitive ageing and the impact of various lesions on cognitive functioning. This does not mean that we cannot learn a great deal from studying the effect of lesions or drug treatments on cognitive functioning in the rodent or monkey. On the other hand, we really do not know what a demented rat looks like in a Morris water maze, or what is the equivalent of word(name)-finding problems in the aged monkey working for a food reward.

It may be that, at least for some forms of memory, one needs the potential for a well-timed emotional response in order to establish a long lasting record of an event in memory. Much recent work of McGaugh and his colleagues illustrates this point very well (e.g. McGaugh et al., 2000). This research also elegantly illustrates how findings from drug and lesion studies with animals can be integrated with drug and brain damage research on human memory.

Clearly, several types of drugs can impair a human's ability to mentally relive past experience. To date, the vast majority of studies have examined the effects of a single dose of a drug on memory. However, these acute effects are often very different from the cognitive changes seen in people under repeated treatment with a drug, or in those who regularly abuse drugs. This is an issue that goes well beyond simple problems of tolerance. For example, totally "naïve" subjects respond quite differently to many drugs, and even a single exposure often has an impact on the cognitive response which differs when subjects are treated a second time with the same drug. A central question for research is, therefore, defining what the neurobiological bases are that differentiate drug-induced acute and chronic cognitive impairments. The answers to this question will be hugely important for understanding changes over time in response to psychiatric drugs, as well as the cognitive and biological processes underpinning the transition from voluntary drug use to drug dependency.

Drug challenge paradigms may offer a useful tool in this and other respects. The interaction of a lesion (disease) and a drug has had some value as a clinical tool and may also be informative about the nature of memory. The notion of a challenge to uncover pathology is certainly well established in medicine (e.g. graded stressors for evaluating the integrity of the cardiovascular system). In psychiatry, several types of drugs have been used to uncover pathology, or risk of pathology, with various degrees of success. In each instance a drug challenge is chosen because it is directly linked to what is believed to be the neurobiological (neurotransmitter-related) basis of psychopathology. Recently, this same logic has been used to study individuals at risk for Alzheimer's disease (i.e. through the use of a cholinergic or glutaminergic challenge), as well as patients with histories of impulsive cognitive styles (using agents that deplete brain serotonin). It is too early to establish the reliability and utility of this approach to the use of drugs in the study of impaired memory.

REFERENCES

Adler, C.M., Goldberg, T.E., Malhotra, A.K. et al. (1998). Effects of ketamine on thought disorder, working memory, and semantic memory in healthy volunteers. *Biological Psychiatry*, **43**, 811–816.

Anderson, M.C., Green, C. & McCulloch, K.C. (2000). Similarity and inhibition in long-term memory: evidence for a two-factor theory. *Journal of Experimental Psychology: Learning, Memory & Cognition*, **26**, 1141–1159.

Andrade, J. (1996). Investigations of hypesthesia: using anesthetics to explore relationships between consciousness, learning and memory. *Consciousness and Cognition*, **5**, 562–580.

Bacon, E., Danion, J.M., Muller, F.K. et al. (1998). Confidence level and feeling of knowing for episodic and semantic memory: an investigation of lorazepam. *Psychopharmacology*, **138**, 318–325.

Baddeley, A. (2000). The episodic buffer: a new component of working memory? *Trends in Cognitive Sciences*, **4**, 417–423.

Bartus, R.T., Dean, R.L., Beer, B. & Lippa, A.S. (1982). The cholinergic hypothesis of geriatric memory dysfunction. *Science*, **217**, 408–14.

Berry, C., Gelder, M.G. & Summerfield, A. (1965). Experimental analysis of drug effects on human performance using information theory concepts. *British Journal of Psychology*, **56**, 255–265.

Bishop, K. & Curran, H.V. (1995). Psychopharmacological analysis of implicit and explicit memory: a study with lorazepam and the benzodiazepine antagonist, flumazenil. *Psychopharmacology*, **121**, 267–278.

Bishop, K. & Curran, H.V. (1998). An investigation of the effects of benzodiazepine receptor ligands and of scopolamine on conceptual priming. *Psychopharmacology*, **140**, 345–353.

Bishop, K.I., Curran, H.V. & Lader, M. (1996). Do scopolamine and lorazepam have dissociable effects on human memory systems? A dose–response study with normal volunteers. *Experimental and Clinical Psychopharmacology*, **4**, 292–299.

Brown, J. & Brown, M.W. (1990). The effects of repeating a recognition test on lorazepam-induced amnesia: evidence for impaired contextual memory as a cause of amnesia. *Quarterly Journal of Experimental Psychology*, **42A**(2), 279–290.

Brown, M.W., Brown, J. & Bowes, J. (1989). Absence of priming coupled with substantially preserved recognition in lorazepam induced amnesia. *Quarterly Journal of Experimental Psychology*, **41A**, 599–617.

Brown, J.M., Brown, J.B. & Bowes, J.B. (1983). Effects of lorazepam on rate of forgetting, on retrieval from semantic memory and manual dexterity. *Neuropsychologia*, **21**, 501–512.

Cahill, L., Prins, B., Weber, M. & McGaugh, J.L. (1994). Beta-adrenergic activation and memory for emotional events. *Nature*, **371**, 702–704.

Cattell, R.B. (1930). The effects of alcohol and caffeine on intelligent and associative performance. *British Journal of Medical Psychology*, **10**, 20–33.

Cotman, C.W. & Monaghan, D.T. (1987). Chemistry and anatomy of excitatory amino acid systems. In H. Meltzer (ed.), *Psychopharmacology: The Third Generation of Progress* (pp. 197–210). New York: Raven Press.

Coull, J.T. (1998). Neural correlates of attention and arousal: insights from electrophysiology, functional neuroimaging and psychopharmacology. *Progress in Neurobiology*, **55**, 343–361.

Coull, J.T., Sahakian, B.J., Middleton, H.C. et al. (1995). Differential effects of clonidine, haloperidol, diazepam and tryptophan depletion on focused attention and attentional search. *Psychopharmacology*, **121**, 222–230.

Cummings, J.L. (2000). Cholinesterase inhibitors: a new class of psychotropic compounds. *American Journal of Psychiatry*, **157**, 4–15.

Curran, H.V. (1991). Benzodiazepines, memory and mood: a review. *Psychopharmacology*, **105**, 1–8.

Curran H.V. (2000a). The psychopharmacology of memory. In E. Tulving & F. Craik (eds), *The Oxford Handbook of Memory* (pp. 539–556) New York: Oxford University Press.

Curran, H.V. (2000b). Is MDMA ("ecstasy") neurotoxic in humans? An overview of evidence and of methodological problems in research. *Neuropsychobiology*, **42**, 34–41.

Curran, H.V. & Birch, B. (1991). Differentiating the sedative and amnestic effects of benzodiazepines: a study with midazolam and the benzodiazepine antagonist, flumazenil. *Psychopharmacology*, **103**, 519–523.

Curran, H.V., Bond, A., O'Sullivan, G. et al. (1994). Memory functions, alprazolam and e.xposure therapy: a controlled longitudinal study of patients with agoraphobia and panic disorder. *Psychological Medicine*, **24**, 969–976.

Curran, H.V., Gardiner, J., Java, R. & Allen, D.J. (1993). Effects of lorazepam on recollective experience in recognition memory. *Psychopharmacology*, **110**, 374–378.

Curran, H.V. & Gorenstein, C. (1993). Differential effects of lorazepam and oxazepam on priming, *International Clinical Psychopharmacology*, **8**, 37–42.

Curran, H.V. & Hildebrandt, M. (1999). Dissociative effects of alcohol on recollective experience. *Consciousness and Cognition*, **8**, 497–509.

Curran, H.V. & Kopelman, M.D. (1996). The cognitive psychopharmacology of Alzheimer's Disease. In R.G. Morris (ed.), *The Neuropsychology of Alzheimer's Disease*. Oxford: Oxford University Press.

Curran, H.V. & Monaghan, L. (2001). In and out of the K hole: a comparison of the acute and residual effects of ketamine in frequent & infrequent ketamine users. *Addiction*, **96**, 749–760.

Curran, H.V. & Morgan, C. (2000). Cognitive, dissociative and psychotogenic effects of ketamine in recreational users on the night of drug use and three days later. *Addiction*, **95**, 575–590.

Curran, H.V., Poovibunsuk, P., Dalton, J. & Lader, M.H. (1998). Differentiating the effects of centrally acting drugs on arousal and memory: an event-related potential study of scopolamine, lorazepam and diphenhydramine. *Psychopharmacology*, **135**, 27–36.

Curran, H.V., Schiffano, F. & Lader, M.H. (1991). Models of memory dysfunction? A comparison of the effects of scopolamine and lorazepam on memory, psychomotor performance and mood. *Psychopharmacology*, **103**, 83–90.

Curran, H.V. & Zangara, A. (2001) A comparison of effects on emotional memory of a benzodiazepine with a beta-blocker (manuscript in preparation).

Danion, J.M., Peretti, S. & Grange, D. (1992). Effects of chlorpromazine and lorazepam on explicit memory, repetition priming and cognitive skill learning in healthy volunteers *Psychopharmacology*, **108**, 345–351.

Drachman, D.A. & Leavitt, J. (1974). Human memory and the cholinergic system. *Archives of Neurology*, **30**, 113–121.

Everitt, B.J. & Robbins, T.W. (1997). Central cholinergic systems and cognition. *Annual Review of Psychology*, **48**: 649–684.

Fillmore, M.T., Vogel-Sprott, M. & Gavrilescu, D. (1999). Alcohol effects on intentional behavior: dissociating controlled and automatic influences. *Experimental & Clinical Psychopharmacology*, **7**, 372–378.

Fletcher, P.C., Frith, C.D., Grasby, P.M. et al. (1996). Local and distributed effects of apomorphine on fronto-temporal function in acute unmedicated schizophrenics *Journal of Neuroscience*, **16**, 7055–7062.

Frith, C.D., Richardson, J.T.E., Samuel, M. et al. (1984). The effects of intravenous diazepam and hyoscine upon human memory, *Quarterly Journal of Experimental Psychology*, **36A**, 133–144.

Ghoneim, M.M. & Mewaldt, S.P. (1975). Effects of diazepam and scopolamine on storage, retrieval and organizational processes in memory, *Psychopharmacologia*, **44**, 257–262.

Ghoneim, M.M. & Mewaldt, S.P. (1977). Studies on human memory: the interactions of diazepam, scopolamine and physostigmine, *Psychopharmacology*, **52**, 1–6.

Ghoneim, M.M. & Mewaldt, S.P. (1990). Benzodiazepines and human memory: a review *Anesthesiology*, **72**, 926–938.

Ghoneim, M.M., Mewaldt, S.P., Berie, J.L. & Hinrichs,V. (1981). Memory and performance effects of single and 3 week administration of diazepam. *Psychopharmacology*, **73**, 147–151.

Gorissen, M.E.E., Curran, H.V. & Ehling, P.A.T.M. (1998). Proactive interference and temporal context encoding after diazepam intake. *Psychopharmacology*, **138**, 334–343.

Gorissen, M.E.E. & Ehling, P.A.T.M. (1998) Dual task performance after diazepam intake: can resource depletion explain the benzodiazepine-induced amnesia? *Psychopharmacology*, **138**, 354–361.

Gray, S.L., Lai, K.V. & Larson, E.B. (1999). Drug-induced cognition disorders in the elderly: incidence, prevention and management. *Drug Safety*, **21**, 101–122.

Harris, E.W., Ganong, A.H. & Cotman, C.W. (1984). Long-term potentiation in the hippocampus involves activation of N-methyl-D-aspartate receptors. *Brain Research*, **323**, 132–137.

Hasselmo, M.E. & Wyble, B.P. (1997). Free recall and recognition in a network model of the hippocampus: simulating effects of scopolamine on human memory function. *Behavioral Brain Research*, **89**, 1–34.

Hetem, L.A., Danion, J.M., Diemunsch, P. & Brandt, C. (2000). Effect of a subanesthetic dose of ketamine on memory and conscious awareness in healthy volunteers. *Psychopharmacology*, **152**, 283–288.

Hommer, D., Weingartner, H. & Breier, A. (1993). Dissociation of benzodiazepine-induced amnesia from sedation by flumazenil. *Psychopharmacology*, **112**, 455–460.

Imperato, A., Dazzi, L., Obinu M.C. et al. (1994). The benzodiazepine receptor antagonist flumazenil increases acetylcholine release in rat hippocampus. *Brain Research*, **647**, 167–171.

Jones, E.E. (1909). The waning of consciousness under chloroform. *Psychological Review*, **16**, 48–54.

Jones, J.R. (1933). The influence of some antipyretic drugs on learning. *Journal of General Psychology*, **9**, 472–475.

Kimberg, D.Y., D'Esposito, M. & Farah, M.J. (1997). Effects of bromocriptine on human subjects depend on working memory capacity. *NeuroReport*, **8**, 3581–3585.

Knopman, D. (1991). Unaware learning vs. preserved learning in pharmacologic amnesia: similarities and differences. *Journal of Experimental Psychology: Learning, Memory and Cognition*, **17**, 1017–1029.

Knopman, D. (1995). Tacrine in Alzheimer's Disease: a promising first step. *Neurologist*, **1**, 86–94.

Kopelman, M.D. & Corn, T. H. (1988). Cholinergic "blockade" as a model for cholinergic depletion. *Brain*, **111**, 1079–1110.

Krystal, J.H., Karper, L.P., Seibyl, J.P. et al. (1994). Subanesthetic effects of the non-competitive NMDA antagonist, ketamine, in humans. *Archives of General Psychiatry*, **51**, 199–214.

Lawrence, A.D. & Sahakian, B.J. (1995). Alzheimer disease, attention and the cholinergic system. *Alzheimer Disease and Associated Disorders*, **9**(S2), 43–49.

Lombardi, W. & Weingartner, H. (1995). Pharmacological treatment of impaired memory function. In A. Baddeley et al. (eds), *Handbook of Memory Disorders* (pp. 577–602). New York: Wiley.

Malenka, R.C. & Nicholl, R.A. (1999). Long-term potentiation—a decade of progress? *Science*, **285**, 1870–1874.

Malhotra, A.K., Pinals, D.A., Weingartner, H. et al. (1996). NMDA receptor function and human cognition: the effects of ketamine in healthy volunteers. *Neuropsychopharmacology*, **14**, 301–307.

Maren, S. (1999). Long-term potentiation in the amygdala: a mechanism for emotional learning and memory. *Trends in Neuroscience*, **22**, 561–567.

Martinez, R., Molchan, S.E., Lawlor, B.A. et al. (1997). Minimal effects of dextroamphetamine on scopolamine-induced cognitive impairments in humans. *Biological Psychiatry*, **41**, 50–57.

Mehta, M.A., Owen, A.M., Sahakian, B.J. et al. (2000). Methylphenidate enhances working memory by modulating discrete frontal and parietal lobe regions in the human brain. *Journal of Neuroscience Online*, **20**(6), RC65.

McDowell, S., Whyte, J. & D'Esposito, M. (1998). Differential effect of a dopaminergic agonist on prefrontal function in traumatic brain injury patients. *Brain*, **121**, 1155–1164.

McGaugh, J.L., Roozendaal, B. & Cahill, L. (2000). Modulation of memory storage by stress hormones and the amygdaloid complex. In Gazzaniga, M. (ed.), *The New Cognitive Neuroscience* (pp. 1081–1098). Cambridge, MA: MIT Press.

Milani, R. & Curran, H.V. (2000). Effects of a low dose alcohol on recollective experience of illusory memory. *Psychopharmacology*, **147**, 397–402.

Mintzer, M.Z. & Griffiths, R.R. (1999). Triazolam and zolpidem: effects on human memory and attentional processes. *Psychopharmacology*, **144**, 8–19.

Mintzer, M.Z. & Griffiths, R.R. (2000). Acute effects of triazolam on false recognition. *Memory & Cognition*, **28**, 1357–1365.

Mintzer, M.Z. & Griffiths, R.R. (2001). Acute dose-effects of scopolamine on false recognition. *Psychopharmacology*, **153**, 425–443.

Molchan, S.E., Martinez, R.A., Hill, J.L. et al. (1992). Increased cognitive sensitivity to scopolamine with age and a perspective on the scopolamine model. *Brain Research Reviews*, **17**, 215–226.

Morgan, M.J. (2000). Ecstasy (MDMA): a review of its possible persistent psychological effects. *Psychopharmacology*, **152**, 230–248.

Muller, D., Joly, M. & Lynch, G. (1988). Contributions of quisqualate and NMDA receptors to the induction and expression of long-term potentiation. *Science*, **242**, 1694–1697.

Newcomer, J.W., Farber, N.B., Jevtovic-Todorovic, V. et al. (1999). Ketamine-induced NMDA receptor hypofunction as a model of memory impairment and psychosis. *Neuropsychopharmacology*, **20**, 106–118.

Nissen, M.J., Knopman, D.S. & Schacter, D.L. (1987). Neurochemical dissociations of memory systems. *Neurology*, **37**, 789–794.

Nordberg, A., Lilja, A., Lundqvist, H. et al. (1992). Tacrine restores cholinergic nicotinic receptors and glucose metabolism in Alzheimer patients as visualized by positron emission tomography. *Neurobiology of Aging*, **13**, 747–758.

Nyberg, L. & Tulving, E. (1996). Classifying human long-term memory: evidence from converging dissociations. *European Journal of Cognitive Psychology*, **8**, 163–183.

O'Carroll, R.E., Drysdale, E., Cahill, L. et al. (1999a). Stimulation of the noradrenergic system enhances and blockade reduces memory for emotional material in man. *Psychological Medicine*, **29**, 1083–1088.

O'Carroll, R.E., Drysdale, E., Cahill, L. et al. (1999b). Memory for emotional material: a comparison of central versus peripheral beta blockade. *Journal of Psychopharmacology*, **13**, 32–39.

Park, S.B., Crull, J.T., McShane, R.H., Young, A.H., Sahakian, B.J., Robbins, T.W. & Cowen, P.J. (1994). Tryptophan depletion in normal volunteers produces selective impairments in learning and memory. *Neuropharmacology*, **33**, 575–578.

Perry, E.K., Tomlinson, B.E., Blessed, G. et al. (1978). Correlation of cholinergic abnormalities with senile plaques and mental test scores in senile dementia. *British Medical Journal*, **2**(6150), 1457–1459.

Perry, E., Walker, M., Grace, J. & Perry, R. (1999). Acetylcholine in mind: a neurotransmitter correlate of consciousness? *Trends in Neuroscience*, **22**, 273–280.

Powell, J.H., al Adawi, S., Morgan, J. & Greenwood, R.J. (1996). Motivational deficits after brain injury: effects of bromocriptine in 11 patients. *Journal of Neurology, Neurosurgery and Psychiatry*, **60**, 416–421.

Preston, G.C., Ward, C., Lines, C.R. et al. (1989). Scopolamine and benzodiazepine models of dementia: cross-reversals by Ro 15–88 and physostigmine. *Psychopharmacology*, **98**, 487–494.

Richards, M. (1997). Neurobiological treatment of Alzheimer's disease. In R.G.M. Morris (ed.), *The Cognitive Neuropsychology of Alzheimer's Disease* (pp. 327–342). Oxford: Oxford University Press.

Riedel, W.J., Klaassen, T., Deutz, N.E. et al. (1999). Tryptophan depletion in normal volunteers produces selective impairment in memory consolidation. *Psychopharmacology*, **141**, 362–369.

Roediger, H.L. & McDermott, K.B. (1995). Creating false memories: remembering words not presented in lists. *Journal of Experimental Psychology: Learning Memory and Cognition*, **21**, 803–814.

Rusted, J.M. (1994). Cholinergic blockade: are we asking the right questions? *Journal of Psychopharmacology*, **8**, 54–59.

Rusted, J.M. & Warburton, D.M. (1988). The effects of scopolamine on working memory in healthy young volunteers. *Psychopharmacology*, **96**, 145–152.

Sahakian, B.J., Owen, A.M., Morant, N.J. et al. (1993). Further analysis of of the cognitive effects of tetrahydroaminoacridine (THA) in Alzheimer's disease: assessment of attentional and mnemonic function using CANTAB. *Psychopharmacology*, **110**, 395–410.

Sarter, M. & Bruno, J.P. (1997). Cognitive functions of cortical acetylcholine: toward a unifying hypothesis. *Brain Research and Brain Research Reviews*, **23**, 28–46.

Sarter, M. & Bruno, J.P. (2000). Cortical cholinergic inputs mediating arousal, attentional processing and dreaming. *Neuroscience*, **95**, 933–952.

Schacter, D.L. (1999). The seven sins of memory. Insights from psychology and cognitive neuroscience. *American Psychologist*, **54**, 182–203.

Schacter, D.L., Verfaellie, M., Anes, M.D. & Racine, C. (1998). When true recognition suppresses false recognition: evidence from amnesic patients. *Journal of Cognitive Neuroscience*, **10**, 668–679.

Sellal, F., Danion, J.M., Kauffmann-Mueller, F. et al. (1992). Differential effects of diazepam and lorazepam on repetition priming in healthy volunteers. *Psychopharmacology*, **108**, 371–379.

Stahl, S. (1996). *Essential Psychopharmacology*. Cambridge: Cambridge University Press.

Starr, J.M. & Whalley, L.J. (1994). Drug-induced dementia. Incidence, management and prevention. *Drug Safety*, **11**, 310–317.

Steinberg, H. & Summerfield, A. (1957). Influence of a depressant drug on acquisition in rote learning. *Quarterly Journal of Experimental Psychology*, **9**, 138–145.

Sunderland, T., Tariot, P., Weingartner, H. et al. (1986). Anticholinergic challenge in Alzheimer patients: a controlled dose-response study. *Progress in Neuropsychopharmacology and Biological Psychiatry*, **10**, 599–610.

Sunderland, T., Molchan, S.E., Little, J.T. et al. (1997). Pharmacologic challenges in Alzheimer disease and normal controls: cognitive modeling in humans. *Alzheimer Disease and Associated Disorders*, **11**(suppl 4), S23–26.

Tulving, E. (1985). How many memory systems are there? *American Psychologist*, **40**, 385–398.

Tulving, E. & Schacter, D.L. (1990). Priming and human memory systems, *Science*, **247**, 301–306.

Vidailhet, P., Kazes, M., Danion, J.M. et al. (1996). Effects of lorazepam and diazepam on conscious and automatic memory processes. *Psychopharmacology*, **127**, 63–72.

Vitiello, B., Martin, A., Hill, J. et al. (1997). Cognitive and behavioral effects of cholinergic, dopaminergic, and serotonergic blockade in humans. *Neuropsychopharmacology*, **16**, 15–24.

Weingartner, H. (1985). Models of memory dysfunctions. *Annals of the New York Academy of Sciences*, **444**, 359–369.

Weingartner, H.J., Sirocco, K., Curran, H.V. & Wolkowitz, O. (1995a). Memory facilitation following the administration of the benzodiazepine triazolam. *Experimental and Clinical Psychopharmacology*, **3**, 298–303.

Weingartner, H.J., Sirocco, K., Rawlings, R. et al. (1995b). Dissociations in the expression of the sedative effects of triazolam. *Psychopharmacology*, **119**, 27–33.

Weingartner, H.J., Rawlings, R., George, D.T. & Eckardt, M. (1998). Triazolam-induced changes in alcoholic thought processes. *Psychopharmacology*, **138**, 311–317.

Wheeler, M.A., Stuss, D.T. & Tulving, E. (1997). Toward a theory of episodic remembering: the frontal lobes and autonoetic consciousness. *Psychological Bulletin*, **121**, 331–354.

Zhang, D.X. & Levy, W.B. (1992). Ketamine blocks the induction of LTP at the lateral entorhinal cortex–dentate gyrus synapses. *Brain Research*, **593**, 124–127.

Varieties of Memory Disorder

CHAPTER 7

The Amnesic Syndrome: Overview and Subtypes

Margaret O'Connor

Beth Israel Deaconess Medical Center, Boston, MA, USA

and

Mieke Verfaellie

Memory Disorders Research Center, Boston, MA, USA

Global amnesia refers to a dense and circumscribed deficit in memory in the context of otherwise preserved intelligence. It encompasses the acquisition of events and facts encountered postmorbidly (anterograde amnesia), as well as the retrieval of information acquired premorbidly (retrograde amnesia). Patients with amnesia are capable of holding a limited amount of information in mind for a very brief period of time, but with increased retention interval or increased interference, their recall and recognition of the information inevitably fails. Anterograde amnesia is usually global, in that memory for all new information is affected—regardless of the nature of the information (i.e. verbal or nonverbal) or the modality in which it is presented (i.e. auditory or visual). In most patients, anterograde amnesia is associated with some degree of retrograde loss, although its extent is more variable. The reverse, however, is not necessarily the case, as some patients have been described who demonstrate relatively focal retrograde amnesia in the absence of anterograde memory loss (Kapur, 1993; Kopelman, 2000).

Although amnesia is characterized by a pervasive and devastating memory loss, it is important to note that some components of memory remain intact. Amnesic patients demonstrate normal performance on tasks of immediate memory and working memory (Cave & Squire, 1992; Parkin & Leng, 1993). This ability to hold and manipulate information "on-line" is critical for performance on a variety of cognitive tasks, ranging from language comprehension to simple arithmetic. Patients with amnesia are also able to retrieve overlearned semantic memories, as evidenced by the fact that their general world knowledge and knowledge of word meanings remains intact. Finally, even within the domain of new learning, some forms of memory are preserved. These include skill learning, classical conditioning and repetition priming, the bias or facilitation in processing a stimulus that results from prior exposure to that same or related stimulus (Squire et al., 1993). These forms of memory have in common the fact that knowledge can be expressed without a need for

The Handbook of Memory Disorders. Edited by A.D. Baddeley, M.D. Kopelman and B.A. Wilson
© 2002 John Wiley & Sons, Ltd.

conscious recollection, and without awareness of the episode in which learning took place. The dissociation between aware (declarative) and unaware (procedural) memory in patients with global amnesia has guided much research into the neural and functional organization of various components of memory (e.g. Gabrieli, 1999; Verfaellie & Keane, 2001).

The memory problem of the amnesic individual must be differentiated from more common forms of memory loss. In order for an individual to be diagnosed with amnesia, there must be evidence of a marked learning deficit and this problem must exist in relative isolation, so that other aspects of cognition remain intact. The severity of the learning deficit is the cardinal feature distinguishing amnesia from milder memory problems, such as those associated with age-related memory decline, depression or developmental learning difficulties. The preservation of attention, working memory and general reasoning abilities differentiate the amnesic patient from the patient who has memory problems in the context of global cognitive decline (e.g. dementia or delirium). It is noteworthy that some amnesics have superior cognitive abilities, a fact that underscores the relative independence of memory and intelligence (e.g. Cermak & O'Connor, 1983). Other amnesic patients show modest reductions on measures of verbal intelligence, but this decline can sometimes reflect decrements in semantic memory (e.g. Stefanacci et al., 2000).

Many clinical and theoretical insights into global amnesia find their origin in the study of patient H.M., a man who became amnesic following bilateral resection of the temporal lobes for treatment of refractory epilepsy (Scoville & Milner, 1957). Although H.M. still serves as a benchmark for characterizing amnesia, it has also become clear that the syndrome is functionally heterogeneous, comprising a number of different patterns of memory loss and associated processing deficits, which may be linked to distinct etiologies and associated patterns of neuroanatomical damage. In addition, it should be kept in mind that premorbid factors, such as baseline intelligence and personality style, can influence a patient's clinical presentation, as may associated neurocognitive problems.

Global amnesia occurs as a result of damage to the medial temporal lobes, the diencephalon and the basal forebrain. Such damage can be caused by a broad array of traumatic, vascular and infectious disease processes, the most common of which are anoxia, encephalitis, cerebrovascular accidents, Korsakoff syndrome and rupture and repair of anterior communicating artery aneurysms. In these conditions, amnesia is usually of a permanent nature. Transient forms of amnesia also occur secondary to seizure activity or temporary disruption of the vascular supply (see Chapter 10, this volume). In what follows, we first review the main etiologies leading to permanent amnesia and their associated neuropsychological profiles. We next consider to what extent each of the main brain regions implicated in amnesia causes a distinct pattern of processing deficits.

NEUROLOGICAL CONDITIONS ASSOCIATED WITH AMNESIA

ENCEPHALITIS

Herpes simplex encephalitis (HSE) occurs as a result of virus-induced hemorrhagic lesions in the brain. In the early stages of the infectious process, patients experience a "flu-like" illness that is often associated with fever, headaches and lethargy. Profound confusion and disorientation may follow and patients often develop other neurocognitive problems, including aphasia, agnosia and amnesia. For some patients these problems persist so that a broad array of cognitive abilities is compromised. For others, disorientation may be followed by complete recovery. A third group of patients presents with focal memory disturbances in the absence of other cognitive deficits. These are the patients who have been of particular interest to memory researchers, because they typically present with very dense amnesic syndromes, quite similar to that of patient H.M. (e.g. Cermak, 1976; Damasio et al., 1985a; Stefanacci et al., 2000).

Like the clinical presentation, the neuroanatomical damage associated with encephalitis is heterogeneous, but typically centers on limbic regions in the temporal lobe, including the hippocampus and adjacent entorhinal, perirhinal and parahippocampal cortices, the amygdala and polar limbic cortices. Damage frequently also extends laterally, resulting in varying degrees of damage to the anterolateral and inferior aspects of the temporal neocortex. Extension of the lesion anteriorly can result in damage to ventromedial areas, such as the insular cortex and basal forebrain (Damasio & Van Hoesen, 1985).

S.S., a patient we have followed for many years, experienced dense memory loss as a result of HSE (Cermak, 1976; Cermak & O'Connor, 1983). S.S.'s initial presentation was noteworthy for lethargy and headaches followed by a 1 month coma. In the acute stage of his illness, S.S. was aphasic and hemiparetic, but these problems resolved and he was left with a dense amnesia associated with bilateral lesions in anterolateral and medial portions of the temporal lobes, the insula and the putamen. S.S.'s anterograde amnesia is profound. He has not been able to form any new declarative memories for the last three decades. He has not retained any episodic information regarding important family matters and is totally unaware of recent public facts or events. He has also failed to acquire any new semantic knowledge. Strikingly, he has not learned any novel vocabulary introduced into the English language since the onset of his illness, even though he has been exposed to these words repeatedly through television programs and newspapers (Verfaellie et al., 1995a). S.S. also has a very extensive retrograde memory loss for autobiographical as well as personal semantic information that encompasses most of his adult life. Despite this dense amnesia, S.S. is of superior intelligence. Even at age 70, 30 years after the onset of his amnesia, he has a Full Scale IQ of 130. He continues to perform in the superior range on tasks of working memory, frontal/executive abilities, language and deductive reasoning skills. Like other amnesic patients who have suffered encephalitis, S.S. has insight into his memory loss, a fact that is likely due to the relative preservation of frontal brain regions.

As with all amnesic etiologies, there are variations in the severity of memory loss. While some patients may be totally unable to benefit from repeated exposure to new material or to benefit from extended study time, others are able gradually to acquire a limited amount of information (e.g. Haslam et al., 1997). This likely reflects the extent of medial temporal damage (Stefanacci et al., 2000). Lesions may be asymmetrical and, as expected, the laterality of lesion affects the nature of the neurobehavioral presentation. Greater damage to right temporal regions has a more pronounced effect on nonverbal/visual memory, such as memory for faces and spatial aspects of stimuli (Eslinger et al., 1993), while disproportionate damage to left temporal regions has a more pronounced effect on verbal memory (Tranel et al., 2000).

The distribution of the encephalitis-induced lesion also affects the nature and severity of the remote memory loss. Patients with extensive retrograde amnesia typically have lesions extending into lateral temporal regions (Damasio et al., 1985a; O'Connor et al., 1992; Stefanacci et al., 2000). Damasio and colleagues attribute the profound loss of remote memories in these patients to the destruction of convergence zones in anterior temporal areas (Tranel et al., 2000). Asymmetrical patterns of damage can result in distinct patterns of remote memory loss. Several case studies have indicated that damage to right anterior temporal regions severely interferes with retrieval of autobiographical memories (O'Connor et al., 1992; Ogden, 1993). Patient L.D., who has been studied extensively by our group, demonstrated a dramatic loss of personal episodic memories, whereas her knowledge of semantic aspects of past memories was preserved. This dissociation took place in the context of pervasive damage to her right temporal lobe vs. much more restricted damage to her left temporal lobe. L.D.'s remote memory was evaluated using various tests of autobiographical memory and public events. Her recollection of personal experiences from childhood years was devastated: she was unable to produce any episodic memories of personal events in response to verbal cues or upon directed questioning. Interestingly, L.D. demonstrated better recall of factually based information (e.g. the name of her first grade teacher, the fact that she owned a poodle). However, she was unable to elaborate upon these facts with experiential information. L.D.'s nonverbal memory and visual imaging problems were examined in relation to her pronounced episodic memory impairment. It was hypothesized that L.D.'s nonverbal memory and imaging deficits augmented her autobiographical memory impairment because visual images provide an organizational framework for retrieval of experiential information.

The reverse pattern, a disproportionate loss of semantic knowledge, occurs in the context of mainly left temporal cortex damage. An illustrative case is that of patient L.P., described by De Renzi and colleagues (1987a). Following an episode of encephalitis, L.P. demonstrated greatly impoverished knowledge of the meaning and attributes of words and pictures. She was severely anomic and unable to define or classify either verbal concepts or their pictorial referents, while non-semantic aspects of language and perception were preserved. Her lesion was centered in the anterior inferotemporal cortex. While L.P. demonstrated semantic difficulties for all types of information, other patients have been described with category-specific deficits. Although such category-specific impairments are rare, a number of cases have been described with differential impairments for concrete vs. abstract concepts, and for animate vs. inanimate concepts (for review, see McKenna & Warrington, 2000).

Anoxia

Anoxic brain injury occurs as a result of reduced oxygen to the brain, due to decreased vascular perfusion or reduced oxygen content in the blood. This may be caused by a variety of conditions, such as cardiac arrest or respiratory distress, which in turn may be a result of severe allergic reactions, strangulation or near-drowning episodes. When the brain is deprived of oxygen, excitatory neurotransmitters are released which are accompanied by increased sodium, cell swelling and neuronal damage. Persistent oxygen deprivation leads to neuronal excitation, which results in increased calcium, and to increased free radicals—events that cause significant cell damage (Caine & Watson, 2000). Specific brain areas are vulnerable to anoxic injury, in part due to their physical location and in part due to their biochemical make-up. Peripheral blood vessels are particularly sensitive to reductions in oxygenation (Brierley & Graham, 1984). Also sensitive to damage are areas with high metabolic demands (Moody et al., 1990). In addition, the neurochemical properties of particular areas render them more vulnerable than others to changes in oxygen content. For instance, the hippocampus is vulnerable to oxygen deprivation due to the neurotoxic effects of excessive release of glutamate and aspartate (Caine & Watson, 2000). It is of interest that anoxic damage affects different parts of the brain over different time courses. While the basal ganglia and cerebral cortex are affected shortly after the anoxic event, hippocampal damage may not occur until days after the initial insult (Kuroiwa & Okeda, 1994; Levine & Grek, 1984).

Studies have shown that initial markers of anoxic insult, such as mental status examination, length of coma and laboratory tests, do not necessarily correlate with long-term indices of behavioral outcome and neuropathological change. Hopkins and colleagues (1995) studied three patients who were severely impaired during the early stage of recovery from anoxia but who presented with very different clinical outcomes. A recent review of 58 studies of cerebral anoxia (Caine & Watson, 2000) discussed the range of neuropathological and neuropsychological outcomes associated with this etiology. This review indicated that the watershed zone of the cerebral cortex and basal ganglia structures are the most common sites of damage. Damage to hippocampal structures was also common, although isolated damage to the hippocampus was seen in only 18% of the cases.

One well-documented example of amnesia following anoxia-induced hippocampal damage is that of patient R.B. (Zola-Morgan et al., 1986). R.B.'s clinical presentation was noteworthy for moderate-level learning difficulties alongside mild remote memory loss covering just a few years preceding the anoxic event. Neuropathological studies revealed that R.B. sustained bilateral damage limited to the CA1 area of the hippocampus. Several other cases of amnesia secondary to anoxia have come to autopsy since then (Rempel-Clower et al., 1996). More extensive lesions beyond CA1, but still limited to the hippocampal formation, appear to produce more severe anterograde memory impairment as well as extensive retrograde amnesia covering up to 15 years or more.

Recently, Vargha-Khadem and colleagues (Gadian et al., 2000; Vargha-Khadem et al., 1997) have drawn attention to the fact that anoxic episodes shortly after birth can lead to a relatively selective form of developmental amnesia. Their most recent report concerned a group of five young patients with amnesia, none of whom demonstrated other signs of neurological dysfunction. Detailed imaging studies confirmed selective bilateral hippocampal atrophy in all cases. Neuropsychological test findings revealed that all of the children performed deficiently on tasks of episodic memory, whereas attention, reasoning abilities and visuospatial skills were intact. Strikingly, these children were able to acquire a considerable amount of new semantic knowledge, as indicated by the fact that they were successfully able to attend mainstream schools. Vargha-Khadem et al. (1997) argued that semantic learning was mediated by preserved subhippocampal cortical areas, including entorhinal and perirhinal cortex. We have recently observed a similar, albeit less striking, dissociation between semantic and episodic learning in P.S., a patient with adult-onset amnesia secondary to anoxic injury (Verfaellie et al., 2000). In line with Vargha-Khadem et al., we ascribed this pattern to relative preservation of subhippocampal cortices.

Although there is clear evidence that anoxia-induced amnesia can result from hippocampal damage (e.g. patient R.B.), it is important to note that damage is not always selective and that lesions often extend beyond the hippocampus to involve other brain areas. Markowitsch et al. (1997) studied a patient with anoxia secondary to a heart attack, in whom PET imaging revealed widespread regions of hypoactivity that could not be predicted from the structural neuroimaging findings. In another study, Reed and colleagues (1999) described thalamic hypometabolism in addition to hippocampal atrophy in a group of four hypoxic patients.

As the review by Caine & Watson (2000) indicates, the neuropathology associated with anoxia is often more widespread, involving the basal ganglia, the thalamus, white matter projections and diffuse cortical areas. Accordingly, many patients present with more generalized cognitive deficits. A number of studies have shown that anoxia is associated with significant changes in frontal/executive abilities, so that the individual's capacities for complex attention (i.e. mental tracking and cognitive flexibility), planning and abstract thinking are compromised (Bengtsson et al., 1969; Volpe & Hirst, 1983). Some patients with extensive posterior neocortical damage have shown visual recognition problems, including prosopagnosia and visual object agnosia (Parkin et al., 1987). Although most anoxic patients present with normal language abilities, there are reports of patients who present with name retrieval difficulties (Bengtsson et al., 1969; Parkin et al., 1987). Tranel and colleagues (2000) have described a patient with diminished lexical and semantic knowledge of concrete items. Other possible sequelae of anoxic brain injury are marked changes in personality, with increased emotional lability and irritability (McNeill et al., 1965), reduced capacity for empathy (Reich et al., 1983) or apathy (Parkin et al., 1987).

Wernicke–Korsakoff Syndrome

Patients with Wernicke–Korsakoff Syndrome (WKS) develop amnesia as a result of the convergent effects of chronic alcohol abuse and malnutrition (Victor et al., 1989). The onset of WKS is usually marked by an acute phase in which the patient is disoriented, confused and apathetic, and unable to maintain a coherent conversation. This confusional state is often accompanied by occulomotor problems and ataxia. Traditionally, this triad of neurological signs was a prerequisite for a diagnosis of Wernicke's encephalopathy, but it is now clear that these problems do not necessarily co-occur in a single patient (Harper et al., 1986). More recently, it has been suggested that the diagnosis of Wernicke's encephalopathy should be based on at least two of the following criteria: (a) dietary deficiencies; (b) occulomotor abnormalities; (c) cerebellar dysfunction; and (d) altered mental status (Caine et al., 1997).

Once the acute confusion clears, the patient is typically left with an enduring dense amnesia, characteristic of the Korsakoff stage of the disorder. Although some patients have been described to recover to a premorbid level of functioning, this is a rare occurrence. Because of considerable variability in its presentation, Wernicke's encephalopathy may at times go unrecognized until autopsy (Harper et al., 1986). Indeed, some patients may evolve to the Korsakoff stage of the disorder without clinical evidence of an antecedent Wernicke encephalopathy.

Neuroanatomical studies of WKS patients have highlighted damage in thalamic nuclei, the mammillary bodies and frontal network systems (Mair et al., 1979; Victor et al., 1989). For many years there was a great deal of controversy regarding the relative contributions of damage to specific thalamic nuclei vs. damage to the mammillary bodies in the etiology of amnesia in this patient group. Many studies were confounded by the poor operational criteria for diagnosis of Korsakoff's syndrome and also by use of inadequate control groups. Chronic alcoholism and Wernicke's encephalopathy cause damage to the entire brain (Kril et al., 1997) and may result in neurodegeneration in specific regions, including the basal forebrain, prefrontal cortex, mammillary nuclei and mediodorsal thalamic nuclei (Cullen et al., 1997; Harding et al., 2000). Hence, inclusion of nonamnesic alcoholics and patients with Wernicke's encephalopathy is necessary in order to examine the neural substrates necessary and sufficient to cause amnesia in the Korsakoff group. A recent comparison (Harding et al., 2000) of Korsakoff patients, patients with Wernicke's encephalopathy and nonamnesic alcoholic controls revealed shared pathology in the hypothalamic mammillary nuclei and in the mediodorsal thalamic nuclei. However, neuronal loss in the anterior thalamic nuclei was found only in the Korsakoff group. The authors therefore concluded that damage to the anterior nucleus of the thalamus is necessary for the amnesic disorder in WKS. Although less emphasis has been placed on the role of hippocampal damage in WKS, several studies have documented hippocampal pathology as well (Jernigan et al., 1991; Sullivan, 2001). However, this is not an invariant finding and other investigators have found that WKS patients do not have reduced medial temporal lobe volume (Colchester et al., 2001). In fact, the latter study documented a double dissociation between WKS and HSE patients: WKS patients demonstrated reduced volume in thalamic structures but no significant atrophy in medial temporal lobe structures, whereas HSE patients showed the reverse pattern.

Patients with WKS amnesia have profound and global learning difficulties that have been viewed as a consequence of increased sensitivity to interference. Patients are able to repeat information in the absence of any delay, but given distracting activity for as little as 9 s, performance can be markedly impaired. Some information may be learned on an initial learning trial, but on subsequent trials marked deficits occur because of interference from information that was presented earlier. Historically, several explanations were proposed for this sensitivity to interference. Butters & Cermak (1980) emphasized the role of superficial and deficient encoding strategies. When left to their own devices, WKS patients process the phonemic and structural aspects of incoming information, rather than more meaningful semantic attributes (Biber et al., 1981; Cermak & Reale, 1978). Others pointed to patients' inability to inhibit competition from irrelevant material at the time of retrieval (Warrington & Weiskrantz, 1970, 1973). More recently, a consensus has emerged that considers the interaction between encoding and retrieval processes as being critical for a full understanding of WKS patients' learning deficit (Verfaellie & Cermak, 1991).

In addition to anterograde amnesia, WKS patients present with a severe retrograde amnesia that is "temporally graded", in that memories from the more recent decades (leading up to the onset of WKS) are more severely affected than very remote memories. There has been controversy regarding the cause of this temporally graded retrograde amnesia. Some investigators conjectured that social deprivation and deficient learning of information in the decades leading up to the onset of WKS contributed to the pattern of impairment (Albert et al., 1981; Cohen & Squire, 1981). However, this interpretation was called into question by the study of P.Z. (Butters & Cermak, 1986), an eminent scientist who had just completed his autobiography prior to the onset of WKS. P.Z.'s writings and his daily log provided comprehensive records regarding his experiences and his knowledge of events that occurred a short while before the onset of his amnesia. P.Z. demonstrated a temporally graded loss for material mentioned in his autobiography. Likewise, he showed a temporally graded loss for knowledge of scientific information that he clearly knew before the onset of amnesia, as indicated by his publications and lecture notes. Thus, it was certain that P.Z.'s temporally graded retrograde amnesia was not due to progressive anterograde memory loss secondary to alcohol abuse. Instead, it was suggested that this pattern might be due to the fact that information from different time periods taps qualitatively different forms of memory. Information from the recent past, which is still anchored in time and space, may tap primarily episodic memory, whereas remote information, which has been rehearsed more frequently, may tap primarily semantic memory. According to this view, a temporally graded pattern would suggest that episodic memories are more vulnerable to disruption in WKS than are semantic memories. Recent evidence, however, suggests that memory for semantic information acquired prior to the onset of amnesia is also impaired in WKS and shows a similar temporal gradient (Verfaellie et al., 1995b). It appears, therefore, that more recent memories, regardless of their episodic or semantic nature, are more vulnerable to disruption than are more remote memories.

We have followed a group of over 20 WKS patients over the last two decades. All of them had significant anterograde amnesia that undermined their management of daily affairs. All demonstrated greatly impaired performance on standard tasks of delayed recall and recognition. However, we have observed variability among patients with regard to how quickly information is lost from memory. Most patients showed deficits on tasks of working memory, such as the Brown–Peterson paradigm (i.e. recall of three items over 0–18 s distractor intervals), whereas several WKS patients demonstrated superior performance on this task. Even though recall has been invariably deficient in our WKS group, in some patients recognition has benefited considerably from extended exposure. Patients have also varied with respect to other aspects of their neuropsychological profiles, such as confabulation, perseveration and executive dysfunction. These latter tendencies are likely linked to frontal brain damage. Whether these tendencies are central features of the WKS syndrome or whether they represent additive neurotoxic effects of alcohol is not certain. Our group of WKS patients vary markedly in their social and psychological dispositions. Many are prone to apathy and low motivation, problems that compound their memory deficits. In addition, there is a great deal of heterogeneity with respect to general intellectual abilities—many, but not all, WKS patients are from educationally deprived backgrounds. Limited academic exposure may confound assessment of baseline intelligence.

Cerebrovascular Accidents

Bilateral posterior cerebral artery (PCA) infarction is a well-recognized cause of amnesia. Because the left and right PCA's originate from a common source, strokes in the posterior circulation system often affect the temporal lobes bilaterally (including the posterior aspect of the hippocampal complex) and may result in severe memory deficits (Benson et al., 1974). Neuroanatomical studies of patients who have suffered PCA infarctions have underscored lesions in the posterior parahippocampus or collateral isthmus (a pathway connecting the posterior parahippocampus to association cortex) as critical in the memory disturbance (Von Cramon et al., 1988). When the lesion extends posteriorly to include occipitotemporal cortices, deficits beyond amnesia are often seen.

As far back as 1900 a patient was described who exhibited severe memory loss in association with bilateral infarction of the PCA (Bechterew, 1900). Since then numerous case reports have documented significant memory disturbances in patients who have suffered similar damage (Benson et al., 1974; Victor et al., 1961). In the early phase of recovery from PCA infarction, patients present with global confusion. This may subsequently resolve into an isolated amnesic syndrome or may be associated with other neuropsychological deficits, such as visual field defects, alexia, color agnosia and anomia (Benson et al., 1974). The memory disturbance of these patients adheres to the classic amnesic profile of consolidation deficits in the context of normal working memory and normal intelligence. Some PCA patients have retrograde memory problems but this is not an invariant feature of the syndrome. Some patients who have suffered PCA infarctions have presented with unusual memory problems. Ross (1980) described the neuropsychological profiles of two patients who sustained bilateral PCA strokes, both of whom had isolated deficits in the domain of visual memory. Their memory for tactile, verbal and nonverbal auditory information remained intact. Imaging studies revealed that both patients had sustained bilateral occipital lobe infarctions and bilateral lesions involving deep white matter in occipital and temporal lobes. Neither patient had lesions in medial temporal areas. The patients' sensory-specific amnesic syndromes were viewed as a consequence of a disconnection between striate cortices involved in visual processing and temporal brain regions involved in learning and memory.

While the majority of cases of amnesia secondary to infarction have involved bilateral hippocampal damage, memory problems have also been described in association with unilateral (primarily left) PCA infarction (Geschwind & Fusillo, 1966; Mohr et al., 1971; Ott & Saver, 1993; Von Cramon et al., 1988). In some of the unilateral PCA patients, the memory deficit has been transient (Geschwind & Fusillo, 1966), whereas permanent memory loss has been present in others (Mohr et al., 1971). Though many of these patients have been labeled "amnesic", there is scant documentation of the extent and nature of their memory problems. Many investigations of patients who sustained unilateral PCA infarction have failed to assess both verbal and nonverbal memory and have not included tests sensitive to rate of forgetting. Consequently, it has been difficult to determine whether the memory deficits of unilateral PCA patients are qualitatively and quantitatively similar to those of other amnesic patients.

One of the more comprehensive studies of patients with left PCA infarction was conducted by De Renzi and colleagues (1987b), who described the neuropsychological profile of 16 PCA patients with damage to left occipitotemporal brain areas. These patients presented with pure alexia, visual naming problems and verbal amnesia. The reading and naming problems were attributed to a disconnection of posterior (occipital) regions from left hemisphere language zones. The most common problem encountered by these patients was verbal amnesia, presumably related to damage in left medial temporal areas. The mnestic abilities of right PCA patients have not been well studied. Von Cramon and colleagues (1988) noted that verbal memory remained intact in 10 right PCA patients, whereas the visual processing abilities of these patients were impaired. Tests of visual memory were not administered as part of the study. Likewise, Goldenberg & Artner (1991) reported that unilateral right PCA infarction may be associated with perceptual discrimination problems but the memory abilities of the patients were not examined.

Thalamic strokes have also been associated with amnesia, although the severity of the memory deficit varies in relation to the site of damage within the thalamus (Graff-Radford et al., 1990; Von Cramon et al., 1985). The small size and close proximity of thalamic nuclei (Jones, 1985) limits analyses based on lesion location. Nonetheless, some conditions, such as lacunar infarctions, result in more spatially restricted lesions in the thalamus, and therefore provide valuable information regarding the differential contributions of specific thalamic nuclei in memory processes.

A recent review (Van der Werf et al., 2000) of 60 patients who sustained damage to the thalamus as a result of infarctions revealed that damage to the mammillo–thalamic tract (MTT) was necessary and sufficient for anterograde amnesia. Since this tract contains fibers bound for the anterior thalamic nucleus, it is to be expected that infarctions that directly affect the anterior nucleus can produce similar deficits.

Others have focused on the role of the medial dorsal nucleus in the memory disturbance of patients who have suffered thalamic strokes. Several patients have been described who demonstrated amnesia following discrete medial dorsal lesions (Isaac et al., 2000; Speedie & Heilman, 1982, 1983), but in other cases of medial dorsal damage, no evidence of a memory impairment was apparent (Kritchevsky et al., 1987; Von Cramon et al., 1985). Based on their review, Van der Werf et al. (2000) concluded that medial dorsal lesions may lead to mild memory disturbances, but that severe amnesia is typically associated with lesions that extend beyond the medial dorsal nucleus to include the MTT or anterior nucleus.

As is to be expected, thalamic amnesia shares many characteristics with the amnesia associated with Korsakoff's syndrome. Patients demonstrate a severe anterograde memory deficit, characterized by increased sensitivity to interference. Impairments in executive functioning frequently accompany the mnestic disturbance (Isaac et al., 2000; Pepin & Auray-Pepin, 1993; Speedie & Heilman, 1982). Deficits in retrograde amnesia also occur in conjunction with thalamic amnesia, but studies have shown that there is variability with respect to the persistence and extent of remote memory loss. In some thalamic patients, retrograde amnesia was seen during the early phases of recovery, but this subsequently resolved (Kapur et al., 1996; Winocur et al., 1984). In other patients, more severe, persistent retrograde deficits were observed (Hodges & McCarthy, 1993; Stuss et al., 1988). Material-specific memory deficits have also been described in association with unilateral thalamic stroke: left-sided damage results in memory deficits on tasks of verbal learning (Sandson et al., 1991; Speedie & Heilman, 1982), whereas right-sided thalamic damage results in nonverbal/visual memory difficulties (Speedie & Heilman, 1983).

Aneurysm Rupture of the Anterior Communicating Artery (ACoA)

Intracranial aneurysms throughout the circle of Willis can result in severe memory problems (Richardson, 1989) but most of the neuropsychological studies over the past few decades have focused on patients who develop amnesia secondary to anterior communicating artery (AcoA) aneuryms. The ACoA and its branches perfuse the basal forebrain, the anterior cingulate, the anterior hypothalamus, the anterior columns of the fornix, the anterior commissure and the genu of the corpus callosum. The behavioral deficits observed following ACoA aneurysm may be a result of infarction, either directly or secondary to subarachnoid hemorrhage, vasospasm and hematoma formation (Alexander & Freedman, 1984; Damasio et al., 1985b).

Because of the various neuropathological sequelae, the cognitive disorders resulting from rupture of ACoA aneurysms are more variable than those seen following diencephalic or medial temporal damage and may be more global in nature (for review, see DeLuca & Diamond, 1995). Nonetheless, memory deficits are often the primary presenting symptom and may range from relatively mild impairments to significant amnesia. Here, we focus on the moderate to severe end of the spectrum of memory disorders to facilitate comparison with other subtypes of amnesia.

In the acute phase of the disorder, patients typically present with a severe confusional state and gross attentional disturbances. When the confusional state clears, significant deficits in new learning become apparent. Patients may be disoriented to time, and there is often a severe retrograde amnesia that appears temporally graded. Confabulation and lack of insight may also occur, especially in patients with additional frontal lobe lesions (D'Esposito et al., 1996; DeLuca, 1993). D'Esposito et al. (1996) observed that executive dysfunction in the early stages of illness was much greater in patients whose lesion extended into the medial frontal lobes than in those whose lesion was restricted to the basal forebrain. Additionally, patients with frontal lesions had more severe retrograde amnesia. Their executive dysfunction and remote memory loss improved significantly by 3 months post-onset, but remained worse than that seen in patients with focal basal forebrain lesions. Anterograde memory loss, however, persisted in both groups and was of equal severity.

During the chronic phase, most patients show preserved immediate memory, as measured by Digit Span Forwards (e.g. Delbecq-Derouesne et al., 1990; DeLuca, 1992; Parkin et al., 1988), but working memory deficits are not uncommon. Several studies have documented impaired performance on the Brown–Peterson distractor paradigm (Corkin et al., 1985; Delbecq-Derouesne et al., 1990; DeLuca, 1992; Parkin et al., 1988; Talland et al., 1967). This impairment may be due to a susceptibility to interference that affects both working memory and long-term memory performance.

The anterograde memory performance of ACoA patients is characterized by severe deficits in recall, especially following a delay, while performance on recognition tasks is often much better preserved. Volpe & Hirst (1983) first drew attention to this pattern, and it has been confirmed in several subsequent studies (Beeckmans et al., 1998; Hanley et al., 1994; Parkin et al., 1988). The disproportionate impairment in recall reflects a disruption of strategic search processes that enable access to information stored in memory.

Not all ACoA patients, however, show a sparing of recognition memory. Particularly striking is the report by Derousne-Delbecque et al. (1990) of a patient whose recognition memory was more severely impaired than his recall. This pattern arose because of the patient's high tendency to produce false alarms in recognition tests. Since then, a number of other patients have been described who show pathological levels of false recognition (Beeckmans et al., 1998; Parkin et al., 1990; Rapscak et al., 1998). This problem is thought to reflect a disruption in the processes that evaluate the outcome of a memory search.

Strategic memory processes are not only important for memory retrieval; they also support adequate encoding of information. In light of the "executive" nature of the memory impairment seen in ACoA patients, it is not surprising to see evidence of inefficient encoding as well. In at least some cases, however, patients' encoding can be supported by the use of strategies. For instance, Parkin et al. (1988) described a patient who performed very poorly when asked to learn paired associates by rote, but whose performance was dramatically improved when given instructions to use imagery to aid encoding. Along the same lines, Diamond et al. (1997) found that in a subgroup of ACoA patients, recall of the Rey Complex Figure could be greatly enhanced by providing an organizational strategy for encoding details of the figure.

ACoA patients also exhibit striking contextual memory deficits. Several studies have demonstrated disproportionate deficits in spatial memory (Mayes et al., 1991; Shoqeirat & Mayes, 1991) and in memory for source (Parkin et al., 1988). Deficits in temporal tagging have also been emphasized (Damasio et al, 1985b; Ptak & Schnider, 1999). Whether these deficits are part of a core basal forebrain amnesia or result from associated frontal deficits remains unclear at present.

It has been difficult to isolate the minimal lesion necessary to cause amnesia in ACoA patients, in part because of clip artifact during scanning. Irle and colleagues (1992) suggested that lesions extending beyond the basal forebrain to include the striatum or frontal regions were necessary to cause amnesia. A number of studies, however, have documented severe amnesia in patients with circumscribed basal forebrain lesions. In several cases lesions have been centered in the septal nuclei (Alexander & Freedman, 1984; Von Cramon et al., 1993) but the nucleus accumbens has also been implicated (Goldenberg et al., 1999). Because several basal forebrain nuclei contain a large number of cholinergic neurons that innervate the hippocampus as well as large sectors of neocortex, the amnesia of ACoA patients may be due, at least in some cases, to disruption of hippocampal functioning caused by basal forebrain damage (Volpe et al., 1984).

SUBTYPES OF AMNESIA

Amnesic patients present with a variety of medical and psychosocial conditions. One approach to dealing with this variability has been to search for specific patterns of memory loss in relation to etiology of amnesia or location of neural damage. A number of investigators have compared the amnesic profiles of patients classified according to site of neural damage (Butters et al., 1984; Huppert & Piercy, 1979; Lhermitte & Signoret, 1972). These early studies suggested that distinct profiles of amnesia were associated with damage in diencephalic and medial temporal brain areas. Patients with diencephalic amnesia were described as having tendencies toward superficial and inefficient encoding, confabulation, diminished insight, sensitivity to interference, and temporally graded retrograde amnesia. Patients with medial temporal amnesia were described as having consolidation deficits, intact insight, lack of confabulation, and limited retrograde amnesia. Studies of patients with basal forebrain amnesia revealed that they displayed many of the same characteristics as the diencephalic group, including limited insight, confabulation, sensitivity to interference, and remote memory problems (DeLuca, 1992; O'Connor et al., 1995).

Despite initial acceptance of amnesia subtypes, questions arose as to whether there were consistent differences in the pattern of memory loss associated with various etiological subgroups (Weiskrantz, 1985). Within the domain of working memory, several studies compared the performance of patients with medial temporal lesions to that of diencephalic patients on the Brown–Peterson task. Leng & Parkin (1988, 1989) found that patients with diencephalic lesions showed disproportionate deficits on this task, but their poor performance was linked to frontal involvement. On the other hand, Kopelman & Stanhope (1997) found no differences on the Brown–Peterson test in their comparison of diencephalic, medial temporal and frontal patients. Hence, differences in the ability to maintain information within working memory did not appear to represent a core distinction between amnesic subtypes.

Within the domain of long-term memory, one area in which differences between groups were initially observed concerns rate of forgetting. Several studies demonstrated that medial temporal patients forget at a faster rate than diencephalic patients (Huppert & Piercy, 1979; Squire, 1981). However, these findings have not stood up to scrutiny (Freed et al., 1987; Kopelman & Stanhope, 1997; McKee & Squire, 1992) and it is now generally accepted that forgetting from long-term memory does not differentiate medial temporal and diencephalic amnesics.

Profiles of retrograde amnesia have also been examined in relation to etiological distinctions. Early studies suggested that diencephalic and medial temporal amnesics differed substantially on tasks of remote memory. Diencephalic patients were described as having extensive "temporally-graded" retrograde amnesia, characterized by relative preservation of early memories (Albert et al., & Levin, 1979; Kopelman, 1989), whereas the retrograde amnesia of the medial temporal group was described as limited (Milner, 1966; Zola-Morgan et al., 1986). More recent studies have indicated significant variability within diencephalic and medial temporal subgroups with respect to the severity and nature of remote memory loss (Kopelman et al., 1999). Patients with focal damage to diencephalic structures secondary to tumors, vascular causes and irradiation have only brief (i.e. less than 3 years) or no remote memory loss, in contrast to WKS patients, who have extensive retrograde amnesia. Within the medial temporal group, some patients have been described who have brief retrograde loss in the context of circumscribed damage to medial temporal structures (Zola-Morgan et al., 1986), whereas more extensive retrograde amnesia has been associated with widespread pathology in bitemporal brain regions (Rempel-Clower et al., 1996).

A number of issues confound comparisons across etiological groups. One of these concerns the fact that some patients have concomitant damage to brain structures that, although not part of the core neural system mediating memory, may nonetheless affect performance on memory tasks. For instance, in patients with WKS, the extensive retrograde amnesia has been attributed to additional frontal pathology, which may contribute to generalized deficits in memory retrieval (Kopelman, 1991; Kopelman et al., 1999). Likewise, frontal damage may explain some of the qualitative differences in performance on new learning tasks in WKS or basal forebrain amnesics compared to medial temporal amnesics. Two studies from our group serve to illustrate this phenomenon. In one study, we (Kixmiller et al., 1995) compared the occurrence of intrusion errors on the Visual Reproduction subtest of the WMS-R among medial temporal amnesics, Korsakoff patients and ACoA patients. Korsakoff patients showed much higher intrusion rates than medial temporal patients. Further, high intrusion rates were also seen in ACoA patients, but only when patients were tested after a delay, when their memory became more clearly depressed. We concluded that the occurrence of intrusions is linked to a combination of severe memory deficits and frontal dysfunction; neither deficit in isolation is sufficient to cause high rates of intrusion errors.

In a second study, Kixmiller et al., (2000) compared the performance of the same three subgroups on the Rey Osterrieth Complex Figure. Even though the Korsakoff patients and medial temporal amnesics were matched in terms of overall severity of amnesia, Korsakoff patients' delayed recall was strikingly worse than that of the medial temporal group. This was ascribed, at least in part, to visual-perceptual and organizational deficits exhibited by the Korsakoff group—deficits that compounded their severe amnesia.

The above studies indicate that nonobligatory frontal deficits in some amnesic patients may account for observed disparities in the memory profile of different etiological groups. Another issue that complicates subtype comparisons concerns selection criteria influencing referral to a memory clinic. In some cases, etiology of amnesia (e.g. a diagnosis of WKS) precipitates such a referral; in other cases, behavioral evidence of significant memory loss may be the reason for referral. Differences in selection factors may influence the nature and severity of the memory deficit exhibited by each etiological group. In addition, it is often the case that subtype comparisons are flawed by between-group differences in level of intelligence. It is well known that intelligence influences performance on a broad array of neuropsychological measures; baseline intellectual abilities may distort the profile of strengths and deficits exhibited by each group.

Table 7.1 Summary of neuropsycholgical characteristics of amnesic patients with medial-temporal (n = 10), diencephalic (n = 10), and basal forebrain (n = 10) damage

| Group | WAIS-R[1] | | WMS-R[2] | | RMT[3] | | BNT[4] | WCST[5] | |
	VIQ	PIQ	Logical Memory I	Logical Memory II	Words	Faces		Categories (n)	Pers. errors (%)
Medial-temporal	103	107	19	3	33	33	52	5	20
Diencephalic	99	100	17	1	34	33	53	5	19
Basal Forebrain	102	103	16	2	37	35	56	4	29

[1] Wechsler Adult Intelligence Scale—Revised.
[2] Wechsler Memory Scale—Revised.
[3] Recognition Memory Test.
[4] Boston Naming Test.
[5] Wisconsin Card Sorting Test.

To examine the memory profiles of different groups of patients while controlling for level of intelligence, we recently reviewed clinical data from 30 patients, selected on the basis of IQ, from a larger group of amnesics at the Memory Disorders Research Center (Table 7.1). Using a traditional lesion-based approach, we compared medial temporal amnesics (i.e. patients with diverse etiologies, such as encephalitis, stroke and anoxia), diencephalic amnesics (i.e. Korsakoff patients) and basal forebrain amnesics (i.e. patients with ACoA aneurysms). All patients underwent comprehensive neuropsychological evaluations and all performed normally on tests of language skills and general reasoning abilities. As we expected, when groups were matched for IQ, their performance on many clinical tests of memory was similar. All three groups demonstrated equivalent forgetting of information from working memory (e.g. recall of items on the Brown Peterson paradigm) and from long-term memory (e.g. delayed recall and recognition of prose stories, word lists, etc.). Analysis of performance on tests of retrograde amnesia (e.g. the Famous Faces Test and the Transient Events Test) also revealed striking similarities across groups. All three groups demonstrated sparse recall and recognition of events from the last three decades and all demonstrated evidence of mild temporal gradients. Because diencephalic and basal forebrain groups often have frontal involvement, we expected that these groups might demonstrate heightened tendencies towards false-positive errors on tests of recognition memory, but this did not turn out to be the case. All groups demonstrated similar rates of false alarms.

Our comparison of amnesic groups suggests that the pattern of performance is largely similar among patients who are matched for baseline intelligence when tests are used that focus on quantitative aspects of performance (i.e. amount of information retained) rather than specific processing strategies. Aside from these clinical comparisons, several studies have compared the performance of medial temporal and diencephalic amnesics on experimental paradigms in an attempt to identify information processing domains in which these subgroups may differ. Most prominently, Parkin and colleagues have suggested that medial temporal and diencephalic amnesics differ in their memory for the temporal context in which target information is presented. In one study (Parkin et al., 1990) they found that diencephalic amnesics performed worse than medial temporal patients on a recognition task that required the encoding of distinctive temporal context to distinguish which stimuli were targets or distractors on any given trial. In another study (Hunkin et al., 1994) they found that diencephalic patients performed worse on a list discrimination task than medial temporal patients, even though their recognition memory was similarly impaired. Although in several studies, memory for temporal context has been linked to frontal dysfunction (Shimamura et al., 1990; Squire, 1982), in neither of the studies by Parkin and colleagues did performance on the temporal memory tasks correlate with performance on frontal tasks. Furthermore, similar impairments in temporal memory were observed in two patients with diencephalic lesions who showed no evidence of impairment on tasks of executive functioning (Parkin et al., 1994; Parkin & Hunkin, 1993). Based on these findings, Parkin and colleagues suggested that amnesics with diencephalic damage present with a qualitatively distinct memory deficit from that seen in amnesics with medial temporal lobe damage. According to their view, structures within the diencephalon, possibly through connections with dorsolateral frontal cortex, may be critically involved in the encoding of temporal information. In the face of diencephalic lesions, contextual input to the hippocampal system is greatly (and selectively) impoverished. In contrast, lesions of the hippocampal system are thought to interfere with consolidation of all types of information, contextual as well as item-related.

More recently, Kopelman et al. (1997) have directly compared memory for temporal and spatial context in patients with medial temporal and diencephalic lesions. Their findings for temporal context were generally consistent with those of Parkin, in that diencephalic patients performed worse than medial temporal patients. The inverse pattern was observed with respect to spatial (position) memory, where the medial temporal group performed worse than the diencephalic group. The latter finding was seen as support for the idea that the hippocampus plays a pivotal role in spatial memory (see also Chalfonte et al., 1996).

Despite reports of some differences between diencephalic and medial temporal amnesic patients, the similarities in the cognitive presentation of these patient groups are striking. Some researchers have argued that these commonalities are to be expected because the medial temporal and diencephalic structures are part of the same functional system required for the encoding of episodic information (Delay & Brion, 1969). Recently, Aggleton & Brown (1999) have argued that the core structures within this system are the hippocampus, fornix, mammillary bodies, anterior thalamus and possibly, more diffusely, the cingulum bundle and prefrontal cortex. According to their model, lesions anywhere in this system can cause deficits in episodic memory. More specifically, these deficits arise because of this system's role in linking target information to the spatial and temporal context that give an event its uniquely episodic character. Aggleton & Brown also postulate the existence of a second memory system, consisting of the perirhinal cortex and its connections to the medial dorsal thalamus. This system is thought to be involved in the detection of stimulus familiarity, a process that can support performance on recognition tasks, but not on recall tasks.

The notion that there are two medial temporal–diencephalic memory circuits that make qualitatively distinct contributions to memory leads to the prediction that patients with lesions restricted to the hippocampal circuit should have normal or near-normal item recognition memory. Aggleton & Shaw (1996) provided evidence in support of this view in a meta-analysis of studies in which the Recognition Memory Test (Warrington, 1984) was given to amnesic patients. They found that patients with lesions restricted to the hippocampus, fornix or mammillary bodies performed at a normal level, even though their recall was as severely impaired as was that of patients with more extensive medial temporal lesions.

A number of other reports of preserved recognition memory in patients with lesions to the hippocampal circuit provide further support for this view. These include several studies of patients with selective fornix lesions (Hodges & Carpenter, 1991; McMakin et al., 1995), a report of three young children who suffered relatively selective hippocampal damage due to anoxic injury early in life (Vargha-Khadem et al., 1997), and the study of a patient with adult-onset selective bilateral hippocampal injury (Mayes et al., in press). Findings in the latter case are especially striking, as the patient was tested on a very extensive battery of recognition tests that varied the nature of to-be-remembered information, list length, retention interval and task difficulty.

Despite this evidence, the notion that different memory circuits subserve qualitatively distinct memory processes remains highly controversial. An alternative view, articulated most forcefully by Squire and colleagues (Squire & Zola, 1998; Zola & Squire, 2000), is that the hippocampus is important not only for recall but also for recognition. By this view, differences between patients with selective hippocampal lesions and more extensive medial temporal lobe lesions are only a matter of severity. Supporting this notion are findings from three patients with selective hippocampal lesions (Reed & Squire, 1997), who showed moderate levels of impairment not only in recall but also in recognition.

In an attempt to reconcile the report by Reed & Squire of impaired recognition following selective hippocampal damage with their own findings of preserved recognition, Mayes and colleagues (in press) have pointed to the possibility of hidden extra-hippocampal damage in Reed & Squire's patients. Further, they raise the possibility that partial damage to the hippocampus may disrupt the functioning of connected structures (such as the perirhinal cortex) more than complete damage. Another possibility, until now not considered, is that the location of lesion within the hippocampus affects the pattern of deficit. Clearly, a resolution of this debate will require convergent evidence from animal and human studies. In this context, careful analysis of patients with selective lesions to the hippocampal circuit, using state-of-the-art measures of structural integrity as well as indices of metabolic activity, will be of great importance.

CONCLUSION

Over the past four decades we have learned a great deal about the diversity of etiologies that may result in amnesia. Initial attempts to classify patients according to site of neuropathology in medial temporal, diencephalic and basal forebrain regions seemed promising, but subsequent investigations revealed that much of the variability between patients was due to extraneous factors rather than core features of the memory disorder. Recent clinical comparisons have emphasized similarities in the neuropsychological profiles of amnesic subgroups. Experimental studies focused on isolated aspects of information processing have revealed only subtle differences between these groups. Against this background, the current emphasis on differentiating the role of specific regions within the medial temporal lobe and its afferents may lead to a more useful framework for patient classification. Regardless of whether this framework turns out to be correct, detailed description of the anatomical and cognitive characteristics of amnesic patients remains an important endeavor. Such studies may lead to better clinical diagnosis and treatment of patients with memory disorders and may contribute a unique source of information to the cognitive neuroscience of memory.

ACKNOWLEDGEMENTS

Preparation of this chapter was supported by Program Project Grant NS 26985 from the National Institute of Neurological Disorders and Stroke and by the Medical Research Service of the U.S. Department of Veterans Affairs.

REFERENCES

Aggleton, J.P. & Brown, M.W. (1999). Episodic memory, amnesia, and the hippocampal–anterior thalamic axis. *Behavioral and Brain Sciences*, **22**, 425–489.

Aggleton, J.P. & Shaw, C. (1996). Amnesia and recognition memory: a re-analysis of psychometric data. *Neuropsychologia*, **34**, 51–62.

Albert, M., Butters, N. & Brandt, J. (1981). Patterns of remote memory in amnesic and demented patients. *Archives of Neurology*, **38**, 495–500.

Albert, M., Butters, N. & Levin, J. (1979). Temporal gradients in the retrograde amnesia of patients with alcoholic Korsakoff's disease. *Archives of Neurology*, **36**, 211–216.

Alexander, M.P. & Freedman, M. (1984). Amnesia after anterior communicating artery rupture. *Neurology*, **34**, 752–759.

Bechterew, W. (1900). Demonstration eines Gehirnes mit Zerstorung der vorderen und inneren Theile der Hirnrinde beider Schlafenlappen. *Neurologisches Zentraltblatt*, **19**, 990–991.

Beeckmans, K., Vancoillie, P. & Michiels, K. (1998). Neuropsychological deficits in patients with an anterior communicating artery syndrome: a multiple case study. *Acta Neurologica Belgica*, **98**, 266–278.

Bengtsson, M., Holmberg, S. & Jansson, B. (1969). A psychiatric–psychological investigation of patients who had survived circulatory arrest. *Acta Scandinavica Psychiatrica*, **45**, 327–346.

Benson, D., Marsden, C. & Meadows, J. (1974). The amnesic syndrome of posterior cerebral artery occlusion. *Acta Neurologica Scandinavia*, **50**, 133–145.

Biber, C., Butters, N., Rosen, J. et al. (1981). Encoding strategies and recognition of faces by alcoholic Korsakoff and other brain damaged patients. *Journal of Clinical Neuropsychology*, **3**, 315–330.

Brierley, J.B. & Graham, D.I. (1984). Hypoxia and vascular disorders of the central nervous system. In W. Blackwood & J. A. N. Corsellis (eds), *Greenfield's Neuropathology* (pp. 125–207). London: Edward Arnold.

Butters, N. & Cermak, L.S. (1980). *Alcoholic Korsakoff's Syndrome: An Information Processing Approach*. New York: Academic Press.

Butters, N. & Cermak, L.S. (1986). A case study of the forgetting of autobiographical knowledge: implications for the study of retrograde amnesia. In D. Rubin (ed.), *Autobiographical Memory* (pp. 253–272). New York: Cambridge University Press.

Butters, N., Miliotis, P., Albert, M. & Sax, D. (1984). Memory assessment: evidence of the heterogeneity of amnesic symptoms. *Advances in Clinical Neuropsychology*, **1**, 127–159.

Caine, D., Halliday, G., Kril, J. & Harper, C. (1997). Operational criteria for the classification of chronic alcoholics: identification of Wernicke's encephalopathy. *Journal of Neurology, Neurosurgery and Psychiatry*, **62**, 51–60.

Caine, D. & Watson, D.G. (2000). Neuropsychological and neuropathological sequelae of cerebral anoxia: a critical review. *Journal of the International Neuropsychological Society*, **6**, 86–99.

Cave, C. & Squire, L. (1992). Intact and long-lasting repetition priming in amnesia. *Journal of Experimental Psychology: Learning, Memory and Cognition*, **1992**, 509–520.

Cermak, L.S. (1976). The encoding capacity of a patient with amnesia due to encephalitis. *Neuropsychologia*, **14**, 311–326.

Cermak, L.S. & Reale, L. (1978). Depth of processing and retention of words by alcoholic Korsakoff patients. *Journal of Experimental Psychology: Human Learning and Memory*, **4**, 165–174.

Cermak, L.S. & O'Connor, M.G. (1983). The anterograde and retrograde retrieval ability of a patient with amnesia due to encephalitis. *Neuropsychologia*, **21**, 213–234.

Chalfonte, B.L., Verfaellie, M., Johnson, M.K. & Reiss, L. (1996). Spatial location memory in amnesia: binding item and location information under incidental and intentional encoding conditions. *Memory*, **4**, 591–614.

Cohen, N. & Squire, L. (1981). Retrograde amnesia and remote memory impairment. *Neuropsychologia*, **19**, 337–356.

Colchester, A., Kingsley, D., Lasserson, B. et al. (2001). Structural MRI volumetric analysis in patients with organic amnesia, 1: methods and comparative findings across diagnostic groups. *Journal of Neurology, Neurosurgery and Psychiatry*, **71**, 13–22.

Corkin, S., Cohen, N.J., Sullivan, E.V. et al. (1985). Analyses of global memory impairments of different etiologies. *Annals of the New York Academy of Sciences*, **444**, 10–40.

Cullen, K.M., Halliday, G.M., Caine, D. & Kril, J.J. (1997). The nucleus basalis (Ch4) in the alcoholic Wernicke–Korsakoff syndrome: reduced cell number in both amnesic and non-amnesic patients. *Journal of Neurology, Neurosurgery and Psychiatry*, **63**, 315–320.

D'Esposito, M., Alexander, M.P., Fisher, R. et al. (1996). Recovery of memory and executive function following anterior communicating artery aneurysm rupture. *Journal of the International Neuropsychological Society*, **2**, 565–570.

Damasio, A.R., Eslinger, P.J., Damasio, H. et al. (1985a). Multi-modal amnesic syndrome following bilateral temporal and frontal damage: the case of patient D.R.B. *Archives of Neurology*, **42**, 252–259.

Damasio, A.R., Graff-Radford, N.R., Eslinger, P.J. et al. (1985b). Amnesia following basal forebrain lesions. *Archives of Neurology*, **42**, 263–271.

Damasio, A.R. & Van Hoesen, G.W. (1985). The limbic system and the localisation of herpes simplex encephalitis. *Journal of Neurology, Neurosurgery and Psychiatry*, **48**, 297–301.

De Renzi, E., Liotti, M. & Nichelli, P. (1987a). Semantic amnesia with preservation of autobiographical memory: a case report. *Cortex*, **23**, 575–597.

De Renzi, E., Zambolin, A. & Crisi, G. (1987b). The pattern of neuropsychological impairment associated with left posterior cerebral artery infarcts. *Brain*, **110**, 1099–1116.

Delay, J. & Brion, S. (1969). *Le Syndrome de Korsakoff*. Paris: Masson.

Delbecq-Derouesne, J., Beauvois, M.F. & Shallice, T. (1990). Preserved recall versus impaired recognition. *Brain*, **113**, 1045–1074.

DeLuca, J. (1992). Cognitive dysfunction after aneurysm of the anterior communicating artery. *Journal of Clinical and Experimental Neuropsychology*, **14**, 924–934.

DeLuca, J. (1993). Predicting neurobehavioral patterns following anterior communicating artery aneurysm. *Cortex*, **29**, 639–647.

DeLuca, J. & Diamond, B.J. (1995). Aneurysm of the anterior communicating artery: a review of neuroanatomical and neuropsychological sequelae. *Journal of Clinical and Experimental Neuropsychology*, **17**, 100–121.

Diamond, B.J., DeLuca, J. & Kelley, S.M. (1997). Memory and executive functions in amnesic and non-amnesic patients with aneurysms of the anterior communicating artery. *Brain*, **120**, 1015–1025.

Eslinger, P.J., Damasio, H., Damasio, A.R. & Butters, N. (1993). Nonverbal amnesia and asymmetric cerebral lesions following encephalitis. *Brain and Cognition*, **21**, 140–152.

Freed, D.M., Corkin, S. & Cohen, N.J. (1987). Forgetting in HM: a second look. *Neuropsychologia*, **25**, 461–471.

Gabrieli, J.D.E. (1999). The architecture of human memory. In J. K. Foster & M. Jelicic (eds), *Memory: Systems, Process or Function?* (pp. 205–231). Oxford: Oxford University Press.

Gadian, D., Aicari, J., Watkins, K. et al. (2000). Developmental amnesia associated with early hypoxic–ischemic injury. *Brain*, **123**, 499–507.

Geschwind, N. & Fusillo, M. (1966). Color naming defects in association with alexia. *Archives of Neurology*, **15**, 137–146.

Goldenberg, G. & Artner, C. (1991). Visual imagery and knowledge about the visual appearance of objects in patients with posterior cerebral lesions. *Brain and Cognition*, **15**, 160–186.

Goldenberg, G., Schuri, U., Gromminger, O. & Arnold, U. (1999). Basal forebrain amnesia: does the nucleus accumbens contribute to human memory? *Journal of Neurology, Neurosurgery and Psychiatry*, **67**, 163–168.

Graff-Radford, N.R., Tranel, D., Van Hoesen, G.V. & Brandt, J. (1990). Diencephalic amnesia. *Brain*, **113**, 1–25.

Hanley, J., Davies, A., Downes, J. & Mayes, A. (1994). Impaired recall of verbal material following rupture and repair of an anterior communicating artery aneurysm. *Cognitive Neuropsychology*, **11**, 543–578.

Harding, A., Halliday, G., Caine, D. & Kril, J. (2000). Degeneration of anterior thalamic nuclei differentiates alcoholics with amnesia. *Brain*, **123**, 141–154.

Harper, C., Giles, M. & Finlay-Jones, R. (1986). Clinical signs in the Wernicke–Korsakoff complex: a retrospective analysis of 131 cases diagnosed at necropsy. *Journal of Neurology, Neurosurgery and Psychiatry*, **49**, 341–345.

Haslam, C., Coltheart, M. & Cook, M.L. (1997). Preserved category learning in amnesia. *Neurocase*, **3**, 337–347.

Hodges, J.R. & Carpenter, K. (1991). Anterograde amnesia with fornix damage following removal of IIIrd ventricle colloid cyst. *Journal of Neurology, Neurosurgery and Psychiatry*, **54**, 633–638.

Hodges, J.R. & McCarthy, R.A. (1993). Autobiographical amnesia resulting from bilateral paramedian thalamic infarction: a case study in cognitive neurobiology. *Brain*, **116**, 921–940.

Hopkins, R., Gale, S., Johnson, S. et al. (1995). Severe anoxia with and without concomitant brain damage. *Journal of the International Neuropsychological Society*, **1**, 501–509.

Hunkin, N.M., Parkin, A.J. & Longmore, B.E. (1994). Aetiological variation in the amnesic syndrome: comparisons using the list discrimination task. *Neuropsychologia*, **32**, 819–825.

Huppert, F.A. & Piercy, M. (1979). Normal and abnormal forgetting in organic amnesia: effects of locus of lesion. *Cortex*, **15**, 385–390.

Irle, E., Wowra, B., Kunert, H. J. et al. (1992). Memory disturbance following anterior communicating artery rupture. *Annals of Neurology*, **31**, 473–480.

Isaac, C., Holdstock, J., Cezayirli, E. et al. (2000). Amnesia in a patient with lesions to the dorsomedial thalamic nucleus. *Neurocase*, **4**, 497–508.

Jernigan, T.L., Shafer, K., Butters, N. & Cermak, L.S. (1991). Magnetic resonance imaging of alcoholic Korsakoff patients. *Neuropsychopharmacology*, **4**, 175–186.

Jones, E. (1985). *The Thalamus*. New York: Plenum.

Kapur, N. (1993). Focal retrograde amnesia in neurological disease: a critical review. *Cortex*, **29**, 217–234.

Kapur, N., Thompson, S., Cook, P. et al. (1996). Anterograde but not retrograde memory loss following combined mammillary body and medial thalamic lesions. *Neuropsychologia*, **43**, 1–8.

Kixmiller, J.S., Verfaellie, M., Chase, K.A. & Cermak, L.S. (1995). Comparison of figural intrusion errors in three amnesic subgroups. *Journal of the International Neuropsychological Society*, **1**, 561–567.

Kixmiller, J.S., Verfaellie, M., Mather, M.M. & Cermak, L.S. (2000). Role of perceptual and organizational factors in amnesics' recall of the Rey–Osterrieth complex figure: a comparison of three amnesic groups. *Journal of Clinical and Experimental Neuropsychology*, **22**, 198–207.

Kopelman, M.D. (1989). Remote and autobiographical memory, temporal context memory and frontal atrophy in Korsakoff and Alzheimer patients. *Neuropsychologia*, **27**, 437–460.

Kopelman, M.D. (1991). Frontal dysfunction and memory deficits in the alcoholic Korsakoff syndrome and Alzheimer-type dementia. *Brain*, **114**, 117–137.

Kopelman, M.D. (2000). Focal retrograde amnesia and the attribution of causality: an exceptionally critical review. *Cognitive Neuropsychology*, **17**, 585–621.

Kopelman, M.D. & Stanhope, N. (1997). Rates of forgetting in organic amnesia following temporal lobe, diencephalic, or frontal lobe lesions. *Neuropsychology*, **11**, 343–356.

Kopelman, M.D., Stanhope, N. & Kingsley, D. (1997). Temporal and spatial context memory in patients with focal frontal, temporal lobe and diencephalic lesions. *Neuropsychologia*, **35**(12), 1533–1545.

Kopelman, M.D., Stanhope, N. & Kingsley, D. (1999). Retrograde amnesia in patients with diencephalic, temporal lobe or frontal lesions. *Neuropsychologia*, **37**, 939–958.

Kril, J.J., Halliday, G.M., Svoboda, M.D. & Cartwright, H. (1997). The cerebral cortex is damaged in chronic alcoholics. *Neuroscience*, **79**, 983–998.

Kritchevsky, M., Graff-Radford, N. & Damasio, A. (1987). Normal memory after damage to the medial thalamus. *Archives of Neurology*, **44**, 959–962.

Kuroiwa, T. & Okeda, R. (1994). Neuropathology of cerebral ischemia and hypoxia: Recent advances in experimental studies on its pathogenesis. *Pathology International*, **44**, 171–181.

Leng, N.R.C. & Parkin, A.J. (1988). Double dissociation of frontal dysfunction in organic amnesia. *British Journal of Clinical Psychology*, **27**, 359–362.

Leng, N.R.C. & Parkin, A.J. (1989). Aetiological variation in the amnesic syndrome: comparisons using the Brown Peterson task. *Cortex*, **25**, 251–259.

Levine, D. & Grek, A. (1984). The anatomic basis of delusions after right cerebral infarction. *Neurology*, **34**, 577–582.

Lhermitte, F. & Signoret, J.L. (1972). Analyse neuropsychologique et differentiation des syndromes amnesiques. *Revue Neurologique*, **126**, 161–178.

Mair, W., Warrington, E. & Weiskrantz, L. (1979). Memory disorder in Korsakoff's psychosis: a neuropathological and neuropsychological investigation of two cases. *Brain*, **102**, 749–783.

Markowitsch, H.J., Weber-Luxemburger, G., Ewald, K. et al. (1997). Patients with heart attacks are not valid models for medial temporal lobe amnesia. A neuropsychological and FDG–PET study with consequences for memory research. *European Journal of Neurology*, **4**, 178–184.

Mayes, A.R., Holdstock, J.S., Isaac, C.L. et al. (in press). Relative sparing of item recognition memory in a patient with adult-onset damage limited to the hippocampus. *Hippocampus*.

Mayes, A.R., Meudell, P.R. & MacDonald, C. (1991). Disproportionate intentional spatial-memory impairments in amnesia. *Neuropsychologia*, **29**, 771–784.

McKee, R.D. & Squire, L.R. (1992). Equivalent forgetting rates in long-term memory in diencephalic and medial temporal lobe amnesia. *Journal of Neuroscience*, **12**, 3765–3772.

McKenna, P. & Warrington, E. (2000). The neuropsychology of semantic memory. In L.S. Cermak (ed.), *Memory and Its Disorders*, 2nd edn, Vol. 2 (pp. 355–382). Amsterdam: Elsevier.

McMakin, D., Cockburn, J., Anslow, P. & Gaffan, D. (1995). Correlation of fornix damage with memory impairment in six cases of colloid cyst removal. *Acta Neurochirurgica*, **135**, 12–18.

McNeill, D.L., Tidmarsh, D. & Rastall, M.L. (1965). A case of dysmnesic syndrome following cardiac arrest. *British Journal of Psychiatry*, **111**, 697–699.

Milner, B. (1966). Amnesia following operation on the temporal lobes. In C.W.M. Whitty & O.L. Zangwill (eds), *Amnesia* (pp. 109–133). London: Butterworths.

Mohr, J., Leicester, J., Stoddard, T. & Sidman, M. (1971). Right hemianopia with memory and color deficits in circumscribed left posterior cerebral artery territory infarction. *Neurology*, **21**, 1104–1113.

Moody, D.M., Bell, M.A. & Challa, R. (1990). Features of the cerebral vascular pattern that predict vulnerability to perfusion or oxygenation deficiency: an anatomic study. *American Journal of Neuroradiology*, **11**, 431–439.

O'Connor, M.G., Butters, N., Miliotis, P. et al. (1992). The dissociation of anterograde and retrograde amnesia in a patient with herpes encephalitis. *Journal of Clinical and Experimental Neuropsychology*, **14**, 159–178.

O'Connor, M.G., Walbridge, M., D'Esposito, M. et al. (1995). *The retrograde memory profile of patients with amnesia secondary to rupture and surgical repair of anterior communicating artery aneurysms*. Paper presented at the International Neuropsychological Society, Seattle, Washington, DC.

Ogden, J.A. (1993). Visual object agnosia, prosopagnosia, achromatopsia, loss of visual imagery, and autobiographical amnesia following recovery from cortical blindness: case M.H. *Neuropsychologia*, **31**, 571–589.

Ott, B.R. & Saver, J.L. (1993). Unilateral amnesic stroke: six new cases and a review of the literature. *Stroke*, **24**, 1033–1042.

Parkin, A.J. & Hunkin, N.M. (1993). Impaired temporal context memory on anterograde but not retrograde tests in the absence of frontal pathology. *Cortex*, **29**, 267–280.

Parkin, A.J., Leng, N.R.C. & Hunkin, N.M. (1990). Differential sensitivity to context in diencephalic and temporal lobe amnesia. *Cortex*, **26**, 373–380.

Parkin, A.J., Leng, N.R.C., Stanhope, N. & Smith, A.P. (1988). Memory impairment following ruptured aneurysm of the anterior communicating artery. *Brain and Cognition*, **7**, 231–243.

Parkin, A.J. & Leng, R.C. (1993). *Neuropsychology of the Amnesic Syndrome*. Hillsdale, NJ: Erlbaum.

Parkin, A.J., Miller, J. & Vincent, R. (1987). Multiple neuropsychological deficits due to anoxic encephalopathy: a case study. *Cortex*, **23**, 655–665.

Parkin, A.J., Rees, J., Hunkin, N. & Rose, P. (1994). Impairment of memory following discrete thalamic infarction. *Neuropsychologia*, **32**, 39–51.

Pepin, E. & Auray-Pepin, L. (1993). Selective dorsolateral frontal lobe dysfunction associated with diencephalic amnesia. *Neurology*, **43**, 733–741.

Ptak, R. & Schnider, A. (1999). Spontaneous confabulations after orbito-frontal damage: the role of temporal context confusion and self-monitoring. *Neurocase*, **5**, 243–250.

Rapscak, S.Z., Kaszniak, A.W., Reminger, S.L. et al. (1998). Dissociation between verbal and autonomic measures of memory following frontal lobe damage. *Neurology*, **50**, 1259–1265.

Reed, J.M. & Squire, L.R. (1997). Impaired recognition memory in patients with lesions limited to the hippocampal formation. *Behavioral Neuroscience*, **111**, 1163–1170.

Reed, L.J., Lasserson, D., Marsden, P. et al. (1999). FDG–PET analysis and findings in amnesia resulting from hypoxia. *Memory*, **7**, 599–612.

Reich, P., Regstein, Q.R., Murawski, B.J. et al. (1983). Unrecognized organic mental disorders in survivors of cardiac arrest. *American Journal of Psychiatry*, **140**, 1194–1197.

Rempel-Clower, N.L., Zola, S.M., Squire, L.R. & Amaral, D.G. (1996). Three cases of enduring memory impairment after bilateral damage limited to the hippocampal formation. *Journal of Neuroscience*, **16**, 5233–5255.

Richardson, J.T. (1989). Performance in free recall following rupture and repair of intracranial aneurysm. *Brain and Cognition*, **9**, 210–226.

Ross, E.D. (1980). Sensory-specific and fractional disorders of recent memory in man: I. Isolated loss of visual recent memory. *Archives of Neurology*, **37**, 193–200.

Sandson, T., Daffner, K., Carvalho, P. & Mesulam, M. (1991). Frontal lobe dysfunction following infarction of the left-sided medial thalamus. *Archives of Neurology*, **48**, 1300–1303.

Scoville, W.B. & Milner, B. (1957). Loss of recent memory after bilateral hippocampal lesions. *Journal of Neurology, Neurosurgery and Psychiatry*, **20**, 11–12.

Shimamura, A.P., Janowski, J.S. & Squire, L.R. (1990). Memory for the temporal order of events in patients with frontal lobe lesions and amnesic patients. *Neuropsychologia*, **28**, 803–813.

Shoqeirat, M. & Mayes, A.R. (1991). Disproportionate incidental spatial-memory and recall deficits in amnesia. *Neuropsychologia*, **29**, 749–769.

Speedie, L.J. & Heilman, K.M. (1982). Amnestic disturbance following infarction of the left dorsomedial nucleus of the thalamus. *Neuropsychologia*, **20**, 597–604.

Speedie, L.J. & Heilman, K.M. (1983). Anterograde memory deficits for visuospatial material after infarction of the right thalamus. *Archives of Neurology*, **40**, 183–186.

Squire, L.R. (1981). Two forms of human amnesia: an analysis of forgetting. *Journal of Neuroscience*, **6**, 635–640.

Squire, L.R. (1982). Comparisons between forms of amnesia: some deficits are unique to Korsakoff's syndrome. *Journal of Experimental Psychology: Learning, Memory and Cognition*, **8**, 560–571.

Squire, L.R., Knowlton, B. & Musen, G. (1993). The structure and organization of memory. *Annual Review of Psychology*, **44**, 453–495.

Squire, L.R. & Zola, S.M. (1998). Episodic memory, semantic memory and amnesia. *Hippocampus*, **8**, 205–211.

Stefanacci, L., Buffalo, E.A., Schmolck, H. & Squire, L.R. (2000). Profound amnesia after damage to the medial temporal lobe: a neuroanatomical and neuropsychological profile of patient E.P. *Journal of Neuroscience*, **20**, 7024–7036.

Stuss, D.T., Guberman, A., Nelson, R. & Larochelle, S. (1988). The neuropsychology of paramedian thalamic infarction. *Brain and Cognition*, **8**, 348–378.

Sullivan, E. (2001). *Equivalent hippocampal volume loss in Korsakoff's syndrome and Alzheimer's disease*. Paper presented at the International Neuropsychological Society, Chicago.

Talland, G.A., Sweet, W.H. & Ballantine, H.T. (1967). Amnesic syndrome with anterior communicating artery aneurysm. *Journal of Nervous and Mental Diseases*, **145**, 179–192.

Tranel, D., Damasio, H. & Damasio, A. (2000). Amnesia caused by herpes simplex encephalitis, infarctions in basal forebrain, and anoxia/ischemia. In L.S. Cermak (ed.), *Handbook of Neuropsychology*, 2nd edn, Vol. 2, pp. 85–110). Oxford: Elsevier.

Van der Werf, Y., Witter, M., Uylings, H. & Jolles, J. (2000). Neuropsychology of infarctions in the thalamus: a review. *Neuropsychologia*, **38**, 613–627.

Vargha-Khadem, F., Gadian, D.G., Watkins, K.E. et al. (1997). Differential effects of early hippocampal pathology on episodic and semantic memory. *Science*, **277**, 376–380.

Verfaellie, M. & Cermak, L.S. (1991). Neuropsychological Issues in Amnesia. In J. L. Martinez & R. P. Kersner (eds), *Learning and Memory: A Biological View* (pp. 467–497). San Diego, CA: Academic Press.

Verfaellie, M. Croce, P. & Milberg, W.P. (1995a). The role of episodic memory in semnatic learning: an examination of vocabulary acquisition in a patient with amnesia due to encephalitis. *Neurocase*, **1**, 291–304.

Verfaellie, M. & Keane, M.M. (2001). Scope and limits of implicit memory in amnesia. In B. De Gelder, E. De Haan & C. Heywood (eds), *Unconscious Minds* (pp. 151–162). Oxford: Oxford University Press.

Verfaellie, M., Koseff, P. & Alexander, M.P. (2000). Acquisition of novel semantic information in amnesia: effects of lesion location. *Neuropsychologia*, **38**, 484–492.

Verfaellie, M., Reiss, L. & Roth, H. (1995b). Knowledge of new English vocabulary in amnesia: an examination of premorbidly acquired semantic memory. *Journal of the International Neuropsychological Society*, **1**, 443–453.

Victor, M., Adams, R.D. & Collins, G.H. (1989). *The Wernicke–Korsakoff Syndrome and Related Neurologic Disorders due to Alcoholism and Malnutrition*, 2nd edn. Philadelphia, PA: Davis.

Victor, M., Angevine, J., Mancall, E. & Fischer, M. (1961). Memory loss with lesions of hippocampal formation. *Archives of Neurology*, **5**, 244–263.

Volpe, B. T., Herscovitch, P. & Raichle, M. E. (1984). Positron emission tomography defines metabolic abnormality in mesial temporal lobes of two patients with amnesia after rupture and repair of anterior communicating artery aneurysm. *Neurology*, **34**, 188.

Volpe, B.T. & Hirst, W. (1983). Amnesia following the rupture and repair of an anterior communicating artery aneurysm. *Journal of Neurology, Neurosurgery and Psychiatry*, **46**, 704–709.

Von Cramon, D., Hebel, N. & Schuri, U. (1985). A contribution to the anatomical basis of thalamic amnesia. *Brain*, **108**, 993–1008.

Von Cramon, D., Hebel, N. & Schuri, U. (1988). Verbal memory and learning in unilateral posterior cerebral infarction. *Brain*, **111**, 1061–1077.

Von Cramon, D.Y., Markowitsch, H.J. & Shuri, U. (1993). The possible contribution of the septal region to memory. *Neuropsychologia*, **31**, 1159–1180.

Warrington, E.K. (1984). 000

Warrington, E.K. & Weiskrantz, L. (1970). Amnesic syndrome: consolidation or retrieval? *Nature*, **228**, 628–630.

Warrington, E.K. & Weiskrantz, L. (1973). An analysis of short-term and long-term memory deficits in man. In J.A. Deutsch (ed.), *The Physiological Basis of Memory* (pp. 365–396). New York: Academic Press.

Weiskrantz, L. (1985). On issues and theories of the human amnesic syndrome. In N. Weinberger, J. McGaugh & G. Lynch (Eds), *Memory Systems of the Brain* (pp. 380–415). New York: Guilford.

Winocur, G., Oxbury, S., Roberts, R. et al. C. (1984). Amnesia in a patient with bilateral lesions to the thalamus. *Neuropsychologia*, **22**, 123–143.

Zola, S.M. & Squire, L.R. (2000). The medial temporal lobe and the hippocampus. In E. Tulving & F. I. M. Craik (Eds), *The Oxford Handbook of Memory* (pp. 485–500). Oxford: Oxford University Press.

Zola-Morgan, S., Squire, L. & Amaral, D. (1986). Human amnesia and the medial temporal region: enduring memory impairment following a bilateral lesion limited to field CA1 of the hippocampus. *Journal of Neuroscience*, **6**, 2950–2967.

CHAPTER 8

Theories of Anterograde Amnesia

Andrew R. Mayes

Department of Psychology, University of Liverpool, UK

Organic amnesia is a syndrome in which four features are present. First, patients are impaired at recalling or recognizing experienced episodes and facts encountered after the onset of their disorder; in other words, they show anterograde amnesia. Second, patients show a variable degree of impairment in their ability to recall and recognize episodes and facts that were encountered and put into memory before the onset of their disorder; in other words, they show retrograde amnesia. Third, patients with these memory disorders can show apparently preserved intelligence. Fourth, patients can also show preservation of working memory; in other words, their recall of information that was encountered in the immediate past is normal. However, patients' anterograde amnesia becomes apparent within seconds of their attention switching from the conscious processing and representation of the information that they have just encountered. Patients who show all these features will be referred to as global amnesics.

This syndrome is caused by lesions that may occur in any one of several distinct, but interconnected regions that lie close to the midline of the brain. Thus, amnesia can be caused by lesions to: (a) the medial temporal lobes; (b) the midline diencephalon; (c) structures in the basal forebrain; and (d) some of the fibre tracts, such as the fornix, which link these regions. In addition, there is some evidence that damage to structures in the ventromedial frontal cortex causes the amnesic syndrome (e.g. Bachevalier & Mishkin, 1986) and that damage to the anterior temporal neocortex, which perhaps has to be accompanied by seizure activity, also causes a form of the syndrome (Kapur et al., 1996). Damage to other structures, such as the retrosplenial cortex (Valenstein et al., 1987), which are connected to some of the above regions may also cause amnesia. Finally, there is evidence that amnesia-like deficits can be caused by posterior neocortex lesions (Rubin & Greenberg, 1998). In such disorders, some of the deficits of amnesia are present, but patients also show other deficits that are not found in global amnesia.

Theories of amnesia are intended to fulfil several goals. The first goal is the precise specification of the functional deficits that underlie the memory impairments shown by patients with the amnesia syndrome. The second goal is the specification of the precise brain damage and dysfunction that causes the functional deficits. The third and longer-term

The Handbook of Memory Disorders. Edited by A.D. Baddeley, M.D. Kopelman and B.A. Wilson
© 2002 John Wiley & Sons, Ltd.

goal is the specification of *how* damage to and dysfunction of these brain regions causes the functional deficits that underlie amnesia. Achievement of this goal depends on specifying how the relevant regions in normal people's brains mediate the functions that are disturbed in amnesia.

How each of these goals will be fulfilled depends on whether the global amnesia syndrome is unitary or comprises several distinct and dissociable disorders. If the syndrome comprises several disorders, then different lesions should cause distinct kinds of functional breakdown that lead to different patterns of memory deficits in amnesic patients. How the brain regions, damage to which causes each distinct kind of functional breakdown, mediate their specific functions will need to be explained on an individual basis, as will how specific lesions disrupt these functions.

It is increasingly believed that the global amnesia syndrome comprises several distinct and dissociable functional deficits, although this belief is controversial and the evidence that supports it needs strengthening. There is a practical and a more theoretical reason why controversy persists. The practical reason is that identifying dissociations usually depends on finding patients with very selective lesions and these patients are extremely rare and have not necessarily shown the same pattern of memory deficits as other patients with apparently the same lesion (see Mayes et al., 2002). The theoretical reason is that the structures, damage to which causes amnesia or an amnesia-like syndrome, are highly interconnected. Although it is widely agreed that these structures must have slightly different information-processing and storage functions and also probably deal with slightly different kinds of information, it does not follow automatically that damage to each of them will disrupt memory in dissociable ways. For example, one structure may pass the results of its processing to another structure, so that damage to either structure prevents a normal output from the second structure and causes the same memory deficit. Our knowledge of the detailed connectivity of the highly interconnected brain structures implicated in global amnesia and of the processing that these structures mediate is still insufficient to allow confident prediction of which lesions will have dissociable effects on memory.

Clearly, identifying whether amnesia is functionally heterogeneous and, if so, in what way, is a fundamental requirement for specifying the key functional deficits that underlie the syndrome, their anatomy, and precisely how this anatomy relates to the functions. In particular, it is critical to know whether anterograde and retrograde amnesia are caused by precisely the same functional deficits and lesions or to what extent they are caused by different functional deficits and lesions. The focus of this chapter is theories of anterograde amnesia, and historically, theories of the amnesia syndrome have mainly concerned what causes anterograde amnesia. Nevertheless, if the same functional deficit(s) cause some aspects of retrograde amnesia as well as anterograde amnesia, theories of anterograde amnesia will need to account for some features of retrograde amnesia. This point is important because it is unlikely that pre- and postmorbid memory deficits will dissociate completely, even in patients with more focal lesions.

The next section will outline what the main features of anterograde amnesia are in the context of global amnesia. How much is known about the precise location of the lesions that cause the deficits of anterograde amnesia will be briefly outlined in the section after this. Evidence that there are several distinct patterns of postmorbid memory impairment, each of which is caused by a specific subset of the lesions that are implicated in the global syndrome, will be considered in the fourth section. In each of these sections, the extent to which there is still disagreement about the evidence will be discussed. The fifth section will outline and critically evaluate the main theories of anterograde amnesia that have been advanced in the past 30 years. The final section will briefly consider more recent developments and discuss what needs to be done in order to advance theoretical understanding of the amnesia syndrome.

THE FEATURES OF ANTEROGRADE AMNESIA

Successful creation of new long-term memories about facts and events that one has experienced requires a sequence of processes to work effectively. Information has to be processed and represented (encoding), that information has to be consolidated into long-term memory (initial consolidation), further storage changes may occur over long periods of time (slow consolidation), perhaps partially to maintain long-term storage and make it more stable, and the stored information has later to be remembered (retrieval). Only encoding and retrieval can be directly measured in humans. Inferences about consolidation and maintenance of long-term memory have to be made indirectly from human data or by extrapolation from animal data about these physiological and biochemical processes (e.g. see Squire & Kandel, 1999).

In this chapter, the term "encoding" is used in the narrow sense that includes only the processes necessary for representing information at input, rather than in the broader sense where it really means "encoding into long-term memory". This broader sense is misleading because it blurs together two separate collections of processes: those involved in representing information at input and those involved in consolidating this represented information into long-term memory. If information is not represented at input, then it cannot later be remembered. Does this failure occur in global amnesics? The preservation of intelligence in these patients argues strongly against the likelihood that this failure is occurring. There is also evidence that, relative to spontaneous encoding, orientating tasks that encourage the encoding of useful semantic information improves explicit memory to the same degree in amnesics as in control subjects, provided that floor, ceiling and subtler scaling effects are avoided by using a matching procedure (for discussion, see Mayes, 1988). Direct assessment of encoding requires testing of what is known immediately after a briefly exposed complex stimulus has been processed, so that normal subjects do not perform at ceiling levels and performance only depends on working memory, at which amnesics are normal. When this was done, global amnesics with medial temporal lobe, midline diencephalic and basal forebrain lesions showed as much knowledge about the spatial, colour, size and semantic features of complex pictures, which they had just studied for 6 s, as did their control subjects (Mayes et al., 1993). The evidence therefore strongly suggests that at least most global amnesics can represent complex information about facts and personally experienced episodes normally.

Despite this normal encoding, after a short filled delay, amnesic patients are impaired at recalling or recognizing information that they have just encountered, processed and represented consciously. The majority of evidence shows that the recognition impairment does not worsen as the length of the delay increases from seconds to minutes, hours, days, and even months (for discussions, see Isaac & Mayes, 1999a, 1999b; Kopelman, 1985; Kopelman & Stanhope, 1997). In other words, although impaired after a short filled delay, the rate of loss of recognition memory is normal in amnesics. There is evidence, however, that the recall deficit, shown by all amnesics after a few seconds of filled delay, gets worse over the first few minutes when rehearsal is prevented (Isaac & Mayes, 1999a, 1999b; Kopelman & Stanhope, 1997). It is impossible to determine whether this accelerated loss of whatever underlies free recall continues beyond a few minutes because amnesic performance drops to chance levels. There is also disagreement about whether the accelerated loss applies to free recall of semantically unrelated word lists as well as to semantically related word lists and stories (Isaac & Mayes, 1999a, 1999b; Green & Kopelman, 2002). The only exception to the generalization that recognition declines at a normal rate over delays that are longer than a few seconds is found with a group of patients most of whom are epileptic and many of whom have damage to the anterior temporal lobes. These patients have been reported to show relatively normal recognition and recall of information that was encountered several hours earlier after which they forget at an accelerated rate over a period that may last for weeks or longer (e.g. Kapur et al., 1996).

Global amnesics show impaired explicit memory (recognition and recall) for postmorbidly encountered facts as well as experienced episodes. However, it has sometimes been suggested that amnesia is a selective impairment of the ability to acquire episodic memories. As global amnesics unquestionably are impaired at acquiring new factual memories, such as memories about the meanings of new terms (e.g. Verfaellie et al., 2000), this suggestion can at best only be true in a restricted sense. Specifically, global amnesics should have impaired explicit memory for postmorbidly acquired facts only when normal subjects' factual memory is facilitated by retrieval of episodic information. Global amnesics should show normal explicit memory for facts when neither they nor their control subjects boost their factual memory by retrieving the context or contexts in which the facts were encountered. Given that context-dependent forgetting is minimal and usually does not occur at all for recognition memory (for review, see Smith, 1988), and global amnesics have severely impaired memory for post-morbidly encountered facts, it is most likely that, even in this restricted sense of factual memory, global amnesia involves factual as well as episodic memory deficits.

Much theoretical thinking about what functional deficits underlie global amnesia has involved the putative distinction between episodic and semantic memory. Use of this distinction has, however, not been heuristically useful in advancing understanding of the causes of amnesia. This is because both episodic and semantic memory are highly complex and each is mediated by a large number of processes. Equally important, the information retrieved when different episodes and facts are remembered is highly variable, and there is a very marked but variable degree of overlap. For example, remembering a sequence from *The Sound of Music* may be an instance of semantic memory if the film has been seen many times, but this memory involves retrieving spatiotemporal context as well as other kinds of visual and auditory perceptual information. These are usually regarded as unique hallmarks of episodic memory. However, if one accepts the example, the only uniquely identifying features of episodic memory may be the storage and retrieval of *events* that include the *rememberer*, i.e. involve self-reference.

It is more heuristically valuable to identify the informational and processing components of the two overlapping kinds of memory in order to determine whether any of these components are specifically affected in global amnesia. As both recall and recognition of facts as well as episodes are impaired in global amnesia, this kind of approach has involved a procedure in which amnesics are given more opportunity than their control subjects to learn specific information. This procedure makes it possible to check whether amnesics remain impaired at one kind of memory, when they do as well as their control subjects at another, in order to support the claim that they are more impaired at the first kind of memory. The procedure is very tricky to execute successfully, because confident interpretation depends on showing that the matching manipulation affects the two kinds of memory to the same extent in normal subjects. If this is not shown, amnesics can falsely appear to be more impaired or not more impaired at one kind of memory than they are at another.

Not surprisingly, use of the matching procedure has produced somewhat conflicting results. There have been two main foci of attention: relative severity of impairment of recall and recognition, and relative severity of impairment of explicit memory for various aspects of context and recognition for items to which attention was paid in the context. Some evidence suggests that free recall of items is more impaired than item recognition in global amnesics (Hirst et al., 1986, 1988), but other evidence suggests that this may not be so, at least for unrelated lists of words (Haist et al., 1992). One resolution of this apparent conflict is that recall is only more impaired than item recognition when it is of semantically related items of the kind that occur in stories or related word lists, and that the greater impairment is caused by amnesics losing their ability to recall, but not to recognize, such items pathologically fast. In support of this resolution, Isaac & Mayes (1999a, 1999b) found that, following extra learning opportunity, global amnesics could recall and recognize studied stories, and semantically related and unrelated word lists, as well as their control subjects after filled delays of 20 s. But following a filled delay of 10 min, although they still recognized all these materials as well as their control subjects and recalled the unrelated words as well, they were clearly impaired at recalling the stories and related words.

The evidence about the relative impairment of explicit memory for context and item recognition memory is also conflicting. However, several studies suggest that global amnesics' explicit memory for several aspects of context is more impaired than their item recognition memory. These aspects of context include spatial location (Chalfonte et al., 1996; Kopelman et al., 1997; Mayes et al., 1991; Shoqeirat & Mayes, 1991), temporal sequence (Downes et al., 2002; Kopelman et al., 1997; Parkin et al., 1990), sensory modality (Pickering et al., 1989), and the kind of interactive context that involves incidentally encoded items that are semantically related to the attended items (Mayes et al., 1992). However, it is disputed whether explicit memory for spatial location is more impaired than item recognition (Cave & Squire, 1991); whether greater impairments of explicit memory for temporal sequence are caused by the lesions that cause amnesia or by frontal lobe damage (e.g. Shimamura et al., 1990); whether all global amnesics or only some show greater explicit memory deficits for temporal sequence (Downes et al., 2002; Parkin et al., 1990); and whether disproportionate explicit spatial memory deficits only occur when associations between locations and items are incidentally encoded (Chalfont et al., 1996; Mayes et al., 1991).

Anterograde amnesia is often described as involving explicit (or declarative) memory, but not implicit (procedural or non-declarative memory). The implicit forms of memory that are claimed to be preserved in anterograde amnesia are heterogeneous, but none are believed to require subjects to feel consciously that they are remembering the learned information. It has been claimed that the preserved forms of implicit memory include various kinds of conditioning, skill memory, some kinds of perceptual memory, and priming (for discussion, see Mayes, 1988). Of these forms of implicit memory, only priming is likely to be able to throw light on what functional deficits cause the impairment in explicit memory that is shown by amnesics. This is because priming is an information-specific form of memory, indicated by an increase in the fluency and accuracy with which the remembered information is processed, that does not depend on consciously remembering the information. However, the information primed involves components of the facts and episodes that cannot be explicitly remembered in anterograde amnesia. If amnesics can be shown to have normal priming of all the kinds of fact and event information they cannot recall and recognize normally, their problem cannot be one of storage.

It is currently controversial to what extent, if at all, amnesics show preserved priming. At one extreme, Ostergaard (1999) has argued that priming for all kinds of information, regardless of whether that information was novel or familiar prior to study, is impaired in global amnesics, although impairments may often be hidden by artefacts of method or analysis. By contrast, others have proposed that all kinds of priming are preserved in amnesia (e.g. Gabrieli, 1998). Arguing that amnesics should be impaired at priming of the kinds of information for which they show impaired explicit memory, Gooding et al. (2000) found, in a recent meta-analysis, that in global amnesics, priming of information (e.g. words) already in memory at study was preserved, but priming of novel items and associations was impaired. Normal subjects' superiority at novel information priming could have resulted from their exploiting their superior explicit memory. However, Chun & Phelps (1999) found that priming of target-spatial context associations that were novel prior to study was impaired in global amnesics, even when their controls showed no explicit memory.

Even when amnesic priming of novel information is completely normal, as was found by Hamann & Squire (1997a, 1997b), this does not necessarily mean that a different storage mechanism underlies priming and recognition of the same information. Hamann & Squire's patients studied novel strings of four consonants. Later, when studied and unstudied strings were very briefly exposed, the patients showed an enhanced identification of the studied strings to the same extent as control subjects, although their recognition of the strings was impaired and not significantly above chance. Kinder & Shanks (2001) have reproduced this pattern of results using a connectionist model, in which amnesia was simulated by a single reduced learning rate and the different testing conditions of priming and recognition were also simulated. These results were found because as "damage" to the model increased and the strength of memory decreased, recognition steadily declined, whereas priming was not affected until memory was markedly reduced, at which point priming rapidly declined.

The idea that priming and explicit memory for the same information depends on the same memory storage processes, as indicated by Kinder & Shanks' model, is seriously challenged by the double dissociation between perceptual priming and recognition. In contrast to global amnesics, two patients with occipital cortex damage have been reported to show impaired perceptual priming, but preserved recognition (Gabrieli et al., 1995; Keane et al., 1995). Both these patients, however, showed evidence of having impaired visual processing (e.g. see Fleischman et al., 1995) and Kinder & Shanks were able to simulate their impaired priming on Hamann & Squire's task with their connectionist model by degrading the input when priming was tested. As exposure to the stimuli was not degraded for recognition because exposure was prolonged, recognition was unaffected.

LOCATION OF THE LESIONS THAT CAUSE ANTEROGRADE AMNESIA

Even with respect to the medial temporal lobes, about which there is most knowledge, there is still poor understanding of the precise damage that causes anterograde amnesia. Much of this knowledge is extrapolated from monkey studies, the precise interpretation of which is controversial. It is agreed that amygdala lesions do not cause a general impairment of recognition and recall for postmorbidly encountered facts and events (Zola-Morgan et al., 1989a). However, amygdala damage does reduce the usual advantage in later memory that is found for information that is associated with emotional arousal at input (Phelps et al., 1998). In monkeys, selective lesions of the parahippocampal and perirhinal cortices cause severe object recognition deficits (Zola-Morgan et al., 1989b), and human patients with Herpes simplex encephalitis, who have large lesions to these two cortices, show very impaired recall and recognition. The effect of hippocampal damage is less severe, and these lesions may only minimally affect item recognition, although this is controversial, as is discussed in the next section.

Midline diencephalic nuclei and fibre tracts are small, but there is evidence from both animal and human studies that selective lesions of the mammillary bodies and anterior thalamus produce impairments of explicit memory (see Aggleton & Saunders, 1997; Mayes & Downes, 1997). The hippocampus is connected to both these diencephalic nuclei via the fornix and there is evidence that selective damage to this fibre tract also impairs explicit memory (e.g. Aggleton et al., 2000). In contrast, the perirhinal cortex is not directly connected to these nuclei, but does have a projection to the magnocellular dorsomedial thalamus (Russchen et al., 1987). Although the evidence is not uniformly supportive, it suggests that a clear anterograde amnesia occurs following sufficiently large, but relatively selective, lesions to either the dorsomedial thalamic nucleus (e.g. see Isaac et al., 1998) or the anterior thalamic nucleus (e.g. see Mark et al., 1970). However, it remains unclear whether damage to other thalamic and hypothalamic nuclei (such as the paratenial and reuniens nuclei) also contributes to anterograde amnesia.

Less is known about the effects of lesions to basal forebrain structures, because the lesions that damage these structures tend to be large in humans. However, as Mayes & Downes (1997) discuss, there is evidence that lesions of the septum, diagonal band of Broca and nucleus accumbens cause anterograde amnesia. Von Cramon & Schuri (1992) have also argued that lesions that disconnect the septum from the hippocampus cause an amnesia-like deficit. It has also been shown that lesions that disconnect the medial temporal lobes and temporal neocortex from the basal forebrain and midbrain by severing the anterior temporal stem, the fornix and pathways that run through and near to the amygdala causes a dense anterograde amnesia in monkeys (Gaffan et al., 2001).

Although the medial temporal lobes and midline diencephalon are linked to the frontal neocortex by complex reciprocal connections, it is widely believed that the role of the frontal neocortex in memory is secondary to its role in mediating executive operations, such as planning, organization of information, monitoring, inhibition, and attentional control. Disruption of such executive operations should clearly reduce the effectiveness of intentional encoding and retrieval, but only mildly impair memory when encoding and retrieval are incidental (Mangels, 1997). Others have argued that the effects of lesions to the frontal neocortex on memory have previously been underestimated (Wheeler et al., 1995), which suggests that not all the memory disruptions produced by frontal neocortex lesions are secondary to executive function deficits. Lesions of the ventromedial frontal cortex (orbitofrontal and anterior cingulate cortices), but not of the dorsolateral frontal cortex, may cause an anterograde amnesia similar to that found following medial temporal and midline diencephalic lesions, as has been claimed on the basis of monkey studies (Bachevalier & Mishkin, 1986). If this is so, then some frontal cortex lesions may impair explicit memory because they disrupt executive processes, whereas other frontal cortex lesions may disrupt explicit memory for the same reasons as medial temporal lobe and midline diencephalic lesions. It is of considerable interest that crossed unilateral frontal cortex and medial forebrain bundle lesions have been found to produce dense amnesia in monkeys (Easton & Gaffan, 2001). Such lesions disconnect these two brain regions and prevent the frontal neocortex from influencing the activity of basal forebrain structures. It seems unlikely that dense amnesia can be produced merely by preventing the intentional executive control of memory, and more likely that these lesions are preventing a tonic as well as a phasic facilitation of memory-related activity in the basal forebrain that is exerted by the frontal neocortex.

EVIDENCE THAT ANTEROGRADE AMNESIA IS FUNCTIONALLY HETEROGENEOUS

Several functional disorders, each caused by lesions to a specific subset of the structures, damage to which produces anterograde amnesia, may be involved in the syndrome. Most prominently, Aggleton & Brown (1999) have argued that lesions of the hippocampus impair recall but leave item recognition relatively intact, provided that successful recognition depends primarily on familiarity. They have also argued that damage to each of the other structures in the Papez circuit causes a similar pattern of impairment to that produced by hippocampal damage. Thus, according to their view, fornix damage, mammillary body damage, or anterior thalamic damage disrupts recall, but leaves item recognition relatively intact. In contrast, they have proposed that damage to the perirhinal cortex severely impairs item recognition as well as recall, and that a milder recognition deficit is produced by lesions of the dorsomedial thalamic nucleus and, possibly, regions of the prefrontal neocortex, to both of which the perirhinal cortex projects. They believe that the item recognition deficit is more severe when these structures are damaged because the lesions impair familiarity as well as recollection, whereas Papez circuit lesions only disrupt recollection.

Brown & Aggleton (2001) have reviewed evidence from animal studies with single unit recording and immediate-early-gene imaging (measurement of the activation of genes that control the transcription of other genes, and hence the production of specific proteins: immediate-early-gene activation correlates with neural activity). This evidence indicates that the perirhinal cortex and adjacent visual association cortex are involved in discriminating between familiar and novel visual objects. In monkeys, the latency of such familiarity judgements and of the perirhinal neural responses to familiarity correspond closely, and the rapidity of the familiarity discrimination makes it unlikely that a top-down input from the hippocampus influences the judgement. Consistent with the results from recording work, immediate-early-gene studies indicate that hippocampal neurons do not significantly discriminate between the familiarity or novelty of individual visual stimuli, but are involved with memory for associations between individual visual stimuli and aspects of their spatial or temporal contexts. In contrast, these studies indicate that the perirhinal cortex is involved in memory for individual items, but not for spatial associations.

Although the above sources of evidence suggest that the perirhinal cortex and hippocampus mediate different explicit memory processes, this does not conclusively prove that selective lesions of these two structures will have clearly dissociable effects on explicit memory. The evidence, which mainly relates to whether hippocampal lesions cause item recognition deficits, is still conflicting and hard to interpret. The majority of animal studies indicate that hippocampal lesions have a minimal effect on object recognition (see Aggleton & Brown, 1999; Brown & Aggleton, 2001). Indeed, it has been argued that although monkey studies indicate that hippocampal lesions mildly disrupt object recognition, there is a negative correlation between the extent of hippocampal damage and the extent of the recognition deficit (Baxter & Murray, 2001a, 2001b), although this view is disputed (Zola & Squire, 2001). The existence of such a negative correlation would imply that complete selective destruction of the hippocampus would have a minimal effect on item recognition, and that small hippocampal lesions might have a larger effect, for any of several reasons (see Mayes et al., 2002), e.g. abnormal outputs from residual hippocampal tissue, which may be greater when there is more such tissue, might disturb the activity of connected structures, such as the perirhinal cortex, that mediate familiarity memory.

A mechanism of this kind might help explain why different human patients with apparently relatively selective hippocampal lesions have shown different patterns of item recognition performance. On the one hand, some patients with either early-onset lesions (Vargha-Khadem et al., 1997) or adult onset lesions (Mayes et al., 2002) have shown relatively normal item recognition across a variety of recognition tasks, but impaired recognition of associations between different kinds of information, particularly those between items and their spatial (Vargha-Khadem et al., 1997) and temporal (Mayes et al., 2001) positions. On the other hand, patients with adult-onset lesions have also been reported to show clear item recognition deficits across a variety of tasks (Manns & Squire, 1999; Reed et al., 1997). The contrasting pattern of deficits shown by these patients is almost certainly related to patient rather than test differences. These patient differences could involve: (a) differing degrees of functional reorganization of the brain; (b) differing degrees of hippocampal damage; or (c) differing degrees of extrahippocampal structural damage (see Mayes et al., 2002). Future resolution of why patients show differing extents of item recognition impairment will require the use of sophisticated structural magnetic resonance imaging (MRI) and functional MRI procedures.

Contrasting patterns of deficits have also been reported in patients who have relatively selective damage to other Papez circuit structures (for discussion, see Mayes, 2000). For example, whereas the colloid cyst patients with fornix damage who were described by McMackin et al. (1995) had relatively intact item recognition, a colloid cyst patient with left fornix section, described by Mayes & Montaldi (1997), had clearly impaired item recognition. Nevertheless, the bulk of the evidence from animal and human studies suggests that lesions of the fornix, mammillary bodies and anterior thalamus leave item recognition relatively intact.

The anterior thalamic nucleus is connected to the retrosplenial cortex, which is one of the two major subdivisions of the posterior cingulate cortex. The retrosplenial cortex is connected to parts of the prefrontal and posterior parietal cortices, and provides a major input to the parahippocampal and entorhinal cortices, as well as to the presubiculum (see Maguire, 2001). There is growing evidence that retrosplenial cortex lesions disrupt explicit memory, although the precise nature of this disruption remains unclear. Maguire argued that examination of human cases with right-sided damage to the retrosplenial cortex indicates that this lesion causes a transient impairment in learning new spatial routes as well as in navigating previously familiar environments.

Whereas the perirhinal cortex receives, from the posterior association neocortex, highly processed information that may be particularly concerned with objects, the parahippocampal cortex receives mainly spatial information from its retrosplenial and posterior parietal cortex inputs. There is evidence that parahippocampal cortex lesions disrupt acquisition of spatial information in new environments more than information about objects (Bohbot et al., 1998; Epstein et al., 2001). In contrast, perirhinal cortex lesions in animals prevent acquisition of new object information, so as to impair intramodal and cross-modal recognition of objects and recognition of object–object associations, but may leave spatial recognition relatively intact (see Aggleton & Brown, 1999; Murray, 1999).

It remains uncertain whether damage to all parts of the Papez circuit disrupt explicit memory in the same way, as Aggleton & Brown (1999) have proposed. The mammillary bodies and anterior thalamus receive fornix projections from the entorhinal and perirhinal cortices, as well as from the hippocampus, and also receive inputs from other brain regions. To the extent that these non-hippocampal inputs are important, damage to other Papez circuit structures may have different effects on memory from those of hippocampal lesions. Although there is no convincing evidence that patients with medial temporal lobe and midline diencephalic lesions show different rates of forgetting (for discussion, see Isaac & Mayes, 1999a, 1999b), Parkin and his colleagues have proposed that lesions to these two sites disrupt contextual memory differently. In support of their proposal, they found that Korsakoff patients were more impaired on tests of memory for temporal order than were post-encephalitic amnesics who had equivalent item recognition memory deficits (e.g. Hunkin et al., 1994). However, like Korsakoff patients, patients with both selective hippocampal (Mayes et al., 2001) and larger medial temporal lobe lesions (Downes et al., 2002) have been shown to be more impaired at memory for temporal order than for item recognition. This does not refute the proposal of Parkin and his colleagues because it remains possible that patients with midline diencephalic lesions are more impaired at temporal order memory tests than are patients with medial temporal lobe lesions who have equivalent levels of item recognition memory. The possibility that midline diencephalic lesions have a slightly different effect from medial temporal lobe lesions on temporal and possibly other kinds of contextual memory requires more investigation. If the possibility is supported, it will need to be shown, however, that the greater effects on context memory of midline diencephalic lesions are not the result of incidental damage to frontal cortex regions concerned with temporal order memory (but see Parkin et al., 1994).

It remains unclear, therefore, whether midline diencephalic and medial temporal lobe lesions produce global amnesic syndromes with slightly different features. In contrast, there is no doubt that the patients described by Kapur and others (e.g. see Kapur et al., 1996) who show retrograde as well as anterograde amnesia have an atypical kind of anterograde amnesia. However, as these patients show normal memory for up to a day or longer after they have encoded new information before forgetting the information pathologically fast over a period of weeks or longer, it might be concluded that they merely have mild impairments rather than qualitatively distinct memory deficits. But this conclusion cannot be correct, because one such patient showed less severe memory deficits than a patient with hippocampal lesions at short delays but markedly more severe ones after delays of weeks or longer (Holdstock et al., 2002a). The neural bases of this disorder are uncertain, but it remains possible that some epileptic seizures contribute to the disorder in some, but not all, cases and that the location of damage may vary across cases.

It is well known, although sometimes disputed, that lateralized damage to the structures implicated in the amnesia syndrome causes material-specific memory deficits (for discussion, see Mayes, 1988). The most probable interpretation of such deficits is not that they constitute different kinds of processing impairment, but that they reflect the same kind of processing deficit of *different kinds of information*. If this interpretation is correct, then lesions which disconnect the input of specific kinds of information into the "memory processing regions" would be expected to cause memory impairments for the disconnected kinds of information (see Mayes, 1988). Ross (1982) has provided examples of memory deficits that show a high degree of material specificity, which are broadly consistent with this interpretation, and there have been reports of anterograde amnesia that is relatively selective for faces (Tippett et al., 2000).

As has already been indicated, theories of anterograde amnesia may also have to explain premorbid memory deficits if these cannot be dissociated from anterograde amnesia. Even if focal retrograde amnesia exists (see Kopelman, 2000), this does not prove that selective lesions can cause anterograde amnesia without some degree of retrograde amnesia. The major evidence for such a possibility would be single cases where it is claimed that the deficit mainly involves anterograde amnesia (e.g. Epstein et al., 2001) or group studies in which there is a negligible correlation between measures of anterograde and retrograde amnesia severity. Unfortunately, such studies have typically been confounded because tests of pre- and postmorbid memory have differed in critical ways, such as with respect to the kinds of information that subjects have to retrieve (for discussion, see Mayes et al., 1997).

WHAT KINDS OF FUNCTIONAL DEFICIT CAUSE ANTEROGRADE AMNESIA?

The amnesia syndrome could occur because information is not encoded properly, is not consolidated and stored properly, is not retrieved properly, or some combination of these problems. These processing deficits could apply to all aspects of episodic and factual information or to specific components of this information. Over the past 30 years, many of these different possible kinds of processing deficit have been proposed as the major cause of anterograde amnesia or even of the whole amnesia syndrome.

Few, however, have proposed that impairments in representing aspects of factual and episodic information at input cause anterograde amnesia. However, Butters & Cermak (1975) postulated that amnesics, or at least Korsakoff patients, do not spontaneously encode semantic features of information to a normal level at input, and that this failure causes patients' later poor memory. Although Gray & McNaughton (2000) have argued that some evidence (e.g. Oscar-Berman & Samuels, 1977) suggests that the proposed semantic encoding deficit may be part of a broader problem in multidimensional stimulus analysis, this possibility has not been developed, whereas the semantic encoding deficit hypothesis has been influential. However, if this hypothesis is proposing that amnesics do not spontaneously represent a normal amount of semantic information about stimuli at input, then it is in tension with patients' preserved intelligence and inconsistent with evidence that their immediate semantic memory is normal (Mayes et al., 1993) and that they benefit normally from semantic orientating tasks (see Mayes, 1988). This tension would be avoided if the hypothesis is construed in the way indicated by Cermak (1997). Cermak wrote that he had intended the hypothesis to postulate that amnesics fail to encode semantic information normally into long-term memory, i.e. at input, patients fail to *consolidate* into long-term memory semantic information that they may have represented normally. Like the encoding (representing at input) hypothesis, such a consolidation hypothesis should predict that purely perceptual explicit memory should be completely normal in amnesics. However, amnesics are clearly impaired at recognition tasks in which foils are so perceptually similar to targets that semantic and verbal memory cannot help performance (see Holdstock et al., 2002b).

On the basis of monkey studies, Murray & Bussey (1999) have, however, argued that a specific lesion that causes severe anterograde amnesia impairs the ability to represent certain kinds of information that are presented visually. They have proposed that perirhinal cortex lesions disrupt not only explicit memory for studied stimuli, but also disrupt the ability to represent certain aspects of high-level visual object information at all, so as to cause a kind of visual agnosia. If they are correct, then monkeys with perirhinal cortex lesions should show impaired perceptual discrimination in visual tests of the appropriate kind, even when memory load is minimized. Even if they are correct that perirhinal cortex lesions have this effect in monkeys, Buffalo et al. (1998) have found that human patients with large bilateral lesions of the medial temporal lobes that include the perirhinal cortex have normal short-term memory, let alone preserved matching abilities, for complex visual stimuli despite having very severe recognition deficits at longer delays. Even if perirhinal cortex lesions do disrupt aspects of perception, it remains unclear how much this encoding deficit contributes to the memory impairment that this lesion causes.

Encoding, or representation at input, should only be impaired in anterograde amnesia when poorly remembered information can only be represented in the critically damaged brain regions. This would be the case if certain kinds of visual object information only converge in the perirhinal cortex and, by extension, if certain kinds of associative information, such as associations between objects and their location, only converge in the hippocampus or entorhinal cortex. However, if the components of the information also converge in the neocortex or elsewhere, then representation should still be possible even when the lesion in question causes amnesia. It remains to be shown that any kind of information is represented *only* within the brain structures, damage to which causes anterograde amnesia. Even if some kinds of information are represented in this way, damage to these regions would cause not only an encoding deficit, but also a storage deficit if a widely held view is correct. This view is that information is stored within the same neural system that represents it at input (see Gaffan & Hornak, 1997). If this is true, then a lesion that destroys the storage site for specific information is also likely to impair the ability to represent that information at input (see Mayes & Roberts, 2002).

The most popular kind of hypothesis about the cause of anterograde amnesia is that patients do not store factual and episodic information properly, even though they can encode this information normally and retrieve it normally provided it is already in storage (e.g. Milner, 1968; O'Keefe & Nadel, 1978). This kind of hypothesis may seem to be in tension with the widely held view that specific information is represented and stored in the same system of neurons. However, this tension may be avoided by certain kinds of storage deficit hypothesis. This is certainly the case with the kind of storage deficit hypothesis which postulates that patients fail to consolidate information into long-term storage in still intact regions of the brain, such as the posterior neocortex. In other words, some or all features of anterograde amnesia are caused by lesions disrupting the facilitatory modulation of the processes that consolidate long-term memory storage *elsewhere* in the brain.

Several different hypotheses have proposed that some or all aspects of anterograde amnesia are caused by a selective disruption of the modulation of consolidation. It has been argued that amygdala damage disrupts a facilitatory modulation of the hippocampus and perhaps other structures when emotional stimuli are processed (Cahill et al., 1996). Amygdala damage may prevent emotional arousal from facilitating the consolidation of stimuli so that the ability to recall these stimuli declines abnormally fast (Phelps et al., 1998). The stimuli could be stored in the medial temporal lobes and parts of the neocortex.

Disconnection of the basal forebrain and midbrain from the medial temporal lobes and temporal neocortex causes a dense amnesia (Gaffan et al., 2001), but it seems very unlikely that factual and episodic information is stored in the basal forebrain and midbrain. It is much more plausible that the basal forebrain and midbrain exert both a tonic and a phasic facilitatory modulation of consolidation that occurs in the medial temporal lobes and temporal neocortex. This lack of facilitatory modulation largely prevents these latter regions from storing new memories, but leaves them still able to represent relatively normally the information that they cannot store.

Gray & McNaughton (2000) have argued that the hippocampus does not store any information related to facts or episodes, and Vinogradova (1975) has proposed that the hippocampus is a comparator that mediates novelty detection. Lesion evidence, which indicates that damage to this structure impairs the attentional arousal that novelty normally produces (e.g. Knight, 1996), supports Vinogradova's proposal. Without such attentional arousal, the consolidation processes that produce long-term storage primarily in the posterior neocortex would not occur normally, and anterograde amnesia would result. However, even if it is correct that hippocampal lesions block the upregulation of the neocortical storage of novel information, this deficit would only partly explain the anterograde amnesia caused by hippocampal lesions. This is because these lesions also impair memory for information that is not novel at input. More seriously, there is not even good evidence that hippocampal lesions impair memory more for information that was novel at input, rather than already familiar.

However, most hypotheses about anterograde amnesia have proposed that key lesions impair initial consolidation because the damaged sites are where some aspects of factual and episodic information are stored for at least some time after input. Theories of this kind are clearly in tension with the widely held view that storage occurs within the system of neurons that represent the stored information. If the view is correct, selective storage deficits, rather than combined storage and encoding deficits, should only be found if: (a) the key information is represented in two sites, but only the site damaged in amnesia is able to store the information or at least to store it rapidly; (b) partial damage to the site implicated in amnesia disrupts storage without disrupting representation. It is unknown whether either of these conditions hold, and the second condition would anyway only allow selective storage deficits to occur when damage to a key structure is less than total.

Two main contrasting selective storage deficit hypotheses have been adopted. The first kind of view, exemplified by the hypothesis of Squire & Alvarez (1995), is that structures in the medial temporal lobes initially consolidate and store key aspects of factual and episodic information but that, through a process of rehearsal and repetition, this information is slowly consolidated into neocortical storage so that the medial temporal lobes, where storage may have faded anyway, cease to be involved in retrieval. The second kind of view, espoused by Nadel & Moscovitch (1997), is that, although semantic memory storage entirely transfers to the neocortex after components of factual information have been initially stored in the medial temporal lobes, there are components of episodic information that remain stored in the medial temporal lobes for as long as episodic memory lasts. With rehearsal and repetition, this second kind of view states that episodic memories become more redundantly stored in the medial temporal lobes.

Both kinds of view allow that some kinds of factual and episodic information are rapidly stored in neocortical sites after relatively limited learning exposures. Other kinds of information are, however, stored at least initially in the medial temporal lobes, and are stored only slowly, if at all, in the neocortex. There have been a variety of hypotheses advanced about what these kinds of information are. It has been proposed that the medial temporal lobes store spatial information of a specific kind (O'Keefe & Nadel, 1978), an index which enables the specific components of episodes that are stored in the neocortex to be reactivated at retrieval (Teyler & Discenna, 1986), contextual information (see Mayes et al., 1985), relational information (Cohen & Eichenbaum, 1993; Cohen et al., 1997) and configural information (Rudy & Sutherland, 1989). All these accounts propose that the medial temporal lobes store some kind of associative information that links together informational components that are rapidly stored in the neocortex after input. The nature of these components is poorly specified. However, those who believe that the form of memory underlying priming is preserved in amnesia could postulate that any information for which patients show normal priming is stored rapidly in the neocortex. Furthermore, they could argue that this rapid storage is not enhanced significantly by processing in the structures that are damaged in amnesia.

Three comments need to be made about views like these, which postulate that associative storage sites are damaged in amnesics. First, as the sceptical views of Gray & McNaughton (2000) illustrate, strong evidence that storage is selectively impaired is hard to find. If certain kinds of information are not stored in amnesia, then one should expect that priming as well as explicit memory for that information should be impaired. As already indicated, there is quite good evidence that this is so. Nevertheless, the possibility that the storage processes underlying certain kinds of priming are preserved in amnesia has still not been conclusively disproved. Equally if storage is directly disrupted, consolidation should also be impaired, and if this occurs, forgetting should be accelerated. Although there is evidence that this occurs with free recall, most evidence indicates that it does not occur with item recognition, so the forgetting rate data are ambivalent. A storage interpretation of a lesion effect would, however, be strongly supported if: (a) the lesion disrupted a memory that had already been formed; and (b) transplanting tissue so that the damaged region returns to normal function, as indicated by restoration of the ability to acquire new memories of the relevant kind, does not restore the lost memory. If, however, transplantation that meets these conditions *does* restore a lost memory, then there is strong reason to believe that the memory was not stored in the damaged structure. This is because the transplanted tissue is unlikely to contain cells carrying the synaptic changes that constitute the lost memory. Precisely this pattern of results has been reported in monkeys for a form of conditional discrimination memory, which was recovered when an excitotoxic lesion of the CA1 field of the hippocampus was followed by a successful transplant of foetal or stem cell tissue (Virley et al., 1999).

Second, if some components of factual and episodic information can be stored rapidly in the neocortex, it is hard to see why more associative kinds of information cannot also be. In other words, it is hard to see why some neocortical learning mechanisms are very slow if others are rapid. Even if, contrary to some of the evidence about priming, rapid learning does not occur in the neocortex, it is still difficult to explain why any neocortical learning is slow. Although McClelland et al. (1995) have provided a computational reason for separating rapid and slow learning mechanisms, it is hard to specify how slow learning mechanisms work. Given that long-term potentiation (LTP) is often treated as a model of long-term memory storage, its rapid development at neocortical sites (Frankland et al., 2001) presents a general problem for the view that neocortical learning is slow. One explanation of why neocortical learning might still be slow has been given by Lisman & Morris

(2001), who argued that LTP involves strengthening synapses that are already present. They propose that sufficient synapses are usually not present at neocortical sites during initial learning and only emerge gradually, so that LTP and memory can only develop slowly through repetition and rehearsal. If there are more synapses linking within neocortical regions than between regions, this proposal could explain rapid neocortical learning of factual and episodic components and slow learning of certain associations.

Third, it remains unresolved whether the hippocampus and other parts of the medial temporal lobes permanently store certain episodic features (e.g. associations between different kinds of information), whether all storage initially mediated by the medial temporal lobes eventually transfers to the neocortex, or indeed whether any episodic or factual information is ever stored in the medial temporal lobes. However, on balance, it seems probable that key episodic and factual information is stored for at least a while within the medial temporal lobes, but despite this it remains controversial whether medial temporal lobe involvement with episodic memory declines over time. Even if temporal gradients of retrograde amnesia exist, memories that were acquired up to decades before the onset of amnesia are often impaired (see Mayes & Roberts, 2002). It seems unlikely that transfer of memories to stable long-term neocortical storage takes decades. More probably, if transfer exists, it occurs over a period of weeks, months or a few years at most. If so, it would be more appropriate to investigate slow consolidation by studying patients of the kind described by Kapur et al. (1996), who develop memory deficits over a period of weeks. It needs to be determined to what kinds of episodic and semantic memory these patients' difficulties apply, and whether their deficits are caused by disordered medial temporal lobe–neocortical interactions and neocortical storage deficits.

It has not often been proposed that amnesics encode and store factual and episodic information at least as well as controls, but this view was advanced by Warrington & Weiskrantz (1970, 1974), although later rejected by them (Warrington & Weiskrantz, 1978), and is still supported by Gray & McNaughton (2000). Based on the use of partial cueing with A–B, A–C learning paradigms that would later be construed as involving priming (but see Mayes et al., 1987), amnesics were found to show normal cued recall of A–B lists, but to show impaired cued recall of A–C lists with abnormal numbers of A–B intrusions (e.g. Warrington & Weiskrantz, 1974). This was interpreted as evidence that amnesics suffer from excessive interference during retrieval and have problems with suppressing incorrect competing responses. According to Gray & McNaughton, amnesics, or at least those amnesics with functional deficits of the same kind that are caused by hippocampal lesions, fail to inhibit competing incorrect responses to the same extent as normal subjects. On their view, the extent of amnesic deficits is a simple function of how much any memory task involves competition between responses rather than specific kinds of memory. In other words, amnesia arises when retrieval fails in certain situations because of a non-memory problem with active response suppression. This view is hard to investigate because very similar findings would be expected if amnesics fail to store certain kinds of information (e.g. contextual associations), so that cues fail to uniquely relate to the correct memory. In other words, failure to store certain information could be causing susceptibility to interference during retrieval, rather than susceptibility to interference causing poor retrieval.

In general, although frontal neocortex lesions can disrupt the search and checking operations that are important for retrieval (Shimamura, 1995), there is little evidence that the main lesions implicated in amnesia disrupt these directed and effortful retrieval processes. The automatic retrieval processes in which cues directly reactivate a memory representation

may well involve the same neurons that mediate storage, so that isolated deficits in such processes should be unlikely to occur. Nevertheless, despite the lack of evidence, there are two
circumstances in which the possible contribution to anterograde amnesia of impairments
to certain kinds of retrieval processes cannot be discounted. First, if a common functional
deficit underlies some aspects of both anterograde and retrograde amnesia, and it turns out
that retrograde amnesia does not involve disruption of previously stored memories, then
deficits in retrieval processes could still be a contributory factor in anterograde amnesia.
Second, if, contrary to much evidence, priming is preserved in amnesia and retrieval is
construed broadly to include processes which signal that a representation is of something
old or familiar, then anterograde amnesia might be caused by a deficit in this signalling
process (see Mayes & Roberts, 2002), rather than in an automatic or effortful search or
monitoring process. However, Buckner & Wheeler (2001) have argued that functional neuroimaging data suggest that this familiarity signal is provided by structures in the parietal
and frontal neocortex, rather than the brain regions usually associated with amnesia.

RECENT DEVELOPMENTS AND THE FUTURE

Several functional deficits, each caused by a distinct pattern of brain lesions, almost certainly contribute to the syndrome of anterograde amnesia. The long-term aim is to identify
all these functional deficits and the lesions or neural dysfunctions which underlie them, and
to create realistic models of how the damage causes the functional deficits. One promising
but controversial first step towards fulfilling this aim has been made by Aggleton & Brown
(1999). According to their hypothesis, intra-item associations are stored in the perirhinal
cortex through interactions with posterior and frontal neocortical as well as midline thalamic structures. Damage to this system should severely impair familiarity memory for
experienced items. In contrast, the hippocampus stores certain kinds of association through
interactions with the medial temporal cortices and other structures in the Papez circuit.
Damage to this system causes impairments in recollection, but not familiarity memory.

A computational neural network model, based on the biological structures of the hippocampus and medial temporal cortices, has been constructed which simulates not only the
recollection and familiarity functions of these structures, but also the effects of selective
lesions (Norman & O'Reilly, 2001). In this model, the hippocampus makes memory representations that emphasize the differences between similar patterns (pattern separation),
whereas the cortices make memory representations that emphasize similarities between
similar patterns. Only pattern separation leads naturally to pattern completion (recall and
recollection) when partial cues are provided at retrieval. This model provides a detailed
mechanism for the processes of recollection/recall and familiarity memory and makes predictions of a kind that cannot be made by neuropsychological hypotheses about the causes
of amnesia.

Future work should test the predictions of models such as that of Norman & O'Reilly, not
only about the effects of lesions but also about the neural activations produced by specific
memory processes. The Norman & O'Reilly model postulates that the hippocampus stores
complex factual and episodic associations in a very specific manner. This is radically different from the proposal of Gray & McNaughton, that the hippocampus stores no episodic
or semantic information even briefly but is critically involved in inhibiting incorrect, competing responses. Hypotheses like these must make conflicting predictions, and only by

testing which predictions are correct will the theoretical understanding of anterograde amnesia be advanced. The key to this understanding is knowing where different components of episodic and semantic information are stored and what brain regions mediate the initial and slow consolidation of such storage. Although there are quite well supported hypotheses, such as that of Aggleton & Brown (1999), the disagreement that remains will only be resolved by developing and testing the predictions of hypotheses that indicate how specific brain regions mediate memory functions and how lesions disrupt these functions. Eventually, such hypotheses must also indicate how functionally distinct regions interact.

REFERENCES

Aggleton, J.P. & Brown, M.W. (1999). Episodic memory, amnesia, and the hippocampal–anterior thalamic axis. *Behavioral and Brain Sciences*, **22**, 425–489.

Aggleton, J.P., McMackin, D., Carpenter, K. et al. (2000). Differential cognitive effects of colloid cysts in the third ventricle that spare or compromise the fornix. *Brain*, **123**, 800–815.

Aggleton, J.P. & Saunders, R.C. (1997). The relationships between temporal lobe and diencephalic structures implicated in anterograde amnesia. *Memory*, **5**, 49–71.

Bachevalier, J. & Mishkin, M. (1986). Visual recognition impairment follows ventromedial but not dorsolateral prefrontal lesions in monkeys. *Behavioral Brain Research*, **20**, 249–261.

Baxter, M.G. & Murray, E.A. (2001). Opposite relationship of hippocampal and rhinal cortex damage to delayed nonmatching-to-sample deficits in monkeys. *Hippocampus*, **11**, 61–71.

Baxter, M.G. & Murray, E.A. (2001b). Effects of hippocampal lesions on delayed nonmatching-to-sample in monkeys: a reply to Zola and Squire, *Hippocampus*, **11**, 201–203.

Bohbot, V., Kalina, M., Stepaknova, K. et al. (1998). Spatial memory deficits in patients with lesions to the right hippocampus and to the right parahippocampal cortex. *Neuropsychologia*, **36**, 1217–1238.

Brown, M.W. & Aggleton, J.P. (2001). Recognition memory: what are the roles of the perirhinal cortex and hippocampus? *Nature Reviews Neuroscience*, **2**, 51–61.

Buckner, R.L. & Wheeler, M.E. (2001). The cognitive neuroscience of remembering. *Nature Reviews Neuroscience*, **2**, 624–634.

Buffalo, E.A., Reber, P.J. & Squire, L.R. (1998). The human perirhinal cortex and recognition memory. *Hippocampus*, **8**, 330–339.

Butters, N. & Cermak, L.S. (1975). Some analyses of amnesic syndromes in brain damaged patients. In R.L. Isaacson & K.H. Pribram (eds), *The Hippocampus*, Vol. 2. New York: Plenum.

Cahill, L., Haier, R.J., Alkire, M.T. et al. (1996). Amygdala activity at encoding correlated with long-term free-recall of emotional information. *Proceedings of the National Academy of Science of the USA*, **93**, 8016–8021.

Cave, C.B. & Squire, L.R. (1991). Equivalent impairment of spatial and nonspatial memory following damage to the human hippocampus. *Hippocampus*, **1**, 329–340.

Cermak, L.S. (1997). A positive approach to viewing processing deficit theories of amnesia. *Memory*, **5**, 89–98.

Chalfonte, B.L., Verfaellie, M., Johnson, M.K. & Reiss, L. (1996). Spatial localization memory in amnesia: binding item and location information under incidental and intentional encoding condition. *Memory*, **4**, 591–614.

Chun, M.M. & Phelps, E.A. (1999). Memory deficits for implicit contextual information in amnesic subjects with hippocampal damage. *Nature Neuroscience*, **2**, 844–847.

Cohen, N.J. & Eichenbaum, H. (1993). *Memory, Amnesia, and the Hippocampal System*. Cambridge, MA: MIT Press.

Cohen, N.J., Poldrack, R.A. & Eichenbaum, H. (1997). Memory for items and memory for relations in the procedural/declarative memory framework. *Memory*, **5**, 131–178.

Downes, J.J., Mayes, A.R., MacDonald, C. & Hunkin, N.M. (2002). Temporal order memory in patients with Korsakoff's syndrome and medial temporal amnesia. *Neuropsychologia*, **40**, 853–861.

Easton, A. & Gaffan, D. (2001). Crossed unilateral lesions of the medial forebrain bundle and either inferior temporal or frontal cortex impair object-reward association learning in Rhesus monkeys. *Neuropsychologia*, **39**, 71–82.

Epstein, R., DeYoe, E.A., Press, D.Z. et al. (2001). Neuropsychological evidence for a topographical learning mechanism in parahippocampal cortex. *Cognitive Neuropsychology*, **18**, 481–508.

Fleischman, D.A., Gabrieli, J.D.E., Reminger, S. et al. (1995). Conceptual priming in perceptual identification for patients with Alzheimer's disease and a patient with right occipital lobectomy. *Neuropsychology*, **9**, 187–197.

Frankland, P.W., O'Brien, C., Ohno, M. et al. (2001). α–CaMKII-dependent plasticity in the cortex is required for permanent memory. *Nature*, **411**, 309–313.

Gabrieli, J.D.E. (1998). Cognitive neuroscience of human memory. *Annual Review of Psychology*, **49**, 87–115.

Gabrieli, J.D.E., Fleischman, D.A., Keane, M.M. et al. (1995). Double dissociation between memory systems underlying explicit and implicit memory in the human brain. *Psychological Science*, **6**, 76–82.

Gaffan, D. & Hornak, J. (1997). Amnesia and neglect: beyond the Delay–Brion system and the Hebb synapse. *Philosophical Transactions of the Royal Society, London B*, **352**, 1481–1488.

Gaffan, D., Parker, A. & Easton, A. (2001). Dense amnesia in the monkey after transection of fornix, amygdala and anterior temporal stem. *Neuropsychologia*, **39**, 51–70.

Gooding, P.A., Mayes, A.R. & van Eijk, R. (2000). A meta-analysis of indirect memory tests for novel material in organic amnesics. *Neuropsychologia*, **38**, 666–676.

Gray, J.A. & McNaughton, N. (2000). *The Neuropsychology of Anxiety*, 2nd edn. Oxford: Oxford University Press.

Green, R. & Kopelman, M.D. (2002). Contribution of context-dependent memory and familiarity judgements to forgetting rates in organic amnesia. *Cortex*, **38**, 161–178.

Haist, F., Shimamura, A.P. & Squire, L.R. (1992). On the relationship between recall and recognition memory. *Journal of Experimental Psychology: Learning, Memory and Cognition*, **18**, 691–702.

Hamann, S.B. & Squire, L.R. (1997a). Intact priming for novel perceptual representations in amnesia. *Journal of Cognitive Neuroscience*, **9**, 699–713.

Hamann, S.B. & Squire, L.R. (1997b). Intact perceptual priming in the absence of conscious memory. *Behavioral Neuroscience*, **111**, 850–854.

Hirst, W., Johnson, M.K., Phelps, E.A. (1986). Recognition and recall in amnesics. *Journal of Experimental Psychology: Learning, Memory and Cognition*, **12**, 445–451.

Hirst, W., Johnson, M.K., Phelps, E.A. & Volpe, B.T. (1988). More on recognition and recall in amnesics. *Journal of Experimental Psychology: Learning, Memory and Cognition*, **14**, 758–762.

Holdstock, J.S., Mayes, A.R., Isaac, C.L. & Roberts, N. (2002a). Differential involvement of the hippocampus and temporal lobe cortices in rapid and slow learning of new semantic information. *Neuropsychologia*, **40**, 748–768.

Holdstock, J.S., Mayes, A.R., Roberts, N. et al. (2002b). Under what conditions is recognition spared relative to recall following selective hippocampal lesions in humans? *Hippocampus*, **12**, 341–351.

Hunkin, N.M., Parkin, A.J. & Longmore, B.E. (1994). Aetiological variation in the amnesic syndrome: comparisons using the list discrimination task. *Neuropsychologia*, **32**, 819–826.

Isaac, C.L., Holdstock, J.S., Cezayirli, E. et al. (1998). Amnesia in a patient with lesions limited to the dorsomedial thalamic nucleus. *Neurocase*, **4**, 497–508.

Isaac, C.L. & Mayes, A.R. (1999a). Rate of forgetting in amnesia 1: recall and recognition of prose. *Journal of Experimental Psychology: Learning, Memory and Cognition*, **25**, 942–962.

Isaac, C.L. & Mayes, A.R. (1999b). Rate of forgetting in amnesia 11: recall and recognition of word lists at different levels of organization. *Journal of Experimental Psychology: Learning, Memory and Cognition*, **25**, 963–977.

Kapur, N., Scholey, K., Moore, E. et al. (1996). Long-term retention deficits in two cases of disproportionate retrograde amnesia. *Journal of Cognitive Neuroscience*, **8**, 416–434.

Keane, M.M., Gabrieli, J.D.E., Mapstone, H.C. et al. (1995). Double dissociation of memory capabilities after bilateral occipital lobe or medial temporal lobe lesions. *Brain*, **118**, 1129–1148.

Kinder, A. & Shanks, D.R. (2001). Amnesia and the declarative/nondeclarative distinction: a recurrent network model of classification, recognition, and repetition priming. *Journal of Cognitive Neuroscience*, **13**, 648–669.

Knight R.T. (1996). Contribution of human hippocampal region to novelty detection. *Nature*, **383**, 256–259.

Kopelman, M.D. (1985). Rates of forgetting in Alzheimer-type dementia and Korsakoff's syndrome. *Neuropsychologia*, **23**, 623–638.

Kopelman, M.D. (2000). Focal retrograde amnesia and the attribution of causality: an exceptionally critical review. *Cognitive Neuropsychology*, **17**, 585–562.

Kopelman, M.D. & Stanhope, N. (1997). Rates of forgetting in organic amnesia following temporal lobe, diencephalic or frontal lobe lesions. *Neuropsychology*, **11**, 343–356.

Kopelman, M.D., Stanhope, N. & Kingsley, D. (1997). Temporal and spatial context memory in patients with focal frontal, temporal lobe and diencephalic lesions. *Neuropsychologia*, **35**, 1533–1545.

Lisman, J. & Morris, R.G.M. (2001). Why is the cortex a slow learner? *Nature*, **411**, 248–249.

Maguire, E.A. (2001). The retrosplenial contribution to human navigation: a review of lesion and neuroimaging findings. *Scandinavian Journal of Psychology*, **42**, 225–238.

Mangels, J.A. (1997). Strategic processing and memory for temporal order in patients with frontal lobe lesions. *Neuropsychology*, **11**, 207–221.

Manns, J.R. & Squire, L.R. (1999). Impaired recognition memory on the Doors and People test after damage limited to the hippocampal region. *Hippocampus*, **9**, 495–499.

Mark, V.H., Barry, H., McLardy, T. & Ervin, F.R. (1970). The destruction of both anterior thalamic nuclei in a patient with intractable agitated depression. *Journal of Nervous and Mental Disorders*, **150**, 266–272.

Mayes, A.R. (1988). *Human Organic Memory Disorders*. Cambridge: Cambridge University Press.

Mayes, A.R. (2000). Effects on memory of Papez circuit lesions. In L.S. Cermak (ed.) *Handbook of Neuropsychology (2nd Edition), Volume 4: Memory and its Disorders*. Amsterdam: Elsevier Sciences.

Mayes, A.R., Daum, I., Markowitsch, H. & Sauter, W. (1997). The relationship between retrograde and anterograde amnesia in patients with typical global amnesia. *Cortex*, **33**, 197–217.

Mayes, A.R. & Downes, J.J. (1997). What do theories of the functional deficit(s) underlying amnesia have to explain? *Memory*, **5**, 3–36.

Mayes, A.R., Downes, J.J., Shoqeirat, M. et al. (1993). Encoding ability is preserved in amnesia: evidence from a direct test of encoding. *Neuropsychologia*, **31**, 745–759.

Mayes, A.R., Holdstock, J.S., Isaac, C.L. et al. (2002). Relative sparing of item recognition memory in a patient with adult-onset damage limited to the hippocampus. *Hippocampus*, **12**, 325–340.

Mayes, A.R., Isaac, C.L., Holdstock, J.S. et al. (2001). Memory for single items, word pairs, and temporal order of different kinds in a patient with selective hippocampal lesions. *Cognitive Neuropsychology*, **18**, 97–123.

Mayes, A.R., MacDonald, C., Donlan, L. et al. (1992) Amnesics have a disproportionately severe memory deficit for interactive context. *Quarterly Journal of Experimental Psychology*, **45A**, 265–297.

Mayes, A.R., Meudell, P.R. & MacDonald, C. (1991). Disproportionate intentional spatial memory impairments in amnesia. *Neuropsychologia*, **29**, 771–784.

Mayes, A.R., Meudell, P.R. & Pickering, A. (1985). Is organic amnesia caused by a selective deficit in remembering contextual information? *Cortex*, **21**, 167–202.

Mayes, A.R. & Montaldi, D. (1997). Neuroradiological approaches to the study of organic amnesia. In A.J. Parkin (ed.), *Case Studies in the Neuropsychology of Memory*. Hove, Sussex: Psychology Press.

Mayes, A.R. & Roberts, N. (2002). Theories of episodic amnesia. *Philosophical Transactions of the Royal Society, London B*, **356**, 1395–1408.

McClelland, J.L., McNaughton, B.L. & O'Reilly, R.C. (1995). Why there are complementary learning systems in the hippocampus and neocortex: insights from the successes and failures of connectionist models of learning and memory. *Psychological Review*, **102**, 419–457.

McMackin, D., Cockburn, J., Anslow, P. & Gaffan, D. (1995). Correlation of fornix damage with memory impairments of six cases of colloid cyst removal. *Acta Neurochirurgie. (Wien)*, **135**, 12–18.

Milner, B. (1968). Preface: material specific and generalized memory loss. *Neuropsychologia*, **6**, 175–179.

Murray, E. (1999). Memory for objects in non-human primates. In M. Gazzaniga (ed.), *The Cognitive Neurosciences*, 2nd edn. Cambridge, MA: MIT Press.

Murray, E.A. & Bussey, T.J. (1999). Perceptual–mnemonic functions of the perirhinal cortex. *Trends in Cognitive Science*, **3**, 142–151.

Nadel, L. & Moscovitch, M. (1997). Memory consolidation, retrograde amnesia and the hippocampal complex. *Current Opinions in Neurobiology*, **7**, 217–227.

Norman, K.A. & O'Reilly, R.C. (2001). Modelling hippocampal and neocortical contributions to recognition memory: a complementary learning systems approach. Technical Report, University of Colorado.

O'Keefe, J. & Nadel, L. (1978). *The Hippocampus as Cognitive Map*. Oxford: Clarendon.

Oscar-Berman, M.O. & Samuels, I. (1977). Stimulus preference and memory factors in Korsakoff's syndrome. *Neuropsychologia*, **15**, 99–106.

Ostergaard, A.L. (1999). Priming deficits in amnesia: now you see them, now you don't. *Journal of the International Neuropsychological Society*, **5**, 175–190.

Parkin, A.J., Leng, N.R.C. & Hunkin, N. (1990). Differential sensitivity to context in diencephalic and temporal lobe amnesia. *Cortex*, **26**, 373–380.

Parkin, A.J., Rees, J.E., Hunkin, N.M. & Rose, P.E. (1994). Impairment of memory following discrete thalamic infarction. *Neuropsychologia*, **32**, 39–52.

Phelps, E.A., LaBar, K.S., Anderson, A.K. et al. (1998). Specifying the contributions of the human amygdala to emotional memory: a case study. *Neurocase*, **4**, 527–540.

Pickering, A., Mayes, A.R., & Fairbairn, A.F. (1989). Amnesia and memory for modality information. *Neuropsychologia*, **27**, 1249–1259.

Reed, J.M. & Squire, L.R. (1997). Impaired recognition memory in patients with lesions limited to the hippocampal formation. *Behavioral Neuroscience*, **111**, 667–675.

Rubin, D.C. & Greenberg, D.L. (1998). Visual memory-deficit amnesia: a distinct amnesic presentation and etiology. *Proceedings of the National Academy of Sciences of the USA*, **95**, 5413–5416.

Rudy, J.W. & Sutherland, R.J. (1989). The hippocampal formation is necessary for rats to learn and remember configural discriminations. *Behavioural Brain Research*, **34**, 97–109.

Russchen, F.T., Amaral, D.G. & Price, J.L. (1987). The afferent input to the magnocellular division of the mediodorsal nucleus in the monkey *Macaca fascicularis*. *Journal of Comparative Neurology*, **271**, 175–210.

Shimamura, A. P. (1995). Memory and frontal lobe function. In M.S. Gazzaniga (ed.), *The Cognitive Neurosciences*. Cambridge, MA: MIT Press.

Shimamura, A., Janowsky, J.S., & Squire, L. (1990). Memory for the temporal order of events in patients with frontal lobe lesions and amnesic patients. *Neuropsychologia*, **28**, 803–813.

Shoqeirat, M. & Mayes, A.R. (1991). Disproportionate incidental spatial memory and recall deficits in amnesia. *Neuropsychologia*, **29**, 749–769.

Smith, S.M. (1988). Environmental context and human memory. In G.M. Davies & D.M. Thomson (eds), *Memory in Context: Context in Memory* (pp. 13–24). New York: Wiley.

Squire, L.R. & Alvarez, P. (1995). Retrograde amnesia and memory consolidation: a neurobiological perspective. *Current Opinion in Neurobiology*, **5**, 169–177.

Squire, L.R. & Kandel, E.R. (1999). *Memory: From Mind to Molecules*. New York: W.H. Freeman.

Teyler, T. & Discenna, P. (1986). The hippocampal memory indexing theory. *Behavioral Neuroscience*, **100**, 147–154.

Tippett, L.J., Miller, L.A. & Farah, M.J. (2000). Prosopamnesia: a selective impairment in face learning. *Cognitive Neuropsychology*, **17**, 241–256.

Valenstein, E., Bowers, D., Verfaellie, M. et al. (1987). Retrosplenial amnesia. *Brain*, **110**, 1631–1646.

Vargha-Khadem, F., Gadian, D.G., Watkins, K.E. et al. (1997). Differential effects of early hippocampal pathology on episodic and semantic memory. *Science*, **277**, 376–380.

Verfaellie, M., Koseff, P. & Alexander, M.P. (2000). Acquisition of novel semantic information in amnesia: effects of lesion location. *Neuropsychologia*, **38**, 484–492.

Vinogradova, O.S. (1975). Functional organization of the limbic system in the process of registration of information: facts and hypotheses. In R.I. Isaacson & K.H. Pribram (eds), *The Hippocampus*. New York: Plenum.

Virley, D., Ridley, R.M., Sinden, J.D. et al. (1999). Primary CA1 and conditionally immortal MHP36 cell grafts restore conditional discrimination learning and recall in marmosets after excitotoxic lesions of the hippocampal CA1 field. *Brain*, **122**, 2321–2335.

von Cramon, D.Y. & Schuri, U. (1992). The septo-hippocampal pathways and their relevance to human memory: a case report. *Cortex*, **28**, 411–422.

Warrington, E.K. & Weiskrantz, L. (1970). Amnesic syndrome: consolidation or retrieval? *Nature*, **228**, 628–630.

Warrington, E.K. & Weiskrantz, L. (1974). The effect of prior learning on subsequent retention in amnesic patients. *Neuropsychologia*, **12**, 419–428.

Warrington, E.K. & Weiskrantz, L. (1978). Further analysis of the prior learning effect in amnesic patients. *Neuropsychologia*, **16**, 169–177.

Wheeler, M.A., Stuss, D.T. & Tulving, E. (1995). Frontal lobe damage produces episodic memory impairment. *Journal of the International Neuropsychological Society*, **I**, 525–536.

Zola, S.M. & Squire, L.R. (2001). Relationship between magnitude of damage to the hippocampus and impaired recognition memory in monkeys. *Hippocampus*, **11**, 92–98.

Zola-Morgan, S., Squire, L.R. & Amaral, D.G. (1989a). Lesions of the amygdala that spare adjacent cortical regions do not impair memory or exacerbate the impairment following lesions of the hippocampus. *Journal of Neuroscience*, **9**, 1922–1936.

Zola-Morgan, S., Squire, L.R., Amaral, D.G. & Susuki, W. (1989b). Lesions of the peripheral and parahippocampal cortex that spare the amygdala and hippocampal formation produce severe memory impairment. *Journal of Neuroscience*, **9**, 4355–4370.

CHAPTER 9

Retrograde Amnesia

Michael D. Kopelman

University Department of Psychiatry and Psychology,
St Thomas's Hospital, King's College London, UK

The study of retrograde amnesia (RA) in brain disease is a fertile topic of research at present. The principal issues at stake will be briefly reviewed, including the relationship of structural brain pathology to RA, dissociations within RA, the associations/correlates of RA and, in particular, the relationship between (and putative independence of) RA and anterograde amnesia (AA). The influence of psychogenic factors on RA will be mentioned only briefly, because this is considered in more detail in Chapter 21. Recent theories of RA will be surveyed.

Methods of Empirical Investigation

In the first modern empirical study of RA in brain-damaged patients, Sanders & Warrington (1971) employed a test requiring subjects to identify the names of famous faces from different time periods, and to provide the answers to a questionnaire about public events from 1930 to 1968. Variants of these tests have been widely employed in subsequent studies, as well as derivative procedures, e.g. identifying pictures of famous news events or the names of US Presidents, and/or identifying whether such people are "dead or alive". By contrast, Zola-Morgan et al. (1983) employed a procedure in which patients were required to produce incidents from their past relating to particular word cues, to describe these incidents in detail, and then to specify when and where they occurred. This latter procedure was based upon earlier investigations in healthy subjects by Galton (1879), Crovitz & Schiffman (1974), and Robinson (1976), and it is now often referred to as the "Crovitz test". In order to make this type of procedure more systematic, tapping incidents and also "personal semantic" facts from specified time-periods, Kopelman et al. (1989, 1990) introduced the Autobiographical Memory Interview (AMI): this requires subjects to produce memories of incidents and personal facts to cue-words relating to these time periods (childhood, early adult life, and "recent"). Other techniques have also been employed, e.g. Fromholt & Larsen (1991, 1992) asked patients to produce a "free narrative" of important personal and public events from their lives. Findings from these different tests will be considered below.

The Handbook of Memory Disorders. Edited by A.D. Baddeley, M.D. Kopelman and B.A. Wilson
© 2002 John Wiley & Sons, Ltd.

STRUCTURAL BRAIN PATHOLOGY
AND RETROGRADE AMNESIA

This topic was considered in some detail by Hodges (1995) in the first edition of this *Handbook*, and it has also been reviewed in detail elsewhere (Kopelman 1993, 2000a; Kapur, 1999).

There is little doubt that large temporal lobe lesions produce an extensive RA (e.g. Cermak & O'Connor, 1983; Wilson & Wearing, 1995). Cermak & O'Connor (1983) studied a patient, S.S., who had suffered herpes encephalitis resulting in bitemporal pathology and a severe anterograde amnesia. On a test of famous faces (Albert et al., 1979), he showed a marked impairment in performance but relative sparing of early memories (a "temporal gradient"). During follow-up over a number of years, there was substantial improvement. Asked about events from his past life (1930s–1970s) on a questionnaire, he showed impairment for the two most recent decades only. Given cue-words, and asked to describe specific episodes from his past relating to those words (the so-called "Crovitz test"), S.S. seemed to display only a "personal pool of generalized knowledge about himself, i.e. his own semantic memory". On the other hand, his past knowledge about physics and laser technology (his profession) appeared to be intact, although he was not able to retain information encountered in a new article about the subject. A further study showed that he was impaired in recalling and recognizing the meaning of words which had come into the language only since the onset of his amnesia (Verfaellie et al., 1995a). Hodges (1995) argued that there was not a temporal gradient in herpes encephalitis patients, but data from the Cermak & O'Connor study and that of Kopelman et al. (1999) suggest that there is, in fact, a weak or "gentle" one. Fujii et al. (2000) placed particular emphasis on the importance of damage to the temporal pole in such patients, arguing that such pathology disconnects pathways between the hippocampi and the temporal lobe neocortex.

Large frontal lobe lesions can also produce retrograde memory loss, particularly if bilateral. Baddeley & Wilson (1986) described impoverished retrieval of autobiographical memories in two such patients and florid confabulation in the retrieval of autobiographical memories in two others. Levine et al. (1998) reported a patient who had a right frontal lesion with a severe and disproportionate retrograde amnesia. These authors emphasized damage to the uncinate fasciculus, causing disconnection between the frontal and temporal lobes. Group studies of patients with neuroradiologically delineated frontal lesions have also demonstrated severe impairments in autobiographical memory retrieval (Della Sala et al., 1993; Kopelman et al., 1999) and knowledge of famous faces or news events (D'Esposito et al., 1996; Mangels et al., 1996; Kopelman et al., 1999).

With respect to diencephalic lesions, there have been many investigations of Korsakoff patients, and there is little doubt that they generally show an extensive RA with a relatively steep temporal gradient (Zola-Morgan et al., 1983; Butters & Cermak, 1986; Kopelman, 1989; Kopelman et al., 1999). Kopelman (1989) found an RA extending back approximately 25 years, and that Korsakoff patients had a steeper temporal gradient than did Alzheimer patients across several different types of remote memory test. Squire et al. (1989) compared the performance of seven patients with the alcoholic Korsakoff syndrome with that of five patients of more acute onset on six tests of remote memory. In both groups, there was a temporally-graded RA extending across a period of about 15 years, and the temporal gradient was closely similar between the two groups. Verfaellie et al. (1995b) examined remote memory for semantic information in Korsakoff and other amnesic patients, using a test of vocabulary for words that had come into the language between 1955 and 1989. They found an impairment in the Korsakoff patients in the recall of these words, and that there was a temporal gradient such that their knowledge of recent words was more impaired than that of remote words. However, the concomitant presence of some degree of frontal lobe atrophy in Korsakoff patients appears to contribute to their RA. This was first postulated on the basis of correlations between RA scores and frontal/executive test performance by Kopelman (1991), who showed that 68% of the variance on remote memory tests could be accounted for by a regression based on executive test scores. Verfaellie et al. (1995b) also obtained a significant correlation between performance on their remote memory test and a "composite" frontal test index.

Findings in patients with diencephalic lesions from vascular aetiology or tumours are more variable. Winocur et al. (1984) did not find RA in a thalamic infarction patient, neither did Graff-Radford et al. (1990) in the majority of their cases, nor did Guinan et al. (1998) and Kopelman et al. (1999) in pituitary tumour cases (despite anterograde memory disorder in pituitary tumour patients, which was sometimes severe). On the other hand, Stuss et al. (1988) reported severe and extensive RA in a patient with bilateral paramedian thalamic infarction, and Hodges & McCarthy (1993) described severe autobiographical memory loss with relatively preserved knowledge of famous people in a somewhat similar patient who showed severe impairments on tests of executive function. Hodges (1995) attributed such RA to a disconnection between frontal (retrieval and initiation) and posterior (storage) components of the memory system.

Most controversial is the issue of whether damage apparently confined to the medial temporal lobes produces an extensive RA. Following a bitemporal lobectomy, patient HM appeared in initial studies to have an RA of only 2–3 years (Milner, 1966, 1972). This appeared to be confirmed on tests of famous faces and famous news events (Marslen-Wilson & Teuber, 1975; Gabrieli et al. 1988), although performance on the Crovitz test suggested a memory impairment extending back 11 years before the operation (Corkin, 1984). Zola-Morgan et al. (1986) found a 2 year RA in a patient with moderately severe AA following hypoxic brain damage to the CA1 regions of the hippocampi bilaterally. In contrast, Nadel & Moscovitch (1997) reviewed reports which suggested that hippocampal pathology alone can produce an extensive RA. Unfortunately, many of the studies they reviewed involved patients with extensive temporal lobe pathology, confounding the interpretation of the findings: this issue will be taken up again below (see section on Theories).

Kopelman et al. (1999) carried out the first study comparing groups of patients with temporal lobe, frontal lobe or diencephalic lesions across several different RA tasks, including recall of autobiographical incidents, personal semantic facts and famous news events. As already mentioned, Korsakoff patients (with combined diencephalic and frontal pathology) showed severe RA across all tasks with a relatively steep temporal gradient, whereas patients who had been treated for pituitary tumours extending into the diencephalon showed moderate or severe AA but no evidence of RA. Patients with temporal lobe pathology also showed a severe RA, although their temporal gradients appeared to be "flatter" than those of Korsakoff patients. Patients with frontal lobe lesions showed severe impairment in the recall of autobiographical incidents and famous news events, but were relatively intact in the retrieval of well-rehearsed personal semantic facts, i.e. this latter group seemed to be particularly impaired where "effortful" or organized retrieval processes were required for reconstructing "old" memories. In general, patients with bilateral frontal lesions performed worse than patients with unilateral frontal lesions. Subsequent analysis has shown significant correlations with quantitative MRI measures of the volume of specific brain structures in these patients, such that 60–68% of the variance on autobiographical memory tasks could be accounted for by changes in these regional brain volumes.

In summary, large temporal lobe or frontal lesions can produce an extensive RA. More controversial are the specific effects of isolated diencephalic or medial temporal lobe pathology. Diencephalic lesions appear to contribute to an extensive RA when there is concomitant frontal pathology or frontal/executive dysfunction. The contribution of medial temporal lobe pathology in isolation remains controversial.

DISSOCIATIONS IN RETROGRADE AMNESIA

Autobiographical vs. Semantic Remote Memory

Autobiographical memory refers to a person's recollection of past incidents and events, which occurred at a specific time and place. Episodic memory is sometimes used in a somewhat broader sense, encompassing autobiographical memory as well as performance on certain learning tasks (e.g. recall of a word list). However, the terms "autobiographical" and "episodic" are often used interchangeably. In the RA literature, autobiographical memory is commonly tested on tasks such as the Crovitz and the AMI. Semantic memory is commonly defined as referring to knowledge of language, concepts, and facts that do not have a specific time or location: they may once have been learned at a particular time and place, but these contextual aspects are not retained. The more semantic aspects of RA are commonly assessed on tests of famous faces, famous names, or famous news events. However, it is important to note that there may be a continuum of knowledge across these domains. First, "personal semantic" facts, such as the names of past schoolteachers or acquaintances, fall midway between the more purely autobiographical and semantic aspects of knowledge. Second, performance on many existing retrograde memory tests, involving famous faces or news events, may involve both autobiographical and more purely semantic knowledge (e.g. a picture of the mangled Mercedes in which Princess Diana died may conjure up simultaneously both the "semantic" facts of the accident and autobiographical information about what you were doing at the time). Third, it is difficult to develop equivalent tests of autobiographical and semantic remote memory for comparative purposes (Kopelman & Kapur, 2001).

Nevertheless, the most common distinction employed in the RA literature is that between autobiographical (episodic) memory and semantic memory (e.g. Kopelman, 1993). Indeed, Kapur (1999) has employed this distinction as the fundamental division within an hierarchical model of retrograde amnesia, in which there are further subdivisions between "pre-ictal" and "extended" episodic RA and between "semantic" knowledge of people and of events.

De Renzi et al. (1987) reported the case of a 44 year-old woman who, following an episode of herpes encephalitis, displayed a severe impairment of semantic knowledge, contrasting with normal memory for autobiographical events. She was impaired at tasks demanding the retrieval of words or of their meaning, e.g. on a confrontation naming test, a sentence verification test, and a test requiring classification of items to categories. More pertinently, she was impaired at knowledge of famous people (including Hitler, Mussolini and Stalin) and at knowledge of public events, e.g. she was unable to provide any information about either the Second World War or the recent (at that time) assassination of the Italian Prime Minister. Cueing helped her in some instances, but she was never able to achieve detailed recollection of these public events. By contrast, not only did she remember personal incidents that had occurred before and after the acute stage of her illness, but she was well informed on current issues in her family, and she could recall the bulk of what had been done from testing session to testing session. A 20-item questionnaire was constructed about autobiographical memories, and her performance was generally very satisfactory. An MRI scan showed a large irregular area of increased signal density extending over the inferior and anterior part of the left temporal lobe, above and lateral to the temporal horn (which was enlarged), involving the amygdala, the uncus, the hippocampus and the parahippocampal gyrus. The frontal lobes and the language areas of the temporal and parietal lobes were spared. In the right hemisphere, there were only minimal signs of increased signal density in the white matter of the inferior temporal lobe.

Subsequent studies have reported disproportionate impairment of knowledge of public events, compared with autobiographical memories, in other patients with left hemisphere pathology, including: a large left parietal lesion following head injury (Grossi et al., 1988); left temporal lobe epilepsy and/or temporal lobectomy (Barr et al., 1990; Kapur et al., 1989); and bilateral irradiation necrosis of anterior/inferior temporal lobe structures (Kapur et al., 1994; Yasuda et al., 1997). Patients with semantic dementia resulting from left temporal lobe atrophy also show disproportionate semantic memory loss. Some studies report preservation of "recent", but not more distant, autobiographical memories in semantic dementia (Snowden et al. 1996; Graham & Hodges, 1997), whereas other investigations find a more uniform impairment of autobiographical memory retrieval, largely secondary to their semantic memory deficit (Moss et al. 2002).

There are other patients who have been reported to show the opposite pattern of performance, i.e. disproportionate autobiographical memory impairment. Dalla Barba et al. (1990) described a female Korsakoff patient with severe episodic memory problems, but who performed well when asked questions about famous people or events. O'Connor et al. (1992) described a patient who had extensive damage to right temporal lobe structures following herpes encephalitis: this resulted in a disproportionately severe impairment in the recall of autobiographical incidents, relative to remote semantic information. This patient also exhibited severe visuoperceptual deficits, and the authors argued that she might have had a particular difficulty in eliciting the visual images necessary for the retrieval of past autobiographical experiences. Ogden (1993) described a head injury patient who also had a severe autobiographical memory loss, associated with prosopagnosia and visual agnosia, with relative preservation of remote semantic knowledge. In this case, the pathology was more posterior, but projections from the right occipital to the right temporal lobe were disrupted. Ogden (1993) suggested, like O'Connor et al. (1992), that a failure in visual imagery might be contributing to the autobiographical memory loss, and both patients manifested a severe impairment in visual, anterograde memory. Rubin & Greenberg (1998) have reviewed a series of similar cases, in whom "visual memory-deficit amnesia" gave rise to apparently disproportionate impairments in autobiographical memory.

However, group studies have indicated that this simple left/semantic vs. right/autobiographical distinction, postulated in single-case reports, does not necessarily hold good. Kopelman et al. (1999) did indeed find particularly severe autobiographical memory loss in patients with right-sided temporal lobe damage from herpes encephalitis, relative to patients with left-sided pathology, consistent with several of the studies cited above (O'Connor et al., 1992; Ogden, 1993; Rubin & Greenberg, 1998). But it should also be noted that the right-sided patients were, in addition, impaired on a measure of famous news events, particularly when this test involved perception of famous faces, suggesting that there were both "episodic" and face recognition components to the test. Left-sided patients were particularly impaired when they had to "complete" the names of famous people from the past from word-stems: this was interpreted as reflecting a deficit in the lexical–semantic labelling of remote memories. There was a statistically significant right/left double dissociation between performance on the autobiographical incidents and famous name-completion tasks (see Figure 9.1). By contrast, Eslinger (1998) also examined patients with left or right temporal pathology, finding that left medial temporal lesions caused time-limited retrograde autobiographical memory changes. More extensive left temporal lobe pathology impaired personal semantic memory, but did not affect recollection of autobiographical incidents. However, right temporal lobe lesions did not appear to affect *either* personal semantic *or* autobiographical incident recall. *Bilateral* temporal lobe lesions seemed to be required to cause extensive autobiographical memory deficits, and Eslinger (1998) postulated that interactions between prefrontal cortex and diverse temporal lobe regions were involved in autobiographical memory retrieval.

In summary, there is some evidence that the more semantic remote memories are dependent upon left temporal lobe function, and that the retrieval of autobiographical incidents is more dependent upon the integrity of right temporal lobe structures. However, this distinction is by no means clear-cut, perhaps reflecting the fact that performance on many remote memory tasks involves aspects of both autobiographical and semantic memory. For example, there is evidence that tests involving identification of famous faces or pictures of famous news events may be sensitive to damage in the right temporal lobe, and that it is tests involving the lexical–semantic labelling of remote memories which are particularly sensitive to left temporal lobe damage.

Explicit vs. Implicit Remote Memory

A different type of dissociation in remote memory was reported by Warrington & McCarthy (1988) and McCarthy & Warrington (1992). They described a 54 year-old man who had suffered herpes encephalitis, resulting in bilateral medial temporal lobe damage as well as generalized signal alteration and atrophy of the right temporal lobe neocortex. This patient showed extensive retrograde amnesia for autobiographical episodes and also for knowledge of public events, famous faces and famous names. Despite this, he performed within normal limits at a word-completion task for famous names, requiring him to give the "completed" name to a picture and a name-stem, and at familiarity judgements for famous faces. The authors proposed a dual system for the semantic representation of names and faces: a vocabulary-like fact memory, which was preserved in this patient, and a cognitive mediation memory system, which was impaired. The implication seemed to be that the former was analogous to so-called "implicit" memory, which is preserved in anterograde amnesia.

Several subsequent studies have employed similar tests. Eslinger et al. (1996) compared the performance of two post-encephalitic patients. One had sustained left inferior and anterior medial temporal lobe damage, together with a small right temporal polar lesion, and

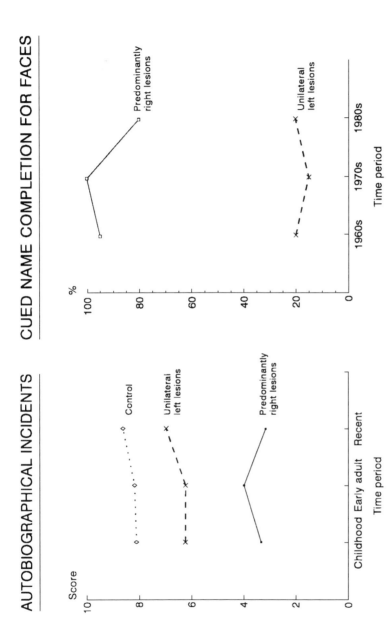

Figure 9.1 Herpes patients with right-sided lesions are severely impaired at recalling autobiographical incidents (left panel) but not at a more semantic remote memory task (right panel). Herpes patients with left-sided lesions are only mildly impaired in recalling autobiographical incidents (left) but are severely impaired at the more semantic task (right). The recall of autobiographical incidents was determined using the Autobiographical Memory Interview (AMI). The more semantic task involved naming famous faces to word-stem cues. Two herpes patients with unilateral left temporal damage were compared with three herpes patients with predominantly right temporal lobe damage

the other showed right-sided inferior and anterior medial temporal lobe pathology. The left-sided patient was substantially impaired at the name-completion task, when the cue was paired with a famous face, whereas the right-sided patient showed only very mild impairment on this test. Similarly, Kopelman et al. (1999) found that two patients with unilateral left temporal lobe pathology from herpes encephalitis were severely impaired at this test, whereas herpes patients with predominantly right-sided temporal lobe pathology were virtually intact on this test (Figure 9.1), consistent with the Warrington & McCarthy (1988) and Eslinger et al. (1996) results. However, Reed & Squire (1998) found impairment in patients with temporal lobe lesions at a more difficult test, in which only the names were presented for completion (in the absence of famous faces), indicating that task difficulty (as well as the side of lesion) may need to be taken into account in evaluating such findings.

In addition, several studies of psychogenic amnesia have addressed the issue of whether there is evidence of preserved "implicit" memory for remote facts or events in the presence of a severe "explicit" retrograde amnesia (see Chapter 21). However, the interpretation of findings in psychogenic amnesia is very difficult in the absence of any very definitive knowledge of whether there is preserved "implicit" RA in organic amnesia.

In summary, it is an attractive idea that there may be preserved implicit memory in retrograde amnesia, analogous to what has been found in anterograde amnesia. However, it is much harder to produce unequivocal evidence of this in RA than in AA. The few studies to date remain vulnerable to alternative interpretations; in particular, that they may have simply demonstrated a cued response in explicit memory.

Brief vs. Extensive Episodic Retrograde Amnesia

As already mentioned, Kapur (1999) distinguished two classes of episodic RA, which he called "preictal" and "extended" RA. The case for qualitatively different types of RA, broadly related to differing time-spans, has also been made by other authors (e.g. Symonds, 1966; Squire et al., 1984). Kapur (1999) proposed four arguments in favour of this distinction:

1. There are qualitative discontinuities in the density of pre-injury memory loss reported by patients, e.g. following head injury, there is commonly a short, virtually complete RA lasting a matter of minutes or (sometimes) hours. In some patients, there is also a far less dense loss of memory for incidents or events over the preceding few weeks (Russell & Nathan, 1946; Williams & Zangwill, 1952).
2. Following a closed head injury, an extensive RA characteristically shrinks to a much briefer period, which may be a matter of minutes, hours or days, depending upon the severity of the injury (Russell & Nathan, 1946; Williams & Zangwill, 1952; Wasterlain, 1971). Kapur (1999) also noted that, following episodes of transient global amnesia (TGA), there is commonly some residual "preictal RA", lasting a matter of minutes or (exceptionally) hours (Fisher, 1982; Hodges, 1991; Kapur et al., 1998).
3. There is a delayed onset to certain types of brief RA. For example, Lynch & Yarnell (1973) studied American footballers who had incurred a mild head injury. These footballers were initially able to describe what had happened just before the blow, but, when re-interviewed some minutes later, they were unable to recall these events. This has usually been interpreted as a failure of memory consolidation following the blow,

resulting in a period of brief RA lasting a matter of minutes. Consistent with this, Russell & Nathan (1946) also noted that, in some patients, pre-traumatic events were briefly recalled in the first few minutes following a head injury, but were then rapidly forgotten.

4. Some experimental studies also support this distinction. Electrical stimulation (under local anaesthetic) of temporal lobe regions in epileptic patients with complex partial seizures produces a period of preictal RA, ranging from a few minutes to a few days or weeks (Bickford et al., 1958). Electroconvulsive therapy (ECT) also gives rise to a brief RA lasting a matter of days (Squire et al., 1981) and complaints of memory loss which may go back 2–3 years (Squire & Slater, 1983).

A fifth argument is that there are at least some patients with lesions confined to the diencephalic/medial temporal lobe structures who have an RA which extends back 2–3 years but no further (Milner, 1966; Zola-Morgan et al., 1986; Dusoir et al., 1990; Graff-Radford et al., 1990; Guinan et al., 1998). This is a controversial topic but, as will be discussed below, one view is that cortical damage seems to be required for an extensive RA going back years or decades, e.g. as seen in the Korsakoff syndrome, herpes encephalitis, or Alzheimer or Huntington's dementia (e.g. Albert et al., 1981; Kopelman, 1989; Wilson et al., 1995; Kopelman et al., 1999).

In summary, the present observations indicate that the nature of RA may vary according to whether it covers a matter of (a) seconds, minutes, or hours; (b) days, weeks, or months up to a period of 2–3 years; or (c) an extensive retrograde memory loss covering years or decades. The precise boundaries of these different types of RA, and whether they should be differentiated into two, three, or more sub-types, remain unclear. To date, most of the neuropsychological literature has concentrated upon an understanding of the nature of extensive RA, but the briefer components are also important.

ASSOCIATIONS/CORRELATES OF RETROGRADE AMNESIA

In interpreting the findings from remote memory tests, it is important to remember that the site or sites of pathology are not the only determinants of performance.

Such factors as age, intelligence, education and media exposure may influence scores, particularly on the more semantic remote memory tasks. Obviously, the subject is more likely to recall correctly those items that he/she has lived through, but there is also some evidence that older amnesic patients (aged 40 or over) are more likely to show a steep temporal gradient following brain damage than patients under 40, particularly in recalling personal semantic facts (Kopelman et al., 1989). Significant correlations have been shown to occur between Full Scale IQ and measures such as recall of famous news events and personalities (Kopelman, 1989), and between a measure of media exposure and recall of public events (Kapur et al., 1999).

Second, as already mentioned, a subject's ability at executive tests may also be an important predictor of remote memory performance, and this may be particularly true of autobiographical recall, where active reconstruction/recollection is required. Kopelman (1991) found that six out of eight executive tests correlated significantly with a "composite" measure of retrograde memory performance, but only one out of eight executive tests correlated significantly with a composite measure of anterograde memory performance. Whereas anterograde memory test scores predicted only 21% of the variance in RA scores, a regression equation based on three of the executive tests predicted 64% of the RA variance. There were also significant correlations between the executive tests and individual autobiographical and semantic remote memory measures. Subsequently, Verfaellie et al. (1995b) and D'Esposito et al. (1996) have also obtained evidence that executive test scores correlate significantly with remote memory performance in Korsakoff and subarachnoid haemorrhage patients, respectively.

In summary, larger-group studies indicate a number of important correlates of remote memory performance. It is important to allow for these in making inferences about dissociations from single-case investigations. The combination of low IQ, poor education, limited media exposure, and relatively mild amnesia may give the impression of disproportionate impairment on the more semantic remote memory tests, whereas the opposite pattern—severe autobiographical memory loss in someone with good background semantic knowledge (high IQ, education, and media exposure)—will give a pattern of performance the other way around.

RETROGRADE VS. ANTEROGRADE AMNESIA

Most studies have found a poor correlation between scores on RA and AA tests. This has been found in Korsakoff patients (Shimamura & Squire, 1986; Kopelman, 1989, 1991; Parkin, 1991), a mixed group of amnesic patients (Mayes et al., 1994), and Alzheimer patients (Kopelman, 1989, 1991; Greene & Hodges, 1996). There is suggestive evidence that the correlation may be higher if equivalent forms of anterograde and retrograde tests are used (Mayes et al., 1997; Poliakoff & Meudell, 2000), but this has yet to be clearly established in large groups of amnesic patients.

It is widely accepted that AA can occur with minimal or no RA, e.g. in some cases of transient global amnesia (Hodges & Ward, 1989), head injury particularly if penetrating (Russell & Nathan, 1946; Dusoir et al., 1990; Lishman, 1968), some cases of thalamic infarction (Dall'Ora et al., 1989; Graff-Radford et al., 1990; Parkin et al., 1994; Winocur et al., 1984), and in certain deep midline tumours (Kapur et al., 1996; Guinan et al., 1998).

Much more contentious is the nature of disproportionate RA, sometimes known as "focal" or "isolated" RA. Many such cases have now been described in the literature, but they differ considerably in the circumstances and features of the onset, clinical diagnosis, findings on neuroimaging, and the postulated site or sites of pathology, as well as in the adequacy of the clinical description given. Two of the better described cases were reported by Kapur et al. (1992) and Levine et al. (1998). Kapur et al. (1992) described a 26 year-old woman who had fallen from a horse, sustaining left and right frontal contusions, evident on CT scan, with subsequent signal alteration at the left and right temporal poles on MRI. The patient was impaired across all the remote memory tests employed with normal performance or only moderate impairment at various anterograde memory tests. Similarly, Levine et al. (1998) described a patient who was involved in a road traffic accident, resulting in a right frontal lesion, implicating the uncinate fasciculus, as well as prefrontal haemorrhages. The patient had an initially severe AA but this resolved, leaving a severe retrograde amnesia.

The underlying nature of focal retrograde amnesia has been debated elsewhere (Kopelman, 2000b, 2000c; Kapur, 2000), and various points have been raised. First, some cases of severe RA cited in this literature were, in fact, accompanied by very poor anterograde memory, especially of visuospatial material: such cases cannot be described as instances of "focal" or "isolated" RA. Second, other cases showed poor anterograde memory in more moderate or subtle form across a number of tests, particularly logical memory, face recognition memory and delayed recall. There are various possible reasons for this, but such findings beg the question of whether "like" has really been compared with "like". Third, patients with "focal RA" commonly cited in this literature encompass cases of specific impairment in autobiographical memory, semantic memory, or both: these are not the same. Fourth, many of the most convincing cases in this literature showed an initially severe AA as well as an extensive RA. However, by the time of their assessment, the RA had remained profound whereas the AA had become only moderate, mild or minimal. In such cases, the issue is not so much whether RA could occur without AA, but what determines differential patterns of recovery—a somewhat different, and poorly understood, issue. Fifth, a further group of patients are those with a diagnosis of transient epileptic amnesia: these patients commonly report "gaps" in their autobiographical memory. This might have resulted from brief ("subclinical") runs of seizure of activity in the past compromising encoding over short periods (Kopelman, 2000b, 2000c) or from current ictal activity inhibiting retrieval processes (Kapur, 2000), an issue which remains unresolved. Finally, it is important to remember that psychogenic amnesia can produce reversed temporal gradients (Kopelman et al., 1994; Kritchevsky et al., 1997), closely similar to those described in focal RA (e.g. Kapur et al., 1992). Psychogenic factors may make an important contribution to the presence of a severe or unusual RA, even in the presence of brain pathology (Kopelman, 2000b).

In summary, the severity and the extent of RA is poorly correlated with the severity of AA. However, most investigations of this topic have studied the more extensive forms of RA, rather than the briefer forms mentioned above. Whilst AA can exist alongside little or no RA, the interpretation of disproportionate RA remains controversial, and several different types of factor may contribute to this phenomenon.

THEORIES OF RETROGRADE AMNESIA

Various theories have been postulated to account for the temporal gradient of RA and for its pattern, severity, and how far back it extends.

One theory of the temporal gradient is that there is a prolonged process of physiological "consolidation" of memories, during which the memories are initially dependent upon the medial temporal lobe system but gradually become established in other areas of the brain ("structural reallocation"). According to this view, there is a gradual reorganization of memory storage, whereby memories that are initially dependent upon the medial temporal lobes eventually do not require this system. A more permanent memory, independent of the medial temporal lobes, gradually develops, presumably in the neocortex (Alvarez & Squire, 1994; Squire & Alvarez, 1995; Murre, 1997). Murre's (2002) TraceLink model is a highly specified account of this, incorporating a trace system (analogous to "neocortex"), a link system (equivalent to the "medial temporal lobes"), and a modulatory system. "Reversed" temporal gradients in semantic dementia patients, in whom the temporal neocortex is severely atrophied with relative sparing of medial temporal lobe structures, have been interpreted as evidence in favour of structural reallocation (Graham & Hodges, 1997; Hodges & Graham, 1998; Murre, 1997, 2002), although there are other, less mechanistic, interpretations of the findings in semantic dementia (Snowden et al., 1996, 1999; Kopelman, 2000b; Moss et al., 2002; Westmacott et al., 2001). A fundamental problem for this theory is that a very extensive temporal gradient, extending back over 20–30 years, would seem to imply that such a process of physiological consolidation must continue for a very long time indeed (Nadel & Moscovitch, 1997).

A second approach has emphasized that, as episodic memories are rehearsed through time, they adopt a more semantic form, which protects them against the effects of brain damage (e.g. Cermak, 1984; Weiskrantz, 1985; Sagar et al., 1988). In other words, the contextual components of these memories become attenuated or lost, making the memories feel much less immediate and vivid, but they are better preserved. This hypothesis is not incompatible with the notion of structural reallocation, proposed in consolidation theory. Although an attractive idea, a problem with this view is that the notion of "semanticization" is poorly specified and, therefore, somewhat unsatisfactory. Moreover, it does not explain why knowledge which is semantic virtually from the outset, such as knowledge of the meaning of new words, also shows a temporal gradient (Verfaellie et al., 1995a).

From a third, more general perspective, Kapur (1999) has argued for a system of representation of memories that is widely distributed as multiple neural networks, containing the substrates of experiences as part of their connectionist structure. He did not provide a theory of the temporal gradient as such, but emphasized that, at least in semantic RA, its presence or absence may relate to matters of patient selection and research method. The variability in findings across studies might result from such factors as: (a) encoding variables (including the novelty, predictability, distinctiveness, cognitive and emotional significance of the event, and how long and how often it has been experienced); (b) lesion variables (including the site, pathology, severity and recency of the lesion, as well as the presence of concomitant cerebral pathology); and (c) retention test variables (including the delay until testing, motivational factors, the sensitivity of test procedures, etc.). The importance of these factors is often underestimated in discussions of RA.

Conway & Fthenaki (2000) have postulated a cognitive model specifically of autobiographical memory organization. In this model, knowledge is structured in an hierarchical fashion: more abstract knowledge (about a lifetime period or general events) provides a context for the retrieval of event-specific knowledge which, in turn, is "near-sensory experience". The lifetime period and general event knowledge have extensive local organization, whereas this is not true of event-specific knowledge. Knowledge held at higher or more abstract levels can be used to access knowledge at more specific levels. Autobiographical memory is considered as a superordinate memory system, in that it takes input from subordinate memory systems and binds together patterns of activation from across those lower-order memory systems into mental representations that are experienced as "autobiographical memory". Because of its superordinate nature, autobiographical memory can be disrupted by lesions at many different sites, resulting in a loss of *access* to autobiographical memory knowledge. Loss of the knowledge itself is predicted to occur less frequently, and to arise from diseases causing widespread damage and degeneration, such as the dementias.

In the same volume, Fujii et al. (2000) presented an updated account of Nadel & Moscovitch's (1997) multiple trace theory of RA. Contrary to the "structural reallocation" hypothesis, Nadel & Moscovitch (1997) postulated that a memory trace for a specific episode is represented by an ensemble of "binding codes" in the hippocampus and by fragments of information in association areas. The binding codes in the hippocampus act as a pointer or index to the neurons in association cortex, or elsewhere, that represent the attended information. Every time a memory is reactivated, new traces will be formed in the hippocampal complex as well as links between it and the association areas: hence, well-established memories are represented by multiple traces, which are protective against brain damage. A prediction is that the greater the damage to the hippocampi, the "flatter" the temporal gradient and the more extensive the RA which results. Some support for this theory has been provided by a study showing a "flat" temporal gradient in patients with "temporal lobe epilepsy" (Viskontas et al., 2000), and by an investigation of a patient with severe, bilateral hippocampal atrophy who showed a severe and extensive RA (Cipolotti et al., 2001; see also Kartsounis et al., 1995). In their review, Fujii et al. (2000) found that damage to the hippocampus proper (the CA fields) did not produce an extensive RA, according to the existing literature, but they argued that damage to the hippocampal formation (the CA fields, dentate gyrus, and the subiculum) or (more definitely) the medial temporal lobes ("hippocampal complex") could produce an autobiographical amnesia extending back 10–50 years. A difficulty is that the neuroimaging procedures or techniques employed in many of the studies reviewed do not allow us to be so precise in the delineation of lesions, and (as already mentioned) there was evidence of more widespread pathology in many of the cases that these authors have cited in support of their theory.

Also in that same volume, Kopelman (2000a) postulated that widespread neural networks within the frontal and temporal neocortex are involved in the storage and retrieval of remote memories, but that there is also evidence of focal or localized contributions within these regions (cf. Kapur, 1999). Studies of focal brain lesions, as well as correlational investigations, have clearly indicated that severe RA could result from frontal pathology, particularly bilateral. It seems likely that the frontal lobes contribute particularly to the planning, monitoring and organization of retrieval processes in remote memory, especially where more "effortful" retrieval or "active" reconstruction is required. As previously discussed, there is evidence that the right temporal lobe appears to be particularly important to those reconstructive processes which engage visual or multi-model imagery, necessary to retrieve autobiographical memories, whereas the left temporal lobe appears to be particularly crucial to the storage and retrieval of remote semantic and lexical–semantic information.

In summary, the temporal gradient has been attributed to a process of long-term consolidation (Alvarez & Squire, 1994), which can be modelled in connectionist networks (Murre, 2002), or memories adopting a more semantic form through time and rehearsal (Cermak, 1984), or memory reactivation and multiple trace formation (Nadel & Moscovitch, 1997), but each of these ideas remains at present poorly specified. Moreover, there is some evidence that the vulnerability to a temporal gradient following brain damage may change with age (Kopelman et al., 1989), in which case the nature of this vulnerability needs further scrutiny. Models of the storage and retrieval of autobiographical memory (Conway & Fthenaki, 2000) and of remote memory more generally (Nadel & Moscovitch, 1997; Fujii et al., 2000) have been postulated; and it seems likely that widespread neural networks are engaged in these processes with some degree of regional specialization (Kapur, 1999; Kopelman, 2000a).

NEUROIMAGING OF REMOTE MEMORY

With these theoretical issues in mind, a number of recent functional imaging (PET, fMRI) studies have examined remote memory retrieval in healthy subjects. Fink et al. (1996) showed widespread activation of right frontal and temporal lobe regions when healthy subjects listened to sentences containing information from their remote past, relative to their brain state when hearing sentences unrelated to their past. Maguire & Mummery (1999) required subjects to listen to statements that differed according to whether or not they constituted autobiographical or general knowledge, and whether or not they had a specific focus in time. There was enhanced activity for time-specific autobiographical events in the left hippocampus, medial prefrontal cortex, and left temporal pole. Bilateral temporoparietal regions were activated preferentially for personal memories, regardless of time specificity. Conway et al. (1999) obtained left frontal, inferior temporal and occipitoparietal activations in verbal cueing of autobiographical memories and, like Ryan et al. (2001) and Maguire et al. (2001), did not obtain any medial temporal differences in retrieving remote or recent memories. On the other hand, Mayes & Roberts, (2001) have found differential patterns of brain activation between remote and recent memory retrieval in a number of conditions, although not all. This issue requires further investigation.

CONCLUSIONS

There is much evidence that there is a broad distinction between the autobiographical and semantic aspects of RA, but this distinction is not always clear-cut, in part because our tests of RA are not very "pure". Large lesions in the temporal or frontal lobes produce RA, but precise delineation in terms of specific structures has not proved possible to date. It is most likely that storage and retrieval of old memories will be found to depend upon a widespread network of neural connections. More particularly, the specific role of the hippocampi and other medial temporal lobe structures remains highly controversial, in part because relatively few patients with very focal pathology have yet been investigated using the most advanced neuroimaging methods and detailed neuropsychological procedures. Moreover, controversies remain concerning the nature of the temporal gradient in RA— whether it results from physiological consolidation and structural reallocation, memories acquiring a more semantic form, or the acquisition of multiple traces within the hippocampal system.

ACKNOWLEDGEMENT

Professor Kopelman's research has been supported by grants from the Wellcome Trust.

REFERENCES

Albert, M.S., Butters, N. & Brandt, J. (1981). Patterns of remote memory in amnesic and demented patients. *Archives of Neurology*, **38**, 495–500.
Albert, M.S., Butters, N. & Levin, J. (1979). Temporal gradients in the retrograde amnesia of patients with alcoholic Korsakoff's disease. *Archives of Neurology*, **36**, 211–216.
Alvarez, P. & Squire, L.R. (1994). Memory consolidation and the medial temporal lobe: a simple network model. *Proceedings of the National Academy of Science of the USA* **91**, 7041–7045.
Baddeley, A.D. & Wilson, B. (1986). Amnesia, autobiographical memory, and confabulation. In D.C. Rubin (ed.), *Autobiographical Memory*. Cambridge: Cambridge University Press.

Barr, W.B., Goldberg, E., Wasserstein, J. & Novelly, R. (1990). Retrograde amnesia following unilateral temporal lobectomy. *Neuropsychologia*, **28**, 243–255.

Bickford, R.G., Mulder, D.W., Dodge, H., Svien, H. & Rome. H.P. (1958). Changes in memory function produced by electrical stimulation of the temporal lobe in man. *Research Publications of the Association for Research in Nervous and Mental Diseases*, **36**, 227–243.

Butters, N. & Cermak, L.S. (1986). A case study of the forgetting of autobiographical knowledge: implications for the study of retrograde amnesia. In D.C.Rubin (ed.), *Autobiographical Memory*. Cambridge: Cambridge University Press.

Cermak, L.S. (1984). The episodic-semantic distinction in amnesia. In L.R. Squire & N. Butters (eds), *The Neuropsychology of Memory*, 1st edn. New York: Guildford.

Cermak, L.S. & O'Connor, M. (1983). The anterograde and retrograde retrieval ability of a patient with amnesia due to encephalitis. *Neuropsychologia*, **21**, 213–234.

Cipolotti, L., Shallice, T., Chan, D. et al. (2001). Long-term retrograde amnesia—the crucial role of the hippocampus. *Neuropsychologia*, **39**, 151–172.

Conway, M.A. & Fthenaki, A. (2000). Disruption and loss of autobiographical memory. In L. Cermak (ed.), *Handbook of Neuropsychology*, 2nd edn, Vol 2 (pp. 281–312). Amsterdam: Elsevier Science.

Conway, M.A., Turk, D.J., Miller, S.L. et al. (1999). A positron emission tomography (PET) study of autobiographical memory retrieval. *Memory*, **7**, 679–702.

Corkin, S. (1984). Lasting consequences of bilateral medial temporal lobectomy: clinical course and experimental findings in H.M. *Seminars in Neurology*, **4**, 249–259.

Crovitz, H.F. & Schifmann, H. (1974). Frequency of episodic memories as a function of their age. *Bulletin of the Psychonomic Society*, **4**, 517–618.

Dalla Barba, G., Cipolotti, L. & Denes, G. (1990). Autobiographical memory loss and confabulation in Korsakoff's syndrome: a case report. *Cortex*, **26**, 525–534.

Dall'Ora, P., Della Sala, S. & Spinnler, H. (1989). Autobiographical memory: its impairment in amnesic syndromes. *Cortex*, **25**, 197–217.

De Renzi, E., Liotti, M. & Nichelli, P. (1987). Semantic amnesia with preservation of autobiographical memory: a case report. *Cortex*, **23**, 575–597.

Della Sala, S., Laiacona, M., Spinnler, H. & Trivelli, C. (1993). Impaired autobiographical recollection in some frontal patients. *Neuropsychologia*, **31**, 823–840.

D'Esposito, M., Alexander, M.P., Fischer, R. et al. (1996). Recovery of memory and executive function following anterior communicating artery aneurysm rupture. *Journal of the International Neuropsychological Society*, **2**, 1–6.

Dusoir, H., Kapur, N., Byrnes, D.P. et al. (1990). The role of diencephalic pathology in human memory disorder: evidence from a penetrating paranasal injury. *Brain*, **113**, 1695–1706.

Eslinger, P.J. (1998). Autobiographical memory after temporal lobe lesions. *Neurocase*, **4**, 481–496.

Eslinger, P.J., Easton, A., Grattan, L.M. & Van Hoesen, G.W. (1996). Distinctive forms of partial retrograde amnesia after asymmetric temporal lobe lesions: possible role of the occipitotemporal gyri in memory. *Cerebral Cortex*, **6**, 530–539.

Fink, G.R., Markowitsch, H.J., Reinkemeier, M. et al. (1996). Cerebral represenation of one's own past: neutral networks involved in autobiographical memory. *Journal of Neuroscience*, **16**, 4275–4282.

Fisher, C.M. (1982). Transient global amnesia. *Archives of Neurology*, **39**, 605–608.

Fromholt, P. & Larsen, S.F. (1991). Autobiographical memory in normal aging and primary degenerative dementia (dementia of Alzheimer type). *Journal of Gerontology and Psychological Science*, **46**, 85–95.

Fromholt, P. & Larsen, S.F. (1992). Autobiographical memory and life-history narratives in aging and dementia. In M.A. Conway, D.C. Rubin, H. Spinnler & W. Wagenaar (eds), *Theoretical Perspectives on Autobiographical Memory* (pp. 413–426). Dordrecht: Kluwer Academic.

Fujii, T., Moscovitch, M. & Nadel, L. (2000). Memory consolidation, retrograde amnesia, and the temporal lobe. In L. Cermak (ed.), *Handbook of Neuropsychology*, 2nd edn, Vol. 2 (pp. 223–250). Amsterdam: Elsevier Science.

Gabrieli, J.D.E., Cohen, N.J. & Corkin, S. (1988). The impaired learning of semantic knowledge following bilateral medial temporal lobe resection. *Brain and Cognition*, **7**, 157–177.

Galton, F. (1879). Psychometric experiments. *Brain*, **2**, 149–162.

Graff-Radford, N.R., Tranel, D, Van Hoesen, G. & Brandt, J.P. (1990). Diencephalic amnesia. *Brain*, **113**, 1–25.

Graham, K.S. & Hodges, J.R. (1997). Differentiating the roles of the hippocampal complex and neocortex in long-term memory storage. Evidence from the study of semantic dementia and Alzheimer's disease. *Neuropsychology*, **11**, 77–89.

Greene, J. & Hodges, J. (1996). Identification of famous faces and famous names in early Alzheimer's disease. Relationship to anterograde episodic and general semantic memory. *Brain*, **119**, 111–128.

Grossi, D., Trojano, L., Grasso, A. & Orsini, A. (1988). Selective "semantic amnesia" after closed-head injury. A case report. *Cortex*, **24**, 457–464.

Guinan, E.M., Lowy, C., Stanhope, C. et al. (1998). Cognitive effects of pituitary tumours and their treatments: two case studies and an investigation of 90 patients. *Journal of Neurology, Neurosurgery and Psychiatry*, **65**, 870–876.

Hodges, J.R. (1991). *Transient Amnesia*. New York: Saunders.

Hodges, J.R. (1995). Retrograde amnesia. In A.D. Baddeley, B.A. Wilson & F.N. Watts (eds), *Handbook of Memory Disorders*, 1st edn (pp. 81–107). New York: Wiley.

Hodges, J.R. & Graham, K.S. (1998). A reversal of the temporal gradient for famous person knowledge in semantic dementia: implications for the neural organization of long-term memory. *Neuropsychologia*, **36**, 803–825.

Hodges, J.R. & McCarthy, R.A. (1993). Autobiographical amnesia resulting from bilateral paramedian thalamic infarction. A case study in cognitive neurobiology. *Brain*, **116**, 921–940.

Hodges, J.R. & Ward, C.D. (1989). Observations during transient global amnesia: a behavioural and neuropsychological study of five cases. *Brain*, **112**, 595–620.

Kapur, N. (1999). Syndromes of retrograde amnesia. A conceptual and empirical synthesis. *Psychological Bulletin*, **125**, 800–825.

Kapur, N. (2000). Focal retrograde amnesia and the attribution of causality: an exceptionally benign commentary. *Cognitive Neuropsychology*, **17**, 623–637.

Kapur, N., Ellison, D., Parkin, A.J. et al. (1994). Bilateral temporal lobe pathology with sparing of medial temporal lobe structures: lesion profile and pattern of memory disorder. *Neuropsychologia*, **23**, 23–38.

Kapur, N., Ellison, D., Smith, M. et al. (1992). Focal retrograde amnesia following bilateral temporal lobe pathology: a neuropsychological and magnetic resonance study. *Brain*, **115**, 73–85.

Kapur, N., Miller, J., Abbott, P. & Carter, M. (1998). Recovery of function processes in human amnesia: evidence from transient global amnesia. *Neuropsychologia*, **36**, 99–107.

Kapur, N., Thompson, S., Cook, P. et al. (1996). Anterograde but not retrograde memory loss following combined mammillary body and medial thalamic lesions. *Neuropsychologia*, **34**, 1–8.

Kapur, N., Thompson, P., Kartsounis. L. & Abbott, P. (1999). Retrograde amnesia: clinical and methodological caveats. *Neuropsychologia*, **37**, 27–30.

Kapur, N., Young, A., Bateman, D. & Kennedy, P. (1989). Focal retrograde amnesia: a long-term clinical and neuropsychological follow-up. *Cortex*, **25**, 387–402.

Kartsounis, L.D., Rudge, P. & Stevens, J.M. (1995). Bilateral lesions of CA1 and CA1 fields of the hippocampus are sufficient to cause a severe amnesic syndrome in humans. *Journal of Neurology, Neurosurgery, and Psychiatry*, **59**, 95–98.

Kopelman, M.D. (1989). Remote and autobiographical memory, temporal context memory, and frontal atrophy in Korsakoff and Alzheimer patients. *Neuropsychologia*, **27**, 437–460.

Kopelman, M.D. (1991). Frontal lobe dysfunction and memory deficits in the alcoholic Korsakoff syndrome and Alzheimer-type dementia. *Brain*, **114**, 117–137.

Kopelman, M.D. (1993). The neuropsychology of remote memory. In F. Boller & H. Spinnler (eds), *Handbook of Neuropsychology*, 1st edn, Vol. 8 (pp. 215–238). Amsterdam: Elsevier Science.

Kopelman, M.D. (2000a). The neuropsychology of remote memory. In L. Cermak (ed.), *Handbook of Neuropsychology*, 2nd edn, Vol. 2 (pp. 251–280). Amsterdam: Elsevier Science.

Kopelman, M.D. (2000b). Focal retrograde amnesia and the attribution of causality: an exceptionally critical review. *Cognitive Neuropsychology*, **17**, 585–621.

Kopelman, M.D. (2000c). Comments on focal retrograde amnesia and the attribution of causality: an exceptionally benign commentary by Narinder Kapur. *Cognitive Neuropsychology*, **17**, 639–640.

Kopelman, M.D., Christensen, H., Puffett, A. & Stanhope, N. (1994). The Great Escape: a neuropsychological study of psychogenic amnesia. *Neuropsychologia*, **32**, 675–691.

Kopelman, M.D. & Kapur, N. (2001). The loss of episodic memories in retrograde amnesia: single-case and group studies. *Philosophical Transactions of the Royal Society, London, B*, **356**, 1409–1421.

Kopelman, M.D., Stanhope, N. & Kingsley, D. (1999). Retrograde amnesia in patients with diencephalic, temporal lobe or frontal lesions. *Neuropsychologia*, **37**, 939–958.

Kopelman, M.D., Wilson, B.A. & Baddeley, A.D. (1990). *The Autobiographical Memory Interview*. Bury St Edmunds: Thames Valley Test Company.

Kopelman, M.D., Wilson, B.A. & Baddeley, A.D. (1989). The Autobiographical Memory Interview: a new assessment of autobiographical and personal semantic memory in amnesic patients. *Journal of Clinical and Experimental Neuropsychology*, **11**, 724–744.

Kritchevsky, M., Zouzounis, J. & Squire, L. (1997). Transient global amnesia and functional retrograde amnesia: contrasting examples of episodic memory loss. *Philosophical Transactions of the Royal Society, London, B*, **352**, 1747–1754.

Levine, B., Black, S., Cabeza, R. et al. (1998). Episodic memory and the self in a case of isolated retrograde amnesia. *Brain*, **121**, 1951–1973.

Lishman, W.A. (1968). Brain damage in relation to psychiatric disability after head injury. *British Journal of Psychiatry*, **114**, 373–410.

Lynch, S. & Yarnell, P.R. (1973). Retrograde amnesia: delayed forgetting after concussion. *American Journal of Psychology*, **86**, 643–645.

Maguire, E.A. & Mummery, C.J. (1999). Differential modulation of a common memory retrieval network revealed by PET. *Hippocampus*, **9**, 54–61.

Maguire, E.A., Henson, R.A., Mummery, C.J. & Frith, C.D. (2001). Activity in prefrontal cortex, not hippocampus, varies parametrically with the increasing remoteness of memory. *NeuroReport*, **12**, 441–444.

Mangels, J.A., Gershberg, F.B., Shimamura, A.P. & Knight, R.T. (1996). Impaired retrieval from remote memory in patients with frontal lobe damage. *Neuropsychology*, **10**, 32–41.

Marslen-Wilson, W. & Teuber, H.L. (1975). Memory for remote events in anterograde amnesia. *Neuropsychologia*, **13**, 353–364.

Mayes, A.R., Daum, I., Markowitsch, H.J. & Sauter, B. (1997). The relationship between retrograde and anterograde amnesia in patients with typical global amnesia. *Cortex*, **33**, 197–217.

Mayes, A.R., Downes, J.J., McDonald, C. et al. (1994). Two tests for assessing remote public knowledge: a tool for assessing retrograde amnesia. *Memory*, **2**, 183–210.

Mayes, A.R. & Roberts, N. (2001). Theories of episodic amnesia. *Philosophical Transactions of the Royal Society, London*, B, **356**, 1395–1408.

McCarthy, R.A. & Warrington, E.K. (1992). Actors but not scripts: the dissociation of people and events in retrograde amnesia. *Neuropsychologia*, **30**, 633–644.

Milner, B. (1966). Amnesia following operation on the temporal lobes. In C.W.M. Whitty & O. Zangwill (eds), *Amnesia*, 1st edn (pp. 109–133). London: Butterworth.

Milner, B. (1972). Disorders of learning and memory after temporal lobe lesions in man. *Clinical Neurosurgery*, **19**, 421–426.

Moss, H., Kopelman, M.D., Cappelletti, M. et al. (2002). Lost for words or loss of memories? Autobiographical memory in semantic dementia. *Cognitive Neuropsychology*, in press.

Murre, J.M.J. (1997). Implicit and explicit memory in amnesia: some explanations and predictions by the TraceLink model. *Memory*, **5**, 213–232.

Murre, J.M.J. (2002). Connectionist models of memory disorders. In A.D. Baddeley, B.A. Wilson & F.N. Watts (eds), *Handbook of Memory Disorders*, 2nd edn. New York: Wiley.

Nadel, L. & Moscovitch, M. (1997). Memory consolidation, retrograde amnesia and the hippocampal complex. *Current Opinion in Neurobiology*, **7**, 217–227.

O'Connor, M., Butters, N., Miliotis, P. (1992). The dissociation of anterograde and retrograde amnesia in a patient with herpes encephalitis. *Journal of Clinical and Experimental Neuropsychology*, **14**, 159–178.

Ogden, J.A. (1993). Visual object agnosia, prosopagnosia, achromatopsia, loss of visual imagery, and autobiographical amnesia following recovery from cortical blindness: Case M.H. *Neuropsychologia*, **31**, 571–589.

Parkin, A.J. (1991). Recent advances in the neuropsychology of memory. In J. Weinman & J. Hunter (eds), *Memory: Neurochemical and Abnormal Perspectives* (pp. 141–162). London: Harwood Academic.

Parkin, A.J., Rees, J.E., Hunkin, N.M. & Rose, P.E. (1994). Impairment of memory following discrete thalamic infarction. *Neuropsychologia*, **32**, 39–52.

Poliakoff, E. & Meudell, P.R. (2000). New learning and remote memory in the same and different domains of experience: implications for normal memory and amnesia. *Cortex*, **36**, 195–212.

Reed, J.M. & Squire, L. (1998). Retrograde amnesia for facts and events: findings from four new cases. *Journal of Neuroscience*, **18**, 3943–3954.

Robinson, J.A. (1976). Sampling autobiographical memory. *Cognitive Psychology*, **8**, 578–595.

Rubin, D. & Greenberg, D. (1998). Visual memory-deficit amnesia: a distinct amnesic presentation and aetiology. *Proceedings of the National Academy of Sciences*, **95**, 5413–5416.

Russell, W.R. & Nathan, P. (1946). Traumatic amnesia. *Brain*, **69**, 280–300.

Ryan, L., Nadel, L., Keil, K. et al. (2001). The hippocampal complex and retrieval of recent and very remote autobiographical memories: evidence from functional magnetic resonance imaging in neurologically intact people. *Hippocampus*, **11**, 707–714.

Sagar, H., Cohen, N., Sullivan, E. et al. (1988). Remote memory function in Alzheimer's disease and Parkinson's disease. *Brain*, **111**, 185–206.

Sanders, H. & Warrington, E. (1971). Memory for remote events in amnesic patients. *Brain*, **94**, 661–668.

Shimamura, A.P. & Squire, L.R. (1986). Korsakoff's syndrome: a study of the relation between anterograde amnesia and remote memory impairment. *Behavioral Neuroscience*, **100**, 165–170.

Snowden, J.S., Griffiths, H.L. & Neary, D. (1996). Semantic-episodic memory interaction in semantic dementia: implications for retrograde memory function. *Cognitive Neuropsychology*, **13**, 1101–1137.

Snowden, J.S., Griffiths, H.L. & Neary, D. (1999). The impact of autobiographical experience on meaning: reply to Graham, Lambon Ralph, and Hodges. *Cognitive Neuropsychology*, **16**, 673–687.

Squire, L.R. & Alvarez, P. (1995). Retrograde amnesia and memory consolidation: a neurobiological perspective. *Current Opinion in Neurobiology*, **5**, 169–177.

Squire, L.R., Cohen, N.J. & Nadel, L. (1984). The medial temporal region and memory consolidation: a new hypothesis. In H. Weingartner & E. Parker (eds), *Memory Consolidation* (pp. 185–210). Hillsdale, NJ: Erlbaum.

Squire, L.R. Haist, F. & Shimamura, A.P. (1989). The neurology of memory: quantitative assessment of retrograde amnesia in two types of amnesic patients. *Journal of Neuroscience*, **9**, 828–839.

Squire, L.R. & Slater, P.C. (1983). ECT and complaints of memory dysfunction: a prospective three-year follow-up study. *British Journal of Psychiatry*, **142**, 1–8.

Squire, L.R., Slater, P.C. & Miller, P.L. (1981). Retrograde amnesia and bilateral electroconvulsive therapy. *Archives of General Psychiatry*, **38**, 89–95.

Stuss, D.T., Guberman, A., Nelson, R. & Larochelle, S. (1988). The neuropsychology of paramedian thalamic infarction. *Brain and Cognition*, **8**, 348–378.

Symonds, C. (1966). Disorders of memory. *Brain*, **89**, 625–644.

Verfaellie, M., Croce, P. & Milberg, W.P. (1995a). The role of episodic memory in semantic learning: an examination of vocabulary acquisition in a patient with amnesia due to encephalitis. *Neurocase*, **1**, 291–304.

Verfaellie, M., Reiss, L. & Roth, H.L. (1995b). Knowledge of new English vocabulary in amnesia: an examination of premorbidly acquired semantic memory. *Journal of International Neuropsychological Society*, **1**, 443–453.

Viskontas, I.V., McAndrews, M.P. & Moscovitch, M. (2000). Remote episodic memory deficits in patients with unilateral temporal lobe epilepsy and excisions. *Journal of Neuroscience*, **20**, 5853–5857.

Warrington, E.K. & McCarthy, R.A. (1988). The fractionation of retrograde amnesia. *Brain and Cognition*, **7**, 184–200.

Wasterlain, C. (1971). Are there two types of post-traumatic retrograde amnesia? *European Neurology*, **5**, 225–228.

Weiskrantz, L. (1985). On issues and theories of the human amnesia syndrome. In N.M. Weinberger, J.L. McGaugh & G. Lynch (eds), *Memory Systems of the Brain* (pp. 380–418). New York: Guilford.

Westmacott, R., Leach, L., Freedman, M. & Moscovitch, M. (2001). Different patterns of autobio-graphical memory loss in semantic dementia and medial temporal lobe amnesia. *Neurocase*, **7**, 37–55.

Williams, M. & Zangwill, O.L. (1952). Memory defects after head injury. *Journal of Neurology, Neurosurgery and Psychiatry*, **13**, 30–35.

Wilson, B.A., Baddeley, A.D. & Kapur, N. (1995). Dense amnesia in a professional musician following herpes simplex virus encephalitis. *Journal of Clinical and Experimental Neuropsychology*, **17**, 668–681.

Wilson, B.A. & Wearing, D. (1995). Prisoner of consciousness: a state of just awakening following herpes simplex encephalitis. In R. Campbell & M.A. Conway (eds), *Broken Memories: Case Studies in the Neuropsychology of Memory*. Oxford: Blackwell.

Winocur, G., Oxbury, S., Roberts, R. et al. (1984). Amnesia in a patient with bilateral lesions to the thalamus. *Neuropsychologia*, **22**, 123–143.

Yasunda, K., Watababe, O. & Ono, Y. (1997). Dissociation between semantic and autobiographic memory: a case report. *Cortex*, **33**, 623–638.

Zola-Morgan, S., Cohen, N.J. & Squire, L.R. (1983). Recall of remote episodic memory in amnesia. *Neuropsychologia*, **21**, 487–500.

Zola-Morgan, S., Squire, L.R. & Amaral, D.G. (1986). Human amnesia and the medial temporal region: enduring memory impairment following a bilateral lesion limited to field CA1 of the hippocampus. *Journal of Neuroscience*, **6**, 2950–2967.

CHAPTER 10

Transient Global Amnesia

Georg Goldenberg

Krankenhaus München Bogenhausen, Münich, Germany

Transient loss of memory has been recognized as a distinct neurological disorder for nearly 50 years (Bender, 1956; Guyotat & Courjon, 1956) The term "Transient Global Amnesia" (TGA) was introduced by Fisher & Adams in 1964. Some 1000 cases have been published and several large studies have investigated the epidemology and prognosis of TGA. It has emerged as a coherent clinical entity and, although its aetiology and pathogenesis are still controversial, the collected clinical and laboratory findings do at least put constraints on theorizing about its cause.

Starting from two typical case reports, this chapter outlines the clinical features, differential diagnosis and definition of TGA. Epidemological, neuropsychological, and neuroradiological and findings are then reviewed. Then follows a discussion of hypotheses on location and aetiology of cerebral dysfunction in TGA.

TWO CASES OF TGA

Case 1 (Goldenberg et al., 1991)

The patient was a 55 year-old female teacher whose medical history was uneventful. She was a moderate smoker, blood pressure was low. At Christmas 1989 she stayed with her husband in their weekend house. One evening, when preparing for bed, her husband asked her to take away a packet of cigarettes she had left on the table. She responded that she did not remember to have left these cigarettes and asked for how long she had been in the weekend house and whether Christmas was already over. She then repeatedly asked these questions and complained that she did not remember when and how she had come to the house. Apart from her loss of memory and her bewilderment, the husband did not note any changes. She recognized the house, him and other relatives who soon came to help. Her blood pressure was found to be elevated to 200/120. She was brought to the Neurological University Clinic.

When arriving at about midnight, her blood pressure was 120/80 and cardiac action rhythmic. Neurological examination was completely normal. She was alert and friendly. Spontaneous speech was normal. She knew that she was in hospital but asked repeatedly

The Handbook of Memory Disorders. Edited by A.D. Baddeley, M.D. Kopelman and B.A. Wilson
© 2002 John Wiley & Sons, Ltd.

how she had come there, and, when given the response, invariably commented that she was sorry to cause troubles to her family. Every few minutes she asked the examiner whether he happened to know her daughter who was a psychiatrist. She was unable to retain new information and did not recognize the examiner when he had been absent for a few minutes. She did not remember public or personal events of the last one and a half years, and gave the age and occupation of her children as they had been before that time. Recall of remote events appeared to be fairly normal but was not tested extensively.

On neuropsychological examination spontaneous speech was normal but confrontation naming was not tested. In her copy of the Rey complex figure she omitted one detail. Immediate recall of the figure was restricted to its gross structure, and delayed recall after 5 min impossible. She did not recognize any of 30 concrete pictures and scored at chance on a multiple-choice recognition trial. The number of words repeated from a 12-word list did not at all improve across five learning trials. When recall was tested after 5 min she denied having heard any words before, and she scored at chance on a multiple-choice recognition trial. By contrast, she markedly improved across three trials of a test of perceptual learning probing the reading of fragmented digits.

Single photon emission tomography (SPECT) was performed the same night. When it was finished about 4 o'clock in the morning, she was still wide awake. Asked about her estimation of the present time she answered that it must be "fairly late, about 8 or 9 in the evening".

She then slept quietly, and the next morning her mental status appeared to be normal again. There was a complete amnesia for the period of TGA and for half an hour preceding the attack. Some patchy recollections started during SPECT data collection but she did not remember at all the injection of the isotope (The distribution of the isotope which is measured by SPECT is accomplished within about two min after injection).

She was reexamined in the afternoon. Confrontation naming was normal, and a copy of the Rey figure perfect. Immediate and delayed recall of the figure were possible but mildly defective, as were memory for concrete pictures and learning of a 15-word list. The patient did not remember having seen the stimuli of the perceptual learning test before, but her performance betrayed complete preservation of the perceptual skill acquired during TGA. She found five out of six possible criteria on a card sorting task. Design fluency was good. When tested for verbal fluency she brought forward a sufficient number of words but produced numerous perseverations in addition.

On a follow-up examination after 10 days the patient reported that the night after the accident she had slept much longer than normal. On neuropsychological testing, recognition memory for pictures was still slightly impaired, but learning of a 15-word list and recall of a complex figure were normal. On both, verbal and design fluency tasks, the number of items produced was well within the normal range but the number of perseverations elevated.

After one month she reported that two weeks after TGA she had experienced during 15 min a blurring of the whole visual field as if it were "covered by lace". All memory tests were now normal. Design fluency was unremarkable too, but the number of perseverations was still elevated in the word-fluency task.

CT, EEG and sonography of the carotid and vertebral arteries were done on the first day after TGA, and MRI 10 days later. All of them were normal. SPECT was performed in the night of the TGA, 12 days later, and 40 days later. During TGA there was a diffuse reduction of cerebral HMPAO uptake. Over and above the global reduction, local flow was severely reduced in the left thalamus, and less severely in the right thalamus. At follow-up, global isotope uptake normalized as well as local flow in the thalami, but there was a persistent hypoperfusion of left frontal areas (Goldenberg et al., 1991; Figure 10.1).

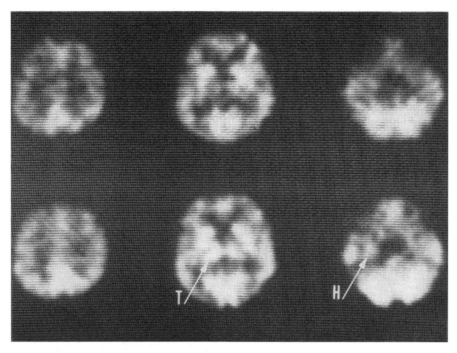

Figure 10.1   99-Tc-HMPAO SPECT studies of Case 1. Upper row: during attack; lower row: at follow-up 12 days later. The left side of the slices corresponds to the left side of the brain. The arrows indicate the location of the left thalamus (T) and of the left hippocampus formation (H). The SPECT images show the distribution of blood flow but not its absolute value. Each row of images is scaled to its own maximum and no correction is made for differences in global blood flow between both studies. A reduction of global blood flow can be deduced from the apparent reduction of brain volume in the study made during the attack and was confirmed by an analysis of absolute HMPAO uptake. During the attack there was a reduction of HMPAO uptake in the thalami over and above the global reduction of cerebral blood flow, which was more marked on the left side. Compared with controls, left frontal flow values were reduced at follow-up. Reproduced by permission from Goldenberg (1995)

Case 2

The second patient was a 75 year-old female retired tailor. Mild hypertension had been treated for 10 years. She had suffered from frequent headaches and occasional attacks of migraine since youth. 30 years ago she had been admitted to a neurological hospital with a suspicion of meningitis because of severe headache. 10 years ago she had been hospitalized with a confusional state lasting two days. In April 1990, in the morning after returning to Vienna from an exhausting bus trip to Budapest, she rose and breakfasted as usual. Her husband then left home to go shopping and when he came back he found her sitting on a chair and complaining: "What's the matter with me, it's starting again, it's like last time". She repeatedly asked where she had been the last days and when she had returned home. When the answer was given she said, "Oh yes, I remember", but asked the same questions again shortly afterwards.

She was brought to the neurological department. When seen there 2 h after her arrival she knew that she was in hospital and that her relatives had brought her there. She knew the month but neither the year nor the day. She had no recollection at all of the time already spent in hospital and did not recognize persons whom she had encountered during that time.

The patient knew that she had returned from a journey one day ago, but she was not sure whether she had been in Budapest or in Tyrol where she actually had spent her last winter holiday. When asked about both of these stays she confounded their circumstances and details. She could neither enumerate a single specific sight seen in Budapest nor recall the name of her hotel there. Her recall of previous hospitalizations and of recent and remote political events was similar in that she confounded their circumstances, and in that she was unable to enumerate specific details. A clear-cut temporal limit of this retrograde memory impairment could not be established, but recall of events up to 1950 appeared unimpaired and was not different from that given at follow-up.

During the examination she would remark with a frequency of up to twice a minute that she was now "starting to have a little headache". Application of analgesics had no influence on the frequency of this complaint. When unable to answer a question she would invariably respond: "I don't know what was yesterday, but I do know what happened 20 years ago".

The neurological examination was normal. On neuropsychological examination sponta-neous speech was normal, and there was no apraxia. A copy of the Rey figure was turned by 90 degrees, and the position of details was distorted. She did not recognize any of 30 concrete pictures and scored at chance on a multiple-choice recognition trial. Across five trials she never could repeat more than 5 words of a 12-word list; 15 mins later she did not remember having heard a word list at all and was at chance level when identifying the words in the multiple choice task. Immediate recall of the Rey figure was restricted to its gross outlines, and delayed recall impossible. On the perceptual learning task probing reading of fragmented digits her score improved across three trials, but after the last trial she thought that she had seen the digits only once or twice. Both verbal and design fluency were reduced and she produced multiple perseverations. On a card sorting task she obtained only one out of six possible criteria and repeated sorting to this criterion three times. In addition, she attempted two illogical sortings. SPECT was performed immediately after the neuropsychological examination.

On the next day her memory appeared to be normal again. She had a complete amnesia for the first three to four hours of the attack and for the morning before. She had some vague recollections of the SPECT examination and of the neuropsychological tests preceding it. Recall of previous events was richer and more orderly than during TGA but details were still lacking and she was insecure with respect to the distinction between events. She still repeatedly commented that "the headache is starting now" and that she did not know what was yesterday but did know what had happened 20 years ago, but the frequency of this repetitive comments was much lower than during the attack. Recognition memory for concrete pictures was at the lower margin of the normal range. Learning and delayed recall of a 15-word list betrayed some storage in secondary memory but was still markedly reduced. When copying the Rey figure she duplicated one detail and omitted another, but preserved the main topological relationships and the orientation, and her score was in the normal range, while reproduction from memory was impoverished. Both verbal and design fluency were in the low normal range. On the perceptual learning task her initial performance was below the final performance of the previous day which was reached only on the second trial.

At follow-up 2 weeks later, she claimed to have regained a recollection of the morning before the spell. Asked about her headache she said that she used to have headaches fre-quently but did not remember a particular aggravation during or after the attack. Her recall of previous events was chronologically correct without confusions, and she recalled without

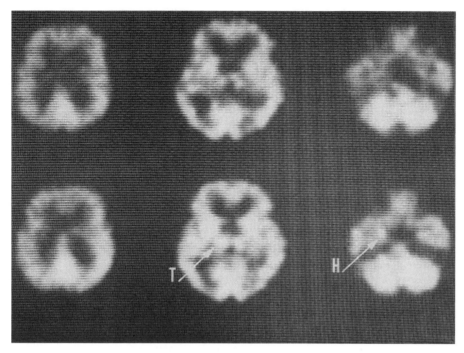

Figure 10.2 99-Tc-HMPAO SPECT studies of Case 2. Upper row: during attack; lower row: at follow-up 2 weeks later. Orientation of the slices and anatomical designations are as in Figure 10.1. Compared with the follow-up study, the study during the attack shows a marked reduction of the volume of both thalami, which presumably indicates local hypoperfusion. There is a diminution of local HMPAO uptake in the left temporal lobe, which extends into the mesial temporal region, in the left frontal lobe and possibly also in the right mesial temporal region. Reproduced by permission from Goldenberg (1995)

hesitation details she had been unable to remember during TGA. On neuropsychological examination recognition memory for concrete pictures was perfect and she scored in the normal range on word list learning and recall of a complex figure. Word fluency had improved while design fluency had remained the same. On the sorting task she now scored two criteria correctly and produced neither perseverations nor alogical sortings. On the perceptual learning task she started at the final level of the last examination and improved further across three trials.

CT on the day of TGA was normal. SPECT done during the attack demonstrated hypoperfusion of both thalami and the left frontal and left temporal lobe (Figure 10.2). The temporal hypoperfusion affected the mesial temporal region, and there was some reduction of local HMPAO uptake also in the right mesial temporal region. A follow-up SPECT 2 weeks later was normal.

CLINICAL FEATURES OF TGA

Complete anterograde amnesia is the most impressive symptom of TGA. As patients are incapable of retaining any record of what is going on, they may be disoriented to time and place. They are, however, able to use contextual clues and general world knowledge for making inferences about their situation. When confronted with a failure of memory, patients may try to guess what they should remember, but they do not spontaneously confabulate. Many patients notice that something is wrong with their mental capacities and are worried about this.

Anterograde amnesia is not the only behavioural abnormality in TGA. Further impressive symptoms are repetitive questioning and repetitive comments. Not only do patients ask the same questions over and over, they frequently use exactly the same wording in each round of questions and give exactly the same comments to the answer. The simple explanation that patients repeat the question because they forget the answer does not hold, as patients repeat the same questions regardless of changing circumstances, and they may repeat questions which are only loosely related to the worry brought forward by the experience of not knowing what is happening to them. Indeed, there are patients who repeat questions over and over in spite of being apparently little concerned or even anosognosic about their disorder (Hodges & Ward, 1989; Stillhard et al., 1990). Repetitive behaviour is not necessarily confined to questions or comments but may also concern senseless motor actions like washing hands (Caplan, 1990), going up and down stairs (Mazzuchi et al., 1980) or jumping up and down from the examination bed (Venneri & Caffarra, 1998). A further behavioural abnormality observed in a significant proportion of patients is either agitation or apathy (Kritchevsky et al., 1988; Hodges & Ward, 1989; Kritchevsky & Squire, 1989; Caplan, 1990; Inzitari et al., 1997), and Case 1 of this chapter would suggest disturbances of sleep–wake rhythm as another possible concomitant of TGA. Some patients complain of headache either during or after the attack, and there may occur vegetative symptoms like sweating, vomiting, diarrhoea, or transient elevations of blood pressure (Caplan, 1985; Stillhard et al., 1990; Hodges, 1991; Inzitari et al., 1997).

In about one-quarter to one-third of patients, TGA appears to be triggered by precipitating events. Most frequent are physical exertion, sexual intercourse, sudden exposure to cold or heat (particularly immersion in cold water), somewhat less frequent are long drives in a motor vehicle and emotional stress associated with quarrel (Caplan, 1990; Miller et al., 1987; Hodges & Warlow, 1990b; Inzitari et al., 1997). The frequency of TGA elicited by sexual intercourse may be higher than indicated by the patients' and their relatives' reports as extraconjugal sex seems to carry a higher risk than conjugal intercourse (Inzitari et al., 1997) possibly due to higher physical effort. TGA can also be triggered by vertebral angiography (Woolfenden et al., 1998) and by painful medical procedures like gastroscopy or dentistry (Inzitari et al., 1997; Tanabe et al. 1999). TGA following head trauma will be considered in the next section.

DIFFERENTIAL DIAGNOSIS OF TGA

The other main conditions to be considered in the differential diagnosis of TGA are post-traumatic amnesia, transient epileptic amnesia, and transient retrograde amnesia.

Posttraumatic Amnesia

Concussion can lead to a transient confusional state whose clinical appearance is very similar to that of TGA, although repetitive questioning is rarely as impressive as in TGA. There are, however, cases of typical TGA following very mild head trauma. Possibly their

TGA was triggered by the emotional stress of the accident rather than by impact on the head. The age of patients with posttraumatic TGA differs from the age of patients with genuine TGA. Posttraumatic TGA affected adolescents and young adults (Haas & Ross, 1986; Haas, 1990; Tosi & Righetti, 1997; Venneri et al., 1998b), whereas patients with genuine TGA are very rarely younger than 40 years (see below).

Transient epileptic amnesia

Epilepsy has once been considered as a possible cause of TGA (Fisher & Adams, 1964). The low recurrence rate of TGA and the absence of epileptic discharges in EEG recordings made during the attack speak against this hypothesis. Rather than as the cause of TGA, epilepsy has to be considered as a differential diagnosis. Postictal amnesia can follow grand mal seizures, while transient epileptic amnesia (TEA) can be the most conspicuous if not the only manifestation of nonconvulsive epilepsy resulting from a focus in the temporal lobe. Like TGA, TEA is a dense anterograde amnesia associated with repetitive questioning and with a patchy retrograde memory loss which may stretch back many years. The age distribution of TEA does not conspicuously differ from that of TGA (Kapur, 1990; Gallassi & Morreale, 1990; Zeman et al., 1998). A suspicion of TEA should be raised if episodes of transient amnesia are shorter than an hour, if they recur within a few weeks, and if they occur on wakening (Hodges & Warlow, 1990b).

Transient Retrograde Amnesia

Recently, attention has been drawn to episodes of retrograde memory loss unaccompanied by anterograde amnesia. The preservation of anterograde memory enables patients to give accurate accounts of the whole episode. Typically, retrograde amnesia is focal, that is, it affects only one domain of previously acquired knowledge. Until now, memory loss has been described for autobiographical memory (Laurent et al., 1990; Venneri & Caffarra, 1998), the topographical layout of familiar surroundings and landmarks (Stracciari et al., 1994; Cammalleri et al., 1996), familiar persons and their names (Kapur et al., 1994), and for the meaning of words (Hodges, 1997). The reported cases are yet too few and too heterogeneous to draw any firm conclusion upon the pathogenetic relationship of transient retrograde amnesia and TGA. The main criterion for differential diagnosis is, of course, the presence or absence of anterograde amnesia.

Fugue States

Fugue states are characterized by a sudded loss of personal identity and of all autobiographical memories, usually associated with a period of wandering, which lasts a few hours or days and for which there is a virtually complete amnesic gap upon recovery. They are generally recognized as being psychogenic (Stengel, 1941; Kopelman et al., 1994a, 1994b). Like TGA fugue states can be triggered by emotionally stressful events or by mild head trauma. Fugue states differ from TGA by the loss of personal identity and by the absence of repetitive questioning and of dense anterograde amnesia. It may, however, be questioned whether cases of transient isolated loss of autobiographical memory (Laurent et al., 1990; Venneri & Caffarra, 1998) should be classified as mild fugue states (Kopelman, 2000).

DEFINITION OF TGA

Criteria have been proposed which should permit a diagnosis of TGA and facilitate the exclusion of other possible causes of transient memory dysfunction (Caplan, 1985):

1. *Information about the beginning of the attack should be available from a capable observer who witnessed the onset.* This criterion is intended to exclude epileptic seizures and concussion as causes of transient amnesia.
2. *The patient should have been examined during the attack to be certain that other neurological symptoms and signs did not accompany the amnesia.*
3. *There should be no important accompanying neurological signs.*

    These criteria are not unequivocal. As will be outlined in the following sections, additional neuropsychological abnormalities are the rule rather than the exception in TGA. As far as the neurological examination is concerned, it must be said that the estimation of, for example, a positive Babinsky sign or a side difference of tendon reflexes is not terribly reliable and may heavily depend on the scrutiny of the examination if not on the expectations of the examiner (Frederiks, 1990). On the other hand there is evidence, reviewed in a later section of this chapter, that accompanying neurological symptoms do have implications for the prognosis and management of TGA. For practice, it seems appropriate to distinguish between "pure TGA" and TGA accompanied by overt neurological symptoms like clouding of consciousness, hemiparesis, ataxia, disturbed oculomotor motility, visual field loss, or aphasia.

4. *The memory loss should be transient.* To be applicable, this criterion should be restricted to the behavioural manifestation of severe amnesia. On neuropsychological testing, restoration of memory proceeds much slower than the rapid restoration of normal behaviour would lead one to assume, and there may even be permanent subtle memory deficits in patients with typical TGA (see below). Usually the length of the spell is in the range of several hours. If the duration is below 1 h or exceeds 24 h, the diagnosis should be questioned.

EPIDEMIOLOGY AND PROGNOSIS OF TGA

Two district based study found the annual incidence of TGA to be 3/100 000 (Hodges, 1991) and 5.2/100 000 respectively (Miller et al., 1987). For most patients TGA remains a unique event, as the annual recurrence rate across several years of follow-up is only 2–5% (Mumenthaler & Treig, 1984; Kushner & Hauser, 1985; Hinge et al., 1986; Miller et al., 1987; Colombo & Scarpa, 1988; Guidotti et al., 1989; Hinge & Jensen, 1990).

The vast majority of patients are aged 50–70 years and the mean age of representative samples of TGA patients is remarkably consistent close to 60 years (Mumenthaler & Treig, 1984; Crowell et al., 1984; Hinge et al., 1986; Miller et al., 1987; Colombo & Scarpa, 1988; Guidotti et al., 1989; Frederiks, 1990; Hodges & Warlow, 1990a; Hodges, 1991; Klotzsch et al., 1996; Inzitari et al., 1997; Schmidtke & Ehmsen, 1998). The incidence of TGA is as high in the sixth decade as it is in the seventh and falls sharply in the eighth. Patients older than 80 are as rare as patients younger than 40 (Caplan, 1985; Hodges, 1991). This contrasts with the incidence of cerebrovascular disease which shows a continuous increase with advancing age as well as with that of migraine which usually starts in adolescence or young adulthood and diminishes with advancing age.

In search for the aetiology of TGA several studies have investigated the prevalence of risk factors for atherosclerosis. In different samples of TGA patients the frequency of arterial hypertension varies widely. It was reported to be only 13% (Hinge et al., 1986), 25–35% (Mumenthaler & Treig, 1984; Matias-Guiu et al., 1986; Miller et al., 1987; Frederiks, 1990; Hodges & Warlow, 1990a), and about 50% (Crowell et al., 1984; Kushner & Hauser, 1985; Colombo & Scarpa, 1988; Guidotti et al., 1989; Zorzon et al., 1995). A history of coronary heart disease was found with frequencies between some 5% (Mumenthaler & Treig, 1984; Hinge et al., 1986; Hodges & Warlow, 1990a) and some 25% (Hinge et al., 1986; Miller et al., 1987; Guidotti et al., 1989; Frederiks, 1990). The frequency of previous cerebrovascular events was reported to be as high as 67% in one study (Kushner & Hauser, 1985), but only 10% or lower in the remainder (Matias-Guiu et al., 1986; Miller et al., 1987; Colombo & Scarpa, 1988; Frederiks, 1990; Hodges & Warlow, 1990a). The prevalence of other risk factors like smoking, diabetes, or hypercholesterolaemia has been reported to be as high as in patients with transient ischaemic attacks by two studies (Kushner & Hauser, 1985; Guidotti et al., 1989), while the majority of studies agreed that it is not higher than in healthy controls and definitely lower than in patients with transient ischaemic attacks (Matias-Guiu et al., 1986; Hinge et al., 1986; Miller et al., 1987; Hodges & Warlow, 1990a; Zorzon et al., 1995; Inzitari et al., 1997). A recent investigation detected a patent foramen ovale in 55% of patients with TGA as compared to 27% of controls (Klotzsch et al., 1996). The foramen ovale connects the right and left atrium of the heart. It normally closes after birth. If it remains patent, emboli from venous thromboses can be propelled into cerebral arteries. This is particularly likely when pressure in pulmonary circulation is elevated by Valsalva-like manoevres, that is, forced expiration against a closed glottis as happens in heavy lifting, coughing, and defecation and may also occur during sexual intercourse.

Whereas there is disagreement as to the frequency of vascular risk factors in patients with TGA, there is unanimity that for mean follow-up periods of about three to four years the risk for transient ischaemic attacks, stroke, or myocardial infarction is not elevated. (Mumenthaler & Treig, 1984; Kushner & Hauser, 1985; Hinge et al., 1986; Miller et al., 1987; Colombo & Scarpa, 1988; Guidotti et al., 1989; Frederiks, 1990; Hinge & Jensen, 1990; Hodges & Warlow, 1990a). A large study which included careful clinical assessment of all TGAs found that the prognosis for subsequent coronary or cerebrovascular ischaemic events was definitely worse in patients in whom TGA was accompanied by other neurological symptoms (Hodges & Warlow, 1990b). These patients also had a higher prevalence of vascular risk factors than those with pure TGA. Another study which did not differentiate between TGA with and without associated neurological symptoms found the prognosis for subsequent cerebrovascular disease to be worse in TGA patients with vascular risk factors than in those without (Jensen & Olivarius, 1981).

A further topic of particular interest for epidemological studies has been the association of TGA with migraine. The given frequency of a history of migraine in patients with TGA varies from 3.6% (Colombo & Scarpa, 1988) to 40% (Crowell et al., 1984). However, some 20% appears to be a reasonable estimate on which several studies accord (Matias-Guiu et al., 1986; Hinge et al., 1986; Hodges & Warlow, 1990a; Inzitari et al., 1997; Schmidtke &

Ehmsen, 1998). The estimate for the prevalence of migraine in an unselected population is 10–20% (Poeck, 1990). Studies which directly compared the frequency of migraine between TGA patients and controls found it to be elevated by 4–15% (Hodges & Warlow, 1990a; Zorzon et al., 1995; Inzitari et al., 1997; Schmidtke & Ehmsen, 1998). Nonetheless, the majority of patients with TGA do not have a history of migraine.

A more impressive difference of premorbid symptoms was reported by Inzitari et al. (1997). They used a phobic attitude scale for assessing a history of agorophobic traits and recorded instances of avoidance behaviour in 82% of TGA patients as compared to only 22% of patients with transient ischemic attacks.

NEUROPSYCHOLOGY OF TGA

During Attack

The clinical impression that patients are completely unable to lay down new permanent memories is confirmed by neuropsychological assessment during the attack. While immediate memory is preserved or only slightly reduced (Hodges & Ward, 1989) the acquisition of information into secondary memory is impossible. Amnesia affects not only verbal and visual, but also olfactory, tactile, and kinaesthetic information and environmental sounds (Shuttleworth & Wise, 1973), and no significant sparing has as yet been observed for any kind of material.

In addition to the complete incapacity to lay down new memories, patients are unable to recall memories which have been at their disposition before the attack. The degree of retrograde amnesia is variable and is more difficult to assess than that of anterograde amnesia as the patient's recall has to be compared with their own premorbid memories in order to estimate the severity of memory loss. There are two types of impaired access to previously acquired memories which are not mutually exclusive:

On the one hand, there may be a loss of any recollection for a limited period of time preceding the attack. Personal and public circumstances are believed to be as they had been before this period which may span up to several years (Case 1; Caffarra et al., 1981; Kritchevsky & Squire, 1989; Goldenberg et al., 1991; Kazui et al., 1996). On the other hand there can be a patchy memory loss which has no clear-cut temporal limit but may stretch back as far as some decades or even to childhood (Case 2: Caffarra et al., 1981; Stracciari et al., 1987; Kritchevsky et al., 1988; Hodges & Ward, 1989; Guillery et al., 2000). Patients are able to recollect major public and personal events but their reports are "curiously empty and lacking in colour, as if reduced to the bare bones of memory" (Hodges & Ward, 1989). A peculiar feature of this type of retrograde amnesia are difficulties with the dating and chronological ordering of recalled events (Case 2: Caffarra et al., 1981; Regard & Landis, 1984; Stracciari et al., 1987; Kritchevsky et al., 1988; Hodges & Ward, 1989).

Semantic memory appears to be less impaired than autobiographical memory. Patients do recognize objects, can use language meaningfully and know how to behave in a civilized way. Normal performance has also been documented on a more demanding test requiring matching of pictures by associative or functional relationships (e.g. selecting whether a lion or a giraffe goes with a clown; Hodges, 1994). Problems might, however, affect the recall of temporally bound public events and of famous personalities (Hodges & Ward, 1989). Patients examined during TGA could normally distinguish real from fictious events, but made more errors than after the TGA when trying to date the events. They were also deficient in the naming of famous faces. It thus seems that the borderline between impaired and preserved retrograde memory is not so much between autobiographical and semantic memory as between recall of specific events or personalities and recall of general knowledge.

The parallel impairment of anterograde and retrograde memory might suggest a retrieval deficit as common source of difficulties, but there are arguments against this explanation. Whereas anterograde amnesia is uniform across patients, the extension and degree of retrograde amnesia varies widely, and retrograde memory can recover while anterograde amnesia is still complete (Kazui et al., 1996; Kapur et al., 1998). Conversely, there are patients with transient retrograde amnesia who can perfectly well recall newly acquired information (see above). These dissociations would suggest that retrograde memory impairment is an independent sequel of cerebral dysfunction which usually accompanies transient global amnesia but is not necessarily bound to it.

Implicit memory, that is the acquisition or modifications of skills, habits and preferences without conscious recollection of the modifying experience, seems not to be affected by TGA. Intact implicit memory has been demonstrated for perceptual learning of recognition of fragmented digits and figures (Goldenberg et al., 1991; Kapur et al., 1996), lexical priming of word stem completion and category decisions (Kazui et al., 1995; Eustache et al., 1997; Beauregard et al., 1997), procedural learning of mirror reading and mirror drawing (Kazui et al., 1995; Eustache et al., 1997) and for acquisition of strategies in the Tower of Toronto puzzle (Kazui et al., 1995).

While simple span is usually normal, more demanding measures of working memory which require simultaneous holding and processing of information, reveal abnormalities in some patients. Digit span backwards can be slightly reduced (Hodges & Ward, 1989; Hodges, 1991). Eustache et al. (1999) asked patients to construct sentences containing a given word. After two sentences patients were asked to repeat the two words given for these sentences. This requires holding of the words in working memory simultaneously with production of sentences. One patient with a TGA had great difficulties with this task while two other patients performed flawlessly.

Careful neuropsychological examination can reveal mild but definite impairments of other cognitive functions than memory. Reduced fluency of production of words or designs has been noted in some patients (Stillhard et al., 1990; Goldenberg et al., 1991; Eustache et al., 1997, 1999) but not in others (Regard & Landis, 1984; Hodges, 1994; Venneri & Caffarra, 1998). Patients may have difficulties with the copy of a complex figure (Case 2: Kritchevsky et al., 1988; Kritchevsky & Squire, 1989). Finally, one study found a slight but statistically significant reduction of correct namings on the Boston Naming Test during TGA as compared to the same patients' performance after TGA (Kritchevsky & Squire, 1989). The prevalence of mild additional cognitive deficits in TGA might be higher than appears from the reported cases, because the memory impairment prevents patients from tackling cognitively demanding tasks by themselves and because many examiners do not probe them.

Neuropsychological examinations thus reveal more deficits than anterograde amnesia in many patients with TGA. There is, however, an essential difference between anterograde amnesia and the other neuropsychological symptoms. Whereas amnesia is complete and uniform, disturbances of retrograde memory, working memory and other cognitive functions are never complete and vary both in type and severity.

Follow-up

TGA leaves a dense amnesic gap for the time of complete amnesia which may extend backwards for up to one hour preceding the attack.

Clinically, TGA is assumed to be over when behaviour and everyday memory are inconspicuous again. Neuropsychological follow-up examinations have established that restoration of memory proceeds much slower than subjectively experienced complaints and that normal performance on memory tests is achieved only after several days or even weeks (Cases 1 and 2: Regard and Landis, 1984; Hodges & Ward, 1989; Stillhard et al., 1990; Goldenberg et al., 1991; Beauregard et al., 1997). Although most patients then reach test results which fall into the range of normality and do not complain about memory loss or other cognitive problems in daily life, comparisons of groups of TGA patients with carefully matched controls suggest some persistent memory impairment even after a single typical TGA (Mazzuchi et al., 1980; Hodges & Oxbury, 1990). A consistent finding has been impaired recall of short stories as used in the logical memory subtest of the Wechsler Memory Scale. Impaired recall of complex geometrical figures has been found in some patients (Mazzuchi et al., 1980; Eustache et al., 1999) but not in others (Hodges & Oxbury, 1990). One study (Hodges & Oxbury, 1990) found impaired naming of famous faces, impaired dating of famous events, and impoverished recall of autobiographical episodes in patients after TGA. These deficits of retrograde memory were not temporally graded.

NEURORADIOLOGY OF TGA

Imaging After Attack

Since the advent of computed tomography, many patients with TGA have undergone CT after the attack. In some 10% of them CT showed cerebral infarctions without relationship to anatomical structures relevant to memory (Miller et al., 1987; Matias-Guiu et al., 1986; Colombo & Scarpa, 1988; Hodges & Warlow, 1990b). There are, however, cases in whom CT after TGA demonstrated ischaemic lesions in either the thalamus (Ladurner et al., 1982; Kushner & Hauser, 1985; Bogousslavsky & Regli, 1988; Colombo & Scarpa, 1988; Raffaele et al., 1995) or the medial temporal lobe (Ladurner et al., 1982; Kushner & Hauser, 1985; Bogousslavsky & Regli, 1988; Tanabe et al., 1991) of one side which was the left more often than the right. The interpretation of these lesions as indicating the cause of TGA is made problematic by the fact that TGA is transient and the lesions are permanent. As the lesions were present when memory was normalized they may have existed already before it became abnormal at all. This scepticism does not, however, apply to one patient in whom CT at the end of a 10-hour episode of TGA disclosed an acute haematoma in the left rostral thalamus (Chen et al., 1996).

Evidence for the location of lesions underlying TGA is also provided by patients in whom TGA is followed by a persistent memory deficit and CT shows lesions in memory-related structures. The occurrence of a permanent memory deficit which correlates with the lesion's location makes it unlikely that the lesion has silently been present before the TGA. It does not, however, exclude more widespread cerebral dysfunction during the TGA. Goldenberg et al. (1983) found a left polar thalamic lesion in a 40 year old patient whose TGA was followed by a predominantly verbal memory deficit and an impairment of autobiographical memory which reached back into school days. Gorelick et al. (1988) reported on a patient who suffered three typical TGAs. Memory recovered completely after the first and the second attack, and a CT after the second attack was normal. After the third attack there remained a persistent, predominantly verbal, memory deficit and CT showed a left polar thalamic infarction.

Cerebral angiography or Doppler sonography in patients after TGA have revealed a considerable incidence of atherosclerotic plaques, stenoses, occlusions and hypoplasias of arteries particularly in the vertebrobasilar territory (Jensen & Olivarius, 1980; Frederiks, 1990; Klotzsch et al., 1996). Again, the causal relationship to TGA is questionable, as the pathogenetic relationship between arterial narrowing and cerebral symptoms is far from being straightforward and as clinically silent stenoses or occlusions of cerebral arteries are a common finding in elderly patients undergoing angiography (Goldenberg & Reisner, 1983).

Imaging During Attack

As TGA is caused by a reversible cerebral dysfunction, the most promising way for finding its anatomical substrate is to acquire measures of local brain function during the attack and afterwards. Table 10.1 gives an overview of such studies. The following section will first consider the diagnostic possibilities and limitations of the methods used, and then discuss what the available data reveal about aetiology and location of cerebral dysfunction in TGA.

Limitations of Methods

Planar 133-Xenon measurement, single photon emission computed tomography (SPECT) and positron emission tomography (PET) have all been applied for measuring regional cerebral blood flow (rCBF). A reduction of rCBF need not necessarily indicate causal ischaemia. It can result as an autoregulatory adaptation to reduced neuronal function. Only PET can distinguish between these possibilities by registering oxygen consumption together with blood flow. In ischaemia but not in primary neuronal dysfunction there is a compensatory increase of oxygen consumption relative to blood flow. Deep brain structures like the thalamus or the mesial temporal lobes are visualized not at all by ^{133}Xenon and with a lower signal to noise ratio than surface structures by SPECT. All three methods are tuned to detect changes in tissue with high blood flow and oxygen consumption, that is grey matter, and do not show subtle abnormalities in blood supply of white matter.

Diffusion weighted magnetic resonance imaging (DW-MRI) shows regions in which the diffusion of interstitial water is reduced due to cell swelling. Cytotoxic cell swelling occurs very early in the course of ischaemia, but may be caused by other pathologies too (Strupp et al., 1998). In contrast to measures of cerebral blood flow, DW MRI is also sensitive to alterations in white matter. Finally, proton magnetic resonance spectroscopy analyses the distribution of metabolites within a selected region of the brain and permits conclusions upon the presence and to some degree also the cause of cellular damage.

Aetiology

PET studies of TGA have demonstrated either a proportional reduction of blood flow and oxygen reduction or more reduction of oxygen consumption than blood flow, and both

Table 10.1 Neuroimaging during TGA

Study	Method	Hippocampus*	Thalamus	Neocortex	Note
Trillet et al., 1987	Xenon	?	?	BIL	
Stillhard et al., 1990	SPECT	BIL	?	BIL	Early recovery
Tanabe et al., 1991	SPECT	BIL	Bil*	–	
Goldenberg et al., 1991	SPECT	BIL	BIL	BIL	Left frontal deficit persistent
Evans et al., 1993	SPECT	BIL	?	–	
Lin et al., 1993	SPECT	L	L	BIL	
Sakashita et al., 1993	SPECT	L	BIL	–	Early recovery, deficits persistent
		R	–	–	Early recovery
Hodges, 1994	SPECT	L	?	?	
Goldenberg, 1995	SPECT	BIL	BIL	L	
Kazui et al., 1995	SPECT	BIL	–	–	Two patients
Jung et al., 1996	SPECT	R*	–	–	Hypoperfusion at follow-up
Sakashita et al., 1997	SPECT	BIL	BIL	BIL	Two patients
		BIL	BIL	BIL	Early recovery
Takeuchi et al., 1998	SPECT	BIL	BIL	?	Early recovery
Schmidtke et al., 1998	SPECT	–	–	BIL	
		BIL	–	BIL	
		BIL	L	BIL	Thalamic and parietal Hyperperfusion at follow-up
		BIL	–	–	Early recovery
		L	–	BIL	Early recovery
		–	BIL*	BIL	Early recovery
Jovin et al., 2000	SPECT	BIL	?	?	
Volpe et al., 1983	PET	BIL	?	BIL	
Baron et al., 1994	PET	–	R	R	Early recovery
Eustache et al., 1997	PET	–	L	L	
Woolfenden et al., 1998	DWMRI	BIL	–	BIL	TGA after cerebral angiography
Ay et al., 1998	DWMRI	L	–	–	Early recovery, no follow-up
Strupp et al., 1998	DWMRI	BIL	–	–	
		BIL	–	–	Two patients, early recovery
		L	–	–	Four patients, early recovery
		–	–	–	Three patients, early recovery
Gass et al., 1999	DWMRI	–	–	–	Two patients
		–	–	–	Four patients, early recovery
Tanabe et al., 1999	DWMRI	BIL	–	–	Early recovery, TGA after cerebral angiography
Zorzon et al., 1998	Spectroscopy	–	?	?	

*Mesial and basal temporal regions including hippocampus.
BIL, bilateral; L, left; R, right; –, normal; ?, not analysed; If not indicated otherwise (*hyperperfusion) the abnormalities are hypoperfusion in Xenon, SPECT, and PET, reduced diffusion of interstitial water in DWMRI, and changed distribution of metabolites in spectroscopy.
"Early recovery" refers to examinations within one day after clinically apparent resolution of complete amnesia. If not indicated otherwise, follow-up examinations of cases with pathological findings were normal.

patterns have been observed to co-occur in different regions of the same patient. (Volpe et al., 1983; Baron et al., 1994; Eustache et al., 1997). This constellation would speak in favour of primarily neuronal dysfunction, although it might also be compatible with early recovery from short lasting ischaemia (Eustache et al., 1997). On the other hand, two DW-MRI studies (Woolfenden et al., 1998; Ay et al., 1998; Tanabe et al., 1999) discovered multiple small foci of cellular damage in cortical and subcortical portions of the vascular territory of the posterior cerebral artery. This distribution of foci is typical of embolism causing local ischaemia.

Location

Table 10.1 lists three types of location of transient abnormalities in TGA: hippocampus formation, thalamus and neocortical areas. Hippocampal abnormalities were demonstrated in 31 patients and excluded in 14, thalamic abnormalities were demonstrated in 13 and excluded in 20, and neocortical abnormalities were demonstrated in 16 and excluded in 23. Unilateral dysfunction was left-sided in 12 patients and right-sided in 3. This statistic would suggest a preponderance of hippocampal over thalamic and neocortical, and of left-sided over right-sided dysfunction, but a more impressive conclusion from inspection of the table is the large variability between patients. On a first inspection one gets the impression that any possible combination of normal and abnormal function in different region is compatible with TGA. On closer scrutiny there are restrictions to this variability: Completely normal images were produced only by DW MRI. As it seems implausible that brain function is completely undisturbed during TGA, the complete absence of any pathological changes in these studies is likely to be due to methodological restrictions. Considering the rCBF studies, there is only one case (Schmidtke et al., 1998, first case) in whom blood flow was normal in both hippocampal regions as well as in both thalami. It thus seems that the minimum condition for TGA is at least unilateral hippocampal or thalamic dysfunction, but in most of the cases this minimum condition is combined with dysfunction in other memory–related deep structures or in the neocortex.

AETIOLOGY OF TGA

The next section will leave the firm ground of established facts and consider hypotheses on the aetiology of cerebral dysfunction in TGA. Before doing so, it might be useful to summarize briefly a few conclusions from the preceding considerations which constitute challenges to a valid explanation of TGA:

- TGA affects patients within a limited age range and has a low recurrence rate. In a significant portion of patients attacks are elicited by specific triggers.
- There is an extraordinary dense and global anterograde amnesia which to all neuropsy-chological experience would point to bilateral dysfunction of memory-related brain structures, but neuroimaging during attacks suggests that the minimum condition for TGA is unilateral dysfunction of the hippocampal formation or thalamus.
- In addition to complete anterograde amnesia there are variable degrees of impairment of retrograde memory, working memory, and other cognitive functions.

There are two classes of hypotheses on the aetiology of TGA. One holds that neuronal dysfunction is a sequel of transient ischaemia whereas the other assumes primary neuronal dysfunction.

Ischaemia

Ischaemia as the cause of TGA can safely be assumed for TGA preceding ischaemic stroke and for those patients in whom DW MRI demonstrated multiple lesions with a typical distribution of embolic infarctions, but it remains open whether this mechanism applies to all cases of TGA and whether it is an expression of atherosclerotic cerebrovascular disease.

Cerebrovascular Disease

The idea that TGA is a sequel of atherosclerotic cerebrovascular disease affecting blood supply to memory-related structures (Frederiks, 1990) does have difficulties with several facts: the incidence of TGA declines at an age when that of other cerebrovascular accidents increases; TGA rarely recurs and does not predict a raised risk for subsequent cerebrovascular accidents in other locations; the triggers of TGA have not been recognised as eliciting cerebral ischaemia.

At least three modified versions of the basic hypothesis have been proposed which preserve the idea that TGA is due to ischaemia to memory-related structures but assume other mechanisms than atherosclerotic cerebrovascular disease as being the cause of ischaemia.

Selective Ischaemia of Paramedian Thalamic Arteries

Goldenberg (1995) sought for the basis of TGA in anatomical peculiarities of blood supply to the polar thalamus. Blood supply for the polar thalamic region is provided by the polar and by the paramedian thalamic arteries. The paramedian arteries arise from the basilar communicating artery which connects the basilar artery with the posterior cerebral arteries. They are the only vessels originating from this small portion of the circle of Willis. As a frequent variation, both paramedian arteries can arise from a common stem on either the left or the right basilar communicating artery (Percheron, 1973).

Being exposed to the high pressure blood stream from the basilar artery, the basilar communicating arteries and the origin of the paramedian arteries are loci of predilection for atherosclerotic plaques (Robinson & Tode, 1989). Both the diameter of the paramedian artery and of the basilar communicating artery vary greatly between individuals (Percheron, 1976a, 1976b). One might easily conceive of anatomical constellations in which mild atherosclerotic changes at or near to the tip of the basilar artery suffice to severely compromise blood flow in a thin paramedian artery at a time when general atherosclerosis is not yet sufficiently advanced to manifest itself by other vascular symptoms. TGA becomes rare when atherosclerosis advances as patients who have the anatomical predisposition for TGA will have suffered the insult already early in the course of atherosclerotic disease. Presumably, paramedian arteries which are thick enough to resist mild atherosclerotic changes supply larger vascular territories. If they happen to be occluded by advanced atherosclerosis, this would lead to amnesic stroke or TGA with associated neurological symptoms rather than to pure TGA.

The plausibility of this hypothesis is endorsed by the demonstration of stroke in the territory of the paramedian thalamic artery in patients with amnesic stroke after TGA. The hypothesis can account for the age distribution of TGA, for its low recurrence rate, and for the low incidence of other cerebrovascular accidents during follow-up periods of three to four years, but has no explanation for the association of TGA with specific triggers. If it is taken to imply that thalamic ischaemia is the only possible cause of TGA, it is severely challenged by those brain imaging studies which demonstrated abnormalities in one or both hippocampal regions but excluded them in both thalami.

Crossed Embolism

Another alternative to atherosclerotic vascular disease as the cause of transient ischaemia is suggested by the raised incidence of patent foramen ovale in patients with TGA (Klotzsch et al., 1996). A crossing over of emboli through the foramen from the right to the left atrium is particularly likely when pressure in the right atrium is elevated due to raised intrathoracal pressure, as occurs in Valsalva-like manoevres. Pressure in the right atrium may also be elevated by an increase of venous inflow from the periphery when superficial veins contract as a reaction to cold or when transport of blood in deep veins is reinforced by muscular activity. Triggering of TGA by physical exertion, sexual intercourse and immersion in cold water would thus find a convenient explanation. Finally, long drives which have also been recognized as a trigger for TGA are frequently associated with immobile sitting and dehydration and are therefore risk factors for venous thrombosis in the leg which may be the source of venous emboli crossing over to the cerebral circulation.

The idea that TGA is caused by crossed embolization through a patent foramen ovale offers an attractive explanation for triggers of TGA but not for the age distribution and low recurrence rate of TGA. As the risk remains the same after a TGA has happened, and as emboli from the heart may as well go to vascular territories unrelated to memory, one should expect a raised rate of subsequent TGA and of cerebrovascular accidents with other symptoms. Finally, the one study on which this hypothesis is based found a patent foramen ovale only in 55% of patients with TGA and no difference in prevalence and type of triggers between TGA patients with or without a patent foramen ovale.

Venous Congestion

A variant of the idea that the source of ischaemia in TGA is to be sought in the venous rather than the arterial portion of circulation was proposed by Lewis (1998). He proposed that ischaemia of the hippocampus or thalamus is caused by a raised venous pressure in the sinus rectus which drains both of these structures. This is turn could be a sequel of increased venous back flow to the superior vena cava from the arms due to muscular activity or of a Valsalva-like manoevre which raises the intrathoracal pressure and hence blocks venous flow from the superior vena cava to the heart. Like the previous hypothesis this one can offer an explanation for the nature of triggers but not for the age distribution or the low recurrence rate of TGA. Furthermore, it does not provide a mechanism explaining how an augmentation of venous pressure lasting seconds or minutes can cause memory dysfunction lasting several hours.

Neuronal Dysfunction

Spreading Depression

The most elaborated and popular variant of the hypothesis that TGA is caused by primary neuronal dysfunction ascribes the memory loss and associated cognitive impairments to spreading depression. Spreading depression (SD) is a phenomenon which has been demonstrated in experimental animals. Local physical or chemical stimuli can induce a depolarization of neurons which spreads to surrounding tissue and temporarily abolishes the functioning of the affected nerve cells (Bures et al., 1992). In human pathology, SD is thought to play a role in the pathogenesis of lasting neuronal damage after ischaemia or head trauma (Somjen et al., 1992). Although primarily a neuronal event, SD is accompanied by changes of rCBF. The spreading wave of SD manifests itself by a short-lasting elevation of blood flow which is followed by a longer lasting period of decreased rCBF. The regional metabolic rates of oxygen and of glucose remain normal, and there are no focal neurological symptoms corresponding to the depression of rCBF (Lauritzen, 1992). Studies of rCBF during the aura symptoms of migraine attacks showed regions of reduced blood flow which moved across the cortex with the same speed as the waves of SD in experimental animals. Because of the similarity of this rCBF depression to the wandering fields of flow reductions following SD, SD has been invoked as being part of the pathogenesis of migraine (Lauritzen et al., 1983; Lauritzen, 1992). Although moving waves of rCBF reduction have not yet been demonstrated in TGA, the finding of diffusely depressed cortical blood flow in several cases of TGA has been estimated to be similar enough to justify the assumption that SD is at work in TGA. The hypothesis has been put forward that stressful stimuli lead to an overstimulation of the hippocampus which provokes local SD inactivating the hippocampus and spreading from there to the cerebral cortex (Olesen & Jorgensen, 1986; Hodges, 1991). The hypothesis thus emphasises a link between migraine and TGA and the emotional valence of triggers of TGA (Caplan et al., 1981; Crowell et al., 1984; Hodges & Warlow, 1990a).

The major strength of the hypothesis is the explanation of the variable additional cognitive deficits accompanying memory loss by variable extension of the wave of spreading depression over the whole cerebral cortex. A major weakness is a lack of explanation for the age distribution and for the low recurrence rate of TGA. It seems implausible that persons who tend to react to emotional stress by spreading depression do so only once in their life and only between the fifth and eighth decade. A further point of concern is that a history of migraine is found only in a minority of patients with TGA. Finally, the link to migraine fits well with neither the age distribution nor the nature of triggers of TGA. Migraine usually starts in adolescence or young adulthood and the frequency of attacks tends to diminish in advanced age. Physical exertion is not very common as a trigger of migraine, the attacks of which may even be aborted by physical exercise (Ziegler & Murrow, 1988; Poeck, 1990). On the other hand, fasting, dietary irregularities, sleep deprivation and excessive sleep which are known as precipitating factors of migraine have not been documented to trigger TGA.

Panic Attack

Another "functional" hypothesis was put forward by Inzitari et al. (1997). As already noted, they found an impressively high prevalence of pre-existent phobic traits in patients with TGA. As phobic attitudes can be associated with panic attacks, they suggested that memory loss and accompanying cognitive deficits in TGA might be a variant of a panic attack triggered either by emotional stress or by hyperventilation and subsequent rise of blood lactate levels in physical exertion.

Similar to the spreading depression hypothesis, this idea gives a satisfactory account of the effect of triggers, but neither of the age distribution nor the low recurrence rate. Furthermore, agitation and vegetative symptoms which are core symptoms of panic attacks (DMS-IV, 1994) accompany TGA only in a portion of patients.

CONCLUSIONS

In spite of the considerable accumulation of data on the epidemology, clinical features, neuropsychology, course, and prognosis of TGA, its aetiology and pathogenesis are still a matter of speculation. None of the hypotheses which have been proposed offers a completely satisfactory account of all aspects of TGA. This should draw attention to the possibility that TGA is not a unitary disorder but can result from a variety of causes which somehow converge on a final mechanism unifiying them in one distinct and well defined clinical disorder. After 50 years of research, the nature of TGA remains elusive.

REFERENCES

Ay, H., Furie, K.L., Yamada, K. & Koroshetz, W.J. (1998). Diffusion-weighted MRI characterizes the ischemic lesion transient global amnesia. *Neurology*, **51**, 901–903.

Baron, J.C., Petit-Taboué, M.C., Le Doze, F. et al. (1994). Right frontal cortex hypometabolism in transient global amnesia: a PET study. *Brain*, **117**, 545–552.

Beauregard, M., Weiner, J., Gold, D. & Chertkow, H. (1997). Word priming during and after transient global amnesia: a case report. *Neurocase*, **3**, 451–459.

Bender, M.B. (1956). Syndrome of isolated episode of confusion with amnesia. *Journal of the Hillside Hospital*, **5**, 212–215.

Bogousslavsky, J. & Regli, F. (1988). Transient global amnesia and stroke. *European Neurology*, **28**, 106–110.

Bures, J., Koroleva, V.I. & Vinogradova, L.V. (1992). Synergetics of spreading depression: reentry waves and reverberators in the rat brain. In R. J. do Carmo (ed.), *Spreading Depression* (pp. 35–48). Berlin: Springer.

Caffarra, P., Moretti, G., Mazucchi, A. & Parma, M. (1981). Neuropsychological testing during a transient global amnesia period and its follow-up. *Acta Neurologica Scandinavica*, **63**, 44–50.

Cammalleri, R., Gangitano, M., D'Amelio, M. et al. (1996). Transient topographical amnesia and cingulate cortex damage: a case report. *Neuropsychologia*, **34**, 321–326.

Caplan, L., Chedru, F., Lhermitte, F. & Mayman, C. (1981). Transient global amnesia and migraine. *Neurology*, **31**, 1167–1170.

Caplan, L.B. (1985). Transient global amnesia. In J.A.M. Frederiks (ed.), *Handbook of Clinical Neurology, Vol. 1(45): Clinical Neuropsychology* (pp. 205–218). Amsterdam: Elsevier Science.

Caplan, L.R. (1990). Transient global amnesia: characteristic features and overview. In H.J. Markowitsch (ed.), *Transient Global amnesia and Related Disorders* (pp. 15–27). Toronto: Hogrefe & Huber.

Chen, W.H., Liu, J.S., Wu, S.C. & Chang, Y.Y. (1996). Transient global amnesia and thalamic hemorrhage. *Clinical Neurology and Neurosurgery*, **98**, 309–311.

Colombo, A. & Scarpa, M. (1988). Transient global amnesia: pathogenesis and prognosis. *European Neurology*, **28**, 111–114.

Crowell, G.F., Stump, D.A., Biller, J. et al. (1984). The transient global amnesia–migraine connection. *Archives of Neurology*, **41**, 75–79.

DMS-IV. (1994). *Diagnostic and Statistical Manual of Mental Disorders*, 4th edn. Washington, DC: American Psychiatric Association.

Eustache, F., Desgranges, B., Laville, P. et al. (1999). Episodic memory in transient global amnesia: encoding, storage, or retrieval deficit? *Journal of Neurology, Neurosurgery, and Psychiatry*, **66**, 148–154.

Eustache, F., Desgranges, B., Petit-Taboué, M.C. et al. (1997). Transient global amnesia: implicit/explicit memory dissociation and PET assessment of brain perfusion and oxygen metabolism in the acute stage. *Journal of Neurology, Neurosurgery, and Psychiatry*, **63**, 357–367.

Evans, J., Wilson, B., Wraight, E.P. & Hodges, J.R. (1993). Neuropsychological and SPECT scan findings during and after transient global amnesia: evidence for the differential impairment of remote episodic memory. *Journal of Neurology, Neurosurgery, and Psychiatry*, **56**, 1227–1230.

Fisher, C.M. & Adams, R.D. (1964). Transient global amnesia. *Acta Neurologica Scandinavica*, **40** (suppl 9), 1–83.

Frederiks, J.A.M. (1990). Transient global amnesia: an amnesic TIA. In H.J. Markowitsch (ed.), *Transient Global Amnesia and Related Disorders* (pp. 28–47). Toronto: Hogrefe & Huber.

Gallassi, R. & Morreale, A. (1990). Transient global amnesia and epilepsy. In H.J. Markowitsch (ed.), *Transient Global Amnesia and Related Disorders* (pp. 58–65). Toronto: Hogrefe & Huber.

Gass, A., Gaa, J., Hirsch, J. et al. (1999). Lack of evidence of acute ischemic tissue change in transient global amnesia on single-shot echo-planar diffusion-weighted MRI. *Stroke*, **30**, 2070–2072.

Goldenberg, G. (1995). Transient global amnesia. In A. Baddeley, B. A. Wilson & F. Watts (eds), *Handbook of Memory Disorders* 1st edn (pp. 109–133). Chichester: Wiley.

Goldenberg, G., Podreka, I., Pfaffelmeyer, N. et al. (1991). Thalamic ischaemia in transient global amnesia: A SPECT study. *Neurology*, **41**, 1748–1752.

Goldenberg, G. & Reisner, T. (1983). Angiographic findings in relation to clinical course and results of computed tomography in cerebrovascular disease. *European Neurology*, **22**, 124–130.

Goldenberg, G., Wimmer, A. & Maly, J. (1983). Amnesic syndrome with a unilateral thalamic lesion: a case report. *Journal of Neurology*, **229**, 79–86.

Gorelick, P.B., Amico, L.A., Ganellen, R. & Benevento, L.A. (1988). Transient global amnesia and thalamic infarction. *Neurology*, **38**, 496–499.

Guidotti, M., Anzalone, N., Morabito, A. & Landi, G. (1989). A case-control study of transient global amnesia. *Journal of Neurology, Neurosurgery, and Psychiatry*, **52**, 320–323.

Guillery, B., Desgranges, B., Piolino, P. et al. (2000). Extensive temporally graded retrograde amnesia for personal-episodic facts in transient global amnesia. *Neurocase*, **6**, 205–210.

Guyotat, J. & Courjon, J. (1956). Les ictus amnésiques. *Journal de Medicine de Lyon*, **37**, 697–701.

Haas, D.C. (1990). Transient global amnesia triggered by mild head trauma: a form of traumatic migraine. In H. J. Markowitsch (ed.), *Transient Global Amnesia and Related Disorders* (pp. 79–88). Toronto: Hogrefe & Huber.

Haas, D.C. & Ross, G.S. (1986). Transient global amnesia triggered by mild head trauma. *Brain*, **109**, 251–257.

Hinge, H.H., Jensen, T.S., Kjaer, M. et al. (1986). The prognosis of transient global amnesia—results of a multicenter study. *Archives of Neurology*, **43**, 673–676.

Hinge, H.H.F. & Jensen, T.S. (1990). The prognosis of transient global amnesia. In H. J. Markowitsch (ed.), *Transient Global Amnesia and Related Disorders* (pp. 172–180). Toronto: Hogrefe & Huber.

Hodges, J.R. (1991). *Transient Amnesia—Clinical and Neuropsychological Aspects*. London: W.B. Saunders.

Hodges, J.R. (1994). Semantic memory and frontal executive function during transient global amnesia. *Journal of Neurology, Neurosurgery, and Psychiatry*, **57**, 605–608.

Hodges, J.R. (1997). Transient semantic amnesia: a new syndrome? *Journal of Neurology, Neurosurgery, and Psychiatry*, **61**, 548–549.

Hodges, J.R. & Oxbury, S.M. (1990). Persistent memory impairment following transient global amnesia. *Journal of Clinical and Experimental Neuropsychology*, **12**, 904–920.

Hodges, J.R. & Ward, C.D. (1989). Observations during transient global amnesia. *Brain*, **112**, 595–620.

Hodges, J.R. & Warlow, C.P. (1990a). The aetiology of transient global amnesia. *Brain*, **113**, 639–657.

Hodges, J.R. & Warlow, C.P. (1990b). Syndromes of transient amnesia: towards a classification. A study of 153 cases. *Journal of Neurology, Neurosurgery, and Psychiatry*, **53**, 834–843.

Inzitari, D., Pantoni, L., Lamassa, M. et al. (1997). Emotional arousal and phobia in transient global amnesia. *Archives of Neurology*, **54**, 866–873.

Jensen, T.S. & Olivarius, B.F. (1980). Transient global amnesia as a manifestation of transient cerebral ischaemia. *Acta Neurologica Scandinavica*, **61**, 115–124.

Jensen, T.S. & Olivarius, B.F. (1981). Transient global amnesia—its clinical and pathophysiological basis and prognosis. *Acta Neurologica Scandinavica*, **63**, 220–230.

Jovin, T.G., Vitti, R.A. & McCluskey, L.F. (2000). Evolution of temporal lobe hypoperfusion in transient global amnesia: a serial single photon emission computed tomography study. *Journal of Neuroimaging*, **10**, 238–241.

Jung, H.H., Baumgartner, R.W., Burgunder, J.M. et al. (1996). Reversible hyperperfusion of the right medial temporal lobe in transient global amnesia. *Journal of Neurology, Neurosurgery, and Psychiatry*, **61**, 654–655.

Kapur, N. (1990). Transient epileptic amnesia: a clinically distinct form of neurological memory disorder. In H. J. Markowitsch (ed.), *Transient Global Amnesia and Related Disorders* (pp. 140–151). Toronto: Hogrefe & Huber.

Kapur, N., Abbott, P., Footitt, D. & Millar, J. (1996). Long-term perceptual priming in transient global amnesia. *Brain and Cognition*, **31**, 63–74.

Kapur, N., Katifi, H., El-Zawawi, H. et al. (1994). Transient memory loss for people. *Journal of Neurology, Neurosurgery, and Psychiatry*, **57**, 862–864.

Kapur, N., Millar, J., Abbott, P. & Carter, M. (1998). Recovery of function processes in human amnesia: evidence from transient global amnesia. *Neuropsychologia*, **36**, 99–108.

Kazui, H., Tanabe, H., Ideda, M. et al. (1995). Memory and cerebral blood flow in cases of transient global amnesia during and after the attack. *Behavioural Neurology*, **8**, 93–101.

Kazui, H., Tanabe, H., Ikeda, M. et al. (1996). Retrograde amnesia during transient global amnesia. *Neurocase*, **2**, 127–133.

Klotzsch, C., Sliwka, U., Berlit, P. & Noth, J. (1996). An increased frequency of patent foramen ovale in patients with transient global amnesia. Analysis of 53 consecutive patients. *Archives of Neurology*, **53**, 504–508.

Kopelman, M.D. (2000). Focal retrograde amnesia and the attribution of causality: an exceptionally critical review. *Cognitive Neuropsychology*, **17**, 585–622.

Kopelman, M.D., Panayiotopoulos, P.C. & Lewis, P. (1994a). Transient epileptic amnesia differentiated from psychogenic "fugue": neuropsychological, EEG, and PET findings. *Journal of Neurology, Neurosurgery, and Psychiatry*, **57**, 1002–1004.

Kopelman, M.D., Christensen, H., Puffett, A. & Stanhope, N. (1994b). The great escape: a neuropsychological study of psychogenic amnesia. *Neuropsychologia*, **32**, 675–692.

Kritchevsky, M. & Squire, L.R. (1989). Transient global amnesia: evidence for extensive, temporally graded retrograde amnesia. *Neurology*, **39**, 213–218.

Kritchevsky, M., Squire, L.R. & Zouzounis, J.A. (1988). Transient global amnesia: characterization of anterograde and retrograde amnesia. *Neurology*, **38**, 213–219.

Kushner, M.J. & Hauser, W.A. (1985). Transient global amnesia: a case-control study. *Annals of Neurology*, **18**, 684–691.

Ladurner, G., Skvarc, A. & Sager, W.D. (1982). Computer tomography in transient global amnesia. *European Neurology*, **21**, 34–40.

Laurent, B., Trillet, M. & Croisile, B. (1990). Atypical semiology in transient global amnesia. In H. J. Markowitsch (ed.), *Transient Global Amnesia and Related Disorders* (pp. 112–120). Toronto: Hogrefe & Huber.

Lauritzen, M. (1992). Cortical spreading depression as a migraine mechanism: clinical and experimental aspects. In R.J. do Carmo (ed.), *Spreading Depression* (pp. 7–16). Berlin: Springer.

Lauritzen, M., Olsen, T.S., Lassen, N.A. & Paulson, O.B. (1983). Changes in regional cerebral blood flow during the course of classic migraine attacks. *Annals of Neurology*, **13**, 633–641.

Lewis, S.L. (1998). Aetiology of transient global amnesia. *Lancet*, **532**, 397–399.

Lin, K.-L., Liu, R.-S., Yeh, T.-P. et al. (1993). Posterior ischaemia during an attack of transient global amnesia. *Stroke*, **24**, 1093–1095.

Matias-Guiu, J., Colomer, R., Segura, A. & Codina, A. (1986). Cranial CT scan in transient global amnesia. *Acta Neurologica Scandinavica*, **73**, 298–301.

Mazzuchi, A., Moretti, G., Caffarra, P. & Parma, M. (1980). Neuropsychological functions in the follow-up of transient global amnesia. *Brain*, **103**, 161–178.

Miller, J.W., Petersen, R.C., Metter, E.J. et al. (1987). Transient global amnesia: clinical characteristics and prognosis. *Neurology*, **37**, 733–737.

Mumenthaler, M. & Treig, T. (1984). Amnestische Episoden—Analyse von 111 eigenen Beobachtungen. *Schweizer Medizinische Wochenschrift*, **114**, 1163–1170.

Olesen, J. & Jorgensen, M.B. (1986). Leao's spreading depression in the hippocampus explains transient global amnesia—a hypothesis. *Acta Neurologica Scandinavica*, **73**, 219–220.

Percheron, G. (1973). The anatomy of the arterial supply of the human thalamus and its use for the interpretation of the thalamic vascular pathology. *Journal of Neurology*, **205**, 1–13.

Percheron, G. (1976a). Les artères du thalamus humain. I. Artère et territoire thalamiques polaires de l'artère communicante postérieure. *Revue Neurologique*, **132**, 297–307.

Percheron, G. (1976b). Les Atères du thalamus humain. II. Artères et territoires thalamiques paramédians de l'artère basilaire communicante. *Revue Neurologique*, **132**, 309–324.

Poeck, K. (1990). *Neurologie*. Berlin: Springer.

Raffaele, R., Tornali, C., Genazzani, A.A., Vecchio, I., & Rampello, L. (1995). Transient global amnesia and cerebral infarct: a case report. *Brain Injury*, **9**, 815–818.

Regard, M. & Landis, T. (1984). Transient global amnesia: neuropsychological dysfunction during attack and recovery in two "pure" cases. *Journal of Neurology, Neurosurgery, and Psychiatry*, **47**, 668–672.

Robinson, M.K. & Toole, J.F. (1989). Ischemic cerebrovascular disease. In R.J. Joynt (ed.), *Clinical Neurology* (pp. 15–15). Philadelphia, PA: J.B. Lippincott.

Sakashita, Y., Kanai, M., Sugimoto, T. et al. (1997). Changes in cerebral blood flow and vasoreactivity in response to azetolamide in patients with transient global amnesia. *Journal of Neurology, Neurosurgery, and Psychiatry*, **63**, 605–610.

Sakashita, Y., Sugimoto, T., Taki, S. & Matsuda, H. (1993). Abnormal cerebral blood flow following transient global amnesia. *Journal of Neurology, Neurosurgery, and Psychiatry*, **56**, 1327–1329.

Schmidtke, K. & Ehmsen, L. (1998). Transient global amnesia and migraine. *European Neurology*, **40**, 9–14.

Schmidtke, K., Reinhardt, M. & Krause, T. (1998). Cerebral perfusion during transient global amnesia: findings with HMPAO–SPECT. *Journal of Nuclear Medicine*, **39**, 155–159.

Shuttleworth, E.C. & Wise, G.R. (1973). Transient global amnesia due to arterial embolism. *Archives of Neurology*, **29**, 340–342.

Somjen, G.G., Herreras, O. & Jing, J. (1992). Spreading depression and neuron damage: a brief review. In R.J. do Carmo (ed.), *Spreading Depression* (pp. 27–34). Berlin: Springer.

Stengel, E. (1941). On the aetiology of the fugue states. *Journal of Mental Science*, **87**, 572–593.

Stillhard, G., Landis, T., Schiess, R. et al. (1990). Bitemporal hypoperfusion in transient global amnesia: 99m-Tc–HM–PAO–SPECT and neuropsychological findings during and after an attack. *Journal of Neurology, Neurosurgery, and Psychiatry*, **53**, 339–342.

Stracciari, A., Lorusso, S. & Pazzaglia, P. (1994). Transient topographical amnesia. *Journal of Neurology, Neurosurgery, and Psychiatry*, **57**, 1423–1425.

Stracciari, A., Rebucci, G.G. & Gallasi, R. (1987). Transient global amnesia: neuropsychological study of a "pure" case. *Journal of Neurology*, **234**, 126–127.

Strupp, M., Brüning, R., Wu, R.H. et al. (1998). Diffusion-weighted MRI in transient global amnesia: elevated signal intensity in the left mesial temporal lobe in 7 of 10 patients. *Annals of Neurology*, **43**, 164–170.

Takeuchi, R., Yonekura, Y., Matsuda, H. et al. (1998). Resting and acetazolamide-challenged technetium-99m-ECD-SPECT in transient global amnesia. *Journal of Nuclear Medicine*, **39**, 1360–1362.

Tanabe, H., Hashiwaka, K., Nakagawa, Y. et al. (1991). Memory loss due to transient hypoperfusion in the medial temporal lobe including hippocampus. *Acta Neurologica Scandinavica*, **84**, 22–27.

Tanabe, M., Watnabe, T., Ishibashi, M. et al. (1999). Hippocampal ischaemia in a patient who experienced transient global amnesia after undergoing cerebral angiography. *Journal of Neurosurgery*, **91**, 347.

Tosi, L. & Righetti, C.A. (1997). Transient global amnesia and migraine in young people. *Clinical Neurology and Neurosurgery*, **99**, 63–65.

Trillet, M., Croisile, B., Phillipon, B. (1987). Ictus amnésique et débits sanguins cérébraux. *Revue Neurologique*, **143**, 536–539.

Venneri, A., Brazzelli, M. & Della Sala, S. (1998). Transient global amnesia triggered by mild head injury. *Brain Injury*, **12**, 605–612.

Venneri, A. & Caffarra, P. (1998). Transient autobiographical amnesia—EEG and single photon emission CT evidence of an organic etiology. *Neurology*, **50**, 186–191.

Volpe, B.T., Herscovitch, P., Raichle, M.E. et al. (1983). Cerebral blood flow and metabolism in human amnesia. *Journal of Cerebral Blood Flow and Metabolism*, **3** (Suppl. 1), S5–S6

Woolfenden, A.R., O'Brien, M.W., Schwartzberg, R.E. et al. (1998). Diffusion-weighted MRI in transient global amnesia precipitated by cerebral angiography. *Stroke*, **28**, 2311–2314.

Zeman, A.Z.J., Boniface, S.J. & Hodges, J.R. (1998). Transient epileptic amnesia: a description of the clinical and neuropsychological features in 10 cases and a review of the literature. *Journal of Neurology, Neurosurgery, and Psychiatry*, **64**, 435–443.

Ziegler, D.K. & Murrow, R.W. (1988). Headache. In R. J. Joynt (ed.), *Clinical Neurology* (pp. 13–13). Philadelphia, PA: J. B. Lippincott.

Zorzon, M., Antonutti, L., Masè, G. et al. (1995). Transient global amnesia and transient ischemic attack—natural history, vascular risk factors, and associated conditions. *Stroke*, **26**, 1356–1542.

Zorzon, M., Longo, R., Mase, G. et al. (1998). Proton magnetic resonance spectroscopy during transient global amnesia. *Journal of the Neurological Sciences*, **156**, 78–82.

CHAPTER 11

Recovery of Memory Function in Neurological Disease

Narinder Kapur
Southampton General Hospital and University of Southampton, UK
and
Kim S. Graham
MRC Cognition and Brain Sciences Unit, Cambridge, UK

The study of recovery of function in brain disorders is a rapidly expanding area of scientific inquiry, bordering as it does on issues relating to brain plasticity and neurological rehabilitation (e.g. Stuss et al., 1999a; Freund et al., 1997; Levin & Grafman, 2000; Wilson, 1998; Shaw & McEachern, 2001). While there have been a number of reviews of recovery of language function following brain pathology (e.g. Kertesz, 1993), there are few corresponding reviews of recovery of memory function. The topic of transient memory disorders itself is covered in more detail elsewhere (Kapur & Wise, 2001), and we will not be covering recovery of function in developmental memory disorders since that is covered in Chapter 24, this volume.

As a preliminary to this review, it should be noted that this chapter deals predominantly with the recovery of human long-term memory after brain damage, in particular episodic memory. The term "episodic memory" has been applied to a broad range of memory processes, ranging from autobiographical memory (the conscious retrieval of personally experienced episodes from the past) to the recall and recognition of recently presented items in laboratory settings. Episodic memory can be distinguished from semantic memory, which refers to information such as our store of knowledge about objects, people and the meanings of words. In this review, we will not be concerned with improvement of memory function after drug intervention, rehabilitation or most surgical procedures, apart from one or two exceptions in the latter case. Recovery of memory function in relation to memory rehabilitation is covered by Wilson in Chapter 30 of this volume and has also been reviewed by D'Esposito & Alexander (1995). We will instead concentrate on a review of (a) single-case and group studies of "dynamic" recovery of function, and (b) instances of longer-term "static" recovery of function, where the emphasis has been on determining

The Handbook of Memory Disorders. Edited by A.D. Baddeley, M.D. Kopelman and B.A. Wilson
© 2002 John Wiley & Sons, Ltd.

which early prognostic indicators, if any, can predict the final level of recovery of residual memory function. By "dynamic" recovery, we mean conditions where there are spontaneous changes in functioning in the acute and post-acute phases after the onset of the brain insult. By "static" recovery, we mean the end-stage of recovery, where there is no longer any naturally occurring improvement in memory functioning. In the final section of the chapter, we will briefly consider methodological factors and key unresolved questions in the field of recovery of memory function.

As a background to some of the articles reviewed in the following sections, it may be worth noting the broad cognitive and anatomical framework in which we consider that human long-term memory should be viewed. At the cognitive level, there would appear to be broad agreement that there are distinctive and dissociable memory systems, and that these include episodic memory, semantic memory, working memory (the active maintenance and processing of information in short-term memory), perceptual representational memory (a representation, usually implicitly assessed, of the sensory features of an earlier experience) and procedural memory (such as memory for elementary and more complex motor sequences). At the anatomical level, there is general agreement that the limbic–diencephalic system, and in particular the hippocampus, is involved in the long-term consolidation of new memories. There is also general agreement that neocortical areas are critically involved in the storage and retrieval of well-established factual knowledge, knowledge that would usually come under the rubric of semantic memory, and also in many aspects of perceptual representational memory and procedural memory. Most researchers would also agree that in the initial consolidation of episodic memories, there is a major degree of interaction between limbic–diencephalic and neocortical structures. There is also increasing recognition that areas adjacent to the hippocampus, such as the entorhinal cortex and the parahippocampal cortex, play a major role in human memory, although the precise parameters of this role remain to be clearly delineated.

SINGLE-CASE STUDIES OF RECOVERY OF MEMORY FUNCTION

In this section, we will concentrate on those single-case studies which have provided detailed recovery of function data relating to particular aspects of memory performance, or those in which the results of serial multiple imaging have suggested possible mechanisms relating to recovery of function. While most of these studies have focused on long-term anterograde or retrograde memory functioning, it is worth noting observations by Wilson & Baddeley (1993) in relation to recovery of short-term memory. Their patient's digit span recovered to normal from an initial span of two that was found 7 years earlier. This improvement was paralleled by an improvement in language comprehension, but not by any major improvement on tests of phonological awareness. This recovery-of-function study therefore highlighted the link between short-term phonological working memory and language comprehension on the one hand, and the dissociation between short-term phonological working memory and phonological awareness on the other hand.

Russell (1935) first reported the condition of "shrinking" of pretraumatic amnesia and described a patient with a closed head injury who had an initial pretraumatic amnesia of at least 5 years which, over a period of 10 weeks, eventually shrank to a matter of a few minutes. Russell & Nathan (1946) confirmed this pattern and found that the recovery of pretraumatic amnesia was in chronological order with items in the distant past recovering first. Williams and Zangwill (1952) pointed to some degree of variability in the chronological sequence of remembered events. They indicated that cueing might often help patients to recover lost memories. Although shrinkage of pretraumatic amnesia usually parallels the resolution of posttraumatic amnesia, the latter may terminate well before pretraumatic amnesia shrinks to its final duration (Russell, 1971), and significant pretraumatic amnesia may remain in a few isolated cases.

Benson & Geschwind (1967), in a widely cited article, brought the phenomenon of shrinkage of retrograde amnesia into the realm of clinical neuroscience, even though the paper was primarily a descriptive report with minimal, formal neuropsychological testing. The patient had a history of occasional alcohol abuse, and although it was assumed that he had drunk heavily before his admission to hospital, there was clear clinical evidence to suggest that he had incurred a severe head injury. On admission, he was stuporous with a mild right hemiparesis. An EEG was abnormal and considered to be compatible with a subdural haematoma. One week after admission, the initial neurological state had improved, but the patient was noted to have a fluent dysphasia, abnormal behaviour and topographical disorientation in the hospital. When assessed 1 month after his admission, he appeared to have a marked anterograde and retrograde amnesia, giving the year as several years previous to the current one, and stating that he was currently working as a bus driver in Washington, DC, rather than living in Boston, where the hospital was located (he had moved from Washington to Boston 2 years earlier). He was uncertain whether the building where he was a patient was a hospital, and could not give a reason as to why he was there. An EEG carried out around 4 weeks after admission showed a left posterior temporal lobe abnormality, and a pneumoencephalogram demonstrated that the left temporal horn was slightly larger than the right. Over the next 2 months, his anterograde memory improved and language function returned to near-normal. Three months post-injury, he could provide eight animal names in 60 s, whereas 1 month after injury he could only offer two names. Over the next few weeks, his retrograde amnesia showed major improvement, and "shrank" from a period of 2 years to a period of 24 h. It would appear that in this instance the sequence of recovery of function was language, followed by anterograde memory, followed by retrograde memory. The authors themselves noted:

> The most dramatic observation was the rather rapid reappearance of the ability to learn new material, followed by a slower but progressive shortening in the duration of the retrograde amnesia (1967, p. 541).

Since only a limited amount of formal cognitive testing was reported, however, this recovery profile needs to be treated with some caution. On the basis of their observations, Benson & Geschwind distinguished between three forms of remote memory loss: that for over-learned knowledge and skills, as was manifest in their patient's aphasia; that for more recently acquired information, such as memory loss for events that occurred in the previous few years and which they considered to be a primary retrieval deficit; and memory loss for events in the preceding minutes and hours before a brain insult, which they regarded as representing a loss of memory consolidation.

One line of research that is relevant to questions about memory recovery comes from patients with the syndrome of transient global amnesia (TGA). The term TGA refers to an abrupt-onset episode of severe anterograde amnesia, confusion and disorientation (Hodges, 1991). The density and relative purity of the amnesia that patients suffer, and the limbic focus of brain abnormalities that have been found in clinical studies (Evans et al., 1993), render TGA a particularly important neurological condition for the study of the evolution and resolution of pure amnesia. Furthermore, single case studies of TGA have the benefit of allowing patients to act as their own controls, which is particularly valuable when memory for public events or autobiographical episodes are sampled. Relatively few studies of TGA, however, have taken advantage of this factor and assessed patients more than once during the amnesic episode, predominantly because memory functioning in patients begins to improve within a few hours of the attack. Kazui et al. (1996) reported two patients who met clinical criteria for TGA. In both cases, there was evidence of a profound anterograde amnesia with an accompanying loss of memory for a few years prior to the onset of the amnesic episode (retrograde amnesia). Kazui et al. observed that retrograde amnesia seemed to recover in advance of the anterograde memory deficits shown on learning of verbal and non-verbal stimuli. The authors also reported that shrinkage of retrograde amnesia was characterized by older memories returning before more recent memories, but noted occasional exceptions to this in their patients. In a few cases, events that were important and/or emotionally significant to the patient returned earlier than older memories. Kazui et al. pointed out, therefore, that the stage at which recovery is assessed in a patient with TGA may strongly influence the profile of memory loss that is found. In a later single case study, Kapur et al. (1998) found that autobiographical memory showed a progressive resolution starting from the early phase of the attack, and that recovery of retrograde amnesia preceded recovery from anterograde amnesia. Resolution of a picture-naming deficit more closely paralleled recovery from retrograde amnesia rather than performance on tests of new learning. Within retrograde amnesia for public events, there was a temporal gradient of memory loss, with more recent events affected to a greater degree than earlier events.

Lee et al. (1992) reported a case of prolonged ictal amnesia that was associated with focal changes in hippocampal regions. The amnesia included marked anterograde memory impairment, and also a retrograde amnesia that stretched back in time for a period of 4 months. Memory functioning returned to normal after the intravenous administration of anticonvulsant medication. Although little detailed anterograde or retrograde memory test data were reported, this case is quite unique in that transient hippocampal abnormalities were visualised during the acute phase of the illness, but these had resolved within a year. In a further case of epilepsy-related memory loss (Mandai et al., 1996), there was deterioration and shrinkage of retrograde memory functioning with increases and reductions in seizure activity, which were in turn accompanied by changes in brain imaging. Although detailed retrograde memory testing that was closely coupled with detailed imaging were not reported, the authors did note that retrograde amnesia appeared to improve more rapidly than anterograde memory, an observation that has been noted in some of the other single-cases studies reviewed here.

Ivanoiu et al. (1998) also described a case that may have been epileptic in origin, although this possibility largely rested on recovery of memory function and resolution of EEG abnormalities in conjunction with the administration of anticonvulsant medication. In the acute stages, the patient had a dense anterograde and retrograde amnesia, both of these largely resolving, such that anterograde memory returned to normal and the patient was left with a retrograde amnesia of approximately 2 months duration and amnesia for a period of 3 weeks following the onset of the illness. An MR scan carried out in the early stages showed left hippocampal abnormality, which later resolved. Recovery of orientation occurred before recovery of performance on episodic memory tasks. Although the former tests included questions with an anterograde component, around half of the items relied on knowledge that predated the onset of the illness, and thus could be classified as "retrograde". To this extent, it would appear that, in line with some other case-studies reviewed in this section, recovery of retrograde memory loss preceded recovery from anterograde amnesia. In another case of selective left medial temporal lobe abnormality, on this occasion secondary to hypoglycaemia, Chalmers et al. (1991) did not carry out as extensive neuropsychological testing as Ivanoiu et al. (1998), but they did observe that recovery of immediate memory impairment occurred 6 months after the onset of amnesia while delayed (30 min) recall and verbal paired-associate learning performance remained severely impaired.

An unusual case of transient amnesia that was probably epileptiform in nature, and which included marked retrograde amnesia and partial anterograde amnesia, was reported by Vuilleumier et al. (1996). The patient was a 41 year-old woman who was found trying to enter a former home where she had not lived for 3 years. When admitted to hospital, she was disoriented in time and profoundly amnesic. In terms of anterograde amnesia, she could not recall any words from a 10-word list after 3 min, and in a recognition memory test for the words she effectively had a score of zero, with one true positive and one false positive response. She also had zero recall of a story after 3 min, and could not give any account of what had happened to her in the previous few days. She could not recall her profession or workplace, nor the names of work colleagues, neighbours and friends. Although she could name her husband, she did not recall divorcing him 3 years previously. Initially, she was not aware of having any children, but then remembered that she had two daughters and a son. She denied any past surgery, even though an abdominal surgical scar was found on examination, and she also denied any previous episodes of acute memory loss. In terms of public events, she could not recall any recent events, nor recognize true from false items in a series of descriptions about local or international news stories. She could not identify any faces from a set of faces that had been famous over the past 40 years, and was not aware of whether the people were dead or alive. On general cognitive testing, no deficits of note were found, apart from some impairment on category word generation. There was also an impairment on Luria's motor tests of frontal lobe function. EEG investigations showed bilateral spike-wave epileptic activity, centred in anterior frontotemporal regions. After an intravenous injection of anticonvulsant medication, she showed a rapid recovery of her amnesia. Not only could she recall factual and event information that could not be retrieved during the attack, she could recount details of the actual amnesic episode—being at her former house, meeting her former neighbours, what they had said, being examined in hospital, etc. Remarkably, she was also now able to recall and recognize some of the words from the word lists that had been given to her 2 h previously. Two days later, a repeat neuropsychological examination showed normal performance on those anterograde and retrograde memory tests which she had previously failed. No abnormality was found on an MRI scan. It subsequently transpired that she had suffered previous amnesic episodes since her teenage years, that they often occurred on awakening, and that they were usually associated with an epigastric aura. The episodes appeared to be characterized by poor retrograde/semantic memory but with preserved memory for ongoing events and actions. They had been labelled as hysterical by her physicians. Although the current episode was initially diagnosed as one of transient global amnesia, the clinical features that made it stand out as different from TGA episodes included the initial manifestation of memory loss (spontaneously presenting herself at her former home), the lack of repetitive questioning, and the profundity of the retrograde amnesia—with loss of a good deal of personal knowledge. The EEG abnormalities, and the subsequent lack of amnesia for the actual episode, are also important differential markers from what one would expect in TGA. The attack could be seen as one that included features of TGA, but where the laying down of very long-term memories was intact. The unusual features of this case suggest caution in the significance that is attached to it. It remains possible that it represents the interaction between a true neurological event that interacted with psychological factors to produce an anomalous pattern of cognitive disturbance, along the lines that have been elegantly outlined by Kopelman (2000).

An example of a study showing preoperative vs. postoperative changes in a patient with a benign space-occupying lesion was that by Ignelzi & Squire (1976). They reported a patient with a cystic craniopharyngioma who had both anterograde and retrograde amnesia as part of his condition, presumably due to pressure on neighbouring limbic–diencephalic structures. Ignelzi & Squire used a range of memory tests, including verbal and nonverbal recognition memory, delayed (24 h) recall of a complex figure and a test of remote memory function. They showed that while there was memory impairment prior to drainage of the cyst, the patient showed a major improvement in memory functioning after drainage of the cyst, being within the normal range on recognition memory and remote memory performance, and close to normal on a test of delayed design recall. The fact that remote memory and new learning improved in parallel allowed the authors the opportunity to speculate on possible common mechanisms underlying both sets of memory processes.

Henke et al. (1999) reported an extensive case-study of a patient who became amnesic following an episode of carbon monoxide poisoning. MR imaging showed selective reductions in hippocampal volume, more in the left than in the right. A wide range of memory tests was given on four test occasions over an 18 month period. Immediate word recall, verbal recognition memory, picture learning and picture memory improved during this time. By contrast, delayed word-list recall, together with most tests of spatial memory, remained reduced apart from maze learning, which showed major improvements over the various test sessions. Retrograde memory was more difficult to assess, in view of the patient's background, but appeared to be relatively mild, covering around a 3–12 month period prior to the illness-onset. It is possible to argue that tests such as immediate story recall and picture memory have a greater cortical than limbic component, compared to verbal free recall and spatial memory, and that the recovery pattern in this case also followed a "lateral-before-medial" rule that we noted above.

A number of single-case studies have documented recovery of function in patients who have shown confabulation as the major feature of their memory disorder. These studies have helped to highlight those neuropsychological functions that *may* be critical and those which are *certain* to be incidental to core deficits in the particular memory distortion under consideration. Kapur & Coughlan (1980) found that their patient, who had incurred a left frontal lesion following a subarachnoid haemorrhage, showed major recovery over a 3–4 month period in the severity of his confabulation. This recovery was paralleled by improvements on tests of executive function, while the pattern and severity of his impairment on memory tests remained largely unchanged. A similar profile of neuropsychological recovery in a confabulatory patient was noted by Hashimoto et al. (2000). In a study of a patient with reduplicative paramnesia following a right frontal vascular lesion, Kapur et al. (1988), found that recovery from the paramnesia was accompanied by selective improvements in neuropsychological functioning—performance improved on verbal and nonverbal reasoning tasks, a complex copying task and a visual design learning test, with a reduction in his left-sided neglect, but he continued to have impairments on tests of faces memory, word-list learning and card sorting. The critical role of components of executive function, in particular self-checking of responses, has been highlighted in a case where recovery of confabulation coincided with the insertion of a shunt to relieve hydrocephalus (Mercer et al., 1977).

GROUP STUDIES OF RECOVERY OF MEMORY FUNCTION

Amongst the first studies to investigate recovery of memory function after an insult to the brain were those examining the effects of electroconvulsive therapy (ECT) on memory functioning (for a review of earlier studies, see Williams, 1966). These studies, and also those reviewed and reported by Daniel & Crovitz (1983a, 1983b), made several important observations: (a) in the post-ictal period, recovery of personal information (e.g. name) preceded recovery of place information (e.g. town, building), which in turn preceded recovery of temporal information (year, day of week, etc.); (b) older material was usually recovered earlier after treatment than material acquired close in time to the ECT treatment; (c) recovery of overlearned material, such as "high-frequency" words, occurred before recovery of "low-frequency" words. Some of these observations have been confirmed in more recent studies, e.g. Lisanby et al. (2000) found that recall of details relating to remote news events showed improvement between 1 week and 2 months post-ECT treatment, while memory for recent events showed much less recovery.

A number of studies have monitored recovery of function after severe head injury. Before discussing these papers, it may be worth briefly noting an unusual phenomenon that has been reported in mild concussion, whereby recall of pre-injury events shortly after a blow to the head is intact, while a few minutes later memory for the events has been lost. The intriguing phenomenon of delayed-onset retrograde amnesia has been found both in animal subjects (e.g. Mactutus & Riccio, 1978) and in a study of sportsmen who incurred a mild head injury (Lynch & Yarnell, 1983). There were similar clinical observations by Russell (1935) in the early stages of recovery from head injury. Russell noted that, in a few cases, pretraumatic events might be remembered in the early posttraumatic period but may then be lost from memory after the period of posttraumatic amnesia.

In the case of recovery of function after more severe head injury, studies are of two types—those that have focused on the early stages of recovery, and those that have monitored recovery of memory function at later stages. In the case of the first type of studies, High et al. (1990) found that the sequence of recovery after severe head injury was similar to that found in studies of the effects of ECT on memory—first person, then place, then time. Similar observations were made in a more recent study by Tate et al. (2000), although with a notable degree of variability between participants in the sequence of recovery, especially *vis-à-vis* recovery of anterograde memory function. As noted by researchers such as Tate et al., orientation to person, time, etc. includes several components and it may be possible to find one aspect of orientation to person (e.g. age) recovering later than one aspect of orientation to time (e.g. year).

Schwartz et al. (1998) also monitored orientation in the early stages of recovery after a severe head injury, and combined this with an assessment of recall and recognition memory for words and for pictures. They found that recovery of orientation returned before recovery of anterograde memory, as did Geffen et al. (1991) in a similar study. Schwartz et al. also noted that recovery of memory for pictures returned approximately 1 day before recovery of memory for words. Since orientation items would generally have sampled pre-injury memories more than new learning of postinjury information, one way of considering the

findings is in terms of the "retrograde before anterograde" sets of findings described previously. Schwartz et al. also noted that recognition memory recovered at around the same
time as orientation, with both of these functions recovering before recall memory, and
they speculated that the degree of cognitive effort required for performance may have been
greater for recall tasks. One could perhaps argue that recall tasks tap medial temporal lobe
functions more than recognition memory tasks, which in turn rely more on neocortical
areas, and that this set of data may reflect in part the "lateral to medial" rule proposed by
Kapur et al. (1998) to account for apparent retrograde before anterograde memory recovery
patterns. Some views of medial temporal lobe contributions to memory, which suggest that
rhinal/parahippocampal areas are more critical for subserving recognition, while hippocampal areas are more crucial for recall (e.g. Aggleton & Brown, 1999), might in fact predict
recovery of recognition before recall, although it would be important to equate difficulty
level across recall and recognition memory tasks.

In a study that looked at a wide range of measures during recovery from post-traumatic
amnesia (PTA), and had the relatively unusual feature of comparing performance with
two groups of control participants who also received repeat testing, Wilson et al. (1999)
found that recall of a word-list on the fourth learning trial and a test of verbal working
memory (backward digit span) were the two memory measures that showed more recovery in
PTA patients than control patients, suggesting that these particular components of memory
function were particularly affected in these patients. The only other neuropsychological
measure that distinguished PTA patients in this way was a simple reaction time task. Stuss
et al. (1999b) also monitored recovery of function in the acute stages of PTA, using a wide
range of memory and attention tasks. They found that the ability to perform simple attention
tasks recovered in advance of less demanding memory tasks that involved a recognition
memory component. They also found that recovery of complex attention tasks recovered
before recall of three words after a 24 h delay.

While most studies have concentrated on recovery of memory function in the early to
medium-term stages of recovery after a head injury, some researchers have noted improvements in memory function at a later stage of recovery. Dikmen et al. (1990) found substantive
recovery in memory functioning 1–12 months after head injury, with more modest recovery
after this period. When recovery profiles on a word-list recall task were compared with
those found on a verbal IQ measure, there was much more variability in memory recovery profiles. Novack et al. (2000) found that memory function improved from testing at
6 months to testing at 12 months, and that this improvement was greater than that found for
other areas of cognitive functioning.

In a study by Lezak (1979), which examined severe head injury patients at regular intervals
over a 3 year period after their trauma, those with less severe head injury appeared more
likely to show improvement on measures of memory, such as delayed recall of a word
list. On some memory measures (backward digit span, components of word list memory),
Lezak also noted a late deterioration in performance 2–3 years postinjury that followed on
from an initial pattern of improvement of memory functioning. Another study by Ruff et al.
(1991) also found evidence of a pattern of improvement and then decline in recovery of
memory function following severe head injury. In all, Ruff et al. found three patterns of
recovery using a multitrial verbal learning test presented shortly after the head injury, at
6 months and then at 1 year. One group of head injury patients, comprising one-third of
the sample, showed an initial improvement from baseline to 6 months but then a decline
in memory performance by 1 year. A second group, comprising just under one-fifth of the

sample, displayed a flat recovery profile, starting off with a relatively low score and showing only a slight improvement over the three testing sessions. A third group, which consisted of around half the sample, showed a steady improvement in memory functioning over the three time periods. A similar degree of diversity in recovery of memory function after severe head injury has been recorded by other researchers. Wilson (1992) compared patients' performance 5–10 years after injury with their performance in the early stages of recovery, usually within the first few months. While around half of the patients showed no change in memory test scores, around one-third of the sample improved and the remainder showed a decline. Lannoo et al. (2001) studied head-injured patients at discharge, at 6 months and at 12 months postinjury. Although they combined memory test scores with other cognitive test indices into an overall neuropsychological impairment index, it is worth noting that they found three patterns of recovery—a slight improvement in cognitive functioning over the retest periods, similar to that found in normal control participants, a marked improvement over the 2 year period, and limited improvement. Some head-injury patients who were severely impaired at 6 months postinjury still showed significant recovery after this time. There was no clear indication as to factors that might determine the variability in recovery profiles found in their study.

Aetiologies other than ECT and head injury have been less frequently investigated, but a few informative studies have been carried out. Hokannen & Launes (1997) carried out prospective cognitive testing in a group of 12 patients (four with confirmed Herpes Simplex Virus) who had significant residual disability following encephalitis. Testing was carried out approximately 3 weeks and then 3 years after the illness-onset. Of the four anterograde memory tests given, only a verbal paired-associate learning test showed significant improvement across the two learning sessions. The two cognitive tasks to show an improvement over the 3 year period were a digit symbol substitution task and a test of verbal fluency. A larger study by Ogden et al. (1993) found significant improvements in memory functioning in a prospective study of 89 patients with subarachnoid haemorrhage (SAH), who were assessed 10 weeks and 12 months after their acute event. Although Ogden et al. found that nonverbal memory, in particular performance on delayed recall of a complex figure, appeared to be more markedly impaired in the early stages of recovery, and to show a slower rate of recovery than verbal memory, this may in part have been accounted for by the greater number of right-sided than left-sided sites of SAH source in her sample.

The topic of confabulation has featured in many single-case studies, but has seldom been the focus of group studies. One exception to this trend is a recent study of recovery of confabulation by Schnider et al. (2000). They found that performance on a test of temporal context memory paralleled recovery of confabulation in a group of patients that primarily included those with head injury and those with subarachnoid haemorrhage. This suggests that temporal context memory mechanisms, which have tended to be associated with frontal lobe functioning, may be critical to processes underlying the occurrence of confabulation.

THE PROGNOSIS OF LONG-TERM RECOVERY OF MEMORY FUNCTION

The prediction of long-term levels of recovery of memory function has both clinical and theoretical import. At the clinical level, patients and their families need to be given as accurate a picture as possible of the type and severity of disabilities that will remain after the patient has recovered from the acute stages of a brain insult; since memory functioning is one of the most sensitive indicators of brain integrity, it is important to know which early indices, if any, are of prognostic value for indicating residual memory impairments. At the theoretical level, prognostic indices may offer clues as to the pathophysiological mechanisms that play a part in contributing to the chronic memory deficits that patients will be left with as part of their residual disability. In this section, we will primarily be dealing with the prognosis of memory function in naturally evolving neurological disease states. The prediction of recovery of memory function after brain surgery, such as for temporal lobe epilepsy, is a major topic in its own right and has been well covered elsewhere (Helmstaedter, 1999; Oxbury, 2000).

In a study of a group of patients that included a variety of aetiologies, Wilson (1991) followed up 54 patients, who initially were seen 3–6 months postinsult for a period of memory rehabilitation and who were reviewed 5–10 years later. She found that scores on the Rivermead Behavioural Memory Test in the early stages were a good predictor of independence at follow-up. When comparisons were made on tests of memory functioning, 60% of the group showed little or no change since completing rehabilitation 5–10 years earlier, while just under one-third showed some improvement.

In the case of head injury patients, most studies have shown a close relationship between degree of residual memory disturbance and duration of posttraumatic amnesia (PTA), whether this is assessed concurrently during the acute phase of recovery or retrospectively some months or years later (for reviews of such studies, see Levin et al., 1987 and Richardson, 2000). By contrast, variables such as duration of coma or particular components of the Glasgow Coma Scale have generally shown an inconsistent relationship with final levels of recovery of memory function. More general pathophysiological indices have also shown a variable relationship with memory outcome, e.g. intracranial hypertension in the acute phase has no clear relationship with longer-term recovery of memory functioning (Levin et al., 1990; Uzzell et al., 1990). Wilson et al. (1988) found that degree of long-term residual memory deficit was not closely related to features of MR scans taken within the first 3 weeks of injury, but was related to more chronic MR indices, such as depth of lesion and degree of ventricular dilatation. In the study noted earlier, Ruff et al. (1991) found that those head injury patients who showed minimal improvement in memory function over a 1 year period after injury were more likely to have sustained acute hypoxic brain damage in the early stages of the head injury.

Fewer studies have been published on acute prognostic indices for recovery of memory function in other aetiologies. In a study that specifically looked at patients who had various forms of encephalitis, Hokkanen & Launes (1997) assessed duration of ictal amnesia once disorientation had subsided, and this turned out to be at a mean of 26 days after the onset of the illness. Their measure of duration of ictal amnesia was akin to duration of posttraumatic amnesia as assessed in head injury patients, but it also included a preictal component. Hokkanen & Launes found that what they therefore termed "transient encephalitic amnesia" (TENA) was closely related to the extent of memory deficit that was found on neuropsychological testing carried out shortly after the time when the estimate of transient amnesia was made. TENA itself was found to be related to the presence of focal lesions on initial CT scanning shortly after illness onset, and also to the presence of epileptic seizure activity in the acute period. To the extent that in this study recovery of memory function was usually assessed in the shorter-term rather than longer-term recovery period, the findings may not be readily comparable with those from the head injury studies reviewed above.

In the Ogden et al. (1993) study referred to earlier, the authors did not find that long-term recovery of memory (at 12 months post-illness) could be predicted from variables in the acute stage, such as vasospasm, site of aneurysm, cerebral ischaemia, or hydrocephalus, although the latter two variables did predict memory recovery after 10 weeks. The authors reported that grade of recovery at discharge from hospital (ranging from alert and orientated to comatose) predicted longer-term level of recovery of memory function at the final 12 month assessment. Site of lesion did, however, appear to play a role in predicting recovery of amnesia and confabulation in the study by Schnider et al., referred to earlier—patients with basal forebrain lesions tended to have poorer recovery than those with orbito-frontal lesions.

BRAIN IMAGING STUDIES OF RECOVERY OF MEMORY FUNCTION

The study of brain imaging correlates of recovery of memory function represents both an exciting and a problematical area of inquiry. While only a limited number of studies that are germane to this topic have been carried out, we thought it would be useful to demarcate this aspect of recovery of memory function and note some recent studies using advanced imaging procedures, if only because of the potential benefits that may accrue for our understanding of the neural mechanisms underlying recovery of memory function. A number of studies of patients with transient global amnesia (TGA) have reported brain imaging abnormalities, such as positron emission tomography (PET) scan or single photon emission tomography (SPECT) findings. These studies have been well reviewed elsewhere (e.g. Brown, 1998), and have usually reported bilateral medial temporal lobe abnormality during the amnesic phase, although unilateral (usually left) temporal lobe hypoperfusion, thalamic changes and frontal abnormalities have also been reported. Since in most TGA studies the second scan and memory test sessions have yielded completely normal findings, TGA studies to date have offered relatively few insights into actual mechanisms underlying recovery of memory functioning.

A study by Jones et al. (1998) on recovery of function in a patient with both anterograde and retrograde amnesia following paraneoplastic limbic encephalitis included a detailed neuropsychological battery and brain imaging. Over a 2 year period, retrograde amnesia but not anterograde amnesia showed major improvements. PET scanning over the same time period showed increases in neocortical metabolic activity but a reduction in medial temporal lobe metabolism, perhaps related to cumulative cell loss in this region. This study, therefore, helps to highlight the distinctive contributions of hippocampal and neocortical mechanisms to anterograde and retrograde memory functioning. A study by Strupp et al. (1998) has provided evidence to show that a sophisticated form of MRI (magnetic resonance imaging), viz. diffusion-weighted imaging (DWI), can reveal focal medial temporal lobe abnormalities in patients up to 38 h after an attack. Of the 10 patients studied, three showed bilateral hippocampal abnormalities, but in four patients the lesion was restricted to the left hippocampus. One of the patients with bilateral hippocampal changes was studied 2 h after the onset of the attack. Strupp et al. hypothesized that the changes seen on scanning may have reflected nerve cell oedema, and that their findings provided support for a particular mechanism, "spreading depression", underlying TGA. It is worth pointing out that although ischaemic-related lesions in association with episodes resembling TGA have been successfully imaged using DWI (Ay et al., 1998; Woolfenden et al., 1997), subsequent reports, such as those of Budson et al. (1999) and Gass et al. (1999), did not find distinctive DWI medial temporal lobe abnormalities in two patients who were studied during the acute stages of a TGA episode. It remains possible, therefore, that the findings reported by Strupp et al. may have been specific to their imaging procedures, may have been specific to their particular patients, or may even have been artefactual. A further "negative" finding of note is that of Zorzon et al. (1998), who carried out MR spectroscopy during and after a TGA episode and did not find any changes that would have been consistent with neurochemical abnormalities in the hippocampus, in particular those relating to N-acetyl aspartate.

A potentially important application of modern brain imaging procedures to the study of recovery of memory function also relates to functional activation studies of those patients who have recovered from an initially dense amnesia, or those who are left with selective memory loss as part of their neurological condition. Such studies may highlight those areas of the brain that act as neural compensatory mechanisms, and so offer clues as to the basis of recovery of function in brain disease. Very few such studies have yet been carried out, but one exception is that by Maguire (2001), in which a patient with developmental amnesia was found to show greater bilateral temporal lobe involvement during an autobiographical memory task compared to matched control participants.

While the emphasis in recent years has been on the application of sophisticated PET and MR procedures, it is worth noting one study that has pointed to the possible value of magnetoencephalography (MEG) to the study of recovery of memory functioning. MEG has the potential to localize neuromagnetic activity related to brain dysfunction with a high degree of temporal resolution. In a recent study of two patients with transient global amnesia, Stippich et al. (2000) found evidence of bilateral medial temporal lobe abnor-mality 4 days after the TGA episode. The advantage of MEG is that it shares with MRI the benefits of repeat scanning with no significant adverse side-effects for the patient. If the finding of subtle brain changes some time after the acute TGA episode are confirmed as reliable findings, this holds out the promise of being able to monitor larger numbers of TGA patients than have hitherto been available for advanced brain imaging, since most SPECT and PET scans have only shown changes during the acute recovery period of 6 hours.

CONCLUSIONS

This review has highlighted a number of methodological issues and key unanswered ques-tions in the area of recovery of memory function. From the methodological point of view, there are a number of factors that need to be borne in mind when studying recovery of function in the dynamic phase:

1. Use of appropriate parallel forms of memory tests, including tasks matched for difficulty (such as when testing recall and recognition memory).
2. The administration of nonmemory tasks, such as tests of attention and executive func-tion, which may help to shed light on the nature of any improvement or absence of improvement in memory functioning.
3. The gathering of data from matched control participants, to ensure that there is appro-priate control for practice effects (cf. Wilson et al., 2000).

4.   Allowance for medical and other variables that may introduce "noise" into the assess-
     ment of memory functioning in the acute phase of recovery. This may range from the
     effects of medication and the presence of seizure activity to tiredness that results from
     disturbed sleep habits in the early stages of an illness/injury.

From the theoretical point of view, the key questions that remain to be answered in the area
of recovery of memory function include the following:

1.   What are the neurobiological mechanisms underlying recovery of memory function?
     Answers to this question will require multidisciplinary approaches that include so-
     phisticated brain imaging techniques and that allow consideration of issues of neural
     plasticity that have emerged in other areas of brain function, such as sensory and motor
     recovery. Evidence that is gathered will help to resolve the related question as to how
     one can explain individual variability in recovery of memory function.
2.   What are the cognitive mechanisms underlying recovery of memory function? An-
     swers to this question will require experimental designs and procedures that allow for
     associations and dissociations to emerge between discrete memory processes, and also
     between memory and nonmemory functions.
3.   What are the natural rates of recovery of memory function in various neurological
     conditions?
4.   Can the natural rate of recovery of memory function be accelerated by physical (e.g.
     pharmacological) or psychological intervention?

   In summary, the area of recovery of memory function remains a relatively uncharted map
in the geography of cognitive neuroscience. As Robertson & Murre (1999) have pointed out,
the benefits that may accrue from the careful scientific study of recovery of function should
help theorists and therapists alike, and will ultimately provide a sound knowledge base
for understanding and effectively treating neurological patients with loss of brain function.
The challenge therefore remains for memory researchers to follow the lead shown by their
colleagues in linguistic neuroscience and to play a part in making the appropriate empirical
and conceptual advances that relate to recovery of memory function.

ACKNOWLEDGEMENTS

We are grateful to Mrs Pat Abbott and Professor Barbara Wilson for their comments on this chapter.

REFERENCES

Ay, H., Furie, K., Yamada, K. & Koroshetz, W. (1998). Diffusion-weighted MRI characterizes the
    ischemic lesion in transient global amnesia. *Neurology*, **51**, 901–903.
Aggleton, J. & Brown, M. (1999). Episodic memory, amnesia, and the hippocampal–anterior thalamic
    axis. *Behavioral and Brain Sciences*, **22**, 425–489.
Budson, A., Schlaug, G. & Briemberg, H. (1999). Perfusion- and diffusion-weighted magnetic reso-
    nance imaging in transient global amnesia. Neurology, **53**, 239–240.
Benson, D.F. & Geschwind, N. (1967). Shrinking retrograde amnesia. *Journal of Neurology,
    Neurosurgery and Psychiatry*, **30**, 539–544.

Brown, A.S. (1998). Transient global amnesia. *Psychonomic Bulletin and Review*, **5**, 401–427.

Chalmers, J., Risk, M.T.A., Kean, D.M. et al. (1991). Severe amnesia after hypoglycemia. *Diabetes Care*, **14**, 922–925.

Daniel, W.F. & Crovitz, H. F. (1983a). Acute memory impairment following electroconvulsive therapy. I. Effects of electrical stimulus wave-form and number of treatments. *Acta Psychiatrica Scandinavica*, **67**, 1–7.

Daniel, W.F. & Crovitz, H.F. (1983b). Acute memory impairment following electroconvulsive therapy. II. Effects of electrical stimulus wave-form and number of treatments. *Acta Psychiatrica Scandinavica*, **67**, 57–68.

Dikmen, S., Machamer, J., Temkin, N. & McLean, A. (1990). Neuropsychological recovery in patients with moderate to severe head injury: 2 year follow-up. *Journal of Clinical and Experimental Neuropsychology*, **12**, 507–519.

D'Esposito, M. & Alexander, M.P. (1995). The clinical profiles, recovery, and rehabilitation of memory disorders. *NeuroRehabilitation*, **5**, 141–159.

Evans, J., Wilson, B., Wraight, E.P. & Hodges, J.R. (1993). Neuropsychological and SPECT scan findings during and after transient global amnesia: evidence for the differential impairment of remote episodic memory. *Journal of Neurology, Neurosurgery and Psychiatry*, **56**, 1227–1230.

Freund, H-J., Sabel, B.A. & Witte, O. (eds) (1997). *Brain Plasticity*. Advances in Neurology, Vol. 73. Lippincott–Raven: New York.

Gass, A., Gaa, J., Hirsch, J. et al. (1999). Lack of evidence of acute ischemic tissue change in transient global amnesia on single-shot echo-planar diffusion-weighted MRI. *Stroke*, **30**, 2070–2072.

Geffen, G.M., Encel, J.S. & Forrester, G. M. (1991). Stages of recovery during post-traumatic amnesia and subsequent everyday memory deficits. *NeuroReport*, **2**, 105–108.

Hashimoto, R., Tanaka, Y. & Nakano, I. (2000). Amnesic confabulatory syndrome after focal basal forebrain damage. *Neurology*, **54**, 978–980.

Helmstaedter, C. (1999). Prediction of memory reserve capacity. In Stefan, H., Andermann, F., Chauvel, P. & Shorvon, S. (eds), *Plasticity in Epilepsy*. Philadelphia, PA: Lippincott Williams & Wilkins.

Henke, K., Kroll, N., Behniea, H. et al. (1999). Memory lost and regained following bilateral hippocampal damage. *Journal of Cognitive Neuroscience*, **11**, 682–697.

High, W.M., Levin, H.S. & Gary, H.E. (1990). Recovery of orientation following closed-head injury. *Journal of Clinical and Experimental Neuropsychology*, **12**, 703–714.

Hodges, J. (1991). *Transient Global Amnesia*. W. B. Saunders: New York.

Hokkanen, L. & Launes, J. (1997). Duration of transient amnesia correlates with cognitive outcome in acute encephalitis. *NeuroReport*, **8**, 2721–2725.

Ignelzi, R.J. & Squire, L.R. (1976). Recovery from anterograde and retrograde amnesia after percutaneous drainage of a cystic craniopharyngioma. *Journal of Neurology, Neurosurgery and Psychiatry*, **48**, 1169–1171.

Ivanoiu, A., Coyette, F., Aubert, G. et al. (1998). A case of long-standing but reversible isolated amnesia of unknown aetiology. *Neurocase*, **4**, 231–243.

Jones, R.D., Grabowski, T.J. & Tranel, D. (1998). The neural basis of retrograde memory: evidence from positron emission tomography for the role of nonmesial temporal lobe structures. *Neurocase*, **4**, 471–479.

Kapur, N. & Coughlan, A.K. (1980). Confabulation and frontal lobe dysfunction. *Journal of Neurology, Neurosurgery and Psychiatry*, **43**, 461–463.

Kapur, N., Turner, A. & King, C. (1988). Reduplicative paramnesia: possible anatomical and neuropsychological mechanisms. *Journal of Neurology, Neurosurgery and Psychiatry*, **51**, 579–581.

Kapur, N., Millar, J., Abbott, P. & Carter, M. (1998). Recovery of function processes in human amnesia: evidence from transient global amnesia. *Neuropsychologia*, **36**, 99–107.

Kapur, N. & Wise, R. (2001). Transient memory disorders. In Cermak, L. (ed.), *Handbook of Neuropsychology, 2nd edn: Memory Disorders* (pp. 85–106). Amsterdam: Elsevier.

Kazui, H., Tanabe, H., Ikeda, M. et al. (1996). Retrograde amnesia during transient global amnesia. *Neurocase*, **2**, 127–133.

Kertesz, A. (1993). Recovery and treatment. In Heilman, K. & Valenstein, E. (eds). *Clinical Neuropsychology*, 3rd edn. Oxford: Oxford University Press.

Kopelman, M. (2000). Focal retrograde amnesia and the attribution of causality: an exceptionally critical review. *Cognitive Neuropsychology*, **17**, 585–621.

Lannoo, E., Colardyn, F., Jannes, C. & De Soete, G. (2001). Course of neuropsychological recovery from moderate-to-severe head injury: a 2-year follow-up. *Brain Injury*, **15**, 1–13.

Lee, B.I., Lee, B.C., Hwang, Y.M. et al. (1992). Prolonged ictal amnesia with transient focal abnormalities on magnetic resonance imaging. *Epilepsia*, **33**, 1042–1046.

Levin, H., Grafman, J. & Eisenberg, L. (eds)(1987). *Neurobehavioral Recovery from Head Injury*. Oxford: Oxford University Press.

Levin, H.S. & Grafman, J. (eds)(2000). *Cerebral Reorganization of Function after Brain Damage*. Oxford: Oxford University Press.

Levin, H., Gary, H., Eisenberg, H. et al. (1990). Neurobehavioral outcome one year after severe head injury: experience of the Traumatic Coma Data Bank. *Journal of Neurosurgery*, **73**, 699–709.

Lezak, M.D. (1979). Recovery of memory and learning functions following traumatic brain injury. *Cortex*, **15**, 63–72.

Lisanby, S., Maddox, J., Prudic, J. et al. (2000). The effects of electroconvulsive therapy on memory for autobiographical and public events. *Archives of General Psychiatry*, **57**, 581–590.

Lynch, S. & Yarnell, P.R. (1983). Retrograde amnesia: delayed forgetting after concussion. *American Psychology*, **86**, 643–645.

Mactutus, C. & Riccio, D. (1978). Hypothermia-induced retrograde amnesia: role of body temperature in memory retrieval. *Physiological Psychology*, **6**, 18–22.

Maguire, E.A. (2001). Neuroimaging studies of autobiographical event memory. *Philosophical Transactions of the Royal Society, London, B* (in press).

Mandai, K., Motomura, N., Yamadori, A. et al. (1996). Expanding and shrinking retrograde amnesia in a case of temporal lobe epilepsy. In Kato, N. (ed.), *The Hippocampus: Functions and Clinical Relevance*. Amsterdam: Elsevier.

Mercer, B., Wapner, W., Gardner, H. & Benson, F. (1977). A study of confabulation. *Archives of Neurology*, **34**, 429–433.

Novack, T.A., Alderson, A.L., Bush, B.A. et al. (2000). Cognitive and functional recovery at 6 and 12 months post-TBI. *Brain Injury*, **14**, 987–996.

Ogden, J., Mee, E. & Henning, M. (1993). A prospective study of impairment of cognition and memory and recovery after subarachnoid hemorrhage. *Neurosurgery*, **33**, 572–586.

Oxbury, S. (2000). Cognitive and memory changes after temporal lobe excision. In Oxbury J., Polkey, C. & Duchowny, M. (eds). *Intractable Focal Epilepsy* (pp. 807–818). New York: W. B. Saunders.

Richardson, J.T.E. (2000). *Clinical and Neuropsychological Aspects of Closed Head Injury*, 2nd edn. Hove: Psychology Press.

Robertson, I. & Murre, J. (1999). Rehabilitation of brain damage: brain plasticity and principles of guided recovery. *Psychological Bulletin*, **125**, 544–575.

Ruff, R.M., Young, D., Gautille, T. et al. (1991). Verbal learning deficits following severe head injury: heterogeneity of recovery over one year. *Journal of Neurosurgery*, **75**, S50–S58.

Russell, W.R. (1935). Amnesia following head injuries. *Lancet*, **ii**, 762–763.

Russell, W.R. (1971). *The Traumatic Amnesias*. New York: Oxford University Press.

Russell, W.R. & Nathan, P. (1946). Traumatic amnesia. *Brain*, **69**, 280–300.

Schnider, A., Ptak, R., von Daniken, C. & Remonda, L. (2000). Recovery from spontaneous confabulations parallels recovery of temporal confusion in memory. *Neurology*, **55**, 74–83.

Schwartz, M.L., Carruth, F., Binns, M.A. et al. (1998). The course of post-traumatic amnesia: three little words. *Canadian Journal of Neurological Sciences*, **25**, 108–116.

Shaw, C.A. & McEachern, J. (eds)(2001). *Toward a Theory of Neuroplasticity*. Hove: Psychology Press.

Stippich, C., Kassubek, J., Kober, H. et al. (2000). Time course of focal slow wave activity in transient ischemic attacks and transient global amnesia as measured by magnetoencephalography. *NeuroReport*, **11**, 3309–3313.

Strupp, M., Bruning, R., Wuh, R. et al. (1998). Diffusion-weighted MRI in transient global amnesia: elevated signal intensity in the left mesial temporal lobe in 7 of 10 patients. *Annals of Neurology*, **43**, 164–170.

Stuss, D.T., Winocur, G. & Robertson, I. H. (eds) (1999a). *Cognitive Neurorehabilitation*. Cambridge: Cambridge University Press.

Stuss, D.T., Binns, M.A., Carruth, F.G. et al. (1999b). The acute period of recovery from traumatic brain injury: posttraumatic amnesia or posttraumatic confusional state? *Journal of Neurosurgery*, **90**, 635–643.

Tate, R.L., Pfaff, A. & Jurjevic, L. (2000). Resolution of disorientation and amnesia during post-traumatic amnesia. *Journal of Neurology, Neurosurgery and Psychiatry*, **68**, 178–185.

Uzzell, B., Dolinskas, C. & Wiser, R. (1990). Relation between intracranial pressure, computed tomographic lesion, and neuropsychological outcome. In Long, D. M. (ed.), *Advances in Neurology: Vol. 52. Brain Oedema: Pathogenesis, Imaging and Therapy* (pp. 269–274). New York: Raven.

Vuilleumier, P., Despland, P.A. & Regli, F. (1996). Failure to recall (but not to remember): pure transient amnesia during nonconvulsive status epilepticus. *Neurology*, **46**, 1036–1039.

Williams, M. & Zangwill, O.L. (1952). Memory defects after head injury. *Journal of Neurology, Neurosurgery and Psychiatry*, **15**, 54–58.

Williams, M. (1966). Memory disorders associated with electroconvulsive therapy. In Whitty, C.W.M. & Zangwill, O. L. (eds), *Amnesia* (pp. 134–149). London: Butterworth.

Wilson, B.A. (1992). Recovery and compensatory strategies in head injured memory impaired people several years after insult. *Journal of Neurology, Neurosurgery and Psychiatry*, **55**, 177–180.

Wilson, B.A., Evans, J.J., Emslie, H. et al. (1999). Measuring recovery from post traumatic amnesia. *Brain Injury*, **13**, 505–520.

Wilson, B.A. (1991). Long-term prognosis of patients with severe memory disorders. *Neuropsychological Rehabilitation*, **1**, 117–134.

Wilson, B.A. (1998). Recovery of cognitive functions following nonprogressive brain injury. *Current Opinion in Biology*, **8**, 281–287.

Wilson, B.A. & Baddeley, A.D. (1993). Spontaneous recovery of impaired memory span: does comprehension recover? *Cortex*, **29**, 153–159.

Wilson, B.A., Watson, P.C., Baddeley, A.D. et al. (2000). Improvement or simply practice? The effects of twenty repeated assessments on people with and without brain injury. *Journal of the International Neuropsychological Society*, **6**, 469–479.

Wilson, J.T.L., Wiedmann, K., Hadley, D. et al. (1988). Early and late magnetic resonance imaging and neuropsychological outcome after head injury. *Journal of Neurology, Neurosurgery and Psychiatry*, **51**, 391–396.

Woolfenden, A., O'Brien, M., Schwartzberg, R. et al. (1997). Diffusion-weighted MRI in transient global amnesia precipitated by cerebral angiography. *Stroke*, **28**, 2311–2314.

Zorzon, M., Longo R., Mase G. (1998). Proton magnetic resonance spectroscopy during transient global amnesia. *Journal of the Neurological Sciences*, **156**, 78–82.

CHAPTER 12

Neuropsychological Impairments of Verbal Short-term Memory

Giuseppe Vallar

and

Costanza Papagno

Università degli Studi di Milano-Bicocca, Milan, Italy

Studies in normal subjects and in patients with brain damage suggest that the system sub-serving retention over short periods of time (seconds) is not unitary, but comprises a number of independent components, which have discrete anatomical correlates. The verbal (phonological) short-term memory system, which has been extensively investigated in patients with brain lesions, is considered in this chapter.

FUNCTIONAL ARCHITECTURE OF PHONOLOGICAL SHORT-TERM MEMORY

Phonological Short-term Store and Rehearsal Process

Since the late 1960s, the psychological features of the system involved in the short-term retention of verbal information have been extensively investigated (see reviews in Baddeley, 1990; Crowder, 1976; Shallice & Vallar, 1990). Short-term retention of verbal material involves the activity of a number of interrelated components. Figure 12.1 shows a model which distinguishes a component devoted to the *storage* of verbal information (phonological short-term store; STS), and a process (*articulatory rehearsal*), which revives the memory trace held in the phonological STS, preventing its decay. The rehearsal process involves the recirculation of information between the phonological STS and a component (phonological output buffer, or assembly system), participating in speech production. This system contributes to the articulatory programming of speech output, storing phonological segments prior to the application of various output processes, such as planning and editing

The Handbook of Memory Disorders. Edited by A.D. Baddeley, M.D. Kopelman and B.A. Wilson
© 2002 John Wiley & Sons, Ltd.

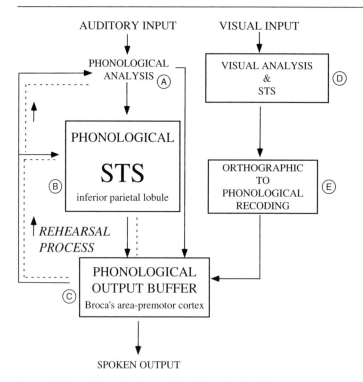

Figure 12.1   A functional model of phonological short-term memory. Auditory–verbal material, after early acoustic and phonological analysis (A), enters the main retention component of the system, the phonological STS (B), where material is coded in a phonological format. The phonological STS is an input system to which auditory material has a direct and automatic access. The process of rehearsal is conceived as involving a recirculation of the memory trace between the phonological STS and a phonological output system, the *phonological output buffer* or *phonological assembly system* (C), primarily concerned with the articulatory programming of speech output, with a recurring translation between input (*acoustic*) and output (*articulatory*) phonological representations. The phonological output buffer provides access for visually presented verbal material to the phonological STS, after *phonological recoding* or *grapheme-to-phoneme conversion* (E). The model also illustrates the multiple-component nature of short-term memory, showing a visual STS (D), where material is likely to be encoded in terms of shape. Reproduced by permission from Vallar & Papagno (1995)

of articulatory procedures (Burani et al., 1991). Auditory–verbal information has a direct access to the phonological STS after phonological analysis. Visual information, by contrast, requires a number of steps before gaining access to the phonological STS: visual analysis, phonological recoding (grapheme-to-phoneme conversion) and articulatory rehearsal. Visual information may be temporarily held in a visual STS system.

The investigation of three variables affecting immediate memory span (phonological similarity, word length and articulatory suppression) has provided the main sources of empirical data, which constrain the structure of this memory system. The data from normal subjects relevant to the interpretation of the pattern of impairment of brain-damaged patients are briefly summarized here (see also Baddeley, Chapter 1, this volume).

- The *phonological similarity effect* (Baddeley, 1966; Conrad, 1964; Conrad & Hull, 1964; Wickelgren, 1965). In immediate serial recall, performance level is greater for lists of phonologically dissimilar stimuli, as compared to similar. This suggests that verbal information held in the STS is coded phonologically. The presence of the effect with both auditory and visual input indicates that written material also gains access to the phonological STS when immediate retention is required.
- The *word length effect* (Baddeley et al., 1975, 1984). In immediate serial recall, span for short words is greater than span for long, with both auditory and visual presentation.
- *Articulatory suppression* (Baddeley et al., 1975, 1984; Levy, 1971; Murray, 1968; Peterson & Johnson, 1971). The continuous uttering of an irrelevant speech sound (e.g. "the, the, the . . . ") has three main effects on immediate memory span:
  — It produces a slight but significant reduction of performance level.
  — It eliminates the effect of phonological similarity when the material has been presented visually, but not with auditory presentation.
  — It abolishes the effect of word length with both auditory and visual presentation.

According to the model shown in Figure 12.1, the phonological similarity effect is not removed by suppression when the stimuli are auditorily presented, because information has a direct access to the phonological STS, without any involvement of the rehearsal process. The persistence of the effect during suppression, when input is auditory, indicates also that information in this system is coded in a phonological nonarticulatory format. By contrast, the disappearance of the effect with visual presentation suggests that written input requires the intermediate step of articulatory rehearsal before gaining access to the phonological STS.

The absence of any significant effect of word length during suppression, with both auditory and visual presentation, argues for an interpretation in terms of the activity of the articulatory rehearsal system. This may be metaphorically described as a time-based tape of fixed length, which recirculates more short words than long.

Finally, the model distinguishes between articulatory rehearsal and phonological recoding, or grapheme-to-phoneme conversion: written material, before entering the rehearsal process, needs to be recoded phonologically. This distinction is based on the observation that in normal subjects phonological tasks, such as homophone judgements on written pairs of letter strings (i.e. deciding whether or not two items, when pronounced, have the same sound), are not interfered with by articulatory suppression. As judgements of this sort involve operations on phonological representations, the absence of interfering effects by suppression implies the existence of nonarticulatory phonological codes, available to written material. By contrast, phonological judgements requiring segmentation and deletion (e.g. rhyme and initial sound) are disrupted by suppression, suggesting the involvement of the rehearsal system (see reviews in Besner, 1987; Burani et al., 1991).

Working Memory and Short-term Memory

The phonological STS and the rehearsal process may be conceived as *working memory spaces*, in which information is temporarily held prior to and during the application of procedures, strategies and analyses, e.g. planning and editing of the articulatory procedures needed for the smooth production of speech may be applied to the phonological segments stored in the output buffer (Burani et al., 1991). The segmentation and deletion procedures required for some phonological judgements are applied to the material held in the output buffer (Besner, 1987; Burani et al., 1991). In sentence comprehension, syntactic and lexical–semantic processes may be applied to material held in the phonological input STS (Martin & Lesch, 1996; Saffran & Martin, 1990b; Vallar et al., 1990). The contribution of the phonological STS to vocabulary acquisition in native and foreign language (Baddeley et al., 1998) may be seen in this perspective: new words are temporarily stored to allow the building up of new phonological representations in long-term memory. This again involves the application of the appropriate procedures to the content of a specific storage system.

In the patients discussed in this chapter, the impairment concerns the storage systems themselves, rather than the procedures and strategies that may be applied to stored information. An illustrative example of this is the performance of patient P.V. in immediate free recall tasks, which in normal subjects produce a recency effect, i.e. a better recall of the final items of the list. P.V.'s defective recency was confined to lists of auditory–verbal words (Basso et al., 1982), but she showed normal recency effects both with visual presentation (Vallar & Papagno, 1986) and in delayed recall tasks (Vallar et al., 1991). P.V. was also able to recall auditory and visual information in the order suggested by the examiner, from the beginning or from the end of the list (Vallar & Papagno, 1986). These data suggest that P.V.'s defective recency does not reflect the impairment of the ordinal and temporally-based retrieval strategies, which underlie the normal advantage of the final items of a list (Baddeley & Hitch, 1993). These preserved procedures, however, cannot be applied to the content of a specific working memory space (the phonological STS), which is selectively damaged in the patient. This brings about a selective deficit of recency in immediate recall of auditory–verbal material.

NEUROANATOMICAL BASIS OF PHONOLOGICAL SHORT-TERM MEMORY

Current information about the neural correlates of phonological short-term memory come from two main sources of evidence: (a) the traditional anatomoclinical correlations (Vallar, 2000) in brain-damaged patients with a selective deficit of this system; and (b) the measurement of regional cerebral activity by PET and fMRI in normal subjects engaged in short-term memory tasks.

The lesion localization in published patients with a selective deficit of auditory–verbal span, and a superior performance level with visual input, is summarized in Table 12.1. It is apparent that, although patients differed in the aetiology of their cerebral disease and in the method of assessment of the lesion, the left parietal region was involved in most cases. More specifically, the lesion data indicate the supramarginal gyrus of the inferior parietal lobule as the crucial region for the function of the phonological STS (Warrington, 1979). It is worth noting that in patients J.O. (Kinsbourne, 1972) and T.O. (Vallar et al., 1997), whose defective span performance may be, at least in part, traced back to output deficits, the lesion was mainly frontal. In patient J.O., anterior damage was also suggested by the neurological examination, which revealed a right hemiparesis without any sensory deficit. This major

Table 12.1   Lesion localization in patients with defective auditory–verbal span

Patient	Atiology	Source	Lesion site			
			Frontal	Temporal	Parietal	Occipital
K.F.	Head injury	Post mortem		x	Inferior	x
J.B.	Meningioma	Surgery		Superior–middle	Inferior	
W.H.	CVA?	Brain scan		x	Inferior	
L.S.	Head injury	Angiography			x	x
I.L.	CVA?	Brain scan?			Posterior	
M.C.	CVA	CT scan		Posterior–superior	Inferior	
P.V.	CVA	CT scan	x	x	x	
E.A.	CVA	CT scan		Posterior	x	
R.A.N.	CVA	CT scan			x	
E.R.	CVA	CT scan		x, insula	x, insula	
R.R.	CVA	CT scan		x	x	
S.C.	CVA	CT scan		x	x	
L.A.	Head injury	MRI		Superior middle	Inferior	
J.O.	CVA?	Brain scan	x	x		
T.O.	CVA	CT scan	Subcortical, premotor, rolandic, anterior insula			

Sources: K.F. (Shallice & Warrington 1980); J.B., W.H. (Warrington et al., 1971); L.S. (Strub & Gardner, 1974); I.L. (Saffran & Marin 1975); MC (Caramazza et al., 1981); P.V. (Basso et al., 1982); E.A. (Friedrich et al., 1984); R.A.N. (McCarthy & Warrington, 1987); E.R. (Vallar et al., 1990); R.R. (Bisiacchi et al., 1989); S.C. (Trojano et al., 1992); L.A. and T.O. (Vallar et al., 1997), J.O. (Kinsbourne, 1972).
Reproduced by permission from Vallar & Papagno (1995)

frontal involvement, which differs from the predominantly parietal damage found in most patients, may represent the anatomical correlate of J.O.'s and T.O.'s output difficulties. These data from individual patients are in line with the results of a group study by Risse et al. (1984). In a series of 20 left brain-damaged patients, defective auditory–verbal span was associated with lesions clustering in the inferior parietal lobule, but not in the frontal lobe or in the basal ganglia. The anatomical evidence concerning the selective impairment of the process of verbal rehearsal is less definite, but one such patient had a lesion involving the left subcortical premotor regions and the anterior insula (patient T.O., see Table 12.1; Vallar et al., 1997). Finally, damage to the right cerebellum may also impair immediate short-term retention, specifically affecting the rehearsal process (Silveri et al., 1998). This neuropsychological result is compatible with the finding that verbal short-term memory tasks activate predominantly the right cerebellum (Smith & Jonides, 1999), consistent with the crossed connections between left cerebrum and right cerebellum.

A number of PET and fMRI studies have investigated, in normal subjects, the anatomical localization of the phonological STS and of the rehearsal process. In PET studies by Paulesu et al. (1993, 1996), the comparison of the patterns of regional cerebral blood flow during a task engaging both components (immediate memory for letter sequences) and a task which involves only the rehearsal process (rhyme judgement for letters: see Burani et al., 1991) suggests a localization of the phonological STS in the left supramarginal gyrus (area 40), and of the rehearsal process in the left premotor frontal regions [Brodmann's areas 44 (Broca's area), 6, and the supplementary motor area]. Converging evidence is provided by

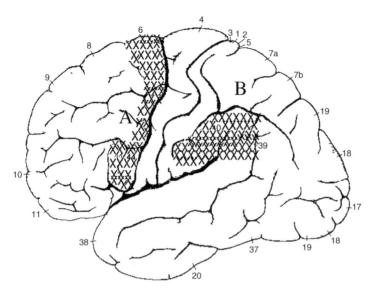

Figure 12.2 The anatomical basis of phonological short-term memory. The system, whose functional architecture is shown in Figure 12.1, is mainly based on left hemisphere networks. (A) Broca's area (Brodmann area 44), the premotor area (Brodmann area 6), and the supplementary motor area are associated with the process of rehearsal. (B) The left inferior parietal lobule (supramarginal gyrus, Brodmann area 40) at the temporoparietal junction, with the phonological STS. These two sets of cerebral regions are likely to be connected through the arcuate fasciculus, and white matter fibre tracts in the insular region

activation studies using fMRI (Henson et al., 2000; Paulesu et al., 1995). This anatomical localization of the rehearsal process is compatible with the view that the recirculation and refreshment of the memory trace held in the phonological STS makes use of systems such as the phonological output buffer, primarily involved in the programming of speech output, rather than requiring actual articulation (Burani et al., 1991; Shallice & Vallar, 1990).

To summarize, as Figure 12.2 shows, two discrete regions in the left hemisphere are the anatomical correlates of the phonological STS, and of the rehearsal process: the inferior parietal lobule (supramarginal gyrus), and the premotor cortex (Brodmann's areas 44 and 6).

PATTERN OF IMPAIRMENT

Clinical Presentation

Patients with defective phonological memory have lesions in the posterior regions of the left hemisphere. They may then show, in addition to the specific disorder of immediate retention, neurological deficits and dysphasia, which are a major problem for everyday life. In most patients the language disorder may be classified, according to the classic taxonomy, as *conduction aphasia*, whose main clinical feature is a disproportionate impairment of repetition (Basso & Cubelli, 1999; Shallice & Warrington, 1977). A few patients have been reported, however, who suffered from a selective impairment of auditory–verbal span without any major associated disorders. The main disability reported by one such patient, J.B. (Warrington et al., 1971, p. 379), was "an impaired memory for spoken names or telephone numbers, even if she attempted to write them down immediately". P.V.'s main subjective report was the inability to *understand* (this was the term she used) even short sequences of digits (prices of goods, telephone numbers) spoken to her. The difficulty was quite minor, however, when such sequences were presented in a written format and she read them. P.V. also complained about her inability to perform mental arithmetic, e.g. when shopping she had problems in checking that she was paying the right amount of money, due to a difficulty in computing change. P.V. also mentioned a difficulty in the acquisition of foreign languages. After the onset of her disease she attempted to resume her study of French, but gave up because it was too difficult (Basso et al., 1982; Papagno & Vallar, 1995a). In patients of this sort the auditory–verbal short-term memory deficit is highly selective and spares long-term episodic memory, visuo–spatial processes and general intelligence. These patients may therefore live on their own, without any specific assistance. J.B. was able to resume her job. P.V. set up as a dealer in pottery painted by herself, and took care of her two sons.

Selective Deficits of Phonological Short-term Memory

Defective Phonological STS

The association between defective auditory–verbal span, left hemisphere damage and dysphasia has long been known (Zangwill, 1946). Selective patterns of impairment were reported only in the late 1960s, however. Luria et al. (1967) described two patients (B. and K.), who had suffered from a traumatic injury in the left temporal lobe. B. and K. had defective repetition of auditory sequences of verbal stimuli (phonemes, words, digits), but their performance level was higher with visual presentation. Luria et al. (1967) explained this deficit in terms of modality-specific disturbances of auditory–verbal memory traces. Warrington & Shallice (1969) reported a selective deficit of auditory–verbal span in patient K.F., and suggested an impairment of auditory–verbal short-term memory. A number of similar patients were subsequently reported. Their pattern of impairment has these main basic features (see also Shallice & Vallar, 1990):

- A selective deficit of span, impairing immediate serial recall of all strings of unconnected auditory–verbal material (digits, letters, words).
- Higher level of performance with visual presentation, as compared with auditory input.
- The deficit arises neither from defective speech perception nor from impaired speech production.

   Table 12.2 shows the results of a meta-analysis of the immediate memory span perfor-mance of 25 patients. When input is auditory, performance level is defective for all stimulus materials. In the series of 1355 Italian normal adult subjects of Orsini et al. (1987), the cut-off score for auditory digit span (adjusted for age and educational level) is 3.75, and no patient included in Table 12.2 has a span above 3.6. In the 16 patients in whom digit, letter and word span were assessed, digit span was higher. This advantage for digits may reflect the reduced number of alternatives in the memory set (9 or 10) and their high frequency, as compared with both letters and words. In line with the results of this meta-analysis, patients

Table 12.2 Average verbal span (range in brackets) in 25 patients with
defective phonological short-term memory, by input modality and stimulus
material. *n* Refers to the number of such patients who were given each
specific span condition. The measure of span is the summed probabilities for
all lengths of lists, where possible. For patients for whom precise information
is unavailable, approximations have been used

Auditory	span		
Digits	Letters	Words	Visual digit span
2.38[a]	1.79[b]	2.00[c]	3.23[d]
(1–3.6)	(1–2.5)	(1.05–3)	(2–6)
[a]$n = 25$, [b]$n = 16$, [c]$n = 19$, [d]$n = 22$			

Auditory vs. visual digit span: paired t-test ($t = 4.44$; d.f. $= 21$; $p = 0.00022$).
Auditory span: one-way analysis of variance: d.f. $= 2$, 30; $F = 19.23$; $p < 0.0001$; Scheffé F-test:
digit vs. letter, and digit vs. word span, $p < 0.05$.
Sources: K.F. (Warrington & Shallice, 1969); J.B., W.H. (Warrington et al., 1971); J.T., J.O. (Kinsbourne,
1972); CA1, CA2, CA2 (Tzortis & Albert, 1974); L.S. (Strub & Gardner, 1974); I.L. (Saffran & Marin,
1975); M.C. (Caramazza et al., 1981); P.V. (Basso et al., 1982); E.A. (Friedrich et al., 1984); R.A.N.,
N.H.A. (McCarthy & Warrington, 1987); T.B. (Baddeley & Wilson, 1988); R.R. (Bisiacchi et al., 1989);
C.N. (Saffran & Martin, 1990a) T.I. (Saffran & Martin, 1990b); E.D.E. (Sloan Berndt & Mitchum, 1990);
E.R. (Vallar et al., 1990); S.C. (Trojano et al., 1992); Ro.L. (Belleville et al., 1992); L.A., T.O. (Vallar
et al., 1997).
Reproduced by permission from Vallar & Papagno (1995)

have been described who were impaired in word repetition but showed a preserved digit
span (Damasio & Damasio, 1980; Shallice et al., 2000).

A final aspect, illustrated by Table 12.2, is the superior span performance when the
material is presented visually. Normal subjects, by contrast, have a better performance
level with auditory input (e.g. Levy, 1971). This dissociation indicates that the defective
system is not a supramodal store (Atkinson & Shiffrin, 1971; Waugh & Norman, 1965),
suggesting instead the existence of discrete auditory (phonological) and visual STSs (see
Figure 12.1). The former system is selectively damaged in these patients, thus accounting
for the auditory–visual dissociation in span. Coding in the visual STS may be in terms
of shape. Warrington & Shallice (1972) showed in patient K.F. a high incidence of visual
errors in visual span (i.e. confusions between visually similar letters, such as OQ and PR).
Unlike K.F., normal subjects show acoustic confusions also in visual span; this indicates
phonological recoding and storage in the phonological STS (see Figure 12.1).

This deficit of auditory-verbal span can not be attributed to impaired phonological analysis. In a number of patients immediate repetition of single stimuli was over 90% correct
or errorless (patient P.V., Basso et al., 1982; patient R.R., Bisiacchi et al., 1989; patient
M.C., Caramazza et al., 1981; patient I.L., Saffran & Marin, 1975; patients K.F., J.B., W.H.,
Warrington et al., 1971). Furthermore, a few such patients also showed normal performance
in tasks requiring phonological analysis but posing minimal demands on immediate retention, such as discrimination between consonant–vowel pairs differing in single distinctive
features (patient T.B., Baddeley et al., 1987; Baddeley & Wilson, 1988; patient E.D.E.,
Sloan Berndt et al., 1990; patient P.V., Vallar & Baddeley, 1984b), or phonemic categorization (patient R.R., Bisiacchi et al., 1989). In patients of this sort, the immediate retention
deficit is *primary*, i.e. it is not produced by processing disorders but reflects the reduced
capacity of the phonological STS.

In other patients with defective auditory–verbal span, phonological analysis is also impaired (patient E.A., Friedrich et al., 1984; patient S.C., Trojano et al., 1992; patient E.R., Vallar et al., 1990). In such patients, the memory disorder may be *secondary*, wholly or in part, to the processing deficit. The pattern of immediate memory impairment in these cases is similar to that of patients with a primary disorder, and it may be difficult to tease apart the relative contributions of the processing and storage deficits (for discussion, see Vallar et al., 1990).

The distinction between storage and processing components outlined in Figure 12.1 is further supported by the observation that *mild* deficits of phonological processing may not impair auditory digit span (patient M.P., Martin & Breedin, 1992). Martin & Breedin account for this dissociation, which contrasts with the case of secondary deficits of auditory span, by suggesting that it reflects a contribution to immediate retention from unimpaired lexical phonological representations (see also Knott et al., 2000). This interpretation predicts that such patients will show some impairment of immediate retention of stimuli such as nonwords that are not represented in the lexicon (see related data in Bisiacchi et al., 1989).

The patients' defective auditory–verbal span does not result from speech production problems, since it does not improve when a nonspeech response is required, such as pointing to the items to be recalled in a multiple choice display (patient P.V., Basso et al., 1982; patient K.F., Warrington & Shallice, 1969). Similarly, the patients' performance remains defective when immediate memory is assessed by matching (patient E.D.E., Sloan Berndt et al., 1990; patients K.F., J.B., W.H., Warrington et al., 1971) or probing techniques (patient K.F., Shallice & Warrington, 1970). In line with the individual case studies, the 24 left brain-damaged patients investigated by Vallar et al. (1992) did not improve their span performance when response was by pointing among alternatives, as compared with oral repetition. The use of methods such as pointing, matching and probe recognition, which do not involve any oral response, has revealed in some patients a definite improvement in immediate memory performance (patient R.L., Caplan et al., 1986; patient J.O., Kinsbourne, 1972; patient G.C., Romani, 1992; patient T.O., Vallar et al., 1997). In these cases the deficit in repetition span is not due simply to a reduced capacity of the phonological STS, but reflects, at least in part, the impairment of processes involved in the production of speech.

The conclusion that the selective impairment of auditory–verbal span cannot be explained in terms of dysfunction of systems participating in speech production, such as the phonological output buffer (see e.g. Ellis, 1979), is further supported by the observation that in such patients oral speech may be entirely spared. A quantitative analysis of pauses, rate of speech and errors in spontaneous speech did not show any abnormality in patient J.B. (Shallice & Butterworth, 1977). Patient P.V. had a normal articulation rate (Vallar & Baddeley, 1984a). Other patients (T.B., Baddeley et al., 1987; Baddeley & Wilson, 1988; I.L., Saffran & Marin, 1975) had normal spontaneous speech on a clinical assessment.

The existence of an auditory–visual dissociation in most patients with defective auditory-verbal span (see Table 12.2) is readily compatible with the hypothesis that the deficit involves an input system, such as the phonological STS. In some patients (T.B., Baddeley et al., 1987; Baddeley & Wilson, 1988; Ro.L., Belleville et al., 1992; C.N., Saffran & Martin, 1990a; T.I., Saffran & Martin, 1990b) span performances were similar, independent of input modality. In patients such as T.B. (Baddeley & Wilson, 1988) and Ro.L. (Belleville et al., 1992), whose visual digit span was 2, this may be explained by an associated impairment of the visual STS (see component *D* of Figure 12.1). This interpretation has some anatomical plausibility: the neural correlates of the two storage systems, putatively impaired in patients T.B. and Ro.L. (phonological and visual STSs) are contiguous, including the posterior regions of the left hemisphere (McCarthy & Warrington, 1990), and may then be disrupted jointly by brain damage. A second factor that may reduce the visual advantage found in most patients (see Table 12.2) is a relatively mild impairment of phonological short-term memory. The auditory digit span of patient T.I. (Saffran & Martin, 1990b) was 3.5, and his visual digit span (about three items) was comparable to the putative capacity of the visual STS, as computed by Zhang & Simon (1985).

The interpretation of the deficit of auditory–verbal span in terms of defective phonological STS is supported by the finding that these patients are also impaired in two other tasks, which reflect the operation of this system. First, when engaged in the verbal interfering activity of counting backwards (Peterson & Peterson, 1959; see Shallice & Vallar, 1990, for a discussion of the utilization of the Peterson–Peterson task in patients with defective auditory–verbal span), these patients exhibited an abnormally steep rate of forgetting of auditorily presented verbal stimuli, such as a single letter; by contrast, forgetting rate was minor with visual presentation (patient P.V., Basso et al., 1982; patients R.A.N., N.H.A., McCarthy & Warrington, 1987; patients K.F., J.B., W.H., Warrington et al., 1971). Second, in immediate free recall of a list of auditorily presented words, they showed a reduced or absent recency effect, the advantage of the final positions of the list (patient P.V., Basso et al., 1982; patient S.C., Trojano et al., 1992; Vallar & Papagno, 1986; patients K.F., J.B., W.H., Warrington et al., 1971). P.V.'s recency remained defective, even when she was specifically instructed to recall the final items first (Vallar & Papagno, 1986). Recency was also absent or reduced in the serial recall of auditory–verbal material (P.V., Basso et al., 1982). The recency effect in immediate recall may, however, be normal when presentation is visual (P.V., Vallar & Papagno, 1986). Long-term recency effects may be also normal: in the delayed recall of a list of solutions of anagrams, P.V., as normal controls, showed a better performance for the final items (Vallar et al., 1991). Taken together, these findings support the view that recency effects reflect the application of temporally-based retrieval strategies to specific components of memory, which implies, in the case of immediate recall of auditory–verbal stimuli, to the content of the phonological STS. The deficit of this system, therefore, selectively disrupts recency in immediate recall of auditory–verbal material (see a general discussion of recency phenomena in Baddeley & Hitch, 1993).

The effects of phonological similarity, word length and articulatory suppression on immediate serial recall have been investigated in a limited number of patients with defective auditory–verbal span. As shown in Table 12.3, most patients showed the effect of phonological similarity with auditory input. Unlike normal subjects, however, the effect was absent with visual presentation. The effect of word length was absent with both auditory and visual presentation. These observations in individual patients are in line with the results of Vallar et al. (1992) who, in 24 left brain-damaged aphasic patients with a defective span, found the effect of phonological similarity with auditory but not with visual presentation.

This pattern is similar to that found in normal subjects during articulatory suppression, which disrupts the operation of the rehearsal process. An impairment of the rehearsal system might then be the core disorder underlying the deficit of auditory–verbal span. This interpretation would account for the persistence of the phonological similarity effect with auditory input, since auditory stimuli would have a direct access to an unimpaired phonological STS. By contrast, the phonological similarity effect with visual input and the

Table 12.3 Phonological similarity and word length effects in brain-damaged patients, and a developmental case (R.E.) with defective auditory–verbal span, by input modality (auditory and visual)

Patient	Phonological similarity effect		Word length effect	
	Auditory	Visual	Auditory	Visual
K.F.	+	−	n.a.	n.a.
P.V.	+	−	−	n.a.
R.E.	+	−	−	−
T.B.	−	−	−	n.a.
E.A.	+	−	−	n.a.
R.R.	+	−	−	−
E.R.	+	−	−	−
E.D.E	+	−	−	n.a.
Ro.L.	+	−	−	−
L.A.	−	−	−	−
T.O.	+	−	−	−

Sources: K.F. (Warrington Shallice, 1972); P.V. (Vallar & Baddeley, 1984a); R.E. (Campbell & Butterworth, 1985); T.B. (Baddeley & Wilson, 1988); E.A. (Martin, 1987); R.R. (Bisiacchi et al., 1989); E.R. (Vallar et al., 1990); E.D.E. (Sloan Berndt & Mitchum, 1990); Ro.L. (Belleville et al., 1992); L.A. and T.O. (Vallar et al., 1997). ±, presence/absence of the effect. n.a., not assessed
Reproduced by permission from Vallar & Papagno (1995)

effect of word length with both input modalities would be abolished by the rehearsal deficit, since they require the integrity of this system (see Figure 12.1).

However, if rehearsal, as discussed above, makes use of a phonological output buffer involved in speech production, then the hypothesis of a defective rehearsal can account neither for the normal speech of some patients with reduced auditory–verbal span, nor for the auditory–visual dissociation in span. The latter finding specifically suggests the impairment of an input, modality-specific system. Alternatively, rehearsal may be an independent process, specifically supporting the phonological STS but not involved in speech production (see a discussion of these two hypotheses in Burani et al., 1991; Shallice & Vallar, 1990). This interpretation also runs into difficulties. In normal subjects suppression has significant but minor detrimental effects: in the study of Baddeley & Lewis (1984), auditory span dropped from 7.96 to 5.79 digits during concurrent articulation. By contrast, the average span of patients with defective phonological short-term memory is about 2.3 (see Table 12.2). Furthermore, patients with defective auditory–verbal span also show a reduced or absent auditory recency effect in immediate free recall, despite the fact that recency involves only a minor contribution from rehearsal (Vallar & Papagno, 1986). Finally, patients P.V. (Vallar & Baddeley, 1984b) and L.A. (Vallar et al., 1997) performed within the normal range on rhyme and stress assignment tasks, which involve the activity of the rehearsal process (Burani et al., 1991). A selective deficit of rehearsal is therefore unable to explain the patients' pathologically low auditory–verbal span.

Vallar & Baddeley (1984a, 1984b), who took the view that rehearsal of information held in the phonological STS makes use of phonological processes involved in speech production, suggested that P.V.'s failure to rehearse was a strategy choice. They reasoned that it is likely to be of little use to convey written material to a damaged phonological STS, and to rehearse traces stored in this system. This hypothesis predicts that articulatory suppression, which has detrimental effects on the recall performance of normal subjects, should not impair immediate memory for written material in patients with a defective auditory–verbal span. Such patients would not make use of the phonological STS, but instead would store visuoverbal information in a nonphonological system, such as the visual STS (patient K.F., Warrington & Shallice, 1972). The absence of detectable effects of suppression on visual span of patients P.V. (Vallar & Baddeley, 1984a) and R.R. (Bisiacchi et al., 1989) confirms this prediction. The unimpaired rehearsal system, however, can be used in order to produce normal speech output (patient J.B., Shallice & Butterworth, 1977; patient P.V., Vallar & Baddeley, 1984a), and to make phonological judgements (Vallar & Baddeley, 1984b; Vallar et al., 1997).

Defective Rehearsal Process

The precise articulatory nature of the rehearsal process has been elucidated by the investigation of anarthric patients, who are unable to articulate any detectable speech sound. A number of such cases have been reported, made anarthric by brainstem (patient C.M., Cubelli & Nichelli, 1992; patient G.F., Vallar & Cappa, 1987) and cortical (patient F.C., Cubelli & Nichelli, 1992; patient E.C., Nebes, 1975; patient M.D.C., Vallar & Cappa, 1987), focal lesions and by diffuse brain damage, such as closed head injury (patient G.B., Baddeley & Wilson, 1985). All these patients have an auditory–verbal span within the normal range, even though response production may be very slow and effortful due to the motor deficit, which may be extremely severe (patient G.F., Vallar & Cappa, 1987). In patient E.C., Nebes (1975) found a normal effect of phonological similarity with written presentation. Similarly, in patient G.B. (Baddeley & Wilson, 1985) and in the patients with brainstem lesions (patient C.M., Cubelli & Nichelli, 1992; patient G.F., Vallar & Cappa, 1987), the effect of phonological similarity was present with both visual and auditory input. The effect of word length was found in patient G.B. (Baddeley & Wilson, 1985) with auditory input, but not in patients G.F. and C.M. (see data and discussion in Cubelli & Nichelli, 1992; Vallar & Cappa, 1987). Bishop & Robson (1989), using visual stimuli (line drawings), found that congenitally anarthric children have preserved memory span and show the normal effects of phonological similarity and word length. Taken together, these findings show that rehearsal does not necessarily require the peripheral (muscular) implementation of the articulatory code (Baddeley & Wilson, 1985; Vallar & Cappa, 1987) but occurs at the more central level of premotor planning of speech output (phonological output buffer; Burani et al., 1991).

A disproportionate impairment of the process of articulatory rehearsal has been described in patient T.O. (Vallar et al., 1997) who, like patient J.O. (Kinsbourne, 1972), showed difficulties in speech production. Compared with patients with a selective impairment of the phonological input store, such as patient L.A. (Vallar et al., 1997), T.O.'s span improved in a pointing task not involving oral repetition. Furthermore, T.O.'s memory performance was disrupted by unattended speech, which interferes with the retention capability of the phonological short-term store (Salamé & Baddeley, 1982). By contrast, the patient's immediate memory was not impaired by articulatory suppression, which affects the rehearsal process. The detrimental effect of unattended speech, together with the absence of effects of suppression, suggests a deficit confined to the rehearsal process, sparing the phonological STS. Third, patient T.O. showed a relatively preserved recency effect in immediate free recall of auditorily presented lists of words, consistent with the view that this phenomenon represents the output of the phonological input STS (Hitch, 1980; Vallar & Papagno, 1986). T.O. was also impaired in phonological judgements (rhyme, initial sound) on written material, which engage the rehearsal process. By contrast, the memory performance of patient L.A. (Vallar et al., 1997) did not improve with a pointing response. The patient's memory performance was affected by articulatory suppression but not by unattended speech, and he did not exhibit any recency effect. L.A. was able to perform the kind of phonological judgements mentioned earlier. These contrasting patterns of performance draw a functional distinction between the input phonological STS and the process of rehearsal. This, as noted earlier, has an anatomical counterpart.

Defective Phonological Recoding

Cortical lesions involving the frontal (prerolandic) regions, which produce anarthria, may, however, selectively impair the phonological recoding process, sparing the phonological STS rehearsal process (see anatomical evidence from an activation paradigm in Henson et al., 2000). Two patients have been described (patient F.C., Cubelli & Nichelli, 1992; patient M.D.C., Vallar & Cappa, 1987) who have a normal auditory–verbal span and similarity and word length effects, with auditory presentation. Such effects are, however, absent with visual input. This modality-dependent dissociation suggests that visual material can not enter an unimpaired rehearsal process. This access failure may be due to a dysfunction of the phonological recoding process, as suggested by MCD's impairment in phonological judgements on written material (Vallar & Cappa, 1987).

The Selectivity of the Deficit of Immediate Verbal Memory

The defective immediate retention of auditory–verbal material can not be attributed to the impairment of memory systems different from phonological short-term memory. A number of such patients have preserved long-term episodic memory for verbal and visuospatial material (patient P.V., Basso et al., 1982; patient R.R., Bisiacchi et al., 1989; patients K.F., J.B., W.H., Shallice & Warrington, 1970; Warrington et al., 1971). Short-term memory may be also spared for auditory nonverbal (patient J.B., Shallice & Warrington, 1974) and visuo-spatial material (patient P.V., Basso et al., 1982; patient S.C., Trojano et al., 1992). Finally, patients with severe deficits of general intelligence (Vallar & Papagno, 1993) or episodic long-term memory (e.g. Baddeley & Warrington, 1970) may exhibit a preserved auditory–verbal span. These components of the cognitive system, therefore, do not provide a crucial contribution to immediate retention. The lexical–semantic system, by contrast, contributes to immediate memory performance, particularly in tasks such as repetition span (Martin & Saffran, 1997; Saffran & Martin, 1990b).

ASSOCIATED DEFICITS: THE USES OF SHORT-TERM MEMORY

Phonological Short-term Memory and Sentence Comprehension

Patients with a selective disorder of auditory–verbal span show an associated deficit of sentence comprehension. This can not be attributed to the defective processing of individual words, which is typically spared (see e.g. Saffran & Marin, 1975; Warrington et al., 1971). The hypothesis of a role of the phonological STS in sentence comprehension is by and large in line with the view that the system has an *input locus*, and is not involved in output processes, such as the programming of oral speech. Most patients show defective sentence comprehension in tasks in which word order is crucial, e.g. they are impaired in the *Token test* (De Renzi & Faglioni, 1978), which includes items such as, "Touch the small green square and the large black circle", and may fail to understand semantically reversible sentences (e.g. "The cat that the dog chased was white"). By contrast, when lexical information constrains sentence interpretation, patients' performance is preserved (see reviews in Caplan & Waters, 1990; Saffran, 1990; Vallar et al., 1990).

A possible interpretation of this pattern of impairment is that phonological memory is the working space of syntactic parsing processes (Caramazza & Berndt, 1985; Clark & Clark, 1977). A pathological reduction of the capacity of this system, produced by brain damage, would interfere with the patients' ability to process syntactic information. Sentence comprehension would be then defective when the linear arrangement of words provides crucial information and lexical–semantic analyses do not constrain meaning, such as in the examples mentioned above. These patients, however, may be successful in deciding whether or not long sentences, exceeding their defective auditory–verbal span, are grammatically correct (patient J.B., Butterworth, Shallice, & Watson, 1990; patient T.I., Saffran & Martin, 1990b; patient P.V., Vallar & Baddeley, 1987). This makes unlikely the hypothesis that phonological memory is an intrinsic part of syntactic processing systems.

According to a number of alternative suggestions, phonological memory may be conceived as an independent system, providing temporary storage of phonological information that may, under specific circumstances, contribute to sentence comprehension. Proposed, non-mutually exclusive functions include:

- A back-up store which allows repeated attempts to understand "complex" sentences (Saffran & Marin, 1975; Shallice, 1979).
- Serving as a *mnemonic window*, which preserves word order by a verbatim phonological record, and hence allows the interpretation of sentences where order is crucial (Baddeley & Wilson, 1988; Vallar & Baddeley, 1984b).
- A system which, in a postinterpretative stage, adjudicates between conflicting interpretations of a given sentence (Caplan & Waters, 1990).
- A system which may allow the appropriate mapping of syntactic descriptions of sentences onto their representations, based on lexical–semantic processes, when this is not specified by lexical–semantic information (Saffran, 1990; Saffran & Martin, 1990b; Vallar et al., 1990).

While these views attempt to elucidate the contribution of phonological memory to sentence comprehension, its precise role remains controversial and a matter of debate.

The hypothesis that phonological memory is involved in sentence comprehension has been supported by a follow-up study in patient T.B. (Baddeley et al., 1987; Baddeley & Wilson, 1988), showing a correlation between memory span and sentence comprehension. Several years after initial testing, which had revealed defective auditory–verbal span and sentence comprehension, T.B.'s digit span recovered from two to nine digits and his performance on a series of sentence comprehension tasks became normal. By contrast, his performance in two tasks requiring phonological judgements remained defective, making unlikely an interpretation in terms of a general and nonspecific recovery (Wilson & Baddeley, 1993).

Phonological Short-term Memory and Vocabulary Acquisition

Patients with defective phonological short-term memory may have preserved performance on standard episodic memory tasks, requiring the acquisition of verbal material. However, learning and retention of new words, i.e. of pronounceable letters strings without any pre-existing lexical–semantic representations, is grossly defective.

In 1988, Baddeley et al. showed that patient P.V. was unable to learn new words (Russian words transliterated into Italian) by a paired-associate paradigm, whereas her learning of pairs of Italian words was entirely preserved. With auditory presentation her learning deficit was complete, with P.V. unable to acquire a single new word. With visual input, some learning was possible but performance was grossly defective. A similar disproportionate difficulty in learning new words was subsequently found by Baddeley (1993) in a 23 year-old graduate student, S.R., who had a span performance (four digits) lower than that of matched controls (fellow students). As with patient P.V., subject S.R. was able to learn pairs of words at a normal rate and had a normal level of general intelligence (full-scale IQ, WAIS-R: 128). At variance with P.V., however, S.R. was not a brain-damaged patient, and showed the effects of phonological similarity and word length, suggesting that the operation of the phonological STS and the rehearsal process was qualitatively normal. Patient S.C. (Trojano et al., 1992), who had a defective auditory–verbal span, was able to learn concrete and abstract nouns, reaching after seven trials the performance level of control subjects, even though his initial learning rate was slower. By contrast, S.C.'s learning of function words was slightly defective. Function words are likely to have a less rich semantic representation, as compared with content words. In this respect, functors may be similar to nonwords: both items receive relatively minor support from semantic long-term memory systems (see Caramazza et al., 1981), placing more emphasis on the role of phonological short-term memory in learning. Finally, S.C.'s slower rate of learning in the initial trials, even when the stimuli were concrete nouns, may reflect the contribution of phonological short-term memory to the early phase of word learning (see converging evidence from normal subjects, in Papagno & Vallar, 1992).

Baddeley et al.'s (1988) conclusion, that phonological short-term memory is involved in the acquisition of vocabulary, was subsequently supported by studies in both normal subjects and children. Phonological similarity, item length and articulatory suppression, which, as discussed earlier, affect memory span, also interfere with the learning of new words, while their effects on word learning are minimal or absent (Papagno et al., 1991;

Papagno & Vallar, 1992). In children, performance on immediate memory tasks, such as repetition of nonwords, predicts subsequent acquisition of vocabulary in both a native (Gathercole & Baddeley, 1989) and a foreign language (Service, 1992). The predictive value of immediate memory performance is higher than that of other factors, such as general intelligence (Gathercole & Baddeley, 1989), syntactic-semantic skills or the ability to copy nonwords (Service, 1992). Polyglot subjects, who were able to learn novel words better than matched nonpolyglots, also had a higher auditory digit span. The two groups of subjects were, however, comparable in their general intelligence, word learning and visuospatial skills (Papagno & Vallar, 1995b). The role of phonological memory in long-term verbal learning is reviewed in detail by Baddeley et al. (1998).

A neuropsychological study by Vallar & Papagno (1993) provides further support for the hypothesis that phonological short-term memory plays a crucial role in the acquisition of new vocabulary. F.F., a 23 year-old subject suffering from Down's syndrome, was able to learn three languages (Italian, English, and French) in spite of defective general intelligence, visuospatial skills and episodic long-term memory. F.F. had an entirely preserved auditory–verbal span, and showed the normal effects of phonological similarity and word length. In contrast to the case of P.V., F.F. was able to learn new words at a normal rate, but her learning of real words was defective. These findings have been replicated in a 20 year-old woman suffering from Williams' syndrome (Barisnikov et al., 1996). These data not only corroborate the view, based on data from patients or subjects with a low auditory–verbal span, that phonological short-term memory plays an important role in vocabulary acquisition, but also indicate that learning of new vocabulary may occur in the presence of severe cognitive deficits, including a dysfunction of long-term episodic memory.

THE ASSESSMENT OF VERBAL SHORT-TERM MEMORY FUNCTION

Immediate Memory Span

This is the most popular and widely used test to assess short-term memory function. In the serial span technique, subjects are presented with a sequence of verbal items, which they attempt to recall in the presentation order. In the original version of the task, simple and highly familiar stimuli, such as auditorily presented digits, have been most often used. Digit span typically ranges between five and nine digits, shows slight but significant age decrements, and is affected by educational level but not by sex (Orsini et al., 1987).

According to the WAIS technique (see Orsini et al., 1987), the examiner recites lists of digits of increasing length, starting with a two-digit sequence, at the rate of one item/s. If subjects do not repeat the first sequence correctly, a second string equal in length is presented. When a string is repeated correctly, the examiner reads the next longer sequence, continuing until the subject fails both sequences of a given length or repeats a nine-digit sequence correctly. The digit span score is the length of the longest correctly recalled sequence. Stimuli different from digits, such as words or letters, can be used (e.g. Spinnler & Tognoni, 1987; Vallar & Baddeley, 1984a), and span should be also tested with visual presentation (e.g. Vallar et al., 1992). Perception and production may be assessed by requiring the repetition of individual items: normal performance suggests that a defective span can not be traced back to a major impairment of acoustic–phonological analysis or of output processes.

Phonological and Word Length Effects in Span Tasks

Auditory–verbal span examines short-term memory performance without distinguishing phonological STS and articulatory rehearsal. The operation of these two components is assessed by testing the effects of phonological similarity (phonological STS) and word length (rehearsal) on span.

Sequences of increasing length (two, three, four, five and six similar letters, or words) are presented to the subject, who has to repeat the items of each sequence in the correct order, immediately after presentation. The same procedure is used for sequences of dissimilar letters or words. Stimulus sets that produce reliable effects of phonological similarity are the following: letters (similar, *B, C, D, V, P, T*; dissimilar, *F, K, Q, R, X, Z*), words (similar, *mad, man, map, can, cad, cap*; dissimilar, *pen, rig, day, bar, cow, sup*) (Baddeley, 1966; Vallar & Baddeley, 1984a). The effect, which should be tested with both visual and auditory presentation, is typically present at span or above-span length of the presented sequence. Two scores are usually noted, the number of correctly recalled *sequences*, and the number of *items* recalled in the appropriate serial position. The presence of the phonological similarity effect with both auditory and visual input indicates that both auditory and visual information have gained access to the phonological STS. The phonological similarity effect with visual input also suggests that the articulatory rehearsal process is qualitatively functioning normally.

The effect of word length is assessed by a span paradigm similar to that used in the case of the phonological similarity effect. In order to obtain a clear-cut effect in the individual case, sets of items that are clearly different in length should be used (e.g. two- vs. four- or five-syllable words; see Vallar & Baddeley, 1984a). The presence of the word length effect indicates the qualitatively normal functioning of the rehearsal process.

Phonological Judgements and Free Recall

The absence of the effects of phonological similarity with visual input and of word length suggests that the patient is not making use of the process of rehearsal in span tasks. This result, however, does not distinguish a strategic choice (rehearsal is preserved, although not utilized in a short-term memory task due to the deficit of the main storage component, the phonological STS) from a primary impairment. It is possible to adjudicate between these two possibilities through phonological tasks which specifically engage the rehearsal process, such as rhyme and stress assignment judgements. Homophone judgements, by contrast, appear to require only minimal involvement of the process of rehearsal (Besner, 1987, for related data in normal subjects; Caplan & Waters, 1995; Vallar et al., 1997). Patients with defective rehearsal are impaired in these tasks, which may be performed normally by patients whose impairment is confined to the phonological STS. Additional information may be provided by the lack of the recency effect in immediate free recall, which suggests a deficit of the phonological STS component of the system (Vallar et al., 1997; Vallar & Papagno, 1986).

Assessment of Phonological Analysis and Speech Production

A few additional tests should be performed to assess whether other deficits are present (phonological processing and speech production disorders), which may bring about defective span performance.

Phonological processing may be assessed by using pairs of consonant–vowel nonsense syllables, which can be identical (e.g. *pa-pa*), differ in voicing, in place, or in both distinctive features (e.g. *pa–ba, pa–ta, pa–ga*). In this discrimination task the subject has to judge whether the two members of the pair are same or different in sound. The diagnosis of a selective and primary deficit of phonological short-term memory (Vallar et al., 1990) requires that performance on phonological discrimination tasks is within the normal range (Vallar & Baddeley, 1984b). Other phonological tasks, such as phonemic categorization, may be also used (Bisiacchi et al., 1989).

The possibility that covert deficits of speech production might impair span performance may be assessed by a recognition paradigm. Patients provide their response by pointing to the correct alternatives in a multiple-choice display, using a response modality that does not require overt articulation (Vallar et al., 1992). If a pointing response is impossible (e.g. due to motor deficits), matching (Sloan Berndt & Mitchum, 1990; Warrington & Shallice, 1972) or probing (Shallice & Warrington, 1970) techniques may be used.

To summarize, span tests may be regarded as the minimal battery that provides a complete assessment of the function of phonological short-term memory. Additional tests, which, as discussed earlier, may offer further evidence, include immediate free recall (recency effect), the Peterson–Peterson paradigm, phonological judgements and learning of new words.

CONCLUSION

The main system involved in the immediate retention of verbal material comprises two components: a *phonological STS* and a *rehearsal process*. The STS is an input store, which provides the main retention capacity. Rehearsal is based on systems primarily concerned with speech production. Its main function is to revive the phonological memory trace, preventing its decay, and to convey visually presented material to the phonological STS. In addition to immediate retention *per se*, a main general role of phonological short-term memory concerns the acquisition of new phonological material, such as unfamiliar sound sequences (new words in a native or foreign language). This system is also involved in certain aspects of speech comprehension. Phonological memory has not only specific functional properties but also specific neural correlates, viz. posterior–inferior parietal and premotor frontal neural networks in the left hemisphere.

REFERENCES

Atkinson, R.C. & Shiffrin, R.M. (1971). The control of short-term memory. *Scientific American*, **225**, 82–90.

Baddeley, A.D. (1966). Short-term memory for word sequences as a function of acoustic, semantic and formal similarity. *Quarterly Journal of Experimental Psychology*, **18**, 362–365.

Baddeley, A.D. (1990). *Human Memory. Theory and Practice*. Hove: Erlbaum.

Baddeley, A.D., Gathercole, S. & Papagno, C. (1998). The phonological loop as a language learning device. *Psychological Review*, **105**, 158–173.

Baddeley, A.D. & Hitch, G. (1993). The recency effect: implicit learning with explicit retrieval? *Memory & Cognition*, **21**, 146–155.

Baddeley, A.D. & Lewis, V. (1984). When does rapid presentation enhance digit span? *Bulletin of the Psychonomic Society*, **22**, 403–405.

Baddeley, A.D., Lewis, V. & Vallar, G. (1984). Exploring the articulatory loop. *Quarterly Journal of Experimental Psychology*, **36A**, 233–252.

Baddeley, A.D., Papagno, C. & Vallar, G. (1988). When long-term learning depends on short-term storage. *Journal of Memory and Language*, **27**, 586–595.

Baddeley, A.D., Thomson, N. & Buchanan, M. (1975). Word length and the structure of short-term memory. *Journal of Verbal Learning and Verbal Behavior*, **14**, 575–589.

Baddeley, A.D., Vallar, G. & Wilson, B. (1987). Sentence comprehension and phonological memory: some neuropsychological evidence. In M. Coltheart (ed.), *Attention and Performance XII. The Psychology of Reading* (pp. 509–529). Hove: Erlbaum.

Baddeley, A.D. & Warrington, E.K. (1970). Amnesia and the distinction between long- and short-term memory. *Journal of Verbal Learning and Verbal Behavior*, **9**, 176–189.

Baddeley, A.D. & Wilson, B. (1985). Phonological coding and short-term memory in patients without speech. *Journal of Memory and Language*, **24**, 490–502.

Baddeley, A.D. & Wilson, B.A. (1988). Comprehension and working memory: a single case neuropsychological study. *Journal of Memory and Language*, **27**, 479–498.

Baddeley, A.D. & Wilson, B.A. (1993). A developmental deficit in short-term phonological memory: implications for language and learning. *Memory*, **1**, 65–78.

Barisnikov, K., Van der Linden, M. & Poncelet, M. (1996). Acquisition of new words and phonological working memory in Williams syndrome: a case study. *Neurocase*, **2**, 395–404.

Basso, A. & Cubelli, R. (1999). Clinical aspects of aphasia. In G. Denes & L. Pizzamiglio (eds), *Handbook of Clinical and Experimental Neuropsychology* (pp. 181–193). Hove: Psychology Press.

Basso, A., Spinnler, H., Vallar, G. & Zanobio, M.E. (1982). Left hemisphere damage and selective impairment of auditory-verbal short-term memory. *Neuropsychologia*, **20**, 263–274.

Belleville, S., Peretz, I. & Arguin, M. (1992). Contribution of articulatory rehearsal to short-term memory: evidence from a case of selective disruption. *Brain and Language*, **43**, 713–746.

Besner, D. (1987). Phonology, lexical access in reading, and articulatory suppression: a critical review. *Quarterly Journal of Experimental Psychology*, **39A**, 467–478.

Bishop, D.V.M. & Robson, J. (1989). Unimpaired short-term memory and rhyme judgement in congenitally speechless individuals: implications for the notion of "articulatory coding". *Quarterly Journal of Experimental Psychology*, **41A**, 123–140.

Bisiacchi, P.S., Cipolotti, L. & Denes, G. (1989). Impairment in processing meaningless verbal material in several modalities: the relationship between short-term memory and phonological skills. *Quarterly Journal of Experimental Psychology*, **41A**, 293–319.

Burani, C., Vallar, G. & Bottini, G. (1991). Articulatory coding and phonological judgements on written words and pictures: the role of the phonological output buffer. *European Journal of Cognitive Psychology*, **3**, 379–398.

Butterworth, B., Shallice, T. & Watson, F.L. (1990). Short-term retention without short-term memory. In G. Vallar & T. Shallice (eds), *Neuropsychological Impairments of Short-term Memory* (pp. 187–213). Cambridge: Cambridge University Press.

Campbell, R. & Butterworth, B. (1985). Phonological dyslexia and dysgraphia in a highly literate subject: a developmental case with associated deficits of phonemic processing and awareness. *Quarterly Journal of Experimental Psychology*, **37A**, 435–475.

Caplan, D., Vanier, M. & Backer, C. (1986). A case study of reproduction conduction aphasia. I. Word production. *Cognitive Neuropsychology*, **3**, 99–128.

Caplan, D. & Waters, G. (1995). On the nature of the phonological output planning processes involved in verbal rehearsal: evidence from aphasia. *Brain and Language*, **48**, 191–220.

Caplan, D. & Waters, G.S. (1990). Short-term memory and language comprehension: a critical review of the neuropsychological literature. In G. Vallar & T. Shallice (eds), *Neuropsychological Impairments of Short-term Memory* (pp. 337–389). Cambridge: Cambridge University Press.

Caramazza, A., Basili, A.G., Koller, J.J. & Sloan Berndt, R. (1981). An investigation of repetition and language processing in a case of conduction aphasia. *Brain and Language*, **14**, 235–271.

Caramazza, A. & Berndt, R.S. (1985). A multicomponent deficit view of agrammatic Broca's aphasia. In M.-L. Kean (ed.), *Agrammatism* (pp. 27–63). Orlando, FL: Academic Press.

Clark, H.H. & Clark, E. (1977). *Psychology and Language. An Introduction to Psycholinguistics*. New York: Harcourt Brace Jovanovich.

Conrad, R. (1964). Acoustic confusions in immediate memory. *British Journal of Psychology*, **55**, 75–84.

Conrad, R. & Hull, A.J. (1964). Information, acoustic confusion and memory span. *British Journal of Psychology*, **55**, 429–432.

Crowder, R.G. (1976). *Principles of Learning and Memory*. Hillsdale, NJ: Erlbaum.

Cubelli, R. & Nichelli, P. (1992). Inner speech in anarthria: neuropsychological evidence of differential effects of cerebral lesions on subvocal articulation. *Journal of Clinical and Experimental Neuropsychology*, **14**, 499–517.

Damasio, H. & Damasio, A.R. (1980). The anatomical basis of conduction aphasia. *Brain*, **103**, 337–350.

De Renzi, E. & Faglioni, P. (1978). Normative data and screening power of a shortened version of the Token Test. *Cortex*, **14**, 41–49.

Ellis, A.W. (1979). Speech production and short-term memory. In J. Morton & J.C. Marshall (eds), *Psycholinguistic Series: Structures and Processes*, Vol. 2 (pp. 157–187). London: Paul Elek.

Friedrich, F.J., Glenn, C.G. & Marin, O.S.M. (1984). Interruption of phonological coding in conduction aphasia. *Brain and Language*, **22**, 266–291.

Gathercole, S.E. & Baddeley, A.D. (1989). Evaluation of the role of phonological STM in the development of vocabulary in children: a longitudinal study. *Journal of Memory and Language*, **28**, 200–213.

Henson, R.N.A., Burgess, N. & Frith, C.D. (2000). Recoding, storage, rehearsal and grouping in verbal short-term memory: an fMRI study. *Neuropsychologia*, **38**, 426–440.

Hitch, G.J. (1980). Developing the concept of working memory. In G. Claxton (ed.), *Cognitive Psychology: New Directions* (pp. 154–196). London: Routledge & Kegan Paul.

Kinsbourne, M. (1972). Behavioral analysis of the repetition deficit in conduction aphasia. *Neurology*, **22**, 1126–1132.

Knott, R., Patterson, K. & Hodges, J.R. (2000). The role of speech production in auditory-verbal short-term memory: evidence from progressive fluent aphasia. *Neuropsychologia*, **38**, 125–142.

Levy, B.A. (1971). Role of articulation in auditory and visual short-term memory. *Journal of Verbal Learning and Verbal Behavior*, **10**, 123–132.

Luria, A.R., Sokolov, E.N. & Klimkowski, M. (1967). Towards a neurodynamic analysis of memory disturbances with lesions of the left temporal lobe. *Neuropsychologia*, **5**, 1–11.

Martin, R.C. (1987). Articulatory and phonological deficits in short-term memory and their relation to syntactic processing. *Brain and Language*, **32**, 159–192.

Martin, N. & Saffran, E.M. (1997). Language and auditory-verbal short-term memory impairments: evidence for common underlying processes. *Cognitive Neuropsychology*, **14**, 641–682.

Martin, R.C. & Breedin, S.D. (1992). Dissociations between speech perception and phonological short-term memory deficits. *Cognitive Neuropsychology*, **9**, 509–534.

Martin, R.C. & Lesch, M.F. (1996). Associations and dissociations between language impairment and list recall: implications for models of STM. In S.E. Gathercole (ed.), *Models of Short-term Memory* (pp. 149–178). Hove: Psychology Press.

McCarthy, R.A. & Warrington, E.K. (1987). The double dissociation of short-term memory for lists and sentences. Evidence from aphasia. *Brain*, **110**, 1545–1563.

McCarthy, R.A. & Warrington, E.K. (1990). *Cognitive Neuropsychology. A Clinical Introduction*. San Diego, CA: Academic Press.

Murray, D.J. (1968). Articulation and acoustic confusability in short-term memory. *Journal of Experimental Psychology*, **78**, 679–684.

Nebes, R. (1975). The nature of internal speech in anarthria. *Brain and Language*, **2**, 489–497.

Orsini, A., Grossi, D., Capitani, E. et al. (1987). Verbal and spatial immediate memory span. Normative data from 1355 adults and 1112 children. *Italian Journal of Neurological Sciences*, **8**, 539–548.

Papagno, C., Valentine, T. & Baddeley, A.D. (1991). Phonological short-term memory and foreign language vocabulary learning. *Journal of Memory and Language*, **30**, 331–347.

Papagno, C. & Vallar, G. (1992). Phonological short-term memory and the learning of novel words: the effects of phonological similarity and word length. *Quarterly Journal of Experimental Psychology*, **44A**, 47–67.

Papagno, C. & Vallar, G. (1995a). To learn or not to learn vocabulary in foreign languages: the problem with phonological memory. In R. Campbell & M. Conway (eds), *Broken Memories* (pp. 334–343). Oxford: Basil Blackwell.

Papagno, C. & Vallar, G. (1995b). Verbal short-term memory and vocabulary learning in polyglots. *Quarterly Journal of Experimental Psychology*, **48A**, 98–107.

Paulesu, E., Connelly, A., Frith, C.D. et al. (1995). Functional MR imaging correlations with positron emission tomography. Initial experience using a cognitive activation paradigm on verbal working memory. *Neuroimaging Clinics of North America*, **5**, 207–225.

Paulesu, E., Frith, C.D. & Frackowiak, R.S.J. (1993). The neural correlates of the verbal component of working memory. *Nature*, **362**, 342–345.

Paulesu, E., Frith, U., Snowling, M. et al. (1996). Is developmental dyslexia a disconnection syndrome? Evidence from PET scanning. *Brain*, **119**, 143–157.

Peterson, L.R. & Johnson, S.T. (1971). Some effects of minimizing articulation on short-term retention. *Journal of Verbal Learning and Verbal Behavior*, **10**, 346–354.

Peterson, L.R. & Peterson, M.J. (1959). Short-term retention of individual verbal items. *Journal of Experimental Psychology*, **58**, 193–198.

Risse, G.L., Rubens, A.B. & Jordan, L.S. (1984). Disturbances of long-term memory in aphasic patients: a comparison of anterior and posterior lesions. *Brain*, **107**, 605–617.

Romani, C. (1992). Are there distinct input and output buffers? Evidence from an aphasic patient with an impaired output buffer. *Language and Cognitive Processes*, **7**, 131–162.

Saffran, E.M. (1990). Short-term memory impairment and language processing. In A. Caramazza (ed.), *Cognitive Neuropsychology and Neurolinguistics: Advances in Models of Cognitive Function and Impairment* (pp. 137–168). Hillsdale, NJ: Erlbaum.

Saffran, E.M. & Marin, O.S.M. (1975). Immediate memory for word lists and sentences in a patient with deficient auditory short-term memory. *Brain and Language*, **2**, 420–433.

Saffran, E.M. & Martin, N. (1990a). Neuropsychological evidence for lexical involvement in short-term memory. In G. Vallar & T. Shallice (eds), *Neuropsychological Impairments of Short-term Memory* (pp. 145–166). Cambridge: Cambridge University Press.

Saffran, E.M. & Martin, N. (1990b). Short-term memory impairment and sentence processing: a case study. In G. Vallar & T. Shallice (eds), *Neuropsychological Impairments of Short-term Memory* (pp. 428–447). Cambridge: Cambridge University Press.

Salamé, P. & Baddeley, A.D. (1982). Disruption of short-term memory by unattended speech: implications for the structure of working memory. *Journal of Verbal Learning and Verbal Behavior*, **21**, 150–164.

Service, E. (1992). Phonology, working memory, and foreign-language learning. *Quarterly Journal of Experimental Psychology*, **45A**, 21–50.

Shallice, T. (1979). Neuropsychological research and the fractionation of memory systems. In L.G. Nillson (ed.), *Perspectives on Memory Research* (pp. 257–277). Hillsdale, NJ: Erlbaum.

Shallice, T. & Butterworth, B. (1977). Short-term memory impairment and spontaneous speech. *Neuropsychologia*, **15**, 729–735.

Shallice, T., Rumiati, R.I. & Zadini, A. (2000). The selective impairment of the phonological output buffer. *Cognitive Neuropsychology*, **17**, 517–546.

Shallice, T. & Vallar, G. (1990). The impairment of auditory-verbal short-term storage. In G. Vallar & T. Shallice (eds), *Neuropsychological Impairments of Short-term Memory* (pp. 11–53). Cambridge: Cambridge University Press.

Shallice, T. & Warrington, E.K. (1970). Independent functioning of verbal memory stores: a neuropsychological study. *Quarterly Journal of Experimental Psychology*, **22**, 261–273.

Shallice, T. & Warrington, E.K. (1974). The dissociation between short-term retention of meaningful sounds and verbal material. *Neuropsychologia*, **12**, 553–555.

Shallice, T. & Warrington, E.K. (1977). Auditory-verbal short-term memory impairment and conduction aphasia. *Brain and Language*, **4**, 479–491.

Shallice, T. & Warrington, E.K. (1980). K.F.: Post-mortem findings. In M. Coltheart, K. Patterson & J.C. Marshall (eds), *Deep Dyslexia* (pp. 411). London: Routledge & Kegan Paul.

Silveri, M.C., Di Betta, A.M., Filippini, V. et al. (1998). Verbal short-term store-rehearsal system and the cerebellum. Evidence from a patient with a right cerebellar lesion. *Brain*, **121**, 2175–2187.

Sloan Berndt, R. & Mitchum, C.C. (1990). Auditory and lexical information sources in immediate recall: evidence from a patient with a deficit to the phonological short-term store. In G. Vallar & T. Shallice (eds), *Neuropsychological Impairments of Short-term Memory* (pp. 115–144). Cambridge: Cambridge University Press.

Smith, E.E. & Jonides, J. (1999). Storage and executive processes in the frontal lobes. *Science*, **283**, 1657–1661.

Spinnler, H. & Tognoni, G. (1987). Standardizzazione e taratura Italiana di Test Neuropsicologici. *Italian Journal of Neurological Sciences (suppl. 8)*.

Strub, R.L. & Gardner, H. (1974). The repetition defect in conduction aphasia: mnestic or linguistic? *Brain and Language*, **1**, 241–255.

Trojano, L., Stanzione, M. & Grossi, D. (1992). Short-term memory and verbal learning with auditory phonological coding defect: a neuropsychological case study. *Brain and Cognition*, **18**, 12–33.

Tzortis, C. & Albert, M.L. (1974). Impairment of memory for sequences in conduction aphasia. *Neuropsychologia*, **12**, 355–366.

Vallar, G. (2000). The methodological foundations of human neuropsychology: studies in brain-damaged patients. In F. Boller & J. Grafman (eds), *Handbook of Neuropsychology*, 2nd edn (pp. 305–344). Amsterdam: Elsevier.

Vallar, G. & Baddeley, A.D. (1984a). Fractionation of working memory: neuropsychological evidence for a phonological short-term store. *Journal of Verbal Learning and Verbal Behavior*, **23**, 151–161.

Vallar, G. & Baddeley, A.D. (1984b). Phonological short-term store, phonological processing and sentence comprehension. *Cognitive Neuropsychology*, **1**, 121–141.

Vallar, G. & Baddeley, A.D. (1987). Phonological short-term store and sentence processing. *Cognitive Neuropsychology*, **4**, 417–438.

Vallar, G., Basso, A. & Bottini, G. (1990). Phonological processing and sentence comprehension. A neuropsychological case study. In G. Vallar & T. Shallice (eds), *Neuropsychological Impairments of Short-term Memory* (pp. 448–476). Cambridge: Cambridge University Press.

Vallar, G. & Cappa, S.F. (1987). Articulation and verbal short-term memory. Evidence from anarthria. *Cognitive Neuropsychology*, **4**, 55–78.

Vallar, G., Corno, M. & Basso, A. (1992). Auditory and visual verbal short-term memory in aphasia. *Cortex*, **28**, 383–389.

Vallar, G., Di Betta, A.M. & Silveri, M.C. (1997). The phonological short-term store-rehearsal system: patterns of impairment and neural correlates. *Neuropsychologia*, **35**, 795–812.

Vallar, G. & Papagno, C. (1986). Phonological short-term store and the nature of the recency effect. Evidence from neuropsychology. *Brain and Cognition*, **5**, 428–442.

Vallar, G. & Papagno, C. (1993). Preserved vocabulary acquisition in Down's syndrome: the role of phonological short-term memory. *Cortex*, **29**, 467–483.

Vallar, G. & Papagno, C. (1995). Neuropsychological impairments of short-term memory. In A.D. Baddeley, B.A. Wilson & F.N. Walts (eds), *Handbook of Memory Disorders*, 1st edn (pp. 135–165) Chichesken: Wiley.

Vallar, G., Papagno, C. & Baddeley, A.D. (1991). Long-term recency effects and phonological short-term memory. A neuropsychological case study. *Cortex*, **27**, 323–326.

Warrington, E.K. (1979). Neuropsychological evidence for multiple memory systems. In G. Wolstenholme & M. O'Connor (eds), *Brain and Mind*. Ciba Foundation Symposium 69 (New Series) (pp. 153–166). Amsterdam: Excerpta Medica.

Warrington, E.K., Logue, V. & Pratt, R.T.C. (1971). The anatomical localisation of selective impairment of auditory verbal short-term memory. *Neuropsychologia*, **9**, 377–387.

Warrington, E.K. & Shallice, T. (1969). The selective impairment of auditory–verbal short-term memory. *Brain*, **92**, 885–896.

Warrington, E.K. & Shallice, T. (1972). Neuropsychological evidence of visual storage in short-term memory tasks. *Quarterly Journal of Experimental Psychology*, **24**, 30–40.

Waugh, N. & Norman, D.A. (1965). Primary memory. *Psychological Review*, **72**, 89–1104.

Wickelgren, W.A. (1965). Short-term memory for phonemically similar lists. *American Journal of Psychology*, **78**, 567–574.

Wilson, B.A. & Baddeley, A.D. (1993). Spontaneous recovery of impaired memory span: does comprehension recover? *Cortex*, **29**, 153–159.

Zangwill, O.L. (1946). Some qualitative observations on verbal memory in cases of cerebral lesion. *British Journal of Psychology*, **37**, 8–19.

Zhang, G. & Simon, H.A. (1985). STM capacity for Chinese words and idioms: chunking and acoustical loop hypotheses. *Memory and Cognition*, **13**, 193–201.

CHAPTER 13

Neuropsychological Impairments of Visual and Spatial Working Memory

Sergio Della Sala

and

Robert H. Logie

Department of Psychology, University of Aberdeen, UK

SPECIFICITY OF VISUOSPATIAL WORKING MEMORY

In Plato's *Meno*, the dialogue between Meno and Socrates (Bluck, 1961; Grube, 1997) describes knowledge as "recollection", i.e. the concept of re-collecting, or "joining together" in new combinations, items of information from the environment or from past experience. In other words, a crucial aspect of memory was seen as an active process of combining, recombining and reinterpreting past and current experience. This is in contrast with Plato's writings in *Theaetetus* (Levett & Burnyeat, 1997), in which memory for past events was seen more in the metaphor of an aviary (storehouse of ideas), with each bird representing an item of information that can be retrieved. Working memory refers to the active processes of memory; the recollection of the birds, forming them into novel groups and generating new insights as well as offering an interpreted snapshot of the current state of our environment. Working memory then is viewed as a set of cognitive functions that are separate from the traces of past experience and accumulated knowledge in long-term memory, but it is also a system than can retrieve and manipulate the activated contents of long-term memory, allowing those contents to be reinterpreted (for contrasting views of working memory, see Miyake & Shah, 1999). The environment and its interpretation within working memory might involve language, or it might involve the layout and identity of objects, or of a sequence of movements required to navigate through the environment and to interact with the objects we encounter. It is these latter, nonlinguistic functions of working memory and their impairments following brain damage that are the focus of this chapter.

Contemporary thinking on the concept of short-term memory has been influenced heavily by the assumption that temporary memory has evolved to support language. Indeed the term "short-term memory" has, until recently, been used to refer solely to verbal

The Handbook of Memory Disorders. Edited by A.D. Baddeley, M.D. Kopelman and B.A. Wilson
© 2002 John Wiley & Sons, Ltd.

temporary storage, e.g. Vallar & Shallice (1990) entitled their seminal text on the impact of brain damage on immediate verbal memory *Neuropsychological Impairments of Short-term Memory*, without feeling the need to state explicitly that the work was focused entirely on verbal temporary memory; short-term memory and verbal short-term memory were seen as synonymous.

It is clear from both neuropsychological reports (e.g. Beyn & Knyazeva, 1962; De Renzi & Nichelli, 1975; Warrington & Rabin, 1971) and experimental studies with healthy adults (e.g. Baddeley & Lieberman, 1980; Farmer et al., 1986; Logie, 1986) that temporary retention and manipulation of visual and spatial information is supported by cognitive functions that are dissociable from verbal short-term memory. Indeed, in the case of patients with verbal short-term memory deficits, such as K.F. (Shallice & Warrington, 1970), I.L. (Saffran & Marin, 1975), or P.V. (Basso et al., 1982), their memory span for visually presented verbal sequences is much higher than their pathological span for aurally presented sequences. This is the converse of the pattern for healthy adults, who typically show higher spans for aurally presented than for visually presented verbal sequences (e.g. Conrad & Hull, 1964; Logie et al., 1996).

The independence of verbal and visual short-term memory has been demonstrated further using interference paradigms with healthy adults, e.g. Baddeley et al. (1975) showed that retaining visuospatial images was disrupted when combined with performing a concurrent perceptuo-motor tracking task. However Baddeley et al. (1986) reported that perceptuo-motor tracking had a minimal impact on concurrent performance with auditory verbal span. In contrast, serial verbal memory span is dramatically disrupted by concurrent generation of an irrelevant, repeated spoken output (articulatory suppression; see Vallar & Papagno, Chapter 12, this volume), whereas articulatory suppression has no impact on a visuospatial manipulation task (Farmer et al., 1986).

The conclusion from the above findings, that verbal and visuospatial short-term memory systems are quite distinct, has been supported by demonstrations of double dissociations within the same studies. In healthy adults, Logie et al. (1990) showed that performing mental arithmetic disrupted performance on a letter immediate memory task, but had little impact on immediate memory for visuospatial material. In a contrasting condition, a concurrent imagery task interfered with retention of a matrix pattern but has little effect on retention of random letter sequences. In a study of a group of Alzheimer patients, Baddeley et al. (1991) reported a clear double dissociation, where some patients showed pathological performance on verbal immediate memory span, but normal performance on memory for a sequence of targeted movements (Corsi blocks; Corsi, 1972; Milner, 1971). Other patients in the same group showed the converse, with very poor Corsi block performance coupled with normal immediate verbal memory span. In summary, there is a growing body of evidence to challenge the assumption that short-term memory is exclusively concerned with temporary retention of verbal material.

Another common assumption is that short-term memory is equivalent to working memory (e.g. Roediger & Goff, 1999; Smith, 1999). It is probably true that working memory as a concept has largely replaced the more traditional concept of short-term memory. However, the concepts differ in important ways. Short-term memory typically refers to passive storage of small amounts of information on a temporary basis. In the case of verbal short-term memory, an example would be retaining a telephone number long enough to make the call. In the case of visual short-term memory, this might involve returning to the correct position on the page after reading has been interrupted. In contrast, working memory refers to both passive, temporary storage of visual or verbal information and the active mental manipulation of that information. In this sense, working memory incorporates short-term memory among its functions. Our focus in this chapter will be on the visuospatial resources of working memory and impairments in its function following brain damage.

One recent example of how working memory might be conceived by the lay public is illustrated in the film *Memento*, directed by Christopher Nolan (2000), where the metaphor of Polaroid photographs is used to convey how visual memories might be formed as the elements of the photograph gradually appear, and how the reverse operation of elements fading from the photograph represents a process of forgetting that is particularly rapid for the main character in the film. This presents forgetting as a passive loss of definition or decay until no information remains. As a metaphor it portrays a commonly-held view. However, for some considerable time research on this topic has shown it to be a metaphor that is very limited and quite misleading (e.g. Kosslyn, 1980). Visuospatial working memory is an active system; it involves manipulating and recombining elements of information from the environment and from prior experience, as well as temporary retention. Moreover, a photograph in itself has no meaning. It is the interpretation by the cognitive system of the contents of the photograph that has meaning, and it is this interpretation that is held within working memory. The objects or the people in the photograph are identified and associated with a lifetime store of knowledge, and one important aspect of forgetting includes the loss or the change of how a scene is interpreted as well as the loss of detailed visual features.

There is now general agreement among researchers that working memory supports visuospatial as well as verbal temporary storage, and that it is an active system. However, the cognitive architecture of working memory, and visuospatial working memory in particular, remains a topic for debate. We will discuss both the experimental and the neuropsycholog-ical evidence that impinge on this debate. First, we address the question of whether or not visuospatial working memory acts as a gateway between perception and long-term memory. This will be followed by a discussion as to whether it is best considered as a unitary system or as a multicomponent system. We will then consider the implications of the impairments of different aspects of visuospatial working memory and the neuroanatomical networks that might be associated with visuospatial working memory functions.

VISUO-SPATIAL WORKING MEMORY: A WORKSPACE, NOT A GATEWAY

Working memory is often viewed as a form of transit lounge or "gateway" that acts to hold sensory input on its way to long-term memory. This was the view in the widely cited model proposed by Atkinson & Shiffrin (1968). Also, it still appears as an assumption in a wide range of contemporary, introductory textbooks, as well as in some contemporary theory, including theories that incorporate multiple components of working memory. An illustration of this form of gateway concept is shown in the upper part of Figure 13.1. However, the transit function for working memory carries with it a number of implications for the status of the information it holds. One implication is that there is no direct access route between sensory input and long-term memory. However, this runs into difficulty when attempting to account for the wide range of evidence for implicit processing of sensory input that arises from studies that we discuss in detail later in the chapter, of patients with blindsight

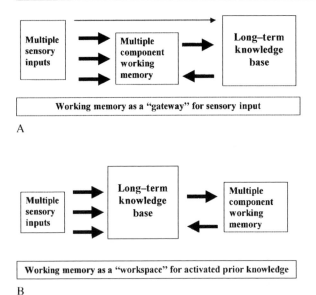

A

B

Figure 13.1   (A) Flow of sensory input through working memory, functioning as a gateway to the long-term store of knowledge and experiences. (B) The flow of sensory input directly activating stored knowledge, with the contents of working memory comprising some of the products of that activation

and with neglect. These data suggest that the gateway can be circumvented under some circumstances, and this additional concept of a "leaky gateway" is illustrated in Figure 13.1 by the arrow at the top of the upper figure. A second implication is that damage to the transit function should result in damage to the processing of sensory input. So, for example, should the visuospatial functions of working memory be damaged as a result of brain injury or disease, and if those visuospatial functions act as a gateway between sensory input and the store of prior knowledge, then the processing of sensory input should be impaired. However, as we discuss later in the chapter, patients that show visual or spatial representational and immediate memory impairments show no evidence of impairments in object identification or naming. This is rather more difficult for the gateway model to address, even with the additional direct route between sensory input and the store of knowledge.

A further implication of working memory as a gateway is that its contents would comprise primarily raw sensory images of edges, contours, light, shade and colour. The successful perception of these raw sensory images as recognizable objects requires access to the store of knowledge that has accumulated from prior experience. However, the contents of working memory appear to comprise identified objects and scenes, rather than raw sensory images. This suggests that sensory input does not pass through working memory prior to the interpretation of that input. This in turn speaks to the view that the primary route for sensory input is that it first activates prior knowledge and experiences in long-term memory, and that it is the product of that activation which is held and manipulated within working memory. This argument is not readily handled by the suggestion that the primary function of working memory is as a gateway (even a leaky gateway), and it is better characterized as a workspace whose primary function is to store on a temporary basis, and to manipulate and recombine the products of the activation of stored knowledge. This alternative view is illustrated in the lower part of Figure 13.1.

If you now close your eyes and consider the objects that are in your immediate environment, then you will draw on the contents of working memory for the recently perceived scene. In reporting the contents of working memory, the objects are identified—as a lamp, a computer screen, a pencil, a book, a grey plastic model of a brain—they are not raw sensory images comprising uninterpreted shades of colour, contrast, texture, edges and contours. It is possible to manipulate these objects in your representation—imagine the book on top of the lamp, the pencil falling on the floor, the model brain growing larger or turning a shade of pink. It is also possible to reach out and physically pick up and manipulate the objects without opening your eyes—physically reach out, pick up and squeeze the model brain, or open the book at the first page. We can perform the same mental operations on the contents of a representation retrieved from our knowledge base of past experience. We can represent mentally objects that are behind us in the immediate, familiar environment of an office, even if they have not been viewed recently—the phrenological head on the bookcase or the painting of the hill of Bennachie. We can also represent and mentally manipulate the landmarks in a familiar square in our home town, or imagine the impact of rearranging the layout of the furniture in our living room. This all points to the idea that working memory cannot be considered as a gateway between sensory input and long-term memory, but more as a system for representing interpreted objects and scenes, allowing us to interact with and mentally manipulate those objects. Visuospatial working memory, therefore, gives us a representation of the environment on which we can act mentally or enact physically.

The idea that visuospatial working memory is best viewed as a workspace rather than a gateway is supported by evidence from experimental psychology, in particular the area of mental discovery. One experimental method for investigation of this topic involves presenting healthy volunteers with the names of a small number of generic shapes, such as "semi-circle, square, figure 8". The volunteers are then required to mentally manipulate the shapes and combine them in such a way as to form a recognizable object. Figure 13.2 shows one example generated by a volunteer contributing to Experiment 2 reported by Barquero & Logie (1999). On the whole, the volunteers were quite good at generating drawings of recognizable objects and allocating labels for their mental constructions (see also Anderson & Helstrup, 1993; Finke & Slayton, 1988; Pearson et al., 1999). However, Barquero & Logie also showed that when volunteers were asked to perform the same task

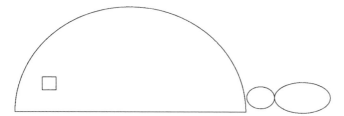

Figure 13.2   Figure generated by a participant in "mental discovery" experiment by Barquero & Logie (1999). Volunteers were provided with the names of generic shapes and their task was to manipulate the shapes mentally and combine them in a recognizable object. In this example, "semi-circle, square, figure 8" were combined to form a mouse

with the shapes of real objects, such as "cigar, bell, ruler", then they had more difficulty in generating recognizable objects mentally, but their ability to reinterpret object shapes as being components of a completely different object improved if they were allowed to sketch their image on paper. These results suggest that healthy adults can use working memory to manipulate shapes and generate new discoveries. However, they also suggest that when people attempt to manipulate mentally the shapes of real objects, then it is difficult to divest the object identity from the object shape. When the shapes are drawn on paper, they can be reinterpreted via the perceptual system. That is, the meaning which arises from object identification through perception becomes part of the mental representation held in working memory. In sum, working memory can aid discovery, but it operates as a workspace, not just a temporary passive storage device. Moreover, working memory is not a gateway: it deals with activated knowledge, not raw sensory images, and the material enters working memory from long-term memory, not directly from sensory input.

IMPLICIT PROCESSING IN PERCEPTUAL NEGLECT AND IN BLINDSIGHT

Evidence that working memory is unlikely to function as a gateway comes from studies of patients with unilateral perceptual neglect. A key deficit in these patients is that they ignore one half of extrapersonal space, most commonly the left, following a lesion in the right parietal lobe (for review, see Robertson & Halligan, 1999). Thus, when asked to copy a picture, they will reproduce only the right half of the picture. When asked to describe their immediate environment, they will describe only the right half of the scene in front of them and, in severe cases, will eat from only the right half of their plate. This deficit does not arise from failure of the visual sensory system, and is generally interpreted as an impairment of the attentional system. Although such patients ignore information on their left side, they nevertheless appear to be affected implicitly by some of the ignored information. A now classic example is that of patient P.S. (Marshall & Halligan, 1988), who was shown a picture of two houses, one above the other. One of the houses looked perfectly symmetrical and normal, while the other house was depicted with flames issuing from a window on the left of the picture. The patient was asked to indicate if she detected whether the two houses were the same, or were different in any way, and consistently reported that the houses were identical. However, when the patient was asked to choose in which house she would prefer to live, she tended to choose the house without the flames while claiming that this was a complete guess.

Similar conclusions can be drawn from studies using pictures of chimeric animals (e.g. Buxbaum & Coslett, 1994; Vallar et al., 1994; Young et al., 1992), i.e. showing one half of an animal joined to half of another animal. In the Vallar et al. (1994, Experiment 1) study, neglect patients were shown pairs of pictures. For one set of picture pairs, two identical animals were shown. For a second set of picture pairs, one picture depicted a normal animal, and the other picture depicted a chimera-like figure (the front halves of two animals joined and facing in opposite directions; see Figure 13.3). The task for the patients was to decide for each pair whether the pictures shown were same or different. One patient in particular, case G.S., is relevant for our discussions. In 100% of trials in which one picture showed a chimeric figure, G.S. indicated that the pictures appeared identical. However, Vallar et al. next presented the picture pairs along with a verbal cue that was the name of the

Figure 13.3 The chimeric figure of a horse, similar to those used by Vallar et al. (1994)

animal depicted on the neglected (left) side, e.g. the word "horse" for the stimulus shown in Figure 13.3. Under these conditions, the patient's performance dramatically improved, responding correctly on 75% of the "different" trials, but despite this she did not become aware of the chimeric nature of the stimuli.

Implicit processing of the unattended half of the space has also been observed in patients with perceptual neglect, using rather different experimental paradigms. When neglect patient F.F. (Cantagallo & Della Sala, 1998) was presented with the drawing of a trombone with a rifle butt coming out from its left side, he spontaneously reported that he was seeing a "trombone which *fired* notes". McGlinchy-Berroth et al. (1993) showed that neglect patients improved their performance in a lexical decision task after they were primed by brief presentation of relevant pictures in their neglected field. All the above cases demonstrate that the information, not available within working memory, was being processed by means of access to stored knowledge in long-term memory (for further discussion see Ellis et al., 1996).

A similar case can be made by drawing on evidence from patients with blindsight. These patients have a lesion in the primary visual cortex, and therefore show the symptoms of blindness in the contralateral hemifield in the absence of damage to the visual sensory system (Weiskrantz, 1986). Despite this inability to report visually presented material in their blind field, they nevertheless show evidence of tacit processing of that material. Thus, for example, they can guess the orientation of a moving light, or the position of a stationary light, and can generate the correct movement and grasp for objects that they are unable to report. The tacit processing appears also for the semantic content of meaningful stimuli in their blind hemifield. For example, interpretation of an ambiguous word (e.g. the word "bank") in their intact hemifield can be influenced by the presentation of a disambiguating stimulus (e.g. the word "river" or the word "money") in the blind hemifield (Marcel, 1998). A similar pattern of findings has been reported using pictures for a speeded object recognition task (Störig, 2000). Specifically, if the target object is presented in the blind field 350 ms before it appears in the unimpaired hemifield, then recognition time is faster than when there is no blind field cue.

Taken together, the data from neglect and from blindsight suggest that sensory inputs are not necessarily held within working memory *en route* to long-term memory. Rather, for those occasions on which a correct or a speeded response is generated, the stimuli activate stored knowledge in long-term memory at a level sufficient to constitute implicit processing.

VISUOSPATIAL WORKING MEMORY AND REPRESENTATIONAL NEGLECT

Neglect is not confined to impairments in reporting details of extrapersonal space. It can also be demonstrated as an impairment of the mental representation of a scene, either recently perceived or drawn from more remote past experience. A number of patients who have been reported with perceptual neglect also present with representational neglect (e.g. Bartolomeo et al., 1994; Bisiach & Luzzatti, 1978), in which only half of the scene represented in a visual image can be reported. Bisiach & Luzzatti asked their two patients to describe, from memory, the Cathedral Square in Milan, or the inside of a room in their home or work place, and to do so from a particular viewpoint (e.g. with their back to the Cathedral). They successfully reported details that would have been on the right from that viewpoint, but reported very few, if any, details on the left. This was not simply because of a general memory problem or because there are few items to report from those locations, because when the patients were asked to describe the scene from the opposite viewpoint (i.e. facing the Cathedral from the other end of the square), they reported details now on their imagined right that had previously been omitted, but failed to report items now on their imagined left that had been reported successfully from the previous imagined viewpoint. Moreover, since these were reports from familiar locations that had been experienced prior to their brain damage, the impairments could not be interpreted as resulting from impoverished perceptual input. Baddeley & Lieberman (1980) suggested that this pattern of impairments might reflect a deficit in the visuospatial system within working memory. This suggestion was reiterated by Bisiach (1993) in a general review of the patients who had been reported as showing both perceptual and representational neglect.

There have been a number of recent reports of patients who present with the representational deficit in the absence of any impairments in perceiving extrapersonal space (Beschin et al., 1997; Coslett, 1997; Denis et al., in press; Guariglia et al., 1993). These are in striking contrast with patients who show clear evidence of perceptual neglect in the absence of any difficulty in generating mental representations and in reporting, from memory, representations of familiar scenes or objects (Bartolomeo et al., 1994; Cantagallo & Della Sala, 1998; Coslett, 1997) or reporting details of recently formed mental representations derived from verbal descriptions of object layouts (Denis et al., 2002). These contrasting cases present a double dissociation between damage to a visual perceptual system and damage to a visuospatial representational system, indicating that these comprise dissociable systems in the healthy brain. This suggests further that the systems cannot be interdependent, as is suggested by the gateway hypothesis depicted in the upper part of Figure 13.1. Were the visuospatial representational system the primary means for initial processing of sensory input, then damage to the representational system might be expected to result in impairments of visual perception. Therefore, the fact that representational neglect can occur in the absence of perceptual neglect, and vice versa, presents a significant challenge for the suggestion that visual perception overlaps substantially with mental representation, as well as for the gateway hypothesis. However, it can be accommodated fairly comfortably with the model of working memory as a workspace, indicated in the lower part of Figure 13.1, by assuming that patients with pure perceptual neglect suffer from impaired activation of the knowledge base from sensory input in their neglected hemifield (arrows on the left of the figure) but have unimpaired access from working memory to previously stored knowledge (arrows on the right of the figure). Patients with pure representational neglect have intact activation of stored knowledge resulting from sensory input, allowing successful object identification or interpretation of a scene. However, because of damage to the part of the system that allows interaction between the knowledge base and working memory, their ability to retain or manipulate information in the absence of sensory input is impaired.

A more detailed discussion of a case of pure representational neglect was based on one of our own patients (Beschin et al., 1997). This patient, N.L., presented with a persistent unilateral neglect limited to visual imagery, with no difficulty in reporting the contents of visually perceived scenes. His deficits appeared in tasks that required access to familiar scenes, such as the Cathedral Square task (Bisiach & Luzzatti, 1978), or drawing from memory, as well as in tasks that required the retention of spatial information over varying delays, of novel scenes or pictures. In order to assess his visuospatial working memory system, we employed a task that has been widely used for this purpose in studies of healthy adults (e.g. Brooks, 1967; Logie et al., 1990; Quinn & Ralston, 1986). N.L. was first shown a printed matrix of sixteen squares arranged in four rows and four columns. The matrix was then removed and N.L. was presented with the description of a path around the matrix, starting in the second row and second column. He was asked to imagine the matrix and to generate a visual image of the pathway as it was being described. For example, in the first square put a 1, in the next square to the right put a 2, in the next square down put a 3, in the next square to the left put a 4 and so on. At the end of the sequence, he was to repeat the sequence of directions moved, based on his visual image. Control subjects in the Beschin et al. study could recall sequences, on average, of around five items. N.L.'s performance on this task was extremely poor, with correct recall of, on average, sequences of just two items. However when N.L. was allowed to look at the blank matrix instead of holding it in an image, his performance was within the normal range. That is, the deficit appeared only when performance relied solely on maintaining and generating a visual image. This difficulty was removed when he could gain external stimulus support through his intact perceptual system, demonstrating that his deficit is most likely in visuospatial working memory that is required for retaining the matrix pattern and for generating the image of the pathway described. This again speaks to the argument that the perceptual system and the representational system can cooperate, but are not as intimately related as is often assumed.

The phenomena linked with representational neglect appear very similar to those reported in cases of "hemi-amnesia" following experimental lesions in monkeys (Gaffan & Hornak, 1997a), and following partial removal in patients of the medial temporal lobe on the left or the right hemisphere (Gaffan & Hornak, 1997b; Hornak et al., 1997). The animals and patients appear to have no difficulty with perceiving and identifying objects. However, following presentation and removal of a complex scene, the animals or patients do not appear to remember that half of the scene which is contralateral to the lesion. That is, it appears that visuo-spatial working memory can be impaired for "half scenes", and further suggests that the mental representation in the healthy brain might be constructed as two mental "hemifields", which are normally experienced as a continuous image.

A particularly intriguing case of neglect was reported by Beschin et al. (2000). Their patient, Signor Piazza (fictitious name), suffered from two consecutive strokes, one in the right thalamus, and the other in the left parietal/occipital lobes. The left hemisphere stroke resulted in a severe perceptual neglect for material presented in the right hemispace, but with no problems in reporting information from memory of the right of previously experienced scenes. In contrast, the right hemisphere stroke resulted in a severe impairment of the patient's ability to report, from memory, details on the left side of a mental representation of a familiar scene, but his ability to perceive and identify objects presented on the left was intact. Moreover, when asked to recall the details of a picture presented either centrally or on the left, his performance was very poor. He could perceive from one hemispace without remembering what he perceived, and could image details in the other "mental" hemisphere from stored information in long-term memory without being able to perceive.

The gateway model of working memory would have great difficulty in accounting for the pattern of deficits found with patients such as N.L. and the "hemi-amnesia" cases, who have normal perceptual input while having demonstrable impairment of their visuospatial working memory system. The model would have even more difficulty accounting for the pattern observed for Signor Piazza, since intact perception resulted in virtually no trace in working memory. The perceptual system does not appear to rely on working memory for intact function. Therefore, working memory, and visuo-spatial working memory in particular, is best seen as a workspace that holds and manipulates information that is interpreted. In other words, perception activates information in long-term memory, and the products of that activation comprise the contents of working memory.

A possible caveat that might arise from basing our argument on neglect and associated disorders is that the impairments are lateralized, with only part of the visual field or of the mental representation disrupted. However, dissociations also arise in patients for whom the damage is bilateral, e.g. Madame D. (Bartolomeo et al., 1998) was severely impaired in identifying visually presented objects, regardless of the visual hemifield, but showed no difficulty in a range of tasks that required visual imagery derived from previously stored knowledge. This pattern contrasts sharply with the pattern of impairment and sparing in patient E.P. (Luzzatti et al., 1998), who had no difficulty in identifying objects in her visual field, but was unable to undertake any form of mental processing on images in the absence of perceptual input.

The pattern of impairment in the patients above has an additional implication, namely that the processes of perception and the cognitive functions that support imagery appear to be less closely linked than is commonly assumed (for discussion, see Denis & Kosslyn, 1999).

NEUROPSYCHOLOGICAL DISSOCIATIONS BETWEEN VISUAL WORKING MEMORY AND SPATIAL WORKING MEMORY

Thus far we have provided neuropsychological evidence to argue that visuospatial working memory is best viewed as an active workspace, rather than a passive memory store, and that it is somewhat distanced from perceptual processes. A range of patient data speak to the notion that visual and spatial working memory might be seen as two distinct but linked components of the cognitive system. For the purposes of this argument, it is important to clarify what we mean by "visual" as opposed to "spatial" properties. By "visual", we refer to the visual appearance of an object or scene, its colour, shape, contrast, size, visual texture and the location of objects relative to one another with respect to a particular viewpoint in a static array. By "spatial" we refer to pathways or sequences of movements from one location to another in the scene, or the processes of change in the perceived relative locations of objects that occur when an observer moves (physically or in a mental image) from one viewpoint to another. There is some ambiguity in the literature as to the use of the word "spatial", which sometimes is used to refer to relative locations or layouts of objects. In the description of neuropsychological impairments that we discuss, it should become clear that it is more useful to think of the "spatial" as referring to the dynamic properties of a scene or representation (e.g. Logie, 1995; Quinn & Ralston, 1986; Smyth & Pendleton, 1990).

The idea that visual and spatial working memory, according to our definitions above, comprise dissociable components of the cognitive system has been supported by a range of studies of healthy participants. For example, in healthy adults visual immediate memory tasks appear to be sensitive to disruption by secondary tasks different from those that disrupt immediate memory for movement sequences (Della Sala et al., 1999; Hecker & Mapperson, 1997; Logie & Marchetti, 1991; Tresch et al., 1993).

This separation in the representations held within working memory is sometimes thought to be similar to a distinction between perceiving object identity and object location derived from single-cell recording in studies of monkeys (Ungerleider & Mishkin, 1982). These studies demonstrated that monkeys attempting to identify an object rely on ventral/temporal pathways, while identifying the location of an object involves dorsal/parietal pathways. There are several problems with the apparently compelling link between the cognitive functions of visuospatial working memory and the neuroanatomical pathways associated with the "what" and the "where" of visual perception. One difficulty arises from the fact that the visual/location/movement distinction within working memory applies to the representation held and manipulated within working memory. It does not refer to the processes of perceiving and identifying an object and its current location. We have already argued that the processes of perception and the operation of working memory are less closely linked than has been widely assumed. Moreover, the ability to detect the location of objects and orientate attention towards them appears to be a fundamental, built-in property of the perception and attention systems. It can be performed by infants who have very limited knowledge and experience of objects. In stark contrast, object identification requires prior experience with objects, their associated labels, uses and properties. However, the information held in working memory incorporates these associated properties along with information about location, again arguing that a separation between "what" and "where" might be relevant for perception but not for visuospatial working memory.

A further problem is that the concept of the so-called "what" and "where" pathways is overly simplistic at a neuroanatomical level. There are multiple connections and pathways involved following initial processing of sensory input within the primary visual cortex (e.g. Hof et al., 1990; Stein, 1992; Zeki & Shipp, 1988; Zeki, cited in Della Sala, 1998). Moreover, the representations that we hold in working memory incorporate information from several sensory modalities (auditory, haptic, kinaesthetic, and possibly even olfactory and gustatory) in addition to elements of prior knowledge not immediately available from the perceived scene.

The apparent similarity has been taken further in linking visual appearance and location information with activation patterns in brain imaging studies using PET and fMRI. For example, Jonides et al. (1993) tested two groups of participants on visual and location immediate memory tasks while undergoing functional brain imaging using PET. In the location task, volunteers were briefly shown dots at random positions on a screen. After a short interval they were shown a visual cue and had to indicate whether or not the cue identified the location of one of the previously presented dots. In the visual task, participants were presented with unfamiliar shapes, and were later shown a second shape. The task was to indicate whether or not the initial and the comparison shape were identical. Both tasks were performed in a memory condition as described above, and in a perceptual condition, in which the target locations or shapes remained on the screen while the comparison took place. When subtracting out the perceptual conditions from the brain activation data, there were clearly different neuroanatomical networks associated with memory for object shape, primarily in the left hemisphere, and memory for object location, primarily in the right hemisphere. Jonides and colleagues (e.g. see Smith & Jonides, 1995) interpreted these different activation patterns as reflecting the operation of the "what" and "where" pathways, and equated different components of working memory with particular sensory input channels.

Subsequent studies with PET and fMRI (e.g. Courtney et al., 1996, 1998; Haxby et al., 2000) using different stimuli, such as faces, have likewise shown a neuroanatomical segregation between memory for object identity (primarily ventral prefrontal cortex), and memory for object location (primarily dorsal prefrontal cortex). It is striking that, although the neuroanatomical correlates show dissociations that echo those found in behavioural data, the locations involved appear to vary from study to study, possibly as a result of the use of rather different materials and procedures that have rather different general cognitive demands. In more recent studies (e.g. Owen et al., 1998; 1999; Petrides, 1996), the general cognitive demands of visual and location tasks were separately manipulated. The more demanding tasks appeared to be associated with the more dorsal areas, while the less demanding tasks were linked with activation in the more ventral areas. However, the same prefrontal areas in both hemispheres were associated with visual and location tasks when the overall task demands were equated, i.e. the neuroanatomical segregation appears to be associated with task demand, and not with a contrast between object identity and object location.

This conclusion raises an important issue with regard to the choice of tasks that are intended to explore distinctions among specialized cognitive resources. Tasks vary between studies, and rarely is there a formal task analysis carried out to ascertain the precise nature as well as the extent of the demands on the cognitive system. Tasks are described as "spatial" or "visual", but there is no guarantee that they are using the cognitive resources that are assumed, and volunteers may adopt a range of cognitive strategies, including verbal labelling of parts of a visual array, or visual encoding of a visually presented verbal sequence for recall (e.g. Logie et al., 2000). The pattern of brain activation will reflect the cognitive processes that volunteers bring to bear when performing each task, and the cognitive strategy that they choose could result in gross differences in the activation patterns observed. In purely behavioural studies, this difficulty is often addressed by testing large numbers of volunteers on multiple trials, so that individual differences in strategy are less influential in the overall data pattern. However, brain imaging studies often use rather small numbers of volunteers, and therefore individual differences in strategies could have a very large influence on the activation patterns observed (Logie et al., in press; Savage et al., 2001). Therefore, we have to be cautious when interpreting brain activation patterns, in the absence of converging evidence from other sources, such as behavioural data from healthy volunteers or from brain-damaged patients for whom the lesion site is known. The brain imaging data are consistent with the notion that locational and visual working memory might be separable, but it is important not to focus too literally on the specific neuroanatomical areas that appear to be active when people perform these tasks. Moreover, it remains unclear precisely what a spatial or visual working memory system might comprise. For example, a requirement to retain locational or movement information might be simply more demanding of cognitive resources than is retention of the visual appearance of an object or shape. The visual/spatial distinction could then reflect a visual memory system coupled with an amodal executive resource that supports retention of novel layouts and sequences of movements (Logie et al., 2001).

The dissociation between visual and spatial working memory has been reported also in studies of nonhuman primates (Goldman-Rakic, 1996; Meunier et al., 1997), electro-physiological studies in healthy adults (Ruchkin et al., 1997; MartinLoeches, 1997) and neuropsychological studies of brain-damaged patients, on whom we will focus.

The experimental dissociations found in healthy volunteers mirror different patterns of impairment and sparing of visual and spatial working memory function found in neuropsychological patients. The dissociations have been shown in contrasts between single cases as well as between groups of patients. The group studies have contrasted performance on a test of visual pattern memory (Phillips & Baddeley, 1971), with retention of targeted movement sequences (Milner, 1971), sometimes referred to as 'Corsi blocks' (Corsi, 1972). Pattern memory involves presenting a matrix of squares, half of which are filled in at random, while avoiding recognizable patterns, such as letter shapes or canonical shapes (see Figure 13.4). The participants are then required to retrieve the patterns. The Corsi task involves the experimenter pointing to a sequence of blocks arranged randomly on a board (see Figure 13.5). The participant has then to repeat from memory the sequence of movements in the same order. One of the group studies (Grossi et al., 1993) examined 39 Alzheimer patients and found two patients, one of whom showed very poor performance on visual pattern memory but had normal memory for retention of targeted movement sequences, while the other showed the converse pattern. Another group study (Della Sala et al., 1999) reported performance

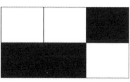

A   B

Figure 13.4   Examples of a simple (A) and a complex (B) matrix pattern, as used in the Visual Patterns Test (Della Sala et al., 1997)

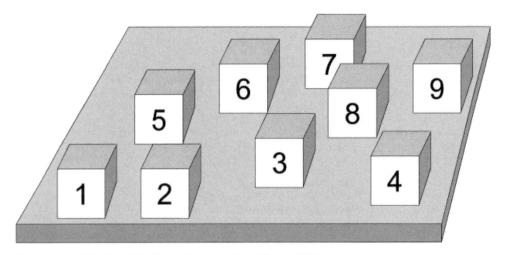

Figure 13.5   The Corsi block test (Corsi, 1972; Milner, 1971)

patterns for 69 patients. Two of the patients performed poorly on retention of targeted movements but were above the median on visual pattern memory, while a further patient showed
the converse. All three patients had a lesion in the left hemisphere.

   Across the whole group of patients, there was no clear link between right or left hemisphere damage and performance on either of the tasks. The same is true of other studies
reporting performance on versions of the Corsi block task. De Renzi & Nichelli (1975)
acknowledged that the size of the lesion, as measured by the presence or absence of a visual
field defect, "not the hemispheric side of the lesion, was a significant factor in impairing the
performance" (p. 346). The results were replicated in a second group study (De Renzi et al.,
1977), in which the authors reported that spatial span, as measured by a version of Corsi
blocks, was "affected by involvement of either side of the posterior region of the brain"
(p. 430). More recently, Feigenbaum et al. (1996) reported performance on a set of three
location and spatial manipulation tasks in a group of 40 neurosurgical patients. Patients with
right hemisphere lesions performed well below the levels observed for healthy controls on
all three tasks, whereas patients with left hemisphere lesions performed poorly overall on
only one of the tasks. However, overall performance levels between the two groups of patients did not differ statistically when they were compared with each other rather than with
controls.

   In summary, the behavioural data from the literature indicate a clear dissociation in
performance of the visual pattern memory and immediate memory for location or mental
spatial manipulation, but there is no clear lateralization of function for movement sequence
memory or for visual pattern memory. This again suggests that a simple mapping of well-
established behavioural dissociations onto neuroanatomy might be too simplistic.

   It is worth noting, too, that different patients could perform poorly on a task for very
different reasons. In addition to being open to the use of different strategies, most tests of
cognitive function require several components of cognition for successful performance, and
damage to any one component could disrupt overall performance on the tasks. For example,
the Corsi blocks task is often assumed to assess a spatial working memory system; however,
retaining a sequence of targeted movements requires memory for observed movement, and

for a pathway between objects. It might also be crucial whether the target positions are coded relative to body position or relative to one another (e.g. Postma et al., 2000). Depending on the nature of the cognitive impairment following brain damage, performance could be poor because of deficits in any or all of the above cognitive functions. Performance could also be poor because of the application of possible compensatory strategies that patients have developed as a result of their impairments. The compensatory strategy that they adopt may be suboptimal for the task concerned. In other words, Corsi blocks cannot be a "pure" test of a spatial working memory system, unless we consider that spatial working memory comprises visual and movement information as well as retention of sequential information, and a decision process that is required as participants choose which block to touch next in the sequence.

Despite the equivocal nature of the possible link between specific neuroanatomical sites and performance on spatial or visual tasks, a number of authors have interpreted patterns from group studies, as well as from single cases, as indicating that damage to the posterior areas of the right hemisphere are linked to poor performance on Corsi blocks and on other location/movement memory tasks (De Renzi, 1982; Nichelli, 1999; Vallar & Papagno, 1995). This contrasts with the brain-imaging data from healthy volunteers, described above, which on the whole indicated involvement of the prefrontal cortex in location memory tasks or in the mental representation of movement. This form of discrepancy is not unique. Analogous discrepancies are apparent when comparing the neuroanatomical correlates of word comprehension and reading in the healthy brain with those identified in neuropsychological patients (Abbott, 2001).

The dissociation between visual- and location/movement-based working memory gains support from the patterns of impairment observed in a number of individual case studies. Farah et al. (1988) reported patient L.H. who, as a result of a closed head injury in an automobile accident, suffered damage in both temporal/occipital areas, in the right temporal lobe and in the right inferior frontal lobe. He performed well on tasks concerned with memory for locations and for pathways, such as letter rotation, 3-D form rotation, mental scanning, and recalling a recently described pathway, but was severely impaired in his ability to remember colours, the relative size of objects and shapes of States in the map of the USA. A similar case was reported more recently by Wilson et al. (1999). Their patient, L.E., was a professional sculptress who, following systemic lupus erythematosus, resulting in diffuse damage to both the cortex and the white matter, was unable to generate visual images of possible sculptures, and had a severe visual short-term memory deficit. Her deficits included very poor performance on the Doors test (Baddeley et al., 1994), which involves recognizing a door amongst very similar distracters, and on retention of visual matrix patterns. However she could draw complex figures that did not rely on memory, and performed within the low normal range for Corsi block span.

Contrasting cases have been reported by Luzzatti et al. (1998) and by Carlesimo et al. (2001). The Luzzatti et al. patient, E.P., mentioned earlier, was affected by a slowly progressive deterioration of the brain and showed a focal atrophy of the anterior part of the right temporal lobe, including the hippocampus. Her performance was flawless on visual imagery tasks, such as making judgements about relative animal size, or the relative shapes or colours of objects. On the other hand, she was impaired on a range of topographical tasks, such as describing from memory the relative locations of landmarks in her home town, as well as in mentally manipulating the contents of images. A similar pattern was reported for the Carlesimo et al. (2001) patient, M.V., who had an ischaemic lesion in the cortical area supplied by the pericallosal artery affecting a diffuse area of the right dorsolateral frontal cortex. The patient performed within the normal range on judging from memory the shapes, colours and sizes of objects and animals, but had pathologically poor performance on mental rotation tasks, on Corsi block span, and on immediate memory for an imagined path around a matrix.

The contrasting patterns shown in the patients above echo dissociations that have been reported for patients with syndromes that are referred to as topographical amnesia and landmark agnosia (for review, see Aguirre & D'Esposito, 1999). Patients with topographical amnesia appear unable to generate or remember routes around towns that were previously very familiar, despite having no difficulty in recognizing familiar buildings and other landmarks. Landmark agnosia is characterized by an inability to recognize familiar buildings, but with an apparently intact ability to remember, generate and follow routes. One crucial point to note, however, is that in the literature describing such patients, the contrast is essentially between a *perceptual* impairment (landmark agnosia) and an impairment of a mental representation (topographical amnesia). Therefore, whether landmark agnosia might bear some similarities to the visual imagery disorders reported for patients L.H. (Farah et al., 1988) and L.E. (Wilson et al., 1999) remains an area for investigation.

The combination of visual and spatial working memory has a long history in neuropsychology as well as in cognitive psychology. A well-established syndrome in classic neuropsychology was known as Charcot–Wilbrand syndrome, and refers essentially to a deficit in visual imagery (for discussion, see Solms et al., 1996). Charcot & Bernard (1883; Young & Van De Wal, 1996) reported a patient, "Monsieur X", who had sudden onset of a clear deficit in forming visual images of objects, such as monuments and buildings, and of familiar people, such as close relatives. He also was unable to use an imagery mnemonic that he had used prior to the brain damage for remembering and reciting poetry. Wilbrand (1887) reported another patient, "Fräulein G", who suffered from an abrupt onset (probably a stroke) of a severe topographical amnesia, e.g. she was unable to report details of locations or routes in her native city of Hamburg, neither could she navigate around this city, in which she had lived for many years. Although the limited formal testing carried out allows only for an educated guess as to the nature of the problems faced by these patients, they do appear to comprise early examples of a dissociation between visual- and location/route-based imagery. However, the characteristic deficits in these patients were considered sufficiently similar for them to be accorded the same eponym. In an analogous fashion, visual and location/movement-based cognition have been combined under the concept of visuospatial working memory. The evidence now available allows us to consider that fractionation of the concept might be useful, theoretically and clinically.

VISUOSPATIAL WORKING MEMORY AND THE CENTRAL EXECUTIVE

Some of the early systematic attempts to assess general intellectual ability were faced with the challenge of devising tasks that did not depend on knowledge of a particular language. This situation arose at Ellis Island in the USA, when psychologists were given the task of assessing the mental abilities of potential immigrants, many of whom did not have English as their native language. Knox (1914)[1] devised and reported a "cube imitation task" that

---

[1] We are grateful to John T.E. Richardson for drawing our attention to the work of Howard A. Knox.

was designed to assess the general intellectual abilities of "illiterate aliens". The Knox test was not dissimilar to the Corsi block test, except that the blocks were presented in a row rather than randomly arranged. The test involved imitating a series of taps on the blocks in the correct sequence, as presented by the examiner. Clearly, what is now referred to as visuospatial cognition was, at that time, considered to be a property of general intelligence.

As discussed above, many current theories view cognition as comprising a range of abilities supported by separate systems, rather than a general intellectual ability, as assumed by Knox and his contemporaries. We have already discussed the range of cognitive functions that might support performance on what appear to be quite simple tasks. A recent line of investigation is beginning to point to the suggestion that temporary visual and spatial temporary memory functions are important, but not sufficient for performance of a range of visuospatial working memory tasks, many of which appear to require additional support from executive resources. For example, Salway & Logie (1995) reported that Brooks' (1967) matrix path memory performance (see earlier discussion) was more sensitive to disruption from a concurrent executive task (random generation of letters) than was performance on an equivalent verbal memory task. A recent series of experiments by Rudkin (2001) has suggested that retention and recall of sequences of movements in variations of the Corsi blocks task appears to be prone to disruption from concurrent random generation of numbers or of time intervals. Both sets of data indicate that the Brooks matrix task and Corsi blocks might not be such pure measures of specifically visuospatial functions as has been assumed. They have been useful in assessing the impact of specific brain damage, and of investigating what are now well-established dissociations between verbal and visuospatial working memory. More recently, the dissociation between Corsi block performance and memory for static matrix patterns has led to the suggestion of a dynamic component of visuospatial working memory supporting the former task, with a more passive component supporting the latter (Della Sala et al., 1999; Logie, 1995; Pickering et al., 2001; Vecchi et al., 2001).

This leads us back to the apparent anomalies between the patterns of brain activation and the lesion sites associated with visuospatial working memory deficits. It is increasingly clear that the tasks used to explore visuospatial working memory function are more complex than first thought, and a patient could fail on the basis of damage to a specialized memory system, or to the executive functions required by the tasks, or indeed any part of the neuroanatomical networks required for performance. Not all of the parts of these networks would necessarily be detected by the subtraction methods used in neuroimaging studies.

CONCLUDING REMARKS

We hope to have demonstrated that visuospatial working memory should be conceived as a theoretical construct in its own right, possibly open to further fractionation, and useful to account for a variety of symptoms shown by neuropsychological patients. Considering visuospatial working memory also as part of a mental workspace has the advantage that it specifies something of the way in which visually presented material can be made available together with other information in working memory. For example, if we see a slice of Gorgonzola cheese, the phonological representation of its name and the associated articulatory codes can form the basis of a trace in the phonological loop, allowing rehearsal and overt articulation of the word. Similarly, on hearing the word, the visual and spatial properties of the word "Gorgonzola" become available, allowing generation of a temporary representation of the visual form of the word which could then be written. Semantic information about cheese, and this cheese in particular, could also be activated, along with a representation of its distinctive odour and taste. The central executive could also draw on all of the available information to carry out further processing on the properties of the visual or phonological representations to allow spelling of the word, its segmentation, as well as imagining the actions associated with consumption of the food to which the word refers.

Future research in visuospatial working memory and its deficits might address the possible resolution of the ambiguity between neuroimaging and neuropsychology findings, the uncertainties with regards to cognitive demands of a range of tasks commonly used in clinical settings, as well as its theoretical development within the context of more general theories of cognition.

REFERENCES

Aguirre, G.K. & D'Esposito, M.D. (1999). Topographical disorientation: a synthesis and taxonomy. *Brain*, **122**, 1613–1628.

Anderson, R.A. & Helstrup, T. (1993). Visual discovery on mind and on paper. *Memory and Cognition*, **21**, 283–293.

Atkinson, R.C. & Shiffrin R.M. (1968). Human memory. A proposed system and its control processes. In K.W. Spence & J.T. Spence (eds), *The Psychology of Learning and Motivation*, Vol. 2 (pp. 89–105). New York: Academic Press.

Baddeley, A.D., Della Sala, S. & Spinnler, H. (1991). The two-component hypothesis of memory deficit in Alzheimer's disease. *Journal of Clinical and Experimental Neuropsychology*, **13**, 372–380.

Baddeley, A.D., Emslie, H. & Nimmo-Smith, I. (1994). *The Doors and People*. Bury St Edmunds: Thames Valley Test Company.

Baddeley, A.D., Grant, W., Wight, E. & Thomson, N. (1975). Imagery and visual working memory. In P.M.A. Rabbitt & S. Dornic (eds), *Attention and Performance V* (pp. 205–217). London: Academic Press.

Baddeley, A.D., & Lieberman, K. (1980). Spatial working memory. In R.S. Nickerson (ed.), *Attention and Performance* (pp. 521–539). Hillsdale, NJ: Erlbaum.

Baddeley, A., Logie, R., Bressi, S. et al. (1986). Senile dementia and working memory. *Quarterly Journal of Experimental Psychology*, **38A**, 603–618.

Barquero, B. & Logie, R.H. (1999) Imagery constraints on quantitative and qualitative aspects of mental synthesis. *European Journal of Cognitive Psychology*, **11**, 315–333.

Bartolomeo, P., Bachoud-Lévi, A.C., de Gelder, B. et al. (1998). Multiple-domain dissociation between impaired visual perception and preserved mental imagery in a patient with bilateral extrastriate lesions. *Neuropsychologia*, **36**, 239–249.

Bartolomeo, P., D'Erme, P. & Gainotti, G. (1994). The relationship between visuo-spatial and representational neglect. *Neurology*, **44**, 1710–1714.

Basso, A., Spinnler, H. Vallar, G. & Zanobio, E. (1982). Left hemisphere damage and selective impairment of auditory verbal short-term memory: a case study. *Neuropsychologia*, **20**, 263–274.

Beschin, N., Basso, A. & Della Sala, S. (2000) Perceiving left and imaging right: dissociation in neglect. *Cortex*, **36**, 401–414.

Beschin, N., Cocchini, G., Della Sala, S. & Logie, R.H. (1997) What the eyes perceive the brain ignores: a case of pure unilateral representational neglect. *Cortex*, **33**, 3–26.

Beyn, E.S. & Knyazeva, G.R. (1962). The problem of protoagnosia. *Journal of Neurology, Neurosurgery and Psychiatry*, **25**, 154–158.

Bisiach. E. (1993). Mental representation in unilateral neglect and related disorders: the twentieth Bartlett memorial lecture. *Quarterly Journal of Experimental Psychology*, **46A**, 435–461.

Bisiach, E. & Luzzatti, C. (1978). Unilateral neglect of representational space. *Cortex*, **14**, 129–133.

Bluck, R.S. (1961). *Plato's Meno*. Cambridge: Cambridge University Press.

Brooks, L.R. (1967) The suppression of visualisation by reading. *Quarterly Journal of Experimental Psychology*, **19**, 289–299.

Buxbaum, L.J. & Coslett, H.B. (1994). Neglect of chimeric figures: two halves are better than a whole. *Neuropsychologia*, **32**, 275–288.

Cantagallo, A. & Della Sala, S. (1998). Preserved insight in an artist with extrapersonal neglect. *Cortex*, **34**, 163–189.

Carlesimo, G., Perri, R., Turriziani, P. et al. (2001). Remembering what but not where: independence of spatial and visual working memory. *Cortex*, **36**, 519–534.

Charcot, J.-M. & Bernard, D. (1883). Un cas de suppression brusque et isolée de la vision mentale des signes et des objects (formes et couleurs). *Le Progrès Médicale*, **11**, 568–571.

Conrad, R. & Hull, A.J. (1964). Information, acoustic confusion and memory span. *British Journal of Psychology*, **55**, 429–432.

Corsi, P.M. (1972). Human Memory and the Medial Temporal Region of the Brain. Unpublished Thesis, McGill University, Montreal.

Coslett, H.B. (1997). Neglect in vision and visual imagery: a double dissociation. *Brain*, **120**, 1163–1171.

Courtney, S.M., Petit, L., Maisog, J.M. et al. (1998). An area specialized for spatial working memory in the human frontal cortex. *Science*, **279**, 1347–1351.

Courtney, S.M., Ungerleider, L.G., Keil, K. & Haxby, J.V. (1996). Object and spatial visual working memory activates separate neural systems in human cortex. *Cerebral Cortex*, **6**, 39–49.

Della Sala, S. (1998) *The Visual Brain in Action*, by A.D. Milner and M.A.Goodale. Book review. *Neuropsychological Rehabilitation*, **8**, 459–464.

Della Sala, S., Gray, C., Baddeley, A. et al. (1999) Pattern span: a tool for unwelding visuo-spatial memory. *Neuropsychologia*, **37**, 1189–1199.

Della Sala, S., Gray, C., Baddeley, A. & Wilson, L. (1997). *The Visual Patterns Test: A New Test of Short-term Visual Recall*. Bury St Edmunds: Thames Valley Test Company.

Denis, M., Beschin, N., Logie, R.H. & Della Sala, S. (2002). Visual perception and verbal descriptions as sources for generating mental representations: evidence from representational neglect. *Cognitive Neuropsychology*, **19**, 97–112.

Denis, M. & Kosslyn, S.M. (1999). Scanning visual mental images: a window on the mind. *Current Psychology of Cognition*, **18**, 409–465.

De Renzi, E. (1982). *Disorders of Space Exploration and Cognition*. Chichester: Wiley.

De Renzi, E., Faglioni, P. & Previdi, P. (1977). Spatial memory and hemisphere locus of lesion. *Cortex*, **13**, 424–433.

De Renzi, E. & Nichelli, P. (1975). Verbal and non-verbal short-term memory impairment following hemispheric damage. *Cortex*, **11**, 341–353.

Ellis, A.X., Della Sala, S. & Logie, R.H. (1996). The bailiwick of visuo-spatial working memory: evidence from unilateral spatial neglect. *Cognitive Brain Research*, **3**, 71–78.

Farah, M.J., Hammond, K.M., Levine, D.N. & Calvanio, R. (1988). Visual and spatial mental imagery: dissociable systems of representation. *Cognitive Psychology*, **20**, 439–462.

Farmer, E.W., Berman, J.V.F. & Fletcher, Y.L. (1986). Evidence for a visuo-spatial scratch-pad in working memory. *Quarterly Journal of Experimental Psychology*, **38A**, 675–688.

Feigenbaum, J.D., Polkey, C.E. & Morris, R.G. (1996). Deficits in spatial working memory after unilateral temporal lobectomy in man. *Neuropsychologia*, **34**, 163–176.

Finke, R. & Slayton, K. (1988) Explorations of creative visual synthesis in mental imagery. *Memory and Cognition*, **16**, 252–257.

Gaffan, D. & Hornak, J. (1997a). Visual neglect in the monkey: representation and disconnection, *Brain*, **120**, 1647–1657.

Gaffan, D. & Hornak, J. (1997b). Amnesia and neglect: beyond the Delay–Brion system and the Hebb synapse. *Philosophical Transactions of the Royal Society, London, B*, **352**, 1481–1488.

Goldman-Rakic, P.S. (1996). The prefrontal landscape: implications of functional architecture for understanding human mentation and the central executive. *Philosophical Transaction of the Royal Society, London, B*, **351**, 1445–1453.

Grossi, D., Becker, J.T., Smith, C. & Trojano, L. (1993). Memory for visuospatial patterns in Alzheimer's disease. *Psychological Medicine*, **23**, 63–70.

Grube, G.M.A. (1997). Meno. In G.M. Cooper (ed.), *Plato: Complete Works* (pp. 870–897). Indianapolis, IN: Hackett.

Guariglia, C., Padovani, A., Pantano, P. & Pizzamiglio, L. (1993). Unilateral neglect restricted to visual imagery. *Nature*, **364**, 235–237.

Haxby, J.V., Petit, L., Ungerleider, L.G. & Courtney, S.M. (2000). Distinguishing the functional roles of multiple regions in distributed neural systems for visual working memory. *NeuroImage*, **11**, 145–156.

Hecker, R. & Mapperson, B. (1997). Dissociation of visual and spatial processing in working memory. *Neuropsychologia*, **35**, 599–603.

Hof, P.R. Bouras, C., Constantinidis, J. & Morrison J.H. (1990.)Selective disconnection of specific visual association pathways in cases of Alzheimer's disease presenting with Balint's syndrome. *Journal of Neuropathology & Experimental Neurology*, **49**, 168–184.

Hornak, J., Oxbury, S., Oxbury, J. et al. (1997). Hemifield-specific visual recognition memory impairments in patients with unilateral temporal lobe removals. *Neuropsychologia*, **35**, 1311–1315.

Jonides, J., Smith, E.E., Koeppe, R.A. et al. (1993). Spatial working memory in humans as revealed by PET. *Nature*, **363**, 623–225.

Knox, H.A. (1914). A scale, based on the work at Ellis Island, for estimating mental defect. *Journal of the American Medical Association*, **62**, 741–747.

Kosslyn, S.M. (1980). *Image and Mind*. Cambridge, MA: Harvard University Press.

Levett, M.J. & Burnyeat, M.F. (1997). *Theaetetus*. In G.M. Cooper (ed.), *Plato: Complete Works* (pp. 157–234). Indianapolis, IN: Hackett.

Logie, R.H. (1986) Visuo-spatial processing in working memory. *Quarterly Journal of Experimental Psychology*, **38A**, 229–247.

Logie, R.H. (1995). *Visuo-spatial Working Memory*. Hove: Erlbaum.

Logie, R.H., Della Sala, S., Laiacona, M., Chalmers, P. & Wynn, V. (1996). Group aggregates and individual reliability: the case of verbal short-term memory. *Memory and Cognition*, **24**, 305–321.

Logie, R.H., Della Sala, S., Wynn, V. & Baddeley, A.D. (2000) Visual similarity effects in immediate verbal serial recall. *The Quarterly Journal of Experimental Psychology*, **53A**, 626–646.

Logie, R.H., Engelkamp, J., Dehn, D. & Rudkin, S. (2001). Actions, mental actions, and working memory. In M. Denis, R.H. Logie, C. Cornoldi et al. (eds), *Imagery, Language and Visuo-spatial Thinking* (pp. 161–184). Hove: Psychology Press.

Logie, R.H. & Marchetti, C. (1991). Visuo-spatial working memory: visual, spatial or central executive? In R.H. Logie & M. Denis (eds), *Mental Images in Human Cognition* (pp. 105–115). Amsterdam: North Holland.

Logie, R.H., Venneri, A., Della Sala, S. et al. (in press). Brain activation and the phonological loop: the impact of rehearsal. *Brain & Cognition*.

Logie, R.H., Zucco, G. & Baddeley, A.D. (1990). Interference with visual short-term memory. *Acta Psychologica* **75**, 55–74.

Luzzatti, C., Vecchi, T., Agazzi, D. et al. (1998) A neurological dissociation between preserved visual and impaired spatial processing in mental imagery. *Cortex*, **34**, 461–469.

Marcel, A.J. (1998). Blindsight and shape perception: deficit of visual consciounsness or of visual function? *Brain*, **121**, 1565–1588.

Marshall, J.C. & Halligan, P.W. (1988). Blindsight and insight in visuo-spatial neglect. *Nature*, **336**, 766–767.

MartinLoeches, M. (1997) Encoding into working memory of spatial location, color, and shape: electrophysiological investigations. *International Journal of Neuroscience*, **91**, 277–294.

McGlinchey-Berroth, R., Milberg, W.P., Verfaellie, M. et al. (1993). Semantic priming in the neglected visual field: evidence from lexical decision task. *Cognitive Neuropsychology*, **10**, 79–108.

Meunier, M., Bachevalier, J. & Mishkin, M. (1997). Effects of orbital frontal and anterior cingulate lesions on object and spatial memory in rhesus monkeys. *Neuropsychologia*, **7**, 999–1015.

Milner, B. (1971). Interhemispheric differences in the localization of psychological processes in man. *British Medical Bulletin*, **27**, 272–277.

Miyake, A. & Shah, P. (1999). *Models of Working Memory*. New York: Cambridge University Press.

Nichelli, P. (1999) Visuospatial and imagery disorders. In L. Pizzamiglio & F. Denes (eds), *Handbook of Clinical and Experimental Neuropsychology* (pp. 453–478). Hove: Psychology Press.

Nolan, C. (2000). *Memento* [film]. Todd S. and Todd J. (Producers).

Owen, A.M., Stern, C.E., Look, R.B. et al. (1998) Functional organization of spatial and nonspatial working memory processing within the human lateral frontal cortex. *Proceedings of the National Academy of Sciences of the USA*, **95**, 7721–7726.

Owen, A.M., Herrod, N.J., Menon, D.K. et al. (1999). Redefining the functional organisation of working memory processes within human lateral prefrontal cortex. *European Journal of Neuroscience*, **11**, 567–574.

Pearson, D.G., Logie, R.H. & Gilhooly, K.J. (1999). Verbal representation and spatial manipulation during mental synthesis. *European Journal of Cognitive Psychology*, **11**, 295–314.

Petrides, M. (1996) Specialized systems for the processing of mnemonic information within the primate frontal cortex. *Philosophical Transactions of the Royal Society, London, B*, **351**, 1455–1461.

Phillips, W.A. & Baddeley, A.D. (1971). Reaction time and short-term visual memory. *Psychonomic Science*, **22**, 73–74.

Pickering, S.J., Gathercole, S.E., Lloyd, S. & Hall, M. (in press). Development of memory for pattern and path: further evidence for the fractionation of visual and spatial short-term memory. *Quarterly Journal of Experimental Psychology*.

Postma, A., Sterken, Y., de Vries, L. & de Haan, E.H.F. (2000). Spatial localization in patients with unilateral posterior left or right hemisphere lesions. *Experimental Brain Research*, **134**, 220–227.

Quinn, J.G. & Ralston, G.E. (1986). Movement and attention in visual working memory. *The Quarterly Journal of Experimental Psychology*, **38A**, 689–703.

Robertson, I.H. & Halligan, P.W. (1999). *Spatial Neglect: A Clinical Handbook for Diagnosis and Treatment*. Hove: Psychology Press.

Roediger, H.L. III & Goff, L.M. (1999). Memory. In W. Bechtel & G. Graham (eds), *A Companion to Cognitive Science* (pp. 250–264). Oxford: Blackwell.

Ruchkin, D.S., Johnson, R., Grafman, J. et al. (1997). Multiple visuo-spatial working memory buffers: evidence from spatio-temporal patterns of brain activity. *Neuropsychologia*, **35**, 195–209.

Rudkin, S. (2001). Executive Processes in Visual and Spatial Working Memory Tasks, Unpublished Phd Thesis, University of Aberdeen, UK.

Saffran, E.M. & Marin, O.S.M. (1975). Immediate memory for word lists and sentences in a patient with deficient auditory short-term memory. *Brain and Language*, **2**, 420–433.

Salway, A.F.S. & Logie, R.H. (1995). Visuospatial working memory, movement control and executive demands. *British Journal of Psychology*, **86**, 253–269.

Savage, C.R., Deckersbach, T., Heckers, S. et al. (2001). Prefrontal regions supporting spontaneous and directed application of verbal learning strategies: evidence from PET. *Brain*, **124**, 219–231.

Shallice, T. & Warrington, E.K. (1970). Independent functioning of verbal memory stores: a neuropsychological study. *Quarterly Journal of Experimental Psychology*, **22**, 261–273.

Smith, E.E. (1999). Working Memory. In R.A. Wilson & F.C. Keil (eds), *The MIT Encyclopedia of the Cognitive Sciences* (pp. 888–890). Cambridge, MA: MIT Press.

Smith, E.E. & Jonides, J. (1995). Working memory in humans: neuropsychological evidence. In M.S. Gazzaniga (ed.), *The Cognitive Neurosciences* (pp. 1009–1020). Cambridge, MA: MIT Press.

Smyth, M.M. & Pendleton, L.R. (1990). Space and movement in working memory. *Quarterly Journal of Experimental Psychology*, **42A**, 291–304.

Solms, M., Kaplan-Solms, K. & Brown, J.W. (1996). Wilbrand's case of "mind-blindness". In C. Code, C.-W. Wallesch, Y. Joanette & A.R. Lecours (eds), *Classic Cases in Neuropsychology* (pp. 89–110). Hove: Psychology Press.

Stein, J.F. (1992). The representation of egocentric space in the posterior parietal cortex. *Behavioral and Brain Sciences*, **15**, 691–700.

Störig, P. (2000). Mind and body. The properties of living organisms. *Proceedings of the Pontifical Academy of Sciences*, **95**, 121–140.

Tresch, M.C., Sinnamon, H.M., & Seamon, J.G. (1993). Double dissociation of spatial and object visual memory: evidence from selective interference in intact human subjects. *Neuropsychologia*, **31**, 211–219.

Ungerleider, L.G. & Mishkin, M. (1982). Two cortical visual systems. In D.J. Ingle, R.J.W. Mansfield & M.S. Goodale (eds), *The Analysis of Visual Behavior* (pp. 549–586). Cambridge, MA: MIT Press.

Vallar, G. & Papagno, C. (1995). Neuropsychological impairments of short-term memory. In A.D. Baddeley, B.A. Wilson & F.N. Watts (eds), *Handbook of Memory Disorders* (pp. 135–165). Chichester: Wiley.

Vallar, G., Rusconi, M.L. & Bisiach, E. (1994). Awareness of controlesional information in unilateral neglect: effects of verbal cueing, tracing, and vestibular stimulation. In C. Umiltà & M. Moscovitch (eds), *Attention and Performance XV* (pp. 377–391). Cambridge: MIT Press.

Vallar, G. & Shallice, T. (1990). *Neuropsychological Impairments of Short-term Memory*. Cambridge: Cambridge University Press.

Vecchi, T., Phillips, L.H. & Cornoldi, C. (2001). Individual differences in visuo-spatial working memory. In M. Denis, R.H. Logie, C. Cornoldi et al. (eds), *Imagery, Language and Visuo-spatial Thinking* (pp. 29–58). Hove: Psychology Press.

Warrington, E.K. & Rabin, P. (1971). Visual span of apprehension in patients with unilateral cerebral lesions. *Quarterly Journal of Experimental Psychology*, **23**, 423–431.

Weiskrantz, L. (1986). *Blindsight*. Oxford: Clarendon.

Wilbrand, H. (1887). *Sie Seelenblindheit als Herderscheinung und ihre Beziehung zur Alexie und Agraphie*. Wiesbaden: Begmann.

Wilson, B., Baddeley, A.D. & Young, A.W. (1999). L.E., a person who lost her "mind's eye". *Neurocase*, **5**, 119–127.

Young, A.W., Hellawell, D.J. & Welch, J. (1992). Neglect and visual recognition. *Brain*, **115**, 51–71.

Young, A.W. & van de Wal, C. (1996). Charcot's case of impaired imagery. In C. Code, C.-W. Wallesch, Y. Joanette & A.R. Lecours (eds), *Classic Cases in Neuropsychology* (pp. 31–44). Hove: Psychology Press.

Zeki, S. & Shipp, S. (1988). The functional logic of cortical connections. *Nature*, **335**, 311–317.

CHAPTER 14

Disorders of Semantic Memory

Julie Snowden

Cerebral Function Unit, Greater Manchester Neuroscience Centre, UK

Semantic memory refers to a person's conceptual knowledge about the world. It includes knowledge of the meaning of words, objects and other stimuli perceived through the senses, as well as a rich abundance of facts and associated information. Semantic knowledge about Paris includes recognizing the verbal label as meaning a place, and as referring to the capital of France. It also includes knowing where Paris is located on a map of France, knowing that the Eiffel Tower, Arc de Triomphe and Notre Dame are situated there, knowing that the river Seine runs through it, knowing that it is where the storming of the Bastille took place, where most people speak French, where some people smoke Gaulloise cigarettes, where people drive on the right, etc. Semantic memory is immensely important because it constitutes the knowledge base that allows us to communicate, use objects, recognize foods, react to environmental stimuli and function appropriately in the world.

In recent years there has been increased clinical recognition of neurological patients who exhibit impaired semantic memory. Although in some patients this constitutes one component of a multifaceted cognitive disorder, in other patients, semantic memory impairment is highly selective and other aspects of cognition are notably spared. The remarkable nature of such circumscribed semantic memory loss has been conveyed eloquently by Patterson & Hodges (1995). Such patients provide the gateway to improved understanding of semantic memory. Their theoretical importance stems from the fact that semantic memory does not break down in an all-or-none fashion. Patients may know some words but not others, may recognize one exemplar of an object but not another, and may retain partial information about a concept while other information is lost. Identification of the underlying principles that govern what is lost and retained has clear implications for how information is organized and represented. Moreover, semantic memory deficits may occur in the context of apparently well preserved day-to-day memorizing, the converse of the situation in classical amnesia. This apparent double dissociation seems, at least at first sight, to provide support for the distinction between semantic and episodic memory (Tulving, 1972) and permits the opportunity to address the relationship between the two.

The Handbook of Memory Disorders. Edited by A.D. Baddeley, M.D. Kopelman and B.A. Wilson
© 2002 John Wiley & Sons, Ltd.

NEUROLOGICAL DISORDERS THAT GIVE RISE TO SEMANTIC MEMORY IMPAIRMENT

Semantic memory impairment is not the exclusive province of a single diagnostic entity. This is because deficits in neuropsychological function depend on the topography of brain lesions, not the underlying aetiology. The diverse conditions associated with impairments of semantic memory include degenerative brain disorders, herpes simplex encephalitis, head trauma and temporal lobe epilepsy, a common underlying feature being disease or injury to the temporal neocortex.

Semantic Dementia

Semantic dementia might reasonably be regarded as the prototypical semantic memory disorder. It is a relatively rare clinical syndrome, resulting from focal degeneration of the temporal neocortex and associated with a non-Alzheimer pathology, in which there is a circumscribed and progressive loss of semantic knowledge. The name "semantic dementia" was introduced in 1989 to encapsulate the multimodal nature of the semantic disorder (Snowden et al., 1989). The designation has been adopted by others (Hodges, et al., 1992a; Saffran & Schwartz, 1994) and criteria for the disorder have been outlined (Neary et al., 1998). Patients with selective semantic loss, described in seminal papers by Warrington (1975) and Schwartz et al. (1979), would now be regarded as examples of semantic dementia. Patients commonly present to medical attention complaining of problems in "memory". However, in keeping with the fact that medial temporal lobe structures are relatively preserved, patients are not amnesic in the classical sense. They remember appointments and day-to-day events and find their way around without becoming lost. Typically, their presenting difficulty is in remembering the meaning of words or in recognizing the faces of acquaintances. On examination they exhibit profound naming difficulties and make semantically related errors (e.g. "dog" for rabbit). They also have difficulty understanding words and may frequently ask what words mean (e.g. "rabbit, what's a rabbit?"). They commonly demonstrate difficulty in recognizing people's names and faces. Although patients' initial symptoms may appear to be predominantly in the verbal or non-verbal domain, semantic deficits are not confined to a single modality. Deficits may include a difficulty in recognizing nonverbal environmental sounds, such as the ring of a doorbell or telephone, visual percepts such as objects, and tactile, gustatory and olfactory stimuli (Snowden et al., 1996b).

It should be emphasized that the problem lies not in the detection or perception of stimuli, but in ascribing meaning to stimuli that are perceived normally. Thus, patients have no difficulty in hearing the sound of the doorbell; they no longer know what that sound signifies. They have no difficulty determining whether two odours are the same or different, yet are unable to match them to the appropriate product in an array. Similarly, they can distinguish the sweet, sour and bitter tastes of orange, lemon and grapefruit juice, yet perform at chance level in matching the taste with the real fruit. They can reproduce accurately line drawings of objects that they do not recognize.

Patients with semantic dementia speak fluently and effortlessly, in grammatically correct sentences. They do not actively search for words or make phonological errors: they simply speak within the constraints of the vocabulary available to them. Over time patients' vocabulary progressively narrows, so that eventually only a few stereotyped phrases remain and patients may show a total absence of language comprehension. Similarly, they may fail to recognize even close family members and common objects. Patients are commonly insightful, and at least in the early stages may spontaneously attempt to relearn words and objects. They may study the dictionary or use a notebook to write words or draw objects that they no longer know. Such self-initiated study typically conveys little practical benefit, because these stimuli, which the patient is capable of remembering by rote, no longer have the connotative associations that are fundamental to understanding.

Semantic dementia is theoretically important because of its highly circumscribed nature. Moreover, the progressive nature of the disorder enables within-subject study of how knowledge breaks down over time.

Alzheimer's Disease

Alzheimer's disease is a primary degenerative brain disease, which leads to progressive impairment of cognitive function. The initial symptom is typically of memory failure (classical amnesia), reflecting early pathological changes in the medial temporal lobes, but patients also characteristically develop perceptuo-spatial and language impairments reflecting atrophy of the temporoparietal cortices. Semantic deficits may be present in Alzheimer's disease, although invariably in the context of other cognitive deficits. It is because of the potential compounding effect of patients' additional difficulties that Alzheimer's disease is a less ideal model than semantic dementia for theoretical understanding of semantic memory. There is nevertheless an extensive literature on semantic impairment in Alzheimer's disease, reflecting the high prevalence and hence clinical importance of this form of dementia. The focus of such studies has largely been to determine whether patients' poor performance on tests of naming or verbal fluency constitute a genuine loss of information from semantic memory or a failure to retrieve information that is potentially available. Some authors (Hodges et al., 1992b, Martin, 1992; Salmon et al., 1999) argue that deficits reflect degradation of knowledge, whereas others favour an interpretation in terms of impaired access (Nebes, 1992; Astell & Harley, 1998; Nebes & Halligan, 1999; Ober & Shenaut, 1999). The continuing debate (e.g. see Ober, 1999) and lack of overall consensus in the literature in part reflects the difficulty in dissecting subcomponents of a multifaceted cognitive disorder. It is likely also to reflect (a) individual differences (Hodges & Patterson, 1995) and (b) stage of disease (Bayles et al., 1999). Some patients show more obvious structural and functional changes in the temporal neocortex than others, so that some patients will have genuine semantic loss, whereas others will not. Moreover, there is spread of pathological change over the course of the disease, so that early changes in the medial temporal lobes may extend over time to the temporal neocortex.

Herpes Simplex Encephalitis

Whereas semantic dementia and Alzheimer's disease are progressive disorders arising from intrinsic changes in brain cells, herpes simplex encephalitis (HSE) is an acute, nonprogressive illness. The viral agent attacks principally the frontotemporal regions, and although about one-third of patients make a full recovery, others are left with permanent residual deficits, reflecting damage to the medial temporal lobes, temporal neocortex and/or the frontal lobes. Semantic deficits occur in those patients with temporal neocortical damage (Pietrini et al., 1988; Sartori & Job, 1988; Warrington & Shallice, 1984). Those deficits may be relatively selective, although they are more usually accompanied by classical amnesia and/or frontal executive and behavioural changes. Hemispheric asymmetry, with greater damage to the left or right temporal lobe, is common. Herpes simplex encephalitis is theoretically important because it may give rise to circumscribed semantic deficits in which certain categories of knowledge appear to be impaired more than others.

Head Trauma

Head trauma, which most commonly results from road traffic accidents, may involve damage to the temporal lobes and, as a consequence, may give rise to deficits in semantic memory. Because the insult to the brain is external and does not respect functional system boundaries, deficits rarely have the degree of selectivity seen in intrinsic brain disorders, such as semantic dementia. Nevertheless, semantic memory deficits may occasionally be a salient presenting feature (Bub et al., 1988; Laiacona et al., 1993; Wilson, 1997).

Temporal Lobe Epilepsy

Semantic memory deficits have been reported in patients with temporal lobe epilepsy and those who undergo anterior temporal lobectomy (Wilkins & Moscovitch, 1978; Ellis et al., 1989) as a surgical treatment for temporal lobe epilepsy. Because surgical excision is selective and restricted to one hemisphere, semantic deficits are typically relatively subtle and not of the magnitude seen in semantic dementia, in which there is extensive and bilateral temporal lobe degeneration.

CONTEMPORARY ISSUES IN NEUROPSYCHOLOGICAL SEMANTIC MEMORY RESEARCH

Several questions have dominated recent research. For the most part these reflect putative dissociations in knowledge observed in patients with semantic memory breakdown.

1. *Superordinate vs. subordinate information.* Is taxonomic category information more resistant to disruption than information about the properties or attributes of an object? Might a patient know that an elephant is an animal, while not knowing that it is large, has a trunk, has tusks, etc? If so, what are the implications for the organization of semantic memory?
2. *Category specificity.* Can semantic memory impairment be confined to specific conceptual categories? Might a patient understand the significance of a hammer, microphone or shuttlecock, but not of an elephant or rabbit? If so, what are the implications for the way categories of information are represented in the brain? Which categories of information are dissociable?

3. *Modality effects.* Can semantic memory deficits be modality-specific? Might one patient understand the significance of a picture of an elephant, while not understanding the verbal label "elephant", and another patient understand the verbal label and not the picture? Do the data support the notion of a single or multiple semantic systems?

4. *Semantic and autobiographical memory relationships.* What is the relationship between semantic and autobiographical memory? Can autobiographical memories support semantic information? What are the implications for the distinction between semantic and episodic memory? Are there separable memory systems?

5. *Context-dependency.* Might a patient understand a word or recognize an object in one context but not another? If so, what are the implications for semantic memory models?

Superordinate vs. Subordinate Information

It is a common clinical observation that semantically impaired patients may classify a word or picture correctly in terms of broad taxonomic category, yet have difficulty discriminating between category exemplars (Warrington, 1975; Warrington & Shallice, 1984; Hodges et al., 1992a). A patient may state that a rabbit is an animal but not know how it differs from a dog or horse, and will make coordinate category errors in naming (e.g "dog" for rabbit). Our own patient, E.B. (Snowden et al., 1996b), was profoundly impaired at matching animal and food words with the corresponding picture. Nevertheless, for all animal words she selected an animal picture and for all food words a food picture, suggesting knowledge of word meaning sufficient to enable superordinate category classification. This apparently greater vulnerability to disruption of subordinate categories has been interpreted by some (Warrington, 1975; Shallice, 1988) as favouring a hierarchical model of semantic memory. In the influential hierarchical network model of Collins & Quillian (1969), it would be assumed that lower levels of the hierarchical tree, representing information about properties or attributes, are most vulnerable to disruption and are damaged first, the higher, superordinate level the last to be lost. Findings from a longitudinal study of naming errors in a semantic dementia patient (Hodges et al., 1995) would be largely consistent with this hierarchical account. Over repeated testing sessions, the patient made progressively fewer coordinate category responses (e.g. "dog" for lion) and more superordinate (e.g. "animal" for lion) and cross-category naming errors (e.g. "vehicle" for fish). However, the hierarchical model as stated does not fully account for patients' pattern of breakdown (Warrington, 1975; Saffran & Schwartz, 1994). According to the model, access from a lower to higher level of the hierarchy requires traversing intervening levels. Knowledge that a robin is an animal is accessed through the intermediate level "bird". A robin should not be correctly classified as an animal if it cannot first be classified as a bird. Yet, patients with semantic disorder do classify robins as animals, without knowing that they are birds.

Alternative explanations (Rapp & Caramazza, 1989, 1993; Tippett et al., 1995) have been advanced, based on a model of semantic memory that assumes concepts to be represented by a network of semantic features (Smith et al., 1974). According to Rapp & Caramazza, if some of those features are lost, then the remaining impoverished information will be better able to support broad (e.g. categorical) rather than fine-grained (i.e. exemplar) distinctions. Impoverished feature knowledge may be sufficient to differentiate an animal from a vegetable, but not a dog from a cat. There is independent evidence that superordinate level information *per se* may not be relatively spared. Funnell (1995) found that a patient's ability to define words did not depend upon the level of generality of the word meaning (i.e. category, basic level or subordinate property). Similarly, Tyler & Moss (1998), using a semantic priming and verification task in a longitudinal study of a patient with semantic dementia, found no support for the view that property information is affected before higher level, category information. Some characteristics of semantic dementia patients' performance are frankly at odds with the notion of a superordinate category superiority. Our own patient, K.E., was better at recognizing her own objects than other examples of the same object (Snowden et al., 1994). Similarly, our patient W.M. (Snowden et al., 1995) understood general words, such as "licence" only in narrow, personalized terms (i.e. "licence" means her own driving licence). Far from having general or broad conceptual understanding, their semantic knowledge appeared to have become limited to the particular, to their own specific experience of the world. Nevertheless, those same patients who demonstrate narrowed, personalized conceptual understanding, showed the usual pattern of errors on naming tasks: e.g. "animal" for horse; or "dog" for horse. We would argue, in line with Rapp & Caramazza, that superordinate category information is not inherently less vulnerable to disruption in a degraded semantic memory system. The patient's overall concept of animals is as severely degraded as of particular exemplars. However, the severely impoverished information available is sufficient to allow a horse to be recognized as an animal (as opposed to a food or an article of clothing), but not sufficient to allow it to be distinguished from a dog.

Category Specificity

In 1984 Warrington & Shallice described four patients recovering from herpes simplex encephalitis who showed a disproportionate impairment in their ability to recognize living things and food compared to inanimate objects. A similar pattern of findings has been reported in other postencephalitic patients (Pietrini et al., 1988; Sartori & Job, 1988; Silveri & Gainotti, 1988; Laiacona et al., 1997) and in some semantic dementia patients (Basso et al., 1988; Breedin et al., 1994; Cardebat et al., 1996; Snowden et al., 1996b). Nevertheless, the notion of category-specific impairments has been controversial. Opponents have argued that category dissociations arise artefactually, as a result of differences in the frequency, familiarity and visual complexity (Stewart et al., 1992; Funnell & Sheridan, 1992) of test stimuli belonging to biological and nonbiological categories. Picture stimuli of inanimate objects are typically high-familiarity items, whereas those of animals are low in familiarity. Members of biological categories are often more visually similar than those of man-made categories. Indeed, normal superiority for man-made artefacts has been demonstrated by some authors (Capitani et al., 1994).

It is certainly the case that some apparent category dissociations disappear when factors such as frequency and familiarity are controlled. However, in other patients the dissociation persists (Sartori et al., 1993a; Sartori et al., 1993b; Farah et al., 1996; Funnell & De Mornay Davies, 1996; Moss et al., 1997). Moreover, category dissociations are not invariably in the same direction. Superior rather than inferior performance for biological categories has been demonstrated in some patients (Warrington & McCarthy, 1983, 1987; Sacchett & Humphreys, 1992) and an identical set of test materials has been shown to elicit opposing patterns of performance in different patients (Hillis & Caramazza, 1991). Such findings provide a persuasive argument that category differences should not be dismissed as mere artefact. A further compelling argument comes from the consistency between pattern of deficit and location of brain lesions (Gainotti et al., 1995). Inferior knowledge of biological categories has invariably been reported in patients with temporal lobe damage, whereas inferior performance for inanimate objects is associated with extensive damage to the frontoparietal lobes of the left hemisphere and occurs in conjunction with global or nonfluent aphasia.

If category dissociations do occur, then how can they be best explained? Alternative explanations have been advanced.

Functional vs. Sensory Attributes of Meaning

The term "category specificity" is in a sense a misnomer. It conveys the impression of exclusive involvement of one category and absolute sparing of another, which is rarely the case. Category differences are typically relative. This suggests that taxonomic category *per se* may not be the crucial factor determining patients' knowledge. A salient view, advanced by Warrington & McCarthy (1987) and Warrington & Shallice (1984), is that category dissociations result from differences in the properties that define a concept, reflecting differences in the sensory processing channels through which information was initially acquired. The conceptual distinction between two inanimate objects, such as a glass and a vase, derives largely from their different functions. Physical properties, such as shape or colour, have relatively little role. Conversely, animals and foods are distinguished predominantly on the basis of sensory properties such as colour, shape, texture, taste and smell. That is, biological categories are weighted towards sensory properties and inanimate objects towards functional properties. A disruption to knowledge about sensory attributes would result in a disproportionately severe impairment for animals compared to household objects, whereas disruption to knowledge about functional attributes would have the opposite effect. This distinction between sensory and functional aspects of knowledge accounts for the otherwise anomalous finding that patients with impaired biological category knowledge typically show relatively preserved knowledge of the biological category of body parts and impaired knowledge of the nonbiological categories of musical instruments and precious stones. Functional properties are salient conceptual attributes of body parts, and sensory properties of musical instruments and precious stones. Although not all authors have framed distinctions in precisely the same terms, distinctions drawn between perceptual and functional (Sartori & Job, 1988), visual and verbal (Silveri & Gainotti, 1988) and perceptual and associative (Chertkow et al., 1992) knowledge essentially parallel the sensory/functional distinction of Warrington and colleagues.

This account of category dissociations is attractive for several reasons. It avoids the seemingly phrenological notion that different categories are stored in separate parts of the brain. Moreover, it makes neuroanatomical sense. The link between perceptual/sensory attributes and the anterior temporal lobes is consistent with the established role of the ventral pathways in the processing of visual information and for object recognition (Mishkin et al., 1983). It has been speculated that the anterior regions of the inferior temporal cortex may be involved in networks at the interface between perception and language (Breedin et al., 1994). The link between functional information and the language areas of the left hemisphere is consonant with the more abstract nature of function information, which may be more closely allied with language. The functional–sensory account is consistent with a distributed model of semantic memory (Allport, 1985), which assumes that properties of an object are encoded across a number of different subsystems or attribute domains (for an excellent discussion of category specificity and implications for models of semantic memory, see Saffran & Schwartz, 1994).

Domain Specificity

Although the functional–sensory distinction has been widely acknowledged as central to understanding category dissociations, there is not always a clear association between category differences and relative disruption to visual and associative–functional information (Caramazza & Shelton, 1998; Lambon Ralph et al., 1998). Some authors have rejected the functional–sensory account and hold that conceptual knowledge is truly organized by category (Caramazza & Shelton, 1998). The argument is that distinct domains of knowledge have developed as an adaptation to evolutionary pressures, which have resulted in allocation of distinct neural networks to the processing of each knowledge domain. On this account, category-specific deficits should selectively impair all information pertaining to the affected domain, while sparing all information pertaining to other knowledge domains. This is certainly sometimes the case, although it is not invariably so. Disproportionate impairment for perceptual over functional properties may be present within as well as across category domains (Farah et al., 1989; De Renzi & Lucchelli, 1994; Gainotti & Silveri, 1996).

Feature Correlation

An intriguing question is why biological category inferiority should be associated more often with herpes simplex encephalitis than semantic dementia, given that both damage the anterior temporal lobes, while sparing traditional language areas. It is plausible that the magnitude of the semantic disorder might be relevant, on the grounds that semantic deficits are commonly less severe in herpes simplex encephalitis than in semantic dementia. An account of category dissociations (Moss et al., 1997; Moss & Tyler, 2000) that differs fundamentally from the functional–sensory and domain-specificity accounts emphasizes the importance of overall severity of the semantic disorder. These authors demonstrated, in a longitudinal study of a patient with an unspecified form of dementia, a crossover from an initial deficit more marked for living things to a later deficit more marked for nonliving concepts. The authors interpreted these data in terms of a connectionist model of conceptual knowledge (Durrant-Peatfield et al., 1997), which assumes concepts to be represented in a network of semantic features. Properties that are shared amongst different concepts and are intercorrelated will be most resilient to disruption. In the case of nonliving concepts, such as artefacts, form (e.g. serrated edge) and function (e.g. can cut) are strongly intercorrelated, giving an initial advantage. However, when damage is more profound and properties more degraded, and the system must rely only on shared properties, then artefacts will be disadvantaged because their shared properties are fewer in number and less densely intercorrelated than those of living things.

   The possible effect of severity warrants further study. However, a number of factors suggest that it is unlikely to provide a general explanation for category dissociations. There is to date no evidence that semantic dementia patients who show an initial disproportionate impairment for biological concepts show a crossover with progression of disease. More-over, semantic dementia and postencephalitic patients typically exhibit a level of semantic impairment that is substantially more profound than that of the patient described by Moss et al. and so, according to their model, ought to exhibit greater deficit for artefacts than living things, which is contrary to what occurs. Furthermore, the severity explanation can-not account for the strong association between pattern of category loss and anatomical site of damage.

Category Impairments: Beyond the Biological–Nonbiological Distinction

Reported category dissociations have focused most frequently on the biological–nonbiological dimension. However, selective impairments of knowledge are not confined to the distinction between knowledge of animals and vegetables on the one hand and knowledge of artefacts on the other. In formulating their interpretation of category-specific impairments, Warrington and colleagues (McCarthy & Warrington, 1988; Warrington & Shallice, 1984; Warrington & McCarthy, 1987) recognized that further fractionations ought to be possi-ble. Fruits, such as an orange and grapefruit, are distinguished by colour, taste and smell, whereas shape is relatively unimportant. By contrast, the distinction between two animals, such as a dog and a horse, depends heavily on shape information, little on colour and smell, and not at all on taste. Some inanimate objects are manipulable, whereas others are not. If the relative weighting on different properties of information underlie category differences then a range of dissociations ought to be possible, reflecting disrupted to particular sensory or nonsensory attributes and relative sparing of others. Indeed, many reported dissociations can be readily accommodated within the functional–sensory framework, which emphasizes a concept's processing requirements. Other dissociations have been interpreted as evidence of domain-specific or category-based representation of knowledge.

Abstract vs. Concrete Concepts

Abstract words would be regarded by most people as more difficult than concrete words to acquire and understand. Yet some patients with semantic disorder show better understanding of abstract than concrete concepts (Warrington, 1975; Warrington & Shallice, 1984; Breedin et al., 1994). The patient A.B. described by Warrington (1975), for example, defined the term "supplication" as, "making a serious request for help"; the term "arbiter" as, "He is the man who tries to arbitrate. Produce a peaceful solution"; and the term "pact" as "friendly agreement". By contrast, his responses to the terms "hay", "poster", "needle" and "acorn" were "I've forgotten", "No idea" or "Don't know". This reversal of the normal advantage for concrete concepts has been interpreted (Breedin et al., 1994) with reference to the functional–sensory distinction, in terms of the qualitative differences between abstract and concrete concepts. Whereas much knowledge about concrete concepts is acquired directly through the senses, knowledge of abstract concepts is acquired in the context of language through their use in sentences and relationship with other concepts. If perceptual–sensory components of semantic representations are disrupted, then this will lead to a disproportionate impairment of concrete concepts, which are partly defined by their sensory properties, compared to abstract concepts, which are devoid of sensory attributes. It is relevant in this regard that abstract word superiority has invariably been demonstrated in patients with temporal lobe pathology, and has been linked also to superior knowledge of artefacts over living things.

Object Knowledge vs. Object Use

Apraxia is the inability to carry out purposeful actions in the absence of weakness or sensory loss. At first sight, consideration of apraxia may seem inappropriate in the context of semantic memory disorders. However, inability to carry out skilled movements can arise for conceptual reasons (De Renzi & Luchelli, 1988; Ochipa et al., 1989; Rothi et al., 1991). A patient may fail to salute or demonstrate the action of combing hair on command because of loss of knowledge of how to carry out the required action. For patients with severe semantic impairment, such as semantic dementia, loss of object knowledge typically entails both an inability to recognize and describe the function of an object, as well as an inability to demonstrate its use. A patient who does not recognize a razor also cannot demonstrate its use by action pantomime. Nevertheless, dissociations between functional knowledge and use can sometimes occur. Moreaud et al. (1998) described a patient who was impaired in his ability to manipulate objects that he could recognize and name. By contrast, a postencephalitic patient described by Sirigu et al. (1991) could manipulate appropriately objects that he could not recognize. Buxbaum et al. (1997) reported a patient with semantic dementia who performed almost normally on single-object use in a naturalistic setting, despite severe loss of functional and associative object knowledge. A contrasting patient, with a frontal executive disorder, showed the opposite effect. In a more recent report Buxbaum et al. (2000) described two apraxic patients with large frontoparietal lesions who showed impaired "manipulation" knowledge about objects, despite relatively preserved "function" knowledge. Importantly, evaluation of that knowledge was independent of patients' gesture production. The patients were simply asked to state which two of three objects were similar, (a) in their manner of manipulation (e.g. typewriter, piano, stove), or (b) in their function (e.g. record player, radio, telephone). The dissociation between manipulation knowledge (knowing how) and function knowledge (knowing what for) is consistent with the formulation of Warrington and colleagues. That is, properties of an object relating to manipulation are lost, whereas properties pertaining to the object's function are retained.

People and Places

Impaired knowledge of famous people, places and monuments is a common feature of semantic memory disorder. Occasionally, it constitutes a relatively selective deficit. An epilepsy patient following temporal lobectomy was reported to show a selective loss of memory for people, famous animals, buildings and product names (Ellis et al., 1989). A postanoxic patient (Kartsounis & Shallice, 1996) demonstrated a specific difficulty in identifying historical figures and famous landmarks. A postencephalitic patient (McCarthy et al., 1996) exhibited defective visual recognition and verbal knowledge of famous buildings and landmarks. A patient reported by Kay & Hanley (1999) showed selective impairment for biographical knowledge of people. A patient reported by Miceli et al. (2000) showed a selective loss of knowledge for names of familiar people. Thus, concepts that represent unique entities (e.g. famous people) may be lost, while concepts that represent nonunique entities (e.g. animals) are spared.

There are compelling evolutionary arguments why specialized neural networks might exist dedicated to the recognition and classification of people, and some authors (Miceli et al., 2000) favour the domain-specific account of their patient's selective loss of knowledge about people. It is less easy to argue why specialized networks should have evolved for places or monuments. Moreover, conceptual loss may be confined to one modality: the patient described by Kartsounis & Shallice (1996) had a difficulty identifying people and landmarks specifically in the visual modality.

Single or Multiple Semantic Systems

There is not an invariable correspondence between impairments of meaning across input modality. A patient may have difficulty understanding the meaning of an object name and yet be able to recognize the corresponding object (Lauro-Grotto et al., 1997; McCarthy & Warrington, 1988). Conversely, a patient may fail to recognize pictures of objects but have no difficulty understanding the corresponding word (McCarthy & Warrington, 1986; Warrington & McCarthy, 1994). In our own series of patients with semantic dementia, patients with more marked left temporal lobe atrophy frequently have greater difficulty in understanding words than drawings of objects, whereas patients with more marked right temporal lobe atrophy may show the opposite effect. One interpretation of such dissociations is that there exist separate modality-specific semantic systems (McCarthy & Warrington, 1988), in which information is stored separately for different input modalities. Dissociations between input modalities are, however, rarely absolute. In most cases, both words and pictorial stimuli are affected, albeit to differing degrees. Moreover, some authors have demonstrated strong correlations between knowledge elicited from pictures and words (Lambon Ralph et al., 1999), which would not be predicted if such knowledge were stored in separate systems. An opposing position is that the semantic system is a unitary amodal storage system, accessible from each input modality (Caramazza et al., 1990; Humphreys & Riddoch, 1988). The finding of superior comprehension for pictures than words has been ascribed to the more direct mapping between surface form and meaning in the case of pictures (Chertkow & Bub, 1990; Lambon Ralph & Howard, 2000): pictures give direct clues to meaning, whereas words are arbitrary labels. The converse finding, of superior knowledge of words than pictures, has been attributed to visual processing deficits occurring at a peripheral, presemantic level (Caramazza et al., 1990; Humphreys & Riddoch, 1988).

The multiple-system account, in its strong form (Warrington & McCarthy, 1994), lacks parsimony as it requires reduplication of information within separate modality-specific systems. A less strong view (Lauro-Grotto et al., 1997) is that the semantic system is a multimodal network, in which different areas are accessed by each modality and store modality-specific information. Under normal circumstances it is assumed that the various components of the net are interconnected, allowing retrieval of the entire representation from any input channel. However, in pathological conditions one or more components of the net can be preferentially damaged, giving rise to the observed dissociations.

The interpretation of modality effects, like category effects, remains controversial. Aside from the notion of one or many systems, the underlying dispute centres on whether semantic knowledge is represented amodally or with regard to input modality. From a purely intuitive point of view, it might be reasonable to argue that one's conceptual representation of an object might be independent of the modality through which it is experienced. On the other hand, a challenge to an amodal view is how knowledge of the smell of peppermint or new-mown grass might be represented, if not by recourse to the modality of smell!

The Relationship between Semantic and Autobiographical Memory

Semantic memory, as originally defined (Tulving, 1972), is information that is typically acquired early in life, shared by individuals within a culture and not tied to a particular temporospatial context. One can know that Paris is the capital of France without remembering when that information was acquired. One can know that a dog is an animal without recalling an individual experience or episode involving dogs. This decontextualized knowledge contrasts with episodic memory, which is context-bound and specific to each individual. The observation of semantic impairments in patients with good day-to-day memory (Snowden et al., 1996b) and the demonstration of double dissociations in performance on semantic and episodic memory tasks (Graham et al., 1997, 2000) appear to provide support for the notion of separable memory systems. The distinction is reinforced by links to different anatomical regions: semantic memory impairment is associated with temporal neocortical damage and episodic memory impairment with medial temporal lobe dysfunction.

Although semantic knowledge must inevitably initially be acquired through individual personal experiences, once acquired it has traditionally been assumed to represent a relatively stable knowledge base, independent of ongoing personal experiences. Feature models of semantic memory reflect this largely static view. Nevertheless, data from patients with semantic memory disorders suggest that traditional assumptions may need to be re-evaluated.

Despite severe impairment on formal tests of naming and word comprehension, patients with semantic dementia sometimes use surprisingly low-frequency vocabulary in their conversation (Snowden et al., 1994). A patient who could not name a flower, pencil or scissors, on visual confrontation or from verbal description, nonetheless uttered sentences such as, "I help prepare the chalice for the Eucharist" and "Anne is catering manager at the agricultural college" (Snowden et al., 1995). How can such an anomaly be explained? We observed that conversation in semantic dementia patients invariably revolves around their personal experience. We hypothesized that concepts relating to patients' daily lives might be available precisely because of their link to preserved experiential autobiographical memories, i.e. in a system that is becoming progressively degraded, what might remain may be those components of knowledge that are linked to individual experiential memories.

Support for this view came from a series of studies that investigated the influence of autobiographical experience on semantic knowledge (Snowden et al., 1994, 1995, 1996a). Patients with semantic dementia showed superior recognition of the names of personal acquaintances than celebrity names (Snowden et al., 1994), a finding not found in control subjects with classical amnesia. Patients better understood place names to mean a place if those place names had personal relevance. A patient, K.E., recognized her own objects significantly better than other examples of the same object. Moreover, her knowledge of an object's function was constrained by her personal usage of that object. She identified a jug as a receptacle for flowers, in keeping with its function in her own home, but she had no idea of alternative possible uses. Another patient identified a clothes peg as the object that she used for closing breakfast cereal packets, but she had no idea of its prototypical use in relation to the drying of clothes. A study of word comprehension (Snowden et al., 1995) yielded complementary findings. A patient's understanding of words that she used entirely appropriately in conversation was found to be limited to the specific personal context in which she used them, e.g. she understood the word "licence" to refer to her own driving licence, but she had no general understanding of licence beyond this specific usage. She appeared to retain that aspect of meaning which pertained to her own current personal experience, but had lost general conceptual knowledge outside her own direct experience. These findings, which complement those of others (De Renzi et al., 1987; Le Moal et al., 1999), were interpreted as evidence that personal experiential memories support patients' semantic knowledge. The findings have fuelled debate as to whether this experience-based knowledge should be considered truly semantic (Graham et al., 1997, 1999a; Snowden et al., 1999). Certainly, it does not conform to traditional notions of semantic memory, which, by definition, imply abstracted knowledge, divorced from specific episodes. On the other hand, it could be argued that knowing that Paris is a place constitutes a semantic fact, regardless of how that information is recalled. Moreover, perhaps in nonneurologically impaired individuals too, recall of semantic facts draws on personal episodes more often than is commonly assumed.

The autobiographical experiential advantage demonstrated in name, place and object recognition (Snowden et al., 1994, 1996a) was most marked for information of current personal relevance. One patient, for example, had no difficulty recognizing faces and names of current acquaintances, including her solicitor and a local shopkeeper, yet showed no recognition of the faces and names of family and friends from the past, including her own (now deceased) parents. To recognize a solicitor of new acquaintance but not one's own parents suggests that the autobiographical effect is not simply one of overall familiarity. The relationship to current daily experience appears critical. The current experience advantage extends, moreover, to recall of specific autobiographical incidents as well as semantic facts (Snowden et al., 1996a; Graham & Hodges, 1997). Patients recall contemporary better than past incidents and events, suggesting a reversal of the temporal gradient of retrograde memory seen in classical amnesia.

We interpreted the findings as evidence of a dynamic, interactive semantic memory system. We proposed that, under normal circumstances, concepts are continually updated through direct experience and abstract neocortical representations of knowledge are altered by the activity of limbic structures. When the neocortical system is damaged, as in semantic dementia, then patients are increasingly dependent upon direct experiential memories, subserved by medial temporal lobe structures, and concepts are limited to the particular exemplars of their own recent experience. The implication is that there is not a simple one-to-one correspondence between temporal neocortical and medial temporal memory systems and semantic and episodic memory (Snowden et al., 1999). Contextualized information, mediated by the medial temporal lobes, includes semantic facts as well as discrete episodes. By contrast, abstracted information, linked to temporal neocortical function, includes past episodes as well as semantic knowledge.

These data complement those found in amnesic patients. Amnesic patients, whose semantic memory for previously acquired information is preserved, nevertheless show impaired learning of new semantic information (Gabrieli et al., 1988; Wilson & Baddeley, 1988). This suggests that acquisition of both semantic and episodic information is dependent upon the functioning of medial temporal lobe structures, and that reported dissociations between preserved semantic and impaired episodic information reflect sparing of old memories rather than fundamentally separate memory systems.

New Learning in Semantic Dementia

If the medial temporal lobes have a role in new learning of semantic information, then it should be possible to demonstrate new learning in semantic dementia patients in whom medial temporal lobe function is preserved. In their daily lives, patients do show evidence of new learning (Snowden et al., 1996b). One patient, on moving house, had no difficulty in learning the names of new neighbours. Another patient had no difficulty learning to use an electric toaster for the first time, despite initial lack of recognition. A patient, reported by Graham et al. (1999b), was able to relearn lost vocabulary. Nevertheless, retention is unstable and information is lost without constant use and rehearsal. Patients retain information only so long as it is linked to ongoing daily experience.

Script Theory and Semantic Memory Loss

The data on semantic–autobiographical interactions point to limitations of cognitive models that represent concepts purely in terms of a static network of properties of words and objects. There are other facets of performance in semantic dementia patients that are not easily accommodated by traditional semantic memory models. One of our patients, L.B., was consistently unable to name a pair of glasses on confrontation. In comprehension tests he would comment, "Glasses, what's glasses? I don't know what that is". He could not match the spoken word with the real object or provide descriptive or gestural information. To all intents and purposes he had total loss of knowledge of the word "glasses". Nevertheless, when intending to read or carry out close work he would remark "I'll just go and get my glasses", would proceed to find his glasses and use them appropriately. Parallel findings have been reported in relation to object use. Objects that fail to be recognized in an artificial test setting may be used normally in a naturalistic setting (Snowden et al., 1994; Buxbaum et al., 1997; Lauro-Grotto et al., 1997; Funnell, 2001).

Why should L.B. fail to name and understand a word in one setting, yet produce that same word with ease in another? Models that view semantic memory in terms of abstracted word and object meanings would have difficulty explaining the context effect. According to the autobiographical experiential account (Snowden et al., 1994), it would be argued that L.B.'s concept of glasses has become progressively diminished and is now limited to his own particular pair of glasses and his own personal use of them. However, L.B. produces the word glasses *only* in the context of expressing the intention of putting on his own glasses. He does not use or understand the word in other circumstances, even when applied to his own glasses. Context appears to be critical. An important development that builds on the experiential account of Snowden et al. comes from Funnell (2001), who noted that the personal experiences that appear to support patients' residual semantic knowledge are typically recurrent personal events rather than discrete episodes. Funnell interpreted performance in semantic dementia patients with reference to script theory (Schank & Abelson,

1977; Schank, 1982), which proposes that people build up schematas or scripts, representing commonly experienced activities or events. Scripts record a particular set of actions that take place in a particular context, with a particular set of objects and in relation to a particular goal. In the case of L.B., the goal-directed activity of putting on glasses would constitute a script that is frequently repeated in his daily life. The verbal expression of his intention would also constitute a well-rehearsed script. Funnell argued that meaning is represented along a continuum of levels of abstraction, from the most context-bound (i.e. tied to specific scripts) to the most abstracted. When semantic memory breaks down, the most context-free levels of knowledge are most compromised. Nevertheless words and objects may continue to be used and recognized within the context of a specific event script. It would be argued that L.B. retains the goal-directed script of putting on glasses in order to read, supporting his continued use of the term "glasses" in that context. However, he has lost knowledge of glasses at an abstract, context-free level.

Scripts are assumed to form the basic level of a dynamic memory system that learns from personal experience. Script theory, like the interactive autobiographical–semantic account, suggests that knowledge is continually updated through personal experience. It assumes that there is not a fundamental dichotomy between a semantic and episodic memory system. Rather, meaning is represented at different levels of generalization in a continuum that connects semantic and episodic characteristics. At one end of the continuum, information is entirely embedded in the physical context of a personal experience. At the other, it is entirely abstracted from context. Complementary findings come from studies of childhood conceptual development (Nelson, 1985; Barrett, 1986), which suggest that in the early stages of development children use words and understand the functions of objects only in the context of particular routines, and cannot generalize to other situations. The implication is that these event scripts form the basic mechanism for concept learning and the foundation upon which abstracted levels of meaning derive.

It remains to be seen whether script theory can provide a full and principled account of the deficits in semantic memory-disordered patients. Its importance lies in the fact that it moves beyond the notion of semantic memory as a static storehouse of words, represented by a set of abstract properties.

THE NEURAL BASIS FOR SEMANTIC MEMORY

The strong association between disorders of the temporal lobes and semantic memory impairments emphasizes the critical role of temporal neocortex in semantic memory. There is converging evidence to implicate the anterior temporal lobes in particular, and the inferior temporal gyri specifically. In semantic dementia, brain imaging shows atrophy of the temporal pole (e.g. Mummery et al., 2000) and particularly involvement of the inferior temporal gyrus (Breedin et al., 1994; Cardebat et al., 1996; Mummery et al., 2000). Autopsy examination (Snowden et al., 1992; Snowden et al., 1996b) has shown atrophy of the inferior and middle temporal gyri with notable sparing of the superior temporal gyri, including Wernicke's area, and medial temporal structures. In herpes simplex encephalitis patients, there is evidence of damage to the inferior temporal neocortex (Pietrini et al., 1988; Sartori & Job, 1988; Silveri & Gainotti, 1988; Sartori et al., 1993a). In a patient with semantic impairment following radionecrosis (Kapur et al., 1994), damage was reported in the anterior inferior temporal cortex. The medial temporal lobes were relatively spared. Similarly, a semantic disorder resulting from a ruptured aneurysm of the left posterior communicating artery (Sartori et al., 1994), was also attributed to damage to the inferior temporal gyrus.

It is undoubtedly the case that both left and right hemispheres contribute to semantic memory function, and that the most severe semantic deficits occur in patients with bilateral disease. Some authors have placed greater emphasis on the importance of the left temporal lobe than the right (Mummery et al., 2000), on the grounds that many patients with semantic dementia show an asymmetrical distribution of atrophy affecting the left side more than the right. However, in our experience, patients with an equally severe semantic memory deficit may exhibit more marked right than left temporal lobe atrophy. Patients with semantic dementia, whose presenting symptom is in naming and word comprehension, typically show more marked left than right temporal atrophy. Conversely, patients in whom face recognition deficits predominate show more marked atrophy in the right temporal lobe. The association between face recognition impairments and the right temporal lobe has also been demonstrated by others (Evans et al., 1995). A patient described by McCarthy et al. (1996) with right temporal lobe damage was particularly impaired in his recognition of pictures of famous buildings and landmarks, suggesting that hemispheric differences may contribute to category effects. The precise role of the two hemispheres remains to be explored.

Notwithstanding the central importance of temporal neocortex, it would be incorrect to assume that semantic memory is localized to this single brain region. The literature on category-specific impairments draws attention to the contribution of diverse brain regions. Those who consider that knowledge is organized by category would argue that specific cortical regions are dedicated to particular domains or categories of knowledge. By contrast, the functional–sensory account would suggest that concepts are represented in a distributed fashion across cortical sites, each representing information about specific attributes. The temporal ventral pathways are particularly important for the processing of visual–sensory information and, according to the functional–sensory account, for the representation of sensory knowledge. By contrast, the frontoparietal lobes are assumed to contribute more to knowledge of functional and abstract linguistic properties. Manipulation knowledge is linked to premotor areas, and topographical knowledge with the parietal lobes. Support for this distributed account has come from functional imaging studies using PET (Martin et al., 1996; Chao et al., 1999). The brain regions active during object identification were found to depend upon the intrinsic properties of the object presented. Thus, for example, naming animals activated occipital regions involved in early visual processing, in addition to the temporal lobes, whereas naming tools activated the left premotor area, involved in object manipulation.

These neocortical sites appear particularly important for knowledge about abstract properties of words and objects. However, the notion that personal experiential memories may support some semantic information, and that event scripts provide the basic mechanism for concept acquisition, suggest a putative role in semantic knowledge, both for the medial temporal lobes, important for event memory, and the frontal neocortex. Goal-directed, purposeful actions are known to be dependent on the frontal lobes, and goal-directed activities break down in patients with frontal lobe lesions (Buxbaum et al., 1997; Godbout & Bouchard, 1999; Schwartz et al., 1995). Patients with semantic dementia, by contrast, frequently have preserved frontal lobe function and are able to establish goals. Aspects of semantic information embedded within a goal-driven action script, subserved by frontal lobe functions, might be preserved, while abstracted knowledge is lost.

CONCLUSION

The last two decades have seen substantial advances in the understanding of semantic memory. Much of this progress can be attributed to the research study of patients with acquired disorders of semantic memory. It has to be said that there is as yet no single consensual account of semantic memory function. Rather, the data derived from patients is gradually constraining both our understanding of what constitutes semantic knowledge and how that knowledge is represented in the brain.

Traditional models of semantic memory have typically viewed semantic knowledge as an encyclopaedia of word and object meanings, represented by a set of properties or attributes. This framework has evident value in accounting for some of the distinctions seen in patients with impaired semantic memory; between words and objects, between different categories of information. Moreover, the notion of different properties reflecting different processing channels is consistent with a distributed model of concept representation and has intuitive appeal. However, patients exhibit patterns of deficit that are sometimes counterintuitive, creating challenges for traditional models. The finding that patients' residual semantic knowledge is influenced by its relevance to personal experience counters the notion of semantic memory as a static store of abstract knowledge, divorced from autobiographical experience. It suggests a more dynamic system, in which there is continual interaction between personal experience and semantic knowledge. Semantic memory is, moreover, as observed by Kintsch (1980), more than an isolated set of word and object meanings. Patients' understanding is influenced by context. A word may be understood and used appropriately in the context of a particular sentence but not in isolation. An object may be recognized in a real-world setting, but not in the artificial setting of a clinical test. Such findings suggest that meaning must be represented, at least to some degree, at levels other than individual word or object. Script theory, which proposes a continuum of levels of meaning, provides a coherent explanation of the context effect. It shows promise, too, in accounting for the clinical observation that patients who perform at floor level on clinical referential tests of word and object meaning may nevertheless function relatively independently in their daily lives.

Patients with disorders of semantic memory provide a natural model for the understanding of semantic memory. Future work needs to go beyond the study of properties of words or objects, and examine patients' real-world knowledge and the conditions under which it breaks down.

REFERENCES

Allport, D.A. (1985). Distributed memory, modular subsystems and dysphasia. In S.K. Newman & R. Epstein (eds), *Current Perspectives in Dysphasia* (pp. 207–244). Edinburgh: Churchill Livingstone.

Astell, A.J. & Harley, T.A. (1998). Naming problems in dementia: semantic or lexical? *Aphasiology*, **12**, 357–374.

Barrett, M.D. (1986). Early semantic representations and early word usage. In S.A. Kuczaj & M.D. Barrett (eds), *The Development of Word Meaning: Progress in Cognitive Development Research* (pp. 39–68). New York: Springer.

Basso, A., Capitani, E. & Laiacona, M. (1988). Progressive language impairment without dementia: a case with isolated category specific semantic defect. *Journal of Neurology, Neurosurgery, and Psychiatry*, **51**, 1201–1207.

Bayles, K.A., Tomoeda, C.K. & Cruz, R.F. (1999). Performance of Alzheimer's disease patients in judging word relatedness. *Journal of the International Neuropsychological Society*, **5**, 668–675.

Breedin, S.D., Saffran, E.M. & Coslett B.H. (1994). Reversal of the concreteness effect in a patient with semantic dementia. *Cognitive Neuropsychology*, **11**, 617–660.

Bub, D., Black, S., Hampson, E. & Kertesz, A. (1988). Semantic encoding of pictures and words: some neuropsychological observations. *Cognitive Neuropsychology*, **5**, 27–66.

Buxbaum, L.J., Schwartz, M.F. & Carew, T.G. (1997). The role of semantic memory in object use. *Cognitive Neuropsychology*, **14**, 219–254.

Buxbaum, L.J., Veramonti, T. & Schwartz, M.F. (2000). Function and manipulation tool knowledge in apraxia: knowing "what for" but not "how". *Neurocase*, **6**, 83–97.

Capitani, E., Laiacona, M., Barbarotto, R. & Trivelli, C. (1994). Living and non-living categories. Is there a "normal" asymmetry? *Neuropsychologia*, **32**, 1453–1463.

Caramazza, A., Hillis, A.E., Rapp, B.C. & Romani, C. (1990). Multiple semantics or multiple confusions? *Cognitive Neuropsychology*, **7**, 161–168.

Caramazza, A. & Shelton, J. (1998). Domain-specific knowledge in the brain: the animate–inanimate distinction. *Journal of Cognitive Neuroscience*, **10**, 1–34.

Cardebat, D., Demonet, J.F., Celsis, P. & Puel, M. (1996) Living/non-living dissociation in a case of semantic dementia: a SPECT activation study. *Neuropsychologia*, **34**, 1175–1179.

Chao, L., Haxby, J. & Martin, A. (1999). Attribute-based neural substrates in temporal cortex for perceiving and knowing about objects. *Nature Neuroscience*, **2**, 913–919.

Chertkow, H. & Bub, D. (1990). Semantic loss in Alzheimer-type dementia. In M.F. Schwartz (ed.), *Modular Deficits in Alzheimer-type Dementia. Issues in the Biology of Language and Cognition*. Cambridge, MA: MIT Press.

Chertkow, H., Bub, D. & Caplan, D. (1992). Constraining theories of semantic memory processing : evidence from dementia. *Cognitive Neuropsychology*, **9**, 327–365.

Collins, A.M. & Quillian, M.R. (1969). Retrieval time from semantic memory. *Journal of Verbal Learning and Verbal Behaviour*, **8**, 240–248.

De Renzi, E., Liotti, M. & Nichelli, P. (1987). Semantic amnesia with preservation of autobiographic memory: a case report. *Cortex*, **23**, 575–597.

De Renzi, E. & Lucchelli, F. (1988). Ideational apraxia. *Brain*, **111**, 1173–1185.

De Renzi, E. & Lucchelli, F. (1994). Are semantic systems separately represented in the brain? The case of living category impairment. *Cortex*, **30**, 3–25.

Durant-Peatfield, M.R., Tyler, L.K., Moss, H.E. & Levy, J. (1997). The distinctiveness of form and function in category structure: a connectionist model. In *Proceedings of the Nineteenth Annual Cognitive Science Conference, University of Stanford*. Mahwah, NJ: Erlbaum.

Ellis A.W., Young, A.W. & Critchley, E.M. (1989). Loss of memory for people following temporal lobe damage. *Brain*, **112**, 1469–1483.

Evans, J.J., Heggs, A.J., Antoun, N. & Hodges, J.R. (1995). Progressive prosopagnosia associated with selective right temporal lobe atrophy. *Brain*, **118**, 1–13.

Farah, M.J., Hammond, K.H., Mehta, Z. & Ratcliffe, G. (1989). Category-specificity and modality-specificity in semantic memory. *Neuropsychologia*, **27**, 193–200.

Farah M.J., Meyer, M.M. & McMullen, P.A. (1996). The living/nonliving dissociation is not an artifact: giving an *a priori* implausible hypothesis a strong test.*Cognitive Neuropsychology*, **13**, 137–154.

Funnell, E. (1995). Objects and properties: a study of the breakdown of semantic memory. *Memory*, **3**, 497–518.

Funnell E. (2001). Evidence for scripts in semantic dementia: implications for theories of semantic memory. *Cognitive Neuropsychology* (in press).

Funnell, E. & De Mornay Davies, P. (1996). JBR: a reassessment of concept familiarity and a category-specific disorder for living things. *Neurocase*, **2**, 135–153.

Funnell, E. & Sheridan, J. (1992). Categories of knowledge? Unfamiliar aspects of living and non-living things. *Cognitive Neuropsychology*, **9**, 135–154.

Gabrieli, J.D., Cohen, N.J. & Corkin S. (1988). The impaired learning of semantic knowedge following bilateral medial temporal-lobe resection. *Brain and Cognition*, **7**, 157–177.

Gainotti, G. & Silveri, M.C. (1996). Cognitive and anatomical locus of lesion in a patient with a category-specific semantic impairment for living beings. *Cognitive Neuropsychology*, **13**, 357–389.

Gainotti, G., Silveri, M.C., Daniele, A. & Giustolisi, L. (1995). Neuroanatomical correlates of category-specific semantic disorders: a critical survey. *Memory*, **3**, 247–264.

Godbout, L. & Bouchard C. (1999). Processing time and space components of semantic memory: a study of frontal-lobe-related impairments. *Brain and Cognition*, **40**, 136–139.

Graham, K.S., Becker, J.T. & Hodges, J.R. (1997). On the relationship between knowledge and memory for pictures: evidence from the study of patients with semantic dementia and Alzheimer's disease. *Journal of the International Neuropsychological Society*, **3**, 534–544.

Graham, K.S. & Hodges, J.R. (1997). Differentiating the roles of the hippocampus complex and the neocortex in long-term memory storage: evidence from the study of semantic dementia and Alzheimer's disease. *Neuropsychology*, 1997, **11**, 77–89.

Graham, K.S., Lambon Ralph, M.A. & Hodges J.R. (1997). Determining the impact of autobiographical experience on "meaning": new insights from investigating sports-related vocabulary and knowledge in two cases with semantic dementia. *Cognitive Neuropsychology*, **14**, 801–837.

Graham, K.S., Lambon Ralph, M.A. & Hodges, J.R. (1999a). A questionable semantics: the interaction beween semantic knowledge and autobiographical experience in semantic dementia. *Cognitive Neuropsychology*, **16**, 689–698.

Graham, K.S., Patterson, K., Pratt, K.H. & Hodges J.R. (1999b). Relearning and subsequent forgetting of semantic category exemplars in a case of semantic dementia. *Neuropsychology*, **13**, 359–380.

Graham, K.S., Simons, J.S., Pratt, K.H. et al. (2000). Insights from semantic dementia on the relationship between episodic and semantic memory. *Neuropsychologia*, **38**, 313–324.

Hillis, A.E. & Caramazza, A. (1991). Category-specific naming and comprehension impairment: a double dissociation. *Brain*, **114**, 2081–2094.

Hodges, J.R. & Patterson, K. (1995). Is semantic memory consistently impaired early in the course of Alzheimer's disease? Neuroanatomical and diagnostic implications. *Neuropsychologia*, **33**, 441–459.

Hodges, J.R., Patterson, K., Oxbury, S. & Funnell, E. (1992a). Semantic dementia. Progressive fluent aphasia with temporal lobe atrophy. *Brain*, **115**, 1783–1806.

Hodges, J.R., Salmon, D.P. & Butters, N. (1992b) Semantic memory impairment in Alzheimer's disease: failure of access of degraded knowledge? *Neuropsychologia*, **30**, 301–314.

Hodges, J.R., Graham, N. & Patterson, K. (1995) Charting the progression in semantic dementia: implications for the organisation of semantic memory. *Memory*, **3**, 463–495.

Humphreys, G. & Riddoch, J. (1988). On the case of multiple semantic systems: a reply to Shallice. *Cognitive Neuropsychology*, **5**, 143–150.

Kapur, N., Ellison, D., Parkin, A.J. et al. (1994). Bilateral temporal lobe pathology with sparing of medial temporal lobe structures: lesion profile and pattern of memory disorder. *Neuropsychologia*, **32**, 23–38.

Kartsounis, L.D. & Shallice, T. (1996). Modality specific semantic knowledge loss for unique items. *Cortex*, **32**, 109–119.

Kay, J. & Hanley, J.R. (1999). Person-specific knowledge and knowledge of biological categories. *Cognitive Neuropsychology*, **16**, 171–180.

Kintsch, W. (1980). Semantic memory: a tutorial. In R.S. Nickerson (ed.), *Attention and Perfomance VIII* (pp. 595–620). Cambridge, MA: Bolt Beranek and Newman.

Laiacona, M., Barbarotto, R. & Capitani, E. (1993). Perceptual and associative knowledge in category specific impairment of semantic memory: a study of two cases. *Cortex*, **29**, 727–740.

Laiacona, M., Capitani, E. & Barbarotto, R. (1997). Semantic category dissociations: a longitudinal study of two cases. *Cortex*, **33**, 441–461.

Lambon Ralph, M.A., Graham, K.S., Patterson, K. & Hodges, J.R. (1999). Is a picture worth a thousand words? Evidence from concept definitions by patients with semantic dementia. *Brain and Language*, **70**, 309–335.

Lambon Ralph, M.A., Howard, D., Nightingale, G. & Ellis, A.W. (1998). Are living and non-living category-specific deficits causally linked to impaired perceptual associative knowledge? Evidence from a category-specific double dissociation. *Neurocase*, **4**, 311–338.

Lambon Ralph, M.A. & Howard, D. (2000). Gogi aphasia or semantic dementia? Simulating and assessing poor verbal comprehension in a case of progressive fluent aphasia. *Cognitive Neuropsychology*, **17**, 437–465.

Lauro-Grotto, R., Piccini, C. & Shallice, T. (1997). Modality-specific operations in semantic dementia. *Cortex*, **33**, 593–622.

Le Moal, S., Lemesle, B., Puel, M. & Cardebat, D. (1999). Semantic–autobiographical memory interactions in severe semantic dementia. A case study. *Brain and Cognition*, **40**, 177–180.

Martin, A. (1992). Degraded knowledge representations in patients with Alzheimer's disease: implications for models of semantic and repetition priming. In L.R. Squire & N. Butters (eds), *Neuropsychology of Memory* (pp. 220–232). New York: Guilford.

Martin, A., Wiggs, C., Ungerleider, L. & Haxby J. (1996). Neural correlates of category-specific knowledge. *Nature*, **379**, 649–652.

McCarthy, R.A., Evans, J.J. & Hodges, J.R. (1996). Topographic amnesia: spatial memory disorder, perceptual dysfunction, or category specific semantic memory impairment? *Journal of Neurology, Neurosurgery and Psychiatry*, **60**, 318–325.

McCarthy, R.A. & Warrington, E.K. (1986). Visual associative agnosia; a clinico-anatomical study of a single case. *Journal of Neurology, Neurosurgery and Psychiatry*, **49**, 1233–1240.

McCarthy, R.A. & Warrington, E.K. (1988). Evidence for modality-specific meaning systems in the brain. *Nature*, **334**, 428–430.

Miceli, G., Capasso, R., Daniele A. et al. (2000) Selective deficit for people's names following left temporal damage: an impairment of domain-specific conceptual knowledge. *Cognitive Neuropsychology*, **17**, 489–516.

Mishkin, M., Ungerleider, L.G. & Macko, K.A. (1983). Object vision and spatial vision: two cortical pathways. *Trends in Neuroscience*, 414–417.

Moreaud, O., Charnallet, A. & Pellat, J. (1998). Identification without manipulation: a study of the relations between object use and semantic memory. *Neuropsychologia*, **36**, 1295–1301.

Moss, H.E. & Tyler, L.K. (2000). A progressive category-specific semantic deficit for living things. *Neuropsychologia*, **38**, 60–82.

Moss, H.E., Tyler, L.K. & Jennings, F. (1997). When leopards lose their spots: knowledge of visual properties in category-specific deficits for living things. *Cognitive Neuropsychology*, **14**, 901–950.

Mummery, C.J., Patterson, K., Price, C.J. et al. (2000). A voxel-based morphometry study of semantic dementia: relationship between temporal lobe atrophy and semantic memory. *Annals of Neurology*, **47**, 36–45.

Neary, D., Snowden, J.S., Gustafson, L. et al. (1998). Frontotemporal lobar degeneration. A consensus on clinical diagnostic criteria. *Neurology*, **51**, 1546–1554.

Nebes, R.D. (1992). Semantic memory dysfunction in Alzheimer's disease: disruption of semantic knowledge or information processing limitation? In L.R. Squire & N. Butters (eds), *Neuropsychology of Memory* (pp. 233–340). New York: Guilford.

Nebes, R.D. & Halligan, E.M. (1999). Instantiation of semantic categories in sentence comprehension by Alzheimer patients. *Journal of the International Neuropsychological Society*, **5**, 685–691.

Nelson, K. (1985). *Making Sense: Development of Meaning in Early Childhood*. New York: Academic Press.

Ober, B. (1999). Symposium. Semantic memory in Alzheimer's disease: loss of knowledge of deficits in retrieval? Introduction from the symposium organizer. *Journal of the International Neuropsychological Society*, **5**, 623–625.

Ober, B. & Shenaut, G.K. (1999). Well-organized conceptual domains in Alzheimer's disease. *Journal of the International Neuropsychological Society*, **5**, 676–684.

Ochipa, C., Rothi, L.J.G. & Heilman, K.M. (1989). Ideational apraxia: a deficit in tool selection and use. *Annals of Neurology*, **25**, 190–193.

Patterson, K. & Hodges J.R. (1995). Disorders of semantic memory. In A.D. Baddeley, B.A. Wilson & F.N. Watts (eds), *Handbook of Memory Disorders*, 1st edn (pp. 167–186). Chichester: Wiley.

Pietrini, V., Nertempi, P., Vaglia, A. et al. (1988). Recovery from herpes simplex encephalitis: selective impairment of specific semantic categories with neuroradiological correlation. *Journal of Neurology, Neurosurgery and Psychiatry*, **51**, 1284–1293.

Rapp, B.A. & Caramazza, A. (1989). General to specific access to word meaning: a claim re-examined. *Cognitive Neuropsychology*, **6**, 251–272.

Rapp, B.A. & Caramazza, A. (1993). On the distinction between deficits of access and deficits of storage: a question of theory. *Cognitive Neuropsychology*, **10**, 113–141.

Rothi, L.J.G., Ochipa, C. & Heilman, K.M. (1991). A cognitive neuropsychological model of praxis. *Cognitive Neuropsychology*, **8**, 443–458.

Sacchett, C. & Humphreys, G.W. (1992). Calling a squirrel a squirrel but a canoe a wigwam: a category specific deficit for artefactual objects and body parts. *Cognitive Neuropsychology*, **9**, 73–86.

Saffran, E.M. & Schwartz, M.F. (1994). Of cabbages and things: semantic memory from a neuropsychological perspective—a tutorial review. In C. Umilta & M. Moscovitch (eds), *Attention and Performance XV: Conscious and Nonconscious Information Processing*. Cambridge, MA: MIT Press.

Salmon, D.P., Heindel, W.C. & Lange, K.L. (1999). Differential decline in word generation from phonemic and semantic categories during the course of Alzheimer's disease: implications for the integrity of semantic memory. *Journal of the Neuropsychological Society*, 5, 692–703.

Sartori, G., Coltheart, M., Miozzo, M. & Job, R. (1994). Category specificity and informational specificity in neuropsychological impairment of semantic memory. In C. Umilta & M. Moscovitch (eds), *Attention and Performance XV: Conscious and Nonconscious Information Processing*. Cambridge, MA: MIT Press.

Sartori, G. & Job, R. (1988). The oyster with four legs: a neuropsychological study on the interaction between vision and semantic information. *Cognitive Neuropsychology*, **5**, 105–132.

Sartori, G., Job, R., Miozzo, M. et al. (1993a) Category-specific form–knowledge deficit in a patient with Herpes Simplex Virus encephalitis. *Journal of Clinical and Experimental Neuropsychology*, **15**, 280–299.

Sartori, G., Miozzo, M. & Job, R. (1993b). Category-specific naming impairments? Yes. *Quarterly Journal of Experimental Psychology*, **46A**, 489–504.

Schank, R.C. (1982). *Dynamic Memory*. Cambridge: Cambridge University Press.

Schank, R.C. & Abelson, R. (1977). Scripts, plans, goals and understanding. Hillsdale, NJ: Erlbaum.

Schwartz, M.F., Marin, O.S.M. & Saffran, E.M. (1979). Dissociations of language function in dementia: a case study. *Brain & Language*, **7**, 277–306.

Schwartz, M., Montgomery, M.W., Fitzpatrick-DeSalme, E.J. et al. (1995). Analysis of a disorder of everyday action. *Cognitive Neuropsychology*, **12**, 863–892.

Shallice, T. (1988). *From Neuropsychology to Mental Structure*. Cambridge: Cambridge University Press.

Silveri, M.C. & Gainotti, G. (1988). Interaction between vision and language in category-specific impairment. *Cognitive Neuropsychology*, **5**, 677–709.

Sirigu, A., Dehamel, J.-R. & Poncet, M. (1991). The role of sensorimotor experience in object recognition. *Brain*, **114**, 2555–2573.

Smith, E.E., Shoben, E.L. & Ripps, L.J. (1974). Structure and process in semantic memory: a featural model for semantic decisions. *Psychological Review*, **81**, 214–241.

Snowden, J.S., Goulding, P.J. & Neary, D. (1989). Semantic dementia: a form of circumscribed cerebral atrophy. *Behavioural Neurology*, **2**, 167–182.

Snowden, J.S., Griffiths, H.L. & Neary, D. (1994). Semantic dementia: autobiographical contribution to preservation of meaning. *Cognitive Neuropsychology*, **11**, 265–288.

Snowden, J.S., Griffiths, H.L. & Neary, D. (1995). Autobiographical experience and word meaning. *Memory*, **3**, 225–246.

Snowden, J.S., Griffiths, H.L. & Neary, D. (1996a). Semantic–episodic memory interactions in semantic dementia: implications for retrograde memory function. *Cognitive Neuropsychology*, **13**, 1101–1137.

Snowden, J.S., Griffiths, H.L. & Neary, D. (1999). The impact of autobiographical experience on meaning: reply to Graham, Lambon Ralph, and Hodges. *Cognitive Neuropsychology*, **16**, 673–687.

Snowden, J.S., Neary, D., Mann, D.M.A., Goulding, P.J. & Testa, H.J. (1992). Progressive language disorder due to lobar atrophy. *Annals of Neurology*, **31**, 174–183.

Snowden, J.S., Neary, D. & Mann, D.M.A. (1996b). *Frontotemporal Lobar Degeneration: Frontotemporal Dementia, Progressive Aphasia, Semantic Dementia*. London: Churchill Livingstone.

Stewart, F., Parkin, A.J. & Hunkin, N.M. (1992). Naming impairments following recovery from herpes simplex encephalitis: category-specific? *Quarterly Journal of Experimental Psychology*, **44**, 261–284.

Tippett L.J., McAuliffe, S. & Farah, M.J. (1995). Preservation of categorical knowledge in Alzheimer's disease: a computational account. *Memory*, **3**, 519–533.

Tulving, E. (1972). Episodic and semantic memory. In E. Tulving & W. Donaldson (eds), *Organization of Memory* (pp. 381–403). New York: Academic Press.

Tyler, L.K. & Moss, H.E. (1998). Going, going, gone . . . ? Implicit and explicit tests of conceptual knowledge in a longitudinal study of semantic dementia. *Neuropsychologia*, **36**, 1313–1323.

Warrington, E.K. (1975). The selective impairment of semantic memory. *Quarterly Journal of Experimental Psychology*, **27**, 635–657.

Warrington, E.K. & McCarthy, R.A. (1983). Category-specific access dysphasia. *Brain*, **106**, 859–878.

Warrington, E.K. & McCarthy, R.A. (1987). Categories of knowledge: further fractionations and an attempted integration. *Brain*, **110**, 1273–1296.

Warrington, E.K. & McCarthy, R.A. (1994). Multiple meaning systems in the brain: a case for visual semantics. *Neuropsychologia*, **32**, 1465–1473.

Warrington, E.K. & Shallice, T. (1984). Category specific semantic impairments. *Brain*, **107**, 829–854.

Wilkins, A. & Moscovitch, M. (1978). Selective impairment of semantic memory after temporal lobectomy. *Neuropsychologia*, **16**, 73–79.

Wilson, B.A. (1997). Semantic memory impairments following non-progressive brain injury: a study of four cases. *Brain Injury*, **11**, 259–269.

Wilson, B. & Baddeley, A. (1988). Semantic, episodic and autobiographical memory in a postmeningitic patient. *Brain and Cognition*, **8**, 31–46.

CHAPTER 15

The Cognitive Neuroscience of Confabulation: A Review and a Model

Asaf Gilboa

and

Morris Moscovitch

Baycrest Center for Geriatric Care, North York, Ontario, Canada

Confabulation may be defined as honest lying. The confabulating patient provides information that is patently false and sometimes self-contradictory without intending to lie. The patient is unaware of the falsehoods, and sometimes will cling to these false beliefs even when confronted with the truth. The patient's underlying false belief is conveyed not only by verbal statements but also by actions. The term "confabulation" is often loosely used to denote a wide range of qualitatively different memory phenomena. On the one hand, it is used to describe mild distortions of an actual memory, such as intrusions, embellishments, elaborations, paraphrasing or high false alarm rates on tests of anterograde amnesia (Kern et al., 1992; Kopelman, 1987; Rapcsak et al., 1998; Tallberg & Almkvist, 2001). On the other hand, it refers to highly implausible bizarre descriptions of false realities, such as claiming to be a pirate on a spaceship (Damasio et al., 1985), being a pilot in Saddam Hussein's air force, forced to eject at 7000 meters and reaching the ground with no parachute (Feinstein et al., 2000), or watching members of one's family being killed (Stuss et al., 1978). Thus, Berlyne (1972) drew the distinction between momentary (or embarrassment) confabulations and fantastic (or productive) ones, the former being commoner, brief and of a variable true content that is displaced in time, the latter being more grandiose and stable in content, and appearing without provocation. Berlyne concluded that fantastic confabulations are a distinct entity, having nothing in common with momentary ones. Kopelman (1987) suggested that a more useful distinction is between spontaneous and provoked types of confabulations, the former being rare and related to an amnesic syndrome superimposed on a frontal dysfunction, while the latter represents a common, normal response to faulty memory.

Clinical observations suggest several characteristics of confabulations (Talland, 1965; Moscovitch, 1989):

The Handbook of Memory Disorders. Edited by A.D. Baddeley, M.D. Kopelman and B.A. Wilson
© 2002 John Wiley & Sons, Ltd.

1. It is a false memory in the context of retrieval, often containing false details within its own context as well: thus, some confabulations may be true memories displaced in time, while others seem to lack any basis in reality.
2. The patient is unaware that he/she is confabulating, and often is unaware even of the existence of a memory deficit (anosognosia). Hence, confabulations are not intentionally produced and are probably not the result of compensatory mechanisms.
3. Patients may act upon their confabulation, reflecting their genuine belief in the false memory. Some researchers (Schnider et al., 1996b) have even based their definition of spontaneous confabulation on this tendency.
4. Confabulations are most apparent when autobiographical recollection is required. However, some cases of spontaneous confabulation have been reported that are not directly related to the patient's own life (e.g. Baddeley & Wilson, 1988) and under certain conditions of testing confabulations may also appear on semantic memory tasks (Moscovitch & Melo, 1997). The preponderance of confabulations in the recall of autobiographical memory, compared to semantic memory, may be a function of a complex narrative structure and its reliance on strategic retrieval processes, which are associated more with autobiographical than with semantic memory (see below).

Confabulation should be distinguished from other related symptoms, such as delusions on the one hand and false recall and false recognition on the other. Berlyne's (1972) definition of confabulation as "a falsification of memory occurring in clear consciousness in association with an organically derived amnesia" was specifically formulated to exclude memory falsifications not associated with organic memory defect, and those due to delirious states. The pathological context constitutes the main distinction between confabulations and delusions, with the latter occurring in the context of psychosis rather than of a neurological insult. Delusions are often bizarre memories that are held by the patient in great confidence, in a manner that is not susceptible to logical persuasion, much as are spontaneous confabulations. Kopelman (1999) suggests, however, that delusions may be more complex, detailed and elaborated than confabulations. He also suggests that delusions may represent a more systematic structure of beliefs (see also Moscovitch, 1995). These distinctions should be considered with care, however, as some confabulations may be quite systematic, persistent and pervasive (e.g. Berlyne, 1972; Burgess & McNeil, 1999; Feinstein et al., 2000) as well as extremely complex and elaborate (Feinstein et al., 2000). An excellent discussion of the distinction between confabulation and related psychiatric and neurological syndromes, such as delirium, confusional states, schizophrenic ideation, Anton's and Capgras syndrome, can be found in DeLuca (2000a, 2000b).

False recognition is often accompanied by confabulation (e.g. Delbecq-Derouesné et al., 1990; Rapcsak et al., 1998), although it may also occur in the absence of substantial confabulatory tendency (Schacter et al., 1996). In contrast to confabulation, false recognition occurs primarily in relation to materials studied after the injury, and episodic autobiographical memory may be relatively spared (Delbecq-Derouesné et al., 1990; Schacter et al., 1996; but see Rapcsak et al., 1998). It may be true to say that false recognition can be elicited readily in many, but not all (e.g. Kapur & Coughlan, 1980; Papagno & Baddeley, 1997), confabulating subjects, though it is not clear that the two phenomena result from the same faulty mechanism (Delbecq-Derouesné et al., 1990).

Neuropathology

Type of Patient

Confabulation often occurs in patients with Korsakoff's syndrome (Benson et al., 1996; Berlyne, 1972; Mercer et al., 1977; Kopelman, 1987; Kopelman et al., 1997; Korsakoff, 1955; Talland, 1965; Victor et al., 1971). It is also commonly found in a subgroup of patients who survived aneurysms of the anterior communicating artery (ACoA; Alexander & Freedman, 1984; Baddeley & Wilson, 1988; Damasio et al., 1985; DeLuca, 1993; DeLuca & Cicerone, 1991; DeLuca & Diamond, 1995; Fischer et al., 1995; Kapur & Coughlan, 1980; Lindqvist & Norlen, 1966; Moscovitch, 1989; Talland et al., 1967; Vilkki, 1985). This subset of patients suffers from what has been termed "ACoA syndrome" (Alexander & Freedman, 1984; Damasio et al., 1985; DeLuca, 1993; Vilkki, 1985), which includes personality changes, an amnesic syndrome and confabulation. However, as pointed out by DeLuca (1993; DeLuca & Diamond, 1995), these symptoms may occur independently of each other, so that confabulation can appear in the absence of personality change, although memory dysfunction is considered a prerequisite for its appearance (see discussion below).

Confabulation also has been reported in association with other etiologies, such as traumatic brain injury (Baddeley & Wilson, 1988; Berlyne, 1972; Box et al., 1999; Moscovitch & Melo, 1997), multiple sclerosis (Feinstein et al., 2000), rupture of a PCoA aneurysm (Dalla Barba et al., 1997a; Mercer et al., 1977), fronto-temporal dementia (Nedjam et al., 2000; Moscovitch & Melo, 1997), herpes simplex encephalitis (Moscovitch & Melo, 1997) and other disorders. Some have reported confabulation in dementia of the Alzheimer type (Nedjam et al., 2000; Kern et al., 1992; Kopelman, 1987; Tallberg & Almkvist, 2001; Dalla-Barba et al., 1999). However, at least in the early stages of the disease, these reports seem to stretch the definition of confabulation to include various types of intrusions, and only rarely is a full-blown confabulatory syndrome seen in these patients (DeLuca, 2000a).

Lesion Location: A Review of 79 Cases

The fact that confabulation is most common among patients with Korsakoff syndrome and those with ruptured aneurysms of the ACoA has implications regarding the brain structures that may be involved in producing the phenomenon. The pathology of alcoholic Wernicke–Korsakoff patients most frequently involves the mammillary bodies, the dorsomedial and anterior thalamic nuclei, as well as structures comprising the basal forebrain and orbitofrontal cortex (Barbizet, 1963; Jernigen et al., 1991; Salmon & Butters, 1987; Torvik, 1987; Victor et al., 1971; Weiskrantz, 1987). The severe amnesia that accompanies the condition is often ascribed to the mammillary bodies and the anterior thalamic lesions, as these structures receive hippocampal afferents via the fornix and are thus considered part of the "extended hippocampal system" (Aggleton & Saunders, 1997). Furthermore, lesions within the basal forebrain itself may cause amnesia, and interruption of pathways connecting basal forebrain with other memory-relevant brain regions, especially the hippocampal formation, may also result in memory impairment.

The dorsomedial thalamic nuclei, on the other hand, are reciprocally connected with the orbitofrontal and the medial aspect of the frontal cortex, and receive input from several

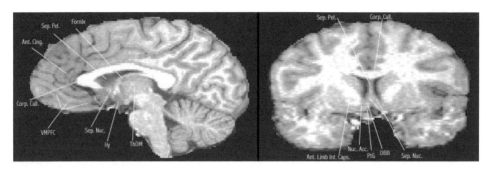

Figure 15.1 Sagittal (left) and coronal (right) slices of MRI scan, showing brain regions that may be implicated in confabulation. Sagittal section shows the location of the thalamus, fornix, hypothalamus, basal forebrain, ventromedial PFC and anterior cingulate. Coronal section, at the level of the anterior commissure, shows some of the major basal forebrain structures. Ant. Cing, anterior cingulate; Ant. Limb Int. Caps., anterior limb of the internal capsule; Corp. Call., corpus callosum; DBB, diagonal band of Broca; Hy, hypothalamus; Nuc. Acc., nucleus accumbens; PtG, paraterminal gyrus; Sep. Nuc., septal nuclei; Sep. pel., septum pellucidum; ThDM, dorsomedial thalamic nucleus; VMPFC, ventromedial prefrontal cortex

cortical and subcortical structures, including the amygdala and structures in the basal fore-brain (e.g. Ray & Price, 1993). Taken together with the evidence of primary degeneration in the basal forebrain and orbitofrontal cortex in Korsakoff syndrome, it may be argued that these structures comprise a second dysfunctional subsystem, which may be more closely related to the production of confabulations in the disease (Salmon & Butters, 1987).

To the best of our knowledge, no study has attempted to differentiate Korsakoff patients who confabulate from those who do not, based on their specific neuropathology. A clue as to which structures may be directly involved is provided in a single-subject follow-up SPECT study by Benson and colleagues (1996). Their results indicated that, as confabulation resolved, so did the hypoperfusion observed in orbitofrontal and medial frontal regions, including the cingulum. The hypoperfusion initially observed in the medial diencephalon, which includes the anterior and dorsomedial nuclei of the thalamus, only slightly improved over this period. This report suggests that it is the second system, i.e. the one comprised of the medial and orbitofrontal cortices and perhaps basal forebrain, that is responsible for confabulation, rather than the classic memory-related structures that remained dysfunctional in this patient (see Figure 15.1).

Several group studies of patients with ruptures of aneurysms of the anterior commu-nicating artery (ACoA) have indicated that the condition is sometimes accompanied by confabulation, and have contrasted those who confabulate with those who do not. Cerebral infarcts following rupture of ACoA aneurysms may appear along the distribution of the anterior cerebral artery, as well as along the arterial branches of the ACoA itself, in and around the basal forebrain (e.g. the septal nuclei, genu of the corpus callosum, anterior cingulum, the fornix, hypothalamus, substantia inominata and more; see Figure 15.1). Why some of these patients are reported to exhibit the "ACoA syndrome" and others not may be related to the exact locus of infarction (DeLuca, 1993). Alexander & Freedman (1984) suggested that damage to the septal nuclei at the basal forebrain might be responsible for this type of amnesia and confabulation. They also report a higher proportion of right anterior cerebral artery infarcts among five of 11 ACoA patients who also confabulated. In another series of five ACoA patients (Vilkki, 1985), the two who had amnesia and also confabulated were noted to have primarily medial and orbitofrontal damage, which was more pronounced on the right for one of them. Based on a study of nine confabulating ACoA patients, DeLuca & Cicerone (1991) proposed a dual-lesion hypothesis, which states that confabulation requires both frontal and basal forebrain damage, or some other damage causing amnesia. DeLuca's hypothesis received confirming evidence in a later study of six ACoA patients (DeLuca, 1993), all of whom had frontal damage but only the three with presumed basal forebrain damage also confabulated (but see contrary evidence, below). Fischer et al. (1995) attempted to differentiate anatomically between ACoA patients who show spontaneous vs. provoked confabulations. They report that of nine confabulating ACoA patients, the five who showed spontaneous confabulations had more extensive medial frontal and striatal pathology, in addition to basal forebrain lesions which were common to all patients.

In an attempt to clarify the relationship between lesion location and confabulation we reviewed 33 studies in which significant imaging or post mortem findings were reported (see Table 15.1). These studies describe 79 confabulating patients whose confabulations may be regarded as spontaneous according to Kopelman's (1987) definition and who were past the confusional state. The majority of patients (47) had ruptures of aneurysms in the ACoA; 14 patients had traumatic brain injury (TBI) and the rest had dementias, other cerebrovascular abnormalities (infarcts, arteriovascular malformations, occlusions, PCoA), multiple sclerosis, encephalitis, meningitis, Korsakoff's syndrome, etc.

In 64 patients (81%) there was damage to the prefrontal cortex (PFC). In nine of the frontal lesions the exact location of the damage was not reported (although two are ACoA patients and it is reasonable to expect medial frontal damage). Of the remaining 55 patients with frontal damage, lesions were located in one or more of the following structures: the dorsolateral PFC (3), polar prefrontal cortex (6), orbitofrontal cortex (25) and medial aspects of the frontal lobe, including the cingulate (49). In 26 patients the frontal lobe damage was restricted to the medial PFC. In all but five patients whose damage was confined to the orbitofrontal cortex and one whose damage was restricted to the polar region, there was also damage to the medial aspect of the PFC. One could also argue that for those patients whose damage was ostensibly restricted to the OFC, there may have been some incursion or overlap with the adjacent ventromedial frontal cortex. *As others have noted before, this analysis suggests that damage to the medial PFC may be crucial in the production of confabulation. There was no evidence of lateralization, as suggested by some researchers (Alexander & Freedman, 1984; Joseph, 1986, 1999), with 13 of the lesions primarily on the left, 11 primarily on the right, and the rest bilateral.*

The other region that had been suggested as crucial for the production of confabulations is the basal forebrain. Twenty-six patients (32%) of the 79 reviewed had damage to this region, in 10 of whom this was the only lesion reported. It should be kept in mind, however, that in 28 of the 47 ACoA patients no damage to the basal forebrain was reported. Although such situations may occur, artifacts produced by surgical clips of the aneurysm may impede the ability to detect such damage (e.g. Alexander & Freedman, 1984; DeLuca, 1993; Eslinger et al., 1984). As far as lateralization of lesion is concerned, of the 26 basal forebrain lesions, five patients had right-sided, two had left-sided and the rest had bilateral or medial lesions. This again does not lend much support to the lateralization hypothesis.

Twenty of the patients with frontal damage (31%) also had basal forebrain damage. Thirteen of the patients who had frontal lobe damage but no basal forebrain damage had other lesions that could produce memory disturbance, such as lesions of the medial temporal lobe or temporal neocortex. The remaining 31 patients (48%) had no lesions in the

Table 15.1 Spontaneous confabulators, etiologies and lesion locations, as reported from imaging and/or post-mortem data

		Lesion location													
		Prefrontal cortex					Basal forebrain								Other
Study	Patient(s) and etiology	NR	DL	OF	M/C	Pol	NR	Sep	GR	SI	NBM	DBB	BG	Th	
Alexander & Freedman, 1984*	1- ACoA														Parietal (R)
	2,3,7- ACoA			R,R,R	R,R,R										
	4- ACoA				B										
	5- ACoA		L												
	6- ACoA				B		B								Temporoparietal (R)
	8,11- ACoA			L,L	L,L										
	9,10- ACoA			B,B	B,B										
	12- ACoA			R	R		R								
	13- ACoA			R	R		B								
Baddeley & Wilson, 1988	RJ- TBI	B	B												
Benson et al., 1996	Korsakoff													B	
Box et al., 1999	IR- TBI		R	B	B										
Conway & Tacchi, 1996	OP- TBI			B		R									Parietal corona radiata
Dab et al., 1999	ACoA				L										Temporal pole and mid-temporal regions
Dalla-Barba et al., 1997a[†]	MG- PCoA														Dilation of occipital horns at admission. None at test
Dalla-Barba et al., 1997b	GA- ACoA			B	B										Anterior Corpus callosum, anterior commissure
Dalla-Barba, 1993b	MB Binswagner's encephalopathy														Subtentorial ventricular expansion, white matter
Damasio et al., 1985	1- ACoA				L		B								
	2- AVM				L		L								
	3- ACoA			R	R		B								
	5- ACoA			R	B	R	B								
Delbecq-Derouesné et al., 1990	RW ACoA			B	B	R							L		Temporal pole (R), fusiform/parahippoeampus
DeLuca & Cicerone, 1991	5 ACoA														Ventricular dilation, hydrocephalus
	8 ACoA				B										
	9 ACoA				B								R		

Study	Case						Location
DeLuca, 1993#	BJ- ACoA	B			B		
	IL- ACoA	L		L			
	OJ- ACoA						
Eslinger & Damasio, 1984*	1- ACoA		L	M	L		
	2-ACoA	R			B		
	3-ACoA	B			B	L	
Feinstein et al., 2000	Multiple sclerosis	B		B			Periventricular white, (primarily frontal)
Fischer et al., 1995	1- ACoA	B			B	R	
	2- ACoA	B			B	L	
	3- ACoA				B	L	
	4- ACoA	B			B		
	5- ACoA	L			B	B	
Hashimoto et al., 2000*	Haemorrhage					R	Nucleus accumbens, preoptic area
Johnson et al., 1997	GS- ACoA	B				R	
	SB- ACoA	L					
Kapur & Coughlan, 1980							
Kopelman et al., 1997	AB-infarct + metastasis		B				Temporoparietal (R), posterior parietal (B)
Manzel et al., 2000	Whipple disease	B			B		MTL (B)
Morris et al., 1992*	Resection of glioma					R	Anterior hypothalamus, lamina terminalis, paraterminal gyrus, nucleus accumbens
Moscovitch & Melo 1997	BR- HSE	B			B		MTL (B)
	JH- TBI	B					Diffuse
	GS- FTD	B					Temporal atrophy (B)
	RC- CVA	B					
	GE- IA occlusion	B	B		B		
	FK-CVA						
	HK- ACoA	B					
Moscovitch, 1989	1-ACoA	B					
Papagano & Baddeley, 1997	MM- haematoma,	B					
	AVM	B				L	

continues overleaf

Table 15.1 (*continued*)

Study	Patient(s) and etiology	Prefrontal cortex					Basal forebrain						BG	Th	Other
		NR	DL	OF	M/C	Pol	NR	Sep	GR	SI	NBM	DBB			
Parkin et al., 1988	JB ACoA				L										
Ptak & Schnider, 1999	ACoA			B			B								
Rapcsak et al., 1998	JS- ACoA		R	B	B	R	B								
Schnider et al. 2000	6- ACoA						B								
	7- TBI						R								Amygdala (R), insula (L), peririhinal (L) DAI
	8- TBI			B	B		B								Peririhinal (R), frontothalamic connections
Schnider et al., 1996b	1- ACoA			B				B		B					Insula (L); corpus callosum
	2-TBI						R	B							Capsular genu (R)
	3-TBI			B											
	4-Infarct														
	5-TBI, frontal contusions		B												
	6-Olfactory meningioma			B											
Shapiro et al., 1981	2- ACoA hydro.				R										Temporal (R)
	3- TBI		L												
	6- TBI		B												
	7- TBI		R												
Stuss et al., 1978	1-TBI		B												
	2- MI				R	L									
	3- ACoA				R								L		Internal capsula
	4- TBI		B												Temporoparietal
Vilkki, 1985	5- ACoA			B											
	3- ACoA			B	B										
	4- ACoA			R	R										

Note: ACoA, anterior communicating artery; AD, Alzheimer's disease; AVM, arteriovenous malformation; B, bilateral; BG, basal ganglia; CVA, cerebral vascular arrest; DAI, diffuse axonal injury; BG, basal ganglia; DBB, diagonal band of Broca; DL, dorsolateral PFC; FTD, fronto-temporal dementia; GR, gyrus rectus; HSE, herpes simplex encephalitis; IA, intercerebral artery; L, left; M/C, medial PFC/cingulate gyrus; M, midline; MI, multiple infarct; MTL, medial temporal lobe; NBM, nucleus basalis of Meinert; NR, not reported (precise location); OF, orbitofrontal; Pol, polar PFC; R, right; Sep, septal nuclei; SI, substantia innominata; TBI, traumatic brain injury; Th, thalamus.

* These authors specifically scrutinized the basal forebrain and anterior hypothalamus region for small lesions, and stress the issue of artifacts from nearby surgical clips obscuring the areas of interest.

This author hypothesizes that the apparent lack of difference in CT results between confabulating and non-confabulating patients is due to artifacts created by clipping of aneurysms and thus an inability to detect possible basal forebrain lesions.

† Although there were no imaging findings at the time of testing of this patient, the data was included because of the special nature of the lesion.

basal forebrain, medial temporal lobes or diencephalic structures associated with memory (although we did not specifically review behavioral data regarding possible memory disturbances). At least from a neuroanatomical point of view, these data lend little support to the dual lesion hypothesis of confabulation (Damasio et al., 1985; DeLuca, 1993; DeLuca & Diamond, 1995; Fischer et al., 1995). *Rather, lesions of the ventromedial aspect of the frontal lobes are sufficient to produce confabulations, even when damage to other regions is minimal or absent.* This view accords with several reports that spontaneous confabulation is present even when anterograde memory impairment is minimal (e.g. Feinstein et al., 2000; Kapur & Coughlan, 1980; Nedjam et al., 2000; Papagno & Baddeley, 1997), although DeLuca (2000a) notes that some memory impairment, especially at long delays, is evident in those cases where such tests were conducted. Damage to regions that cause an amnesic syndrome may promote the production of confabulations but is not a necessary condition for their occurrence. It is possible that damage to the basal forebrain alone could produce confabulation, but the weight of the evidence suggests that confabulations may occur as a result of secondary dysfunction of the medial prefrontal cortex, which is highly interconnected to the basal forebrain.

An alternative interpretation is that damage to any part of the anterior limbic system is sufficient to produce confabulation (Schnider et al., 1996b, 2000). Although the medial frontal lobe is the pre-eminent structure affected, damage to other structures, such as the basal forebrain, anterior insula, capsular genu, amygdala, perirhinal cortex and hypothalamus, may also lead to confabulation (see details below).

It is important to note that structural damage alone cannot account entirely for the production of confabulation and its evolution during recovery. Spontaneous confabulation often subsides within a few weeks or months (e.g. Box et al., 1999; DeLuca & Diamond, 1995; Mercer et al., 1977; Shapiro et al., 1981; Stuss et al., 1978), which suggests an underlying dynamic mechanism, rather than a static one. This could very well be related to metabolic or other neurochemical processes (Box et al., 1999; DeLuca & Cicerone, 1991; Kopelman, 1999) interacting with the site of lesion, or to psychological processes that inhibit confabulation under most circumstances, e.g. patients may learn over time not to confabulate spontaneously because such utterances are neither believed nor reinforced. Our own observation is that confabulations may nonetheless be induced in these individuals long after spontaneous confabulation has subsided.

Theories of Confabulation

Compensation

Early investigators of confabulation considered them a reflection of psychological defense mechanisms, activated in response to embarrassment or a need to cover up lapses in memory or fill in gaps of knowledge (e.g. Weinstein & Kahn, 1955; Zangwill, 1953; for discussion, see Berlyne, 1972; DeLuca, 2000a, 2000b; Mercer et al., 1977). These concepts are also reflected in the DSM-IV (American Psychiatric Association, 1994) as part of the associated features of amnesic disorders. Experimental data, however, provide little empirical evidence to support this view (e.g. Dalla-Barba, 1993a; Kopelman et al., 1997; Mercer et al., 1977; Schnider et al., 1996b). Furthermore, one of the most apparent characteristics of confabulating patients is their unawareness of their memory disorder or lack of appreciation of

its severity and implications. Many of these patients, who suffer injury to the medial aspect of the frontal lobes, are also apathetic and indifferent about their situation and about
social interactions. It is unlikely that someone who is unaware of a deficit and seems to
be indifferent to it would feel a need to resort to confabulation in order to alleviate anxiety
associated with embarrassment or memory lapses. Stuss et al. (1978) have even postulated
that the lack of concern about performance is one of the frontal characteristics necessary to
produce confabulation. DeLuca (2000a) points out that confabulation often tends only to
appear early following the injury, while the amnesic disorder is long-lasting, raising the
question of why should patients only fill in gaps early in their illness. These clinical observations, however, do not rule out the possibility that a tendency to fill in gaps in memory
plays some role in confabulations.

Another psychological mechanism proposed by Williams & Rupp (1938) to be associated
with confabulation was increased suggestibility and a greater tendency to utilize external
cues for memory retrieval. This idea, again, did not receive empirical support in the study
of Mercer et al. (1977) (see later), who conclude that proclivity towards suggestibility is
not a major factor in the incidence of confabulation, and that it is more parsimonious to
think of apparent suggestibility as secondary to a general tendency towards confabulation.
The same may be true of filling in memory gaps as an impetus to confabulate. Based on
their findings, Mercer et al. (1977) suggest that confabulators are aware when an answer is
not expected and do not confabulate excessively in response to questions for which they do
not believe they should know the answer. Moscovitch (1989) suggested that confabulations
occur to questions for which the patient has some general knowledge about the topic (e.g.
what is the capital of Australia?) but not the correct answer, whereas confabulations do not
occur to questions where the patient's general knowledge is absent (e.g. what is the capital
of Senegal?).

To conclude, it seems that a tendency to fill in gaps in memory and an increased suggestibility cannot account for the phenomenon of confabulation. Neither, however, can they
be entirely ruled out as underlying some instances of it.

Temporal Disorder

Another hypothesis proposed to account for confabulation is that patients have a disturbed
sense of chronology, so that they can remember the content of events but not their order
of occurrence. As a result, they misattribute aspects of events that occurred at one time to
other events that occurred at another time. This hypothesis, proposed initially by Korsakoff
(1889/1955) and others (Talland, 1965; Victor et al., 1971), also figures in a number of
current theories (Dalla Barba, 1993a, 1993b; Nedjem et al., 2000; Ptak & Schnider, 1999;
Schnider et al., 1996a, 1996b).

Schnider et al. (1996b, 2000; Ptak & Schnider, 1999) identify a subset of confabulating patients who tend on some occasions to act upon their confabulatory beliefs. They distinguish
these confabulators from others, based on the quality of errors they make, which they term
"temporal context confusion" (TCC). TCC is a tendency to use information that may have
been relevant in a previous context and interject it in a current context when it is no longer
relevant or appropriate. They hypothesize that increased TCC emanates from an inability
to suppress previously activated, but currently irrelevant, memory traces (Schnider & Ptak,
1999). They distinguish this type of automatic temporal confusion from source memory

deficits (Johnson et al., 1993) present in other frontal lobe patients with dorsolateral lesions, which depend more on strategic evaluative processes (Schnider & Ptak, 1999; and p. 329 below).

Dalla Barba et al. (1997b, 1999; Nedjam et al., 2000; Dalla Barba, 1993a, 1993b, 1999, 2000) offer a different view of confabulation as a disorder in temporality. They suggest three dimensions of temporality: past, present and future, which may be related to three types of confabulation with regard to past episodic memory, time–place disorientation and future plans, respectively. They hypothesize the existence of two modes of consciousness—a knowing consciousness and a temporal consciousness, which represent two modes of relating to objects—as an undetermined categorical entity (i.e. habits and semantics) and a determined specific entity (i.e. personal events). Only the latter has a temporal dimension. These classifications resemble Tulving's (1985) distinction among anoetic (procedures), noetic (semantics) and autonoetic (episodic) consciousness. Confabulation, by this account, affects all three time dimensions and therefore may be conceptualized as a deficit in temporal consciousness, which is responsible for the ability to ascribe memory representations to particular moments in time. Confabulation is a product of a failure of temporal consciousness to conduct a fine-grained search through long-term memory. As a result, habits and semantic knowledge are apprehended as personal events. Dalla-Barba and colleagues further suggest that confabulation in the semantic domain should be interpreted as arising from a dysfunctional (but not totally lost) knowing consciousness. This term roughly coincides with Tulving's (1985) noetic consciousness and refers to the subjective experience associated with semantic memory retrieval. Cases of completely lost knowing consciousness would result in omissions, rather than confabulations, in the semantic domain. They argue that, contrary to Schnider et al.'s notion of a disorder in temporality, their formulation also accounts for confabulations associated with future plans. However, one should remember that Schnider et al.'s conception of spontaneous confabulation by definition incorporates future plans, since patients act on their (erroneous) beliefs. which arise from erroneous memories.

The notion of some kind of disturbance in temporality as an underlying mechanism for confabulation is appealing, in that many confabulations can be traced back to real memories which are misplaced in time (e.g. Kopelman et al., 1997). However, some of the more bizarre instances may not necessarily conform to this rule. Although one might argue that even the most bizarre ideas and beliefs patients hold may have originated from dreams, fantasies or current perceptions, this argument is impossible to prove and may not lend support to the idea of temporal confusion, but rather speak to a deficit in source monitoring (see below). Furthermore, accounts that rely solely on deficits in temporality run into trouble when accounting for confabulation associated with semantic memory. Most of the temporality hypotheses refer to distortions in a personal temporal frame of reference, which should lead to confabulations that are restricted to the episodic domain. Evidence is accumulating, however, that confabulation may occur in semantic as well as episodic retrieval (Delbecq-Derouesné et al., 1990; Dalla-Barba et al., 1998; Moscovitch & Melo, 1997; Kopelman et al., 1997). Dalla-Barba et al.'s contention that semantic confabulations arise from a partially dysfunctional "knowing consciousness" is poorly defined at best, as it is not clear what constitutes such a partially dysfunctional entity. Furthermore, Dalla-Barba's (1993a) suggestion that, in cases of semantic deficits, confabulations should carry a bizarre and fantastic quality based on such a deficit, is not supported by empirical evidence (Moscovitch & Melo, 1997; Kopelman et al., 1997). Moreover, Moscovitch & Melo (1997) showed that the number of confabulations associated with distortion of content can exceed those on which there is distortion of time, although the two likely interact with one another.

Source Monitoring

A more general case of the temporality theory is that confabulation results from an inability to determine the source of one's memories. This may result from confusion in terms of time and context (source monitoring), or even in terms of whether they refer to experienced events or merely imagined ones (reality monitoring; Johnson et al., 1993, 1997). Failure of several different mechanisms might underlie the production of confabulation, including failure in encoding, retrieval, motivation and evaluative processes (Johnson et al., 1997; Johnson & Raye, 1998). Thus, for example, deficits in judgment or even motivation could lead to the use of lenient decision criteria for the reality of an event. Equally, disruption in retrieval processes could result in faulty access to stored information that could potentially be helpful in identifying the source of a particular event. Finally, faulty acquisition could produce memories that lack the type of cues, such as perceptual details, that help determine source in normal memory processes (Johnson & Raye, 1998). These processes are not viewed as mutually exclusive, and it is suggested that a confluence of factors may produce different kinds of confabulations, differing on aspects such as plausibility. For example, failing to distinguish dreams from real events may result in highly implausible confabulations, while confusing different real events may yield believable confabulations. It should be noted, however, that deficits in source monitoring can occur in patients who show little if any spontaneous confabulation, suggesting that additional or different processes from source moitoring are implicated (see Schnider et al., 1996b).

Retrieval Deficit

Because confabulation affects remote memories acquired long before brain damage occurred as much as recent, anterograde memories that were acquired subsequently, many theorists have concluded that confabulation is related to a deficit in retrieval rather than encoding. Two types of retrieval are distinguished: (a) *associative-cue-dependent* or *direct retrieval*, in which a cue elicits a memory almost automatically and which is thought to be dependent primarily on the medial temporal lobes and related structures (e.g. "Were you ever in France?"); (b) *strategic* or *indirect retrieval*, in which the target memory is not elicited immediately by the cue but which needs to be recovered through a strategic search process akin to problem solving (e.g. as in "Who won the World Cup before the current champions?" or "Who won the Academy Award for best movie 2 years ago?"). These strategic retrieval processes operate at input to frame the memory problem and initiate search, constrain it, and guide it towards local, proximal cues that can activate associative memory processes. Once a memory is recovered, strategic processes operate at output to monitor the recovered memory and determine whether it is consistent with the goals of the memory task and with other knowledge, thereby verifying whether the recovered memory is likely true or false. Finally, the recovered memory must be placed in the proper temporal–spatial context in relation to other memories (Burgess & Shallice, 1996; Conway, 1996; Moscovitch, 1995; Moscovitch & Melo, 1997). Moscovitch & Melo (1997) conclude that the search component is probably one of the defective processes in confabulators, based primarily on the finding that prompting led to a substantial increase in both veridical and false memories in confabulators, but not in non-confabulating amnesics or normal controls. Interestingly,

Burgess & Shallice (1996) reach a similar conclusion, based on studies of retrieval processes in healthy adults. It appears that as well as having a severe strategic search deficit, confabulators also have a monitoring deficit. Monitoring may involve two separate processes: (a) keeping track of actions and of expected events so as not to repeat them, which perhaps is mediated by the mid-dorsolateral prefrontal region, closely related to regions involved in making decisions about temporal order; (b) editing memories and inhibiting false ones, and perhaps initiating search process that are mediated by the ventromedial prefrontal cortex (see Schnider & Ptak, 1999, for a related distinction; and a recent paper by Moscovitch & Winocur, 2002, for an elaboration on this idea).

To sum up, confabulations are thought to be the result of: (a) a faulty memory system creating faulty cue–memory associations; (b) faulty search strategies causing both omissions and commissions as misleading proximal cues are accessed; (c) the above two are necessary but not sufficient conditions for confabulations; defective monitoring and failure to edit out faulty memories constitute a third component leading to confabulation (cf. Burgess & Shallice, 1996, for a related model based on retrieval processes in normal subjects).

A number of investigators have proposed that the same strategic processes used in other domains are also implicated in memory (Moscovitch, 1992; Moscovitch & Umiltá, 1991). The major objection to the strategic retrieval view is based on this assertion. Confabulating patients have been reported who have intact executive functions, as determined by their performance on a variety of nonmemory tasks sensitive to frontal damage (e.g. Dalla-Barba, 1993a; Nedjam et al., 2000). To counter this objection, Moscovitch & Melo (1997) suggested that the crucial lesion in the medial frontal cortex may not affect performance on standard tests of executive function which typically are more sensitive to lateral frontal lesions (see also Schnider et al., 1996a, 1996b; Kopelman et al., 1997; Kopelman, 1999).

Review of Recent Empirical Evidence for Theories of Confabulation

Considering the large literature on confabulation, it is surprising that only a few studies have attempted to investigate experimentally the underlying mechanisms of the disorder. This scarcity may be attributed to two primary types of difficulty. Methodological issues, such as finding a sufficiently large sample of subjects with well-defined confabulation make it difficult to run large-scale well-controlled studies. This problem is compounded by the temporal dynamics of the disorder, which tends to resolve within a few months in most cases. Furthermore, experimental manipulations and between-subject comparisons are difficult to perform, because confabulation is a positive sign that may or may not be produced, even in the same patient under the same conditions, and because confabulations are unique to the individual and rich in content that is often personal. It may be for these reasons that most studies in the field are single-case studies that are often descriptive in nature, at least with respect to the confabulations themselves. However, there are several group and single-case studies in which experimental manipulations have been attempted.

Compensation

One of the early questions to receive experimental attention was whether confabulation reflects a need to cover up gaps in memory that arise from amnesia. This is an important issue, as it addresses the distinction between confabulation as a secondary emotional response to a primary memory deficit and confabulation as a primary neuropsychological disorder. A common method used to investigate the issue of compensation is to present questions for which the expected answer is "I don't know" (e.g. "Do you remember what you did on 13 March 1985?"; Dalla-Barba, 1993a; Mercer et al., 1977) or questions regarding non-existent items, to which there is no answer (e.g. "what is a water-cove"; Schnider et al., 1996b). This approach has yielded mixed results, with some patients tending to provide the appropriate answer, "I don't know" (Dalla-Barba et al., 1993a, 1997a, 1997b; Schnider et al., 1996b), while others confabulate (Dalla-Barba et al., 1998; Kopelman et al., 1997; Papagno & Baddeley, 1997; Schnider et al., 1996b). The results from Schnider et al. (1996) are illustrative of this variation in response pattern. Although the authors rightly conclude, based on analysis of means of wrong answers, that gap filling is not a common mechanism of either provoked or spontaneous confabulations, they do not discuss the great variability in responses within each group. For example, one of their spontaneous confabulators produced confabulations on 8/15 items, while two others had 0/15. This result is similar to differences found between patients in different studies on Dalla-Barba's questionnaire. Furthermore, normal controls and non-confabulating amnesics also sometimes confabulate on such items, producing 5–30% confabulations on average (Kopelman et al., 1997; Schnider et al., 1996b).

A related question, examined by Mercer et al. (1977), is whether confabulation reflects the patients' suggestibility. They made patients believe that they had previously given a response to some questions to which they had actually responded with "I don't know" and asked them to reproduce their answer. Both severe and mild confabulators mostly adhered to their previous "I don't know" response, and did not differ on a tendency to provide an answer to these questions.

The findings suggest that confabulations that are produced because of suggestion or a memory lapse may not be directly related to the neurological condition, but rather may arise from aspects of personal style, such as leniency, the need to conform to apparent social demand, etc. From clinical observation, it seems that compensation does not occur as a primary cause of spontaneous confabulation, but comes into play once confabulation has begun and the individual becomes aware (or is made aware) that the responses given are implausible or inconsistent (Moscovitch, 1989). We refer to these as *secondary confabulations*. *Primary confabulations* may be associated with a poor sense of temporal order or of the source of one's memories, or with poor strategic retrieval. Thus, if a patient produces an erroneous memory (either spontaneously or in response to a prompt), this memory is considered a primary confabulation; it has no compensatory function and merely reflects the defective neuropsychological processes associated with confabulation. It is important to note that the patient genuinely believes that the memory is true. Even when the memory is implausible, the patient resists abandoning it.

One account for this strong belief in the confabulation is that this false memory is as vivid (Dalla-Barba, 1993b) or as impoverished in detail (Johnson et al., 1997; see later) as real memories. Dalla-Barba (1993b) administered a remember–know judgment paradigm to a confabulating patient. "Remember" judgments refer to memories whose source and context is retrieved, whereas "know" judgments are indicative of memories lacking such information. This patient gave "remember" judgments for all of the confabulations he produced, a finding that is indicative of an abundance of episodic details that accompanies the recall of these false memories (although for contradictory observations, see Papagno & Baddeley, 1997). At times, however, these beliefs may be so blatantly illogical, or the patient may be presented with contradictory evidence, that additional confabulations may arise in order to reconcile, often clumsily, the apparent contradiction while maintaining the strong belief in the original memory. These attempts often give rise to *secondary confabulation* and may have the same underlying mechanisms that promote gap-filling of the type seen in both confabulators and controls.

Temporality and Source Monitoring

Another hypothesis that has attracted much research is the *temporality hypothesis* discussed earlier. This research has evolved from the frequent observation that confabulations can be traced to an original true memory that is misplaced in time or in context. Research paradigms conducted from this perspective have usually focused on experimental tasks believed to represent the type of cognitive processing involved in time perception and judgment. In a series of studies on temporal context, Schnider et al. (1996b, 2000; Ptak & Schnider, 1999) used two runs of a continuous recognition paradigm, separated by 1 h, to test patients' ability to differentiate currently relevant stimuli from those which were previously studied. The results showed no difference between confabulating and non-confabulating amnesics in the ability to store new information, but what distinguished the two groups was that confabulating amnesics erroneously chose targets that were relevant on the previous list, but not the current one. Schnider et al. argue that their performance on this task is indicative of their temporal confusion, which leads to their conflating memories from widely dispersed time periods.

Schnider and colleagues termed the deficit "temporal context confusion" (TCC; see above), which is defined as an inability to suppress memory traces that are currently irrelevant but were once important. In contrast with most source memory tests, the subject is not required to indicate explicitly the origin of an item, a fact the authors take to mean that the task probes a feeling of current relevance, rather than an explicit cognitive process of the type usually involved in time-related cognition (Friedman, 1993; Johnson et al., 1993).

Schnider et al. (1996a, 1996b, 2000; Ptak & Schnider, 1999) suggested that temporal context confusion arises from lesions in anterior limbic structures as diverse as posterior orbitofrontal cortex, basal forebrain, amygdala, perirhinal cortex, or medial hypothalamus, which they refer to as the anterior limbic system. They further suggest that the more extensive the damage, the more persistent the confabulation, proposing that the ability to suppress irrelevant memories is distributed over many structures in the system. Damage to any one of these regions could lead to a temporary condition of confabulation, but only the destruction of all of these regions or their connection with executive structures at the dorsolateral prefrontal cortex would result in persistent confabulation (Schnider et al., 2000). They further relate their neuropsychological model to animal studies on the role of the posterior medial orbitofrontal cortex in reward behavior, which is specifically related to extinction. Animals with ablations to the posterior medial orbitofrontal cortex continue to respond to cues that are no longer rewarded, i.e. they fail to adapt their behavior to the new stimulus value. They suggest that a similar failure, different in complexity but not in quality, is the basic mechanism of confabulation, based on the assumption that human behavior in general is motivated by future incentives (Schnider et al., 1999, 2000).

The theoretical construct of temporal context confusion as an underlying mechanism of confabulation is well conceptualized, from both a psychological and an anatomical point of view. Empirically, the paradigm used to operationalize this construct yields robust results, in that confabulators consistently and specifically fail on the second run of the continuous recognition task. The paradigm, however, is overly reliant on false-positives as an indication of confabulation, a common experimental bias which probably originates from the difficulty in studying the mechanisms of confabulations in all their complexity. What is measured is a single response to a recently studied item, rather than the contextually-rich, elaborate responses that comprise confabulations, and that are often derived from knowledge or memories acquired long before the injury. The relation between spontaneous confabulations and failure on Schnider's task is attributed to the same underlying cause, namely failure to discount irrelevant memories or temporal confusion, although there is no evidence yet of a direct causal relation between the two. Furthermore, poor performance on Schnider's task may result from inefficient search and undifferentiated monitoring, rather than from TCC. For example, it may be that the inability to specify the particular temporal context of a memory trace is but one manifestation of a more general failure to specify the parameters that define the relevance of the memory trace to task demands. This would be equivalent to a failure in "descriptor" processes (Burgess & Shallice, 1996, see below) or the processes involved in the search component (i.e. initiating a search, constraining it and guiding it towards a proximal cue) of the strategic retrieval hypothesis of Moscovitch (e.g. Moscovitch & Melo, 1997). As yet, the question of which of these hypotheses provides the best account of the data is unresolved.

The idea of temporal context confusion as but one factor in many that lead to confabulation was also suggested by Kopelman et al. (1997). These authors studied a confabulating patient and compared her to three normal controls, a frontal-lobe patient and a temporal-lobe patient, using the Autobiographical Memory Interview (AMI, Kopelman et al., 1990), Dalla-Barba's (1993a) confabulation battery, an informal interview and a range of neuropsychological tests. Although their study did not specifically address the issue of temporality, their findings and conclusions are relevant to it. They report a "temporal gradient" in the accuracy of autobiographical memories, as revealed by the AMI, the confabulation battery and the interview (see Dalla-Barba et al., 1998, for similar findings in a study that used personal photos). Tracing the source of confabulatory responses of their patient led them to the conclusion that temporal confusion within the episodic domain was only one of a number of factors that contributed to her confabulation. Other factors were: (a) executive dysfunction, although not necessarily a pervasive one but rather a specific failure related to frontal dysfunction; (b) cues from the immediate environment, which either cause confabulations or influences their content (see Stuss et al., 1978, for a similar suggestion; but Mercer et al., 1977 for contradictory evidence); (c) perseverations were also noted as a causative factor, particularly in the semantic domain, a finding that resonates with previous research by Mercer et al. (1977) and by Shapiro et al. (1981), who found it to be a major factor in confabulation.

Deficit in *source monitoring* has also been offered as a cause of confabulation by Johnson (1991) and investigated by several researchers (Dab et al., 1999; Dalla-Barba et al., 1997b; Johnson et al., 1997; Nedjam et al., 2000). Johnson et al. (1997) tested temporal memory (duration and order), source memory (temporal and speaker identification) and reality monitoring (actual vs. imagined autobiographical vignettes) in G.S., a confabulating patient. They compared his performance to that of matched frontal-lobe patients who do not confabulate, and to normal controls. Additionally, they tested qualitative aspects, such as references to actions, people, objects, emotions and temporal information of a single recurring confabulation and a real memory. Their findings indicated that G.S.'s deficits on most source memory indices were similar to those of nonconfabulating frontal patients, except for his temporal ordering ability, which was preserved. They do note, however, that in comparison to controls and other frontal patients, G.S. had more details on imagined vignettes than on real ones, as well as impoverished autobiographical memory and an absence of temporal information in these memories. The recurring confabulation received a similar score on the amount and kind of details provided as did the real memory. Johnson et al. (1997) conclude that, although deficits in source monitoring may be a factor in confabulation, they contribute only in interaction with other factors, such as vivid imagination and an inability to retrieve autobiographical memories systematically (see Kopelman et al., 1997, for a similar conclusion).

Another drawback for the hypothesis that source memory is at the root of confabulation is the discrepancy between brain regions implicated in source memory and those identified whose damage is crucial for confabulation. Most of the evidence regarding the neuroanatomical substrate of source monitoring and memory implicate dorsolateral prefrontal regions (most often around Brodmann's area 10/46), as revealed in both neuroimaging and lesion studies (for review, see Johnson & Raye, 1998). Confabulation, on the other hand, is strongly associated with orbitomedial and ventromedial damage. It has never been reported with damage confined to the dorsolateral prefrontal cortex. Together with the evidence of the lack of specificity of source memory deficits in confabulators, this raises the question of the exact relationship between source memory deficits and confabulation. One possibility is that source monitoring deficits serve as one component of a collection of processes that eventually lead to confabulations (Johnson et al., 1997; Kopelman et al., 1997). This hypothesis leaves open the question whether it is a necessary component, or whether confabulation may also occur in the context of intact source memory. Most studies that tested source and reality monitoring in confabulation found deficits on some, although not necessarily on all, measures of source memory (see Johnson et al., 1997, on the usefulness of considering different source attributes separately). As mentioned earlier, G.S. had intact temporal ordering ability, while other source memory functions were compromised. Dab et al. (1999) report similar findings of preserved temporal ordering and deficits on contextual source in their patient. Nedjam et al.'s (2000) frontotemporal dementia patient, O.I., showed only mild deficits on a reality monitoring task, while their Alzheimer's disease patient showed severe deficits. Finally, patient H.W. (Moscovitch, 1989) did not show deficits on the source memory task used by Schacter et al. (1984) (Moscovitch, unpublished data). The evidence is currently too sparse to determine whether source memory deficits are indeed necessary components for confabulation, and if so which attributes of source memory might be the crucial ones. Alternatively, it may be that source memory deficits are epiphenomenal to confabulation, arising from damage caused either directly or indirectly by disrupting pathways to the dorsolateral cortex in confabulating patients. Cognitively, it could be that both these kinds of deficits are manifestations of a more general deficit in frontal memory processes which may or may not co-occur.

It is interesting to note that the bulk of the evidence for a temporality factor, whether as part of the TCC hypothesis or the source memory hypothesis, is derived from confabulations in the episodic domain. In the semantic domain, content errors are just as prevalent (Delbecq-Derouesné et al., 1990; Kopelman et al., 1997; Moscovitch & Melo 1997; Papagno & Baddeley, 1997). This could lead one to hypothesize that the predominance of time-related errors in episodic confabulations is an artifact of testing methods and the nature of episodic memory. Confabulations are often true memories that are erroneously or inappropriately recalled in the context of retrieval. Within the episodic domain, such erroneous memories are, by definition, tied to a particular moment in time. Within the semantic domain, however, memories are not tied to a particular moment in time and content-related confabulations can be detected. Episodic confabulations, even if they arise from a confusion in content, may be attributed to a confusion in time, as content and time in the episodic domain are confounded.

Strategic Retrieval

Like Johnson et al. (1997) and Kopelman et al. (1997; Kopelman, 1999), proponents of the strategic retrieval hypothesis believe that a confluence of factors lead to confabulation, only they relegate them to the realm of memory retrieval. Based on an analysis of the protocols of healthy volunteers' autobiographical recollections, Burgess & Shallice (1996) proposed a strategic retrieval model of confabulation that emphasizes the relation between control processes and memory processes. Specifically, self-reflections and errors of normal individuals during retrieval of recent everyday autobiographical episodes were analyzed and compared to error patterns found in confabulators. Three components of a model of strategic retrieval, corresponding to three different patterns of self-reflective comments or errors made by the volunteers, were identified:

1. *Description processes*, which specify the type of trace that would satisfy the demands of the retrieval task. Self-reflective comments, such as, "Thinking now about meetings I have been to recently . . . ", are thought to represent this type of process. They proposed that failure in descriptor processes would result in intrusion of generic or highly practiced memories, as could be seen on some of their volunteers' protocols. Some evidence for such failures underlying confabulations was later obtained in two case-reports of confabulating patients (Burgess & McNeil, 1999; Dab et al., 1999).
2. *Memory-editing processes*, which are continuously implicated in checking that the various outputs of memory search fit with each other and with the overall task requirements. Trying to recall an event that happened in January, one of their volunteers said: "I comp . . . I completed a major sale. No! . . . . . I didn't sell anything at all in January because I remember looking at the board and it was blank" (Burgess & Shallice, 1996, p. 382).
3. *Mediator processes* are general strategic and problem-solving procedures, which are used to monitor the adequacy and plausibility of retrieved memories, but are not memory-specific processes, e.g. " . . . well, it wouldn't have been an Indonesian because I hate peanut butter, and it's unlikely to have been a chicken place because my company was vegetarian . . . " (Burgess & Shallice, 1996, p. 410). Burgess & Shallice (1996) propose that severe damage to these processes may result in bizarre or fantastic confabulations, such as described by Damasio et al. (1985).

Burgess & Shallice's model is consistent with Moscovitch's proposal that confabulation is associated with deficits in strategic retrieval, which implicate defective search and monitoring. Moscovitch (1989) and Moscovitch & Melo (1997) provide evidence to support the strategic retrieval hypothesis derived from performance of confabulators on various memory tasks. Moscovitch & Melo (1997) compared a group of eight confabulating patients with a group of non-confabulating amnesics and controls on a variant of the Crovitz cue-word test (Crovitz & Schiffman, 1974). Subjects were required to produce personal memories to poorly specified cue words, such as "letter" or "broken". Three things distinguished confabulating from nonconfabulating amnesics:

1. Confabulating amnesics produced fewer memories overall, which is indicative of poor search strategies.
2. Confabulating amnesics benefited more from prompts that aided retrieval, thereby confirming that their search was defective. These results are in accord with informal observations in the patient H.W. (Moscovitch, 1989). When required to rely on strategic retrieval processes in response to non-specific cues, H.W. performed poorly. When, however, retrieval cues were specific, and triggered cue-dependent associative retrieval processes, he often could provide the correct response. For example, when asked to name the Canadian teams in the National Hockey League, H.W. insisted that there were only two, Toronto and Montreal. However, when given a more specific cue, and asked to complete the name of a team such as the "Vancouver _____" he would supply the correct name, protesting that he was merely guessing.
3. When a memory was recovered, poor monitoring led to a greater number of confabulations among the confabulating patients than in other amnesics. Indeed, prompting led to an increase in both veridical memories and erroneous ones in confabulating patients. Moscovitch & Melo (1997) also noted that confabulations were more likely to be about content than about temporal order (see Figure 15.2).

Similar results were obtained when subjects were required to recount historical events that occurred before they were born in response to non-specific cues, such as "battle" or "king". The latter finding indicated that confabulations can be associated as much with general (semantic) memories as with personal (episodic) memories as long as they both have a narrative structure, which likely implicates strategic retrieval processes more than the retrieval of semantic facts in response to direct questions. These findings highlight the importance of differentiating between *knowledge* and the *process* of retrieving that knowledge. The fact that confabulations are more common in episodic than semantic memory may not result from something intrinsic to the memories themselves, but rather because the process of strategic retrieval is implicated more in the recovery of episodic than of semantic memories.

Dalla-Barba and colleagues (1997b, 1999) dispute the idea that confabulation rates on semantic tasks may be low because of poor involvement of strategic retrieval on these tasks. In a single-case study of G.A., an ACoA patient, Dalla-Barba et al. (1997b) were not able to replicate the findings from Moscovitch & Melo (1997) using the semantic version of the Crovitz test. They concluded that even when strategic retrieval demands are equated, confabulation may be restricted to the episodic domain, in which G.A. did produce confabulations. They reach a similar conclusion based on the performance of 17 patients with mild Alzheimer's disease (Dalla-Barba et al., 1999), although in the latter case it is unclear that the patients could be considered as displaying a full confabulatory syndrome.

Dalla-Barba et al.'s (1997b) evidence against the strategic retrieval hypothesis is weak. It appears from the overall memory score for details that a large number of omissions, primarily on the semantic task, characterized their patient's performance. Furthermore, on

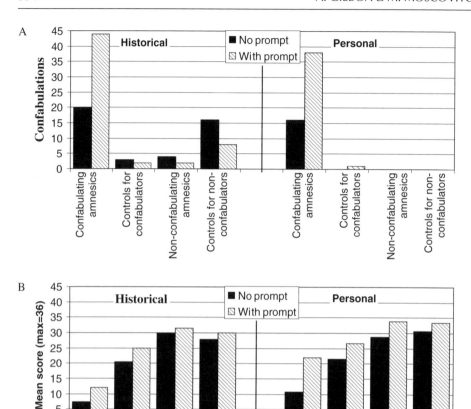

Figure 15.2 Total number of confabulations (A) and mean detail score (B), with and without prompt, for confabulating and non-confabulating amnesics and their respective controls on the Crovitz personal and historical cue-word test (from Moscovitch & Melo, 1997)

the items for which she did provide an answer, it was apparently very poor in detail. Thus, on a detail-scale of 0–2, where 0 is an omission and 2 is a very detailed response, GA scored an average of 0.6, which was 6 SDs lower than the average score of 1.8 in the controls. A slightly higher detail score was reported on the episodic version (0.9), which was accompanied with a low rate of confabulation (13%) compared to G.A.'s general tendency to confabulate. Indeed, as mentioned earlier, Moscovitch & Melo (1997) found that confabulating patients had the most difficulty in recovering memories in response to the minimal cues, which they ascribe to a deficit in the initiation and execution of search processes. They also found that prompting led to a substantial increase in both veridical memories and confabulations (see Figure 15.2). Unfortunately, Dalla-Barba and colleagues did not use the prompting technique in their study and it is unclear whether their task truly tapped strategic post-retrieval processes such as monitoring, or merely demonstrated the poor search ability of their patient.

Moscovitch & Melo (1997) implicate the ventromedial prefrontal cortex and adjacent regions as crucial for editing memories and inhibiting false ones (the primary feature of confabulation by this account), as well as for initiating search processes. More recently, Moscovitch & Winocur (2002) have differentiated between the functions of the ventro-medial PFC and the adjacent regions (see later). That the ventromedial and adjacent cortex should have some specialization in memory-related processes is strongly supported by the neuroanatomical connections of the caudal orbitofrontal and medial prefrontal cortices. These cortices receive input from the anterior inferior temporal cortices, perirhinal, entorhi-nal and parahippocampal cortices, as well as the hippocampus itself (for recent reviews, see Barbas, 2000; Öngur & Price, 2000). Robust projections from the thalamic midline nuclei, and in particular the dorsomedial thalamic nucleus, which is strongly implicated in memory functions (Victor & Adams, 1971), also attest to this region's role in memory. That the specific role in memory would be editing the content of retrieval is also plausible from an anatomical point of view. Cortico–cortical connections from these limbic cortices orig-inate predominantly in deep cortical layers, and are directed at the outer layers of diverse neocortical regions, a fact that has some functional implications. Specifically, in the sensory cortices, afferent neurons from deep layers that terminate on outer layers are believed to have a feedback role, suggesting that this may also be the role of the ventromedial and caudal orbitofrontal neurons in relation to neocortical ones (Barbas, 2000).

There are also good anatomical and neurobehavioral reasons to assume that the medial prefrontal cortex and adjacent structures may be involved in the initiation of search pro-cesses. One of the most prominent neurobehavioral consequences of insult to the medial prefrontal cortex is apathy and severe reduction in volition (Cummings, 1995; Devinsky et al., 1995; Stuss et al., 2000). Stuss et al. (2000) defined such apathy as an absence of responsiveness to stimuli and lack of self-initiated action. This may be related to the spe-cific pattern of input to this region, which includes afferents from brainstem structures, such as the lateral tegmental nucleus, as part of a circuit that regulates levels of arousal and exploratory behavior in animals (for review, see Gold & Chrousos, 1999). It is also inter-connected with subcortical structures, such as the dorsomedial thalamus and basal ganglia, that may also play a role in self-initiation of behavior (Stuss et al., 2000). An analogy to deficits in the initiation of search in the memory domain is not a far stretch in cases of confabulation, especially in the light of the apparent lack of concern about performance often observed in these patients (Moscovitch, 1989; Stuss et al., 1978).

It may be that different subregions of the ventromedial prefrontal cortex are responsible for these two different components of the strategic retrieval process. A more dorsal sub-genual region and anterior cingulate cortex may be responsible for the initiation of search, and a more ventral region closely related to the caudal medial orbitofrontal cortex region is probably related to the monitoring component (cf. Schnider et al., 1996a, 1996b, for a related view of this second component).

Damage to the dorsolateral prefrontal cortex may also be involved in the production of confabulations through its role in other, more controlled executive processes, either of the type described by Burgess & Shallice's (1996) mediator processes, or as part of the source monitoring processes (Johnson et al., 1993, 1997). Lesion studies in both humans and primates indicate that the mid-dorsolateral prefrontal cortex (areas 46/9) is crucial for the type of monitoring that involves keeping track of actions and of expected events, so as not to repeat them (Petrides, 1995). There is evidence (cited above) that perseveration may be an important mechanism in the production of some confabulations, primarily in the semantic domain (Kopelman et al., 1997; Mercer et al., 1977; Shapiro et al., 1981). It is thus reasonable to assume that damage to this region, or to its afferent pathways passing in the vicinity of the ventromedial prefrontal cortex, would lead to the breakdown of such memory control mechanisms. These regions closely adjoin the regions that are usually implicated in studies of temporal order judgments (Milner et al., 1991) and source monitoring (Johnson & Raye, 1998), processes which may also enhance the tendency to confabulate when they are impaired. Additionally, damage to the dorsolateral prefrontal cortex, primarily on the left, has also been noted to produce executive apathy and lack of responsiveness (Stuss et al., 2000), although probably to a lesser degree than anterior cingulate lesions. A model relating these cognitive processes and neuroanatomical regions is presented below.

Memory as Reconstruction: A Neuropsychological Model

Confabulation provides some of the best evidence that memory is a reconstructive process that becomes impaired, not only when acquisition and storage are defective but also when strategic retrieval processes needed for proper reconstruction are impaired. These principles are captured by the following neuropsychological model (Moscovitch, 1992; Moscovitch & Winocur, 1992) and has much in common with similar proposals by a number of investigators, including Conway (1992; Conway & Tacchi, 1996), Schacter et al. (1998) and Burgess & Shallice (1996).

Encoding and Storage

Any event that is experienced consciously is automatically picked up by the hippocampus and related limbic structures in the medial temporal lobe (hippocampal complex) and diencephalon. These structures help form a memory trace, which consists of an ensemble of neocortical neurons that mediate the conscious experience, bound together by the hippocampal complex. Memory traces are laid down randomly; except for simultaneity or immediate temporal contiguity, they are not organized by theme or temporal order with regard to any other event. With respect to hippocampal–neocortical ensembles which form memory traces, there is no past, present, or future.

Retrieval

Recovery of memory traces can be associative cue-dependent, in which case the cue directly activates the hippocampal–neocortical ensemble or memory trace. Alternatively, the frontal lobes act as "working-with-memory" structures that initiate and organize strategic retrieval search when the associative cue is inadequate. The frontal lobes are also involved in monitoring, evaluating and verifying recovered memory traces in accordance with the goals of the memory task, and in organizing memory traces into the correct context by theme and temporal order. Each of these functions is accomplished by different regions of a network in prefrontal cortex which work cooperatively with each other.

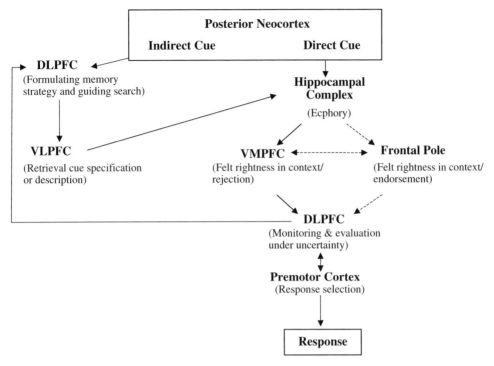

Figure 15.3 Proposed neuropsychological model of strategic retrieval (see text for details) (from Moscovitch & Winocur, 2002)

Recently, Moscovitch & Winocur (2002) have proposed a model elaborating on the hypothetical roles of different subregions of the prefrontal cortex in strategic memory retrieval, or "working-with-memory" functions, and their interaction with the hippocampal complex (see Figure 15.3). They base their model on converging evidence regarding the function of different regions within the prefrontal cortex (PFC) derived from animal and human lesion and neuroimaging literature. Briefly, the model suggests that if external or internal cues cannot elicit a memory directly, retrieval is initiated by the dorsolateral prefrontal cortex, which establishes a retrieval mode by setting the goals of the task. The ventrolateral prefrontal cortex plays a role in specifying, and describing the cues needed to gain access to and interact with the code in the hippocampal complex that elicits the memory trace. This is a reiterative process, which continues until a sufficiently specific cue activates the memory trace.

Once a memory trace is activated (either directly or via the PFC-mediated process), the information is passed on to the ventromedial prefrontal cortex, which signals endorsement or rejection based on an intuitive "felt rightness" quality of the recovered memory. This region may play the inhibitory (rejecting) role in a dual process, in which the reciprocal endorsement role is played by the frontal pole. Further processing and strategic deliberation is mediated by the dorsolateral prefrontal cortex, which interacts with posterior neocortex and ventrolateral cortex to determine the compatibility of the recovered memory with other knowledge and influence the decision of whether to accept it for further processing and response selection.

The model can account for the production of both spontaneous and provoked confabulation. As mentioned earlier, spontaneous confabulation may arise in the background of faulty associative cue-dependent retrieval, giving rise to an erroneous memory trace, although this stage is not a necessary condition for confabulation. Errors in cue-dependent retrieval are quite common among persons with an intact neurological system (Burgess & Shallice, 1996). The indirect route, which begins with the formulation of memory search strategy by the dorsolateral prefrontal cortex, then needs to be initiated. The initiation of this search is often faulty in confabulators, leading to the high rate of omissions. This may be the result of a dysfunction of either the dorsolateral prefrontal cortex itself or the anterior cingulate in the medial prefrontal cortex (currently not included in the model). Poor specification of cues by the ventrolateral prefrontal region may lead to activation of memories that are incompatible with the memory task within the hippocampal complex. This would normally lead to a repetition of the process. However, lesions to the ventromedial prefrontal cortex, which are crucial for confabulation to occur, lead to the indiscriminate acceptance of activated memories and so, in cases of erroneous traces, to the output of confabulation. This may also explain why, in the face of contradictory evidence, confabulators continue to adhere to their original memory and instead produce secondary confabulations in an attempt to reconcile the inconsistencies.

Source monitoring deficits (Johnson et al., 1997) and temporal context confusions (Schnider et al., 1996b) can be considered specific instances of such failures. The former may be more related to the faulty search strategy, as it appears that a sense of chronology is heavily dependent on active inferential reconstructive processes associated with the dorsolateral PFC (Friedman, 1993; Moscovitch, 1989; Moscovitch & Melo, 1997). Temporal context confusion, especially as construed by Schnider et al. (1996b) as a failure in suppressing erroneous memories, is likely one of the processes involved in the monitoring and editing out of memory search results associated with ventromedial regions (see above; see also Burgess & Shallice, 1996, for a related view and empirical evidence).

CONCLUSION

Until recently, neuropsychological studies of memory disorders focused on the limbic system, which includes structures in the medial temporal lobes and diencephelon. Memory loss resulting from damage to these structures was typically interpreted as being related to deficits in consolidation and storage. The prefrontal cortex did not figure much in most theories of memory, although some investigators, such as Brenda Milner (1982) and Alexander Luria (1976), did note its contribution.

Although confabulation is not common, more than any other condition it highlights the important role that the prefrontal cortex plays in memory. Attempts to account for confabulation have led to a shift in the focus of theories of memory from concerns with consolidation and storage, in which organizational processes play a minor role, to concerns with encoding and more so with retrieval, in which organizational and strategic processes play a major role. Faulty interaction between a cue and stored information is common among individuals who are neurologically intact, and is of course greatly enhanced when the associative retrieval system is damaged, as in the case of amnesia. Poor strategic search leads both to increased instances of omission (i.e. in cases when the correct cue–trace association exists but the patient fails to arrive at the correct cue) and to exacerbation of the problem of faulty output when the wrong proximal cue is selected or used. These instances, however, tend to go unnoticed when the monitoring component of the frontal strategic retrieval system functions properly, as they are quickly recognized and their output is inhibited, eliciting either omissions or the start of a new search. The unedited faulty output of the associative cue-dependent system attests to the failure of this editing component in confabulating patients.

The frontal lobes convert memory from a mere reflexive response to appropriate cues to a reflective activity that is guided by ongoing concerns and informs future plans and actions. Memory recovery itself is viewed primarily as a reconstructive process, mediated in large part by the frontal lobes but drawing on information represented in the medial temporal lobes and neocortex. The burgeoning neuroimaging studies of memory have confirmed the importance of the frontal lobes as working-with-memory structures. Activation of the prefrontal cortex is ubiquitous at both encoding and retrieval, and activation is greatest when strategic processes are emphasized.

ACKNOWLEDGEMENT

Preparation of this paper and some of the research reported here was supported by a Canadian Institute of Health Research grant to M.M. and Gordon Winocur.

REFERENCES

Aggleton, J.P. & Saunders, R.C. (1997). The relationships between temporal lobe and diencephalic structures implicated in anterograde amnesia. *Memory*, **5**(1–2), 49–71.

Alexander, M.P. & Freedman, M. (1984). Amnesia after anterior communicating artery aneurysm rupture. *Neurology*, **34**(6), 752–757.

American Psychiatric Association. (1994). *DSM-IV: Diagnostic and Statistical Manual of Mental Disorders*. Washington, DC: American Psychiatric Association.

Baddeley, A. & Wilson, B. (1988). Frontal amnesia and the dysexecutive syndrome. *Brain and Cognition*. **7**(2), 212–230.

Barbas, H. (2000). Complementary roles of prefrontal cortical regions in cognition, memory, and emotion in primates. *Advances in Neurology*, **84**, 87–110.

Barbizet, J. (1963). Defect of memorizing of hippocampal mammillary origin. *Journal of Neurology, Neurosurgery, and Psychiatry*, **26**, 127–135.

Benson, D.F., Djenderedjian, A., Miller, B.L. et al. (1996). Neural basis of confabulation. *Neurology*, **46**(5), 1239–1243.

Berlyne, N. (1972). Confabulation. *British Journal of Psychiatry*, **120**(554), 31–39.

Box, O., Laing, H. & Kopelman, M. (1999). The evolution of spontaneous confabulation, delusional misidentification and a related delusion in a case of severe head injury. *Neurocase*, **5**, 251–262.

Burgess, P.W. & McNeil, J.E. (1999). Content-specific confabulation. *Cortex*, **35**(2), 163–182.

Burgess, P.W. & Shallice, T. (1996). Confabulation and the control of recollection. *Memory*, **4**(4), 359–311.

Conway, M.A. (1992). A structural model of autobiographical memory. In M.A. Conway, D.C. Rubin, H. Spinnler & W.A. Wagenaar (eds), *Theoretical Perspectives on Autobiographical Memory* (pp. 167–194). Dordrecht: Kluwer Academic.

Conway, M.A. & Tacchi, P.C. (1996). Motivated confabulation. *Neurocase*, **2**, 325–345.

Crovitz, H.F. & Schiffman, H. (1974). Frequency of episodic memories as function of their ages. *Bulletin of the Psychonomics Society*, **4**, 517–518.

Cummings, J.L. (1995). Anatomic and behavioral aspects of frontal–subcortical circuits. *Annals of New York Academy of Sciences*, **15**, 769, 1–13.

Dab, S., Claes, T., Morais, J. & Shallice, T. (1999). Confabulation with a selective descriptor process impairment. *Cognitive Neuropsychology* (Special Issue: The Cognitive Neuropsychology of False Memories), **16**(3–5), 215–242.

Dalla Barba G. (1993a). Different patterns of confabulation. *Cortex*, **29**(4), 567–581.

Dalla Barba, G. (1993b). Confabulation: knowledge and recollective experience. *Cognitive Neuropsychology*, **10**(1), 1–20.

Dalla Barba, G. (2000). Memory, consciousness, and the brain. *Brain and Cognition*, **42**(1), 20–22.

Dalla Barba, G., Boisse, M.F., Bartolomeo, P. & Bachoud-Levi, A.C. (1997a). Confabulation following rupture of posterior communicating artery. *Cortex*, **33**(3), 563–570.

Dalla Barba, G., Cappelletti, J.Y., Signorin, M. & Denes, G. (1997b). Confabulation: remembering "another" past, planning "another" future. *Neurocase*, **3**, 425–436.

Dalla Barba, G., Mantovan, M.C., Cappelletti, J.Y. & Denes, G. (1998). Temporal gradient in confabulation. *Cortex*, **34**(3):417–426.

Dalla Barba, G., Nedjam, Z. & Dubois, B. (1999). Confabulation, executive functions, and source memory in Alzheimer's disease. *Cognitive Neuropsychology* (Special Issue: The Cognitive Neuropsychology of False Memories), **16**(3–5), 385–398.

Damasio, A.R., Graff-Radford, N.R., Eslinger, P.J. et al. (1985). Amnesia following basal forebrain lesions. *Archives of Neurology*, **42**(3), 263–271.

Delbecq-Derouesné, J., Beauvois, M.F. & Shallice, T. (1990). Preserved recall versus impaired recognition. *Brain*, **113**, 1045–1154.

DeLuca, J. (1993). Predicting neurobehavioral patterns following anterior communicating artery aneurysm. *Cortex*, **29**(4), 639–647.

DeLuca, J. (2000a). A cognitive neuroscience perspective on confabulation. *Neuropsychoanalysis*, **2**, 119–132.

DeLuca, J. (2000b). Confabulation: response to expert commnetators. *Neuropsychoanalysis*, **2**, 167–170.

DeLuca, J. & Cicerone, K.D. (1991). Confabulation following aneurysm of the anterior communicating artery. *Cortex*, **27**(3), 417–423.

DeLuca, J. & Diamond, B.J. (1995). Aneurysm of the anterior communicating artery: a review of neuroanatomical and neuropsychological sequelae. *Journal of Clinical and Experimental Neuropsychology*, **17**(1), 100–121.

Devinsky, O., Morre, M. & Vogt, B.A. (1995). Contribution of anterior cingulate cortex to behavior. *Brain*, **118**(1), 279–306.

Eslinger, P. & Damasio, A.R. (1984). Behavioral disturbances associated with rupture of anterior communicating artery. *Seminars in Neurology*, **4**(3), 385–389.

Feinstein, A., Levine, B. & Protzner, A. (2000). Confabulation and multiple sclerosis: a rare association. *Multiple Sclerosis*, **6**(3), 186–191.

Fischer, R.S., Alexander, M.P., D'Esposito, M. & Otto, R. (1995). Neuropsychological and neuroanatomical correlates of confabulation. *Journal of Clinical and Experimental Neuropsychology*, **17**(1), 20–28.

Friedman, W.J. (1993). Memory for the time of past events. *Psychological Bulletin*, **113**, 44–66.

Gold, P.W. & Chrousos, G.P. (1999). The endocrinology of melancholic and atypical depression: relation to neurocircuitry and somatic consequences. *Proceedings of the Association of American Physicians*, **111**(1), 22–34.

Hashimoto, R., Tanaka, Y. & Nakano, I. (2000). Amnesic confabulatory syndrome after focal basal forebrain damage. *Neurology*, **54**(4), 978–980.

Jernigan, T.L., Schafer, K., Butters, N. & Cermak, L.S. (1991). Magnetic resonance imaging of alcoholic Korsakoff patients. *Neuropsychopharmacology*, **4**(3), 175–186.

Johnson, M.K. (1991). Reality monitoring: evidence from confabulation in organic brain disease patients. In G.P. Prigatano & D.L. Schacter (eds), *Awareness of Deficit after Brain Injury: Clinical and Theoretical Issues* (pp. 176–197). New York: Oxford University Press.

Johnson, M.K., Hashtroudi, S. & Lindsay, D.S. (1993). Source monitoring. *Psychological Bulletin*, **114**, 3–28.

Johnson, M.K., O'Connor, M. & Cantor, J. (1997). Confabulation, memory deficits, and frontal dysfunction. *Brain and Cognition*, **34**(2), 189–206.

Johnson, M.K. & Raye, C.L. (1998). False memories and confabulation. *Trends in Cognitive Sciences*, **2**, 137–145.

Joseph, R. (1986). Confabulation and delusional denial: frontal lobe and lateralized influences. *Journal of Clinical Psychology*, **42**(3), 507–520.

Joseph, R. (1999). Frontal lobe psychopathology: mania, depression, confabulation, catatonia, perseveration, obsessive compulsions, and schizophrenia. *Psychiatry*, **62**(2), 138–172.

Kapur, N. & Coughlan, A.K. (1980). Confabulation and frontal lobe dysfunction. *Journal of Neurology, Neurosurgery and Psychiatry*, **43**(5), 461–463.

Kern, R.S., Van Gorp, W.G., Cummings, J.L. et al. (1992). Confabulation in Alzheimer's disease. *Brain and Cognition*, **19**, 172–182.

Kopelman, M.D. (1987). Two types of confabulation. *Journal of Neurology, Neurosurgery and Psychiatry*, **50**(11), 1482–1487.

Kopelman, M.D. (1999). Varieties of false memory. *Cognitive Neuropsychology* (Special Issue: The Cognitive Neuropsychology of False Memories), **16**(3–5), 197–214.

Kopelman, M.D., Ng, N. & Van den Brouke, O. (1997). Confabulation extending across episodic memory, personal and general semantic memory. *Cognitive Neuropsychology*, **14**, 683–712.

Kopelman, M.D., Wilson, B. & Baddeley, A.D. (1990). *The Autobiographical Memory Interview*. Bury St Edmonds: Thames Valley Test Company.

Korsakoff, S.S. (1955). Psychic disorder in conjunction with peripheral neuritis (transl. M. Victor & P.I. Yakovlev). *Neurology*, **5**, 394–406 (original work published in 1889).

Lindqvist, G. & Norlen, G. (1966). Korsakoff's syndrome after operation on ruptured aneurysm of the anterior communicating artery. *Acta Psychiatrica Scandinavica*, **42**(1), 24–34.

Luria, A. (1976). *The Neuropsychology of Memory*. New York: Wiley.

Manzel, K., Tranel, D. & Cooper, G. (2000). Cognitive and behavioral abnormalities in a case of central nervous system Whipple disease. *Archives of Neurology*, **57**(3), 399–403.

Mercer, B., Wapner, W., Gardner, H. & Benson, D.F. (1977). A study of confabulation. *Archives of Neurology*, **34**(7), 429–433.

Milner, B. (1982). Some cognitive effects of frontal-lobe lesions in man. *Philosophical Transactions of The Royal Society of London*, **298**(1089), 211–226.

Milner, B., Corsi, P. & Leonard, G. (1991). Frontal-lobe contribution to recency judgements. *Neuropsychologia*, **29**(6), 601–618.

Morris, M.K., Bowers, D. Chatterjee, A. & Heilman, K.M. (1992). Amnesia following a discrete basal forebrain lesion. *Brain*, **115**(6), 1827–1847.

Moscovitch, M. (1989). Confabulation and the frontal systems: strategic versus associative retrieval in neuropsychological theories of memory. In H.L. Roediger III & F.I.M. Craik (eds), *Varieties of Memory and Consciousness: Essays in Honor of Endel Tulving* (pp. 133–160). Hillsdale, NJ: Erlbaum.

Moscovitch, M. (1992). Memory and working with memory: a component process model based on modules and central systems. *Journal of Cognitive Neuroscience*, **4**, 257–267.

Moscovitch, M. (1995). Confabulation. In D.L. Schacter (ed.), *Memory Distortion: How Minds, Brains, and Societies Reconstruct the Past* (pp. 226–251). Cambridge: Harvard University Press.

Moscovitch, M. & Melo, B. (1997). Strategic retrieval and the frontal lobes: evidence from confabulation and amnesia. *Neuropsychologia*, **35**(7), 1017–1034.

Moscovitch, M. & Umiltá, C. (1991). Modularity and neuropsychology: modules and central processes in attention and memory. In Lister, R.G. & Weingartner, H.J. (eds), *Perspectives on Cognitive Neuroscience* (pp. 229–266). New York: Oxford University Press.

Moscovitch, M. & Winocur, G. (1992). The neuropsychology of memory and aging. In F.I.M. Craik & T.A. Salthouse (eds), *The Handbook of Aging and Cognition* (pp. 315–372). Hillsdale, NJ: Erlbaum.

Moscovitch, M. & Winocur, G. (2002). The frontal cortex and working with memory. In D. Stuss & R. Knight (eds), *Principles of Frontal Lobe Function*. New York: Oxford University Press.

Nedjam, Z., Dalla Barba, G. & Pillon, B. (2000). Confabulation in a patient with fronto-temporal dementia and a patient with Alzheimer's disease. *Cortex*, **36**(4), 561–577.

Öngur, G. & Price, J.L. (2000). The organization of networks within the orbitofrontal and medial prefrontal cortex of rats, monkeys and humans. *Cerebral Cortex*, **10**, 206–219.

Papagno, C. & Baddeley, A. (1997). Confabulation in a dysexecutive patient: implication for models of retrieval. *Cortex*, **33**(4), 743–752.

Parkin, A.J., Leng, N.R., Stanhope, N. & Smith, A.P. (1988). Memory impairment following ruptured aneurysm of the anterior communicating artery. *Brain and Cognition*, **7**(2), 231–243.

Petrides, M. (1995). Functional organization of the human frontal cortex for mnemonic processing. Evidence from neuroimaging studies. *Annals of the New York Academy of Science*, **769**, 85–96.

Ptak, R. & Schnider, A. (1999). Spontaneous confabulation after orbitofrontal damage: the role of temporal context confusion and self-monitoring. *Neurocase*, **5**, 243–250.

Rapcsak, S.Z., Kaszniak, A.W., Reminger, S.L., Glisky, M.L., Glisky, E.L. & Comer, J.F. (1998). Dissociation between verbal and autonomic measures of memory following frontal lobe damage. *Neurology*, **50**, 1259–1265.

Ray, J.P. & Price, J.L. (1993). The organization of projections from the mediodorsal nucleus of the thalamus to orbital and medial prefrontal cortex in macaque monkeys. *Journal of Comparative Neurology*, **337**, 1–31.

Schacter, D.L., Curran, T., Galluccio, L. et al. (1996). False recognition and the right frontal lobe: a case study. *Neuropsychologia*, **34**(8), 793–808.

Schacter, D.L., Harbluk, J.L. & McLachlan, D.R. (1984). Retrieval without recollection: an experimental analysis of source amnesia. *Journal of Verbal Learning and Verbal Behavior*, **23**(5), 593–611.

Schacter, D.L., Norman, K.A. & Koutstaal, W. (1998). The cognitive neuroscience of constructive memory. *Annual Review of Psychology*, **49**, 289–318.

Salmon, D. & Butters, N. (1987). Etiology and neuropathology of the alcoholic Korsakoff syndrome. Some evidence for the role of the basal forebrain. In M. Galanter (ed.), *Recent Developments in Alcoholism*, Vol. 5 (pp. 27–58). New York: Plenum.

Schnider, A., Gutbrod, K., Hess, C.W. & Schroth, G. (1996a). Memory without context: amnesia with confabulations after infarction of the right capsular genu. *Journal of Neurology, Neurosurgery and Psychiatry*, **61**(2), 186–193.

Schnider, A., Ptak, R., von Daniken, C. & Remonda, L. (2000). Recovery from spontaneous confabulations parallels recovery of temporal confusion in memory. *Neurology*, **55**(1), 74–83.

Schnider, A. & Ptak, R. (1999). Spontaneous confabulators fail to suppress currently irrelevant memory traces. *Nature Neuroscience*, **2**(7), 677–681.

Schnider, A., von Daniken, C. & Gutbrod, K. (1996b). The mechanisms of spontaneous and provoked confabulations. *Brain*, **119**(4), 1365–1375.

Shapiro, B.E., Alexander, M.P., Gardner, H. & Mercer, B. (1981). Mechanisms of confabulation. *Neurology*, **31**(9), 1070–1076.

Stuss, D.T., Alexander, M.P., Lieberman, A. & Levine, H. (1978). An extraordinary form of confabulation. *Neurology*, **28**(11), 1166–1172.

Stuss, D.T., Van Reekum, R. & Murphy, K.J. (2000). Differentiation of states and causes of apathy. In *The Neuropsychology of Emotion*. New York: Oxford University Press.

Talland, G.A. (1965). *Deranged Memory*. New York: Academic Press.

Talland, G.A., Sweet, W.H. & Ballantyne, H.T. Jr (1967). Amnesic syndrome with anterior communicating artery aneurysm. *Journal of Nervous and Mental Disorders*, **145**, 179–192.

Tallberg, I.M. & Almkvist, O. (2001). Confabulation and memory in patients with Alzheimer's disease. *Journal of Clinical and Experimental Neuropsychology*, **23**(2), 172–184.

Torvik, A. (1987). Topographic distribution and severity of brain lesions in Wernicke's encephalopathy. *Clinical Neuropathology*, **6**(1), 25–29.

Tulving, E. (1985). Memory and consciousness. *Canadian Psychology*, **26**, 1–12.

Victor, M., Adams, R.D. & Collins, G.H. (1971). *The Wernicke–Korsakoff Syndrome*. Philadelphia, PA: Davis.

Vilkki, J. (1985). Amnesic syndromes after surgery of anterior communicating artery aneurysms. *Cortex*, **21**(3), 431–444.

Weinstein, E.A. & Kahn, R.L. (1955). *Denial of Illness: Symbolic and Psychological Aspects*. Springfield, IL: Charles C. Thomas.

Weiskrantz, L. (1987). Neuroanatomy of memory and amnesia: a case for multiple memory systems. *Human Neurobiology*, **6**(2), 93–105.

Williams, H.W. & Rupp, C. (1938). Observation on confabulation. *American Journal of Psychiatry*, **95**: 395–405.

Zangwill, O.L. (1953). Disorientation for age. *Journal of Mental Science*, **99**, 698–701.

CHAPTER 16

The Cognitive Neuropsychology of False Memories: Theory and Data

Chad S. Dodson
University of Virginia, Charlottesville, VA, USA
and
Daniel L. Schacter
Harvard University, Cambridge, MA, USA

Memory for past events can differ, sometimes in striking ways, from how they were initially experienced (Bartlett, 1932; Kopelman, 1999; Loftus et al., 1978; Neisser, 1967; Roediger, 1996; Schacter, 1995, 2001). Even exceptionally vivid and emotional memories, such as "flashbulb memories", are not immune from memory distortion. Schmolck, Buffalo, and Squire (2000) examined individuals' memory for the events surrounding their learning the verdict of the O.J. Simpson trial, such as where they were, who they were with, what they felt, etc. They tested their participants' memory 3 days after the announcement of the verdict and then either 15 months or 32 months later. Surprisingly, nearly 43% of the individuals tested at the 32 month interval reported memories that contained major distortions, as compared to the account they gave just 3 days after learning the verdict. For instance, one individual reported at the 3 day interval that he learned about the verdict while in a lounge at college. When tested 32 months later, this individual remembered being at home with his sister and father when he learned about the verdict. Ironically, many individuals expressed confidence in the accuracy of their recollection, despite its actual inaccuracy (for similar results, see Bohannon & Symons, 1992; Neisser & Harsch, 1992).

How can a remembered episode differ so dramatically from how that episode was initially experienced? As Roediger & McDermott (2000, p. 149) ask in their review of memory distortion, "Where would the recollection come from, if not from stored traces of actual events?" This chapter will review cognitive and neuropsychological research that illustrates mechanisms that promote or minimize the occurrence of distorted memories. First, we will outline a general framework for understanding the processes that contribute to constructive memory phenomena. We then will consider how false memories are influenced by factors operating primarily at the encoding or retrieval stages of memory.

The Handbook of Memory Disorders. Edited by A.D. Baddeley, M.D. Kopelman and B.A. Wilson
© 2002 John Wiley & Sons, Ltd.

A CONSTRUCTIVE MEMORY FRAMEWORK

Our view of constructive memory, which we refer to as the constructive memory framework (CMF; see also Schacter et al. 1998a), draws on the ideas of several investigators, including Johnson et al. (1993), McClelland et al. (1995), Moscovitch (1994), Norman & Schacter (1996), Reyna & Brainerd (1995) and Squire (1992), among others. This framework focuses on key encoding and retrieval processes that contribute to both accurate and inaccurate memories.

Memories of past events consist of a pattern of features that constitute a record of the processes that were active during the encoding of these events (e.g. Johnson et al., 1993; Johnson & Raye, 1981), e.g. some features in the pattern would represent the output of different sensory processes, whereas others would reflect the output of conceptual processes. This pattern of features is widely distributed across different parts of the brain, such that no single location contains a complete record of the trace or engram of a specific experience (Damasio, 1989; Squire, 1992). In short, the memory representation of an event is this distributed pattern of features. Remembering this event, therefore, involves a process of reactivating the features constituting the desired memory representation. In other words, remembering is a process of pattern completion (McClelland et al., 1995) in which a retrieval cue activates a subset of the features comprising a particular past experience, and activation spreads to the rest of the constituent features of that experience.

There are several problems that must be solved in order for the foregoing memory system to represent past events relatively accurately. First, during the encoding of an event, the features making up the corresponding memory representation must be connected or bound together to form a "coherent" representation (i.e. the feature binding process; see Johnson & Chalfonte, 1994; Moscovitch, 1994; Schacter, 1989). If the feature binding process is incomplete because the individual is distracted, for instance, then he/she may subsequently remember fragments or particular features of the episode but not the entire pattern (Johnson et al., 1993; Schacter et al., 1984; Squire, 1995). Inadequate feature binding can contribute to source memory failure, in which an individual fails to remember the conditions under which an event was acquired, such as remembering a fact but failing to remember the journal that contained this bit of information. A second problem that must be solved at encoding is keeping the bound representations or patterns separate from each other. There must be a process of pattern separation (McClelland et al., 1995), e.g. if an individual regularly has breakfast with a friend, then the memory representations for these different episodes will share many characteristics. The patterns comprising the separate memories of these episodes will overlap. If the patterns overlap extensively with one another, then the person may subsequently only recall the general similarities (Hintzman & Curran, 1994) or gist (Reyna & Brainerd, 1995) common to the many episodes. In other words, if there is a failure in pattern separation, then an individual may fail to recollect distinctive, item-specific information that distinguishes one episode from another.

The memory system must solve similar problems at retrieval in order to reconstruct relatively accurate memories of past events. A common assumption of most memory theorists is that the likelihood of retrieving a past event depends on the degree to which features of the retrieval cue match features of the memory representation (e.g. Bower, 1967; Hintzman, 1988; Johnson & Raye, 1981; Tulving, 1983; Underwood, 1969). One problem is that retrieval cues can potentially match representations other than the one that is desired (Dodson &

Shimamura, 2000; Nystrom & McClelland, 1992). For instance, if given the retrieval cue "having breakfast with a friend", there could be countless memories that contain this characteristic and that would potentially be remembered. To solve this problem, there is often an initial stage of retrieval, referred to as focusing (Norman & Schacter, 1996), in which the rememberer forms a more refined description of the characteristics of the episode to be retrieved (Burgess & Shallice, 1996; Norman & Bobrow, 1979). Poor retrieval focus can lead to recollection of information that does not pertain to the target episode. However, the process of focusing means that how people are oriented to assess their memories can influence what is remembered. This is indeed what is found, e.g. the particular kind of memory test, such as an old–new recognition or a source monitoring test, can affect the probability of making a source misattribution (e.g. Dodson & Johnson, 1993; Lindsay & Johnson, 1989; Marsh & Hicks, 1998; Multhaup, 1995; Zaragoza & Lane, 1994).

Once memorial information has been retrieved, the memory system faces an additional problem, referred to by Johnson (1992) as the source monitoring problem. A decision must be made about whether the activated information is a veridical recollection of a previously experienced event, or whether it is a fantasy or a memory of an earlier imagined event (Johnson & Raye, 1981). This phase of retrieval involves a criterion-setting process: the rememberer needs to consider the diagnostic value of perceptual vividness, semantic detail and other kinds of information for determining the origin of the retrieved pattern (Johnson et al., 1993). It is also during this stage that an individual's expectations, metamemorial beliefs and strategies influence how the remembered information is evaluated (e.g. Dodson & Johnson, 1996; Dodson & Schacter, 2001, 2002, and in press).

Although many brain areas are involved in the preceding memory processes, two brain regions are especially relevant to constructive memory: the medial temporal area, including the hippocampal formation, and the prefrontal cortex. Many researchers view the hippocampus as implementing feature binding and pattern separation (cf. McClelland et al., 1995; Squire & Alvarez, 1995; Treves & Rolls, 1994). According to this view, distributed patterns of activity in the neocortex, constituting the memory representations for different episodes, are linked to sparse neuronal representations in region CA3 of the hippocampus, such that each episode is assigned its own hippocampal "index". To the extent that the hippocampus is able to assign nonoverlapping CA3 representations to different episodes, pattern separation is achieved, which will facilitate remembering distinctive characteristics about particular episodes.

The medial temporal region also contributes to pattern completion at retrieval (e.g. Moscovitch, 1994). According to McClelland et al. (1995; see also Squire, 1992), during retrieval of relatively recent episodes (for which there is still a hippocampal index corresponding to the episode), cues activate the episode's index in region CA3 of the hippocampus, and activation spreads from the index to all the features comprising that episode. Once an episode has been consolidated in the neocortex, however, activation can spread directly between the episode's features, and the hippocampus no longer plays an important role in pattern completion (for a contrasting view on consolidation and the medial temporal lobe, see Nadel et al., 2000). Relevant evidence is provided by Teng & Squire (1999) concerning a patient, E.P., with profound amnesia resulting from bilateral damage to the hippocampus and surrounding structures. E.P. is severely impaired at remembering recent events. Nonetheless, he is able to retrieve remote memories about the spatial layout of the city where he grew up as well as controls who also lived in the same city as E.P. during the same time period and for about the same length of time. Thus, although the medial temporal lobe plays a critical role in the formation of episodic memories, it does not appear to be a necessary part of the retrieval of remote episodic memories, at least spatial memories (cf. Rosenbaum et al., 2000, for a patient with more extensive damage who shows dissociations between different types of remote spatial memories; for neuroimaging evidence indicating hippocampal activation during retrieval of remote memories, see Nadel et al., 2000).

The prefrontal cortex also plays a role in the retrieval of memories (for review, see Shimamura, 2000). Patients with frontal lobe damage have shown difficulty remembering the source of previously learned facts (e.g. Janowsky et al., 1989a), reconstructing the order of a recently studied list of words (e.g. Shimamura et al., 1990), determining the relative recency of items (e.g. Milner, 1971) and so forth. In addition, neuroimaging studies consistently have shown prefrontal activity during episodic retrieval, often in a right anterior frontal region (for reviews, see Buckner, 1996; Nyberg et al., 1996; Tulving et al., 1994). Although the exact nature of the functions indexed by these activations remains open to debate, they appear to tap effortful aspects of retrieval (Schacter et al., 1996a) related to focusing or entering the "retrieval mode" (Lepage et al., 2000; Nyberg et al., 1995), post-retrieval monitoring and criterion setting (Rugg et al., 1996; Schacter et al., 1997) or both (Norman & Schacter, 1996).

In the remainder of the chapter we will consider both cognitive and neuropsychological evidence focusing on false memories, particularly occurrences of false recognition. We will attempt to explain these occurrences of memory in terms of malfunctioning processes operating at encoding and/or retrieval.

MEMORY DISTORTION AND FALSE RECOGNITION

One often investigated kind of memory distortion, known as false recognition, occurs when individuals report incorrectly that they previously encountered a novel event (e.g. Deese, 1959; Underwood, 1965). False recognition responses reflect, to some degree, a tendency to endorse items that are similar to what was studied, e.g. individuals are likely to falsely recognize: (a) objects that resemble many earlier-studied objects (e.g. Franks & Bransford, 1971; Posner & Keele, 1968, 1970); (b) words that are semantically related to earlier presented words (e.g. Underwood, 1965); or (c) sentences that match the implied meaning of studied sentences (e.g. Bransford & Franks, 1971; Johnson et al., 1973). Interestingly, Johnson et al.'s study indicates that individuals occasionally go beyond the information given in the studied sentence (e.g. Bruner, 1986), i.e. one's preexisting knowledge—and hence, expectancies—can introduce distortion. For example, after listening to the sentence, "the spy threw the secret document into the fireplace just in time, since 30 seconds longer would have been too late", participants on a later recognition test were likely to claim that they had heard "the spy had burned the secret document" (Johnson et al., 1973). Furthermore, becoming more knowledgeable about a topic—increasing one's expertise—does not necessarily reduce memory errors. In fact, Arkes & Freedman (1984) show that, compared to novices, experts were more likely to falsely recognize statements that matched the implied meaning of events in a previously read story. These kinds of errors indicate that distorted memories are occasionally a byproduct of comprehension in which a representation is created that is based on both the information provided and general knowledge (however, see Alba & Hasher, 1983; Brewer, 1977).

During the past several years, a paradigm developed by Deese (1959) and modified by Roediger & McDermott (1995; see also Read, 1996) has attracted much attention because it produces very high levels of false memories. The Deese/Roediger–McDermott (DRM) paradigm consists of presenting individuals with a list of words (e.g. one list might consist of the words truck, bus, train, automobile, vehicle, drive, jeep, Ford, race, keys, garage, highway, sedan, van, and taxi) that are all semantically related to a lure word that was not presented in the list (e.g. car). Subsequently, when asked to recall the presented words individuals frequently report having studied the non-presented lure word (e.g. car) (e.g. Deese, 1959; McDermott, 1996; Read, 1996; Roediger & McDermott, 1995; Smith & Hunt, 1998; Toglia et al., 1999). Similarly, if individuals are asked to distinguish between studied words and new words, they often falsely recognize the related lure word. In fact, false recognition rates to the non-presented lure words are so high that they are often indistinguishable from the correct recognition rates to words that were actually studied (Dodson & Schacter, 2001; Mather et al., 1997; Norman & Schacter, 1997; Payne et al., 1996; Roediger & McDermott, 1995; Schacter et al., 1996c; cf. Miller & Wolford, 1999; Roediger & McDermott, 1999; Wixted & Stretch, 2000).

Although there are a variety of factors contributing to this false memory effect, such as how deeply the items were encoded or whether people were distracted during the study phase, one important variable is the number of related items that were studied (e.g. Seamon et al., 1998; Smith & Hunt, 1998; Toglia et al., 1999). Individuals are more likely to falsely recognize a related new word when they have studied many, rather than few, associates of the item (e.g. Arndt & Hirshman, 1998; Robinson & Roediger, 1997; Shiffrin et al., 1995), e.g. Arndt & Hirshman presented participants with lists that contained either 4 or 16 associated words (filler words were included to equate list lengths). On a later memory test, studied words from the small and large lists of associates were recognized at comparable rates (58% for the 4-associate-word lists and 61% for the 16-associate-word lists). By contrast, new words were much more likely to be falsely recognized when they were related to the large list of associates (67%) than to the small list of associates (41%).

There have been three general accounts of this false recognition effect. The first explanation involves the increased activation, or familiarity, of the lure word (e.g. car) that is a consequence of having studying many related words (e.g. truck, bus, train) (see Arndt & Hirshman, 1998, for a fuller discussion). Specifically, the related new word's familiarity is determined by the degree to which it is similar to or matches earlier studied items. Thus, increasing the number of similar words that are studied will increase the activation and the false recognition rate of the related new word. Related to this account, the activation/monitoring framework of Roediger, McDermott and colleagues views the activation of the lure word as occurring during the study phase (e.g. McDermott & Watson, in press; Roediger et al., in press), i.e. studying the related words (e.g. bed, tired, dream, etc.) activates, via a lexical/semantic network, the lure word (e.g. sleep), thus enhancing its likelihood of false recall and false recognition. A second account of this false memory effect, represented by the CMF (and also by Brainerd & Reyna's "fuzzy trace" theory), proposes that it is a byproduct of pattern separation failure (e.g. Schacter et al., 1998a), i.e. when many related words have been studied there may be very high levels of overlap among the corresponding memory representations. This failure to keep representations separate will result in good memory for what the items have in common, but there will be poor memory for the specific details about each item. However, this difficulty in recollecting specific information about the studied items may encourage responding on the basis of the test item's overall familiarity or the degree to which it matches the gist of what was studied (Brainerd & Reyna, 1998; Payne et al., 1996; Schacter et al., 1996c). A third explanation of this false memory effect involves a process of "implicit associative responses" (Underwood, 1965), in which studying many related words (e.g. truck, bus, train, etc.) may lead individuals to produce on their own the new lure word (i.e. car). On a subsequent memory test, individuals may experience source confusion with the lure words and mistakenly believe that they have studied this word, when in fact it was one that they had generated (e.g. Johnson et al., 1993).

These accounts of the false memory effect in the DRM paradigm are not exclusive, of course, and may even interact with each other. For example, according to Roediger, McDermott and colleagues' activation/monitoring framework, studying many associated words activates the related lure word to such a degree that individuals occasionally think of the lure word (Roediger et al., in press). In other words, the activation of the lure word contributes to the occurrence of an implicit associative response. Moreover, if individuals do consciously generate the lure word during the study episode, then as it is rehearsed with the other studied words the lure word may acquire some of the features that are shared by the other studied words. Thus, according to this framework rehearsal processes during the study phase contribute to "remember" responses on the later memory test, whereby people recollect specific features about the lure word, such as the quality of the voice that spoke it (e.g. Payne et al., 1996).

Koutstaal & Schacter (1997) have provided evidence that activation and/or pattern-separation related processes, instead of implicit associative responses, can produce false recognition. Participants in their study were presented with numerous pictures from various categories, such as different kinds of shoes and cars. On a later memory test, participants often falsely recognized new pictures that were similar to studied pictures, such as a new picture of a shoe. Koutstaal & Schacter reasoned that it is unlikely that participants produced the new picture during the study phase as an implicit associative response. Instead, false recognition responses to the new pictures were likely a result of some combination of the first two accounts: (a) associative activation processes, in which related pictures are falsely recognized because they match many studied pictures; and/or (b) pattern separation failure, whereby individuals have difficulty remembering features about specific studied pictures but do remember what the pictures have in common (i.e. the gist) and, therefore, respond accordingly.

The foregoing studies indicate that memory distortion can result from a variety of factors that operate at both encoding and at retrieval. As many have noted, distorted memories are, in part, a by-product of comprehension processes as the mind attempts to integrate what is perceived with what is known (for review and discussion, see Alba & Hasher, 1983; Schacter, 1996). However, as we will discuss later, how events are remembered does not depend solely on the processes occurring during perception and comprehension. For both the source monitoring framework of Johnson and colleagues and the CMF of Schacter and colleagues, retrieval strategies and how individuals are oriented to examine their memories can influence what is remembered about past events (e.g. Dodson & Johnson, 1993, 1996; Hasher & Griffin, 1978; Johnson et al., 1993; Lindsay & Johnson, 1989; Schacter et al., 1998a).

FALSE RECOGNITION AND AMNESIA

Neuropsychologists have recently begun to intensify their efforts to examine memory distortion and the underlying brain systems that give rise to false memories (for reviews, see

Kopelman, 1999; Schacter et al., 1998). In this section we focus on patients with amnesia and the contributions to our understanding of constructive memory that have been provided by studying amnesic patients. Patients with damage to the temporal lobes and related structures in the diencephalon usually exhibit problems in remembering recent events, despite showing relatively intact perceptual, linguistic and general intellectual abilities (e.g. Parkin & Leng, 1993; Squire, 1992).

Schacter et al. (1996c) used the DRM paradigm to investigate memory distortion in amnesics. Amnesics (of varying etiologies) and control subjects studied lists of semantically related words (e.g. bed, tired, dream) and then completed a recognition test containing studied words (e.g. bed), new related words (e.g. sleep), and new unrelated words (e.g. point). As expected, amnesics recognized fewer studied items than did the matched controls. However, they also falsely recognized fewer related lure words than did the controls (for an extension, see Melo et al., 1999). In a follow-up experiment, Schacter et al. (1997) showed that amnesics' reduced false recognition of related lure items extends to perceptual materials. After studying perceptually related words (e.g. fade, fame, face, fake, mate, hate, late, date, and rate) amnesics were less likely than controls both to correctly recognize studied words and to falsely recognize perceptually related lure words (e.g. fate). Thus, for amnesics the same processes that support accurate recognition of studied words also contribute to the false recognition of critical lures that are semantically or perceptually related to earlier studied items (see Koutstaal et al., 1999b, in press, for similar patterns of reduced false recognition in amnesics with different types of pictorial stimuli).

Subsequent experiments using the DRM paradigm have identified conditions in which amnesics show comparable or higher than normal false recognition rates to related lure words. In a study by Schacter et al. (1998b), both amnesic patients (both Korsakoff and amnesics of mixed etiology) and matched controls studied DRM lists of semantically related words and then made old–new recognition judgments about studied words, new related words, and new unrelated words. The key feature of this paradigm was that this study and test procedure was repeated five times, with the same study and test items in all trials. As seen in panels A and C of Figure 16.1, both amnesics and controls correctly recognized increasingly more studied words with repeated study and testing. Panels B and D of Figure 16.1 show the false recognition rates to the related lure words. Across the five study-test trials, control subjects falsely recognized fewer related lure words (see also McDermott, 1996; McKone & Murphy, 2000), whereas the Korsakoff amnesics falsely recognized increasingly more related lure words (Panel B) and the mixed amnesics showed fluctuating levels of false recognition (Panel D). Control subjects presumably encoded more distinct features of the studied words with repeated study and testing, causing their representations to overlap less and less. Moreover, their increasingly better memory for studied words—and the greater pattern separation—heightened the probability that control subjects would notice a difference between the studied words and the related lure word, thus diminishing the false recognition rate across study-test trials.

The Korsakoff amnesics, by contrast, were not able to suppress false recognition responses to the related lures with repeated study and testing. In terms of the CMF, the Korsakoff amnesics formed additional memory representations, and enriched existing ones, with repeated study and testing. However, these representations were not enriched to such an extent that there was a substantial increase in pattern separation. Consequently, there was an increase in false recognition responses across the study-test trials because these amnesics were unable to remember specific information about the studied items to oppose falsely recognizing the

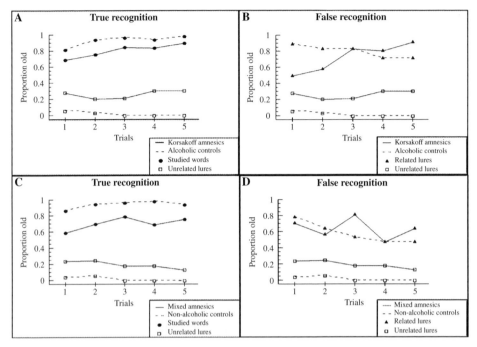

Figure 16.1 Proportions of old responses to studied words (A, C), related lures (B, D) and unrelated lures (A–D) in the two subgroups of amnesics (Korsakoff and mixed) and their respective control groups (alcoholic and nonalcoholic) as a function of study-test trial. Korsakoff and mixed amnesics showed similarly impaired true recognition. However, Korsakoff patients showed increasing false recognition across trials, whereas mixed amnesics showed a fluctuating pattern across trials

lures (for a similar pattern in patients with memory disorders attributable to Alzheimer's disease, see Budson et al., 2000). In sum, these data highlight the importance in healthy individuals of recollecting detailed information for resisting the tendency to falsely recognize similar items.

In contrast to the preceding findings of reduced false recognition by amnesics in the DRM paradigm, when there is a single study and test trial, an earlier study by Cermak et al. (1973) used a different paradigm and showed that amnesics produced *increased* levels of false recognition as compared to control subjects. Cermak et al. presented a series of words to Korsakoff amnesics and alcoholic controls and instructed them to indicate for each word whether or not they had seen it before in the list (i.e. a continuous recognition task). Some words in the series were lures that were semantically or acoustically related to earlier seen words, such as initially seeing "hare" and then later seeing in the list the new lure word "hair". Cermak et al. found that amnesics were more likely than controls to falsely recognize the lure words (see Kroll et al., 1996, who also found that amnesics with either left or right hippocampal damage had higher than normal false recognition rates).

Different processes likely contribute to amnesics' higher than normal false recognition rates in the Cermak et al. (1973) paradigm, but lower than normal false recognition rate in the DRM paradigm. In the Cermak et al. study, the number of items separating a word from its lure (i.e. the lag) may have been sufficiently small that control subjects recollected the initial study word when seeing the lure. For instance, when confronted with the new lure word "hair", the control subjects may have remembered that they had earlier seen "hare" and thus concluded that although "hair" is familiar it does not match the initially studied word. Amnesics, by contrast, have difficulty reactivating earlier studied words (e.g. Johnson & Chalfonte, 1994). This deficiency would have hindered their use of recollection to counter the familiarity of the new lure word, and consequently contributed to their higher than normal false recognition rate in the Cermak et al. paradigm.

In the DRM paradigm, however, the amnesics' lower than normal false recognition rate may have had less to do with recollective deficiencies and more to do with the processes that contribute to a related lure item's feeling of familiarity. That is, the amnesics' low false (and true) recognition rate is likely attributable to the reduced amount of activation (and therefore, familiarity) that is generated by studying the related words. Amnesics' inability to associate the related studied items, and construct an organized representation of the list, may have diminished the activation of the lure items and therefore produced the low false recognition rate.

The preceding studies illustrate two processes that contribute to reports of false memories. First, false recognition responses are influenced by variables, such as how many related items have been studied, that contribute to the familiarity of related lure items. Second, recollecting specific information about past events can counteract false recognition responses. As suggested by the Cermak et al. study, the amnesics' deficiency in remembering item-specific information may have contributed to their higher than normal false recognition rate. Thus, healthy individuals may become more vulnerable to distorted memories as they fail to recollect the discriminative features of past events (e.g. Riccio et al., 1994). In short, memory distortion depends upon a dynamic interaction between processes contributing to familiarity and memory for item-specific information.

THE DISTINCTIVENESS HEURISTIC AND FALSE RECOGNITION

Remembering past events is an active process that is influenced by a variety of factors, such as an individual's expectations, metamemorial beliefs, and even the particular way that memory is queried (e.g. Dodson & Johnson, 1993, 1996; Dodson & Schacter, 2001, 2002; Johnson et al., 1993; Koutstaal et al., 1999a; Lindsay & Johnson, 1989; Marsh & Hicks, 1998; Multhaup, 1995; Schacter et al., 1999; Strack & Bless, 1994). According to both the CMF and the SMF of Johnson and colleagues, individuals can recruit a variety of different decision strategies when making memory judgments. In this section, we will focus on the influence of a retrieval strategy, known as the distinctiveness heuristic, that has been effective at reducing false recognition errors (Dodson & Schacter, 2001, submitted; Israel & Schacter, 1997; Schacter et al., 1999, 2001). The distinctiveness heuristic refers to a mode of responding in which people expect to remember vivid details of an experience and make recognition decisions based on this metacognitive expectation. When a novel event lacks the expected distinctive information, individuals can use this absence of critical evidence to reject the item.

Recently, we have shown that people can use the distinctiveness heuristic to suppress the large false recognition rate of lure words in the DRM false memory paradigm (Dodson &

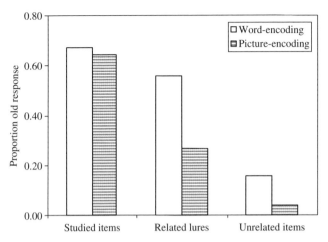

Figure 16.2 Proportions of old responses to studied words, related lures and unrelated lures in the two groups of participants who encoded the words by hearing them either with or without a picture

Schacter, 2001; Israel & Schacter, 1997; Schacter et al., 1999, 2001). Recall that in the DRM paradigm participants initially study lists of words that are associatively related to a nonpresented lure word. On a subsequent old–new recognition test, participants frequently judge the related lure words as having been studied before. However, as seen in Figure 16.2, studying the same items with an accompanying picture, instead of words alone, dramatically reduces false recognition rates to the related lure words (Israel & Schacter, 1997; Schacter et al., 1999, submitted). Schacter et al. argued that the success in rejecting related lure words after picture-plus-word encoding, as compared to word-only encoding, stems from participants' metamemorial belief that they ought to remember the distinctive pictorial information. Participants invoke a distinctiveness heuristic whereby they demand access to pictorial information as a basis for judging items as previously studied; the *absence* of memory for this distinctive information indicates that the test item is new. By contrast, participants who studied only words would not expect detailed recollections about studied items and, thus, would not base recognition decisions on the presence or absence of memory for distinctive information. We (Dodson & Schacter, 2001) reported a similar reduction in false recognition responses to related lures in a condition where participants themselves actually said aloud the target words on the study lists, compared to when they simply heard the target words (participants also saw the studied words in both conditions). Paralleling the reasoning regarding distinctive pictorial information, we suggested that participants who actually said words at study employed a distinctiveness heuristic during the recognition test, demanding access to the distinctive "say" information in order to judge an item as "old". Although the related lure words may feel familiar, the lure words should not evoke the distinctive information associated with actually having said a word out loud, and consequently, can be identified as "new".

Thus far, we have examined the distinctiveness heuristic in a situation in which the studied items share considerable conceptual similarity with one another. However, an important question is whether this retrieval strategy is effective in reducing false recognition rates in situations where the items are unrelated. We (Dodson & Schacter, 2002, in press) examined this question by modifying a "repetition lag" paradigm initially reported by Jennings & Jacoby (1997). In this paradigm, participants study either a list of unrelated words or a list of unrelated pictures, and then make old–new recognition judgments about previously studied items and new words. On the test, the studied items appear once, whereas the new words appear twice, with a varying lag (i.e. number of intervening items) between its first and second occurrence. The new words repeat at lags of either 4, 12, 24, or 48. Participants are instructed to say "old" to studied words only, and to say "new" to non-studied words, even when they repeat. Although participants are explicitly told that if a word occurs twice on the test they can safely conclude that it is a new word, participants in the word-encoding condition nonetheless incorrectly respond "old" to the repeated new words, especially when they repeat at the longer lags. Presumably, individuals mistake the familiarity of the repeated new words—derived from their earlier exposure on the test—for prior presentation in the *study* phase. By contrast, we found that encoding pictures during the study phase, compared to encoding words, reduced the false recognition rate to new words that were repeated during the recognition test. Apparently, participants in the picture-encoding condition, as in the DRM paradigm, used a distinctiveness heuristic during the test, responding "old" only when they could recollect pictorial information about the test items.

The distinctiveness heuristic is one mechanism that has proven useful for minimizing false memories. In terms of the CMF, the distinctiveness heuristic operates on how retrieved information is evaluated. This heuristic depends on the metamemorial knowledge about the kind of events that are likely to be remembered, such as having said something earlier. Based on this knowledge, people are able to infer that the absence of memory for this expected characteristic is diagnostic that an event did not actually occur, despite how familiar it may feel. The distinctiveness heuristic is similar to retrieval strategies that operate in three other paradigms. First, Johnson and colleagues observe that participants use the perceived memorability of studied items to attribute a test item to a particular source, such as inferring that something must have been heard earlier based on the absence of expected memorial information about having generated the item (e.g. Anderson, 1984; Foley et al., 1983; Hashtroudi et al., 1989; Hicks & Marsh, 1999; Johnson et al., 1981). Second, Collins and colleagues argue that a "lack of knowledge" inference contributes to how people answer questions, such as inferring that you have not met Bill Clinton because you would expect to remember this event (e.g. Collins et al., 1975; Gentner & Collins, 1981). Third, and similar to the above, others have argued that especially salient new test items, relative to less salient new items, are correctly rejected because of the expectation of remembering these particularly salient items, i.e. a "I-would-have-seen-it-if-it-had-been-there" strategy (e.g. Brewer and Treyens, 1981; Brown et al., 1977; Strack & Bless, 1994: cf. Rotello, 1999; Wixted, 1992). In sum, our results in combination with existing findings suggest that there is a fundamental metacognitive inference process, based on the absence of memory for expected information, that contributes to retrieval in a variety of situations.

THE FRONTAL LOBES AND FALSE RECOGNITION

Patients with frontal lobe damage can experience a wide range of disorders involving inhibitory processes, language, memory, motor control, personality and general executive functions (e.g. Luria, 1966; Schacter, 1987; Shimamura, 1995, 2000). Several studies document that patients with frontal lobe damage exhibit pathologically high false recognition rates (e.g. Curran et al., 1997; Delbecq-Derouesne et al., 1990; Rapcsak et al., 1999; Schacter et al., 1996b; Schnider & Ptak, 1999; Ward et al., 1999).

Recently, Schnider and colleagues (2000) have observed abnormally high false recognition rates by patients with damage to the orbital frontal cortex or to areas connected to it, such as the basal forebrain, capsular genu, amygdala, perirhinal cortex and hypothalamus. Schnider et al. use a paradigm in which patients and control subjects are presented with a series of pictures, such as pictures of an airplane, bicycle, ball, etc. (Schnider & Ptak, 1999; Schnider et al. 1996a, 1996b, 2000). Some of the pictures repeat in the series, whereas others occur only once. Participants are instructed that the goal of this task is to respond "yes" only to pictures that repeat (i.e. hit) and "no" to pictures that are appearing for the first time. The critical feature of this paradigm is that after viewing the series of pictures, individuals are exposed to the *same* set of pictures again, with a different subset of the pictures repeating, e.g. if airplane and ball had repeated during the first run, then a different set of items would repeat during the second run, such as the picture of the bicycle. By the end of the experiment, individuals have seen multiple runs of the same series of pictures with different subsets of the pictures repeating in a given run.

Schnider & Ptak (1999) compared healthy controls with frontal patients and patients with medial temporal lobe damage. Overall, hit rates—correctly identifying repeating pictures—were not significantly different between the two patient groups, although both patient groups made significantly fewer hits than did control subjects. With repeated exposures to the same series of pictures, the control subjects and the patients with medial temporal lobe damage were no different in correctly rejecting pictures that occurred for the first time within a given run. By contrast, the frontal patients were increasingly vulnerable to falsely recognizing pictures with repeated exposures, e.g. on the final run patients with frontal damage falsely recognized nearly 36% of the pictures, whereas the matched controls and the medial temporal lobe patients falsely recognized less than 5% of the pictures.

The abnormal false recognition rate on the part of the frontal patients may reflect a defective process of remembering source information or specific item information (e.g. Johnson et al., 1993). These patients may have trouble distinguishing between memories for events that occurred earlier in the current run from memories for events that occurred in previous runs. As Schnider & Ptak (1999) report, their patients with frontal damage "fail to suppress mental associations that do not pertain to the present; memories thus seem to be as real and pertinent for present behavior as representations of current reality" (p. 679). Failing to distinguish between items repeating in the current run from items that were seen in earlier runs may leave the frontal patients prone to relying on an item's overall familiarity as a basis for a response, thus contributing to their high false recognition rate.

Swick & Knight (1999) have also observed elevated false recognition rates, compared to controls, in a group of patients with focal unilateral lesions of the lateral prefrontal cortex. In their study, both frontal patients and controls completed a continuous recognition test: participants saw a series of words and pronounceable nonwords and pushed one button for items occurring for the first time (new items) and another button for items that repeat in the series (old items). Whereas the frontal patients were no different from controls in their recognition rates to old items, they were much more likely to falsely recognize new items.

Like the findings of Schnider and colleagues and Swick & Knight, there are a growing number of case studies of individuals with frontal lobe damage who exhibit pathologically high false recognition rates (e.g. Delbecq-Derouesne et al., 1990; Rapcsak et al., 1999;

Schacter et al., 1996b; Ward et al., 1999). Schacter et al. (1996b) and Curran et al. (1997) described a patient, B.G., with right frontal damage who is generally alert, attentive and cooperative. B.G. shows no signs of amnesia but he is prone to extremely high rates of false recognition, e.g. after studying a series of unrelated words, B.G. recognized studied words at a rate comparable to normal control subjects, but B.G. was much more likely than controls to respond that new test words had also been studied (Schacter et al., 1996b). Interestingly, a subsequent experiment identified a condition in which B.G. was able to reduce his high false recognition rate. B.G. and control subjects studied pictures of inanimate objects and then completed a memory test in which the distractors were either related or unrelated to studied items. Some distractors were similar to the studied pictures in that both were from the same semantic category, such as pictures of tools or toys. Other distractors were taken from a semantic category that had not been studied, such as a picture of an animal (Schacter et al., 1996b). As in the prior studies, B.G. recognized the studied items at a rate comparable to controls and showed an abnormally high false recognition rate for related distractors. By contrast, B.G. almost never falsely recognized distractors that were from a different semantic category.

Schacter et al. (1996b) proposed that B.G. uses inappropriate decision criteria during the test. In terms of the CMF, his pathological false recognition rate stems from an excessive reliance on information about the general correspondence between a test item and earlier studied words. Responding on the basis of overall similarity led B.G. to exhibit very high false recognition rates to similar distractors, but not to dissimilar distractors. Alternatively, it is possible that B.G. fails to encode specific features of items at study, so that he is forced to rely on overall similarity. That is, the memory representations of the items do not include enough item-specific information so that at test they can be identified on the basis of this specific information. Moreover, encoding items in a vague manner would result in feelings of familiarity for features that are common to many items, including both studied and new lure items that contain these features (see Curran et al., 1997).

Rapcsak et al. (1999) discuss two other frontal lobe patients that exhibit a pattern of false recognition that is similar to that of B.G. J.S. sustained bilateral damage to the basal forebrain/septal area and the ventromedial frontal region; B.W. is characterized by widespread damage to the right frontal lobe. Both patients show high false recognition rates and, like B.G., are able to lessen their false recognition rates when presented with new items that are substantially different from studied items, e.g. both frontal patients and control subjects recognized previously studied faces at roughly similar rates (94% vs. 81%, respectively) and, as expected, the frontal patients were more likely to falsely recognize the distractor faces than were the control subjects (42% vs. 11%, respectively). Consistent with the behavior of B.G., the frontal patients made many more false alarms to the similar distractor faces (i.e. other white males) than to the dissimilar distractor faces (i.e. white females and non-white males). Apparently, the frontal patients, as Rapscak et al. suggest, use overall familiarity as a basis for a response.

Subsequent experiments by Rapcsak et al. (1999) examined whether the frontal patients' reliance on familiarity stems primarily from deficient encoding of specific item information. Alternatively, there may be a bias at retrieval to rely on familiarity as a basis for a response. J.S., B.W. and healthy controls were given a famous faces test: they were presented a series of famous faces (politicians, entertainers, etc.) intermingled with nonfamous faces and were instructed to respond "yes" when the face was that of a famous person, and "no" when it was not. This test probes memory for information that was learned long before the patient's brain damage and, thus, specifically taps processes operating during retrieval. The frontal patients and control subjects identified comparable numbers of faces that were actually famous (94% vs. 85%, respectively). However, J.S. and B.W. showed a much greater tendency to respond that the nonfamous faces were also famous (52%) than did the controls (6%).

In a follow-up experiment, the same famous faces were intermixed with a new set of unfamiliar faces and all subjects were instructed to base fame judgments solely on whether or not they could remember the name and occupation of the person. With these instructions, the false recognition rates of the nonfamous faces dropped down to normal levels for the frontal patients (i.e. 6% false alarm rate for frontal patients and 1% for controls). Hit rates to the famous faces were also no different for the frontal patients and control subjects. The finding that test instructions greatly improved the frontal patients' performance is consistent with the results of group studies of patients with prefrontal cortex damage (Gershberg & Shimamura, 1995; Hirst & Volpe, 1988).

The preceding studies suggest that, in part, the pathological false recognition rate associated with frontal damage stems from a bias at retrieval to rely on overall familiarity or similarity as a basis for a response. Interestingly, performance improves dramatically when the patients are instructed to respond on the basis of more specific memorial information. In terms of the CMF, a malfunctioning focusing mechanism can explain the behavior of B.G. and the frontal patients of Rapcsak et al. (1999; see Curran et al., 1997; Norman & Schacter, 1996; and Schacter et al., 1996b, for further discussion of B.G.'s memory deficit). That is, the frontal patients may generate a search description that is extremely vague, such as whether or not the test item is a member of one of the studied categories of items. This vague description is sufficient for correctly rejecting distractors that are from nonstudied categories, but it does not exclude similar distractors from studied categories. In the Rapcsak et al. study, the instructions to base fame judgments on the retrieval of specific information about the person may have the effect of focusing or refining the search description. Interestingly, when they are instructed to do so, these frontal patients are capable of focusing their search description and relying on more specific information, since they performed as well as the control subjects in this condition.

One reason for frontal patients' bias to rely on overall familiarity as a basis for a response comes from a study by Janowsky et al. (1989b). Janowsky et al. required frontal patients and matched controls to learn a series of sentences, e.g. "Mary's garden was full of marigolds". On a subsequent cued recall test (e.g. "Mary's garden was full of ____"), all participants gave a "feeling-of-knowing" score for each item that they could not recall, e.g. if an individual failed to recall "marigolds" to the above cue then he/she would predict how likely he/she would be able to recognize the answer on a multiple-choice test—the feeling-of-knowing judgment. Recall and recognition performance was comparable between the two groups, but the frontal lobe patients were at chance levels in their feeling-of-knowing judgments, whereas the control subjects achieved much higher scores. Interestingly, the frontal patients attained poor feeling-of-knowing scores because they tended to overestimate their knowledge. Specifically, the frontal patients only recognized 27% of the unrecalled items that they were moderately or highly confident of subsequently recognizing, whereas the control subjects recognized 42% of these items. This tendency on the part of frontal patients to overestimate their knowledge could contribute to abnormally high false recognition rates. Their apparent overconfidence that an item's familiarity means that it must have been studied earlier may have lead them *not* to use a more focused search description (e.g. search memory for more specific item information) and rely on a test item's familiarity.

CONCLUSION

A basic strategy in cognitive neuropsychology and cognitive neuroscience is to examine how mental processes malfunction in order to increase understanding of how they work. This strategy has proved quite useful in uncovering basic memory mechanisms of encoding, storage and retrieval, and more recently has begun to yield insights into various kinds of memory errors (e.g. Schacter, 1999, 2001). We have examined memory distortion in various kinds of brain-damaged patients from the perspective of the CMF. The reviewed studies indicate that healthy individuals are susceptible to falsely recognizing items when they fail to recollect detailed item information. This may occur when there is a pattern separation failure and the representations of similar studied items overlap, such as in the DRM paradigm. The medial temporal lobes appear to be important for storing and/or retaining both familiarity information and more specific information about an item. False recognition also can be a byproduct of the retrieval process—e.g. when patients (or healthy controls) use lax criteria to search memory, such as when they accept memories as true that are only vaguely familiar. Conversely, a retrieval strategy such as the distinctiveness heuristic can be a powerful mechanism for reducing false recognition responses. Some of the evidence we considered indicates that the frontal lobes are implicated in the criteria and strategies people use to search and evaluate their memories. In short, a variety of brain mechanisms are likely responsible for the occurrence of both true and false memories.

ACKNOWLEDGEMENT

We gratefully acknowledge the support provided by grants from the National Institute on Aging (AG08441), National Institute of Mental Health (NS60941) and National Institute of Neurological Disorders and Stroke (NS26985).

REFERENCES

Alba, J.W. & Hasher, L. (1983). Is memory schematic? *Psychological Bulletin*, **93**, 203–231.

Anderson, R.E. (1984). Did I do it or did I only imagine doing it? *Journal of Experimental Psychology: General*, **113**, 594–613.

Arkes, H.R. & Freedman, M.R. (1984). A demonstration of the costs and benefits of expertise in recognition memory. *Memory & Cognition*, **12**, 84–89.

Arndt, J. & Hirshman, E. (1998). True and false recognition in MINERVA2: explanations from a global matching perspective. *Journal of Memory and Language*, **39**, 371–391.

Bartlett, F.C. (1932). *Remembering*. Cambridge: Cambridge University Press.

Bohannon, J.N. & Symons, L.V. (1992). Flashbulb memories: confidence, consistency, and quantity. In E. Winograd & U. Neisser (eds), *Affect and Accuracy in Recall: Studies of "Flashbulb" Memories* (pp. 65–91). Cambridge: Cambridge University Press.

Bower, G.H. (1967). A multi-component theory of the memory trace. In K.W. Spence & J.T. Spence (eds), *Coding Processes in Human Memory* (pp. 85–123). Washington DC: V.H. Winston.

Brainerd, C.J. & Reyna, V.F. (1998). When things that were never experienced are easier to "remember" than things that were. *Psychological Science*, **9**, 484–489.

Bransford, J.D. & Franks, J.J. (1971). The abstraction of linguistic ideas. *Cognitive Psychology*, **2**, 331–350.

Brewer, W.F. (1977). Memory for the pragmatic implications of sentences. *Memory & Cognition*, **5**, 673–678.

Brewer, W.F. & Treyens, J.C. (1981). Role of schemata in memory for places. *Cognitive Psychology*, **13**, 207–230.

Brown, J., Lewis, V.J. & Monk, A.F. (1977). Memorability, word frequency and negative recognition. *Quarterly Journal of Experimental Psychology*, **29**, 461–473.

Bruner, J. (1986). *Actual Minds, Possible Words*. Cambridge, MA: Harvard University Press.

Budson, A.E., Daffner, K.R., Desikan, R. & Schacter, D.L. (2000). When false recognition is unopposed by true recognition: Gist-based memory distortion in Alzheimer's disease. *Neuropsychology*, **14**, 277–287.

Burgess, P.W. & Shallice, T. (1996). Confabulation and the control of recollection. *Memory*, **4**, 359–411.

Buckner, R.L. (1996). Beyond HERA: contributions of specific prefrontal brain areas to long-term memory retrieval. *Psychonomic Bulletin and Review*, **3**, 149–158.

Cermak, L.S., Butters, N. & Gerrein, J. (1973). The extent of the verbal encoding ability of Korsakoff patients. *Neuropsychologia*, **11**, 85–94.

Collins, A., Warnock, E.H., Aiello, N. & Miller, M.L. (1975). Reasoning from incomplete knowledge. In D. Bobrow & A. Collins (eds), *Representation & understanding: Studies in cognitive science*. New York: Academic Press.

Curran, T., Schacter, D.L., Norman, K.A. & Galluccio, L. (1997). False recognition after a right frontal lobe infarction: memory for general and specific information. *Neuropsychologia*, **35**, 1035–1049.

Damasio, A.R. (1989). Time-locked multiregional retroactivation: a systems-level proposal for the neural substrates of recall and recognition. *Cognition*, **33**, 25–62.

Deese, J. (1959). On the prediction of occurrence of particular verbal intrusions in immediate recall. *Journal of Experimental Psychology*, **58**, 17–22.

Delbecq-Derouesne, J., Beauvois, M.F. & Shallice, T. (1990). Preserved recall versus impaired recognition. *Brain*, **113**, 1045–1074.

Dodson, C.S. & Johnson, M.K. (1993). Rate of false source attributions depends on how questions are asked. *American Journal of Psychology*, **106**, 541–557.

Dodson, C.S. & Johnson, M.K. (1996). Some problems with the process dissociation approach to memory. *Journal of Experimental Psychology: General*, **125**, 181–194.

Dodson, C.S. & Schacter, D.L. (2001). "If I had said it I would have remembered it": reducing false memories with a distinctiveness heuristic. *Psychonomic Bulletin and Review*, **8**, 155–161.

Dodson, C.S. & Schacter, D.L. (2002). When false recognition meets metacognition: the distinctiveness heuristic. *Journal of Memory and Language*, **46**, 782–803.

Dodson, C.S. & Schacter, D.L. (in press). Aging and strategic retrieval processes: the suppresssion of false memories with a distinctiveness heuristic. *Psychology and Aging*.

Dodson, C.S. & Shimamura, A.P. (2000). Differential effects of cue dependency on item and source memory. *Journal of Experimental Psychology: Learning, Memory, and Cognition*, **26**, 1023–1044.

Foley, M.A., Johnson, M.K. & Raye, C.L. (1983). Age-related changes in confusion between memories for thoughts and memories for speech. *Child Development*, **54**, 51–60.

Franks, J.J. & Bransford, J.D. (1971). Abstraction of visual patterns. *Journal of Experimental Psychology*, **90**, 65–74.

Gentner, D. & Collins, A. (1981). Studies of inference from lack of knowledge. *Memory & Cognition*, **9**, 434–443.

Gershberg, F.B. & Shimamura, A.P. (1996). The role of the frontal lobes in the use of organizational strategies in free recall. *Neuropsychologia*, **13**, 1305–1333.

Hasher, L. & Griffin, M. (1978). Reconstructive and reproductive processes in memory. *Journal of Experimental Psychology: Human Learning and Memory*, **8**, 318–330.

Hashtroudi, S., Johnson, M.K. & Chrosniak, L.D. (1989). Aging and source monitoring. *Psychology and Aging*, **4**, 106–112.

Hicks, J.L. & Marsh, R.L. (1999). Attempts to reduce the incidence of false recall with source monitoring. *Journal of Experimental Psychology: Learning, Memory, and Cognition*, **25**, 1195–1209.

Hintzman, D.L. (1988). Judgments of frequency and recognition memory in a multiple-trace memory model. *Psychological Review*, **95**, 528–551.

Hintzman, D.L. & Curran, T. (1994). Retrieval dynamics of recognition and frequency judgments: evidence for separate processes of familiarity and recall. *Journal of Memory and Language*, **33**, 1–18.

Hirst, W. & Volpe, B.T. (1988). Memory strategies and brain damage. *Brain and Cognition*, **8**, 379–408.

Israel, L. & Schacter, D.L. (1997). Pictorial encoding reduces false recognition of semantic associates. *Psychological Bulletin and Review*, **4**, 577–581.

Janowsky, J.S., Shimamura, A.P. & Squire, L.R. (1989a). Source memory impairment in patients with frontal lobe lesions. *Neuropsychologia*, **27**, 1043–1056.

Janowsky, J.S., Shimamura, A.P. & Squire, L.R. (1989b). Memory and metamemory: comparisons between patients with frontal lobe lesions and amnesic patients. *Psychobiology*, **17**, 3–11.

Jennings, J.M. & Jacoby, L.L. (1997). An opposition procedure for detecting age-related deficits in recollection: telling effects of repetition. *Psychology and Aging*, **12**, 352–361.

Johnson, M.K. (1992). MEM: mechanisms of recollection. *Journal of Cognitive Neuroscience*, **4**, 268–280.

Johnson, M.K., Bransford, J.D. & Solomon, S.K. (1973). Memory for tacit implications of sentences. *Journal of Experimental Psychology*, **98**, 203–205.

Johnson, M.K. & Chalfonte, B.L. (1994). Binding complex memories: the role of reactivation and the hippocampus. In D.L. Schacter & E. Tulving (eds), *Memory Systems 1994* (pp. 311–350). Cambridge, MA: MIT Press.

Johnson, M.K., Hashtroudi, S. & Lindsay, D.S. (1993). Source monitoring. *Psychological Bulletin*, **114**, 3–28.

Johnson, M.K. & Raye, C.L. (1981). Reality Monitoring. *Psychological Review*, **88**, 67–85.

Johnson, M.K., Raye, C.L., Foley, H.J. & Foley, M.A. (1981). Cognitive operations and decision bias in reality monitoring. *American Journal of Psychology*, **94**, 37–64.

Kopelman, M.D. (1999). Varieties of false memory. *Cognitive Neuropsychology*, **16**, 197–214.

Koutstaal, W., & Schacter, D.L. (1997). Gist-based false recognition of pictures in older and younger adults. *Journal of Memory and Language*, **37**, 555–583.

Koutstaal, W., Schacter, D.L., Galluccio, L. & Stofer, K.A. (1999a). Reducing gist-based false recognition in older adults: encoding and retrieval manipulations. *Psychology and Aging*, **14**, 220–237.

Koutstaal, W., Schacter, D.L., Verfaellie, M., Brenner, C. & Jackson, E.M. (1999b). Perceptually-based false recognition of novel objects in amnesia: effects of category size and similarity to category prototypes. *Cognitive Neuropsychology*, **16**, 317–342.

Koutstaal, W., Verfaellie, M. & Schacter, D.L. (in press). Recognizing identical vs. similar categorically related common objects: further evidence for degraded gist-representations in amnesia. *Neuropsychology*.

Kroll, N.E.A., Knight, R.T., Metcalfe, J. et al. (1996). Cohesion failure as a source of memory illusions. *Journal of Memory and Language*, **35**, 176–196.

Lepage M., Ghaffar, O., Nyberg, L. & Tulving, E. (2000). Prefrontal cortex and episodic memory retrieval mode. *Proceedings of the National Academy of Sciences of the USA*, **97**, 506–511.

Lindsay, D.S. & Johnson, M.K. (1989). The eyewitness suggestibility effect and memory for source. *Memory & Cognition*, **17**, 349–358.

Loftus, E.F., Miller, D.G. & Burns, H.J. (1978). Semantic integration of verbal information into a visual memory. *Journal of Experimental Psychology: Human Learning and Memory*, **4**, 19–31.

Luria, A.R. (1966). *Higher Cortical Functions in Man*. New York: Basic Books.

Marsh, R.L. & Hicks, J.L. (1998). Test formats change source-monitoring decision processes. *Journal of Experimental Psychology: Learning, Memory, and Cognition*, **24**, 1137–1151.

Mather, M., Henkel, L.A. & Johnson, M.K. (1997). Evaluating the characteristics of false memories: remember/know judgments and memory characteristics questionnaire compared. *Memory and Cognition*, **25**, 826–837.

McClelland, J.L., McNaughton, B.L. & O'Reilly, R.C. (1995). Why there are complementary learning systems in the hippocampus and neocortex: insights from the successes and failures of connectionist models of learning and memory. *Psychological Review*, **102**, 419–457.

McDermott, K.B. (1996). The persistence of false memories in list recall. *Journal of Memory and Language*, **35**, 212–230.

McDermott, K.B. & Watson, J.M. (in press). The rise and fall of false recall: the impact of presentation duration. *Journal of Memory and Language*.

McKone, E. & Murphy, B. (2000). Implicit false memory: effects of modality and multiple study presentations on long-lived semantic priming. *Journal of Memory and Language*, **43**, 89–109.

Melo, B., Winocur, G. & Moscovitch, M. (1999). False recall and false recognition: an examination of the effects of selective and combined lesions to the medial temporal lobe/diencephalon and frontal lobe structures. *Cognitive Neuropsychology*, **16**, 343–359.

Miller, M.B. & Wolford, G.L. (1999). Theoretical Commentary: the role of criterion shift in false memory. *Psychological Review*, **106**, 398–405.

Milner, B. (1971). Interhemispheric differences in the localization of psychological processes in man. *British Medical Bulletin*, **27**, 272–277.

Moscovitch, M. (1994). Memory and working-with-memory: evaluation of a component process model and comparisons with other models. In D.L. Schacter & E. Tulving (eds), *Memory Systems 1994* (pp. 311–350). Cambridge, MA: MIT Press.

Multhaup, K.S. (1995). Aging, source, and decision criteria: when false fame errors do and do not occur. *Psychology and Aging*, **10**, 492–497.

Nadel, L, Samsonovich, A, Ryan. L. & Moscovitch M. (2000). Multiple trace theory of human memory: Computational, neuroimaging, and neuropsychological results. *Hippocampus*, **10**, 352–368.

Neisser, U. (1967). *Cognitive Psychology*. New York: Appleton-Century-Crofts.

Neisser, U. & Harsch, N. (1992). Phantom flashbulbs: false recollections of hearing the news about Challenger. In E. Winograd & U. Neisser (eds), *Affect and Accuracy in Recall: Studies of "Flashbulb" Memories* (pp. 9–31). Cambridge: Cambridge University Press.

Norman, D.A. & Bobrow, D.G. (1979). Descriptions: an intermediate stage in memory retrieval. *Cognitive Psychology*, **11**, 107–123.

Norman, K.A. & Schacter, D.L. (1996). Implicit memory, explicit memory, and false recollection: a cognitive neuroscience perspective. In L.M. Reder (ed.), *Implicit Memory and Metacognition* (pp. 229–259). Hillsdale, NJ: Erlbaum.

Norman, K.A. & Schacter, D.L. (1997). False recognition in young and older adults: exploring the characteristics of illusory memories. *Memory and Cognition*, **25**, 838–848.

Nyberg, L., Cabeza, R. & Tulving, E. (1996). PET studies of encoding and retrieval: the HERA model. *Psychonomic Bulletin and Review*, **3**, 135–148.

Nyberg, L., Tulving, E., Habib, R. et al. (1995). Functional brain maps of retrieval mode and recovery of episodic information. *NeuroReport*, **6**, 249–252.

Nystrom, L.E. & McClelland, J.L. (1992). Trace synthesis in cued recall. *Journal of Memory and Language*, **31**, 591–614.

Parkin, A.J., Ward, J., Bindschaedler, C. et al. (1999). False recognition following frontal lobe damage: the role of encoding factors. *Cognitive Neuropsychology*, **16**.

Parkin, A.J. & Leng, N.R.C. (1993). *Neuropsychology of the Amnesic Syndrome*. Hillsdale, NJ: Erlbaum.

Payne, D.G., Elie, C.J., Blackwell, J.M. & Neuschatz, J.S. (1996). Memory illusions: recalling, recognizing, and recollecting events that never occurred. *Journal of Memory and Language*, **35**, 261–285.

Posner, M.I. & Keele, S.W. (1968). On the genesis of abstract ideas. *Journal of Experimental Psychology*, **77**, 353–363.

Posner, M.I. & Keele, S.W. (1970). Retention of abstract ideas. *Journal of Experimental Psychology*, **83**, 304–308.

Rapcsak, S.Z., Reminger, S.L., Glisky, E.L. et al. (1999). Neuropsychological mechanisms of false facial recognition following frontal lobe damage. *Cognitive Neuropsychology*, **16**.

Read, J.D. (1996). From a passing thought to a false memory in 2 minutes: confusing real and illusory events. *Psychonomic Bulletin and Review*, **3**, 105–111.

Reyna, V.F. & Brainerd, C.J. (1995). Fuzzy-trace theory: an interim synthesis. *Learning and Individual Differences*, **7**, 1–75.

Riccio, D.C., Rabinowitz, V.C. & Axelrod, S. (1994). Memory: when less is more. *American Psychologist*, **49**, 917–926.

Roediger, H.L. III (1996). Memory illusions. *Journal of Memory and Language*, **35**, 76–100.

Roediger, H.L. III & McDermott, K.B. (1995). Creating false memories: remembering words not presented in lists. *Journal of Experimental Psychology: Learning, Memory, and Cognition*, **21**, 803–814.

Roediger, H.L. III & McDermott, K.B. (1999). False alarms about false memories. *Psychological Review*, **106**, 406–410.

Roediger, H.L. III & McDermott, K.B. (2000). Distortions of memory. In E. Tulving & F.I.M. Craik (eds), *The Oxford Handbook of Memory* (pp. 149–162). New York: Oxford University Press.

Roediger, H.L. III, Watson, J.M., McDermott, K.B. & Gallo, D.A. (in press). Factors that create false recall. *Psychonomic Bulletin & Review*.

Robinson, K.J. & Roediger, H.L. III. (1997). Associative processes in false recall and false recognition. *Psychological Science*, **8**, 231–237.

Rosenbaum, R.S., Priselac, S., Kohler, S. et al. (2000). Remote spatial memory in an amnesic person with extensive bilateral hippocampal lesions. *Nature Neuroscience*, **3**, 1044–1048.

Rotello, C.M. (1999). Metacognition and memory for nonoccurrence. *Memory*, **7**, 43–63.

Rugg, M.D., Fletcher, P.C., Frith, C.D. et al. (1996). Differential response of the prefrontal cortex in successful and unsuccessful memory retrieval. *Brain*, **119**, 2073–2083.

Schacter, D.L. (1987). Memory, amnesia and frontal lobe dysfunction. *Psychobiology*, **15**, 21–36.

Schacter, D.L. (1989). On the relation between memory and consciousness. In H.L. Roediger III & F.I.M. Craik (eds), *Varieties of Memory and Consciousness: Essays in Honor of Endel Tulving* (pp. 355–389). Hillsdale, NJ: Erlbaum.

Schacter, D.L. (1995). Memory distortion: history and current status. In D.L. Schacter (ed.), *Memory Distortion: How Minds, Brains and Societies Reconstruct the Past* (pp. 1–43). Cambridge, MA: Harvard University Press.

Schacter, D.L. (1996). *Searching for Memory: The Brain, the Mind, and the Past*. New York: Basic Books.

Schacter, D.L. (1999). The seven sins of memory: insights from psychology and cognitive neuroscience. *American Psychologist*, **54**, 182–203.

Schacter, D.L. (2001). *The Seven Sins of Memory: How the Mind Forgets and Remembers*. Boston, MA: Houghton Mifflin.

Schacter, D.L., Alpert, N.M., Savage, C.R. et al. (1996a). Conscious recollection and the human hippocampal formation: evidence from positron emission tomography. *Proceedings of the National Academy of Sciences of the USA*, **93**, 321–325.

Schacter, D.L., Buckner, R.L., Koutstaal, W. et al. (1997). Late onset of anterior prefrontal activity during true and false recognition: an event-related FMRI study. *NeuroImage*, **6**, 259–269.

Schacter, D.L., Cendan, D.L., Dodson, C.S. & Clifford, E.R. (2001). Retrieval conditions and false recognition: testing the distinctiveness heuristic. *Psychonomic Bulletin & Review*, **8**, 824–833.

Schacter, D.L., Curran, T., Galluccio, L. et al. (1996b). False recognition and the right frontal lobe: a case study. *Neuropsychologia*, **34**, 793–808.

Schacter, D.L., Harbluk, J.L. & McLachlan, D.R. (1984). Retrieval without recollection: an experimental analysis of source amnesia. *Journal of Verbal Learning and Verbal Behavior*, **23**, 593–611.

Schacter, D.L., Israel, L. & Racine, C.A. (1999). Suppressing false recognition in younger and older adults: the distinctiveness heuristic. *Journal of Memory and Language*, **40**, 1–24.

Schacter, D.L., Norman, K.A. & Koutstaal, W. (1998a). The cognitive neurosciences of constructive memory. *Annual Review of Psychology*, **49**, 289–318.

Schacter, D.L., Verfaellie, M. & Anes, M.D. (1997). Illusory memories in amnesic patients: conceptual and perceptual false recognition. *Neuropsychology*, **11**, 331–342.

Schacter, D.L., Verfaellie, M., Anes, M.D. & Racine, C. (1998b). When true recognition suppresses false recognition: evidence from amnesic patients. *Journal of Cognitive Neuroscience*, **10**, 668–679.

Schacter, D.L., Verfaellie, M. & Pradere, D. (1996c). The neuropsychology of memory illusions: false recall and recognition in amnesic patients. *Journal of Memory and Language*, **35**, 319–334.

Schmolck, H., Buffalo, E.A. & Squire, L.R. (2000). Memory distortions develop over time: recollections of the O.J. Simpson trial verdict after 15 and 32 months. *Psychological Science*, **11**, 39–45.

Schnider, A. & Ptak, R. (1999). Spontaneous confabulators fail to suppress currently irrelevant memory traces. *Nature Neuroscience*, **2**, 677–681.

Schnider, A., Ptak, R., von Daniken, C. & Remonda, L. (2000). Recovery from spontaneous confabulations parallels recovery of temporal confusion in memory. *Neurology*, **55**, 74–83.

Schnider, A., von Daniken, C. & Gutbrod, K. (1996a). The mechanisms of spontaneous and provoked confabulations. *Brain*, **119**, 1365–1375.

Schnider, A., von Daniken, C. & Gutbrod, K. (1996b). Disorientation in amnesia: a confusion of memory traces. *Brain*, **119**, 1627–1632.

Seamon, J.G., Luo, C.R. & Gallo, D.A. (1998). Creating false memories with or without recognition of list items: evidence for nonconscious processes. *Psychological Science*, **9**, 20–26.

Shiffrin, R.M., Huber, D.E. & Marinelli, K. (1995). Effects of category length and strength on familiarity in recognition. *Journal of Experimental Psychology: Learning, Memory and Cognition*, **21**, 267–287.

Shimamura, A.P. (1995). Memory and frontal lobe function. In M.S. Gazzaniga (ed.), *The Cognitive Neurosciences* (pp. 803–813). Cambridge, MA: MIT Press.

Shimamura, A.P. (2000). The role of the prefrontal cortex in dynamic filtering. *Psychobiology*, **28**, 207–218.

Shimamura, A.P., Janowsky, J.S. & Squire, L.R. (1990). Memory for the temporal order of events in patients with frontal lobe lesions and amnesic patients. *Neuropsychologia*, **28**, 803–813.

Smith, R.E. & Hunt, R.R. (1998). Presentation modality affects false memory. *Psychonomic Bulletin & Review*, **5**, 710–715.

Squire, L.R. (1992). Memory and the hippocampus: a synthesis from findings with rats, monkeys, and humans. *Psychological Review*, **99**, 195–231.

Squire, L.R. (1995). Biological foundations of accuracy and inaccuracy in memory. In D.L. Schacter, J.T. Coyle, G.D. Fischback et al. (eds), *Memory Distortion: How Minds, Brains and Societies Reconstruct the Past*. Cambridge, MA: Harvard University Press.

Squire, L.R. & Alvarez, P. (1995). Retrograde amnesia and memory consolidation: a neurobiological perspective. *Current Opinions in Neurobiology*, **5**, 169–177.

Strack, F. & Bless, H. (1994). Memory for nonoccurrences: metacognitive and presuppositional strategies. *Journal of Memory and Language*, **33**, 203–217.

Swick, D. & Knight, R.T. (1999). Contributions of prefrontal cortex to recognition memory: electrophysiological and behavioral evidence. *Neuropsychology*, **13**, 155–170.

Teng, E. & Squire, L.R. (1999). Memory for places learned long ago is intact after hippocampal damage. *Nature*, **400**, 675–677.

Toglia, M.P., Neuschatz, J.S. & Goodwin, K.A. (1999). Recall accuracy and illusory memories: when more is less. *Memory*, 7, 233–256.

Treves, A. & Rolls, E.T. (1994). Computational analysis of the role of the hippocampus in memory. *Hippocampus*, **4**, 374–391.

Tulving, E. (1983). *Elements of Episodic Memory*. Oxford: Clarendon.

Tulving, E., Markowitsch, H.J., Kapur, S. et al. (1994). Novelty encoding networks in the human brain: positron emission tomography data. *NeuroReport*, **5**, 2525–2528.

Underwood, B.J. (1965). False recognition produced by implicit verbal responses. *Journal of Experimental Psychology*, **70**, 122–129.

Underwood, B.J. (1969). Attributes of memory. *Psychological Review*, **76**, 559–573.

Ward, J., Parkin, A.J., Powell, G. et al. (1999). False recognition of unfamiliar people: "seeing film stars everywhere." *Cognitive Neuropsychology*, **16**.

Wixted, J.T. (1992). Subjective memorability and the mirror effect. *Journal of Experimental Psychology: Learning, Memory and Cognition*, **18**, 681–690.

Wixted, J.T. & Stretch, V. (2000). The case against a criterion-shift account of false memory. *Psychological Review*, **107**, 368–376.

Zaragoza, M.S. & Lane, S.M. (1994). Source misattributions and the suggestibility of eyewitness memory. *Journal of Experimental Psychology: Learning, Memory, and Cognition*, **20**, 934–945.

CHAPTER 17

Frontal Lobes and Memory

Juliana V. Baldo
Scripps College, Claremont, CA, USA
and
Arthur P. Shimamura
University of California, Berkeley, CA, USA

Casual observations of patients with focal frontal lobe lesions often reveal little if any cognitive impairment (Fuster, 1989; Hebb, 1945). At the same time, such patients display an assortment of cognitive deficits upon neuropsychological assessment (Janowsky et al., 1989c; Luria, 1980; Stuss & Benson, 1984). With respect to memory, focal frontal injury does not produce a severe amnesic disorder, such as that observed in patients with medial temporal damage, but it can cause more subtle, yet definable, memory deficits. These deficits take the form of an impairment in the *control* of memory (Moscovitch, 1992; Shimamura, 1995, 2000a), i.e. the prefrontal cortex appears to be crucial for the monitoring and control of memory processes, both at the time of encoding and at the time of retrieval. In this chapter, we describe patterns of memory impairment associated with focal damage to the prefrontal cortex. Specifically, we review the role of the prefrontal cortex in learning and recall, memory for contextual information, metamemory and retrieval from remote memory. We then relate these long-term memory deficits to impairments in on-line processing associated with working memory and attention. Finally, we put these deficits in the context of a more global view of prefrontal function.

LEARNING AND RECALL

Clinically, patients with focal prefrontal lesions do not exhibit an "amnesic syndrome". This term has been reserved for the debilitating, new learning disorder associated with medial temporal damage (Gershberg & Shimamura, 1998; Squire, 1992). Moreover, standard clinical tests of learning and memory are often not sensitive to prefrontal lesions (Incisa della Rocchetta & Milner, 1993; Janowsky et al., 1989c), e.g. recognition memory in frontal patients is often not significantly different than that of controls (Janowsky et al., 1989c). Nonetheless, experimental studies of new learning in patients with frontal lobe lesions have identified specific memory deficits. The pattern of these deficits suggests that frontal patients suffer from a failure to utilize memory strategies to enhance encoding and retrieval.

The Handbook of Memory Disorders. Edited by A.D. Baddeley, M.D. Kopelman and B.A. Wilson
© 2002 John Wiley & Sons, Ltd.

Free Recall and Semantic Organization

Recall tasks require the ability to organize, encode and retrieve information with minimal external aids. Patients with prefrontal lesions exhibit significant memory impairment on tasks involving free recall of word lists (Baldo et al., 2002; Dimitrov et al., 1999; Gershberg & Shimamura, 1995; Hildebrandt et al., 1998; Janowsky et al., 1989c; Stuss et al., 1994). These deficits are quite apparent on tests of delayed free recall and can also be observed on tests of cued recall, in which participants are presented with a cue at test (e.g. a category cue). However, when information is embedded within a rich, well-organized context, such as learning a story, frontal patients show relatively good recall (Incisa della Rocchetta & Milner, 1993; Janowsky et al., 1989c). Also, tasks that put minimal demands on effortful retrieval, such as word stem completion and category exemplar priming, are not sensitive to frontal lesions (Gershberg & Shimamura, 1998; Shimamura et al., 1992).

Several studies have shown that free recall impairment in frontal patients is due to a failure to make use of semantic organization inherent in list material (Hildebrandt et al., 1998; Hirst & Volpe, 1988; Jetter et al., 1986; Kopelman & Stanhope, 1998; Stuss et al., 1994). Semantic encoding has been assessed experimentally by comparing patients' memory for related vs. unrelated lists. Related lists consist of several exemplars (e.g. table, chair, uncle, mother) from different semantic categories (e.g. furniture, relatives), usually presented in a random order. In normal controls, recall for related lists is superior, because semantic associations within the list facilitate organization during learning and can act as a retrieval cue at test. In contrast, Hirst & Volpe (1988) found that frontal lobe patients did not show a benefit on related vs. unrelated lists during recall. Moreover, patients did not spontaneously use the semantic categories in the related lists to aid their performance. In a subsequent condition, frontal patients were directed to use the categories and were given explicit and lengthy instructions on how to encode related items. In this condition, frontal patients' performance rose to that of the control participants, demonstrating that frontal patients possess the ability to utilize semantic cues but do not do so spontaneously. In contrast, amnesic patients (mixed etiology) spontaneously made use of and benefited from categorization but, despite this, their performance across conditions was much lower overall compared to frontal patients and controls.

Other studies have assessed organizational strategies in frontal patients by manipulating the presence of category cues at encoding and retrieval. Incisa della Rocchetta & Milner (1993) tested patients on related lists and showed that organizational cues provided at encoding (blocked vs. random order) as well as at retrieval improved frontal patients' performance. Similarly, Gershberg & Shimamura (1995) provided category cues during learning and/or at test and found that frontal patients' performance improved significantly. These findings suggest that both encoding and retrieval are disrupted in frontal patients due to poor (spontaneous) utilization of strategic cues.

Semantic organization during memory encoding has also been assessed using semantic clustering measures. Given a related list of words, an effective strategy is to recall groups or clusters of items from each category. Patients with frontal lobe lesions exhibit reduced levels of semantic clustering (Baldo et al., 2002; Gershberg & Shimamura, 1995). These studies have shown that reduced semantic clustering is present in both initial list-learning trials and on tests of delayed recall. Other studies, however, have not found strong evidence for impaired semantic clustering in frontal patients (see Jetter et al., 1986; Stuss et al., 1994). One possible explanation for this discrepancy is the manner in which semantic clustering is computed. A recent study has called into question former methods for computing this factor and proposes a more sensitive formula for doing so (Stricker et al., 2002). Using this method, Stricker et al. found that a group of patients with prefrontal lesions did indeed show impaired semantic clustering compared to control participants.

Other strategies for learning word lists include subjective and serial organization. Subjective organization is the tendency for an individual to cluster items across test trials, even when there is no apparent semantic association between the items, e.g. a participant might recall the words "table" and "dollar" in succession across several trials, even though these two words were never presented together in the list. Like semantic clustering, subjective organization involves reorganization or reencoding of list items. Not surprisingly, patients with frontal lobe lesions exhibit reduced subjective organization across learning trials of unrelated word lists (Eslinger & Grattan, 1994; Gershberg & Shimamura, 1995; Stuss et al., 1994). Another strategy for encoding is serial organization, or the tendency to recall words in the same order in which they were presented. Such a strategy is less effective, because it is based simply on the surface structure of list order. Patients with frontal lobe lesions and control participants do not differ in the use of serial organization (Baldo et al., 2002; Gershberg & Shimamura, 1995).

In short, these findings suggest that recall deficits in frontal patients are related to their reduced use of semantic and subjective organization, both at encoding and retrieval. Moreover, these studies support the notion that the learning process itself may not be fundamentally impaired. Instead, it is the monitoring and control of information during encoding and retrieval that is compromised in these patients.

Susceptibility to Interference

Experimental studies of learning and memory have assessed the impact of interference on frontal patients' ability to retrieve newly learned information. Frontal patients have been shown to exhibit interference, as evidenced by increased intrusions and cross-list interference during recall (Baldo et al., 2002; Gershberg & Shimamura, 1995; Shimamura et al., 1995). In a paired-associate paradigm, Shimamura et al. (1995) had participants learn related word pairs (e.g. "lion–hunter"). Following learning of this AB list, a second list (AC) was learned in which the same cue words were paired with different responses (e.g. "lion–circus"). Patients with frontal lobe lesions exhibited intact learning for the first set of pairs (AB list) but exhibited impairment in learning the second list (AC list), in part due to increased intrusions from the first list.

Incisa della Rocchetta & Milner (1993) assessed interference effects using a part-list-cueing paradigm, in which presentation of part of a word list at test actually disrupts normal recall. In their study, left frontal patients showed an exaggerated part-list-cueing effect, suggesting that they were most susceptible to the interference effect. In contrast, left temporal patients were minimally affected. Such findings suggest that frontal patients are impaired in their ability to select and manipulate information and that this leads to significant problems when highly salient but irrelevant information is activated.

Recognition Memory

Tests of recognition memory do not require participants to generate information, but rather rely more on familiarity. Traditionally, recognition memory has been thought to be intact in patients with frontal lesions (Janowsky et al., 1989c). Recently, however, Wheeler et al. (1995) performed a meta-analysis of studies that assessed memory performance in patients with frontal lesions. Across these studies, significant impairment was observed on tests of free recall (80% of studies), cued recall (50% of studies) and even on tests of recognition (8% of studies). They suggested that the inconsistency in findings on tests of recognition is due to the lack of statistical power in studies with small numbers of patients available for testing. Despite this inconsistency, Wheeler et al. concluded that these data were evidence for the presence of an episodic memory impairment in frontal patients, rather than simply a deficit in organizational and strategic control.

Other findings have suggested that impaired recognition (as well as recall) may be due to subclinical language impairment. Stuss et al. (1994) reported that frontal patients were impaired on an overall recognition score and that this recognition impairment correlated with the degree of anomia in left frontal patients. They hypothesized that reduced verbal elaboration at encoding (due to language deficits) was in part responsible for subsequent recognition deficits (but see Vilkki et al., 1998). In keeping with this, Vogel et al. (1987) found that aids that increased depth of processing improved memory performance in frontal patients. This factor is crucial to consider, as many left frontal patients included in studies may have been acutely aphasic and may possess a residual, although mild, anomia. Indeed, studies of new learning often report greater impairment in left than right frontal patients (Dimitrov et al., 1999).

To what extent does impaired recognition performance reflect problems in organizing information during encoding and retrieval? In a recent study, Baldo et al. (in press) found significant impairment in yes–no recognition memory, based on the tendency of frontal patients to false-alarm to semantically related distractors. On a forced-choice recognition procedure, however, frontal patients made no errors; but on this task, the distractor items were semantically unrelated and easily dismissed. This pattern of errors in frontal patients was distinct from that of an amnesic patient with medial temporal injury who, in addition to poor performance on yes–no recognition (worse than frontals), made several errors on the same forced-choice recognition paradigm that was trivially easy for frontal patients.

Further evidence for this dissociation comes from Swick & Knight (1999), who tested frontal and hippocampal patients on a continuous recognition memory paradigm. They reported a double dissociation, such that frontal patients exhibited a normal hit rate but an inflated false alarm rate compared to controls, while hippocampal patients exhibited a reduced hit rate (especially at long lags) but a normal false alarm rate. They concluded that frontal patients do not show a "simple" memory deficit but rather have impairments due to poor use of strategy, source monitoring errors and working memory impairments.

Severe recognition impairment following frontal injury has been reported by Schacter and colleagues in case studies of patient B.G., who incurred an extensive, right posterior frontal lesion (Curran et al., 1997; Schacter, 1996; Schacter et al., 1996). B.G. exhibited a "pathological" false recognition syndrome for semantically related distractors and would even claim to recall details of learning certain items that had not been presented. Interestingly, this false recognition syndrome was ameliorated when he studied a categorized list and the distractor items on the subsequent recognition task were from novel categories.

Schacter and colleagues concluded that B.G. exhibited an "over-responsivity to a memory signal based on the general similarity of test items to studied items" (Curran et al., 1997, p. 1047; also see Schacter, Chapter 16, this volume). Again, B.G.'s deficits demonstrate that memory impairments in frontal patients stem from an inability to control and sort newly-learned information, but that this impairment does not exist when critical cues are provided for the patient as a memory aid.

Findings on tests of recognition memory traditionally supported the view that recognition was relatively unimpaired in frontal patients. However, more recent findings suggest that this view may be incorrect, as recognition is sometimes found to be impaired, e.g. when distractors are semantically related to target items. As in new learning and recall, such recognition deficits in frontal patients are ameliorated under certain conditions. This pattern of memory impairments and residual abilities is best explained by a general deficit in strategic encoding and retrieval, rather than a fundamental learning deficit. Further support for this notion comes from evidence of similar deficits in other aspects of memory described in the following sections.

MEMORY FOR CONTEXTUAL INFORMATION

In addition to deficits in new learning and recall, frontal patients have a reduced ability to recollect contextual information (Janowsky et al., 1989a; Shimamura et al., 1990; Smith & Milner, 1988). Contextual information refers to the spatiotemporal aspects of an event (e.g. when and where you saw a recent movie), as opposed to its semantic content (e.g. the plot of a movie; see Johnson et al., 1993). Retrieving such information requires the reconstruction of episodic information from long-term memory.

The first demonstration of an impairment of this type was a study of verbal and nonverbal recency memory in frontal and temporal lobe patients (Corsi, as described in Milner, 1971). Patients with frontal lobe lesions were impaired when they had to determine which of two items was presented more recently. Specifically, left frontal patients exhibited a recency deficit for words, whereas right frontal patients exhibited a recency deficit for nonverbal stimuli. In contrast, temporal lobe patients were impaired at making old–new judgments about the items but did not exhibit disproportionate impairment on recency judgments.

Studies of temporal order memory have also supported the proposition that patients with frontal lobe damage are impaired at retrieving spatiotemporal information. Shimamura et al. (1990) tested frontal lobe patients' memory for temporal order, using a sequence reconstruction test in which items were displayed in a random array and participants were asked to reconstruct the study order. Patients with frontal lobe lesions were significantly impaired at reconstructing the order of both recently presented word lists and at reconstructing the chronological order of public events. In a similar study, Mangels (1997) tested focal frontal patients on a series of temporal order tasks that involved both intentional and incidental learning conditions. In each condition, patients were shown a series of words and 1 min later were asked to reconstruct the word sequence. Frontal patients were impaired relative to controls in the *intentional* learning condition, but they performed as well as controls in the *incidental* learning condition, i.e. frontal patients were inferior to controls only when participants were told that their memory would later be tested. Mangels concluded that frontal patients possess the ability to form "basic temporal codes" but are not able to engage additional strategies needed to enhance performance.

Other studies have shown that patients with frontal lobe lesions are impaired in another aspect of temporal coding known as frequency estimation, which involves estimating how often an event has occurred. Smith & Milner (1988) showed that patients with right and left frontal, but not temporal, lesions were impaired on a test of frequency estimation using abstract designs. Importantly, a recognition test demonstrated an impairment only in right temporal lobe patients, which suggested that the performance of patients with frontal lobe lesions could not be attributed to an impairment of discrimination or recognition of the designs.

Source memory (i.e. recalling the source of learned information) has also been shown to be disproportionately impaired in patients with frontal lobe lesions. In one study, participants were asked a series of trivial questions (e.g. "What is the name of the dog on the Cracker Jacks box?"; Janowsky et al., 1989a). On those questions that they could not answer correctly, participants were given the correct answer (e.g. "Bingo") and asked to repeat and memorize it. Several days later, participants returned and were tested on the previously learned items, along with new (filler) items. They were tested for their ability to recall the answer to each question and to determine the source of the information (i.e. whether they heard it during the experimental session or at some other time). Patients with frontal lobe lesions were not impaired on tests of item recall or recognition. They were, however, poor at determining the source of a correctly answered question. That is, they made source errors by stating that filler items were learned during the previous session and by misattributing information learned during the previous session to their own general knowledge.

To what extent does impaired source memory in frontal patients reflect a basic deficit in representing source and temporal information? Some have suggested that episodic memory (and thus, contextual information) is an inherent property of the prefrontal cortex (Tulving et al., 1994; Wheeler et al., 1995). Alternatively, it may be that retrieval of contextual information, like free recall, requires extensive manipulation and control of memory processes. Findings by Mangels (1997), demonstrating intact memory for temporal order under incidental learning conditions, show that when strategic processing is reduced, frontal patients do not exhibit deficits in temporal order memory. Also, McAndrews & Milner (1991) addressed this issue by facilitating attentional control in frontal patients during learning. Participants were presented with objects and asked to perform a task with each one (e.g. "bounce the ball"). Later, participants were given a recency judgment test in which pairs of objects were presented, and they were asked to determine which of the two was presented more recently. Patients with frontal lobe lesions exhibited intact recency memory for manipulated stimuli but impaired performance for objects that were shown but not manipulated. In sum, these findings suggest that patients with frontal lobe lesions have the capacity to retrieve contextual, spatiotemporal information, depending on the attentional demands during learning.

METACOGNITION AND MEMORY

Metacognition refers to the ability to reflect upon one's own thoughts, memories, and knowledge (see Metcalfe & Shimamura, 1994). This ability depends in part on the status of the prefrontal cortex (Janowsky et al., 1989b; Metcalfe & Shimamura, 1994; Shimamura, 2000b). Similar to other aspects of memory discussed thus far, metacognition depends upon strategic, explicit retrieval of information from long-term memory.

Hirst & Volpe (1988, Experiment 1) tested metacognition by questioning patients about memory strategies (e.g. how would they go about learning a list of categorizable words) and by having patients judge the relative difficulty of different memory tasks. This experiment revealed that frontal lobe patients were not very sophisticated in their metacognitive knowledge and had little awareness of their memory deficits, e.g. they did not realize the importance of item repetition or extra study time. In contrast, amnesic patients were relatively sophisticated in their knowledge of memory strategies and were aware of their deficits.

A well-studied technique that involves the use of metacognitive processes is the "feeling-of-knowing" paradigm. In this paradigm, participants make predictions about future performance on a memory test. In one study, Janowsky et al. (1989b) assessed feeling-of-knowing judgments in patients with frontal lesions and amnesic patients (including Korsakoff patients). Participants learned sentences such as, "Mary's garden was full of marigolds". Following a retention interval (5 min–3 days), patients were shown the sentences with the final word missing and were asked to supply that word. If they could not recall the word, they rated how likely they could recognize the word if given some choices. Frontal patients performed like controls at the short delay but exhibited impaired feeling-of-knowing at long (1–3 days) delays. That is, they were not accurate at predicting the likelihood that they could recall the target word.

Another way of testing metacognition is by asking individuals to make inferences using basic knowledge. Shallice & Evans (1978) used questions such as, "How tall is a bus?" or "How long is the average man's necktie?". Since such answers are rarely known directly, they involve estimations based on strategic analysis of memory and inferential reasoning. Shallice & Evans assessed frontal and nonfrontal patients on a series of such cognitive estimation questions, as well as on arithmetic and nonverbal reasoning tests. They found that frontal patients were impaired on the cognitive estimation questions but not on the latter two tests, which suggested that general problem-solving ability could not account for their metacognitive deficit. Similarly, Smith & Milner (1984) found that patients with frontal lesions were impaired in their ability to make reasonable estimations of prices of objects. The largest impairment was observed in right frontal patients, and performance on the task correlated with lesion size in left frontal patients.

Metacognition has been construed specifically as the monitoring and control of information processing (see Nelson & Narens, 1994; Shimamura, 1994, 2000b). Findings from patients with frontal lobe lesions suggest that they lack such an ability to use and manipulate memories. These deficits may be part of a general deficit in selecting, organizing and manipulating information in working memory, e.g. in an attempt to recall some information, one might retrieve partial information and, based on this information, decide to spend extra time trying to develop associative strategies to retrieve further information. Frontal patients' poor metacognitive awareness, coupled with retrieval deficits discussed above, make such an effortful search unlikely to be successful.

RETRIEVAL FROM REMOTE MEMORY

In most studies of memory, such as list-learning experiments, it is difficult to distinguish between deficits at the time of learning from deficits at the time of retrieval. One way to isolate retrieval deficits is to assess memory for remote information that was presumably learned before the onset of neurological damage. Mangels et al. (1996) tested frontal patients' recall and recognition for remote public events (e.g. "Who killed John Lennon?") and for the names of famous faces. Frontal patients performed more poorly than controls on free recall for public events, but they exhibited normal performance on a four-choice recognition task (e.g. "Was it John Hinkley, Sarah Jane Moore, Mark Chapman or David Roth?"). On the famous faces test, frontal patients were impaired on both free recall of the names of famous people and cued (phonemic and semantic) recall, but again, there was no difference between frontal patients and controls on a four-choice recognition task. Interestingly, unlike in amnesia, where retrieval is often better for very remote information vs. information learned closer to the time of injury, frontal patients exhibited a consistent recall deficit across all time periods tested. Similar findings were reported by Kopelman et al. (1999), who found that frontal patients were impaired at retrieval for autobiographical and news events and that cueing and recognition tasks improved performance.

Similar retrieval deficits have been observed in other modalities. Baldo & Shimamura (1995) tested frontal patients' ability to recall and recognize the names of common odors (e.g. smoke, cinnamon, orange). Frontal patients were significantly worse than controls at retrieving the names of odors, especially when odors were presented monorhinally to the lesioned hemisphere. In contrast to recall performance, frontal patients' performance improved significantly with a recognition task, i.e. when they were given a choice of four odor names from which to choose.

Another way of assessing retrieval from remote memory is analysis of performance on fluency tasks. Fluency tasks require patients to make a strategic search through memory for words that meet certain criteria, e.g. words belonging to a particular category (e.g. "animals") or words beginning with a particular letter. A large number of studies have shown that both letter and category fluency are disrupted in patients with right and left frontal lesions (Baldo & Shimamura, 1998; Benton, 1968; Janowsky et al., 1989c; Miceli et al., 1981; Miller, 1984; Milner, 1964; Perret, 1974).

Like new learning, fluency deficits appear to be due to an impairment in strategic retrieval rather than to a loss of semantic knowledge (Baldo et al., 1997). Troyer et al. (1998) showed that frontal patients' impaired performance on fluency tasks was due to their tendency to perseverate on a subcategory, rather than switch to a new subcategory to enhance output (e.g. normals might switch from land animals to water animals to birds to maximize their output). Importantly, Baldo et al. showed that, while frontal patients were impaired at retrieval of animal names on a category fluency task, the same patients exhibited a normal "semantic space" of animal names using a triadic comparison task. This finding supports the notion that frontal patients' semantic networks are generally intact, despite their poor retrieval. When left and right frontal patients were analyzed separately for the quality of their responses, right frontal patients tended to produce more typical word profiles, while left frontal patients generated highly atypical word profiles (Schwartz & Baldo, 2001). These results suggested that the left frontal lobe is more involved in the retrieval of highly typical associations, while right frontal processes support more remote and/or idiosyncratic associations.

As this review indicates, patients with frontal lobe lesions exhibit marked impairment on a variety of tests involving long-term memory. Deficits are observed on tests involving list learning, source memory, metacognition and retrieval of information from remote memory. However, frontal patients can exhibit intact memory when the demands on attention are reduced and/or retrieval strategies are provided (Hirst & Volpe, 1988; Mangels, 1997; McAndrews & Milner, 1991).

WORKING MEMORY

Frontal patients exhibit deficits on tests of new learning and retrieval when there are high demands on monitoring and controlling memory. As such, these deficits in long-term memory can be construed as directly related to deficits in the executive control of working memory. In a seminal analysis of working memory, Baddeley (1986) characterized frontal lobe impairment as a "dysexecutive" syndrome and offered a concise interpretation of the relationship between working memory and long-term memory disorders associated with frontal lobe damage (see also Moscovitch, 1992,1994).

It is well documented that patients with frontal lobe lesions exhibit deficits in the on-line control of information in short-term memory. Such working memory processes have been tested using a variety of stimuli, including digits, locations, colors and sounds (Baldo & Shimamura, 2000; Chao & Knight, 1996; Freedman & Oscar-Berman, 1986; Goldman & Rosvold, 1970; Jacobsen, 1936; Mishkin & Pribram, 1956; Petrides et al., 1993; Ptito et al., 1995). These findings are consistent with experimental studies of prefrontal damage in monkeys using delayed response paradigms (Fuster, 1989; Goldman-Rakic, 1987; Jacobsen, 1936). In the delayed response task, food is concealed in one of two locations and, after a brief delay, the animal selects the location in which the food reward was placed. Jacobsen (1936) first showed that performance on this task is impaired after bilateral lesions of prefrontal cortex but not after temporal, premotor, postcentral or parietal lesions.

Several studies have used delayed response paradigms to assess working memory in neurologic patients. One of the first studies, however, reported negative results. Ghent et al. (1962) tested frontal patients' ability to recall (following a short delay) the angle of tilt of visual and tactile stimuli, as well as their own body tilt. In addition, they tested short-term memory for digit and block design sequences. Patients with frontal damage were not impaired on any of these tasks. In contrast, Lewinsohn et al. (1972) reported that patients with frontal damage were impaired on a similar series of tasks, in which patients had to match visual, auditory, and tactile stimuli. Importantly, unlike the study by Ghent et al., this study required participants to count out loud during the delay interval to prevent rehearsal. Freedman & Oscar-Berman (1986) showed that patients with bilateral frontal lobe lesions were impaired on two types of simple delayed response tasks, the classic delayed response task and a delayed alternation task, in which the target alternated between two spatial locations. These researchers suggested that negative results from previous studies (e.g. Ghent et al., 1962) were due to the fact that they did not use populations with bilateral lesions.

A similar finding was reported by Milner et al. (1985), who used a delayed match-to-sample task with a 60 s delay. In one condition, all objects in a block of trials were different; in another condition, some objects were repeated on subsequent trials. Patients with frontal damage were only impaired in the latter condition, namely when objects appeared more than once. Milner et al. concluded that this impairment was due to interference arising from the repetition of objects and to patients' inability to segregate trials into temporally-unique events. These findings are consistent with deficits in spatiotemporal coding and increased susceptibility to interference, as discussed above.

More complex tasks of working memory have also been shown to be sensitive to frontal lobe impairment. These tasks require not only maintenance but also manipulation of information in working memory. In the self-ordered task developed by Petrides & Milner (1982), participants are presented with a matrix of stimuli (e.g. words or abstract designs);

these stimuli are presented in different positions across trials and, on each trial, participants are asked to point to a different item. Thus, the participant must not only maintain information in working memory but must also update information on each trial. Petrides & Milner found that the patients with left frontal lesions were impaired on both verbal and nonverbal conditions of the self-ordered task, while patients with right frontal lesions were moderately impaired in a nonverbal condition. Petrides & Milner thus suggested that the left frontal lobe is crucial for mediating verbal rehearsal and manipulating information in working memory. In both neuroimaging and animal studies, Petrides (1998) has identified the dorsolateral prefrontal cortex (areas 9 and 46) as critical for performance on the self-ordered pointing task.

A series of studies by Owen et al. (1990, 1995, 1996) have shown that patients with frontal lobe lesions are impaired on a complex spatial working memory paradigm. In this task, participants attempted to determine in which of several locations a token was hidden. A strategy measure was computed, based on the assumption that the optimal strategy (the one most controls employ) is to begin each search in the same location. Owen and colleagues showed that patients with frontal lobe lesions were impaired on this spatial working memory task, not because of a short-term memory deficit *per se*, but rather because of a deficient searching strategy. In contrast, Owen et al. (1996) found that frontal lobe patients had normal spatial spans. Such a pattern of findings suggests that the prefrontal cortex subserves more complex working memory functions than simply maintaining information in short-term memory.

A recent study (Baldo, in preparation) assessed frontal patients and controls on a two-back working memory paradigm, similar to that used in recent functional neuroimaging studies (e.g. Awh et al., 1996). In this type of task, participants are presented with a continuous series of stimuli and they have to decide whether the current stimulus is the same as that presented two trials previously. In this way, participants have to keep updating in working memory what the comparison (two-back) stimulus was. Patients and controls were tested on three conditions of the two-back task, where the stimuli were visually presented words, nonwords and phonologically similar words (e.g. lap, sat, back, pat, etc.). Frontal patients were impaired compared to controls across all three conditions of the two-back task, making a large percentage of errors that consisted mostly of false alarms.

In short, a large body of literature supports the association between working memory and frontal cortex. Findings suggest that patients with frontal lobe lesions exhibit deficits, not simply in the maintenance of information but more so in the manipulation and updating of information in working memory.

NEUROIMAGING FINDINGS: CORROBORATION AND EXTENSION

Over the past decade, our understanding of memory processes has benefited significantly from advances in functional neuroimaging. Techniques such as positron emission tomography (PET) and functional magnetic resonance imaging (fMRI) have allowed us to identify neural networks that are particularly active during memory tasks (D'Esposito, 2000; D'Esposito et al., 2000; Poldrack & Gabrieli, 1997). A number of neuroimaging studies have corroborated findings from memory studies with focal frontal patients. Others have offered a more detailed analysis of the cortical and subcortical networks that support mnemonic processes.

In terms of new learning and long-term memory, neuroimaging studies have shown that the dorsolateral prefrontal cortex plays a critical role in organizational processes (e.g. during list learning), while the ventral prefrontal cortex is activated during encoding more generally (Fletcher et al., 1998). Other studies have shown that source memory judgments activate left and bilateral prefrontal regions, while simple recognition judgments activate a subset of these regions (Rugg et al., 1999). Individual and retrospective analyses of PET data have suggested that the left prefrontal cortex is preferentially activated during encoding of episodic memories, while retrieval of episodic information is associated with bilateral but predominantly right prefrontal activation (Andreasen et al., 1995; Lepage et al., 2000; Tulving et al., 1994; but see Swick & Knight, 1996).

In terms of working memory, many neuroimaging studies have demonstrated that the lateral prefrontal cortex is activated as part of a large network of cortical regions (D'Esposito et al., 2000; Smith & Jonides, 1999). Some studies have reported a distinction between right and left hemisphere activation for spatial vs. object working memory, respectively (e.g. Smith et al., 1995), while others have not observed such a clear distinction (e.g. McCarthy et al., 1996). Other studies have focused on the neural components of verbal working memory and have reported activation of Broca's area, as well as the dorsolateral prefrontal cortex, with such tasks (Awh et al., 1996; Fiez et al., 1996; Grasby et al., 1993; Paulesu et al., 1993).

Activation of the prefrontal regions has also been observed with more complex, "executive" tasks associated with the frontal lobe, e.g. self-ordered and dual-task paradigms (Petrides & Milner, 1982; Moscovitch, 1994; Petrides et al., 1993). D'Esposito et al. (1995) reported significant activation of area 46 bilaterally when participants performed two tasks simultaneously (mental rotation and semantic judgment), but observed no frontal activation when they performed either of these tasks alone. D'Esposito et al. concluded that the prefrontal cortex is necessary for the allocation of attentional resources under such demanding conditions. Moreover, Prabhakaran et al. (2000) reported that the prefrontal cortex (especially the right) was activated preferentially when participants had to maintain in working memory integrated spatial and nonspatial information (e.g. holding in mind *what AND where* a stimulus was), while the posterior regions supported maintenance of nonintegrated information (e.g. holding in mind *what* OR *where* a stimulus was).

While functional neuroimaging studies can elaborate on brain regions implicated in focal lesion studies, it is important to distinguish between regions that play critical roles in memory and regions that are merely correlated with memory tasks. Ideally, functional neuroimaging and focal lesion studies will continue to complement each other, as neuroimaging studies detect large networks of cortical and subcortical regions involved in memory, and patient studies provide information about the extent to which those regions are critical to mnemonic processes.

DYNAMIC FILTERING THEORY OF FRONTAL LOBE FUNCTION

Deficits in executive control appear to play a role in memory impairments observed in patients with frontal lobe lesions. Shimamura (1995, 2000a) developed dynamic filtering theory as a way of linking cognitive dysfunction associated with prefrontal damage to an impairment in a neurobiological gating mechanism. This view suggests that the prefrontal cortex acts to filter or gate to neural activity arising in posterior cortical regions. This filtering mechanism increases activity selected by the prefrontal cortex and at the same time actively inhibits extraneous or irrelevant activity. In essence, dynamic filtering increases the signal-to-noise ratio by enabling top-down control of information processing. This gating mechanism can account for four basic aspects of executive control—selecting, maintaining, updating and rerouting (Shimamura, 2000a). When these processes are disrupted following frontal injury, the result is executive dyscontrol that then leads to deficits in a number of areas, including memory.

A number of studies have provided physiological evidence for the role of the prefrontal cortex in dynamic filtering and inhibitory gating. Knight and colleagues have reported a series of studies in which they recorded event related potentials (ERPs) in patients with frontal lobe lesions (Knight et al., 1989, 1999; Yamaguchi & Knight, 1990). They have shown that frontal lobe patients exhibit exaggerated ERPs to sensory information, e.g. auditory and somatosensory stimuli, suggesting that prefrontal cortex damage leads to some form of "disinhibition" in responding to environmental stimuli. In other words, frontal lobe lesions resulted in the failure to gate activity arising in posterior cortex. Moreover, patients with frontal lesions did not show normal inhibition of irrelevant stimuli (as measured by ERPs) when they were attending to target stimuli. Further support for this theory comes from neuroimaging studies with normal individuals. In a PET study of word finding (Frith et al., 1991), increased activity in the dorsolateral prefrontal cortex correlated with decreased activity in posterior cortical regions. Also, an fMRI study reported that inhibitory mechanisms were associated with dorsolateral prefrontal cortex activation in a go–no go task (Konishi et al., 1999; see also Dolan & Fletcher, 1997).

Behavioral findings are also consistent with the dynamic filtering hypothesis (Bartus & Levere, 1977; Blake et al., 1966; Knight & Grabowecky, 1995; Malmo, 1942; Shimamura, 1995, 2000a). Early studies of the prefrontal cortex noted that both monkeys and humans with frontal lesions were highly susceptible to extraneous stimuli (Brickner, 1936; Jacobsen, 1936). Jacobsen observed the following:

> The operated animal seems more distractable in contrast to the sustained, directed behaviour of the normal subject. Behaviour, instead of being directed by a balance of immediate, recent and temporally remote stimulation, is dominated by present external stimuli and the stable habit systems . . . the mnemonic influence of immediately past experience is lacking (p. 52).

A number of experimental findings in both animals and humans have corroborated these behavioral observations (Baldo & Shimamura, 2000; Bartus & Levere, 1977; Chao & Knight, 1996; Malmo, 1942; Ptito et al., 1995). Working memory studies have shown that patients with frontal lobe lesions are disproportionately impaired when there is some form of distraction during the delay interval. This delay period interference may be in the form of irrelevant auditory distractors (Chao & Knight, 1996) or a secondary task (Baldo & Shimamura, 2000; Ptito et al., 1995). Other support for the failure to inhibit extraneous information comes from studies of response inhibition, as frontal patients show increased interference on go–no go tasks (Drewe, 1975) and the Stroop effect (Perret, 1974).

In short, both physiological and behavioral evidence are consistent with the notion that a basic disruption of inhibitory gating results from frontal injury, and that such disruption can result in impaired performance in a number of domains, including memory.

CONCLUSIONS

Over the past decade, resurgent interest in the role of the frontal lobes in memory has led to extraordinary advances. Neuropsychological and neuroimaging studies indicate that prefrontal cortex contributes to a variety of memory processes, including learning, recall, source memory, metacogntion and remote retrieval. These long-term memory mechanisms place heavy demands on executive processes, such as working memory and attention, which are also compromised in this patient group. With respect to global processing, the prefrontal cortex appears to act as a gating mechanism that monitors and controls information processing represented in other brain regions. Future studies will need to better characterize the complex, dynamic relationship between the prefrontal cortex and the medial temporal regions in order to have a more complete understanding of the neurobiological substrates and cognitive mechanisms underlying human memory.

REFERENCES

Andreasen, N.C., O'Leary, D.S., Arndt, S. et al. (1995). Short-term and long-term verbal memory: a positron emission tomography study. *Proceedings of the National Academy of Sciences*, **92**, 5111–5115.

Awh, E., Jonides, J., Smith, E. et al. (1996). Dissociation of storage and rehearsal in verbal working memory: evidence from positron emission tomography. *Psychological Science*, **7**, 25–31.

Baddeley, A. (1986). *Working Memory*. Oxford: Oxford University Press.

Baldo, J.V. (in preparation). Two-back working memory in patients with focal frontal lesions.

Baldo, J.V., Chen, C.-Y. & Shimamura, A.P. (1997). Impaired memory retrieval in frontal lobe patients, despite intact semantic space. *Society for Neuroscience Abstracts*, **23**, 1579.

Baldo, J.V., Delis, D., Kramer, J. & Shimamura, A.P. (2002). Memory performance on the California Verbal Learning Test II: findings from patients with focal frontal lesions. *Journal of the International Neuropsychological Society*, **8**, 539–546.

Baldo, J.V. & Shimamura, A.P. (1995). Performance of patients with dorsolateral frontal lesions on an olfactory identification task. *Society for Neuroscience Abstracts*, **21**.

Baldo, J.V. & Shimamura, A.P. (1998). Letter and category fluency in patients with frontal lobe lesions. *Neuropsychology*, **12**, 259–267.

Baldo, J.V. & Shimamura, A.P. (2000). Spatial and color working memory in patients with lateral prefrontal cortex lesions. *Psychobiology*, **28**, 156–167.

Bartus, R. & Levere, T. (1977). Frontal decortication in rhesus monkeys: a test of the interference hypothesis. *Brain Research*, **119**, 233–248.

Benton, A. (1968). Differential behavioral effects of frontal lobe disease. *Neuropsychologia*, **6**, 53–60.

Blake, M., Meyer, D. & Meyer, P. (1966). Enforced observation in delayed response learning by frontal monkeys. *Journal of Comparative and Physiological Psychology*, **61**, 374–379.

Brickner, R. (1936). *The Intellectual Functions of the Frontal Lobes*. New York: Macmillan.

Chao, L. & Knight, R. (1996). Human prefrontal lesions increase distractibility to irrelevant sensory inputs. *NeuroReport*, **6**, 45–50.

Curran, T., Schacter, D.L., Norman, K.A. & Galluccio, L. (1997). False recognition after a right frontal lobe infarction: memory for general and specific information. *Neuropsychologia*, **35**, 1035–1049.

D'Esposito M. (2000). Functional neuroimaging of cognition. *Seminars in Neurology*, **20**, 487–498.

D'Esposito, M, Postle, B.R. & Rypma, B. (2000). Prefrontal cortical contributions to working memory: evidence from event-related fMRI studies. *Experimental Brain Research*, **133**, 3–11.

D'Esposito, M., Detre, J., Alsop, D. et al. (1995). The neural basis of the central executive system of working memory. *Nature*, **378**, 279–281.

Dimitrov, M., Granetz, J., Peterson, M. et al. (1999). Associative learning impairments in patients with frontal lobe damage. *Brain and Cognition*, **41**, 213–230.

Dolan, R.J. & Fletcher, P.C. (1997). Dissociating prefrontal and hippocampal function in episodic memory encoding. *Nature*, **388**, 582–585.

Drewe, E. (1975). Go-no go learning after frontal lobe lesions in humans. *Cortex*, **11**, 8–16.

Eslinger, P.J. & Grattan, L.M. (1994). Altered serial position learning after frontal lobe lesion. *Neuropsychologia*, **32**, 729–739.

Fiez, J., Raife, E., Balota, D.et al. (1996). A positron emission tomography study of the short-term maintenance of verbal information. *Journal of Neuroscience*, **16**, 808–822.

Fletcher, P.C., Shallice, T. & Dolan, R.J. (1998). The functional roles of prefrontal cortex in episodic memory. *Brain*, **121**, 1239–1248.

Freedman, M. & Oscar-Berman, M. (1986). Bilateral frontal lobe disease and selective delayed response deficits in humans. *Behavioral Neuroscience*, **100**, 337–342.

Frith, C., Friston, K., Liddle, P. & Frackowiak, R. (1991). A PET study of word finding. *Neuropsychologia*, **29**, 1137–1148.

Fuster, J. (1989). *The Prefrontal Cortex*. New York: Raven.

Gershberg, F.B. & Shimamura, A.P. (1995). Impaired use of organizational strategies in free recall following frontal lobe damage. *Neuropsychologia*, **13**, 1305–1333.

Gershberg, F.B. & Shimamura, A.P. (1998). The neuropsychology of human learning and memory. In J.L. Martinez Jr. & R.P. Kesner (eds), *Neurobiology of Learning and Memory*. San Diego, CA: Academic Press.

Ghent, L., Mishkin, M. & Teuber, H. (1962). Short-term memory after frontal lobe injury in man. *Journal of Comparative and Physiological Psychology*, **55**, 705–709.

Goldman, P. & Rosvold, E. (1970). Localization of function within the dorsolateral prefrontal cortex of the rhesus monkey. *Experimental Neurology*, **27**, 291–304.

Goldman-Rakic, P. (1987). Circuitry of primate prefrontal cortex and regulation of behavior by representational memory. In F. Plum (ed.), *Handbook of Physiology; Nervous System, Vol. V: Higher Functions of the Brain, Part 1*, (pp. 373–417). Bethesda, MD: American Physiological Society.

Grasby, P., Frith, C., Friston, K. et al. (1993). Functional mapping of brain areas implicated in auditory–verbal memory function. *Brain*, **116**, 1–20.

Hebb, D. (1945). Man's frontal lobes. *Archives of Neurology and Psychiatry*, **54**, 10–24.

Hildebrandt, H., Brand, A. & Sachsenheimer, W. (1998). Profiles of patients with left prefrontal and left temporal lobe lesions after cerebrovascular infarctions on California Verbal Learning Test-like indices. *Journal of Clinical and Experimental Neuropsychology*, **20**, 673–683.

Hirst, W. & Volpe, B.T. (1988). Memory strategies with brain damage. *Brain and Cognition*, **8**, 379–408.

Incisa della Rocchetta, I. & Milner, B. (1993). Strategic search and retrieval inhibition: the role of the frontal lobes. *Neuropsychologia*, **31**, 503–524.

Jacobsen, C. (1936). Studies of cerebral functions in primates. *Comparative Psychology Monographs*, **13**, 1–60.

Janowsky, J.S., Shimamura, A.P., Kritchevsky, M. & Squire, L.R. (1989c). Cognitive impairment following frontal lobe damage and its relevance to human amnesia. *Behavioral Neuroscience*, **103**, 548–560.

Janowsky, J.S., Shimamura, A.P. & Squire, L.R. (1989a). Source memory impairment in patients with frontal lobe lesions. *Neuropsychologia*, **27**, 1043–1056.

Janowsky, J.S., Shimamura, A.P., & Squire, L.R. (1989b). Memory and metamemory: comparisons between frontal lobe lesions and amnesic patients. *Psychobiology*, **17**, 3–11.

Jetter, W., Poser, U., Freeman, R.B. & Markowitsch, H.J. (1986). A verbal long-term memory deficit in frontal lobe damaged patients. *Cortex*, **22**, 229–242.

Johnson, M.K., Hashtroudi, S. & Lindsay, D.S. (1993). Source monitoring. *Psychological Bulletin*, **114**, 3–28.

Knight, R. & Grabowecky, M. (1995). Escape from linear time: prefrontal cortex and conscious experience. In M. Gazzaniga (ed.), *The Cognitive Neurosciences*. Cambridge, MA: MIT Press.

Knight, R.T., Staines, W.R., Swick, D. & Chao, L.L. (1999). Prefrontal cortex regulates inhibition and excitation in distributed neural networks. *Acta Psychologica*, **101**, 59–78.

Knight, R.T., Scabini, B. & Woods, D.L. (1989). Prefrontal cortex gating in auditory transmission in humans. *Brain Research*, **504**, 338–342.

Konishi, S., Nakajima, K., Uchida, I. et al. (1999). Common inhibitory mechanism in human inferior prefrontal cortex revealed by event-related functional MRI. *Brain*, **122**, 981–991.

Kopelman, M.D. & Stanhope, N. (1998). Recall and recognition memory in patients with focal frontal, temporal lobe and diencephalic lesions. *Neuropsychologia*, **36**, 785–796.

Kopelman, M.D., Stanhope, N. & Kingsley, D. (1999). Retrograde amnesia in patients with diencephalic, temporal lobe or frontal lesions. *Neuropsychologia*, **37**, 939–958.

Lepage, M., Ghaffar, O., Nyberg, L. & Tulving, E. (2000). Prefrontal cortex and episodic memory retrieval mode. *Proceedings of the National Academy of Sciences of the USA*, **97**, 506–511.

Lewinsohn, P., Zieler, R., Libet, J. et al. (1972). Short-term memory: a comparison between frontal and nonfrontal right- and left-hemisphere brain-damaged patients. *Journal of Comparative and Physiological Psychology*, **81**, 248–255.

Luria, A. (1980). *Higher Cortical Functions in Man*. New York: Consultants Bureau.

McAndrews, M.P. & Milner, B. (1991). The frontal cortex and memory for temporal order. *Neuropsychologia*, **29**, 849–859.

McCarthy, G., Puce, A., Constable, R. et al. (1996). Activation of human prefrontal cortex during spatial and nonspatial working memory tasks measured by functional MRI. *Cerebral Cortex*, **6**, 600–611.

Malmo, R. (1942). Interference factors in delayed response in monkeys after removal of frontal lobes. *Journal of Neurophysiology*, **5**, 295–308.

Mangels, J. (1997). Strategic processing and memory for temporal order in patients with frontal lobe lesions. *Neuropsychology*, **11**, 207–221.

Mangels, J.A., Gershberg, F.B., Shimamura, A.P. & Knight, R.T. (1996). Impaired retrieval from remote memory in patients with frontal lobe damage. *Neuropsychology*, **10**, 32–41.

Metcalfe, J. & Shimamura, A.P. (1994). *Knowing about Knowing*. Cambridge, MA: MIT Press.

Miceli, G., Caltagirone, C., Gainotti, G. et al. (1981). Neuropsychological correlates of localized cerebral lesions in non-aphasic brain-damaged patients. *Journal of Clinical Neuropsychology*, **3**, 53–63.

Miller, E. (1984). Verbal fluency as a function of a measure of verbal intelligence and in relation to different types of cerebral pathology. *British Journal of Clinical Psychology*, **23**, 53–57.

Milner, B. (1964). Some effects of frontal lobectomy in man. In J. Warren & K. Akert (eds), *The Frontal Granular Cortex and Behavior* (pp. 313–331). New York: McGraw-Hill.

Milner, B. (1971). Interhemispheric differences in the localization of psychological processes in man. *British Medical Bulletin*, **27**, 272–277.

Milner, B., Petrides, M. & Smith, M. (1985). Frontal lobes and the temporal organization of memory. *Human Neurobiology*, **4**, 137–142.

Mishkin, M. & Pribram, K. (1956). Analysis of the effects of frontal lesions in monkey: I. Variations of delayed response. *Journal of Comparative and Physiological Psychology*, **49**, 36–40.

Moscovitch, M. (1992). Memory and working-with-memory: a component process model based on modules and central systems. *Journal of Cognitive Neuroscience*, **4**, 257–267.

Moscovitch, M. (1994). Cognitive resources and dual-task interference effects at retrieval in normal people: the role of the frontal lobes and medial temporal cortex. *Neuropsychology*, **8**, 524–534.

Nelson, T.O. & Narens, L. (1994). Why investigate metacognition? In J. Metcalfe & A.P. Shimamura (eds), *Metacognition: Knowing about Knowing*. Cambridge, MA: MIT Press.

Owen, A., Downes, J., Sahakian, B. et al. (1990). Planning and spatial working memory following frontal lobe lesions in man. *Neuropsychologia*, **28**, 1021–1034.

Owen, A., Sahakian, B., Semple, J. et al. (1995). Visuo-spatial short-term recognition memory and learning after temporal lobe excisions, frontal lobe excisions or amygdalo-hippocampectomy in man. *Neuropsychologia*, **33**, 1–24.

Owen, A., Morris, R., Sahakian, B. et al. (1996). Double dissociations of memory and executive functions in working memory tasks following frontal lobe excisions, temporal lobe excisions or amygdalo-hippocampectomy in man. *Brain*, **119**, 1597–1615.

Paulesu, E., Frith, C. & Frackowiak, D. (1993). The neural correlates of the verbal component of working memory. *Nature*, **362**, 342–345.

Perret, E. (1974). The left frontal lobe of man and the suppression of habitual responses in verbal categorical behavior. *Neuropsychologia*, **12**, 323–330.

Petrides, M. (1998). Specialized systems for the processing of mnemonic information within the primate frontal cortex. In A.C. Roberts, T.W. Robbins et al. (eds), *The Prefrontal Cortex: Executive and Cognitive Functions*. New York: Oxford University Press.

Petrides, M., Alivisatos, B., Evans, A. & Meyer, E. (1993). Dissociation of human mid-dorsolateral from posterior dorsolateral frontal cortex in memory processing. *Proceedings of the National Academy of Science of the USA*, **90**, 873–877.

Petrides, M. & Milner, B. (1982). Deficits on subject-ordered tasks after frontal- and temporal-lobe lesions in man. *Neuropsychologia*, **20**, 249–262.

Poldrack, R.A. & Gabrieli, J.D. (1997). Functional anatomy of long-term memory. *Journal of Clinical Neurophysiology*, **14**, 294–310.

Prabhakaran, V., Narayanan, K., Zhao, Z. & Gabrieli, J.D. (2000). Integration of diverse information in working memory within the frontal lobe. *Nature Neuroscience*, **3**, 85–90.

Ptito, A., Crane, J., Leonard, G. et al. (1995). Visual-spatial localization by patients with frontal-lobe lesions invading or sparing area 46. *NeuroReport*, **6**, 1781–1784.

Rugg, M.D., Fletcher, P.C., Chua, P. M-L. & Dolan, R.J. (1999). The role of the prefrontal cortex in recognition memory and memory for source: an fMRI study. *NeuroImage*, **10**, 520–529.

Schacter, D.L. (1996). Illusories memories: a cognitive neuroscience analysis. *Proceedings of the National Academy of Sciences of the USA*, **93**, 13527–13533.

Schacter, D.L., Curran, T., Galluccio, L. et al. (1996). False recognition and the right frontal lobe: a case study. *Neuropsychologia*, **34**, 793–808.

Schwartz, S. & Baldo, J.V. (2001). Distinct patterns of word retrieval in right and left frontal lobe patients: a multidimensional perspective. *Neuropsychologia*, **39**, 1209–1213.

Shallice, T. & Evans, M. (1978). The involvement of the frontal lobes in cognitive estimation. *Cortex*, **14**, 294–303.

Shimamura, A.P. (1994). The neuropsychology of metacognition. In J. Metcalfe & A.P. Shimamura (eds), *Metacognition: Knowing about Knowing*. Cambridge, MA: MIT Press.

Shimamura, A. (1995). Memory and frontal lobe function. In M. Gazzaniga (ed.), *The Cognitive Neurosciences*. Cambridge, MA: MIT Press.

Shimamura, A.P. (2000a). The role of the prefrontal cortex in dynamic filtering. *Psychobiology*, **28**, 207–218.

Shimamura, A.P. (2000b). Toward a cognitive neuroscience of metacognition [comment]. *Consciousness and Cognition*, **9**, 313–326.

Shimamura, A.P., Gershberg, F.B., Jurica, P.J. et al. (1992). Intact implicit memory in patients with frontal lobe lesions. *Neuropsychologia*, **30**, 931–937.

Shimamura, A., Janowsky, J. & Squire, L. (1990). Memory for the temporal order of events in patients with frontal lobe lesions and amnesic patients. *Neuropsychologia*, **28**, 803–813.

Shimamura, A.P., Jurica, P.J., Mangels, J.A. et al. (1995). Susceptibility to memory interference effects following frontal lobe damage: findings from tests of paired-associate learning. *Journal of Cognitive Neuroscience*, **7**, 144–152.

Smith E.E. & Jonides, J. (1999). Storage and executive processes in the frontal lobes. *Science*, **283**, 1657–1661.

Smith, E., Jonides, J., Koeppe, R. et al. (1995). Spatial versus object working memory: PET investigations. *Journal of Cognitive Neuroscience*, **7**, 337–358.

Smith, M.L. & Milner, B. (1984). Differential effects of frontal-lobe lesions on cognitive estimation and spatial memory. *Neuropsychologia*, **22**, 697–705.

Smith, M. & Milner, B. (1988). Estimation of frequency of occurrence of abstract designs after frontal or temporal lobectomy. *Neuropsychologia*, **26**, 297–306.

Squire, L.R. (1992). Memory and the hippocampus: synthesis of findings with rats, monkeys, and humans. *Psychological Review*, **99**, 195–231.

Stricker, J.L., Brown, G.G., Wixted, J. et al. (2002). New semantic and serial clustering indices for the California Verbal Learning Test—second edition: background, rationale, and formulae. *Journal of the International Neuropsychological Society*, **8**, 425–435.

Stuss, D.T., Alexander, M.P., Palumbo, C.L. et al. (1994). Organizational strategies of patients with unilateral or bilateral frontal lobe injury in word list learning tasks. *Neuropsychology*, **8**, 355–373.

Stuss, D. & Benson, D. (1984). Neuropsychological studies of the frontal lobes. *Psychological Bulletin*, **95**, 3–28.

Swick, D. & Knight, R.T. (1996). Is prefrontal cortex involved in cued recall? A neuropsychological test of PET findings. *Neuropsychologia*, **34**, 1019–1028.

Swick, D. & Knight, R.T. (1999). Contributions of prefrontal cortex to recognition memory: electro-physiological and behavioral evidence. *Neuropsychology*, **13**, 155–170.

Troyer, A., Moscovitch, M., Winocur, G. et al. (1998). Clustering and switching on verbal fluency: the effects of focal frontal- and temporal-lobe lesions. *Neuropsychologia*, **36**, 499–504.

Tulving E., Kapur S., Craik, F.I. et al. (1994). Hemispheric encoding/retrieval asymmetry in episodic memory: positron emission tomography findings. *Proceedings of the National Academy of Sciences*, **91**, 2016–2020.

Vilkki, J., Servo, A. & Surma-aho, O. (1998). Word list learning and prediction of recall after frontal lobe lesions. *Neuropsychology*, **12**, 268–277.

Vogel, C., Markowitsch, H., Hempel, U. & Hackenberg, P. (1987). Verbal memory in brain damaged patients under different conditions of retrieval aids: a study of frontal, temporal, and diencephalic damaged subjects. *International Journal of Neuroscience*, **33**, 237–256.

Wheeler, M., Stuss, D. & Tulving, E. (1995). Frontal lobe damage produces episodic memory impairment. *Journal of the International Neuropsychological Society*, **1**, 525–536.

Yamaguchi, S. & Knight, R.T. (1990). Gating of somatosensory input by human prefrontal cortex. *Brain Research*, **521**, 281–288.

CHAPTER 18

Posttraumatic Amnesia and Residual Memory Deficit after Closed Head Injury

Harvey S. Levin

and

Gerri Hanten

*Department of Physical Medicine and Rehabilitation,
Baylor College of Medicine, Houston, TX, USA*

Early concepts of amnesia following closed-head injury (CHI) can be traced to ancient descriptions (for review see Levin et al., 1983). However, detailed serial observations of resolving anterograde and posttraumatic amnesia following CHI were first widely disseminated in the nineteenth century reports (Brodie, 1854), which influenced the theoretical writings by Ribot (1882) on dissolution of memory. In this review of research on memory disorder after CHI, we will use studies from our laboratory and other centers to illustrate recent advances in understanding the consequences of CHI on different aspects of memory performance.

PATHOPHYSIOLOGIC FEATURES CONTRIBUTING TO MEMORY DEFICIT

Brain damage associated with CHI can be classified as primary or secondary (Graham et al., 2000). Primary brain damage, which occurs or is initiated at the time of injury, includes focal brain lesions, diffuse axonal injury (DAI) and intracranial hemorrhage.

Focal brain lesions, including contusions and intracranial hematomas, primarily occur in the frontal and temporal lobes in association with a wide spectrum of CHI severity (Adams et al., 1980; Eisenberg et al., 1990; Levin et al., 1987). Temporal lobe hematomas and contusions have been implicated in residual memory disturbance after CHI (Jennett, 1969; Levin et al. 1982), which is consistent with amnesic disorder arising from other etiologies of mesial temporal lobe damage (Scoville & Milner, 1957). During the past 20 years, studies of patients with focal brain lesions arising from various etiologies have elucidated the role

The Handbook of Memory Disorders. Edited by A.D. Baddeley, M.D. Kopelman and B.A. Wilson
© 2002 John Wiley & Sons, Ltd.

of the prefrontal cortex in declarative memory. Patients with frontal lesions have been shown to exhibit impaired knowledge and deployment of memory strategies (Shimamura et al., 1991). Consistent with frontal lobe involvement in declarative memory, prefrontal activation on positron emission tomography (PET) occurs with memory retrieval in neurologically intact adults (Lepage et al., 2000). In agreement with the focal lesion and functional brain imaging literatures, a recent volumetric magnetic resonance imaging (MRI) study showed that frontal lesion volume (but not extrafrontal lesion volume) was predictive of recall of categorized words by children and adolescents who had sustained CHI that ranged from mild to severe in acute severity (DiStefano et al., 2000). Distefano et al. found that the volume of frontal lesion was related to total recall across five recall trials of the California Verbal Learning Test—Children's Version (CVLT-C; Delis et al., 1994), using a regression analysis that first adjusted for the effects of overall CHI severity and the patient's age (Figure 18.1).

In addition to focal lesions involving the frontal and temporal lobes, the hippocampus is especially vulnerable to the effects of ischemia (Adams et al., 1980). Neuropathological studies have documented hippocampal damage in more than 90% of fatal cases of CHI (Kotapka et al., 1994).

Frontotemporal connections, which are postulated to mediate strategic aspects of declarative memory, such as rehearsal and selective processing of rewarded items (Miller, 2000), can presumably be disrupted by DAI even in the absence of focal lesions. However, the relationship between structural brain imaging findings and memory functioning has been inconsistent across studies (Wilson et al., 1988; Levin et al., 1992), suggesting that areas of cerebral dysfunction can be larger than the lesions detected by conventional CT and MRI. This interpretation has been supported by metabolic imaging, in which abnormalities in neurotransmitters (N-aspartate, choline), detected in lesion-free brain regions such as the frontal white matter by MRI, corresponded to neuropsychological outcome in chronic survivors of CHI (Friedman et al., 1998; Garnett et al., 2000). Regional cerebral glucose metabolism, as measured by PET in adult CHI patients without cortical contusions on MRI, were studied between 2 and 12 months postinjury (Fontaine et al., 1999). Fontaine et al. found that verbal memory was correlated with glucose metabolism primarily in the left mesial prefrontal region, the left dorsolateral prefrontal area and the left posterior cingulate gyrus. In addition, less robust correlations with verbal memory were found with glucose metabolism in the left anterior cingulate gyrus, the orbitofrontal cortex and the right mesial prefrontal cortex. Preliminary findings using functional MRI (fMRI) to study working memory after mild CHI (McAllister et al., 1999) suggest that altered patterns of brain activation might elucidate the mechanisms mediating memory disorder in more severe injuries.

Secondary brain insult, including hypoxia and hypotension, also complicate efforts to isolate the effects of focal brain lesions on memory. Secondary brain damage, which also arises during the first few hours after CHI from a cascade of excitotoxic neurotransmitters such as glutamate, can lead to cellular injury or death, even in patients without evidence of structural brain lesions on CT (Bullock et al., 1998). Programmed cell death, or apoptosis, also contributes to diffuse brain damage (Graham et al., 2000; Kochanek et al., 2000). Other forms of secondary brain injury associated with CHI include increased intracranial pressure, swelling, ischemia and infection. Secondary brain injury occurs more frequently with moderate to severe CHI, but delayed brain swelling and/or hematomas can develop occasionally in patients who initially have mild impairment of consciousness. Although the distinctive

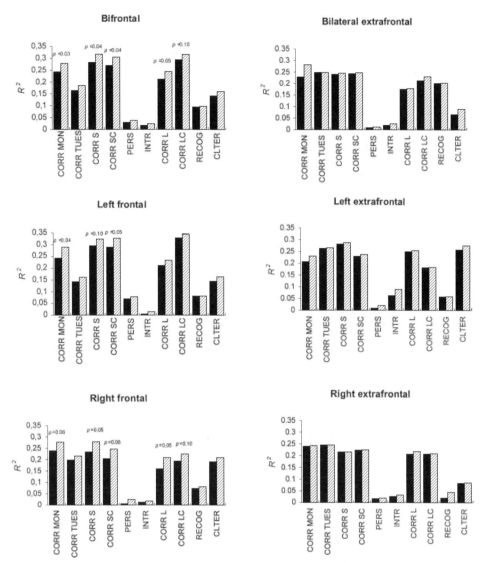

Figure 18.1 Summary of the results of hierarchical multiple regression that evaluated the incremental contributions of bilateral frontal (top left), bilateral extrafrontal (top right), left frontal (middle left), left extrafrontal (middle right), right frontal (bottom left) and right extrafrontal (bottom right) lesions to predicting the verbal learning and memory test scores after entering the severity of injury and age at testing alone. Closed bars indicate R^2 when entering GCS score and age at testing into the regression equation; hatched bars indicate incremental R^2 when additionally entering lesion size into regression equation. CORR MON, correct words on Monday list; CORR TUES, correct words on Tuesday list; CORR S, correct words on short delay free recall; CORR SC, correct words on short delay cued recall; PERS, perseverations on Monday list recall; INTR, intrusions on Monday list recall; CORR L, correct word on long delay free recall; CORR LC, correct word on long delay cued recall; RECOG, correct recognitions; CLTER, clusters on Monday list recall. Reproduced by permission from DiStefano et al. (2000). © 2000, BMJ Publishing Group

contribution of specific pathophysiologic features to residual memory disturbance is difficult to isolate because of the heterogeneity of injury in patient samples and the confounding by co-morbidities such as alcohol abuse in some studies, several pathophysiologic features of CHI have been implicated in producing memory deficit.

In addition to the primary vs. secondary distinction, brain damage produced by CHI includes focal brain lesions and diffuse brain insult. Investigating the relationship between localization of traumatic focal lesions and memory disorder is complicated by variation across patients in type and size of lesion, in addition to concomitant diffuse and multifocal neuropathology in many cases. Further, the weak correlation between structural damage detected by imaging and performance on neuropsychological tests (Wilson et al., 1988; Levin et al., 1992) suggests that areas of cerebral dysfunction are more extensive than the abnormalities detected by conventional imaging procedures. This interpretation has been supported by evidence from metabolic imaging, in which abnormalities detected with MRI corresponded to neuropsychological outcome in chronic survivors of traumatic brain injury (Langfitt et al., 1986; Friedman et al., 1998; Garnett et al., 2000).

POSTTRAUMATIC AMNESIA

Measurement of Posttraumatic Amnesia

Posttraumatic amnesia (PTA), an early stage of recovery during which the patient fails to retain information about ongoing events, is a characteristic feature of CHI which can occur even in mild injuries which produce no coma (Ommaya & Gennarelli, 1974; Russell, 1932). Apart from anterograde amnesia, PTA also involves a variable constellation of behavioral disturbances, including defective attention, agitation, lethargy, inappropriate and disinhibited behavior and speech. Early reports of PTA duration (Russell, 1971; Russell & Nathan, 1946; Russell & Smith, 1961) were based on the patient's retrospective estimate due to circumstances of assessing injured servicemen evacuated after the acute injury phase to the Oxford Hospital for Head Injury. However, subsequent research has shown that objective, serial assessment of mild CHI patients, beginning in the emergency room, yields durations of PTA which are discrepant from later subjective estimates by the patients (Gronwall & Wrightson, 1980). In contrast to Russell's inclusion of the comatose period in estimating PTA duration, widespread use of the Glasgow Coma Scale (GCS) of Teasdale & Jennett (1974) has facilitated separate assessment of the acute amnesic period after the patient begins to follow commands consistently.

In response to the aforementioned problem in retrospective estimates of PTA (see Schacter & Crovitz, 1977), Levin et al. (1979) developed the Galveston Orientation and Amnesia Test (GOAT), a brief bedside evaluation of orientation and retention of ongoing events. The test includes items from a temporal orientation questionnaire (Benton et al., 1964), recall of the first postinjury event and the last event that occurred prior to the injury. Error points are awarded for each item and deducted from 100, yielding a total score that we found to range from 75 to 100 in patients who had recovered from a mild CHI. Duration of PTA, which was operationally defined by the interval from injury to the point of reaching a stable score within the normal range on this brief test, was related to both the severity of initial injury and the outcome of head injury 6 months later (Levin et al., 1979). Ellenberg

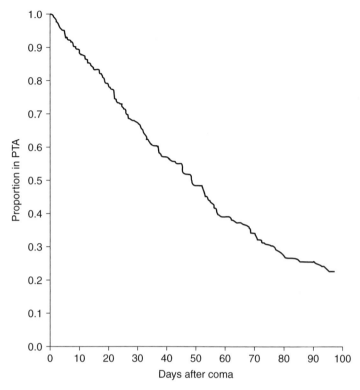

Figure 18.2 Kaplan–Meier survival curve for time to resolution of posttraumatic amnesia (PTA) as defined by achieving a Galveston Orientation and Amnesia Test score of 75 or more after termination of coma. At 30 days, approximately 65% of the cohort remained in PTA. At 65 days after awakening from coma, approximately 35% were still in PTA. Reproduced by permission from Ellenberg et al. (1996). © 2000, American Medical Association

et al. (1996) accessed the National Institutes of Health Traumatic Coma Data Bank to plot a survival curve for the proportion of severe CHI patients remaining in PTA with a GOAT score of 75 or higher as the criterion for recovery. Ellenberg et al. found that half of the patients were still in PTA at 50 days after recovery of consciousness and that PTA duration was predictive of 6 months outcome after taking into account the duration of coma. Initial postresuscitation GCS score, pupillary reactivity, coma duration and use of phenytoin were all predictive of PTA duration, as measured by serial administration of the GOAT (Figure 18.2).

A second method of directly assessing PTA was developed by Artiola et al. (1980) of the Neuropsychology Unit at Oxford. This method defined resolution of PTA according to recall of three pictures, the examiner's name and the examiner's face on the day after the previous assessment. If recall was not perfect, recognition memory was tested. The Westmead Test, a variant of the Oxford procedure, has also been published (Shores et al., 1986). The Oxford and Westmead procedures offer the advantage of more specific testing of declarative memory, exclusive of orientation, as compared to the GOAT. As described

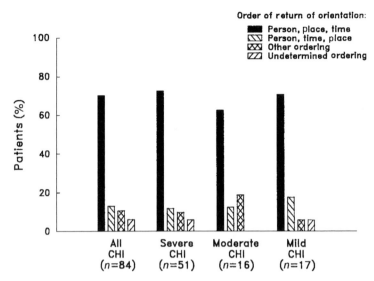

Figure 18.3   Order of return of orientation shown for the closed head-injured patients, combined and separately, according to severity of injury as assessed by the Glasgow Coma Scale. Reproduced by permission from High et al. (1990). © 1990, Swets Zeitlinger

below, the decision regarding measurement method should be based on the specific clinical or research application and practical issues.

Features of Posttraumatic Amnesia

Sequence of Recovery

Recovery of orientation during PTA was studied by High et al. (1990) in a series of 84 survivors of CHI of varying severity who were serially tested during their acute hospitalization. As shown in Figure 18.3, orientation recovered in the sequence of person, place and time in the majority (70%) of patients. Estimates of the date were displaced backward in time (up to 5 years for severe injuries), and the discrepancies between the estimate and the actual date diminished as orientation improved. This receding of retrograde amnesia was observed for moderate and severe but not mild head injuries. Accordingly, the investigators postulated that backward displacement of time may shrink in parallel with the resolution of loss of information for events preceding the injury. This pattern of recovery of orientation was corroborated in a study of 31 severely injured patients which also compared the results of the GOAT with the Westmead and Oxford procedures (Tate et al., 2000).

In contrast to the finding that orientation recovered before recognition memory of items presented on the preceding day to patients recovering from mild CHI (Gronwall & Wrightson, 1980), Tate et al. (2000) found that recognition of three line drawings of concrete items presented on the preceding day improved to a normal level before temporal disorientation resolved in adults following severe CHI. Orientation to place recovered before free recall of the three items and the examiner's name, but there was no significant difference between the duration of PTA, as measured by the GOAT, and time to recover free recall. The inconsistency in findings obtained in these studies might reflect the patient samples with a mild CHI group studied by Gronwall & Wrightson, as compared to severe CHI patients assessed by Tate et al.

Attentional Disturbance or Memory Deficit?

Descriptions of recovery of CHI patients initially after they began comprehending commands and opening their eyes have implicated attentional disturbance concomitant with memory and learning problems (Russell, 1971; Russell & Nathan, 1946; Russell & Smith, 1961). Experimental support for the role of attentional disturbance in PTA was obtained by Stuss and co-workers (1999), who serially administered attention tests of varying complexity, the GOAT, and recognition memory to patients during the early stage of recovery from mild, moderate or severe CHI. Stuss et al. found that performance on attention control tasks, such as reciting overlearned sequences (counting forward, months of year), typically recovered concurrent with improvement in scores to within the normal range on the GOAT, whereas recovery on these simple attention tasks preceded resolution of PTA as defined by the GOAT in severely injured patients. Parallel investigation of recognition and recall memory generally showed a pattern of earlier recovery on less effortful tasks, followed by improved memory performance on more difficult measures (Stuss et al., 1999). Analysis of the sequence of recovery of attention, memory and performance on the GOAT generally reflected a closer correspondence between changes on the GOAT and the attentional measures with later improvement on the memory tests.

To summarize, there is general agreement that resolution of PTA as measured by the GOAT is paralleled by improvement in performance on simple attentional and memory tests. Although the findings reported by Tate et al. indicate that the GOAT might be sufficient to measure PTA duration, it is apparent from Stuss et al.'s findings that recovery measured by more challenging tests of recall will be delayed after patients attain a normal score on the GOAT. From a cognitive perspective it is appropriate to differentiate PTA from residual memory disorder. For clinical applications, it is important to determine the complexity of bedside testing that is relevant to monitoring recovery and planning rehabilitation in relation to the time required for assessment and the effort asked of the patient.

Frequency, Specificity and Impact of Residual Memory Disorder

Russell (1971) reported that residual memory disturbance (i.e. persisting after resolution of PTA) was present in 23% of the 1000 servicemen he examined while they were convalescing from a CHI. This figure rose to 50% of the severely injured patients. Interviews with survivors of severe CHI and their families have corroborated the results of Russell's clinical examinations, indicating a high frequency of residual memory impairment observed in performance of daily activities. Oddy et al. (1985) found that 53% of patients and 79% of their families reported that memory deficit was still present 7 years after injury. This was the most common problem mentioned by the patients and their relatives. Other studies have found that survivors of CHI frequently underestimate the severity of their memory deficit, as measured by experimental tests (Baddeley et al., 1987b; Sunderland et al., 1983). More recently, Brooks et al. (1987) identified verbal memory deficit as one of the two neurobehavioral sequelae (the other being slowed information-processing rate) which were most strongly related to unemployment 7 years after severe head injury.

Whether memory deficit can persist as a relatively specific sequel of CHI or is invariably a manifestation of global cognitive impairment was addressed by Gronwall & Wrightson (1980), who were able to show that verbal memory deficit was dissociable from information-processing rate on a test of paced auditory addition. To further address the specificity of memory impairment after head injury, we analyzed the findings of 87 young adults and adolescents who had sustained moderate or severe CHI and who participated in a prospective outcome study (Levin et al., 1988a). Memory was assessed for two postinjury intervals (5–15 months, 16–42 months) using the Verbal Selective Reminding Test (Buschke & Fuld, 1974) and the Continuous Memory Test (Hannay et al., 1979), which involved recognition of recurring line drawings of familiar living things. To evaluate the presence of a dissociation between intellectual function and memory, the analysis was confined to patients (about two-thirds of the series) whose Wechsler Verbal and Performance IQs were at least 85 at the time of the follow-up examination. The number of words consistently recalled across trials (CLTR) and d', an index of memory sensitivity, were the dependent measures for selective reminding and recognition memory tests, respectively. To facilitate within-subjects comparison of intellectual and memory functioning, the raw scores of the memory tests were transformed into standard scores (i.e. a mean of 100 and a standard deviation of 15) based on normative data obtained from a sample of 50 young adults.

Figures 18.4A and 18.4B are box-plots showing the distribution of IQ and transformed memory scores for controls, moderate and severe head-injured patients. It is seen that intellectual functioning in these groups did not significantly differ, whereas severely injured patients exhibited impaired verbal memory (Selective Reminding Test) relative to the moderate CHI and control groups who did not differ from each other. A similar pattern emerged for visual recognition memory, but the group differences did not reach statistical significance. To evaluate the presence of a relatively specific impairment of memory, a disparity of at least 15 standard score points was used to compare verbal memory with verbal intelligence quotient (VIQ) and visual recognition memory with performance intelligence quotient (PIQ).

Disproportionate memory impairment, defined by standard scores on both memory tests that were below 85 and at least 15 points less than the corresponding VIQ or PIQ score (VIQ > CLTR, PIQ > d'), was present in about 15% of the moderate and 30% of the severe head-injured patients whose intellectual level had recovered to within the normal range. The feature of verbal memory that most consistently distinguished the memory-impaired patients from the other head-injured patients with normal intellectual function (who comprised about one-half of the total sample at each interval) was their difficulty in recalling the test words after a 30 min delay. About one-third of the total series had global cognitive impairment (i.e. IQ below 85, associated with poor memory). These patients had more severe injuries than the patients with IQ 85 and above, as reflected by the degree and duration of impaired consciousness and their frequency of nonreactive pupils during the acute stage of injury. In contrast, the indices of CHI severity of the patients with a relatively specific memory deficit did not significantly differ from the patients who recovered to the normal range of both intellectual and memory functions.

A

5–15 months postinjury

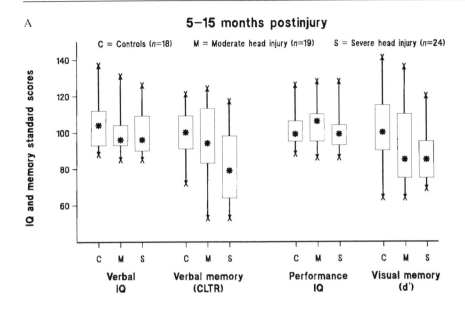

B

16–42 months postinjury

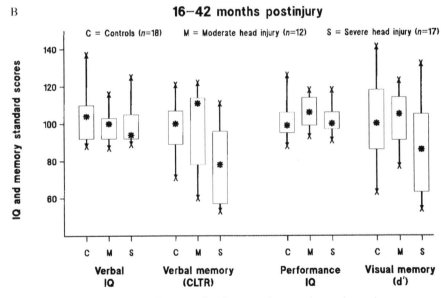

Figure 18.4 (A) Box-plots showing distribution of IQ and transformed memory scores for controls, moderate and severe head-injured patients who obtained IQ scores within the normal range (<85) at 5–15 months after injury. (B) IQ and transformed memory test data obtained at 16–42 months postinjury. Each asterisk signifies the median, upper and lower horizontal lines of each bar indicate the 75th and 25th centile scores, respectively, and the maximum and minimum scores are depicted by the letter "X". Reproduced by permission from Levin et al. (1988b). © 1988, BMJ Publishing Group

PATTERNS OF MEMORY DEFICIT AFTER CLOSED HEAD INJURY

In recent years memory theorists have come to substantial agreement that human memory is not a unitary construct, but rather is made up of dissociable components sensitive to differing stimulus characteristics and demands (see Baddeley, 1998). Much of the progress in this area has resulted from cognitive neuropsychological studies of individuals who have demonstrated differential patterns of performance on tests of memory subsequent to brain injury. The precise nature of the components has yet to be completely specified, and discussion of the various theories relating to memory components and systems, although beyond the scope of this chapter, are addressed in other chapters in this volume. However, in reporting research concerning the effects of traumatic brain injury on memory, we will make certain assumptions based on widely reported functional dissociations in memory performance, e.g. there is ample evidence from both the neuropsychological and the normal cognitive literature to support a functional distinction between short-term memory and long-term memory, regardless of theoretical approach. In addition to discussing aspects of short- and long-term memory performance, we will also report recent findings on the effect of CHI on some "hybrid" memorial abilities, specifically prospective memory and metacognition, illustrated by descriptions of studies from our laboratory and others where appropriate.

Impairments of Working Memory

The term "working memory" as used here refers to a limited capacity system for the temporary storage of information held for further manipulation (Baddeley, 1986). Working memory is central to performance in many cognitive domains, including learning, planning and problem solving, as well as language acquisition, comprehension and production. The effect of traumatic brain injury on task performance has been investigated for various forms of memory, including verbal and nonverbal memory, spatial memory, and phonological and semantic components of working memory.

Auditory–Verbal Memory Deficits

Probably the most well-characterized area of cognitive impairment after traumatic brain injury is auditory–verbal memory. Many studies have directly or indirectly investigated the characteristics of auditory–verbal memory after CHI using recall, cued recall or recognition tests. The tests employed have frequently been standardized list-learning tests using the repeated presentation and recall of a single supraspan list of related words, such as the California Verbal Learning Test (Delis et al., 1986, 1991, 1994) or the Auditory–Verbal Learning Test (Rey, 1964), although other types of tests, such as the Selective Reminding Test (Buschke & Fuld, 1974) and the Continuous Recognition Memory Test (Hannay et al., 1979), have also been used.

   The general finding is that both adults and children who have had severe CHI and are in the postacute stages of injury show deficits in immediate and delayed recall (e.g. Baddeley et al., 1987a; Brooks, 1975; Crosson et al., 1988; Hanten & Martin, 2000; Jaffe et al.,

1992; Levin, 1989; Levin et al., 1979, 1982, 1988a, 2000; Reid & Kelly, 1993; Roman et al., 1998; Wiegner & Donders, 1999; Yeates et al., 1995). Tests of recognition memory and cued recall also generally show that persons with severe CHI are impaired relative to uninjured controls (Baddeley et al., 1987; Dennis & Barnes, 1990; Levin et al., 1988a; Roman et al., 1998). In some studies persons with severe CHI have been found to show increased errors in recall, including intrusions and perseverations, and impairment in the ability to utilize semantic information to aid recall (Hanten & Martin, 2000; Levin et al., 1996, 2000; Levin & Goldstein, 1986). This will be discussed in more detail later.

Specific Components of STM

Essential to the eventual development of effective intervention techniques is the elucidation of the specific underlying causes of impairment. Although various studies have used cluster analyses in order to determine factors that contribute to the impairments in verbal learning exhibited by CHI patients (Wiegner & Donders, 1999; Gardner & Vrbancic, 1998; Millis, 1995; Wilde & Boake, 1994), the factors used in such analyses tend to be general. As clinical research tools, verbal learning tests, such as the CVLT, have proved useful in identifying general verbal learning impairment in various populations, including CHI. However, one of the disadvantages of such tests is that they do not provide measures of specific memory processes in isolation. The variables are usually complex, and therefore difficult to dissociate into discrete components. Experimental neuropsychological studies of individuals who have short-term memory deficits have been more successful in isolating specific components of short-term memory (Baddeley & Wilson, 1993; Hulme et al., 1993; Jarrold et al., 1999; Martin et al., 1994; Saffran & Martin, 1990). Using this approach, studies of adult patients with brain injury have revealed individuals with severely reduced memory span whose impairments appear to arise from a phonological short-term memory deficit (see Shallice & Vallar, 1990). Other recent studies have elucidated that there are separable components of phonological and semantic short-term memory, and that brain damage can selectively affect these components (Hanten & Martin, 2000, 2001; Martin & Romani, 1994; Saffran & Martin, 1990; Shelton et al., 1992). One recent study (Hanten & Martin, 2000), investigating the short-term memory and sentence-processing abilities of two children who had sustained severe CHI, found a dissociation in performance, such that one child appeared to have a relatively pure phonological STM deficit, whereas the other child showed a pattern of performance, consistent with a deficit in semantic STM coupled with a milder impairment of phonological STM. Such studies may provide a clearer understanding of the specific functional impairment underlying memory deficits and may be important in terms of remediation efforts.

Non-verbal/Visual Memory Deficits

A number of group studies have investigated memory deficits after head injury using visual, non-verbal stimuli. Many studies have found that individuals with severe CHI are impaired on recognition tests of nonverbal memory, using abstract, nonverbalizable stimuli (Brooks, 1974, 1976; Reid & Kelly, 1993; Shum et al., 2000), drawings of nameable objects (Hannay et al., 1979; Levin et al., 1988b) and unfamiliar faces (Millis & Dijkers,

1993). In studies that have looked at individual performance, dissociations in patterns of impairment have been found with recognition or matching of faces dissociated from facial expression recognition (Parry et al., 1991). In studies requiring recall of an unnameable object, as in the Rey Complex figure (Rey, 1964), some group studies have shown no persistent impairment (Hellawell et al., 1999), although other studies have revealed impairments (Donders, 1993). A study done by Spikeman et al. (1995) may shed some light on the conditions under which recognition memory may be preserved or impaired. They found that 22 adults with severe CHI demonstrated preserved recognition memory for complex pictorial scenes but impaired recognition memory for unfamiliar faces. The authors of the study noted that the two sets of visual stimuli varied in at least one notable way. The pictures of faces used in the task comprised a set of common features that varied from face to face; thus, recognition had to be based on subtle differences among common features. On the other hand, the complex pictures had different and distinct features from picture to picture, and thus had more unique information to support recognition. The difference in recognition performance in the two conditions suggests that the patients may have utilized the distinctive features in the complex pictures as an aid in recognition, but in the absence of such supporting features showed impairment in face recognition performance. A recent study in our laboratory using non-verbal stimulus items is consistent with this interpretation. We investigated the ability of adults with severe CHI to perform an ongoing task that required the subject to select each member of a full set of abstract stimulus items during a series of trials in a sequence of their choice without pointing to the same alternative twice (adapted from Petrides & Milner, 1982). The number of designs that had to be kept in mind increased with each successful trial, thus increasing the working memory load. The task was untimed, and responses were made by pointing to the items, thus eliminating speed of cognitive processing and language as contributing factors to impaired performance. Importantly, in this study, the stimulus items, although easily discriminable, shared many features, and the stimulus items themselves were randomly rearranged between trials; thus, neither unique features nor spatial context could contribute to performance. The results of the study indicated that adults with severe CHI made significantly more errors (Figure 18.5)

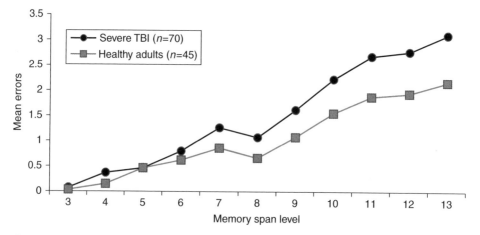

Figure 18.5 Average errors per trial by memory load in persons with severe TBI and age-matched uninjured controls. From Stallings et al. (submitted)

and achieved a lower memory span than did age- and education-matched uninjured control subjects.

This and other studies showing impaired recognition in the absence of context but spared recognition under conditions of rich contextual support (Mangels et al., 2000; Tsukiura et al., 2000) suggests that persons with CHI may be able to use contextual support as an aid in memory performance.

In summary, most studies of auditory–verbal memory and working memory in persons with CHI indicate that memory impairment is a likely consequence of severe head injury. In addition, the magnitude of the impairment has been found to be related to the severity of the injury, as determined by the GCS (Levin et al., 1988a). Studies of components of working memory have indicated that it may be possible to isolate impairments of specific components of working memory.

Impairment of Long-term and Remote Memory

Various aspects of long-term memory after traumatic brain injury have been investigated, including varieties of knowledge (semantic, declarative, procedural), autobiographical and remote memory, and memory for names of familiar objects or faces. Within the semantic/declarative knowledge domain, studies have tended to look at either the ability to acquire knowledge or the selective loss or preservation of (presumably) already existing knowledge. In the procedural knowledge domain, most studies have focused only the ability to acquire knowledge, rather than on the selective loss or preservation of specific areas of procedural knowledge.

Semantic/Declarative Knowledge

Selective impairments of semantic knowledge have been reported in patients with acquired brain damage arising from various etiologies; however, such deficits have not been commonly reported in studies of CHI. However, many studies of memory deficits after CHI employ group study designs, which may occlude relatively rare semantic deficits. In studies that have reported deficits on tasks that assess semantic knowledge, the impairments tend to be revealed in tasks that require the spoken output of a lexical item. In a study comparing the nature of semantic deficits exhibited by nonprogressive brain injury (CHI) as compared to progressive brain injury, Wilson (1997) described two CHI patients who appeared to have semantic knowledge deficits. The deficits were similar to those reported for patients with dementia but appeared to be limited to tasks in which spoken output of the actual lexical item was required. The patients were very impaired on a verbal fluency test, in which they produced exemplars from specific categories, and on naming to pictures and descriptions of exemplars. However, they performed normally on picture sorting for both superordinate and subordinate categories and on picture–word matching for nonliving categories, and were only mildly impaired on picture–word matching for living categories. This pattern of impaired verbal production of exemplars with spared semantic knowledge is consistent with other studies investigating semantic impairments after CHI (Haut et al., 1991; Hough et al., 1997; Lohman et al., 1989; Levin et al., 1996; Levin & Goldstein, 1986). It should be noted that when generating words beginning with a specified letter, CHI subjects have been found to produce significantly fewer items than normal controls (Adamovich & Henderson, 1984; Crowe, 1992; Levin et al., 1981; Sarno, 1984), suggesting that at least a portion of the reported impairments may be accounted for by lexical factors unrelated to semantic organization.

Although patients with CHI may display relatively spared semantic knowledge, there is evidence that the mechanism of access is not only slowed or very effortful, but may be qualitatively different than in uninjured persons (Goldstein et al., 1990; Haut et al., 1991). Several investigators have reported that CHI patients at varying levels of functioning and time postinjury produce excessive intrusions on tests of verbal recall (Hough et al., 1997; Levin, 1989; Richardson, 1984). Further, the ability to either benefit from or use semantic information to facilitate recall has been shown to be impaired in children (Hanten & Martin, 2000; Levin et al., 1996) and adults with CHI (Gruen et al., 1990; Levin & Goldstein, 1986). A further issue to be addressed is the ability of persons with CHI to acquire categorical knowledge, separate from the ability to make use of preserved categorical knowledge. Although we are not aware of any studies specifically investigating this aspect of memory after CHI, the ability of persons with amnesia from various etiologies to acquire categorical knowledge has been studied. Knowlton & Squire (1993) found that after training on sets of dot patterns to learn "categories", amnesic patients and control subjects performed similarly when asked to decide if novel patterns belonged to the same category as the set of training patterns. In contrast, the amnesic subjects were impaired relative to the controls at recognizing which dot patterns had been presented for training, thus demonstrating preserved category acquisition in the presence of impaired recognition. Other studies have investigated category knowledge acquisition with more life-like stimulus items with similar results (Reed et al., 1999). These results are suggestive of categorical knowledge acquisition relying on preserved implicit learning in amnesic patients. It remains to be determined whether a similar pattern is present for patients with CHI.

Episodic/Remote/Autobiographical Memory

One variety of long-term memory is that for personally experienced events. Falling under the general rubric of episodic memory, i.e. memory for events (Tulving, 1983), it has sometimes been called "remote" memory for events having to do with historical events, and "autobiographical" memory when the memory episodes are personal in nature. As mentioned above, temporary retrograde amnesia occurs as an immediate consequence of brain trauma, and usually gradually resolves until the patient can remember all but the very immediate moments prior to the trauma. Less common is more persistent retrograde amnesia, in which loss of memory from events in the past may be experienced for much longer duration, up to years or even permanently. Deficits of remote and autobiographical memory have been described in which patients with brain injury from various etiologies (including CHI) show selective loss of memory for specific time periods (Albert et al., 1979; Barr et al., 1990; Ellis et al., 1989; Evans et al., 1993; Markowitsch et al., 1993; McCarthy & Warrington, 1992; Squire, 1974). Memory loss has been reported to occur in a temporal gradient, with memory for more remote events better than memory for recent events (e.g. Albert et al., 1979). This phenomenon has been explained as a disruption by trauma of the "consolidation" of immediate memory (Squire, 1992; Squire & Zola-Morgan, 1988). However, methodological issues somewhat cloud this area of research. Primarily, in the absence of a measure of the premorbid state of

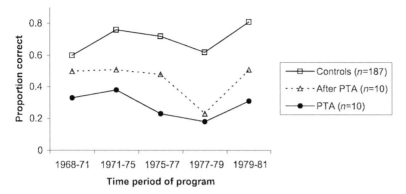

Figure 18.6 Mean proportion of correct recognition of titles of television programs, plotted across the time period of broadcast for oriented (after PTA) and amnesic (PTA) head-injured patients and control subjects. Reproduced by permission from Levin et al. (1985b). © 1985, BMJ Publication Group

remembering of an individual for a specific event, it is difficult to determine how memorial abilities or knowledge has been changed as a consequence of trauma. This is compounded for events that are autobiographical in nature, as the events themselves are difficult to verify. A second problem relating to the measurement of temporal gradients in remote memory is the difficulty in equating the salience of memory items across chronological intervals. As has been pointed out by McCarthy & Warrington (1992), items that are remembered from the remote past might be of higher salience than those from the recent past. Methodological issues aside, impairments for remote/autobiographical memory do appear to accompany brain injury, although only a few studies have focused on the consequences of traumatic brain injury. Studies done by Levin et al. (1977, 1984, 1985a) investigated the remote memory of oriented (After) and amnesic (PTA) head-injured patients by testing their memory on a questionnaire for television programs that had been shown for only one season, thus equating the difficulty of the items to be remembered (Squire & Slater, 1975). The amnesic CHI patients showed a clear impairment in recognition memory, but no evidence for a temporal gradient (Figure 18.6).

Similarly, Leplow et al. (1997) investigated remote memory for patients with CHI and two other patient groups, as well as a large control group of 214 persons. To control for the increased salience effect, the authors tested memory for events across six decades that had been on the front page of the newspapers for 3 days. Further, the study was confined to people who had not left the geographical area for more than 6 months throughout their lifetime. The results of the recall and recognition tests for events and people indicated that the patients with CHI were very impaired in remote memory, especially in recall, when compared to the controls. However, as in the studies by Levin, there was no indication of a memory gradient for more impairment for more recent events, and in fact, performance was slightly better for recent as compared to more remote events.

Levin et al. (1985a) also investigated recall of autobiographic events in survivors of moderate to severe CHI undergoing inpatient rehabilitation. In contrast to the lack of a temporal gradient for salience-matched remote memory on the questionnaire of television programs (Figure 18.6), Levin et al. (1985a) found relative preservation of recall for autobiographical events from the primary school years, as compared to later development periods, in these

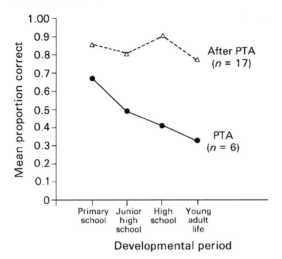

Figure 18.7   Mean proportion of correct recall of autobiographical events, compiled for developmental periods of the head-injured patients during and after PTA. Reproduced by permission from Levin et al. (1985b). © 1985, BMJ Publication Group

young adult patients (Figure 18.7). The temporal gradient obtained for autobiographical events is similar to the sparing of memory for faces of famous persons and retention of public events from the remote past, which has been reported in amnesics with alcoholic Korsakoff syndrome (Albert et al., 1979).

Methodological issues notwithstanding, the studies described above suggest that loss of memory for remote and for autobiographical memory is associated with CHI. However, the findings of a temporal gradient for preserved distant memory with loss for recent memory, although theoretically plausible, is yet not consistent and requires further investigation.

Naming

There have been a number of studies that have found impaired naming of people and objects after CHI. Specific naming impairments have been described in the presence of the ability to produce accurate and specific semantic knowledge of the people that could not be named (Brooks et al., 1984; Carney & Temple, 1993; Fery et al., 1995; Hittmaier-Delazer et al., 1994; Lucchelli & de Renzi, 1992; Parry et al., 1991; Sunderland et al., 1983). Impaired naming of familiar objects following closed head injury has also been found to be relatively frequent in adults with CHI, e.g. Levin et al. (1977) found impaired object naming in 40% of the 50 patients they studied in whom PTA had resolved. Similar findings have been reported in other studies of adults with CHI (Hellawell et al., 1999; Kerr, 1995; Mattson et al., 2000), e.g. Mattson et al. (2000) reported a case of prosopagnosia following moderate CHI with left hemisphere focal lesion. Color vision was intact on screening, although shape detection was borderline. Impairments in higher order visual perception were evident to varying degrees on nonfacial tasks. Matching of unfamiliar faces was very slow but accurate, and identification of characteristics of faces (gender, age) and identification and matching of facial expressions were relatively intact. However, the patient showed a marked impairment in the ability to recognize familiar faces and learn new face–name associations relative to healthy control subjects.

In summary, research on the long-term memory consequences has demonstrated that deficits in declarative knowledge can be a consequence of traumatic brain injury, especially under conditions that require naming of an item. Although semantic category information is generally reported to be intact, there is some evidence that the acquisition of new categorical knowledge may be impaired.

PRODEDURAL KNOWLEDGE

Within the procedural memory domain, most studies have focused only on the acquisition of knowledge, rather than systematically testing loss or preservation of knowledge. Studies of the ability to acquire procedural knowledge (i.e. learning "how to" do something) after CHI have generally shown intact procedural learning, even in the presence of impaired verbal learning, e.g. Ewert et al. (1989) investigated the acquisition of procedural knowledge as compared to declarative knowledge in adults with severe CHI. They reported that individuals with CHI were impaired on declarative learning tasks relative to a group of matched uninjured adults but they showed learning across sessions on all procedural memory tasks. Timmerman & Brouwer (1999) used reaction time tasks to evaluate the effect of task difficulty on performance in acquiring declarative and procedural knowledge. They found that patients with CHI were generally slower than controls on both declarative and procedural tasks, but task difficulty affected performance only on the declarative tasks. Further, analysis of errors indicated that only on the declarative tasks did the CHI patients make more errors than the controls. However, it should be noted that both of the declarative knowledge tasks were machine-paced. One of the procedural tasks was self-paced and the other task, although machine paced, had a presentation time substantially longer than for the declarative tasks. Because no distinction was made between omission of responses and incorrect responses, it is possible that some of the differences observed may be accounted for by slowed processing. Nonetheless, the finding that task difficulty affected only declarative knowledge supports the general results of other studies that the ability to acquire procedural knowledge is less susceptible to disruption by traumatic brain injury than is declarative knowledge.

IMPLICIT MEMORY

Implicit memory occurs when the response to a stimulus is influenced by previous experience in the absence of intentional, conscious recollection of that experience (Roediger, 1990; Schacter, 1987). The findings that implicit memory was spared in persons with dense amnesia (Warrington & Weiskrantz, 1968) incited a riot of recent research on the dissociation between explicit and implicit memory in both normal and patient populations (e.g. Bassili et al., 1989; Challis & Brodbeck, 1992; Craik et al., 1994; Gabrieli et al., 1995; Graf & Masson, 1993; Graf et al., 1985; Jacoby & Dallas, 1981; Rajaram & Roediger, 1993; Roediger & Blaxton, 1987; Roediger et al., 1992; Schacter, 1987; Schacter & Church, 1992). In the studies investigating memory deficits, the general finding is that patients who show impairment on explicit tests of memory perform normally on implicit tests of memory. This pattern has been shown for a wide variety of stimulus materials, including verbal, nonverbal, procedural and even memory for context (McAndrews et al., 1987; Vakil et al., 1998). Studies with memory-impaired patients in various populations have indicated that priming for words (used to measure implicit learning) in word-stem completion tasks is spared in patients with frontal lesions (Shimamura et al., 1992), and supports previous neuropsychological and PET findings, which indicate that word priming depends critically on posterior cortical areas (e.g. Dhond et al., 2001). Although studies directly comparing implicit and explicit tests of memory in CHI patients are relatively sparse, such studies that have been done suggest that implicit memory is more resistant to impairment after CHI than is explicit memory in both adults (Ewert et al., 1989; Glisky, 1993; Shum et al., 1996; Watt et al., 1999) and children (Shum et al., 1999a), e.g. Shum et al. (1999a) investigated the abilities of 12 children with severe CHI and 12 matched uninjured children on a picture fragment completion task under explicit or implicit instructions. In the study phase of both conditions the children were shown complete pictures in a naming task, after which there was a filled delay. Under implicit instructions, the children were shown fragments of the pictures that had been presented in the study phase intermixed with non-studied picture fragments. Without reference to the previous study stage, the children were asked to identify pictures from the fragments. Under explicit instructions, the children were shown fragments and were asked to identify pictures from the fragments, but were told that they had seen the pictures earlier in the testing session. The authors found that the children with CHI performed similarly to the uninjured control children in the implicit task, but were significantly impaired on the explicit task.

IMPAIRMENTS OF METACOGNITION

The term "metacognition" has been applied to different processes. Some theorists (Flavell, 1981; Flavell et al., 1970; Metcalfe & Shimamura, 1996) have used the word to mean conscious awareness of one's cognitive abilities, in other words, what we know about what we know. A different use of the term metacognition is a product of the information-processing approach to theoretical models of cognition, which assume a system whose activities and resources are monitored by a central executive. In these models, metacognition refers to the self-regulatory activities of the cognitive system (Brown, 1978; Brown & Deloache, 1978). This aspect might be conceptualized as what we *do* about what we know. As has been alluded to above, successful memorial performance involves more than the passive registration and retrieval of information. It can also involve strategic manipulation of information, assessment of ongoing processes, monitoring of performance or appraisal of feedback. There is a rich tradition of metacognitive research—mostly metamemory—in normal adults and children (e.g. Flavell, 1981; Flavell et al., 1970; Hart, 1967), which has been extended to neuropsychological research (e.g. Mazzoni & Nelson, 1998; Metcalfe & Shimamura, 1996). Studies of individuals with CHI have revealed that in performance of memory tasks they may fail to apply the appropriate metacognitive processes, e.g. studies of verbal learning using the CVLT-C have shown that children with head injury show increased numbers of intrusions and perseverations in list recall (Levin et al., 1996) and in procedural learning (Beldarrain et al., 1999), suggesting a failure of metacognitive monitoring and control processes. Adults with CHI have also demonstrated a passive learning strategy with semantically related lists, leading to poorer recall (Levin & Goldstein, 1986). In studies that have directly investigated metacognition, previous research in adults with acquired brain damage has shown that feeling-of-knowing judgments (the ability to judge whether one can recognize a previously unrecallable target item) are impaired in individuals with frontal lobe damage (Janowsky et al., 1989; Shimamura et al., 1991; Shimamura & Squire, 1986). These impairments in metacognitive abilities were evident even when item recall level was matched across groups. Thus, the impairment in metacognitive processing in these patients was apparently not related to any general memory impairment, but rather to an impairment of executive level monitoring processes. In studies that have directly addressed metacognitive processing in persons with CHI, deficits have been reported in "feeling-of-knowing" judgments in adults and children (Hanten et al., 2000; Jurado et al., 1998). In our laboratory we have investigated metacognitive control within the memory domain in children with CHI and in uninjured children using a modification of a selective learning task for adults (Watkins & Hanten, unpublished manuscript). In this task we tested children's ability to selectively learn high-value items over low-value items in list recall (Hanten et al., 2001).

We studied 13 children with chronic severe CHI, ages 9–15, and 24 normally developing uninjured children matched for age and parental education. The children were presented lists of 16 words, of which eight words are designated as "high-value" words, and eight words are "low-value" words, with value indicated by category membership. The subjects were to make as high a score as possible by learning the words in the list. The measure of metacognitive control was the *selective efficiency* demonstrated in learning the words of differing value, independent of the number of words recalled. Children with CHI appeared to recall slightly fewer words than did control children (Figure 18.8A), although the difference was not significant. In contrast, the children with CHI were impaired relative to the control children on the measure of selective efficiency (Figure 18.8B). The different pattern of performance demonstrated for memory span and the measure of selective learning may be interpreted as a dissociation in memory capacity and metacognitive control in children with CHI.

Although research investigating the relationship between metacognition and memory performance after CHI is in the early stages, such results as have been reported suggest that impairments in metacognitive monitoring and control are a possible consequence of CHI and may interact with memory processes. Such interactions may have implications for outcome after CHI.

PROSPECTIVE MEMORY

Prospective memory, the recall of future intentions or actions to be performed, is a hybrid or multicomponent form of memory. Prospective memory has a "declarative" component (the *what* element to be recalled, which in this case is an action or intention), and also has a temporal–contextual element (the *when* and sometimes *where* the intention or action is to be executed). Relatively little research has been conducted on prospective memory after CHI. Self-reports on a questionnaire of memory failures indicate that adult CHI patients report significantly impaired prospective memory compared to uninjured adults (Mateer et al., 1987). In studies utilizing experimental tasks to investigate prospective memory in adults after CHI, impairments have been reported after short delay (Shum et al., 1999b) but not long delay (Hannon et al., 1995; Kinsella et al., 1996). In our laboratory, we studied the prospective memory performance of children with severe CHI and normally developing children (McCauley & Levin, 2000). Children were tested on several versions of event-based

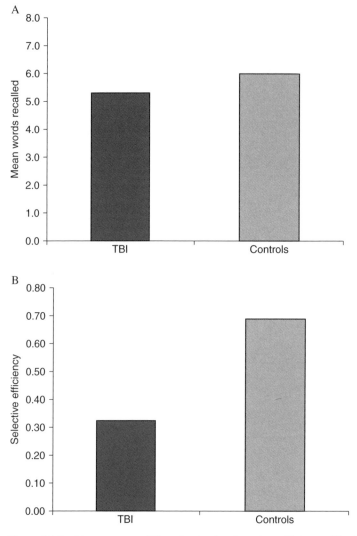

Figure 18.8 Memory span (A) and selective learning efficiency (B) of children with TBI and uninjured control children. From Hanten et al. (2001)

(EB) and activity-based (AB) prospective memory tasks. The tasks were designed to be ecologically valid and included such tasks as requiring the child to place his/her hands in his/her lap as quickly as possible (in spite of any ongoing activity) at the sound of a bell, or to pick up an envelope and give it to his/her parent at the conclusion of the testing session. We found that children with CHI were impaired relative to the control children on both EB and AB prospective memory tasks (Figure 18.9). These results support the hypothesis that severe CHI in children can result in prospective memory deficits across a variety of ecologically valid prospective memory tasks.

To summarize, neuropsychological findings in consecutive admissions for moderate to severe CHI support the impression that memory disturbance is a frequent and perhaps the

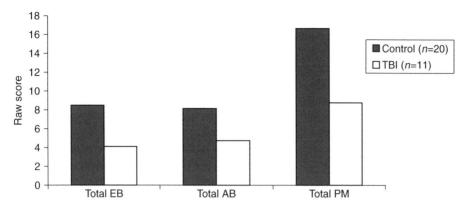

Figure 18.9 Raw score for tests of prospective memory in children with severe TBI and age-matched control children. In these tasks, a higher score indicates better performance. From McCauley & Levin (2000)

most prominent residual cognitive deficit after CHI. These results are also consonant with reports by patients and their families indicating that memory deficit is a common, persisting complaint (Oddy et al., 1985).

SEVERITY AND CHRONICITY OF HEAD INJURY

Numerous studies have documented the relationship between severity of acute CHI and the degree and persistence of the resulting memory deficit (Brooks, 1974, 1975; Dikmen et al., 1987; Levin et al., 1987, 1988a). The influence of chronicity of injury is particularly apparent in recovery from an initial memory deficit in patients examined within the first week after sustaining a mild head injury (Levin et al., 1987). In a three-center study, Levin et al. (1987) found that an initial impairment of verbal learning and memory resolved between 1 and 3 months after a mild head injury characterized at the time of hospital admission by brief loss of consciousness, normal neurologic findings and confusion, with preserved eye opening and ability to follow commands. This recovery pattern is depicted by the box plots shown in Figure 18.10. Support for our conclusion was provided by Dikmen et al. (1987), who found evidence of residual memory deficit in patients tested a year after sustaining a severe, but not a mild, injury. Findings from the Traumatic Coma Data Bank have documented remarkable individual variation in memory recovery curves among a cohort of severe CHI patients studied serially over 2 years (Levin et al., 1990; Ruff et al., 1991). These investigators found subgroups that exhibited recovery of verbal memory to within the normal range, as opposed to relatively flat functions showing minimal or no improvement over time, and a subgroup that showed evidence of deterioration in performance.

Analysis of the 1 year neurobehavioral follow-up data collected in the Traumatic Coma Data Bank has provided an opportunity to investigate the relationship between acute neurologic indices of severe CHI and later memory functioning (Levin et al., 1990). The lowest postresuscitation GCS score was predictive of verbal memory (Selective Reminding Test) 1 year later in patients who also had nonreactive pupils during their initial hospitalization. In contrast, the GCS score was unrelated to memory performance in patients who had normal

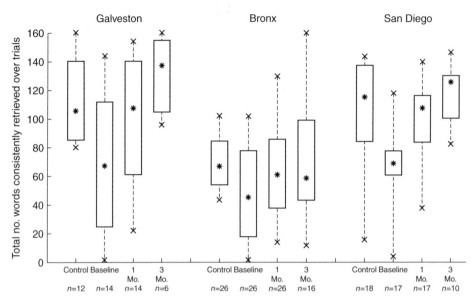

Figure 18.10   Box-plot showing the distribution of verbal memory retrieval scores by the controls and mild head-injured group studied in Galveston, the Bronx and San Diego. The distributions of scores are given for the head-injured groups at baseline (within 1 week postinjury) and at 1 and 3 months (Mo.) after injury; n = number of patients. See Figure 18.4A for explanation of symbols. Reproduced by permission from Levin et al. (1987). © 1987 *Journal of Neurosurgery*

pupillary reactivity in the emergency room and throughout their initial hospitalization. Levin et al. interpreted this interaction as evidence for long-term consequences of severely impaired consciousness on memory, provided that it is accompanied by other signs of neurologic deterioration, as reflected by abnormal pupillary reactivity. In contrast, recovery of verbal memory within 1 year after a severe CHI appears to be unrelated to the lowest GCS score, provided that there is no other evidence of neurologic deterioration. Further analysis of the interrelationships among indices of acute brain injury could potentially elucidate the wide variation in recovery of memory observed among survivors of severe CHI.

IMPLICATIONS FOR REHABILITATION

Memory theorists and clinical neuropsychologists have published case reports and studies of small groups of CHI patients that lend support to various remedial techniques for memory disorder (Crosson & Buenning, 1984; Crovitz et al., 1979; Glasgow et al., 1977; Glisky & Schacter, 1988; Glisky et al., 1986; Harris & Sunderland, 1981; Richardson, 1979; Wilson & Moffat, 1984). Although visual imagery and semantic elaboration techniques have received preliminary support (Glasgow et al., 1977; Kovner et al., 1983), evidence from controlled clinical trials is limited to a single study that evaluated the efficacy of a total program, rather than a specific technique (Prigatano et al., 1984). Apart from the modest empirical support for remediation of memory deficit, practical issues include the compliance of severely brain-injured patients with unfamiliar techniques, such as bizarre imagery. Other limitations include the lack of generalization across situations and erosion of gains after termination of training (Crosson & Buenning, 1984, Crovitz et al., 1979).

A primary objection to attempts to "retrain" memory through role experience is that repeatedly tested amnesics, such as patient H.M., have exhibited no improvement despite exhaustive practice and exposure to various mnemonic techniques (Milner et al., 1968). Similarly, we have reported that survivors of severe CHI frequently exhibit persistent impairment of memory, despite intensive rehabilitation (Levin et al., 1985a).

In recent years a broader spectrum of rehabilitation techniques has been explored, in part as a consequence of expanding knowledge of physiology and neurochemistry of the brain, as well as advances in understanding of the mechanisms underlying basic cognitive processes. Traditional psychological approaches to rehabilitation have employed compensatory strategies, such as utilization of internal or external memory cues or memory aid devices, with variable results (for review, see Sohlberg & Mateer, 1989). More recently, researchers have taken the approach of devising strategies that build on preserved cognitive components, such as procedural and/or implicit memory (e.g. Evans et al., 2000; Glisky, 1993; Glisky & Schacter, 1988; Thoene & Glisky,1995; Wilson & Evans, 1996). As with more traditional approaches, the results of these types of strategies are inconclusive. More research is needed to specify the conditions under which such interventions are effective. Several more biological approaches to rehabilitation have shown promise when implemented in animal models, including methods to stimulate regeneration or reorganization of brain structure (e.g. Kolb et al., 1997; McEwen & Wooley, 1994), and intracerebral transplantation (see Dickinson-Anson et al., 1999). In humans, pharmacological agents have been used to mitigate the effects of brain trauma (e.g. Arnsten & Smith, 1999; McIntosh, 1993; McIntosh et al., 1996; Stein et al., 1999; Zhu et al., 2000) with some success, although experimental evidence for the efficacy of such treatments is at present equivocal.

ACKNOWLEDGEMENT

Research presented in this chapter was supported by grants NS21889, H133B990014, and H133A980073. The authors are indebted to Angela D. Williams for word processing and editorial assistance.

REFERENCES

Adamovich, B. & Henderson, J. (1984). Can we learn more from word fluency measures with aphasic, right brain-injured, and closed head trauma patients? In R. Brookshire (ed.), *Clinical Aphasiology Conference Proceedings* (pp. 124–131). Minneapolis, MN: BRK.

Adams, J.H., Graham, D., Scott, G. et al. (1980). Brain damage in fatal non-missile head injury. *Journal of Clinical Pathology*, **33**, 1132–1145.

Albert, M.S., Butters, N. & Levin, J. (1979). Temporal gradients in the retrograde amnesia of patients with alcoholic Korsakoff's disease. *Archives of Neurology*, **36**, 211–216.

Arnsten, A.F.T. & Smith, D.H. (1999). Pharmacological strategies for neuroprotection and rehabilitation. In D.T. Stuss, G. Winocur & I.H. Robertson (eds), *Cognitive Neurorehabilitation* (pp. 113–135). Cambridge: Cambridge University Press.

Artiola, L., Fortuny, I., Briggs, M. et al. (1980). Measuring the duration of post-traumatic amnesia. *Journal of Neurology, Neurosurgery, and Psychiatry*, **43**, 377–379.

Baddeley, A. (1986). *Working Memory*. Oxford: Clarendon/Oxford University Press.

Baddeley, A. (1998). Recent developments in working memory. *Current Opinion in Neurobiology*, **8**(2), 234–238.

Baddeley, A., Harris, J., Sunderland, A. et al. (1987). Closed head injury and memory. In H.S. Levin, J. Grafman & H.M. Eisenberg (eds), *Neurobehavioral Recovery from Head Injury* (pp. 295–316). Oxford: Oxford University Press.

Baddeley, A. & Wilson, B.A. (1993). A developmental deficit in short-term phonological memory: implications for language and reading. *Memory*, **1**, 65–78.

Barr, W.B., Goldberg, E., Wasserstein, J. & Novelly, R.A. (1990). Retrograde amnesia following unilateral temporal lobectomy. *Neuropsychologia*, **28**, 243–255.

Bassili, J.N., Smith, M.C. & MacLeod, C.M. (1989). Auditory and visual word-stem completion: separating data-driven and conceptually driven processes. *Quarterly Journal of Experimental Psychology, A Human Experimental Psychology*, **41**, 439–453.

Beldarrain, M., Grafman, J., Pascual-Leone, A. & Garcia-Monco, J.C. (1999). Procedural learning is impaired in patients with prefrontal lesions. *Neurology*, **52**, 1853–1860.

Benton, A.L., Van Allen, M.W. & Fogel, M.L. (1964). Temporal orientation in cerebral disease. *Journal of Nervous and Mental Disorders*, **139**, 110–119.

Brodie, B. (1854). *Psychological Enquiries*. London: Longman.

Brooks, D.N. (1974). Recognition memory and head injury. *Journal of Neurology, Neurosurgery, and Psychiatry*, **37**, 224–230.

Brooks, D.N. (1975). Long- and short-term memory in head injured patients. *Cortex*, **11**, 329–340.

Brooks, D.N. (1976). Recognition memory after head injury: a signal detection analysis. *Cortex*, **10**, 224–230.

Brooks, D.N., Deelman, B.G., van Zomeren, A.H. et al. (1984). Problems in measuring cognitive recovery after acute brain injury. *Journal of Clinical Neuropsychology*, **6**(1), 71–85.

Brooks, N., McKinlay, W., Simington, C., Beattie, A. & Campsie, L. (1987). Return to work within the first seven years of severe head injury. *Brain Injury*, **1**, 5–19.

Brown, A.L. (1978). Knowing when, where, and how to remember: a problem of metacognition. In R. Glaser (ed), *Advances in Instructional Psychology* (pp. 367–406). Hillsdale, NJ: Erlbaum.

Brown, A.L. & DeLoache, J.S. (1978). Skills, plans, and self-regulation. In R. Siegler (ed.), *Children's Thinking: What Develops?* Hillsdale, NJ: Erlbaum.

Bullock R., Zauner A., Woodward, J.J. et al. (1998). Factors affecting excitatory amino acid release following severe human head injury. *Journal of Neurosurgery*, **89** (4), 507–518.

Buschke, H. & Fuld, P.A. (1974). Evaluating storage, retention, and retrieval in disordered memory and learning. *Neurology*, **14**, 1019–1025.

Carney, R. & Temple, C.M. (1993). Prosopagnosia: a possible category specific anomia for faces. *Cognitive Neuropsychology*, **10**, 185–195.

Challis, B.H. & Brodbeck, D.R. (1992). Level of processing affects priming in word fragment completion. *Journal of Experimental Psychology: Learning, Memory, and Cognition*, **18**, 595–607.

Craik, F.I.M., Moscovitch, M. & McDowd, J.M. (1994). Contribution of surface and conceptual information to performance on implicit and explicit memory tasks. *Journal of Experimental Psychology: Learning, Memory, and Cognition*, **20**, 864–875.

Crosson, B. & Buenning, W. (1984). An individualized memory retraining program after closed head injury: a single-case study. *Journal of Clinical Neuropsychology*, **6**, 287–301.

Crosson, B., Novack, T.A., Trenerry, M.R. & Craig, P.L. (1988). California Verbal Learning (CVLT) performance in severely head-injured and neurologically normal adult males. *Journal of Clinical and Experimental Neuropsychology*, **10**, 754–768.

Crovitz, H.F., Harvey, M.T. & Horn, R.W. (1979). Problems in the acquisition of imagery mnemonics: three brain-damaged cases. *Cortex*, **15**, 225–234.

Crowe, S.F. (1992.) Dissociation of two frontal lobe syndromes by a test of verbal fluency. *Journal of Clinical and Experimental Neuropsychology*, **14**, 327–339.

Delis, D.C., Kramer, J.H., Kaplan, E. et al. (1986). *The California Verbal Learning Test, research edition*. New York, NY: Psychological Corporation.

Delis, D.C., Kramer, J.H., Kaplan, E. & Ober, B.A. (1994). *The California Verbal Learning Test, Children's Version Manual*. San Antonio, TX: Psychological Corporation.

Delis, D.C., Massman, P.J., Butters, N. et al. (1991). Profiles of demented and amnesic patients on the California Verbal Learning Test: implications for the assessment of memory disorders. *Psychological Assessment*, **3**, 19–26.

Dennis, M. & Barnes, M.A. (1990). Knowing the meaning, getting the point, bridging the gap, and carrying the message: aspects of discourse following closed head injury in childhood and adolescence. *Brain and Language*, **39**, 428–446.

Dhond, R.P., Buckner, R.L., Dale., A.M. et al. (2001). Spatiotemporal maps of brain activity underlying word generation and their modification during repetition priming. *Journal of Neuroscience*, **21**, 3564–3571.

Dickinson-Anson, H., Aubert, I. & Gage, F.H. (1999). Intracerebral transplantation and regeneration: practical implications. In D.T Stuss & G. Winocur (eds), *Cognitive Neurorehabilitation* (pp. 26–46). New York: Cambridge University Press.

Dikmen S., Temkin, N., McLean, A. et al. (1987). Memory and head injury severity. *Journal of Neurology, Neurosurgery and Psychiatry*, **50**, 1613–1618.

DiStefano, G., Bachevalier, J., Levin, H.S. et al. (2000). Volume of focal brain lesions and hippocampal formation in relation to memory function after closed head injury in children. *Journal of Neurology, Neurosurgery, and Psychiatry*, **69**, 210–216.

Donders J. (1993). Memory functioning after traumatic brain injury in children. *Brain Injury*, **7**, 431–437.

Eisenberg, H.M., Gary, H.E. Jr, Aldrich, E.F. et al. (1990). Initial CT findings in 753 patients with severe head injury: a report from the NIH Traumatic Coma Data Bank. *Journal of Neurosurgery*, **73**, 688–698.

Ellenberg, J.H., Levin, H.S. & Saydjari, C. (1996). Posttraumatic amnesia as a predictor of outcome after severe closed head injury: prospective assessment. *Archives of Neurology*, **53**, 782–786.

Ellis, A.W., Young, A.W. & Critchley, M.R. (1989). Loss of memory for people following temporal lobe damage. *Brain*, **112**, 1469–1483.

Evans, J.J., Wilson, B.A., Schuri, U. et al. (2000). A comparison of "errorless" and "trial-and-error" learning methods for teaching individuals with acquired memory deficits. *Neuropsychological Rehabilitation*, **10**, 67–101.

Evans, J., Wilson, B., Wright, E. & Hodges, J.R. (1993). Neuropsychological and SPECT scan findings during and after transient global amnesia: evidence for the differential impairment of remote episodic memory. *Journal of Neurology, Neurosurgery, and Psychiatry*, **56**, 1227–1230.

Ewert, J., Levin, H.S., Watson, M.G. & Kalisky, Z. (1989). Procedural memory during posttraumatic amnesia in survivors of closed head injury: implications for rehabilitation. *Archives of Neurology*, **46**, 911–916.

Fery, P., Vincent, E. & Brédart, S. (1995). Personal name anomia: a single case study. *Cortex*, **31**, 191–198.

Flavell, J.H. (1981). Cognitive monitoring. In W.P. Dickson (ed.), *Children's Oral Communication Skill*. New York: Academic Press.

Flavell, J.H., Friedrichs, A. & Hoyt, J. (1970). Developmental changes in memorization processes. *Cognitive Psychology*, **1**, 324–340.

Fontaine, A., Azouvi, P., Remy, P. et al. (1999). Functional anatomy of neuropsychological deficits after sever traumatic brain injury. *American Academy of Neurology*, **53**, 1963–1968.

Friedman, S.D., Brooks, W.M., Jung, R.E. et al. (1998). Proton MR spectroscopic findings correspond to neuropsychological function in traumatic brain injury. *American Journal of Neuroradiology*, **19**, 1879–1885.

Gabrieli, J.D.E., Fleischman, D.A., Keane, M.M. et al. (1995). Double dissociation between memory systems underlying explicit and implicit memory in the human brain. *Psychological Science*, **6**, 76–82.

Gardner, S.D. & Vrbancic, M.I. (1998). Which California Verbal Learning Test factors discriminate moderate and severe head injury from normals? *Brain and Cognition*, **37**, 10–13.

Garnett, M.R., Blamire, A.M., Rajagopalan B. et al. (2000.). Evidence for cellular damage in normal-appearing white matter correlates with injury severity in patients following traumatic brain injury. A magnetic resonance spectroscopy study. *Brain*, **123**, 1403–1409.

Glasgow, R.E., Zeiss, R. A., Barreara, M. Jr & Lewinsohn, P.M. (1977). Case studies on remediating memory, deficits in brain-damaged individuals. *Journal of Clinical Psychology*, **33**, 1049–1054.

Glisky, E. (1993). Computer-assisted instructions for patients with traumatic brain injury: teaching of domain-specific knowledge. *Journal of Head Trauma Rehabilitation*, **7**, 1–12.

Glisky, E.L. & Schacter, D.L. (1988). Long-term retention of computer learning by patients with memory disorders. *Neuropsychologia*, **26**, 173–178.

Glisky, E.L., Schacter, D.L. & Tulving, E. (1986.) Computer learning by memory-impaired patients: acquisition and retention of complex knowledge. *Neuropsychologia*, **24**, 313–328.

Goldstein, F.C., Levin, H.S., Boake, C., Lohrey, J.H. (1990). Facilitation of memory performance through induced semantic processing in survivors of closed head injury. *Journal of Clinical and Experimental Neuropsychology*, **12**, 286–300.

Graf, P. & Masson, E. (eds) (1993). *Implicit Memory: New Directions in Cognition, Development, and Neuropsychology.* Hillsdale, NJ: Erlbaum.

Graf, P., Shimamura, A.P. & Squire, L.R. (1985). Priming across modalities and priming across category levels: extending the domain of preserved function in amnesia. *Journal of Experimental Psychology: Learning, Memory, & Cognition*, **11**, 386–396.

Graham, D.I., McIntosh, T.K., Maxwell, W.L. & Nicoll, J.A.R. (2000). Recent advances in neuro-trauma. *Journal of Neuropathology and Experimental Neurology*, **59**, 641–651.

Gronwall, D. & Wrightson, P. (1980). Duration of post-traumatic amnesia after mild head injury. *Journal of Clinical Neuropsychology*, **2**, 51–60.

Gruen, A.K., Frankle, B.C. & Schwartz, R. (1990). Word fluency generation skills of head-injured patients in an acute trauma center. *Journal of Communication Disorders*, **23**, 163–170.

Hannay, H.J., Levin, H.S. & Grossman, R.G. (1979). Impaired recognition memory after head injury. *Cortex*, **15**, 269–283.

Hannon, R., Adams, P., Harrington, S. et al. (1995). Effects of brain injury and age on prospective memory self-rating and performance. *Rehabilitation Psychology*, **40**, 289–298.

Hanten, G., Bartha, M. & Levin, H.S. (2000). Metamemory following pediatric traumatic brain injury: a preliminary study. *Developmental Neuropsychology*, **18**, 383–390.

Hanten, G., Dennis, M. & Levin, H.S. (2001). Knowing about knowing: metacognition after childhood closed head injury. In M. Dennis (Chair), *Neurobehavioral Outcome of Traumatic Brain Injury in Children*. Symposium conducted at the 29th Annual Meeting of the International Neuropsychological Society, Chicago, IL, February.

Hanten, G. & Martin, R. C. (2000). Contributions of phonological and semantic short-term memory to sentence processing: evidence from two cases of closed head injury in children. *Journal of Learning and Memory*, **43**, 335–361.

Hanten, G. & Martin, R.C. (2001). A developmental phonological short-term memory deficit: a case study. *Brain and Cognition*, **45**, 164–188.

Harris, J.E. & Sunderland, A. (1981). A brief survey of the management of memory disorders in rehabilitation units in Britain. *International Journal of Rehabilitation Medicine*, **3**, 206–209.

Hart, J.T. (1967). Memory and the memory-monitoring process. *Journal of Verbal Learning and Verbal Behavior*, **6**, 685–691.

Haut, M.W., Petros, T.V., Frank, R.G. & Haut, J.S. (1991). Speed of processing within semantic memory following severe closed head injury. *Brain and Cognition*, **17**, 31–41.

Hellawell, D.J., Taylor, R.T. & Pentland, B. (1999). Cognitive and psychosocial outcome following moderate or severe traumatic brain injury. *Brain Injury*, **13**, 489–504.

High, W.M. Jr, Levin, H.S. & Gary, H.E. Jr. (1990). Recovery of orientation and memory following closed-head injury. *Journal of Clinical and Experimental Neuropsychology*, **12**, 703–714.

Hittmaier-Delazer, M., Denes, G., Semenza, C. & Mantovan, M.C. (1994). Anomia for proper names. *Neuropsychologia*, **32**, 465–476.

Hough, M.S. (1993). Categorization in aphasia: access and organization of goal-derived and common categories. *Aphasiology*, **7**, 335–357.

Hough, M, S., Pierce, R.S, Difilippo, M. & Pabst, MJ. (1997). Access and organization of goal-derived categories after traumatic brain injury. *Brain Injury*, **11**, 801–814.

Hulme, C., Lee, G., Brown, G.D. (1993). Short-term memory impairments in Alzheimer-type dementia: evidence for separable impairments of articulatory rehearsal and long-term memory. *Neuropsychologia*, **31**(2), 161–172.

Jacoby, L.L. & Dallas, M. (1981). On the relationship between autobiographical memory and perceptual learning. *Journal of Experimental Psychology: General*, **110**, 306–340.

Jaffe, K.M., Fay, G.C., Polissar, N.L. et al. (1992). Severity of pediatric traumatic brain injury and early neurobehavioral outcome: a cohort study. *Archives of Physical Medicine and Rehabilitation*, **73**, 540–547.

Janowsky, J.S., Shimamura, A.P. & Squire, L.R. (1989). Memory and metamemory: comparisons between patients with frontal lobe lesions and amnesic patients. *Psychobiology*, **17**, 56–61.

Jarrold, C., Baddeley, A.D. & Hewes, A.K. (1999). Genetically dissociated components of working memory: evidence from Down's and Williams' syndrome. *Neuropsychologia*, **37**, 637–651.

Jennett, W.B. (1969). Head injuries and the temporal lobe. R.N. Herrington (ed). *Current Problems in Neuropsychiatry. British Journal of Psychiatry*, special publication No. 4. Ashford, Kent, UK: Headly Brothers, Ltd.

Jurado, M.A., Junque, C., Vendrell, P. et al. (1998). Overestimation and unreliability in "feeling-of-doing" judgments about temporal ordering performance: impaired self-awareness following frontal lobe damage. *Journal of Clinical and Experimental Neuropsychology*, **20**, 353–364.

Kerr, C. (1995). Dysnomia following traumatic brain injury: an information-processing approach to assessment. *Brain Injury*, **9**, 777–796.

Kinsella, G., Murtagh, D., Landry, A. et al. (1996). Everyday memory following traumatic brain injury. *Brain Injury*, **10**, 499–507

Knowlton B.J. & Squire L.R. (1993). The learning of categories: parallel brain systems for item memory and category knowledge. *Science,* **10**, 1747–1749.

Kochanek, P.M., Clark, R.S.B., Ruppel, R.A. et al. (2000). Biochemical, cellular and molecular mechanisms in the evolution of secondary damage after severe traumatic brain injury in infants and children: lessons learned from the bedside. *Pediatric Critical Care Medicine*, **1**, 4–19.

Kolb, B., Cote, S., Ribeiro-da-Silva, A. & Cuello, A.C. (1997). NGF stimulates recovery of function and dendritic growth after unilateral motor cortex lesion in rats. *Neuroscience*, **76**, 1139–1151.

Kotapka, M.J., Graham, D.I., Adams, J.H. et al. (1994). Hippocampal pathology in fatal human head injury without high intracranial pressure. *Journal of Neurotrauma*, **11**, 317–324.

Kovner, R., Mattis, S., Goldmeier. E. (1983). A technique for promoting robust free recall in chronic organic amnesia. *Journal of Clinical Neuropsychology*, **5**(1), 65–71.

Langfitt, T.W., Obrist, W.D., Alavi, A. et al. (1986). Computerized tomography, magnetic resonance imaging and positron emission tomography in the study of brain trauma: preliminary observations. *Journal of Neurosurgery*, **64**, 760–767.

Lepage, M., Ghaffar, O., Nyberg, L. & Tulving, E. (2000). Prefrontal cortex and episodic memory retrieval mode. *Proceedings of the National Academy of Sciences*, **97**(1), 506–511.

Leplow, B., Dierks, C.H., Lehnung, M. et al. (1997). Remote memory in ptients with acute brain injuries. *Neuropsychologia*, **35**, 881–892.

Levin, H.S. (1989). Memory deficit after closed head injury. *Journal of Clinical and Experimental Neuropsychology*, **12**, 129–153.

Levin, H.S., Benton, A.L. & Grossman, R.G. (1982). *Neurobehavioral Consequences of Closed Head Injury*. New York: Oxford University Press.

Levin, H.S., Fletcher, J.M., Kusnerik, L. et al. (1996). Semantic memory following pediatric head injury: relationship to age, severity of injury, and MRI. *Cortex*, **32**, 461–478.

Levin H.S., Gary, H.E., Eisenberg, H.M. et al. (1990). Traumatic Coma Data Bank Research Group. Neurobehavioral outcome 1 year after severe head injury: experience of the Traumatic Coma Data Bank. *Journal of Neurosurgery*, **73**, 699–709.

Levin, H.S. & Goldstein, F.C. (1986). Organization of verbal memory after severe closed head injury. *Journal of Clinical and Experimental Neuropsychology*, **8** (6), 643–656.

Levin, H.S., Goldstein, F.C., High, W.M. Jr & Eisenberg, H.M. (1988a). Automatic and effortful processing after severe closed head injury. *Brain and Cognition*, **7**, 283–297.

Levin, H.S., Goldstein, F.C., High, W.M. Jr & Eisenberg, H.M. (1988b). Disproportionately severe memory deficit in relation to normal intellectual functioning after closed head injury. *Journal of Neurology, Neurosurgery, and Psychiatry*, **51**, 1294–1301.

Levin, H.S., Grossman, R.G. & Kelly, P.J.(1977). Aphasic disorder in patients with closed head injury. *Journal of Neurology, Neurosurgery, and Psychiatry*, **39**,1062–1070.

Levin, H.S., Grossman, R., Sarwar, M. et al. (1981). Linguistic recovery after closed head injury. *Brain and Language*, **12**, 360–374.

Levin, H.S., Handel, S.F., Goldman, A.M. et al. (1985a). Magnetic resonance imaging after "diffuse" nonmissile head injury. *Archives of Neurology*, **42**, 963–968.

Levin, H.S., High, W.M. Jr, Meyers, C.A. et al. (1985b). Impairment of remote memory after closed head injury. *Journal of Neurology, Neurosurgery and Psychiatry*, **45**, 556–563.

Levin, H.S., High, W.M., Ewing-Cobbs, L. et al. (1988c). Memory functioning during the first year after closed head injury in children and adolescents. *Neurosurgery*, **22**, 1043–1052.

Levin, H.S., Mattis, S., Ruff, R.M. et al. (1987). Neurobehavioral outcome following minor head injury: a three-center study. *Journal of Neurosurgery*, **66**, 234–243.

Levin, H.S., O'Donnell, V.M. & Grossman, R.G. (1979). The Galveston Orientation and Amnesia Test: a practical scale to assess cognition after head injury. *Journal of Nervous and Mental Disease*, **167**, 675–684.

Levin, H.S., Papanicolaou, A.C. & Eisenberg, H.M. (1984). Observations of amnesia after nonmissile head injury. In: L.R. Squire and N. Butters (eds), *Neuropsychology of Memory* (pp. 247–257). New York: Guilford.

Levin, H.S., Peters, B.H. & Hulkonen, D.A. (1983). Early concepts of anterograde and retrograde amnesia. *Cortex*, **19**, 427–440.

Levin, H.S., Song, J., Scheibel, R.S. et al. (2000) Dissociation of frequency and recency processing from list recall after severe closed head injury in children and adolescents. *Journal of Clinical and Experimental Neuropsychology*, **22**, 1–15.

Levin H.S., Williams, D.H., Eisenberg, H.M. et al.(1992). Serial MRI and neurobehavioral findings after mild to moderate closed head injury. *Journal of Neurology, Neurosurgery, Psychiatry*, **55**, 255–262.

Lohman, T., Ziggas, D. & Pierce, R.S. (1989). Word fluency performance on common categories by subjects with closed head injuries. *Aphasiology*, **3**, 685–693.

Lucchelli, F. & de Renzi, E. (1992). Proper name anomia. *Cortex*, **28**, 221–230.

Mangels, J., Craik, F., Levine, B. et al. (2000). Chronic deficits in item and context memory following traumatic brain injury: a function of attention and injury severity. *Brain and Cognition*, **44**, 98–112.

Markowitsch, H.J., Calabrese, P, Liess, J. et al. (1993). Retrograde amnesia after traumatic brain injury of the frontal temporal cortex. *Neurology, Neurosurgery, and Psychiatry*, **56**, 988–992.

Martin, R.C. & Romani, C. (1994). Verbal working memory and sentence comprehension: a multiple components view. *Neuropsychology*, **8**, 506–523.

Martin, R.C., Shelton, J.R. & Yaffee, L.S. (1994). Language processing and working memory: neuropsychological evidence for separate phonological and semantic capacities. *Journal of Memory and Language*, **33**, 83–111.

Mateer, C.A., Sohlberg, M.M. & Crinean, J. (1987). Focus on clinical research: perceptions of memory function in individuals with closed-head injury. *Journal of Head Trauma Rehabilitation*, **2**, 74–84.

Mattson, A.J., Levin, H.S. & Grafman J. (2000). A case of prosopagnosia following moderate closed head injury with left hemisphere focal lesion. *Cortex*, **36**, 125–137.

Mazzoni, G. & Nelson, T.O. (eds) (1998). Metacognition and cognitive neuropsychology: monitoring and control processes (pp. 212). Mahwah, NJ: Erlbaum.

McAllister, T.W., Saykin, A.J., Flashman, L.A. et al. (1999). Brain activation during working memory 1 month after mild traumatic brain injury: a functional MRI study. *Neurology*, **121**,1300–1308.

McAndrews, M.P., Glisky, E.L. & Schacter, D.L. (1987). When priming persists: long-lasting implicit memory for a single episode in amnesic patients. *Neuropsychologia*, **25**, 497–506.

McCarthy, R.A. & Warrington, E.K. (1992). Actors but not scripts: the dissociation of people and events in retrograde amnesia, *Neuropsychologia*, **30**, 633–644.

McCauley, S.R. & Levin, H.S. (2000). Prospective memory deficits in children and adolescents sustaining severe closed-head injury. Presentation at the 7th Annual Meeting of the Cognitive Neuroscience Society, San Francisco, CA.

McEwen, B.S. & Wooley, C.S. (1994). Estradial and progesterone regulate neuronal structure and synaptic connectivity in adult as well a developing brain. *Experimental Gerontology*, **29**, 431–436.

McIntosh, T.K. (1993). Novel pharmacologic therapies in the treatment of experimental traumatic brain injury: a review. *Journal of Neurotrauma*, **10**, 215–361.

McIntosh, T.K., Smith, D.H., Voddi, M. et al. (1996). Riluzole, a novel neuroprotective agent, attenuates both neurologic motor and cognitive dysfunction following experimental brain injury in the rat. *Journal of Neurotrauma*, **13**, 767–780.

Metcalfe, J. & Shimamura, A.P. (eds.) (1996). *Metacognition: Knowing about Knowing*. Cambridge, MA: MIT Press.

Miller, E.K. (2000). The prefrontal cortex and cognitive control. *Nature Reviews*, **1**, 59–65.

Millis, S.R. (1995). Factor structure of the California Verbal Learning Test in moderate and severe closed brain injury. *Perceptual and Motor Skills*, **80**, 219–224.

Millis, S.R. & Dijkers, M. (1993). Use of the Recognition Memory Test in traumatic brain injury: preliminary findings. *Brain Injury*, **7**, 53–58.

Milner, B., Corkin, S. & Teuber, H.L. (1968). Further analysis of the hippocampal amnesic syndrome: 14-year follow-up study of H.M. *Neuropsychologia*, **6**, 215–234.

Oddy, M. Coughlan, T., Tyerman, A. & Jenkins, D. (1985). Social adjustment after closed head injury: A further follow-up seven years after injury. *Journal of Neurology, Neurosurgery and Psychiatry*, **48**, 564–568.

Ommaya, A.D. & Gennarelli, T.A. (1974). Cerebral concussion and traumatic unconsciousness: correlation of experimental and clinical observations on blunt head injuries. *Brain*, **97**, 633–654.

Parry, F.M., Young, A.W., Saul, J.S.M. & Moss, A. (1991). Dissociable face processing impairments after brain injury. *Journal of Clinical and Experimental Neuropsychology*, **13**, 545–558.

Petrides, M. & Milner, B. (1982). Deficits on subject-ordered tasks after frontal and temporal-lobe lesions in man. *Neuropsychologia*, **20**, 249–262.

Prigatano, G.P., Fordyce, D.J., Zeiner, H.K. et al. (1984). Neuropsychological rehabilitation after closed head injury in young adults. *Journal of Neurology, Neurosurgery, and Psychiatry*, **47**, 505–513.

Rajaram, S. & Roediger, H.L. (1993). Direct comparison of four implicit memory tests. *Journal of Experimental Psychology: Learning, Memory, & Cognition*, **19**, 765–776.

Reed, J.M., Squire, L.R., Patalano, A.L. et al. (1999). Learning about categories that are defined by object-like stimuli despite declarative memory. *Behavioral Neuroscience*, **113**, 411–419.

Reid, D.B. & Kelly, M.P. (1993). Weschler Memory Scale—Revised in closed head injury. *Journal of Clinical Psychology*, **49**, 245–254.

Rey, A.L. (1941). Examen psychologique dans les cas d'encephalopathie traumatique. *Archives de Psychologie*, **28**, 286–340.

Rey, A. (1964). *L'examen clinique en psychologie*. Paris: Presses Universitaires de France.

Ribot, T. (1882). *Diseases of Memory: An Essay in the Positive Psychology*. New York: Appleton.

Richardson, J.T.E. (1979). Mental imagery, human memory, and the effects of closed head injury. *British Journal of Social and Clinical Psychology*, **18**, 319–327.

Richardson, J.T.E. (1984). The effects of closed head injury upon intrusions and confusions in free recall. *Cortex*, **20**, 413–420.

Roediger, H.L. (1990). Implicit memory: retention without remembering. *American Psychologist*, **45**, 1043–1056.

Roediger, H.L. & Blaxton, T.A. (1987). Effects of varying modality, surface features, and retention interval on priming in word-fragment completion. *Memory and Cognition*, **15**, 379–388.

Roediger, H.L., Weldon, M.S., Stadler, M.L. & Riegler, G.L. (1992). Direct comparison of two implicit memory tests: word fragment and word stem completion. *Journal of Experimental Psychology: Learning, Memory, & Cognition*, **18**, 1251–1269.

Roman, M.J., Delis, D.C., Willerman, L. et al. (1998). Impact of pediatric traumatic brain injury on components of verbal memory. *Journal of Clinical and Experimental Neuropsychology*, **20**(2), 245–258.

Ruff R.M., Young D., Levin H.S. et al. (1991). Verbal learning deficits following severe head injury: heterogeneity in recovery over one year. *Journal of Neurosurgery* **75** *(suppl.)*, S50–S58.

Russell, W.R. (1932). Cerebral involvement of head injury. *Brain*, **55**, 549–603.

Russell, W.R. (1971). *The Traumatic Amnesias*. New York: Oxford University Press.

Russell, W.R. & Nathan, P.W. (1946). The traumatic amnesias. *Brain*, **69**, 183–187.

Russell, W.R. & Smith, A. (1961). Post-traumatic amnesia in closed head injury. *Archives of Neurology*, **5**, 4–17.

Saffran, E.M. & Martin, N. (1990). Neuropsychological evidence for lexical involvement in short-term memory. G. Vallar & T. Shallice (eds), *Neuropsychological Impairments of Short-term Memory* (pp. 145–166). New York: Cambridge University Press.

Sarno, M. (1984). Verbal impairment after closed head injury: report of a replication study. *Journal of Nervous and Mental Disease*, **172**, 475–479.

Schacter, D.L. (1987). Implicit memory history and current status: learning, memory, and cognition. *Journal of Experimental Psychology*, **13**, 501–518.

Schacter, D.L. & Church, B.A. (1992). Auditory priming: Implicit and explicit memory for words and voices. *Journal of Experimental Psychology: Learning, Memory, & Cognition*, **18**, 915–930.

Schacter, D.L. & Crovitz, H.F. (1977). Memory function after closed head injury: a review of the quantitative research. *Cortex*, **8**, 150–176.

Scoville, W.B. & Milner, B., (1957). Loss of recent memory after bilateral hippocampal lesions. *Journal Neurology, Neurosurgery and Psychiary*, **20**, 11–21.

Shallice, T. & Vallar, G. (1990). The impairment of auditory-verbal short-term storage. In G. Vallar & T. Shallice (eds), *Neuropsychological Impairments of Short-term Memory* (pp. 11–53). Cambridge: Cambridge University Press.

Shelton, J.R., Martin, R.C. & Yaffee, L.S. (1992). Investigating a verbal short-term memory deficit and its consequences for language processing. In Margolin, D. I. (Ed.), *Cognitive Neuropsychology in Clinical Practice* (pp. 131–167). New York: Oxford University Press.

Shimamura, A.P., Gershberg, F.B., Jurica, P.J. et al. (1992). Intact implicit memory in patients with frontal lobe lesions. *Neuropsychologia*, **30**, 931–937.

Shimamura, A.P., Janowsky, J.S. & Squire, L.R. (1991). What is the role of frontal lobe damage in amnesic disorders? In H.S. Levin, H.M. Eisenberg & A.L. Benton (eds), *Frontal Lobe Function and Dysfunction* (pp.173–195). New York: Oxford University Press.

Shimamura, A.P. & Squire, L.R. (1986). Memory and metamemory: a study of the feeling-of-knowing phenomenon in amnesic patients. *Journal of Experimental Psychology: Learning, Memory, and Cognition*, **12**, 452–560.

Shores, E.A., Marosszeky, J.E., Sandanam, J. et al. (1986). Preliminary validation of a clinical scale for measuring the duration of post-traumatic amnesia. *Medical Journal of Australia*, **144**, 569–572.

Shum, D., Harris, D. & O'Gorman, J.G. (2000). Effects of severe traumatic brain injury on visual memory. *Journal of Clinical and Experimental Neuropsychology*, **22**(1), 25–39.

Shum, D., Jamieson, E., Bahr, M. & Wallace, G. (1999a). Implicit and explicit memory in children with traumatic brain injury. *Journal of Clinical & Experimental Neuropsychology*, **21**, 149–158.

Shum, D., Sweeper, S. & Murray, R. (1996). Performance on verbal implicit and explicit memory tasks following traumatic brain injury. *Journal of Head Trauma Rehabilitation*, **11**, 43–53.

Shum, D., Valentine, M. & Cutmore, T. (1999b). Performance of individuals with severe long-term traumatic brain injury on time-, event-, and activity-based prospective memory tasks. *Journal of Clinical and Experimental Neuropsychology*, **21**(1),49–58.

Sohlberg, M.M. & Mateer, C.A. (1989). *Introduction to Cognitive Rehabilitation. Theory and Practice*. New York: Guilford.

Spikeman, J.M., Berg, I.J. & Deelman, B.G. (1995). Spared recognition capacity in elderly and closed-head-injury subjects with clinical memory deficits. *Journal of Clinical & Experimental Neuropsychology*, **17**(1), 29–34.

Squire, L.R. (1974). Remote memory as affected by ageing. *Neuropsychologia*, **12**, 429–435.

Squire, L.R. (1992). Memory and hippocampus: a synthesis from findings with rats, monkeys and humans. *Psychological Review*, **2**, 195–231.

Squire, L.R. & Slater, P.G. (1975). Forgetting in very long-term memory as assessed by an improved questionnaire technique. *Journal of Experimental Psychology: Human Learning and Memory*, **1**, 50–54.

Squire, L.R. & Zola-Morgan, S. (1988). Memory: brain systems and behavior. *Trends in Neuroscience*, **11**, 170–175.

Stallings, G.A., Hanten, G., Song, J.X. et al. Subject Ordered pointing task performance following severe traumatic brain injury in adults. (submitted). Paper presented at the Annual meeting of the International Neuropsychological Association meeting, Denver, CO.

Stein, D.G., Roof, R.L. & Fulop, Z.L. (1999). Brain damage, sex hormones and recovery. In D.T. Stuss, G. Winocur & I.H. Robertson (eds), *Cognitive Neurorehabilitation* (pp. 73–93). Cambridge: Cambridge University Press.

Stuss, D.T., Binns, M.A., Carruth, F.G. et al. (1999). The acute period of recovery from traumatic brain injury: posttraumatic amnesia or posttraumatic confusional state? *Journal of Neurosurgery*, **90**, 635–643.

Sunderland, A., Harris, J.E. & Baddeley, A.D. (1983). Do laboratory tests predict everyday memory? A neuropsychological study. *Journal of Verbal Learning and Verbal Behavior*, **22**, 341–357.

Tate, R.L., Pfaff, A. & Jurjevic, L. (2000). Resolution of disorientation and amnesia during posttraumatic amnesia. *Journal of Neurology, Neurosurgery and Psychiatry*, **68**,178–185.

Teasdale, G. & Jennett, B. (1974). Assessment of coma and impaired consciousness: a practical scale. *Lancet*, **2**, 81–84.

Thoene, A.I. & Glisky, E.L. (1995). Learning of name-face associations in memory impaired patients: a comparison of different training procedures. *Journal of the International Neuropsychological Society*, **1**(1), 29–38.

Timmerman, M.E. & Brouwer, W.H. (1999). Slow information processing after very severe closed head injury: Impaired access to declarative knowledge and intact application and acquisition of procedural knowledge. *Neuropsychologia*, **37**, 467–478.

Tsukiura, T., Otsuka, Y., Miura, R. et al. (2000). Remote memory for items, contents, and contexts: a case study for post-traumatic amnesia. *Brain and Cognition*, **44**, 98–112.

Tulving, E. (1983). *Elements of Episodic Memory*. New York: Oxford University Press.

Vakil, E., Golan. H., Grunbaum, E. et al. (1998). Direct and indirect measures of contextual information in brain-injured patients. *Neuropsychiatry, Neuropsychology, & Behavioral Neurology*, **9**,176–181.

Warrington, E.K. & Weiskrantz, L. (1968). New method of testing long-term retention with special reference to amnesic patients. *Nature*, **217**, 972–974.

Watkins, M.J. & Hanten, G. (unpublished manuscript). Selective remembering in visual short-term memory.

Watt, S., Shores, E.A. & Kinoshita, S. (1999). Effects of reducing attentional resources on implicit and explicit memory after severe traumatic brain injury. *Neuropsychology*, **13**, 338–349.

Wiegner, S. & Donders, J. (1999). Performance on the California Verbal Learning Test after traumatic brain injury. *Journal of Clinical and Experimental Neuropsychology*, **21**, 159–170.

Wilde, M.C. & Boake, C. 1994. Factorial validity of the California Verbal Learning Test in head injury. *Archives of Clinical Neuropsychology*, **9**, 202.

Wilson, B.A. (1997).Semantic memory impairments following non-progressive brain injury: a study of four cases. *Brain Injury*, **11**, 259–269

Wilson, B.A. & Evans, J.J. (1996). Error-free learning in the rehabilitation of people with memory impairments. *Journal of Head Trauma Rehabilitation*, **11**(2), 54–64.

Wilson, B.A. & Moffat, N. (eds) (1984). *Clinical Management of Memory Problems*. Rockville, MD: Aspen.

Wilson, J.T., Wiedmann, K.D., Hadley, D.M. et al.(1988). Early and late magnetic resonance imaging and neuropsychological outcome after head injury. *Journal of Neurology, Neurosurgery, Psychiatry*, **51**, 391–396.

Yeates, K.O., Blumenstein, E., Patterson, C.M. & Delis, D.C. (1995). Verbal learning and memory following pediatric closed-head injury. *Journal of the International Neuropsychological Society*, **1**, 78–87.

Zhu, J., Hamm, R.J., Reeves, T.M. et al. (2000). Postinjury administration of L-deprenyl improves cognitive function and enhances neuroplasticity after traumatic brain injury. *Experimental Neurology*, **166**,136–152.

CHAPTER 19

Schizophrenia

Peter McKenna
Fulbourn Hospital, Cambridge, UK
Tisha Ornstein
Department of Psychiatry, University of Cambridge, UK
and
Alan D. Baddeley
Department of Experimental Psychology, University of Bristol, UK

Schizophrenia is customarily described as a disorder where there are major disturbances in thought, emotion and behaviour, leading in many cases to a state of permanent deterioration. Defined more precisely, it is characterized by a range of "positive" symptoms, including delusions, hallucinations and incoherence of speech, which occur against a background of "negative" symptoms consisting of social withdrawal, lack of motivation and emotional unresponsiveness. Positive symptoms typically fluctuate and may drop out of the clinical picture altogether, but the negative symptoms are almost always enduring. A minority of patients who become schizophrenic recover or remain relatively well most of the time. More often there are regular relapses and remissions accompanied by occupational and social decline. In the worst-affected cases, patients become unable to care for themselves, may suffer continual psychotic symptoms, and are quite likely to require indefinite care and supervision.

The cause or causes of schizophrenia remain, after decades of research, largely unknown. For much of the twentieth century, psychoanalytic and psychosocial theories held sway, and at one time the whole construct of the disorder as an illness was called into question. Currently, however, it is widely believed that schizophrenia is a biological brain disease. Originally based on evidence for a hereditary factor in the disorder, this became the dominant view with the discovery in 1952 that dopamine receptor-blocking drugs (antipsychotics or neuroleptics) were an effective treatment. This latter finding led to the hypothesis that schizophrenia is caused by a functional excess of brain dopamine, which became for a time the major force motivating research, but which ultimately had disappointing results. More recent biological investigations have demonstrated that the disorder is associated with at least one structural brain abnormality, lateral ventricular enlargement. Functional imaging has also revealed evidence of brain abnormality, albeit less consistently.

Somewhat surprisingly in view of its devastating effects on sufferers' ability to function and the evidence that it is a brain disease, the time-honoured view has been that schizophrenia

The Handbook of Memory Disorders. Edited by A.D. Baddeley, M.D. Kopelman and B.A. Wilson
© 2002 John Wiley & Sons, Ltd.

does not affect cognitive function. While it is true that many, even most, schizophrenic patients are not obviously intellectually impaired in the same way as individuals with brain damage or dementia, over the years neuropsychological deficits ranging from the subtle to the quite marked have been increasingly recognized. Memory impairment has been found to make an important contribution to the pattern of poor performance, and it may be that this is sometimes pure and pronounced enough to constitute a "schizophrenic amnesia".

COGNITIVE IMPAIRMENT IN SCHIZOPHRENIA

Kraepelin (1913) and Bleuler (1911), the psychiatrists who originated the concept of schizophrenia, were also responsible for the view that intellectual function was not affected. Kraepelin believed that the dementia of his term dementia praecox predominated in the emotional and volitional spheres and that memory, in particular, was "comparatively little disordered". Part of Bleuler's stated reason for renaming dementia praecox as schizophrenia was that he considered the connotation of intellectual impairment to be misleading. According to him, lack of motivation, withdrawal, distraction by psychotic symptoms and other more esoteric factors could and did cause patients to perform poorly on certain tests at certain times, but all mental faculties remained fundamentally intact underneath. With respect to memory, Bleuler (1911) was emphatic:

> The patients are able to recall, as well as any healthy person, their experiences and the events of the time before and during their illness—in many instances the latter much better than the healthy, since they can register things almost like a camera.

Notwithstanding these assertions, psychological studies carried out in the early part of the century quickly established that patients with schizophrenia performed more poorly than normal individuals on virtually every cognitive task (see Chapman & Chapman, 1973). Later, IQ testing revealed that schizophrenic patients had lower IQs than the rest of the population. As a group, the disadvantage was minor, on average of the order of four points, but patients with severe and chronic forms of illness were found to have a mean IQ of just over 80 (Payne, 1973). Later still, poor performance was found on neuropsychological tests. Three reviews of such studies published in the same year (Goldstein, 1978; Heaton et al., 1978; Malec, 1978) found that groups of acute, mixed and chronically hospitalized schizophrenic patients were increasingly difficult to distinguish from patients with brain damage on a wide range of tests, and that for the last group a meaningful differentiation was not possible.

The range and severity of neuropsychological test impairment in schizophrenia is well illustrated in a recent meta-analysis by Heinrichs & Zakzanis (1998). These authors collected 204 studies carried out between 1980 and 1997 which compared schizophrenic patients and normal controls, and which covered areas of memory, motor skills, attention, intelligence, visual and visuospatial function, executive function, language and tactile perception. The findings are shown in Table 19.1, from which it can be seen that the effect sizes for impairment were all moderate or large, ranging from 0.46 (for WAIS Block Design) to 1.41 (for verbal memory). The degree of nonoverlap between the schizophrenic patients and the normal controls varied from 30% to 70% on different tests. Heinrichs & Zakzanis (1998) concluded that schizophrenic cognitive impairment affects most areas of function and takes the form of a continuum from a mild impairment overlapping with the levels of function

Table 19.1 Effect sizes for neuropsychological test impairment in schizophrenia

Test	Effect size	No. of studies	Patients below median (%)
Global verbal memory	1.41	31	78
Bilateral motor skill	1.30	5	77
Performance IQ	1.26	17	77
Continuous Performance Test	1.16	14	75
Word fluency	1.15	29	75
Stroop	1.11	6	74
WAIS-R IQ	1.10	35	74
Token Test	0.98	7	71
Tactile-transfer	0.98	12	71
Selective verbal memory	0.90	7	70
Wisconsin Card Sort	0.88	43	69
Verbal IQ	0.88	27	69
Unilateral motor skill	0.86	6	69
Trail Making, part B	0.80	15	68
Nonverbal memory	0.74	14	67
Trail Making, part A	0.70	12	66
Facial recognition	0.61	8	64
Digit span	0.61	18	64
Line orientation	0.60	4	64
Non-WAIS-R IQ	0.59	43	64
Vocabulary	0.53	38	62
Block Design	0.46	12	61

seen in many healthy individuals, to the kind of severe dysfunction found in patients with central nervous system disease.

It is not likely that the poor performance found in these studies was due to antipsychotic drug treatment. In general, administration of these drugs to normal individuals has been found to have only minor effects on cognitive function (King, 1990). Higher dose and longer treatment in schizophrenic patients appears, if anything, to improve their test performance (King, 1990; Mortimer, 1997). Additionally, several studies (Saykin et al., 1991, 1994; Blanchard & Neale, 1994) have examined drug-free or never-treated schizophrenic patients on batteries of neuropsychological tests and have found much the same pattern and degree of impairment as in treated patients.

MEMORY IMPAIRMENT IN SCHIZOPHRENIA

Credit for the first detailed exploration of memory in schizophrenia belongs to Calev and co-workers (Calev, 1984a, 1984b; Calev et al., 1983, 1987a, 1987b). In a series of studies carried out mainly on chronic schizophrenic patients, they found evidence of substantial impairment in verbal and nonverbal episodic memory tasks. The deficits affected both recall and recognition, although the former appeared to be of considerably greater magnitude. Evidence of retrograde amnesia was also found.

Since then numerous studies have been carried out, almost all of which have continued to find evidence of impairment. McKenna et al. (2000) reviewed 10 recent studies that used modern diagnostic criteria for schizophrenia and compared patients with well-matched normal controls on a range of memory measures. Eight of the 10 studies found significantly impaired performance on some or all of the tests used (Calev et al., 1987b; Gruzelier et al., 1988; Gold et al., 1992b; Goldberg et al., 1993; Landro et al., 1993; Elliott et al., 1995; Paulsen et al., 1995; Rushe et al., 1999) and only two studies failed to find any differences (Shoqeirat & Mayes, 1988; Morrison-Stewart et al., 1992).

In a meta-analysis of 70 studies carried out between 1975 and 1998, Aleman et al. (1999) also found that memory was significantly impaired in schizophrenia. The effect sizes were uniformly moderate or large, ranging from 0.61 for verbal recognition to 1.21 for a composite measure of recall.

Typical of the findings is that of McKenna et al. (1990). They used the Rivermead Behavioural Memory Test (RBMT) (Wilson et al., 1985, 1989), a simple and relatively undemanding test of "everyday" memory functioning. This was administered to a sample of 60 schizophrenic patients aged 18–68 who were selected to be representative of the disorder as a whole: they were drawn in approximately equal numbers from acute wards and outpatient clinics; from a rehabilitation service for chronically ill patients; and from long-stay wards that house the most severely disabled patients. Performance on the RBMT was expressed as a screening score, the number of tests passed out of a maximum of 12. As shown in Figure 19.1, the schizophrenic patients' performance was obviously poorer than that of 118 normal individuals of comparable age range, with nearly half scoring 7 or fewer, compared to less than 5% of the controls. In fact their performance was not discernibly different than that of a further comparison sample of 176 patients with moderate or severe brain injury.

As with general intellectual impairment, it is difficult to attribute poor memory performance in schizophrenia to antipsychotic drug treatment. Memory impairment has been found in studies carried out on drug-free or never-treated schizophrenic patients (Saykin et al., 1991, 1994; Blanchard & Neale, 1994). Also, in the meta-analysis of Aleman et al.

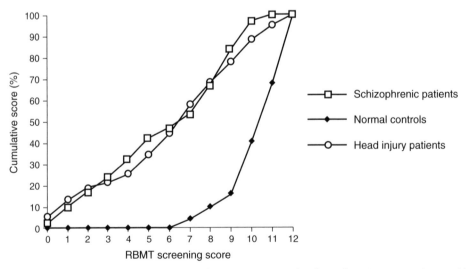

Figure 19.1 Cumulative RBMT scores for 60 patients with schizophrenia, 176 patients with head injury and 118 normal controls. Reproduced by permission from McKenna et al. (1990)

(1999), status as treated or untreated was not found to be a significant moderator of the effect size for memory impairment. There is likewise little evidence that memory impairment is related to the anticholinergic drug treatment that schizophrenic patients commonly take to combat the parkinsonian side-effects of antipsychotic drugs. Deficits have been documented in patients who were not taking such drugs at the time of testing (Calev, 1987a; Goldberg et al., 1993), and the degree of impairment has been found not to differ between patients who were on and off such medication (Calev et al., 1987b; McKenna et al., 1990; Duffy & O'Carroll, 1994; Rushe et al., 1999).

It is also difficult to ascribe poor memory performance in schizophrenia to factors like poor motivation, lack of cooperation or the distracting effects of psychotic symptoms. McKenna et al. (1990) found that excluding 16 of their 60 patients in whom poor cooperation was evident at the time of testing made little difference to the mean RBMT screening score—there was an improvement of less than one point. In a replication of this study, Duffy & O'Carroll (1994) rated motivation and cooperation on a five-point scale and found no relationship between this and their patients' memory performance.

SCHIZOPHRENIC MEMORY IMPAIRMENT: A SPECIFIC NEUROPSYCHOLOGICAL DEFICIT?

It is clear that memory impairment in schizophrenia is present against a background of overall intellectual impairment, which can be quite severe in some patients. In these circumstances the question arises whether the memory deficit is merely part of a pattern of generally poor cognitive performance, which would show itself on any test, or whether it is present over and above this, and hence sometimes appears as a relatively circumscribed deficit.

Studies relevant to this issue have had mixed findings. McKenna et al. (1990), in the study described above, found that whereas nearly half of their sample fell into the moderately or severely impaired range on the RBMT, only 19% fell into the mildly or severely demented range on a brief test of general intellectual function, the Mini-Mental State Examination (MMSE) (Folstein et al., 1975). This crude finding gained support in a study by Saykin et al. (1991): they administered a wide-ranging battery of neuropsychological tests to a group of 36 schizophrenic patients and 36 normal controls and converted their raw scores into z-scores based on the control group's means and standard deviations (SDs). On most tests, the schizophrenic patients' mean scores fell between one and two SDs below those of the controls. Only the scores on three memory measures—composite scores for verbal memory, visual memory and learning—provided an exception, performance on these being depressed to nearly three SDs below the control group mean.

Saykin et al. (1994), however, failed to fully replicate their own findings in a similar study using a larger sample of patients. On this occasion they found a disproportionate impairment in verbal memory but not visual memory. Braff et al. (1991) and Blanchard & Neale (1994) also failed to find any evidence of differential memory impairment in similarly designed studies.

A further, psychometrically robust method of comparing memory and general intellectual function is by means of Weschler IQ and memory scales. As well as being equivalently standardized, performance on these two scales is highly correlated in normal individuals, so that in clinical groups an IQ–MQ discrepancy of more than 12–15 points is considered to be

Table 19.2 Performance of 45 schizophrenic patients
on the WAIS-R and Wechsler Memory Scale—Revised

	Mean	SD
Estimated premorbid IQ		
WRAT-R Reading*	95.6	14.4
Current IQ		
WAIS-R Full Scale IQ	86.8	12.1
WAIS-R Verbal IQ	90.0	12.9
WAIS-R Performance IQ	84.8	11.1
Memory		
WMS-R General Memory Index	78.1	18.4
WMS-R Verbal Memory Index	81.8	17.2
WMS-R Visual Memory Index	81.5	20.5
WMS-R Attention Index	80.0	16.7
WMS-R Delayed Memory Index	81.6	20.5

*Wide Range Achievement Test—Revised, reading subscale.
Reproduced by permission from Gold et al. (1992a). © 1992 Swets
Zeitlinger

a good indicator of selective memory deficit. Gold et al. (1992a) administered the WAIS-R
and WMS-R to a sample of 45 chronic schizophrenic patients. Their mean scores are shown
in Table 19.2, from which it can be seen that premorbid IQ, estimated using a reading test,
was higher than current Full Scale IQ, which in turn was higher than the General Memory
Index (the equivalent of MQ in the original WMS). The mean difference between the latter
two measures was 8.6 points, which was significant at $p < 0.0001$; 33% of the patients had
discrepancies of 15 points or more, and 23% had discrepancies of 20 or more points.

THE PATTERN OF MEMORY IMPAIRMENT: THE CASE
FOR A SCHIZOPHRENIC AMNESIA

It is almost a requirement of clinical memory disorders to show dissociations, i.e. a pattern
of impairment and preservation of function across the different subdivisions of memory.
However, the fact that memory impairment in schizophrenia commonly occurs against a
background of some degree of general intellectual impairment will tend to obscure any
such pattern, since scoring on all tests will be depressed to some extent. This "noise" can
be reduced by controlling for general intellectual function in the analysis, or alternatively
by testing only patients who meet some criterion of overall intellectual intactness. A further
strategy that has occasionally been employed is to select patients on the basis that they
show substantial levels of general memory impairment and then examine them for areas of
spared function.

Long-term Memory

There is no controversy that this memory store is affected by schizophrenia. The vast
majority of studies have included (and have often relied exclusively on) long-term memory

measures, and, as noted above, almost all of these have found evidence of impairment. For example, in the review of studies comparing patients with well-matched controls carried out by McKenna et al. (2000), all of the eight which found significant impairment, found this on long-term memory measures (Calev et al., 1987b; Gruzelier et al., 1988; Gold et al., 1992b; Goldberg et al., 1993; Landro et al., 1993; Elliott et al., 1995; Paulsen et al., 1995; Rushe et al., 1999).

Several early studies (e.g. Bauman & Murray, 1968; Nachmani & Cohen, 1969; Koh, 1978) found that schizophrenic patients showed impairment on tests of recall but not recognition. Goldberg et al. (1989) later replicated this finding and interpreted it as suggesting that schizophrenic memory impairment was secondary to executive impairment (see below). Other studies, however, have documented impairment on recognition memory tests (Tamlyn et al., 1992; Gold et al., 1992b; Clare et al., 1993; Elliott et al., 1995; Paulsen et al., 1995). Recognition tasks are typically much easier than recall tasks and so it is quite possible that some of the earlier positive findings reflected differences in task difficulty, rather than a true neuropsychological dissociation. Two studies by Calev et al. (1984a, 1984b) addressed this issue, using recall and recognition tests which were matched for difficulty. In both cases it was found that, although relatively worse at recall, the schizophrenics also had significantly poorer recognition than normal controls.

Aleman et al. (1999) found evidence for a recognition memory deficit in schizophrenia in their meta-analysis; the effect size for combined verbal and nonverbal recognition memory impairment was a respectable 0.64. However, this was of lesser magnitude than the effect size for combined verbal and nonverbal recall, which was 1.21.

Short-term Memory

In contrast to studies of long-term memory in schizophrenia, studies of short-term memory have had inconsistent findings. Several studies have reported that forward digit span remains intact (Kolb & Whishaw 1983; Park & Holzman, 1992; Tamlyn et al., 1992; Goldberg et al., 1993; Duffy & O'Carroll, 1994; Morice & Delahunty, 1996; Salame et al., 1998; Stone et al., 1998), whereas others have found impairment (Gruzelier et al., 1988; Brebion et al., 1997; Gold et al., 1997; Conklin et al., 2000). In these latter studies the differences have been relatively small, usually of the order of one digit, and in three of them the patients and controls were not well matched, particularly for education. Nevertheless, the meta-analysis of Aleman et al. (1999) once again found evidence for impairment in forward digit span, but at 0.71 the effect size was smaller than that for long-term recall.

Corsi block span has been more consistently found to be impaired in schizophrenia (Rizzo et al., 1996; Pantelis et al., 1997; Fleming et al., 1997; Hutton et al., 1998; Salame et al., 1998), although there have been a significant number of negative findings (Kolb & Whishaw, 1983; Nelson et al., 1990; Goldberg et al., 1993). Performance on another nonverbal span task, visual pattern span, was also found to be impaired in schizophrenic patients by Salame et al. (1998).

Three studies have examined the influence that the general level of intellectual functioning might be exerting on the short-term memory findings in schizophrenia. Rushe et al. (1999) found that 58 schizophrenic patients had a mean digit span of 5.44, compared to 6.05 for 53 normal controls. However, the patients had a significantly lower premorbid IQ than the controls (105.7 vs. 111.6), as estimated using the National Adult Reading Test (NART)

(Nelson, 1982), and when this was controlled for the difference in span scores no longer reached significance—although significant impairment remained on long-term memory measures. In contrast, Stirling et al. (1997) compared 27 schizophrenic patients and 19 normal controls who were matched for NART-estimated premorbid IQ and found the mean forward digit span to be 5.77 in the patients and 6.89 in the controls. In this study the groups differed in current IQ, but the difference in digit span survived controlling for this. Finally, Elliott et al. (1998) examined 12 schizophrenic patients with preserved IQ (as defined by NART-estimated premorbid IQ/current IQ discrepancies of less than 10 points) and found that they were significantly impaired compared to well-matched controls on a computerized version of the Corsi blocks. However, the degree of impairment expressed in terms of z-scores was only half as great as on a spatial recognition memory task.

Working Memory

The first study of working memory in schizophrenia was carried out by Park & Holzman (1992): 12 schizophrenic patients and 12 normal controls viewed a black circle, which appeared briefly at different points in their visual fields. After a delay of 5 or 30 s, during which a distractor task was performed, they had to select the location of the circle from an array of eight possibilities. The schizophrenic patients were significantly impaired compared to the controls at both delay intervals, but were unimpaired on a control task where the target stimulus remained in view at all times. Subsequently Fleming et al. (1997) found that schizophrenic patients were impaired on a similar but somewhat more difficult visuospatial task, at both 0 and 7 s (unfilled) delay intervals.

The tasks used by Park & Holzman (1992) and Fleming et al. (1997) were designed to be analogous to delayed response and delayed alternation tasks in nonhuman primates, and were based on a definition of working memory (Goldman-Rakic, 1991) which is somewhat different from the human cognitive psychological construct of Baddeley (1986). These studies are perhaps best viewed as testing the latter model's visuospatial sketchpad. Studies which have specifically examined the central executive component of working memory in schizophrenia are shown in Table 19.3 (a more inclusive review has been provided by Keefe, 2000). Included are versions of span tasks, such as reverse digit span and the letter-number span task incorporated into the most recent versions of the WAIS and WMS, plus dual-task performance and one or two miscellaneous procedures. It can be seen that, while many of the studies found impairment, a minority found normal function or only a trend towards poorer performance. The studies finding preserved function tended to employ controls who were matched for age and education or IQ; however, some studies which found impairment were also well controlled.

Two of the above studies were carried out on intellectually preserved patients, defined on the basis of lack of discrepancy between NART-estimated premorbid IQ and current IQ. Elliott et al. (1998) used the CANTAB spatial working memory task, in which subjects have to touch boxes presented on a computer screen to find tokens while avoiding locations where these have already been found. They found only a trend towards impairment in 12 intellectually preserved schizophrenic patients, compared to well-matched controls. Iddon et al. (1998) employed a task in which subjects had to generate sequences of responses while remembering those they had already used. Twenty intellectually preserved schizophrenic patients and 20 controls matched for age and NART IQ were required to touch each of

Table 19.3 Studies of working memory in schizophrenia

Study	Sample	Matching	Task	Findings	Comment
Goldberg et al. (1993)	24 Patients 24 Controls	Controls were unaffected identical twins	Reverse digit span	Trend to impairment	–
Condray et al. (1996)	25 Patients 11 Controls	Age Education	Sentence span[1]	Impaired	–
Morice & Delahunty (1996)	17 Patients 17 Controls	Age Sex NART IQ	Reverse digit span Alphabet span[2] Sentence span[1]	Normal Impaired Impaired	Patients had significantly lower WAIS IQ
Brebion et al. (1997)	38 Patients 38 Controls	Age Education	Reverse digit span	Impaired	
Fleming et al. (1997)	32 Patients 27 Controls	Reading ability	Reverse block tapping span	Impaired	Patients older, less educated and had lower WAIS IQ
Gold et al. (1997)	36 Patients 30 Controls	Reading ability	Letter-number span	Impaired	Patients older, less educated and had lower WAIS IQ
Iddon et al. (1998)	20 Patients 20 Controls	Age NART IQ	Generating spatial sequences[3]	Normal	Patients were intellectually intact
Pantelis et al. (1997)	36 Patients 31 Controls	Age Sex NART IQ	CANTAB spatial working memory[4]	Impaired	
Spindler et al. (1997)	14 Patients 12 Controls	Age NART IQ	Non-verbal equivalent of letter-number span	Impaired	–
Stirling et al. (1997)	27 Patients 19 Controls	Age NART IQ	Reverse digit span	Impaired	Difference remained significant after co-varying for current IQ
Stratta et al. (1997)	30 Patients 25 Controls	Age Education	Reverse digit span Finding pairs of matching cards[5]	Impaired Impaired	
Hutton et al. (1998)	30 Patients 30 Controls	Age NART IQ	CANTAB spatial working memory[4]	Impaired	Patients only impaired at hardest levels of task
Salame et al. (1998)	27 Patients 20 Controls	Age Education	Dual task performance	Normal	–
Stone et al. (1998)	18 Patients 15 Controls	Age	Reverse digit span Sentence span[6] Computation span	Impaired Impaired Impaired	Patients less educated and had lower WAIS IQ
Wexler et al. (1998)	38 Patients 39 Controls	Age Sex Education	Word serial position[7] Tone serial position[7]	Impaired Impaired	–
Conklin et al. (2000)	52 Patients 73 Controls	Age	Reverse digit span	Impaired	Differences remained significant after co-varying for education

[1] Requires verification of progressively longer sets of sentences as true or false plus recall of last word of each in any order.
[2] Word span task requiring reproduction in alphabetical order.
[3] See text.
[4] See text.
[5] Subject has to turn over pairs of cards from each of two sets of 12 cards in order to find identical pairs in as few trials as possible.
[6] Requires recall of last word of sentence after each presentation following short distractor task.
[7] Requires subjects to retain series of four words or tones and indicate position of one of the words when it is repeated after delay of 1, 5 or 9 s.

four boxes arranged in a diamond shape on a computer screen, following as many different sequences as possible. No significant difference was found between the two groups on the score achieved or the number of trials before a sequence was repeated. However, after both groups had been given training to help them generate sequences more effectively, the controls improved their performance, whereas the schizophrenic patients failed to do so.

Semantic Memory

An earlier generation of studies investigating the concept of "overinclusive thinking" in schizophrenia provided some of the best-replicated evidence of psychological abnormality in the disorder (see Payne, 1973). Many of these studies strayed into the territory of semantic memory, as they examined word meaning, categorization and the relationship between concepts. More recently, Cutting & Murphy (1988) found that schizophrenic patients showed surprising deficits on a questionnaire testing elementary practical and social knowledge.

The first of a number of recent studies designed specifically to examine semantic memory in schizophrenia was carried out by Tamlyn et al. (1992). They used the semantic processing test of Collins & Quillian (1969) (developed by Baddeley et al., 1992, as part of the Speed and Comprehension of Language Processing Battery), in which subjects have to indicate whether each of 50 simple sentences, such as "Rats have teeth" and "Onions crush their prey" are true or false. Speed of verification is the usual measure and errors are rarely made by normal individuals. The performance of a mixed group of 53 acute and chronic schizophrenic patients on this task was compared with that of 38 normal individuals of comparable age distribution. Speed of semantic processing was significantly slower for the schizophrenic patients and, more surprisingly, they also made considerable numbers of errors: 14 (26%) of the patients made three or more verification errors, with five of them making more than 10. This was in contrast to the controls, none of whom made more than two errors.

Duffy & O'Carroll (1994) replicated this finding of impairment on the semantic processing test, and Clare et al. (1993) found additional impairment on tests of vocabulary and categorization of words. Laws and co-workers (1998, 2000) have also documented impairment of naming of objects and knowledge about famous people in chronic schizophrenic patients, which was marked in some cases. However, one further study using a version of the "silly sentences" test (Rossell et al., 1998) failed to find a higher rate of errors (time measures were not made). This last study was carried out on outpatients and acutely ill inpatients, whereas all the other studies included at least some chronically hospitalized patients, and so it is possible that the failure to find semantic memory impairment was a consequence of the patients' lesser severity of illness.

How far semantic memory impairment is a function of general intellectual impairment in schizophrenia has been investigated in a single study. McKay et al. (1996) administered the battery of semantic tests devised by Hodges et al. (1992) to 46 patients and 40 normal controls. This battery probes knowledge of well-known living and man-made items, such as "fox" and "toaster", in a variety of ways, e.g. by requiring subjects to name the items, to sort them into categories and to give definitions of them. The schizophrenic patients showed impairment on almost all the subtests (only word–picture matching was unaffected). Significant impairment with the same pattern continued to be found in patients who were intellectually intact, as defined by having current IQs of 85 or greater (i.e. within 1 SD of the population mean) or by having estimated premorbid/current IQ discrepancies of 15 points or less.

Procedural and Implicit Memory

Granholm et al. (1993) compared the performance of seven schizophrenic patients and 11 controls on the prototypical test of motor skill learning, the pursuit rotor. As shown in Figure 19.2, although the patients' level of performance was (nonsignificantly) lower than that of the controls at the beginning and the end of the study, there was no difference in the rate of acquisition of the skill. Goldberg et al. (1993) replicated this finding in a study of identical twins, one member of whom had schizophrenia; this was despite the patients showing significantly poorer episodic memory performance than their unaffected co-twins. Two further studies used the pursuit rotor, but varied the design so that the turntable speed was adjusted individually in order to give the same initial mean time on target for patient and control groups. One of these studies (Kern et al., 1997) again found no difference between patients and controls. The other (Schwartz et al., 1996) found that schizophrenic patients learnt significantly more slowly than controls, despite the fact that they were in effect performing an easier version of the task. Schwartz et al.'s findings are also illustrated in Figure 19.2, from which it can be seen that the learning curves were virtually parallel after the first trial, perhaps calling into question the validity of matching for initial performance.

Almost all studies of implicit memory in schizophrenia have found it to be intact. Five out of six studies using word-stem completion tasks found normal performance, usually in the setting of significant impairment on free recall of the same words (Schmand et al., 1992; Gras-Vincendon et al., 1994; Bazin & Perruchet, 1996; Brebion et al., 1997; Kazes et al., 1999). The remaining study (Randolph et al., 1993) found impaired implicit memory performance in 10 schizophrenic patients, compared to 10 age- and educationally-matched controls, when the subjects had to rate the words for likability when they were first presented. However, their performance was no different from the controls in a second condition, where the words had first not only to be rated for likability but also defined and used in a sentence.

Schwartz et al. (1993) found normal priming in schizophrenia in a study that compared recall of words when cued by semantic categories or primed with the same semantic categories. Normal implicit learning has also been demonstrated using a variety of other procedures. Green et al. (1997) used the Serial Reaction Time task, in which subjects had repetitively to press one of four keys corresponding to stimuli which appeared in one of four positions on a screen. Unknown to them, the correct key presses occurred in repeated sequences of 10, and their speed of responding therefore progressively increased. A group of schizophrenic patients was found to show comparable rates of improvement to normal controls. Keri et al. (2000) found evidence of normal implicit rule learning on a probabilistic classification task, where the subjects had to decide whether a set of four geometrical shapes, presented alone or in combination, were predictive of hypothetical weather conditions of rain or shine. Schizophrenic patients showed a similar degree of improvement over trials to controls, despite having significantly poorer knowledge of what weather conditions the cues were associated with at the end of the study. Finally, O'Carroll et al. (1999) took advantage of the "errorless learning" procedure developed by Baddeley & Wilson (1994), which has

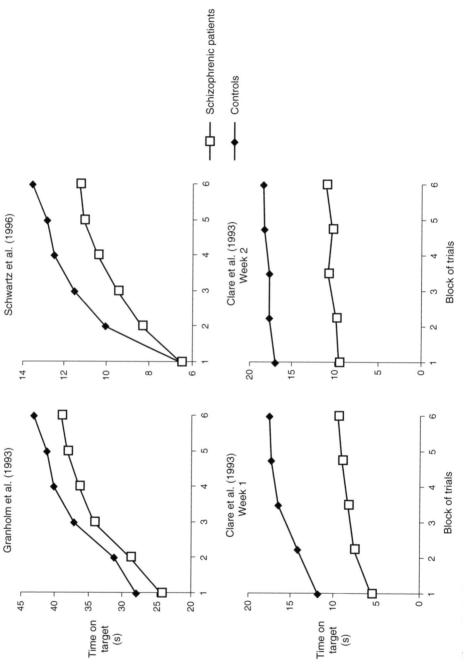

Figure 19.2 Pursuit rotor performance in different studies of schizophrenic patients

been found to be effective in improving memory performance in amnesic patients. This involves preventing subjects from guessing during learning trials, and its success is thought to be due to the fact that in the traditional trial-and-error approach erroneous responses are remembered implicitly and interfere with conscious recall of target items. Groups of schizophrenic patients with and without memory impairment were found to perform more poorly than the controls in the errorful condition, but were not significantly different from them at all points in the errorless condition.

The sparing of procedural and implicit memory in schizophrenia appears to hold true when patients with substantial degrees of general memory impairment are considered. Clare et al. (1993) tested 12 schizophrenic patients who scored in the moderately or severely impaired range on the RBMT and 12 controls matched for age, sex and NART-estimated premorbid IQ on three procedural memory tasks: pursuit rotor, repeatedly completing a child's jigsaw and learning to read mirror writing. The patients showed poorer initial and final performance than the controls on all three procedural tasks (which was significant for pursuit rotor and jigsaw completion). However, in each case the rate of acquisition of the skill was comparable, and the gains made were retained to a comparable extent across two test sessions a week apart. The findings for pursuit rotor are shown in Figure 19.2, which illustrates both the patients' generally lower level of performance and their comparable acquisition of the skill. An obvious interpretation of this pattern is that the poor overall performance reflects the schizophrenic tendency to general intellectual impairment, against the background of which certain functions—in this case procedural memory—are preserved.

Clare et al. (1993) also administered an implicit memory task to their 12 generally memory-impaired patients, priming in homophone spelling. In this, both groups were first primed for the less frequently occurring spelling of homophones of words (e.g. buoy, wring), and were then asked to spell a list of words, some of which contained the 10 primed homophones. Both the patients and controls showed similar priming on the homophone task in week one, and in both groups this was less marked but still evident a week later.

Taken together, these findings indicate that memory impairment in schizophrenia shows dissociations, but has its own unique pattern of these which differ, for example, from those seen in the classical amnesic syndrome. Episodic long-term memory is impaired to a degree which, while highly variable across patients, is on average substantial. This is coupled with short-term memory performance which has sometimes been found to be preserved or relatively preserved, and which at worst appears to be impaired to a considerably lesser extent than long-term memory. Interestingly, short-term memory impairment is most consistently found on visuospatial short-term memory tasks, which current evidence suggests places a heavier load on the central executive component of working memory than the phonological loop (e.g. Smith & Jonides, 1999). The central executive itself has been repeatedly found to be impaired in schizophrenia, but there are enough instances of normal or marginally poor performance to suggest that the deficit is not as marked as that in long-term memory. As in most if not all clinical memory disorders, procedural and implicit memory are preserved in schizophrenia, even when the episodic memory deficit is quite severe. Unlike most other memory disorders, though, semantic memory appears to be a major area of impairment, with the deficit extending to knowledge, such as the meaning of words, which was presumably acquired long before the onset of illness.

THE ROLE OF EXECUTIVE FUNCTION IN SCHIZOPHRENIC MEMORY IMPAIRMENT

In recent years the concept of abnormal frontal lobe function has dominated schizophrenia research, with most if not all current theoretical approaches invoking some form of executive impairment (e.g. Weinberger, 1987; Gray et al., 1991; Frith, 1992; Andreasen, 1999). The origins of this view can be traced back to claims for "hypofrontality" in functional imaging studies which began to be carried out in the 1980s. These were followed by a number of structural imaging studies which claimed to find reduced frontal lobe volume in schizophrenic patients. Ten years on, it is apparent that hypofrontality was only ever found in a minority of studies under resting conditions (Chua & McKenna, 1995), and it seems likely that any frontal lobe volume reductions in schizophrenia are no greater than those for the brain as a whole (Lawrie & Abukmeil, 1998; Wright et al., 2000). What survives is a somewhat more consistent body of evidence supporting task-related hypofrontality in schizophrenia, i.e. reduced prefrontal cortex activation on functional imaging when schizophrenic patients perform an executive task (see Chua & McKenna, 1995; Weinberger & Berman, 1996).

Neuropsychological studies of executive function appeared late in the course of the frontal initiative in schizophrenia research, almost, as it were, as an afterthought. Poor performance was documented on a wide range of executive tasks (e.g. Goldberg et al., 1987, 1988; Morice, 1990; Liddle & Morris, 1991), but it was—and is—less clear whether this represented a specific deficit. Some studies have found evidence that the executive impairment is disproportionate to the overall level of intellectual impairment (Shallice et al., 1991; Crawford et al., 1993; Elliott et al., 1995; Evans et al., 1997), but several have failed to do so (Braff et al., 1991; Saykin et al., 1991, 1994). Laws (1999) meta-analysed studies using the Wisconsin Card Sorting Test and found that the effect size for impairment on this task was smaller than that for IQ in schizophrenia.

Disproportionate or not, executive impairment is part of the profile of deficits in schizophrenia, and it therefore becomes legitimate to ask to what extent memory impairment might be secondary to it. Memory problems have been recognized in the frontal lobe syndrome for a long time, but until relatively recently these were thought to reflect the patients "forgetting to remember" because of indifference, inattention and lack of foresight (e.g. Luria, 1971; Stuss & Benson, 1984). Baddeley & Wilson (1988) first clearly defined what they termed "frontal amnesia" in a single-case study of a patient with a dysexecutive syndrome secondary to trauma to the frontal lobes. This patient was severely impaired on long-term memory tests, including both recall and recognition and paired-associates learning. However, short-term memory, as assessed by digit span, was intact. In a subsequent group study, Kopelman et al. (1999) demonstrated deficits affecting remote memory tests, semantic memory, autobiographical memory and recall of current events.

Nathaniel-James et al. (1996) tested the hypothesis that schizophrenic memory impairment is a form of frontal amnesia. They found that a group of 25 schizophrenic patients were significantly impaired compared to controls on three executive tests, and also showed impairment of recall but not recognition memory—a pattern which, like Goldberg et al. (1989), they argued was consistent with frontal lobe damage. However, when they went on to examine the correlations between memory and executive measures, they found that only few of these were significant (11/63 on various measures derived from the tests). Two other studies (Elliott et al., 1995; Evans et al., 1997) also failed to find significant correlations between measures of executive function and memory in chronic schizophrenic patients. In the latter of these studies, the authors were additionally able to isolate individual patients who showed normal performance on the RBMT but impairment on a battery of tests of everyday executive function, the Behavioural Assessment of the Dysexecutive Syndrome (Wilson et al., 1996), and vice versa.

Rightly or wrongly, the idea that schizophrenic memory impairment can be understood as an example of frontal amnesia has fallen into disfavour. The most widely held current view seems to be that while executive function and memory are both conspicuous areas of deficit in schizophrenia, they are more closely related to the general intellectual impairment which also characterizes the disorder than they are to each other.

THE FUNCTIONAL CONSEQUENCES OF MEMORY IMPAIRMENT IN SCHIZOPHRENIA

While poor performance on memory, executive and other cognitive tests is established beyond reasonable doubt in schizophrenia, the degree to which this translates into corresponding failures in daily life is less certain. This is not an trivial issue, because for most of the twentieth century it was believed that there was no genuine cognitive impairment in the disorder, a dogma that was undoubtedly shored up by a lack of obvious forgetfulness or other cognitive difficulties in the majority of patients encountered in everyday clinical practice. This could, of course, merely reflect the fact that memory impairment only becomes obvious in the most severely and chronically ill patients, where it is easy to overlook amidst their multiple other symptoms. But other interpretations are possible, one of which is Bleuler's (1911) original assertion that cognitive impairment in schizophrenia is fundamentally different in nature from that seen in brain damage or dementia.

Green (1996; Green et al., 2000) reviewed studies that examined the relationship of cognitive deficits in schizophrenia to what he termed functional outcome—the skills necessary for successful functioning in the community. He found that the 30 or so studies exploring this issue were generally underpowered and preliminary. Nevertheless, verbal memory and vigilance, and somewhat less strongly executive function, emerged as predictors of performance in daily living skills such as self-care, transportation, finances, social skills and shopping.

To date, only one study has examined the relationship between memory test performance in schizophrenia and memory failures in daily life. Ornstein et al. (submitted) administered the RBMT to 30 chronic schizophrenic patients and 23 patients with frontal or temporal brain damage, mainly due to strokes or following neurosurgery. Carers of both groups of patients were also asked to complete a checklist of their memory failures over the last month. This was based on a questionnaire designed by Sunderland et al. (1983), which was used by Wilson et al. (1985, 1989) in the original validation of the RBMT, and consisted of statements such as, "Did he/she forget where things are normally kept or look for things in the wrong places?", "Did he/she get details of what someone had said confused?" and "Did you observe him/her getting lost on a journey or in a building where he/she has been before?".

The mean RBMT screening score was 5.93 in the schizophrenic patients and 6.33 in the brain-damaged patients. These scores were not significantly different from each other, but were significantly poorer than the mean of 9.17 for a group of 30 age-matched normal controls. Carer ratings for the schizophrenic and the brain-damaged patients are shown in

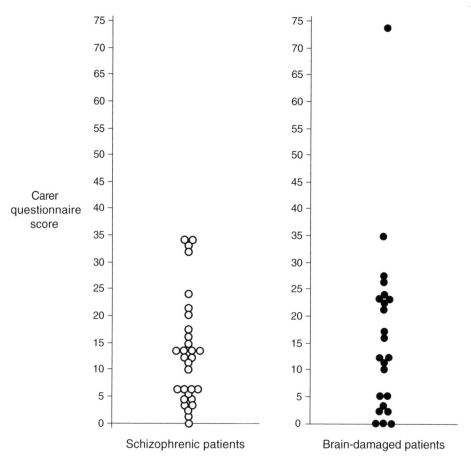

Figure 19.3 Distribution of scores on a carer questionnaire for everyday memory failures in 30 schizophrenic patients and 23 patients with brain damage

Figure 19.3, from which it can be seen that some patients in both groups were rated as having severe problems, while others showed few or no difficulties. Although the score range was wider in the brain-damaged patients, this was due to a single outlier who received a very high rating, and the means of the two groups were not significantly different (schizophrenic patients 12.90; brain damage patients 16.09). In both groups, RBMT screening scores also correlated significantly with carer ratings of memory failures ($r = 0.57$ for the schizophrenic patients and 0.48 brain-damaged patients).

CONCLUSION

Nowadays, there can be no real doubt that "memory belongs to the cognitive domains which show major impairment in schizophrenia", as Aleman et al. (1999) concluded in their meta-analysis. Whether in this case "major" means disproportionate to the general intellectual impairment also found in the disorder is a question that remains at the present time unanswered. Schizophrenic memory impairment does, however, appear to be specific in another sense, that of showing a pattern of dissociations, with impairment in episodic long-term memory being coupled with preservation of function in areas such as procedural and implicit memory and perhaps also short-term memory, especially verbal short-term memory.

Beyond this, considerably less is known. The available evidence suggests that cognitive impairment appears to represent an independent dimension of pathology in schizophrenia, which is a function of severity and chronicity of illness but is not closely linked to positive or negative symptoms (Mortimer & McKenna, 1994; De Vries et al., 2001). It is also an enduring feature of the disorder that, as far as is known, does not change significantly over time. A typical profile of IQ and neuropsychological test impairment has been found to be present at the time of first onset of illness, and follow-up studies have uniformly failed to find that the deficits worsen over time, at least in the short or medium term (Russell et al., 1997; Rund, 1998; Heaton et al., 2001). These findings have given rise to a paradox: memory and other cognitive deficits can be so marked in some patients that it seems unlikely that they could have been present and escaped notice prior to illness. Yet at the same time, all attempts to demonstrate progressive deterioration in cognitive function after the onset of illness have proved unsuccessful. To date, this paradox remains unresolved.

After an intensive search for brain pathology in schizophrenia over the last 25 years, it has been established that there are structural abnormalities in the disorder, taking the form of a modest degree of lateral ventricular enlargement (of around 25%) plus much smaller reductions (of the order of 2–3%) of brain substance (Harrison, 1999; Wright et al., 2000). No correlations between these structural abnormalities and any type of cognitive deficit have been demonstrated (Chua & McKenna, 1995), however, and patients with the most severe cognitive impairment do not stand out from the remainder in terms of their CT scan appearances (Owens et al., 1985; De Vries et al., 2001). Neither is there anything to be found at post mortem: the brains of elderly schizophrenic patients who were cognitively impaired in life show no excess of Alzheimer's, Pick's or Lewy body pathology, and no increase in any other marker for brain damage or dementia (see Harrison, 1999).

While, as described earlier, functional imaging carried out under resting conditions has failed to reveal consistent evidence of abnormality in schizophrenia, most of around 10 studies measuring blood flow or metabolism during performance of an executive task have found evidence for task-related or activation hypofrontality (see Weinberger & Berman, 1996). In contrast, studies using memory tasks, which also activate the prefrontal cortex, have generally found only marginal evidence of hypofrontality (Ganguli et al., 1997; Crespo-Facorro et al., 1999; Heckers et al., 1999). One study (Heckers et al., 1998) found that schizophrenic patients showed reduced hippocampal activation during a word recall task, but in several studies there have been no differences from normal subjects (Gur et al., 1994; Busatto et al., 1994; Fletcher et al., 1998). Surprising though it seems, schizophrenic patients appear on the whole to show a pattern of memory-associated brain activation that is qualitatively and quantitatively much the same as in normal subjects, even while they are performing poorly on the task.

A possible explanation of cognitive impairment in schizophrenia might be that it has a neurochemical basis. For a long time the leading biological approach to schizophrenia was a neurochemical one, the dopamine hypothesis, but direct evidence for increased brain dopamine in the disorder ultimately proved elusive (see McKenna, 1994). There is evidence that altered dopamine function can lead to worsening of cognitive function, e.g. in patients with Parkinson's disease in whom L-DOPA has been withdrawn (Lange, et al., 1992). However, the effects of dopamine agonist (e.g. Elliott et al., 1997; Kimberg et al., 1997) and antagonist drugs (e.g. Green et al., 1996; Mehta et al., 1999) on normal subjects have generally been found to be complex and not marked. Many other neurotransmitters have been proposed as candidates for abnormality in schizophrenia, but the current favourite is glutamate—this is based largely on the fact that glutamate antagonist drugs, such as phencyclidine and ketamine, can induce schizophrenia-like symptoms in normal individuals, and worsen existing symptoms in schizophrenic patients (see Hirsch et al., 1997). Interestingly, administration of ketamine to normal subjects has been found to produce quite marked impairment on memory, executive and other tests (Krystal et al., 1994; Newcomer et al., 1999).

An intriguing aspect of schizophrenic memory impairment, which sets it apart from that seen in the classical amnesic syndrome and most other types of amnesia, is the involvement of semantic memory. As one of the striking characteristics of schizophrenic patients is their disturbed knowledge about at least some aspects of the world, this raises the possibility that their symptoms might reflect a disturbance of semantic memory. Findings to date do not suggest that semantic memory impairment is related to schizophrenic symptoms in any direct way (e.g. Tamlyn et al., 1992; Duffy & O'Carroll, 1994). However, two recent studies have raised the possibility that in patients with delusions, semantic memory is disturbed in areas of knowledge that touch on their abnormal beliefs (Laws et al., 1995; Rossell et al., 1998). There are also claims that schizophrenic patients show increased semantic priming, which is particularly associated with the symptom of incoherence of speech (thought disorder or loosening of associations) (see Spitzer, 1997). Goldberg & Weinberger (2000) have argued that these and a number of other findings are robust enough to justify the claim that "thought disorder . . . is associated with and may result from semantic processing abnormalities".

REFERENCES

Aleman, A., Hijman, R., de Haan, E.H.F. & Kahn, R.S. (1999). Memory impairment in schizophrenia: a meta-analysis. *American Journal of Psychiatry*, **156**, 1358–1366.

Andreasen, N.C. (1999). A unitary model of schizophrenia: Bleuler's "fragmented phrene" as schizencephaly. *American Journal of Psychiatry*, **156**, 781–787.

Baddeley, A.D. & Wilson, B. (1988). Frontal amnesia and the dysexecutive syndrome. *Brain and Cognition*, **7**, 212–230.

Baddeley, A.D. & Wilson, B. (1994).When implicit learning fails: amnesia and the problem of error elimination. *Neuropsychologia*, **32**, 53–68.

Baddeley, A.D. (1986). *Working Memory*. Oxford: Clarendon Press.

Baddeley, A.D., Emslie, H. & Nimmo-Smith, I. (1992). *The Speed and Capacity of Language Processing (SCOLP) Test*. Bury St Edmunds: Thames Valley Test Co.

Bauman, E. & Murray, D.J. (1968). Recognition vs. recall in schizophrenia. *Canadian Journal of Psychology*, **22**, 18–25.

Bazin, N. & Perruchet, P. (1996). Implicit and explicit associative memory in patients with schizophrenia. *Schizophrenia Research*, **22**, 241–248.

Blanchard, J. & Neale, J. (1994). The neuropsychological signature of schizophrenia: generalized or differential deficit? *American Journal of Psychiatry*, **151**, 40–48.

Bleuler, E. (1911). *Dementia Praecox, or the Group of Schizophrenias* (translated 1950 by J. Zinkin). New York: International Universities Press.

Braff, D.L., Heaton, R., Kuck, J. et al. (1991). The generalized pattern of neuropsychological deficits in outpatients with chronic schizophrenia with heterogeneous Wisconsin Card Sorting Test results. *Archives of General Psychiatry*, **48**, 891–898.

Brebion, G., Amador, X., Smith, M.J. & Gorman, J.M. (1997). Mechanisms underlying memory impairment in schizophrenia. *Psychological Medicine*, **27**, 383–393.

Busatto, G.F., Costa, D.C., Ell, P.J. et al. (1994). Regional cerebral blood flow (rCBF) in schizophrenia during verbal memory activation: a ^{99m}Tc-HMPAO single photon emission tomography (SPET) study. *Psychological Medicine*, **24**, 463–472.

Calev, A. (1984a). Recall and recognition in mildly disturbed shcizophrenics: the use of matched tasks. *Psychological Medicine*, **14**, 425–429.

Calev, A. (1984b). Recall and recognition in chronic nondemented schizophrenics: use of matched tasks. *Joumal of Abnormal Psychology*, **93**, 172–177.

Calev, A. Berlin, H. & Lerer, B. (1987a). Remote and recent memory in long-hospitalised chronic schizophrenics. *Biological Psychiatry*, **22**, 79–85.

Calev, A. Korin, Y., Kugelmass, S. & Lerer, B. (1987b). Performance of chronic schizophrenics on matched word and design recall tasks. *Biological Psychiatry*, **22**, 699–709.

Calev, A., Venables, P.H. & Monk, A.F. (1983). Evidence for distinct memory pathologies in severely and mildly disturbed schizophrenics. *Schizophrenia Bulletin*, **9**, 247–264.

Chapman, L.J. & Chapman, J.P. (1973). *Disordered Thought in Schizophrenia*. New York: Appleton-Century-Crofts.

Chua, S.E. & McKenna, P.J. (1995). Schizophrenia—a brain disease? A critical review of structural and functional cerebral abnormality in the disorder. *British Journal of Psychiatry*, **166**, 563–582.

Clare, L., McKenna, P.J., Mortimer, A.M. & Baddeley, A.D. (1993). Long-term memory in schizophrenia: what is impaired and what is preserved? *Neuropsychologia*, **31**, 1225–1241.

Collins, A.M. & Quillian, M.R. (1969). Retrieval time from semantic memory. *Journal of Verbal Learning and Verbal Behavior*, **8**, 240–247.

Condray, R., Steinhauer, S.R., van Kammen, D.P. & Kasparek, A. (1996). Working memory capacity predicts language comprehension in schizophrenic patients. *Schizophrenia Research*, **20**, 1–13.

Conklin, H., Clayton, E., Katsanis, J. & Iacono, W. (2000). Verbal working memory impairment in schizophrenia patients and their first-degree relatives: evidence from the digit span task. *American Journal of Psychiatry*, **157**, 275–277.

Crawford, J.R., Obonsawin, M.C. & Bremner, M. (1993). Frontal lobe impairment in schizophrenia: relationship to intellectual functioning. *Psychological Medicine*, **23**, 787–790.

Crespo-Facorro, B., Paradiso, S., Andreasen, N.C. et al. (1999). Recalling word lists reveals "cognitive dysmetria" in schizophrenia: a positron emission tomography study. *American Journal of Psychiatry*, **156**, 386–392.

Cutting, J. & Murphy, D. (1988). Schizophrenic thought disorder: a psychological and organic interpretation. *British Journal of Psychiatry*, **152**, 310–319.

de Vries, P.J., Honer, W.G., Kemp, P.M. & McKenna, P.J. (2001). Dementia as a complication of schizophrenia. *Journal of Neurology, Neurosurgery and Psychiatry*, **70**, 588–596.

Duffy, L. & O'Carroll, R. (1994). Memory impairment in schizophrenia—a comparison with that observed in the alcoholic Korsakoff syndrome. Psychological Medicine, **24**, 155–165.

Elliott, R., McKenna, P.J., Robbins, T.W. & Sahakian, B.J. (1995). Neuropsychological evidence of frontostriatal dysfunction in schizophrenia. *Psychological Medicine*, **25**, 619–630.

Elliott, R., Sahakian, B.J., Matthews, K. et al. (1997). Effects of methylphenidate on spatial working memory and planning in healthy young adults. *Psychopharmacology*, **131**, 196–206.

Elliott, R., McKenna, P.J., Robbins, T.W. & Sahakian, B.J. (1998). Specific neuropsychological deficits in schizophrenic patients with perserved intellectual function. *Cognitive Neuropsychiatry*, **3**, 45–70.

Evans, J., Chua, S., McKenna, P. & Wilson, B. (1997). Assessment of dysexecutive syndrome in schizophrenia. *Psychological Medicine*, **27**, 635–646.

Fleming, K., Goldberg, T.E., Binks, S. et al. (1997). Visuospatial working memory in patients with schizophrenia. *Biological Psychiatry*, **41**, 43–49.

Fletcher, P.C., McKenna, P.J., Frith, C.D. et al. (1998). Neural responses in schizophrenia during a graded memory task studied with functional neuroimaging. *Archives of General Psychiatry*, **55**, 1001–1009.

Folstein, M.F., Folstein, S.E. & McHugh, P.R. (1975). "Mini-Mental State": a practical method for grading the cognitive state of patients for the clinician. *Journal of Psychiatric Research*, **12**, 189–198.

Frith, C.D. (1992). *The Cognitive Neuropsychology of Schizophrenia*. Hove: Erlbaum.

Ganguli, R., Carter, C., Mintun, M. et al. (1997). PET brain mapping study of auditory verbal supraspan memory versus visual fixation in schizophrenia. *Biological Psychiatry*, **41**, 33–42.

Gold, J.M., Randolph, C., Carpenter, C.J. et al. (1992b). Forms of memory failure in schizophrenia. *Journal of Abnormal Psychology*, **101**, 487–494.

Gold, J.M., Randolph, C., Carpenter, C.J. et al. (1992a). The performance of patients with schizophrenia on the Wechsler Memory Scale—Revised. *Clinical Neuropsychologist*, **6**, 367–373.

Gold. J.M., Carpenter, C., Randolph, C. et al. (1997). Auditory working memory and Wisconsin Card Sorting Test performance in schizophrenia. *Archives of General Psychiatry*, **54**, 159–165.

Goldberg, T., Torrey, E., Gold, J. et al. (1993). Learning and memory in monozygotic twins discordant for schizophrenia. *Psychological Medicine*, **23**, 71–85.

Goldberg, T.E. & Weinberger, D.R. (2000). Thought disorder in schizophrenia: a reappraisal of some older formulations and an overview of some recent studies. *Cognitive Neuropsychiatry*, **5**, 1–20.

Goldberg, T.E., Kelsoe, J.R., Weinberger, D.R. et al. K.R. (1988). Performance of schizophrenic patients on putative neuropsychological tests of frontal lobe function. *International Journal of Neuroscience*, **42**, 51–58.

Goldberg, T.E., Weinberger, D.R., Berman, K.F. et al. (1987). Further evidence for dementia of prefrontal type in schizophrenia? A controlled study of teaching the Wisconsin Card Sorting Test. *Archives of General Psychiatry*, **44**, 1008–1014.

Goldberg, T.E., Weinberger, D.R., Pliskin, N.H. et al. (1989). Recall memory deficit in schizophrenia: a possible manifestation of prefrontal dysfunction. *Schizophrenia Research*, **2**, 251–257.

Goldman-Rakic, P.S. & Friedman, H.R. (1991). The circuitry of working memory revealed by anatomy and metabolic imaging. In H.S. Levin, H.M. Eisenberg & A.L. Benton (eds), *Frontal Lobe Function and Dysfunction*. Oxford: Oxford University Press.

Goldstein, G. (1978). Cognitive and perceptual differences between schizophrenics and organics. *Schizophrenia Bulletin*, **4**, 160–185.

Granholm, E., Bartzokis, G., Asarnow, R.F. & Marder, S.R. (1993). Preliminary associations between motor procedural learning, basal ganglia T_2 relaxation times, and tardive dyskinesia in schizophrenia. *Psychiatry Research: Neuroimaging*, **50**, 33–44.

Gras-Vincendon, A., Danion, J.-M., Grange, D. et al. (1994). Explicit memory, repetition priming, and cognitive skill learning in schizophrenia. *Schizophrenia Research*, **13**, 117–126.

Gray, J.A., Rawlins, J.N.P., Hemsley, D.R. & Smith, A.D. (1991). The neuropsychology of schizophrenia. *Behavioral and Brain Sciences*, **14**, 1–84.

Green, M. F. (1996). What are the functional consequences of neurocognitive deficits in schizophrenia? *American Journal of Psychiatry*, **153**, 321–330.

Green, M., Kern, R., Braff, D. & Mintz, J. (2000). Neurocognitive deficits and functional outcome in schizophrenia: are we measuring the "right stuff". *Schizophrenia Bulletin*, **26**, 119–136.

Green, M.F., Kern, R.S., Williams, O. et al. (1997). Procedural learning in schizophrenia: evidence from serial reaction time. *Cognitive Neuropsychiatry*, **2**, 123–134.

Gruzelier, J., Seymour, K., Wilson, L. et al. (1988). Impairment on neuropsychological tests of temporohippocampal and frontohippocampal function in remitting schizophrenia and affective disorders. *Archives of General Psychiatry*, **45**, 623–629.

Gur, R.E., Jaggi, J.L., Shtasel, D.L. et al. (1994). Cerebral blood flow in schizophrenia: effects of memory processing on regional activation. *Biological Psychiatry*, **35**, 3–15.

Harrison, P. (1999). The neuropathology of schizophrenia: a critical review of the data and their interpretation. *Brain*, **122**, 593–624.

Heaton, R.K., Baade, L.E. & Johnson, K.L. (1978). Neuropsychological test results associated with psychiatric disorders in adults. *Psychological Bulletin*, **85**, 141–162.

Heaton, R.K., Gladsjo, J.A., Palmer, B.W. et al. (2001). Stability and course of neuropsychological deficits in schizophrenia. *Archives of General Psychiatry*, **58**, 24–32.

Heckers, S., Goff, D., Schacter, D.L. et al. (1999). Functional imaging of memory retrieval in deficit vs. nondeficit schizophrenia. *Archives of General Psychiatry*, **56**, 1117–1123.

Heckers, S., Rauch, S.L., Goff, D. et al. (1998). Impaired recruitment of the hippocampus during conscious recollection in schizophrenia. *Nature Neuroscience*, **1**, 318–323.

Heinrichs, R.W. & Zakzanis, K.K. (1998). Neurocognitive deficit in schizophrenia: a quantitative review of the evidence. *Neuropsychology*, **12**, 426–445.

Hirsch, S.R., Das, I., Garey, J.L. & Belleroche, J. (1997). A pivotal role for glutamate in the pathogenesis of schizophrenia and its cognitive dysfunction. *Pharmacology, Biochemistry and Behavior*, **56**, 797–802.

Hodges, J.R., Salmon, D.P. & Butters, N. (1992). Semantic memory impairment in Alzheimer's disease: failure of access or degraded knowledge? *Neuropsychologia*, **30**, 301–314.

Hutton, S.B., Puri, B.K., Duncan, L.J. et al. (1998). Executive function in first-episode schizophrenia. *Psychological Medicine*, **28**, 463–473.

Iddon, J., McKenna, P.J, Sahakian, B.J. & Robbins, T.W. (1998). Impaired generation and use of strategy in schizophrenia: evidence from visuospatial and verbal tasks. *Psychological Medicine*, **28**, 1049–1062.

Kazes, M., Berthet, L., Danion, J.M. et al. (1999). Impairment of consciously controlled use of memory in schizophrenia. *Neuropsychology*, **13**, 54–61.

Keefe, R.S.E. (2000). Working memory dysfunction and its relevance to schizophrenia. In T. Sharma & P. Harvey (eds), *Cognition in Schizophrenia*. Oxford: Oxford University Press.

Keri, S. Kelemen, O., Szekeres, G. et al. (2000). Schizophrenics know more than they can tell: probabilistic classification learning in schizophrenia. *Psychological Medicine*, **30**, 149–155.

Kern, R.S., Green, M.S. & Wallace, C.J. (1997). Declarative and procedural learning in schizophrenia: a test of the integrity of divergent memory systems. *Cognitive Neuropsychiatry*, **2**, 39–50.

Kimberg, D., D'Esposito, M. & Farah, M. (1997). Effects of bromocriptine on human subjects depend on working memory capacity. *Neuroreport*, **8**, 3581–3585.

King, D.J. (1990). The effect of neuroleptics on cognitive and psychomotor function. *British Journal of Psychiatry*, **157**, 799–811.

Koh, S.D. (1978). Remembering of verbal materials by schizophrenic young adults. In S. Schwartz (ed.), *Language and Cognition in Schizophrenia*. New York: Wiley.

Kolb, B. & Whishaw, I.Q. (1983). Performance of schizophrenic patients on tests sensitive to right or left frontal, temporal or parietal function in neurological patients. *Journal of Nervous and Mental Disease*, **171**, 435–443.

Kopelman, M.D., Stanhope, N. & Kingsley, D. (1999). Retrograde amnesia in patients with diencephalic, temporal lobe or frontal lesions. *Neuropsychologia*, **37**, 939–958.

Kraepelin, E. (1913). *Dementia Praecox and Paraphrenia* (translated 1919 by R.M. Barclay). Edinburgh: Livingstone.

Krystal, J.H., Karper, L.P., Seibyl, J.P. et al. (1994). Subanesthetic effects of the noncompetitive NMDA antagonist, ketamine, in humans. *Archives of General Psychiatry*, **51**, 199–214.

Landro, N.I., Orbeck, A.L. & Rund, B.R. (1993). Memory functioning in chronic and non-chronic schizophrenics, affectively disturbed patients and normal controls. *Schizophrenia Research*, **10**, 85–92.

Lange, K.W., Robbins, T.W., Marsden, C.D. et al. (1992). L-Dopa withdrawal in Parkinson's disease selectively impairs cognitive performance in tests sensitive to frontal lobe dysfunction. *Psychopharmacology*, **107**, 394–405.

Lawrie, S.M. & Abukmeil, S.S. (1998). Brain abnormality in schizophrenia. A systematic and quantitative review of volumetric magnetic resonance imaging studies. *British Journal of Psychiatry*, **172**, 110–120.

Laws, K. (1999). A meta-analytic review of Wisconsin Card Sort studies in schizophrenia: general intellectual deficit in disguise. *Cognitive Neuropsychiatry*, **4**, 1–35.

Laws, K., McKenna, P.J. & McCarthy, R.A. (1995). Delusions about people. *Neurocase*, **1**, 349–362.

Laws, K.R., Al-Uzri, M. & Mortimer, A.M. (2000). Lexical knowledge degradation in schizophrenia. *Schizophrenia Research*, **45**, 123–131.

Laws, K.R., McKenna, P.J. & Kondel, T.K. (1998). On the distinction between access and store disorders in schizophrenia: a question of deficit severity? *Neuropsychologia*, **36**, 313–321.

Liddle, P.F. & Morris, D.L. (1991). Schizophrenic symptoms and frontal lobe performance. *British Journal of Psychiatry*, **158**, 340–345.

Luria, A.R. (1971). Memory disturbance in local brain lesions. *Neuropsychologia*, **9**, 376–376.

Malec, J. (1978). Neuropsychological assessment of schizophrenia vesus brain damage: a review. *Journal of Nervous and Mental Disease*, **166**, 507–516.

McKay, A.P., McKenna, P.J., Mortimer, A.M. et al. (1996). Semantic memory is impaired in schizophrenia. *Biological Psychiatry*, **39**, 929–937.

McKenna, P.J. (1994). *Schizophrenia and Related Syndromes*. Oxford: Oxford University Press.

McKenna, P.J., McKay, A.P. & Laws, K. (2000). Memory in functional psychosis. In G.E. Berrios & J.R. Hodges (eds), *Memory Disorders in Clinical Practice*. Cambridge: Cambridge University Press.

McKenna, P.J., Tamlyn, D., Lund, C.E. et al. (1990). Amnesic syndrome in schizophrenia. *Psychological Medicine*, **20**, 967–972.

Morice, R. & Delahunty, A. (1996). Frontal/executive impairments in schizophrenia. *Schizophrenia Bulletin*, **22**, 125–137.

Morice, R. (1990). Cognitive inflexibility and prefrontal dysfunction in schizophrenia and mania. *British Journal of Psychiatry*, **157**, 50–54.

Morrison-Stewart, S.L., Williamson, P.C., Corning, W.C. et al. (1992). Frontal and non-frontal neuropsychological test performance and clinical symptomatology. *Psychological Medicine*, **22**, 353–359.

Mortimer, A.M & McKenna, P.J. (1994). Levels of explanation: symptoms, neuropsychological deficits and morphological abnormalities in schizophrenia. *Psychological Medicine*, **24**, 541–546.

Mortimer, A.M. (1997). Cognitive function in schizophrenia: do neuroleptics make a difference? *Pharmacology, Biochemistry and Behavior*, **56**, 789–795.

Nachmani, G. & Cohen, B.D. (1969). Recall and recognition free learning in schizophrenics. *Journal of Abnormal Psychology*, **74**, 511–516.

Nathaniel-James, D.A., Brown, R. & Ron. M.A. (1996). Memory impairment in schizophrenia: its relationship to executive function. *Schizophrenia Research*, **21**, 85–96.

Nelson, H., Pantelis, C., Carruthers, K. et al. (1990). Cognitive functioning and symptomatology in chronic schizophrenia. *Psychological Medicine*, **20**, 357–365.

Nelson, N.E. (1982). *The National Adult Reading Test (NART)*. Windsor: NFER-Nelson.

Newcomer, J.W., Farber, N.B., Jevtovic-Todorovic, V. et al. (1999). Ketamine-induced NMDA receptor hypofunction as a model of memory impairment and psychosis. *Neuropsychopharmacology*, **20**, 106–118.

O'Carroll, R., Russell, H.H., Lawrie, S.M. & Johnstone, E.C. (1999). Errorless learning and the cognitive rehabiliation of memory-impaired schizophrenic patients. *Psychological Medicine*, **29**, 105–112.

Ornstein, T.J., Sahakian, B.J. & McKenna, P.J. The stability and functional implications of memory and executive impairment in schizophrenia (submitted for publication).

Owens, D.G.C., Johnstone, E.C., Crow, T.J. et al. (1985). Lateral ventricular size in schizophrenia: relationship to the disease process and its clinical manifestations. *Psychological Medicine*, **15**, 27–41.

Pantelis, C., Barnes, T., Nelson, H. et al. (1997). Frontal-striatal cognitive deficits in patients with chronic schizophrenia. *Brain*, **120**, 1823–1843.

Park, S. & Holzman, P. (1992). Schizophrenics show spatial working memory deficits. *Archives of General Psychiatry*, **49**, 975–982.

Paulsen, J.S., Heaton, R.K., Sadek, J.R. et al. (1995). The nature of learning and memory impairments in schizophrenia. *Journal of the International Neuropsychological Society*, **1**, 88–99.

Payne, R.W. (1973). Cognitive abnormalities. In H.J. Eysenck (ed.), *Handbook of Abnormal Psychology*. London: Pitman.

Randolph, C., Gold, J.M, Carpenter, C.J. et al. (1993). Implicit memory in patients with schizophrenia and normal controls: effects of task demands and susceptibility to priming. *Journal of Clinical and Experimental Neuropsychology*, **15**, 853–866.

Rizzo, L., Danion, J.-M., Van der Linden, M. et al. (1996). Impariment of memory for spatial context in schizophrenia. *Neuropsychology*, **10**, 376–384.

Rossell, S.L., Shapleske, J. & David, A.S. (1998). Sentence verification and delusions: a content-specific deficit. *Psychological Medicine*, **28**, 1189–1198.

Rund, B.R. (1998). A review of longitudinal studies of cognitive functions in schizophrenia. *Schizophrenia Bulletin*, **24**, 425–436.

Rushe, T.M., Woodruff, P.W.R., Murray, R.M. & Morris, R.G. (1999). Episodic memory and learning in patients with chronic schizophrenia. *Schizophrenia Research*, **35**, 85–96.

Russell, A.J., Munro, J.C., Jones, P.B. et al. (1997). Schizophrenia and the myth of intellectual decline. *American Journal of Psychiatry*, **154**, 635–639.

Salame, P., Danion, J.M., Peretti, S. & Cuervo, C. (1998). The state of functioning of working memory in schizophrenia. *Schizophrenia Research*, **30**, 11–29.

Saykin, A., Shtasel, D., Gur, R. et al. (1994). Neuropsychological deficits in neuroleptic naive patients with first-episode schizophrenia. *Archives of General Psychiatry*, **51**, 124–131.

Saykin, A.J., Gur, R.C., Gur, R.E. et al. (1991). Neuropsychological function in schizophrenia: selective impairment in memory and learning. *Archives of General Psychiatry*, **48**, 618–624.

Schmand, B., Kop, W.J., Kuipers, T. & Bosveld, J. (1992). Implicit learning in psychotic patients. *Schizophrenia Research*, **7**, 55–64.

Schwartz, B.L., Rosse, R.B. & Deutsch, S.I. (1993). Limits of the processing view in acounting for dissociations among memory measures in a clinical population. *Memory and Cognition*, **21**, 63–72.

Schwartz, B.L., Rosse, R.B., Veazey, C. & Deutsch, S.I. (1996). Impaired motor skill learning in schizophrenia: implications for corticostriatal dysfunction. *Biological Psychiatry*, **39**, 241–248.

Shallice, T., Burgess, P.W. & Frith, C.D. (1991). Can the neuropsychological case-study approach be applied to schizophrenia? *Psychological Medicine*, **21**, 661–673.

Shoqeirat, M.A. & Mayes, A.R. (1988). Spatiotemporal memory and rate of forgetting in acute schizophrenia. *Psychological Medicine*, **18**, 843–853.

Smith, E.E. & Jonides, J. (1999). Storage and executive processes in the frontal lobes. *Science*, **283**, 1657–1661.

Spindler, K.A., Sullivan, E.V., et al. Menon, V. et al. (1997). Deficits in multiple systems of working memory in schizophrenia. *Schizophrenia Research*, **27**, 1–10.

Spitzer, M. (1997). A cognitive neuroscience view of schizophrenic thought disorder. *Schizophrenia Bulletin*, **23**, 29–50.

Stirling, J.D., Hellewell, J.S.E. & Hewitt, J. (1997). Verbal memory impairment in schizophrenia: no sparing of short-term recall. *Schizophrenia Research*, **25**, 85–95.

Stone, M., Gabrieli, J.D.E., Stebbins, G.T. & Sullivan, E. (1998). Working and strategic memory deficits in schizophrenia. *Neuropsychology*, **12**, 278–288.

Stratta, P., Daneluzzo, E., Prosperini, P. et al. (1997). Is Wisconsin Card Sorting Test Performance related to "working memory" capacity? *Schizophrenia Research*, **27**, 11–19.

Stuss, D.T. & Benson, D.F. (1984). Neuropsychological studies of the frontal lobes. *Psychological Bulletin*, **95**, 3–28.

Sunderland, A., Harris, J.E. & Baddeley, A.D. (1983). Do laboratory tests predict everyday memory? A neuropsychological study. *Journal of Verbal Learning and Verbal Behavior*, **22**, 341–357.

Tamlyn, D., McKenna, P.J., Mortimer, A.M. et al. (1992). Memory impairment in schizophrenia: its extent, affiliations and neuropsychological character. *Psychological Medicine*, **22**, 101–115.

Weinberger, D.R. & Berman, K.F. (1996). Prefrontal function in schizophrenia: confounds and controversies. *Philosophical Transactions of the Royal Society of London (B)*, **351**, 1495–1503.

Weinberger, D.R. (1987). Implications of normal brain development for the pathogenesis of schizophrenia. *Archives of General Psychiatry*, **448**, 660–669.

Wexler, B.E., Stevens, A.A., Bowers, A.A. et al. (1998). Word and tone working memory deficits in schizophrenia. *Archives of General Psychiatry*, **55**, 1093–1096.

Wilson, B.A., Alderman, N., Burgess, P.W. et al. (1996). *Behavioural Assessment of the Dysexecutive Syndrome*. Bury St. Edmunds: Thames Valley Test Co.

Wilson, B.A., Cockburn, J.M. & Baddeley, A.D. (1985). *The Rivermead Behavioural Memory Test*. Bury St Edmunds: Thames Valley Test Co.

Wilson, B.A., Cockburn, J.M., Baddeley, A.D. & Hiorns, R. (1989). The development and validation of a test battery for detecting and monitoring everyday memory problems. *Journal of Clinical and Experimental Neuropsychology*, **11**, 855–870.

Wright, I.C., Rabe-Hesketh, S., Woodruff, P.W. et al. (2000). Meta-analysis of regional brain volumes in schizophrenia. *American Journal of Psychiatry*, **157**, 16–25.

CHAPTER 20

Memory and Emotional Disorder

Tim Dalgleish
and
Sally G. Cox
MRC Cognition and Brain Sciences Unit, Cambridge, UK

Clients with clinical levels of emotional distress often complain of day-to-day problems with basic mental processes, such as memory and concentration (Watts & Sharrock, 1985). These difficulties fall into two broad categories. The first concerns the effects of emotional distress on general memory functioning (see Burt et al., 1995; Ellis & Ashbrook, 1989; for reviews, see Ellis & Moore, 1999; Watts, 1993). The second concentrates on the effects of emotional distress on memory for emotional material (see Blaney, 1986; Dalgleish & Watts, 1990; Matt et al., 1992; Teasdale & Barnard, 1993: for reviews, see Ellis & Moore, 1999; Williams et al., 1997). A consideration of these two themes and their theoretical and clinical implications forms the bulk of the present chapter.

Understanding more about the relationship between emotional problems and memory is important for a variety of reasons. First, accurate knowledge about the type and severity of cognitive problem associated with mood disturbances is often an important component in differential clinical diagnosis. In the most extreme cases, it is important to ascertain whether the client is suffering primarily from a memory disorder or is struggling with memory problems secondary to emotional distress; e.g. differentially diagnosing major depressive disorder (MDD) and senile dementia of the Alzheimer's type (SDAT) in elderly clients is notoriously difficult (e.g. Cummings, 1989; desRosier, 2000). Second, a number of intervention packages have been developed that focus on problems with basic cognitive processes such as memory (e.g. Fogler & Stern, 1987), and the use of these with mood-disturbed clients is dependent on a thorough understanding of the problems with which such individuals are grappling. Third, a number of psychological therapies, such as cognitive behavioural therapy (CBT; e.g. Beck, 1976) involve a substantive mnemonic component, both in the generation of material to work within the therapeutic session and prospectively for remembering to carry out homework assignments. It is therefore important to have a handle on the memory difficulties that may impinge on the therapeutic process.

The Handbook of Memory Disorders. Edited by A.D. Baddeley, M.D. Kopelman and B.A. Wilson
© 2002 John Wiley & Sons, Ltd.

Researchers have generally utilized a number of methodologies in examining memory–
emotion relations. Self-report techniques invariably reveal a high level of perceived memory
problems associated with emotional distress. However, it is unclear whether this reflects a
response bias towards the presentation of problems and difficulties, as opposed to a genuine
memory impairment. In parallel with self-report methods, a number of objective tests of
memory have been applied, using either emotionally neutral material (e.g. Hertel & Hardin,
1990) or hedonically toned material (e.g. Neshat-Doost et al., 1998). Such methodologies
have been applied to a range of participant groups; most usually, clinically diagnosed
participants have been compared with nonclinical controls (e.g. Watts et al., 1990). More
rarely, a clinical control group has been included (e.g. Gotlib, 1981). In some studies, clinical
individuals have been followed up and tested again following recovery or remission and
have thereby acted as their own controls (e.g. Stromgren, 1977). Finally, several studies
have examined analogues of clinical levels of emotional distress, such as major depressive
disorder (APA, 1994), in the form of subclinically distressed individuals and/or individuals
who have received some form of negative emotion induction.

Each of these objective approaches also has its particular difficulties. Comparisons of
clinical individuals with controls sheds little light on the specificity of any memory impairments to the particular clinical diagnosis. The use of clinical individuals as their own
controls runs the risk of practice effects and of statistical regression to the mean in an
initially below-average group, thus obscuring the true picture (e.g. Watts, 1993). The use
of analogue groups leaves the question of the generalizability of any findings to clinical
populations. Finally, many of the objective approaches potentially suffer from problems of
ecological validity. Performance on such memory tests may not be a valid reflection of day-
to-day mnemonic experience. Participants might be able to perform above their day-to-day
level for a short period of time, or they may be able to summon up uncharacteristic levels of
motivation for a formal test. All of these issues represent important caveats when it comes
to translating results from the laboratory into practice in the clinic.

Much of the work in the area of memory and emotional distress has focused on clinical
depression and/or depressed mood. For this reason, the present chapter uses depression as
a vehicle to examine the relationship between emotional distress and the following aspects
of memory: general memory functioning; memory for emotionally-valenced information;
the nature and style of autobiographical memory; and a brief note on memory intrusions.
In some of these domains there is an extensive literature focusing on emotional problems
other than depression and, where relevant, appropriate examples will be discussed.

GENERAL MEMORY PERFORMANCE

Depression seems linked to self-reported memory problems (e.g. Watts & Sharrock, 1985).
However, this association appears to be far stronger than that between depression and levels
of memory performance on objective tests (e.g. Kahn et al., 1975; O'Hara et al., 1986;
O'Connor et al., 1990; Scogin, 1985; Scogin et al., 1985; West et al., 1984). For example,
Kahn et al. (1975) studied participants with differing degrees of depression severity and
found a strong relationship between self-reported memory problems and level of depression,
but no correlation between level of depression and memory performance on objective tests.
Furthermore, certain neuropsychological tests, such as the Mental State Questionnaire,
predicted levels of objective memory performance but not the level of memory complaints.

A related issue was investigated by Scogin et al. (1985), who demonstrated that a structured memory training package had a beneficial effect on objective memory performance but not on memory complaints or, indeed, on levels of depressed mood.

This apparent finding of a discrepancy between self-reported memory problems and levels of performance on objective memory tests in depressed individuals clearly does not mean that depression is unassociated with memory impairments. There is a wealth of evidence that demonstrates impairments in general memory in depressed subjects relative to other groups (for a comprehensive listing, see Burt et al., 1995). For example, a seminal study by Cronholm & Ottosson (1961) compared depressed individuals with matched surgical patient controls on memory for word pairs, simple figures, and personal data about fictitious people, using both immediate and delayed memory tests. The depressed individuals showed significantly poorer memory on all three tests at both immediate and delayed testing relative to the controls, and these findings were replicated by Sternberg & Jarvik (1976). Deficits have also been found on tests of prospective memory. For example, Rude et al. (1999) showed that depressed participants were impaired, relative to controls, on a time-based prospective memory task.

In a meta-analysis of studies of depression and memory impairment on objective tests, Burt et al. (1995) concluded: "depression and memory impairment are significantly associated . . . a great amount of research with results contrary to those of the studies reviewed would be required to alter this conclusion". In fact, as Watts (1993) notes, a disproportionate number of the studies that do not reveal generic memory impairments in depressed groups have involved a comparison of older adult depressed participants with non-depressed older-adult controls—a comparison group in which the baseline level of memory difficulties may already be quite high (e.g. Hart et al., 1987; Whitehead, 1973). Other factors may also figure in the nonappearance of depression-related memory impairments including relatively easy memory tasks and the operation of mood repair processes such as increased attention (Ellis & Moore, 1999).

Burt et al. (1995) also included a number of moderator variables in their meta-analysis. The effects of the majority of these are difficult to interpret (e.g. depression subtype, medication status, stimulus type, and retention interval on the memory task). However, there are clear effects of patient status, with inpatients exhibiting a greater association between depression and memory performance than outpatients, and of age, with a greater association in younger depressives than in older subjects, where again the residual level of memory problems associated with depression in older populations seems the most likely explanatory factor (Watts, 1993).

In sum, there seems to be clear evidence of an association between depression and generic memory impairments. Indeed, there is a similar association in the literature between levels of generic memory impairment and clinical anxiety (for review, see Eysenck, 1992).This raises the questions of why this should be the case and what aspects of memory are impaired. Perhaps the most influential theory of general memory deficits in depression (and other emotional problems) is the Resource Allocation Model (RAM; Ellis & Ashbrook, 1988; see Ellis & Moore, 1999). The central thesis of RAM is a simple one, affective states reduce the amount of processing resources available for a given task. Thus, in the memory domain, the suggestion is that less resources are available for the elaboration, organization, encoding and retrieval of material into and out of memory. Much of the support for this approach is provided by studies with analogue populations (e.g. Ellis et al., 1984; Leight & Ellis, 1981). However, there are also a number of compelling studies with clinically depressed individuals. For example, Potts et al. (1989) (replicating a previous study by Ellis et al. 1984) took advantage of a finding from earlier research that recall is greater for material presented in a context that requires high levels of elaboration at encoding vs. one that requires low levels of elaboration (Stein & Bransford, 1979). Potts et al. found that this elaboration advantage was eliminated in depressed patients, suggesting that depression interferes with elaborative processing of neutral material. Other studies testing predications of RAM have produced more equivocal findings, e.g. Weingartner et al. (1981) reported no differences between clinically depressed participants and healthy controls on recall of structured word lists, but clear differences for the same material presented in an unstructured format, implying that depressed subjects may not have the resources to organize material at encoding. However, Levy & Maxwell (1968) using approximation-to-text as a method of structuring prose material found that depressed individuals benefited less from increased structure. Finally, Watts et al. (1990) found that depressed participants performed optimally when the material was of medium text approximation.

It seems that the RAM struggles to account for all of the available data, but this is perhaps not surprising as the model is somewhat underspecified. For example, Ellis (1990) has proposed that the RAM is completely agnostic as to where the depressed mood states have their effect. It is also unclear what is the underlying reason for a reduction in available processing resources. It may be because resources are employed in processing task-irrelevant depressogenic thoughts or, more simply, a general resource depletion. These more specific issues are increasingly the subject of research. For example, Ellis et al. (1990) provide evidence for higher levels of task-irrelevant unfavourable thoughts associated with depressed mood.

A somewhat different line on the depression and general memory literature has been provided by Paula Hertel and colleagues (e.g. Hertel & Hardin, 1990; Hertel & Rude, 1991). She suggests that depressed individuals are exhibiting a deficit in initiative rather than simply resource allocation; in other words, depressed individuals are less likely to initiate strategies or to generate appropriate hypotheses when performing unstructured tasks. In a set of experiments investigating this, Hertel & Hardin (1990) showed that depressed participants show no performance deficits relative to controls when provided with a clear task structure, thus indicating that the resources to perform the task are available if the depressed individuals are guided to the right strategies. Perhaps not surprisingly, Ellis & Moore (1999) have suggested that such choice of strategy and initiative is itself resource-dependent and that Hertel's findings present no problems for RAM.

Differential Diagnosis of Emotion-related Memory Problems vs. Organic Memory Problems

In elderly emotionally distressed populations (especially those with depression), a particular difficulty in the assessment and evaluation of memory difficulties is the possibility that the patients may be in the early stages of an organic illness such as dementia. The basic facts are that, first, emotional distress, especially depression, is associated with memory difficulties. Second, ageing itself is associated with memory difficulties. Third, memory difficulties in elderly emotionally distressed populations can therefore be reasonably severe. Fourth, a number of organic conditions are associated with memory difficulties. Finally, a proportion of elderly depressed patients (with memory difficulties) will indeed also be in the early stages of a progressive organic illness such as dementia (for review, see desRosiers, 2000).

The challenge for the clinician is, therefore, to differentiate between memory difficulties that are associated with emotional distress and that are therefore reversible (sometimes called depressive pseudodementia), memory difficulties that are associated with an organic illness that are nonreversible, and memory difficulties that are associated with both emotional distress and the early stages of an organic illness, and that are therefore partly reversible.

To meet this challenge, a considerable amount of research effort has been involved in finding measures that can reliably aid the diagnostician. To date, despite some strong claims in the literature, it is probably true to say that profiles on diagnostic tests cannot reliably distinguish between reversible, partly reversible and irreversible memory problems. Furthermore, it is therefore questionable whether such profiles can be used to avoid misdiagnosing patients as depressed and/or suffering from a progressive organic disorder (desRosiers et al., 1995).

In summary, there are clear generic mnemonic deficits associated with depression. This association is stronger for self-reported memory difficulties but remains substantial, even on objective memory tests with a stronger relationship being found in younger depressed subjects and in inpatients relative to outpatients. In elderly participants, great care has to be taken with the differential diagnosis of memory difficulties associated primarily with emotional distress vs. those due to a progressive organic disorder. Theoretical accounts of general memory deficits associated with emotional distress, such as Ellis & Ashbrook's Resource Allocation Model, have proved useful in setting the research agenda. However, they are perhaps underspecified and the time has come for more tightly defined theoretical frameworks. There is some light on the horizon here with the advent of multirepresentational theories of emotion, such as interacting cognitive subsystems (ICS; Teasdale & Barnard, 1993) and schematic, propositional, associative and analogue representational systems (SPAARS; Power & Dalgleish, 1997); however, the complex nature of these models precludes any detailed discussion in the present chapter.

MEMORY FOR VALENCED MATERIAL

Mood-congruent Memory

Mood-congruence effects refer to a memory bias where affectively toned material is more easily remembered if it is congruent with the individual's mood during retrieval. Unlike state-dependent memory (SDM) effects, when material which is learned in a particular mood is more likely to be recalled when in that same mood at retrieval, mood-congruency effects are agnostic to mood at encoding. SDM effects have often proved elusive (Bower et al., 1978) and, although robust, tend to be found only under very limited conditions (e.g. Schare et al., 1984).

Empirically, mood congruency and SDM are difficult to disentangle. This issue is particularly relevant if the researcher is unaware of mood at encoding, as is the case with recall of autobiographical memories. Hence, it is unreasonable to rule out a putative role of SDM in mood-congruency studies, and vice versa. It is perhaps therefore safer to assume that, in some studies, both of these processes may operate in combination.

Clearly, the idea of memory bias in favour of material that is congruent with the emotional state has clinical implications. In terms of maintenance, any distortions in cognitive processing that favour material that is likely to have a negative impact on mood are likely to maintain negative mood states and, in the worst cases, emotional disorder. Furthermore, biased processing in favour of mood-congruent emotional material is likely to be a problem for any talking therapy aimed at examining nonmood-congruent information as a strategy for treatment (e.g. CBT).

Mood-congruent memory is therefore a phenomenon that has been studied in depth and has been demonstrated with a wide variety of cognitive tasks, materials and subject samples (including naturally occurring mood in clinically depressed and subclinically depressed populations and induced moods) and has produced "relatively robust findings in clinical and experimental investigation" (Blaney, 1986).

The prototypical method of investigation in studies of mood-congruence involves exposing the participant to material with an affective valence and probing for memory of it in the same or different mood states. Memory is indexed through the speed and/or accuracy of recall/recognition. The main finding of interest, with relevance to depression, is that a depressed mood leads to lower levels of recall of positive material and in some cases facilitated recall of negative material relative to the performance of healthy controls, although the latter effect is less common. In a day-to-day situation the to-be-remembered material is most likely to be memories for events in the individual's life. In an attempt to see whether an emotional memory bias could be found under experimental conditions, Teasdale & Fogarty (1979) provided a sample of nondepressed participants with a list of neutral words to act as cues for the recall of positive or negative memories. They then induced an elated mood in half of the participants and a depressed mood in the remainder (Velten, 1968). Teasdale & Fogarty found that latencies to remember positive events were increased in the depressed group, relative to the controls. Clark & Teasdale (1982) asked a sample of clinically depressed individuals characterized by diurnal mood swings to retrieve positive or negative memories at different times in the daily cycle. Negative memories were more easily retrieved than positive memories in the more depressed mood and the opposite was true when in the less depressed mood. Finally, a biasing effect of mood on autobiographical memories using various mood induction techniques (e.g. hypnosis, success vs. failure on a laboratory task, music and naturally occurring depressed mood) has proved robust and has been found both with participants in an induced mood and clinically depressed individuals (e.g. Lloyd & Lishman, 1975; Gilligan & Bower, 1984; Teasdale et al., 1980; Williams & Scott, 1988).

The most common criticism of mood-congruence studies using autobiographical memories has been that the mood at encoding is unknown ensuring that one cannot reliably distinguish between SDM and mood-congruent effects. Furthermore, the relative balance of positive and negative memories for a given participant is an unknown. It is therefore not possible to say whether memory effects represent a genuine bias or merely reflect the profile of the embedded material. One way of avoiding this confound is to move away from the autobiographical domain and provide the to-be-learned material in the experiment proper, e.g. Bradley & Mathews (1983) supplied clinically depressed and nondepressed participants with lists of affectively valenced (positive and negative) words. The depressed group showed lower recall of positive material relative to controls. Memory bias effects using variations of this kind of paradigm have been shown in a large number of studies with subclinically (e.g. Gotlib & McCann, 1984; Ingram et al., 1983) and clinically depressed patients (e.g. Dunbar & Lishman, 1984; Neshat-Doost et al., 1998; McDowall, 1984, Study 1). The majority of these studies reveal that depressed participants either remember less positive material or more negative material, compared with controls.

A remaining issue reflects the relative contributions of mood at encoding and mood at retrieval to the memory bias, and mood induction studies have been used in an attempt to separate out the relative contributions of these two mnemonic operations, e.g. Isen et al. (1978) gave participants in a neutral mood a list of positive and negative personality trait words to learn. Participants were then randomly allocated to one of two groups. Both groups then played a game in which, by design, one group was bound to be successful and the other group was bound to fail. Participants in the "success" condition recalled more positive words, but subjects in the "failure" condition did not recall more negative words. This suggests that it is mood-biasing effects occurring at retrieval that underlie the mood and memory effect. However, Bower et al. (1981) suggested that mood-congruence effects also may involve a bias at encoding. In their study, a story including an equal number of happy and sad statements was read by participants, this time in a hypnotically-induced happy or sad mood. Mood-congruence effects were revealed, but there was *no* effect of mood at retrieval. Various reasons have been suggested for the lack of mood-congruent retrieval effects in Bower's study. It may be due to associations being made between items of opposite valence within the story or because the fictional material was not self-referent, as in other studies, e.g. Isen et al. (1978; see also e.g. Teasdale & Russel, 1983). Research consistently suggests that mood-congruence effects are obtainable only under self-referent conditions (Williams & Scott, 1988). It has been shown that if self-referencing is actively discouraged, mood-congruence effects are almost impossible to demonstrate (e.g. see Gotlib & Hammen, 1992).

There are a few studies which have failed to show mood-congruence effects associated with depression and/or depressed mood and it has been suggested that this is due to problems in experimental design or with the material used. Ellis & Ashbrook (1989), for example, have suggested that highly structured material, such as narrative passages with the to-be-learned material embedded within them (e.g. Hasher et al., 1985), are impervious to mood-congruent effects. It has also been argued that mood-congruence effects may not involve only purely automatic processes. Thus, individuals in a depressed mood may actively try to avoid negative material or retrieve happy memories, thereby overriding, to a greater or lesser extent, the automatic impact of mood-congruent accessibility, thereby leading to mood-incongruent effects (Singer & Salovey, 1988). Matt et al. (1992) have pointed out that mood-congruence studies have failed to consider that mood-congruent memory effects may vary in magnitude. In their review of a subset of the published research, they suggested that failure to find a mood-congruent effect may have been due to a lack of statistical power.

One paradoxical finding by researchers has been that there is no correlation between the level of depressed mood and differential recall of congruent material within a particular mood (Mathews & Bradley, 1983; Riskind, 1983). It has been suggested that this is due to the complex nature of cognitive states, and therefore it may not be mood *per se* that is responsible for mood-congruence effects, but perhaps processes involving priming of specific cognitive themes. Alternatively, mood states may be confounded with other characteristics of being in a particular mood, e.g. certain personality traits (Mayer & Salovey, 1988) and it is these that influence processing of information.

Although mood-congruent memory effects are a relatively robust finding in association with depression, the evidence with respect to anxiety and anxiety disorders is far less clear cut. There seems to be some evidence for a memory bias in favour of threatening information in panic disorder patients (e.g. Becker et al., 1999) and patients with PTSD (e.g. Moradi et al., 2000). However, the data for high levels of subclinical/trait) anxiety and for generalized anxious states such as generalized anxiety disorder (GAD) is much weaker (for review, see Williams et al., 1997).

As with the effects of emotional distress on general memory, various models have attempted to explain mood-congruence effects. There are often variations on a theme, and the intention here is to provide a brief overview of the most widely recognized and most elaborately developed of these approaches. The most commonly used model to explain mood-congruence is Bower's Associated Network Theory of Affect (e.g. Bower, 1981). This theory describes an associative network of nodes. Each emotion is represented as a central node in this network and can be activated by physiological or symbolic verbal means, and is linked to all associated aspects of that emotion; i.e. related ideas, events of corresponding valence, associated semantic material, autonomic activity and expressive behaviours. Bower suggests that mood-congruence effects occur owing to affectively valenced words being associated with the congruent emotion node; hence, at retrieval, when in a given mood the activated emotion node leads to a biased search and increased availability of mood-congruent materials due to spreading activation. However, this model is not able to explain many complex aspects of the data (such as the lack of reliable mood-congruency effects associated with anxiety), even with *post hoc* additions to the theory, and a major disadvantage of this model is that emotion is represented in the same network as semantic meaning (Dalgleish & Watts, 1990).

An alternative approach is based on schema theory, as applied by Beck and colleagues to depression (e.g. Beck, 1976; Beck et al., 1979). Beck proposes that, when an individual is in a prevailing mood (e.g. a depressed mood), a schema which is consistent with that mood state organizes and processes all new information in a biased, schema-congruent way. In the case of depression, the schema is purportedly concerned with negative aspects of the self, world and future, and consequently influences the retrieval of specific memories congruent with those themes. However, again, schema-based approaches, such as this, struggle with the fact that mood-congruent effects associated with anxiety are unreliable.

More sophisticated accounts of memory bias phenomena are offered by multirepresentational models such as ICS (Teasdale & Barnard, 1993) and SPAARS (Power & Dalgleish, 1997). However, the predictions of these theories are broadly in line with the simpler models of Bower and Beck and no discussion of the details of their respective architectures and processing parameters will therefore be offered.

In sum, research on mood-congruence effects suggests that individuals in a depressed mood remember relatively more negative and relatively less positive material than controls, but that this effect is considerably weaker, if not absent, in anxious individuals (with the possible exception of patients with panic disorder or PTSD).

AUTOBIOGRAPHICAL MEMORY STYLE

The majority of the research on both general memory processes and mood-congruent memory in individuals experiencing emotional distress has been concerned with the amount of material of particular types that is recalled. However, more recently researchers have also turned their attention to aspects of memory style, i.e. the structure of the recalled material. Perhaps the most carefully researched aspect of memory style has been the generality/specificity of autobiographical memories. Williams and colleagues (for review, see Healy & Williams, 1999) have found that emotionally distressed individuals have relative difficulty in generating specific autobiographical memories to emotional cue words, i.e. memories referring to events that happened on a particular day. Instead they tend to generate relatively more "overgeneral" memories that are categorical in nature, e.g. to the cue word "party", instead of saying, "I remember my best friend's 30th birthday party when we all went out for a meal", they might say, "All of the parties I've been to in the last 5 years have made me miserable". This tendency to generate overgeneral autobiographical memories seems to be a relatively robust finding (Healy & Williams, 1999). Perhaps more importantly, the number of overgeneral memories generated while an individual is in an emotionally distressed state seems to predict poorer long-term outcome, over and above baseline symptom measures (Brittlebank et al., 1993; Dalgleish et al., 2001). These data suggest that the tendency to generate overgeneral memories is not just an epiphenomenon of emotional distress, but rather reflects something more fundamental about the maintenance of distressed states. As was the case with mood-congruent memory, overgeneral memory effects are more reliably associated with depression than with anxiety. Overgeneral memory seems to be a feature of PTSD (e.g. McNally et al., 1995) but not more generally anxious states, such as GAD (Burke & Mathews, 1992).

A NOTE ON INTRUSIVE MEMORIES

As well as difficulties with the intentional recall of either general or emotionally valent materials, individuals in emotional distress are characterized by unintentional (intrusive) memories of past experiences (e.g. Uleman & Bargh, 1989). For certain disorders, such as PTSD, acute stress disorder and adjustment disorder, intrusive experiences are part of the diagnostic profile (APA, 1994). For other types of emotional distress, such as depression, intrusive memories are common (e.g. Brewin et al., 1996) but are not necessary for a diagnosis.

SUMMARY AND CLINICAL IMPLICATIONS

What are the clinical implications of the memory difficulties associated with emotional distress? The first is diagnostic. As already discussed, emotionally distressed individuals, because of the memory problems we have highlighted, may overlap in presentation with individuals with organic or neuropsychologically-based memory difficulties. Care is therefore called for in differential diagnosis, especially in the elderly population (e.g. Cummings, 1989).

The second issue concerns day-to-day therapeutic management of mood disorders. The pattern of memory problems, e.g. in depression, suggests that work on timetabling and diary management would not only be pragmatically helpful but would also mitigate against further damage to self-esteem arising from the forgetting of important information. Similarly, cognitive therapy with mood-disordered individuals revolves around working with autobiographical material and using it to challenge core beliefs and assumptions about the self. If mnemonic access to this material is slanted in a negative direction in mood-disordered individuals, then extra therapeutic work is indicated to generate positive memories for use in the cognitive therapy process.

The third issue relates to the research techniques themselves as much as to the findings they have generated. Cognitive psychology paradigms, such are those described in the present chapter, may provide a useful objective measure of mood disorder and may have potential applications in assessment and measurement of outcome. Admittedly, there is a long way to go from the sort of group effects that have been reviewed here to the development of cognitive tools which can be used reliably on an individual basis, and the jury is still out on this issue.

To summarize, in this chapter there has been an endeavour to do justice to the wealth of literature on mood and memory. It has been possible to offer only the briefest of summaries of the many studies in this area. However, it is hoped that the spirit of the findings has been captured, if not the letter, in our conclusion that high levels of emotional distress appear to be associated with deficits in general memory performance, mnemonic biases in favour of negative material and "away from" positive material, overgenerality of autobiographical memories, and high levels of unwanted and intrusive emotional memories.

REFERENCES

American Psychiatric Association (1994) . *Diagnostic and Statistical Manual for Mental Disorders*, 4th edn. Washington, DC: APA.
Becker, E.S., Roth, W.T., Andrich, M. & Margraf, J. (1999). Explicit memory in anxiety disorders. *Journal of Abnormal Psychology*, **108**, 153–163.
Beck, A.T. (1976). *Cognitive Therapy and the Emotional Disorders*. New York: Meridian.
Beck, A.T., Rush, A.J., Shaw, B.F. & Emery, G. (1979). *Cognitive Therapy of Depression*. New York: Guilford.
Blaney, P.H. (1986). Affect and memory: a review. *Psychological Bulletin*, **99**, 229–246.
Bower, G.H. (1981). Mood and memory. *American Psychologist*, **36**, 129–148.
Bower, G.H., Monteiro, K.P. & Gilligan, S.G. (1978). Emotional mood as a context for learning and recall. *Journal of Verbal Learning and Verbal Behaviour*, **17**, 573–587.
Bower, G.H., Gilligan, S.G. & Monteiro, K.P. (1981). Selectivity of learning caused by affective states. *Journal of Experimental Psychology: General*, **110**, 451–473.
Bradley, B. & Mathews, A. (1983). Negative self-schemata in clinical depression. *British Journal of Clinical Psychology*, **22**, 173–181.
Brewin, C.B., Phillips, E., Carroll, O. & Tata, P. (1996). Intrusive memories in depression. *Psychological Medicine*, **26**, 1271–1276.
Brittlebank, A. D., Scott, J., Williams, J. M. G. & Ferrier, I. N. (1993). Autobiographical memory in depression: state or trait marker? *British Journal of Psychiatry*, **162**, 118–121.
Burke, M. & Mathews, A. (1992). Autobiographical memory and clinical anxiety. *Cognition and Emotion*, **6**, 23–35.
Burt, D.B., Zembar, M.J. & Niederehe, G. (1995). Depression and memory impairment: a meta-analysis of the association, its pattern and specificity. *Psychological Bulletin*, **117**, 285–305.
Clark, D.M. & Teasdale, J.D. (1982). Diurnal variation in clinical depression and accessibility of memories of positive and negative experiences. *Journal of Abnormal Psychology*, **91**, 87–95.
Cronholm, B. & Ottosson, J.O. (1961). The experience of memory function after electroconvulsive therapy. *British Journal of Psychiatry*, **109**, 251–258.
Cummings. J.L. (1989) Dementia and depression: an evolving enigma. *Journal of Neuropsychiatry*, **1**, 236–242.
Dalgleish, T. & Watts, F.N. (1990). Biases of attention and memory in disorders of anxiety and depression. *Clinical Psychology Review*, **10**, 589–604.
Dalgleish, T., Spinks, H., Yiend, J. & Kuyken, W. (2001). Autobiographical memory style in seasonal affective disorder and its relationship to future symptom remission. *Journal of Abnormal Psychology*, **110**, 335–340.
desRosiers, G. (2000). Depressive pseudodementia. In G.E. Berrios & J.R. Hodges (eds), *Memory Disorders in Psychiatric Practice*. Cambridge: Cambridge University Press.
desRosiers, G., Hodges, J.R. & Berrios, G.E. (1995). The neuropsychological diffentiation of patients with very mild Alzheimer's disease and/or major depression. *Journal of American Geriatric Society*, **43**, 1256–1263.

Dunbar, G.C. & Lishman, W.A. (1984). Depression, recognition-memory and hedonic tone: a signal detection analysis. *British Journal of Psychiatry*, **144**, 376–382.

Ellis, H.C. (1990). Depressive deficits in memory: processing initiative and resource allocation. *Journal of Experimental Psychology: General*, **119**, 60–62.

Ellis, H.C. & Ashbrook, P.W. (1989). The "state" of mood and memory research: a selective review. Special Issue: Mood and memory: theory, research and applications. *Journal of Social Behaviour and Personality*, **4**, 1–21.

Ellis, H.C. & Moore, B.A. (1999). Mood and memory. In T. Dalgleish & M. Power (eds), *Handbook of Cognition and Emotion*. Chichester: Wiley.

Ellis, H.C., Thomas, R.L. & Rodriguez, I.A. (1984). Emotional mood states and memory: elaborative encoding, semantics processing, and cognitive effort. *Journal of Experimental Psychology: Learning, Memory, and Cognition*, **10**, 470–482.

Ellis, H.C., Seibert, P.S. & Herbert, B.J. (1990). Mood state effects on thought listening. *Bulletin of the Psychonomic Society*, **28**, 147–150.

Eysenck, M.W. (1992). *Anxiety: The Cognitive Perspective*. Hove, U.K.: Lawrence Erlbaum Associates.

Fogler, J. & Stern, L. (1987). *Memory Improvement Programs for Older Adults: A Training Manual*. Ann Arbor, MI: University of Michigan Turner Geriatric Clinic.

Gilligan, S.G. & Bower, G.H. (1984). Cognitive consequences of emotional arousal. In C. Izard, J. Kagen & R. Zajonc (eds), *Emotions, Cognitions and Behaviour*. (pp. 547–548). New York: Cambridge University Press.

Gotlib, I.H. (1982). Self-reinforcement and recall: differential deficits in depressed and non-depressed psychiatric inpatients. *Journal of Abnormal Psychology*, **90**, 521–530.

Gotlib, I.H. & McCann, C.D. (1984). Construct accessibility and depression: an examination of cognitive and affective factors. *Journal of Personality and Social Psychology*, **47**, 427–439.

Gotlib, I.H. & Hammen, C.L. (1992). *Psychological Aspects of Depression: Toward a Cognitive–Interpersonal Integration*. Chichester: Wiley.

Hart, R., Kwentus, A., Taylor, R. & Harkins, S.W. (1987). Rate of forgetting in dementia and depression. *Journal of Consulting and Clinical Psychology*, **55**, 101–105.

Hasher, L., Rose, K.C., Zacks, R.T. et al. (1985). Mood, recall, and selectivity in normal college students. *Journal of Experimental Psychology: General*, **114**, 104–118.

Healy, H. & Williams, J.M.G. (1999). Autobiographical memory. In T. Dalgleish & M. J. Power (eds), *Handbook of Cognition and Emotion*. Chichester: Wiley.

Hertel, P.T. & Hardin, T.S. (1990). Remembering with and without awareness in a depressed mood: evidence of deficits in initiative. *Journal of Experimental Psychology: General*, **119**, 45–59.

Hertel, P.T. & Rude, S.S. (1991). Recalling in a state of natural or experimental depression. *Cognitive Therapy and Research*, **15**, 103–127.

Ingram, R.E., Smith, T.W. & Brehm, S.S. (1983). Depression and information processing: self-schemata and the encoding of self-referent information. *Journal of Personality and Social Psychology*, **45**, 412–420.

Isen, A.M., Shalker, T.E., Clark, M. & Carp, L. (1978). Affect, accessibility of material in memory, and behaviour: a cognitive loop. *Journal of Personality and Social Psychology*, **36**, 1–12.

Kahn, R.L., Zarit, S.H., Hilbert, N.M. & Niederehe, G. (1975). Memory complaint and impairment in the aged: the effect of depression and altered brain function. *Archives of General Psychiatry*, **32**, 1569–1573.

Leight, K.A. & Ellis, H.S. (1981). Emotional mood states, strategies and state-dependency in memory. *Journal of Verbal Learning and Verbal Behaviour*, **20**, 251–266.

Levy, R. & Maxwell, A.E. (1968). The effect of verbal context on the recall of schizophrenics and other psychiatric patients. *British Journal of Psychiatry*, **114**, 311–316.

Lloyd, G.G. & Lishman, W.A. (1975). Effect of depression on the speed of recall of pleasant and unpleasant experiences. *Psychological Medicine*, **5**, 173–180.

McDowall, J. (1984). Recall of pleasant and unpleasant words in depressed subjects. *Journal of Abnormal Psychology*, **93**, 401–407.

McNally, R. J., Lasko, N. B., Macklin, M. L. & Pitman, R. K. (1995). Autobiographical memory disturbance in combat-related post-traumatic stress disorder. *Behaviour Research and Therapy*, **33**, 619–630.

Mathews, A. & Bradley, B. (1983). Mood and the self-referenced bias in recall. *Behaviour, Research and Therapy*, **21**, 233–239.

Matt, G.E., Vázquez, C. & Campbell, W.K. (1992). Mood-congruent recall of affectively toned stimuli: a meta-analytic review. *Clinical Psychology Review*, **12**, 227–255.

Mayer, J.D. & Salovey, P. (1988). Personality moderates the interaction of mood and cognition. In K. Fiedler & J. Forgas (eds), *Affect, Cognition and Social Behaviour* (pp. 87–99). Toronto: Hogrefe.

Moradi, A., Taghavi, R., Neshat-Doost, H. et al. (2000). Memory bias for emotional information in children and adolescents with PTSD: a preliminary study. *Journal of Anxiety Disorders*, **14**, 521–534.

Neshat-Doost, H., Taghavi, R., Moradi, A. et al. (1998). Memory for emotional trait adjectives in clinically depressed youth. *Journal of Abnormal Psychology*, **107**, 642–650.

O'Connor, D.W., Pollitt, P.A., Roth, M. et al. (1990). Memory complaints and impairment in normal, depressed and demented elderly persons identified in a community survey. *Archives of General Psychiatry*, **47**, 224–227.

O'Hara, M.W., Hinrichs, J.V., Kohout, F.J. et al. (1986). Memory complaint and memory performance in the depressed elderly. *Psychology and Aging*, **1**, 208–214.

Potts, R., Camp, C. & Coyne, C. (1989). The relationship between naturally occurring dysphoric moods, elaborative encoding and recall performance. *Cognition and Emotion*, **3**, 197–205.

Power, M. & Dalgleish, T. (1997). *Cognition and Emotion: From Order to Disorder*. Hove: Psychology Press.

Riskind, J.H. (1983). Nonverbal expressions and the accessibility of life experience memories: a congruency hypothesis. *Social Cognition*, **2**, 62–86.

Rude, S.S., Hertel, P.T., Jarrold, W. et al. (1999). Depression related impairments in prospective memory. *Cognition & Emotion*, **13**, 267–276.

Schare, M.L., Lishman, S.A. & Spear, N.E. (1984). The effects of mood variation on state-dependent retention. *Cognitive Therapy and Research*, **8**, 387–408.

Scogin, F. (1985). Memory complaints and memory performance: the relationship re-examined. Special Issue: Ageing and mental health. *Journal of Applied Gerontology*, **4**, 79–89.

Scogin, F., Storandt, M. & Lott, L. (1985). Memory skills training, memory complaints, and depression in older adults. *Journal of Gerontology*, **40**, 562–568.

Singer, J.A. & Salovey, P. (1988). Mood and memory: evaluating the network theory of affect. *Clinical Psychology Review*, **8**, 211–251.

Stein, B.S. & Bransford, J.D. (1979). Constraints on effective elaboration: effects of precision and subject generation. *Journal of Verbal Learning and Verbal Behaviour*, **18**, 769–777.

Sternberg, D.E. & Jarvik, M.E. (1976). Memory functions in depression. *Archives of General Psychiatry*, **33**, 219–224.

Stromgren, L.S. (1977). The influence of depression on memory. *Acta Psychiatrica Scandinavica*, **56**, 109–128.

Teasdale, J.D. & Fogarty, S.J. (1979). Differential effects of induced mood on retrieval of pleasant and unpleasant events from episodic memory. *Journal of Abnormal Psychology*, **88**, 248–257.

Teasdale, J.D. & Russel, M.L. (1983). Differential effects of induced mood on the recall of positive, negative and neutral words. *British Journal of Clinical Psychology*, **22**, 163–171.

Teasdale, J.D. & Barnard, P.J. (1993). *Affect, Cognition and Change: Remodelling Depressive Thought*. Hove: Erlbaum.

Teasdale, J.D., Taylor, R. & Fogarty, S.J. (1980). Effects of induced elation-depression on the accessibility of memories of happy and unhappy experiences. *Behaviour Research and Therapy*, **18**, 339–346.

Uleman, J.S. & Bargh, J.A. (eds)(1989). *Unintended Thought*. New York: Guilford.

Velten, E. (1968). A laboratory task for induction to mood states. *Behaviour Research and Therapy*, **6**, 473–482.

Watts, F.N. (1993). Problems of memory and concentration. In C.G. Costello (ed.), *Symptoms of Depression*, New York: Wiley.

Watts, F.N. & Sharrok, R. (1985). Description and measurement of concentration problems in depressed patients. *Psychological Medicine*, **15**, 317–326.

Watts, F.N., Dalgleish, T., Bourke, P. & Healy, D. (1990). Memory deficit in clinical depression: processing resources and the structure of materials. *Psychological Medicine*, **20**, 345–349.

Weingartner, H., Cohen, R.M., Murphy, D.L. et al. (1981). Cognitive processes in depression. *Archives of General Psychiatry*, **38**, 42–47.

West, R.L., Boatwright, L.K. & Schleser, R. (1984). The link between memory performance, self-assessment, and affective status. *Experimental Ageing Research*, **10**, 197–200.

Whitehead, A. (1973). Verbal learning and memory in elderly depressives. *British Journal of Psychiatry*, **123**, 203–208.

Williams, J.M.G. & Scott, J. (1988). Autobiographical memory in depression. *Psychological Medicine*, **18**, 689–695.

Williams, J.M.G., Watts, F.N., MacLeod, C. & Mathews, A. (1997). *Cognitive Psychology and Emotional Disorders*, 2nd edn. Chichester: Wiley.

CHAPTER 21

Psychogenic Amnesia

Michael D. Kopelman

*University Department of Psychiatry and Psychology,
St Thomas's Hospital, King's College London, UK*

Psychologically-based amnesia encompasses instances of persistent memory impairment, such as occurs in depression or (in extreme form) in a depressive pseudodementia. Alternatively, it can entail transient or discrete episodes of memory loss. The effects of depression on memory are considered in Chapter 20, and transient episodes of psychogenic memory loss are the subject of the present account. Such transient amnesias can be situation-specific, as occurs in amnesia for offences, fragments of recall in posttraumatic stress disorder, and in amnesia for childhood sexual abuse. In other cases, the transient amnesia can involve a more global memory deficit, often accompanied by a loss of the sense of personal identity, such as occurs in a psychogenic "fugue" state. Whilst these latter instances are the stuff of film and fiction (usually in grossly distorted form), it is important to recognize that situation-specific amnesia is much more commonplace, coming to the attention of clinical and forensic psychologists, psychiatrists and neurologists.

Various forms of terminology are commonly used in discussing this issue. The present writer favours the term "psychogenic amnesia", because it does not make any assumptions about mechanism (as does "dissociative amnesia") or about the degree to which memory loss results from unconscious processes ("hysterical amnesia"), rather than motivated/deliberate/conscious processes ("factitious" or exaggerated amnesia). The term "functional amnesia" is somewhat unsatisfactory in that there are, of course, deficits in function (or "processing") in organic amnesia, and the salient feature of psychogenic amnesia is that, in some sense, it is always "dysfunctional". On the other hand, it can be argued that the term "psychogenic" makes assumptions about underlying aetiology and begs questions about when, and in what circumstances, a psychological stress is sufficient to become "psychogenic". However, similar criticisms can be made in cases of "organic" amnesia, where the markers of pathophysiology are not necessarily clear-cut; and the necessary and sufficient criteria for the attribution of causality to any given "lesion" have been insufficiently addressed in the neuropsychological literature (Kopelman, 2000a).

The present chapter will discuss examples of situation-specific and global psychogenic amnesia in turn.

The Handbook of Memory Disorders. Edited by A.D. Baddeley, M.D. Kopelman and B.A. Wilson
© 2002 John Wiley & Sons, Ltd.

SITUATION-SPECIFIC PSYCHOGENIC AMNESIA

Situation-specific psychogenic amnesia refers to a brief, discrete episode of memory loss, usually relating to a traumatic event in the individual's personal history: this is known as "dissociative amnesia" in DSM-IV (American Psychiatric Association, 2000).

Amnesia for Offences

This is important because, although controversial (Schacter, 1986a, 1986b, 1986c; Kihlstrom & Schacter, 2000), clinical and forensic psychologists, psychiatrists and neurologists are often asked to assess defendants claiming amnesia for their alleged crimes. Whilst there is a burgeoning experimental literature on eyewitness testimony, there is a relative dearth of experimental studies investigating this intriguing form of forgetting.

Amnesia has been reported most commonly in cases of homicide. In six studies conducted between 1948 and 1985, it was found that 23–47% of those convicted of homicide claimed amnesia for the killing (Leitch, 1948; Guttmacher, 1955; O'Connell, 1960; Bradford & Smith, 1979; Taylor & Kopelman, 1984; Parwatikar et al., 1985). In a recent study of all offenders given life sentences in 1994, Pyszora et al. (2002) found that 31% of convicted homicide cases had claimed amnesia at trial. Amnesia also arises following other types of crime, but three studies carried out in very different settings showed a clear relationship with the violence of the offence: these studies were carried out in a maximum security hospital (Hopwood & Snell, 1933), a forensic psychiatry outpatient service in Canada (Lynch & Bradford, 1980), and in a remand prison in the UK (Taylor & Kopelman, 1984). Studies of the victims and eyewitnesses of offences have also revealed that impaired recall is related to the violence of the crime (e.g. Kuehn, 1974; Clifford & Scott, 1978; Yuille & Cutshall, 1986).

In the absence of a substantive, prospective study of this topic, there are conflicting views about the persistence of such amnesia (Leitch, 1948; O'Connell, 1960; Bradford & Smith, 1979). In a retrospective study, Pyszora et al. (2002) found that, at 3 year follow-up, 33% of an amnesic sample were reported to have complete return of memory, 26% had partial return, and 41% no return of memory.

Amnesia for offences appears to occur in four main types of circumstance:

1. *Crimes of passion.* Amnesia appears to be particularly important in homicide cases where the offence was unpremeditated and took place in a state of extreme emotional arousal, the victim usually being closely related to the offender—a wife, lover, close friend or family member. There is often an accompanying diagnosis of depression and occasionally of schizophrenia (Hopwood & Snell, 1933; O'Connell, 1960; Bradford & Smith, 1979; Taylor & Kopelman, 1984).

   > A 40-year-old Egyptian was married to an English woman with two young children. When he discovered that his wife was having an affair with a musician, he became depressed, and he was treated with an antidepressant as an outpatient at his local hospital. During the afternoon of the offence, he had a furious row with his wife, during which he threatened to kill the musician. Later, he could recall going to kiss his daughter good night, but he could not remember anything after that until the police arrived. However, in the meantime, he had telephoned the police, and he was subsequently charged with the murder of his wife by stabbing.

2. *Alcohol abuse and intoxication*. There is commonly a history of chronic alcohol abuse and/or intoxication at the time of the offence in amnesic subjects (O'Connell, 1960; Bradford & Smith, 1979; Taylor & Kopelman, 1984; Parwatikar et al., 1985). In three of these studies, other drugs were also implicated, although the types of substance were not specified. Alcohol could produce amnesia either from a so-called "blackout" or as a state-dependent phenomenon (Goodwin et al., 1969).

> A 20-year-old man had consumed eight or more pints of beer plus three whiskies in the course of an evening. The last thing he could recall was being in a night-club with friends, who had been threatened by a rival gang, and who were then pacified by attendants. Continuous memory returned early the following morning, whilst he was being interviewed in the police station, although there were "islets" of preserved memory in between: peering down from a roof above a shop, being kicked by a policeman whilst up on the roof, being made to descend a ladder with handcuffs on. He had no idea how he had climbed up the roof or why. The accused was charged with assaulting a police officer whilst under the influence of alcohol. Eight months after the offence, there had been some infilling of memory between the "islets", and shrinkage of the amnesic gap from about 6 h to approximately 2 h.

3. *Psychosis/delusional memory*. Some studies report that a small group of patients are found to have committed offences during floridly psychotic episodes (Taylor & Kopelman, 1984). These offences often consist of criminal damage or minor acts of aggression, but the account given of them by their perpetrator, although stated with apparent conviction, is at complete variance with what others had observed. Occasionally, such anomalous or even delusional memories may result in charges being brought inappropriately.

> A young man, who had a history of recurrent hospital admissions for schizophrenia, reported that he had gone into a fish-and-chip shop, that he had looked into the eyes of a Chinese serving woman, and that he had asked for cod roe. He said the lights had then become bright, and that he had fainted, and he could not remember anything else. In fact, there had been no loss of consciousness or altercation—he had suddenly picked up a bar and started smashing the ovens.

4. *Brain disorder/automatism*. As in the case of severe intoxication, this is not "psychogenic" but it is very important to differentiate from the psychogenic forms of memory loss in this context because, in the UK and in many other jurisdictions, amnesias resulting from an organic factor may have important legal implications. Although lawyers are very much aware of this, it should be noted that automatisms are a very rare cause of amnesia for an offence, and they did not feature in at least two surveys of this topic (Bradford & Smith, 1979; Taylor & Kopelman, 1984).

Epileptic automatisms or postictal confusional states occasionally result in crime. When this occurs, EEGs subsequently reveal that the seizure activity has involved the hippocampal and parahippocampal structures bilaterally as well as the mesial diencephalon (Fenton, 1972). As these structures are crucial for memory formation, amnesia for the period of automatic behaviour is always present and is usually complete (Knox, 1968). There is no automatism without amnesia. Consequently, assessment requires a convincing history of both epilepsy and amnesia. Since the case of *R. vs. Sullivan* (reported by Fenwick, 1990), the English courts have regarded epileptic automatisms as a form of "insane automatism", resulting from "intrinsic" brain disease, liable to recur and therefore requiring compulsory psychiatric treatment, often in a secure hospital.

Hypoglycaemia can result from insulin-treated diabetes, alcohol intoxication, insulinoma, insulin abuse, or the "dumping" syndrome. Insulin abuse has been implicated in a number of serious offences, including violent crimes against children (Scarlett et al., 1977; Lancet, 1978). Where hypoglycaemia has resulted from the administration of an "extrinsic" agent such as insulin, the case for a "sane" automatism can be argued, potentially resulting in acquittal (in England and Wales and many other jurisdictions). The present author managed to argue successfully for an acquittal in the case of a young diabetic man who delayed taking a meal after self-administering his insulin because he had become interested in a television programme; subsequently, he killed a friend without any apparent motivation, and he was clearly hypoglycaemic when the police arrived.

Sleepwalking or somnambulism has also been used as grounds for automatism. It occurs most commonly in childhood and adolescence, and occasionally in adult life when precipitated by fatigue, mental stress, sleep deprivation, drugs or alcohol, or a change in the sleeping environment (Kales et al., 1980; Howard & d'Orbán, 1987; Fenwick, 1990). It most commonly occurs within 2 h of falling asleep, and episodes last only a few minutes. There are a substantial number of case-reports in the medical and legal literature of violent attacks during sleepwalking, often involving strangulation, attempted strangulation or the use of available implements as weapons with a sleeping partner as the victim (Howard & d'Orbán, 1987; Fenwick, 1990). Most commonly in these case-reports, there has not been any hostility between the offender and the victim and the behaviour is entirely out of character. Characteristically, episodes of violence accompanying sleepwalking terminate in the subject appearing confused on awakening, recalling relatively little of any accompanying dream, but being aware of a sense of acute dread or terror in such a dream (so-called "night terrors"). This arises because sleepwalking and night terrors characteristically occur in stage 4 of slow-wave sleep, shortly before the transition to rapid-eye-movement (REM) sleep. It used to be thought that violent offences could not occur in association with REM sleep because the subject was paralysed and could not sleepwalk; however, since the identification of REM sleep behaviour disorder (Schenck et al., 1986), episodes of lashing out or more organized violence against a sleeping partner have indeed been reported.

Authentic Amnesia or Deliberate Malingering?

Many observers consider that the amnesia claimed by offenders is a deliberate strategy to try to avoid the legal consequences of their offence (e.g. Schacter, 1986a). In view of this, Hopwood & Snell (1933) conducted a retrospective review of follow-up information in the case-notes of 100 Broadmoor high-security patients who, at the time of their trials, had claimed amnesia for their offences; they concluded that 78% of the amnesias had been "genuine", 14% had been "feigned", and 8% were "doubtful". However, there are a number of other reasons for supposing that many cases of amnesia are authentic, even though this is always hard (if not impossible) to prove.

First, many offenders give a very similar account of their memory loss, viz. a brief "amnesic gap" lasting an hour or less for the period of the offence. Some use phrases somewhat similar to those employed by fugue patients (e.g. Kopelman & Morton, 2001) to describe their memory loss. For example, O'Connell (1960) described amnesic offenders who reported having "buried everything about (the) case" and feeling that recollection would be "so . . . horrifying . . . that I just can't remember anything" or that "there is something in my mind . . . it seems to be forming a picture and then . . . my head hurts . . . [and] it gets all jumbled up again".

Second, many amnesic cases have been described in the literature who either have reported their own crime or failed to take measures to avoid their capture (Hopwood & Snell, 1933; Leitch, 1948; Gudjonsson & Mackeith, 1983; Taylor & Kopelman, 1984; Gudjonsson & Taylor, 1985). This makes an account of amnesia as simulation in order to avoid punishment seem less plausible. This was true of the Egyptian's case-history given above, and Gudjonsson & MacKeith (1983) reported a similar incident:

> A 67-year-old man had apparently battered his wife to death without any obvious motive, before telephoning the police and giving himself up. On their arrival, he reported that he had no memory of the actual attack, but that he recalled standing over the body realizing that he had been responsible for his wife's death. His memory had not cleared by the time of the Court hearing.

Third, it should be noted that the factors which have been associated with amnesia in offenders overlap with those that have been implicated in cases of impaired recall by the victims or eyewitnesses of crime—in particular, violent crime, extreme emotional arousal and alcohol intoxication (e.g. see Kuehn, 1974; Clifford & Scott, 1978; Yuille & Cutshall, 1986; Deffenbacher, 1988; Yuille, 1987). Nobody questions the motivation of eyewitnesses or victims whose recall is impaired.

Fourth, it should be reiterated that, in English law (and in many other, but not all, jurisdictions), amnesia *per se* does not constitute either a barrier to trial or any defence. For amnesia to contribute to the question of responsibility, other issues have to be raised, such as epilepsy or other forms of organic brain disease. Most lawyers are aware of this but, nevertheless, their clients continue to plead amnesia even in instances where recall of what actually happened would be helpful to their cause.

Posttraumatic Stress Disorder (PTSD)

Posttraumatic stress disorder (PTSD) can occur in association with head injury, road traffic accidents, being the victim of a violent crime, or a major disaster (e.g. the sinking of the *Herald of Free Enterprise* at Zeebrugge, or the King's Cross fire in the London Underground). As is well known, it is characterized by intrusive thoughts and memories ("flashbacks") about the traumatic experience, as well as anxiety and avoidance phenomena, a startle reaction, and a variety of other cognitive and somatic complaints (Raphael & Middleton, 1988). However, there may be instances of partial memory loss ("fragmentary" memory), distortions, or even frank confabulations.

Most commonly, there is disorganization in the retrieval of memory for the trauma, evident as gaps in recall and difficulty in producing a coherent narrative: this disorganization may partially explain the tendency for PTSD patients in psychotherapy to recall progressively additional detail of their traumatic experience as therapy progresses (Harvey & Bryant, 2001; Brewin, 2001). With regard to confabulation, the present author saw a victim of the *Herald of Free Enterprise* at Zeebrugge, who described trying to rescue a close friend whilst still on board the ship, when other witnesses reported that this close friend had not been seen from the moment that the ship turned over. Although factors such as head injury or hypothermia may confound the interpretation of such cases, it is of interest that PTSD symptoms have been reported to occur even when the subject appears to have been completely amnesic for the episode (McNeil & Greenwood, 1996; Harvey et al., 2001). Moreover, PTSD victims may show deficits in anterograde memory on formal tasks many years after the original trauma (Bremner et al., 1993), and there are claims that they show a loss of hippocampal volume on MRI brain scan (Bremner et al., 1995), which has been attributed to effects on glucocorticoid levels (Markowitsch, 1996). However, these MRI findings have to be interpreted with caution in view of the rather crude measurements employed, as even the control values were a long way out-of-line with those of most other investigations (Colchester et al., 2001).

A recent review (Brown et al., 1999) documented evidence of amnesia in the victims of lightening flashes, flood disasters, pipeline explosions, earthquakes, concentration camp and holocaust survivors, refugees, and traumatized soldiers from the two world wars and Vietnam. Other reviews have cited instances of kidnap and torture (Van der Kolk & Fisler, 1995). The psychological impact of a road traffic accident may also give rise to amnesia (Harvey, 2000; Kopelman, 2000b), although it may be difficult to separate this from the effects of concussion.

Harvey (2000) reported a personal instance of memory loss for the events of a life-threatening accident in the absence of any apparent concussion or violent acceleration/deceleration forces. He concluded that this was a "posttraumatic amnesia in which the trauma was wholly psychological". It is to be noted that he could recall that the front seat passenger was wearing a flowery hat in the car that had swerved across the road in front of him, that the car was a small red Honda saloon, and that a black and white soft toy was dangling in the rear window, but he forgot what happened after he noticed this. It is characteristic that, in trauma, some memories are enhanced, detailed, and may be re-called intrusively thereafter, whereas other items are forgotten. Similarly, in head injury, Russell & Nathan (1946) referred to memories with the quality of "visions" arising from a brief "lucid interval" before the onset of posttraumatic amnesia, e. g. the screech of brakes or the flashing of ambulance lights. In head injury, amnesia predominates and such vivid memories are infrequent, whereas in PTSD intrusive memories predominate and memory lapses are less common. Nevertheless, the two seem to lie at the extremes of a continuum: what is poorly understood in both instances is why certain things are forgotten, whereas others are vividly remembered.

In this connection, Brewin et al. (1996; Brewin, 2001) have produced a dual representation theory of PTSD. According to this, memories of a personally experienced traumatic event can be of two distinct types, stored in different representational formats. One type of format ("verbally accessible memory" or VAM) supports ordinary autobiographical memories that can be retrieved either automatically or using deliberate strategic processes. VAM memories can be edited and interact with the rest of autobiographical memory, so that the trauma is represented within a complete personal context comprising past, present, and future. Such memories contain information that the individual attended to before, during, and after the traumatic event, and which received sufficient conscious processing to be transferred to a long-term memory store in a form that can be deliberately retrieved at a later date, but which are also subject to normal processes of forgetting. The second type of format ("situationally accessible memory" or SAM) supports the specific trauma-related "flashbacks" and dreams that are characteristic of PTSD. The SAM system contains information that has been obtained from more extensive lower-level perceptual processing of the traumatic scene with little conscious processing, including the person's autonomic and motor responses to the scene. This results in flashbacks being more detailed and affect-laden than ordinary memories. Because the SAM system does not use verbal codes, these memories are difficult to communicate to others, and they do not necessarily interact with other autobiographical memories. They are also difficult to control, because people cannot always regulate their exposure to sights, sounds, smells, etc., which act as cues to these flashbacks.

Child Sexual Abuse

The fraught issue of memory for child sexual abuse can be viewed as an aspect of this topic. For many years, child psychologists and child psychiatrists have reported that abused children or adolescents appear amnesic for what has happened, but, in the last decade, this has become a hugely controversial topic. In reviewing the literature, Pope & Hudson (1995) found only four investigations bearing upon this issue, and they criticized these studies on the basis that *either* the original abuse had not been corroborated *or* the findings were heavily dependent upon self-report, in which case a report of past forgetting needed to be corroborated. On the other hand, even the most forthright protagonists of "false memory" have found that 19% of victims of abuse have reported forgetting at some time in the past (Loftus et al., 1994), and Brown et al. (1999) claimed that there was evidence of forgetting in all 68 studies they reviewed on this topic. Whilst there are indeed problems in evaluating self-reports of amnesia for child abuse, some smaller-scale studies have examined the corroborative evidence for the trauma and the subsequent forgetting in some detail (Schooler et al., 1997). Other researchers have suggested that the memories for abuse are never actually completely forgotten, but that they are retained in a vague unelaborated form, poorly located in temporal and spatial context (Schacter, 1996; Shimamura, 1997). Such memories would be vulnerable to the normal processes of decay and interference as well as to conscious avoidance and suppression. Appropriate cueing or triggers might result in the re-retrieval of these memories (Andrews et al., 2000), but the "weak trace" would make them particularly vulnerable to distortion and augmentation.

Trauma as Cause or Coincidence?

More recently, Kihlstrom & Schacter (2000) have queried the nature of the association between trauma and amnesia. In part, their argument reflects the fact that there is a dearth of controlled studies and that, more typically, traumatic memories are held with enhanced intensity. However, they also make the important point that "in the final analysis, the fact that functional amnesia often occurs in association with trauma does not mean that trauma causes amnesia, either directly (like the mental equivalent of a concussive blow to the head) or through some psychological process (like repression or dissociation)".

It is certainly true that trauma does not necessarily cause amnesia: there are many cases where people survive trauma without any memory loss. Against this, it can be pointed out that a severe precipitating stress appears to be a prerequisite for the onset of "fugue" (see below), that amnesia for offences shows characteristic features as described above, and that

PTSD and the resulting disorganization and disruption of memory (as described by Brewin, 2001) appear to be very common phenomena—certainly much more common than multiple personality disorder, which Kihlstrom & Schacter (2000) appear to accept. It needs to be acknowledged, however, that a person's cognitive response to trauma—determining whether or not amnesia develops—is likely to be influenced by factors such as his/her current mood state, past experience of memory loss, and underlying personality traits (see below).

GLOBAL PSYCHOGENIC AMNESIA

Psychogenic Fugue

A "fugue state" refers, in essence, to a syndrome consisting of a sudden loss of all autobiographical memories and the sense of self or personal identity, usually associated with a period of wandering, for which there is a subsequent amnesic gap upon recovery. Kihlstrom & Schacter (2000) point out that there is often a brief delay or lag between the end of the period of wandering and recovery of memory for personal identity. Fugue states usually last a few hours or days only, and they appear to have occurred more commonly earlier in the century, particularly during war time (Hunter, 1964). Where a fugue lasts much longer than this, the possibility of deliberate simulation must be strongly considered. Psychogenic fugues are classified in DSM-IV (American Psychiatric Association, 2000) as "dissociative fugues", and they have also been labelled as "functional retrograde amnesia" (RA) (Schacter et al., 1982).

> Schacter et al. (1982) described a young man who developed "functional RA" after attending the funeral of his grandfather, to whom he had been very close. When asked to retrieve autobiographic memories to cue-words, the median age of his retrieved memories was very brief, relative to both healthy controls and his own subsequent (post-recovery) performance. However, there were some preserved "islands" of autobiographical memory evident when he was "constrained" to produce memories from his earlier life: it emerged that these "islands" of preserved memory came from what he subsequently described as the happiest period of his life. He recovered his memories after seeing a television programme in which a funeral was shown.
>
> Kopelman et al. (1994a) described a 40-year-old woman who "came round" on the London Underground, unaware of who or where she was. She carried a bag, containing some clothes and an envelope addressed to a name (which subsequently turned out not to be hers). It eventually emerged that, following a marital crisis, this woman had disappeared from her home and had taken a flight across the Atlantic. There was a persistent amnesic gap for a 1 week period, which was thought to reflect an authentic fugue state, although this lady was shown to be at least partially simulating some 3 months after being first seen. During that period, she showed a "reversed" temporal gradient on standardized tests of autobiographical and public event remote memory.
>
> Kopelman et al. (1994b) described a 55-year-old man who, after being confronted with embezzlements he was alleged to have made from his work place, disappeared from his home the following morning, emerging in the railway station of the city where he grew up (500 miles away) that evening. He also disappeared for a briefer period 3 months later, the day after the police had searched his home. In this case, these episodes of undoubted fugue (in which personal identity was lost) emerged against a background of mild-to-moderate organic memory impairment of vascular aetiology.

Kapur & Abbott (1996) described a 19-year-old male university student who was found in a city park a few days before his university examinations were due to start. In addition to the likely stress resulting from his pending examinations, the patient's grandmother had died 8 months earlier, and the patient had been quite close to her. Witness accounts were obtained from people who had observed the episode from the onset, and the authors monitored the acute stages of recovery of memory function over the next 4 weeks. The memory loss was characterized by impaired performance on both autobiographical and public events memory tests in the context of normal anterograde memory scores. Shrinkage of RA took place over a 4 week period with the autobiographical and public events components of retrograde memory recovering at the same rate.

Markowitsch et al. (1997) described a 37-year-old man who experienced a "fugue" episode lasting 5 days when out bicycling, and who then had a persistent loss of autobiographical memory lasting 8 months or more. During this period, the patient was required to listen to sentences containing information about his past, either preceding or following the onset of amnesia, whilst undergoing a 15-oxygen positron emission tomography (PET) scan. The authors found reduced right hemisphere activation for remote memories, relative to healthy controls performing a similar task.

Reviews of the earlier literature on psychogenic fugue states (Kopelman, 1987, 1995) have suggested that three main factors predispose to such episodes. *First*, fugue states are always preceded by a severe precipitating stress, such as marital or emotional discord (Kanzer, 1939), bereavement (Schacter et al., 1982), financial problems (Kanzer, 1939), a charge of offending (Wilson et al., 1950) or stress during wartime (Sargant & Slater, 1941; Parfitt & Gall, 1944). *Second*, depressed mood is an extremely common antecedent for a psychogenic fugue state. Berrington et al. (1956) wrote:

In nearly all fugues, there appears to be one common factor, namely a depressive mood. Whether the individual in the fugue is psychotic, neurotic, or even psychopathic, a depression seems to start off the fugue".

For example, Schacter et al.'s (1982) patient was in a depressed mood because he had just attended the funeral of his grandfather, of whom he had been particularly fond. In fact, many patients in a fugue have been contemplating suicide just before the episode, or do so following recovery from it (Abeles & Schilder, 1935; Stengel, 1941), e.g. Abeles & Schilder (1935) described a woman who deserted her husband for another man: after a week she determined to return to her family but, as she descended into the railway underground station, she was contemplating suicide. The authors tersely reported that "instead, amnesia developed". The *third* factor which commonly precedes a fugue state is a history of a transient, organic amnesia: Stengel (1941) reported that 10% of his sample had a history of epilepsy, and Berrington et al. (1956) reported that 16 of their 37 cases had previously experienced a severe head injury, and a further three cases had suffered a head injury of unknown severity. In brief, it appears that patients who have experienced a previous, transient organic amnesia and who have become depressed and/or suicidal are particularly likely to go into a fugue in the face of a severe, precipitating stress.

A confounding factor, however, is that several authors have noted that some of their patients appeared to be somewhat unreliable personalities with a possible legal motive for wanting to claim amnesia (Stengel, 1941; Wilson et al., 1950; Berrington et al., 1956). Kopelman (1987) gave the example of a man who reported about 10 or 12 fugue episodes, several of which were well-documented in medical records, and who also had a past history of depression and suicide attempts as well as transient amnesia following epileptic seizures and ECT. This gentleman claimed amnesia for a period of a few hours during which he was involved in a motor accident whilst driving when disqualified, without any insurance, whilst under the influence of alcohol, making assessment (for a medico-legal report) particularly difficult.

The clinical and neuropsychological phenomena of fugue episodes often bear interesting resemblances to organic amnesia, e.g. there may be islets or fragments of preserved memory within the amnesic gap. A woman, who was due to meet her husband to discuss divorce, re-called that she was "supposed to meet someone" (Kanzer, 1939; cf. also Schacter et al., 1982, above). The subject may adopt a detached attitude to these memory fragments, describing them as "strange and unfamiliar" (Coriat, 1907). In many cases, semantic knowledge re-mains intact (e.g. foreign languages, and the names of streets, towns, and famous people; Kanzer, 1939; Schacter et al., 1982). Consistent with this, IQ scores are characteristically unaffected (Schacter et al., 1982; Kopelman et al., 1994a, 1994b). In other cases, there are suggestions that semantic memory has been affected over-and-above the self-referential component (Kihlstrom & Schacter, 2000), which constitutes the sense of personal identity. Similarly, performance at verbal learning tests has been reported as unaffected (Abeles & Schílder, 1935; Kopelman et al., 1994a), mildly impaired (Schacter et al., 1982), or more severely affected (Gudjonsson & Taylor, 1985). Memory for skills has been relatively little investigated, but appears often to be preserved (e.g. Coriat, 1907). In the Padola hearing in 1959 (Bradford & Smith, 1979), retention of a rudimentary knowledge of aerodynamics and of other skills (e.g. solving jigsaw puzzles) was taken as evidence against an organic amnesia—a frankly erroneous interpretation in the light of contemporary findings demon-strating preserved procedural memory in organic amnesia. Kihlstrom & Schacter (1995, 2000) have provided examples of instances where subjects have appeared to show some "implicit" knowledge of events in the absence of explicit recollection. These included the case described by Christianson & Nilsson (1989), who studied a woman who developed amnesia after an assault and rape. She became extremely upset when taken back to the scene of the assault, even though she did not explicitly remember what had happened or where. In the first edition of this volume, Kopelman (1995) provided a model of hierarchies of awareness in psychogenic amnesia, analogous to that described in normal memory and organic amnesia (see Figure 21.1).

Memory retrieval may be facilitated by chance cues in the environment (e.g. Abeles & Schílder, 1935; Schacter et al., 1982). Kopelman (1995) gave the example of a man who, on seeing the author's name on the spine of a book in a medical ward, remembered that a close friend of that name had recently been admitted to hospital with terminal cancer. On transfer to a psychiatric ward, this same patient remembered that he had been briefly admitted to another psychiatric unit some years earlier. After recovery of these two memories, his other memories rapidly returned. On the other hand, deliberate cueing, such as taking a patient back to the site(s) where he/she had been found or lived or suffered trauma, is often unsuc-cessful in cueing memory retrieval (Coriat, 1907; Kanzer, 1939; Christianson & Nilsson, 1989; Kopelman et al., 1994a). Hypnosis and/or interview under sodium amylobarbitone (amytal) have commonly been used, but are often disappointing (Lennox, 1943; Adatto, 1949; Kopelman et al., 1994a, 1994b); and there is a dearth of substantive clinical trials sup-porting their efficacy (Patrick & Howells, 1990). On the other hand, such strategies may be useful to allow a patient to "recover" without loss of face, where there is background informa-tion about the patient and some degree of simulation is suspected (Kopelman et al., 1994a).

Normal memory/ organic amnesia	Psychogenic amnesia
Conscious recollection of event or incident (remembering)	Deliberate simulation of memory loss in the presence of conscious recollection
↑ ↓	↑ ↓
"Knowing" that event/ incident happened without explicit recollection	"Knowing" that event/ incident happened without explicit recollection
↑ ↓	↑ ↓
Familiarity judgements ("recognition") but no explicit recollection	Familiarity judgements ("recognition") but no explicit recollection
↑ ↓	↑ ↓
Implicit ("unaware") memory: -priming -skill learning (procedural) -conditioning	No awareness of memory (unconscious mechanisms postulated i.e. traditional notion of "hysterical amnesia")

Figure 21.1 Level of awareness in memory and amnesia: normal memory/organic amnesia and psychogenic amnesia

In differentiating psychogenic fugue from a transient organic amnesia, such as transient global amnesia (TGA), clinical factors may be important indicators, such as the rate and the circumstances of the onset of the memory loss, whether there is loss of the sense of personal identity (rare in organic amnesia except for advanced dementia), and whether new learning is affected (often spared in psychogenic amnesia, although not necessarily). In TGA and organic confusional states, repetitive questioning (e.g. "Where am I?" or "What am I doing here?") is a characteristic feature, whereas personal identity is seldom lost (Hodges & Ward, 1989). By contrast, in psychogenic fugue, personal identity is lost but repetitive questioning is rare (Kopelman et al., 1994c). If TGA attacks are frequent and brief (an hour or less), they are likely to have an epileptic basis (Hodges & Warlow, 1990), which Kapur (1990) has termed "transient epileptic amnesia" (TEA). On the other hand, TGA episodes are preceded by a precipitating stress in 14–33% of cases (Hodges & Ward, 1989; Miller et al., 1987), and it is misleading to assume that such stressors mean that an amnesia must necessarily be psychogenic. An important feature, although seldom assessed clinically, is the slope (temporal gradient) of the remote memory curve during the attack. Kritchevsky et al. (1997) obtained a pronounced recency effect on a cued autobiographical memory task in nine patients with "functional RA" (cf. Kopelman et al., 1994a), whereas TGA patients showed a conventional Ribot temporal gradient (i.e. sparing of early memories) during an attack.

Psychogenic Focal Retrograde Amnesia

This is a contentious topic, which has given rise to recent debate (Kopelman, 2000a, 2000c; Kapur, 2000). However, the present author would argue that many of these cases are likely to have had a psychogenic origin, even where there has been some evidence of organic brain pathology. Kapur (1999) has also acknowledged that psychogenic retrograde amnesia can occur in either the absence or the presence of concomitant brain pathology, and Kapur (2000) was brave and honest enough to acknowledge that psychological factors now appeared contributory in a patient previously described as having focal RA as a result of definite brain pathology (Kapur et al., 1992). Since this latter case was one of the better-described cases in the literature, the discovery of these putatively psychogenic factors must raise question marks about other cases in whom all physical investigations have been normal, but in whom underlying organic pathology was inferred (Stracciari et al., 1994; Lucchelli et al., 1995; De Renzi et al., 1995).

In focal RA, the subject characteristically loses memories for the entirety of his/her previous life. However, current new learning is preserved, and these patients often show only minor impairments on formal measures of anterograde amnesia. There is not necessarily any loss of the sense of personal identity, nor is there a period of wandering, although occasionally focal RA may follow a more typical "fugue" episode (Kopelman et al., 1994a; Markowitsch et al., 1997). However, the present author has noted that it seems to be very common, at least in the early stages, for these patients to complain that they cannot recognize their spouses and/or other close family members and, later, they say that they have "relearned" whom these people are. Two features make these patients particularly difficult to diagnose and manage. First, the underlying stressor or stressors are often not clearly apparent, as the patient and/or family are often reluctant to discuss them. The family may indeed reinforce the patient's adopting and maintaining a "sick role". Only later, after the patient's trust has been engaged, and new information has emerged, will underlying issues become evident, as in Kapur's (2000) case (see also Kopelman, 2000a). Second, as already mentioned, there may be concomitant brain pathology. This is usually minor, and the disorder often seems to follow mild concussion (Kopelman, 2000a), but occasionally it can be more serious (Stuss & Guzman, 1988; Binder, 1994).

> Barbarotto et al. (1996) described a 38-year-old woman who slipped and fell in her office, losing consciousness for an unknown period of time and who, upon recovery, showed an apparently complete loss of explicit autobiographical memory. The authors favoured the possibility that this was "a psychogenic block in a person with a hysterical personality structure", but emphasized that the patient was able to show implicit knowledge of information to which she apparently lacked explicit access—as demonstrated on tests requiring familiarity judgements and in her rate of relearning facts about her past.

> Della Sala et al. (1996) described a 33-year-old man who suffered a loss of autobiographical memory following a fall down some stairs at his parent-in-laws' home, resulting in concussion. Despite this patient's severe loss of explicit, autobiographical recall, and an initial loss of personal identity as well as a failure to recognize his wife, relatives and friends, there was substantial evidence of preserved implicit/procedural memories, including the ability to access secret codes on his computer. The authors considered the possibility of a psychogenic amnesia, although they favoured the more neutral term "functional amnesia". It is of interest that, although no formal psychiatric disorder was diagnosed, the patient had shown progressively less interest in his young wife over the preceding months, joined an unusual role-playing group from which he excluded his wife, started to collect sadomasochistic pornography, became involved in a homosexual relationship, and subsequently pursued a divorce.

Papagno (1998) described a 26-year-old man who fell from a scaffold no higher than 2 metres. He briefly lost consciousness, but he could not remember his name, what he was doing there, or any autobiographical detail. He failed to recognize his relatives, including his mother. He appeared unconcerned by his memory loss. There were no focal neurological signs; CT scan and MRI were normal; an EEG showed mild left temporal changes only. Although "no abnormalities" were detected during a psychiatric interview, there was a history that his girlfriend had broken off their relationship the previous December, leaving him very depressed, irritable, and quarrelsome with everybody. He made every possible attempt to meet his ex-girlfriend again, whilst she tried to avoid him. On one occasion, he had left home suddenly without warning; 3 days later he telephoned his ex-girlfriend from Rome, saying he was sleeping on the road and out of money. On his return, his mother described him as "out of his mind", threatening to kill his girlfriend as well as threatening suicide. One night he awoke and broke some of his home furniture. Apparently, he had stopped speaking about his girlfriend a month before the present accident and he "seemed" to have accepted the situation. Papagno postulated a primary retrieval deficit, i.e. "an inhibition (psychogenic and/or organic) of retrieval without a storage deficit". It should be noted that, in this case, psychological factors were present and acknowledged by the author, despite a report that there were "no pathological traits" by a psychiatrist.

MacKenzie Ross (2000) described a 56-year-old woman who, following a minor head injury at work, developed a profound RA for both public events and autobiographical memories spanning her entire life. The accident occurred shortly after the patient had returned to England to live with a fiancé, only to discover that he was already living with someone else. MacKenzie Ross emphasized that hospital and general practitioner records described repeated complaints of anxiety and depression, going back many years, and a "tendency to make mountains out of molehills". Mackenzie Ross argued for a "functional" disorder of memory retrieval, whilst acknowledging the putative importance of psychological factors in this case.

Kopelman (2000a) described a 55-year-old man who collapsed at work during early 1998 with a transient left-sided weakness and a complete loss of autobiographical memory. At initial admission, this patient was disorientated in time and place as well as person, and there was a mild loss of power in the left arm and leg with an equivocally upgoing left plantar response. A CT scan was normal, but an MRI brain scan showed evidence of a few pinpoint regions of altered signal bilaterally, consistent with a history of previously diagnosed hypercholesteraemia and diabetes. However, the physicians attending this man felt confident that his memory loss was entirely disproportionate to his neurological signs, which rapidly resolved. The patient did not recognize his wife, and he could not remember the names and ages of his children. He claimed to have "relearned" language and mental calculation, and that "each day I remember more of the day before". On formal tests, he showed severe and extensive autobiographical and remote memory loss with intact anterograde memory. When first seen, he and his family were extremely angry at any suggestion that there might be a psychological component to his memory loss. However, during the succeeding weeks, his wife provided information about an emotionally deprived childhood, abuse, and subsequent psychological problems. The initial onset had occurred after the patient had been confronted about "moonlighting" in two employments, from which he had been dismissed. After being seen on a regular basis for several weeks, he was more willing to accept a psychological contribution to his RA and, following an amytal interview, virtually all of this patient's memories were recovered.

There is evidence that the implicit component of memory may be relatively intact in such patients:

Campodonico & Rediess (1996) administered a measure of indirect remote memory to a patient with "profound psychogenic retrograde amnesia". The patient showed more rapid learning of famous identities relative to novel ones, comparable with controlled subjects, despite having been unable to name the famous faces at baseline. She also recalled the names and occupations of famous people better than she did those for novel items. The authors interpreted these findings as evidence for preserved "implicit" remote semantic knowledge.

One further study pointed to possible underlying brain mechanisms:

> Costello et al. (1998) described a man in his 40s who, following a left superior dorsolateral prefrontal haemorrhage, developed a dense RA for 19 years preceding the stroke. However, the authors considered that "a purely organic account of the condition does not seem very plausible". They carried out a PET activation study, in which the subject attempted to recall events using family photographs as stimuli in three conditions— events for which he was amnesic but at which he had been present, events from the amnesic period at which he was not present, and events outside the amnesic period. In the "amnesic-present" condition, activation was increased in the precuneus, but diminished in the right posterior ventrolateral frontal cortex and a region close to the site of haemorrhage. The finding of reduced right ventrolateral frontal activation was broadly consistent with Markowitsch et al.'s (1997) finding of diminished right hemisphere activation (see above).

This last finding indicates that psychogenic phenomena may produce their effect upon mechanisms operating in normal memory retrieval, which can of course also be affected by brain damage. Kopelman (2000a) proposed a model of how psychosocial factors and brain systems may influence autobiographical memory retrieval and personal identity (Figure 21.2) (cf. Markowitsch, 1996). The relevant psychosocial factors are indicated in the ovals, and are derived largely from the literature on fugue. The brain systems are indicated in the rectangular boxes. The model postulated that psychosocial stresses affect frontal control/executive systems, such that there is inhibition in the retrieval of autobiographical and episodic memories. As indicated in the model, this inhibition will be exacerbated, or made more likely, when a subject is extremely aroused or very depressed, or when there is a past "learning experience" of transient amnesia (see above, p. 459). When such stresses are severe, the inhibition may even affect a "personal semantic belief system", resulting in a transient loss of knowledge of self and identity (dashed arrow). Despite this suppression of autobiographical memory retrieval by these frontal inhibitory mechanisms, anterograde learning (and "new" episodic memory retrieval) can occur from "normal" environmental stimuli via the intact medial temporal/diencephalic system.

Multiple Personality Disorder

Multiple personality disorder (MPD), known as "dissociative identity disorder" in DSM-IV, has been described as the "crown jewel of the dissociative disorders and also of the functional amnesias" by Kihlstrom & Schacter (2000). By contrast, Merskey (1992, 1995) regarded the widely varying geographical prevalence of this disorder as almost certainly reflecting differences in the reinforcing behaviour of doctors, psychologists, and the outside world. Kihlstrom & Schacter (2000) noted that, of almost 2000 papers on this topic, approximately two-thirds appeared between 1989 and 2000. However, these authors themselves acknowledged that "the features of amnesia observed in experimental studies of MPD patients may be influenced to varying degrees by iatrogenic and sociocultural factors".

According to Kihlstrom & Schacter (2000), a cardinal symptom of this disorder is the between-personality amnesia. The amnesia often appears to be asymmetrical, in that at least

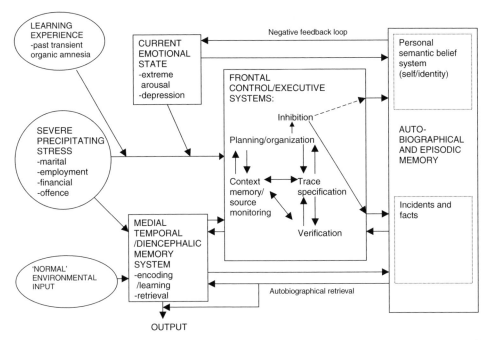

Figure 21.2 Social factors and brain systems influencing autobiographical memory retrieval and personal identity. The relevant social and psychological factors are indicated in the ovals. The brain systems are indicated in the rectangular boxes. Severe stress affects frontal control/executive system, thereby inhibiting the retrieval of autobiographical/episodic memories. This is more likely if the subject is extremely aroused, very depressed, or if there is past experience of a transient organic amnesia. If the stress is severe, there may even be a transient loss of knowledge of self and identity (dashed arrow). Reproduced by permission of Psychology Press Ltd., Hove, UK, from Kopelman (2000a)

one personality shows dense amnesia for the experiences of the others, while one or more personalities typically have unimpaired access to the experience of some or all the other personalities. Kihlstrom & Schacter (1995, 2000) have described a number of experimental studies in such patients.

Nissen et al. (1988) examined a 45-year-old woman with 22 diagnosed personalities. The authors focused upon eight mutually amnesic personalities who could each be elicited in response to an appropriate request by the experimenter. Target materials were studied by one personality (elicited by the patient's psychiatrist) and, after retention intervals of approximately 5–10 min, another personality was elicited for memory testing. Little or no evidence of between-personality explicit memory was observed across a variety of tests. However, on a word-fragment completion test, one personality's performance was indeed facilitated or primed by previous exposure of the words to another personality, and similar cross-personality implicit memory effects were observed on other tasks which required perceptual identification of briefly exposed words.

Schacter et al. (1989) studied I.C., a 24-year-old married woman, who manifested four other personalities. The authors used a variant of the Crovitz procedure, previously employed in a fugue patient (Schacter et al., 1982). In marked contrast to the performance of age-matched control subjects, I.C. produced almost no memories from the first 14 years of her life, and her earliest recollection was dated to age 12. When instructed to confine her responses to childhood, all of her memories were dated from years 10–12, again in marked contrast to controls. The authors suggested that I.C.'s current personality had, in fact, first emerged around the time of adolescence.

Eich et al. (1996) examined nine patients with MPD. Explicit tests of free and cued recall gave strong evidence of interpersonality amnesia. However, implicit memory was spared on a test of picture-fragment completion, but not on a test of word-fragment completion, indicating that implicit memory is not always or uniformly spared in such patients.

Such patients are rare, and they may be particularly vulnerable to suggestions from clinicians and researchers. The present author has noted that some of his fugue patients have used their fugue episode as a means of adopting a new way of life (Kopelman et al., 1994a; Kopelman & Morton, 2001) and several fugue patients have asked the author whether he "believes in" multiple personality disorder—as if they were seeking ways of experimenting with other alternatives.

THE NATURE OF PSYCHOGENIC AMNESIA

Leaving aside deliberate simulation, various mechanisms have been proposed to account for psychogenic amnesia. These include repression, dissociative states, failure of initial encoding, an encoding–retrieval interaction, and state or context-dependent retrieval deficits. These various theories can be grouped into those that place emphasis on the failure of memory at the time of initial encoding, which may be particularly true of amnesic offenders where severe alcohol or drug intoxication is implicated, and those that place emphasis on a failure of memory retrieval. The latter is possibly more true of those unpremeditated homicide cases, which take place in a state of extreme emotional arousal, although compromised encoding and avoidance of rehearsal (cf. O'Connell, 1960) may also be important factors contributing to subsequent difficulties in retrieval. Figure 21.2 has provided a model in which frontal control mechanisms, operating within a particular psychosocial environment, inhibit the retrieval of autobiographical memories and even of personal identity, whilst new learning remains intact. Anderson & Green (2001) have recently reported evidence that executive mechanisms can indeed be recruited to prevent unwanted memories from entering awareness, and that repeated use of this strategy inhibits the subsequent recall of the suppressed memories.

In the present author's experience, a complete absence of any recollection is very rare, where organic brain disease, intoxication, or obvious simulation have been excluded. On detailed assessment, subjects often show some degree of "knowledge" or "recognition" of certain memories without explicit recollection, in a manner analogous to that seen in studies of amnesic patients or healthy controls who have failed to remember something (Gardiner & Parkin, 1990; see also Figure 21.1). For example, as discussed above, O'Connell (1960) pointed to the qualitative similarities between what he called the "passive disregard" of those who deliberately put an unpleasant or traumatic memory to the back of their mind, and those subjects who, although claiming amnesia, described the memory as being on the verge of "forming a picture". The Egyptian homicide case, cited above, and Gudjonsson & Mackeith's (1983) case both "knew" that they must have committed their respective offences (although, in part, this was from the evidence before their eyes). Patient A.T. (Kopelman et al., 1994a) "recognized" a hotel she had stayed in when she was taken back there, but she could recollect nothing about her time there, even after recovery of most of her earlier memories. Kihlstrom & Schacter (1995, 2000) have given examples of other evidence of preserved implicit memory in the absence of explicit recollection.

CONCLUSIONS

In summary, psychogenic amnesia encompasses situation-specific and global forms of memory loss. The former includes amnesia for offences and memory loss (or "fragmentation") arising in PTSD and for childhood sexual abuse. The latter entails fugue episodes, cases of psychogenic focal retrograde amnesia, and cases of multiple personality disorder (even though the last may often be iatrogenically determined). Knowledge of the circumstances in which amnesia for an offence arises is important for its assessment; and investigations of PTSD are beginning to shed light on why certain images show enhanced recall, whilst other features are forgotten. Studies of fugue episodes and psychogenic focal retrograde amnesia indicate features in common with organic amnesia—such as preserved memory "fragments" and some evidence of preserved implicit and semantic components—although the temporal gradient is characteristically "reversed" (a strong recency effect in psychogenic amnesia; a Ribot gradient in TGA and other forms of organic amnesia). It seems likely that psychosocial influences exert their effects upon brain mechanisms that have been implicated in studies of normal memory and organic amnesia: the present chapter has provided a model to take account of this phenomenon.

ACKNOWLEDGEMENT

Professor Kopelman's research has been supported by grants from the Wellcome Trust.

REFERENCES

Abeles, M. & Schílder, P. (1935). Psychogenic loss of personal identity. *Archives of Neurology and Psychiatry*, **34**, 587–604.

Adatto, C.P. (1949). Observations on criminal patients during narcoanalysis. *Archives of Neurology and Psychiatry*, **62**, 82–92.

American Psychiatric Association (2000). *Diagnostic and Statistical Manual of Mental Disorders (DSM-IV)*. Washington, DC: APA.

Anderson, M.C. & Green, C. (2001). Suppressing unwanted memories by executive control. *Nature*, **410**, 366–369.

Andrews, B., Brewin, C.R., Ochera, J. et al. (2000). The timing, triggers and qualities of recovered memories in therapy. *British Journal of Clinical Psychology*, **39**, 11–26.

Barbarotto, R., Laiacona, M. & Cocchini, G. (1996). A case of simulated, psychogenic or focal pure retrograde amnesia: did an entire life become unconscious? *Neuropsychologia*, **34**, 575–585.

Berrington, W.P., Liddell, D.W. & Foulds, G.A. (1956). A revaluation of the fugue. *Journal of Mental Science*, **102**, 281–286.

Binder, L.M. (1994). Psychogenic mechanisms of prolonged autobiographical retrograde amnesia. *Clinical Neuropsychologist*, **8**, 439–450.

Bradford, J. & Smith, S.M. (1979). Amnesia and homicide: the Padola case and a study of thirty cases. *Bulletin of the American Academy of Psychiatry and the Law*, **7**, 219–231.

Bremner, J.D., Scott, T.M., Delaney, R.C. et al (1993). Deficits in short-term memory in posttraumatic stress disorder. *American Journal of Psychiatry*, **150**, 1015–1019.

Bremner, J.D., Randall, P., Scott, T.M. et al. (1995). Memory-based measurement of hippocampal volume in patients with combat-related posttraumatic stress disorder. *American Journal of Psychiatry*, **152**, 973–981.

Brewin, C.R. (2001). A cognitive neuroscience account of posttraumatic stress disorder and its treatment. *Behavioural Research and Therapy*, **39**, 373–393.

Brewin, C.R., Dalgleish, T. & Joseph, S. (1996). A dual representation of posttraumatic stress disorder. *Psychological Review*, **103**, 670–686.

Brooks, D.N. (1984). Cognitive deficits after head injury. In D.N. Brooks (ed.), *Closed Head Injury: Psychological, Social and Family Consequences* (pp. 44–73). Oxford: Oxford University Press.

Brown, D., Scheflin, A.W. & Whitfield, C.L. (1999) Recovered memories: the current weight of the evidence in science and in the courts. *Journal of Psychiatry and Law.* **27**, 5–156.

Campodonico, J.R. & Rediess, S. (1996). Dissociation of implicit and explicit knowledge in a case of psychogenic retrograde amnesia. *Journal of the International Neuropsychological Society*, **2**, 146–158.

Christianson, S-A. & Nilsson, L.G. (1989). Hysterical amnesia: a case of aversively motivated isolation of memory. In T. Archer & L.G. Nilsson (eds), *Aversion, Avoidance, and Anxiety* (pp. 289–310). Hillsdale, NJ: Erlbaum.

Clifford, B.R. & Scott, J. (1978). Individual and situational factors in eyewitness testimony. *Journal of Applied Psychology*, **63**, 852–859.

Colchester, A., Kingsley, D., Lasserson, D. et al. (2001). Structural MRI volumetric analysis in patients with organic amnesia, 1: methods and comparative findings across diagnostic groups. *Journal of Neurology, Neursurgery, and Psychiatry*, **71**, 13–22.

Coriat, I.H. (1907). The Lowell case of amnesia. *Journal of Abnormal Psychology*, **2**, 93–111.

Costello, A., Fletcher, P.C., Dolan, R.J. et al. (1998). The origins of forgetting in a case of isolated retrograde amnesia following a haemorrhage: evidence from functional imaging. *Neuroscase*, **4**, 437–446.

Deffenbacher, K. (1988). Eyewitness research: the next ten years. In M. Gruneberg, P. Morris & R. Sykes (eds), *Practical Aspects of Memory*, Vol. 1 (pp. 20–26). Chichester: Wiley.

Della Sala, S., Freschi, R., Lucchelli, F. (1996). Retrograde amnesia: no past, new life. In P.W. Halligan & J.C. Marshall (eds), *Method in Madness: Case Studies in Cognitive Neuropsychiatry* (pp. 209–233). Hove: Psychology Press.

De Renzi, E., Lucchelli, F., Muggia, S. & Spinnler, H. (1995). Persistent retrograde amnesia following a minor trauma. *Cortex*, **31**, 531–542.

Eich, E., McCaulay, D., Lowenstein, R.J. & Dihle, P.H. (1996). Memory, amnesia, and dissociative identity disorder. *Psychological Science*, **8**, 417–422.

Fenton, G.W. (1972). Epilepsy and automatism. *British Journal of Hospital Medicine*, **7**, 57–64.

Fenwick, P. (1990). Automatism, medicine and the law. *Psychological Medicine Monographs*, suppl. 17. Cambridge: Cambridge University Press.

Gardiner, J.M. & Parkin, A.J. (1990). Attention and recollective experience. *Memory and Cognition*, **18**, 579–583.

Goodwin, D.W., Crane, J.B. & Guze, S.E. (1969). Phenomenological aspects of the alcoholic "blackout". *British Journal of Psychiatry*, **115**, 1033–1038.

Gudjonsson, G.H. & MacKeith, J. (1983). A specific recognition deficit in case of homicide. *Medicine, Science and the Law*, **23**, 37–40.

Gudjonsson, G.H. & Taylor, P.J. (1985). Cognitive deficit in a case of retrograde amnesia. *British Journal of Psychiatry*, **147**, 715–718.

Guttmacher, M.S. (1955). *Psychiatry and the Law.* New York: Grune & Stratton.

Harvey, P. (2000). Fear can interrupt the continuum of memory. *Journal of Neurology, Neurosurgery and Psychiatry*, **69**, 431–432.

Harvey, A.G. & Bryant, R.A. (2001). Reconstructing trauma memories: a prospective study of "amnesic" trauma survivors. *Journal of Traumatic Stress*, **14**, 277–282.

Harvey, A.G., Brewin C.R. & Kopelman, M.D. (2001). Co-existence of posttraumatic stress disorder and traumatic brain injury: resolving the paradox. *Journal of International Neuropsychological Society* (accepted subject to amendments).

Hodges, J.R. & Ward C.D. (1989). Observations during transient global amnesia: a behavioural and neuropsychological study of the five cases. *Brain*, **112**, 595–620.

Hodges, J. & Warlow, C.P. (1990). The aetiology of transient global amnesia. *Brain*, **113**, 639–657.

Hopwood, J.S. & Snell, H.K. (1933). Amnesia in relation to crime. *Journal of Mental Science*, **79**, 27–41.

Howard, C. & d'Orbán, P.T. (1987). Violence in sleep: medico-legal issues and two case reports. *Psychological Medicine*, **17**, 915–925.

Hunter, I.M.L. (1964). *Memory*. Harmondsworth: Penguin.

Kales, A., Soldatos, C.R., Caldwell, A.B. et al. (1980). Somnambulism. *Archives of General Psychiatry*, **37**, 1406–1410.

Kanzer, M. (1939). Amnesia: a statistical study. *American Journal of Psychiatry*, **96**, 711–716.

Kapur, N. (1990). Transient epileptic amnesia: a clinically distinct form of neurological memory disorder. In H.J. Markowitsch (ed.), *Transient Global Amnesia and Related Disorders*. Lewiston, NY: Hogrefe and Huber.

Kapur, N. (1999). Syndromes of retrograde amnesia: conceptual and empirical synthesis. *Psychological Bulletin*, **125**, 800–825.

Kapur, N. (2000). Focal retrograde amnesia and the attribution of causality: an exceptionally benign commentary. *Cognitive Neuropsychology*, **17**, 623–637.

Kapur, N. & Abbot, P. (1996). A study of recovery of memory function in a case of witnessed functional retrograde amnesia. *Cognitive Neuropsychiatry*, **1**, 247–258.

Kapur, N., Ellison, D., Smith, M. et al. (1992). Focal retrograde amnesia following bilateral temporal lobe pathology: a neuropsychological and magnetic resonance study. *Brain*, **116**, 73–86.

Kihlstrom, J.F. & Schacter, D. (1995). Functional disorders of autobiographical memory. In A.D. Baddeley, B.A. Wilson & F.N. Watts (eds), *Handbook of Memory Disorders*, Ist edn (pp. 337–364). Chichester: Wiley.

Kihlstrom, J.F. & Schacter, D.L. (2000). Functional amnesia. In L. Cermak (ed.), *Handbook of Neuropsychology*, 2nd edn, Vol. 2. (pp. 409–427). Amsterdam: Elsevier Science.

Knox, S.J. (1968). Epileptic automatism and violence. *Medicine, Science and the Law*, **8**, 96–104.

Kopelman, M.D. (1987). Amnesia: organic and psychogenic. *British Journal of Psychiatry*, **150**, 428–442.

Kopelman, M.D. (1995). Assessment of psychogenic amnesia. In A.D. Baddeley, B.A. Wilson & F.N. Watts (eds), *Handbook of Memory Disorders*, 1st edn (pp. 427–448). Chichester: Wiley.

Kopelman, M.D. (2000a). Focal retrograde amnesia and the attribution of causality: an exceptionally critical review. *Cognitive Neuropsychology*, **17**, 585–621.

Kopelman, M.D. (2000b). Editorial commentary: fear can interrupt the continuum of memory. *Journal of Neurology, Neurosurgery and Psychiatry*, **69**, 431–432

Kopelman, M.D. (2000c). Comments on focal retrograde amnesia and the attribution of causality: an exceptionally benign commentary by Narinder Kapur. *Cognitive Neuropsychology*, **17**, 639–640.

Kopelman, M.D., Christensen, H., Parfitt, A. & Stanhope, N. (1994a). The Great Escape: a neuropsychological study of psychogenic amnesia. *Neuropsychologia*, **32**, 675–691.

Kopelman, M.D., Green, R.E.A., Guinan, E.M. (1994b). The case of the amnesic intelligence officer. *Psychological Medicine*, **24**, 1037–1045.

Kopelman, M.D. & Morton, J. (2001). Psychogenic amnesia—functional memory loss. In G. Davies & T. Dalgleish (eds), *Recovered Memories: The Middle Ground*. Chichester: Wiley (pp. 219–243).

Kopelman, M.D., Panayiotopoulos, C.P. & Lewis, P. (1994c). Transient epileptic amnesia differentiated from psychogenic "fugue": neuropsychological, EEG and PET findings. *Journal of Neurology, Neurosurgery, and Psychiatry*, **57**, 1002–1004.

Kritchevsky, M., Zouzounis, J. & Squire, L. (1997). Transient global amnesia and functional retrograde amnesia: Contrasting examples of episodic memory loss. *Philosophical Transactions of the Royal Society of London, Series B, Biological Sciences*, **352**, 1747–1754.

Kuehn, L.L. (1974). Looking down a gun barrel: person perception and violent crime. *Perceptual and Motor Skills*, **39**, 1159–1164.

Lancet (1978). Editorial: Factitious hypoglycacmia. *Lancet*, **I**, 1293.

Leitch, A. (1948). Notes on amnesia in crime for the general practitioner. *Medical Press*, **219**, 459–463.

Lennox, W.G. (1943). Amnesia, real and feigned. *American Journal of Psychiatry*, **99**, 732–743.

Loftus, E.F., Polonsky, S. & Fullilove, M.T. (1994). Memories of childhood sexual abuse: remembering and repressing. *Psychology of Women*, **18**, 67–84.

Lucchelli, F., Muggia, S. & Spinnler, H. (1995). The "Petites Madeleines" phenomenon in two amnesic patients. Sudden recovery of forgotten memories. *Brain*, **118**, 167–183.

Lynch, B.E. & Bradford, J.M.W. (1980). Amnesia—its detection by psychophysiological measures. *Bulletin of the American Academy of Psychiatry and the Law*, **8**, 288–297.

Markowitsch, H.J. (1996). Organic and psychogenic retrograde amnesia: two sides of the same coin? *Neurocase*, **2**, 357–371.

Markowitsch, H.J., Fink, G., Thone, A. et al. (1997). A PET study of persistent psychogenic amnesia covering the whole life span. *Cognitive Neuropsychiatry*, **2**, 135–158.

MacKenzie Ross, S. (2000). A process of discovery: profound retrograde amnesia following mild head injury: organic or functional? *Cortex*, **36**, 521–538.

Merskey, H. (1992). The manufacture of personalities: the production of multiple personality disorder. *British Journal of Psychiatry*, **160**, 327–340.

Merskey, H. (1995). Multiple personality disorder and false memory syndrome. *British Journal of Psychiatry*, **166**, 281–283.

McNeil, J.E. & Greenwood, R. (1996). Can PTSD occur with amnesia for the precipitating event? *Cognitive Neuropsychiatry*, **1**, 239–246.

Miller, J.W., Petersen, R.C., Metter, E.J. et al. (1987). Transient global amnesia: clinical characteristics and prognosis. *Neurology*, **37**, 733–737.

Nissen, M.J., Ross, J.L., Willingham, D.B. et al. (1988). Memory and awareness in a patient with multiple personality disorder. *Brain and Cognition*, **8**, 21–38.

O'Connell, B.A. (1960). Amnesia and homicide. *British Journal of Delinquency*, **10**, 262–276.

Papagno, C. (1998). Transient retrograde amnesia associated with impaired naming of living categories. *Cortex*, **34**, 111–121.

Parfitt, D.N. & Gall, C.M.C. (1944). Psychogenic amnesia: the refusal to remember. *Journal of Mental Science*, **90**, 511–527.

Parwatikar, S.D., Holcomb, W.R. & Meninger, K.A. (1985). The detection of malingered amnesia in accused murderers. *Bulletin of the American Academy of Psychiatry and the Law*, **13**, 97–103.

Patrick, M. & Howells, R. (1990). Barbiturate-assisted interviews in modern clinical practice. *Psychological Medicine*, **20**, 763–765.

Pope, H.G. & Hudson, J.I. (1995). Can memories of childhood sexual abuse be repressed? *Psychological Medicine*, **25**, 121–126.

Pyszora, N., Barker, A. & Kopelman, M.D. (2002). Amnesia for criminal offences: a study of life sentence prisoners (submitted).

Raphael, B. & Middleton, W. (1988). After the horror. *British Medical Journal*, **296**, 1142–1144.

Russell, W.R. & Nathan, P.W. (1946). Traumatic amnesia. *Brain*, **69**, 280–300.

Sargant, W. & Slater, E. (1941). Amnesic syndromes in war. *Proceedings of the Royal Society of Medicine*, **34**, 757–764.

Scarlett, J.A., Mako, M.E., Rubenstein, A.H. et al. (1977). Factitious hypoglycaemia. *New England Journal of Medicine*, **297**, 1029–1032.

Schacter, D.L. (1986a). Amnesia and crime: how much do we really know? *American Psychologist*, **41**, 286–295.

Schacter, D.L. (1986b). On the relation between genuine and simulated amnesia. *Behavioural Sciences and the Law*, **4**, 47–64.

Schacter, D.L. (1986c). Feelings-of-knowing ratings distinguish between genuine and simulated forgetting. *Journal of Experimental Psychology: Learning, Memory and Cognition*, **12**, 30–41.

Schacter, D.L., Wang, P.L., Tulving, E. & Freeman, M. (1982). Functional retrograde amnesia: a quantitative case study. *Neuropsychologia*, **20**, 523–532.

Schacter, D.L. (1996). *Searching for Memory: the Brain, the Mind, and the Past*. New York: Basic Books.

Schacter, D.L., Kihlstrom, J.F., Kihlstrom, L. & Berren, M. (1989). Autobiographical memory in a case of multiple personality disorder. *Journal of Abnormal Psychology*, **98**, 508–514.

Schenck, C.H., Bundlie, S., Ettinger, M. & Mahowald, M. (1986). Chronic behaviour disorders of human REM sleep: a new category of parasomnia: *Sleep*, **9**: 293–308.

Schooler, J.W., Bendiksen, M. & Ambadar, Z. (1997). Taking the middle line: can we accommodate both fabricated and recovered memories of sexual abuse? In M.A. Conway (ed.), *Recovered Memories and False Memories*. New York: Oxford University Press.

Shimamura, A.P. (1997). Neuropsychological factors associated with memory recollection: what can science tell us about reinstated memories? In J.D. Read & D.S. Lindsay (eds), *Recollections of Trauma: Scientific Research and Clinical Practice* (pp. 253–272). New York: Plenum.

Stengel, E. (1941). On the aetiology of the fugue states. *Journal of Mental Science*, **87**, 572–599.

Stracciari, A., Ghidoni, E., Guarino, M. et al. (1994). Post-traumatic retrograde amnesia with selective impairment of autobiographic memory. *Cortex*, **30**, 459–468.

Stuss, D. & Guzman, D. (1988). Severe remote memory loss with minimal anterograde amnesia: a clinical note. *Brain and Cognition*, **8**, 21–30.

Taylor, P.J. & Kopelman, M. (1984). Amnesia for criminal offences. *Psychological Medicine*, **14**, 581–588.

Van der Kolk, B.A. & Fisler, R. (1995). Dissociation and the fragmentary nature of traumatic memories: overview and exploratory study. *Journal of Trauma and Stress*, **8**, 505–525.

Wilson, G., Rupp, C. & Wilson, W.W. (1950). Amnesia. *American Journal of Psychiatry*, **106**, 481–485.

Yuille, J.C. (1987). The effects of alcohol and marijuana on eyewitness recall. Paper presented at the Conference on Practical Aspects of Memory, Swansea, UK (unpublished).

Yuille, J.C. & Cutshall, J.L. (1986). A case study of eye-witness memory of a crime. *Journal of Applied Psychology*, **71**, 291–301.

Development and Memory

CHAPTER 22

Memory Development During the Childhood Years

Susan E. Gathercole
Department of Psychology, University of Bristol, UK

This chapter provides an overview of some of the major changes in memory function that occur during the childhood period. Understanding the developmental processes by which mature memory function is achieved is crucial to theories of memory in adults as well as children. There are more practical reasons, too, why we need to know about memory in childhood. Large individual differences exist in children's memory capacities, with poor memory function often compromising learning and scholastic achievements. The assessment of memory abilities is therefore important for understanding learning difficulties. Also, effective methods of education depend upon teachers understanding the capacities of children of different ages to learn and remember information. Finally, the reliability of children's memories is becoming an increasingly important issue as more children are providing testimony in the courtroom. These issues of current educational and psycholegal relevance underscore the impact of understanding children's memory in everyday life as well as in the psychological laboratory.

One of the undoubted facts to emerge from the study of human memory over the past 40 years is that no single memory system underpins all mnemonic experience. Instead, there exist many separable systems that are distinguishable in terms of both their neural circuitry and cognitive structure, and that can function relatively independently of one another. The organization of this review reflects widely accepted distinctions between the following memory systems: short-term or working memory, and two long-term memory systems—episodic memory, and autobiographical memory. In each case, major qualitative and quantitative changes that take place in both cognitive structure and neuroanatomy during development are identified. Where relevant, developmental pathologies of memory, links between memory and other aspects of cognition, and methods of assessing each aspect of memory function during childhood, are discussed.

The Handbook of Memory Disorders. Edited by A.D. Baddeley, M.D. Kopelman and B.A. Wilson
© 2002 John Wiley & Sons, Ltd.

SHORT-TERM AND WORKING MEMORY

The term "short-term memory" refers to memory for events that occurred in the very recent past, when the delay between presentation of the material to-be-remembered and remembering is measured in terms of seconds and possibly minutes rather than hours or days. Evidence from a wide range of sources indicates that short-term memory is itself fractionated, being served by a number of separate temporary memory systems with distinct neuranatomical loci (see Gathercole, 1999, for review). The working memory model originally advanced by Baddeley & Hitch (1974) is the most influential theoretical account of short-term memory. Although originally devised to account for adult short-term memory performance, this model has proved to be of great value in characterizing the development of short-term memory during the childhood years, and is used to guide the analysis provided here.

The standard working memory model (e.g. Baddeley, 1986) comprises three components: the central executive, the phonological loop and the visuospatial sketchpad. The latter two components, the phonological loop and the visuospatial sketchpad, are slave systems specialized for the processing and manipulation of limited amounts of information within highly specific domains. Material is stored in the phonological loop in terms of its phonological qualities, whereas the sketchpad has the capacity to maintain the spatial and visual properties of limited amounts of information.

In contrast to the highly specific informational domains in which these two slave systems operate, the central executive is capable of performing a range of high-level functions. Functions ascribed to the central executive include the coordination of performance on different tasks, the control of action, switching retrieval plans or strategies, controlled attention and inhibition, and the storage and maintenance of temporarily activated information from long-term memory (Baddeley, 1986; Baddeley et al., 1998a). An important recent development in the working memory model is the identification of a new subcomponent, the episodic buffer (Baddeley, 2000). This is a limited-capacity storage system capable of integrating information from a variety of sources, using a multidimensional code. The buffer functions as an interface between the slave systems and long-term memory, and can be conceived as a fractionation of the central executive.

In the sections below, some of the major changes in functioning of the cerebral executive, the phonological loop and the visuospatial sketchpad of working memory are identified. More detailed coverage on various aspects of of the development of short-term and working memory is provided by Cowan et al. (1998), Gathercole (1999), Gathercole and Baddeley (1993), Gathercole & Hitch (1994) and Pickering (2001).

Verbal Short-term Memory

Development

Phonological short-term memory is usually measured using a serial recall paradigm, in which a series of verbal items arranged in arbitrary sequence are remembered, e.g. the digit sequence 4, 7, 2, 5, 9 might be presented, and the task is to recall the sequence in the original order. Children's performance on such tests increases dramatically over the early and middle years of childhood (e.g. Hulme et al., 1984). Memory span (a measure of the maximum number of items that can be remembered in correct sequence) shows an average two-fold

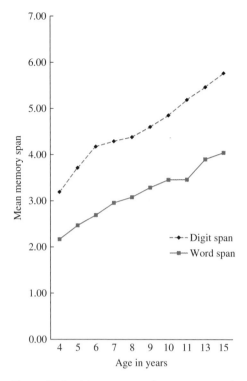

Figure 22.1 Memory span for sequences of words and digits as a function of age. Data from Pickering & Gathercole (2001)

increase from 5 to 14 years of age. Figure 22.1 illustrates this developmental function with data from two auditory serial recall measures: digit span and word span.

According to the working memory model, performance on verbal short-term memory tasks is mediated largely by the phonological loop (Baddeley, 1986; Baddeley & Hitch, 1974). This system consists of two subcomponents: a phonological store and a subvocal rehearsal process. Information gains access to the phonological store, either directly, via auditory presentation of speech stimuli, or indirectly via internally generated phonological codes for nonauditory inputs, such as printed words or familiar visual objects. Phonological representations of memory items decay rapidly in the phonological store, and typically become indiscriminable within about 2 seconds if unrehearsed (Baddeley et al., 1975). Subvocal rehearsal occurs serially and in real time, and acts to refresh decaying representations in the phonological store. In this way, decay of representations within the phonological store can be offset if the entire contents of the store can be rehearsed within 2 seconds. The rehearsal process is also used to recode stimuli, such as printed words and pictures that have verbal labels, into a phonological form suitable for representation in the phonological short-term store.

Recent neuroimaging studies indicate that the neural circuitry of the phonological loop is located within the left hemisphere (for overviews, see Gupta & MacWhinney, 1997; Smith & Jonides, 1998). Phonological short-term storage is associated with activity in posterior parietal areas, whereas rehearsal is served by more anterior regions, including Broca's area, premotor cortex and supplementary motor cortex.

Specific experimental techniques have been developed to tap these two subcomponents of the phonological loop. The phonological short-term store is highly sensitive to phonological similarity, with better recall of lists containing memory items that are phonologically distinct from one another (e.g. X, R, W, Q, J) than those that are phonological distinct (e.g. B, C, V, G, D). The rehearsal process, on the other hand, is impaired by increasing the articulatory duration of the to-be-remembered items, e.g. by comparing recall of lists of words each containing either five syllables or one syllable (Baddeley et al., 1975). Subvocal rehearsal is completely eliminated by continuously articulating irrelevant information (such as "the, the, the") during a memory test (Baddeley et al., 1975, 1984).

Two changes in phonological loop function with age have been identified which may contribute to the developmental function illustrated in Figure 22.1. One qualitative change relates to the age-related emergence of the subvocal rehearsal strategy. As indexed by the phonological similarity effect with auditorily presented material, the phonological short-term store appears to be in place by the youngest age at which serial recall tasks can be reliably performed, at around 3 or 4 years (Ford & Silber, 1994; Hitch et al., 1989a). Spontaneous use of subvocal rehearsal, on the other hand, is not detectable in the form of a sensitivity to the word length of the memory list items presented in pictorial form until about 7 years of age (Hitch & Halliday, 1983; see also Palmer, 2000). Other findings, too, fit well with this view, that young children fail to exploit a rehearsal strategy for nonauditory memory stimuli. One of the earliest methods of identifying rehearsal was to observe whether children performing immediate memory tasks produced any overt signs of rehearsal, such as lip movements and whispering, in the interval between memory presentations. Using this technique, Flavell et al. (1966) failed to find any evidence for rehearsal in children below the age of 7. Interestingly, there are some close links between the acquisition of literacy and the emergence of a rehearsal strategy (Palmer, 2000).

Successful subvocal rehearsal guards the traces in the phonological store against decay, and so should result in improved serial recall accuracy. However, the emergence of subvocal rehearsal as a strategy alone seems unlikely to account for the whole developmental increase in memory span, which extends from (at least) 4 to 15 years of age. A further quantitative change in the phonological loop with age results from increases in the speed of rehearsal and hence in the efficiency of maintaining material in the phonological store in older children. Rehearsal speed, as indexed by overt rate of articulation, is strongly associated with memory span in older children and adults (e.g. Cowan et al., 1998; Gathercole et al., 1994). Thus, at least part of the developmental increase in serial recall performance beyond 7 years of age probably reflects the increases in covert rate of rehearsal, and hence functional capacity, of the phonological store with age. Consistent with the view that young children do not rehearse, articulation rate and memory span scores are significantly correlated in children below 7 years of age (Cowan et al., 1994; Gathercole & Adams, 1993; Gathercole et al., 1994; Henry, 1994).

Other factors, too, may play a crucial role in the dramatic changes in serial recall abilities with age. Speed of recall as well as rehearsal may be important. It is known that memory sequences that take more time to articulate at the time of recall are more poorly remembered, probably as a consequence of increased opportunity for decay from the phonological store (Cowan et al., 1992). The slow rates of articulation in very young children may therefore result in greater decay of memory items in the phonological store prior to output than in their faster-speaking older peers. This factor may underpin some of the early developmental changes in verbal memory seen prior to the onset of rehearsal.

Another speed factor operating at output may also contribute to age-related changes in verbal short-term memory. In a detailed analysis of potential contributors to memory development, Cowan et al. (1998) found evidence that the duration of pauses during recall, a measure that was independent of articulation rate, was an important predictor of memory span (see also Fry & Hale, 2000). These researchers proposed that a rapid memory search process operates at the time of retrieval, and that the speed of this process constrains memory accuracy.

A further source of developmental change has been identified in behavioural analyses of the microstructure of serial recall that have been motivated by the development of computational models of verbal short-term memory (Burgess & Hitch, 1992, 1998; Page & Norris, 1999). On the basis of findings that the magnitude of order errors in serial recall (i.e. the distance that the items deviate in the output protocol from their original position in the sequence) decreases with age, McCormack et al. (2000) proposed that there are developmental improvements in the time-based signals involved in representing the serial order of items.

Finally, it has been suggested that the contribution from long-term lexical knowledge to immediate memory may increase with age. The dependence of serial recall on lexical representations as well as temporary phonological storage is well established: immediate memory is much more accurate for familiar words, such as "gorilla", "radio" and "botany", than unfamiliar phonological forms such as "taffost", "crepog" and "teggid" (Hulme et al., 1991). This phenomenon is known as the lexicality effect, and is suggested to arise from the use of primed lexical phonological representations to fill in incomplete information in representations of words in the phonological store, in a process described as redintegration (Gathercole et al., 1999; Hulme et al., 1991). As nonword stimuli have no lexical representations with which to recover missing information in the phonological trace, they fail to benefit from redintegration and hence are more poorly recalled.

Roodenrys et al. (1993) found some evidence for an increased lexical contribution to serial recall in older children. Ten year-old children showed a greater lexicality effect than young children, although the changes in magnitude failed to reach statistical significance. We have recently had the opportunity to explore further the development of the lexicality effect in the course of standardizing the Working Memory Test Battery for Children (Gathercole & Pickering, 2001; Pickering & Gathercole, 2001). The battery includes tests of immediate serial recall of one-syllable words and nonwords, and has been normed in large samples of children aged 5–15 years (n = 750 in total). The data are quite clear. Although the memory span advantage to words over nonwords increased in absolute magnitude with age, the proportionate cost of including nonwords rather than words in the memory sequence shows no consistent increase with age, remaining more or less invariant at around 32%. Children as young as 4 years of age therefore appear to able to exploit fully long-term lexical knowledge to reconstruct partial memory traces, indicating that developmental changes in the extent or efficiency of this redintegrative process do not contribute to the developmental improvements in serial recall.

In summary, many processes contribute to immediate verbal memory performance, as illustrated by the complexity of computational models of short-term memory (Burgess & Hitch, 1998; Page & Norris, 1999). The steady increase in immediate serial recall performance across the childhood years probably originates from multiple sources. The subvocal rehearsal process changes both qualitatively and quantitatively with age: it is not used to maintain representations in the phonological store or to recode nonauditory material into phonological form until around 7 years of age, and its speed and hence efficiency at preventing decay in the phonological store increases over the remaining years through to early adulthood. Other age-related factors that may influence the developmental function include changes in the efficiency of serial order mechanisms and in the speed of memory search. In concert, these developments combine to yield a robust and highly specialized system for retaining sequences of phonological material, which undergoes a lengthy period of development spanning the childhood years.

Developmental Impairments of Verbal Short-term Memory

One notable feature of children's performance on tests of phonological short-term memory is the high degree of variability across individuals. Although memory span increases regularly across age when assessed on the basis of group data at each chronological point, very large differences are found in span estimates for individual children at any one age. For unselected cohorts of young children, these differences in phonological memory capacity have been found to relate closely to two important aspects of language development: vocabulary acquisition (e.g. Avons et al., 1998; Gathercole & Baddeley, 1989, 1993; Gathercole et al., 1992; Michas & Henry, 1994) and speech production (Adams & Gathercole, 1995, 1996; Blake et al., 1994; Speidel, 1989, 1991).

These and related findings have led to the proposal that a primary function of the phonological loop is to support language learning (Baddeley et al., 1998b; Gathercole & Baddeley, 1993). Consistent with this view, children with *specific language impairment* (SLI) have been found to have extremely poor phonological short-term memory function. The evidence for phonological memory deficits in children with this disorder, and for the possible role of these deficits in the symptomology of the disorder, is briefly considered below.

SLI is a term applied to the estimated 5–7% of children in the general population who fail to develop language normally despite normal levels of general intellectual attainment and in the absence of any other problems of a physical, social or emotional nature (Stevenson & Richman, 1976). This developmental pathology is associated with persisting deficits in the production and comprehension of language, including in particular poor vocabulary development, immature syntax and impaired grammatical morphology. For many children diagnosed as specific language-impaired, a genetic origin seems likely (Gopnik & Crago, 1991; Bishop et al., 1996). On tests of verbal short-term memory, SLI children have been consistently found to underperform even younger control children matched on general language ability. Their deficit is particularly marked when procedures such as nonword repetition, which use phonologically unfamiliar stimuli, are employed (Gathercole & Baddeley, 1990; Gillam & van Kleeck, 1996; Gillam et al., 1995; James et al., 1994; Kail et al., 1984; Montgomery, 1995), e.g. the SLI group studied by Gathercole & Baddeley (1990) had a mean chronological age of 8 years, performed at the level of an average 6 year-old on standardized language tests of vocabulary knowledge, language comprehension and reading, but had the nonword repetition skills of a 4 year-old child. The problems in nonword repetition of this SLI group therefore far outweigh even their poor performance on language measures which are the criterion variables for specific language impairment. A twin study involving children with a language impairment diagnosis and their co-twins by Bishop et al. (1996) yielded high heritability estimates for nonword repetition which, the authors suggest, may provide an excellent phenotypic marker for the SLI condition.

We have suggested that these deficits arise from extreme limitations in phonological loop capacity, probably located in the phonological store rather than in the subvocal rehearsal process, which appears to operate at a language-appropriate level in SLI children (Baddeley et al., 1998b; Gathercole & Baddeley, 1990). It is this poor temporary storage of incoming speech stimuli, we propose, that may lie at the root of the difficulties encountered by SLI children in establishing durable long-term phonological representations of novel words (e.g. Dollaghan, 1987; Ellis-Weismer & Hesketh, 1996; Rice et al., 1991). The phonological storage deficit may also contribute to the impaired abilities of SLI children to learn complex syntactic patterns, in the manner suggested by Adams & Gathercole (1995, 1996) and Speidel (1991). Thus, the suggestion is that impairments in a child's ability to store phonological material temporarily may be sufficient to disrupt many different aspects of language development to a sufficient degree to yield a profile of specific language impairment.

Detailed analysis of memory deficits associated with other kinds of learning disabilities is provided by Vicari & Carlesimo (Chapter 23, this volume).

Assessment of Verbal Short-term Memory

Forward digit span is the most widely used technique for assessing verbal short-term memory ability in children, due largely to its presence in large-scale intelligence test batteries, such as the Wechsler Intelligence Scales for Children—III UK (Wechsler, 1991), and the British Ability Scales II (Elliott, 1996). The Test of Memory & Learning (Reynolds & Bigler, 1994) includes standardized assessments of forward recall of both digits and letter sequences.

Measures of serial recall incorporating stimuli from a highly familiar item pool, such as digits and letters, may in fact be rather less sensitive to basic phonological storage capacities than other measures, as a consequence of its use of digit names as the to-be-remembered items (Gathercole et al., 1994). Digit sequences, for example, offer the rememberer opportunities to chunk or recode sequences of digits into higher-order number patterns, and also are so highly familiar and phonologically redundant that for most items, retention of the vowel sound will be sufficient to allow correct guessing of the whole item. For this reason, it may be advisable to combine this standard method of assessment with other immediate memory measures, such as serial recall of open sets of words or nonwords (Working Memory Test Battery for Children; Pickering & Gathercole, 2001) or nonword repetition (Gathercole & Baddeley, 1996).

Visuospatial Short-term Memory

Visuospatial short-term memory supports our capacities to remember and manipulate mentally the physical features and dimensions of events such as shape, colour and movement. Logie (1994) has recently proposed that the sketchpad consists of two primary subcomponents: a visual store, in which the physical characteristics of objects and events can be represented, and a spatial mechanism that can be used for planning movements and which may also serve a rehearsal function by reactivating the contents of the visual store. Although in practice very little memory material is either purely visual or purely spatial, the visuospatial distinction is supported by several reported neuropsychological dissociations (Della Sala et al., 1999; Farah et al., 1988; Hanley et al., 1991). Neuroimaging studies have identified cortical activity in frontal and parietal sites of the right hemisphere during visuospatial memory tasks (Smith & Jonides, 1998; O'Reilly et al., 1999). The detailed mechanisms involved in visuospatial short-term memory are discussed by Della Sala and Logie (Chapter 13, this volume).

Development of Visuospatial Short-term Memory

Like the phonological loop, the visuospatial sketchpad markedly increases in capacity during the childhood years. In order to assess this subsystem of working memory adequately, it is necessary to employ stimuli that cannot be verbally recoded in order to gain access to the phonological loop, a common strategy in children beyond about 7 years of age (Hitch et al., 1989a, 1989b). Further information on suitable methods for assessing visuospatial short-term memory are provided by Della Sala et al. (1999), Pickering (in press) and Pickering & Gathercole (2001).

The precise mechanisms underpinning the developmental improvements in visuospatial short-term memory are as yet not fully understood. One debate concerns whether or not there are separable visual and spatial memory systems that undergo independent development (Logie & Pearson, 1997; Pickering et al., 2001). Other research has indicated that at least part of the sizeable improvements in visuospatial short-term memory function with age reflects increasing dependence on either the central executive (Wilson et al., 1987) or the phonological loop (Miles et al., 1996). Detailed discussion of these and other possible nonvisual recoding strategies contributing to the development of visuospatial short-term memory is provided by Pickering (2001).

The Central Executive

In adults, central executive activity has been found to be strongly associated with bilateral activity in the dorsolateral prefrontal cortex (e.g. O'Reilly et al., 1999). Interestingly, the frontal lobe undergoes more extended development than other areas (e.g. Diamond, 1990), with metabolic activity not reaching adult levels until adolescence (Elman et al., 1998).

Development of the Central Executive

The capacity of the central executive, like that of the other two components of working memory, undergoes an extended period of development during the childhood years. Central executive function is typically assessed using tasks, also termed "complex working memory tasks", which have significant processing and storage loads. An example of such a task is listening span, in which an individual has to verify some feature of each of a series of spoken sentences at the same time as retaining the sequence of the final words of the preceding sentences (Daneman & Carpenter, 1980). Another memory task considered to have a significant central executive component is backward digit recall, which involves recalling a digit sequence in the reverse order to its original presentation. Each of these tasks clearly requires processing and/or transformation of material as well as storage. Performance of children on versions of these two tasks is shown in Figure 22.2.

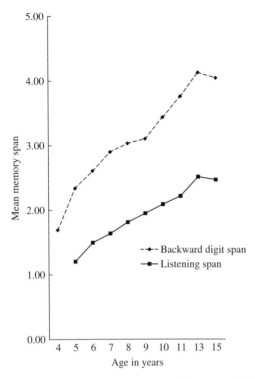

Figure 22.2 Listening span and backward digit span as a function of age. Data from Pickering & Gathercole (2001)

The two major classes of explanation that have been advanced for these developmental changes have emerged largely from a school of North American research focusing on general working memory. For the present purposes, the terms "central executive" and "working memory" can be used more or less synonymously, although they have emerged from two quite distinct empirical and theoretical traditions. The major distinction between the two frameworks is the extent to which the major constraint on working memory is viewed as either the processing demands of specific activities or a general capacity for controlling attention.

According to Daneman, Carpenter and colleagues (e.g. Daneman & Carpenter, 1980; Just & Carpenter, 1992), working memory is fuelled by a limited capacity processing resource which can be flexibly allocated to meet the processing and storage demands of complex cognitive activities. Thus, in tasks in which processing and storage demands exceed the available capacity, there will be a tradeoff between processing and storage activities: the greater the resource devoted to ongoing processing, the less that there will be available to dedicate to storing the products of processing activities. Using this framework, Case et al. (1980) proposed that, during the childhood years, the total amount of processing resource available to support these activities remains constant but the efficiency of processing activities increases. Thus, as the child grows older and more skilled at processing and manipulating information, the amount of resource required to support processing decreases and memory storage capacity increases.

This singular view of development as reflecting different points in a tradeoff function between processing and storage has recently been challenged by Towse et al. 1998). They demonstrated that performance on complex working memory tasks is strongly influenced by the time over which children must store items in short-term memory, with greater memory delays being associated with increased storage decrements. This feature of memory performance cannot readily be accommodated by a processing/storage tradeoff account. Instead, it points to the possibility of age-related changes in task-switching behaviour and in decay functions as possible origins of the striking differences found in complex working memory performance at different points in childhood.

An alternative conceptualization of complex working memory emphasizes selective attention rather than processing efficiency *per se* as the major constraint on task performance. Engle and colleagues (Cantor & Engle, 1993; Engle et al., 1999) have argued that working memory consists of domain-general controlled attention which is applied to activated long-term memory structures. Findings of close associations between estimates of working memory capacity for different domains of activity (e.g. Jurden, 1995)are consistent with this view that working memory performance is constrained by a single general factor, rather than by processing expertise in particular domains.

Although this framework has primarily been developed and applied to the understanding of individual differences in complex working memory, rather than development, there is evidence for age-related changes in attention underpinning the improved working memory capacities in older children. Swanson (1999) conducted a large-scale study of individuals aged 6–57 years in which working memory performance was assessed under a variety of access, storage and processing conditions for both verbal and visuospatial material. The results showed that age-related changes in performance were not specific to either verbal or visuospatial domains, and were related to the memory access and storage demands of the activities, rather than to processing demands. Swanson argues on this basis that the amount of activation of long-term structures changes with age, due to increase availability of attentional resources as children grow older.

It should be noted that the view that individual differences in complex working memory have their source in the capacity of general controlled attention, rather than in more domain-specific processing and storage constraints, is not uncontentious. Evidence from other research groups points to limitations in working memory capacity that are highly specific to particular knowledge and processing domains (e.g. Shah & Miyake, 1996). There is also concern about the extent to which contrasting verbal and visuospatial tasks used in some studies truly tap distinct underlying domains, and so have the power to test the domain-specificity of working memory.

Developmental Impairments of the Central Executive

In the past decade close links have been established between central executive capacities and attainments in many key intellectual domains during childhood. Central executive function is closely associated with the comprehension of both written and spoken language in both children and adults (Daneman & Merikle, 1996), and with mathematical abilities (Bull & Johnston, 1997; Furst & Hitch, 2000; McLean & Hitch, 1999). Furthermore, children with reading disabilities show significant impairments of complex memory capacity. Recent evidence indicates that this is a genuine causal link rather than a simple association (Engle et al., 1999). Individuals with good working memory abilities are also particularly good at acquiring the conceptual aspects of vocabulary acquisition (Daneman & Green, 1986).

The development of mathematical ability is constrained by central executive capacity. While it is certainly the case that working memory (as well as phonological short-tem memory) can play a crucial role in supporting on-line mental arithmetic in both children and adults (Adams & Hitch, 1997; Logie et al., 1994), evidence that either system is crucial to the acquisition of arithmetic ability over the entire childhood period is inconsistent(Bull & Johnston, 1997; Bull et al., 1999; McLean & Hitch, 1999). This may possibly reflect the fact that, whereas working memory is important for components of mathematical ability, such as mental arithmetic, it may play a relatively minimal role in supporting the understanding of conceptual aspects of mathematics, which are crucial at other points in a child's mathematical education.

Studies of adult participants have established links between complex working memory capacity and many high-level cognitive abilities, including following directions, note-taking, writing, reasoning and complex learning (see Engle et al., 1999). It might therefore be expected that children with compromised central executive function will be educationally disadvantaged at school. There is accumulating evidence that this is indeed the case. Children who performed below expected levels of attainment in National Curriculum assessments in English and maths at 7 years had significant deficits on central executive tasks relative to their normally achieving peers (Gathercole & Pickering, 2000). These data indicate that the consequences of compromised central executive function may be far-reaching for young children. More severe central executive deficits may lead to significant learning difficulties. Gathercole & Pickering (2001) found that central executive measures were highly effective in identifying 6- and 7-year-old children who were currently recognized by their schools as having special educational needs arising from learning difficulties. These measures also successfully discriminated children whose special needs were not acknowledged until more than a year after the memory assessment. In addition to providing support for the contention that working memory is a key system in supporting learning in an educational context, these findings suggest that working memory assessments may provide a valuable means of identifying children at present and future educational risk.

The Episodic Buffer

Current thinking about the development of the central executive is clearly challenged by the recent expansion of the working memory model to include an episodic buffer, which acts as an interface between the slave systems and long-term memory (Baddeley, 2000). In the new model, it is the episodic buffer, rather than the central executive, which integrates and stores information from different cognitive systems. The combined processing and storage measures that are widely used as methods of assessing individual differences and developmental changes in central executive capacity may therefore need to be re-conceptualized as measures of the storage capacity of the episodic buffer.

Perhaps, then, it is the episodic buffer rather than the central executive that supports learning and the acquisition of complex cognitive skills during childhood. This seems quite plausible. A common feature of the mental activities involved in the process of acquiring complex cognitive skills during childhood is the need to integrate information from temporary memory and long-term memory systems at particular points in time. This multimodal storage is, for example, a crucial feature of mental arithmetic, when the child needs to store the partial products of computations while accessing and applying learned rules relating to number. Similarly, a child using context to guide interpretation of the unfamiliar ortho- graphic form of a new word in text needs to store the propositional or semantic attributes of the prior text while attempting to decode, using either phonological or orthographic strategies, the novel string.

The multimodal nature of the representational code employed by the episodic buffer potentially provides an ideal medium for the temporary storage burdens encountered in young children when acquiring skills in complex domains, such as literacy and mathematics. It may therefore be relatively unsurprising that a child with relatively poor episodic buffer capacity would encounter significant difficulties in progressing in these key educational domains.

Assessment of the Central Executive

Versions of listening span, counting span and backward digit recall have recently been standardized for children (Pickering & Gathercole, 2001). Pennington & Ozonoff (1996) provide information concerning methods for assessing higher-order executive functions, such as set switching and inhibition.

LONG-TERM MEMORY

We have seen above that children, like adults, have well-marked capacities to retain and manipulate many different types of information in short-term memory, and that differences in these capacities may have direct consequences for the individual child's abilities to learn in many different ways. So, there appear to be important links between short-term memory and long-term learning. But what about children's long-term memory? The term is used here to refer to memory for events that occurred hours, days, months and years ago. What distinguishes long-term memory used in this way from learning is that it refers not to memory for repeated events, but instead for single distant episodes. This type of memory is almost always incomplete, and is not typically associated with any conscious attempt to learn.

The Development of Episodic Memory

Over relatively short periods, such as hours and days, adults are rather good at being able to retrieve information about mundane aspects of our lives, such as the food we ate at a particular meal, and where the car was parked. At longer intervals—weeks or years—we are unlikely to remember the details of such events, or even to judge whether or not they happened. This most recent type of long-term memory is referred to as episodic memory (Tulving, 1972).

How episodic memory develops during childhood is an issue that has greatly interested experimental and developmental psychologists. The dependence on verbal reports in as- sessing episodic memory has made it difficult to assess episodic memory prior to about

3 years of age using conventional procedures. Nonverbal techniques suitable for use with infants have been developed, although whether or not such techniques tap episodic memory remains a matter of debate (Bauer & Mandler, 1989; Meltzoff, 1988; Nelson, 1994). More detailed coverage of findings using such techniques is provided by Gathercole (1998).

Beyond the infancy years, most research on the development of episodic memory has emerged from the burgeoning eyewitness memory tradition. The need to understand the quality of children's memory for distant events has become an imperative as a consequence of increasing dependence on testimony provided by child witnesses in the courtroom, in cases relating to child abuse, domestic violence and crime in schools. The interpretation of such evidence clearly requires scientific evaluation of the reliability of children's memory and of the developmental changes that occur. The principal issues guiding research in this area concern whether there are age differences in the reliability of children's memory for experienced events, whether there are age differences in the susceptibility of children to misleading suggestions made by others, and which are the best methods of obtaining unbiased memories in children.

Most research on children's eyewitness memory uses episodic memory-type paradigms in which the child either sees an enactment of an event or hears a story in which he/she is not an active participant. Consistent with the investigations of children's autobiographical memories reviewed above, young children (and especially, preschool children) in these tasks recall considerably less of the target events than either older children or adults (e.g. Cohen & Harnick, 1980; King & Yuille, 1987; Oates & Shrimpton, 1991; Ornstein et al., 1992). It has been suggested that the reason is that young children have relatively impoverished memory representations of events that may arise from poor understanding of the causal structure of the events (Pillemer et al., 1994).

Adults' memory for witnessed events is fallible, too, and has been shown on many occasions to be liable to distortion by misleading postevent information. Using the eyewitness testimony paradigm developed by Loftus (1979), in which a memory event is followed by some questions which incorporate inaccurate information, it has been found that children below 7 years are even more vulnerable to distortion following exposure to misleading information about the memory event than older children and adults, e.g. Ceci et al. (1987) presented to children a story about a girl who had a stomachache from eating her breakfast too fast. Subsequently, the children were asked a biased question: "Do you remember the story about Loren, the girl who had a headache because she ate her cereal too fast?" Still later, the children were given a forced-choice recognition task involving two pictures; in one, Loren was eating her cereal and in the other (incorrect one) she had a headache. In this experiment, the probability of making correct recognition judgments was lower for such biased than unbiased information, and the extent of the biasing decrement decreased regularly from the younger (3–4 years) to the older (10–12 years) children. In a recent review, Ceci & Bruck (1993) found such evidence of increased suggestibility to misleading information in younger children in 88% of such eyewitness testimony studies. According to Ceci (1995), "there are reliable age differences in suggestibility, with preschool children's reports being more readily impeded by the presence of erroneous suggestions by an interviewer than older children's reports" (p. 155).

These findings suggest that the integrity of young children's memories for real-life events is unlikely to survive detailed questioning in and out of the courtroom. Ceci et al. (1994) attempted to simulate this by asking children to think, repeatedly over a 10-week period, about both real events and events that never happened, e.g. a false event could be cued by the interviewer saying to the child, "Think real hard, and tell me if this ever happened to you. Can you ever remember going to hospital with a mousetrap on your finger?" Over the period of the study, 58% of preschool children produced false narratives and at least one false event description, and one-quarter of the children responded with "memories" to the majority of the fictionalized event descriptions. So, mere exposure to adults asking you about events which did not take place is clearly sufficient under some circumstances to yield false memories. Possibly most troubling of all, Ceci et al. video-taped the children in this experiment being given a forensic-style interview about both real and false events, and showed the tapes to psychologists specializing in children's testimony. These professionals were no better than chance at discriminating children's recounting of true than false memories.

The evidence reviewed so far indicates that young children have both relatively poor event memory and are highly suggestible (to misleading information). For a detailed analysis of the roots of this comparatively low reliability of preschoolers' memories, it is useful to consider possible mechanisms for suggestibility effects. Loftus et al. (1985) suggested that postevent information (such as a biasing question) may destructively update the original memory trace, replacing the original target information with the later biasing information. Quite plausibly, it could be argued that the lower levels of organization and integration of information within the original in younger children might be particularly low in resistance to such updating. Another mechanism considered by Loftus et al. is that the subsequent biased material is retained in a coexisting memory with the original information but that, possibly as a consequence of its more recent date, it suppresses access to incompatible material in the earlier memory trace and hence leads to biasing errors. To account for the greater degree of suggestibility of young children via this mechanism, it would be necessary to make the rather arbitrary assumption that the inhibitory effect of the later memory on access to the original memory trace is more severe in younger children.

Other accounts of memory suggestibility effects make less strong claims about the impact of later events on original memory representations. McCloskey & Zaragoza (1985; see also Zaragoza & Lane, 1994) suggested that the later biased information neither distorts nor denies access to the original memory information, but instead is used to fill in gaps in incompletely specified memory traces. Thus, in very young children, who are already known to have particularly poorly specified memories, the probability of misleading information being used in this way to complete earlier memories will be particularly high.

A related view is that the increased suggestibility of young children reflects their response to the demand characteristics of the memory situation, in which the child is provided with new information by the adult experimenter, an authority figure (Poole & Lindsay, 1995). Thus the child may assume that the postevent suggestions are valid and so consciously base his/her responses on the suggestions rather than the original, and possibly conflicting, memories. In Ceci et al.'s (1994) simulated false memory situation, the child may simply assume that if the experimenter thinks that he/she went to hospital attached to a mousetrap, it must be right. Consistent with this compliance view, the impact of biasing postevent information on young children is now known to be reduced if its source is another child, rather than an adult (Ceci et al., 1993).

A further possibility is that the young child remembers both the critical detail of the original event and the content of the postevent suggestion (in the example of the Ceci et al., 1987, study, this would be the stomachache and the headache), but is uncertain as to which detail occurred in the original story. This represents a failure of what has come to be known as source monitoring, or the ability to discriminate between memories from different sources. Young children have been found to make more errors than adults in discriminating between performed and imagined actions (Foley & Johnson, 1985; Foley et al., 1983; Lindsay et al., 1991), although these developmental differences in monitoring do appear somewhat inconsistent across studies (e.g. Roberts & Blades, 1995; Foley et al., 1991). There is certainly direct evidence that source confusions in eyewitness testimony tasks are greater in younger than older children (Ackil & Zaragoza, 1995), lending further weight to this suggestion that very young children are not necessarily unduly misled, but instead are often unable to remember what detail was supplied by what source.

In summary, the vulnerability of preschool children to misinformation after the memory event is widely accepted but the causes for the apparent memory distortions are still open to debate. It certainly seems plausible that much of the apparent distortion of their memories does not necessarily reflect alterations in the original memory representation but rather other factors, such as compliance to the suggestions of adult authority figures and uncertainty about the precise source of the remembered information. Practical implications follow from this analysis. In particular, incorporating source-monitoring questions (e.g. "Did you see that happen, or did somebody tell you that it happened?") into interviews with child witnesses should lead to an increase in the reliability of their testimony (Poole & Lindsay, 1995).

The Development of Autobiographical Memory

In real life, of course, specific events are remembered over much longer periods than are tapped in the experimental paradigms discussed in the previous section—for years and decades, in some cases. We can often recall some features of salient events which took place a long time ago, such as moving house, a particularly impactful conversation with a colleague, a wedding, or a car accident. Our memories of such events is almost always incomplete, in that we remember much less material than we would if the event had taken place earlier today. Some important information, however, endures over a long period of time and allows us to reminisce. This type of remembering of genuine events which can take place over many years is termed "autobiographical memory". Autobiographical memory is high in self-reference, and frequently accompanied by a personal interpretation, in contrast to laboratory-tested episodic memory described above (Conway, 1990, 1996). There appear to be at least three highly significant aspects of autobiographical memory knowledge: specific events, general classes of events, and lifetime periods, which are organized hierarchically (Conway, 1990). These different sources of knowledge are combined at time of remembering to construct the dynamic representations of specific events which correspond to our phenomenological experience of being able to remember a distant event (Conway, 1996; Conway & Rubin, 1993; Neisser, 1962).

One extremely important feature of the development of autobiographical memory is childhood amnesia: the inability of older children and adults to retrieve memories about events which took place before 2 years of age, and the relative infrequency of recall of memories for the period between about 2 and 5 years are relatively infrequent. Pillemer & White (1989) estimated the average age of the earliest retrieved memory as 3.5 years.

This scarcity of memories for events in the earliest years of life has been attributed to a variety of different factors. One theory is that adults' failures to retrieve memories from early childhood and infancy reflects inaccessibility rather than absence of memory traces for very early events. Remembering personal events which occurred many years ago is not simply a passive act of retrieval, but is instead a reconstructive process in which different types of knowledge about the structure of events and one's life is applied to incomplete memory traces to generate a stable representation (Conway, 1996; Neisser, 1962). Neisser suggested that the adult "schemata" applied at retrieval will fail to make sense of the fragments available for early childhood events, and that this "schema-mismatch" is the source of childhood amnesia.

Other more specific accounts of the changes in children's memories during the early part of life and the ways in which these changes may contribute to childhood amnesia have been advanced in recent years. Nelson and associates have proposed that autobiographical memories are not formed during the childhood amnesia period, and that this is why they are not subsequently available for retrieval in childhood (Nelson & Gruendel, 1981). Analyses of children's memories for events within this critical period of late infancy and the preschool years provide some support for this view. Young children are better at describing the features of familiar, repeated events, such as going to nursery and having lunch at MacDonald's, than at recalling details of specific incidents which occurred just once (Hudson, 1986; Hudson & Nelson, 1986; Nelson, 1978; Nelson & Gruendel, 1981; Nelson & Ross, 1980). This finding has prompted the proposal that during the early years of life, children incorporate their ongoing experiences into frames of knowledge for familiar events or scripts, such as going to nursery and eating at MacDonalds, but do not (unlike older children and adults) retain detailed of specific incidents. By this account, information about specific details of events that depart from the routine are only retained in an emerging autobiographical memory system by about 4 years of age, when the child has developed an extensive repertoire of generic knowledge about the event structure of his/her life. Nelson (1993a, 1993b) argues that such an evolving system is an efficient use of the child's cognitive resources, since before such generic knowledge has been accumulated, it is not possible for the child to judge what is and what is not unusual, and therefore he/she cannot effectively judge what features of an episode to store in memory.

The view that children do not have detailed autobiographical memories for specific incidents during the period of childhood amnesia is that it is at odds with a considerable amount of other evidence. Nelson's (1989) transcripts and analysis of the bedtime talk of an infant, Emily, between the ages of 19 and 37 months show that over short timescales of a day or less, Emily was able to recall many detailed features of the day's activities. On a larger timescale, Fivush & Hamond (1990) found that at 2 years, many children had memories of events which took place 6 months previously and that at 4 years, some children were able to recall events from 2 years earlier.

To account for such findings, Nelson (1993a, 1993b) proposed that children's early memories of recent events are served not by autobiographical memory but by a short-term holding system, episodic memory. Emily's crib talk reflects use of this system. How then can children, on occasion, remember details of events over much longer periods, as Fivush & Hamond (1990) have shown? Nelson suggests that this might be achieved by the reinstatement of previous event contexts, which appears to prolong very substantially, even in young infants, the amount of time that information can be preserved in episodic memory. Several studies have now demonstrated that reinstatement, or the re-presentation of an earlier event some time after its initial occurrence, will effectively extend a child's memory for that event (Bauer et al., 1995; Boller et al., 1996; Fivush & Hamond, 1989; Rovee-Collier et al., 1980).

Pre-autobiographical system

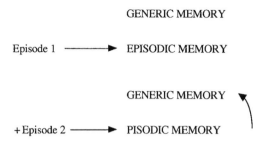

Post-autobiographical system

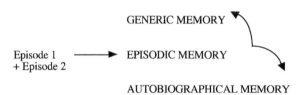

AUTOBIOGRAPHICAL MEMORY

Figure 22.3 Schematic representation of developmental changes to long-term memory, according to and adapted from Nelson (1993a)

Nelson's (1993a, 1993b) views of the changes that take place in the types of memory knowledge or systems available to support remembering of distant events are summarized schematically in Figure 22.3. In the pre-autobiographical stage that characterizes the infancy and preschool period, memory is supported by two systems, episodic memory and generic memory. Repeated encounters with similar events allow access to the generic memory system. In the subsequent postautobiographical system, autobiographical memory emerges and interacts with semantic, generic and episodic memory to provide a dynamic and flexible system for remembering both recent and distant events.

Fivush, Nelson and colleagues suggest that autobiographical memory emerges at this point because children have learned how to talk about their memories, and specifically how to formulate memories as narratives. Fivush et al. (1996) provide evidence that although adults engage children in conversations involving reminiscence of shared events as young as 2 years and below, the young child makes little substantive contribution to the collective activity of remembering, even when cued. By 4 years, however, the typical child is competent in talking within the narrative structure appropriate for shared reminiscence (Fivush et al., 1995). Fivush et al. (1996) identify two possible contributors to this emerging competence. Firstly, adults gradually introduce children to more rich and complex ways of talking about earlier events. Secondly, the child's increasing facility at language provides the opportunity for restructuring and understanding past experiences in a way that more closely approximates to the adult narrative form. Through these and other processes, it is proposed that a coherent and organized autobiographical memory system can eventually be developed and used from 4 years onwards, with increasing effectiveness for supporting memory for distant events.

In an important test of whether narrative coherence in talking about memories heralds the end of childhood amnesia, Pillemer et al. (1994) provided a detailed investigation of whether the degree of narrative structuring of young children's memory for a recent autobiographical event predicts the likelihood of recall of the same event 7 years later. The children participating in the Pillemer study had attended a preschool center and had experienced an unusual event in which a fire alarm went off, caused by burning popcorn in another part of the building. The children duly evacuated the building, following the emergency procedure. Pillemer et al. tested the children's memories for this exciting event 2 weeks later and then again after a delay of 7 years. The most interesting aspect of the findings related to the subdivision of the children according to their age at the time of the original event. Seven years later, 57% of the 4 year-old group produced either an intact or fragmentary memory of the event, whereas only 18% of the children who were 3 years at the time of the event were able to do so. Similarly, whereas 86% of the older group selected the correct location of classroom from which they were evacuated in a forced-choice test, the younger children performed at chance level on this measure. Thus, despite the very long period intervening between the event and the later unexpected memory test, the 1 year age difference at original experience between the younger and older preschool children had powerful consequences for the much later memory of this real-life event.

Pillemer et al. (1994) accommodates these findings in a cognitive developmental approach to childhood amnesia (Pillemer, 1992; Pillemer & White, 1989; Usher & Neisser, 1993). According to this, the possibility and quality of later recall is dependent upon the degree of correspondence between the cognitive mechanisms in place at the time of experiencing the original event and attempting to recollect it. Pillemer et al. suggest that the principal constraining factor at original experience was the degree of causal understanding of the narrative structure of the event, with the older children showing superior understanding of relationship of the different components of the event to one another. The greater the narrative coherence at the time, the more organized the resulting memory trace and the closer the match with the narrative schemas applied to interpret the incomplete memory traces many years later.

A different perspective on the development of autobiographical memory was advanced by Howe & Courage (1997). They propose that autobiographical memory emerges between 18 and 24 months, as soon as the awareness of oneself as having specific cognitive capacities (termed the "cognitive self"). According to this account, there is no developmental discontinuity in memory systems prior and subsequent to the emergence of autobiographical memory. Rather, basic memory systems are in place from early infancy, and the organizing structure of the cognitive self acts upon these to generate autobiographical memories. Increases in the accuracy of autobiographical memory subsequent to 2 years are attributed by Howe and Courage to a variety of developmental changes, including increased linguistic proficiency, narrative knowledge and memory storage capacity.

In addition to these general developmental factors, which appear to govern the quality and quantity of autobiographical memories in childhood, emotional experience appears to play a critical role in the establishment of enduring autobiographical memories during childhood. The degree of trauma associated with a personally-experienced event has a substantial impact on a young child's subsequent memories. Ornstein (1995) found superior recall in children of experiencing an unpleasant medical procedure than of a routine visit to a doctor. Similarly, Hamond & Fivush (1990) obtained recall protocols from young children for their experience of Hurricane Andrew, which contained over twice the degree of detail as a comparable group of children's recall of a family trip to Disneyworld. These and other findings indicate that in children as in adults, the degree of personal involvement and emotional experience accompanying events are important determinants of the memorability of the event (Conway, 1995).

There are clearly major developmental changes in the organization of autobiographical memory in the early childhood years. As adults we remember very little from these years (childhood amnesia). Children do remember some specific details of distant events during the period of up to 4 years or so, but their recall of the memories tends to be either lacking in specific detail or fragmentary and disorganized at this time. Theorists disagree, however, about whether the changes over these years reflect the initial absence and then eventual emergence of an autobiographical memory system (Nelson, 1993a, 1993b) or gradual changes to the ways in which the child organizes his/her experience (Howe & Courage, 1997; Usher & Neisser, 1993).

Assessment of Long-term Memory

There are many tests available for assessing episodic memory function in childhood. These range from measures of delayed and repeated free recall of words, to memory for faces and other nonverbal stimuli, for stories, for routes and for future actions. There are relevant subtests on the Test of Memory and Learning (Reynolds & Bigler, 1994), and the Children's Memory Scale (Cohen, 1997). The Rivermead Behavioural Memory Test for Children (Wilson et al., 1991) also provides a valuable tool for evaluating a broad range of real life memory function.

CONCLUSIONS

Memory performance in each of the basic memory systems reviewed in this chapter improves dramatically during the years spanning infancy and early adulthood. Evidence from many sources converges on the view that the developmental gains observed cannot be accounted for in terms of any single maturational process. First, different memory systems have distinct neuroanatomical bases, with dissociable developmental trajectories in terms of both neural structure and metabolic activity (Cycowicz, 2000; Elman et al., 1998; Nelson, 1995). Second, age-related changes in multiple rather than single processes give rise to the deceptively smooth developmental function. This point is perhaps most clearly illustrated in the analysis of the development of a relatively simple memory system whose theoretical underpinnings are well understood—verbal short-term memory. Third, developmental changes are qualitative as well as quantitative in nature. As children grow older, they increasingly depend on strategies to promote memory and learning, often aided by emerging metamemory skills (for review, see Pressley & Schneider, 1997). Fourth, individual differences in memory are highly specific to memory systems: a child with deficits in one aspect of memory function may nonetheless perform normally in other memory domains (for further examples, see Temple, Chapter 24, this volume).

The importance of memory function during childhood cannot be underestimated. The complex and idiosyncratic memory profiles characterizing individual children directly influence crucial aspects of their day-to-day experiences and longer-term achievements: memory skills constrain not only the quality of explicit memory reports, but also the acquisition of higher-order abilities in a variety of domains. Analysis of children's memory function therefore represents a vital step in understanding their cognitive development.

REFERENCES

Ackil, J.K. & Zaragoza, M.S. (1995). Developmental differences in eyewitness suggestibility and memory for source. *Journal of Experimental Child Psychology*, **60**, 57–83.

Adams, A.-M. & Gathercole, S.E. (1995). Phonological working memory and speech production in preschool children. *Journal of Speech and Hearing Research*, **38**, 403–414.

Adams, A.-M. & Gathercole, S.E. (1996). Phonological working memory and spoken language development in young children. *Quarterly Journal of Experimental Psychology*, **49A**, 216–233.

Adams, J.W. & Hitch, G.J. (1997). Working memory in children's mental arithmetic. *Journal of Experimental Child Psychology*, **67**, 21–38.

Avons, S.E., Wragg, C.A. & Cupples, I. (1998. Measures of phonological short-term memory and their relationship to vocabulary development. *Applied Psycholinguistics*, **19**, 583–601.

Baddeley, A.D. (1986). *Working Memory*. Oxford: Oxford University Press.

Baddeley, A.D. (2000). The episodic buffer: a new component of working memory? *Trends in Cognitive Sciences*, **4**, 417–422.

Baddeley, A.D., Emslie, H., Kolodny, J. & Duncan, J. (1998a). Random generation and the executive control of working memory. *Quarterly Journal of Experimental Psychology*, **51A**, 819–852.

Baddeley, A.D., Gathercole, S.E. & Papagno, C. (1998b). The phonological loop as a language learning device. *Psychological Review*, **105**, 158–173.

Baddeley, A.D. & Hitch, G. (1974). Working memory. In G.A. Bower (ed.), *Recent Advances in Learning and Motivation*, Vol. 8. New York: Academic Press.

Baddeley, A.D., Lewis, V.J. & Vallar, G. (1984). Exploring the articulatory loop. *Quarterly Journal of Experimental Psychology*, **36**, 233–252.

Baddeley, A.D., Thomson, N. & Buchanan, M. (1975). Word length and the structure of short-term memory. *Journal of Verbal Learning and Verbal Behavior*, **14**, 575–589.

Bauer, P.J., Hertsgaard, L.A. & Wewerka, S.S. (1995). Effects of experience and reminding on long-term recall in infancy: remembering not to forget. *Journal of Experimental Child Psychology*, **59**, 260–298.

Bauer, P. & Mandler, M.M. (1989). One thing follows another: effects of temporal structure on 1- to 2 year-olds' recall of events. *Developmental Psychology*, **25**, 197–206.

Bishop, D.V.M, North, T. & Donlan, C. (1996). Nonword repetition as a behavioural marker for inherited language impairment: evidence from a twin study. *Journal of Child Psychology & Psychiatry*, **37**, 391–404.

Blake, J., Austin, W., Cannon, M. et al., (1994). The relationship between memory span and measures of imitative and spontaneous language complexity in preschool children. *International Journal of Behavioural Development*, **17**, 91–107.

Boller, K., Rovee-Collier, C., Gulya, M. & Prete, K. (1996). Infants' memory for context: timing effects of postevent information. *Journal of Experimental Child Psychology*, **63**, 583–602.

Bull, R. & Johnston, R.S. (1997) Children's arithmetic difficulties: contributions from processing speed, item identification, and short-term memory. *Journal of Experimental Child Psychology*, **65**, 1–24.

Bull, R., Johnston, R.S. & Roy, J.A. (1999) Exploring the roles of the visuospatial sketchpad and central executive in children's arithmetical skills: views from cognition and developmental neuropsychology. *Developmental Neuropsychology*, 15, 421–442.

Burgess, N. & Hitch, G.J. (1992). Toward a network model of the articulatory loop. *Journal of Memory and Language*, **31**, 429–460.

Burgess, N. & Hitch, G.J. (1998). Memory for serial order: a network model of the phonological loop and its timing. *Psychological Review*, **106**, 551–581.

Cantor, J. & Engle, R.W. (1993) Working memory capacity as long-term activation: an individual differences approach. *Journal of Experimental Psychology: Learning, Memory, & Cognition*, **19**, 1101–1114.

Case, R., Kurland, D.M. & Goldberg, J. (1982). Operational efficiency and the growth of short-term memory span. *Journal of Experimental Child Psychology*, **33**, 386–404.

Ceci, S.J. (1995). False beliefs: some developmental and clinical considerations. In D.L. Schacter (ed.), *Memory Distortion* (pp. 91–128). Cambridge, MA: Harvard University Press.

Ceci, S.J. & Bruck, M. (1993). The suggestibility of the child witness: a historical review and synthesis. *Psychological Bulletin*, **113**, 403–439.

Ceci, S.J., Huffman, M.L.C. & Smith, E. (1994). Repeatedly thinking about a non-event: source misattributions among preschoolers. *Consciousness and Cognition*, **3**, 388–407.

Ceci, S.J., Leichtman, M., Putnick, M. & Nightingale, N. (1993). Age differences in suggestibility. In D. Cicchetti & S. Toth (eds), *Child Abuse, Child Development, and Social Policy* (pp. 117–137). Norwood, NJ: Ablex.

Ceci, S.J., Ross, D.F. & Toglia, M.P. (1987). Suggestibility of children's memory: psycholegal implications. *Journal of Experimental Psychology: General*, **116**, 38–49.

Cohen, M.J. (1997). *Children's Memory Scale*. San Antonio, TX: Psychological Corporation.

Cohen, R.L. & Harnick, M.A. (1980). The susceptibility of child witnesses to suggestion. *Law and Behavior*, **4**, 201–210.

Conway, M.A. (1990). *Autobiographical Memory: An Introduction*. Milton Keynes: Open University Press.

Conway, M.A. (1995). *Flashbulb Memories*. Hove: Psychology Press.

Conway, M.A. (1996). Autobiographical knowledge and autobiographical memories. In D.C. Rubin (ed.), *Remembering Our Past: Studies in Autobiographical Memory* (pp. 67–93). Cambridge, MA: Cambridge University Press.

Conway, M.A. & Rubin, D.C. (1993). The structure of autobiographical memory. In A. Collins, S.E. Gathercole, M.A. Conway & P.E. Morris (eds), *Theories of Memory* (pp. 103–138). Hove: Erlbaum.

Cowan, N., Day, L., Saults, J.S. et al. (1992). The role of verbal output time in the effects of word length on immediate memory. *Journal of Memory & Language*, **31**, 1–17.

Cowan, N., Keller, T.A., Hulme, C. et al. (1994). Verbal memory span in children: speech timing cues to the mechanisms underlying age and word length effects. *Journal of Memory and Language*, **33**, 234–250.

Cowan, N., Wood, N.L., Wood, P.K. et al. (1998). Two separate verbal processing speeds contributing to verbal short-term memory span. *Journal of Experimental psychology: General*, **127**, 141–160.

Cycowicz, Y.M. (2000). Memory development and event-related brain potentials in children. *Biological Psychology*, **54**, 89–109.

Daneman, M. & Carpenter, P.A. (1980) Individual differences in working memory and reading. *Journal of Verbal Learning and Verbal Behavior*, **19**, 450–466.

Daneman, M. & Merikle, P.M. (1996). Working memory and language comprehension: a meta-analysis. *Psychonomic Bulletin & Review*, **3**, 422–433.

Daneman, M. & Green, I. (1986). Individual differences in comprehending and producing words in context. *Journal of Memory and Language*, **25**, 1–18.

Della Sala, S., Gray, C., Baddeley, A.D. et al. (1999). Pattern span: a tool for unwelding visuospatial memory. *Neuropsychologia*, **37**, 1189–1199.

Diamond, A. (1990) Developmental time course in human infants and infant monkeys, and the neural bases, of inhibitory control in reaching. In A. Diamond (ed.), *The development and Neural Bases of Higher Cognitive Functions*. New York: Annals of the New York Academy of Sciences, **608**, 394–426.

Dollaghan, C. (1987). Fast mapping in normal and language-impaired children. *Journal of Speech and Hearing Disorders*, **52**, 218–222.

Elliott, C.D. (1996). *British Abilities Scales II*. Windsor: NFER Nelson.

Ellis-Weismer, S. & Hesketh, L.J. (1996). Lexical learning by children with specific language impairment: Effects of linguistic input presented at varying speaking rates. *Journal of Speech and Hearing Research*, **39**, 177–190.

Elman, J.L., Bates, E.A., Johnson, M.H. et al. (1998). *Rethinking Innateness*. Cambridge, MA: MIT Press.

Engle, R.W., Kane, M.J. & Tuholski, S.W. (1999) Individual differences in working memory capacity and what they tell us about controlled attention, general fluid intelligence, and functions of the prefrontal cortex. In A. Miyake & P. Shah (eds), *Models of Working Memory*. (pp. 102–134). New York: Cambridge University Press.

Farah, M.J., Hamond, K.M., Levine, D.L. & Calvanio, R. (1988). Visual and spatial mental imagery: Dissociable systems of representation. *Cognitive Psychology*, **20**, 439–462.

Fivush, R., Haden, C. & Adam, S. (1995). Structure and coherence of preschoolers' personal narratives over time: implications for childhood amnesia. *Journal of Experimental Child Psychology*, **60**, 32–56.

Fivush, R., Haden, C. & Reese, E. (1996). Autobiographical knowledge and autobiographical memories. In D.C. Rubin (ed.), *Remembering Our Past: Studies in Autobiographical Memory* (pp. 341–359). New York: Cambridge University Press.

Fivush, R. & Hamond, N.R. (1989). Time and again: effects of repetition and retention interval on 2 year-olds' event recall. *Journal of Experimental child Psychology*, **47**, 259–273.

Fivush, R. & Hamond, N.R. (1990). Autobiographical memory across the preschool years: towards reconceptualising childhood amnesia. In R. Fivush & J.A. Hudson (eds), *Knowing and Remembering in Young Children* (pp. 223–248). New York: Cambridge University Press.

Flavell, J.H., Beach, D.R. & Chinsky, J.M. (1966). Spontaneous verbal rehearsal in a memory task as a function of age. *Child Development*, **37**, 283–299.

Foley, M.A., Durso, F.T., Wilder, A. & Friedman, R. (1991). Developmental comparisons of the ability to discriminate between memories from symbolic play enactments. *Developmental Psychology*, **30**, 206–217.

Foley, M.A. & Johnson, M.K. (1985). Confusions between memories for performed and imagined actions: a developmental comparison. *Child Development*, **54**, 1145–1155.

Foley, M.A., Johnson, M.K. & Raye, C.L. (1983). Age-related changes in confusion between memories for thoughts and memories for speech. *Child Development*, **54**, 51–60.

Ford, S. & Silber, K.P. (1994). Working memory in children: a developmental approach to the phonological coding of pictorial material. *British Journal of Developmental Psychology*, **12**, 165–175.

Furst, A.J. & Hitch, G.J. (2000). Separate roles for executive and phonological components of working memory in mental arithmetic. *Memory & Cognition*, **28**, 774–782.

Fry, A.F. & Hale, S. (2000). Relationships among processing speed, working memory, and fluid intelligence in children. *Biological Psychology*, **54**, 1–34.

Gathercole, S.E. (1998). The development of memory. *Journal of Child Psychology and Psychiatry*, **39**, 3–27.

Gathercole, S.E. (1999). Cognitive approaches to the development of short-term memory. *Trends in Cognitive Science*, **3**, 410–418.

Gathercole, S.E. & Adams, A. (1993). Phonological working memory in very young children. *Developmental Psychology*, **29**, 770–778.

Gathercole, S.E., Adams, A.-M. & Hitch, G.J. (1994). Do young children rehearse? An individual differences' analysis. *Memory and Cognition*, **22**, 201–207.

Gathercole, S.E. & Baddeley, A.D. (1989). Evaluation of the role of phonological STM in the development of vocabulary in children: a longitudinal study. *Journal of Memory and Language*, **28**, 200–213.

Gathercole, S.E. & Baddeley, A.D. (1990). Phonological memory deficits in language-disordered children: is there a causal connection? *Journal of Memory and Language*, **29**, 336–360.

Gathercole, S.E. & Baddeley, A.D. (1993). *Working memory and language*. Hove: Erlbaum.

Gathercole, S.E. & Hitch, G.J. (1993). Developmental changes in short-term memory: a revised working memory perspective. In A. Collins, S.E. Gathercole, M.A. Conway & P.E. Morris (eds), *Theories of Memory* (pp. 189–210). Hove: Erlbaum.

Gathercole, S.E. & Pickering, S.J. (2000). Working memory deficits in children with low achievements in the national curriculum at seven years of age. *British Journal of Educational Psychology*, **70**, 177–194.

Gathercole, S.E. & Pickering, S.J. (in press). Working memory deficits in children with special educational needs. *British Journal of Special Education*.

Gathercole, S.E. & Pickering, S.J. (in preparation). The lexicality effect is impervious to age.

Gathercole, S.E., Pickering, S.J., Hall, M. & Peaker, S.J. (2001). Dissociable lexical and phonological influences on serial recognition and serial recall. *Quarterly Journal of Experimental Psychology*, **54A**, 1–30.

Gathercole, S.E., Willis, C., Emslie, H. & Baddeley, A.D. (1992). Phonological memory and vocabulary development during the early school years: a longitudinal study. *Developmental Psychology*, **28**, 887–898.

Gathercole, S.E., Willis, C.S., Baddeley, A.D. & Emslie, H. (1994). The Children's Test of Nonword Repetition: a test of phonological working memory. *Memory*, **2**, 103–127.

Gillam, R., Cowan, N. & Day, L. (1995). Sequential memory in children with and without language impairment. *Journal of Speech and Hearing Research*, **38**, 393–402.

Gillam, R.B. & van Kleeck, A. (1996). Phonological awareness training and short-term working memory: clinical implications. *Topics in Language Disorders*, **17**, 72–81.

Gopnik, M. & Crago, M.B. (1991). Familial aggregation of a developmental language disorder. *Cognition*, **39**, 1–50.

Gupta, P. & MacWhinney, B. (1997). Vocabulary acquisition and verbal short-term memory: computational and neural bases. *Brain & Language*, **59**, 267–333.

Hamond, N.R. & Fivush, R. (1990). Memories of Mickey Mouse: young children recount their trip to Disneyworld. *Cognitive Development*, **6**, 433–448.

Hanley, J.R., Young, A.W. & Pearson, N.A. (1991). Impairment of the visuospatial sketchpad. *Quarterly Journal of Experimental Psychology*, **43A**, 101–126.

Henry, L.A. (1994). The relationship between speech rate and memory span in children. *International Journal of Behavioral Development*, **17**, 37–56.

Hitch, G.J. & Halliday, M.S. (1983). Working memory in children. *Philosophical Transactions of the Royal Society of London*, **B302**, 324–340.

Hitch, G.J., Halliday, M.S., Dodd, A. & Littler, J.E. (1989a). Development of rehearsal in short-term memory: differences between pictorial and spoken stimuli. *British Journal of Developmental Psychology*, **7**, 347–362.

Hitch, G.J., Woodin, M.E. & Baker, S. (1989b). Visual and phonological components of working memory in children. *Memory & Cognition*, **17**, 175–185.

Howe, M.L. & Courage, M.L. (1997). The emergence and early development of autobiographical memory. *Psychological Review*, **104**, 499–523.

Hudson, J.A. (1986). Memories are made of this: general event knowledge and the development of autobiographical memory. In K. Nelson (ed.), *Event Knowledge: Structure and Function in Development* (pp. 97–118). Hillsdale, NJ: Erlbaum.

Hudson, J.A. & Nelson, K. (1986). Repeated encounters of a similar kind: effects of familiarity on children's autobiographical memory. *Cognitive Development*, **1**, 253–271.

Hulme, C., Maughan, S. & Brown, G.D.A. (1991). Memory for familiar and unfamiliar words: evidence for a long-term memory contribution to short-term memory span. *Journal of Memory & Language*, **30**, 685–701.

Hulme, C., Muir, C., Thomson, N. & Lawrence, A. (1984). Speech rate and the development of short-term memory span. *Journal of Experimental Child Psychology*, **38**, 241–253.

James, D., van Steenbrugge, W. & Chiveralls, K. (1994). Underlying deficits in language-disordered children with central auditory processing difficulties. *Applied Psycholinguistics*, **15**, 311–328.

Jurden, F.H. (1995). Individual differences in working memory and complex cognition. *Journal of Educational Psychology*, **87**, 93–102.

Just, M.A. & Carpenter, P.A. (1992). A capacity theory of comprehension: individual differences in working memory. *Psychological Review*, **99**, 122–149.

Kail, R., Hale, C.A., Leonard, L.B. & Nippold, M.A. (1984). Lexical storage and retrieval in language-impaired children. *Applied Psycholinguistics*, **5**, 37–49.

King, M. & Yuille, J. (1987). Suggestibility and the child witness. In S.J. Ceci, M. Leichtman, & M. Putnick (eds), *Social and Cognitive Factors in Early Deception* (pp. 47–62). Hillsdale, NJ: Erlbaum.

Lindsay, D.S., Johnson, M.K. & Kwon, P. (1991). Developmental changes in memory for source monitoring. *Journal of Experimental Child Psychology*, **52**, 297–318.

Loftus, E.F. (1979). *Eyewitness Testimony*. Cambridge, MA: Harvard University Press.

Loftus, E.F., Schooler, J. & Wagenaar, W. (1985). The fate of memory: comment on McCloskey & Zaragoza. *Journal of Experimental Psychology: General*, **114**, 375–380.

Logie, R.H. (1994). *Visuospatial Working Memory*. Hove: Erlbaum.

Logie, R.H., Gilhooly, K. & Wynn, V. (1994). Counting on working memory in arithmetic problem solving. *Memory & Cognition*, **22**, 395–410.

Logie, R.H. & Pearson, D.G. (1997). The inner eye and the inner scribe of visuospatial working memory: evidence from developmental fractionation. *European Journal of Cognitive Psychology*, **9**, 241–257.

McCloskey, M. & Zaragoza, M. (1985). Misleading postevent information and memory for events: arguments and evidence against memory impairment hypotheses. *Journal of Experimental Psychology: General*, **114**, 1–16.

McCormack, T., Brown, G.D.A., Vousden, J.I. & Henson, R.N.A. (2000). Children's serial recall errors: impliations for theories of short-term memory development. *Journal of Experimental Psychology*, **76**, 222–252.

McLean, J.F. & Hitch, G.J. (1999). Working memory impairments in children with specific learning difficulties. *Journal of Experimental Child Psychology*, **74**, 240–260.

Meltzoff, A.N. (1988). Infant imitation after a 1-week delay: long-term memory for novel acts and multiple stimuli. *Developmental Psychology*, **24**, 470–476.

Montgomery, J.W. (1995). Examination of phonological working memory in specifically language-impaired children. *Applied Psycholinguistics*, **16**, 355–378.

Michas, I.C. & Henry, L.A. (1994). The link between phonological memory and vocabulary acquisition. *British Journal of Developmental Psychology*, **12**, 147–164.

Miles, C., Morgan, M.J., Milne, A.B. & Morris, E.D.M. (1996). Developmental and individual differences in visual memory span. *Current Psychology*, **15**, 53–67.

Neisser, U. (1962). Cultural and cognitive discontinuity. In T.E. Gladwin & W. Sturtevant (eds), *Anthropology and Human Behavior*. Washington, DC: Anthropological Society of Washington.

Nelson, K. (1978). How children represent knowledge of their world in and out of language. In R.S. Siegler (ed.), *Children's Thinking: What Develops?* (pp. 225–273). Hillsdale, NJ: Erlbaum.

Nelson, K. (1989). *Narratives from the crib*. Cambridge, MA: Harvard University Press.

Nelson (1993a). Explaining the emergence of autobiographical memory in early childhood. In A. Collins, S.E. Gathercole, M.A. Conway & P.E. Morris (eds), *Theories of Memory* (pp. 355–385). Hove: Erlbaum.

Nelson (1993b). The psychological and social origins of autobiographical memory. *Psychological Science*, **4**, 7–14.

Nelson, K. (1994). Long-term retention of memory for preverbal experience: evidence and implications. *Memory*, **2**, 467–475.

Nelson, K. & Gruendel, J. (1981). Generalised event representations: basic building blocks of cognitive development. In M.A. Lamb & A. Brown (eds), *Advances in Developmental Psychology*, Vol. 1. Hillsdale, NJ: Erlbaum.

Nelson, K. & Ross, G. (1980). The generalities and specifics of long-term memory in infants and young children. In M. Perlmutter (ed.), *Children's Memory: New Directions for Child Development* (pp. 87–101). San Francisco, CA: Jossey-Bass.

Oates, K. & Shrimpton, S. (1991). Children's memories for stressful and non-stressful events. *Medicine, Science and the Law*, **31**, 4–10.

Ornstein, P.A. (1995). Children's long-term retention of salient personal experiences. *Journal of Traumatic Stress*, **8**, 581–606.

O'Reilly, R.C., Braver, T.S. & Cohen, J.D. (1999). In A. Miyake & P. Shah (eds), *Models of Working Memory*. (pp. 375–411). New York: Cambridge University Press.

Ornstein, P.A., Gordon, B.N. & Larus, D. (1992). Children's memory for a personally experienced event: implications for testimony. *Applied Cognitive Psychology*, **6**, 49–60.

Page, M.P.A. & Norris, D. (1998). The primacy model: a new model of immediate serial recall. *Psychological Review*, **105**, 761–781.

Palmer, S. (2000). Working memory: a developmental study of phonological recoding. *Memory*, **8**, 179–194.

Pennington, B.F. & Ozonoff, S. (1996). Executive functions and developmental pathology. *Journal of Child Psychology and Psychiatry*, **37**, 51–87.

Pickering, S.J. (2001). The development of visuospatial short-term memory. *Memory*, **9**, 423–432.

Pickering, S.J. & Gathercole, S.E. (2001). *The Working Memory Test Battery for Children*. Psychological Corporation UK.

Pickering, S.J., Gathercole, S.E., Hall, M. & Lloyd, S.A. (in press). Development of memory for pattern and path: further evidence for the fractionation of visuospatial memory. *Quarterly Journal of Experimental Psychology*, **54**, 397–420.

Pillemer, D.B. (1992). Preschool children's memories of personal circumstances: the fire alarm study. In E. Winograd & U. Neisser (eds), *Affect and Accuracy in Recall: Studies of 'Flashbulb' Memories*. New York: Cambridge University Press.

Pillemer, D.B., Picariello, M.L. & Pruett, J.C. (1994). Very long-term memories of a salient preschool event. *Applied Cognitive Psychology*, **8**, 95–106.

Pillemer, D.B. & White, S.H. (1989) Childhood events recalled by children and adults. In H.W. Reese (ed.), *Advances in Child Development and Behavior*, Vol. 21 (pp. 297–340). New York: Academic Press.

Poole, D.A. & Lindsay, D.S. (1995). Interviewing preschoolers: effects of nonsuggestive techniques, parental coaching, and leading questions on reports of nonexperienced events. *Journal of Experimental Child Psychology*, **60**, 129–154.

Pressley, M. & Schneider, W. (1997). *Introduction to Memory Development during Childhood and Adolescence*. Mahwah, NJ: Erlbaum.

Reynolds, E.R., & Bigler, E.D. (1994). *Test of Memory and Learning*. Austin, TX: Pro-Ed.

Rice, M.L., Buhr, J.C. & Nemeth, M. (1991). Fast mapping word learning abilities of language-delayed preschoolers. *Journal of Speech and Hearing Disorders*, **55**, 33–42.

Roberts, K.P. & Blades, M. (1995). Children's discrimination of memories for actual and pretend actions in a hiding task. *British Journal of Developmental Psychology*, **13**, 321–333.

Roodenrys, S., Hulme, C. & Brown, G. (1993). The development of short-term memory span: separable effects of speech rate and long-term memory. *Journal of Experimental Child Psychology*, **56**, 431–442.

Rovee-Collier, C., Sullivan, M.W., Enright, M., Lucas, D. & Fagen, J.W. (1980). Reactivation of infant memory. *Science*, **208**, 1159–1161.

Shah, P. & Miyake, A. (1996). The separability of working memory resources for spatial thinking and language processing: an individual differences approach. *Journal of Experimental Psychology: General*, **125**, 4–27.

Smith, E.E. & Jonides, J. (1988). Neuroimaging analyses of working memory. *Proceedings of the National Academy of Science USA*, **95**, 12061–12068.

Speidel, G.E. (1989). Imitation: a bootstrap for learning to speak? In G.E. Speidel & K.E. Nelson (Eds), *The Many Faces of Imitation in Language Learning* (pp. 151–179). New York: Springer-Verlag.

Speidel, G.E. (1991). Phonological short-term memory and individual differences in learning to speak: a bilingual case study. *First Language*, **13**, 69–91.

Stevenson, J. & Richman, M. (1976). The prevalence of language delay in a population of 3-year old children and its association with general retardation. *Developmental Medicine and Child Neurology*, **18**, 431–441.

Swanson, H.L. (1999). What develops in working memory? A life span perspective. *Developmental Psychology*, **35**, 986–1000.

Towse, J.N., Hitch, G.H. & Hutton, U. (1998). A reevaluation of working memory capacity in children. *Journal of Memory and Language*, **39**, 195–217.

Tulving, E. (1972). Episodic and semantic memory. In E. Tulving & W. Donaldson (eds), *Organization of Memory*. New York: Academic Press.

Usher, J.A. & Neisser, U. (1993). Childhood amnesia and the beginnings of memory for four early life events. *Journal of Experimental Psychology: General*, **122**, 155–165.

Wechsler, D. (1986). *Wechsler Intelligence Scale for Children–Revised*. New York: Psychological Corporation.

Wilson, B., Ivani-Chalian, R. & Aldrich, F. (1991). *The Rivermead Behavioural Memory Test for Children*. Bury St. Edmunds: Thames Valley Test Company.

Wilson, J.T.L., Scott, J.H. & Power, K.G. (1987). Developmental differences in the span of visual memory for pattern. *British Journal of Developmental Psychology*, **5**, 249–255.

Zaragoza, M.S. & Lane, S.M. (1994). Source misattributions and the suggestibility of eyewitness memory. *Journal of Experimental Psychology: Learning, Memory, & Cognition*, **20**, 934–945.

CHAPTER 23

Children with Intellectual Disabilities

Stefano Vicari

Ospedale Pediatrico Bambino Gesù, Rome, Italy

and

Giovanni Augusto Carlesimo

Clinica Neurologia, Università Tor Vergata and I.R.C.C.S. Fondazione Santa Lucia, Rome, Italy

MENTAL RETARDATION

The most recent and widely accepted definition of mental retardation (MR) was developed by the American Association on Mental Retardation (1992) as:

> Mental retardation refers to the substantial limitations in present functioning. It is characterized by significantly subaverage functioning, existing concurrently with related limitation in two or more of the following applicable adaptive skills areas: communication, self-care, home living, social skills, community use, self-direction, health and safety, functional academics, leisure and work. Mental retardation manifests before age 18 (p. 1).

The American Psychiatric Association (DSM-IV, 1994) stated that the essential feature of MR is significantly subaverage general intellectual functioning (Criterion A). However, from the point of view of cognitive psychology, the nature of the intellectual deficit is still a matter of debate. According to one line of thought (Zigler, 1969; Zigler & Balla, 1982), cognitive development in MR follows the same developmental stages as in normal children, although more slowly and with a precocious arrival at the asymptote. Thus, MR is characterized by a homogeneous slowing down in the development of cognitive skills, subtended by the deficit of a *G factor* of general intelligence (Spearman, 1923). Instead, other authors hold that cognitive maturation requires the development of a complex system of correlated, but also relatively independent, functions (Ellis, 1969; Ellis & Cavalier, 1982) and that in MR the prevalent impaired development of some functions rather than others may be at the base of the general intellectual deficit.

Various authors (Detterman, 1987; Vicari et al., 1992) showed that verification of the above-mentioned theoretical premises necessitates adequate investigative instruments.

The Handbook of Memory Disorders. Edited by A.D. Baddeley, M.D. Kopelman and B.A. Wilson
© 2002 John Wiley & Sons, Ltd.

In particular, the traditional psychometric evaluation instruments (e.g. the Wechsler or Stanford–Binet intelligence scales), conceived for identifying mental age and respective intelligence quotient (IQ), are not suitable for the qualitative analysis of single functions. On the contrary, neuropsychological evaluation instruments specifically created for the functional analysis of the various components comprising the cognitive system can offer invaluable information for the development of adequate interpretative models of MR. In recent years, neuropsychological research has permitted the definition of different cognitive profiles for persons with MR of varying aetiology. Characteristic patterns of neuropsychological impairment have been described, among others, in genetic syndromes such as Down's and Williams's syndromes, as well as in abnormalities of acquired brain development, such as that determined by maternal alcohol abuse during pregnancy (Pulsifer, 1996). Different cognitive profiles have been described, not only among individuals affected by genetic or acquired syndromes of varying nature, but also among individuals with global cognitive (IQ) deficits of comparable severity (Vicari et al., 1992) or even within the same aetiopathological group (Pezzini et al., 1999).

Overall, these observations seem to support the theoretical approach that considers the intellectual disorder in MR persons not as a mere slowing down of normal cognitive development, but as a picture characterized by a qualitative lack of homogeneity that confers specific peculiarities to each subject (Vicari et al., 1992; Volterra et al., 1996, et al., 1999; Pezzini et al., 1999). Following this theoretical perspective, which suggests the need for strongly individualized rehabilitative treatment protocols adapted to the cognitive characteristics of each child, many recent studies have tried to better define the impaired cognitive capacities of each individual, as well as their respective "areas of strength" or relatively preserved abilities. Studies describing individual cognitive abilities have multiplied; among these, researches aimed at describing the mnesic abilities of MR individuals are particularly important. In fact, it is easy to understand that altered development of the memory function can seriously interfere with adequate maturation of general intellectual abilities, thus interfering with the possibility of learning and of modifying behaviour on the basis of experience.

This chapter is dedicated to reviewing the neuropsychological literature regarding the memory performances of MR individuals. First, the characteristics of short-term and working memory will be discussed, followed by a review of the experimental evidence dealing with long-term memory processes in persons with cognitive disabilities.

SHORT-TERM MEMORY

Verbal Short-term Memory

Much of the neuropsychological investigation on the development of the mnesic function in MR has been directed toward evaluating short-term memory (STM). Studies on this topic have often documented a reduced STM span in MR individuals and in those with Down's syndrome in particular, compared to groups of mental age-matched controls (Dodd, 1975; Ellis, 1978; McDade & Adler, 1980; Marcell & Weeks, 1988; Hulme & Mackenzie, 1992; Kay-Rayning Bird & Chapman, 1994; Jarrold & Baddeley, 1997; Jarrold et al., 1999, 2000).

A more qualitative analysis of the verbal STM disorder in MR was made by Hulme & Mackenzie (1992) in a study based on the cognitive model of working memory developed by Baddeley & Hitch (1974) and Baddeley (1986). In their study, Hulme & Mackenzie (1992) administered span tests for phonologically similar verbal sequences and for words of increasing length to groups of individuals with Down's syndrome and with MR of varied aetiology and to a group of mental age-matched normal children. They also evaluated articulatory speed using vocalization of syllable sequences. The results showed that MR individuals (Down's and non-Down's) had reduced spans compared to the normal children and, furthermore, that phonological similarity and word length effects were absent in these persons; there was also a nonsignificant correlation between articulatory speed and size of the span (which, in contrast, was significant in the group of normal children). Hulme & Mackenzie (1992) interpreted these data as the expression of a reduced contribution of the articulatory loop to the verbal span of the MR persons. In particular, the disabled persons showed little evidence of verbally rehearsing the sequences, which would thus decay rapidly from the phonological store (reduced span) and show little effect of manipulations involving word length and phonological structure.

More recently, Jarrold et al. (2000) explored the efficiency of the articulatory loop in a group of 14 children with Down's syndrome and an equal number of mental age-matched controls. Although the children with Down's syndrome always obtained a shorter span than the controls, in none of the groups were subvocal repetition processes demonstrated. This latter result raises problems for the assumption of impaired repetition as the basis of the verbal working memory deficit in individuals with Down's syndrome. However, they do not exclude the possible impairment of the other cognitive components of working memory, i.e. the phonological store and the central executive system. A possible involvement of the phonological store in the verbal STM deficit of children with Down's syndrome is consistent with their difficulties in auditory phonological analysis (Chapman, 1995; Fowler, 1995). Nevertheless, the currently available data (see e.g. Jarrold et al., 2000 and also Vicari et al., 2000b) raise many questions regarding interpretation, making further experimental investigation necessary.

There are also very few data regarding the functioning of the central executive system in Down's individuals. As far as we know, the only work present in the literature is a study conducted by Vicari et al. (1995). One reason for this apparent lack of interest may be related to the methodological difficulties in assessing the functioning of the executive system. In healthy adults, the availability of processing resources in the central executive is generally investigated by measuring the decrement of accuracy or speed in a primary task while performing a secondary task (Baddeley & Hitch, 1974). In persons with MR, however, possible floor effects of performance in the primary task drastically reduce the possibility of executing dual task paradigms. An alternative experimental approach for exploring the functioning of the executive system was devised for use with demented patients, and simply consists of contrasting performances in the forward and backward versions of the memory span tasks (Carlesimo et al., 1994). The articulatory loop is suited to maintaining strings of items in the same presentation order, as is appropriate for forward span (Orsini et al., 1988). By contrast, backward spans require a more complex manipulation of mental data to reproduce the sequence in the reversed order. As a consequence, greater involvement of the central executive resources is expected in managing this kind of task. In our study (Vicari et al., 1995), we presented forward digit and spatial (Corsi's block) span tasks and backward digit and spatial span tasks (in which the subject had to repeat the numbers or reproduce the spatial sequence in the reverse order) to groups of Down's individuals, MR persons of various aetiology, and mental age-matched normal persons. The results showed lower performance in Down's individuals on backward span tasks compared to both normal children and to MR persons of various aetiologies, thus suggesting that the resources of the executive system are one feature of poor STM in persons with Down's syndrome.

In conclusion, compared to mental age-matched children with normal cognitive development, the verbal STM of Down's syndrome children seems to be independent of the articulatory difficulty they often present. Instead, greater responsibility should be attributed to input processes of phonological analysis or, even more, to deficits of the central executive system. Other studies, able to simultaneously evaluate the contribution of each component of the model of working memory and phonological discrimination, could perhaps clarify the actual cause of the deficit in verbal STM in Down's syndrome individuals.

Recent evidence suggests that verbal STM is not equally impaired in all individuals with intellectual disability. Particularly relevant in this regard are the findings reported in children with Williams's syndrome. This is another genetic condition with an incidence estimated at 1 in 20 000 live births typified by a number of severe medical anomalies, including mental retardation, facial dysmorphology and abnormalities of the cardiovascular system, as well as of the renal, musculoskeletal, endocrine and other organ systems. Williams's syndrome is associated with a microdeletion on chromosome 7q11.23 (Frangiskakis et al., 1996; Ewart et al., 1993; Tassabehji et al., 1997; Botta et al., 1999). In previous studies it was claimed that the syndrome presents not only specific clinical features but also a major dissociation in cognitive functioning: (a) severe cognitive deficits co-occurring with relatively spared language; and (b) severe difficulties in spatial cognition and numbering but excellent facial recognition (Bellugi et al., 1988; Bellugi et al., 1994, 1999; Reilly et al., 1990). In children with Williams's syndrome, phonological STM is usually at the level of their mental age (Udwin & Yule, 1990; Vicari et al., 1996a) or higher than their mental age (Mervis et al., 1999). Furthermore, Wang & Bellugi (1994) and, more recently, Jarrold et al. (1999), demonstrated opposite patterns of memory span, namely, better verbal span in children with Williams's syndrome and, conversely, better visuospatial span in children with Down's syndrome.

Wang & Bellugi (1994) discussed these data in light of the working memory model and suggested better preservation of the articulatory loop in Williams's children but better preservation of the visuospatial sketchpad (the slave system devoted to the processing of visual and spatial data) in Down's children. This kind of interpretation is in line with the particular neuropsychological pattern exhibited by children with Williams's syndrome. Indeed, as we reported above, these persons are relatively proficient in language and face recognition abilities, but exhibit severe difficulties in other visuospatial tasks as well as in numbering (Bellugi et al., 1988, 1994, 1999; Reilly, et al. 1990).

Other researchers suggest a more complex neuropsychological profile, with nonhomogeneous development not only across but also within cognitive domains (Pezzini et al., 1999; Paterson et al., 1999; Bishop, 1999; Jarold et al., 1999; Karmiloff-Smith et al., 1997). In particular, some dissociation was demonstrated in visuospatial abilities, where visual perception is relatively preserved and spatial processing is more severely impaired (Atkinson et al., 1997; Bellugi et al., 1994, 1990), as well as in the verbal domain, where phonological processing of words is preserved but grammatical and semantic aspects of language are impaired (Pezzini et al., 1999; Mervis et al., 1999; Volterra et al., 1996).

Following this last finding, Vicari et al. (1996b) investigated the contribution of phonological and semantic processes to verbal span in children with Williams's syndrome. In particular, they explored phonological similarity and length and frequency effects in a verbal span task in groups of children with Williams's syndrome and mental age-matched normal controls. The participants with Williams's syndrome showed normal similarity and length effects in their performance, supporting the hypothesis of relatively preserved phonological competencies in children with this syndrome. However, the authors found a reduced frequency effect in the verbal span of these persons compared to the group of normally developing children. Although both groups repeated high-frequency words better than low-frequency words, this effect was smaller in the Williams's syndrome group.

The reduced frequency effect in these children may be the result of a rigid use of phonological recoding strategy for both high and low frequency words. The dissociation between normal phonological encoding and the reduced contribution of lexical–semantic encoding mechanisms to word span in children with Williams's syndrome is particularly interesting in light of their pattern of linguistic abilities. As we have seen, in fact, several studies have demonstrated that children with Williams's syndrome present impaired lexical–semantic and grammatical abilities in the presence of well-preserved phonological processes (Volterra et al., 1996; Grant et al., 1997; Karmiloff-Smith et al., 1997, 1998; Pezzini et al., 1999; Mervis et al., 1999). This challenges the popular view that Williams's syndrome individuals present a simple dissociation between relatively preserved linguistic abilities and visual–spatial deficits.

Visual and Spatial Short-term Memory

There are very few data available on the functioning of the visuospatial sketchpad system of working memory in children with intellectual disabilities. As we have seen, some authors (Wang & Bellugi, 1994; Vicari et al., 1996a; Jarrold et al., 1999) have shown that, contrary to what is observed in Down's syndrome children, the performances of Williams's syndrome children do not differ from those of mental age-matched normal controls on verbal memory tests, although they are deficient on visuospatial memory tests. However, the impairment of these abilities in children with Williams's syndrome is not uniform. In fact, they have specific difficulties in executing purely spatial tasks, while their performances in visual–perceptual tests, such as recognizing faces, is quite normal (Bellugi et al., 1990, 1994; Atkinson et al., 1997). On the basis of these observations, particularly due to the marked difficulty Williams's syndrome persons have in spatial processing, they could provide a "natural" example of a possible dissociation between visual and spatial memory. In fact, on the basis of clinical and experimental data, evidence has recently emerged affirming the hypothesis that the temporary memory for visual material (such as colours and shapes) and spatial material (such as the localization of objects and sequences of movement) is actually supported by different, but complementary, cognitive systems (for review, see Logie, 1995). Therefore, identifying a difference in performance in the two STM tasks (visual and spatial) in a group of subjects characterized by a common genetic syndrome could provide further confirmation of the hypothesis that the visuospatial sketchpad is organized in two distinct subsystems. For this reason, in a recent study of our group (Vicari et al., submitted) we administered visual and spatial span tests to a group of 13 children with Williams's syndrome and 26 normal mental age-matched controls (7 years and 1 month). The two tests involved studying the same complex, non-verbalizable figures and using the same response modality (pointing to targets on the screen). The crucial experimental variable was that in one case the position

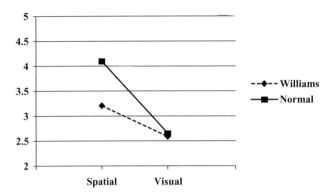

Figure 23.1 Performance profiles of Williams's syndrome children and normal controls on two STM tasks (visual and spatial)

where the figure appeared on the screen had to be recalled; in the other case, the physical aspect of the figure studied had to be recalled.

The results show a different performance profile in the two groups of children examined (Figure 23.1). In fact, although the normal and the Williams's syndrome children performed analogously in the visual span test, the spatial span performances of the Williams's syndrome children were significantly lower than those of the controls. A two-way mixed analysis of variance (group × test) confirmed what was reported, showing a significant group × test interaction, $F(1,37) = 16.11, p < 0.001$.

Although these data are preliminary, they are consistent with the results of several other studies that documented more difficulty on tests of spatial than visual processing in children with Williams's syndrome (Bellugi et al., 1999; Mervis et al., 1999; Pezzini et al., 1999). In an attempt to describe the biological bases of this deficit, Atkinson et al. (1997) studied a group of 15 children with Williams's syndrome and 30 children with normal cognitive development. They administered psychophysical tests considered to be indices of the integrity of cortical pathways responsible for the visual processing of the *spatial* characteristics (*dorsal cortical stream*) and *visual* characteristics of objects (*ventral cortical stream*). The results showed that the performance of the Williams's syndrome children was deficient in tasks involving the spatial dorsal stream, although they performed in the normal range on tests involving visual information processing.

LONG-TERM MEMORY

People with MR learn and successively retain new information less efficiently than age-matched normally developed individuals. Although this statement may seem trivial, awareness of the central role that long-term memory (LTM) impairment presumably plays in the emergence of learning difficulties and adaptation problems of MR people has prompted a large body of experimental literature, aimed at clarifying the qualitative characteristics and basic mechanisms of this deficit.

The major questions relevant for better understanding the LTM deficit of MR people can be summarized as follows. First, in view of the multicomponential structure of the

LTM function in humans (Squire, 1987; Tulving & Schacter, 1990), it is relevant to know whether the impairment in MR individuals affects all components of the LTM architecture homogeneously or whether some components are more disrupted than others. A second topic of interest is the salience the memory impairment assumes in the context of the global cognitive deficit suffered by MR people. In particular, is the memory deficit in MR individuals proportionate to their overall deficient cognitive functioning, or is it disproportionately more severe, thus conferring a peculiar position in the cognitive derangement of these patients to the LTM impairment?

Once the qualitative and quantitative features of the LTM deficit are ascertained in MR persons, the third topic of interest is the search for the basic mechanisms of this deficit. In this regard, the debate between the sustainers of the "information processing" or "structural" deficits at the base of the memory difficulties of MR persons is particularly relevant. Finally, recent contributions have raised the hypothesis that, as in STM, severity, qualitative features and, possibly, basic mechanisms of the LTM impairment are not homogeneous across all MR subjects but may be differentiated (among other variables) by the aetiology of the deranged brain development. In this vein, a comparison of qualitative profiles of memory impairment exhibited by different aetiological groups of MR persons is important both for a better description of their neuropsychological deficit and for gaining new insights about the neural substrate underlying the memory impairment in these clinical populations. The remaining part of this chapter will be devoted to reporting and discussing the main experimental data relevant to the topics mentioned above.

Weaknesses and Strengths in the LTM Performance of MR Individuals

In 1979, Detterman put forward the "everything hypothesis" to describe the pervasive impairment of memory functions in MR. According to this author, MR individuals are poor in virtually every type of memory task, so any effort to find islands of relative weakness and strength in their memory performance is doomed to end in frustration.

In the same years, neuropsychological investigation was reaching somewhat opposite conclusions in the description of the deficit suffered by adult brain-damaged patients with memory problems. As early as the 1960s, it had become evident that not all aspects of LTM are impaired in amnesic patients. In fact, it was repeatedly demonstrated that these patients show normal learning of a number of visuomotor skills, such as pursuit rotor performance (Corkin, 1968), and cognitive skills, such as reading mirror-reversed words (Cohen & Squire, 1980). Such patients also show normal priming by previous exposure to visuoverbal or visuoperceptual stimuli (Graf et al., 1984; Warrington & Weiskrantz, 1968). A further refinement of the taxonomy of LTM processes was provided by the discovery that, in the domain of implicit memory, a double dissociation can be found between performance on skill-learning and repetition-priming tests. In particular, while brain diseases affecting the basal ganglia (e.g. Huntington's disease) or the cerebellar structures may impair the learning of visuomotor or cognitive skills, leaving unaffected the susceptibility to be primed by previous exposure to relevant material (Salmon & Butters, 1995), the opposite dissociation (i.e. normal skill-learning but reduced repetition-priming) may be found in mildly demented Alzheimer's patients. This is a condition characterized by the early involvement of hippocampal and neocortical associative structures but substantial sparing of the cerebellum-basal ganglia circuitry (Eslinger & Damasio, 1986; Fleischman & Gabrieli, 1998).

The first reports of dissociable performance in MR individuals on LTM tasks supposed to tap theoretically distinguishable memory processes date back to the late 1980s. Ellis and co-workers (Ellis & Allison, 1988; Ellis et al., 1989; Katz & Ellis, 1991) reported a series of experiments contrasting the performance of MR and chronological age-matched individuals on memory tasks intended to investigate effortful or automatic memory processes in the context of an influential theoretical framework proposed by Hasher & Zacks (1979, 1984). According to these latter authors, critical differences between effortful memory tasks (e.g. the traditional free recall and recognition procedures) and automatic memory tasks (e.g. tests of frequency judgement and spatial location) reside in the amount of attentional resources and elaborative encoding implicated, which are maximal for the first type of memory task and minimal for the second. Hasher & Zacks (1979, 1984) theoretically argued (and in part experimentally demonstrated) that performance levels on effortful and automatic memory tasks may be dissociated by the use of dual task paradigms, which affect effortful but not automatic memory. This was done by manipulating the level of stimulus processing during the study phase (with effortful but not automatic memory processes taking advantage of elaborative encoding) and, critically for our purpose, by comparing people with different overall levels of cognitive efficiency on the two kinds of tasks (with intelligence expected to be related to performance on effortful but not on automatic memory tasks). As partial support for this latter claim, Ellis & Allison (1988) reported that individuals with MR are significantly poorer than normal controls in the free recall of lists of words and pictures and in the frequency judgement of pictures but are as accurate as normal controls in the frequency judgement of words. In a different experimental paradigm, individuals with mild MR (IQ 56–75) were poor in the free recall of a list of pictures but were as accurate as normal controls in relocating the pictures on the pages of a cartoon book in the same positions they occupied during the study phase (Ellis et al., 1989; Katz & Ellis, 1991). The pattern of results on this task is somewhat complicated by the fact that people with a more severe level of MR (IQ 29–59) were less accurate than chronological age-matched normal on both the free recall and spatial relocation tests (Dulaney et al., 1996; Ellis et al., 1989; Katz & Ellis, 1991). Moreover, a group of mildly retarded individuals with a maternal history of alcohol abuse during pregnancy showed the opposite pattern to the mild MR individuals described by Ellis and co-workers. They did not differ from the normal controls on the free recall but scored significantly lower on the spatial relocation test (Uecker & Nadel, 1998).

A different approach was used by Burack & Zigler (1987) in the search for LTM processes possibly spared in MR individuals. These authors compared groups of organic MR, familial MR and mental age-matched individuals on episodic memory tests. These varied depending on whether the examiner's instructions during the study phase were directed toward producing intentional or incidental stimulus learning. The distinction between intentional and incidental learning is a different one from that between implicit and explicit retrieval. The former refers to the intentionality of memorizing the information at the time of study, the latter to the intentionality of deliberately recollecting the information at the time of test. In a free recall test of an intentionally learned word list, normal children scored higher than familial MR individuals who, in turn, scored higher than organic MR individuals. In contrast, in a paired-associate task in which no instruction to learn was given during the study phase (incidental learning), the two MR groups and the group of normal controls scored similarly.

In the last few years, some experimental data have been reported regarding the possible extension to MR individuals of the dissociation between explicit and implicit memory processes so frequently described in brain-damaged adults with memory disorders. As previously noted, the various types of implicit learning involve the functioning of different parts of the brain, which happen to have in common the fact that they do not rely on the hippocampal–temporal lobe circuit that is responsible for explicit episodic memory (see also Baddeley, Chapter 1, this volume). For this reason, it is not expected that MR subjects will behave in the same manner in tasks tapping the various forms of implicit memory.

In the case of *repetition priming*, studies investigating facilitation in identifying perceptually degraded pictures induced by the previous exposure to the same pictures have consistently reported a comparable priming effect in MR individuals and normal subjects matched for chronological age (Takegata & Futuruka, 1993; Wyatt & Conners, 1998) or mental age (Perrig & Perrig, 1995). On the other hand, a quite complex and somewhat contradictory pattern of results emerged from studies investigating repetition priming of verbal material. Most of these studies were based on the stem completion procedure in which subjects are requested to complete a list of stems (i.e. the first three letters) with the first word that comes to mind. The priming effect is revealed by a bias in completing the stems with words that have been previously studied rather than unstudied ones. Carlesimo et al. (1997) and Vicari et al. (2000a, 2001) reported a priming effect with this procedure in various groups of MR individuals (aetiologically unspecified, Down's syndrome and Williams's syndrome) comparable to that of mental-age matched normal subjects. However, Mattson & Riley (1999) compared a group of individuals with MR resulting from a fetal alcoholic syndrome and a group of individuals with Down's syndrome to a group of chronological age-matched individuals and found normal stem completion priming in the first MR group and reduced priming in the Down's syndrome group. One possible reason for these discrepant results is that, in MR persons, verbal repetition priming varies as a function of global intellectual efficiency, being normal in mildly retarded and poor in moderately retarded persons. Indeed, in Mattson & Riley's study (1999), the two groups of MR individuals were matched for chronological age but not for mental age; Down's syndrome individuals, who had deficient priming, had lower IQs than individuals with fetal alcoholic syndrome, who had normal priming.

Another source of potential variability in the verbal repetition priming performance of MR individuals was suggested by Komatsu et al. (1996). These authors contrasted the repetition priming evoked by a Word Fragment Completion procedure in groups of MR and chronological age-matched individuals. In that study, the level of processing during the study phase was manipulated by giving half of the words to be read and half to be generated starting from a sentence in which they were embedded. MR individuals displayed a priming level comparable to that of normal controls for the words that had been previously read, but less than normal priming for the words that had been generated. These results suggest a dissociation in MR individuals between normal perceptual priming (a kind of facilitation elicited by perceptually reprocessing a given item in the same physical format as in a previous presentation) and deficient conceptual priming (a kind of priming produced by reprocessing the semantic identity of an item without any overlapping between the perceptual formats of the study and test presentations).

Less experimental work has been devoted to investigating the ability of MR individuals to learn *visuomotor* or *cognitive skills*. In a first study, Vakil et al. (1997) compared the improvement in accuracy displayed by groups of MR and mental age-matched individuals on successive trials of the Tower of Hanoi and the Porteus Maze tests. The MR individuals performed both tests at a significantly lower level of accuracy than the normal controls. However, while in the first test (which requires completing a spatial pattern according to a series of predetermined rules) the rate of trial-to-trial improvement was higher in the normal than in the MR group, in the Porteus Maze test (which requires solving a series of mazes with the least number of errors possible) the two groups improved at the same rate. Recently, Vicari and co-workers suggested an intriguing difference in the skill-learning abilities of two genetically distinct groups of MR individuals. In the first study (Vicari et al., 2000a), a group of Down's syndrome individuals showed the same rate of improvement as a group of mental age-matched normal children across successive trials of the Tower of London test (analogous to the Tower of Hanoi) and in the comparison of the repeated vs. random blocks of a facilitated version of the Serial Reaction Time test (requiring implicit learning of the sequential order of a series of visual events) devised by Nissen & Bullemer (1987). In the second study, however, a group of children with Williams's syndrome showed significantly less procedural learning than normal children on both of these tests (Vicari et al., 2001).

In summary, the overall pattern of results that emerges from the literature is quite inconsistent; some studies report normal and others deficient performance in MR individuals. When performance inconsistency emerges from exactly the same memory tests (e.g. the Spatial Relocation test devised by Ellis and co-workers and the stem completion priming), the main source of variability is likely to be the overall level of cognitive efficiency of the MR groups investigated, with less compromised individuals achieving performance levels similar to age-matched controls and more severely retarded persons scoring less well. In other cases (e.g. skill learning), different aetiological groups of MR individuals may show discrepant performance patterns on the same memory task, probably reflecting a different neurobiological substrate for their mental deficiency. Finally, when discrepant results emerge from distinct memory tasks (e.g. various repetition priming procedures), it may be the nature of the memorandum (e.g. visuoperceptual vs. verbal) or the type of stimulus processing (perceptually-driven vs. conceptually-driven) that makes the difference. In any case, although these results are inconclusive, they permit the rejection of Detterman's (1979) "everything hypothesis". In fact, a quite evident contrast emerges in the memory performances of MR individuals as a function of experimental manipulation of both learning and retrieval conditions. On the one hand, there is absolute consistency in the experimental literature that when the deliberate retrieval of intentionally and/or effortfully encoded information is requested, the performance of MR individuals as compared to chronological age-matched normal subjects is poor. In contrast, when the memory of previously experienced procedures or information is tested implicitly, or when the task calls for the intentional retrieval of incidentally and/or automatically encoded information, the performance of MR persons (at least those in the mild range of cognitive dysfunction) is not infrequently in the range of normal controls.

Relevance of Memory Impairment in the Overall Cognitive Deficit of People with MR

In the previous section, we argued that MR people (even in the mild range of retardation) are definitely poorer than age-matched normal subjects in the deliberate retrieval of information learned intentionally and/or effortfully. Thus, the next question is whether such a deficit is proportional to the overall cognitive dysfunction suffered by these patients or whether it is more severe than expected, simply on the basis of general mental efficiency. If we were able to demonstrate that the available evidence supports this second alternative, this would suggest that the memory impairment has a special role in the neuropsychological profile and, probably, in the occurrence of functional problems in these individuals.

One approach frequently utilized with MR individuals to evaluate the importance of their memory deficit in the context of their overall cognitive dysfunction is to compare their memory performance to that of normal individuals, matched not for chronological age but for absolute level of cognitive development (mental age). The rationale underlying this kind of approach is the following. If memory in MR develops as slowly as general cognition, then no difference should emerge from a comparison of the memory profiles of MR and mental age-matched normal subjects. If, in contrast, memory in MR people develops more slowly than general mental efficiency, then quantitative and/or qualitative differences in the memory performance of retarded individuals and normally developing children should be found. Unfortunately, findings from experimental studies using this kind of approach are not homogeneous. A rather contradictory picture emerges from a review of 11 papers concerned with the comparison of MR and mental age-matched subjects on a variety of episodic memory measures; approximately the same number of studies report no difference between MR and normal mental age-matched individuals (Fletcher & Bray, 1995; Schultz, 1983; Spitz, 1966; Spitz et al., 1975; Turnure, 1991; Winters & Semchuk, 1986) or, in contrast, significantly lower performance in MR than in normal subjects (Burack & Zigler, 1987; Carlesimo et al., 1997; Vakil et al., 1997; Vicari et al., 1996a, 2000a). Reliance on different experimental instruments for evaluating the memory function can hardly be used to account for such contradictory results. The wide variety of tests used make generalization difficult, but even when analysis is limited to specific testing instruments common to several of these studies, a contradictory pattern of results still emerges, e.g. the learning of word lists across successive presentation trials was used in both studies that did not report differences (e.g. Spitz, 1966; Spitz et al., 1975) and studies that found significantly lower performances in MR than in normal children (e.g. Burack & Zigler, 1987; Carlesimo et al., 1997).

Perhaps a more fruitful approach to identifying the source of the discrepancy in the experimental results would be to search for possible sampling differences between the different studies. In this regard, it is interesting to note that larger discrepancies were found between the chronological and mental ages of MR individuals who participated in the five studies reporting intergroup differences in the memory performances of MR individuals and normal children (average IQ range = 34–56) than in the subjects investigated in studies which did not find differences between general intelligence and memory development in MR (in this case, the average IQ range = 59–72). So, it could be the case that rate of memory development closely parallels global cognitive development in subjects in the mild range of MR, but that it deviates toward a particularly slow developmental trend in more severely retarded individuals.

In conclusion, currently available evidence does not permit straightforward conclusions about the role of experimental or sampling factors in the prediction of the rate of memory development in MR people compared to the rate of their overall cognitive maturation. Further work is needed in which these different factors are independently manipulated in order to gain new insights into this controversial issue.

Basic Mechanisms of Poor LTM in MR Individuals

The debate about basic mechanisms of poor episodic LTM in people with MR has been largely dominated by the controversy between proponents of the information-processing deficit hypothesis and those proposing a structural deficit in the memory system of these subjects. The first theory postulates that MR individuals are specifically poor in spontaneously engaging in those strategic behaviours that, at the time of study, permit normal people to achieve a richer encoding of the memorandum and, as a consequence, more effective recovery of the information at the time of testing. They suggest that once the information has been effectively encoded, the structural mechanisms devoted to consolidating the memory trace function normally in MR persons, thus allowing for normal long-term maintenance of the record of the experience. Authors who support the second theory argue that in MR subjects, structural memory mechanisms are also defective, thus resulting in abnormally fast forgetting.

Two main lines of evidence suggest deficient spontaneous reliance of people with MR on effective mnemonic strategies at the time of study. The first one deals with the above-reported dissociation in these subjects between consistently poor performance in traditional episodic memory tests (such as free and cued recall and recognition) and tests of unintentional retrieval of previously experienced information or intentional retrieval of incidentally or automatically encoded information. One way to interpret this dissociation rests on the different benefit these various kinds of memory tests gain from the use of mnemonic strategic behaviours at the time of learning. As discussed by Baddeley (Chapter 1, this volume), accuracy of retrieval in traditional episodic memory tests is largely a function of the quality of stimulus encoding at the time of study (Craik & Lockhart, 1972). In contrast, the accuracy of intentional retrieval of automatically encoded information or the degree of repetition priming (at least when it is based on perceptually reprocessing visual information) are generally unaffected by manipulations of encoding conditions of stimuli (Hasher & Zacks, 1979; Kirsner et al., 1983). In view of this, the dissociated performance in MR people between different kinds of LTM tasks can not be due to the reliance of these different tests on the functioning of distinct memory systems, some of which are functioning normally in MR people and some of which are not. It appears rather to depend on the fact that, within a unitary memory system, some of the tests (particularly those that are impaired in MR people) benefit from strategic mnemonic behaviours, while others (those which are preserved in MR individuals) are not sensitive to the quality of stimulus encoding.

The second line of evidence, supporting the hypothesis of deficient information processing as the basis of poor episodic memory in MR individuals, rests on the direct observation of a lack, or reduction, of mnemonic strategic behaviours in these subjects at the time of learning or retrieval. Two kinds of strategic behaviours known to affect performance accuracy in explicit memory tasks have been more extensively investigated in people with MR. The first one is cumulative rehearsal; the second is elaborative encoding of the semantic characteristics of the memorandum. There is experimental evidence that people with MR are defective in virtually all of the behavioural manifestations of cumulative rehearsal, e.g. they exhibit reduced strategic variation of pause duration during self-paced learning of word lists (Belmont et al., 1982; Turner et al., 1996). Moreover, a clear primacy effect is frequently lacking in the serial position curves derived from the free recall of word lists of MR individuals (Ellis, 1970; Spitz et al., 1975). Finally, in the free recall of word lists, MR individuals do not benefit from slower presentation rates at the time of initial presentation (Ellis, 1970). All of these suggest an absence of normal rehearsal strategies.

Elaborative encoding of the semantic aspects of information is a critical factor in predicting the quality of stimulus retrieval (Butters & Cermak, 1975; Craik & Lockhart, 1972). The experimental approach most used for investigating the efficiency of elaborative encoding in MR people is the measurement of the organizational strategies in the free recall of semantically categorizable word lists. Normal young adults recall semantically categorizable word lists more efficiently than noncategorizable ones (Spitz, 1966). Moreover, the extent of the recall advantage for the semantically-related over the unrelated word list is generally a function of the use of a strategic behaviour characterized by the clustering of stimulus words according to the taxonomic category at the time of retrieval (Spitz, 1966). In a number of studies, MR people have revealed the complete absence or, at the very least, severely defective clustering behaviour in word list recall (Spitz, 1966; Turner et al., 1996; Winters & Semchuck, 1986).

The integrity of structural memory mechanisms devoted to consolidating the memory traces of past experiences is generally investigated by comparing the rates of forgetting in normal and experimental subjects. Katz & Ellis (1991) reported more forgetting in the 24 h delayed recall of a list of pictures by a sample of MR individuals compared to a group of chronological age-matched subjects. In contrast, other authors described comparable rates of forgetting passing from immediate to delayed recall in MR individuals and normal age matches (e.g. Carlesimo et al., 1997; Vicari et al., 1996a). However, these studies can be criticized because baseline performance (i.e. immediate retrieval) greatly differs between normal and memory-disordered patients, thus leading to an estimation of the forgetting rate at different levels on the measurement scale. Since one cannot assume that the retention scale is linear, it is difficult to interpret a numerical difference in amount of forgetting. When degree of initial learning is equated, rates of forgetting in adult amnesic patients is equivalent to that of control subjects scale (Huppert & Piercy, 1979; Kopelman, 1985; McKee & Squire, 1992). McCartney (1987) investigated the immediate and delayed recognition of unknown faces in groups of MR and chronological age-matched individuals. By varying the number of times the individual faces were presented during the study phase, McCartney was able to match the immediate recognition performances in two subgroups of MR and normal matches. Performance after 1 day, 7 days and 6 months revealed equivalent forgetting curves in these two subgroups.

In conclusion, the available evidence suggests that MR people are poor in the spontaneous use of mnemonic strategies at the time of stimulus encoding. It is not clear, however, whether such poor encoding abilities are sufficient to account for their reduced learning rate. If it was the case, then experimental manipulations inducing these subjects to effectively process the incoming information should be able to equate their initial learning levels to those of normal people. To our knowledge, such evidence has never been reported, thus leaving the problem of the basic mechanism underlying the impaired acquisition of information in MR people substantially unresolved. In contrast, the normal forgetting rate reported by McCartney (1987) suggests that, once a high level of initial learning in MR individuals has been obtained, then the memory for learned information dissipates in these subjects at the same rate as in normal individuals. However, the conclusion that there is a normal forgetting rate in MR individuals is based on the results of a single study. These data should be replicated before this view can be considered as definitively supported.

Contrasting LTM Performance in Distinct Aetiological Groups of MR

Studies of LTM performance in groups of aetiologically specific MR individuals are potentially of great interest. By restricting behavioural observation to groups of patients that are presumably homogeneous for the quality and localization of abnormal brain development, direct relationships can potentially be inferred between deranged memory functioning and anomalous maturation of specific cerebral structures.

As in the case of STM, Down's syndrome is the aetiological group that has been most extensively investigated. Individuals with Down's syndrome performed more poorly than groups with MR of unspecified aetiology, or mental age-matched normal children, on tests of free recall of word lists and of a short story, and on the reproduction of Rey's figure from memory (Carlesimo et al., 1997). In the same study, individuals with aetiologically unspecified MR showed more semantic clustering during the free recall of a categorizable word list, and better recall of the categorizable than the uncategorizable list compared to individuals with Down's syndrome. However, the two MR groups and the normal children's group scored the same on a test of yes/no recognition of an uncategorized word list.

Implicit memory has also been experimentally investigated in people with Down's syndrome. Stem completion repetition priming has been found to be comparable to that of mental age-matched normal individuals in two studies (Carlesimo et al., 1997; Vicari et al., 2000a) but deficient with respect to normal individuals of the same chronological age in a third study (Mattson & Riley, 1999). Vicari et al. (2000a) also investigated the skill-learning abilities of MR people with Down's syndrome in some detail, and found that these persons improved at the same rate as mental age-matched normal controls across successive trials of the Tower of London task and in the repeated vs. random blocks of the serial reaction time task. To summarize, the available evidence suggests a dissociation in people with Down's syndrome between substantially spared implicit learning but particularly poor performance on episodic LTM tests. The lack of an evident semantic clustering behaviour in the recall of word lists and the relatively better performance on recognition than free recall tests (Carlesimo et al., 1997) suggest that poor episodic memory in Down's syndrome individuals may be related to deficient semantic processing of verbal information, and to a problem in accessing the memory representations in LTM.

Two experimental studies investigated the explicit and implicit LTM performance of MR individuals with Williams's syndrome. In the first study, Vicari et al. (1996a) documented poor performance of these children compared to a group of mental age-matched normal children in both the free recall and recognition of a word list and in the immediate and delayed reproduction of Rey's figure. In the second study (Vicari et al., 2001), MR children with Williams's syndrome displayed a level of stem completion repetition priming comparable to that of normal children. However, they exhibited deficient skill learning in the same two tests (Tower of London and serial reaction time) which, in a previous study, had elicited a normal learning pattern in people with Down's syndrome (Vicari et al., 2000a). Commenting on the pattern of LTM impairment exhibited by persons with Down's syndrome, Carlesimo et al. (1997) suggested that their particularly poor explicit memory could be related to the marked reduction of hippocampal volume reported by Jernigan & Bellugi (1990). The dissociation between the skill-learning abilities displayed by the individuals with Down's syndrome and those with Williams's syndrome is particularly relevant to the search for the underlying brain pathology subtending abnormal development of this ability. As previously noted, neuropsychological investigation in brain-damaged adult individuals established the critical role of the basal ganglia and cerebellum in the normal learning of visuomotor and cognitive skills (Salmon & Butters, 1995). The brain development of children with Williams's syndrome is characterized by atrophy of the basal ganglia (Jernigan & Bellugi, 1990) and by a reduction of the neurotransmitter N-acetylaspartate in the cerebellum (Rae et al., 1998). Persons with Down's syndrome, in turn, show marked atrophy of the cerebellum but substantially normal volumes of basal ganglia structures (Jernigan & Bellugi, 1990). The normal skill learning displayed by Down's syndrome individuals and the deficient learning exhibited by Williams's syndrome individuals suggest a role for basal ganglia development in the normal maturation of procedural memory.

A last aetiological group of studies concerns individuals with a maternal history of alcohol abuse during pregnancy. Animal models suggest a particular vulnerability of the hippocampus to gestational alcohol exposure (Abel et al., 1983), leading to particularly poor performance of these on spatial learning tasks (Blanchard et al., 1987). Uecker & Nadel (1996, 1998) hypothesized that there is more severe spatial than verbal and visual memory impairment in individuals with fetal alcohol syndrome. Consistent with the hypothesis, these individuals scored at the same level as chronological age-matched normal controls on the free recall of verbalizable pictures, but were significantly poorer than controls when requested to indicate the location in which each picture had been originally studied (Uecker & Nadel, 1996, 1998). However, further work, possibly correlating neuropsychological data with morphometric analysis of cerebral structures, is clearly needed.

CONCLUSIONS

The review of the neuropsychological literature presented here clearly suggests deficient development of the memory function in MR. In the case of STM, it is quite firmly established that the deficit is heterogeneous across the various clinical groups examined. In Down's syndrome individuals, both the peripheral systems and the central systems governing information processing seem deficient, whereas visual and spatial memories do not seem particularly impaired. In contrast, persons with Williams's syndrome show relative preservation of the functioning of the articulatory loop and impairment of the visual–spatial sketchpad, or at least of the spatial component. It is interesting to note that impairment of STM has been related to the more general intellectual development of these subjects. It has been suggested that the phonological loop has a close functional relation to language learning (Baddeley, 1990; Gathercole & Baddeley, 1993), while the processing ability of the executive system is certainly of critical importance in determining the efficiency of processes of logical reasoning and problem-solving (Baddeley & Hitch, 1974).

In the context of LTM, the performance of MR individuals seems to dissociate as a function of encoding and retrieval demands of the memory task. As for basic mechanisms of the episodic memory deficit in MR individuals, experimental results are substantially inconclusive. These subjects are definitely impaired in the spontaneous utilization of elaborative strategies at the time of stimulus encoding. However, this deficit may not fully account for their poor level of initial learning. Indeed, experimental manipulations aimed to facilitate the full processing of characteristics of memorandum have consistently failed to equate the learning levels of MR subjects to those of healthy subjects. On the other hand, although available evidence seems to suggest a substantial preservation of the mechanisms for consolidating and recovering the memory trace once it has been effectively stored, further experimental work is needed to confirm this conclusion. Data collection for delineating possible differential patterns of LTM impairment across different aetiological groups of MR persons is just beginning. The parallel evaluation of scores on neuropsychological tests and of morphovolumetric and neurofunctional data in specific aetiological MR groups seems a promising avenue for establishing possible correlates between deranged memory development and abnormal maturation of the brain.

From a practical point of view, these data can provide invaluable information allowing educational psychologists and teachers to plan rationally grounded interventions to alleviate the learning difficulties and social maladjustment of these individuals. In the case of long-term memory, for example, while children with Down's syndrome might learn more proficiently by applying implicit than explicit learning techniques, children with Williams's syndrome seem to show the opposite pattern, with explicit procedures more easily learned than implicit. While such examples are speculative, increasing knowledge of the memory abilities of special populations promises to change the traditional approach to the cognitive rehabilitation of children with learning disabilities.

REFERENCES

Abel, E.L., Jacobson, S. & Sherwin, B.T. (1983). *In utero* alcohol exposure: functional and structural brain damage. *Neurobehavior Toxicology and Teratology*, **5**, 363–366.

American Association on Mental Retardation (1992). *Mental Retardation: Definition, Classification, and Systems of Support*, 9th edn. Washington, DC: American Association on Mental Retardation.

American Psychiatric Association (APA) (1994). *Diagnostic and Statistical Manual of Mental Disorders*, 4th edn (DSM-IV). Washington, DC: APA.

Atkinson, J., King, J., Braddick, O. et al. (1997). Specific deficit of dorsal stream function in Williams syndrome. *NeuroReport* **8**, 1919–1922.

Baddeley, A.D. & Hitch, G. (1974). Working memory. In G.H. Bower (ed.), *The Psychology of Learning and Motivation*, Vol. **8** (pp. 47–90).

Baddeley, A.D. (1986). *Working Memory*. London: Oxford University Press.

Baddeley, A.D. (1990). *Human Memory: Theory and practice*. London: Erlbaum.

Bellugi, U., Marks, S., Bihrle, A.M. & Sabo, H. (1988). Dissociation between language and cognitive functions in Williams' syndrome. In J. Stiles, M. Kritchevsky & U. Bellugi (eds), *Spatial Cognition: Brain Bases and Development* (pp. 273–298). Hillsdale, NJ: Erlbaum.

Bellugi, U., Bhirle, A., Jernigan, T., Trauner, D. & Doherty, S. (1990). Neuropsychological, neurological and neuroanatomical profile of Williams' syndrome. *American Journal of Medical Genetics*, **6**, 115–125.

Bellugi, U., Wang, P.P. & Jernigan, T.L. (1994). Williams's syndrome: an unusual neuropsychological profile. In S.H. Broman & J. Grafman (eds), *Atypical Cognitive Deficits in Developmental Disorders: Implications for Brain Function* (pp. 23–56). Hillsdale, NJ: Erlbaum.

Bellugi, U., Mills, D., Jernigan, T., Hickock, G. & Galaburda, A. (1999). Linking cognition, brain structure, and brain function in Williams' syndrome. In H. Tager-Flusberg, (ed.), *Neurodevelopmental Disorders* (pp. 111–154). Cambridge, MA: MIT Press.

Belmont, J.M., Ferretti, R.P. & Mitchell, D.W. (1982). Memorizing: a test of untrained mildly mentally retarded children's problem-solving. *American Journal of Mental Deficiency*, **87**, 197–210.

Bishop, D. (1999). An innate basis for language, *Science*, **286**, 2283–2284.

Blanchard, B.A., Riley, E.P. & Hannigan, J.H. (1987). Deficits on a spatial navigation task following prenatal exposure to ethanol. *Neurotoxicology and Teratology*, **9**, 906–911.

Botta, A., Sangiuolo, F., Calza, L., Giardino, L. et al. (1999). Expression analysis and protein localization of the human HPC-1/syntaxin 1A, a gene deleted in Williams' syndrome, *Genomics*, **15**, 525–528.

Burack, J.A. & Zigler, E. (1987). Intentional and incidental memory in organically mentally retarded, familial retarded, and nonretarded individuals. *American Journal on Mental Retardation*, **94**, 532–540.

Butters, N. & Cermak, L.S. (1975). Some analyses of amnesic syndromes in brain damaged patients. In R.L. Isaacson & K.H. Pribram (eds), *The Hippocampus*. New York: Plenum.

Carlesimo, G.A., Fadda, L., Lorusso, S. & Caltagirone, C. (1994). Verbal and spatial memory spans in Alzheimer's and multi-infarct dementia. *Acta Neurologica Scandinavica*, **89**, 132–138.

Carlesimo, G.A., Marotta, L. & Vicari, S. (1997). Long-term memory in mental retardation: evidence for a specific impairment in subjects with Down's syndrome. *Neuropsychologia*, **35**, 71–79.

Chapman, R.S. (1995). Language development in Children and Adolescents with Down's syndrome. In P. Fletcher & B. MacWhinney (eds), *The Handbook of Child Language* (pp. 641–663). Oxford: Blackwell.

Cohen, N.J. & Squire, L.R. (1980). Preserved learning and retention of pattern-analyzing skill in amnesia: dissociation of knowing how and knowing that. *Science*, **210**, 207–210.

Corkin, S. (1968). Acquisition of motor skill after bilateral medial temporal-lobe excision. *Neuropsychologia*, **6**, 255–265.

Craik, F.I.M. & Lockhart, R.S. (1972). Levels of processing: a framework for memory research. *Journal of Verbal Learning and Verbal Behavior*, **11**, 671–684.

Detterman, D.K. (1979). Memory in the mentally retarded. In N.R. Ellis (ed.), *Handbook of Mental Deficiency, Psychological Theory and Research*, 2nd edn (pp. 727–760). Hillsdale, NJ: Erlbaum.

Detterman, D.K. (1987). Theoretical notions of intelligence and mental retardation. *American Journal of Mental Deficiency*, **92**, 2–11.

Dodd, B. (1975). Recognition and reproduction of words by Down's syndrome and non-Down's syndrome retarded children. *American Journal of Mental Deficiency*, **80**, 306–11.

Dulaney, C.L., Raz, N. & Devine, C. (1996). Effortful and automatic processes associated with Down's syndrome and nonspecific mental retardation. *American Journal on Mental Retardation*, **100**, 418–423.

Ellis, N.R. (1969). A behavioral research strategy in mental retardation: defense and critique. *American Journal of Mental Deficiency*, **73**, 557–567.

Ellis, N.R. (1970). Memory processes in retardates and normals. In N.R. Ellis (ed.), *International Review of Research on Mental Retardation* (pp. 1–32). New York: Academic Press.

Ellis, N.R. (1978). Do the mentally retarded have poor memory? *Intelligence*, **2**, 41–54.

Ellis, N.R. & Allison, P. (1988). Memory for frequency of occurrence in retarded and nonretarded persons. *Intelligence*, **12**, 61–75.

Ellis, N.R. & Cavalier, A.R. (1982). Research perspectives in Mental Retardation. In E. Zigler & D. Balla (eds), *Mental Retardation: The Development–Difference Controversy* (pp. 121–152). Hillsdale, NJ: Erlbaum.

Ellis, N.R., Woodley-Zanthos, P. & Dulaney, C.L. (1989). Memory for spatial location in children, adults, and mentally retarded persons. *American Journal on Mental Retardation*, **93**, 521–527.

Eslinger, P.J. & Damasio, A.R. (1986). Preserved motor learning in Alzheimer's disease: implications for anatomy and behavior. *Journal of Neuroscience*, **6**, 3006–3009.

Ewart, A.K., Morris, C.A., Atkinson, D. et al. (1993). Hemizygosity at the elastin locus in a developmental disorder, Williams' syndrome. *Nature Genetics*, **5**, 11–16.

Fleischman, D.A. & Gabrieli, J.D.E. (1998). Repetition priming in normal aging and Alzheimer's disease: a review of findings and theories. *Psychology and Aging*, **13**, 88–119.

Fletcher, K.L. & Bray, N.W. (1995). External and verbal strategies in children with and without wild mental retardation. *American Journal of Mental Retardation*, **99**, 363–375.

Frangiskakis, J.M., Ewart, A.K., Morris, C.A. et al. (1996). Lim-kinase-1 hemizygosity implicated in impaired visuospatial constructive cognition. *Cell*, **86**, 59–69.

Fowler, A.E. (1995). Language variability in persons with Down's syndrome. In L. Nadel & D. Rosenthal (eds), *Down's Syndrome: Living and Learning in the Community*, New York: Wiley-Liss.

Gathercole, S.E. & Baddeley, A. (1993). *Working Memory and Language*. Hove, UK: Lawrence Erlbaum Associates.

Graf, P., Squire, L.R. & Mandler, G. (1984). The information that amnesic patients do not forget. *Journal of Experimental Psychology: Learning, Memory and Cognition*, **10**, 164–178.

Grant, J., Karmiloff-Smith, A., Gathercole, S.A. et al. (1997). Phonological short-term memory and its relationship to language in Williams' syndrome. *Cognitive Neuropsychiatry*, **2**, 81–99.

Hasher, L. & Zacks, R.T. (1979). Automatic and effortful processes in memory. *Journal of Experimental Psychology: General*, **108**, 356–388.

Hasher, L. & Zacks, R.T. (1984). Automatic processing of fundamental information. *American Psychologist*, **39**, 1372–1388.

Hulme, C. & Mackenzie, S. (1992) *Working Memory and Severe Learning Difficulties*. Hove: Erlbaum.

Huppert, F.A. & Piercy, M. (1979). Normal and abnormal forgetting in amnesia: effect of locus of lesion. *Cortex*, **15**, 385–390.

Jarrold, C. & Baddeley, A.D. (1997). Short-term memory for verbal and visuospatial information in Down's syndrome. *Cognitive Neuropsychiatry*, **2**, 101–122.

Jarrold, C., Baddeley A.D. & Hewes, A.K. (1999). Dissociating working memory: evidence from Down's and Williams' Syndrome. *Neuropsychologia*, **37**, 637–651.

Jarrold, C., Baddeley A.D. & Hewes, A.K. (2000). Verbal short-term memory deficits in Down's syndrome: a consequence of problems in rehearsal? *Journal of Child Psychology and Psychiatry*, **40**, 233–244.

Jernigan, T.L. & Bellugi, U. (1990). Anomalous brain morphology on magnetic resonance images in Williams' syndrome and Down's syndrome. *Archives of Neurology*, **47**, 529–533.

Karmiloff-Smith, A., Grant, J., Berthoud, I. et al. (1997). Language and Williams' syndrome: how intact is "intact"? *Child Development*, **68**, 274–290.

Karmiloff-Smith, A., Tyler, L.K., Voice, K. et al. (1998). Linguistic dissociation in Williams' syndrome: evaluating receptive syntax in on-line and off-line tasks. *Neuropsychologia*, **36**, 343–351.

Katz, E.R. & Ellis, N.R. (1991). Memory for spatial location in retarded and nonretarded persons. *Journal of Mental Deficiency Research*, **35**, 209–229.

Kay-Raining Bird, E. & Chapman, R.S. (1994). Sequential recall in individuals with Down Syndrome. *Journal of Speech and Hearing Research*, **37**, 1369–1380.

Kirsner, K., Milech, D. & Stander, P. (1983). Common and modality-specific processes in the mental lexicon. *Memory and Cognition*, **11**, 621–630.

Komatsu, S., Naito, M. & Fuke, T. (1996). Age-related and intelligence-related differences in implicit memory: effects of generation on a word-fragment completion test. *Journal of Experimental Child Psychology*, **62**, 151–172.

Kopelman, M.D. (1985). Rates of forgetting in Alzheimer-type dementia and Korsakoff's syndrome. *Neuropsychologia*, **23**, 623–638.

Logie, R.H. (1995). *Visuospatial Working Memory*. Hove: Erlbaum.

Marcell, M.M. & Weeks, S.L. (1988). Short-term memory difficulties and Down's syndrome. *Journal of Mental Deficiency Research*, **32**, 153–162.

Mattson, S.N. & Riley, E.P. (1999). Implicit and explicit memory functioning in children with heavy prenatal alcohol exposure. *Journal of the International Neuropsychological Society*, **5**, 462–471.

McCartney, J.R. (1987). Mentally retarded and nonretarded subjects' long-term recognition memory. *American Journal of Mental Retardation*, **92**, 312–317.

McDade, H.L. & Adler, S. (1980). Down's syndrome and short-term memory impairment: a storage or retrieval deficit? *American Journal of Mental Deficiency*, **84**, 561–567.

McKee R.D. & Squire R.L. (1992). Equivalent forgetting rates in long-term memory for diencephalic and medial temporal lobe amnesia. *Journal of Neuroscience*, **12**, 3765–3772.

Mervis, C.B., Morris, C.A., Bertrand, J. & Robinson, B.F. (1999). Williams' syndrome: findings from an integrated program of research. In H. Tager-Flusberg (ed.), *Neurodevelopmental Disorders* (pp. 65–110). Cambridge, MA: MIT Press.

Nissen, M.J. & Bullemer, P. (1987). Attentional requirements of learning: evidence from performance measures. *Cognitive Psychology*, **19**, 1–32.

Orsini, A., Trojano, L., Chiaccio, L. & Grossi, D. (1988). Immediate memory span in dementia. *Perceptual and Motor Skills*, **67**, 267–272.

Paterson, S.J., Brown, H.J., Gsödl, M.K. et al. (1999). Cognitive modularity and genetic disorders, *Science*, **286**, 2355–2358.

Perrig, P. & Perrig, W.J. (1995). Implicit and explicit memory in mentally retarded, learning disabled, and normal children. *Swiss Journal of Psychology*, **54**, 77–86.

Pezzini, G., Vicari, S., Volterra, V. et al. (1999). Children with Williams Syndrome: Is there a unique neuropsychological profile? *Developmental Neuropsychology*, **15**, 141–155.

Pulsifer, M.B. (1996). The neuropsychology of mental retardation. *Journal of the International Neuropsychological Society*, **2**, 159–176.

Rae, C., Karmiloff-Smith, A., Lee, M.A. et al. (1998). Brain biochemistry in Williams' syndrome: evidence for a role of the cerebellum in cognition? *Neurology*, **51**, 33–40.

Reilly, J., Kline, E.S. & Bellugi, U. (1990). Once more with feeling: affect and language in atypical populations. *Development and Psychopathology*, **2**, 367–391.

Salmon, D.P. & Butters, N. (1995). Neurobiology of skill learning. *Current Opinion in Neurobiology*, **5**, 184–190.

Schultz, E.E. (1983). Depth of processing by mentally retarded and MA-matched nonretarded individuals. *American Journal of Mental Deficiency*, **88**, 307–313.

Spearman, C. (1923). *The Nature of Intelligence and the Principles of Cognition*. London: Macmillan.

Spitz, H.H. (1966). The role of input organization in the learning and memory of mental retardates. In N.R. Ellis (ed.), *International Review on Mental Retardation*, vol. **2** (pp. 29–56). New York: Academic Press.

Spitz, H.H., Winters, J.J., Shirley, J.J. & Carrlo, J.C. (1975). The effects of spatial, temporal, and control variables on the free-recall serial position curve of retardates and equal-MA normals. *Memory and Cognition*, **3**, 107–112.

Squire, L.R. (1987). *Memory and Brain*. New York: Oxford University Press.

Takegata, R. & Furutuka, T. (1993). Perceptual priming effect in mentally retarded persons: implicit and explicit remembering. *Japanese Journal of Educational Psychology*, **41**, 176–182.

Tassabehji, M.K., Karmiloff-Smith, A., Grant, J. et al. (1997). Genotype phenotype correlation in Williams' syndrome. *American Journal of Human Genetics*, **61**, 11.

Tulving, E. & Schacter, D.L. (1990). Priming and human memory systems. *Science*, **247**, 301–306.

Turner, L.A., Hale, C.A. & Borkowski, J.G. (1996). Influence of intelligence on memory development. *American Journal on Mental Retardation*, **100**, 468–480.

Turnure, J.E. (1991). Long-term memory in mental retardation. In N.W. Bray (ed.), *International Review of Research on Mental Retardation*, vol. **17** (pp. 193–217). New York: Academic Press.

Udwin, O. & Yule, W. (1990). Expressive language of children with Williams' syndrome. *American Journal of Medical Genetics (suppl.)*, **6**, 108–114.

Uecker, A. & Nadel, L. (1996). Spatial locations gone awry: object and spatial memory deficits in children with fetal alcohol syndrome. *Neuropsychologia*, **34**, 209–223.

Uecker, A. & Nadel, L. (1998). Spatial but not object memory impairments in children with fetal alcohol syndrome. *American Journal of Mental Retardation*, **103**, 12–18.

Vakil, E., Shelef-Reshef, E. & Levy-Shiff, R. (1997). Procedural and declarative memory processes: individuals with and without mental retardation. *American Journal of Mental Retardation*, **102**, 147–160.

Vicari, S., Albertini, G. & Caltagirone, C. (1992). Cognitive profiles in adolescents with mental retardation. *Journal of Intellectual Disability Research*, **36**, 415–423.

Vicari, S., Bellucci, S. & Carlesimo, G.A. (2000a). Implicit and explicit memory: a functional dissociation in persons with Down's syndrome. *Neuropsychologia*, **38**, 240–251.

Vicari, S., Bellucci, S. & Carlesimo, G.A. (2001). Procedural learning deficit in children with Williams' syndrome. *Neuropsychologia*, **39**, 665–677.

Vicari, S., Bellucci, S. & Carlesimo, G.A. (submitted). Visual and spatial working memory dissociation: evidence from Williams' syndrome. *Developmental Medicine and Child Neurology*.

Vicari, S., Carlesimo, G.A. & Caltagirone, C. (1995). Short-term memory in persons with intellectual disabilities and Down's syndrome. *Journal of Intellectual Disabilities Research*, **39**(6), 532–537.

Vicari, S., Brizzolara, D., Carlesimo, G.A. et al. (1996a). Memory abilities in children with Williams' syndrome. *Cortex*, **32**, 503–514.

Vicari, S., Carlesimo, G.A., Brizzolara, D. & Pezzini, G. (1996b). Short-term memory in children with Williams' syndrome: a reduced contribution of lexical–semantic knowledge to word span. *Neuropsychologia*, **34**, 919–925.

Vicari, S., Marotta, L., Menghini, D. & Carlesimo, G.A. (2000b). Working memory and speech fluency in subjects with Down's syndrome. Abstracts of the 11th World Congress of the International

Association for the Scientific Study of Intellectual Disabilities (IASSID), August 1–6 2000, Seattle, WA, USA. *Journal of Intellectual Disability Research*, **44**, 504.

Volterra, V., Capirci, O., Pezzini, G. et al. (1996). Linguistic abilities in Italian children with Williams' syndrome. *Cortex*, **32**, 663–677.

Volterra V., Longobardi E., Pezzini G. et al. (1999). Visuospatial and linguistic abilities in a twin with Williams' syndrome. *International Journal of Intellectual Disabilities*, **43**(4), 294–305.

Wang, P.P. & Bellugi, U. (1994). Evidence from two genetic syndromes for a dissociation between verbal and visual-spatial short-term memory. *Journal of Clinical Experimental Neuropsychology*, **16**, 317–322.

Warrington, E.K. & Weiskrantz, L. (1968). A new method of testing long-term retention with special reference to amnesic patients. *Nature*, **217**, 972–974.

Winters, J.J. & Semchuk, M.T. (1986). Retrieval from long-term store as a function of mental age and intelligence. *American Journal of Mental Deficiency*, **90**, 440–448.

Wyatt, B.S. & Conners, F.A. (1998). Implicit and explicit memory in individuals with mental retardation. *American Journal on Mental Retardation*, **102**, 511–526.

Zigler, E. (1969) Developmental vs. difference theories of mental retardation and the problem of motivation. *American Journal of Mental Deficiency*, **73**, 536–556.

Zigler, E. & Balla, D. (1982) Introduction: the developmental approach to mental retardation. In E. Zigler & D. Balla (eds), *Mental Retardation: The Developmental Difference Controversy* (pp. 3–8). Hillsdale, NJ: Erlbaum.

CHAPTER 24

Developmental Amnesias and Acquired Amnesias of Childhood

Christine M. Temple

Developmental Neuropsychology Unit, University of Essex, Colchester, UK

BACKGROUND ISSUES

Selective impairments of literacy or language in children of otherwise good intelligence have been well documented in both acquired and developmental forms. There has also been recognition that there are other selective impairments of cognitive development which may coexist with intact intelligence and may be manifest in developmental or acquired form, e.g. disorders of face recognition (de Haan & Campbell, 1991; Temple, 1992a; Young & Ellis, 1989) or disorders of executive skill (Marlowe, 1992; Williams & Mateer, 1992; Temple, 1997a). The first detailed case analyses were presented 10–15 years ago of both acquired amnesia in childhood (Ostergaard, 1987) and developmental amnesia (De Renzi & Lucchelli, 1990), with both individuals displaying normal intelligence. There was relatively limited discussion of these conditions in the 1990s, but there is now an expanding literature that indicates not only that these disorders may be more common than had been recognized but also that they have interesting implications for discussions of memory systems in adults as well as children. They provide models of memory development with unusual constraints, which affect theorizing about distinctions between component processes in adult memory systems, e.g. there are issues in the adult literature about the relationship between episodic and semantic memory. Dissociations may be seen in childhood that are not evident in adulthood but are directly relevant to such issues. Disorders of memory in childhood also provide information about the normal development of memory and are relevant to theoretical debates about prescribed or emergent modularity in development (Bishop, 1997; Temple, 1997a, 1997b). They are also significant from a more applied perspective, since children with amnesia yet normal intelligence constitute a group whose education is being accommodated within normal classrooms, despite limited recognition of the form of their difficulties.

The idea that memory impairments might be present in those of limited intellectual skills gained earlier credence than the idea that they might occur in those of normal intelligence.

The Handbook of Memory Disorders. Edited by A.D. Baddeley, M.D. Kopelman and B.A. Wilson
© 2002 John Wiley & Sons, Ltd.

Ribot (1882, cited by Maurer, 1992) argued that "idiots", "imbeciles" and some "cretins" have "a general debility of memory". More explicitly, it has been suggested that in children with general learning disabilities, the later stages of memory may be intact but the ability to code information effectively for storage may be impaired. However, as Maurer (1992) emphasizes, memory can also seem to be well developed in some "idiots savants" who are able to use efficient mnemonic strategies. The apparent dissociation of memory skills from many aspects of intellectual development becomes evident, however, in the cases of developmental and acquired amnesia that are discussed below.

There are a variety of potential aetiologies for memory impairments in childhood. Traditionally, disorders in children are divided into those that are acquired and those that are developmental (Temple, 1992b). In acquired disorders, a child has a normally developing skill, then sustains injury or disease and the development of the skill or its subsequent progress is impaired. In developmental disorders, the child has never learnt the skill and has not sustained a known injury, the disorder simply becoming manifest as the child acquires and develops cognitive competence.

In practice, this division for memory impairments, as for other disorders in childhood, may not be straightforward, e.g. epilepsy, which is often associated with memory impairments, may be a developmental or an acquired disorder. Recently, Vargha-Khadem et al. (1997) and Gadian et al. (2000) have also discussed children with memory impairments who have had hypoxic-ischaemic episodes at or shortly after birth. These children are referred to as having acquired amnesias and the disorders are acquired, in the sense that there has been injury or disease and pathology is identified in the hippocampus. However, the children have not had a period of normal skill development that has been interrupted, and their development from the outset is with an impaired substrate for memory. Within child neuropsychology, it has not simply been the occurrence of an acquired lesion that has led to a classification as an acquired disorder. In Landau–Kleffner syndrome, so-called "acquired aphasia of childhood", there is a period of normal development followed by declining and then severely impaired language function but no episode of injury or disease.

Thus, we see classification as an acquired disorder in childhood either where there is a known lesion or where a period of normal development is followed by decline and impairment. The issue of classification becomes significant if developmental amnesias and acquired amnesias of childhood differ in their characteristics and if the pattern of memory impairment differs, dependent upon the age of onset of the impairment. Effects of age of onset would be predicted by a number of developmental models, within which systems evolve but would be predicted less by developmental frameworks which incorporate more preformist views of the underlying functional architecture.

Acquired memory impairments in children may follow closed head injury or encephalitis, exhibiting similar symptomatology to adults (Herkowitz & Rosman, 1982). However, additional cognitive impairments are common in these cases, which may sometimes make the study of the effect of the memory impairments itself difficult to disentangle form other cognitive loss. Cases of more selective acquired amnesia have been described following anoxia, to which it appears that the large mitochondria of the hippocampi may be particularly vulnerable, and in temporal lobe epilepsy similar circuitry may be affected. Developmental amnesias may occur in association with epilepsy, family history suggesting a genetic vulnerability, or in the absence of any explicit predisposing factor.

In the analysis of memory impairments in children, an issue arises that differs from their study in adulthood. This relates to the potential effects of memory impairments upon the acquisition of skill or knowledge in other cognitive domains, e.g. adults with classical amnesia typically have normal language skills. In contrast, if a child acquires amnesia before language is fully established or has developmental amnesia, then the memory impairment itself could affect the subsequent development of semantic or other memory stores which may underpin language. Thus, for example, Julia (Temple, 1997a), discussed below in the section on developmental amnesia, also had a developmental anomia, which was a disorder resulting from failure to establish knowledge of vocabulary items, rather than a straightforward retrieval difficulty. Thus, children with developmental disorders of memory provide knowledge not only about the structure of developing memory systems but also about the relationship between memory and other skills, as learning and development take place.

In disorders of naming in childhood, a distinction has been drawn between *semantic representation anomia* (Temple, 1997a), in which naming difficulties are associated with apparent failure to establish a semantic representations for the word, reflected in similarly impaired receptive vocabulary, and *semantic access anomia* (Van Hout, 1993; Temple, 1997a), in which there is evidence of an intact representation for the word but difficulties with lexical retrieval of its name. The former disorder may be associated with more generalized memory impairments. The latter disorder has been described by Van Hout (1993) in parallel developmental and acquired forms.

ACQUIRED AMNESIA IN CHILDREN

An early case of acquired amnesia in a child, following ECT, is reported by Geschwind (1974). The 10-year-old child had normal language prior to the ECT but subsequently developed both memory and language impairment. Geschwind attributed the language impairment to a retrograde amnesia which extended back into the period of language acquisition. An alternative explanation would be that the acquired amnesia and acquired dyphasia were distinct disorders. However, Geschwind argued that an acquired memory impairment in childhood may not only affect the acquisition of subsequent skills, as discussed above, but may also affect skills that have been previously acquired if the amnesia disrupts the storage, consolidation or subsequent retrieval of previously learnt material.

Ostergaard (1987) presented the first detailed analysis of a child with acquired amnesia. The 10-year-old child, C.C., developed amnesia following an episode of anoxia following water intoxication in the treatment of diabetic ketoacidosis, resulting in severe left hippocampal damage and at least partial right hippocampal damage. The child remained of normal intelligence but many memory skills were impaired. Ostergaard (1987) made the first attempt to determine the components of memory that might be affected and spared in such cases. He argued that the distinction between the skills that were impaired and those that were intact related to a procedural–declarative dimension, with declarative memory impaired and procedural memory intact.

Within declarative memory, both semantic and episodic memory was impaired. Knowledge of semantic memory for facts was impaired, as reflected by scores on the Information subtest of the WISC-R (Wechsler, 1974). The impairment in semantic memory also extended to vocabulary skills in tasks of lexical decision, semantic classification and verbal fluency. In lexical decision, accuracy was good, indicating development of lexical representations, but responses were very slow, suggesting access difficulties, and there was a significantly elevated priming effect of a related preceding word. In semantic classification, Ostergaard (1987) divided words by age of acquisition into three groups, 0–4 years, 4–8 years and over 8 years. He found a much sharper than normal temporal gradient to performance in terms of response speed, with words acquired early being responded to more quickly than those acquired later. He argued that this reflected a retrograde amnesia with a temporal gradient.

Impaired episodic memory was seen on immediate and delayed story recall, design recall and delayed free recall of word lists, although immediate free recall of words was within the normal range. Reading and spelling were also impaired and there was the suggestion of some retrograde loss, with teachers reporting normal reading prior to illness, yet reading and spelling ages 6 months after illness were found to be 9–14 months below chronological age at time of illness.

However, like cases of acquired amnesia in adulthood, C.C. had intact procedural memory for skills, such as learning a computer video-attack game. Like acquired amnesic patients, Ostergaard (1987) also showed that C.C. could learn and retain skills on the Gollin incomplete pictures tests, where pictures depicting an item become progressively more complete. Repeat testing 24 h later showed much improved skills for both C.C. and controls and the improvement was sustained on further retesting 8 days later. Follow-up at age 15 indicated a similar pattern, with a distinction between declarative and procedural memory skills. There was some limited progress in reading and spelling but much less than would be expected from a normal child.

Vargha-Khadem et al. (1992) reported, in an abstract, a case of acquired amnesia in a child, J.L., where they also found impaired performance in declarative memory but normal performance on procedural memory. J.L. developed amnesia after surgery for a craniopharyngioma. There was ventral diencephalic pathology encompassing the mammillary bodies. Some scholastic skills were nevertheless attained and reading developed to age level.

A further case of acquired amnesia is described in a 9-year-old child, T.C., who had acute encephalopathy, possibly as a result of herpes simplex encephalitis, resulting in diffuse cerebral injury (Wood et al., 1982, 1989). T.C. had severely impaired semantic memory in relation to facts about the world and severely impaired episodic memory impairment affecting both story recall and autobiographical day-to-day memory. However, Woods et al. (1987) argued that their case did not conform to the procedural–declarative distinction of the Ostergaard case, since T.C. made some scholastic progress through the school years, although a dense amnesia remained in both clinical and psychometric terms. However, Ostergaard & Squires (1990) argued, in response, that some scholastic progress would be expected in the absence of declarative memory on the basis of automated procedures or conceptual development. They also emphasized that the distinction they had proposed was based upon relative rather than absolute impairment, with studies of even acquired amnesia in adults discussing "differential susceptibility of these systems to amnesia" (Squire & Cohen, 1984). C.C.'s declarative skills were severely impaired and were much more impaired than procedural memory skills. Similarly, for T.C., declarative knowledge at age 20 remained severely impaired, with inability to report events of the last hour and memory for verbal and visual material "essentially absent", but there were some miminal skills, e.g. with some words recalled on repeated exposure with the Rey Auditory Verbal Learning task. Ostergaard & Squire (1990) argued that minimal residual declarative skills in C.C. or T.C. could enable some limited acquisition of skills contributing to scholastic progress, without difficulty for the Ostergaard (1987) proposal. They point out that in the cases of both C.C.

and T.C. scholastic progress in literacy and arithmetic was abnormally slow, although the Vargha-Khadem et al. (1992) case of J.L., mentioned above, illustrates that impairment in literacy is not a necessary concomitant of a declarative impairment.

Subsequent to this debate, Brainerd & Reyna (1992) argued that children's logical and mathematical skills and ability to make pragmatic inferences are not dependent upon memory in terms of reactivation of previously encoded traces. This would permit progress in these scholastic areas despite memory impairment. Wood et al. (1989) had reported above-average skills for T.C. in general problem-solving ability on the Porteus mazes, and a further pattern of this sort was confirmed by Broman et al. (1997), who reported the case of a child, M.S., with an acquired amnesia that followed respiratory arrest and consequent anoxic encephalopathy at the age of 8 years. MRI indicated loss of volume in bilateral hippocampal and medial temporal grey areas, with no evidence of amygdalar atrophy.

The child was followed up into adulthood and assessed in detail at the age of 28. Intelligence on Progressive Matrices was normal. In contrast, declarative memory was severely impaired. His profile on the Wechsler Intelligence Scales indicated that as an adult his weakest subtest scores were attained on Information, which assesses the factual general knowledge established in semantic memory, and on Vocabulary, which assesses the knowledge of words established in semantic memory. On further formal testing, he was impaired in episodic recall of words, stories and patterns. He was also impaired in learning paired associates and delayed recall of a route. His memory impairment extended to both anterograde and retrograde loss as he was unable to remember any events more than 6–9 months prior to the anoxia.

Recognition memory for words, faces and doors on the WRMB (Warrington, 1984) and the Doors and People Test (Baddeley et al., 1994) was impaired but immediate recognition memory for patterns on Benton's Visual Retention Test was normal. Short-term memory, as assessed by digit span, was also normal. Consistent with the view of Brainerd & Reyna (1992), some mathematical and logical skills had become established, e.g. he developed algorithms to derive the multiplication tables he was unable to memorise by rote. With lengthy perseverance, he could solve puzzles like Rubic's cube and some computer games. On the Wechsler Intelligence Scales, Picture Completion, Object Assembly and Block Design were entirely normal, indicating intact skills of logical analysis, nonverbal reasoning and construction. He could also assemble items in real life, e.g. a canopy tent, and he could recite the tune and lyrics to the signature songs for his favourite television programmes. Thus, some automated and procedural memory skills had also been acquired. Within language, comprehension of syntax of varying complexity and comprehension of the sentences comprising the verbal ideational material taken from the BDAE (Goodglass & Kaplan, 1983), which incorporate adult logical complexity, were both at an average level for an adult. In contrast, receptive vocabulary was impaired and was at an average 9-year-old level; naming was also impaired to the expected level relative to his receptive vocabulary. Thus, he has a semantic representation anomia as discussed above. Reading and spelling remained at an 8-year-old level, hence whilst syntactic and logical reasoning skills in language had developed to an adult level, knowledge of word meanings and ability to read or spell words had remained severely impaired.

Broman et al. (1997) noted the difference in the patterns of deficit in the reported cases of acquired amnesia in childhood with respect to language and literacy development, with the degree of reading difficulty for M.S. being more extreme than that of C.C. (Ostergaard, 1987) or T.C. (Woods et al., 1982, 1989). Reviewing the identified lesions, he proposed that for those cases involving the hippocampus and its circuitry, language development and skills were also affected to a degree, which might vary dependent upon the degree of the amnesia. In cases like that of J.L (Vargha-Khadem et al., 1992), where the damage was to the diencephalic structures including the mammillary bodies, language and reading appear to develop normally, since reading was at the expected level for chronological age.

However, in contrast to this view, Vargha-Khadem et al. (1997) reported a further three cases of amnesic impairment in children following early hippocampal pathology. In each case they argued that language and literacy were in the low-average to average range and that episodic memory was much more significantly affected than semantic memory. Despite the bilateral hippocampal pathology, they argue for the development of semantic skills. These are the first cases of acquired amnesia in childhood in which it is argued that semantic skills are normal for both knowledge of words and factual knowledge of the world, and that some declarative skills are intact despite episodic impairment.

The first of Vargha-Khadem et al.'s (1997) three cases was a 14-year-old girl, Beth. After birth Beth remained without a heartbeat for 7–8 min before resuscitation. Memory difficulties were noticed on entrance into mainstream school. The second case, Jon, was a 19-year-old boy. He had been delivered prematurely at 26 weeks, had breathing difficulties and was in an incubator, on a ventilator, for 2 months. At the age of 4, he had two protracted seizures. Memory difficulties were noted by his parents at age 5.5 years. The third case was a 22-year-old, Kate, who for 3 days at the age of 9 had received a toxic dose of theophylline, a drug being given for her asthma. This led to respiratory arrest and loss of consciousness. Upon physical recovery, she displayed amnesia.

In support of competent semantic skills, Vargha-Khadem et al. (1997) discuss both the Information and Vocabulary subtests on the WISC-III (Wechsler, 1992) and predicted reading and spelling skills on the basis of IQ. They argue that there is a pronounced disparity between attainments on these measures and a severe amnesia for everyday life. In relation to the Information subtest, Beth and Jon attain normal scaled scores, although Kate has a scaled score of 6, indicative of a degree of impairment and equivalent to the level of performance taken to indicate impairment in the Ostergaard (1987) study. Scores on Vocabulary for all three children were within the normal range. Reading scores for all three children were commensurate with predictions from IQ, although for Beth, where intellectual skills were a standard deviation below average, these attainments were equivalently below average. Spelling was similarly at the predicted level for Beth and Kate, although this was more markedly impaired for Jon. Thus, whilst semantic memory is not intact for all skills in all three cases, there is clear evidence that it is has developed to a substantive degree.

For all three cases, immediate episodic memory for a word list was normal, as was digit span and Corsi span. Thus, short-term memory appeared normal. However, delayed recall of both verbal and nonverbal material was severely impaired. There was also parental complaint of severe difficulties with day-to-day memory to a degree that significantly affects their day-to-day abilities. This was confirmed for all three children by their very weak scores on the Rivermead Behavioural Memory Test (Vargha-Khadem et al., 1997). Thus, episodic memory is severely impaired and is much less well developed than semantic memory skills.

This inequality of sparing might result from independent storage, with the more significant impact upon episodic rather than semantic stores in these cases of bilateral hippocampal pathology, being similar to that seen in acquired amnesia. Another possibility that Vargha-Khadem et al. (1997) discuss is that, whilst episodic memory is impaired, it might be sufficiently preserved to enable the acquisition of knowledge to which there is repeated exposure in different contexts, and therefore enable context-free linguistic and factual knowledge. This would enable preservation of the theory of acquired amnesia for both adults and children, and would argue that both episodic memory and semantic memory are a single process mediated by the hippocampal system. However, Vargha-Khadem et al.'s (1997) proposal is that the underlying sensory memory functions of the perirhinal and entorhinal cortices may be sufficient to support context-free semantic memories, but not context-rich episodic memories, for which hippocampal circuitry is required. For both semantic and episodic memory to be affected severely, the hippocampi and underlying cortices would then require to be damaged.

Both Beth and Jon (Vargha-Khadem et al., 1997) had hypoxic–ischaemic episodes at or shortly after birth without showing any subsequent hard neurological signs. A further three similar cases are also presented by Gadian et al. (2000). In each of these five cases, the authors argue for the relative preservation of semantic memory over episodic memory. In each case, the Information and Vocabulary subtest scores on the WISC-III (Wechsler, 1992) are normal, and in each case basic reading is in line with IQ, episodic memory in terms of delayed story recall, delayed recall of listed words and delayed recall of the Rey figure is very poor, and day-to-day memory is impaired, based on both parental report and psychometric assessment. MRI scans indicate visible bilateral hippocampal atrophy in all cases and quantitative measures also indicate reduced grey matter in the putamen, with abnormality in the thalamus and midbrain.

Of further interest in the Gadian et al. (2000) paper is the parental comment, "Although his understanding of language is good, his use of language is often simplistic and he gropes for words". This suggests possible anomic difficulties in the use of language and, whilst name retrieval has not been explored in the cases of acquired amnesia discussed above, it has been found to be impaired in some of the cases of developmental amnesia outlined below (Temple, 1997a; Casalini et al., 1999).

A more detailed investigation of Jon, one of the hypoxic–ischaemic cases of Gadian et al. (2000), is given by Baddeley et al. (2001). Baddeley et al. (2001) established that, despite the very weak episodic recall skills, recognition memory for both visual and verbal material might nevertheless be normal. Recognition skills at a normal level were demonstrated on a range of tasks, including those which involved different speeds of presentation and those involving recognition after a 2 day delay. The only example of good recall came from material presented on a newsreel studied four times over a 2 day period, the conditions most like those involved in the acquisition of semantic memory. As Baddeley et al. (2001) note, Jon is an intelligent and highly motivated subject, so an above-average level of performance might have been expected. Thus, they do not argue that recognition is definitely normal but they do demonstrate convincingly that recognition is very significantly better than recall, even when scores are scaled to take account of the generally greater ease of recognition over recall. The enhancement of recognition over recall for Jon is of a degree that would not be typical of peer performance or the performance of adults with memory disorders.

Thus it would appear, from cases such as Jon's, that memory is being encoded and stored and that whilst the recollective process of episodic memory is impaired, this is not necessary for the acquisition of semantic knowledge or for recognition memory. This negates the view that semantic memory is simply the derivative of many episodes (e.g. Baddeley, 1997; Squire, 1992), a view derived from adult studies, where impaired episodic memory generally coexists with failure to update semantic memory, although Tulving (1972; Tulving & Markovitch, 1998) has argued otherwise for many years. It also indicates a more focal pattern of impairment in these cases of developmental amnesia than is typically seen in acquired amnesia. In acquired amnesia, recognition is usually, although not always, impaired (Aggleton & Brown, 1999; Holdstock et al., 2000) and, whilst semantic memory for facts acquired prior to injury is intact, there is difficulty in upgrading semantic information. In amnesic cases like Jon, recognition memory is good and semantic memory stores are upgraded, despite severe episodic memory impairment.

The idea of a developmental disorder being more focal than a similar acquired disorder in adulthood is interesting, given the view often argued that abnormalities in development have a pervasive and generalized impact because the system is adapting and formulating without prespecified functional architecture. Jon's case of amnesia from an early age demonstrated the potentially focal impact of a developmental memory impairment, with a pattern of performance entirely consistent with a modular view of the developing memory system.

Tulving (1985) defined episodic memory in a more focal way than it is often used now. He stressed the subjective experience of recollection in episodic memory. Thus, he distinguished between "remembering" and simply "knowing". Recognition memory is also argued to reflect these two processes of "remembering" and "knowing" (Tulving, 1985). Baddeley et al. (2001) argue that when Jon recognizes information, he "knows" he has seen it before but he does not "remember" the experience of having seen it before. In their terms, he lacks the ability to recollect the contextual detail which would be necessary for a "remember" response. Thus, the memory impairment is truly episodic in the original Tulving (1972, 1985) meaning of the term.

A further case of acquired amnesia, in which there are retrieval difficulties of a more unusual form, is described by Vargha-Khadem et al. (1994) in a 14-year-old boy, Neil. The amnesia followed successful treatment the preceding year with radiotherapy and chemotherapy for a tumour in the pineal region of the posterior third ventricle. Neil retained normal verbal intelligence, attaining scores of 111/109 on the verbal scale of the Wechsler Intelligence Scales. Although Performance IQ was significantly impaired, block design scores were normal. Retrograde memory was normal but episodic memory was impaired. Memory assessed on the Wechsler Memory Scales was very poor, with a MQ of 59 attained. Neil could copy a complex design well but delayed recall was severely impaired. With spoken verbal response, the verbal memory impairment appeared to be pervasive. There was also both agnosia and alexia. Although he could recognize familiar objects when they were in their customary place in his home, he was unable to recognize any of them when they were placed on a table directly in front of him. Yet, he could produce precise and intricate drawings of imagined objects and scenes and had intact and detailed visual memories for these items. Writing was also intact and he could produce accurate written responses for some information that he could not access in oral form, thereby indicating some ability to learn and retain new information. He was not always aware of his correct written responses. Thus, the recall is not linked to explicit awareness.

These abilities argued for separate stores and/or retrieval modalities for verbal material, one oral and one orthographic. His ability to use orthographic output included information taught in a verbal format at school but also included recall of day-to-day events. In the case of Jon (Baddeley et al., 2001), overt recall was problematic but recognition was much better. In the case of Neil (Vargha-Khadem et al., 1994), overt oral recall is problematic but written recall is much better. In both cases, it appears that memory is being encoded and stored but the recollective process of episodic memory is impaired and, without that episodic process, one may "know" rather than "remember", as in the case of Jon (Baddeley et al., 2001), or one may not have conscious awareness of "knowing", as in the case of Neil (Vargha-Khadem et al., 1994), despite explicit response accuracy with orthographic output.

REYE'S SYNDROME

A seemingly quite different form of acquired memory impairment despite intact intellectual skills is documented as a consequence of Reye's syndrome (RS; Quart et al., 1987). RS is most common in children aged 5–15 years (Nelson et al., 1979). It occurs in children who have previously been healthy. The child may appear to have a viral infection from which he/she seems to be recovering. RS has also been linked to ingestion of 5-aminosalicylates (5-ASA), or to both viral infection and 5-ASA ingestion. The child then develops a serious acute encephalopathy linked to liver disease and severe disturbance of intracellular metabolism (Meekin et al., 1999). Behaviourally, there is vomiting, lethargy, personality change and disorientation. The disease differs in severity from mild personality changes in an otherwise oriented child (Stage 1) to coma (Stage 5) (Lovejoy et al., 1974). Changes to the brain include astrocyte swelling, myelin bleb formation and damage to neuron mitochondria (Partin et al., 1978). There is diffuse encephalopathy with cerebral oedema and raised intracranial pressure, causing tissue displacement and reduced cerebral perfusion pressure. This occasionally leads to death (Sarnaik, 1982) but more commonly there is recovery, with intact intelligence but specific neuropsychological impairment (Quart, 1984).

The position of the temporal lobes is thought to make them particularly vulnerable to the effects of oedema and raised intracranial pressure in RS and elsewhere (Quart et al., 1987). However, a single MRI case study indicated compressed ventricles and lesions of the thalamus, mesencephalon and pons, with the thalamic lesion persisting for 2 months as the others resolved. When the age of onset is below a year, the incidence of neurological impairment is higher (Meekin et al., 1999). Thus, in similar fashion to Landau–Kleffner syndrome with language (Bishop, 1985), earlier onset is associated with poorer prognosis (Davidson et al., 1978), the reverse of the normal expectation from developmental plasticity.

Quart et al. (1987) report a study of 26 children with RS, with a mean age of 12.9 and a range of 7–18 years. They were aged at least 3 when they became ill. Controls were matched by age, race, sex, socioeconomic status and receptive vocabulary score on the PPVT, which provided an estimate of intelligence levels. The children with RS were significantly poorer than controls on the children's version of the Wechsler Memory Scales. The mean MQ–IQ difference for the RS group was also significantly greater than for controls. No details are given about semantic memory skills, except that since PPVT scores are normal, it appears that semantic memory for words has developed normally. The memory impairment for the children with RS included verbal and visual episodic memory, as reflected in immediate and delayed recall of stories and designs. Working memory as assessed by digit span forward was also impaired. In contrast, paired associate learning was not significantly different from normal.

Quart et al. (1987) carried out a "levels of processing" experiment. In the face section, 30 unfamiliar faces were presented and the children either had to make a "superficial" judgement by indicating whether the person was "male" or "female", or they had to engage in "deep" processing and indicate whether the person was "nice" or "not nice". For a parallel words version, the superficial judgement was whether the word was printed in "small letters" or "capitals", and the deep processing occurred in indicating whether the thing was "alive" or "not alive". On the face section, there was no difference between the groups. However, on the word section, whilst there was no difference in responses for the items which had been superficially cued, the RS group missed significant words that had been deeply processed. Only the control group benefited from deep processing. Semantic activation did not assist the verbal memory of the children with RS.

A further difference between the children with RS and controls was in the use of other memory techniques. None of the children with RS outwardly demonstrated the use of mnemonic strategies, whereas nine of the 26 controls used techniques such as chunking, rehearsing digits and words, drawing designs in the air when the design card was exposed and verbalizing associations to go with difficult pairs of words. Quart et al. (1987) suggest that there is less active involvement in the effort to retain information. They also suggest that the children with RS are less good as organizing visual designs, with almost half failing to perceive the overall design, in contrast to 15% of the control group. These failures in encoding and organization of memory are reminiscent of the discussion of frontal amnesia by Luria (1966, 1973), discussed further by Warrington & Weiskrantz (1982).

In acquired amnesia in adults and in some of the cases of acquired amnesia in children, with onset later than infancy, there is evidence that memory is intact for events before a point in time and impaired for subsequent points. Maurer (1992) suggests that in such cases registration is normal but retention abnormal. In the cases of Jon and Neil, discussed above, both registration and retention appear to be normal but there is difficulty with episodic retrieval and normal free recall. However, with diffuse pathology, such as Reye's syndrome, there may be impairment in registration as well as retention and recall (Lishman, 1987; Maurer, 1992).

TEMPORAL LOBECTOMIES AND TEMPORAL LOBE SURGERY

Temporal lobectomies in children are carried out for the relief of intractable epilepsy, in cases where there is a temporal lobe focus. Dennis et al. (1988) report a study of the effects of temporal lobectomies in adolescent and young adults. Those with left-sided lobectomies showed impairments in verbal recognition memory. However, Dennis et al. (1988) also found complex interactions between side of surgery, age at onset and seizure type which are difficult to interpret. Meyer et al. (1986) also report complex effects of surgery in a study of 50 children aged under 18 years. IQ was not significantly affected by the surgery. Overall, there were no significant effects in memory scores. However, boys were significantly more likely to show memory impairment after surgery and girls were significantly more likely to show memory improvement. Sex differences in memory skill have received little attention in other studies.

Temporal lobe surgery is also carried out for lateralized tumours of the temporal lobes. Cavazzutti et al. (1980) discuss a study in which 60% of the subjects were aged 3–19. Those who had left temporal lobe surgery had increased verbal dysfunction and reduced verbal memory quotient but had improved nonverbal memory. Those who had right temporal lobe surgery had improved verbal skills and verbal learning. The improvements in skill were interpreted as reflecting the removal of the inhibitory effects of the pathological areas upon intact systems in the contralateral hemisphere via the commissural connections.

Carpantieri & Mulhern (1993) also reported memory impairments in 50% of children surviving temporal lobe tumours. They found that the earlier the age of diagnosis, and therefore presumably the earlier the tumour developed, the more severe the long-term memory deficits. However, the greatest memory impairments were seen in those who had radiation therapy, and in such cases memory impairments were probable, even if intelligence was well-preserved. Reading and spelling were significantly correlated with verbal memory performance.

Memory impairment following radiation treatment at the age of 5.6 for a tumour of unspecified location is also reported by Morrow et al. (1989). They briefly described a child, K.I., whose memory for the time around the treatment was intact, as was the knowledge that she had at that time, suggesting intact semantic memory. However, she became "almost completely unable to encode or retrieve long-term memories ... she became unable to add new information", suggesting severely impaired episodic memory. Although intellectual development was age-appropriate, a year and a half after treatment it failed to rise as fast as chronological age, so that by the age of 8.3 her mental age on the WISC-R was below expectation at 7.2. By the age of 12.8, there had been essentially no intellectual development and, if anything, a slight decline. Mental age on the WISC-R had dropped to 6.8. Cognitive measures had plateaued. Thus, although intelligence seemed age-appropriate immediately after treatment, impairment became more evident over time. It is not clear whether such a pattern relates to long-term effects of the memory impairment itself or to the more generalized impairment to the substrate for cognition, caused by the radiation treatment.

DEVELOPMENTAL AMNESIA

Maurer (1992) described a child, N.S., with developmental amnesia, which he termed "congenital amnesia". CT scan at the age of 9 years revealed low-density areas in both temporal fossae, indicating absence of the left temporal lobe and the pole and mesial parts of the right temporal lobe. These abnormalities were thought to result from prenatal events, possibly as the result of a stroke *in utero*. The memory impairment of N.S. is described as resembling H.M. (Scoville & Milner, 1957). Since in H.M. there is a disorder of declarative memory but procedural memory is intact, Maurer (1992) attempted remediation based on embedding responses within actions that were trained as habits. The information that N.S. was to learn was imbedded in stimulus–response sets of pairings, which were then trained by repetition day after day. N.S. had difficulty in learning the names of the people she met everyday. Every time she met the person she was cued to say "Hello" and then the name of the person. The remediation was effective and N.S. was able to learn some names. Moreover, she was then able to use these names effectively in other contexts. Using similar procedures, which are not given in detail, Maurer (1992) reports that she was taught to read.

Vargha-Khadem et al. (1994) report brief details in an abstract of a case, J.F., of developmental amnesia in childhood. The child had seizures from the age of 4. A memory difficulty was recognized at the age of 8 years. There was no mention of any loss of previously acquired skills. MRI showed bilateral mesial temporal sclerosis and intact mammillary bodies. The development of some verbal skills and reading was impaired.

The first extensive analysis of a case of developmental amnesia is given by De Renzi & Lucchelli (1990), who describe a 22-year-old man, M.S. M.S. was born early at 7 months of gestation with a birth weight of 2500 g. CT scan was normal but EEG indicated bilateral bursts of theta and delta waves, with a left frontotemporal prevalence. He was of normal intelligence, with a Verbal IQ of 110 and a Performance IQ of 111. Oral language, visual perception, praxis and attention were normal. M.S. complained that he had had memory difficulties since earliest childhood. He complained of extreme difficulty in remembering the names of familiar people, places, foreign language words and mathematical formulae and tables. He had never managed to learn the lyrics of a song or a poem by heart. He also reported that he had difficulty in remembering faces and his day-to-day memory created everyday problems for him.

On formal assessment, semantic memory for past events and famous names was impaired, as was recognition memory for famous faces. However, vocabulary levels were normal. M.S. was also found to have severe impairment of episodic memory, with difficulty in learning new verbal or nonverbal material. Story recall and paired associate learning were at an amnesic level. In relation to automated series, he was unable to recite the alphabet or the months of the year. There was also difficulty in recognition memory for newly learnt, previously unfamiliar faces. There was a severe reading and spelling difficulty throughout development, which persisted into adulthood, when reading remained slow and laborious. Memory for recurring items was impaired for verbal material but surprisingly unimpaired for nonverbal material.

A further case of developmental amnesia, Julia, was reported by Temple (1997a). Julia was born at 40 weeks' gestation. She smiled at 6 weeks, walked at 13 months and could dress herself at 2 years, indicating good milestones. There was a family history of convulsions and specific learning difficulties with language and reading. All of the family was right-handed but Julia was left-handed. Both memory difficulties and delayed language development were noted in the preschool years. At the age of 3.9, naming skills were at the first centile for age. At the age of 6, temporal lobe epilepsy developed. CT scan was normal. Difficulties with both word recognition and word finding were noted in the speech therapist's report at this time. When she was 7, Julia's class teacher noted that she "sometimes has difficulty remembering words or what a word actually means". Assessed at the age of 12, on the WISC-R, there was a wide scatter in subtests with half in the 7–10 score range, i.e. within 1 SD of the mean for age. The weakest subtests were Information, reflecting established semantic memory for facts about the world (scaled score 1), and Vocabulary, reflecting established semantic knowledge of word meanings (scaled score 3). She was also unable to answer correctly any factual questions about contemporary events that would have been familiar to most children. The impairment of semantic memory encompassed both factual general knowledge about the world and knowledge of words. Language was characterized by an anomia, such that at the age of 12.8 her naming age was 5.3. Further analysis of this anomia indicated a pattern of consistency in the items found to be difficult, with identical errors being generated across trials in many cases. Further, receptive vocabulary was no better than naming skills. There was no significant difference in Julia's ability to comprehend the names of clothes, animals and foodstuffs than her ability to name these items. The naming impairment was not thus a modality-specific access difficulty. Further, it seemed to reflect impaired establishment of knowledge of words, i.e. a *semantic representation anomia* (Temple, 1997a). There was also impairment in episodic memory and the acquisition of new verbal and nonverbal material. She was impaired in story recall, both when a story was read to her and when she read the story herself. She was also impaired in the recall of patterns and designs. Procedural knowledge, as reflected by knowledge and recall of automated sequences, counting, alphabet and days of the week, was normal, quick and accurate. Recognition memory for words on Warrington's Recognition Memory Battery [WRMB] was very good, with a score of 49/50, which is near ceiling. In contrast, recognition memory for faces was entirely random, with a score of 25/50 in this forced-choice paradigm.

Thus, in Julia's case, there is a severe semantic memory impairment for both facts and word meanings. There is episodic memory impairment for both verbal material and designs. Procedural memory appears intact, as does recognition memory for words, but recognition memory for faces is very impaired. There is an immediate contrast between M.S. (De Renzi & Lucchelli, 1990) and Julia (Temple, 1997a). Whilst both cases have severe impairment of semantic and episodic memory, M.S. has developed normal language, although he continues to have difficulty in learning proper names and foreign language words. Thus, for M.S. the semantic memory impairment does not extend to semantic memory for the majority of vocabulary. For Julia there is a marked anomia, which takes the form of a semantic representation anomia, in which the semantic memory for words is impoverished. A further contrast between the two cases lies in procedural memory, as assessed by memory of automated series. There is impairment and failure to learn these series for M.S. but development of automated series is intact for Julia.

Casalini et al. (1999) report a further case of developmental amnesia, in a 9-year-old girl, O.N. There were no neurological symptoms but there was a positive family history, with O.N.'s father reported to have similar difficulties. Her semantic memory was impaired, with poor established knowledge for facts. Like Julia, discussed above, O.N. also had difficulties in naming, which affected spontaneous speech, and there was poor semantic knowledge of vocabulary. There was also episodic memory impairment, with difficulty in learning new verbal material. Autobiographical memory for past events was also poor. However, there were some material-specific effects; since nonverbal learning and memory were unimpaired. Thus, whilst O.N. is like Julia in having a semantic memory impairment which extends to knowledge of vocabulary, she is unlike Julia in having intact nonverbal memory skills.

The possibility that developmental amnesia may be relatively common and found in the normal classroom population has been explored recently in a study from our Unit (Temple & Richardson, in preparation). Normal children were screened for both semantic knowledge reflected in knowledge of facts about the world, using the *Information* subtest of the WISC-III (Wechsler, 1992), and for episodic memory, using a word recall task; 3–4% of the children screened were found to have memory difficulties (see Table 24.1). Children were also identified who had normal average intelligence, defined strictly as an IQ within 1 SD of the mean (i.e. 85–115), but who nevertheless had selective impairments of either semantic or episodic memory (see Table 24.1). These children had average IQs but scored below the 5th centile

Table 24.1 Incidence of memory difficulties in a sample of normal children

	8–9 Years	11–12 Years
Children screened (*n*)	239	70
Memory difficulties (%)	3.4	4.3
Average children (*n*)	134	52
(IQ 85–115)		
Average children with specific memory difficulties (%)	5.9	5.8

on the memory screening tests. Temple & Richardson (in preparation) describe the pattern of memory development in one of these screened cases for whom no explicit aetiology is known. C.L. was aged 8.11. He was compared to 10 control children who also had IQs in the 85–115 range but who had memory screening scores within 1 SD of the mean. C.L. was therefore matched to the controls for age and IQ, yet he was significantly impaired in comparison to them in terms of semantic memory for facts. Despite this impairment, given forced-choice response of possible alternatives, C.L. was no longer significantly different from normal, indicating a retrieval difficulty in semantic memory. There was also impairment in semantic knowledge of words, with significant impairment in both lexical decision and receptive vocabulary. In oral fluency, there was a sharp dissociation between retrieval on the basis of initial letters, where's C.L. performance was at the mean level for controls, and retrieval on the basis of semantic category, where performance was significantly impaired.(C.L., 26; controls, 45.6; SD, 6.13; range, 38–56). Unlike all the other cases of developmental amnesia discussed above, episodic recall and recognition was normal. Paired associate learning was also normal. Autobiographical memory was normal and Behavioural Memory on the Rivermead was normal. Procedural memory showed normal learning on the first few trials, although later in the series the skill tailed off and performance levels fell, whilst controls improved.

The picture was thus of a selective semantic memory impairment with other memory systems intact. The pattern of semantic impairment but intact episodic skill is a new dissociation in developmental amnesia and forms a double dissociation to the cases of Gadian et al. (2000), where episodic skill is impaired but semantic knowledge is intact. C.L. was also dyslexic, with significant impairment in word recognition skills in comparison to controls. The pattern of reading was that of surface dyslexia, with normal reading of nonwords, impaired reading of irregular words and homophone confusion. This pattern of reading is typically interpreted as reflecting impairment of the lexico–semantic reading route, and in this case the impairment within this route would be localized to retrieval from the semantic system itself.

MEMORY IN EPILEPSY

The areas of the brain within which it is most likely that an epileptic seizure will be sustained are the temporal lobes, which has been attributed to their proximity to the hippocampus. Invasive EEG monitoring has indicated that idiopathic temporal lobe seizures are predominantly of hippocampal origin (Spencer et al., 1990; Wyler et al., 1988). Thus, the most epileptogenic areas of the brain are those known to be intimately involved in memory and it is possible that the underlying characteristics which make them appropriate for memory encoding and storage are also characteristics that make them susceptible to seizures. In both cases, distributed networks are involved and critical steady states are attained (Temple, 1997a). However, when the steady states associated with the occurrence of seizures are active, they prohibit the generation of the steady states required for memory encoding or consolidation.

Memory impairments are common in those who suffer from epilepsy (Loiseau et al., 1988), particularly those who have temporal lobe epilepsy (TLE), who comprise one-third of those who have epilepsy. There are at least four reasons why those with epilepsy may have memory impairments. First, there may be underlying pathology in the temporal lobes or the hippocampi which lie beneath them, which leads to an impaired substrate for memory encoding and storage and which also leads to less stable circuitry more prone to generate seizures. Thus, underlying pathology may create both memory impairment and seizures, e.g. hippocampal sclerosis is evident in medial TLE (Engel, 1996) and may contribute to both seizures and memory impairment.

Secondly, ongoing seizures or subclinical interictal activity may interfere with the processes of memory consolidation (Glowinski, 1973; O'Connor et al., 1997). In the case of J.T. (O'Connor et al., 1997), retention for hours and days was accurate for new material but there was then rapid forgetting. Increased seizures increased the forgetting, and medication that reduced seizures reduced the forgetting. O'Connor et al. (1997) argue that this provides evidence that consolidation occurs over a long period of time. A similar case is described by Kapur et al. (1997). Their patient with TLE displayed normal episodic retention on immediate and half-hour delay measures, but 40 days later had dense amnesia for the information, whereas controls could remember much of it. Behaviourally, their patient complained of amnesia for events 3–24 months previously. MRI scans and EEG maps showed left temporal pathology and a possible left anterior hippocampus focus. Kapur et al. (1997) argued that the data support a long-term consolidation process, rather than a single-stage unitary consolidation process.

A third reason for memory impairment in epilepsy is that anticonvulsive medication, such as phenobarbital, phenytoin and primidone, may exacerbate impairments in memory (Trimble & Reynolds, 1976). Finally, repeated seizures in which there are extended periods of status epilepticus may cause structural damage to the areas affected by the seizures, thereby damaging one of the substrates employed in memory (Reynolds et al., 1983).

A specific memory impairment has been found in children with TLE, in contrast to normal memory skills in centrencephalic epilepsy. Early studies demonstrated that children with left TLE are worse than those with right TLE on memory for factual material (e.g. Fedio & Mirsky, 1969). In particular, medial left TLE, which begins around the age of 4–8 years (Adam et al., 1996), is linked to verbal memory impairment. In contrast, those with right TLE have poorer delayed recall for unfamiliar faces than those with left TLE (Beardsworth & Zaidel, 1994) and poorer spatial memory (Abrahams et al., 1999). Using combined data from TLE and temporal lobectomies. Helmstaedter et al. (1997) argue that material-specific acquisition is mediated by neocortical structures, which demonstrate laterality effects, whilst long-term consolidation/retrieval is mediated by temporomesial structures, which are material-nonspecific.

EXECUTIVE IMPAIRMENT IN MEMORY

Cornoldi et al. (1999) report impairment in strategic memory in children with ADHD. They found that, in comparison to controls, children with ADHD had weak recall and many intrusion errors. However, when they were given a strategy to use, their performance improved to become as good as controls. They had to be shown how to use the strategy, as otherwise their recall remained poor. Cornoldi et al. (1999) interpreted these results as reflecting an executive impairment in memory. They also gave the children with ADHD and controls other executive tasks to perform and found that performance on the other executive tasks predicted memory skills. These strategic difficulties with memory may be similar to some of the difficulties discussed above in relation to Reye's syndrome.

MATERIAL-SPECIFIC IMPAIRMENT OF MEMORY

Temple (1992b) described Dr S., an intelligent and highly educated lady, who had sustained no neurological injury or disease and was in good health. However, throughout her life she had experienced severe difficulties with memory for faces and visual patterns. Another member of her family is also reported to have similar difficulties. Dr S. had high academic attainments, reflecting good semantic memory. She also had a well-developed vocabulary. Further, her episodic memory for the stories in the Wechsler Memory Battery was very good. However, she had a severe impairment in memory for faces, houses, buildings and visual patterns. The impairment in memory for faces produced a specific form of developmental prosopagnosia. The pattern of her difficulties on face processing was interpreted in relation to the model of Bruce & Young (1986). In relation to this model, it was suggested that Dr S. had specific difficulty in retaining or making use of the face recognition units needed to activate person identity information. Since verbal memory is good, she thus has a material-specific impairment in memory affecting visuospatial material. This focal impairment has been a lifelong deficit coexisting with a successful professional career.

Bishop et al. (2000) described material-specific memory impairments in Turner's syndrome (TS). TS is a genetic disorder in females, in which the second X chromosome is absent or abnormal. Intelligence spans the normal range but there is a set of specific learning difficulties. Cerebral glucose metabolism studies of brain activation and MRI studies suggest bilateral, parietal and occipital lobe involvement in TS (Clark et al., 1989; Elliott et al., 1996; Murphy et al., 1993; Reiss et al., 1993). However, Murphy et al.'s (1993) study also indicated bilateral involvement of the hippocampi. In a MRI study of monozygotic twins discordant for TS, Reiss et al. (1993) concurred with the parieto–occipital locus on the right with a parietal–perisylvian locus on the left. However, in addition, they found marked discrepancies between the twins in right prefrontal areas.

Impairment in visual memory has been documented in a number of studies (Alexander et al., 1966; Clark et al., 1989; Lahood & Bacon, 1985; Lewandowski et al., 1985; Riess et al., 1993; Rovet & Netley, 1981; Silbert et al., 1977; Waber, 1979). Pennington et al. (1985) reported either a verbal or a nonverbal memory deficit in 8/10 cases of TS. Surprisingly, since some theoretical interpretations of TS have implicated the right hemisphere, Pennington et al. (1985) found that 7/10 cases had episodic verbal memory impairments, whilst impairment in nonverbal episodic memory was found in only 4/10.

However, Bishop et al. (2000) argue that the pattern of memory performance varied, depending upon whether the single X came from the mother (X^m) or the father (X^p). She reported that for immediate verbal recall, both TS groups obtained significantly higher scores than control boys, and the X^p group also outscored control girls. This result is consistent with a number of studies indicating elevated verbal skills in TS (Shaffer, 1962; Lahood & Bacon, 1985; Temple, 1996, 2002; Temple & Carney, 1996). However, in relation to the elevated immediate recall level, the X^m group showed enhanced verbal forgetting. Thus, although both immediate and delayed recall scores were in the normal range, Bishop et al. (2000) argued that the relationship between the two was abnormal, with the $45X^m$ group showing elevated immediate recall but then disproportionate forgetting with delay. In a visual memory task, both groups performed poorly on the initial copy of a design, and both were significantly impaired on delayed recall of the design. However, Bishop et al. (2000) argued that the X^p group, who appeared marginally better than the X^m on the initial copy, had nevertheless forgotten a disproportionate amount with delay interpreted as enhanced spatial forgetting.

As Maurer (1992) pointed out, many learning disabilities can be recast as disorders of material-specific memory. Exploring this idea within the framework of developmental cognitive neuropsychology provides a number of examples. Temple (1986, 1995) described the case of a developmental anomic, John, who had particular difficulty in naming animals in comparison to indoor objects. The impairment with animals was pervasive across tasks and at least part of his difficulty appeared to arise from a failure to establish effective semantic representations for animals, and may therefore be thought of as a selective impairment of the semantic system and thereby memory.

The reading disorder, surface dyslexia (e.g. Coltheart et al., 1983; Castles & Coltheart, 1993, 1996), is characterized by relatively good phonological reading skills and ability to read nonwords but poor development of the lexico–semantic reading route employed in the reading of irregular words and the reading of highly familiar established words. This difficulty could be characterized as a difficulty in developing the memory that enables word recognition. The surface dyslexic fails to recognize words that would be recognized with ease by his peers.

Similarly, in surface dysgraphia, there can be well-developed phonological spelling systems associated with using the sound of the word to analytically determine its spelling. In contrast, there is difficulty with the memory for spelling patterns, which is essential for the spelling of irregular words in English and for spelling the many words for which the representation of the vowel is ambiguous with multiple possibilities.

Number fact dyscalculia (Temple, 1991, 1994, 1997b) is a selective impairment which affects the development of factual knowledge about arithmetic and tables, with intact development of number processing and knowledge of arithmetic procedures. This could be considered a material-specific impairment of memory for arithmetical facts. Other aspects of semantic memory can be quite normal (Temple, 1997a).

However, formulating these selective disorders as material-specific impairments of memory is, to some extent, simply redescribing their problems without addressing anything more fundamental. It may be more constructive to continue to discuss such disorders in relation to the cognitive domain within which they occur.

CONCLUDING COMMENTS

At the outset it was suggested that the study of developmental amnesia may provide evidence relevant to: (a) models of normal development; (b) theorizing about adults; and (c) education of children with memory difficulties. It is evident from the work discussed above that there are many forms that the developmental amnesias and acquired amnesias of childhood may take.

In relation to both models of normal development and theorizing about adults, one may ask: are there any double dissociations evident? In the studies of Vargha-Khadem et al. (1997) and Gadian et al. (2000), semantic memory is intact but episodic memory is impaired. In the developmental anomic, C.L. (Temple & Richardson, in preparation), episodic memory is intact but semantic memory is impaired. In both cases, memory has been abnormal throughout development. In neither case has memory been partially established with subsequent impairment. The contrasting patterns argue for the relative independence of episodic and semantic memory during development and further argue that neither is critically dependent upon the other.

Within semantic memory, semantic knowledge for facts may be impaired and may coexist with impaired or intact semantic knowledge about words. A double dissociation would require semantic representation anomia in the absence of semantic memory impairment for facts, a dissociation not yet reported and hence not explored.

There is a double dissociation between M.S. (De Renzi & Lucchelli, 1990) and Julia (Temple, 1997a) between semantic knowledge for words and procedural knowledge, indicating an unsurprising distinction between these systems in development. With the exception of M.S., in almost all the cases of amnesia reported procedural memory is intact.

There are further single dissociations that justify Tulving's proposal for episodic memory, where there is a sense not only of "knowing" but also of "remembering" specific elements of the personal experience.

There are also distinctions in the memory processes that may be impaired. There appears to be impairment of memory encoding in Reye's syndrome (Quart et al., 1987), memory storage as a result of failure of consolidation in TLE, and impairment of retrieval processes for Jon (Baddeley et al., 2001), where recognition memory is intact, and for Neil (Vargha-Khadem et al., 1994), where orthographic retrieval is superior to oral.

In relation to classroom implications, the results are less clear, for it seems that the developmental amnesias and acquired amnesias of childhood do not take one prescribed form for which a specialized remedial programme could be recommended. Rather, the disorders have a variety of forms, and the pattern of intact skills to be utilized in establishing new strategies and impaired skills to be targeted in remedial learning vary sharply from case to case, and require individual case analysis for their identification.

REFERENCES

Abrahams, S., Morris, R.G., Polkey, C.E. et al. (1999). Hippocampal involvement in spatial and working memory: a structural MRI analysis of patients with unilateral mesial temporal lobe sclerosis. *Brain & Cognition*, **41**, 39–65.

Adam, C., Clemenceau, S., Semah, F. et al. (1996). Variability of presentation in medial temporal lobe epilepsy: a study of 30 operated cases. *Acta Neurolica Scandinavica*, **94**, 1–11.

Aggleton, J.P. & Brown, M.W. (1999). Episodic memory, amnesia and the hippocampal–anterior thalamic axis. *Behavioural & Brain Sciences*, **22**, 425–490.

Alexander, D., Ehrhardt, A. & Money, J. (1966). Defective figure drawing, geometric and human in Turner's syndrome. *Journal of Nervous & Mental Diseases*, **142**, 161–167.

Baddeley, A., Emslie, H. & Nimmo-Smith, I. (1994). *The Doors & People Test*. Bury St. Edmunds: Thames Valley Test Company.

Baddeley, A. (1997). *Human Memory: Theory & Practice* (revised edn) Hove: Psychology Press.

Baddeley, A., Vargha-Khadem, F. & Mishkin, M. (2001). Preserved recognition in a case of developmental amnesia: implications for the acquisition of semantic memory. *Journal of Cognitive Neuroscience*, **13**, 357–369.

Beardsworth, E.D. & Zaidel, D.W. (1994). Memory for faces in epileptic children before and after brain surgery. *Journal of Clinical & Experimental Neuropsychology*, **16**, 589–596.

Bishop, D.V.M. (1985). Age of onset and outcome in acquired aphasia with convulsive disorder (Landau–Kleffner syndrome).*Developmental Medicine & Child Neurology*, **27**, 705–712.

Bishop, D.V.M. (1997). Cognitive neuropsychology and developmental disorders: Uncomfortable bedfellows. *Quarterly Journal of Experimental Psychology*, **50A**, 899–923.

Bishop, D.V.M., Canning, E., Elgar, K. et al. (2000). Distinctive patterns of memory function in subgroups of females with Turner syndrome: evidence for imprinted loci on the X-chromosome affecting neurodevelopment. *Neuropsychologia*, **38**, 712–721.

Brainerd, C.J. & Reyna, V.F. (1992). Explaining "memory free" reasoning. *Psychological Science*, **3**, 332–339.

Broman, M., Rose, A.L., Hotson, G. & Casey, C.M. (1997). Severe anterograde amnesia with onset in childhood as a result of anoxic encephalopathy. *Brain*, **120**, 417–433.

Bruce, V. & Young, A. (1986). Understanding face recognition. *British Journal of Psychology*, **77**, 305–327.

Carpantieri, S.C. & Mulhern, R.K. (1993). Patterns of memory dysfunction among children surviving temporal lobe tumors. *Archives of Clinical Neuropsychology*, **8**, 345–357.

Casalini, C., Brizzolara, D., Cavallaro, M.C. & Cipriani, P. (1999). Developmental dysmnesia: a case report. *Cortex*, **35**, 713–727.

Castles, A. & Coltheart, M. (1993). Varieties of developmental dyslexia. *Cognition*, **47**, 149–180.

Castles, A. & Coltheart, M. (1996). Cognitive correlates of developmental surface dyslexia: a single case study. *Cognitive Neuropsychology*, **13**, 25–50.

Cavazzutti, V., Winston, K., Baker, R. & Welch, K. (1980). Psychological changes following surgery for tumours in the temporal lobes. *Journal of Neurosurgery*, **53**, 618–626.

Clark, C., Klonoff, H. & Hayden, M. (1990). Regional cerebral glucose metabolism in Turner's syndrome. *The Canadian Journal Neurological Sciences*, **17**, 140–144.

Coltheart, M., Masterson, J., Byng, S. et al. (1983). Surface dyslexia. *Quarterly Journal of Experimental Psychology*, **35**, 469–496.

Cornoldi, C., Barbieri, A., Gaiani, C. & Zocchi, S. (1999). Strategic memory deficits in attention deficit disorder with hyperactivity participants: the role of executive processes. *Developmental Neuropsychology*, **15**, 53–71.

Davidson, P.W., Wiloughby, L.A., O'Tuama, L.A. et al. (1978). Neurological and intellectual sequelae of Reye's syndrome. *American Journal of Mental Deficiencies*, **82**, 535–541.

De Haan, E. & Campbell, R. (1991). A fifteen year follow-up of a case of developmental prosopagnosia. *Cortex*, **27**, 489–509.

Dennis, M., Farrell, K., Hoffman, H.J. et al. (1988). Recognition memory of item, associative and serial-order information after temporal lobectomy for seizure disorder. *Neuropsychologia*, **26**, 55–65.

De Renzi, E. & Lucchelli, F. (1990). Developmental dysmnesia in a poor reader. *Cortex*, **113**, 1337–1345.

Dupont, S., Van de Moortele, P., Samson, S. et al. (2000). Episodic memory in left temporal lobe epilepsy: a functional MRI study. *Brain*, **123**, 1722–1732.

Elliott, T.K., Watkins, J.M., Messa, C. et al. (1996). Positron emission tomography and neuropsychological correlations in children with Turner's syndrome. *Developmental Neuropsychology*, **12**, 365–386.

Engel, J. (1996). Surgery for seizures. *New England Journal of Medicine*, **334**, 647–652.

Fedio, P. & Mirsky, A. (1969). Selective intellectual deficits in children with temporal lobe or centrencephalic epilepsy. *Neuropsychologia*, **3**, 287–300.

Gadian, D.G., Aicardi, J., Watkins, K.E. et al. (2000). Developmental amnesia associated with early hypoxic-ischaemic injury. *Brain*, **123**, 499–507.

Geschwind, N. (1974). Disorders of higher cortical function in children. In N. Geschwind (ed.), *Selected Papers on Language and the Brain. Boston Studies in the Philosophy of Science*, Vol. XVI. Boston: Reidel.

Glowinski, H. (1973). Cognitive deficits in temporal lobe epilepsy: an investigation of memory functioning. *Journal of Nervous & Mental Diseases*, **157**, 129–137.

Goodglass, H. & Kaplan, E. (1983). *The Assessment of Aphasia and Related Disorders*, 2nd edn. Philadelphia, PA: Lea & Febiger.

Helmstaedter, C., Grunwald, T., Lehnertz, K. (1997). Differential involvement of left temporolateral and temporomesial structures in verbal declarative learning and memory: evidence from temporal lobe epilepsy. *Brain & Cognition*, **35**, 110–131.

Herkowitz, J. & Rosman, N.P. (1982). *Pediatrics, Neurology and Psychiatry—Common Ground: Behavioural, Cognitive, Affective and Physical Disorders in Childhood and Adolescence.* New York: Macmillan.

Holdstock, J.S., Mayes, A.R., Cezayirli, E. et al. (2000). A comparison of egocentric and allocentric spatial memory in a patient with selective hippocampal damage. *Neuropsychologia*, **38**, 410–425.

Kapur, N., Millar, J., Colbourn, C. et al. (1997). Very long-term amnesia in association with temporal lobe epilepsy: evidence for multiple-stage consolidation processes. *Brain & Cognition*, **35**, 58–70.

Lahood, B.J. & Bacon, G.E. (1985). Cognitive abilities of adolescent Turner's syndrome patients. *Journal of Adolescent Health Care*, **6**, 358–364.

Lewandowski, L., Costenbader, V. & Richman, R. (1985). Neuropsychological aspects of Turner's syndrome. *International Journal of Clinical Neuropsychology*, **7**, 144–147.

Lishman, W.A. (1987). *Organic Psychiatry: The Psychological Consequences of Cerebral Disorder*, 2nd edn. Oxford: Blackwell Scientific.

Loiseau, P., Strube, E. & Signoret, J.-L. (1988). Memory and epilepsy. In M.R. Trimble & E.H. Reynolds (eds), *Epilepsy, Behaviour and Cognitive Function.* Stratford-upon-Avon: Wiley.

Lovejoy, F.H., Smith, A.L., Bresnan, M.J. et al. (1974). Clinical staging in Reye's syndrome. *American Journal of Diseases in Children*, **128**, 36–41.

Luria, A.R. (1966). *The Higher Cortical Function of Man.* New York: Basic Books.

Luria, A.R. (1973). *The Working Brain.* New York: Penguin.

Marlowe, W.B. (1992). The impact of a right prefrontal lesion on the developing brain. *Brain & Cognition*, **20**, 205–213.

Maurer, R.G. (1992). Disorders of memory and learning. In S.J. Segalowitz & I. Rapin (eds), *Handbook of Neuropsychology, Vol. 7: Child Neuropsychology.* Amsterdam: Elsevier.

Meekin, S.L., Glasgow, J.F.T., McCusker, C.G. & Rooney, N. (1999). A long-term follow-up of cognitive, emotional and behavioural sequelae to Reye syndrome. *Developmental Medicine & Child Neurology*, **41**, 549–553.

Meyer, F., Marsh, R., Laws, E. & Sharborough, F. (1986). Temporal lobectomy in children with epilepsy. *Journal of Neurosurgery*, **64**, 371–376.

Morrow, J., O'Connor, D., Whitman, B. & Accardo, P. (1989). CNS Irradiation and memory deficit. *Developmental Medicine & Child Neurology*, **31**, 690–692.

Murphy, D., DeCarli, C., Daly, E. et al. (1993). X-chromosome effects on female brain: a magnetic resonance imaging study of Turner's syndrome. *Lancet*, **342**, 1197–1200.

Nelson, D.B., Sullivan-Bolyai, J.Z., Marks, J.S. et al. (1989). Reye's syndrome: an epidemiologic assessment based on national surveillance, 1977–1978 and a population-based study in Ohio 1973–1977. In J.F.S. Croker (ed.), *Reye's Syndrome II* (pp. 33–49). New York: Grune & Stratton.

O'Connor, M., Sieggreen, M.A., Ahern, G. et al. (1997). Accelerated forgetting in association with temporal lobe epilepsy. *Brain & Cognition*, **35**, 71–84.

Ostergaard, A.L. (1987). Episodic, semantic and procedural memory in a case of amnesia at an early age. *Neuropsychologia*, **25**, 341–357.

Ostergaard, A.L. & Squire, L. (1990). Childhood amnesia and distinctions between forms of memory: a comment on Wood, Brown & Felton. *Brain & Cognition*, **14**, 127–133.

Partin, J.S., McAdams, J.J., Partin, J.C. et al. (1978). Brain ultrastructure in Reye's disease II. *Journal of Neuropathology & Experimental Neurology*, **37**, 796–819.

Pennington, B.F., Heaton, R.K., Karzmark, P. et al. (1985). The neuropsychological phenotype in Turner syndrome. *Cortex*, **21**, 391–404.

Quart, E.J. (1984). Memory and attention in children recovering from Reye's syndrome. *Dissertation Abstracts International*, **45**, 711-B (University Microfilms No 22185).

Quart, E.J., Buchtel, H.A. & Sarnaik, A.P. (1987). Long lasting memory deficits in children recovering from Reye's syndrome. *Journal of Clinical & Experimental Neuropsychology*, **10**, 409–420.

Reiss, A.L., Freund, L., Plotnick, L. et al. (1993). The effects of X monosomy on brain development: monozygotic twins discordant for Turner's syndrome. *Annals of Neurology*, **34**, 95–107.

Reynolds, E.H., Elwes, R.D.C. & Shorvon, S.D. (1983). Why does epilepsy become intractable? Prevention of chronic epilepsy. *Lancet*, **2**, 952–954.

Ribot, T.R. (1882). *Diseases of Memory.* New York: Appleton & Co.

Rovet, J. & Netley, C. (1981). Turner syndrome in a pair of dizygotic twins: a single case study. *Behavior Genetics*, **11**, 65–72.

Sarnaik, A. (1982). Diagnosis and management of Reye's syndrome. *Comprehensive Therapy*, **8**, 47–53.

Scoville, W.B. & Milner, B. (1957). Loss of recent memory after bilateral hippocampal lesions. *Journal of Neurology, Neurosurgery & Psychiatry*, **20**, 11–21.

Shaffer, J. (1962). A specific cognitive deficit observed in gonadal aplasia (Turner's syndrome). *Journal of Clinical Psychology*, **18**, 403–406.

Silbert, A., Wolff, P.H. & Lilienthal, J. (1977). Spatial and temporal processing in patients with Turner's syndrome. *Behaviour Genetics*, **7**, 11–21.

Spencer, S.S., Spencer, D.D., Williamson, P.D. & Mattson, R. (1990). Combined depth and subdural electrode investigation in uncontrolled epilepsy. *Neurology*, **40**, 74–79.

Squire, L. (1992). Declarative and non-declarative memory: multiple brain systems supporting learning and memory. *Journal of Cognitive Neuroscience*, **4**, 232–243.

Squire, L.R. & Cohen, N.J. (1984). Human memory and amnesia. In G. Lynch, J.L. McGaugh & N.M. Weinberger (eds), *Neurobiology of Learning and Memory*. New York: Guilford.

Temple, C.M. (1986). Anomia for animals in a child. *Brain*, **109**, 1225–1242.

Temple, C.M. (1991). Procedural dyscalculia and number fact dyscalculia: double dissociation in developmental dyscalculia. *Cognitive Neuropsychology*, **8**, 155–176.

Temple, C.M. (1992a). Developmental and acquired disorders in children. In S.J. Segalowitz & I. Rapin (eds), *Handbook of Neuropsychology, Vol 7: Child Neuropsychology*. Amsterdam: Elsevier.

Temple, C.M. (1992b). Developmental memory impairment: faces and patterns. In R. Campbell (ed), *Mental Lives: Case Studies in Cognition* (pp. 199–215). Oxford: Blackwell.

Temple, C.M. (1994). The cognitive neuropsychology of the developmental dyscalculias. *Cahiers de Psychologie Cognitive/ Current Psychology of Cognition*, **133**, 351–370.

Temple, C.M. (1995). The kangaroo's a fox. In R. Campbell (ed.), *Broken Memories* (pp. 383–396). Oxford: Blackwell.

Temple, C.M. (1996). Language ability and disability in Turner's syndrome. Paper presented at the XXVI International Congress of Psychology, Montreal. *International Journal of Psychology*, **31**, 3644 [Abstract].

Temple, C.M. (1997a). *Developmental Cognitive Neuropsychology*. Hove: Erlbaum.

Temple, C.M. (1997b). Cognitive neuropsychology and its application to children. *Journal of Child Psychology & Psychiatry*, **38**, 27–52.

Temple, C.M. (2002). Oral fluency and narrative production in children with Turner's syndrome. *Neuropsychologia*, **40**, 1419–1427.

Temple, C.M. & Carney, R. (1996). Reading skills in children with Turner's Syndrome: an analysis of hyperlexia: *Cortex*, **32**, 335–345.

Temple, C.M. & Richardson, P. (in preparation). Developmental amnesia: a case of selective impairment of semantic memory with intact episodic memory.

Trimble, M.R. & Reynolds, E.H. (1976). Anticonvulsant drugs and mental symptoms. *Psychological Medicine*, **6**, 169–178.

Tulving, E. (1972). Episodic and semantic memory. In E. Tulving & W. Donaldson (eds), *Organization of Memory* (pp. 381–403). New York: Academic Press.

Tulving, E. (1985). Memory and consciousness. *Canadian Psychologist*, **26**, 1–12.

Tulving, E. & Markovitch, H.J. (1998). Episodic and declarative memory: the role of the hippocampus. *Hippocampus*, **8**, 198–204.

Vargha-Khadem, F., Isaacs, E.B. & Watkins, K.E. (1992). Medial temporal lobe vs. diencephalic amnesia in childhood. *Journal of Clinical & Experimental Neuropsychology*, **14**, 371–372.

Vargha-Khadem, F., Gadian, D.G., Watkins, K.E. et al. (1997). Differential effects of early hippocampal pathology on episodic and semantic memory. *Science*, **277**, 376–380.

Vargha-Khadem, F., Isaacs, E.B. & Mishkin, M. (1994). Agnosia, alexia and a remarkable form of amnesia in an adolescent boy. *Brain*, **117**, 683–703.

Van Hout, A. (1993). Acquired aphasia in childhood and developmental dysphasias: are the errors similar? Analysis of errors made in confrontation naming tasks. *Aphasiology*, **7**, 525–531.

Waber, D. (1979). Neuropsychological aspects of Turner's Syndrome. *Developmental Medicine & Child Neurology*, **31**, 58–70.

Warrington, E.K. (1984). *Recognition Memory Battery*. Windsor: NFER, Nelson.

Warrington, E.K. & Weiskrantz, L. (1982). Amnesia: a disconnection syndrome. *Neuropsychologia*, **20**, 233–249.

Wechsler, D. (1974). *Wechsler Intelligence Scale for Children—Revised*. New York: Psychological Corporation.

Wechsler, D. (1992). *Wechsler Intelligence Scale for Children*, 3rd edn (UK edn). London: Psychological Corporation.

Williams, D. & Mateer, C.A. (1992). Developmental impact of frontal lobe injury in middle childhood. *Brain & Cognition*, **20**, 196–204.

Wood, F.B., Brown, I.S. & Felton, R.H. (1989). Long-term follow-up of a childhood amnesic syndrome. *Brain & Cognition*, **10**, 76–89.

Wood, F.B., Ebert, V. & Kinsbourne, M. (1982). The episodic–semantic memory distinction in memory and amnesia: clinical and experimental observations. In L.S. Cermak (ed.), *Human Memory and Amnesia*. Hillsdale, NJ: Erlbaum.

Wyler, A.R., Walker, G., Richey, E.T. & Hermann, B.P. (1988). Chronic subdural strip electrode recording for difficult epileptic problems. *Journal of Epilepsy*, **1**, 71–78.

Young, A.W. & Ellis, H.D. (1989). Childhood propospagnosia. *Brain & Cognition*, **9**, 16–47.

CHAPTER 25

Memory in Elderly People

Jill D. Kester
Aaron S. Benjamin
Alan D. Castel
and
Fergus I.M. Craik
Department of Psychology, University of Toronto, Canada

THEORETICAL BACKGROUND

Memory difficulty is one of the most common complaints of older adults (e.g. Hertzog & Dixon, 1994), so the study of age-related changes in memory function is motivated by practical as well as theoretical considerations. This chapter reviews the major empirical findings in memory and aging research, with particular emphasis on recent work. In order to provide a contemporary context for understanding and evaluating the many results, we first summarize four major theoretical approaches to understanding memory and aging. At the end of the paper we will spell out the theories more fully, and discuss the extent to which each theory is able to accommodate current findings.

The four theoretical approaches are a decline in processing speed, reduced processing resources, age-related inhibitory deficits, and decreased cognitive control. The slowing of behavior in old age is widely accepted and well documented (Birren, 1965; Salthouse, 1991, 1996). The basic notion is that decreased speed of mental processing underlies many if not all age-related cognitive deficits, either directly (i.e. behavior is slow and inefficient) or indirectly by disrupting the timing of a complex sequence of mental operations. Within this framework, then, age-related decrements in memory performance are not attributed to impaired memory processes per se, but to a generalized age difference in speed of processing.

A somewhat different viewpoint from the speed of processing framework suggests that aging is accompanied by a depletion of attentional resources available for cognitive processing (Craik & Byrd, 1982). An underlying assumption of the reduced resources perspective is that attention is required to carry out cognitive tasks, and difficult tasks require more attentional capacity than simpler tasks. Thus, age-related reductions in attentional resources will impair older adults' ability to carry out cognitively demanding processes, such as the deep, elaborative encoding operations known to facilitate learning, or strategic search at retrieval.

The Handbook of Memory Disorders. Edited by A.D. Baddeley, M.D. Kopelman and B.A. Wilson
© 2002 John Wiley & Sons, Ltd.

Hasher & Zacks (1988) introduced a third important framework for memory and aging research with their proposal that older adults are less efficient at inhibiting partially activated representations. Inhibitory function is putatively important for at least three processes relevant to memory. First, it provides control over access to working memory, thus restricting access to task-relevant information. Second, it supports the deletion of no-longer relevant information from working memory. Third, it provides for the restraint of strong but situationally inappropriate responses (Hasher et al., 1999; Zacks et al., 2000).

The fourth framework encompasses notions from both the reduced resources and the inhibitory deficit perspective in the idea that older adults suffer from an impairment in executive control of cognitive processing. This notion relies heavily on the distinction between automatic processing, which requires little attentional capacity and occurs without intent, and controlled processing, which is effortful, consciously controlled, and requires intent (Hasher & Zacks, 1979; see also Hay & Jacoby, 1999). Automatic processing is assumed to be immune to the effects of aging, while controlled processing declines with age. An age-related deficit in controlled processing affects both the initiation of cognitively effortful processing such as that required by deep, elaborative encoding and strategic search at retrieval, and the inhibition of irrelevant information or processes. It is possible of course that aspects of all four of these approaches may play some part in age-related memory decline.

EMPIRICAL FINDINGS

A distinction can be drawn between direct memory tests that require subjects to verbally report information from memory, and indirect memory tests in which memory is inferred from changes in behavior as a result of previous experiences. In a typical test of indirect memory subjects are unaware that their memory is being tested. The dichotomy between direct and indirect memory tests is closely related to theoretical distinctions that have been drawn between memory systems (declarative vs. nondeclarative; implicit vs. explicit) and memory processes (conscious vs. nonconscious; controlled vs. automatic). A discussion of the merits of these various taxonomies of memory is beyond the scope of this chapter; we have thus attempted to organize the empirical data according to the nature of the task used to assess memory, without appealing to any one theory of systems or processes. Indirect tests of memory reviewed here include motor learning, visuospatial memory and priming. In the second section, we review direct tests of memory, including semantic, episodic, working, prospective and source memory tasks as well as false memory and metamemory.

Indirect Memory Tests

Motor Learning

Older adults are clearly impaired on most features of motor performance, including speed of movement, perceptual functioning, target tracking, use of spatially incompatible stimulus-response mapping, and so forth (Welford, 1985). What is less clear, however, is the effect of old age on the ability to learn and retain new motor skills. The performance of older subjects appears to improve at approximately the same rate as younger adults on some tasks, while lagging behind on other tasks (see Willingham, 1998, for a more comprehensive review of the data and various theoretical accounts).

One common task used to study motor learning involves a pursuit rotor, or a computerized analogue thereof. In that task, the subject is instructed to keep the tip of a hand-held stylus in continuous contact with a moving target. Motor skill is measured by the proportion of time that the subject can in fact keep the stylus in contact with the target during a time-limited trial; motor learning is evidenced by increased time-on-target across repeated trials. Older adults demonstrate learning at a slower rate than younger adults (Ruch, 1934; Wright & Payne, 1985). Similar tasks, where subjects are only able to view their hand and the tracking target in a mirror (Ruch, 1934; Wright & Payne, 1985) also show age-related impairments in learning.

A potential confound plaguing these studies concerns the fact that the experimenter controls the pace in each of the tasks. Given that older adults tend to be slower at performing motor tasks, experimenter paced tasks may put older adults at a disadvantage relative to younger adults, thereby making it difficult to determine whether age-related impairments in learning are due to memory difficulties or more peripheral motor difficulties.

In contrast, age differences have not been found on tasks where the task is subject paced, and requires learning of a sequence of motor movements or a new stimulus-response mapping, e.g. Wishart & Lee (1997) required subjects to produce a continuous movement comprising three distinct spatial segments, each with specific timing requirements. Learning was assessed by rate of initial acquisition and subsequent reacquisition, as well as transfer to a similar task. Although older adults performed less accurately and consistently on the task, there were no age-related differences on any of the three measures of learning.

Similar results have been found with the serial four-choice response time task in which the stimuli appear in a repeating sequence. Subjects pace the task themselves: the next stimulus in the sequence is not presented until the subject responds. Even though subjects are often unaware of the repeating sequence, learning is evidenced by decreased reaction times after several repetitions. Older adults show normal learning in this task (Howard & Howard, 1989), even when the stimulus and response are spatially incompatible, thus requiring new stimulus-response mapping (Willingham & Winter, 1995). Stimulus–response mapping must also be learned in tasks where subjects are required to navigate a maze presented on a computer screen, utilizing either a computer keyboard or mouse. Again, no age-related differences in learning have been found, even when the older adults had never used a computer mouse before (Willingham & Winter, 1995).

Thus it seems that although older adults are not as adept as younger adults at performing motor tasks, they are equally skilled in learning, retaining, and transferring motor skills–if they are allowed to pace themselves during learning. A possible exception to this conclusion is a finding by Harrington & Haaland (1992). The researchers used a serial response time task, but instead of pressing a key, subjects had to respond to each stimulus with a different hand posture. Unlike younger adults, older adults failed to show learning. Willingham (1998) argued that age differences on this task could be explained in terms of speed of processing limitations. Even though the task is subject paced, subjects are required to maintain multiple cognitive processes simultaneously in order to both learn the repeating sequence and map the stimuli onto the appropriate hand posture. According to the "simultaneity mechanism" (Salthouse, 1996), products of an early mental operation that are needed for a later operation may be lost due to slowness in executing the later operation. Through this mechanism limitations on processing speed may hamper the ability to coordinate multiple streams of processing.

Visuospatial Memory

Closely related to motor learning is memory for visuospatial information. Age-related decline in memory for spatial location has been widely reported in the literature (e.g. Naveh-Benjamin, 1987; Zelinski & Light, 1988; Uttl & Graf, 1993; Foisy, 1994). Experiments have looked at memory for the spatial location of objects (e.g. Rutledge et al., 1997; Desrocher & Smith, 1998) as well as route learning (e.g. Wilkniss et al., 1997; Newman & Kaszniak, 2000). Several recent studies have incorporated ecologically valid procedures that require subjects to move about during encoding, allowing the integration of sensorimotor information. Rutledge et al. (1997) conducted a study in which participants viewed 20 common objects in one of four rooms, and were later asked to place the object in the room and location in which they had previously seen it after a retention interval of 3, 15 or 30 min. Older adults demonstrated significantly less accurate spatial memory than younger subjects following a 30 min retention interval, whereas the age-difference was non-significant (although of a small to moderate effect size) at the two shorter retention intervals.

Wilkniss et al. (1997) had subjects follow an experimenter along a novel route in order to examine age-related differences in memory for spatial information. Older adults were impaired at retracing the route and ordering landmarks, but unimpaired at recognizing landmarks. In a second task, subjects were allowed to study a two-dimensional map of a route, and then navigate the route from memory. Older adults had more difficulty than young adults in memorizing and navigating the route. Janowsky et al. (1996) examined whether age-associated memory impairments were comparable in the verbal and non-verbal domains by asking participants to learn the identity and location of objects. Later, participants were asked to verbally recall the objects as well as their spatial location. The researchers found that verbal memory was disproportionately impaired relative to spatial memory.

Several studies have demonstrated that age-related differences in visuo-spatial memory can be greatly reduced (Cherry & Park, 1993; Park et al., 1990) or even eliminated (Sharps, 1991) by a visually distinctive context. This is consistent with Craik's (1986) environmental support theory, which proposes that age-related memory impairments can be ameliorated by supportive contexts that reduce the need for self-initiated processing. On the other hand, Arbuckle et al. (1994) presented evidence that spatial layouts inconsistent with well-established schemas are in fact more difficult for older adults to learn and remember, perhaps because of a decreased ability to inhibit prepotent information. These seemingly inconsistent conclusions could potentially be reconciled by appealing to the process of forming internal spatial representations. Sharps (1998) has suggested that age-related impairments in visuospatial memory are underscored by a diminished ability to represent and process visual images. Spatial layouts unsupported by well-learned schemas would be particularly difficult to form internal representations of; however, distinctive visual features may be able to support memory performance in the absence of a well-integrated representation of the space. This analysis suggests that when age deficits are observed in visuospatial memory, they may be attributable to impaired encoding due to difficulties in perceptual processing.

Priming

Priming is observed when the processing of a stimulus is influenced by past experience with that stimulus or related stimuli, and is often measured as a change in response accuracy, reaction time, or response bias. Performance on priming tasks has often been equated with implicit memory, but explicit processes can also influence performance on priming tasks. This indirect measure of memory has received considerably more attention from aging researchers than motor memory or visuospatial memory. The general finding is that older adults show strong priming effects, and age differences are notably smaller than on comparable direct tests of memory, often failing to reach statistical significance (for more comprehensive reviews, see Light & La Voie, 1993; La Voie & Light, 1994; and Fleischman & Gabrieli, 1998).

Light & Singh (1987) illustrated this pattern using the word stem completion task. Both younger and older adults showed priming effects when they were given the first few letters of a word and asked to complete the stem with the first word that came to mind; all subjects were more likely to complete the stems of previously studied words than unstudied words, and the slight age difference was not significant. However, when subjects were asked to use the stems consciously and deliberately to retrieve studied words (cued recall—a direct test of memory), young subjects were now significantly superior. Interestingly, these results parallel those found when comparing amnesic patients to normal controls (e.g. Graf et al., 1984). A second example is provided by a study of skill learning reported by Hashtroudi et al. (1991). Participants were presented with a series of inverted words (each for 450 ms) and asked to identify the words by saying them aloud. On some trials, words were repeated, allowing for an examination of priming effects for the two age groups. The results revealed that older adults showed less improvement in the skill of reading inverted words relative to the younger adults, but the priming effect did not differ between the two age groups. However, when older adults were presented with the word stimuli for 900 ms, the age-deficit in skill learning was eliminated. Thus, similar to motor skill learning, age-related impairments in learning a cognitive skill such as inverted reading may be more attributable to limitations on speed of processing or perceptual difficulties, rather than to memory problems *per se*.

Researchers have made the distinction between various types of priming, including perceptual and conceptual priming (Roediger & McDermott, 1993) and item and associative priming. Perceptual priming tasks, such as picture naming and perceptual identification, are presumed to rely heavily on processing of perceptual features, whereas conceptual priming tasks, such as general knowledge questions and generation of category exemplars, rely more on processing of stimulus meaning. Item priming refers to facilitation in the processing of individual stimuli, as is seen in word stem completion tasks, while associative priming involves learning of novel associations between stimuli, such as word pairs, nonwords constructed from word parts, and novel compound words. Although the results of experiments comparing these different types of priming have been somewhat inconsistent (Jelicic et al., 1996; Cherry & St. Pierre, 1998), in general it appears that age effects are similar for perceptual and conceptual priming (La Voie & Light, 1994; Jelicic, 1995; Fleischman & Gabrieli, 1998), as well as for item and associative priming (La Voie & Light, 1994; Light et al., 1995, 1996).

The failure to find a disproportionate age deficit in associative priming is in marked contrast to the clear age deficit in associative learning found using direct memory measures (Kausler, 1994; Naveh-Benjamin, 2000). In a similar vein, Vakil et al. (1996) reported age differences in memory for context when measured directly, but no differences when measured indirectly. Subjects were presented with pictures of one common object on top of another common object (e.g. a book on a chair), and instructed to remember the top object (e.g. the book). Later, recognition memory was tested with the target object (book) in the same context (chair), a neutral context (white background), or new context (different background object). Recognition of the context objects (e.g. chair) was also tested. While older adults showed impaired recognition of the context objects, both older and younger adults showed the same benefit of context reinstatement when recognizing the target objects. This contrast between direct and indirect memory measures has been taken as evidence that age-impairments in learning of new associations seen on direct tests reflect deficits at retrieval, rather than at encoding.

Direct Memory Tests

Semantic Memory

Semantic memory tasks probe subjects' knowledge of the world, including facts, concepts, propositions, and the meaning of words. Intact conceptual priming in older adults (see previous section) has been taken as evidence for the preservation of conceptual knowledge into old age (Laver & Burke, 1993). Direct tests of semantic memory seem to paint a similar picture. Older adults show minimal declines in vocabulary (Giambra et al., 1995), knowledge of historical facts (Perlmutter et al., 1980), knowledge of concepts (Eustache et al., 1998), and production of category exemplars (Mayr & Kliegl, 2000). One difficulty in measuring long-term memory for facts is the influence of cohort effects: the seemingly poor performance of young adults might be a function of the fact that they have not been exposed to or learned the information. However, age differences remain minimal even when efforts are made to correct for cohort differences in the knowledge base (Lachman & Lachman, 1980).

Charness (2000) proposed that a preserved knowledge base might compensate for age-related declines in other areas of memory and cognitive functioning. Evidence suggests that prior knowledge can in fact compensate for declines in episodic memory (Gillund & Perlmutter, 1993), memory for scene information (Hess & Slaughter, 1990), face recognition (Bäckman & Herlitz, 1990) and comprehension and memory for textual information (Radvansky, 1999) and spoken language (Wingfield, 2000). On the other hand, domain specific expertise (e.g. knowing how to play a musical instrument or fly planes) benefits memory for domain-relevant information in both younger and older adults, but has not been found to reliably attenuate age differences (Morrow et al., 1994; Meinz & Salthouse, 1998). Similarly, studies comparing university professors to blue collar workers (e.g. Christensen et al., 1997) have found that the high academic ability is not associated with slower rates of decline in memory performance.

All of the studies referenced so far examined older adults' ability to retrieve already learned information from semantic memory. Age effects on new learning of semantic information have received considerably less attention. Work by Hasher and colleagues suggests that new learning of semantic information may also remain relatively intact in old age. In one study (Rahhal et al., 2002), subjects listened to multiple spoken statements that were identified as either true or false. Older adults were impaired at later recalling which speaker stated each item, but did not differ from younger adults in labeling statements as true or false. More research is needed directly addressing age effects on acquisition of new semantic information.

An important exception to the general finding of preserved semantic memory in old age is an age related deficit in the retrieval of familiar words. Older adults are less accurate than younger adults on picture naming tasks (Bowles et al., 1989) and in producing words in response to definitions (Bowles & Poon, 1985). When recalling a sequence of videotaped events (Heller et al., 1992) or a memorable personal experience (Ulatowska et al., 1986), older adults produce more pronouns and other ambiguous references. Measures involving speed of retrieval or speed of decision are particularly vulnerable; e.g. Madden & Greene (1987) showed that lexical decision times increased with age, and Madden (1985) found that synonym decisions were slower in older than in younger adults. However, later work by Mayr & Kliegl (2000) suggests that the age-related difficulty is in the nonsemantic components rather than in the semantic components of retrieval.

The most dramatic example of older adults' word-finding difficulties is their increased susceptibility to tip-of-the-tongue (TOT) states. A TOT state involves the inability to recall a sought-after word, combined with a strong feeling that the word is in fact known. Older adults generally experience more TOTs (both naturally occurring and laboratory induced), report less partial information about the target word (such as number of syllables, stress pattern, initial sound), and take longer to resolve TOT states, relative to younger adults (Burke et al., 1991). Proper names are the most common category of words for which TOTs occur, for both younger and older adults, and the relative proportion of proper name TOTs appears to be greater for older adults (although see Maylor, 1997). The available evidence suggests that TOT states reflect a selective failure in accessing phonological information, and that providing phonological cues is equally beneficial to both older and younger adults in preventing and resolving TOT states (James & Burke, 2000).

Episodic Memory

Episodic memory refers to the ability to recall specific events and is typically measured by either recognition or recall of materials presented in the laboratory. Age effects on memory for autobiographical events occurring outside the laboratory have received less attention, and involve less controlled techniques, such as asking subjects to generate memories in response to cue words, and examining the distribution of memories across the lifespan. In a series of studies, Rubin and colleagues (Rubin & Schulkind, 1997a, 1997b; Rubin et al., 1986) utilized this technique with various age groups. The distribution of memories from the most recent 10–20 years of life did not differ across age groups: recent memories were the most available, and retention decreased monotonically with increasing time since the event occurred. It has also been found that memories from early childhood are distributed similarly across age groups (Waldfogel, 1948; Crovitz & Harvey, 1979; Crovitz et al., 1980), with very few memories from before the age of four or five. This pattern of results is consistent with the notion that once level of learning is equated, age-related differences in retention are negligible. Older adults' distribution of memories differs from young and middle aged adults in the existence of a so-called reminiscence bump—a disproportionate number of memories from early adulthood (Rubin et al., 1986). Several explanations have been proposed for the existence of the bump, including peak cognitive performance during early adulthood and a greater number of significant life events occurring at that time. It is likely that this bump is overshadowed in middle-aged adults by memories for recent events.

In contrast to memory for well learned life events, episodic memory tasks that measure memory for events occurring in the past few minutes, hours, or days, show more marked age deficits, e.g. Zelinski & Burnight (1997) reported the results of a 16 year longitudinal study that incorporated measures of recall and recognition. They found that participants who were aged 55 years and older at the beginning of the study showed reliable 16-year declines in both text recall and word list recall, but not in recognition memory. Participants who were aged 30–36 years at the start showed a decline in text recall only, so this measure appears to be the most sensitive to the effects of aging.

It has been known for some time that age-related declines in recognition memory are less severe than the comparable declines in recall. The effect was first documented by Schonfield & Robertson (1966) and has been noted by various other researchers since then (for review, see Craik & Jennings, 1992). Reduced processing resources (Craik & Byrd, 1982) have been proposed as a theoretical framework for interpreting the differential effects of aging on recall and recognition. The notion is that recall demands more attentional resources than does recognition, creating difficulty for resource-depleted older adults. Recognition tasks, where the same item is presented at study and test, provide high levels of environmental support (Craik, 1986), thereby minimizing age related decrements in performance. Support for this account is provided by the results of a study by Craik & McDowd (1987) in which subjects performed a secondary reaction-time (RT) task concurrently with recall or recognition. Recall was associated with greater RT costs (i.e. greater slowing of the RT task) than was recognition, and these costs were particularly high in older adults. Anderson and her colleagues (Anderson, 1999; Anderson et al., 1998; see also Whiting & Smith, 1997) reported similar results using a choice RT task as the concurrent secondary task at both encoding and retrieval. RT costs were greater at retrieval than at encoding, and were again greatest for older adults during the retrieval phase of a free recall task. Secondary task costs declined from free recall to cued recall to recognition, in line with the notion that the greater provision of environmental support at retrieval reduces the need to expend processing resources, and that this benefit is especially useful to older adults.

Bäckman & Small (1998) extended this line of thinking to include patients with Alzheimer's Disease (AD). They tested a large sample of residents from a section of Stockholm on two occasions, 3 years apart. The memory task was free recall of a word list, and the potential supports to performance included: (a) more time to encode the words; (b) the provision of words that could be organized by category; and (c) the provision of cues at retrieval. Normal older people were able to improve their performance using all three types of support; AD patients benefited only from cues at retrieval, and participants who were free of dementia on the first test but diagnosed with AD on the second test responded to all three types of support on the first test, but only to retrieval cues on the second test. It thus seems that the gradual loss of ability to utilize some types of cognitive support is a hallmark of AD.

It should be emphasized that although most studies have reported greater age-related losses in recall than in recognition, this result is not always found (Salthouse, 1991), e.g. Baddeley (1996) reported a study in which the difficulty of recall and recognition test was equated, and found equivalent age-related losses in the two types of test. Clearly, task difficulty is a factor that should be taken into account before reaching a firm theoretical conclusion. It is also the case that small age-related decrements in recognition memory are typically reported (e.g. Verhaeghen, 1999). Such decrements are often most apparent as age-related increases in the liability to make false-positive errors (Schacter et al., 1997a), although it is also possible to reduce this liability by inducing richer encoding of perceptual features at encoding and more careful scrutiny of each item at retrieval (Koutstaal et al., 1999).

Finally, Baddeley's (2000) recent proposal of an "episodic buffer" component in his model of memory suggests some interesting lines of research in the present context. If episodic memory for recent material is more vulnerable to loss in the elderly, e.g. it would be expected that delayed recall would show greater age-related losses than immediate recall.

Working Memory and Executive Processes

In the original model of working memory proposed by Baddeley & Hitch (1974) the central executive system was supported by relatively automatic modality-specific "slave systems", such as the articulatory loop and the visuo-spatial sketchpad. Adult age differences in these slave systems are slight, so tasks that require only brief holding and verbatim repetition of a string of words, letters or digits show comparatively small age-related decrements (for review, see Craik & Jennings, 1992). Floden et al. (2000) illustrated this result using the Brown–Peterson paradigm in which sets of three consonants are presented and then recalled after intervals of 0–60s. Floden and her colleagues adjusted the difficulty of the distractor task, used to prevent rehearsal during the retention interval, until it was equivalent for all participants. Using this technique, unadjusted scores showed a faster rate of forgetting for older than for younger participants, but decomposition of the total score into primary memory and secondary memory components showed that this effect was due entirely to a lower probability of recall from long-term or secondary memory; the forgetting rate from primary memory was identical for younger and older participants.

Two recent studies have provided further useful information about age-related differences in short-term or working memory. The first involved a modified version of the reading span paradigm, in which participants read a list of two, three or four sentences and then attempt to recall the last words from each sentence (Daneman & Carpenter, 1980). Typically, list lengths are tested in ascending order; thus a good deal of proactive inhibition may accumulate by the time longer lists are tested. May et al. (1999) showed that age-related decrements in reading span were greatly reduced (although not entirely eliminated) first by providing breaks between trials, and second by presenting the sequences in descending order of list length (i.e. testing the longest list first). The result of their study strongly suggests that proactive inhibition is a factor in reading span performance, and that older participants are more vulnerable to such inhibitory effects. The second study, by Murphy et al. (2000) showed that the impaired performance of older participants on a short-term recall task involving five word pairs can be mimicked in younger adults by presenting the pairs to be remembered auditorily and in a noisy background. The researchers concluded that the results demonstrated either that the sensory input to older participants was weak and "noisy", or that both normal aging and the addition of noise in younger participants reduced the effectiveness of encoding processes and thus reduced later retrieval performance.

These results notwithstanding, many researchers have shown that performance on working memory tasks, requiring online manipulation as well as passive storage, declines across the adult lifespan (Bäckman et al., 2000; Verhaeghen et al., 1993; Zacks et al., 2000). The factors responsible for this decline are still under active debate. One such factor is likely to be the greater vulnerability of older adults to interference from irrelevant or distracting information (e.g. May et al., 1999). It is unlikely that an age-related decline in inhibitory processes is the whole story, however; older adults also show difficulties in the self-initiation of novel patterns of thought and action, and in boosting task-appropriate responses as well as inhibiting task-inappropriate responses (Craik, 1986; Hay & Jacoby, 1999). Such find-ings suggest strongly that the central executive component of working memory declines in efficiency with increasing age, and this decline in turn likely reflects the reduced efficiency of frontal lobe processes in older adults (Glisky et al., 1995). In line with the notion that normal aging is associated with reduced frontal lobe functioning, one study found that the performance of older adults on a word list learning task resembled the pattern shown by young adults with lesions in the right dorsolateral prefrontal cortex (Stuss et al., 1996).

A further area of general agreement is that normal aging is accompanied by a reduction in the efficiency with which the various aspects of an encoded event are bound together to form an integrated, coherent episode. One account of this age-related failure attributes it to the declining efficiency of consciously experienced reflective processes in working memory (Mitchell et al., 2000). Other theorists have described the problem as a difficulty in the integration of focal items with their context (Smith et al., 1998), as a deficit in ensemble processing (Bayen et al., 2000) or, most generally, as an age-related deficit in associative processing (Naveh-Benjamin, 2000).

One final set of results in this area concerns the difficulties experienced by older adults in dealing with divided attention or dual-task situations. Such difficulties are also reflective of the declining efficiency of executive processes. Studies by Nyberg et al. (1997) and by Anderson et al. (1998) found that when a memory task is carried out simultaneously with a secondary task, memory performance declined by a similar absolute amount in younger and older adults relative to the memory task performed on its own, but that secondary task performance declined much more in the older group. This pattern was especially pronounced during the retrieval phase of the memory task. In an interesting variant of this procedure, Lindenberger et al. (2000) measured walking accuracy and speed in younger and older adults while they attempted to memorize a list of words. The researchers found greater dual-task costs in the older group, and attributed this result to the greater need for executive processes in older adults, partly to carry out the appropriate memory encoding processes, but also because the sensorimotor processes governing walking require greater degrees of cognitive control and supervision in the elderly. Interestingly, this current suggestion is very much in line with proposals put forward some years ago by Welford in his classic monograph, Ageing and Human Skill (1958).

Prospective Memory

"Prospective memory" (PM) refers to situations in which a person forms the intention to carry out an action at some future time, and then either remembers or forgets to carry out that action. The topic has received a lot of attention recently (e.g. Brandimonte et al., 1996), especially in the context of studies of aging. Some initial reports using laboratory-based techniques suggested that age differences were minimal in PM (Einstein & McDaniel, 1990), but further studies have shown, on the contrary, that age-related impairments in PM can be substantial (Cockburn & Smith, 1991). Such failures have important real-life consequences—forgetting to take medications, for example, or to lock doors or to turn off the stove. One large-scale study that demonstrated a clear age-related decline in such abilities was reported by Mäntylä & Nilsson (1997). Their study involved 100 subjects in each of 10 age cohorts ranging from 35–80 years, and the task was to remind the experimenter at the end of a testing session that the subjects should sign a form. Performance on this simple task dropped from 61% of subjects aged 35–45 remembering successfully, to 25% of subjects aged 70–80. This age-related decline is greater in people of lower ability (Cherry & Le Compte, 1999).

PM tasks may be classified as either time-based (e.g. remembering to make a phone call at 2.30 p.m.) or event-based (e.g. remembering to ask John a question when you next meet him). Einstein et al. (1995) found age-related decrements in time-based but not event-based tasks, and suggested that this pattern may be attributable to the greater demands for self-initiated processing on time-based tasks, which lack any external reminders. This suggestion is in line with Craik's (1986) proposal that self-initiated processing declines with age as a consequence of a decline in attentional resources, or possibly reflects an age-related decline in frontally-mediated cognitive control (West, 1996). Other studies have shown age-related declines in both event-based tasks as well as in time-based tasks (e.g. Maylor, 1996) although the decline may be greater in the latter (Park et al., 1997). At least one study has shown the opposite result (d'Ydewalle et al., 1999), so it may well be the case that the pattern of results is less dependent on the category of task (e.g. time-based or event-based) than on such aspects as the salience of event-based cues, the difficulty of the ongoing background activity and the number of PM intentions to be borne in mind.

Some evidence on these modulating variables comes from recent studies. Both Kidder et al. (1997) and Einstein et al. (1997) demonstrated that age-related decrements in a PM task were greater when the background task (the ongoing activity) was more demanding. The study of Einstein et al. (1997) also found that increasing background task demands at encoding decreased performance equally for younger and older adults, but that increasing demands at retrieval penalized older participants in particular. In general, it makes sense that PM failures are likely to be greater when the ongoing background activity is interesting and absorbing. It also seems possible that older adults (like patients with frontal dysfunction) have greater difficulty in switching their attention from the background task to the PM task. Some portion of age-related PM failures may reflect a failure to remember the action to be performed, but such impairments of retrospective memory cannot account for all cases (Park et al., 1997).

Maylor (1996) found that participants of all ages show fluctuations in their ability to remember a series of PM activities; that is, success on one trial may be followed by failure on a subsequent trial (forgetting), or failure may be followed by success (recovery). Maylor found that such fluctuations were more common in older people, who thus show a greater tendency to experience "momentary lapses of intention" (Craik & Kerr, 1996). West & Craik (1999) explored this phenomenon further and concluded that older adults retain their sensitivity to PM cues, but show a decline in accessibility of the appropriate cue-action pairing. In general, PM situations are often those in which habitual behavior on the background task dominates thought and action, especially for older people. In this sense an age-related reduction in self-initiated processing (Craik, 1986) will contribute to the failure to break such automatic modes of behaviour, although Zacks et al. (2000) make the useful point that some instances of PM success appear to involve little deliberate attentional processing; rather, the intention simply seems to "pop to mind".

Finally, there is an interesting discrepancy between laboratory-based and real-life PM tasks, in that large age-related decrements are typically found in the former but not in the latter. In a particularly convincing study, Rendell & Thomson (1999) found that adults in their 60s and 80s performed better than a group in their 20s on PM tasks taking place in the course of daily living, although the same groups of older adults performed less well than the younger group on laboratory-based PM tasks. Rendell & Craik (2000) hypothesized that the superiority of older adults on real-life tasks might reflect their more structured daily lives, and attempted to tap this greater structure in a laboratory board game called "Virtual Week". However, the results showed that older adults performed less well than their younger counterparts on the board game although they again outperformed the young group in real life. It is unlikely that this latter superiority is due simply to older adults relying more on external aids, since all participants in both of Rendell's studies were instructed not to use aids, and later reported compliance with this instruction. The superiority of older adults on real-life PM tasks may thus be attributable to such factors as greater motivation, more adequate learning, or greater compliance on the part of older adults. In any event, it is encouraging to find at least one class of memory task in which older adults consistently do better than their younger counterparts.

Source Memory

The capacity to accurately remember the origin of our knowledge allows us to evaluate the relevance of that knowledge for a given task or situation. In this section, we review multiple sources of evidence that the elderly suffer disproportionately from an inability to remember the context of material that they have learned.

The prototypical task used in source memory experiments involves external source monitoring (Johnson et al., 1993); in which the subject must select a correct contextual detail about the prior physical presentation of a stimulus. Often this task is combined with an item memory task, in which the subject is simply asked to recall or recognize studied stimuli prior to the source memory decision (see previous section on episodic memory). A wide variety of studies have demonstrated greater impairment of source than item memory in the elderly, with physical contextual characteristics including the color of words and pictures (Park & Puglisi, 1985), typeface (Kausler & Puckett, 1980; Naveh-Benjamin & Craik, 1995), and presentation modality (Light et al., 1992; McIntyre & Craik, 1987). The deficit in source memory even arises under conditions in which item memory is equated (Ferguson et al., 1992; Schacter et al., 1991) or the relationship between item memory and age is partialled out statistically (Erngrund et al., 1996).

Some authors have suggested that this deficit simply reflects group perceptual differences, whereby the elderly are less able to distinguish between multiple perceptually similar sources than are the young. Consistent with this view, Ferguson et al. (1992; see also Schacter et al., 1991) found that making the sources more distinctive—such as using one male and one female voice, as opposed to two female voices—eliminated age differences in source memory. This view is also consistent with the arguments sometimes forwarded by those who study cognition from an individual differences perspective and call attention to the large proportion of age-related variance in memory performance that covaries with perceptual acuity (Baltes & Lindenberger, 1997; Frieske & Park, 1999).

However, other results are inconsistent with a purely perceptual explanation, e.g. source memory deficits can be shown when the sources are not primarily perceptual in origin. Tasks that involve internal source monitoring (Johnson et al., 1993) require the subject to distinguish between sources that are not physical, such as doing versus imagining (Cohen & Faulkner, 1989), and the results suggest that the age-related effects on such tasks are no different than on tasks involving external sources (Brown 1995). Some authors have even shown age-related deficits in internal, but not external, source monitoring (Degl'Innocenti & Bäckman, 1996).

There is also evidence from the "false-fame" task (e.g. Jacoby et al., 1989) that is inconsistent with a perceptual explanation of source memory deficits. In that task, subjects are asked to evaluate the fame of names, some of which had been previously viewed. The typical finding is that variables that decrease the probability of remembering the earlier presentation of the name increase the likelihood of attributing fame to a previously seen nonfamous name. One such variable is age: The elderly show much larger false-fame effects than do the young (Bartlett et al., 1991; Dywan & Jacoby, 1990). Such results indicate that older subjects perceive the studied materials adequately, otherwise the names would not be sufficiently familiar to evoke mistaken feelings of fame! Yet those same subjects were unable to accurately attribute the basis for those feelings of familiarity to the prior exposure, indicating a deficit specific to source monitoring.

Similar evidence is provided by older adults' performance on exclusion tasks, in which subjects are required to endorse only one subset of the previously studied items. Manipulations that enhance memory for the eventually to-be-rejected items, such as repetition (Jacoby, 1999) or spacing (Benjamin & Craik, 2001), increase the probability of correct rejection in the young but increase the probability of incorrect endorsement (i.e. false alarms) in the elderly. This pattern of errors could arise only if the elderly perceive the stimuli well enough to encourage their (correct) belief that they were studied, but fail to remember the correct source.

It is worth noting that, although the aforementioned results are largely inconsistent with the hypothesis that a failure to adequately perceive and encode contextual dimensions underlies source memory deficits in the elderly, they are not inconsistent with other perceptually-based hypotheses. It may be the case, for example, that older adults do indeed perceive the contextual elements perfectly well, but that the greater effort it takes to do so (because of declining perceptual faculties) draws resources away from the mnemonic processes that would help them recover the source later.

Several authors have attempted to link source memory deficits in the elderly to frontal dysfunction. Frontal patients show many of the same characteristic deficits as the elderly (e.g. Janowsky 1989), and several authors have found correlations between frontal function and source memory performance (Craik et al., 1990; Glisky et al., 2001; Parkin & Walter, 1992). However, others have failed to find any such relation (Degl'Innocenti & Bäckman, 1996; Dywan et al., 1994; Spencer & Raz, 1994).

Schacter et al. (1994) proposed that the apparent source memory deficit with aging reflects the fact that most source memory experiments used many-to-one fact-to-source mapping. They suggested that older people might simply be more prone to the effects of cue overload, and ran an experiment in which each item was accompanied by a combination of cues yielding a unique presentation context. Disproportionate impairment of source memory was still evident, suggesting that the particular mapping between items and sources was not central to the source memory deficit (see also Glisky, 2001).

Although these results suggest that the source memory impairment in the elderly is indeed a memory deficit—and not a perceptual or attentional capacity deficit—there are variables that reduce or even eradicate the difference between old and young. As mentioned earlier, making the sources highly perceptually distinct benefits the elderly (Ferguson et al., 1992), as does encouraging subjects to consider the factual and not the emotional aspects of previously uttered statements (Hashtroudi et al., 1994), using statements that have personal rather than general relevance (Brown et al., 1995), using source dimensions that are associated with truth value or personality characteristics (Rahhal et al., 2002), and utilizing contextual dimensions that are less peripheral to the task (Spencer & Raz, 1995). Consistent with the idea that older subjects employ different bases for evaluating fame, Multhaup (1995) showed that encouraging them to adopt stringent criteria reduced false-fame effects.

In sum, these results seem to indicate that source memory deficits in the elderly are reliable and at least in part mnemonic in origin. However, the numerous manipulations that attenuate or even eliminate the effects suggest that such deficits do not necessarily implicate a separate and impaired source memory system, but rather reflect the different ways in which the elderly strategically deploy their more limited mnemonic skills.

False Memory

The previous section on source memory delineated ways in which older subjects have particular difficulty with remembering the context in which information was learned, and some examples of false memory are a natural consequence of this inability, e.g. older subjects are more susceptible to misleading postevent suggestion (Cohen & Faulkner, 1989; Schacter et al., 1997b). A natural interpretation of such results is that the elderly fail to remember whether their memory for the suggested information came from the postevent period or from the event itself. Similarly, the enhanced false-fame effects in the elderly described earlier can be explained by the inability to localize the source of a name's familiarity to the study episode, rather than the popular media.

Other findings are somewhat more complex. Older adults are more likely to falsely recall and recognize stimuli that are highly related to previously studied materials, regardless of whether that relationship is semantic (Norman & Schacter, 1998; Rankin & Kausler, 1979; Smith, 1975; Tun et al., 1998) or phonological (Watson et al., 2001) and even when the stimuli are pictures (Koutstaal & Schacter, 1997; for review, see Schacter et al., 1997a). One interpretation of these effects is consistent with the source memory deficit discussed above; namely, that subjects covertly "generate" plausible foils when studying highly related stimuli, and that their later memory for them is an example of a reality monitoring deficit: they fail to attribute their memory for the item to their imagination, rather than to a physical presentation. This hypothesis is inconsistent with several results, however.

The encoding-based explanation of false-memory effects predicts that manipulations that enhance learning of the study materials should also increase false-memory effects. On the contrary, a persistent finding in the literature is that, in general, increased learning increases true but decreases false recognition (Benjamin, 2001; McDermott, 1996; Schacter et al., 1998), and that groups (such as the elderly) that show poorer veridical memory also show greater false memory (e.g. Watson et al., 2001). These findings are most interpretable in the context of a regularity in recognition memory known as the mirror effect. This effect refers to the general tendency of increases in veridical memory performance (i.e. hit rate) to be accompanied by decreases in false memory (i.e. false-alarm rate). Numerous theories have been advanced to account for these findings (e.g. Benjamin et al., 1998; Glanzer et al., 1993) but a review of such theories is outside the scope of this review.

What is of present interest, however, is the failure to find a mirror effect for the elderly (Benjamin, 2001). In that experiment, subjects studied lists of words either once or thrice, and both veridical and false memory for the lists was assessed. For the young subjects, multiple study-list exposures increased true memory and decreased false memory. For the old subjects, multiple exposures increased both true and false memory, suggesting that, although semantic priming and activation is intact in the elderly (e.g. Balota & Duchek, 1991; Duchek & Balota, 1993), the inability to attribute that activation to likely sources and thereby set appropriate decision criteria leads them to be more prone to false memory.

Metamemory

There are several partially overlapping literatures that address metacognition, or knowledge about memory. These topics can be roughly categorized as follows:

- General beliefs about the structure and function of memory.
- Assessment of memory self-efficacy.
- Monitoring of memory performance.
- Strategic use of memory.

In this section, we briefly review key findings from these domains. Understanding metacognition in the elderly is particularly important because of its link with memory training and rehabilitation, in which strategies that circumvent or obviate memory deficits are taught.

Older people consistently complain that their ability to learn and remember information has declined (e.g. Hertzog & Dixon, 1994). In longitudinal studies subjects report deteriorating faculties regardless of whether they show an increase in self-reported forgetting over that time frame (Zelinski et al., 1993) or not (Taylor et al., 1992). This result suggests that memory complaints are based at least in part on an implicit theory that is held about the nature of memory decline, rather than strictly on an evaluation of their own memory performance (McDonald-Miszczak et al., 1995).

If older adults maintain a bleaker view of their own memory ability than do the young, and indeed even more so than is warranted by their performance, then they may set their goal levels unnecessarily low and thus engage in suboptimal strategy use (see e.g. Berry & West, 1993). Several sets of findings bear this hypothesis out. First, programs aimed at increasing memory self-efficacy improve memory performance (e.g. Lachman et al., 1992), as does simply providing older adults experience with the use of effective strategies on a memory task (Welch & West, 1995), although it should be noted that such strategies improve the performance of young adults too—sometimes even more than the performance of older adults (Kliegl et al., 1989). Such training appears to have long-lived consequences, up to 3 years or greater (Neely & Bäckman, 1993). Second, de-emphasizing the "memory" component and emphasizing the "knowledge" component of memory tasks reduces or even eliminates age differences on tasks such as remembering the truth value of a fictitious trivia statement (Rahhal et al., 2001). Such findings illustrate that stereotypes about memory in the elderly may play a limiting role in older adults' performance. For more comprehensive reviews on metacognition and aging, the reader is directed to Cavanaugh (1996), Dunlosky & Hertzog (1998), Hertzog & Dixon (1994), and Verhaeghen et al. (1992).

SUMMARY AND CONCLUSIONS

As is clearly demonstrated by the preceding review, age-related effects on memory performance are not uniform across tasks. Aspects of memory performance that appear to hold up well to the aging process include the following: motor learning, priming, semantic memory (with the exception of word-finding difficulties), episodic memory for well-learned life-events, passive short-term storage of information (primary memory), recognition memory, and prospective memory in everyday life.

More substantial age-related decrements are seen in three main areas of memory processing. First, older adults seem particularly impaired at tasks that require online processing to be carried out while simultaneously holding information in mind, as evidenced by their poor performance on working memory tasks (Zacks et al., 2000). Secondly, older adults appear to have difficulties with encoding of new information in a deep and elaborative manner, most likely due to inefficiencies in processing related to lack of cognitive control and suboptimal strategy selection. Finally, the elderly experience trouble retrieving information from memory, particularly when retrieval requires effortful processing, as in uncued recall, prospective memory tasks, or recovery of specific details, as in source memory tasks.

The challenge presented to a scholar of memory and aging is thus the development of a theoretical framework that can parsimoniously explain why age related deficits are quite significant on some tasks, and minimal or even non-existent on others. How well do each of the theoretical frameworks outlined at the beginning of the chapter accommodate the pattern of findings described here?

Speed of Processing

Explanations based on speed of processing limitations work best for memory tasks in which speed clearly plays a role, such as experimenter-paced motor learning tasks (e.g. Wright & Payne, 1985), or tasks that require timely coordination of multiple processes (Harrington & Haaland, 1992). Salthouse (1996) suggests that age-related impairments on tasks that do not have an obvious speed component, such as free recall tasks, can be explained via the simultaneity mechanism: the products of earlier processes are lost before later processes are carried out. While it is compelling to note that much of the age related variance on free recall tasks can be explained by decreased speed of processing, it is not clear either what exactly the "earlier" and "later" processes involved in free recall are, or what the optimal timing for these processes should be. Moreover, correlations between measured speed and memory performance do not necessarily imply that speed logically precedes memory ability; it is quite possible that both effects derive from some other source, such as widespread neurological changes associated with aging. Additionally, Rabbitt (1993) has presented evidence to show that aging is related strongly to memory performance independently of changes in speed of information processing. Until the subprocesses involved in tasks such as free recall are specified to a greater degree and related more directly to speed of processing, the usefulness of generalized slowing as an explanatory concept in memory and aging research remains in question.

Reduced Processing Resources

The finding that older adults have particular difficulties on tasks that demand a great deal of cognitive effort, such as free recall (e.g. Zelinski & Burnight, 1997), prospective memory (e.g. Mäntylä & Nilsson, 1997) and source memory (e.g. Naveh-Benjamin & Craik, 1995), fits nicely with the notion that aging is accompanied by a depletion of attentional resources. Also consistent with this framework is the finding that environmental supports such as re-presentation of studied items (as in recognition tasks: Craik & Jennings, 1992), distinctive perceptual cues (e.g. Ferguson et al., 1992), and supportive contexts (e.g. Rendell & Thomson, 1999) can greatly reduce age-related differences in performance. Finally, preservation into old age of some memory processes that are presumed to be automatic and therefore require few attentional resources, such as priming (Fleischman & Gabrieli, 1997) provide further support for the reduced resources hypothesis. However, other memory processes, such as spatial learning, are also presumed to be automatic in nature, and yet show substantial age-related decrements (e.g. Wilkniss et al., 1997). Perhaps the most potent criticism of the reduced resources framework is the nebulous nature of its core construct: attentional resources. Working memory tasks have been proposed as a potential measure of attentional capacity (Park, 2000); however the central executive component of working memory has likewise been criticized for its vague formulation.

Inhibitory Deficit

Many of the findings regarding age-differences in working memory functioning can be easily explained within the framework of age-related inhibitory deficits. For example, when age differences are found on span tasks, they may be attributable, at least in part, to interference from items activated on successive trials, but not subsequently deleted from working memory by the elderly (May et al., 1999). The inhibitory deficit hypothesis deserves further credit for sparking interest in how the contents of working memory, as well as the capacity, may differ between old and young. However, it is less clear how inhibitory deficits can explain age-related differences in tasks such as free recall, where there appears to be a failure of activation rather than inhibition. Nor does it explain deficits in source memory— if older adults are less able to inhibit irrelevant information, one would expect that they would encode more peripheral details of the context than younger adults. It seems sensible to postulate that efficient information processing requires control over both the activation and suppression of information, and that aging is accompanied by a reduction in both kinds of control.

Control

The theoretical proposal of an age-related decrement in executive control over cognitive processes combines the explanatory power of the reduced resources and inhibitory deficit frameworks by postulating that older adults have difficulty both with the initiation of effortful processing, such as required by deep and elaborative encoding and strategic retrieval searches, and with the active suppression of task irrelevant information. It is thereby able to accommodate much of the data pointing to age differences in working memory, episodic memory, source memory, prospective memory, and false memory. However, the concept of an executive dysfunction suffers from the same criticism as reduced resources: What exactly is meant by the terms "executive functioning" or "controlled processing?" The finding that tasks proposed to be heavily reliant on executive functioning are especially sensitive to frontal lobe functioning (e.g. Stuss et al., 1996) provides some support for the view that executive functions are a discrete subset of cognitive processing, subserved by a particular region of the brain. The ability of the impaired executive control framework to account for a wide variety of findings in the field of aging and memory underscores the need for further research aimed at illuminating the nature or executive functioning, its relation to memory performance, and the aging process.

ACKNOWLEDGEMENT

Preparation of this chapter was facilitated by support from the National Institute of Aging to ASB and from the Natural Sciences and Engineering Research Council of Canada to FIMC.

REFERENCES

Anderson, N.D., Craik, F.I.M. & Naveh-Benjamin, M. (1998). The attentional demands of encoding and retrieval in younger and older adults: I. Evidence from divided attention costs. *Psychology & Aging*, **13**, 405–423.

Anderson, N.D. (1999). The attentional demands of encoding and retrieval in younger and older adults: 2. Evidence from secondary task reaction time distributions. *Psychology & Aging*, **14**, 645–655.

Arbuckle, T.Y., Cooney, R., Milne, J., & Melchior, A. (1994). Memory for spatial layouts in relation to age and schema typicality. *Psychology & Aging*, **9**, 467–480.

Bäckman, L. & Herlitz, A. (1990). The relationship between prior knowledge and face recognition memory in normal aging and Alzheimer's disease. *Journals of Gerontology*, **45**, P94–P100.

Bäckman, L. & Small, B.J. (1998). Influences of cognitive support on episodic remembering: tracing the process of loss from normal aging to Alzheimer's disease. *Psychology & Aging*, **13**, 267–276.

Bäckman, L., Small, B.J., Wahlin, A. & Larsson, M. (2000). Cognitive functioning in very old age. In F.I.M. Craik & T.A. Salthouse (eds), *The Handbook of Aging and Cognition 2nd edn* (pp. 499–558). Mahwah, NJ: Erlbaum.

Baddeley, A. (1996). Applying the psychology of memory to clinical problems. In D.J. Herrmann, C.L. McEvoy, C. Hertzog et al. (eds), *Basic and Applied Memory Research: Theory in Context* (pp. 195–219). Mahwah, NJ: Erlbaum.

Baddeley, A. (2000). The episodic buffer: a new component of working memory? *Trends in Cognitive Sciences*, **4**, 417–423.

Baddeley, A. & Hitch, G. (1974). Working memory. In G. Bower (ed.), *Recent Advances in Learning and Motivation*, Vol. 8 (pp. 47–89). New York: Academic Press.

Balota, D.A. & Duchek, J. (1991). Semantic priming effects, lexical repetition effects, and contextual disambiguation effects in healthy aged individuals and individuals with senile dementia of the Alzheimer's type. *Brain and Language*, **40**, 181–201.

Baltes, P.B. & Lindenberger, U. (1997). Emergence of a powerful connection between sensory and cognitive functions across the adult life span: a new window into the study of cognitive aging? *Psychology & Aging*, **12**, 12–21.

Bartlett, J.C., Strater, L. & Fulton, A. (1991). False recency and false fame of faces in young adulthood and old age. *Memory & Cognition*, **19**, 177–188.

Bayen, U.J., Phelps, M.P. & Spaniol, J. (2000). Age-related differences in the use of contextual information in recognition memory: a global matching approach. *Journals of Gerontology: Psychological Sciences*, **55B**, P131–P141.

Benjamin, A.S. (2001). On the dual effects of repetition in false recognition. *Journal of Experimental Psychology: Learning, Memory, and Cognition*, **27**, 941–947.

Benjamin, A.S., Bjork, R.A. & Hirshman, E. (1998). Predicting the future and reconstructing the past: a Bayesian characterization of the utility of subjective fluency. *Acta Psychologica*, **98**, 267–290.

Benjamin, A.S. & Craik, F.I.M. (in press). Parallel effects of aging and time pressure on memory for source: evidence from the spacing effect. *Journal of Experimental Psychology: Learning, Memory, and Cognition*.

Berry, J.M. & West, R.L. (1993). Cognitive self-efficacy in relation to personal mastery and goal setting across the life span. *International Journal of Behavioral Development*, **16**, 351–379.

Birren, J.E. (1965). Age changes in speed of behavior: its central and neurophysiological correlates. In A.T. Welford & J.E. Birren (eds), *Behavior, Aging and the Nervous System* (pp. 191–216). Springfield, IL: Charles C. Thomas.

Bowles, N.L. & Poon, L.W. (1985). Aging and retrieval of words in semantic memory. *Journal of Gerontology*, **40**, 77.

Bowles, N.L., Obler, L.K. & Poon, L.W. (1989). Aging and word retrieval: naturalistic, clinical and laboratory data. In L.W. Poon, D.C. Rubin & B.A. Wilson (eds), *Everyday Cognition in Adulthood and Late Life* (pp. 244–264). Cambridge: Cambridge University Press.

Brandimonte, M., Einstein, G.O. & McDaniel, M.A. (1996). *Prospective Memory: Theory and Applications*. Mahwah, NJ: Erlbaum.

Brown, A.S., Jones, E.M. & Davis, T.L. (1995). Age differences in conversational source monitoring. *Psychology & Aging*, **10**, 111–122.

Burke, D.M., MacKay, D.G., Worthley, J.S. & Wade, E. (1991). On the tip of the tongue: what causes word finding failures in young and older adults. *Journal of Memory and Language*, **30**, 542–579.

Cavanaugh, J.C. (1996). Memory self-efficacy as a moderator of memory change. In F. Blanchard-Fields & T.M. Hess (eds), *Perspectives on Cognitive Change in Adulthood and Aging* (pp. 488–507). New York: McGraw-Hill.

Charness, N. (2000). Can acquired knowledge compensate for age-related declines in cognitive efficiency? In S.H. Qualls & N. Abeles (eds), *Psychology and the Aging Revolution: How We Adapt to Longer Life* (pp. 99–117). Washington, DC: American Psychological Association.

Cherry, K.E. & Park, D.C. (1993). Individual differences and context variables influence spatial memory in younger and older adults. *Psychology & Aging*, **8**, 526.

Cherry, K.E. & St Pierre, C. (1998). Age-related differences in pictorial implicit memory: role of perceptual and conceptual processes. *Experimental Aging Research*, **24**, 53–62.

Cherry, K.E. & LeCompte, D.C. (1999). Age and individual differences influence prospective memory. *Psychology & Aging*, **14**, 60–76.

Christensen, H., Henderson, A.S., Griffiths, K. & Levings, C. (1997). Does ageing inevitably lead to declines in cognitive performance? A longitudinal study of elite academics. *Personality and Individual Differences*, **23**, 67–78.

Cockburn, J. & Smith, P.T. (1991). The relative influence of intelligence and age on everyday memory. *Journal of Gerontology: Psychological Sciences*, **46**, P31–36.

Cohen, G. & Faulkner, D. (1989). Age differences in source forgetting: effects on reality monitoring and on eyewitness testimony. *Psychology & Aging*, **5**, 148–151.

Craik, F.I.M. & Byrd, M. (1982). Aging and cognitive deficits: the role of attentional resources. In F.I.M. Craik & S. Trehub (eds), *Aging and Cognitive Processes* (pp. 191–211). Hillsdale, NJ: Erlbaum.

Craik, F.I.M. (1986). A functional account of age differences in memory. In F. Klix & H. Hagendorf (eds), *Human Memory and Cognitive Capabilities* (pp. 409–422). Amsterdam: Elsevier.

Craik, F.I.M. & McDowd, J.M. (1987). Age differences in recall and recognition. *Journal of Experimental Psychology: Learning, Memory & Cognition*, **13**, 474–479.

Craik, F.I.M., Morris, L.W., Morris, R.G. & Loewen, E.R. (1990). Relations between source amnesia and frontal lobe functioning in older adults. *Psychology & Aging*, **5**, 148–151.

Craik, F.I.M. & Jennings, J.M. (1992). Human memory. In F.I.M. Craik & T.A. Salthouse (eds), *The Handbook of Aging and Cognition* (pp. 51–110). Hillsdale, NJ: Erlbaum.

Craik, F.I.M. & Kerr, S.A. (1996). Commentary: prospective memory, aging, and lapses of intention. In M. Brandimonte, G.O. Einstein, & M.A. McDaniel (eds), *Prospective Memory: Theory and Applications* (pp. 227–237). Mahwah, NJ: Erlbaum.

Crovitz, H.F. & Harvey, M.T. (1979). Early childhood amnesia: a quantitative study with implications for the study of retrograde amnesia after brain injury. *Cortex*, **15**, 331–335.

Crovitz, H.F., Harvey, M.T. & McKee, D.C. (1980). Selecting retrieval cues for early childhood amnesia: implications for the study of shrinking retrograde amnesia. *Cortex*, **16**, 305–310.

Daneman, M. & Carpenter, P.A. (1980). Individual differences in working memory and reading. *Journal of Verbal Learning and Verbal Behavior*, **19**, 450–466.

Degl'Innocenti, A. & Bäckman, L. (1996). Aging and source memory: influences of intention to remember and associations with frontal lobe tests. *Aging, Neuropsychology and Cognition*, **3**, 307–319.

Desrocher, M. & Smith, M.L. (1998). Relative preservation of egocentric but not allocentric spatial memory in aging. *Brain and Cognition*, **37**, 91–93.

Duchek, J. & Balota, D.A. (1993). Sparing of activation processes in older adults. In J. Cerella & W. Hoyer (eds), *Adult Information Processing: Limits on Loss* (pp. 383–406). San Diego, CA: Academic Press.

Dunlosky, J. & Hertzog, C. (1998). Training programs to improve learning in later adulthood: helping older adults educate themselves. In D.J. Hacker, J. Dunlosky & A.C. Graesser (eds), *Metacognition in Educational Theory and Practice* (pp. 249–275). Mahwah, NJ: Erlbaum.

Dywan, J. & Jacoby, L.L. (1990). Effects of aging on source monitoring: differences in susceptibility to false fame. *Psychology & Aging*, **3**, 379–387.

Dywan, J., Segalowitz, S.J. & Williamson, L. (1994). Source monitoring during name recognition in older adults: psychometric and electrophysiological correlates. *Psychology & Aging*, **9**, 568–577.

d'Ydewalle, G., Luwel, K. & Brunfaut, E. (1999). The importance of ongoing concurrent activities as a function of age in time- and event-based prospective memory. *European Journal of Cognitive Psychology*, **11**, 219–237.

Einstein, G.O. & McDaniel, M.A. (1990). Normal aging and prospective memory. *Journal of Experimental Psychology: Learning, Memory & Cognition*, **16**, 717–726.

Einstein, G.O., McDaniel, M.A., Richardson, S.L. et al. (1995). Aging and prospective memory: examining the influences of self-initiated retrieval processes. *Journal of Experimental Psychology: Learning, Memory & Cognition*, **21**, 996–1007.

Einstein, G.O., Smith, R.E., McDaniel, M.A. & Shaw, P. (1997). Aging and prospective memory: the influence of increased task demands at encoding and retrieval. *Psychology & Aging*, **12**, 479–488.

Erngrund, K., Mäntylä, T. & Nilsson, L.G. (1996). Adult age differences in source recall: a population-based study. *Journals of Gerontology: Series B: Psychological Sciences and Social Sciences*, **51B**, P335–P345.

Eustache, F., Desgranges, B., Jacques, V. & Platel, H. (1998). Preservation of the attribute knowledge of concepts in normal aging groups. *Perceptual and Motor Skills*, **87**, 1155–1162.

Ferguson, S.A., Hashtroudi, S. & Johnson, M.K. (1992). Age differences in using source-relevant cues. *Psychology & Aging*, **7**, 443–452.

Fleischman, D.A. & Gabrieli, J.D.E. (1998). Repetition priming in normal aging and Alzheimer's disease: a review of findings and theories. *Psychology & Aging*, **13**, 88–119.

Floden, D., Stuss, D.T. & Craik, F.I.M. (2000). Age differences in performance on two versions of the Brown–Peterson task. *Aging, Neuropsychology and Cognition*, **7**, 245–259.

Foisy, P. (1994). Age-related deficits in intentional memory for spatial location in small-scale space: a meta-analysis and methodological critique. *Canadian Journal on Aging*, **13**, 353–367.

Frieske, D.A. & Park, D.C. (1999). Memory for news in young and old adults. *Psychology & Aging*, **14**, 90–98.

Giambra, L.M., Arenberg, D., Zonderman, A.B. & Kawas, C. (1995). Adult life span changes in immediate visual memory and verbal intelligence. *Psychology & Aging*, **10**, 123–139.

Gillund, G. & Perlmutter, M. (1993). Episodic memory and knowledge interactions across adulthood. In L.L. Light & D.M. Burke (eds), *Language, Memory and Aging* (pp. 191–208). New York: Cambridge University Press.

Glanzer, M., Adams, J.K., Iverson, G.J. & Kim, K. (1993). The regularities of recognition memory. *Psychological Science*, **100**, 546–567.

Glisky, E.L., Polster, M.R. & Routhieaux, B.C. (1995). Double dissociation between item and source memory. *Neuropsychology*, **9**, 229–235.

Glisky, E.L., Rubin, S.R. & Davidson, P.S. (2001). Source memory in older adults: an encoding or retrieval problem? *Journal of Experimental Psychology: Learning, Memory & Cognition*, **27**, 1131–1146.

Glisky, E.L. (2001). Source memory, aging, and frontal lobes. In M. Naveh-Benjamin, H.L. Roediger III & M. Moscovitch (eds), *Perspectives on Human Memory and Cognitive Aging: Essays in Honour of Fergus Craik*. Philadelphia, PA: Psychology Press.

Graf, P., Squire, L. R. & Mandler, G. (1984). Information that amnesic patients do not forget. *Journal of Experimental Psychology: Learning, Memory & Cognition*, **10**, 164–178.

Harrington, D.L. & Haaland, K.Y. (1992). Skill learning in the elderly: diminished implicit and explicit memory for a motor sequence. *Psychology & Aging*, **7**, 425–434.

Hasher, L. & Zacks, R.T. (1979). Automatic and effortful processes in memory. *Journal of Experimental Psychology: General*, **108**, 356–388.

Hasher, L. & Zacks, R.T. (1988). Working memory, comprehension and aging: a review and a new view. In G. Bower (ed.), *The Psychology of Learning and Motivation*, Vol. 22 (pp. 193–225). New York: Academic Press.

Hasher, L., Zacks, R.T. & May, C.P. (1999). Inhibitory control, circadian arousal, and age. In D. Gopher & A. Koriat (eds), *Attention and Performance XVII: Cognitive Regulation of Performance: Interaction of Theory and Application* (pp. 653–675). Cambridge, MA: MIT Press.

Hashtroudi, S., Chrosniak, L.D. & Schwartz, B.L. (1991). Effects of aging on priming and skill learning. *Psychology & Aging*, **6**, 605–615.

Hashtroudi, S., Johnson, M.K., Vnek, N. & Ferguson, S.A. (1994). Aging and the effects of affective and factual focus on source monitoring and recall. *Psychology & Aging*, **9**, 160–170.

Hay, J.F. & Jacoby, L.L. (1999). Separating habit and recollection in young and older adults: effects of elaborative processing and distinctiveness. *Psychology & Aging*, **14**, 122–134.

Heller, R.B., Dobbs, A.R. & Rule, B.G. (1992). Age differences in communication: evidence from an on-line video description task. Paper presented at the 4th Biennial Cognitive Aging Conference, Atlanta, GA.

Hertzog, C. & Dixon, R.A. (1994). Metacognitive development in adulthood and old age. In J. Metcalfe & A. Shimamura (eds), *Metacognition: Knowing about Knowing* (pp. 227–251). Cambridge, MA: MIT Press.

Hess, T.M. & Slaughter, S.J. (1990). Schematic knowledge influences on memory for scene information in young and older adults. *Developmental Psychology*, **26**, 855–865.

Howard, D.V. & Howard, J.H.J. (1989). Age differences in learning serial patterns: evidence from direct and indirect tests. *Psychology & Aging*, **4**, 364.

Jacoby, L.L., Woloshyn, V. & Kelley, C.M. (1989). Becoming famous without being recognized: unconscious influences of memory produced by dividing attention. *Journal of Experimental Psychology: General*, **118**, 115–125.

Jacoby, L.L. (1999). Ironic effects of repetition: Measuring age-related differences in memory. *Journal of Experimental Psychology: Learning, Memory & Cognition*, **25**, 3–22.

James, L. & Burke, D.M. (2000). Phonological priming effects on word retrieval and tip-of-the-tongue experiences in young and older adults. *Journal of Experimental Psychology: Learning, Memory & Cognition*, **26**, 1378–1391.

Janowsky, J.S., Shimamura, A. & Squire, L.R. (1989). Source memory impairment in patients with frontal lobe lesions. *Neuropsychologia*, **27**, 1043–1056.

Janowsky, J.S., Carper, R.A. & Kaye, J.A. (1996). Asymmetrical memory decline in normal aging and dementia. *Neuropsychologia*, **34**, 527–535.

Jelicic, M. (1995). Aging and performance on implicit memory tasks: a brief review. *International Journal of Neuroscience*, **82**, 155–161.

Jelicic, M., Craik, F.I.M. & Moscovitch, M. (1996). Effects of ageing on different explicit and implicit memory tasks. *European Journal of Cognitive Psychology*, **8**, 225–235.

Johnson, M.K., Hashtroudi, S. & Lindsay, D.S. (1993). Source monitoring. *Psychological Bulletin*, **114**, 3–28.

Kausler, D.H. & Puckett, J.M. (1980). Adult age differences in recognition memory for a nonsemantic attribute. *Experimental Aging Research*, **7**, 117–125.

Kausler, D.H. (1994). *Learning and Memory in Normal Aging*. San Diego, CA: Academic Press.

Kidder, D.P., Park, D.C., Hertzog, C. & Morrell, R.W. (1997). Prospective memory and aging: the effects of working memory and prospective memory task load. *Aging, Neuropsychology and Cognition*, **4**, 93–112.

Kliegl, R., Smith, J. & Baltes, P.B. (1989). Testing-the-limits and the study of adult age differences in cognitive plasticity of a mnemonic skill. *Developmental Psychology*, **25**, 247–256.

Koutstaal, W. & Schacter, D.L. (1997). Gist-based false recognition of pictures in older and younger adults. *Journal of Memory and Language*, **37**, 555–583.

Koutstaal, W., Schacter, D.L., Galluccio, L. & Stofer, K.A. (1999). Reducing gist-based false recognition in older adults: encoding and retrieval manipulations. *Psychology & Aging*, **14**, 220–237.

La Voie, D. & Light, L.L. (1994). Adult age differences in repetition priming: a meta-analysis. *Psychology & Aging*, **9**, 539–553.

Lachman, J.L. & Lachman, R. (1980). Age and the actualization of world knowledge. In L.W. Poon, J.L. Fozard, L.S. Cermak et al. (eds), *New Directions in Memory and Aging: Proceedings of the George A. Talland Memorial Conference* (pp. 285–343). Hillsdale, NJ: Erlbaum.

Lachman, M.E., Weaver, S.L., Bandura, M. et al. (1992). Improving memory and control beliefs through cognitive restructuring and self-generated strategies. *Journals of Gerontology: Psychological Sciences*, **47**, 293–299.

Laver, G.D. & Burke, D.M. (1993). Why do semantic priming effects increase in old age? A meta-analysis. *Psychology & Aging*, **8**, 34–43.

Light, L.L., Kennison, R., Prull, M.W. et al. (1996). One-trial associative priming of nonwords in young and older adults. *Psychology & Aging*, **11**, 417–430.

Light, L.L., La Voie, D., Valencia-Laver, D. et al. (1992). Direct and indirect measures of memory for modality in young and older adults. *Journal of Experimental Psychology: Learning, Memory & Cognition*, **18**, 1284–1297.

Light, L.L. & La Voie, D. (1993). Direct and indirect measures of memory in old age. In P. Graf & M.E.J. Masson (eds), *Implicit Memory: New Directions in Cognition, Development and Neuropsychology* (pp. 207–230). Hillsdale, NJ: Erlbaum.

Light, L.L., La Voie, D. & Kennison, R. (1995). Repetition priming of nonwords in young and older adults. *Journal of Experimental Psychology: Learning, Memory & Cognition*, **21**, 327–346.

Light, L.L. & Singh, R. (1987). Implicit and explicit memory in young and older adults. *Journal of Experimental Psychology: Learning, Memory & Cognition*, **13**, 531–541.

Lindenberger, U., Marsiske, M. & Baltes, P. B. (2000). Memorizing while walking: increase in dual-task costs from young adulthood to old age. *Psychology & Aging*, **15**, 417–436.

Madden, D.J. (1985). Age-related slowing in the retrieval of information from long-term memory. *Journal of Gerontology*, **40**, 208–210.

Madden, D.J. & Greene, H.A. (1987). From retina to response: contrast sensitivity and memory retrieval during visual word recognition. *Experimental Aging Research*, **13**, 15–21.

Mäntylä, T. & Nilsson, L.G. (1997). Remembering to remember in adulthood: a population-based study on aging and prospective memory. *Aging, Neuropsychology and Cognition*, **4**, 81–92.

May, C.P., Hasher, L. & Kane, M.J. (1999). The role of interference in memory span. *Memory & Cognition*, **27**, 759–767.

Maylor, E.A. (1996). Age-related impairment in an event-based prospective-memory task. *Psychology & Aging*, **11**, 74–78.

Maylor, E.A. (1997). Proper name retrieval in old age: converging evidence against disproportionate impairment. *Aging, Neuropsychology and Cognition*, **4**, 211–266.

Mayr, U. & Kliegl, R. (2000). Complex semantic processing in old age: does it stay or does it go? *Psychology & Aging*, **15**, 29–43.

McDermott, K.B. (1996). The persistence of false memories in list recall. *Journal of Memory and Language*, **35**, 212–230.

McDonald-Miszczak, L., Hertzog, C. & Hultsch, D.F. (1995). Stability and accuracy of metamemory in adulthood and aging: a longitudinal analysis. *Psychology & Aging*, **10**, 553–564.

McIntyre, J.S. & Craik, F.I.M. (1987). Age differences in memory for item and source information. *Canadian Journal of Psychology*, **41**, 175–192.

Meinz, E.J. & Salthouse, T.A. (1998). The effects of age and expertise on memory for visually presented music. *Journals of Gerontology: Psychological Sciences*, **53B**, P60–P69.

Mitchell, K.J., Johnson, M.K., Raye, C.L. et al. (2000). Aging and reflective processes of working memory: binding and test load deficits. *Psychology & Aging*, **15**, 527–541.

Morrow, D.G., Leirer, V.O., Altieri, P.A. & Fitzsimmons, C. (1994). When expertise reduces age differences in performance. *Psychology & Aging*, **9**, 134–148.

Multhaup, K.S. (1995). Aging, source, and decision criteria: when false fame errors do and do not occur. *Psychology & Aging*, **10**, 492–497.

Murphy, D.R., Craik, F.I.M., Li, K.Z.H. & Schneider, B.A. (2000). Comparing the effects of aging and background noise of short-term memory performance. *Psychology & Aging*, **15**, 323–334.

Naveh-Benjamin, M. (1987). Coding of spatial location information: an automatic process? *Journal of Experimental Psychology: Learning, Memory & Cognition*, **13**, 595–605.

Naveh-Benjamin, M. & Craik, F.I.M. (1995). Memory for context and its use in item memory: comparisons of younger and older persons. *Psychology & Aging*, **10**, 492–497.

Naveh-Benjamin, M. (2000). Adult age differences in memory performance: tests of an associative deficit hypothesis. *Journal of Experimental Psychology: Learning, Memory & Cognition*, **26**, 1170–1187.

Neely, A.S. & Bäckman, L. (1993). Long-term maintenance of gains from memory training in older adults: two 3-year follow-up studies. *Journals of Gerontology: Psychological Sciences*, **48**, 233–237.

Newman, M.C. & Kaszniak, A.W. (2000). Spatial memory and aging: performance on a human analog of the Morris water maze. *Aging, Neuropsychology and Cognition*, **7**, 86–93.

Norman, K.A. & Schacter, D.L. (1998). False recognition in younger and older adults: exploring the characteristics of illusory memories. *Memory & Cognition*, **25**, 838–848.

Nyberg, L., Nilsson L.-G., Olofsson, U. & Bäckman, L. (1997). Effects of division of attention during encoding and retrieval on age differences in episodic memory. *Experimental Aging Research*, **23**, 137–143.

Park, D.C. & Puglisi, J.T. (1985). Older adults' memory for the colors of pictures and words. *Journal of Gerontology*, **40**, 198–204.

Park, D.C., Cherry, K.E., Smith, A.D. & Lafronza, V.N. (1990). Effects of distinctive context on memory for objects and their locations in young and elderly adults. *Psychology & Aging*, **5**, 250–255.

Park, D.C., Hertzog, C., Kidder, D.P. et al. (1997). Effect of age on event-based and time-based prospective memory. *Psychology & Aging*, **12**, 314–327.

Park, D.C. (2000). The basic mechanisms accounting for age-related decline in cognitive function. In D.C. Park & N. Schwarz (eds), *Cognitive Aging: A Primer* (pp. 3–21). Philadelphia, PA: Psychology Press/Taylor & Francis.

Parkin, A.J. & Walter, B.M. (1992). Recollective experience, normal aging, and frontal dysfunction. *Psychology & Aging*, **7**, 290–298.

Perlmutter, M., Metzger, R., Miller, K. & Nezworski, T. (1980). Memory of historical events. *Experimental Aging Research*, **6**, 60.

Rabbitt, P. (1993). Does it all go together when it goes? The nineteenth Bartlett Memorial Lecture. *Quarterly Journal of Experimental Psychology*, **46A**, 385–434.

Radvansky, G.A. (1999). Aging, memory, and comprehension. *Current Directions in Psychological Science*, **8**, 49–53.

Rahhal, T.A., Hasher, L. & Colcombe, S.J. (2001). Instructional manipulations and age differences in memory: now you see them, now you don't. *Psychology & Aging*, **16**, 697–706.

Rahhal, T.A., May, C.P. & Hasher, L. (2002). Truth and character: sources that older adults can remember. *Psychological Science*, **13**, 101–105.

Rankin, J.L. & Kausler, D.H. (1979). Adult age differences in false recognition. *Journal of Gerontology*, **34**, 58–65.

Rendell, P.G. & Craik, F.I.M. (2000). Virtual week and actual week: age-related differences in prospective memory. *Applied Cognitive Psychology*, **14**, S43–S62.

Rendell, P.G. & Thomson, D.M. (1999). Aging and prospective memory: differences between naturalistic and laboratory tasks. *Journal of Gerontology: Psychological Sciences*, **54B**, 256–269.

Roediger, H.L. III & McDermott, K.B. (1993). Implicit memory in normal human subjects. In F. Boller & J. Grafman (eds), *Handbook of Neuropsychology*, Volume 8 (pp. 63–131). Amsterdam: Elsevier.

Rubin, D.C., Wetzler, S.E. & Nebes, R.D. (1986). Autobiographical memory across the adult life-span. In D.C. Rubin (ed.), *Autobiographical Memory* (pp. 202–221). Cambridge: Cambridge University Press.

Rubin, D.C. & Schulkind, M.D. (1997a). The distribution of autobiographical memories across the lifespan. *Memory & Cognition*, **25**, 859–866.

Rubin, D.C. & Schulkind, M.D. (1997b). Properties of word cues for autobiographical memory. *Psychological Reports*, **81**, 47–50.

Ruch, F.L. (1934). The differential effects of age upon human learning. *Journal of General Psychology* **11**, 286.

Rutledge, P.C., Hancock, R.A. & Walker, L. (1997). Effects of retention interval length on young and elderly adults' memory for spatial information. *Experimental Aging Research*, **23**, 163–177.

Salthouse, T.A. (1991). *Theoretical Perspectives on Cognitive Aging*. Hillsdale, NJ: Erlbaum.

Salthouse, T.A. (1996). General and specific speed mediation of adult age differences in memory. *Journals of Gerontology: Series B: Psychological Sciences and Social Sciences*, **51B**, P30–P42.

Schacter, D.L., Kaszniak, A.W., Kihlstrom, J.F. & Valdiserri, M. (1991). The relation between source memory and aging. *Psychology & Aging*, **6**, 559–568.

Schacter, D.L., Osowiecki, D., Kaszniak, A.W. et al. (1994). Source memory: extending the boundaries of age-related deficits. *Psychology & Aging*, **9**, 81–89.

Schacter, D.L., Koutstaal, W. & Norman, K.A. (1997a). False memories and aging. *Trends in Cognitive Science*, **1**, 229–236.

Schacter, D.L., Koutstaal, W., Johnson, M.K. et al. (1997b). False recollection induced by photographs: a comparison of older and younger adults. *Psychology & Aging*, **12**, 203–215.

Schacter, D.L., Verfaellie, M., Anes, M.D. & Racine, C. (1998). When true recognition suppresses false recognition: evidence from amnesic patients. *Cognitive Neuroscience*, **10**, 668–679.

Schonfield, D. & Robertson, B.A. (1966). Memory storage and aging. *Canadian Journal of Psychology*, **20**, 228–236.

Sharps, M.J. (1991). Spatial memory of young and old adults: category structure of stimulus sets. *Psychology & Aging*, **6**, 312.

Sharps, M.J. (1998). Age-related change in visual information processing: toward a unified theory of aging and visual memory. *Current Psychology: Developmental, Learning, Personality, Social*, **16**, 284–307.

Smith, A.D. (1975). Partial learning and recognition memory in the aged. *International Journal of Aging & Human Development*, **6**, 359–365.

Smith, A.D., Park, D.C., Earles, J.L.K. & Whiting, W.L.I. (1998). Age differences in context integration in memory. *Psychology & Aging*, **13**, 21–28.

Spencer, W.D. & Raz, N. (1995). Differential effects of aging on memory for content and context: a meta-analysis. *Psychology & Aging*, **10**, 527–539.

Stuss, D.T., Craik, F.I.M., Sayer, L. et al. (1996). Comparison of older people and patients with frontal lesions: evidence from word list learning. *Psychology & Aging*, **11**, 387–395.

Taylor, J.L., Miller, T.P. & Tinklenberg, J.R. (1992). Correlates of memory decline: a 4-year longitudinal study of older adults with memory complaints. *Psychology & Aging*, **7**, 185–193.

Tun, P.A., Wingfield, A., Rosen, M.J. & Blanchard, L. (1998). Older adults show greater susceptibility to false memory than young adults: temporal characteristics of false recognition. *Psychology & Aging*, **13**, 230–241.

Ulatowski, H.K., Hayashi, M.M., Cannito, M.P. & Flemming, S.G. (1986). Disruption of reference in aging. *Brain and Language*, **28**, 24–41.

Uttl, B. & Graf, P. (1993). Episodic spatial memory in adulthood. *Psychology & Aging*, **8**, 257–273.

Vakil, E., Melamed, M.D. & Even, N. (1996). Direct and indirect measures of contextual information: older vs. young adult subjects. *Aging, Neuropsychology and Cognition*, **3**, 30–36.

Verhaeghen, P., Marcoen, A. & Goossens, L. (1992). Improving memory performance in the aged through mnemonic training: a meta-analytic study. *Psychology & Aging*, **8**, 176–186.

Verhaeghen, P., Marcoen, A. & Gossens, L. (1993). Facts and fiction about memory aging: a quantitative integration of research findings. *Journals of Gerontology*, **48**, P157–P171.

Verhaeghen, P. (1999). The effects of age-related slowing and working memory on asymptotic recognition performance. *Aging, Neuropsychology and Cognition*, **6**, 201–213.

Waldfogel, S. (1948). The frequency and affective character of childhood memories. *Psychological Monographs: General and Applied*, **62** (291).

Watson, J.M., Balota, D.A. & Sergent-Marshall, S.D. (2001). Semantic, phonological, and hybrid veridical and false memories in healthy older adults and in dementia of the Alzheimer's type (submitted for publication).

Welch, D.C. & West, R.L. (1995). Self-efficacy and mastery: its application to issues of environmental control, cognition, and aging. *Developmental Review*, **15**, 150–171.

Welford, A.T. (1958). *Ageing and Human Skill*. London: Oxford University Press.

Welford, A.T. (1985). Changes of performance with age: an overview. In N. Charness (ed.), *Aging and Human Performance* (pp. 333–369). Chichester: Wiley.

West, R.L. (1996). An application of prefrontal cortex function theory to cognitive aging. *Psychological Bulletin*, **120**, 272–292.

West, R. & Craik, F.I.M. (1999). Age-related decline in prospective memory: the roles of cue accessibility and cue sensitivity. *Psychology and Aging*, **14**, 264–272.

Whiting, W.L.I. & Smith, A.D. (1997). Differential age-related processing limitations in recall and recognition tasks. *Psychology & Aging*, **12**, 216–224.

Wilkniss, S.M., Jones, M.G., Korol, D.L. & Gold, P.E. (1997). Age-related differences in an ecologically based study of route learning. *Psychology & Aging*, **12**, 372–375.

Willingham, D.B. (1998). Implicit learning and motor skill learning in older subjects: an extension of the processing speed theory. In M.A. Stadler & P.A. Frensch (eds), *Handbook of Implicit Learning* (pp. 573–594). Thousand Oaks, CA: Sage.

Willingham, D.B. & Winter, E. (1995). Comparison of motor skill learning in elderly and young human subjects. *Society for Neuroscience Abstracts*, **21**, 1440.

Wingfield, A., Lindfield, K.C. & Kahana, M.J. (1998). Adult age differences in the temporal characteristics of category free recall. *Psychology & Aging*, **13**, 256–266.

Wingfield, A. (2000). Speech perception and the comprehension of spoken language in adult aging. In D. C. Park & N. Schwarz (eds), *Cognitive Aging: A Primer* (pp. 175–195). Philadelphia, PA: Psychology Press/Taylor & Francis.

Wishart, L.R. & Lee, T.D. (1997). Effects of aging and reduced relative frequency of knowledge of results on learning a motor skill. *Perceptual and Motor Skills*, **84**, 1107–1122.

Wright, B.M. & Payne, R.B. (1985). Effects of aging on sex differences in psychomotor reminiscence and tracking proficiency. *Journal of Gerontology*, **40**, 184.

Zacks, R.T., Hasher, L. & Li, K.Z.H. (2000). Human memory. In F.I.M. Craik & T.A. Salthouse (eds.), *The Handbook of Aging and Cognition* (pp. 293–357). Mahwah, NJ: Erlbaum.

Zelinski, E.M. & Light, L.L. (1988). Young and older adults' use of context in spatial memory. *Psychology & Aging*, **3**, 99–101.

Zelinski, E.M., Gilewski, M.J. & Schaie, K.W. (1993). Individual differences in cross-sectional and 3-year longitudinal memory performance across the adult life span. *Psychology & Aging*, **8**, 176–186.

Zelinski, E.M. & Burnight, K.P. (1997). Sixteen-year longitudinal and time lag changes in memory and cognition in older adults. *Psychology & Aging*, **12**, 503–513.

CHAPTER 26

The Memory Deficit in Alzheimer's Disease

James T. Becker

and

Amy A. Overman

Western Psychiatric Institute and Clinic, University of Pittsburgh, PA, USA

Patients diagnosed with Alzheimer's disease (AD) suffer from a devastating and progressive loss of memory (APA, 1987; McKhann et al., 1984). At the earliest stages of the illness, the patient may forget day-to-day events, misplace money or car keys, fail to pay bills on time, or even to remember the day of the week, all of which significantly affects their daily lives. The failure to establish and retrieve these personally relevant, context-dependent memories—so-called *episodic* memories (Tulving, 1972)—is one of the hallmarks of AD. Although this loss of episodic memories is common among progressive dementias of the elderly, it is by no means the only memory dysfunction suffered by these patients. Perhaps equally important in terms of functional adaptation is the loss of what Tulving referred to as *semantic* memory—the lexicon of facts, words, concepts and ideas that form the basis of our world knowledge and language. Defects in the retrieval of semantic memories can affect not only communication (both expressive and receptive) but also the patient's sense of self.

Episodic memory is the result of the encoding, storage and retrieval of temporally and spatially defined events, and the temporal and spatial relationships among them (Tulving, 1984). The study of these kinds of engrams has been, and probably will remain, the focus of most research on memory (Tulving, 1972) and memory disorders. By contrast, semantic memory is that information necessary for language, a "mental thesaurus" including not only lexical information (i.e. word meaning and concepts) but also facts and general world knowledge. Although Tulving (1987) assumed that episodic and semantic memory are functionally independent systems, others suggest that while these concepts are useful heuristic devices, the evidence that they are independent functional systems is less compelling (Baddeley, 1986; Baddeley et al., 1986; Squire, 1992; Squire & Zola-Morgan, 1991). It is now clear from a variety of neuropsychological studies that these systems interact a great deal, especially at the encoding and retrieval stages. Nevertheless, for the sake of this discussion, we assume that these are functionally distinct systems, and that their dysfunction in AD results from the breakdown of anatomically independent systems.

There is, however, a third memory system that plays a key role in our understanding of the memory loss in AD—working memory. Unlike other models of memory that were popular in the late 1960s and early 1970s (e.g. Atkinson & Shiffrin, 1968), Baddeley & Hitch (1974) concluded that a system of *active* processors (i.e. a *working* memory, WM) was needed for the encoding and retrieval of information over short delays. Memory is, in their view, a set of multiple, interacting processes and WM has a role in cognition generally, rather than only in "memory" itself (Baddeley, 2000).

At the core of the WM model are two verbal subsystems, and a system dedicated to the processing of nonverbal, imagery-based information. The verbal subsystems, the articulatory loop and phonological input store, are thought of as relatively automatic processors which can thus function without much direct control; the visuospatial scratchpad was thought of as the nonverbal analog of the two verbal systems. Neuropsychological data suggest that these systems are, indeed, interdependent and interactive (Baddeley & Wilson, 1988; Farah et al., 1985; Shallice & Warrington, 1970; Vallar & Baddeley, 1984). However, in addition to these apparently automatic information processors, the model also proposes the existence of a central executive system (CES), similar to the supervisory attentional system of Norman & Shallice (1980), that provides attentional control to WM.

Although the WM system has been successful in accounting for a wide variety of data in cognitive psychology, neuropsychology and cognitive neuroscience, there were a range of phenomena not so easily explained (for review, see Baddeley, 2000). The problems could largely be subsumed under the general notion of the need for a storage system that was intimately associated with WM but was not the phonological loop. Although earlier versions of the model had ascribed some limited capacity storage to the CES, this had been rejected (Baddeley et al., 1999; Baddeley, 1986). Recently, however, Baddeley (2000) has proposed the concept of the *episodic buffer* (EB) to serve as a processor that acts as a kind of intermediary between WM and the component subsystems, and long-term memory (cf. Ericsson & Kintsch, 1995). The EB is thought to integrate information from WM and long-term memory, but is of limited capacity. It has a role in binding information from separate cognitive systems (and, it is assumed, different sensory and perceptual representations) into a coherent whole. The CES plays an important role in this binding process, but needs the EB to maintain such complex representations. Thus, the EB is also accessible to the CES, and the CES can affect the content of the store by attending to a different source of information (either as an external percept or as a representation from one of the subsystems of WM or from long-term memory). This concept of a binding process (and of a neuroanatomical structure needed for the process) is strongly reminiscent of the theories of McClelland and colleagues as they relate to the hippocampus (McClelland, 1998). The EB might therefore be seen not only as a bridge between WM and long-term memory, but also between frontal/parietal systems and the mesial temporal lobe.

Thus, WM has a role not only in the short-term processing and retention of incoming information but also in the longer-term memory processes. It may very well then serve, to some extent, as a link between the more permanent episodic memories and semantic memory. Thus, each of the memory systems interacts with the other, and their breakdown results in the characteristic memory loss of AD. By understanding the pattern of cognitive dysfunction and the neuroanatomical abnormalities that lead to them, we will have a better understanding of the neuropsychology of AD.

THE MEMORY DEFICIT IN ALZHEIMER'S DISEASE

Working Memory in AD

The verbal subsystems of working memory appear to function normally in AD patients. Although performance is clearly poorer than normal, the qualitative aspects of performance suggest that the same factors that influence the performance of healthy subjects also influence that of AD patients. Thus, the phonological store and articulatory loop appear intact in AD patients (Morris, 1986; Morris & Baddeley, 1988). The CES, by contrast, does *not* appear to function normally in AD patients, especially when their performance is compared with that of old and young normal control subjects on concurrent tasks (Baddeley et al., 1986). The subjects were required first to demonstrate a stable level of performance on a manual tracking task and a digit span task. After having established the baseline performance, the subjects were then required to perform the two tasks concurrently. The older control subjects were no less competent than the younger controls at combining the two tools. By contrast, the AD patients were dramatically impaired. Their performance on both the tracking and repetition tasks fell significantly, and the authors interpreted these data to suggest that the AD patients were suffering from a CES defect. (In practice, many although not all patients will trade off their performance on one of the tasks to "protect" the performance of the other (A.D. Baddeley, personal communication)). However, when the executive defect is sufficiently severe, this sort of trade-off does not occur and the patient seems at a loss as to how to proceed (J.T. Becker, unpublished observation).

Based on these data and the previous suggestions by Morris & Kopelman (1986), we tested the hypothesis that AD patients suffer from two independent syndromes, an "amnesic syndrome", identical to that seen in patients with focal amnesic syndromes, and a "dysexecutive syndrome", resulting from a defective CES (Becker et al., 1988, 1992a). We argued, on the basis of the pattern of impairment in AD patients, that we should be able to identify individual patients with "focal" amnesic and dysexecutive syndromes. We analyzed the performance of 194 AD patients on measures of verbal fluency (Benton 1968; Benton et al., 1983), verbal similarities (Wechsler, 1945), card sorting (Weigl, 1927) and letter cancellation (Diller et al., 1979) relative to their performance on secondary episodic memory tasks (paired-associate learning and free recall). We were able to identify eight patients with dysexecutive syndromes and 24 with amnesic syndromes (Becker et al., 1992a), confirming an observation that this functional dissociation is possible (Becker, 1988). Baddeley et al. (1991) independently identified patients with relatively focal impairments in memory or executive function. These studies also demonstrated that these dissociations were not merely the result of the random assortment of symptoms, but rather followed the predictions of the two-component model. However, Baddeley et al. (1991) also found other dissociations, and certainly careful neuropsychological assessment can reveal a variety of such differential patterns of impairment (e.g. Williams et al., 1996; see also discussion of other such groups, below).

Episodic Memory in Alzheimer's Disease

The earliest symptoms of AD include an impairment in episodic memory (Huff et al., 1987; Kaszniak, 1988; Kaszniak et al., 1986; Kopelman, 1985b; Welsh et al., 1992). One influential neuropathological model of the progression of the senile plaques and neurofibrillary tangles in AD has emphasized that early in the disease it is the mesial temporal regions, including the hippocampal formation and related structures, that are most heavily affected (Braak & Braak, 1991). Among patients with mild cognitive impairment (Morris et al., 2001; Petersen et al., 1999) it is hippocampal atrophy that distinguishes these patients from healthy controls (independently of symptoms of memory loss) (Jack et al., 1999, 1997; Johnson et al., 1998), whereas among AD patients the neuropathology has progressed to include perihippocampal temporal neocortex and, to a lesser extent, the parietal lobes (Ouchi et al., 1998; Stout et al., 1999). Indeed, it is likely that a disconnection of these brain regions from associated cortex is responsible for the episodic memory loss (Geula, 1998; Hyman 1984, 1986, 1990).

Functional and structural neuroimaging studies emphasize the association between the integrity of these mesial temporal regions and episodic memory function in AD, e.g. Ouchi et al. (1998) noted both structural and metabolic abnormalities in AD patients relative to controls, and Stout et al. (1999) reported correlations between verbal memory test scores and the volume (i.e. inverse of atrophy) of both the mesial temporal and diencephalic gray matter. In a separate study comparing probable AD with "questionable" AD, Johnson et al. (1998) noted lower cerebral perfusion values (using SPECT imaging) in the hippocampal–amygdaloid area of the probable AD cases. Again, there was a significant association between perfusion values and memory test scores. Furthermore, consistent with other data (Ouchi et al., 1998), these investigators noted decreased perfusion of the temporoparietal region *only* in the probable AD cases, emphasizing the importance of the mesial temporal pathology at the earliest stage of the dementia.

Because of the prominent temporal lobe damage early in AD and the resulting impairment in episodic memory, much attention has focused on this symptom cluster. Indeed, the ability to learn and remember new information is a highly sensitive marker of dementia (Delis et al., 1991; Huff et al., 1987; Kaszniak et al., 1986). In one of the first reports to arise from the Center to Establish a Registry of Alzheimer's Disease, Welsh and associates reported that delayed recall memory testing was a highly accurate method for differentiating mildly demented subjects from normal elderly (Welsh et al., 1991). Indeed, memory measures are consistently better at such case identification than measures of other cognitive functions (Flicker et al., 1991; Morris et al., 1991; Troster et al., 1993).

The episodic memory defect in AD is similar to that of patients with other types of memory disorders, but differs qualitatively from patients with dementia syndromes arising from pathology in subcortical regions (e.g. Huntington's disease, Parkinson's disease, progressive supranuclear palsy, Lewy body dementia). In AD, the extent of the memory deficit is evident from the virtually flat learning curves in any list-learning procedures; the relatively little information that is remembered usually comes from working memory, with little if any information more permanently encoded (e.g. Buschke & Fuld, 1974; Moss et al., 1986; Wilson et al., 1983b), e.g. early in AD the primacy effect in free recall is minimized as less information is transferred into longer-term storage and sensitivity to interference effects increases (Miller, 1971; Pepin & Eslinger, 1989; Wilson et al., 1983b). As the disease progresses, the primacy effect is virtually eliminated and the recency effect is also reduced. Estimates of the *capacity* of primary or working memory in AD patients remain stable even into the moderate stage of severity (i.e. 2.5–3.5 items).

A striking qualitative difference between the memory loss in AD and that seen in other dementias was first documented by Delis et al. (1991). These investigators found that although the overall *quantitative* performance of AD and Huntington's disease (HD) patient subgroups were similar using many standard measures (e.g. delayed recall), there were certain *qualitative* features that could distinguish them. Specifically, the rate of intrusion errors (i.e. reporting a word that was not on the to-be-remembered list) was higher among the AD patients and recognition memory test performance was poorer. The latter measure is particularly important, since recognition memory testing minimizes the retrieval demands of the task and thus it is often interpreted as a more direct measure of memory storage. The reliability and validity of this qualitative analysis has been demonstrated by, among other methods, showing that patients with dementia disorders due to conditions other than AD or HD can be meaningfully classified. Thus, HIV/AIDS patients with impaired California Verbal Learning Test (CVLT) performance are classified as having the HD-like pattern of retrieval failure (Becker et al., 1995), and Salmon et al. (1996) reported the subcortical pattern of performance in patients with Lewy body dementia. It should be noted that while many authors will describe these qualitatively different patterns of memory abnormalities as "cortical" (typical AD) or "subcortical" (as in HD or Parkinson's disease), it is probably more helpful (and at least as accurate) to consider the one pattern to reflect more of an encoding and storage deficit (with less effect on retrieval) as compared with a deficit primarily in memory retrieval (with less effect on encoding and storage). Obviously, these neuropsychological patterns are not "process pure" and neither is the neuropathological substrate of the respective dementia syndromes (Whitehouse, 1986).

In spite of the fact that intrusion errors are relatively common in AD, the specificity of the error type to this disease is not high (Butters et al., 1986a, 1986b; Fuld et al., 1982; Kopelman, 1985a; Kramer et al., 1988), i.e. patients with memory disorders arising from other conditions can also have increased rates of intrusion errors, e.g. AD patients remember few facts and make numerous prior-story and extra-story intrusion errors when recalling a short prose passage (Butters et al., 1986b). However, patients with amnesic Korsakoff's syndrome (KS) also produce intrusion errors, show an increased sensitivity to proactive interference and manifest perseverative errors on a letter fluency test. The parallel performance of AD and KS patients led Butters et al. (1986b) to suggest this was due to an anatomical lesion that was common to both diseases, namely damage to the nucleus basalis of Meynert. Further, in the majority of AD patients, senile plaques and neurofibrillary tangles are found in the mammillary bodies, hypothalamus and dorsomedial nucleus of the thalamus (Grossi et al., 1989), which are structures heavily affected in KS (Mair et al., 1979; Victor et al., 1971). Thus, the overlap in neuropsychological symptoms between AD and KS—in this case, errors of intrusion—are likely due to common disruptions of the circuits responsible for normal memory retrieval processes. These findings thus presaged the neuroimaging studies that showed that subcortical structures—specifically the midline thalamus—are involved in memory processes in an important way in AD (Stout et al., 1999).

One aspect of episodic memory in AD that has received considerable attention has to do with the rate at which information is lost over time, e.g. AD patients were given a recognition memory test for photographs and their performance was compared to that of normal controls immediately after presentation of the list (Kopelman, 1985a). The exposure to the pictures had been adjusted (i.e. lengthened) so that the AD patients performed as well as the controls at the short interval (i.e. 5 min), and their recognition memory was re-evaluated up to 24 h later. Under these conditions, the rate of decay of information from long-term memory was normal. In a separate study, we examined the ability of patients to remember a short 18 item story and a modified 24 item Rey–Osterreith complex figure (Becker et al., 1987). The rate of decay of information from immediate to delayed recall did not differ between the patients and controls; i.e. they did not have an abnormally rapid rate of forgetting (Becker et al., 1987). However, the AD patients did lose significantly more information between the figure copy and immediate recall conditions, suggesting a deficit in the encoding of the stimulus. This would be consistent with Kopelman's suggestion that any accelerated forgetting in AD occurs very soon after stimulus presentation (i.e. 2–3 s) and that the rate of loss is normal thereafter (Greene et al., 1996; Kopelman, 1985a, 1989; cf. Christensen et al., Owen, 1998).

At least some of the difficulty that AD patients have with long-term episodic memory is due to processing defects earlier in the chain of events, and several lines of evidence support this conclusion. Unlike control subjects, AD patients' secondary memory is significantly correlated with their primary memory capacity (Kramer et al., 1989; Wilson et al., 1983b), i.e. the ability (or inability) of the patients to maintain information in primary memory limits their performance on the secondary memory component of the task. Morris (1986) and Morris & Kopelman (1986) reached a similar conclusion, that AD patients suffer from a defect in the ability to transfer information from primary memory into secondary memory, due at least in part to an abnormally rapid rate of decay from primary memory. Greene et al. (1996) assessed episodic memory in 33 AD patients using a variety of measures, including recall of a prose passage, word list learning, and the Doors and People test. Detailed data analysis revealed that defects in primary memory played a substantial role in the AD patient's difficult time with immediate memory. Furthermore, these investigators did not find that memory was more disrupted using recall, as opposed to recognition procedures, suggesting that the AD patient's difficulties occur due to weaknesses in the initial learning of the items.

Reductions in elaborative stimulus encoding by AD patients severely limits their recall of newly learned information. Granholm & Butters (1988) presented subjects with associative cues during encoding and retrieval of word lists. Unlike HD patients and normal controls, AD patients only benefited from the use of strong associative cues at the time of recall (and not at input), suggesting not only that the patients failed to encode and/or utilize the semantic association of the to-be-remembered words and the cue words, but that when they did appear to use these links, it was based almost exclusively on free associations with cue words. Several reports of performance on verbal recognition memory tasks also support the hypothesis that poor initial encoding and the severity of language impairment may account for some of the deficit in verbal memory in AD patients (Kaszniak et al., 1986; Wilson et al., 1983a, 1983b). These findings indicate that impairments in semantic memory limit the verbal encoding and make a significant contribution to the word recognition impairment. By contrast, face recognition performance seemed not to be affected by verbal semantic limitations (Wilson et al., 1982). All of these findings are consistent with the growing body of evidence from functional neuroimaging studies about the importance of mesial temporal lobe structures, including the hippocampus, parahippocampal gyrus and fusiform cortex, for the initial encoding of stimulus materials (e.g. Schacter et al., 1999; Wagner et al., 1998; see also Martin & Chao, 2001). Given that it is these structures that are affected early in AD, it is not surprising to find that these encoding defects occur early in AD.

Of particular relevance to understanding the clinical manifestations of the episodic memory loss in AD is the notion of subgroups of patients (Jorm, 1985); these consist of individuals with islands of preserved function in the context of a syndrome that meets the criteria for probable AD. The importance of this type of analysis has been discussed in detail by Martin (1990) and it is important to emphasize that these patterns are not simply the result of random co-occurances of cognitive impairments but that they likely relate to the underlying neuroanatomical disruption caused by the disease. There are specific subgroups of AD patients (Becker, 1988; Becker et al., 1992a, 1992b; Becker & Lopez, 1992; Butters et al., 1996); not only can subgroups of AD patients be defined based on differences in degree of impairment *between* cognitive domains (e.g. visuospatial and language; Becker et al., 1988; Martin, 1987; Martin et al., 1986), but these subgroups exist *within* domains, e.g. memory (Becker et al., 1992b). Thus, a "global" degenerative disease such as AD can have breakdowns in cognition that affect one cognitive domain more than another, and these patterns of breakdown can inform us about the basis of the memory disorder (e.g. Martin et al., 1985).

Of particular interest to this review, because it involves the breakdown of both episodic and semantic memory, was the identification of the "temporal lobe variant" of AD (Butters et al., 1996). These are patients who present for evaluation with complaints of progressive memory loss. Careful neuropsychological examination reveals that memory is impaired: delayed recall of pictures and stories is abnormal. Semantic memory is also affected: visual confrontation naming and word fluency are reduced. However, other cognitive functions are either normal (e.g. visuospatial) or only mildly affected (e.g. executive functions). Thus, temporal lobe functions are prominently affected, but cognitive functions normally localized outside of the temporal lobes are not. What is important about these patients is that their rate of decline over time is very slow. Families typically describe changes over a matter of 3–5 years, rather than the more typical 12–18 months.

These findings of subgroups of AD patients motivated a novel statistical analysis of the neuropsychological test performances of 180 AD patients and 1010 normal elderly subjects (Salthouse & Becker, 1998). The purpose of that study was to determine whether the cognitive dysfunction seen in AD was the additive effect of several independent domain-specific impairments (as would be predicted by the subgroup analyses), or whether there was a single core element that could account for the variability in patterns of impairment. The analysis technique, called single common factor analysis (SCFA), essentially determined what all of the neuropsychological tests had in common and then, after controlling for this common factor, determined the relationship between each test variable and group (i.e. patient or control). Because all of the variables had moderate-to-high loadings on the common factor, this indicated that they shared substantial variance and were not independent. However, a subset of the tests also had a substantial independent relationship, and these tests shared the feature that they all involved episodic memory. These findings not only emphasize the importance of the episodic memory loss in AD as a core component of the syndrome, but also that once the common factor is accounted for, there are no further effects of importance on 75% of the test variables. The results of this analysis do not invalidate the subgroup analyses reported above but do suggest that, for the majority of patients, there is but a single common factor that plays a critical role in the cognitive expression of the disease.

Functional Neuroimaging Studies of Episodic Memory in Alzheimer's Disease

Over the past decade, the use of functional neuroimaging techniques as tools for the neuropsychological evaluation of cognitive dysfunction has flourished. Although the field is still in its infancy, functional neuroimaging has greatly aided our understanding of disordered cognition. In one series of studies (Becker et al., 1994b, 1996; Herbster et al., 1996), we documented the changes in brain regional activation that occurs in AD while the patients were performing a verbal free recall task. Although crude by current technological standards (due to improvement in both PET scanning technology and data analysis procedures) these studies pointed out that, at least early in the disease, AD patients had a normal pattern of brain regional activity during verbal free recall. Indeed, the patients had what appeared to be a paradoxical hyperactivation of the functional network during recall of three- and eight-word lists of words. Initially, we interpreted this finding as a compensatory reallocation of resources to allow the patients the opportunity to perform the task regardless of the level of performance. However, the development of latent structure statistical analysis techniques led us to other conclusions.

In order to understand the relationships *among* the brain regions activated during the performance of memory tasks, and whether there were differences in these relationships between AD patients and normal elderly subjects, we examined the functional connectivity among brain regions (Friston, 1997; Friston & Frith, 1995; Friston et al., 1993; Herbster et al., 1996). Whereas *t*-tests are useful for determining regional activity that occurs above a given threshold (*functional specialization*), a network of functionally associated regions may exist within the dataset that can be revealed by analyses that emphasize *functional integration* (Friston et al., 1993). We used an analysis that focused on the pattern of regional covariation of relative cerebral blood flow, a procedure similar to principal components analysis. We extended this analysis to find the pattern of distributed brain activity that was most prevalent in one subject group and least prevalent in the other (Friston, 1997; Friston & Frith, 1995). The pattern of connectivity that maximally differentiated the AD patients and controls reflected, in general, the memory circuits displayed by the normal controls, i.e. the difference in functional connectivity between the patients and controls on the verbal episodic memory recall tasks is related not to the connections themselves but rather to the extent to which they are expressed. As such, the functional network is normal, but is simply differentially active in the two study groups. Indeed, as we noted previously (Herbster et al., 1996), the patients expressed the matrix *more than* the controls. This finding is important because it suggests that, at least for this episodic memory functional network, the basic structure is intact.

In retrospect, the functional activation that we observed, especially in the eight-word recall condition, was more related to the retrieval aspects of the task than to encoding. In addition, the dorsal parietal and prefrontal circuit that was identified seems to suggest a high degree of attentional load, even though the task was auditory (and that loop is usually associated with visual attention) (Posner & Petersen, 1990). Thus, further research is needed to determine the nature and extent of any compensatory response in AD patients using cognitive probes that more carefully dissect the memory circuits.

Semantic Memory Loss in AD

The performance of AD patients on tests that require semantic memory, such as visual confrontation naming or word generation, is often severely impaired (Hodges et al., 1990), whereas the performance of patients with some other dementias, e.g. HD, is relatively normal (Butters et al., 1988). Thus, consistent with the growing body of neuropsychological, behavioral, neurological and neuroimaging data, the loss of semantic knowledge may be peculiar to those pathological states that affect the functional integrity of the temporal lobes (Hodges & Patterson, 1995; Hodges et al., 1999). This position is supported by the descriptions of *semantic dementia*, a condition occurring in the context of a progressive aphasia and marked by a profound loss of semantic knowledge (e.g. Graham et al., 1997a, 1997b; Hodges et al., 1992; Neary et al., 1993; Snowden et al., 1992). Structural and functional imaging studies demonstrate that these conditions are associated with severe disruption of the function of the language-dominant temporal lobe (Mummery et al., 1999, 2000).

Early in the course of their dementia, AD patients have difficulty performing many tests that rely on semantic memory (Nebes & Brady, 1989); even "minimally" impaired patients have significant impairments in category fluency, confrontation naming, naming to description, and answering questions about semantic features (Hodges & Patterson, 1995) (although some mild AD patients can have normal semantic memory, cf. Becker et al., 1988; Martin et al., 1986). However, it is still not clear whether these difficulties reflect a disruption of the patients' semantic knowledge (i.e. an actual loss of information), a disruption of their ability to access or use that knowledge base, or both. As noted by Perry & Hodges (1996), there is considerable variability in the nature and extent of semantic memory dysfunction, especially early in the course of the dementia (Hodges & Patterson, 1995), and there is evidence to support models that differentially emphasize storage loss, retrieval defects and alterations in the basic structure of semantic memory (Bayles et al., 1991; Chan et al., 1995b; Chertkow & Bub, 1990).

Although early in AD visual confrontation naming can be relatively preserved, as the disorder progresses patients have more and more difficulty with this function (Becker et al., 1994a, 1988). Typically, the use of semantic cues is not helpful to AD patients, whereas a phonemic cue can elicit the correct response (at least early in the disease course). In terms of word generation, category fluency (e.g. animals) is typically more impaired than letter fluency (e.g. CFL) early in the disease, but with increasing severity this distinction is blurred. If a patient is asked about subcategories (e.g. birds or dogs) he/she can also have a significant defect, even when the superordinate (i.e. animals) was not appreciably affected. Even with a general category cue, e.g. the Supermarket Task from the Mattis (1976) dementia rating scale, it is possible to show that there are fewer exemplars from subcategories (e.g. meat, vegetables/fruits; Martin & Fedio, 1983). By contrast, patients with frontal lobe lesions are quantitatively similar to AD patients (i.e. same total number of words generated), but they achieve this by sampling from fewer subcategories and generating more words from each. This finding, as well as the *relative* sparing of letter (vs. category) fluency in AD, emphasizes the importance of the temporal lobe pathology (as opposed to any frontal system dysfunction) in explaining the nature of the semantic memory loss.

It is reasonable to ask whether the poor performance of AD patients on a given semantic memory task is the result of an actual semantic memory deficit, or stems from a problem in more general information-processing operations; e.g. is the visual naming defect that is so characteristic of AD patients due to knowledge lost about the semantic features that define different lexical referents (Bayles & Tomoeda, 1983), or is it because AD patients cannot carry out the needed perceptual analysis of the object (Kirshner et al., 1984), or cannot access the name (Barker & Lawson, 1968)? Although the first of these potential mechanisms would involve a deficit in semantic knowledge, the latter two would represent situations in which a failure on a "semantic" test would result from limitations in *non*semantic cognitive operations necessary for the appropriate use of an intact semantic knowledge base.

A number of investigators have suggested that AD patients' knowledge of concept meaning is impaired (Chertkow et al., 1989; Huff et al., 1986; Martin & Fedio, 1983; Troster et al., 1989). They claim that although AD patients usually retain knowledge of the semantic category to which a concept belongs, they lose information about its specific attributes. In confrontation naming, AD patients often misname objects, using their category names or the names of other items from the same category. They also have a great deal of difficulty recognizing the name of a pictured object in a multiple-choice task when the distractors are drawn from the same category as the target object, but not when they are drawn from other categories (Chertkow et al., 1989; Huff et al., 1986). This pattern of performance may reflect a preservation of category information, coupled with a loss of those specific attributes that make it possible to differentiate semantically related objects—hence the confusion with other items from the same category. Perhaps the most impressive evidence for a loss of specific attribute information in AD comes from several studies that have asked subjects direct questions about an item's category membership and its attributes. AD patients can accurately answer a question about an object's category but have a great deal of difficulty in answering questions about its physical features or functions (Martin & Fedio, 1983). Even when given multiple-choice questions (e.g. "Do you use this object to lift things or to cut things?"), AD patients are much more impaired on questions about an object's attributes than on questions about its category membership (Chertkow et al., 1989).

Other evidence suggests that AD patients *retain* their knowledge of the semantic attributes of concepts. Demented patients can be quite accurate (95% correct) when asked to recognize features that were attributes of a target (Grober et al., 1985). Nebes & Brady (1988) used a task in which they measured the time it took normal elderly and AD patients to decide whether a given stimulus word was related to a target word. If AD patients have actually lost knowledge of the features and functions of objects, or find such knowledge differentially difficult to access, then they should be slower and less accurate in making decisions about a target's features and actions than about its category membership and associations. However, the difference in response time between AD patients and the normal elderly was, if anything, smaller for decisions about features and actions than for decisions about categories and associates. The AD patients made very few errors, and there was no evidence that decisions about a concept's action or feature were significantly more difficult. These results, unlike others (Chertkow et al., 1989; Martin & Fedio, 1983), suggest that AD patients are aware of the relationship between concepts and their attributes.

Innovative work by Chan and colleagues, however, has shown that the structure of the semantic networks is perturbed in AD. These studies used a variety of latent structure techniques, including multidimensional scaling, to analyze the organization of information in semantic memory, e.g. using the method of triads (and a multidimensional scaling analysis), they compared and contrasted the semantic organization of the concept of "animal" in AD patients and elderly controls (Chan et al., 1993a, 1993b, 1995a). AD patients and normal controls used the same dimensions to distinguish among the animals (i.e. domestic, predatory, size); however, the patients tended to use the more concrete concept of physical size in their categorization, whereas the controls primarily used the more abstract concept of domestication. In addition, relationships among the stimuli along the multidimensional axes also differed between the patients and controls.

How are we to reconcile these contradictory conclusions about concept knowledge in AD? Nebes (1992) has argued that one possible source for this discrepancy lies in the differing cognitive demands imposed by the experimental tasks. When AD patients are asked a direct question about a concept's attributes, they perform poorly; by contrast, if they are asked merely to decide whether a concept and one of its attributes are related, they do very well. Therefore, what appears in some studies to be an impairment in the structure of semantic memory in AD (i.e. a loss of knowledge of concept attributes or their relative importance) may instead reflect a failure of more general-purpose cognitive operations, such as those involved in intentionally accessing and evaluating information (e.g. response search and response selection). If the need for these cognitive operations is minimized, AD patients may show a pattern of performance similar to that seen in normal control subjects. Thus, before we attribute poor semantic memory in AD to an actual semantic deficit, it is important to be sure that performance is not limited by a nonsemantic processing impairment.

In their longitudinal study of semantic memory in AD, Hodges & Patterson tested knowledge about specific items using a variety of different techniques in different test modalities. While not minimizing the nonsemantic processing demands of individual tasks, consistent findings across several tasks would point toward a degradation of semantic knowledge. Indeed, their data demonstrate a high reliability between tests (and within items), e.g. if an AD patient was unable to spontaneously name an object, he/she was also unlikely, to be able to describe it or to pick it out using a multiple choice format (Hodges et al., 1996; Lambon-Ralph et al., 1997).

In sum, there is evidence for a multicomponent breakdown in semantic memory in AD. This may reflect, in part, the multifactorial aspects of semantic memory, and may also reflect the fact that various aspects of semantic memory function are subsumed in different neuroanatomical regions. The heterogeneity of symptoms and symptom clusters may reflect both cognitive and pathological variation.

Neuroimaging Studies of Semantic Memory in AD

There have been relatively few studies of the functional neuroanatomical basis of semantic memory function and dysfunction in AD patients. Indeed, there have been relatively few published functional neuroimaging studies involving AD patients at all (e.g. Becker et al., 1996; Herbster et al., 1996; Hirono et al., 2001; Kessler et al., 1991, 1996; Rombouts et al., 2000) and fewer that use fMRI to study semantic memory in AD (Saykin et al., 1999b; cf. Mummery et al., 1999). However, these data all suggest that there are abnormalities in the functional networks involved in semantic memory retrieval in AD. Saykin et al. (1999a) reported the differences in brain regional activation between AD patients and normal controls when performing two semantic decision tasks relative to a phonological decision task. Although the AD patients were selectively impaired in performing the semantic tasks relative to the phonological task, it was nevertheless possible to obtain meaningful data. Both AD patients and controls activated the left inferior frontal cortex, but the patients had additional activation in the left dorsolateral prefrontal cortex and the superior temporal gyrus. As we had reported earlier for episodic memory tasks (Becker et al., 1996; Herbster et al., 1996), these investigators found that the spatial extent of the activations by the patients were greater than those observed in the controls for their semantic memory task. This finding, coupled with a specific association between right medial prefrontal activation and performance in the patients but not the controls, is further evidence for some form of compensatory response in the AD patients.

One way to examine the pathological locus responsible for a specific cognitive defect in AD is to study structure–function relationships with structural neuroimaging data. In

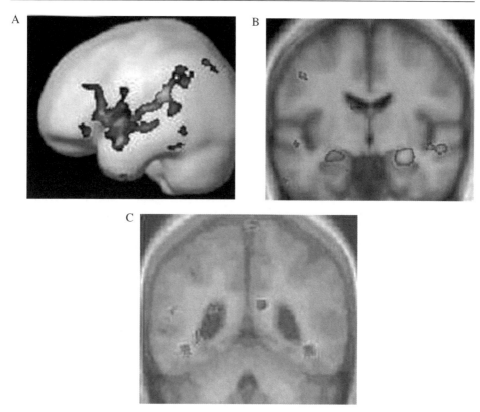

Figure 26.1 Brain structural differences between probable AD patients and normal controls. (A) Cortical atrophy in the left hemisphere, with typical gray matter loss. (B) Coronal plane view showing tissue loss in the inferior temporal lobe and hippocampus. (C) Errors/no errors.

our own studies of the neuroanatomical basis of the semantic memory loss in AD, we have adopted the voxel-based morphometry methods used by Mummery et al. (1999) in their studies of semantic dementia. High-resolution structural MR images are spatially normalized using a nonlinear algorithm and then segmented into gray matter and white matter images (Ashburner & Friston, 1997; Mazziotta et al., 1997). For our studies, the focus is on the grey matter and these images are smoothed (using a 3-D Gaussian filter) and analyzed using a between-group analysis to identify the voxels with significant differences in intensity, reflecting differences in brain volumes (see also Sowell et al., 1999).

Figure 26.1 (top) shows the results of an analysis comparing the brain structural differences between probable AD patients and normal, elderly control subjects (S.B. McGinty, personal communication). The left-hand image shows the cortical atrophy in the language-dominant left hemisphere, with the typical temporoparietal gray matter loss. The right-hand image shows a view in the coronal plane, demonstrating the tissue loss in the inferior temporal lobe and hippocampus.

In the bottom pair of images, we show the results of an analysis of AD patients who were divided into two groups based on their object-naming performance: those who made no naming errors, and those who did make naming errors on the relevant section of the AD Assessment Scale. There were no significant differences between groups in education or on overall cognitive impairment, but the groups did differ significantly on age.

The analysis revealed a significant difference in the gray matter volume of several temporal lobe structures. In particular, Brodmann area 37 in the posterior temporal lobe showed a significant reduction in volume in the AD patients with poor visual naming, compared with patients with good visual naming. In addition, middle inferior regions of the temporal lobe, the fusiform gyrus and parahippocampal gyrus, also had significant differences in density between groups, such that the patients with poor naming had reduced volumes relative to those with good naming.

These structural data are consistent with the existing functional neuroimaging and neuropsychological studies that have demonstrated the critical role of the temporal lobe in the processes needed to execute semantic memory tasks. There is reliable functional activation of the left temporal lobe during object-naming tasks (Martin et al., 1996; Vandenberghe et al., 1996; Zelkowicz et al., 1997), and structural imaging studies have shown that temporal lobe volume is abnormal in AD patients compared with the normal aged (Jernigan et al., 1991; Killiany et al., 1993). Knowing that AD patients have these structural changes not only helps explain the basis of their naming impairment, but also helps understand the functional basis of visual object naming.

The results in this study extend those of Mummery et al. (1999), who found that in semantic dementia the site of significant atrophy was the anterolateral temporal lobe. However, a functional neuroimaging analysis of a semantic task revealed activity in the left posterior inferior temporal gyrus, and they suggested that the decreased functional activation found in these patients was due to lack of input from the atrophied anterior temporal lobe to the posterior inferior temporal gyrus, and not due to atrophy of the posterior inferior temporal gyrus. Our data suggest, therefore, that the anatomical basis for the naming impairment in AD is different from that seen in semantic dementia, which is commonly associated with Pick's disease and other variants of frontotemporal lobe dementia (FTD), i.e. the more posterior temporal regions may be directly involved in the semantic processing of visual objects, and these are directly affected in AD, but only indirectly affected in FTD (by virtue of disruption of upstream connections from the anterior temporal lobe). Thus, while there appears to be a common final pathway to explain the naming defect, the *cause* of that defect differs between diseases.

Analysis of the neuroanatomical abnormalities in patients with language disturbance associated with frontotemporal dementia (Snowden et al., 1992) reveals the different functional loci that can produce impaired processing in dementia, e.g. patient G.C. has a semantic dementia syndrome (Graham et al., 1997a; Hodges et al., 1992), and has been followed by our group for more than 5 years. Figure 26.2 shows the brain regional atrophy (projected onto an average brain image) in G.C. relative to controls (top row of images). What is striking is the significant left temporal lobe atrophy. Specifically, superior and middle temporal cortex are affected, as well as the hippocampus and peri-hippocampal regions. When this is compared with the atrophy seen in AD patients relative to controls (Figure 26.1), the focal nature of the defect in semantic dementia can be appreciated.

Patient S.M., by contrast, has little impairment in semantics *per se*, but rather has significant abnormalities in word retrieval and word production. He is able to perform a variety of tasks that require semantic memory (e.g. the Vocabulary subtest of the Wechsler Adult Intelligence Scale—Revised; Pyramids and Palm Trees (Howard & Patterson, 1992),

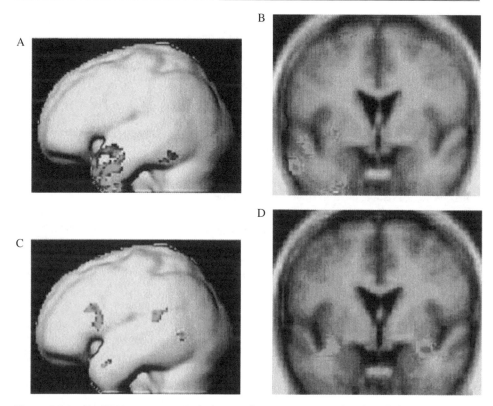

Figure 26.2 (A, B) Neuroanatomical abnormalities in a patient (G.C) with language disturbance associated with frontotemporal dementia, showing brain in regional atrophy. In patient
S.M. (C, D), there are significant abnormalities in word retrieval and word production; the
figures show a small region of atrophy in left frontal cortex near Broca's area, with no significant atrophy in the temporal lobe.

word-picture matching (Kay et al., 1992), but has significant impairments when required to
generate words (e.g. visual naming, fluency tasks). A voxel-based morphometric analysis
of his MRI scan (relative to age- and education-appropriate normal elderly) revealed a small
region of significant atrophy in the left frontal cortex, around Broca's area (see bottom row,
Figure 26.2), with no significant atrophy in the temporal lobe.

The results of these three morphometric analyses allow several conclusions about the
functional basis of the semantic memory loss in AD. First, the inferior temporal lobe, and
perhaps most importantly the parahippocampal gyrus, is critical for the ability to successfully name objects. However, the ability to effectively retrieve the names of objects appears
to be related to atrophy in the frontal cortex, BA44/45. The data further imply, although this
has not been directly tested, that even early in AD there is sufficient atrophy in the frontal
cortex to explain at least part of AD patients' defects in verbal fluency. Finally, as was shown
by G.C., the extent of temporal atrophy can be quite profound, but this nevertheless does
not affect cognitive processes that do not require the extensive memory functions subsumed
by these brain regions.

SUMMARY

Although the cognitive dysfunction associated with AD is often described as generalized, it is perhaps more accurate and meaningful to describe it as multifocal; the development of CNS dysfunction in AD appears to progress such that some cognitive systems are more or less affected than others. Thus, at various points during the progression of the disease, the neuropsychological profile will reflect the relative impairments and sparing of cognitive functions, based on the underlying patterns of neuropathological change. These patterns of impairments should, and do, follow the "natural fracture lines of behavior" (Thomas et al., 1968), reflecting the way in which normal memory processes are organized. By understanding better the nature of the breakdown of these multiple processes, it will be possible to inform the development of rational behavioral and pharmacological treatment and management of AD.

ACKNOWLEDGEMENT

J.T.B. is the recipient of a Research Scientist Development Award (Level II) from the National Institute of Mental Health (MH03177). The authors are grateful to R.D. Nebes for discussion about semantic memory in AD, and to S. Bell McGinty for comments on an earlier version of this manuscript.

REFERENCES

American Psychiatric Association (APA). (1987). *Diagnostic and Statistical Manual of Mental Disorders—Revised (DSM-III-R)*, 3rd (revised) edn. Washington, DC: American Psychiatric Press.

Ashburner, J. & Friston, K.J. (1997). Spatial transformation of images. In R.S.J. Frackowiak, K.J. Friston, C.D. Frith et al. (eds), *Human Brain Function* (pp. 43–58). San Diego, CA: Academic Press.

Atkinson, R.C. & Shiffrin, R.M. (1968). Human memory: a proposed system and its control processes. In K.W. Spence & J.T. Spence (eds), *The Psychology of Learning and Motivation: Advances in Research and Theory*, Vol. 2 (pp. 89–195). New York: Academic Press.

Baddeley, A. (2000). The episodic buffer: a new component of working memory? *Trends in Cognitive Science*, **4**(11), 417–423.

Baddeley, A., Cocchini, G., Della Sala, S. et al. (1999). Working memory and vigilance: evidence from normal aging and Alzheimer's disease. *Brain and Cognition*, **41**(1), 87–108.

Baddeley, A.D. (1986). *Working Memory*. Oxford: Clarendon.

Baddeley, A.D., Bressi, S., Della Salla, S. et al. (1986). Senile dementia and working memory. *Quarterly Journal of Experimental Psychology*, **38A**, 603–618.

Baddeley, A.D., Della Salla, S. & Spinnler, H. (1991). The two-component hypothesis of memory deficit in Alzheimer's disease. *Journal of Clinical and Experimental Neuropsychology*, **13**, 372–380.

Baddeley, A.D. & Hitch, G. (1974). Working memory. In G.H. Bower (ed.), *The Psychology of Learning and Motivation*, Vol. 8 (pp. 47–90). San Diego, CA: Academic Press.

Baddeley, A.D. & Wilson, B.A. (1988). Frontal amnesia and dysexecutive syndrome. *Brain and Cognition*, **1**, 212–230.

Barker, M.G. & Lawson, J.S. (1968). Nominal aphasia in dementia. *British Journal of Psychiatry*, **114**, 1351–1356.

Bayles, K.A. & Tomoeda, C.K. (1983). Confrontation naming in dementia. *Brain and Language*, **19**, 98–114.

Bayles, K.A., Tomoeda, C.K., Kaszniak, A.W. & Trosset, M.W. (1991). Alzheimer's disease effects on semantic memory: loss of structure or impaired processing. *Journal of Cognitive Neurosciences*, **3**, 166–182.

Becker, J.T. (1988). Working memory and secondary memory deficits in Alzheimer's disease. *Journal of Clinical and Experimental Neuropsychology*, **10**, 739–753.

Becker, J.T., Bajulaiye, O. & Smith, C. (1992a). Longitudinal analysis of a two-component model of the memory deficits in Alzheimer's disease. *Psychological Medicine*, **22**, 437–446.

Becker, J.T., Boller, F., Lopez, O.L. et al. (1994a). The natural history of Alzheimer's disease: description of study cohort and accuracy of diagnosis. *Archives of Neurology*, **51**, 585–594.

Becker, J.T., Boller, F., Saxton, J. & McGonigle-Gibson, K. (1987). Normal rates of forgetting of verbal and non-verbal material in Alzheimer's disease. *Cortex*, **23**, 59–72.

Becker, J.T., Caldararo, R., Lopez, O.L. et al. (1995). Qualitative features of the memory deficit associated with HIV infection and AIDS: cross-validation of a discriminant function classification scheme. *Journal of Clinical and Experimental Neuropsychology*, **17**, 134–142.

Becker, J.T., Huff, F.J., Nebes, R.D. et al. (1988). Neuropsychological functioning in Alzheimer's disease: pattern of impairment and rates of progression. *Archives of Neurology*, **45**, 263–268.

Becker, J.T. & Lopez, O.L. (1992). Episodic memory in Alzheimer's disease: breakdown of multiple memory processes. In L. Backman (ed.), *Memory Functioning in Dementia* (pp. 27–44). Amsterdam: North Holland.

Becker, J.T., Lopez, O.L. & Wess, J. (1992b). Material specific memory loss in probable Alzheimer's disease. *Journal of Neurology Neurosurgery & Psychiatry*, **55**, 1177–1181.

Becker, J.T., Mintun, M.A., Aleva, K. et al. (1996). Compensatory reallocation of brain resources supporting verbal episodic memory in Alzheimer's disease. *Neurology*, **46**, 692–700.

Becker, J.T., Mintun, M.A., Diehl, D.J. et al. (1994b). Functional neuroanatomy of verbal free recall: a replication study. *Human Brain Mapping*, **1**, 284–292.

Benton, A.L. (1968). Differential behavioral effects in frontal lobe disease. *Neuropsychologia*, **6**, 53–60.

Benton, A.L., Hamsher, K., Varney, N.R. & Spreen, O. (1983). *Contributions to Neuropsychological Assessment. A Clinical Manual*. New York: Oxford University Press.

Braak, H. & Braak, E. (1991). Neuropathological staging of Alzheimer-related changes. *Acta Neuropathologica*, **82**, 239–259.

Buschke, H. & Fuld, P.A. (1974). Evaluating storage, retention, and retrieval in disoriented memory and learning. *Neurology*, **24**, 1019–1025.

Butters, M.A., Lopez, O.L. & Becker, J.T. (1996). Focal temporal lobe dysfunction in probable Alzheimer's disease predicts a slow rate of cognitive decline. *Neurology*, **46**, 692–700.

Butters, N., Granholm, E.L., Salmon, D.P. et al. (1986a). Episodic and semantic memory: a comparison of amnesic and demented patients. *Journal of Clinical and Experimental Neuropsychology*, **9**, 479–497.

Butters, N., Salmon, D.P., Heindel, W. & Granholm, E. (1988). Episodic, semantic and procedural memory: some comparisons of Alzheimer's and Huntington's disease patients. In R. D. Terry (ed.), *Aging and the Brain* (pp. 63–87). New York: Raven.

Butters, N., Wolfe, J., Granholm, E. & Martone, M. (1986b). An assessment of verbal recall, recognition and fluency abilities in patients with Huntington's disease. *Cortex*, **22**, 11–32.

Chan, A.S., Butters, N., Paulsen, J.S. et al. (1993a). An assessment of the semantic network in patients with Alzheimer's disease. *Journal of Cognitive Neuroscience*, **5**, 254–261.

Chan, A.S., Butters, N., Salmon, D.P. & Johnson, S.A. (1995a). Semantic network abnormality predicts rate of cognitive decline in patients with probable Alzheimer's disease. *Journal of the International Neuropsychological Society*, **1**, 297–303.

Chan, A.S., Butters, N., Salmon, D.P. et al. (1995b). Comparison of the semantic networks in patients with dementia and amnesia. *Neuropsychology*, **9**, 177–186.

Chan, A.S., Butters, N., Salmon, D.P. & McGuire, K.A. (1993b). Dimensionality and clustering in the semantic network of patients with Alzheimer's disease. *Psychology and Aging*, **8**, 411–419.

Chertkow, H. & Bub, D. (1990). Semantic memory loss in dementia of Alzheimer's type. What do various measures measure? *Brain*, **113**(2), 397–417.

Chertkow, H., Bub, D. & Seidenberg, M. (1989). Priming and semantic memory loss in Alzheimer's disease. *Brain and Language*, **36**, 420–446.

Christensen, H., Kopelman, M.D., Stanhope, N. et al. (1998). Rates of forgetting in Alzheimer dementia. *Neuropsychologia*, **36**(6), 546–557.

Delis, D.C., Massman, P.J., Butters, N. et al. (1991). Profiles of demented and amnesic patients on the California Verbal Learning Test: implications for the assessment of memory disorders. *Psychological Assessment: A Journal of Consulting and Clinical Psychology*, **3**, 19–26.

Diller, L., Ben-Yishay, Y., Gerstman, L.J. et al. (1979). *Studies in Cognition and Rehabilitation in Hemiplegia (Rehabilitation Monograph No. 50)*. New York: New York University.

Ericsson, K.A. & Kintsch, W. (1995). Long-term working memory. *Psychological Review*, **102**(2), 211–245.

Farah, M.J., Gazzaniga, M.S., Holtzman, J.D. & Kosslyn, S.M. (1985). A left-hemisphere basis for visual imagery. *Neuropsychologia*, **23**, 115–118.

Flicker, C., Ferris, S.H. & Reisberg, B. (1991). Mild cognitive impairment in the elderly: predictors of dementia. *Neurology*, **41**(7), 1006–1009.

Friston, K.J. (1997). Characterizing distributed functional systems. In R.S.J. Frackowiak, K.J. Friston, C.D. Frith et al. (eds), *Human Brain Function* (pp. 107–126). San Diego, CA: Academic Press.

Friston, K.J. & Frith, C.D. (1995). Schizophrenia: a disconnection syndrome? *Clinical Neuroscience*, **3**, 89–97.

Friston, K.J., Frith, C.D., Liddle, P.F. & Frackowiak, R.S.J. (1993). Functional connectivity: the principal-component analysis of large (PET) data sets. *Journal of Cerebral Blood Flow and Metabolism*, **13**, 5–14.

Fuld, P.A., Katzman, R., Davies, P. & Terry, R.D. (1982). Intrusions as a sign of Alzheimer's dementia: Chemical and pathological verification. *Annals of Neurology*, **11**, 155–159.

Geula, C. (1998). Abnormalities of neural circuitry in Alzheimer's disease: hippocampus and cortical cholinergic innervation. *Neurology*, **51**(suppl 1), S18–S29.

Graham, K.S., Becker, J.T. & Hodges, J.R. (1997a). On the relationship between knowledge and memory for pictures: evidence from the study of patients with semantic dementia and Alzheimer's disease. *Journal of the International Neuropsychological Society*, **3**(6), 534–544.

Graham, K.S., Becker, J.T., Patterson, K. & Hodges, J.R. (1997b). Lost for words: a case of primary progressive aphasia. In A. Parkin (ed.), *Case Studies in the Neuropsychology of Memory* (pp. 83–110). Hove.

Granholm, E. & Butters, N. (1988). Associative encoding and retrieval in Alzheimer's and Huntington's disease. *Brain and Cognition*, **7**, 335–347.

Greene, J.D., Baddeley, A.D. & Hodges, J.R. (1996). Analysis of the episodic memory deficit in early Alzheimer's disease: evidence from the Doors and People Test. *Neuropsychologia*, **34**(6), 537–551.

Grober, E., Buschke, H., Kawas, C. & Fuld, P. (1985). Impaired ranking of semantic attributes in dementia. *Brain and Language*, **26**, 276–286.

Grossi, D., Lopez, O.L. & Martinez, A.J. (1989). The mammillary bodies in Alzheimer's disease. *Acta Neurological Scandinavica*, **80**, 41–45.

Herbster, A.N., Nichols, T., Wiseman, M.B. et al. (1996). Functional connectivity in auditory verbal short-term memory in Alzheimer's disease. *NeuroImage*, **4**, 67–77.

Hirono, N., Mori, E., Ishii, K. et al. (2001). Neuronal substrates for semantic memory: a positron emission tomography study in Alzheimer's disease. *Dementia and Geriatric Cognitive Disorders*, **12**(1), 15–21.

Hodges, J.R. & Patterson, K. (1995). Is semantic memory consistently impaired early in the course of Alzheimer's disease? Neuroanatomical and diagnostic implications. *Neuropsychologia*, **33**, 441–460.

Hodges, J.R., Patterson, K., Garrard, P. (1999). The differentiation of semantic dementia and frontal lobe dementia (temporal and frontal variants of frontotemporal dementia) from early Alzheimer's disease: a comparative neuropsychological study. *Neuropsychology*, **13**, 31–40.

Hodges, J.R., Patterson, K., Graham, N. & Dawson, K. (1996). Naming and knowing in dementia of Alzheimer's type. *Brain and Language*, **54**, 302–325.

Hodges, J.R., Patterson, K., Oxbury, S. & Funnell, E. (1992). Semantic dementia: progressive fluent aphasia with temporal lobe atrophy. *Brain*, **115**, 1783–1806.

Hodges, J. R., Salmon, D.P. & Butters, N. (1990). Differential impairment of semantic and episodic memory in Alzheimer's and Huntington's disease: a controlled prosepective study. *Journal of Neurology Neurosurgery and Psychiatry*, **53**, 1089–1095.

Howard, D. & Patterson, K. (1992). *The Pyramid and Palm Trees Test: A Test of Semantic Access from Words and Pictures*. Bury St Edmunds: Thames Valley Test Company.

Huff, F.J., Becker, J.T., Belle, S. et al. (1987). Cognitive deficits and clinical diagnosis of Alzheimer's. *Neurology*, **37**, 1119–1124.

Huff, J.F., Corkin, S. & Growdon, J.H. (1986). Semantic impairment and anomia in Alzheimer's disease. *Brain and Language*, **28**, 235–249.

Hyman, B.T., Van Hoesen, G.W. & Damasio, A.R. (1984). Alzheimer's disease: cell-specific pathology isolates the hippocampal formation. *Science*, **225**, 1168–1170.

Hyman, B.T., Van Hoesen, G.W. & Damasio, A.R. (1990). Memory-related neural systems in Alzheimer's disease: an anatomic study. *Neurology*, **40**, 1721–1730.

Hyman, B.T., Van Hoesen, G.W., Kromer, L.J. & Damasio, A.R. (1986). Perforant pathway changes and the memory impairment of Alzheimer's disease. *Annals of Neurology*, **20**, 472–481.

Jack, C.R., Petersen, R.C., Xu, Y.C. et al. (1999). Prediction of AD aith MRI-based hippocampal volume in mild cognitive impairment. *Neurology*, **52**(7), 1397–1403.

Jack, C.R., Petersen, R.C., Xu, Y.C. et al. (1997). Medial temporal atrophy on MRI in normal aging and very mild Alzheimer's disease. *Neurology*, **49**, 786–794.

Jernigan, T.L., Salmon, D.P., Butters, N. & Hesselink, J.R. (1991). Cerebral structure on MRI: II. specific changes in Alzheimer's and Huntington's diseases. *Biological Psychiatry*, **29**, 68–81.

Johnson, K.A., Jones, K., Holman, B.L. et al. (1998). Preclinical prediction of Alzheimer's disease using SPECT. *Neurology*, **50**, 1563–1571.

Jorm, A.F. (1985). Subtypes of Alzheimer's dementia: a conceptual analysis and critical review. *Psychological Medicine*, **15**, 543–553.

Kaszniak, A.W. (1988). Cognition in Alzheimer's disease: theoretic models and clinical implications. *Neurobiology of Aging*, **9**(1), 92–94.

Kaszniak, A.W., Poon, L.W. & Riege, W. (1986). Assessing memory deficits: an information-processing approach. In L.W. Poon (ed.), *Handbook for Clinical Memory Assessment of Older Adults*. Washington: American Psychological Association.

Kay, J., Lesser, R. & Coltheart, M. (1992). *PALPA: Psycholinguistic Assessments of Language Processing in Aphasia*. Hove: Erlbaum.

Kessler, J., Ghaemi, M., Mielke, R. et al. (1996). Visual vs. auditory memory stimulation in patients with probable Alzheimer's disease: a PET study with 18 FDG. *Annals of the New York Academy of Science*, **777**, 233–238.

Kessler, J., Herholz, K., Grond, M. & Heiss, W.-D. (1991). Impaired metabolic activation in Alzheimer's disease: a PET study during continuous visual recognition. *Neuropsychologia*, **29**(3), 229–243.

Killiany, R.J., Moss, M.B., Albert, M.S. et al. (1993). Temporal lobe regions on magnetic resonance imaging identify patients with early Alzheimer's disease. *Archives of Neurology*, **50**, 949–954.

Kirshner, H.S., Webb, W.G. & Kelly, M.P. (1984). The naming disorder of dementia. *Neuropsychologia*, **22**, 23–30.

Kopelman, M.D. (1985a). Multiple memory deficits in Alzheimer-type dementia: implications for pharmacotherapy. *Psychological Medicine*, **15**, 527–541.

Kopelman, M.D. (1985b). Rates of forgetting in Alzheimer-type dementia and Korsakoff's syndrome. *Neuropsychologia*, **23**, 623–638.

Kopelman, M.D. (1989). Remote and autobiographical memory, temporal context memory and frontal atrophy in Korsakoff and Alzheimer patients. *Neuropsychologia*, **27**, 437–460.

Kramer, J.H., Delis, D.C., Blusewitz, M.J. et al. (1988). Verbal memory errors in Alzheimer's and Huntington's dementias. *Developmental Neuropsychology*, **4**, 1–15.

Kramer, J.H., Levin, B.E., Brandt, J. & Delis, D.C. (1989). Differentiation of Alzheimer's, Huntington's, and Parkinson's disease patients on the basis of verbal learning characteristics. *Neuropsychology*, **3**, 111–120.

Lambon-Ralph, M.A., Patterson, K. & Hodges, J.R. (1997). The relationship between naming and semantic knowledge for different categories in dementia of Alzheimer's type. *Neuropsychologia*, **35**(9), 1251–1260.

Mair, W.P., Warrington, E.K. & Weiskrantz, L. (1979). Memory disorders in Korsakoff's psychosis: a neuropathological and neuropsychological investigation of two cases. *Brain*, **102**, 749–783.

Martin, A. (1987). Representation of semantic and spatial knowledge in Alzheimer's patients: implication for models of preserved learning in amnesia. *Journal of Clinical and Experimental Neuropsychology*, **9**, 191–224.

Martin, A. (1990). Neuropsychology of Alzheimer's disease: the case for subgroups. In M. F. Schwartz (ed.), *Modular Deficits in Alzheimer's-type Dementia* (pp. 143–176). Cambridge, MA: Bradford/MIT.

Martin, A., Brouwers, P., Lalonde, F. et al. (1986). Towards a behavioral typology of Alzheimer's patients. *Journal of Clinical and Experimental Neuropsychology*, **8**, 594–610.

Martin, A. & Chao, L.L. (2001). Semantic memory and the brain: structure and processes. *Current Opinions in Neurobiology*, **11**, 194–201.

Martin, A., Cox, C., Brouwers, P. & Fedio, P. (1985). A note on the different patterns of impaired and preserved cognitive abilities and their relation to episodic memory deficits in Alzheimer's patients. *Brain and Language*, **25**, 323–341.

Martin, A. & Fedio, P. (1983). Word production and comprehension in Alzheimer's disease: the breakdown of semantic knowledge. *Brain and Language*, **19**, 124–141.

Martin, A., Wiggs, C.L., Ungerleider, L.G. & Haxby, J.V. (1996). Neural correlates of category-specific knowledge. *Nature*, **379**, 649–652.

Mattis, S. (1976). Mental status examination for organic mental syndrome in the elderly patient. In L. Bellak & T.B. Karuso (eds), *Geriatric Psychiatry*. New York: Grune & Stratton.

Mazziotta, J.C., Toga, A., Evans, A. et al. (1997). Brain maps: linking the present to the future. In R.S.J. Frackowiak, K.J. Friston, C.D. Frith et al. (eds), *Human Brain Function* (pp. 429–466). San Diego, CA: Academic Press.

McClelland, J.L. (1998). Complementary learning systems in the brain: a connectionist approach to explicit and implicit cognition and memory. *Annals of the New York Academy of Science*, **843**, 153–169.

McKhann, G., Drachman, D.A., Folstein, M.F. (1984). Clinical diagnosis of Alzheimer's disease: report of the NINCDS–ADRDA Work Group under the auspices of the Department of Health and Human Services Task Force on Alzheimer's disease. *Neurology*, **34**, 939–944.

Miller, E. (1971). On the nature of the memory disorder in presenile dementia. *Neuropsychologia*, **9**, 75–81.

Morris, J.C., McKeel, D.W., Storandt, M. et al. (1991). Very mild Alzheimer's disease: informant-based clinical psychometric and pathological distinction from normal aging. *Neurology*, **41**, 469–478.

Morris, J.C., Storandt, M., Miller, J.P. et al. (2001). Mild cognitive impairment represents early-stage Alzheimer disease. *Archives of Neurology*, **58**, 397–405.

Morris, R.G. (1986). Short-term forgetting in senile dementia of the Alzheimer type. *Cognitive Neuropsychology*, **3**, 77–97.

Morris, R.G. & Baddeley, A. D. (1988). A review of primary and working memory functioning in Alzheimer-type dementia. *Journal of Clinical and Experimental Neuropsychology*, **10**, 279–296.

Morris, R.G. & Kopelman, M.D. (1986). The memory deficits in Alzheimer-type dementia: a review. *Quarterly Journal of Experimental Psychology*, **38**, 575–602.

Moss, M.B., Albert, M.S., Butters, N. & Payne, M. (1986). Differential patterns of memory loss among patients with Alzheimer's disease, Huntington's disease, and alcoholic Korsakoff's syndrome. *Archives of Neurology*, **43**, 239–246.

Mummery, C.J., Patterson, K., Price, C.J. et al. (2000). A voxel-based morphometry study of semantic dementia: relationship between temporal lobe atrophy and semantic memory. *Annals of Neurology*, **47**(1), 36–45.

Mummery, C.J., Patterson, K., Wise, R.J.S. et al. (1999). Disrupted temporal lobe connections in semantic dementia. *Brain*, **122**, 61–73.

Neary, D., Snowden, J.S. & Mann, D.M.A. (1993). Familial progressive aphasia: its relationship to other forms of lobar atrophy. *Journal of Neurology Neurosurgery and Psychiatry*, **56**, 1122–1125.

Nebes, R.D. (1992). Semantic memory dysfunction in Alzheimer's disease: disruption of semantic knowledge or information-processing limitation? In L.R. Squire & N. Butters (eds), *Neuropsychology of Memory*, 2nd edn. New York: Guilford.

Nebes, R.D. & Brady, C.B. (1988). Integrity of semantic fields in Alzheimer's disease. *Cortex*, **24**, 291–300.

Nebes, R.D. & Brady, C. B. (1989). Focused and divided attention in Alzheimer's disease. *Cortex*, **25**, 305–315.

Norman, D.A. & Shallice, T. (1980). *Attention to Action: Willed and Automatic Control of Behavior.* CHIP Report No. 99. San Diego, CA: University of California.

Ouchi, Y., Nobezawa, S., Okada, B.A. et al. (1998). Altered glucose metabolism in the hippocampal head in memory impairment. *Neurology*, **51**, 136–142.

Pepin, E.P. & Eslinger, P.J. (1989). Verbal memory decline in Alzheimer's disease: a multiple-process deficit. *Neurology*, **39**(1477–1482).

Perry, R.J. & Hodges, J.R. (1996). Spectrum of memory dysfunction in degenerative disease. *Current Opinion in Neurology*, **9**, 281–285.

Petersen, R.C., Smith, G.E., Waring, S.C. et al. (1999). Mild cognitive impairment: clinical characterization and outcome. *Archives of Neurology*, **56**, 303–308.

Posner, M.I. & Petersen, S.E. (1990). The attention system of the human brain. *Annual Review of Neuroscience*, **13**, 25–42.

Rombouts, S.A., Barkhof, F., Veltman, D.J. et al. (2000). Functional MR imaging in Alzheimer's disease during memory encoding. *American Journal of Neuroradiology*, **21**(10), 1869–1875.

Salmon, D.P., Galasko, D., Hansen, L.A. et al. (1996). Neuropsychological deficits associated with diffuse Lewy body disease. *Brain and Cognition*, **31**(2), 148–165.

Salthouse, T.A. & Becker, J.T. (1998). Independent effects of Alzheimer's disease on neuropsychological functioning. *Neuropsychology*, **12**(2), 242–252.

Saykin, A.J., Flashman, L.A., Frutiger, S.A. et al. (1999a). Neuroanatomic substrates of semantic memory impairment in Alzheimer's disease: patterns of functional fMRI activation. *Journal of the International Neuropsychological Society*, **5**, 377–392.

Saykin, A.J., Johnson, S.C., Flashman, L.A. et al. (1999b). Functional differentiation of medial temporal and frontal regions involved in processing novel and familiar words: an fMRI study. *Brain*, **122**, 1963–1971.

Schacter, D.L., Curran, T., Reiman, E.M. et al. (1999). Medial temporal lobe activation during episodic encoding and retrieval: a PET study. *Hippocampus*, **9**(5), 575–581.

Shallice, T. & Warrington, E.K. (1970). Independent functioning of verbal memory stores: a neuropsychological study. *Quarterly Journal of Experimental Psychology*, **22**, 261–273.

Snowden, J.S., Neary, D., Mann, D.M.A. et al. (1992). Progressive language disorder due to lobar atrophy. *Annals of Neurology*, **31**, 174–183.

Sowell, E.R., Thompson, P.M., Holmes, C.J. et al. (1999). *In vivo* evidence for post-adolescent brain maturation in frontal and striatal regions. *Nature Neuroscience*, **2**(10), 859–861.

Squire, L.R. (1992). Memory and the hippocampus: a synthesis from findings with rats, monkeys, and humans. *Psychological Review*, **99**, 195–231.

Squire, L.R. & Zola-Morgan, S. (1991). The medial temporal lobe system. *Science*, **253**, 1380–1386.

Stout, J.C., Bondi, M.W., Jernigan, T.L. et al. (1999). Regional cerebral volume loss associated with verbal learning and memory in dementia of the Alzheimer type. *Neuropsychology*, **13**(2), 188–197.

Thomas, G., Hostetter, G. & Barker, D.J. (1968). Behavioral function of the limbic system. In E. Stellar & J.M. Sprague (eds), *Progress in Physiological Psychology*, Vol. 2. New York: Academic Press.

Troster, A.I., Butters, N., Salmon, D.P. et al. (1993). The diagnostic utility of savings scores: differentiating Alzheimer's and Huntington's diseases with the Logical Memory and Visual Reproduction tests. *Journal of Clinical and Experimental Neuropsychology*, **15**(5), 773–788.

Troster, A.L., Salmon, D.P., McCullough, D. & Butters, N. (1989). A comparison of category fluency deficits associated with Alzheimer's and Huntington's disease. *Brain and Language*, **37**, 500–513.

Tulving, E. (1972). Episodic and semantic memory. In E. Tulving & W. Donaldson (eds), *Organization of Memory*. New York: Academic Press.

Tulving, E. (1984). Relations among components and processes of memory. *Behavior and Brain Science*, **1**, 257–268.

Tulving, E. (1987). Multiple memory systems and consciousness. *Human Neurobiology*, **6**, 67–80.

Vallar, G. & Baddeley, A.D. (1984). Fractionation of working memory: neuropsychological evidence for a phonological short-term store. *Journal of Verbal Learning and Verbal Behavior*, **23**, 151–161.

Vandenberghe, R., Price, C., Wise, R. et al. (1996). Functional anatomy of a common semantic system for words and pictures. *Nature*, **383**, 254–256.

Victor, M., Adams, R. D. & Collins, G. H. (1971). *The Wernicke–Korsakoff Syndrome*. Philadelphia, PA: Davis.

Wagner, A.D., Schacter, D.L., Rotte, M. et al. (1998). Building memories: remembering and forgetting of verbal experiences as predicted by brain activity. *Science*, **281**(5380), 1188–1191.

Wechsler, D. (1945). A standardized memory scale for memory use. *Journal of Psychology*, **19**, 87–95.

Weigl, E. (1927). On the psychology of so-called process of abstraction. *Journal of Abnormal Social Psychology*, **36**, 3–33.

Welsh, K., Butters, N., Hughes, J. (1991). Detection of abnormal memory decline in mild cases of Alzheimer's disease using CERAD neuropsychological measures. *Archives of Neurology*, **48**, 278–281.

Welsh, K.A., Butters, N., Hughes, J.P. (1992). Detection and staging of dementia in Alzheimer's disease: use of neuropsychological measures developed for the consortium to establish a registry for Alzheimer's disease. *Archives of Neurology*, **49**, 448–452.

Whitehouse, P.J. (1986). The concept of subcortical and cortical dementia: another look. *Annals of Neurology*, **19**, 1–6.

Williams, R.N., MacIntosh, D.E., Eells, G.T. (1996). Neuropsychological subgroups of dementia of the Alzheimer's type. *International Journal of Neuroscience*, **87**(1–2), 79–90.

Wilson, R.S., Bacon, L.D. & Fox, J.H. (1983a). Primary memory and secondary memory in dementia of the Alzheimer type. *Journal of Clinical and Experimental Neuropsychology*, **5**(4), 337–344.

Wilson, R.S., Bacon, L.D. & Fox, S.H. & Kaszniak, A.W. (1983b). Word frequency effect and recognition memory in dementia of the Alzheimer type. *Journal of Clinical and Experimental Neuropsychology*, **5**, 97–104.

Wilson, R.S., Kaszniak, A.W., Bacon, L.D. et al. (1982). Facial recognition memory in dementia. *Cortex*, **18**, 329–336.

Zelkowicz, B.J., Herbster, A.N., Nebes, R.D. et al. (1997). An examination of regional cerebral blood flow during object naming tasks. *Journal of the International Neuropsychological Society*, **4**, 160–166.

CHAPTER 27

Memory Disorders in Subcortical Dementia

Jason Brandt

and

Cynthia A. Munro

Johns Hopkins University School of Medicine, Baltimore, MD, USA

Contemporary discussions of "subcortical dementia" often cite the work of Albert et al. (1974) on progressive supranuclear palsy and/or McHugh & Folstein (1975) on Huntington's disease as the origin of the concept. However, descriptions of what would come to be known as *subcortical dementia* actually appeared in the medical literature at least as early as the mid-nineteenth century (Mandell & Albert, 1990). The term itself was not coined until 1932, when "subcorticale demenz" was used to describe the cognitive impairments associated with encephalitis (von Stockert, 1932). Thus, research on subcortical dementia may have a short history, but the concept has a long past.

Subcortical dementia is a neuropsychological/neuropsychiatric syndrome. It consists of slowed mentation (bradyphrenia), sustained attention and working memory deficits, forgetfulness, impaired planning and judgment, and changes in drive and/or mood states (with apathy, irritability and depression being most common). Since subcortical dementia is usually seen in diseases that also feature prominent movement disorders, dysarthric speech and psychomotor slowing, and problems with motor set acquisition and switching are typically seen as well. In contrast to the clinical presentation of cortical dementia (the prototype of which is seen in Alzheimer's disease), frank aphasia, apraxia, agnosia and amnesia are rare (Lovell & Smith, 1997; Darvesh & Freedman, 1996; Cummings & Benson, 1984).

Almost since its rediscovery a quarter-century ago, the term "subcortical dementia" has been the subject of controversy. In fact, criticisms of the concept are so widespread that virtually every time the term appears in the literature, its authors seem almost apologetic and justify using the term by appealing to its history and its clinical usefulness. Opponents of the concept argue that describing some dementia syndromes as "cortical" and others as "subcortical" ignores the fact that subcortical nuclei and pathways are affected in diseases like Alzheimer's disease (AD) and, conversely, that cortical changes are seen in conditions like Huntington's disease (HD) and Parkinson's disease (PD) (Whitehouse, 1986). Furthermore, even if the neuropathology of so-called subcortical dementias were confined

The Handbook of Memory Disorders. Edited by A.D. Baddeley, M.D. Kopelman and B.A. Wilson
© 2002 John Wiley & Sons, Ltd.

to specific striatal, thalamic, cerebellar or brainstem nuclei, the cognitive impairments may be a manifestation of impaired cortical activity via the disruption of corticostriatothala-mocortical loops (Crosson, 1992; Domesick, 1990). Accordingly, the term "subcortical dementia", as used in this chapter, should not be interpreted literally. It should be construed as a clinical entity found most prominently in diseases with severe subcortical neuropathol-ogy, and not as a precisely specified, anatomically defined entity (Cohen & Freedman, 1995; Cummings, 1993).

CONCEPTUAL AND METHODOLOGICAL ISSUES IN STUDYING MEMORY IN SUBCORTICAL DEMENTIA

Definition of Dementia

To appreciate what the existing literature does and does not reveal about memory impair-ments in subcortical dementia, a number of conceptual issues need to be considered. The first of these is the very definition of "dementia". The *Diagnostic and Statistical Manual of Mental Disorders* (DSM-IV) criteria for dementia require impairment in memory and at least one other cognitive domain, as well as impairment in social or occupational func-tioning (American Psychiatric Association, 1994). Whereas the requirement of disordered memory is quite appropriate for the dementia of AD, it may not be appropriate for diseases of subcortical brain structures. Much neuropsychological evidence (discussed later in this chapter) suggests that impaired performance on tests of new learning and episodic recall in subcortical dementia are not due to failures in memory encoding and storage, but rather are attributable to deficits in attention or central executive functions. Thus, one might argue that memory *per se* is less clearly affected in these conditions, and therefore the diagnosis of "dementia" might not be appropriate.

Another problem with the DSM-IV definition of *dementia* concerns the criterion of impaired social or occupational functioning. If a disease affecting subcortical structures causes impairment in everyday functioning, but this impairment is due to a movement dis-order rather than cognitive deficits, is the diagnosis of dementia appropriate? For example, PD, by virtue of its motor features, causes clear impairment in social and/or occupational functioning. Although there may be pervasive cognitive deficits in PD, these are often mild and, in and of themselves, might not impair social/occupational functioning. Is it legitimate to diagnose very mild dementia in such patients, even if daily functioning is not yet affected or is impaired only by bradykinesia? Finally, requiring that social role functioning be impaired for the diagnosis of dementia complicates empirical investigation of the differential impact of various dementias on individuals, families, organizations and society.

Severity of Dementia and Group Matching

A second conceptual and methodological issue that needs to be addressed when studying memory (or any other cognitive) impairment across dementia syndromes is that of matching individuals or groups for overall severity of dementia. In order to conclude that a particular aspect of memory is differentially impaired in one patient population compared to another (i.e. that there is a *selective* deficit), one must eliminate the possibility that one patient group is simply more impaired overall (i.e. that there is a *generalized* deficit). How one accomplishes this is not a simple matter. Matching study groups for mean score and variance on the Mini-Mental State Exam (MMSE) (Folstein et al., 1975) is problematic because the test has a heavy language loading and is known to be relatively insensitive to the subcortical dementias (Rothlind & Brandt, 1993; Brandt, 1994). As a result, it is difficult to construct groups with AD and HD, for example, matched for MMSE score. Any such groups will consist of very early AD patients and very advanced HD patients (e.g. Brandt et al., 1992). The Dementia Rating Scale (DRS) (Mattis, 1988) has also been used for this purpose (e.g. Heindel et al., 1989; Paulsen et al., 1995) and is subject to the same limitations. Matching groups on functional disability is an alternative strategy but is likely to yield very mild subcortical dementia patients, since movement disorders are typically a major source of their disability.

Rather than attempt group matching, many studies have dealt with differences between groups by using statistical procedures (e.g. analysis of covariance) to "correct" for nuisance variables. These approaches are also problematic for a variety of technical reasons (Adams et al., 1985). In addition, they have the potential to create groups that simply do not exist in nature.

Disease Heterogeneity

A third issue to consider in discussions of subcortical dementia is disease heterogeneity. Although the bulk of the research on subcortical dementia has been in HD and PD, more than a dozen disorders, each with a unique morbid anatomy and physiology, have been described as causing this syndrome. Grouping all these disorders under the single category "subcortical dementia" is likely to obfuscate important differences among them (Pillon et al., 1991). In addition, there is significant heterogeneity *within* clinically defined disease entities. For example, among patients with Wilson's disease there may be at least two distinct subtypes—those who have neurological deficits and dementia and those who do not—that may reflect genuine biological subtypes (i.e. different genotypes). Among the spinocere-bellar ataxias, at least 12 genetically distinct subtypes have been identified. Several of these have neuropathology extending beyond the cerebellum, and almost all of them produce some cognitive changes of the subcortical type. Identifying the sources of such heterogeneity is a major task for the clinical neurosciences in the twenty-first century.

SPECIFIC DISORDERS CAUSING SUBCORTICAL DEMENTIA

Disorders of the Basal Ganglia

The basal ganglia consist of the striatum (caudate nucleus and putamen) and globus pallidus. Since these forebrain nuclei have intricately-patterned connections to many other brain regions, many authors include highly interrelated structures, especially the subthalamic nucleus and substantia nigra, in discussions of the basal ganglia.

Through their interconnections with thalamic, cerebellar and cortical motor areas, the basal ganglia are thought to modulate movement (Benecke et al., 1987; Middleton & Strick, 2000). As such, diseases of the basal ganglia, including HD, basal ganglia calcification, neuroacanthocytosis and Wilson's disease, typically present with movement disorders. Only more recently have the interconnections of basal ganglia with association cortices, and their implications for memory and cognition, been appreciated.

Huntington's Disease

This inherited neurodegenerative disease is characterized by the full "subcortical triad" of movement disorder, dementia and emotional disorder (McHugh, 1989). The onset of HD is insidious, with symptoms typically emerging between ages 35 and 45 (Folstein, 1989). Involuntary movements of the upper limbs and face are often early signs, progressing to more generalized choreic and athetoid movements. Neuropathologically, the disease is characterized by neuronal death in the head of the caudate nucleus and putamen, progressing in later stages to the cerebral cortex (Vonsattel et al., 1985).

Memory functioning in HD has been the focus of numerous investigations, and several consistent findings have emerged. First, at any given level of dementia (defined by MMSE or DRS), episodic memory appears to be less severely impaired in HD than in AD (Brandt et al., 1988; Salmon et al., 1989). Second, HD patients typically have impairments in retrieval (i.e. the organization and execution of effortful memory search) that are manifest most clearly on tests of free recall. This contrasts with their normal, or near-normal, performance on tests of yes/no or multiple-choice recognition (Butters et al., 1978; Caine et al., 1978; Pillon et al., 1993; Rohrer et al., 1999; Weingartner et al., 1979). A comparison of 23 patients with HD and 23 with AD, equated for total score on the DRS, found performance on the Memory subtest of the DRS to be worse in AD and performance on the Initiation/Perseveration subtest to be worse in HD (Salmon et al., 1989). This was later found to be the case even for patients with advanced dementia (Paulsen et al., 1995). Pillon et al. (1993) found that the memory performance of HD patients was more highly correlated with performance on tests of executive function (including the Initiation subtest of the DRS, Wisconsin Card Sorting Test, and initial letter fluency) than was the case in AD. Pillon and associates concluded that the learning and memory deficit of HD patients may be more apparent than real.

Another consistent finding in HD is a deficit in particular types of perceptual and motor learning. In one of the first studies exploring these phenomena, Martone et al. (1984) administered a task requiring the rapid reading of mirror-reversed words to patients with HD and amnesic patients with alcoholic Korsakoff syndrome. Subjects were administered this task three times, one day apart, with a recognition trial administered following the last trial. The Korsakoff amnesics demonstrated normal ability to learn the skill of mirror reading, but were severely impaired on the recognition portion of the task. In contrast, HD patients exhibited normal word recognition, but had much slower rates of perceptual skill acquisition. Defects in perceptual adaptation have also been demonstrated in HD (Heindel et al., 1991; Paulsen et al., 1993).

Heindel et al. (1988) compared procedural learning (using the pursuit rotor task) and declarative learning (using the Verbal Recognition Span Test; Moss et al., 1986) in HD and AD. The HD patients were severely impaired on the pursuit rotor task, improving much less over learning trials than did the AD patients. In contrast, the HD group's performance was superior to that of the AD group on the verbal recognition span test. These findings support a role for the striatum in motor skill learning, a system dissociable from the temporal–limbic explicit memory system impaired in AD.

In a more recent study, Gabrieli et al. (1997) examined procedural learning in HD using two psychomotor tasks. HD patients performed worse than a normal control group on the pursuit rotor task; however, they performed as well as the normal subjects on a mirror-tracing task. The authors concluded that the basal ganglia, affected in HD, are involved in the learning of repetitive motor sequences (as on the rotary pursuit task) but not with the learning of new mappings between visual cues and motor responses (as on the mirror-tracing task). Several studies further specify the motor learning deficit in HD as involving impaired ability to benefit from the predictability of movement sequences (Bylsma et al., 1990; Brandt, 1994; Knopman & Nissen, 1991; Willingham et al., 1996).

Basal Ganglia Calcification

This syndrome, first described in the mid-nineteenth century (Delacour, 1850; cited in Klein & Vieregge, 1998), is characterized by parkinsonian symptoms as well as seizures, ataxia and dementia. Basal ganglia calcification (BGC) can be caused by a number of conditions, including anoxia, radiation, infections and metabolic disturbances (Lopez-Villegas et al., 1996). Idiopathic BGC, also known as Fahr's disease, is usually familial and is associated with dementia and schizophreniform psychosis (Cummings et al., 1983). Neuropathologically, BGC is characterized by mineral deposits in the putamen, globus pallidus, thalamus, corona radiata, cerebellar dentate nuclei and cerebellar white matter (Hier & Cummings, 1990).

In the few studies on cognition in BGC, deficits are usually found on tests of memory, visuospatial processing and aspects of executive function (Lopez-Villegas et al., 1996; Cummings et al., 1983). In perhaps the most comprehensive study to date, Lopez-Villegas et al. (1996) compared the performance of 18 BGC patients to that of 16 normal control subjects matched for age, education, sex and estimated premorbid IQ on a battery of neuropsychological tests. The BGC patients performed worse than the control subjects on several tests of motor skills and executive functions. Memory was assessed with the Visual Reproduction subtest of the Wechsler Memory Scale, the multiple-choice version of the Benton Visual Retention Test, the Rey Auditory Verbal Learning Test (RAVLT), the Digit Span subtest from the Wechsler Adult Intelligence Scale, the Corsi span test, and 30-min recall of the Rey Complex Figure Test. Only degree of improvement over the five learning trials of the RAVLT differed between the patient and control groups. Lopez-Villegas et al. (1996) concluded that the memory impairment of BGC is characterized by poor free recall with relative preservation of recognition. Furthermore, they conceptualized this memory deficit as based on dysfunction of the frontal-subcortical circuits that impair retrieval, and noted that this pattern is similar to that observed among patients with other basal ganglia diseases. To explore the possibility of subtypes of BCG, the researchers stratified the patients by presence/absence of neurological signs (seizures, parkinsonism, dysarthria, and orthostatic hypotension), by presumed etiology, and by extent of calcification, i.e. limited to the lenticular nucleus (putamen and globus pallidus) or more widespread. There were few meaningful differences in cognition between these subgroups of BCG and the sample as a whole.

Neuroacanthocytosis

This rare, presumably autosomal-recessive degenerative disorder is clinically and pathologi-cally similar to HD. The disease usually first presents at ages 30–50 years. It is characterized by choreiform movements but can often be distinguished from HD by its prominent orofacial dyskinesia, including involuntary vocalizations and biting of the lips and tongue (Quinn & Schrag, 1998; Kutcher et al., 1999). Pathologically, neuroacanthocytosis (NA) is associated with neuronal loss in the caudate, putamen, pallidum and substantia nigra, without involve-ment of the locus coeruleus, cerebral cortex, brainstem or cerebellum (Hardie et al., 1991; Brooks et al, 1991; Rinne et al., 1994).

Only a single study could be found that attempted to identify the cognitive profile of patients with NA. In a chart review of 10 NA patients who received neuropsychological assessments, Kartsounis & Hardie (1996) found that all 10 had evidence of executive dys-function (measured by various tests considered to be sensitive to frontal lobe dysfunction), whereas only half demonstrated memory impairment. The latter was assessed using the Recognition Memory Test (Warrington, 1984) and a three-choice test of recognition mem-ory (Warrington, 1995, unpublished data). Because patients' memories were tested only with recognition procedures, it cannot be determined whether NA patients, like those with other subcortical syndromes, would have greater impairments in free recall.

Wilson's Disease

Also known as progressive hepatolenticular degeneration, Wilson's disease (WD) is inher-ited as an autosomal recessive trait. It is caused by a mutated gene on chromosome 13 that results in the absence of a copper-carrying protein, resulting in copper deposits in the liver, cornea and basal ganglia (Scheinberg & Sternlieb, 1984; Wilson, 1912). Clinically, WD patients may be neurologically asymptomatic. When they do display symptoms, dysarthria, flapping tremor, rigidity, drooling, gait disturbance and bradykinesia are common (Hefter et al., 1993; Lang et al., 1990).

Brain-imaging studies in WD often reveal focal abnormalities in the brainstem, white matter and subcortical nuclei. Bilaterally symmetrical changes in the basal ganglia, par-ticularly, the putamen, are common, as is some degree of cortical atrophy (Hefter et al., 1993; Chen et al., 1983; Williams & Walshe, 1981). Neuropathological studies have found accumulations of copper in the striatum and globus pallidus (Scheinberg & Sternlieb, 1984). Vascular changes, including perivascular thickening in the basal ganglia, have also been found (Scheinberg & Sternlieb, 1984).

Whether the cognitive deficits that accompany WD constitute a full-blown dementia is a matter of some debate (cf. Lang, 1989; Medalia, 1991). In his original description of the condition, Wilson (1912) noted mental status changes and a "narrowing of the mental horizons", but did not believe that his patients were "demented" (Hier & Cummings, 1990). In a report on 31 WD patients, Starosta-Rubenstein et al. (1987) commented that dementia was "rare", although neither the exact prevalence nor the way in which dementia was assessed was reported. Lang (1989) reported no memory impairment in his sample of 15 WD patients, whereas Medalia (1991) maintains that memory impairment is common, at least among those with other signs of neurologic involvement. The cognitive impairments in WD have been shown to lessen following treatment with penicillamine, a copper-chelating agent (Hach & Hartung, 1979; Lang et al., 1990).

Because cognitive impairment seems to occur only among those who have other neurological signs of the illness (Lang, 1989; Medalia, 1991), most studies categorize patients into those with and without such signs (Medalia et al., 1988; Isaacs-Glaberman et al., 1989). In spite of this, there appears to be little correlation between the severity of neurological deficits and cognitive impairments, except for the effect of motor performance on neuropsychological test performance (Medalia, 1991). Performance on tests of memory, for example, is generally not correlated with the extent of neurological impairment (Medalia, 1991).

Medalia et al. (1992) administered a battery of neuropsychological tests to 31 patients with WD and reported the number of patients who fell below established cutoffs on the tests. Among the 12 neurologically asymptomatic WD patients, two (16%) had performances below the cutoff for impairment on the DRS and the Rey Auditory Verbal Learning Test, and three (25%) were impaired on the Trail Making Test. Roughly 30% of the 19 neurologically symptomatic patients were impaired on every test in the battery (Medalia et al., 1992).

Among neurologically symptomatic WD patients, motor slowing and memory deficits are the most common findings (Isaacs-Glaberman et al., 1989). The memory impairment has been demonstrated on tests of free recall for short stories, list of words and geometric designs (Rosselli, 1987). Isaacs-Glaberman et al. (1989) administered the RAVLT to 19 neurologically symptomatic WD patients and 15 normal control subjects. The patients recalled fewer words than the control group on the RAVLT, but performed as well as the control group on the recognition trial. On other memory tests, the WD patients demonstrated normal rates of learning and forgetting and were aided by recognition cues. These findings, combined with the patients' impaired performance on a word list generation task, led the authors to conclude that the memory deficit in WD is due to a retrieval deficit. The qualitative similarities in memory characteristics between patients with WD and those with HD are obvious.

Disorders of Brainstem Nuclei

Parkinson's Disease

First described by James Parkinson in 1817, PD is one of the earliest characterized neurodegenerative diseases affecting primarily subcortical brain areas. Despite its long recognition by the medical and scientific communities, its etiology remains incompletely understood. Abnormalities of movement, primarily resting tremor, stooped and unstable posture, rigidity and slowness, are the most common, and typically the earliest, manifestations of PD. Onset of PD is typically at age 40–70, with average age of onset in the 50s (Freedman, 1990). Neuropathologic studies reveal loss of dopamine-producing neurons and the presence of Lewy bodies in the substantia nigra and locus coeruleus. Dopamine depletions in the head of the caudate nucleus and the frontal cortex are common (Kish et al., 1986; Kish et al., 1988a). Neuronal loss is also frequently seen in the nucleus basalis of Meynert, a major source of cholinergic innervation to the forebrain (Adams & Victor, 1985; Whitehouse et al., 1982).

A relatively consistent finding in early studies comparing memory in PD to that in HD is that PD patients are less severely impaired on tests of word list recall and recognition (Drebing et al., 1993; Caine et al., 1977; Fisher et al., 1983; Kramer et al., 1989). Several of these studies could be criticized, however, for neglecting to match patient groups for age, sex, presumed premorbid intelligence and other factors that influence verbal memory performance. To remedy this, Massman et al. (1990) compared well-matched groups of PD patients, HD patients and normal control subjects on the California Verbal Learning Test (CVLT). Immediate recall (Trial 1 of List A) did not differ between the HD and PD groups, but both were worse than the control group. However, rate of learning over trials was significantly higher in PD than in HD. Performance of the PD group was also better than that of the HD group on the delayed recall trials. The yes/no recognition performance of both groups was mildly impaired. These results led Massman et al. to conclude that verbal memory in PD is characterized by a retrieval deficit that is less severe than that seen in HD, but not qualitatively different.

As in HD, there are selective impairments in procedural learning and implicit memory in PD (Saint-Cyr et al., 1988; Harrington et al., 1990; Heindel et al., 1989). Harrington et al. (1990) found PD patients to be impaired in learning the pursuit rotor task, but normal on a more perceptually-based implicit memory task (reading mirror-reversed text). Bondi & Kazniak (1991) also found PD patients to perform normally in reading mirror-reversed text, but their patients, carefully screened for the absence of frank dementia, also improved at a normal rate over trials on the pursuit rotor task. A selective impairment on the skill-learning component of a fragmented pictures test was the only implicit memory deficit that could be discerned.

In an attempt to further characterize the motor-learning deficit in PD, Haaland et al. (1997) compared the performance of 40 patients with PD to 30 normal control subjects on the pursuit rotor task. Patients were assigned to one of two conditions. In one condition, the speed of the rotating target varied randomly across trials. In the other condition, speed was fixed within blocks of trials and varied across blocks. The PD patients were impaired only in the varied speed condition of this task. The authors concluded that PD patients display their procedural learning deficit only when required to rapidly adjust their motor programming to changing environmental demands.

Progressive Supranuclear Palsy

Progressive supranuclear palsy (PSP) is a rare degenerative disorder of unknown etiology. Also known as Steele–Richardson–Olszewski syndrome, PSP was first described as a distinct disorder in the mid-1960s (Steele et al., 1964). The disease is characterized by parkinsonism, including axial rigidity, gait disturbance, bradykinesia and profound ophthalmoplegia, but absent a resting tremor. Neuropathological changes associated with PSP include neurofibrillary tangles in the basal ganglia, brainstem and cerebellar nuclei (Steele et al., 1964). PSP is perhaps the prototypical subcortical dementia, as the cerebral cortex appears to remain intact even late in the course of the disease (Jellinger & Bancher, 1992). Structural brain imaging studies are often normal (Grafman et al., 1990; Zakzanis et al., 1998), but sometimes reveal midbrain atrophy (Soliveri et al., 1999). PET imaging often shows hypometabolism in the frontal lobes, presumably due to disrupted subcortical projections (Blin et al., 1992).

Whether PSP is invariably associated with memory impairment has not been firmly established. A review of early clinical descriptions led Albert and colleagues (1974) to conclude that there is indeed a "dementia" in this illness, but also that "memory as such may not be truly impaired" (p. 126). Grafman et al. (1990) found that scores on the Wechsler Memory Scale (WMS; Wechsler, 1945) were lower among 12 PSP patients than among 12 normal control subjects. The authors attributed the deficits to deficient subcortical input to the frontal lobes. In this study, however, the memory scores of both the patient and control groups were consistent with their IQ scores. Thus, it is difficult to make the case for a selective memory impairment in the PSP group.

Milberg & Albert (1989) studied nine PSP patients and compared them to 16 patients with AD and 23 normal control subjects. They found no impairment in the PSP group on tests of new learning and memory (Logical Memory and Visual Reproduction subtests of the WMS) or semantic memory (Boston Naming Test; Kaplan et al., 1983). Van der Hurk & Hodges (1995) also found that episodic memory, measured by the Logical Memory subtest of the WMS and the word list learning task from the CERAD battery (Welsh et al., 1994), was preserved in PSP. However, they found that semantic memory, assessed with the Synonym Judgment subtest of the Action for Dysphasic Adults Battery (Franklin et al., 1992) and the Pyramids and Palm Trees Test (Howard & Patterson, 1982), was as impaired in PSP as it was in AD. The authors attempted to reconcile their findings with those of Milberg & Albert (1989) by suggesting that their patients were more cognitively impaired overall. A comparison of total DRS scores between the two studies, however, reveals that is not the case. Patient heterogeneity and/or differences in the sensitivity of the semantic memory tests used are likely sources of the discrepant findings. Nevertheless, van der Hurk & Hodges (1995) suggested that the difficulty with semantic memory among those with PSP is not due to a loss of stored information as it is in AD. Rather, they posited faulty retrieval due to a functional deactivation of the prefrontal cortex secondary to subcortical pathology.

In a truly comparative neuropsychological study of subcortical dementia, Pillon et al. (1994) compared 15 patients with PSP to equal numbers of PD, HD and AD patients as well as 19 normal control subjects. Although a few minor differences among the three subcortical groups were found on the CVLT and the Grober–Buschke category-cued recall test (Grober et al., 1988), the authors concluded that, "their [the groups'] similarities ... are more impressive than their differences ...".

A recent meta-analysis of 23 studies of PSP published between 1984 and 1997 led Zakzanis et al. (1998) to conclude that memory impairment is not a "core" feature of PSP. Rather, they maintained, the disease is characterized primarily by impaired ability to manipulate acquired knowledge and to process information rapidly, resulting in a sluggish and inefficient memory system.

Disorders of Thalamic Nuclei

Thalamic Degeneration

Selective thalamic degeneration is a rapidly progressing disorder, which can be inherited as an autosomal dominant trait (Lugaresi et al., 1986). It appears to be an extremely rare condition, with fewer than 50 cases in the world's literature. Neuropathological studies have revealed degeneration almost exclusively in the anterior and dorsomedial nuclei of the thalamus (Lugaresi et al., 1986), with up to 90% reduction in cell counts.

Because of its rarity, thalamic degeneration has been the focus of very few neuropsychological or neuropsychiatric studies. Those reports that exist describe profound apathy, psychomotor retardation, deficits in attention and concentration, and forgetfulness, without aphasia, apraxia or agnosia (McDaniel, 1990). In other words, the picture appears to be one of classic subcortical dementia.

The rapidity with which the thalamic degeneration progresses, coupled with its attendant profound deficits in arousal and attention, render formal neuropsychological study of these patients difficult. A single report of three patients with familial thalamic degeneration is perhaps the most comprehensive attempt to date to characterize the cognitive abilities in this disorder (Gallassi et al., 1992). In this study, repeated cognitive assessments were conducted on each patient, but the tests administered varied among them. In general, immediate and short-term memory were less impaired than was memory after a delay. Verbal memory was deficient relatively early in the course of the disease, whereas spatial memory did not become impaired until later. Finally, tests of semantic memory and procedural memory were performed normally. The authors attributed the memory impairment of these patients to deficits in the encoding and manipulation of information and in the ordering of events. They concluded that the primary neuropsychological deficits in thalamic degeneration are in attention, working memory and planning, with preservation of memory stores.

Disorders of Cerebral White Matter

Ischemic Vascular Disease

Small vessel disease in the periventricular and deep white matter can produce cognitive impairment (Libon et al., 1993; Rao, 1996). Ischemic vascular disease (IVD) is a subtype of vascular dementia (VaD), a category that also includes multi-infarct dementia and strategic single-infarct dementia (Román et al., 1993). Included under the classification of IVD is Binswanger's disease, a disorder characterized by numerous areas of demyelination and infarction in the cerebral white matter.

In one of the early neuropsychological studies of IVD, Kertesz et al. (1990) compared the MRI findings and cognitive functioning of 11 VaD patients, 27 AD patients and 15 control subjects. The patient groups were matched for DRS scores. Fewer than half (11 of 27) of the AD patients had white matter changes, compared to eight of the 11 VaD patients. The Logical Memory, Visual Reproduction and Paired Associates subtests of the WMS were all better among patients with white matter changes than in those without, regardless of diagnosis. In contrast, tests of attention and comprehension were worse in those with periventricular hyperintensities. This general finding, that subcortical hyperintensities are associated with better memory performance but poorer executive control, has since been replicated (Libon et al., 1997). A similar study by Bernard et al. (1990) found that patients with Binswanger's disease performed better than DRS-matched AD patients on a verbal recognition memory test, but worse on a conceptual reasoning task.

Lafosse et al. (1997) compared 32 IVD patients to an equal number of AD patients, matched for dementia severity by MMSE scores, on performance on the Memory Assessment Scale (MAS) (Williams, 1991). The IVD group performed better on delayed free recall, produced fewer intrusions on the cued recall trial, and had better recognition discrimination than the AD patients. The authors highlighted the much better score of the IVD group on recognition compared to free recall, and attributed this to retrieval difficulties. Among the IVD patients, greater white matter abnormalities were associated with poorer free recall, whereas ventricular enlargement was related to poorer delayed cued recall. In a very similar investigation, Libon et al. (1997) compared CVLT performance of 33 AD and 27 IVD patients, matched on MMSE score. Although the groups did not differ in immediate free recall (measured by trials 1–5 of list A and list B), differences were found on delayed free recall, cued recall and recognition, with the IVD group faring better in all cases. Libon et al. concluded that the memory performance in IVD could be distinguished from that of AD, and is qualitatively similar to that seen in PD and HD.

Reed et al. (2000) compared regional glucose metabolism using PET imaging in IVD and AD during a continuous recognition memory task. Fifteen AD patients and 15 IVD patients, matched for MMSE score, identified visually-presented words as "old" or "new", depending whether they had seen the words before. Performance on the task was worse in both patient groups than in normal subjects but the IVD and AD groups did not differ between themselves. Lower metabolism in the prefrontal cortex was associated with the memory impairment in IVD but not AD, whereas lower metabolism in the left hippocampus and left medial temporal gyrus was associated with memory impairment in AD but not IVD. Because the continuous recognition task requires both working and episodic memory, the authors concluded that the frontal dysfunction observed in IVD impairs the task via its effects on attention, working memory or other executive abilities.

To determine whether a double dissociation between IVD and AD could be elicited from a comparison of declarative and procedural memory performance, Libon et al. (1998) used methodology borrowed from Butters et al. (1990). They compared 16 AD patients to 14 IVD patients, matched for disease severity by MMSE score, on the CVLT and the pursuit rotor learning task. There was no difference between groups on CVLT free recall (trials 1–5 on list A), but the IVD group made fewer intrusion errors and had better recognition discrimination. In contrast, the AD group outperformed the IVD group on the pursuit rotor task, as measured by both total time on target and slope of the learning curve over trials. Furthermore, severity of white matter pathology was associated with greater pursuit rotor learning impairment. Like HD patients, patients with IVD demonstrated impaired procedural learning on the pursuit rotor task, with preserved recognition (relative to free recall) on the CVLT (Libon et al., 1998).

Multiple Sclerosis

The cognitive characteristics of multiple sclerosis (MS) have been described since the nineteenth century (Peyser & Poser, 1986; Rao, 1990). While the cause of MS remains unknown, the neuropathology is well described. The disease consists of patchy areas of demyelination in the cerebrum, brainstem, cerebellum and spinal cord (Rao, 1990). Selective degeneration of the corpus callosum has also been recognized (Brownell & Hughes, 1962). Extreme variability in clinical course distinguishes MS from most other subcortical dementias; symptoms can exacerbate and remit at unpredictable times and for unpredictable durations. Whereas some investigators have found more severe cognitive impairment in chronic-progressive MS than in relapsing–remitting MS (Heaton et al., 1985), this is not always the case (e.g. Beatty et al., 1990). In addition, no consistent relationship has been found between duration of illness and cognitive test performance (Ivnik, 1978; Rao et al., 1984).

Some type of memory impairment is often reported in patients with MS (Ruchkin et al., 1994). There is some debate, however, as to whether the memory impairment in MS is due to an encoding or a retrieval deficit (DeLuca et al., 1994; Arnett et al., 1997). Ruchkin et al. (1994) compared 10 patients with MS to 10 normal control subjects with the goal of identifying the neurophysiological substrate of working memory deficits. Although the groups did not differ significantly on most tests of episodic memory (Logical Memory, Visual Paired Associates, Visual Reproduction, and Digit Span from the WMS-R), the MS patients performed more poorly than the control group on tests of working memory (WAIS-R Digit Symbol and articulation of irregular words). The authors interpreted these performance deficits as reflecting a defect in the phonological loop of the working memory system (Baddeley, 1986). Furthermore, they suggested that this defect is related to the often-observed pathology in the corpus callosum in MS.

Wishart & Sharpe (1997) conducted a meta-analysis of 37 studies comparing the neuropsychological functioning of MS patients to that of normal control subjects conducted between 1974 and 1994. They found that no cognitive domains were spared in MS. Within the domain of memory, the effect sizes for visual and verbal learning were greater than for delayed visual recall and recognition. Additionally, the effect size for immediate recall for verbal information was larger than that for delayed recall for visual information. Taken together, these results suggest that recognition memory does appear to be affected in MS, although less so than free recall. Wishart & Sharpe also opined that the contribution of both processing speed and working memory must be considered in understanding the recognition failures in MS.

HIV-related Dementia

The neuropsychology of acquired immune deficiency syndrome (AIDS) is distinguished from that of other diseases associated with subcortical pathology by virtue of its youth; the first cases of AIDS were reported just a decade or so ago (Navia, 1990). In spite of this (or perhaps because of it), several different terms have been used to refer to cognitive impairment associated with the human immunodeficiency virus (HIV) and the resulting illness (AIDS). *AIDS dementia complex* (ADC) requires cognitive, motor and behavioral dysfunction (Navia et al., 1986b; Price, 1996), whereas a more recent term, *AIDS-related dementia* (ARD) refers to AIDS dementia without motor impairment (Price, 1996). Since there may be neurocognitive and neuromotor abnormalities in patients infected with the virus who do not meet clinical criteria for AIDS, the terms "HIV-related dementia" and "HIV-related cognitive impairment" may be preferred terms. Neuropathological studies of HIV-related dementia have found lesions in the basal ganglia, thalamus, brainstem and central periventricular white matter (Navia et al., 1986a; Lang et al., 1989). The presence of opportunistic infections in AIDS complicates investigations of the effects of the HIV virus itself.

Early in its course, HIV-related dementia produces impairments in sequential problem solving, fine manual dexterity and motor speed (summarized by Navia, 1990). Other studies find impairment on tests of executive function (Wisconsin Card Sorting Test), memory (Selective Reminding Test recall, but not recognition) and complex attention (Trail Making Test, Symbol Digit Modalities Test, Digit Span backwards) (Maruff et al., 1994). With disease progression, additional impairments are seen in word-list generation and constructional praxis, as well as more pervasive verbal and spatial memory deficits. Because HIV-related cognitive impairment has been shown to be more similar to that found in HD than AD, many consider it a subcortical dementia (Van Gorp et al., 1992). White et al. (1995) critically reviewed the literature on cognitive impairment in asymptomatic, HIV-seropositive persons, and concluded that these individuals have a rate of cognitive impairment three times that of seronegative control subjects.

Systemic Lupus Erythematosus

Systemic lupus erythematosus (SLE), or lupus, is an autoimmune disorder that affects multiple organ systems. It was first described in 1833 by the French dermatologist Laurent Biett, although the term "lupus erythemateux" was not coined until almost 20 years later (Benedek, 1997). SLE can sometimes produce frank neurological and/or psychiatric signs, including stroke, seizures, sensory and motor neuropathies and psychosis, clearly indicating central nervous system involvement (Denburg & Denburg, 1999; Kozora et al., 1996; West, 1996). The presence of such neuropsychiatric signs reliably predicts cognitive impairment in SLE (Carlomagno et al., 2000; Kozora et al., 1998). However, even patients without such signs (i.e. "non-CNS" SLE) often complain of, and can have, significant cognitive impairment (Leritz et al., 2000; Denburg & Denburg, 1999).

Structural imaging studies of non-CNS SLE are often inconclusive, but some have revealed white matter lesions as well as increased ventricle:brain ratios (Chinn et al., 1997; Kozora et al., 1996). Functional imaging studies have proven more sensitive in detecting abnormalities associated with SLE, but their findings have been inconsistent with regard to the specific regions involved. SPECT studies, for example, have revealed hypometabolism in the basal ganglia and thalamus, but also in multiple regions of the neocortex (Kao et al., 1999; Falcini et al., 1998).

While some investigators have suggested that memory is particularly vulnerable in non-CNS SLE (Denburg & Denburg, 1999), others have found no memory impairment (Ginsburg et al., 1992; Skeel et al., 2000). Kozora et al. (1996) compared 51 patients with non-CNS SLE to 29 patients with rheumatoid arthritis (RA) and 27 healthy control subjects. RA is a well-suited clinical control group for SLE because it is rarely associated with CNS abnormalities. A comparable proportion of both patient groups (approximately 30%) demonstrated overall cognitive impairment, defined as scoring 2 SDs below the mean in at least two of eight cognitive domains. However, the proportion of patients who were impaired in the learning domain, assessed by the Story and Figure Memory Tests (Heaton et al., 1991) and the CVLT (Delis et al., 1987), was greater in SLE than in RA.

In one of the largest studies of its type, Denburg et al. (1997) investigated the relationship of antiphospholipid antibodies to cognitive function in 118 SLE patients with and without CNS signs and symptoms. Antiphospholipid antibodies are immunoglobulins in the bloodstream that react with specific fat molecules and predispose the patient to thromboembolic events. The authors found that roughly half of SLE patients testing positive for these antibodies demonstrated cognitive impairment (defined as having at least 3/18 cognitive summary scores below the 5th percentile), whereas only 25% of the antibody-negative patients were cognitively impaired. Presence of antibodies predicted cognitive impairment, even in non-CNS patients. Verbal memory, assessed with WMS Logical Memory and Paired-Associate Learning, and trials 1–5 of the RAVLT, was one of three domains in which the antibody-positive patients performed worse than antibody-negative patients (the others being cognitive flexibility and psychomotor speed).

Although the cognitive impairment associated with SLE is suggestive of a subcortical dementia, the variability of cognitive deficits makes the identification of a "typical" pattern of impairments difficult. In a recent investigation, Leritz et al. (2000) used the algorithm developed by Brandt et al. (1988) to classify the performance of non-CNS SLE patients on the MMSE as suggestive of "cortical" or "subcortical" dysfunction. Of the 93 patients, 95% were categorized as having "subcortical" deficits, whereas 5% were categorized as having "cortical" deficits. The authors concluded that even among a group of SLE patients without gross neurological impairment, the pattern of cognitive performance reflects subtle disturbances in attention, working memory and mental tracking.

Dementia of Depression

Several recent neuroimaging and neuropathological studies have suggested that patients with major depressive disorder often have localized metabolic abnormalities or structural lesions in the subcortical nuclei (including the striatum and locus coeruleus) and/or cerebral white matter (Baxter et al., 1985; O'Connell et al., 1989; Coffey et al., 1989).

It has long been recognized that the cognitive deficits observed among patients with major depression can be differentiated from those seen in AD. Whitehead (1973) reported that their new learning and memory is less variable and less prone to false-positive errors than is the case in AD. Since that time, a consistent finding is that of mild anterograde amnesia, typically not as severe as in early-stage AD and without semantic deficits (Weingartner, 1986; Hart et al., 1987). King & Caine (1990) were among the first to note the similarity of the dementia of depression to the dementia of HD and other subcortical dementias.

Clinical and neuroradiological variability among patients with depression has led to the suggestion that there are subtypes of depression, some of which are associated with dementia and others which are not. Massman et al. (1992) used discriminant function analysis to classify 49 patients with major depression into like-HD, like-AD, and normal groups, based on their performance on the CVLT and other neuropsychological tests. Whereas 29% were classified as like HD, none were classified as like AD, suggesting that at least a subset of depressed patients have a subcortical dementia profile.

Disorders of the Cerebellum

Although the cerebellum is most clearly implicated in the coordination of movement, its role in cognition is becoming more widely recognized (Rapoport et al., 2000). Cerebellar lesions can arise acutely, as in stroke, or as part of a neurodegenerative process, as in the inherited spinocerebellar ataxias. A functional disconnection of the cerebellum from the cerebrum, especially the prefrontal cortex (via the basal ganglia and thalamus), is often implicated in these higher cognitive impairments (Botez et al., 1991a). Neurochemical abnormalities of the cholinergic system (Kish et al., 1987) and of the dopaminergic system (Botez et al., 1991b) have also been suggested as contributing to the cognitive disorder of some cerebellar patients.

Patients with cerebellar disease may suffer from a variety of cognitive and affective impairments (Schmahmann & Sherman, 1998), with particularly prominent disorders of executive functioning (Grafman et al., 1992). Schmahmann & Sherman (1998) studied a heterogeneous group of 20 patients with isolated cerebellar pathology. Most prominent among the cognitive deficits and emotional disturbances found were impairments in executive functioning, including deficits in working memory (assessed with backward digit span).

Spinocerebellar Ataxias

The autosomal dominant cerebellar ataxias (ADCAs), also known as the spinocerebellar ataxias (SCAs), are a group of inherited movement disorders, several of which, like HD, are caused by triplet repeat (*CAG*) mutations coding for glutamine. This group of disorders overlaps with the entity known as olivopontocerebellar atrophy (OPCA), a disease that occurs sporadically as well as familially and is caused by progressive degeneration of the cerebellar cortex, pons and inferior olives. Kish et al. (1988) studied 11 OPCA patients with standardized cognitive tests and found prominent impairments in the recall of stories (WMS Logical Memory subtest), as well as deficits in verbal and nonverbal intelligence and executive functions. Because these patients were not aphasic, apractic or agnosic, the authors described their mental state as a mildly disabling subcortical dementia. In contrast, Berent et al. (1990) reported no cognitive performance differences between 39 OPCA patients (ill for an average of 6 years) and education-matched control subjects. In a follow-up study of 43 patients with a variety of SCAs, ill for an average of 11 years, Kish et al. (1994) found mildly ataxic patients to perform near-normally on a battery of neuropsychological tests. Moderately ataxic patients in this study displayed executive functioning deficits and mild memory deficits (WMS Mental Control and Logical Memory subtests, and Memory Quotient) that could not be explained by depression, whereas severely ataxic patients had more pervasive deficits but were nonetheless nonaphasic.

On verbal list-learning tasks, deficient immediate and delayed free recall with preservation of yes/no or forced-choice recognition is often taken as the *sine qua non* of subcortical dementia. This is generally what has been found among patients with spinocerebellar degeneration (Hirono et al., 1991).

In one of the most comprehensive memory studies of cerebellar patients to date, Appollonio et al. (1993) studied both effortful and automatic aspects of explicit memory performance in 11 patients with isolated cerebellar degeneration. The patients performed worse than normal control subjects on the DRS (Mattis, 1988) and word-list generation tasks, as well as free recall of word lists (Hasher frequency monitoring task; Hasher & Zacks, 1984) and a paired-associate learning task using both word and picture stimuli. Importantly, the patients were not impaired on the cued recall or recognition portion of either task. Neither were they impaired in their incidental monitoring of frequency of occurrence or modality of stimuli, two measures of automatic processing. Implicit memory was also investigated by Appollonio et al. (1993). Cerebellar patients and normal control subjects displayed equivalent improvement over trials on both a word fragment completion test and an identification of incomplete pictures test. The results led the authors to conclude that only attention-demanding cognitive processes are impaired in patients with pure cerebellar pathology, and these contribute to their "frontal-like" executive dysfunction.

The cognitive processing deficit(s) underlying the dysexecutive syndrome and mild subcortical dementia seen in cerebellar patients has also been the subject of several other investigations. In many cases, a defect in some aspect of sequencing or timing has been implicated (Ivry & Keele, 1989; Botez-Marquard & Routhier, 1995). Possibly related to this, it is well established that cerebellar lesions severely impair classical conditioning of the eyeblink response (Daum & Schugens, 1996; Woodruff-Pak et al., 1996), known to depend on precise timing of conditioned and unconditioned stimuli.

CONCLUSIONS

"Subcortical dementia" is simultaneously a much revered and much maligned concept in neuropsychology and behavioral neurology. It is a syndrome that is clearly more difficult to define than it is to apply. It implies anatomical delineations that fall apart on close scrutiny and a clinical phenotype that is overly broad and imprecise. Nonetheless, several relatively consistent themes emerge from the literature reviewed here:

1. Impairments in anterograde learning and memory, to the extent that they exist in diseases affecting primarily subcortical nuclei and pathways, are relatively milder than those seen in AD.
2. Tests of free recall are more sensitive to the new learning deficits of these patients than are tests of recognition. While this is likely true for most, if not all, conditions, the relative difference between recognition and recall is greater in the subcortical dementias than, for example, in AD.
3. Fluency/generativity and working memory are typically more impaired than memory storage, and may contribute to performance deficits on episodic memory tests.
4. There are probably subtypes of many subcortical diseases; some of them are associated with memory impairment and others not.
5. Memory impairments are usually most significant in patients with clear signs and symptoms of neurological disease (e.g. sensory or motor deficits).

Methodological advances in brain imaging and neuropathology have increased our understanding of the differences in pathological anatomy and chemistry underlying specific diseases affecting primarily the brainstem nuclei, cerebellum, thalamus, basal ganglia and subcortical white matter. Unfortunately, the same level of detail is often lacking when discussing the mental states of these patients. Most clinicians and scientists will agree that the term "subcortical dementia" is too coarse for further progress to be made in this field. The term will almost certainly give way eventually to the more precise delineation of specific cognitive syndromes linked to specific neurobiological entities.

ACKNOWLEDGEMENTS

Preparation of this chapter was supported, in part, by Grants AG05146 and NS16375 from the National Institutes of Health, USA.

REFERENCES

Adams, R.D. & Victor, M. (1985). *Principles of Neurology*, 3rd edn. New York: McGraw-Hill.
Adams, K.M., Grant, I. & Brown, G.G. (1985). The use of analysis of co-variance as a remedy for demographic group mismatch: some sobering simulations. *Journal of Clinical and Experimental Neuropsychology*, **7**, 445–462.

Albert, M.L., Feldman, R.G. & Willis, A.L. (1974). The "subcortical dementia" of progressive supranuclear palsy. *Journal of Neurology, Neurosurgery, and Psychiatry*, **37**, 121–130.

American Psychiatric Association. (1994). *Diagnostic and Statistical Manual of Mental Disorders*, 4th edn. Washington, DC: American Psychiatric Association.

Appollonio, I.M., Grafman, J., Schwartz, V. et al. (1993). Memory in patients with cerebellar degeneration. *Neurology*, **43**, 1536–1544.

Arnett, P.A., Higginson, C.I., Voss, W.D. et al. (1997). Working memory span and long-term memory in multiple sclerosis [Abstract]. *Journal of the International Neuropsychological Society*, **2**, 19.

Baddeley, A. (1986). *Working Memory*. Oxford: Clarendon.

Baxter, L.R., Phelps, M.E., Mazziotta, J.C. et al. (1985). Cerebral metabolic rates for glucose in mood disorders: studies with positron emission tomography and fluorodeoxyglucose F18. *Archives of General Psychiatry*, **46**, 243–250.

Beatty, W.W., Goodkin, D.E., Hertsgaard, D. & Monson, N. (1990). Clinical and demographic predictors of cognitive performance in multiple sclerosis. Do diagnostic type, disease duration, and disability matter? *Archives of Neurology*, **47**, 305–308.

Benecke, R., Rothwell, J.C. & Dick, J.P. (1987). Disturbance of sequential movements in patients with Parkinson's disease. *Brain*, **110**, 361–379.

Benedek, T. (1997). Historical background of discoid and systemic lupus erythematosus. In D.J. Wallace & B.H. Hahn (eds), *Dubois' Lupus Erythematosus* (pp. 3–16). Baltimore, MD: Williams & Wilkins.

Berent, S., Giordani, B., Gilman, S. et al. (1990). Neuropsychological changes in olivopontocerebellar atrophy. *Archives of Neurology*, **47**, 997–1001.

Bernard, B.A., Wilson, R.S., Gilley, D.W. et al. (1990). Performance of patients with BD and AD on the Mattis Dementia Rating Scale [Abstract]. *Journal of Clinical and Experimental Neuropsychology*, **12**, 22.

Blin, J., Ruberg, M. & Baron, J.C. (1992). Positron emission tomography studies. *Progressive Supranuclear Palsy: Clinical and Research Approaches* (pp. 155–168). New York: Oxford University Press.

Bondi, M.W. & Kazniak, A.W. (1991). Implicit and explicit memory in Alzheimer's disease and Parkinson's disease. *Journal of Clinical and Experimental Neuropsychology*, **13**, 339–358.

Botez, M.I., Léveillé, J., Lambert, R. & Botez-Marquard, T. (1991a). Single photon emission computed tomography (SPECT) in cerebellar disease: cerebello-cerebral diaschisis. *European Neurology*, **31**, 405–412.

Botez, M.I., Young, N.S., Botez-Marquard, T. & Pedraza, O.L. (1991b). Treatment of heredodegenerative ataxias with amantadine hydrochloride. *Canadian Journal of Neurological Sciences*, **18**, 307–311.

Botez-Marquard, T. & Routhier, I. (1995). Reaction time and intelligence in patients with olivopontocerebellar atrophy. *Neuropsychiatry, Neuropsychology, and Behavioral Neurology*, **8**, 168–175.

Brandt, J., Folstein, S.E. & Folstein, M.F. (1988). Differential cognitive impairment in Alzheimer's disease and Huntington's disease. *Annals of Neurology*, **23**, 555–561.

Brandt, J. (1994). Cognitive investigations in Huntington's disease. In L. Cermak (ed.), *Neuropsychological Explorations of Memory and Cognition: Essays in Honor of Nelson Butters* (pp. 135–146). New York: Plenum.

Brandt, J., Corwin, J. & Krafft, L. (1992). Is verbal recognition memory really different in Alzheimer's and Huntington's disease? *Journal of Clinical and Experimental Neuropsychology*, **14**, 773–784.

Brooks, D.J., Ibanez, V., Playford, E.D. et al. (1991). Presynaptic and postsynaptic striatal dopaminergic function in neuroacanthocytosis: a positron emission tomographic study. *Annals of Neurology*, **30**, 166–171.

Brownell, B. & Hughes, J.F. (1962). The distribution of plaques in the cerebrum in multiple sclerosis. *Journal of Neurology, Neurosurgery, and Psychiatry*, **25**, 315–320.

Butters, N., Sax, D., Montgomery, K. & Tarlow, S. (1978). Comparison of the neuropsychological deficits associated with early and advanced Huntington's disease. *Archives of Neurology*, **35**, 585–589.

Butters, N., Heindel, W.C., & Salmon, D.P. (1990). Dissociation of implicit memory in dementia: neurological implications. *Bulletin of the Psychonomic Society*, **28**, 359–366.

Bylsma, F.W., Brandt, J. & Strauss, M.E. (1990). Aspects of procedural memory are differentially impaired in Huntington's disease. *Archives of Clinical Neuropsychology*, **5**, 287–297.

Caine, E.D., Hunt, R.D., Weingartner, H. & Ebert, M.H. (1978). Huntington's dementia: clinical and neuropsychological features. *Archives of General Psychiatry*, **35**, 377–384.

Caine, E.D., Ebert, M.H. & Weingartner, H. (1977). An outline for the analysis of dementia. The memory disorder of Huntington's disease. *Neurology*, **27**, 1087–1092.

Carlomagno, S., Migliaresi, S., Ambrosone, L. et al. (2000). Cognitive impairment in systemic lupus erythematosus: a follow-up study. *Journal of Neurology*, **247**, 273–279.

Chinn, R.J.S., Wilkinson, I.D., Hall-Craggs, M.A. et al. (1997). Magnetic resonance imaging of the brain and cerebral proton spectroscopy in patients with systemic lupus erythematosus. *Arthritis and Rheumatism*, **40**, 36–46.

Chen, X.R., Shen, T.Z., Li, N.Z. & Liu, D.K. (1983). Computed tomography in hepatolenticular degeneration (Wilson's disease). *Computed Radiology*, **7**, 361–364.

Coffey, C.E., Figiel, G.S., Djang, W.T. et al. (1989). White matter hyperintensity on magnetic resonance imaging: clinical and neuroanatomic correlates in the depressed elderly. *Journal of Neuropsychiatry and Clinical Neurosciences*, **3**, 18–22.

Cohen, S. & Freedman, M. (1995). Cognitive and behavioural changes in Parkinson-plus syndromes. In W.J. Weiner & A.E. Lang (eds), *Advances in Neurology: Behavioral Neurology of Movement Disorders*, Vol. 65 (pp.139–157). New York: Raven.

Crosson, B. (1992). *Subcortical Functions in Language and Memory*. New York: Guilford.

Cummings, J.L., Gosenfeld, L.F., Houlihan, J.P. & McCaffrey, T. (1983). Neuropsychiatric disturbances associated with idiopathic calcification of the basal ganglia. *Biological Psychiatry*, **18**, 591–601.

Cummings, J.L. (1993). Frontal-subcortical circuits and human behavior. *Archives of Neurology*, **50**, 873–880.

Cummings, J.L. & Benson, D.F. (1984). Subcortical dementia. Review of an emerging concept. *Archives of Neurology*, **41**, 874–879.

Darvesh, S. & Freedman, M. (1996). Subcortical dementia: a neurobehavioral approach. *Brain and Cognition*, **31**, 230–249.

Daum, I. & Schugens, M.M. (1996). On the cerebellum and classical conditioning. *Current Directions in Psychological Science*, **5**, 58–61.

Delis, D.C., Kramer, J.H., Kaplan, E. & Ober, B.A. (1987). *California Verbal Learning Test*. New York: Psychological Corporation.

DeLuca, J., Barbieri-Berger, S. & Johnson, S.K. (1994). The nature of memory impairments in multiple sclerosis: acquisition vs. retrieval. *Journal of Clinical and Experimental Neuropsychology*, **16**, 183–189.

Denberg, S.D., Carbotte, R.M. & Denberg, J.A. (1987). Cognitive impairment in systemic lupus erythematosus: a neuropsychological study of individual and group deficits. *Journal of Clinical and Experimental Neuropsychology*, **9**, 323–339.

Denburg, S.D., Carbotte, R.M., Ginsberg, J.S. & Denburg, J.A. (1997). The relationship of antiphospholipid antibodies to cognitive function in patients with systemic lupus erythematosus. *Journal of the International Neuropsychological Society*, **3**, 377–386.

Denburg, S.D. & Denburg, J.A. (1999). Cognitive dysfunction in systemic lupus erythematosus. In D.J. Walace & B.H. Hahn (eds), *Dubois' Lupus Erthematosus* (pp. 611–629). Philadelphia, PA: Lea & Febiger.

Domesick, V.B. (1990). Subcortical anatomy: the circuitry of the striatum. In J.L. Cummings (ed.), *Subcortical Dementia* (pp. 31–43). New York: Oxford University Press.

Drebing, C.E., Moore, L.H., Cummings, J.L. et al. (1993). Patterns of neuropsychological performance among forms of subcortical dementia: a case study approach. *Neuropsychiatry, Neuropsychology, and Behavioral Neurology*, **7**, 57–66.

Falcini, F., DeCristofaro, M.T., Ermini, M. et al. (1998). Regional cerebral blood flow in juvenile systemic lupus erythematosus: a prospective SPECT study. *Journal of Rheumatology*, **25**, 583–588.

Fisher, J.M., Kennedy, J.L., Caine, E.D. & Shoulson, I. (1983). Dementia in Huntington's disease: a cross-sectional analysis of intellectual decline. *Advances in Neurology*, **38**, 229–238.

Folstein, S.E. (1989). *Huntington's Disease: A Disorders of Families*. Baltimore, MD: Johns Hopkins University Press.

Folstein, M.F., Folstein, S.E. & McHugh, P.R. (1975). Mini-Mental State: a practical method of grading the cognitive state of patients for the clinician. *Journal of Psychiatric Research*, **12**, 189–198.

Franklin, S., Turner, J.E. & Ellis, A.W. (1992). *The ADA Comprehension Battery*. University of York: Human Neuropsychology Laboratory.

Freedman, M. (1990). Parkinson's Disease. In J.L. Cummings (ed.), *Subcortical Dementia* (pp. 71–86). New York: Oxford University Press.

Gabrieli, J.D.E., Stebbins, G.T., Jaswinder, S. et al. (1997). Intact mirror-tracing and impaired rotary-pursuit skill learning in patients with Huntington's disease: evidence for dissociable memory systems in skill learning. *Neuropsychology*, **11**, 272–281.

Gallassi, R., Morreale, A., Montagna, P. et al. (1992). Fatal familial insomnia: neuropsychological study of a disease with thalamic degeneration. *Cortex*, **28**, 175–187.

Ginsburg, K.S., Wright, E.A., Larson, M.G. et al. (1992). A controlled study of the prevalence of cognitive dysfunction in randomly selected patients with systemic lupus erythematosus. *Arthritis and Rheumatism*, **35**, 776–782.

Grafman, J., Litvan, I., Massaquoi, S. et al. (1992). Cognitive planning deficit in patients with cerebellar atrophy. *Neurology*, **42**, 1493–1496.

Grafman, J., Litvan, I., Gomez, C. & Chase, T.N. (1990). Frontal lobe function in progressive supranuclear palsy. *Archives of Neurology,* **47**, 553–558.

Grober, E., Buschke, H., Crystal, H. et al. (1988). Screening for dementia by memory testing. *Neurology*, **38**, 900–903.

Haaland, K.Y., Harrington, D.L., O'Brien, S. & Hermanowicz, N. (1997). Cognitive-motor learning in Parkinson's disease. *Neuropsychology*, **11**, 180–186.

Hach, B. & Hartung, M.L. (1979). The effect of penicillamine on the mental disorders associated with Wilson's disease (in German). *Nervenarzi*, **50**, 115–120.

Hardie, R.J., Pullon, H.W.H., Harding, A.E. et al. (1991). Neuroacanthocytosis: a clinical, haematological and pathological study of 19 cases. *Brain*, **114**, 13–49.

Harrington, D.L., Haaland, K.Y., Yeo, R.A. & Marder, E. (1990). Procedural memory in Parkinson's disease: impaired motor but not visuoperceptual learning. *Journal of Clinical and Experimental Neuropsychology*, **12**, 323–339.

Hart, R.P., Kwentus, J.A., Taylor, J.R. & Harkins, S.W. (1987). Rate of forgetting in dementia and depression. *Journal of Consulting and Clinical Psychology*, **55**, 101–105.

Hasher, L. & Zacks, R. (1984). Automatic processing of fundamental information: the case of frequency of occurrence. *American Psychologist*, **39**, 1372–1388.

Heaton, R.K., Grant, I. & Matthews, C.G. (1991). *Comprehensive Norms for an Extended Halstead Reitan Battery*. Odessa, FL: Psychological Assessment Resources.

Heaton, R.K., Nelson, L.M., Thompson, D.S. et al. (1985). Neuropsychological findings in relapsing-remitting and chronic-progressive multiple sclerosis. *Journal of Consulting and Clinical Psychology*, **53**, 103–110.

Hefter, H., Arendt, G., Stremmel, W. & Freund, H.-J. (1993). Motor impairment in Wilson's disease: slowness of voluntary limb movements. *Acta Neurologica Scandinavia*, **87**, 133–147.

Heindel, W.C., Salmon, D.P. & Butters, N. (1991). The biasing of weight judgments in Alzheimer's and Huntington's disease: a priming or programming phenomenon? *Journal of Clinical and Experimental Neuropsychology*, **13**, 189–203.

Heindel, W.C., Butters, N. & Salmon, D.P. (1988). Impaired learning of a motor skill in patients with Huntington's disease. *Behavioral Neuroscience*, **102**, 141–147.

Heindel, W.C., Salmon, D.P., Shults, C.W. et al. (1989). Neuropsychological evidence for multiple implicit memory systems: a comparison of Alzheimer's, Huntington's, and Parkinson's disease patients. *Journal of Neuroscience*, **9**, 582–587.

Hier, D.B. & Cummings, J.L. (1990). Rare acquired and degenerative subcoirtical dementias. In J.L. Cummings (ed.), *Subcortical Dementia* (pp. 199–217). New York: Oxford University Press.

Hirono, N., Yamadori, A., Kameyama, M. et al. (1991). Spinocerebellar degeneration (SCD): cognitive disturbances. *Acta Neurologica Scandinavica*, **84**, 226–230.

Howard, D. & Patterson, K. (1992). *The Pyramids and Palm Trees Test*. Bury St. Edmunds: Thames Valley Test Co.

Isaacs-Glaberman, K., Medalia, A. & Scheinberg, H. (1988). Verbal recall and recognition abilities in patients with Wilson's disease. Paper read at the 16th annual meeting of the International Neuropsychological Society, New Orleans, January.

Ivnik, R.J. (1978). Neuropsychological test performance as a function of the duration of MS-related symptomatology. *Journal of Clinical Psychiatry*, **39**, 304–307.

Ivry, R.B. & Keele, S.W. (1989). Timing functions of the cerebellum. *Journal of Cognitive Neurosciences*, **1**, 136–152.

Jellinger, K.A. & Bancher, C. (1992). Neuropathology. In *Progressive Supranuclear Palsy: Clinical and Research Approaches* (pp. 44–88). New York: Oxford University Press.

Kao, C-H., Ho, Y-J., Lan, J-L. et al. (1999). Discrepancy between regional cerebral blood flow and glucose metabolism of the brain in systemic lupus erythematosus patients with normal brain magnetic resonance imaging findings. *Arthritis and Rheumatism*, **42**, 61–68.

Kaplan, E.F., Goodglass, H. & Weintraub, S. (1983). *The Boston Naming Test*. Philadelphia, PA: Lea & Febinger.

Kartsounis, L.D. & Hardie, R.J. (1996). The pattern of cognitive impairments in neuroacanthocytosis: a frontosubcortical dementia. *Archives of Neurology*, **53**(1), 77–80.

Kertesz, A., Polk, M. & Carr, T. (1990). Cognition and white matter changes on magnetic resonance imaging in dementia. *Archives of Neurology*, **47**, 387–391.

King, D.A. & Caine E.D. (1990). Depression. In J.L. Cummings (ed.), *Subcortical Dementia* (pp. 218–230). New York: Oxford University Press.

Kish, S.J., Rajput, A., Gilbert, J. et al. (1996). Elevated GABA level in striatal but not extrastriatal brain regions in Parkinson's disease: correlation with striatal dopamine loss. *Annals of Neurology*, **20**, 26–31.

Kish, S.J., Shannak, K. & Hornykiewicz, O. (1988a). Uneven pattern of dopamine loss in the striatum of patients with idiopathic Parkinson's disease: pathophysiologic and clinical implications. *New England Journal of Medicine*, **318**, 876–880.

Kish, S.J., El-Awar, M., Stuss, D. et al. (1994). Neuropsychological test performance in patients with dominantly inherited spinocerebellar ataxia: Relationship to ataxia severity. *Neurology*, **44**, 1738–1746.

Kish, S.J., Currier, R.D., Schut, L. et al. (1987). Brain choline acetyltransferase reduction in dominantly inherited olivopontocerellar atrophy. *Annals of Neurology*, **22**, 272–275.

Kish, S.J., El-Awar, M., Schut, L. et al. (1988b). Cognitive deficits in olivopontocerebellar atrophy: Implications for the cholinergic hypothesis of Alzheimer's disease. *Annals of Neurology*, **24**, 200–206.

Klein, C. & Vieregge, P. (1998). Fahr's disease—far from a disease. *Movement Disorders*, **13**, 620–621.

Knopman, D.S. & Nissen, M.J. (1991). Procedural learning is impaired in Huntington's disease: evidence from the serial reaction time task. *Neuropsychologia*, **29**, 245–254.

Kozora, E., Thompson, L., West, S.G. & Kotzin, B.L. et al. (1996). Analysis of cognitive and psychological deficits in systemic lupus erythematosus patients without overt central nervous system disease. *Arthritis & Rheumatism*, **39**, 2035–2045.

Kozora, E., West, S.G., Kotzin, B.L. et al. (1998). Magnetic resonance imaging abnormalities and cognitive deficits in systemic lupus erythematosus patients without overt central nervous system disease. *Arthritis and Rheumatism*, **41**, 41–47.

Kramer, J.H., Levin, B.E., Brandt, J. & Delis, D.C. (1989). Differentiation of Alzheimer's, Huntington's, and Parkinson's disease patients on the basis of verbal learning characteristics. *Neuropsychology*, **3**, 111–120.

Kutcher, J.S., Kahn, M.J., Andersson, H.D. & Foundas, A.L. (1999). Neuroacanthocytosis masquerading as Huntington's disease: CT/MRI findings. *Journal of Neuroimaging*, **9**, 187–189.

Lafosse, J.M., Reed, B.R., Mungas, D. et al. (1997). Fluency and memory differences between ischemic vascular dementia and Alzheimer's disease. *Neuropsychology*, **11**, 514–522.

Lang, C., Müller, D., Claus, D. & Druschky, K.F. (1990). Neuropsychological findings in treated Wilson's Disease. *Acta Neurologica Scandinavica*, **81**, 75–81.

Lang, C. (1989). Is Wilson's disease a dementing condition? *Journal of Clinical and Experimental Neuropsychology*, **14**, 569–570.

Lang, W., Miklossy, J., Deruaz, J.P. et al. (1989). Neuropathology of the acquired immune deficiency syndrome (AIDS): a report of 135 consecutive autopsy cases from Switzerland. *Acta Neuropathologica*, **77**, 379–390.

Leritz, E., Brandt, J., Minor, M. et al. (2000). "Subcortical" cognitive impairment in patients with systemic lupus erythematosus. *Journal of the International Neuropsychological Society*, **6**, 821–825.

Libon, D.J., Bogdanoff, B., Bonavitak, J. et al. (1997). Dementia associated with periventricular and deep white matter alterations: a subtype of subcortical dementia. *Archives of Clinical Neuropsychology*, **12**, 239–250.

Libon, D.J., Bogdanoff, B., Cloud, B.S. et al. (1998). Declarative and procedural learning, quantitative measures of the hippocampus, and subcortical white alterations in Alzheimer's disease and ischaemic vascular dementia. *Journal of Clinical and Experimental Neuropsychology*, **20**, 30–41.

Libon, D.J., Swenson, R., Malamut, B.L. et al. (1993). Periventricular white matter alterations, Binswanger's disease, and dementia. *Developmental Neuropsychology*, **9**, 87–102.

Lopez-Villegas, D., Kulisevsky, J., Deus, J. et al. (1996). Neuropsychological alterations in patients with computed tomography-detected basal ganglia calcification. *Archives of Neurology*, **53**, 251–256.

Lovell, M.R. & Smith, S.S. (1997). Neuropsychological evaluation of subcortical dementia. In P. David (ed.), *Handbook of Neuropsychology and Aging. Critical Issues in Neuropsychology* (pp. 189–200). New York: Plenum.

Lugaressi, E., Medori, R., Montagna, P. et al. (1986). Fatal familial insomnia and dysautonimia with selective degeneration of thalamic nuclei. *New England Journal of Medicine*, **315**, 997–1003.

Mandell, A.M. & Albert, M.L. (1990). History of subcortical dementia. In J.L. Cummings (ed.), *Subcortical Dementia* (pp. 17–30). New York: Oxford University Press.

Martone, M., Butters, N., Payne, J. et al. (1984). Dissociations between skill learning and verbal recognition in amnesia and dementia. *Archives of Neurology*, **41**, 965–970.

Maruff, P., Currie, J., Malone, V. et al. (1994). Neuropsychological characterization of the AIDS dementia complex and rationalization of a test battery. *Archives of Neurology*, **51**, 689–695.

Massman, P.J., Delis, D.C., Butters, N. et al. (1990). Are all subcortical dementias alike? Verbal learning and memory in Parkinson's and Huntington's disease patients. *Journal of Clinical and Experimental Neuropsychology*, **12**, 729–744.

Massman, P.J., Delis, D.C., Butters, N. et al. (1992). The subcortical dysfunction hypothesis of memory deficits in depression: neuropsychological validation in a subgroup of patients. *Journal of Clinical and Experimental Neuropsychology*, **14**, 687–706.

Mattis, S. (1988). *Dementia Rating Scale: Professional Manual*. Odessa, FL: Psychological Assessment Resources.

McDaniel, K.D. (1990). Thalamic degeneration. In J.L. Cummings (ed.), *Subcortical Dementia* (pp. 132–144). New York: Oxford University Press.

McHugh, P.R. (1989). The neuropsychiatry of basal ganglia disorders: a triadic syndrome and its explanation. *Neuropsychiatry, Neuropsychology, and Behavioral Neurology*, **2**, 239–246.

McHugh, P.R. & Folstein, M.F. (1975). Psychiatric syndrome of Huntington's chorea: a clinical and pharmacologic study. In D.F. Benson & D. Blumer (eds), *Psychiatric Aspects of Neurologic Disease*. New York: Grune & Stratton.

Medalia, A., Isaacs-Glaberman, K. & Scheinberg, I.H. (1988). Neuropsychological impairment in Wilson's disease. *Archives of Neurology*, **45**, 502–504.

Medalia, A., Galynker, I. & Scheinberg, H. (1992). The interaction of motor, memory, and emotional dysfunction in Wilson's disease. *Biological Psychiatry*, **31**, 823–826.

Medalia, A. (1991). Memory deficit in Wilson's disease: a response to Lang. *Journal of Clinical and Experimental Neuropsychology*, **13**(2), 359–360.

Middleton, F.A. & Strick, P.L. (2000). Basal ganglia and cerebellar loops: motor and cognitive circuits. *Brain Research Reviews*, **31**, 236–250.

Milberg, W. & Albert, M. (1989). Cognitive differences between patients with progressive supranuclear palsy and Alzheimer's disease. *Journal of Clinical and Experimental Neuropsychology*,
11(5), 605–614.

Moss, M.D., Albert, M.S., Butters, N. & Payne, M. (1986). Differential patterns of memory loss among
patients with Alzheimer's disease, Huntington's disease, and alcoholic Korsakoff's syndrome.
Archives of Neurology, **43**, 239–246.

Navia, B.A., Cho, E.S., Petito, C.K. & Price, R.W. (1986a). The AIDS dementia complex: II. Neuropathology. *Annals of Neurology*, **19**(6), 525–535.

Navia, B.A., Jordan, B.D. & Price, R.W. (1986b). The AIDS dementia complex. I. Clinical features.
Annals of Neurology, **19**, 517–524.

Navia, B.A. (1990). The AIDS dementia complex. In J.L. Cummings (ed.), *Subcortical Dementia*
(pp. 181–198). New York: Oxford University Press.

O'Connell, R.A., Van Heertum, R.L., Billick, S.B. et al. (1989). Single photon emission computed
tomography (SPECT) with [^{123}I] IMP in the differential diagnosis of psychiatric disorders. *Journal
of Neuropsychiatry and Clinical Neurosciences*, **1**, 145–152.

Paulsen, J.S., Butters, N., Salmon, D.P. et al. (1993). Prism adaptation in Alzheimer's and Huntington's
disease. *Neuropsychology*, **1**, 73–81.

Paulsen, J.S., Butters, N., Sadek, J.R. et al. (1995). Distinct cognitive profiles of cortical and subcortical
dementia in advanced illness. *Neurology*, **45**, 951–956.

Peyser, J.M. & Poser, C.M. (1986). Neuropsychological correlates of multiple sclerosis. In S.B.
Filskov & T.J. Boll (eds), *Handbook of Clinical Neuropsychology*, Vol. 2 (pp. 364–397). New
York: Wiley.

Pillon, B., Deweer, B., Michon, A. et al. (1994). Are explicit memory disorders of progressive supranuclear palsy related to damage to striatofrontal circuits? *Neurology*, **44**, 1264–1270.

Pillon, B., Deweer, B., Agid, Y. & Dubois, B. (1993). Explicit memory in Alzheimer's, Huntington's,
and Parkinson's diseases. *Archives of Neurology*, **50**, 374–379.

Pillon, B., Dubois, B., Ploska, A. & Agid, Y. (1991). Severity and specificity of cognitive impairment in Alzheimer's, Huntington's, and Parkinson's diseases and progressive supranuclear palsy.
Neurology, **41**, 634–643.

Price, R.W. (1996). AIDS dementia complex: a complex, slow virus "model" of acquired genetic
neurodegenerative disease. *Cold Spring Harbor Symposium on Quantitative Biology*, **61**, 759–
770.

Quinn, N. & Schrag, A. (1998). Huntington's disease and other choreas. *Journal of Neurology*, **245**,
709–715.

Rao, S.M. (1996). White matter disease and dementia. *Brain and Cognition*, **31**, 250–268.

Rao, S.M., Hammeke, T.A., McQuillen, M.P. et al. (1984). Memory disturbance in chronic progressive
multiple sclerosis. *Archives of Neurology*, **41**, 625–631.

Rao, S.M. (1986). Neuropsychology of multiple sclerosis: a critical review. *Journal of Clinical and
Experimental Neuropsychology*, **8**, 503–542.

Rapoport, M., van Reekum, R. & Mayberg, H. (2000). The role of the cerebellum in cognition
and behavior: a selective review. *Journal of Neuropsychiatry and Clinical Neurosciences*, **12**,
193–198.

Reed, B.R., Eberling, J.L., Mungas, D. et al. (2000). Memory failure has different mechanisms in
subcortical stroke and Alzheimer's disease. *Annals of Neurology*, **48**, 275–284.

Rinne, J.O., Daniel, S.E., Scaravilli, F. et al. (1994). The neuropathological features of neuroacanthocytosis. *Movement Disorders*, **9**, 297–304.

Rohrer, D., Salmon, D.P., Wixted, J.T. & Paulsen, J.S. (1999). The disparate effects of Alzheimer's
disease and Huntington's disease on semantic memory. *Neuropsychology*, **13**, 381–388.

Román, G.C., Tatemichi, T.K., Erkinjuntti, T. et al. (1993). Vascular dementia: diagnostic criteria for
research studies. Report of the NINDS–AIREN International Workshop. *Neurology*, **43**, 250–260.

Rosselli, M. (1987). Wilson's disease, a reversible dementia: case report. *Journal of Clinical and
Experimental Neuropsychology*, **9**, 399–406.

Rothlind, J. & Brandt, J. (1993). Validation of a brief assessment of frontal and subcortical functions
in dementia. *Journal of Neuropsychiatry and Clinical Neurosciences*, **5**, 73–77.

Ruchkin, D.S., Grafman, J., Krauss, G.L. et al. (1994). Event-related brain potential evidence for a
verbal working memory deficit in multiple sclerosis. *Brain*, **117**, 289–305.

Saint-Cyr, J.A., Taylor, A.E. & Lang, A.E. (1988). Procedural learning and neostriatal dysfunction in man. *Brain*, **111**, 941–959.

Salmon, D.P., Kwo-on-Yuen, P.F., Heindel, W.C. et al. (1989). Differentiation of Alzheimer's disease and Huntington's disease with the Dementia Rating Scale. *Archives of Neurology*, **46**, 1204–1208.

Scheinberg, I.H. & Sternlieb, I. (1984). *Wilson's Disease*. Philadelphia, PA: Saunders.

Schmahmann, J.D. & Sherman, J.C. (1998). The cerebellar cognitive affective syndrome. *Brain*, **121**, 561–576.

Skeel, R.J., Johnstone, B., Yangco, D.T. et al. (2000). Neuropsychological deficit profiles in systemic lupus erythematosus. *Applied Neuropsychology*, **7**, 96–101.

Soliveri, P., Monza, D., Paridi, D. et al. (1999). Cognitive and magnetic resonance imaging aspects of corticobasal degeneration and progressive supranuclear palsy. *Neurology*, **53**, 502–507.

Starosta-Rubinstein, S., Young, A.B., Kluin, K. et al. (1987). Clinical assessment of 31 patients with Wilson's disease. *Archives of Neurology*, **4**, 365–370.

Steele, J.C., Richardson, J.C. & Olszewski, J. (1964). Progressive supranuclear palsy: a heterogeneous degeneration involving the brain stem, basal ganglia, and cerebellum, with vertical gaze and pseudobulbar palsy, nuclear dystonia, and dementia. *Archives of Neurology*, **10**, 339–359.

van der Hurk, P.R. & Hodges, J.R. (1995). Episodic and semantic memory in Alzheimer's disease and progressive supranuclear palsy: a comparative study. *Journal of Clinical and Experimental Neuropsychology*, **17**, 459–471.

Van Gorp, W.G., Mandelkern, M.A., Gee, M. et al. (1992). Cerebral metabolic dysfunction in AIDS: Findings in a sample with and without dementia. *Journal of Neuropsychiatry and Clinical Neuroscience*, **4**, 280–287.

Von Stockert, F.G. (1932). Subcorticale demenz. *Archives of Psychiatry*, **97**, 77–100.

Vonsattel, J.P., Myers, R.H., Stevens, T.J. et al. (1985). Neuropathological classification of Huntington's disease. *Journal of Neuropathology and Experimental Neurology*, **44**, 559–577.

Warrington, E.K. (1984). *Recognition Memory Test*. Windsor: NFER-Nelson.

Wechsler, D. (1945). A standardized memory scale for clinical use. *Journal of Psychology*, **19**, 87–95.

Weingartner, H. (1987). Automatic and effort-demanding cognitive processes in depression. In J.W. Poon & T. Crook (eds), *Handbook of Clinical Memory Assessment of Older Adults* (pp. 218–225). Washington, DC: American Psychological Association.

Weingartner, H., Caine, E.D. & Ebert, M.H. (1979). Imagery, encoding, and retrieval of information form memory: some specific encoding-retrieval changes in Huntington's disease. *Journal of Abnormal Psychology*, **88**, 52–58.

Welsh, K.A., Butters, N., Mohs, R.C. et al. (1994). The Consortium to Establish a Registry for Alzheimer's Disease (CERAD). Part V. A normative study of the neuropsychological battery. *Neurology*, **44**, 609–614.

West, S.G. (1996). Lupus and the central nervous system. *Current Opinion in Rheumatology*, **8**, 408–414.

White, D.A., Heaton, R.K., Monsch, A.U. & the HNRC Group. (1995). Neuropsychological studies of asymptomatic Human Immunodeficiency Virus Type-1 infected individuals. *Journal of the International Neuropsychological Society*, **1**, 304–315.

Whitehead, A. (1973). Verbal learning and memory in elderly depressives. *British Journal of Psychiatry*, **123**, 203–208.

Whitehouse, P.J., Price, D.L., Struble, R.G. et al. (1982). Alzheimer's disease and senile dementia: loss of neurons in the basal forebrain. *Science*, **215**, 237–239.

Whitehouse, P.J. (1986). The concept of subcortical and cortical dementia: another look. *Annals of Neurology*, **19**, 1–6.

Williams, J.M. (1991). *Memory Assessment Scales Manual*. Odessa, FL: Psychological Assessment Resources.

Williams, F.J.B. & Walshe, J.M. (1981). Wilson's disease—an analysis of the cranial computerized tomography appearances found in 60 patients and the changes in response to treatment with chelating agents. *Brain*, **104**, 735–752.

Willingham, D.B., Koroshetz, W.J. & Peterson, E.W. (1996). Motor skills have diverse neural bases: Spared and impaired skill acquisition in Huntington's disease. *Neuropsychology*, **10**, 315–321.

Wilson, S.A.K. (1912). Progressive lenticular degeneration: a familiar nervous disease associated with cirrhosis of the liver. *Brain*, **34**, 294–507.

Wishart, H. & Sharp, D. (1997). Neuropsychological aspects of multiple sclerosis: a quantitative review. *Journal of Clinical and Experimental Neuropsychology*, **19**, 810–824.

Woodruff-Pak, D.S., Papka, M. & Ivry, R.B. (1996). Cerebellar involvement in classical eyeblink conditioning in humans. *Neuropsychology*, **10**, 443–458.

Zakzanis, K.K., Leach, L. & Freedman, L. (1998). Structural and functional meta-analytic evidence for fronto-subcortical system deficit in progressive supranuclear palsy. *Brain and Cognition*, **38**, 283–296.

Assessment and Management of Memory Problems

CHAPTER 28

Assessment of Memory Disorders

Barbara A. Wilson

MRC Cognition and Brain Sciences Unit, Cambridge, and Oliver Zangwill Centre for Cognitive Rehabilitation, Ely, UK

This chapter is concerned with the assessment of memory disorders in people whose problems follow an injury or insult to the brain. Assessment can be taken to mean the systematic collection, organisation and interpretation of information about a person and his/her situation. It is also concerned with the prediction of future behaviour in new situations (Sundberg & Tyler, 1962).

Ways in which information is collected, organized and interpreted will depend on reasons why the information is needed. Assessments carried out for research purposes may require a different approach from assessments carried out for clinical purposes. Both research and clinically-orientated assessments will differ further, depending on the nature of the question or questions each is asking. So, for example, someone interested in the underlying processes involved in memory would carry out a different assessment procedure from someone interested in whether or not a memory impaired patient can return to work. An example of the former might be to find out whether or not part of a theoretical model is true, e.g. Baddeley et al. (1986) wanted to support or refute the hypothesis that patients with Alzheimer's disease had a deficit in the central executive component of the working memory model (Baddeley & Hitch, 1974). An example of the latter might be to identify the tasks involved in a particular job and observe whether or not a memory-impaired person could do those tasks in various situations, at different times of day and with increasing amounts of distraction. Mayes (1986, 1995) discusses the different concerns of researchers and clinicians.

This chapter focuses on clinical assessments and how clinically-orientated questions can be answered. Some can be answered using standardized tests, while others require a more functional or behavioural approach. Standardized tests are appropriate for certain questions and answer these reasonably well. As assessment of memory is typically part of a broader cognitive assessment, important questions might include the following:

- What is this person's general level of intellectual functioning?
- What was the probable level of premorbid functioning?

The Handbook of Memory Disorders. Edited by A.D. Baddeley, M.D. Kopelman and B.A. Wilson
© 2002 John Wiley & Sons, Ltd.

- Does this person have an organic memory deficit?
- Is there a difference in ability between recognition and recall tasks?
- Is there a difference between verbal and visual memory ability?
- To what extent are the memory problems due to language, perceptual or attention deficits?
- How do these scores compare with people of the same age in the general population?

These and similar questions can, on the whole, be answered by the administration of standardized tests, e.g. there are adequately normed, reliable and valid tests available to answer each of the above questions. It is when we turn to treatment or rehabilitation issues that standardized tests are perhaps less satisfactory. They are less effective in telling us how memory deficits identified on tests affect everyday life. Standardized tests tend to be more concerned with the structure of memory, rather than the manifestations of memory difficulties in real life. Furthermore, they do not take into account factors such as premorbid lifestyle, personality, motivation, family support and so forth.

The kind of questions people in rehabilitation want answered include the following:

- What problems are causing the greatest difficulty for this person and the family?
- What coping strategies are used?
- Are the problems exacerbated by anxiety or depression?
- Can this person return home/to school/to work?
- Should we try to restore lost functioning or teach compensatory strategies?

Although results from standardized tests can throw light on some of these questions (e.g. someone with widespread cognitive deficits plus a severe memory impairment is unlikely to return to work), they do not directly answer them. Instead, a more behavioural or functional approach is required, such as that provided by direct observation, self-report measures (usually from relatives or therapists) or interviews.

In concluding this introduction, it needs to be pointed out that the two methodologies are not in opposition to each other. In fact, they are complementary and can be combined in order to plan treatment strategies (see Chapter 30).

MODELS OF ASSESSMENT

Current assessment procedures in neuropsychology have been influenced by several theoretical models or approaches. Perhaps the most widely known is the psychometric approach, based on statistical analysis. Test development typically involves establishing a procedure for administration, collecting norms from a representative population, developing a scoring procedure, and determining the reliability and validity of the test. Although other models of assessment may include many of these features, the rationale behind them is not based solely on statistical analysis. Anastasi (1982), Lezak (1995) and Evans et al. (1996) provide accounts of the characteristics of psychometric tests. The revised Wechsler Memory Scales (Wechsler, 1987, 1997) are examples of psychometrically-influenced memory tests.

Another approach to assessment is the localisation model, whereby the examiner attempts to assess damage to a particular part of the brain, such as the frontal lobes or the hippocampus. Until about 20 years ago, one of the main purposes of a neuropsychological assessment was to identify damage of this kind in order to help neurologists or neurosurgeons obtain a diagnosis. With the advent of scanners, this is no longer the case. Less often used in clinical memory assessments, localisation models have been traditionally associated with the detection of frontal lobe damage rather than other areas of the brain. The Halstead–Reitan battery (Halstead, 1947; Reitan & Davison, 1974) is a classic example of this approach, and was originally used to discriminate between patients with frontal lobe damage and with controls.

Researchers interested in the anatomy of memory are, perhaps, more concerned with localisation than clinicians. Markowitsch (1998) discusses different types of memory problems associated with particular anatomical sites. Some believe that the left frontal lobe is particularly involved with encoding of information, while the right is more concerned with retrieval of information (see e.g. Shallice et al., 1994; Tulving et al., 1994). In short, people with typical episodic anterograde amnesia are likely to have lesions in and around the hippocampal area (i.e. the medial temporal lobes). Those with confabulation, poor attention or encoding, poor retrieval and prospective memory difficulties are likely to have frontal lobe damage.

Working memory deficits are associated with frontal lobe lesions (Goldman-Rakic & Friedman, 1991), although they may also be associated with other areas. One component of working memory, the phonological loop, appears to involve several sites, such as the left basal frontal, the parietal and the superior temporal areas (Vallar & Papagno, 1995). Another working memory component, the visuospatial sketchpad, appears to involve the right occipital, parietal and prefrontal areas (Baddeley, 1999). Semantic memory deficits are associated with damage to the lateral temporal neocortex, with the hippocampal areas being relatively unaffected (Graham et al., 1997). Procedural memory appears to depend on the basal ganglia and cerebellar regions (Markowitsch, 1998; Tranel & Damasio, 1995). Recall and recognition deficits may follow both hippocampal and frontal lobe damage, although recognition may be less impaired in frontal patients. This is because such patients are likely to have poor retrieval skills and recognition tasks avoid the need for retrieval strategies.

Retrograde amnesia is believed to result from lesions in different areas of the brain from those causing anterograde amnesia. Medial temporal lobe structures are responsible for anterograde memory, and anterolateral temporal lobe areas, especially on the right, are thought to be critical for the retrieval of anterograde factual knowledge (Calabrese et al., 1996; Jones et al., 1998). Another paper, by Eslinger (1998), argues for both left and right temporal lobe involvement in one component of retrograde memory, namely autobiographical memory, with more severe impairment following bilateral damage.

Although researchers are interested in the anatomy of memory, assessments are not always administered to identify location of lesion. Instead, lesions are used to confirm the functional distinctions of memory. In clinical memory assessments, the localisation approach is perhaps mostly associated with: (a) whether or not a client has a pure amnesic syndrome (associated with hippocampal damage) or more widespread damage, in which case there will be additional cognitive deficits; and (b) whether the memory deficit is due to hippocampal or frontal lobe damage. Hippocampal damage results in a different pattern of memory deficits than frontal lobe damage. Within the frontal lobes there are several systems involved in memory. Some argue that they have an indirect rather than a direct role in memory, and exert their influences through processes such as attention, encoding and problem solving (see Tranel & Damasio, 1995; for discussion, see Chapter 2, this volume). What is clear is that memory disorders associated with damage to the frontal lobes are different from those that occur with medial temporal lobe damage.

Frontal lobe memory deficits include poor prospective memory, problems in judging how recently or how frequently something has happened, confabulation, poor retrieval problems, and difficulty in linking various components of a memory together, so that mismatching may occur (i.e. components from different memories may be incorrectly linked together).

A third approach to the assessment of memory derives from theoretical models from cognitive psychology and cognitive neuropsychology. Models of language, reading, perception and attention have provided a rich source of ideas for assessment procedures. In memory, the working memory model of Baddeley & Hitch (1974) has had a big influence on the assessment of people with organic memory impairment. At one time, memory was assessed either as if it were one skill or function or as if the subdivisions were gross, e.g. the first Wechsler Scale (Wechsler, 1945) did not include delayed recall. Since the working memory and other memory models appeared, clinicians have become increasingly likely to separate assessments into visual and verbal, semantic and episodic, and short- and long-term memory. Furthermore, it is now routine to examine phonological loop, visual spatial sketchpad and central executive deficits, although it was unheard of to do this when I first entered neuropsychology in the mid-1970s. These models enable us to predict patterns of functioning and explain phenomena that on the surface might appear improbable, e.g. that someone should have an excellent digit span but fail to recall anything of a story after 20 s. Wilson & Patterson (1990) discuss this in more detail.

One of the latest memory assessments to appear, based on the visual–verbal and recall–recognition distinctions within memory, is "Doors and People: a test of visual and verbal recall and recognition" (Baddeley et al., 1994), which is described in more detail below. Other recent, theoretically-driven assessments include the Camden Memory Test (Warrington, 1996) and the Visual Patterns Test (Della Sala et al., 1997).

One of the earliest approaches to neuropsychological assessment involves defining a condition through the exclusion of other possible explanations. Thus, to determine whether someone has visual agnosia, it is necessary to exclude poor eyesight and anomia as explanations for the problem. Although such definition by exclusion is not directly relevant to the assessment of memory, as we typically determine memory impairment through test scores, the exclusion approach is used indirectly, e.g. when assessing a memory-impaired person, we need to know whether the problems observed can be explained wholly or in part by poor attention, perception or language. We therefore assess these functions and, if necessary, exclude them as explanations for the results. Howieson & Lezak (Chapter 29, this volume) address this issue when they discuss "separating memory from other cognitive disorders".

The final model of assessment described in this section involves an ecological approach whereby the main focus of interest is in predicting the problems that are likely to occur in everyday life. If someone scores in the impaired range on a standardized memory test, we do not necessarily learn that he/she will have problems coping in real life, e.g. one of my ex-patients, J.C., is a densely amnesic young man who is able to live alone, hold down a job and fill in his own tax forms, despite scoring zero on all tests of delayed, episodic memory (see Wilson & Hughes, 1997). V.K., on the other hand, achieves scores in the normal or mild range on the same delayed, episodic memory tests, yet she cannot live alone, is unemployed and needs help with many of her activities. The main reason for the difference between these two clients is that J.C. has a pure amnesia, his other cognitive functions are intact, he is of above average intelligence and he can compensate well for his memory problems. V.K., on the other hand, has diffuse brain damage and widespread cognitive impairments.

In many assessments, particularly if one is concerned with rehabilitation or helping people manage their memory difficulties, one needs to predict the nature, frequency and severity of everyday problems. This is often best done through a more functional assessment (discussed in the following section). However, there are tests specifically designed to predict everyday problems. The first memory test designed to do this was probably the Rivermead Behavioural Memory Test (RBMT: Wilson et al., 1985).

The RBMT grew out of the need to provide professionals working in rehabilitation with functionally relevant information. When I first began working in rehabilitation in 1979 I would carry out assessments I had been taught and report the findings at the weekly ward rounds, using such terminology as, "She is two standard deviations below the mean on the Rey–Osterreith figure", or "He is below the fifth percentile on the story recall". The response from the other staff was often, "But can she return to work?" or "Is he safe to go home?". I could not answer such questions because the tests I gave were not representative of the problems faced in real life. The priorities of patients, family and other rehabilitation staff were different from mine. I set about designing a test that would predict everyday memory problems, based partly on observations of the real-life memory problems exhibited by patients and partly on some earlier work by Sunderland et al. (1983), in which they had found that, although some standardized tests were good at distinguishing between head injured patients and controls, they were not good at predicting the kinds of everyday problems reported by patients or their relatives. In collaboration with Alan Baddeley and Janet Cockburn, we carried out 5 years of research to produce the RBMT, which proved useful in predicting independence and employability (Schwartz & McMillan, 1989; Wilson, 1991) as well as correlating very well with observed memory failures (Wilson et al., 1989b). A more difficult version, the RBMT-E (extended), appeared in 1999 to assess people with more subtle memory deficits (Wilson et al., 1999b).

The RBMT was not the first ecologically valid test. In 1980, Holland published the Test of Functional Communication for Aphasic Adults (Holland, 1980), based on the principle that scores from conventional tests do not give sufficient information about real-life competencies or difficulties faced by people who have sustained an insult to the brain. Several other ecologically valid tests have appeared in recent years including the Behavioural Inattention Test for unilateral neglect (Wilson et al., 1988), the Test of Everyday Attention (Robertson et al., 1994), the Behavioural Assessment of the Dysexecutive Syndrome (Wilson et al., 1996a) and the Wessex Head Injury Matrix (Shiel et al., 2000).

Ecologically valid tests may never provide sufficient information on their own but they can provide complementary information to other tests in our "toolbox". We need a complete range of neuropsychological assessments to provide the clearest picture of a person's strengths and weaknesses. It is unhelpful for neuropsychologists who ask a particular set of questions to attack other neuropsychologists who ask a different set of questions. Some questions are answered best by theoretically-driven assessment procedures and others by more practically orientated procedures. To return to my earlier statement, much depends upon reasons why information is needed.

Standardized and Behavioural (Functional) Assessment Procedures

In order to obtain the broadest picture of deficit and impairment we need to collate information from all sources. If we want to plan, implement and evaluate a rehabilitation programme (see Chapter 30, this volume) we must include information from all forms of assessment available to us. Ecological tests may be relatively good at predicting whether or not everyday problems are likely to occur, but they may not provide sufficient detail about an individual's specific problems requiring isolation for treatment. For example, one problem that frequently arises and causes great irritation to families is repetition on the part of the patient of previously told stories or statements. People with severe memory problems are likely to repeat a question, story or joke over and over again. Although this may sound trivial, it can drive staff and relatives to breaking point. Standardized tests will neither identify this problem nor measure its frequency. Furthermore, standardized tests cannot detect whether certain situations or people make the repetition better or worse, neither can they detect the level of distress caused to family members.

Standardized tests can build up a picture of an individual's cognitive profile and this is important in planning treatment. We need to know that we are not asking the cognitively impossible, that instructions or requests are understood, that material can be perceived or read and so forth. However, they are insufficient on their own for all questions needing to be answered about a memory-impaired individual. A behavioural assessment involves an analysis of the relationship between a person's behaviour, its antecedents and its consequences. There are several ways this can be carried out, including direct observations, self-report measures and interviews.

Direct observations of everyday memory failures may be carried out in real-life settings or in analogue situations. In the example of repetition given above, one could observe the client during therapy sessions, on the ward, at home or at work, whatever is appropriate. It may be possible to follow the client around for several hours a day for a period of time or it may only be practical to see him/her for half an hour a day for several days or weeks. The crucial thing is to ensure there is a stable baseline. It is also helpful to recruit a colleague or student to do the same recording for some of the time to check for inter-rater reliability.

If the person conducting the observation (e.g. a relative, therapist or work colleague) is present, when the observations are taking place, then the observer is said to be dependent. The advantage of a dependent observer is that the person being observed is with a familiar person and less likely to change his/her natural behaviour. The disadvantage here is that certain targeted behaviours may be missed because the relative, therapist or colleague is engaged in his/her own activities. If the observer is specially recruited to carry out the observations, and is not there for any other purpose, then he/she is said to be an independent observer. The advantage of an independent observer is that all attention can be focused on the client. The disadvantage is that the client may be aware of being observed and may consequently change or modify behaviour under observation.

Given the fact that direct observations are time consuming, it is not always possible for busy clinicians to engage in them. An alternative is to set up an analogue situation, either through role-play or through simulating a particular setting, e.g. role-play could be employed to find out information about how the memory-impaired person copes with passing on messages. A therapist could be recruited to play the person giving the message and the memory-impaired client could be asked to role-play how he/she would deal with the situation. The assessor might want to find out whether the client wrote down or tape-recorded the information, or repeated it back. A simulated setting might be employed to see how a person copes at work. A mock office or shop could be set up and certain tasks given to the client to see what kinds of problem occur. With all direct observations the assessor should carry out the observations several times to check for consistency.

Another approach to collecting information about everyday memory failures is to use self-report measures, such as questionnaires, checklists, rating scales and diaries. It has been known for a number of years that there is poor agreement between self-report measures and traditional or laboratory memory tasks, e.g. Sunderland et al. (1984) designed a study to look at the relationship between laboratory tests of memory and subjective reports of memory difficulties by brain-injured people and their relatives. Questionnaires were used to investigate the type and frequency of memory lapses noted in everyday life after a severe brain injury. Correlations with objective tests were low. However, relatives' responses had a greater relationship to the test than responses by the brain-injured people themselves. This was explained as a result of the fact that people with memory problems cannot remember their own memory failures. A related study (Sunderland et al., 1983) found that daily checklists kept by the patients related better to objective test results than did responses to questionnaires, possibly because filling in a checklist provides a more immediate evaluation of problems.

Although self-report measures are a quick way to identify everyday problems and can target relevant issues, it is important to remember that filling in the measures is, in itself, a memory task, so one should not expect accuracy from the memory-impaired person. Nevertheless, such measures are useful because they give us insight into the patients' perceptions and understanding of their problems. Perhaps more importantly, however, one can give the measures to relatives and members of staff to complete on behalf of the memory-impaired person in order to get a more accurate picture. Thus, it is usual, at least in the settings where I work, to administer measures to the client and to an independent other who knows the memory-impaired person well. Examples of self-report measures can be found in Wilson (1999).

The main differences between standardized and the more functional or behavioural assessments include the following. First, standardized tests tend to tell us what a person *has*, e.g. a person might have a severe memory impairment or a visuospatial memory deficit. Behavioural assessments, on the other hand, tend to tell us what a person *does*. Thus, a person might forget to put her wheelchair brakes on when transferring to the toilet, or asks the same question 50 times each hour.

Second, in standardized tests, behaviours observed are typically *signs* of a disorder, so for example, if someone fails to recall a prose passage after a delay, this can be taken as a sign of memory impairment. In behavioural assessments, however, the behaviours observed are seen as *samples* of performance, so we might sample a person's remembering or forgetting performance.

Third, standardized tests are usually carried out in *one situation*, typically the neuropsychologist's office; whereas behavioural assessments are more likely to be carried out in a *number of situations*, such as the hospital ward, occupational therapy, at home or at work.

Fourth, standardized tests are carried out as part of a *diagnosis*: we want to find out whether there is organic memory impairment or whether there are additional cognitive problems. In contrast, behavioural assessments are usually implemented to *help select or plan treatment*, e.g. we need to know whether the problems are particularly likely to occur in certain situations or at certain times of day.

Fifth, the standardized tests have an *indirect relationship to treatment*. We need to know as much as possible about the nature of the memory deficit and of other cognitive functions but we do not (or should not) treat the inability to do well on a memory test. Behavioural assessments, on the other hand, have a *direct relationship to treatment*.

Finally, standardized tests are typically carried out prior to treatment (or perhaps post-treatment) but they are *not part of the treatment process itself*. In contrast, behavioural assessments may well be carried out during treatment and are therefore *part of the treatment process*. If we are trying to ensure, for example, that wheelchair brakes are applied by a patient, or the repetition of a question decreases, we need to measure these behaviours during treatment. Although there are fundamental differences between standardized test and behavioural assessments, both are important and provide complementary information. We need standardized test results to build up a cognitive map of strengths and weaknesses; we need behavioural assessments to clarify everyday problems, set goals for and evaluate treatment.

ASPECTS OF MEMORY TO BE ASSESSED

Leaving aside behavioural assessments of memory problems (see Chapter 30 for more on this), what should be included in a clinical memory assessment? Not every person referred for memory assessment will need to be assessed in great detail. Again, the nature of the question(s) one is trying to answer will determine this. Sometimes a quick screening test might suffice. If, for example, one is looking for signs of organic memory impairment, then one of the existing tests, such as WMS-R/WMS III, might provide evidence of this. If the pattern of results is consistent with organic memory impairment (e.g. normal forward digit span, poor delayed memory and problems with paired-associate learning particularly hard verbal pairs), then one could conclude there is evidence of organic memory impairment.

Frequently, however, testers will need a more thorough and fine-grained assessment, particularly for people who are referred for rehabilitation. In such cases, one may want to look at a wide range of memory functions, together with other cognitive functions In these cases, as far as memory is concerned, one will probably need to look at:

1. Orientation for time, place and person.
2. Immediate memory, including verbal, visual and spatial short-term/immediate memory.
3. Delayed episodic memory, including visual recall, visual recognition, verbal recall and verbal recognition.
4. New episodic learning, including verbal, visual and spatial.
5. Implicit memory, including, perhaps, motor, verbal and visual aspects of implicit memory.
6. Remote memory, to look at retrograde amnesia—one may want to subdivide this into personal/autobiographical memory and memory for public information.
7. Prospective memory, perhaps subdivided into remembering to do things (a) at a given time, (b) within a certain time interval, and (c) when a certain event happens.
8. Semantic memory, for both verbal and visual material.

How should these aspects of memory be assessed?

Most of the subtypes of memory functioning above will be able to be measured by one or more of the many published memory tests. A number of the published tests are described in Lezak (1995) and Spreen & Strauss (1998). Orientation should be included in all memory assessments (Erickson & Scott, 1977) and it is easy to find tests containing orientation questions (e.g. The Wechsler Scales, the RBMT and the Randt et al. (1980) test. People with organic memory impairment are almost always orientated for person and most will be able to give their date of birth. Problems may arise with orientation for time and place. If someone does not know what year it is, it is difficult to work out how old one is, so it is not uncommon to find memory-impaired patients who do not know their current age unless they are given the date and can thus work it out. Immediate memory for verbal material is almost always assessed clinically with forward digit span. Test items, age-related norms and percentiles can be found in the Wechsler Memory Scales and in the Wechsler Adult Intelligence Scales. It is less clear what is being measured by backward digit span, although it is often used to assess attention. Immediate visuospatial span can be measured by the visual memory span tasks in the Wechsler Memory Scales and a purer measure of visual memory by the Visual Patterns Test (Della Sala et al., 1997). Some studies have shown double dissociations between the visual and spatial aspects of immediate memory. Thus, there may be differences between the Visual Patterns Test, which reduces the spatial component, and the Wechsler Memory Scales visual tapping tasks (Della Sala et al., 1999; Wilson et al., 1999a).

Other ways of testing immediate memory can be employed. These include:

- The recency effect in free recall. The testee is requested to recall a list of words in any order. If the last word(s) are consistently recalled (i.e. a recency effect is found), one can conclude that there is normal short-term/immediate memory.
- Other pattern recognition tasks, such as those used by Phillips (1974).
- The Token Test (De Renzi, 1982). Although this is normally used as a test of comprehension, it is also sensitive to deficits of immediate memory span.

Delayed/long-term episodic memory can be subdivided into (a) verbal recall, (b) verbal recognition, (c) visual recall and (d) visual recognition. Verbal recall tasks are among the most frequently used of all memory tests and prose recall passages among the most sensitive tests for detecting organic impairment (Sunderland et al., 1984). The stories from the Wechsler Memory Scales, the Adult Memory and Information Processing Battery (AMIPB; Coughlan & Hollows, 1984, 1985) and the Rivermead Behavioural Memory Test all provide prose passages for verbal recall.

One widely used test of recognition, at least in the UK, is the Recognition Memory Test (Warrington, 1984). This is in two parts — Recognition Memory for Words (i.e. verbal recognition) and Recognition Memory for Faces (i.e. visual recognition). The new Camden Memory Tests (Warrington, 1996) include a short recognition memory test for words and faces.

Among the best known visual recall tests are the Rey–Osterreith Complex Figure (Rey, 1958), the Benton Visual Retention Test (BVRT; Benton, 1974) and the Visual Reproduction Tests from the Wechsler Memory Scales. The AMIPB also has a complex figure analogous to the Rey figure. Participants are required to copy the figure first (with the exception of the BVRT) and recall after a delay. Participants with planning, visuospatial or apraxic difficulties may have problems copying these figures and this, in turn, could affect their delayed recall. Another potential disadvantage of these figures is that the scoring is not always straightforward, e.g. at least two scoring methods exist for the Rey figure (see Lezak, 1995) and some of the drawings/figures are, at least partly, verbalisable. With the Rey, the overall figure looks rather like a flag, there are vertical, horizontal and diagonal lines with triangles and a component resembling a face.

Recognition memory for faces has already been mentioned. The Camden (Warrington, 1996) also includes a topographical and a pictorial recognition task, as does the RBMT and RBMT-E. Baddeley et al. (1994) produced a test that includes all four components in one battery. This is the Doors and People: a test of visual and verbal recall and recognition. This is a theoretically-derived, broad-based test, using ecologically plausible material which provides a number of scores. Results can be used to derive: (a) a single overall age-scaled score; (b) a verbal memory score; (c) a visual memory score; (d) a recognition memory score; (e) a recall memory score; and (f) a forgetting score. In the visual recall task, participants copy the figures first, so it is possible to ensure there are no problems with the execution of the design. Although the visual material is verbalisable (e.g. "door" or "cross"), in practice this is of little help as all the other material also consists of a "door" or a "cross", so one has to rely on visual detail. Finally, scoring problems are considerably reduced through clear examples and instructions.

New episodic learning can also be subdivided into verbal and visual (or visuospatial learning). The Wechsler Scales include subtests to look at both visual and verbal learning. For verbal learning there is the paired associate learning task. Eight pairs of words are presented, with four pairs having a logical match (e.g. metal–iron) and four pairs having no logical connection (e.g. cabbage–pen). Everyone finds the nonlogical pairs harder to learn but people with organic memory deficits find this task almost impossible, even over several trials. The Wechsler visual paired-associate task involves learning to match a colour with a symbol. Again, this is extremely difficult for memory-impaired people.

A number of other verbal paired-associate learning tasks are available. These include the Camden (Warrington, 1996), the Test for Longitudinal Measurement of Mild to Moderate Deficits (Randt et al., 1980), and the paired-associate learning tests of Inglis (1957) and Walton & Black (1957). Not all new verbal learning tests are paired-associates. The Rey Auditory–Verbal Learning Test (RAVLT; Rey, 1964) and The California Verbal Learning Test (CVLT; Delis et al., 1987) are both readily available and useful tests to include in one's repertoire. In both these tests, the testee is required to listen to a list of 15 or 16 words and repeat back as many as possible in any order. The list is repeated four more times. Each time, free recall is required. There is then a distraction list, followed by recall of the original list. The CVLT (Delis et al., 1987) has some advantages over the RAVLT, e.g. it includes a short delayed recall and a long (20 min) delayed recall. It also provides category cues to aid recall, e.g. "Tell me all the tools that you can recall". Finally, the CVLT enables one to score several different aspects of memory. The Selective Reminding Test (Buschke & Fuld, 1974) is another test of verbal learning and one that is claimed to separate out retention, storage and retrieval (Lezak, 1995); however, as (Lezak, 1995) says, this is a procedure rather than a test and is given in a number of ways, so it is hard to compare different findings.

Apart from the visual paired associates in the WM Scales, tests to assess nonverbal, episodic learning are harder to find. Wilson et al. (1989a) describe a test of new learning in which participants are given three trials to learn a six-step task. The testee is required to put the date and time into an electronic memory aid. All 50 normal control participants learned the task in three trials (and most in one trial), whereas less than 44% of the people with brain injury learned the task in three trials.

Both the RBMT and the RBMT-E include learning a new route (both immediate and delayed recall are required) and a model version of the route in the RBMT-E has recently been published (Clare et al., 2000). The RBMT-E routes combine visuospatial and verbal learning as they attempt to replicate real-life learning of new routes.

A recently published test of visuospatial learning, designed specifically for use with older adults and individuals with dementia or suspected dementia, is the Location Learning Test

(LLT; Bucks et al., 2000). The LLT uses an array on which 10 pictures of everyday items have been placed. The participant is required to learn the location of the pictures over five trials. Rather than using a number correct score for each trial, the LLT is calculated in terms of displacement error, thus allowing for a more sensitive measure of learning.

One final approach to non-verbal learning, which is easy to administer, is a visual-span plus two task. This can be given with the Corsi blocks (described by Milner, 1971), the visual tapping from the WM Scales and the Visual Patterns test. Once span has been established in the usual way, the tester adds two more blocks or squares. Thus if the span is a typical five, the learning sequence of seven is administered and repeated until the participant can reproduce it correctly or until 25 (or even 50) trials have been given. Although norms do not appear to exist, most without brain injury people would learn this within three (and certainly within five) trials, whereas people with a dense amnesia fail to learn the sequence even after 50 trials.

Although implicit memory, or memory without awareness, is of great interest to researchers into theoretical models of memory, implicit memory is not regularly assessed by clinicians. This may be due to the fact that standardized assessments are not available, so each battery or test has to be made separately or obtained from colleagues working in the area. Another reason for the haphazard inclusion of these tasks is that it is not clear how implicit memory relates to everyday problems or rehabilitation goals (although see Chapter 30 for further discussion). As long ago as 1988, Baddeley & Wilson suggested that poor procedural memory (one aspect of implicit memory) in people with organic memory impairment could be a poor prognostic sign (Baddeley & Wilson, 1988). Implicit memory is not a unitary concept, however (Wilson et al., 1996b), and one should probably look at a number of aspects, including implicit memory for motor verbal and visual tasks.

Another way to subdivide implicit memory is to look at tasks involving procedural memory, priming and stem completion. One task for looking at motor implicit or procedural memory is the pursuit rotor task, a visual-motor tracking task. People with organic memory deficits typically improve the percentage of time on target, despite (in some cases) being unable to recognize that they have been tested on the task previously. A variation on pursuit rotor is the mirror tracing task, in which the testee is required to trace a pattern with a light pen. The pattern cannot be seen directly and has to be viewed through a mirror. Woodworth & Schlosberg (1954) report a large practice effect with nonbrain-injured people on this task and improvement has also been shown with people who are amnesic. Wilson et al. (1996b) gave a mirror tracing task to 110 control participants and 12 amnesic participants aged 20–55 years. These results can be seen in Figure 28.1. Thus, it can be seen that although the people with amnesia were slower than controls, the pattern of improvement was similar.

Clinically, the best way to measure motor memory is probably to use a computerized visual tracking task, such as that used by Baddeley et al. (1986) in their study of Alzheimer's disease. The problem with this is that participants would have to be used as their own controls. This would allow one to see whether or not they improved over time, but not how such improvement compared to a normal control group.

One verbal implicit memory task frequently used in theoretical studies is stem completion or verbal priming. This involves the presentation of a list of words and then the presentation of a stem (the first two or three letters). The testee is then required to say the first word that comes to mind when he/she sees the stem. So, for example, if the words CHOKE, TRUST and WHEAT are presented and a few seconds later CH is shown and the testee asked for the first word that comes to mind, the response (even among people with amnesia) is likely

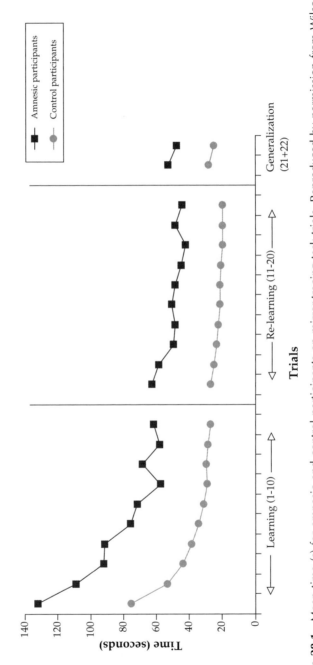

Figure 28.1 Mean time (s) for amnesic and control participants on mirror-tracing task trials. Reproduced by permission from Wilson et al. (1996). © 1996, Swets Zeitlinger

to be CHOKE rather than CHEESE or CHALK (see Davis & Bernstein, 1982; Graf et al., 1984; Chapter 30, this volume, for further discussion). Baddeley & Wilson (1994) used a stem completion task to compare errorful and errorless learning (again, see Chapter 30, this volume).

Perceptual priming involving visual implicit memory is another kind of task employed in a number of studies. Fragmented pictures (degraded from a greater to a lesser degree) are presented until the testee can identify the picture. Originally employed by Warrington & Weiskrantz (1968), it was shown that people with amnesia showed savings, i.e. recognized the pictures earlier in the sequence when these were shown a second time despite having no episodic memory of seeing the pictures earlier. Wilson et al. (1996b), using a computerized method to fragment the pictures based on Snodgrass et al. (1987), administered fragmented pictures to 136 control participants and 16 people with amnesia. The people with amnesia were poorer at recognizing the sequences but showed savings compared to a baseline condition. An auditory priming task was also included in the Wilson et al. (1996b) study. This was a replication of a study by Johnson et al. (1985), whereby melodies heard several times were preferred to melodies heard only once. There was no difference between the controls and the people with amnesia on the preference (implicit memory) task, despite a significant difference on a recognition (explicit memory) task. The Wilson et al. (1996b) study also showed dissociations among people with amnesia in that "normal" performance (compared to controls) on one type of implicit memory task did not guarantee "normal" performance on another. This supported the view that implicit memory is not unitary and can be fractionated like episodic, explicit memory tasks. The time is right for a published standardized test battery to appear for the assessment of several aspects of implicit memory.

Remote memory is another aspect of memory functioning that is rarely assessed routinely in clinical practice, despite having important implications for real life problems. In 1986, Baddeley & Wilson suggested that impaired autobiographical memory can result in anxiety, depression and other problematic behaviours (Baddeley & Wilson, 1986). In order to know who we are, we need a past. People with long periods of retrograde amnesia are frequently angry or bewildered by what seems to them an unexpectedly high cost of living, change in political and geographical circumstances or the loss of several years from their lives. For a description of one man with a very long retrograde amnesia (RA), bewilderment and confusion, see Wilson (1999, Chapter 6).

It is possible to find people whose RA for public events is greater than that for personal events and vice versa (see Hodges & McCarthy, 1993; Kapur, 1993, 1999), although it is more typical to find impairments in both. There is a published semistructured interview to assess autobiographical memory. This is the Autobiographical Memory Interview (AMI; Kopelman et al., 1989b). The AMI encompasses two aspects of autobiographical memory, viz. personal semantic memory, i.e. memory for facts (e.g. names of friends, addresses and schools attended) and memory for specific autobiographical incidents (e.g. something that happened at one's wedding or when one went on holiday). Each of these aspects covers three broad time bands: childhood, early adult life and recent time, i.e. the past year.

Kopelman et al. (1989a) believe that it is useful to assess autobiographical memory for at least three reasons: to understand the nature of the memory deficit, to allow for more adequate counselling and to provide an individual focus for treatment. Baddeley & Wilson (1986) found that subjects who are very similar on intelligence and memory test scores may differ markedly on ability to recall events from their own past life. The AMI has been subject to a number of research studies, e.g. Evans et al. (1993) found that a woman assessed during an episode of Transient Global Amnesia (TGA) achieved a reasonable score on the personal semantic sections but scored poorly on the autobiographical incidents. When reassessed following recovery from the TGA, she scored normally on both personal semantic and autobiographical questions. In contrast, Graham & Hodges (1997) found that patients with semantic dementia (at least in the earlier stages) showed the reverse pattern, i.e. they were poor at the personal semantic sections but relatively unimpaired on the autobiographical incidents.

Famous faces, famous names and famous events from different decades are most often used in assessing remote memory for public events. However, there is not one readily available test for the assessment of public events. Although a number of tools have been developed as research instruments, including a Retrograde Amnesia Battery by Butters & Albert (1982), all such tests need regular updating, so any published RA test is only valid for a couple of years or so. Other problems include: (a) differences in the level of interest, so that people who have always been interested in the news are likely to show a different pattern to those who have shown little interest; (b) cultural specificity, so British politicians or sports stars may have had little exposure in the USA; and (c) differences in exposure, so Charlie Chaplin, dead many years, will still be recognized by many, whereas Lord Mountbatten, who died much more recently, will be recognized by far fewer people. There have been attempts to develop other tests of remote memory, e.g. the Prices Test (Wilson & Cockburn, 1988) in which people are asked to estimate the cost of some common items; and the Dead-and-Alive Test (referred to in Kapur et al., 1996), in which people have to say whether or not a famous person is dead or alive (and if dead, when and how the death occurred). The aforementioned problems still apply, however, and it will probably always be necessary to produce one's own materials and/or modify material regularly.

Prospective memory involves remembering to perform previously planned actions at the right time (e.g. "at 8 pm tonight telephone your sister") or within the right time interval (e.g. "post a letter before leaving work today") or when a certain event takes place (e.g. "when you next see your colleague pass on a message"). These actions should take place while the person concerned is engaged in other activities. One of the commonest complaints of people with memory problems is forgetting to do things (prospective memory failures), yet once again, this aspect of memory is not always assessed. Mateer et al. (1987) showed that people both with and without brain injury perceive themselves as having more trouble with prospective memory tasks than with other memory tasks, and went on to develop a Prospective Memory Screening tool (PROMS; Sohlberg & Mateer, 1989) to look at the ability to remember to carry out tasks after 60 s, 2 min, 10 min, 20 min, and 24 h. The only other tests to formally include prospective memory items appear to be the RMBT and the RMBT-E. The original RBMT has three (out of 12) items concerned with prospective memory. Participants have to remember to: (a) ask, at the end of the test, for a belonging that was placed out of sight at the beginning of the test; (b) ask about the next appointment when an alarm rings; and (c) deliver a message to a predetermined place during the immediate and delayed recall of a new route. These prospective memory items seem to account for some of the sensitivity of the RBMT, e.g. Cockburn & Smith (1989) found that prospective memory items significantly discriminated between two groups of older subjects living in the community: a "young" old group aged 55–70 years and an "old" old group aged 71–90 years.

The RBMT-E has similar prospective memory items but as this test places a greater load on memory, the items are consequently more demanding. Thus two belongings are hidden at the beginning of the test instead of one, two questions are asked when the alarm rings and two messages have to be delivered during the immediate and delayed recall of the route.

As screening tests the RBMT and RBMT-E adequately cover the assessment of prospective memory. However, a more detailed assessment of prospective memory would appear to be clinically useful and work on this is well under way. We are developing a clinical, ecologically valid test of prospective memory in Cambridge, covering time-based prospective memory tasks (e.g. "In 15 min time remind me not to forget my key") and event-based tasks (e.g. "When the alarm rings please open the window").

A pilot study with 36 people with brain injury and 28 people with no known brain injury, showed that: (a) the new test of prospective memory discriminated between those with and without brain injury; (b) time-based tasks were more difficult for both groups than event-based tasks; and (c) people who took notes/wrote down information scored significantly better than those who did not take notes (Groot et al., in press). We expect the final version of this test to be ready in 2002.

Tulving (1972) first suggested that semantic and episodic memory should be distinguishable. Semantic memory is the system we use to store knowledge about the world. We refer to our semantic store when answering such questions as "Does a rabbit have prick ears?", "What does the word 'happy' mean?" and "What shape is Italy?" We have a huge store of information as to what things mean, look like, sound like, smell like and feel like. Damage to this store or impaired access to this store may follow brain damage, e.g. Warrington (1975) suggests that visual object agnosia is a deficit of the visual semantic memory system. Furthermore, some patients lose the ability to recognize living things but are still able to recognize non-living things. They are said to have a category-specific disorder (Warrington & Shallice, 1984). Hillis & Caramazza (1991) and Sacchett & Humphreys (1992) describe the reverse, i.e. people who show greater knowledge of living than of non-living or manufactured objects. Patients with semantic memory deficits are likely to have problems recognizing objects in the real world and problems expressing themselves, and may be considered stupid because of the errors they make.

Semantic memory may be assessed in a variety of ways, including spoken and single-word comprehension, category fluency and general knowledge. Hodges et al. (1992a, 1992b) describe a semantic memory test battery designed to assess semantic knowledge in patients with dementia of the Alzheimer type and patients with progressive semantic dementia. Wilson (1997) also administered the battery, with broadly similar results, to people with non-progressive brain injury. The battery has the major advantage of employing one set of stimulus items designed to assess input to and output from a central store of representational knowledge. Thus, the same group of items is used as stimuli and assessed using different sensory modalities. The battery contains 48 items, representing three categories of manufactured items matched for prototypicality. The three living categories are land animals, water creatures and birds. The three manufactured categories are household items, vehicles and musical instruments. Knowledge of these items is assessed in several ways, namely fluency, naming, picture–word matching, picture sorting and naming to description. Although a considerable amount of work has been carried out on this battery, it has not yet been published as a test. One semantic memory battery that has been published is the Category-Specific Names Test (McKenna, 1998), a test of naming objects and of matching objects with their names in four semantic categories.

In conclusion to this section, it must be pointed out that the above list of potential clinical memory tests is by no means exhaustive. Readers can find details about other tests in Lezak (1995) and Spreen & Strauss (1998).

General Principles in the Assessment of Memory Disorders

Failure to select, administer and interpret tests appropriately can have serious consequences, e.g. a problem that exists might be missed, incorrect administration can invalidate results, and misinterpretation of results may lead to incorrect conclusions being drawn and, perhaps, inappropriate treatment offered. All people administering tests need to ensure they are competent to do so. Not only is it imperative to know how to administer and score tests, but the tester should also know how to put the person being tested at ease, how to feed back the results to the patient, family member, therapy staff and referring agents. Confidentiality needs to be ensured and the tester needs to know when it is appropriate and inappropriate to disclose information. Guidelines on selecting, administering and interpreting cognitive tests can be found in Evans et al. (1996). Further issues on assessment are dealt with in Lezak (1995) and Spreen & Strauss (1998).

Another factor that may be forgotten in assessment is the effect of practice. If there is an improvement in test scores, does this mean that the person being tested has really improved or that the change reflects the fact that the test is now no longer novel? Similarly, if there is no change in scores, does this mean the patient has stayed at the same level, or that practice effects have masked any decline? These are very real issues in assessment. Practice effects are different for different tests, e.g. there is virtually no practice effect on forward digit span but a large one on verbal fluency (Wilson et al., 2000). Some tests, such as the RBMT, have several parallel versions, while others, such as the WMS-R, have only one version. This, too, influences results on repeated assessments. Practice effects are also different for people with and without brain injury (Wilson et al., 2000).

Memory assessment, and assessment of other cognitive functions, is not something to be approached in a casual manner. A test is as good as its developers, designers and administrators. All three owe it to the people being tested to do the best job possible. Used responsibly and ethically, good assessments can contribute to the understanding and well-being of memory-impaired people referred to us.

REFERENCES

Anastasi, A. (1982). *Psychological Testing*, 5th edn. New York: Collier/Macmillan.

Baddeley, A.D. (1999). *Essentials of Human Memory*. Hove: Psychology Press.

Baddeley, A.D., Emslie, H. & Nimmo-Smith, I. (1994). *Doors and People: A Test of Visual and Verbal Recall and Recognition*. Bury St Edmunds: Thames Valley Test Company.

Baddeley, A.D. & Hitch, G. (1974). Working memory. In G. H. Bower (ed.), *The Psychology of Learning and Motivation*, Vol. 8 (pp. 47–89). New York: Academic Press.

Baddeley, A.D., Logie, R., Bressi, S. et al. (1986). Dementia and working memory. *Quarterly Journal of Experimental Psychology*, **38**, 603–618.

Baddeley, A.D. & Wilson, B.A. (1986). Amnesia, autobiographical memory and confabulation. In D. Rubin (ed.), *Autobiographical Memory* (pp. 225–252). New York: Cambridge University Press.

Baddeley, A.D. & Wilson, B.A. (1988). Frontal amnesia and the dysexecutive syndrome. *Brain and Cognition*, **7**, 212–230.

Baddeley, A.D. & Wilson, B.A. (1994). When implicit learning fails: amnesia and the problem of error elimination. *Neuropsychologia*, **32**, 53–68.

Benton, A.L. (1974). *The Revised Visual Retention Test: Clinical and Experimental Applications*. New York: Psychological Corporation.

Bucks, R.S., Willison, J.R. & Byrne, L.M.T. (2000). *Location Learning Test*. Bury St Edmunds: Thames Valley Test Company.

Buschke, H. & Fuld, A.P. (1974). Evaluating storage, retention and retrieval in disordered memory and learning. *Neurology*, **24**, 1019–1025.

Butters, N. & Albert, M.L. (1982). Processes underlying failures to recall remote events. In L. Cermak (ed.), *Human Memory and Amnesia* (pp. 257–274). Hillsdale, NJ: Erlbaum.

Calabrese, P., Markowitsch, H.J., Durwen, H.F. et al. (1996). Right temperofrontal cortex as critical locus for the ecphory of old episodie memories. *Journal of Neurology, Neurosurgery and Psychiatry*, **61**, 304–310.

Clare, L., Wilson, B.A., Emslie, H. (2000). Adapting the Rivermead Behavioural Memory Test Extended Version (RBMT-E) for people with restricted mobility. *British Journal of Clinical Psychology*, **39**, 363–369.

Cockburn, J. & Smith, P. (1989). *The Rivermead Behavioural Memory Test. Supplement* 3: *Elderly People*. Bury St Edmunds: Thames Valley Test Company.

Coughlan, A.K. & Hollows, S.E. (1984). Use of memory tests in differentiating organic disorder from depression. *British Journal of Psychiatry*, **145**, 164–167.

Coughlan, A.K. & Hollows, S. (1985). *The Adult Memory and Information Processing Battery (AMIPB)*. Leeds: A. Coughlan, St James University Hospital.

Davis, H.P. & Bernstein, P.A. (1982). Age-related changes in explicit and implicit memory. In L.R. Squire & N. Butters (eds), *Neuropsychology of Memory*, 2nd edn (pp. 249–261). New York: Guilford.

De Renzi, E. (1982). *Disorders of Space Exploration and Cognition*. Chichester: Wiley.

Delis, D., Kaplan, E., Kramer, J. & Ober, B. (1987). *California Verbal Learning Test*. San Antonio, TX: Psychological Corporation.

Della Sala, S., Gray, C., Baddeley, A.D. et al. (1999). Pattern span: a tool of unwelding visuospatial memory. *Neuropsychologia*, **37**, 1189–1199.

Della Sala, S., Gray, C., Baddeley, A.D. & Wilson, L. (1997). *Visual Patterns Test*. Bury St Edmunds: Thames Valley Test Company.

Erickson, R.C. & Scott, M.L. (1977). Clinical memory testing: a review. *Psychological Bulletin*, **84**, 1130–1149.

Eslinger, P.J. (1998). Autobiographical memory after temporal lobe lesions. *Neurocase*, **4**, 481–495.

Evans, J.J., Wilson, B.A. & Emslie, H. (1996). *Selecting, Administering and Interpreting Cognitive Tests: Guidelines for Clinicians and Therapists*. Bury St Edmunds: Thames Valley Test Company.

Evans, J.J., Wilson, B.A., Wraight, E.P. & Hodges, J. (1993). Neuropsychological and SPECT scan findings during and after transient global amnesia: evidence for differential impairment of remote episodic memory. *Journal of Neurology, Neurosurgery and Psychiatry*, **56**, 1227–1230.

Goldman-Rakic, P.S. & Friedman, H.R. (1991). The circuitry of working memory revealed by anatomy and metabolic imaging. In H.S. Levin, H.M. Eisenberg & A.L. Benton (eds), *Frontal Lobe Function and Dysfunction* (pp. 72–91). New York: Oxford University Press.

Graf, P., Squire, L.R. & Mandler, G. (1984). The information that amnesic patients do not forget. *Journal of Experimental Psychology: Learning, Memory, and Cognition*, **10**, 164–178.

Graham, K.S., Becker, J.T. & Hodges, J.R. (1997). On the relationship between knowledge and memory for pictures: evidence from the study of patients with semantic dementia and Alzheimer's disease. *Journal of the International Neuropsychological Society*, **3**, 534–544.

Graham, K.S. & Hodges, J.R. (1997). Differentiating the roles of the hippocampal complex and the neocortex in long-term memory storage: evidence from the study of semantic dementia and Alzheimer's disease. *Neuropsychology*, **11**, 77–89.

Groot, Y.C.T., Wilson, B.A., Evans, J. & Watson, P. (in press). Prospective memory functioning in people with and without brain injury. *Journal of the International Neuropsychological Society*.

Halstead, W.C. (1947). *Brain and Intelligence*. Chicago, IL: University of Chicago Press.

Hillis, A.E. & Caramazza, A. (1991). Category-specific naming and comprehension impairment: a double dissociation. *Brain*, **114**, 2081–2094.

Hodges, J.R. & McCarthy, R.A. (1993). Autobiographical amnesia resulting from bilateral paramedian thalamic infarction. A case study in cognitive neurobiology. *Brain*, **116**, 921–940.

Hodges, J.R., Patterson, K., Oxbury, S. & Funnell, E. (1992b). Semantic dementia: progressive fluent aphasia with temporal lobe atrophy. *Brain*, **115**, 1783–1806.

Hodges, J., Salmon, D.P. & Butters, N. (1992a). Semantic memory impairment in Alzheimer's disease: failure of access or degraded knowledge? *Neuropsychologia*, **30**, 301–314.

Holland, A.L. (1980). *CADL—Communicative Abilities in Daily Living: A Test of Functional Communication for Aphasic Adults.* Baltimore, MD: University Park Press.

Inglis, J. (1957). An experimental study of learning and "memory function" in elderly psychiatric patients. *Journal of Mental Science*, **103**, 796–803.

Johnson, M.K., Kim, J.K. & Risse, G. (1985). Do alcoholic Korsakoff's syndrome patients acquire affective reactions? *Journal of Experimental Psychology: Learning, Memory, and Cognition*, **11**, 22–36.

Jones, R.D., Grabowski, T.J. & Tranel, D. (1998). The neural basis of retrograde memory: evidence from positron emission tomography for the role of non-mesial temporal lobe structures. *Neurocase*, **4**, 471–479.

Kapur, N. (1993). Focal retrograde amnesia in neurological disease: a critical review. *Cortex*, **29**, 217–234.

Kapur, N. (1999). Syndromes of retrograde amnesia: a conceptual and empirical synthesis. *Psychological Bulletin*, **125**, 800–825.

Kapur, N., Thompson, S., Cook, P. et al. (1996). Anterograde but not retrograde memory loss following combined mammillary body and medial thalamic lesions. *Neuropsychologia*, **34**, 1–8.

Kopelman, M., Wilson, B.A. & Baddeley, A.D. (1989a). The Autobiographical Memory Interview: a new assessment of autobiographical and personal semantic memory in amnesic patients. *Journal of Clinical and Experimental Neuropsychology*, **11**, 724–744.

Kopelman, M., Wilson, B.A. & Baddeley, A.D. (1989b). *The Autobiographical Memory Interviews.* Bury St Edmunds: Thames Valley Test Company.

Lezak, M. (1995). *Neuropsychological Assessment*, 3rd edn. New York: Oxford University Press.

Markowitsch, H.J. (1998). Cognitive neuroscience of memory. *Neurocase*, **4**, 429–435.

Mateer, C.A., Sohlberg, M.M. & Crinean, J. (1987). Perceptions of memory functions in individuals with closed head injury. *Journal of Head Trauma Rehabilitation*, **2**, 74–84.

Mayes, A.R. (1986). Learning and memory disorders and their assessment. *Neuropsychologia*, **24**, 25–39.

Mayes, A.R. (1995). *Human Organic Memory Disorders.* Cambridge: Cambridge University Press.

McKenna, P. (1998). *The Category-specific Names Test.* Hove: Psychology Press.

Milner, B. (1971). Interhemispheric differences in the localisation of psychological processes in man. *British Medical Bulletin: Cognitive Psychology*, **27**, 272–277.

Phillips, W.A. (1974). On the distinction between sensory storage and short-term visual memory. *Perception and Psychophysics*, **16**, 283–290.

Randt, C.T., Brown, E.R. & Osborne, D.P. (1980). A memory test for longitudinal measurement of mild to moderate deficits. *Clinical Neuropsychology*, **2**, 184–194.

Reitan, R.M. & Davison, L.A. (1974). *Clinical Neuropsychology: Current Status and Applications.* New York: Hemisphere.

Rey, A. (1958, 1964). *L'Examen Clinique en Psychologie.* Paris: Universitaires de France.

Robertson, I.H., Ward, T., Ridgeway, V. & Nimmo-Smith, I. (1994). *The Test of Everyday Attention.* Bury St Edmunds: Thames Valley Test Company.

Sacchett, C. & Humphreys, G.W. (1992). Calling a squirrel a squirrel but a canoe a wigwam: a category-specific deficit for artifactual objects and body parts. *Cognitive Neuropsychology*, **9**, 73–86.

Schwartz, A.F. & McMillan, T.M. (1989). Assessment of everyday memory after severe head injury. *Cortex*, **25**, 665–671.

Shallice, T., Fletcher, P., Frith, C.D. et al. (1994). Brain regions associated with acquisition and retrieval of verbal episodic memory. *Nature*, **368**, 633–635.

Shiel, A., Wilson, B.A., McLellan, L. et al. (2000). *The Wessex Head Injury Matrix (WHIM).* Bury St Edmunds: Thames Valley Test Company.

Snodgrass, J.G., Smith, B., Feenan, K. & Corwin, J. (1987). Fragmenting pictures on the Apple Macintosh computer for experimental and clinical applications. *Behavior Research Methods, Instruments, and Computers*, **19**, 270–274.

Sohlberg, M.M. & Mateer, C. (1989). Training use of compensatory memory books: a three-stage behavioural approach. *Journal of Clinical and Experimental Neuropsychology*, **11**, 871–891.

Spreen, O. & Strauss, E. (1998). *A compendium of neuropsychological tests*, 2nd edn. New York: Oxford University Press.

Sundberg, N.S. & Tyler, L.E. (1962). *Clinical Psychology*. New York: Appleton-Century-Crofts.

Sunderland, A., Harris, J.E. & Baddeley, A.D. (1983). Do laboratory tests predict everyday memory? A neuropsychological study. *Journal of Verbal Learning and Verbal Behavior*, **22**, 341–357.

Sunderland, A., Harris, J.E. & Gleave, J. (1984). Memory failures in everyday life after severe head injury. *Journal of Clinical Neuropsychology*, **6**, 127–142.

Tranel, D. & Damasio, A.R. (1995). Neurobiological foundations of human memory. In A. D. Baddeley, B. A. Wilson & F. N. Watts (eds), *Handbook of Memory Disorders*, 1st edn (pp. 27–50). Chichester: Wiley.

Tulving, E. (1972). Episodic and semantic memory. In E. Tulving & W. Donaldson (eds), *Organization of Memory* (pp. 381–403). New York: Academic Press.

Tulving, E., Kapur, S., Craik, F.I.M. et al. (1994). Hemispheric encoding/retrieval asymmetry in episodic memory: positron emission tomography findings. *Proceedings of the National Academy of Sciences of the USA*, **91**, 2016–2020.

Vallar, G. & Papagno, C. (1995). Neuropsychological impairments of short-term memory. In A.D. Baddeley, B.A. Wilson & F.N. Watts (eds), *Handbook of Memory Disorders, 1st edn* (pp. 135–165). Chichester: Wiley.

Walton, D. & Black, D.A. (1957). The validity of a psychological test of brain damage. *British Journal of Medical Psychology*, **30**, 270–279.

Warrington, E.K. (1975). The selective impairment of semantic memory. *Quarterly Journal of Experimental Psychology*, **27**, 635–657.

Warrington, E.K. (1984). *The Recognition Memory Test*. Windsor: NFER-Nelson.

Warrington, E. (1996). *Camden Memory Tests*. Hove: Psychology Press.

Warrington, E.K. & Shallice, T. (1984). Category-specific semantic impairments. *Brain*, **107**, 829–854.

Warrington, E.K. & Weiskrantz, L. (1968). New method of testing long-term retention with special reference to amnesic patients. *Nature*, **217**, 972–974.

Wechsler, D. (1945). A standardized memory scale for clinical use. *Journal of Psychology*, **19**, 87–95.

Wechsler, D. (1987). *The Wechsler Memory Scale—Revised*. San Antonio, TX: Psychological Corporation.

Wechsler, D. (1997). *Wechsler Memory Scale III*. San Antonio, TX: Psychological Corporation.

Wilson, B.A. (1991). Theory, assessment and treatment in neuropsychological rehabilitation. *Neuropsychology*, **5**, 281–291.

Wilson, B.A. (1997). Semantic memory impairments following non-progressive brain damage: a study of four cases. *Brain Injury*, **11**, 259–269.

Wilson, B.A. (1999). *Case Studies in Neuropsychological Rehabilitation*. New York: Oxford University Press.

Wilson, B.A., Alderman, N., Burgess, P. et al. (1996a). *Behavioural Assessment of the Dysexecutive Syndrome*. Bury St Edmunds: Thames Valley Test Company.

Wilson, B.A., Baddeley, A.D. & Cockburn, J. (1989a). How do old dogs learn new tricks? Teaching a technological skill to brain-damaged people. *Cortex*, **25**, 115–119.

Wilson, B.A., Baddeley, A.D. & Young, A.W. (1999a). L.E., a person who lost her "mind's eye". *Neurocase*, **5**, 119–127.

Wilson, B.A., Clare, L., Baddeley, A.D. et al. (1999b). *The Rivermead Behavioural Memory Test—Extended Version*. Bury St Edmunds: Thames Valley Test Company.

Wilson, B.A. & Cockburn, J. (1988). The Prices Test: a simple test of retrograde amnesia. In M.M. Gruneberg, P.E. Morris & R.N. Sykes (eds), *Practical Aspects of Memory: Current Research and Issues*, Vol. 2 (pp. 46–51). Chichester: Wiley.

Wilson, B.A., Cockburn, J. & Baddeley, A.D. (1985). *The Rivermead Behavioural Memory Test*. Bury St Edmunds: Thames Valley Test Company.

Wilson, B.A., Cockburn, J., Baddeley, A.D. & Hiorns, R. (1989b). The development and validation of a test battery for detecting and monitoring everyday memory problems. *Journal of Clinical and Experimental Neuropsychology*, **11**, 855–870.

Wilson, B.A., Cockburn, J. & Halligan, P.W. (1988). *The Behavioural Inattention Test*. Bury St Edmunds: Thames Valley Test Company.

Wilson, B.A., Green, R., Teasdale, T. et al. (1996b). Implicit learning in amnesic subjects: a comparison with a large group of normal control subjects. *Clinical Neuropsychologist*, **10**, 279–292.

Wilson, B.A. & Patterson, K.E. (1990). Rehabilitation and cognitive neuropsychology: does cognitive psychology apply? *Journal of Applied Cognitive Psychology*, **4**, 247–260.

Wilson, B.A., Watson, P.C., Baddeley, A.D. et al. (2000). Improvement or simply practice? The effects of twenty repeated assessments on people with and without brain injury. *Journal of the International Neuropsychological Society*, **6**, 469–479.

Wilson, J.C. & Hughes, E. (1997). Coping with amnesia: the natural history of a compensatory memory system. *Neuropsychological Rehabilitation*, **7**, 43–56.

Woodworth, R.S. & Schlosberg, H. (1954). *Experimental Psychology*, revised edn. London: Methuen.

CHAPTER 29

Separating Memory from Other Cognitive Disorders

Diane B. Howieson

and

Muriel D. Lezak

Oregon Health Sciences University, Portland, OR, USA

The clinician is often asked to evaluate patients' memory or learning problems, even when memory is not the actual problem. It is not uncommon for patients and the people close to them to attribute a variety of cognitive and behavioral problems to failing memory. A spouse brings her husband for evaluation complaining that he does not remember to do anything she has asked. When it turns out that the memory problem is confined to this one category of information, the clinician begins to suspect that the problem lies elsewhere. More often, the complaint is difficulty remembering the names of new acquaintances. In these circumstances the social encounter may provide ample distraction for not properly registering the name at the introduction.

Memory complaints provide fascinating and sometimes amusing insights into the complexities and vagaries of human relationships as well as the human mind, but they can present neuropsychologists with serious diagnostic challenges. In this chapter we will focus on the variety of cognitive problems that (secondarily) produce what patients experience or those dealing with them describe as poor memory. As more is learned about how the brain functions, it becomes increasingly difficult to distinguish between theoretical concepts of memory and other cognitive functions (Damasio et al., 1990; Kosslyn & Thompson, 2000; Lezak, 1995). At the practical level, however, the clinician is able to make distinctions that have important implications for counseling and remediation.

The major sources of the *experience* of memory impairment when new learning and retention actually are spared are *information registration deficits*, which can be due to impaired attention or information processing, and *executive function disorders* (see Figure 29.1). These neuropsychological abnormalities can occur discretely or in combination to affect the efficiency of the learning/memory system. Obviously, the more the problem is compounded, the more impaired will be the patient's memory performance.

The Handbook of Memory Disorders. Edited by A.D. Baddeley, M.D. Kopelman and B.A. Wilson
© 2002 John Wiley & Sons, Ltd.

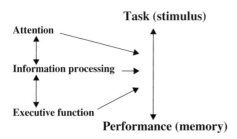

Figure 29.1   Cognitive processes that affect memory as well as other areas of cognition

INFORMATION REGISTRATION

Memory functions are dependent on attention and information processing for proper registration of information to be learned (Curran, 2000; Fischler, 1998; Pashler, 1998). "Attention" refers to the several abilities involved in attending to and grasping all of a specific stimulus (Parasuraman, 1998). "Information processing" refers to the ability to extract the meaning of the stimulus based on past experiences. Some types of information processing are relatively automatic while others require effort and strategies. Reductions in attention and information processing produce marked limitations on memory. The cognitive inefficiencies consequent to attention and information processing deficits are frequently mis-interpreted by patients and those close to them as "memory" problems (e.g. see Di Stefano & Radanov, 1996).

Attention

Many diffusely brain-injured patients have impaired attention (Gasquoine, 1997; Morrow, Robin et al., 1992; Rao, 1996; van Gorp et al., 1989). Their deficit may be obvious only on examination because they appear to attend adequately to tasks. Patients may be limited in attentional capacity, in the ability to direct attention, in the ability to divide attention to more than one stimulus, or in the ability to sustain attention. As attentional tasks increase in complexity, they are often referred to as "tests of concentration" and "mental tracking" or "mental manipulation" (Lezak 1995; Weintraub, 2000). Although many of them involve more complex mental operations as well, attention is a prominent contributing process.

Attentional Capacity

Simple attention span is most frequently examined with a digit repetition task, which tests how many numbers a person can attend to at once and repeat in sequence. The Digit Span tests from the Wechsler Intelligence Scales (WIS) (Wechsler, 1955, 1981, 1997) and the Wechsler Memory Scales (WMS) (Wechsler, 1945, 1987, 1997) assess repetition of digits both forward and backward. The latter task involves a mental tracking component that distinguishes it from the simple span measure. A more subtle disorder may be detected by increasing the demands of the task, such as using a sentence repetition task, which increases the informational load (Benton & Hamsher, 1989; Spreen & Strauss, 1998). A visual measure of attention span may be obtained by the Corsi Cube Test (Milner, 1971) or the WMS Spatial Span Test (Wechsler, 1987, 1997), in which the patient reproduces spatially arranged patterns of increasing length, as demonstrated by the examiner.

These tests of attention require intact short-term memory. Most patients with brain disorders have intact short-term memory when recall follows reception immediately, with neither delay nor interference. When their attention is directed away from tasks by an interpolated activity, retention, even for relatively brief intervals, becomes tenuous. Patients with actual short-term memory impairment do exist but it is relatively rare (e.g. Vallar & Shallice, 1990; Warrington & Shallice, 1984), so this possibility should be evaluated. Poor performance on a simple digit span task is more likely to be representative of an attentional impairment rather than a true memory impairment.

Attentional capacity is resistant to the effects of many brain disorders. It may be restricted in the first months following head trauma but it is likely to return to normal during later states (Bazarian et al., 1999; Lezak, 1979; Ponsford & Kinsella, 1992). Most mildly demented Alzheimer's patients have normal capacity for reciting a string of digits (Pachana et al., 1996; Rubin et al., 1998), although not as the dementia progresses (Freed et al., 1989; Storandt et al., 1992). However, when the information becomes more complex, as in sentence span tests, or more information is presented than can normally be grasped at once, as in supraspan tests (Benton et al., 1983; Milner, 1970; see also Lezak, 1995), the reduced attentional capacity of many brain-injured persons becomes evident.

> A 55-year-old advertising executive had his first symptoms of multiple sclerosis 20 years before he was examined for suspected cognitive deficits. At this examination he was confined to a wheelchair, having use of only his left hand. His highest test scores were on a recognition vocabulary test (93rd percentile) and a test of practical reasoning based on well-established information (90th percentile). Working memory, measured by Auditory Consonant Trigrams, was intact. However, he had difficulty repeating sentences of more than 19 syllables accurately (e.g. his recall of "Yesterday he said he would be near the village station before it was time for a train to come" was "Yesterday he said he would be before the station where the train was to come").

Directed Attention

In most settings an individual attending to a task must direct attention to the relevant material and ignore extraneous information, e.g. that required to read a book while riding a crowded bus. Normally, the clinician examines the patient in an environment relatively free from distractions in order to minimize this factor. Although ideal in one respect and expected when administering standardized tests, this arrangement differs, often radically, from the clatter and clutter of most patients' everyday situations and may mask the problem to be assessed. Therefore, the clinician may wish to interact with the patient in an environment with extraneous noise or activity and observe the patient's ability to be free from distraction. Some tests are designed with distractions included for this reason.

The Stroop Test (Dodrill, 1978; Posner & DiGirolamo, 2000; Stroop, 1935) is a difficult task involving directed attention in addition to other processes. As a baseline measure of speed of responding, the patient is asked to read a page of color names. For the critical condition, the patient is instructed to name the color in which color words are presented, such as saying "green" when the word "red" is printed in green ink. For literate adults, reading the words is prepotent over naming the ink color: therefore, attention must be directed to the color in which the words are printed while inhibiting the prepotent response.

Sustained Attention

Another aspect of attention that may be disrupted by brain injuries frequently involving the frontal lobes, such as that incurred in a moving vehicle accident (Ponsford, 1995; Wrightson & Gronwall, 1999), is the ability to sustain attention (Parasuraman et al., 1998; Swick & Knight, 1998). Many neuropsychological tests require this ability. The WMS Mental Control tests and Subtracting Serial Sevens (Strub & Black, 2000) provide measures of sustained attention as well as other mental operations.

Clinical evaluations of sustained attention often involve vigilance tasks in which stimuli both targets and foils) are presented over an extended period of time and the patient must indicate each target occurrence (Rosvold et al., 1956). Paper and pencil versions are usually in the form of cancellation tests consisting of rows of letters or numbers with instructions to the patient the cross out the target item. Auditory forms are available in which subjects tap or press a computer key when they hear the designated target letter or word. Complex variations may be devised by asking the patient to indicate when two or more conditions have been fulfilled, such as when two numbers occur in succession on a tape presentation. The Letter Cancellation Test (Diller et al., 1974) and Vigilance Test (Strub & Black, 2000) are examples of this kind of test.

Divided Attention

Divided attention, or the ability to attend to more than one stimulus simultaneously, is yet another aspect of attention that is sensitive to brain injury (Nestor et al., 1991; Raskin & Mateer, 2000; Stuss et al., 1989) or normal aging (Baddeley, 1986; Greenwood & Parasuraman, 1991). Practically, problems in this area show up in inability to follow a recipe while the children are talking or difficulty following a conversation when surrounded by a chattering crowd. However, deficiencies in divided attention may also be at the heart of the "misplaced keys (or wallet, or glasses, etc.)" complaint: upon entering their homes these are patients who become immediately distracted by something (the dog, the mail on the hall table, the children) and lay down their keys without registering where they have put them. Almost inevitably, they attribute this latter problem to "poor memory".

Oral arithmetic stories provide one means of examining this problem, as subjects must perform a second or third set of operations while keeping practical solutions in mind. Take the problem, "Mary has 13 stamps and Jane has five. How many would Mary have to give to Jane for them to have the same number?" To solve this, several sequential calculations must be performed while retaining the question.

Difficulties in doing more than one thing at a time may also show up on list producing tasks, whether they involve learning a series of items or generating items *de novo*. On these tasks patients who may be having no difficulty fulfilling the task requirements, whether they be to learn words or generate line patterns (e.g. Ruff Figural Fluency Test: Ruff et al., 1987), will repeat an abnormally large number of responses just given within the last minute or even the last 10–15 seconds. In these repetitions, the patients demonstrate difficulty in keeping track of their responses while performing an ongoing task. These repetitions are distin-guishable from true perseverations, as perseverating patients typically produce very few different responses, and once they begin perseverating, some if not all of the elements of succeeding responses will be perseverations.

The Trail Making Test (Lezak, 1995) is a frequently used test of divided attention or mental tracking. In part A in this timed task, the patient is asked to draw a line connecting in sequence a random display of numbered circles. The level of difficulty is increased in the second part (B) by having the patient again sequence a random display of circles with numbers and letters, going from 1 to A to 2 to B to 3 and so forth. The patient must be able to keep both sequences in mind to perform the task efficiently and quickly. The test also requires visual scanning, flexibility in shifting from set to set, and fine motor coordination and speed. Problems with divided attention show up in abnormally slowed performances on the more complex part B relative to part A.

A working memory test that uses a distractor condition involving divided attention is the "Brown–Peterson technique", the "Peterson task" (Peterson & Peterson, 1959), which is also referred to as "auditory consonant trigrams " (Mitrushina et al., 1999; Spreen & Strauss, 1998). The patient hears three consonants presented at the rate of 1/s, is asked to count backward from a given number until signaled to stop counting, and then to report the stimulus items, e.g. the examiner says, "P R L 126" and the subject begins counting, "125, 124" etc., until told "stop" at the end of the predesignated number of seconds and is expected to recall the three letters. Mental tracking problems may also show up, as some patients lose track of numbers as they count backwards (e.g. ". . . 123, 122, 121, 130, 129", etc.).

Everyday Attention

Daily activities place a heavy demand on many aspects of attention. The Test of Everyday Attention is designed to assess attentional demands of common tasks, such as searching maps, looking through telephone directions and listening to lottery number broadcasts (Crawford et al., 1997; Robertson et al., 1996). The eight tasks measure selective atten-tion, sustained attention, attentional switching and divided attention with activities that are meaningful to the patient.

Contributions to Memory

It is often difficult to distinguish between a primary memory disorder and a more general impairment in attention or concentration secondarily disrupting memory. Several theorists (Luria, 1971; Petrides, 1998; Stuss et al., 1997) have described the frontal lobe memory disorder as more a deficit in attention and other control functions than memory *per se*. Some cases sort themselves out, such as when a patient performs well on one class of tests and not on the other. Some amnesic patients appear to have normal attention and several studies have shown that the memory deficit in mild Alzheimer's disease occurs in patients without impaired sustained attention (Lines et al., 1991) or directed attention (Lafleche & Albert, 1995; Nebes & Brady, 1989). Often patients perform poorly on both attentional and memory tasks, thus making the distinction more difficult. Reductions in attentional capacity as well as memory may be seen in patients with diffuse brain dysfunction, such as from severe closed head injury, schizophrenia, metabolic encephalopathy, or dementia of the Alzheimer's type. One method for identifying components of complex cognitive disorders is to examine the correlation between performances on memory tests and other cognitive tests, e.g. performance on a word-list learning task by a group with mixed neurological disorders was related to performance on tests of attention and mental tracking (Vanderploeg et al., 1994). Using between-group comparisons, rumination in patients with dysphoric mood was associated with deficits in both focused attention and memory not seen in subjects who were not dysphoric (Hertel, 1998).

Some memory tasks place heavy demands on attention. Lengthy memory tasks require intact sustained attention, e.g. in continuous memory recognition tests (Tombaugh, 1996; Trahan & Larrabee, 1988; Warrington, 1984) patients see a long sequence of items out of which they must identify those already seen. Any loss of attention during the early, acquisition phase of the task could affect performance on the remainder of the task. The performance demands of some visuographic memory tasks are substantial and may divide attention. Drawing geometric designs from memory would be expected to produce interference for those patients who labor with the drawing component of the task (Taylor, 1992).

The clinician may choose to minimize the influence of attentional factors by test selection. Some tests are constructed to ensure that the patient overtly attends to material to be learned. The CERAD Word List Task (Morris et al, 1989) requires that the patient read aloud each of the to-be-recalled words, which requires registration of the words. One could argue that the act of reading divides the patient's attention between the performance and memory requirements of the test. However, reading is relatively automatic and the interference would be expected to be small. The examiner may wish to select a memory test with a simple response mode, e.g. rather than having patients draw geometric designs, visuospatial memory can be examined by having patients place items in their learned position on a spatial grid. The original 7/24 (Barbizet & Cany, 1968) and modified 7/24 Spatial Recall (Rao et al., 1984) tests, as well as the Visual Spatial Learning Test (Malec et al., 1991) and the Visual Recognition tasks of the Memory Assessment Battery (Williams, 1991), examine memory for the location of stimulus items on a grid.

Information Processing

Many traumatically brain-injured patients, especially those whose damage is diffusely distributed, have reduced ability to process information as rapidly as it is presented to them. They may fail to recall elements of a conversation or the evening's news because they have not been able to assimilate the information as it was presented. Others with more focal and lateralized lesions may no longer be able to process verbal or nonverbalizable information adequately. If not properly examined, these deficits can be misinterpreted as due to memory failures.

It is generally accepted that memory deficits that are specific to either verbal or nonverbal material cut across sensory modalities. Most memory tests in clinical use confound the type of material to be learned (verbal and nonverbal) with modality of presentation (aural or visual), i.e. most verbal memory tests consist of having the patient recall material that has been read by the examiner and most nonverbal tasks require the patient to draw from memory or recognize visually presented material. It is possible to dissociate these two factors, such as asking the patient to recall the names of a set of visually presented objects or pictures or to recall a series of familiar sounds, such as a bell, birdsong and paper rustling.

Speed

Information processing speed can be assessed using timed tasks. Timed performances on commonly used mental tracking tasks, such as serial subtraction of sevens, proved to be effective measures of speed of information processing in cardiac transplant patients (Williams et al., 1996). One of the more demanding of these is the Paced Auditory Serial Addition Task (PASAT) (Gronwall, 1977; Gronwall & Sampson, 1974), which has been used extensively to detect subtle disorders in patients with mild brain dysfunction. Although originally developed for patients with mild traumatic brain injury, the PASAT has also been used in other conditions in which brain damage tends to be diffuse, such as AIDS, toxic encephalopathy, and multiple sclerosis. The task requires that the patient report aloud the sum of consecutive pairs of numbers presented at a fixed rate by a tape recorder, e.g. if the numbers, "2–7–4–1" are heard in that sequence, the subject should say "9" after hearing the "7", then "11" after hearing the "4", and so on. The task difficulty results from the necessity to inhibit the easier response of adding the last number presented on the tape with the last summation generated by the patient. The level of difficulty can be heightened by speeding up the rate of presentation of numbers. Like most complex tasks, it requires a number of cognitive operations in addition to information processing: sustained as well as divided attention, calculation, and inhibition of a prepotent response.

Verbal Deficits

Patients may have deficits that are specific to the nature of the information to be learned (Fuster, 1995). Many patients with left hemisphere lesions have language impairments and patients with right hemisphere lesions often have visuospatial impairment. Even patients with intact fluent speech who appear to follow a casual conversation may have subtle language-processing deficits. The Token Test (Boller & Vignolo, 1966; Spreen & Strauss, 1998) is sensitive to disrupted language processing that is not readily recognizable (Lezak, 1995; Weintraub, 2000). The test consists of series of oral commands, using "tokens" of varying shapes, sizes and colors. The patient follows commands of increasing length and syntactic complexity. Unlike most information conveyed in social conversations, the commands given during this test lack contextual cuing or redundancy of information, thus bringing to light even fairly subtle comprehension problems. Similarly, reading comprehension tests may identify language-processing deficits that might not be obvious (Greenwald, 2000).

Nonverbal Deficits

Likewise, patients may have deficits that are specific to processing of visuospatial information (Ogden, 1996; Robertson & Rafal, 2000). The WIS subtests include constructional tasks involving reconstructing designs with blocks and assembling puzzle pieces

(Wechsler, 1944, 1955, 1981, 1997). The Complex Figure Test requires more complex visuospatial processing by the drawing from memory of this difficult geometric design (Corwin & Bylsma, 1993; Rey, 1964) or one of the alternative forms (Spreen & Strauss, 1993; Taylor, 1979). Lesions of the posterior cerebral cortex tend to be associated with the greatest difficulty with constructions, with right hemisphere lesions producing greater deficits than left hemisphere lesions. The geometric designs used in some memory tests, such as the Benton Visual Retention Test (Benton, 1974; Sivan, 1991) lend themselves to verbal labels and thus are not useful measures of nonverbal functions.

Contributions to Memory

Speed of information processing influences memory as well as other cognitive abilities, e.g. age-related changes in memory are related to changes in speed of processing (Birren et al., 1980; Bryan & Luszcz, 1996; Salthouse, 1996; Verhaeghen & Salthouse, 1997) and memory performance is related to processing speed in patients with Parkinson's disease (Stebbins et al., 1999) and multiple sclerosis (De Luca et al., 1994). Slower processing speed can limit the capacity of working memory (Grigsby, et al., 1994); Salthouse & Babcock, 1991) and reduce the amount of elaboration or formation of associations that are involved in encoding to-be-remembered information (Salthouse, 1994).

The role of slow information processing on memory performance can be examined by comparing performances on tests in which speed is essential and in which speed is relatively irrelevant. Many patients react as though overwhelmed when presented with story recall tasks, such as in the WMS. They experience it as too much information too fast. Presentation rates that are too fast hinder recall in intact persons (Shum et al., 1997) and this effect would be expected to be greatest in the elderly and in patients with brain disorders, whose information processing is slow. To test the limits on such a task, the examiner should slow down the pace, particularly pausing between sentences. Ideally, story recall tests would allow ample information processing by presenting the story more than once, such as with the Heaton Story Recall format (Heaton et al., 1991) or Story B of the WMS-III (Wechsler, 1997). Patients may show better performance on a word-list learning task, in which the pace of presentation is naturally slower and the material is repeated three or more times.

Material-specific processing deficits affect performance on memory tests in which language or visuospatial information is to be learned. Aphasic patients often perform poorly on verbal memory tests, which require both language and memory capacities. Language impairment can affect the patient's comprehension of the material or ability to produce the correct verbal response (Wilshire & Coslett, 2000). Aphasic stroke patients with extensive damage to the left temporal lobe involving both language areas on the convexity and memory structures more anterior and mesial may sustain both memory and language impairments. Both of these areas play important but different roles in the verbal memory impairment. Aphasic patients tend to perform more poorly on word-list learning, paired word associates learning, and prose recall tasks than nonaphasic patients (Fuster, 1995). However, some aphasic patients perform better on the prose tasks because they benefit from contextual information. Others process the grammatical and syntactical information too slowly and perform better on word-list tasks.

For some patients it may be impossible to assess the relative contribution of language impairment on verbal memory performance. One attempt consists of assessing memory with tasks with minimal verbal characteristics, such as memory for complex geometric designs or for faces (Warrington, 1984). Aphasic patients are at a disadvantage even on these tasks because of their disrupted ability to encode material using verbal mediation as well as visual imagery. The difference in performance of a language-impaired patient on a verbal memory task compared with a nonverbal memory task will provide an indication of the material-specificity of the impairment.

Patients with visuospatial disorders who have difficulty in drawing a geometric design will be disadvantaged in recalling the design, because here memory becomes confounded with processing demands. Some examiners have advocated calculating the memory score in relation to the copy score (Brooks, 1972; Kuehn & Snow, 1992), thereby factoring out as much as possible the constructional component from the memory performance. However, if a patient is unable to copy the design within at least the *low average* range, a subsequent recall score is of dubious value. Some frequently used memory tests require the copying of relatively simple geometric designs, thereby minimizing the processing and constructional requirements of the test. The Benton Visual Retention Test and, to a lesser extent, the WMS Visual Reproduction Test fall into this category. However, even the Visual Reproduction Test designs are too difficult for healthy very elderly persons (Howieson et al., 1991). Some memory recognition tests have a spatial as well as pattern or picture component (e.g. Trahan & Larrabee, 1988; Williams, 1991)

EXECUTIVE FUNCTIONS

The distinction between memory and other cognitive functions is perhaps most difficult when describing the motivating, control and regulatory behaviors that are necessary for all goal-directed activities, including memory. In neuropsychological terms, executive functions refer to those abilities necessary to formulate goals and effectively carry them out (Lezak, 1982; Stuss & Benson, 1987). These are difficult tasks for many patients with extensive frontal lobe or diffuse brain injuries (Damasio & Anderson, 1993; Eslinger & Geder, 2000; Luria, 1980). Executive deficits also can be found in patients with disorders involving subcortical structures and connections (Huber & Shuttleworth, 1990) and right hemisphere damage (Cutting, 1990; Pimental & Kingsbury, 1989). The major categories of executive behaviors are: (a) volition; (b) planning; (c) executing activities; and (d) self-monitoring (Lezak, 1995). A deficiency in any of these task-orientating behaviors can interfere with the ability to succeed in all but the simplest of cognitive tasks. Some executive functions have particular bearing on memory performance.

Volition

An individual must be aware of his/her self and surroundings in order to have the capacity to formulate a goal and exercise self-will. The ability to create motives involves an interaction of an appreciation of personal or social needs based on past experiences and self-identity and the capacity to be motivated (Lezak, 1982). Some patients with brain disorders have greatly diminished capacity for self-generating activity, which may be reflected in diminished spontaneous memory retrieval (Markowitsch, 2000). They may have a reasonable plan of action but fail to initiate the plan. These patients typically look their best in a formal evaluation where they can respond to the structure and motivation provided by the examiner (Damasio & Anderson, 1993; Eslinger & Geder, 2000). By their very nature, most examiner-administered tests require little self-generation by the patient (Lezak, 1982). Left on their own, these patients lack the capacity to carry on and appear apathetic (Habib, 2000; Knight & Grabowecky, 2000). Descriptions of patients' self-initiated activities from persons close to them can provide important information.

Planning

Tasks that best assess executive functions are sufficiently complex to require planning or strategies to maximize performance. Examples include mazes, constructional tasks including free drawing (e.g. of a bicycle), and complex problem-solving tests, such as the Twenty Questions parlor game, which was modified for neuropsychological use by Laine & Butters (1982). This task requires the subject to identify an object the examiner has in mind by asking questions that can only be answered by "yes" and "no". The object is to identify the task with as few questions as possible. A successful strategy uses questions that include or exclude as many items as possible in one question, e.g. the first question might be, "Is it living?" and, if the answer is "No", a follow-up question, "Is it bigger than a car (or whatever comparison nearly equally divides the inanimate objects)?" The tower puzzles, such as the Tower of London task (Shallice, 1982), are solved successfully by planning the movement of rings from one peg to another to achieve a particular display of rings in the fewest moves (Lezak, 1995). Patients who have difficulties on these tests may also fail to use strategies to facilitate their recall during memory testing.

Executing

Carrying out activities requires the capacities to initiate behavior and modify that behavior through switching, maintaining or stopping behavior in an integrated manner, according to an analysis of appropriate actions (Lezak, 1982). The Brixton Spatial Anticipation Test (Burgess & Shallice, 1996a), the Category Test (Halstead, 1947) and the Wisconsin Card Sorting Test (Berg, 1948; Grant & Berg, 1948; Heaton et al., 1993) are designed to measure rule attainment, flexibility of thinking and appropriate switching of behavior. They present patterns of stimuli and require the patients to select a response based on a principle or concept learned through feedback about the correctness of previous responses. The patients must realize when a shift in principles occurs and act accordingly. These tasks also assess capacity for concept formation. Deficits in modulation of behavior may result in inconsistent responses, perseverations and impersistence. Using six tests that are more exemplary of everyday tasks, the Behavioural Assessment of the Dysexecutive Syndrome (BADS) examines cognitive flexibility, novel problem solving, planning, judgment and estimation, and behavioural regulation (Wilson et al., 1996). It is designed to predict patients' abilities to handle problems that are likely to be encountered in daily activities.

Some brain-injured patients lack the ability to persist with lengthy or complex tasks. There are few open-ended tests that measure persistence directly. However, a fluency task can be used to measure persistence (Lezak, 1995; Spreen & Strauss, 1998). Patients may be asked to name all the words they can think of beginning with a designated letter of the alphabet. Impaired patients will think of a few that come to mind and stop generating items prematurely. These patients often will perform adequately if frequently prompted by the examiner. The Tinkertoy Test (Bayless et al., 1989; Lezak, 1982, 1995) was designed to measure planning and persistence. Patients are simply instructed to make what they want with these simple construction materials and thus must decide what to build and how to design it. Severely impaired patients begin the task without a plan and their final product may be the result of serendipity.

Self-monitoring

Another executive function necessary for successful performance on cognitive tasks is the capacity to monitor and self-correct spontaneously and reliably. The person who is able to regulate the relevance and accuracy of their responses on tests will have an advantage over those who make careless errors or contaminate their performance with perseverative or extraneous responses. Some patients with brain disorders, particularly those with frontal lobe damage, are impulsive and may trade accuracy of performance for speed (Knight & Grabowecky, 2000; Ogden, 1996).

Impulsivity occurs when inhibiting an undesirable, often easy, behavior fails. It can be seen on the Trail Making Test, Part B, when a patient fails to shift set and gives the easier, same-set response. Maze-tracing tests may also elicit impulsivity as the patient charges into turns that lead to blind alleys. The Stroop Test requires inhibiting an easy response, as the patient is asked to state the color of ink in which a conflicting color word is printed. After asking the patient to supply a reasonable word for the missing last word in a series of sentences, the Hayling Sentence Completion Test then asks the patient to complete each sentence with a word that is unrelated to the sentence in every way (Burgess & Shallice, 1996b). Success requires inhibition of meaningful associations that the sentence activates and use of a strategy to generate unconnected responses. Observations of test-taking behavior differentiate those patients who regularly check their work, such as a reconstructed design on WIS Block Design test or copy of the Complex Figure, from those who do not. Requiring patients to complete a page of arithmetic calculations at their leisure (e.g. see Lezak, 1995) frequently brings out carelessness tendencies in patients who demonstrate adequate arithmetic skills but make (*and leave*) small computational errors on the page.

Contribution to Memory

When are deficits in volition, planning, persistence or self-monitoring on memory tests a primary feature of the memory disorder, and when are they associated impairments? The executive deficit might be primary, but it can also occur in conjunction with a true memory disorder. The difficulty in making this distinction is illustrated by Baddeley & Wilson (1988) in their analysis of man with a frontal syndrome due to a closed head injury sustained in a traffic accident. They concluded that this patient's memory disorder resembled a classic memory disorder but that it occurred in combination with a frontal syndrome. Trauma patients might be expected to have frontal syndromes because many sustain damage to the frontal lobes as well as to memory areas of the anterior/medial temporal lobes. It has been proposed that memory disorders of frontal patients are related to problems in attention, susceptibility to interference, and problems with planning and organization needed for retrieval, rather than deficits in storage or consolidation as seen in memory-impaired patients with medial temporal lobe and diencephalic areas (Shimamura et al., 1991; Smith et al., 1995; Stuss et al., 1997).

Perhaps the best example of the interaction of executive and memory deficits occurs with Korsakoff's syndrome. The Korsakoff's patient has a severe memory impairment that dramatically interferes with daily activities, but it is the pervasive executive disorders that render them socially dependent and unable to carry out ordinary constructive activities (Lezak, 1995). Memory impairment is presumably related to lesions of primary memory areas, the dorsal-medial nucleus of the thalamus and mammillary bodies, but Korsakoff patients have frontal atrophy as well (Shimamura et al., 1991). Moscovitch (1982) showed that the Korsakoff's patient's poor performance on one memory task, release from proactive interference, is related more to impairment of frontal functions than to the amnesic disorder.

Failure to use strategies to manipulate and organize information will also limit recall on memory tests. These strategies may include chunking information (e.g. digits to recall), making meaningful associations between unrelated items to be recalled (e.g. difficult paired associates), or using semantic attributes to facilitate recall of related bits of information (e.g. words from a list). Several memory tests developed for clinical applications provide useful information about the use of strategies. The California Verbal Learning Test (Delis et al., 1983, 1986, 1987) and the California Verbal Learning Test, 2nd edn (Delis et al., 2000) assess the patient's use of semantic categorizing in the course of memory testing. The items to be learned are 16 words, four from of each of four object categories, such as fruits or clothing. The items are presented in random order with both uncued and category-cued recall trials. The uncued performances can be evaluated for semantic clustering, an effective recall strategy. Thus, patients who cluster according to categories tend to perform better than those who do not. Patients with left hemisphere lesions show impaired semantic clustering and better (although still impaired) recall with category cues (Hildebrandt et at., 1998). Parkinson's patients are impaired when forced to rely on internally generated strategies and function normally when provided with category cues (Knoke et al., 1998). Using similarly constructed word lists, Stuss et al. (1996) found that patients with frontal lesions and adults over the age of 65 perform worse than younger participants on memory measures of strategy, monitoring, and efficiency. Absence of semantic strategy may also reflect a breakdown in semantic knowledge, such as with Alzheimer's disease.

A less structured word list also can provide important information about the use of memory strategies. The commonly used Auditory Verbal Learning Test (Lezak, 1995; Rey, 1964) consists of 15 unrelated words that the patient hears in the same order for each of five trials, with no restriction on order of recall. On first hearing the list, intact subjects show both recency and primacy effects, recalling most often the first few words and the last few words, with perhaps a few in the middle. As trials are repeated, most intact subjects begin to organize the words according to associations and their recall demonstrates these clusters. They also begin to recall first the words they have not given before so they make sure not to forget them. These self-employed strategies assist the patient. We advocate inquiring of the patient who performs poorly on such a task whether they used any particular method for learning the words.

Deficits in self-monitoring can play havoc with memory. Both psychiatric patients and frontal lobe-injured patients may have difficulty distinguishing accurate memories from internal associations (Schacter & Curran, 2000). Some patients elaborate a completely faulty ending to a story they have been asked to remember, or interject associative material here and there. In some instances, if the examiner questions their response, these patients are able to specify the elaborated portion, thereby displaying some capacity to distinguish between external stimuli and their mental contents. Most people have a relatively strong sense of confidence about accuracy of memories, often referred to as the "feeling-of-knowing", and inhibit irrelevant or erroneous associations (Hintzman, 2000).

Impersistence can also result in poor memory performance. Patients may readily recall a few elements of a story to be learned and then stop, sometimes stating and sometimes implying that "that's enough" without attempting to expand the recall.

CONCLUSIONS

Most cognitive tasks involve a composite of mental operations, so that it is often difficult to specify where one ends and the other takes over. Several models have been proposed to relate the cognitive functions discussed in this chapter. The information-processing model proposed by Schneider & Shiffrin (1977) relates attention and information processing by suggesting that divided attention is dependent on adequate speed of information processing. In fact, models of information processing include a stage in which stimuli are compared with memory stores for familiarity. Information processing also is a key element of some theories of memory (Cermak, 1972; Craik & Lockhart, 1972). Shallice (1982) has proposed a model of executive control over attentional resources that regulates the use of attentional resources in a goal-directed fashion, while Baddeley (1986, 1994) has proposed a model of working memory that includes inherent attentional and executive functions.

Memory tasks certainly have multiple demands and it is not always easy to dissociate memory from other cognitive functions (Fuster, 1995; Schachter et al., 2000). Clearly, some patients' cognitive impairments are restricted to memory alone. However, the majority of patients with memory impairment have other cognitive deficits as well, e.g. if the patient has difficulty with attention or self-monitoring across a range of tasks, then poor performance on memory tests may be at least partly attributable to these other cognitive problems. Some distinctions are difficult, such as between poor memory retrieval and general impersistence. The clinician is challenged with making the correct distinctions so that necessary counseling and possibly remediation can be accurately directed.

REFERENCES

Baddeley, A.D. (1986). *Working Memory*. Oxford: Oxford University Press.

Baddeley, A.D. (1994). Working memory: the interface between memory and cognition. In D.L. Schacter & E. Tulving (eds), *Memory Systems 1994* (pp. 351–376). Cambridge, MA: MIT Press.

Baddeley, A. & Wilson, B. (1988). Frontal amnesia and the dysexecutive syndrome. *Brain and Cognition*, **7**, 212–230.

Barbizet, J. & Caney, E. (1968). Clinical and psychometrical study of a patient with memory disturbances. *International Journal of Neurology*, **7**, 44–54.

Bayless, J.D., Varney, N.R. & Roberts, R.J. (1989). Tinker Toy Test performance and vocational outcome in patients with closed head injuries. *Journal of Clinical and Experimental Neuropsychology*, **11**, 913–917.

Bazarian, J.J., Wong, T., Harris, M. et al. (1999). Epidemiology and predictors of post-concussive syndrome after minor head injury in an emergency population. *Brain Injury*, **13**, 173–189.

Benton, A.L. (1974). *The Revised Visual Retention Test*. New York: Psychological Corporation.

Benton, A.L. & Hamsher, K. de S. (1989). *Multilingual Aphasia Examination*. Iowa City, IA: AIA Associates.

Benton, A.L., Hamsher K. de S., Varney N.R. & Spreen, O. (1983). *Contributions to Neuropsychological Assessment*. New York: Oxford University Press.

Berg, E.A. (1948). A simple objective test for measuring flexibility in thinking. *Journal of General Psychology*, **39**, 15–22.

Boller, F. & Vignolo, L.A. (1966). Latent sensory aphasia in hemisphere-damaged patients: an experimental study with the Token Test. *Brain*, **89**, 815–831.

Birren, J., Woods, A.M. & Williams, M.V. (1980). Behavioral slowing with age: causes, organization and consequences. In L.W. Poon (ed.), *Aging in the 1980s* (pp. 293–308). Washington, DC: American Psychological Association.

Brooks, D.N. (1972). Memory and head injury. *Journal of Nervous and Mental Disease*, **155**, 350–355.

Bryan, J. & Luszcz, M.A. (1996). Speed of information processing as a mediator between age and free-recall performance. *Psychology and Aging*, **11**, 3–9.

Burgess, P.W. & Shallice, T. (1996a) Bizarre responses, rule detection and frontal lobe lesions. *Cortex*, **32**, 241–259.

Burgess, P.W. & Shallice, T. (1996b) Response suppression, initiation, and strategy use following frontal lobe lesions. *Neuropsychologia*, **34**, 263–273.

Cermak, L.S. (1972). *Human Memory; Research and Theory*. New York: Ronald Press.

Corwin, J. & Bylsma, F.W. (1993). Translations of excerpts from André Rey's "Psychological examination of traumatic encephalopathy" and P.A. Osterrieth's "The Complex Figure Copy Test". *Clinical Neuropsychologist*, **7**, 4–21.

Craik, F.I.M. & Lockhart, R.S. (1972). Levels of processing: framework for memory research. *Journal of Verbal Learning and Verbal Behavior*, **11**, 671–684.

Crawford, J.R., Sommerville, J. & Robertson, I.H. (1997) Assessing the reliability and abnormality of subtest differences on the Test of Everyday Attention. *British Journal of Clinical Psychology*, **36**, 609–617.

Curran, H.V. (2000). Psychopharmacological approaches to human memory. In M.S. Gazzaniga (ed.), *The New Cognitive Neurosciences*, 2nd edn (pp. 797–804). Cambridge, MA: MIT Press.

Cutting, J. (1990). *The Right Cerebral Hemisphere and Psychiatric Disorders*. Oxford: Oxford University Press.

Damasio, A.R. & Anderson, S.W. (1993). The frontal lobes. In K.M. Heilman & E. Valenstein (eds), *Clinical Neuropsychology*, 3rd edn (pp. 409–460). New York: Oxford University Press.

Damasio, A.R., Damasio, H. & Tranel, D. (1990). Impairments in visual recognition as clues to the processes of memory. In G.M. Edelman et al. (eds), *Signal and Sense. Local and Global Order in Perceptual Maps* (pp. 451–473). New York: Wiley-Liss.

Delis, D.C., Kaplan, E., Kramer, J.H. & Ober, B.A. (2000). *California Verbal Learning Test—Second Edition (CVLT-II) Manual*. San Antonio, TX: The Psychological Corporation/Harcourt Brace Jovanovich.

Delis, D.C., Kramer, J.H., Kaplan, E. & Ober, B.A. (1986). *California Verbal Learning Test*. San Antonio, TX: Psychological Corporation/Harcourt Brace Jovanovich.

Delis, D.C., Kramer, J.H., Kaplan, E. & Ober, B.A. (1983, 1987). *California Verbal Learning Test, Form II (Research edn)*. San Antonio, TX: The Psychological Corporation/Harcourt Brace Jovanovich.

De Luca, J., Barbieri-Berger, S. & Johnson, S.K. (1994). The nature of memory impairments in multiple sclerosis: acquisition vs. retrieval. *Journal of Clinical and Experimental Neuropsychology*, **16**, 183–189.

Diller, L., Ben-Yishay, Y., Gerstman, L.J. et al. (1974). *Studies in Cognition and Rehabilitation in Hemiplegia* (Rehabilitation Monograph No. 50). New York: New York University Medical Center Institute of Rehabilitation Medicine.

Di Stefano, G. & Radanov, B.P. (1996). Quantitative and qualitative aspects of learning in common whiplash patients: a 6-month follow-up study. *Archives of Clinical Neuropsychology*, **11**, 661–676.

Dodrill, C.B. (1978). A neuropsychological battery for epilepsy. *Epilepsia*, **19**, 611–623.

Eslinger, P.J. & Geder, L. (2000). Behavioral and emotional changes after focal frontal lobe damage. In J. Bogousslavsky & J.L. Cummings (eds), *Behavior and Mood Disorders in Focal Brain Lesions* (pp. 217–260). Cambridge: Cambridge University Press.

Fischler, I. (1998). Attention and language. In R. Parasuraman (ed.), *The Attentive Brain* (pp. 381–399). Cambridge, MA: MIT Press.

Freed, D.M., Corkin, S., Growdon, J.H. & Nissen, M.J. (1989). Selective attention in Alzheimer's disease: characterizing cognitive subgroups of patients. *Neuropsychologia*, **27**, 325–339.

Freides, D. & Avery, M.E. (1972). Narrrative and visual spatial recall: assessment incorporating learning and delayed retention. *Clinical Neuropsychologist*, **5**, 338–344.

Fuster, J.M. (1995). *Memory in the Cerebral Cortex*. Cambridge, MA: MIT Press.

Gasquoine, P.G. (1997). Postconcussion symptoms. *Neuropsychological Review*, **7**, 77–85.

Grant, D.A. & Berg, E.A. (1948). A behavioral analysis of degree of reinforcement and ease of shifting to new responses on a Weigl-type card-sorting problem. *Journal of Experimental Psychology*, **38**, 404–411.

Greenwald, M.L. (2000). The acquired dyslexias. In S.E. Nadeau et al. (eds), *Aphasia and Language. Theory to Practice* (pp. 159–183). New York: Guilford.

Greenwood, P. & Parasuraman, R. (1991). Effects of aging on the speed of attentional cost of cognitive operations. *Developmental Neuropsychology*, **7**, 421–434.

Grigsby, J., Kaye, K. & Busenbark, D. (1994). Alphanumeric sequencing: a report on a brief measure of information processing used among persons with multiple sclerosis. *Perceptual and Motor Skills*, **78**, 883–887.

Gronwall, D.M.A. (1977). Paced auditory serial-addition task: a measure of recovery from concussion. *Perceptual and Motor Skills*, **44**, 367–373.

Gronwall, D.M.A. & Sampson, H. (1974). *The Psychological Effects of Concussion*. Auckland: University Press/Oxford University Press.

Habib, M. (2000). Disorders of motivation. In J. Bogousslavsky & J.L. Cummings (eds), *Behavior and Mood Disorders in Focal Brain Lesions* (pp. 261–284). Cambridge: Cambridge University Press.

Halstead, W.C. (1947). *Brain and Intelligence*. Chicago: University of Chicago Press.

Heaton, R.K., Chelune, G.J., Talley, J.L. et al. (1993). *Wisconsin Card Sorting Test Manual: Revised and Expanded*. Odessa, FL: Psychological Assessment Resources.

Heaton, R.K., Grant, I. & Matthews, C.G. (1991). *Comprehensive Norms for an Expanded Halstead–Reitan Battery: Demographic Corrections, Research Findings, and Clinical Applications*. Odessa, FL: Psychological Assessment Resources.

Hertel, P.T. (1998). Relation between rumination and impaired memory in dysphoric moods. *Journal of Abnormal Psychology*, **107**, 166–172.

Hildebrandt, H., Brand, A. & Sachsenheimer, W. (1998). Profiles of patients with left prefrontal and left temporal lobe lesions after cerebrovascular infarctions on California Verbal Learning Test-like indices. *Journal of Clinical and Experimental Neuropsychology*, **20**, 673–683.

Hintzman, D.L. (2000). Memory judgments. In E. Tulving & F.I.M. Craik (eds), *The Oxford Handbook of Memory* (pp. 165–177). New York: Oxford University Press.

Howieson, D.B., Kaye, J. & Howieson, J. (1991). Cognitive status in healthy aging. *Journal of Clinical and Experimental Neuropsychology*, **13**, 28.

Huber, S.J. & Shuttleworth, E.C. (1990). Neuropsychological assessment of subcortical dementia. In J.L. Cummings (ed.), *Subcortical Dementia* (pp. 71–86.) New York: Oxford University Press.

Kapur, N. (1988). Pattern of verbal memory deficits in patients with bifrontal pathology and patients with third ventricle lesions. In M.M. Gruneberg, P.E. Morris & R.N. Sykes (eds), *Practical Aspects of Memory: Current Research and Issues*, Vol. 2 (pp. 10–15). New York: Wiley.

Knight, R.T. & Grabowecky, M. (2000). Prefrontal cortex, time, and consciousness. In M.S. Gazzaniga (ed.), *The New Cognitive Neurosciences*, 2nd edn (pp. 1319–1339). Cambridge, MA: MIT Press.

Knoke, D., Taylor, A.E. & Saint-Cyr, J.A. (1998). The differential effects of cueing on recall in Parkinson's disease and normal subjects. *Brain and Cognition*, **38**, 261–274.

Kosslyn, S.M. & Thompson, W.L. (2000). Shared mechanisms in visual imagery and visual perception: Insights from cognitive neuroscience. In M.S. Gazzaniga (ed.), *The New Cognitive Neurosciences*, 2nd edn (pp. 975–985). Cambridge, MA: MIT Press.

Kuehn, S. & Snow, W.G. (1992). Are the Rey and Taylor figures equivalent? *Archives of Clinical Neuropsychology*, **7**, 445–448.

LaBerge, D. (2000). Networks of attention. In M.S. Gazzaniga (ed.), *The New Cognitive Neurosciences*, 2nd edn (pp. 711–724). Cambridge, MA: MIT Press.

LaFleche, G. & Albert, M. (1995). Executive function in mild Alzheimer's disease. *Neuropsychology*, **9**, 313–320.

Laine, M. & Butters, N. (1982). A preliminary study of problem solving strategies of detoxified long-term alcoholics. *Drug & Alcohol Dependence*, **10**, 235–242.

Lezak, M.D. (1979). Recovery of memory and learning functions following traumatic brain injury. *Cortex*, **15**, 63–70.

Lezak, M.D. (1982). The problem of assessing executive functions. *International Journal of Psychology*, **17**, 281–297.

Lezak, M.D. (1994). Domains of behavior from a neuropsychological perspective: the whole story. In W. Spaulding (ed.), *41st Nebraska Symposium on Motivation* (pp. 23–55). Lincoln, NE: University of Nebraska.

Lezak, M.D. (1995). *Neuropsychological Assessment*, 3rd edn. New York: Oxford University Press.

Lines, C.R., Dawson, C., Preston, G.C. et al. (1991). Memory and attention in patients with senile dementia of the Alzheimer's type and in normal elderly subjects. *Journal of Clinical and Experimental Neuropsychology*, **13**, 691–702.

Luria, A.R. (1971). Memory disturbance in local brain lesions. *Neuropsychologia*, **9**, 367–376.

Luria, A.R. (1980). *Higher Cortical Functions in Man*, 2nd edn. New York: Basic Books.

Malec, J.F., Ivnik, R.J. & Hinkeldey, N.S. (1991). Visual spatial learning test. *Psychological Assessment*, **3**, 82–88.

Markowitsch, H.J. (2000). Memory and amnesia. In M.-M. Mesulam (ed.), *Principles of Behavioral and Cognitive Neurology*, 2nd edn (pp. 257–293). New York: Oxford University Press.

Milner, B. (1970). Memory and the medial regions of the brain. In K.H. Pribram & D.E. Broadbent (eds), *Biology of Memory* (pp. 29–50). New York: Academic Press.

Milner, B. (1971). Interhemispheric differences in the localization of psychological processes in man. *British Medical Bulletin*, **27**, 272–277.

Mitrushina, M.N., Boone, K.B. & D'Elia, L.F. (1999). *Handbook of Normative Data for Neuropsychological Assessment*. New York: Oxford University Press.

Morris, J.C., Heyman, A., Mohs, R.C. et al. (1989). The consortium to establish a registry for Alzheimer's disease (CERAD). Part I. Clinical and neuropsychological assessment of Alzheimer's disease. *Neurology*, **39**, 1159–1165.

Morrow, L.A., Robin, N., Hodgson, M.J. & Kamis, H. (1992). Assessment of attention and memory efficiency in persons with solvent neurotoxicity. *Neuropsychologia*, **30**, 911–922.

Moscovitch, M. (1982). Multiple dissociations of function in amnesia. In L.S. Cermak (ed.), *Human Memory and Amnesia* (pp. 337–370). Hillsdale, NJ: Erlbaum.

Nebes, R.D. & Brady, C.B. (1989). Focused and divided attention in Alzheimer's disease. *Cortex*, **25**, 300–315.

Nestor, P.G., Parasuraman, R. & Haxby, J.V. (1991). Speed of information processing and attention in early Alzheimer's dementia. *Developmental Neuropsychology*, **7**, 242–256.

Ogden, J.A. (1996). *Fractured Minds* (pp. 125–153). New York: Oxford University Press.

Parasuraman, R. (1998). Issues and prospects. In R. Parasuraman (ed.), (pp. 381–399). *The Attentive Brain*. Cambridge, MA: MIT Press.

Pachana, N.A., Boone, K.B., Miller, B.L. et al. (1996). Comparison of neuropsychological functioning in Alzheimer's disease and frontotemporal dementia. *Journal of the International Neuropsychological Society*, **2**, 505–510.

Pashler, H.E. (1998*). The Psychology of Attention*. Cambridge, MA: MIT Press.

Peterson, L.R. & Peterson, M.J. (1959). Short-term retention of individual verbal items. *Journal of Experimental Psychology*, **58**, 193–198.

Petrides, M. (1998). Specialized systems for the processing of mnemonic information. In A.C. Roberts, T.W. Robbins et al. (eds), *The Prefrontal Cortex. Executive and Cognitive Functions* (pp. 103–116). London: Oxford University Press.

Pimental, P.A. & Kingbury, N.A. (1989). The injured right hemisphere: Classification of related disorders. In P.A. Pimental & N.A. Kingsbury (eds), *Neuropsychological Aspects of Right Brain Injury* (pp. 19–64). Austin, TX: PRO-ED.

Ponsford J. (1995). *Traumatic Brain Injury*. Hove: Erlbaum.

Ponsford, J. & Kinsella, G. (1992). Attentional deficits following closed-head injury. *Journal of Clinical and Experimental Neuropsychology*, **14**, 822–838.

Posner, M.I. & DiGirolamo, G.J. (2000). In M.S. Gazzaniga (ed.), *The New Cognitive Neurosciences*, 2nd edn (pp. 623–631). Cambridge, MA: MIT Press.

Rao, S.M. (1996). White matter disease and dementia. *Brain and Cognition*, **31**, 250–268.

Rao, S.M., Hammeke, T.A., McQuillen, M.P. et al. (1984). Memory disturbance in chronic progressive multiple sclerosis. *Archives of Neurology*, **41**, 625–631.

Raskin, S.A. & Mateer, C.A. (2000). *Neuropsychological Management of Mild Traumatic Brain Injury*. New York: Oxford University Press.

Rey, A. (1964). *L'examen Clinique en Psychologie*. Paris: Presses Universitaries de France.

Robertson, I.H., Ward, T., Ridgeway, V. & Nimmo-Smith, I. (1996) Structure of normal human attention: the Test of Everyday Attention. *Journal of the International Neuropsychological Society*, **2**, 525–534.

Robertson, L.C. & Rafal, R. (2000). Disorders of visual attention. In M.S. Gazzaniga (ed.), *The New Cognitive Neurosciences*, 2nd edn (pp. 633–649). Cambridge, MA: MIT Press.

Rosvold, H.E., Mirsky, A.F., Sarason, I. et al. (1956). A continuous performance test of brain damage. *Journal of Consulting Psychology*, **20**, 343–350.

Rubin, E.H., Storandt, M., Miller, J.P. et al. (1998). A prospective study of cognitive function and onset of dementia in cognitively healthy elders. *Archives of Neurology*, **55**, 395–401.

Ruff, R.M., Light, R.H. & Evans, R.W. (1987). The Ruff Figural Fluency Test: a normative study with adults. *Developmental Neuropsychology*, **3**, 37–52.

Salthouse, T.A. (1996). The processing-speed theory of adult age differences in cognition. *Psychological Review*, **103**, 403–428.

Salthouse, T.A. & Babcock, R.L. (1991). Decomposing adult age differences in working memory. *Developmental Psychology*, **27**, 763–776.

Salthouse, T.A. (1994). Aging associations: influence of speed on adult age differences in associative learning. *Journal of Experimental Psychology: Learning, Memory and Cognition*, **20**, 1486–1503.

Schachter, D.L. & Curran, T. (2000). Memory without remembering and remembering without memory: Implicit and false memories. In M.S. Gazzaniga (ed.), *The New Cognitive Neurosciences*, 2nd edn (pp. 829–840). Cambridge, MA: MIT Press.

Schachter, D.L., Wagner, A.D. & Buckner, R.L. (2000). Memory systems of 1999. In E. Tulving & F.I.M. Craik (eds), *The Oxford Handbook of Memory* (pp. 627–643), New York: Oxford University Press.

Schneider, W. & Shiffrin, R.M. (1977). Controlled and automatic human information processing: I. Detection, search and attention. *Psychological Review*, **84**, 1–66.

Shallice, T. (1982). Specific impairments of planning. In D.E. Broadbent & L. Weiskrantz (eds), *The Neuropsychology of Cognitive Function* (pp. 199–209). London: The Royal Society.

Shimamura, A.P., Janowsky, J.S. & Squire, L.R. (1991). What is the role of frontal lobe damage in memory disorders. In H.M. Levin, H.M. Eisenberg & A.L. Benton (eds), *Frontal Lobe Function and Dysfunction* (pp. 173–195). New York: Oxford University Press.

Shum, D.H.K., Murray, R.A. & Eadie, K. (1997). Effect of speed of presentation of administration of the Logical Memory subtest of the Wechsler Memory Scale—Revised. *Clinical Neuropsychologist*, **11**, 188–191.

Sivan, A.B. (1991). *Benton Visual Retention Test*, 5th edn. San Antonio, TX: Psychological Corporation.

Smith, M.L., Leonard, G., Crane, J. & Milner, B. (1995). The effects of frontal- or temporal-lobe lesions on susceptibility to interference in spatial memory. *Neuropsychologia*, **33**, 275–285.

Spreen, O. & Strauss, E. (1998). *A Compendium of Neuropsychological Tests*, 2nd edn. New York: Oxford University Press.

Stebbins, G.T., Gabrieli, J.D., Masciari, F. et al. (1999). Delayed recognition memory in Parkinson's disease: a role for working memory? *Neuropsychologia*, **37**, 503–510.

Storandt, M., Morris, J.C., Rubin, E. (1992). Progression of senile dementia of the Alzheimer's type on a battery of psychometric tests. In L. Baeckman (ed.), *Memory Functioning in Dementia* (pp. 207–226). Amsterdam: Elsevier Science.

Stroop, J.R. (1935). Studies of interference in serial verbal reactions. *Journal of Experimental Psychology*, **18**, 643–662.

Strub, R.L. & Black, F.W. (2000) *Mental Status Examination in Neurology,* 3rd edn. Philadelphia, PA: F.A. Davis.

Stuss, D.T., Alexander, M.P. & Benson, D.F. (1997). Frontal lobe functions. In M.R. Trimble & J.L. Cummings (eds), *Contemporary Behavioral Neurology* (pp. 141–158). Boston, MA: Butterworth-Heinemann.

Stuss, D.T. & Benson, D.F. (1987). The frontal lobes and control of cognition and memory. In E. Perecman (ed.) *The Frontal Lobes Revisited* (pp. 141–158). New York: IRBN Press.

Stuss, D.T., Craik, F.I., Sayer, L. et al. (1996). Comparison of older people and patients with frontal lesions: evidence from word list learning. *Psychology and Aging*, **11**, 387–395.

Stuss, D.T., Stethem, L.L., Hugenholtz, H. et al. (1989). Reaction time after head injury: fatigue, divided and focused attention, and consistency of performance. *Journal of Neurology, Neurosurgery, and Psychiatry*, **52**, 742–748.

Swick, D. & Knight, R.T. (1998). Cortical lesions and attention. In R. Parasuraman (ed.), *The Attentive Brain* (pp. 143–162). Cambridge, MA: MIT Press.

Taylor, R. (1992). Art training and the Rey figure. *Perceptual and Motor Skills*, **74**, 1105–1106.

Tombaugh, T. (1996). *Test of Memory Malingering*. North Tonawanda, NY: Multi-Health Systems.

Trahan, D.E. & Larrabee, G.J. (1988). *Continuous Visual Memory Test*. Odessa, FL: Psychological Assessment Resources.

Vallar, G. & Shallice T. (1990). *Neuropsychological Impairments of Short-Term Memory*. Cambridge: Cambridge University Press.

Vanderploeg, R.D., Schinka, J.A. & Retzlaff, P. (1994). Relationships between measures of auditory verbal learning and executive functioning. *Journal of Clinical and Experimental Neuropsychology*, **16**, 243–252.

Van Gorp, W.G., Miller, E.N., Satz, P. & Visscher, B. (1989). Neuropsychological performance in HIV-1 immunocompromised patients. *Journal of Clinical and Experimental Neuropsychology*, **11**, 763–773.

Verhaeghen, P. & Salthouse, T.A. (1997). Meta-analyses of age-cognition relations in adulthood: estimates of linear and nonlinear age effects and structural models. *Psychological Bulletin*, **122**, 231–249.

Warrington, E.K. (1984). *Recognition Memory Test*. Windsor: National Foundation for Educational Research-Nelson.

Warrington, E.K. & Shallice, T. (1984) Category specific semantic impairments. *Brain*, **107**, 829–854.

Wechsler, D. (1944). *The Measurement of Adult Intelligence*, 3rd edn. Baltimore, MD: Williams & Wilkins.

Wechsler, D. (1945). A standardized memory scale for clinical use. *The Journal of Psychology*, **19**, 87–95.

Wechsler, D. (1955). *WAIS Manual*. New York: Psychological Corporation.

Wechsler, D. (1981). *WAIS-R Manual*. New York: Psychological Corporation.

Wechsler, D. (1987). *Wechsler Memory Scale—Revised: Manual*. San Antonio, TX: Psychological Corporation/Harcourt Brace Jovanovich.

Wechsler, D. (1997). *WAIS-III Administration and Scoring Manual*. San Antonio, TX: Psychological Corporation/Harcourt Brace Jovanovich.

Weintraub, S. (2000). Neuropsychological assessment of mental state. In M.-M. Mesulam (ed.), *Principles of Behavioral and Cognitive Neurology*, 2nd edn (pp. 121–173). New York: Oxford University Press.

Williams, J.M. (1991). *Memory Assessment Scales*. Odessa, FL: Psychological Assessment Resources.

Williams, M.A., LaMarche, J.A., Alexander, R.W. et al. (1996). Serial 7s and alphabet backwards as brief measures of information processing speed. *Archives of Clinical Neuropsychology*, **11**, 651–659.

Wilshire, C.E. & Coslett, H.B. (2000). Disorders of word retrieval in aphasia: theories and potential applications. In S.E. Nadeau, R. Gonzalez, J. Leslie et al. (eds), *Aphasia and Language. Theory to Practice* (pp. 40–81). New York: Guilford.

Wilson, B.A., Alderman, N., Burgess, P.W. et al. (1996). *Behavioural Assessment of the Dysexecutive Syndrome*. Bury St Edmunds: Thames Valley Test Company.

Wrightson, P. & Gronwall, D. (1999). *Mild Head Injury*. Oxford: Oxford University Press.

CHAPTER 30

Management and Remediation of Memory Problems in Brain-injured Adults

Barbara A. Wilson

MRC Cognition and Brain Sciences Unit, Cambridge, and Oliver Zangwill Centre for Cognitive Rehabilitation, Ely, UK

> Because I've got a bad memory, it doesn't mean I'm intellectually impaired. People talk down to me, they see the handicap and not the person (Alex, in Wilson, 1999, p. 66).

The statement by the young man quoted above illustrates how people with memory problems can suffer distress caused by the misunderstanding of others. Problems experienced by memory-impaired people in their daily interaction with people who do not have, and perhaps cannot appreciate, the effects of memory loss, can sometimes be regarded as reflecting stupidity or laziness. Too much might be expected from the memory-impaired person—or indeed too little, with the effect, either way, of causing them unhappiness. The situation is compounded by the fact that few people are offered appropriate rehabilitation to help them compensate for their cognitive problems and reduce the social and emotional consequences of brain injury.

There are large numbers of people like Alex in our society. Some 36% of people with severe head injury will have significant and permanent memory impairments. In the UK these figures reflect about 2500 new cases each year, and over four times that number in the USA.

Some 10% of people over the age of 65 years have dementia, with memory impairment an almost inevitable consequence. About 34% of people with multiple sclerosis have moderate or severe memory problems, as do 70% of people with AIDS, 70% of people who survive encephalitis, and 10% of people with temporal lobe epilepsy. In addition, memory impairment is commonly seen after Korsakoff's syndrome and is not uncommon after stroke, cerebral tumour, myocardial infarction, meningitis and carbon monoxide poisoning. Despite these large numbers, and the severity of impairment experienced by people with brain damage, few will receive help in managing problems they will confront each day of

The Handbook of Memory Disorders. Edited by A.D. Baddeley, M.D. Kopelman and B.A. Wilson
© 2002 John Wiley & Sons, Ltd.

their lives, few will be given guidance as to how to reduce the effect of their handicap on their everyday functioning.

Among neurologists, and many neuropsychologists working with these patients, the prevailing attitude seems to suggest that little or nothing can be done to alleviate the problems of brain-injured people. In contrast, relatives live in the hope, and sometimes indeed the expectation, that memory functioning can be restored if the right drug or relevant set of exercises can be administered. Neither of these views is correct: although at present it is not possible to *restore* memory functioning in people with organic amnesia once the period of natural recovery is over, it is nevertheless true that these people and their families can be helped to *cope with* everyday difficulties they are likely to experience. The lives of brain-injured people can be made much more tolerable by teaching them, for example, to bypass certain problems, compensate for them, or use their residual skills more efficiently.

THE CONSEQUENCES OF MEMORY PROBLEMS FOR PATIENTS AND THEIR FAMILIES

Not only are memory problems common following brain injury, they are also among the most handicapping of cognitive deficits, often preventing return to work or independent living, and causing considerable stress to brain-injured people and their families. Some brain-injured people feel they are going crazy or believe that other people regard them as insane. They frequently refer to isolation and loneliness. A large proportion of families and caregivers become infuriated, for example, at the constant repetition of a story, joke or question that is proffered by amnesic people who forget they have said the same thing earlier or forget that an answer has been supplied. One mother of a memory-impaired son once said to me, "If he tells me that story once more. I'll kill him". When their loss of memory causes such effects on others who are close to them, it is hardly surprising that some brain-injured people, fearing they might repeat something they have said perhaps on a number of other occasions, end up remaining very quiet. A woman who survived herpes simplex encephalitis said, "In company I'm very quiet. I'm afraid of repeating myself so I don't say anything".

A typical account of the kinds of everyday problems faced by families is provided by the mother of a young man, Jack, whose memory problems followed an attempted suicide by carbon monoxide poisoning. She said:

> He never remembers where the car is parked and gets embarrassed if he has to look in his book. He gets confused about arrangements with his friends. He double-books: e.g. he records one appointment at home and then meets someone in the street and arranges another meeting with that person. He loses everything, pencils, his wallet—everything. It would be worse, except I move things to obvious places. He never remembers what he has spent his money on and he forgets to carry out any plans he has made for himself, like sorting out his video tapes.

Wearing (1992) graphically illustrates the very limited understanding many people, including Health Service staff, have of memory impairments when she writes:

> One mother in Manchester told me that her daughter, amnesic since an aneurysm at age 19, was to attend a day centre at a psychiatric hospital. She spent a couple of hours in discussion with the staff to make sure they understood her daughter's amnesia. After the

first day she went to collect her but arrived to find that she was lost. "Well", explained a staff member, "we told her the way to lunch but she never arrived". Naturally the poor girl had forgotten the directions almost immediately and had no idea where she was supposed to go, or why, or what she was doing there. So she found herself in the alcoholics' clinic and sat there for she knew not how long, in the expectation that somehow her mother would eventually find her [one of very many similar incidents] (Wearing, 1992, pp. 280–281).

Although severe memory impairment is always distressing for family members and carers, their feelings of distress are not always shared by the person with the impairment. Usually, lack of concern on the patient's part is associated with poor insight that can follow from the original injury. Not surprisingly, on the other hand, those with greater awareness of their difficulties are typically distressed and/or depressed. They may feel that their memory disorder looks like stupidity in the eyes of others, or they may believe that other people will regard them as mentally unstable. Some memory-impaired people report that life is like a dream, and one young woman did in fact repeat to me several times each day the words, "This is a dream, I am going to wake up". Some people, aware of the effect they have on others, become very withdrawn and socially isolated because of their reluctance to bore and irritate their families and friends.

Because of the stressful efforts required to cope with daily living and the need to participate in compensatory behaviour in order to get through each day, the effects of amnesia can be exhausting for both relatives and the memory-impaired person. People with amnesia are also frustrated by frequent and sometimes humiliating failures and constant misunderstandings. As one young man said, "Frustration is constantly waiting in the wings". Tate (Chapter 35, this volume) discusses emotional aspects of memory impairment in more detail.

RECOVERY OF MEMORY FUNCTION AFTER BRAIN INJURY

Particularly in the early stages of an insult to the brain, families are keenly if not anxiously interested in the extent of possible recovery and improvement of memory functioning. When asked questions about recovery, however, it is likely that most health service professionals hedge their bets by suggesting that some improvement will take place while avoiding pronouncements on the extent of such improvement.

One problem associated with prognosis in cases of brain injury is that recovery means different things to different people. Some clinicians focus on survival rates, some on biological recovery, such as repair of brain structures, and others are interested in recovery of cognitive functions. The differences do not end there. Some clinicians interpret *recovery* as a complete regaining of identical functions that were lost or impaired as a result of the brain injury (Finger & Stein, 1982). Recovery of memory functioning, in this sense, is rarely achievable for people with brain injury. Others regard good recovery as resumption of normal life, even though there may be minor neurological and psychological deficits (Jennett & Bond, 1975). Such resumption is possible for some memory-impaired people (see e.g. "Alex" and "Jay", described in Wilson, 1999). Another interpretation of recovery regards it as the reduction of impairments in functioning over time (Marshall, 1985); and this is certainly applicable to the majority of memory-impaired people (see e.g. Wilson, 1991). Kolb (1995) believes that recovery typically involves partial recovery of function together with considerable *substitution* of function, i.e. learning to do things in a different way.

Wilson (1998) defines cognitive recovery operationally as "a complete or partial resolution of cognitive deficits incurred as a result of an insult to the brain" (p. 281).

How does this discussion relate to memory-impaired people referred for help with their memory problems? On the one hand, we have studies that show families reporting a high incidence of memory problems several years after the insult (e.g. Brooks, 1984; Brooks et al., 1987; Oddy, 1984; Stilwell et al., 1999). On the other hand, we have studies showing significant recovery of memory functioning taking place during the first year after brain injury (Lezak, 1979). We know that one densely amnesic patient, H.M., did not show recovery or indeed improvement over a 30 year period (Freed et al. 1998; Scoville & Milner, 1957); and that another patient, T.B., showed a dramatic recovery at least 2 years after insult (Wilson & Baddeley, 1993). Victor et al. (1989) found that 74% of a sample of 104 Korsakoff patients showed some degree of recovery over a 3 year period following admission, and 21% of their sample seemed to show a more or less complete recovery. Kapur & Graham (Chapter 11, this volume) provide a more comprehensive discussion of recovery of memory functions.

What should we say to those who ask us about improvement or recovery? The answer depends, in part, on the cause of the memory impairment. We would not expect improvement in people with Alzheimer's or Huntington's disease, although it may prove possible to slow down the rate of deterioration, either with drugs or cognitive strategies or a combination of both. Fetal, stem cell or neural transplants, too, may eventually be able to reverse deterioration (for discussion, see Barker & Dunnett, 1999). Caution must be exercised when responding to questions from families, as people with progressive conditions, while failing to improve, may nevertheless be able to learn new skills or information, e.g. new learning and maintenance of this learning was observed by Clare et al. (1999, 2000) in patients with Alzheimer's disease (see also Chapter 32, this volume).

In contrast, patients in posttraumatic amnesia (PTA) following head injury may show complete or considerable recovery, depending on the length of PTA (Wilson et al., 1999b). Even when patients are several months postinjury and out of PTA, improvement for some may be considerable. In one study of 43 brain-injured people referred for memory therapy during 1979–1985 and followed up 5–12 years later, just over 30% showed a substantial improvement on memory test scores, 60% remained virtually unchanged and just over 9% had declined. In addition to the 43 seen and reassessed, a further seven had died (including two suicides) three could not be contacted and one refused to take part in the study (Wilson, 1991). Although only one-third had improved since the end of rehabilitation, many had improved *during* rehabilitation. In addition, most subjects were using more aids, strategies and techniques to compensate for difficulties compared to the period before and at the end of rehabilitation. Those people who were using six or more strategies were significantly more likely to be independent (defined as in paid employment or living alone or in full-time education) than those using less than six strategies ($\chi^2 = 10.87$, $p < 0.001$).

Most people in the 1991 study, including those who had improved, were left with residual memory deficits, so they had not achieved their pre-injury levels. Nevertheless, the long-term prognosis was less bleak than had been believed several years earlier. Only nine of the 43 were in long-term care (despite the fact that most of the 43 had very significant cognitive problems), while 15 were in paid employment. Most were coping better than when last seen. These figures should not, however, hide the fact that some individuals in the group were lonely, unhappy and still very handicapped by their brain injury and their memory impairment.

It is probably true to say that people whose memory problems follow encephalitis and anoxia are likely to reach their final level of recovery earlier than those who have sustained a severe head injury, who may continue to show some recovery for a long period. Even with damage that occurred in childhood, little change may be seen. Vargha-Khadem et al. (1997) followed three children with early bilateral hippocampal damage from anoxic episodes for several years. The children showed reasonable levels of language functioning and general knowledge but their memory deficits remained severe. Broman et al. (1997) report on a boy who became severely amnesic following a cardiac arrest when he was 8 years old. He was followed for 19 years and his memory functioning remained severely impaired. He was described as being similar to H.M. (Scoville & Milner, 1957).

An adult patient, C.W., who became densely amnesic following herpes simplex encephalitis in 1985, showed no recovery of memory functioning over a 10 year period (Wilson et al., 1995). Funnell & De Mornay Davies (1996) also report on an encephalitic patient who showed little change over time. On the face of it, then, it looks as if restoration of memory functioning is unlikely following certain types of neurological damage. Kolb (1995) believes that language functions are more likely to show recovery than other cognitive functions, including memory. Yet a paper by Eriksson et al. (1998) suggests that regeneration of hippocampal cells can occur, even in the adult human brain: the authors found post-mortem evidence for neurogenesis in the dentate gyrus of the hippocampus in five patients who died of cancer. The authors were appropriately cautious about the practical implications of their findings and, to date, it is not clear whether such cells can survive in sufficient numbers and integrate in ways to improve everyday functioning.

What is clear, however, is that intervention and rehabilitation can reduce some of the everyday problems faced by people with memory problems. This appears to work through one of the following mechanisms: (a) reducing the load on memory through organizing or structuring the environment; (b) enabling people to learn more efficiently; and/or (c) teaching people to compensate for deficits. Each of these areas will be discussed later.

HELPING MEMORY-IMPAIRED PEOPLE AND THEIR FAMILIES

When first seeing someone who requires memory therapy, a good approach is to begin by formally interviewing the person and one or more relatives. Ask about the precipitating accident or illness and question them about resultant problems as they are manifested in everyday life. Also ask what they hope to achieve as a result of the referral. Questioning along these lines usually opens up an opportunity to explain that, although it may not be possible to restore or retrain memory functioning lost through certain accidents and illnesses, there may well be actions we can take that will help the patient manage his/her everyday life more successfully.

The nature of these actions will depend on a number of factors, including the nature and severity of the deficit (e.g. whether the memory impairment is due to a degenerative condition), the presence or absence of additional cognitive impairments, the current social and vocational situation of the patient, and the environmental demands of the patient's lifestyle.

A neuropsychological assessment will provide a picture of the patient's cognitive strengths and weaknesses (see Howieson & Lezak, Chapter 29, this volume). This should be supplemented by a more direct assessment of everyday problems, using procedures such as interviews, questionnaires, rating scales, checklists, memory diaries and direct observation (see Wilson, Chapter 28, this volume; Wilson, 1999).

Combining information from different assessments will highlight problems that need tackling, thus enabling realistic treatment programmes to be designed in such a way that they are both relevant to the life of the patient and match the neuropsychological demands suggested by cognitive test results. Of course, treatment programmes should be within the capabilities of the patient, e.g. we should not expect memory-impaired people to remember arguments made in a previous session about the value of using external memory aids. Neither should we confuse patients having visuospatial difficulties by employing spatial terms when teaching routes. Those who are very ataxic will not be able to write quickly or even at all. People with deep dyslexia will have problems comprehending verbs, prepositions and abstract nouns. The message here is that our own treatment programmes should aim to bypass those areas that might rely on strengths or aptitudes that are themselves damaged in any particular patient.

Having identified particular problem areas and assessed cognitive functioning, a decision has to be made as to which of the problems should be tackled. Apart from the provisos listed immediately above, there is no right or wrong way of doing this. However, treatment planners will be influenced by the wishes of the patient, relatives and other staff members. Some patients are quite specific about the kind of help they want: e.g. they may say, "I can't remember my partners' names when playing bridge" or "I always forget where I have parked the car". Others are more vague and might say something like, "It's just everything, I can't remember a thing". Yet others will deny they have memory problems: "There's nothing wrong with my memory, it's people like you who are destroying my confidence". Relatives will also vary according to the clarity or vagueness of their descriptions of problems.

Future plans and placement will also influence the choice of problems to be tackled. For people planning to return to education, the choice might involve teaching study techniques to improve verbal recall (see Wilson, 1987a) or teaching the use of one of the electronic personal organizers (see Wilson, Chapter 30 and Woods, Chapter 33, this volume). For someone going into long-term care the focus might be on teaching how to transfer from a wheelchair to an ordinary chair, or teaching the location of the toilet.

Another question concerns the number of problems to be tackled at any one time. This will depend on factors such as the patient's general intellectual level, the level of insight into physical and mental status, degree of motivation, the amount of involvement of others in the programme, and, of course, time available. For a person with a pure amnesia, having good intellectual functioning, good insight and high motivation, and whose family is willing to assist, it might be possible to work on four to six problems at any one time. With someone who is of poor intellectual functioning, with little insight or motivation and without family support, tackling one problem at a time is more appropriate.

When planning a treatment programme to overcome these problems, one can follow a behavioural approach using the steps involved in behaviour modification programmes (for a more detailed discussion, see Wilson, 1992). Working in this way provides a structure for the psychologist or therapist when attempting to get to grips with a difficult area: it enables him/her to measure the problem(s) and to determine whether goals have been achieved. There is a saying that "structure reduces anxiety", and this is true not only for brain-injured patients but also for those treating them.

The behavioural structure is adaptable to a wide range of patients, problems and settings, the goals are small and specific, treatment and assessment are inseparable, and there is continuous monitoring of results. Evidence that this approach is effective has been supplied by Wilson (1987a) and Moffat (1989). The number of steps in a behavioural programme may vary but can include as many as 11:

- Define the problem.
- (An operational definition may be required).
- Set goals (may need both short- and long-term).
- Measure the problem (take baseline).
- Consider reinforcers or motivators.
- Plan treatment.
- Begin treatment.
- Monitor progress.
- Evaluate.
- Change if necessary.
- Plan for generalization.

Examples of successful treatment programmes using this structure can be found in Wilson (1987b, 1992).

Another approach is to follow a holistic programme (Ben-Yishay, 1978; Diller, 1976; Prigatano, 1987, 1999). Followers of this approach believe that rehabilitation should consider cognitive, social and emotional aspects together, so one would not just treat memory problems in isolation but would include accompanying social and emotional consequences. Holistic programmes include group and individual therapies aimed at: (a) increasing awareness of what has happened; (b) achieving acceptance and understanding of one's difficulties; (c) providing cognitive remediation for memory and other deficits; (d) developing compensatory skills; and (e) offering vocational counselling. For further details on how this approach works in practice, see Prigatano (1999) and Wilson et al. (2000). Ben-Yishay (1996) also provides an interesting historical account of the origins of this approach.

MANAGING THE EMOTIONAL CONSEQUENCES OF MEMORY IMPAIRMENT

Clare & Wilson (1997) argue that:

> Memory is a very important part of our sense of who we are...It is no surprise that memory problems often have major emotional consequences, including feelings of loss and anger and increased levels of anxiety (p. 41).

People with severe memory difficulties may become frightened, isolated, withdrawn or worried about making mistakes. As Jack (already mentioned) wrote in a letter to me:

> I can't perform basic sociable tasks, such as taking orders to buy a round of drinks or noting the names and faces of new acquaintances. In fact, I am sure that on many occasions I have met people who are not aware of my condition, and then upon not recognizing them on a second meeting, will have appeared rude and impolite (Wilson, 1999, p. 42).

Another young man with memory impairment told me that he was exhausted with making an effort to remember, and yet another that trying to be normal wore him out.

Evans & Wilson (1992) found anxiety levels high in people attending a memory group, while Kopelman & Crawford (1996) found depression present in over 40% of 200 consecutive referrals to a memory clinic. Reducing distress, anxiety and depression, together with increasing awareness and understanding, should be part of every memory rehabilitation programme. Giving people the chance to talk, ask questions and express their feelings may ease the distress and frustration and help them to accept the strategies we can offer.

One inexpensive and easily implemented strategy for reducing anxiety is to provide information. Questions such as, "Why does she ask the same question over and over again?" or "Why can he remember things that happened years ago but not what happened this morning?" deserve explanations. Some people are happy with simple explanations, e.g. "She isn't doing it to annoy you, she has simply forgotten how many times she asked the question" or "old memories are stored differently in the brain from new memories". Others will want access to references providing more detailed information. Simply being reassured that the behaviours seen are normal in people with memory problems may reduce anxiety for both relatives and memory-impaired people. Written information should supplement oral explanations, as even those with good memories find it harder to remember when preoccupied or distressed. Clare & Wilson (1997) wrote a short book for people with memory impairments, their relatives, friends and carers. This book contains general information about memory as well as suggestions as to how to deal with specific problems. A useful reference on self-help and support groups is Wearing (1992).

Relaxation therapy is also useful for people under stress. Even if those with memory problems do not remember that they have taken part in relaxation exercises, the effects may well remain. Individual relaxation therapy is fairly easy to organize and one can make tapes for individuals to take away and practice at home. Group relaxation therapy is sometimes carried out at rehabilitation centres. In addition, memory groups may have an indirect effect on reducing anxiety. Evans & Wilson (1992) felt that reduction in anxiety was one of the main benefits of their memory groups. Reduction in social isolation was another benefit for those attending outpatient groups. Wilson & Moffat (1992) describe the structure of memory groups in more detail.

Depression can also impair memory functioning (see Dalgleish & Cox, Chapter 20, this volume). Cognitive-behavioural therapy and psychological support can be offered. Even though memory-impaired people may not remember much of the discussions that take place, they can be given handouts, notes and revision sessions. Group work to increase awareness and reduce emotional stress is common in holistic rehabilitation programmes (Prigatano, 1999).

Reminiscence therapy is a way of encouraging older memory-impaired people to remember experiences and incidents from the past by using reminders, such as old songs, newspaper articles and photographs. Reminiscence groups may also help to reduce anxiety and depression and improve mood. Because remembering old songs, advertisements, newspaper cuttings, etc. are typically easier for older people to recall and to engage in, the enjoyment experienced may improve their mood. Although reminiscence therapy is typically used with older people and in groups, it can be adapted for younger people and/or for individuals.

Finally, psychologists and other therapists engaged in memory therapy can act as a resource for putting families in touch with the right services. Given that emotional problems after a neurological insult may result from loss of income, loss of structure in one's life and loss of enjoyment from leisure or work, there is nothing to stop us telling families how to approach local social services or self-help societies, or how to access the right kind of assessment or treatment packages.

GUIDELINES FOR HELPING PEOPLE WITH MEMORY DIFFICULTIES

In 1991, Berg et al. described a memory group in The Netherlands. The participants were told, "Try to accept that a deficient memory cannot be cured: make a more efficient use of your remaining capacities; use external aids when possible; pay more attention; spend more time; repeat; make associations; organize; link input and retrieval situations" (p. 101). These general guidelines were given to brain-injured people in the form of a textbook and illustrated with examples. In addition, participants tackled real-life problems in their sessions and were given homework to enable them to practise and rehearse the strategies they were taught. For each participant, about three real-life problems were selected and worked on in an 18 session therapy programme. In the short term, participants in the memory rehabilitation group did better than those in the control group, although a follow-up 4 years later showed that the control group had caught up (Milders et al., 1995).

Others have also taught general strategies to memory-impaired people to try to enable them to cope in real-life situation. Lawson & Rice (1989), for example, were working with a 15 year-old boy who had sustained a severe head injury some 4 years earlier. They taught him a strategy to cope with his memory problems. First, he had to recognize that he had memory problems. Then he was taught to say, "I have a plan for helping me to work on a memory problem. It's WSTC". "WSTC" referred to a series of steps to follow: W stood for *What* (what are you asked to do?); this was regarded as the analysis of the problem. S stood for *Select* (select a strategy for the task); this was seen as strategy selection. T stood for *Try* (try out the strategy); this was seen as the strategy initiation stage. Finally, C stood for *Check* (check how the strategy is working); this was seen as the monitoring stage. The young man was able to employ the WSTC strategy in test situations and maintain the ability to do this up to 6 months posttraining. Unfortunately there was no attempt to generalize this training to real-life tasks or to monitor the extent to which he applied the strategy learning to real-life situations. Similar training in strategy application has been used in other areas of cognitive rehabilitation, e.g. Von Cramon & Matthes-von Cramon (1992) used problem-solving therapy for clients with dysexecutive syndrome, and Levine et al. (2000) used a somewhat similar strategy training programme to help people with memory and attention disorders.

The advantage of general strategy training is that it enables memory-impaired people to deal with whatever difficulties come their way. Ideally, of course, this is what all of us in memory rehabilitation would like. In practice, we may need to set our sights a little lower with those clients who have more widespread cognitive difficulties (say a combination of memory, attention, planning and organizational problems), or who are so severely impaired that it is difficult to teach them to remember to apply a strategy.

There are general guidelines that psychologists, therapists, family members and others can apply to help memory-impaired people *take in*, *store* and *retrieve* information more successfully. While these guidelines will not solve memory problems, they may improve or ease situations for those with impaired memory functioning. The guidelines themselves are the result of theoretical experiments to determine whether the amnesic syndrome is due to a deficit of (a) encoding, or (b) storage, or (c) retrieval). Although accounts to explain amnesia as a failure in only one of these processes are insufficient in themselves, experiments trying to prove or disprove these views have provided us with a number of useful pointers.

People are more likely to encode (i.e. take in) information efficiently if:

- The information is simplified (it is easier to remember short words than long words and jargon should be avoided).
- They are required to remember one thing at a time (do not present three or four names/instructions/words at once).
- The information is understood (ask the memory-impaired person to repeat the information back in his/her own words to check for understanding).
- The information is linked or associated with something already known (e.g. when trying to remember the name Molly, you could check if they have an Aunt Molly, or if they know the song "Good Golly Miss Molly" or "Molly Malone".
- The "little and often" or distributed practice rule is followed (have frequent breaks when teaching new information or a new skill).
- The information is processed or manipulated in some way (don't let your memory-impaired clients be passive recipients of the information, instead ask them to think about it, question it, do something with it, to ensure they process the information).

Once the information is encoded, it has to be stored. Rehearsal, practice and testing can all be used to try to ensure the information remains in storage. The method known as "spaced retrieval" (also called "expanding rehearsal") is a good testing procedure to follow. Present the information, test immediately, test again after a very brief delay and so forth. The retention interval is gradually increased. This method will be discussed in more detail later in the chapter.

Another problem, faced at times by all of us, is retrieving the information from memory when it is required. Some memory-impaired people seem to have particular problems with retrieval. If we can provide a hook in the form of a cue or prompt, they may be able to retrieve the information more readily. The first letter of a word or name to be recalled can be a powerful retrieval cue. The problem here, of course, is that someone needs to be available to provide the first letter. Some people, including some memory-impaired people, learn to go through the alphabet systematically to try to find their own first letter cue. Even for these people, however, the system is haphazard and unreliable.

Perhaps the best way to improve retrieval is to avoid context specificity, i.e. if material is learned in one situation, it is recalled better in the same situation (Godden & Baddeley, 1975; Watkins et al.,1976). Most of us will have experienced this phenomenon. You may, for example, know a work colleague very well and be able to greet him/her by name at work without a second thought. However, if you meet that colleague in a different situation, say at a shopping centre, the name may become inaccessible because of the change of context. In rehabilitation it is not uncommon to find clients who use a notebook in occupational therapy but do not use it elsewhere, or who can tell you the name of their physiotherapist in the gym but not elsewhere. The answer here is to avoid such context-specific learning by teaching the use of the notebook not only in occupational therapy but also in a number of other situations. Similarly, the physiotherapist will need to be met and interacted with in other settings.

Another general guideline when working with severely memory-impaired people is to avoid trial-and-error learning. As errorless learning is such a large part of current memory rehabilitation, it deserves a section to itself and will be discussed at some length later.

In the final part of this section on general strategies, a series of steps is provided by Schuri et al. (1996). These are described as the basic steps to follow in memory rehabilitation.

Step 1   Assess the memory functions and associated cognitive deficits. Standardized tests should be used (to understand the client's cognitive strengths and weaknesses) and behavioural measures to see how the problems are manifested in everyday life.
Step 2   Inform the clients and their families and caregivers about the functional deficits and possible consequences in everyday life. Clients should be provided with practical experience relevant to "real-life" situations.
Step 3   Agree on the goals of therapy and on which specific problems should be treated.
Step 4   Select the most appropriate external and/or internal strategies for the specific problems to be treated.
Step 5   Teach the clients to use the strategies themselves, or use the strategies in therapy to achieve a treatment goal (e.g. learn a specific piece of information or change a piece of behaviour).
Step 6   Evaluate treatment effectiveness (in terms of the goals achieved). If necessary, change the procedure.

The next three sections will discuss more specific strategies for improving everyday life situations for people with memory impairment.

ENVIRONMENTAL ADAPTATIONS

One of the simplest ways to help people with memory impairment is to arrange the environment so that they rely less on memory. Examples include labelling doors for a person who cannot remember which room is which, or labelling cupboards in the kitchen or beds in a hospital ward. Other examples include drawing arrows or lines to indicate routes round a building, or positioning objects so they cannot be missed or forgotten (e.g. tying a front door key to a waist belt). Making rooms safer for confused, brain-injured people is also possible by altering the environment.

Sometimes it is possible to avoid irritating or problematic behaviours by identifying and then changing the environmental triggers of the behaviour, e.g. people who constantly ask the same question may be responding to something said to them, such as a greeting or request.

There are a few reports of environmental changes in the management of memory problems, e.g. Harris (1980) describes a geriatric unit where the rate of incontinence was reduced by the simple strategy of painting all lavatory doors a different colour from other doors, thus making them easier to distinguish. Kapur, et al. (Chapter 34, this volume) also discuss environmental adaptations.

Lincoln (1989) reports how one woman was able to keep track of whether she had taken her medication by placing a chart next to the bottle of tablets rather than in another room. Lincoln also provides suggestions for further environmental adaptations. She notes that most hospital staff wear name badges that may be too small for elderly people to read, and contain surnames rather than first names, which are used more frequently on the ward.

The most densely amnesic person seen by the present author is C.W., a musician who developed herpes simplex encephalitis in 1985. The only strategies that seem to help this man are environmental adaptations. He has an unusual form of epilepsy that takes the form of jerking movements and belching. These occur with greater frequency when C.W. is under stress or agitated. A behavioural analysis undertaken by Avi Schmueli (personal communication) showed that the seizures were far more likely to occur when there was a change in activity, e.g. when changing from one test to another during assessment, or when an additional person entered the room. Although it was not possible or indeed ethical to prevent all such changes in activity or personnel, some changes were introduced to reduce the frequency of this man's seizures.

Because C.W. was unable to remember any of the people involved in his care, he considered them all to be strangers and disliked being treated informally by them as though they were well known to him. Consequently, he was not called by his first name, as was usual with long-stay patients. Demonstrations of affection also caused him fear and distress, e.g. one nurse who had known C.W. for 4 years, went on holiday for 2 weeks and on returning she approached C.W. to give him a hug. He saw what was for him a total stranger bear down upon him with open arms and panicked. Again, a more formal approach can reduce the number of occasions resulting in panic.

C.W. also repeats certain phrases scores of times in the course of each day, the most frequent stating that he has just that moment woken up. Every few minutes during a conversation or assessment he says something along the lines of, "This is the first time I've been awake, this is the first taste I've had, the first time I've seen anything or heard anything. It's like being dead. I don't remember you coming into the room but now for the first time, I can see." Sympathizing with these statements or trying to offer explanations seems to increase his agitation and cause an escalation of the number of repetitions. Distracting him by introducing another topic of conversation results in calmer behaviour.

For people with severe intellectual deficits or progressive deterioration or very dense amnesia, environmental adaptations may be the best we can offer to enable them to cope and reduce some of their confusion and frustration. Few studies have discussed ways in which environments can be designed to help people with severe memory impairment, although it would seem to be a fruitful area for psychologists, engineers, architects and designers to join forces.

Modification or restructuring the environment means that problems due to memory impairment can be avoided. The origins of this approach can be found within the field of behaviour modification, especially in the area of severe learning disability (Murphy & Oliver, 1987). Despite being, at times, an effective and rapid way of reducing problems, this approach does not always work. For example, people have to be able to understand the labels and the signposts; some repetitious behaviours are not triggered by external events and the notebook clipped to a belt is no good if it is never used. In addition, one has to be aware of possible ethical considerations of an environment that is too restrictive. Therefore, it might be possible to avoid any demands on memory by placing someone in an environment where every move is supervised by a staff member, leaving the person with memory problems completely unable to exercise any choice. Like other psychiatric and psychological methods of management, environmental control is open to abuse. Nevertheless, there is little doubt that for some people with severe and widespread cognitive impairments, environmental restructuring or modification probably provides the best chance of some degree of independence.

ERRORLESS LEARNING IN REHABILITATION

Errorless learning is a teaching technique whereby people are prevented, as far as possible, from making mistakes while they are learning a new skill or acquiring new information. Instead of teaching by demonstration, which may involve the learner in trial-and-error, the experimenter, therapist or teacher presents the correct information or procedure in ways that minimize the possibility of erroneous responses.

There are two theoretical backgrounds to investigations of errorless learning in people with organic memory impairment. The first is the work on errorless discrimination learning from the field of behavioural psychology, first described by Terrace (1963, 1966). Terrace was working with pigeons and found it was possible to teach pigeons to discriminate a red key from a green key with a teaching technique whereby the pigeons made no (or very few) errors during learning. Furthermore, pigeons learning via errorless learning were reported to show less emotional behaviour than pigeons learning with trial-and-error.

Sidman & Stoddard (1967) soon applied errorless learning principles to children with developmental learning difficulties. They were able to teach these children to discriminate ellipses from circles. Others soon took up the idea (e.g. Cullen, 1976; Jones & Eayrs, 1992; Walsh & Lamberts, 1979).

Cullen (1976) believed that if errors were made during learning it was harder to remember just what had been learned. He also pointed out that more reinforcement occurred during errorless learning as only successes occurred, never failures. To this day errorless learning is a frequently used teaching technique for people with developmental learning difficulties.

The second theoretical impetus came from studies of implicit memory and implicit learning from cognitive psychology and cognitive neuropsychology (e.g. Brooks & Baddeley, 1976; Graf & Schacter, 1985; Tulving & Schacter, 1990; and many others). Although it has been known for decades that memory-impaired people can learn some skills and information normally through their intact (or relatively intact) implicit learning abilities, it has been difficult to apply this knowledge to reduce real-life problems encountered by people with organic memory deficits.

Glisky and colleagues (Glisky & Schacter, 1987; Glisky et al., 1986) tried to capitalize on intact implicit abilities to teach people with amnesia computer terminology, using a technique they called "the method of vanishing cues". Despite some successes, the method of vanishing cues involved considerable time and effort from both experimenters and people with amnesia. Implicit memory or learning, on the other hand, does not involve effort, as it occurs without conscious recollection. This, together with certain other anomalies seen during implicit learning (such as the observation that in a fragmented picture/perceptual priming procedure, if an amnesic patient mislabels a fragment during an early presentation, the error may "stick" and be repeated on successive presentations), led Baddeley & Wilson (1994) to pose the question, "Do amnesic patients learn better if prevented from making mistakes during the learning process?" In a study with 16 young and 16 elderly control participants, and 16 densely amnesic people, employing a stem completion procedure, it was found that every one of the amnesic people learned better if prevented from making mistakes during learning.

Baddeley & Wilson (1994) believed that errorless learning was superior to trial-and-error learning because it depended on implicit memory. As the amnesic people could not use explicit memory effectively, they were forced to rely on implicit memory. This system is not designed to eliminate errors, so it is better to prevent the injection of errors in the first place. In the absence of an efficient episodic memory, the very fact of making an incorrect response may strengthen or reinforce the error.

Errorless learning principles were quickly adopted in the rehabilitation of memory-impaired people. Wilson et al. (1994) described a number of single-case studies in which amnesic people were taught several tasks, such as learning therapists' names, learning to programme an electronic organizer and learning to recognize objects. Each participant was taught two similar tasks in an errorful or an errorless way. In each case errorless was superior to errorful learning. Wilson & Evans (1996) provided further support for these findings. Squires et al. (1996) taught a man with amnesia to use a notebook with an errorless learning procedure. The same group (Squires et al., 1997, 1998) found that errorless learning procedures enabled amnesic people to learn novel associations and to acquire word-processing skills. More recently, these principles have been used successfully for people with Alzheimer's disease (Clare et al., 1999, 2000).

As stated above, Baddeley & Wilson (1994) believed that errorless learning was effective for people with amnesia because it capitalized on their intact implicit memory capacities. Hunkin et al. (1998) believed that errorless learning capitalized on the impoverished, residual, explicit memory capacities. Ongoing and, as yet unpublished, investigations in Cambridge suggest that both these explanations may be correct. For very severely amnesic people with virtually no explicit memory, it would appear that errorless learning is succesful because it capitalizes on their implicit abilities. For those with some, albeit weak, explicit/episodic memory, then errorless learning is beneficial for both memory systems.

OTHER WAYS OF IMPROVING LEARNING

There are a number of strategies that can help memory-impaired people learn more efficiently. These include spaced retrieval (otherwise known as expanding rehearsal) and mnemonics.

Spaced retrieval involves the presentation of material to be remembered (e.g. a new telephone number) followed by immediate testing. People with a normal digit span will, for example, be able to repeat back a seven figure number. The tester then waits for a second or two and requests the number again. The test interval is very gradually increased until the number is learned. New names, short addresses, items of general knowledge can also be taught in this way. Spaced retrieval is a form of distributed practice, i.e. distributing the learning trials over a period of time rather than massing them together in one block. Massed practice is a less efficient learning strategy than distributed practice (Baddeley, 1999), a phenomenon that has been known since the 1930s (Baddeley & Longman, 1978; Lorge, 1930). Landauer & Bjork (1978) showed that name learning proceeds faster with expanding rehearsal/spaced retrieval and from that time the procedure has been used in memory rehabilitation (Camp, 1989; McKitrick & Camp, 1993; Moffat, 1989; Schacter et al., 1985). Although most published studies describe using spaced retrieval with people with dementia, the technique has been used with people with other conditions, such as traumatic brain injury (see Wilson, 1989).

Mnemonic systems are those that enable people to organize, store and retrieve information more efficiently. Sometimes the term "mnemonics" is used to refer to anything that helps people to remember, including external memory aids. Usually, however, the term is used for methods involving mental manipulation of material, e.g. in order to remember how many days there are in each month, most people use a mnemonic. In the USA and the UK this is typically the rhyme, "Thirty days hath September, April, June and November..." and so forth. In other parts of the world people use their knuckles and the dips in between to remember the long and the short months, or else they have different suffixes and prefixes to distinguish them. Every country using our calendar system appears to have a mnemonic for remembering the long and the short months. Mnemonics are also employed to learn notes of music, colours of the rainbow, cranial nerves, and other ordered material.

Mnemonics can be employed to help people with memory impairments learn new information (see Wilson, 1987a, for a series of studies using a variety of mnemonics). It is usually best for the psychologist, therapist or carer to work out the mnemonic (perhaps together with the memory-impaired person) and work through this together. People with organic memory deficits often find it difficult to devise their own mnemonics, or they may forget to employ them, or forget to use them spontaneously in novel situations. This is not always the case, as some people can be taught to use them in new situations (Kime et al., 1996). The real value of mnemonics, however, is that they are useful for teaching new information to people with memory difficulties, and they almost always lead to faster learning than rote rehearsal (Clare et al., 1999; Moffat, 1989; West, 1995; Wilson, 1987a). Clare et al. (1999) employed a combination of strategies, including a visual mnemonic, spaced retrieval and errorless learning to reteach the names of people at a social club to a man with Alzheimer's disease.

EXTERNAL MEMORY AIDS

Helping people to compensate for their memory deficits through the use of external memory aids is one of the most effective methods of rehabilitation. External memory aids enable us to remember by using systems to record or access information. Diaries, notebooks, lists, alarm clocks, wall charts, calendars, tape recorders and personal organizers are all examples of external memory aids. Almost every one of us makes use of these at one time or another. Such aids are likely to be the most helpful method of compensating for difficulties encountered by memory-impaired people (Wilson, 1991), but, unfortunately, it is often difficult for memory-impaired people to learn to use these aids, because they forget to record or access information. They may use the aids in a disorganized way or they may be embarrassed to use aids in the presence of others. The trouble with external memory aids is that their use involves memory. Thus, the very people who need external memory aids the most have the greatest difficulty in learning to use them.

Despite these problems, there is evidence that some memory-impaired people use external aids effectively, e.g. people with a pure amnesic syndrome tend to be able to use them reasonably well (Wilson & Watson, 1996). A good example is J.C. (see Wilson & Hughes, 1997a), who had a haemorrhage caused by a ruptured posterior cerebral artery aneurysm when he was 20 years old. As a result he became severely amnesic and remains so to this day, 15 years later. Despite this, he is able to live alone, earn his own living, complete his own tax forms and remain completely independent. He developed (and continues to develop) a sophisticated system of compensatory strategies. Soon after his haemorrhage he started writing notes on scraps of paper. Over the years he has progressed to using a number of different aids. The most often used include a databank watch, a personal organizer and a small tape recorder. These are supported by a number of additional strategies, used less often. J.C. records most information he needs to remember in at least two systems, so that if he fails to access it one way, he has a back-up.

The first 10 years of the development of his system is described in Wilson et al. (1997a). It was possible to describe this natural history of a compensatory system, as J.C. kept a journal over this period; his aunt kept details of how she helped J.C., and I kept records of my assessments. By combining information from these three sources, we were able to trace the increasing sophistication of J.C.'s use of strategies.

Another study describing how a densely amnesic young woman was taught to use a memory notebook is that of Kime et al. (1996). The young woman became amnesic following status epilepticus. After 20 months she was admitted to a rehabilitation programme. A complex memory book was provided for her and over a period of weeks she was taught to use the book, containing details of her programme, local transport, important people, locations in the neighbourhood, a things-to-do list and so forth. Initially, the woman was never allowed to fail (so inadvertently an errorless learning approach was employed). She was always prompted and guided to go to the right section and do the right thing. Gradually, the prompts were faded out until she was using the book reliably and systematically. Furthermore, she demonstrated generalization of this behaviour by employing the aids in new environments and for new problems. Following discharge from rehabilitation she was able to obtain paid employment and use the memory book effectively.

One recently developed and successful memory aid that has been helping people with widespread cognitive deficits is NeuroPage® (Hersh & Treadgold, 1994). NeuroPage® is a simple and portable paging system with a screen that can be attached to a belt. Larry Treadgold, the engineer father of a head-injured son, and Neil Hersh, a neuropsychologist, combined their skills to produce a programmable messaging system that utilizes an arrangement of microcomputers linked to a conventional computer memory and, by telephone, to a paging company.

The scheduling of reminders or cues for each individual is entered into the computer and from then on no further human interfacing is necessary. On the appropriate date and time, NeuroPage® accesses the user's data files, determines the reminder to be delivered, transmits the information by modem to the terminal, where the reminder is converted, and transmits, as a wireless radio signal, to only that receiver corresponding to the particular user. The user is alerted to an incoming reminder by a flashing, light-emitting diode and an audible "chirp". The reminder is graphically displayed on the screen of the receiver. Once the message appears, users are requested to telephone a person or an answer service to confirm the message. Without this confirmation, the message is repeated.

Users of NeuroPage® can control everything with one rather large button, easy to press even for those having motor difficulties. It avoids most of the problems of existing aids. It is highly portable, unlike many computers. It has an audible alarm that can be adapted to vibrate if required, together with an accompanying explanatory message, unlike many watch alarms. It is not embarrassing for the majority of users and indeed may convey prestige. Perhaps the biggest advantage of the NeuroPage® is that once it has been programmed it is easy to use. Most other systems require considerable time for memory-impaired people to learn how to handle them.

We began evaluating NeuroPage® in the UK in 1994. Using an ABA single case experimental design, we started with 15 neurologically impaired people, all of whom had significant everyday memory problems because of organic memory impairment or because of problems with planning and organization resulting from frontal lobe damage. We found a statistically significant improvement between the baseline and treatment phases for each of the 15 clients. In this study, clients selected their own target behaviours (e.g. "take medication; feed the dog; pack your spectacles for work"). The mean success rate for the group as a whole was just over 37% of targets achieved during a 4–6 week baseline. This rose to over 85% during the 12 week treatment phase, i.e. when subjects were provided with a pager and reminded to carry out the target behaviours. During the second (posttreatment) baseline phase, the overall percentage of targets achieved was 74%. In fact, some clients learned their routines during the baseline while others did not. This suggests that for some clients, the pager may only be needed for a short while in order to establish certain behaviours. Others, particularly those with executive deficits, may need the reminding service on a longer-term basis.

We have also published two single case studies using NeuroPage®. The first (Evans et al., 1998) is a treatment study with a stroke patient who had considerable problems with planning and organization. The second (Wilson et al., 1999a) is an account of a very amnesic young man who was enabled to live independently with the help of NeuroPage®. Health and Social Services saved considerable amounts of money on these clients following the implementation of the pager (Wilson & Evans, in press).

Following the success of the pilot study (Wilson et al., 1997b), we carried out a further investigation with NeuroPage® (Wilson et al., 2001) involving 143 clients, even more impaired (as a group) than those in the pilot study. Some were referred by other therapists who were feeling some desperation because all else had failed. We employed a randomized control trial in the larger study whereby, following a 2 week baseline, clients were allocated to either the treatment group (pager) or to a waiting list control group. After a further 7 weeks, those on the waiting list were given a pager and those who had been using the pager were taken off the paging service. After a further 5 weeks, target behaviours were monitored for a final 2 weeks. The results can be seen in Figure 30.1.

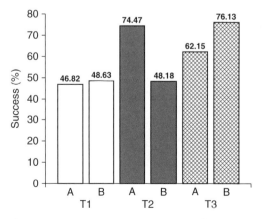

Figure 30.1 Percentage success rate for participants in Group A (pager first) and Group B (pager later) at Time 1 (baseline); Time 2 (weeks 8 and 9) and Time 3 (weeks 15 and 16). Reproduced by permission from Wilson et al. (2001). © 2001, BMJ publishing group

There were no significant differences between groups A and B during baseline. Group A then went on to receive the pager while group B members were on the waiting list. At time 2 (weeks 6 and 7), following the end of baseline, there was a significant difference in favour of group A. Group B participants were then given a pager with group A returning their pagers. At time 3 (weeks 6 and 7 following the changeover), there was a significant difference in the number of target behaviours achieved in favour of group B. The main findings then were broadly similar to those in the pilot study.

One big advantage of a system like NeuroPage® is that it is adaptable and suitable for a wide range of people and problems, from different diagnostic groups and at different times postinsult. The main disadvantage is that people cannot programme the system themselves and have to telephone or otherwise contact a centre so that the messages can be entered on to a computer and, on the right date and time, be transmitted to the individual pager.

There are, of course, systems to bypass these problems, e.g. "Reminder system" (Davis, D., personal communication, 16 July 1999) enables people to programme their own messages via the World Wide Web. A study comparing two different keyboards of microcomputers found some people preferred one system while others preferred the other. Both, however, allowed clients to programme their own reminders (Wright et al., 2000; in press).

The use of pagers, computers and other technological aids in memory rehabilitation is likely to expand in the future, given the current growth in information technology. One of the first studies to use an electronic aid with a brain-injured person was that of Gouvier (1982). A small portable timer was used to remind a memory-impaired man to check his memory book. More sophisticated technology in the form of computers came later in the 1980s. Although computers have been used in cognitive rehabilitation since the 1970s, these were used, on the whole, to provide exercises, in the belief that exercising an impaired function such as memory would lead to an improvement in that function (Gianutsos, 1980; see also Wilson, 1997, for a critique of this approach). Computers as a compensatory aid arrived a little later (see e.g. Bergman, 1991; Kim et al., 1999; Kirsch et al., 1987, 1992). Another series of studies using computers is that of Glisky and colleagues (Glisky, 1995; Glisky & Schacter, 1986, 1987, 1989). The very latest in technology is the use of virtual reality systems in rehabilitation (see Brooks et al., 1999; Rizzo et al., 1997; Rose, et al., 1996). Kapur et al., (Chapter 34, this volume) discusses the use of computers and other external memory aids in detail.

In conclusion to this section, compensating for memory problems is probably one of the best strategies for improving quality of life for people with significant memory impairment. The principle here is to try to find an alternative means to achieve a goal. This idea can be traced back to Zangwill (1947), when he discussed his principle of compensation, and is also similar to Luria's (1963) principle of functional adaptation, i.e. if you cannot achieve something one way, try to find an alternative way to achieve the goal. Frequently, however, psychologists and therapists need to spend time finding the best aids for a particular client and then teaching the use of those aids. One paper describing in some detail how to teach use of a memory aid is that of Sohlberg & Mateer (1989), in which they describe a three-stage procedure for teaching the use of compensatory memory books. The three stages are acquisition, application and adaptation. The authors state correctly that often compensatory notebooks are provided with minimal instruction or without formal training in their use. Furthermore, memory books are frequently rejected by clients or only used for a short time. Sohlberg & Mateer believe that the notebook must be tailored for the individual client, so the content or sections of the book will differ, e.g. some clients will require an orientation section containing personal, autobiographical information and details about the brain injury, whereas others will not need this.

In the acquisition stage clients learn the different sections and the purpose of each section. A question-and-answer format is used to teach this and 100% success is required before moving to the second stage—application. In this stage clients learn appropriate methods of recording in their notebooks. Role-play situations are used to teach the skill and success is defined as 100% accuracy in three role-play situations without cueing on two consecutive days. The final stage is adaptation. Here clients have to demonstrate appropriate notebook use in naturalistic settings. Training is in the community (e.g. a shop or cafeteria) and a certain score from the clinician accompanying the client is required on two consecutive days before the client is considered to be efficient at this stage.

The Sohlberg & Mateer (1989) description is clinically useful, flexible and suitable for a wide range of clients. They provide ideas on how to adapt the training to inpatients in the acute stage and for clients who are unable to write. This paper is important in stressing that many, if not most, memory-impaired people will need to undergo training if they are to use their compensatory strategies or external aids efficiently.

In a study comparing four different memory improvement strategies, namely written rehearsal, verbal rehearsal, acronym formation and memory notebook logging, Zencius et al. (1991) found that only memory notebook logging was effective in increasing recall of classroom material. A more recent account of training in the use of memory journals, using a five-step approach, can be found in Donaghy & Williams (1998). Ownsworth & McFarland (1999) also found diary training with self-instructional training led to better diary use than diary training alone.

So, do memory-impaired people use aids in their everyday lives and, if so, what aids are used? In the long-term follow-up study mentioned earlier (Wilson, 1991), it was found that most subjects were using more aids, strategies and techniques to compensate for their difficulties, compared with the numbers they were using before and immediately at the end of rehabilitation. Of the 44 people for whom information was available, 38 of them were using compensations. The remaining six, who were not using anything, were all in long-term care. A further three people in long-term care were using memory compensations. Those using six or more aids, strategies or techniques were significantly more likely to be independent (i.e. in paid employment, or living alone or in full-time education) than those using five or less.

A more recent study interviewed 94 people with memory problems (Evans et al., submitted) and once again found that 92 of the participants were using at least some form of memory aid or strategy, and use of these correlated with independence, i.e. people who used six or more aids were significantly more likely to be independent. This confirmed the results of the earlier study by Wilson & Watson (1996). The number and type of aids used by people in the Evans et al. (submitted) study can be found in Table 30.1.

In the first edition of this *Handbook*, Kapur (1995) said:

> The contribution of aids to memory rehabilitation holds considerable promise but many questions remain unanswered. We need to know which memory aids benefit which memory problems in which memory-disordered clients. Memory aids may often best be used in combination and we need to know the optimal combinations for particular clinical needs. We also need to know if the magnitude of any benefit to clients is significant and makes a meaningful difference to their everyday adjustment, if the change is permanent and if it is cost-effective in terms of money and in therapists' time (p. 550).

Table 30.1   Number of participants using particular memory aids/strategies

Remembering strategy	Number of sample using the strategy (n = 94)
Wall calendar/wall chart	68
Notebook	60
List	59
A diary	51
Asking others to remind	46
Mental retracing	45
Alarm clock (wake up)	38
Objects in unusual places	33
Notes in special places	32
Repetitive practice	28
Writing on hand	23
Making associations	20
Watch with date/timer	17
Daily routine	17
Personal organizer	16
Journal	15
Daily timetable	14
Alarm clock/timer	9
Visual imagery	9
Weekly routine	9
Alphabetic searching	7
Electronic organizer	7
TV guide (annotated)	7
First-letter mnemonics	5
Pager	5
Recipe cards or books	5
Pleasantness rating	3
Key chain	3
Pocket phone book	3
Mobile phone	3
Dictaphone/tape recorder	2
Rhymes	2
Knot in handkerchief	2
Orientation of medication	2
Dictionary	2
Chunking	1
Phone numbers/address on key ring	1
Home filing system	1
Home accounts	1
Information for work on wall	1
Organizer handbag	1
Buying small quantities	1
Clock–calendar combination	1

While endorsing Kapur's views, examples such as J.C. and the Kime et al. (1996) client, described above, would appear to be cost-effective in that both these young people were in paid employment. Nevertheless, we need to address Kapur's point in future studies of external aids in rehabilitation (see Chapter 34, this volume).

GENERALIZATION ISSUES

Generalization of principles, techniques and strategies practised or learned in rehabilitation to situations outside rehabilitation is of crucial importance. There are several kinds of generalization, such as across subjects, across behaviours or across settings. Our concern here is with generalization as it refers to transfer of training, i.e. generalization across settings and generalization across behaviours.

Generalization across settings refers to a situation where a strategy taught in one setting is applied to other settings. An example would be where a patient is taught to use an electronic aid or particular mnemonic in one setting (say in the clinical psychology department) and then uses the aid or the mnemonic at home or at school.

Generalization across behaviours refers to situations in which a strategy taught to help with one problem is used to assist with another problem. An example would be teaching a person to use a technique for remembering current events in the newspapers, and finding that the person used the method for school work. Once again, there is little evidence that this occurs spontaneously in adults with acquired brain damage. If generalization is considered desirable (as it usually is in treatment), then it should be built into the treatment programme in the same way as it is built into programmes with people with developmental learning difficulties (Zarkowska, 1987).

To promote generalization across settings we can use a variety of places as part of the treatment. For example, when teaching the use of a personal organizer, we might begin in the clinical psychology department and, once the patient is proficient at recording and referring to the organizer in this setting, the psychologist could see the patient in the occupational therapy department and, if necessary, reteach the use of the organizer there. The next step might be to repeat the procedure in physiotherapy, then speech therapy, on the ward, at home and so forth. The wider the range of settings, the more likelihood there is of the strategy generalizing to other settings (Zarkowska, 1987).

Similarly, to encourage generalization across behaviours, a patient could be taught how to use a strategy for remembering some of the content in newspaper articles, then encouraged or taught to use that same strategy for remembering magazine stories, then chapters in books, and even studying for examinations.

Persuading patients to put into practice strategies they have been taught may be more difficult. Again several options are open. It is possible to put some patients on a behaviour programme to reinforce the use of memory aids and mnemonics. Practical goals could be formulated in ways similar to the following examples: "Teaching Mrs X to refer to her notebook after each meal" or "Increasing the number of times Mr Z uses a particular study technique spontaneously when he is revising for examinations". The use of timers, together with prompting and fading, would perhaps be one way of achieving success, e.g. a timer could be set to ring at the end of each meal. Initially, when the timer sounds the therapist or psychologist may need to prompt (or remind) Mrs X to check her notebook. Gradually the verbal reminders could be abbreviated and eventually stopped. Later still, the timer could be omitted as the meal-time setting itself becomes the reminder to check the notebook. Alternatively, a chaining method could be used whereby a particular task is broken down into a series of smaller units and taught one at a time, e.g. if a patient is required to learn a new route, it should be possible to break the route down into sections. One section of the route could be taught, then section two added to section one, then section three added to sections one and two, and so forth.

In other cases it might be necessary to allow more time before expecting strategies to be used spontaneously. Some patients who are slow to start can sometimes begin to put into practice the skills they have been taught previously when they are given sufficient time. One amnesic man frequently argued with his wife over whether or not he had taken a bath. Because of his amnesia he could not remember and therefore insisted he had bathed recently. His wife knew better but could not convince him. It was suggested that he kept a "bath diary" in which he recorded dates and times of baths. However, he kept forgetting to record times. With the help of his wife, frequent reminding and keeping the diary above the sink in the bathroom, he began to note his bath times and now he continues to bathe regularly.

It may be necessary to abandon a particular strategy in favour of another if a patient shows signs of distress when participating in therapy, e.g. one man hated visual imagery and his comment every time he worked with imagery was, "Where's the logic in that?". Although he learned the names of staff by using imagery, he became angry whenever the method was presented. He was much happier using first-letter cueing, as he could see "the logic in it". In his case, visual imagery was not recommended to his relatives when the time came for his discharge from the centre. At what point a therapist abandons a strategy in favour of another will usually be guided by observation, clinical experience and intuition, but there is little doubt that a method that causes a patient some discomfort and even distress will be unlikely to produce a favourable outcome.

In ending this section on generalization, it should be emphasized again that generalization must not be expected to occur automatically. When it does occur spontaneously it is a bonus, but to increase the chances of it happening more regularly we must ensure that planning for generalization is always part of any treatment programme. If it is not possible to teach generalization, then relatives and staff can be taught to implement the procedure if necessary, e.g. in the use of visual imagery for names, it can be explained to the relatives that if the memory-impaired person needs to learn, for example, the names of neighbours, they can teach these names by converting each name into a picture, drawing the picture, and teaching one name at a time. The principles of errorless learning and expanding rehearsal can be explained too, so these can be incorporated. Finally, all explanations should be written down for the relatives as they, too, are likely to forget what has been said to them.

SUMMARY AND FUTURE DIRECTIONS

Although people with memory impairment and their families should not be led to believe that significant improvement in memory can occur once the period of natural recovery is over, they can nevertheless be helped to understand, manage, cope with or bypass problems arising from the impairment. Such help will normally be given to individual patients and their families by therapists and psychologists. They can also be put in touch with local and national self-help groups.

Indirect or emotional consequences of brain injury and cognitive deficit should be addressed by counsellors, psychologists and psychotherapists, so that anxiety management and cognitive therapy programmes can be introduced. When planning for a memory therapy programme, results from a neuropsychological assessment should be combined with more direct assessment of everyday problems, obtained by observation, interviewing, rating scales and questionnaires. Neuropsychological assessment will identify cognitive strengths and weaknesses, while direct assessment will highlight everyday problems requiring treatment.

In addition to treatment of specific problems revealed by neuropsychological assessment, more general guidelines are recommended to improve encoding, storage and retrieval. In view of the findings of recent research studies, which indicate that people learn better when prevented from making errors, it is probably best to avoid trial-and-error learning for people with organic memory deficits.

Specific problems can be dealt with in a number of ways, including environmental adaptations, teaching the use of external aids as compensatory strategies and using mnemonics as a faster route to learning new information. Planning and imagination should be brought into play when teaching the use of external aids. Although mnemonics may not be used spontaneously by memory-impaired people, their teachers, therapists and psychologists can use them to enhance learning by the memory impaired.

Memory groups have certain advantages. They are useful in reducing anxiety and depression, in increasing social contacts, and in introducing and practising the use of external aids. Memory-impaired group members may be more willing to imitate their peers than the non-impaired professionals running a group.

People with severe memory problems will probably need help in generalizing from one setting to another, and from one problem to another. It is therefore recommended that the teaching of generalization is an integral part of any rehabilitation programme.

At present, drugs are of rather limited value in enhancing memory functioning (see Chapter 6). However, this disappointing situation may change in the future. If it does, a combination of pharmacological and psychological treatments is likely to enhance performance in everyday life. It is also possible that neural transplants in people with Huntington's disease may lead to better memory performance, although here again the recipients may need to be taught to use their memories to the best advantage by employing memory rehabilitation strategies.

In the immediate future advances are likely to be made in better design and implementation of external aids and better structuring of the environment, hence reducing the load on memory. Meanwhile, further development of the errorless learning technique described above, and perhaps other ways of improving learning, can be implemented to teach people to use their prosthetic memory more efficiently.

REFERENCES

Baddeley, A.D. (1999). *Essentials of Human Memory*. Hove: Psychology Press.

Baddeley, A.D. & Longman, D.J.A. (1978). The influence of length and frequency of training sessions on the rate of learning to type. *Ergonomics*, **21**, 627–635.

Baddeley, A.D. & Wilson, B.A. (1994). When implicit learning fails: amnesia and the problem of error elimination. *Neuropsychologia*, **32**, 53–68.

Barker, R.A. & Dunnett, S.B. (1999). *Neural Repair, Transplantation and Rehabilitation*. Hove: Psychology Press.

Ben-Yishay, Y. (ed.) (1978). *Working Approaches to Remediation of Cognitive Deficits in Brain-damaged Persons* (Rehabilitation Monograph). New York: New York University Medical Center.

Ben-Yishay, Y. (1996). Reflections on the evolution of the therapeutic milieu concept. *Neuropsychological Rehabilitation*, **6**, 327–343.

Berg, I.J., Koning-Haanstra, M. & Deelman, B.G. (1991). Long-term effects of memory rehabilitation: a controlled study. *Neuropsychological Rehabilitation*, **1**, 97–111.

Bergman, M.M. (1991). Computer-enhanced self sufficiency: Part 1. Creation and implementation of a text writer for an individual with traumatic brain injury. *Neuropsychology*, **5**, 17–24.

Broman, M., Rose, A.L., Hotson, G. & Casey, C.M. (1997). Severe anterograde amnesia with onset in childhood as a result of anoxic encephalopathy. *Brain*, **120**, 417–433.

Brooks, D.N. (1984). *Closed Head Injury: Psychological, Social and Family Consequences*. Oxford: Oxford University Press.

Brooks, B.M., McNeil, J.E., Rose, D.F. et al. (1999). Route learning in a case of amnesia: a preliminary investigation into the efficacy of training in a virtual environment. *Neuropsychological Rehabilitation*, **9**, 63–76.

Brooks, D.N. & Baddeley, A.D. (1976). What can amnesic patients learn? *Neuropsychologia*, **14**, 111–122.

Brooks, D.N., Campsie, L. & Symington, C. (1987). The effects of severe head injury upon patient and relative within seven years of injury. *Journal of Head Injury Trauma Rehabilitation*, **2**, 1–13.

Camp, C.J. (1989). Facilitation of new learning in Alzheimer's disease. In G. Gilmore, P. Whitehouse & M. Wykle (eds), *Memory and Aging: Theory, Research and Practice* (pp. 212–225). New York: Springer.

Clare, L. & Wilson, B.A. (1997). *Coping with Memory Problems: A Practical Guide for People with Memory Impairments, Relatives, Friends and Carers*. Bury St Edmunds: Thames Valley Test Company.

Clare, L., Wilson, B.A., Breen, E.K. & Hodges, J.R. (1999). Errorless learning of face-name associations in early Alzheimer's disease. *Neurocase*, **5**, 37–46.

Clare, L., Wilson, B.A., Carter, G. et al. (2000). Intervening with everyday memory problems in dementia of Alzheimer type: an errorless learning approach. *Journal of Clinical and Experimental Neuropsychology*, **22**, 132–146.

Cullen, C.N. (1976). Errorless learning with the retarded. *Nursing Times*, 25 March.

Diller, L.L. (1976). A model for cognitive retraining in rehabilitation. *Clinical Psychologist*, **29**, 13–15.

Donaghy, S. & Williams, W. (1998). A new protocol for training severely impaired patients in the usage of memory journals. *Brain Injury*, **12**, 1061–1076.

Eriksson, P.S., Perfilieva, E., Bjork-Eriksson, T. et al. (1998). Neurogenesis in the adult human hippocampus. *Nature Medicine*, **4**, 1313–1317.

Evans, J.J., Emslie, H. & Wilson, B.A. (1998). External cueing systems in the rehabilitation of executive impairments of action. *Journal of the International Neuropsychological Society*, **4**, 399–408.

Evans, J.J. & Wilson, B.A. (1992). A memory group for individuals with brain injury. *Clinical Rehabilitation*, **6**, 75–81.

Evans, J.J., Wilson, B.A., Needham, P. & Brentnall, S. (2001). Who makes good use of memory-aids: results of a survey of 100 people with acquired brain injury (manuscript submitted).

Finger, S. & Stein, D.G. (1982). *Brain Damage and Recovery: Research and Clinical Perspectives*. New York: Academic Press.

Freed, D.M., Corkin, S. & Cohen, N.J. (1998). Forgetting in H.M.: a second look. *Neuropsychologia*, **25**, 461–471.

Funnell, E. & De Mornay Davies, P. (1996). JBR: a reassessment of concept familiarity and a category-specific disorder for living things. *Neurocase*, **2**, 461–474.

Gianutsos, R. (1980). What is cognitive rehabilitation? *Journal of Rehabilitation*, **1**, 37–40.

Glisky, E.L. (1995). Computers in memory rehabilitation. In A.D. Baddeley, B.A. Wilson & F.N. Watts (eds), *Handbook of Memory Disorders*, 1st edn (pp. 557–575). Chichester: Wiley.

Glisky, E.L. & Schacter, D.L. (1986). Long-term retention of computer learning by patients with memory disorders. *Neuropsychologia*, **26**, 173–178.

Glisky, E.L. & Schacter, D.L. (1987). Acquisition of domain-specific knowledge in organic amnesia: training for computer-related work. *Neuropsychologia*, **25**, 893–906.

Glisky, E.L. & Schacter, D.L. (1989). Extending the limits of complex learning in organic amnesia: computer training in a vocational domain. *Neuropsychologia*, **27**, 107–120.

Glisky, E.L., Schacter, D.L. & Tulving, E. (1986). Computer learning by memory impaired patients: acquisition and retention of complex knowledge. *Neuropsychologia*, **24**, 313–328.

Godden, D. & Baddeley, A.D. (1975). Context-dependent memory in two natural environments: on land and under water. *British Journal of Psychology*, **66**, 325–331.

Gouvier, W.D. (1982). Using the digital alarm chronograph in memory retraining. *Behavioral Engineering*, **7**, 134.

Graf, P. & Schacter, D.L. (1985). Implicit and explicit memory for new associations in normal and amnesic subjects. *Journal of Experimental Psychology: Learning, Memory, and Cognition*, **11**, 501–518.

Harris, J.E. (1980). We have ways of helping you remember. *Concord: The Journal of the British Association of Service to the Elderly*, **17**, 21–27.

Hersh, N. & Treadgold, L. (1994). NeuroPage: the rehabilitation of memory dysfunction by prosthetic memory and cueing. *NeuroRehabilitation*, **4**, 187–197.

Hunkin, M.M., Squires, E.J., Parkin, A.J. & Tidy, J.A. (1998). Are the benefits of errorless learning dependent on implicit memory? *Neuropsychologia*, **36**, 25–36.

Jennett, B. & Bond, M. (1975). Assessment of outcome after severe brain injury. *Lancet*, **1**, 480–484.

Jones, R.S.P. & Eayrs, C.B. (1992). The use of errorless learning procedures in teaching people with a learning disability. *Mental Handicap Research*, **5**, 304–312.

Kapur, N. (1995). Memory aids in the rehabilitation of memory disordered patients. In A.D. Baddeley, B.A. Wilson & F.N. Watts (eds), *Handbook of Memory Disorders*, 1st edn (pp. 533–556). Chichester: Wiley.

Kim, H.J., Burke, D.T., Dowds, M.M. & George, J. (1999). Utility of a microcomputer as an external memory aid for a memory-impaired head injury patient during inpatient rehabilitation. *Brain Injury*, **13**, 147–150.

Kime, S.K., Lamb, D.G. & Wilson, B.A. (1996). Use of a comprehensive program of external cuing to enhance procedural memory in a patient with dense amnesia. *Brain Injury*, **10**, 17–25.

Kirsch, N.L., Levine, S.P., Fallon-Krueger, M. & Jaros, L.A. (1987). The microcomputer as an "orthotic" device for patients with cognitive deficits. *Journal of Head Trauma Rehabilitation*, **2**, 77–86.

Kirsch, N.L., Levine, S.P., Lajiness O'Neill, L. & Schnyder, M. (1992). Computer assisted interactive task guidance: facilitating the performance of a simulated vocational task. *Journal of Head Trauma Rehabilitation*, **7**, 13–25.

Kolb, B. (1995). *Brain Plasticity and Behavior*. Mahwah, NJ: Erlbaum.

Kopelman, M. & Crawford, S. (1996). Not all memory clinics are dementia clinics. *Neuropsychological Rehabilitation*, **6**, 187–202.

Landauer, T.K. & Bjork, R.A. (1978). Optimum rehearsal patterns and name learning. In M.M. Gruneberg, P.E. Morris & R.N. Sykes (eds), *Practical Aspects of Memory* (pp. 625–632). London: Academic Press.

Lawson, M.J. & Rice, D.N. (1989). Effects of training in use of executive strategies on a verbal memory problem resulting from closed head injury. *Journal of Clinical and Experimental Neuropsychology*, **11**, 842–854.

Levine, B., Robertson, I.H., Clare, L. et al. (2000). Rehabilitation of executive functioning: an experimental–clinical validation of Goal Management Training. *Journal of the International Neuropsychological Society*, **6**, 299–312.

Lezak, M.D. (1979). Recovery of memory and learning functions following traumatic brain injury. *Cortex*, **15**, 63–72.

Lincoln, N.B. (1989). Management of memory problems in a hospital setting. In L.W. Poon, D.C. Rubin & B.A. Wilson (eds), *Everyday Cognition in Adulthood and Late Life* (pp. 639–658). Cambridge: Cambridge University Press.

Lorge, I. (1930). *Influence of Regularly Interpolated Time Intervals upon Subsequent Learning*. Quoted in H.H. Johnson & R.L. Solso (1971) *An Introduction to Experimental Design in Psychology: A Case Approach*. New York: Harper & Row.

Luria, A.R. (1963). *Restoration of Function after Brain Injury*. New York: Pergamon.

Marshall, J.F. (1985). Neural plasticity and recovery of function after brain injury. *International Review of Neurobiology*, **26**, 201–247.

McKitrick, L.A. & Camp, C.J. (1993). Relearning the names of things: the spaced-retrieval intervention implemented by a caregiver. *Clinical Gerontologist*, **14**, 60–62.

Milders, M.V., Berg, I.J. & Deelman, B.G. (1995). Four-year follow-up of a controlled memory training study in closed head injured patients. *Neuropsychological Rehabilitation*, **5**, 223–238.

Moffat, N. (1989). Home-based cognitive rehabilitation with the elderly. In L.W. Poon, D.C. Rubin & B.A. Wilson (eds), *Everyday Cognition in Adulthood and Late Life* (pp. 659–680). Cambridge: Cambridge University Press.

Murphy, G. & Oliver, C. (1987). Decreasing undesirable behaviour. In W. Yule & J. Carr (eds), *Behaviour Modification for People with Mental Handicaps* (pp. 102–142). London: Croom Helm.

Oddy, M. (1984). Head injury and social adjustment. In D.N. Brooks (ed.), *Closed Head Injury: Psychological, Social and Family Consequences*. Oxford: Oxford University Press.

Ownsworth, T.L. & McFarland, K. (1999). Memory remediation in long-term acquired brain injury: two approaches in diary training. *Brain Injury, 13*, 605–626.

Prigatano, G. (1999). *Principles of Neuropsychological Rehabilitation*. New York: Oxford University Press.

Prigatano, G.P. (1987). Recovery and cognitive retraining after craniocerebral trauma. *Journal of Learning Disabilities, 20*, 603–613.

Rizzo, A.A., Buckwalter, J.G. & Neumann, U. (1997). Virtual reality and cognitive rehabilitation: a brief review of the future. *Journal of Head Trauma Rehabilitation, 12*, 1–15.

Rose, F.D., Attree, E.A. & Johnson, D.A. (1996). Virtual reality: an assistive technology in neurological rehabilitation. *Current Opinion in Neurology, 9*, 461–467.

Schacter, D.L., Rich, S.A. & Stampp, M.S. (1985). Remediation of memory disorders: experimental evaluation of the spaced-retrieval technique. *Journal of Clinical and Experimental Neuropsychology, 7*, 79–96.

Schuri, U., Wilson, B.A. & Hodges, J. (1996). Memory disorders. In T. Brandt, L.R. Caplan, J. Dichgans et al. (eds), *Neurological Disorders: Course and Treatment* (pp. 223–230). San Diego, CA: Academic Press.

Scoville, W.B. & Milner, B. (1957). Loss of recent memory after bilateral hippocampal lesions. *Journal of Neurology, Neurosurgery, and Psychiatry, 20*, 11–21.

Sidman, M. & Stoddard, L.T. (1967). The effectiveness of fading in programming simultaneous form discrimination for retarded children. *Journal of Experimental Analysis of Behavior, 10*, 3–15.

Sohlberg, M.M. & Mateer, C. (1989). Training use of compensatory memory books: a three-stage behavioural approach. *Journal of Clinical and Experimental Neuropsychology, 11*, 871–891.

Squires, E.J., Aldrich, F.K., Parkin, A.J. & Hunkin, N.M. (1998). Errorless learning and the acquisition of word processing skills. *Neuropsychological Rehabilitation, 8*, 433–449.

Squires, E.J., Hunkin, N.M. & Parkin, A.J. (1996). Memory notebook training in a case of severe amnesia: generalising from paired associate learning to real life. *Neuropsychological Rehabilitation, 6*, 55–65.

Squires, E.J., Hunkin, N.M. & Parkin, A.J. (1997). Errorless learning of novel associations in amnesia. *Neuropsychologia, 35*, 1103–1111.

Stilwell, P., Stilwell, J., Hawley, C. & Davies, C. (1999). The National Traumatic Brain Injury Study: assessing outcomes across settings. *Neuropsychological Rehabilitation, 9*, 277–293.

Terrace, H.S. (1963). Discrimination learning with and without "errors". *Journal of Experimental Analysis of Behavior, 6*, 1–27.

Terrace, H.S. (1966). Stimulus control. In W.K. Honig (ed.), *Operant Behavior: Areas of Research and Application* (pp. 271–344). New York: Appleton-Century-Crofts.

Tulving, E. & Schacter, D.L. (1990). Priming and human memory systems. *Science, 247*, 301–306.

Vargha-Khadem, F., Gadian, D.G., Watkins, K.E. et al. (1997). Differential effects of early hippocampal pathology on episodic and semantic memory. *Science, 277*, 376–380.

Victor, M., Adams, R.D. & Collins, G.H. (1989). *The Wernicke–Korsakoff Syndrome and Related Neurological Disorders Due to Alcoholism and Malnutrition*, 2nd edn. Philadelphia, PA: F.A. Davis.

von Cramon, D.Y. & Matthes-von Cramon, G. (1992). Reflections on the treatment of brain injured patients suffering from problem-solving disorders. *Neuropsychological Rehabilitation, 2*, 207–230.

Walsh, B.F. & Lamberts, F. (1979). Errorless discrimination and fading as techniques for teaching sight words to TMR students. *American Journal of Mental Deficiency, 83*, 473–479.

Watkins, M.J., Ho, E. & Tulving, E. (1976). Context effects in recognition memory for faces. *Journal of Verbal Learning and Verbal Behavior, 15*, 505–517.

Wearing, D. (1992). Self-help groups. In B.A. Wilson & N. Moffat (eds), *Clinical Management of Memory Problems*, 2nd edn (pp. 271–301). London: Chapman & Hall.

West, R.L. (1995). Compensatory strategies for age-associated memory impairment. In A.D. Baddeley, B.A. Wilson & F.N. Watts (eds), *Handbook of Memory Disorders*, 1st edn (pp. 481–500). Chichester: Wiley.

Wilson, B.A. (1987a). *Rehabilitation of Memory*. New York: Guilford.

Wilson, B.A. (1987b). Single-case experimental designs in neuropsychological rehabilitation. *Journal of Clinical and Experimental Neuropsychology*, **9**, 527–544.

Wilson, B.A. (1989). Models of cognitive rehabilitation. In R.L. Wood & P. Eames (eds), *Models of Brain Injury Rehabilitation* (pp. 117–141). London: Chapman & Hall.

Wilson, B.A. (1991). Long-term prognosis of patients with severe memory disorders. *Neuropsychological Rehabilitation*, **1**, 117–134.

Wilson, B.A. (1992). Memory therapy in practice. In B.A. Wilson & N. Moffat (eds), *Clinical Management of Memory Problems*, 2nd edn (pp. 120–153). London: Chapman & Hall.

Wilson, B.A. (1997). Cognitive rehabilitation: how it is and how it might be. *Journal of the International Neuropsychological Society*, **3**, 487–496.

Wilson, B.A. (1998). Recovery of cognitive functions following non-progressive brain injury. *Current Opinion in Neurobiology*, **8**, 281–287.

Wilson, B.A. (1999). *Case Studies in Neuropsychological Rehabilitation*. New York: Oxford University Press.

Wilson, B.A. & Baddeley, A.D. (1993). Spontaneous recovery of digit span: does comprehension recover? *Cortex*, **29**, 153–159.

Wilson, B.A., Baddeley, A.D., Evans, J.J. & Shiel, A. (1994). Errorless learning in the rehabilitation of memory impaired people. *Neuropsychological Rehabilitation*, **4**, 307–326.

Wilson, B.A., Baddeley, A.D. & Kapur, N. (1995). Dense amnesia in a professional musician following Herpes Simplex Virus encephalitis. *Journal of Clinical and Experimental Psychology*, **17**, 668–681.

Wilson, B.A., J.C. & Hughes, E. (1997a). Coping with amnesia: the natural history of a compensatory memory system. *Neuropsychological Rehabilitation*, **7**, 43–56.

Wilson, B.A., Emslie, H., Quirk, K. & Evans, J. (1999a). George: learning to live independently with NeuroPage®. *Rehabilitation Psychology*, **44**, 284–296.

Wilson, B.A. Emslie, H.C., Quirk, K. & Evans, J.J. (2001). Reducing everyday memory and planning problems by means of a paging system: a randomised control crossover study. *Journal of Neurology, Neurosurgery, and Psychiatry*, **70**, 477–482.

Wilson, B.A. & Evans, J. (in press). Does cognitive rehabilitation work? Clinical and economic considerations and outcomes. In G. Prigatano (ed.), *Clinical Neuropsychology and Cost–Outcome Research: An Introduction*. Hove: Psychology Press.

Wilson, B.A. & Evans, J.J. (1996). Error-free learning in the rehabilitation of individuals with memory impairments. *Journal of Head Trauma Rehabilitation*, **11**, 54–64.

Wilson, B.A. Evans, J., Brentnall, S. et al. (2000). The Oliver Zangwill Centre for Neuropsychological Rehabilitation: a partnership between health care and rehabilitation research. In A.-L. Christensen & B.P. Uzzell (eds), *International Handbook of Neuropsychological Rehabilitation* (pp. 231–246). New York: Kluwer Academic/Plenum.

Wilson, B.A., Evans, J.J., Emslie, H. et al. (1999b). Measuring recovery from post traumatic amnesia. *Brain Injury*, **13**, 505–520.

Wilson, B.A., Evans, J.J., Emslie, H. & Malinek, V. (1997b). Evaluation of NeuroPage: a new memory aid. *Journal of Neurology, Neurosurgery, and Psychiatry*, **63**, 113–115.

Wilson, B.A. & Moffat, N. (1992). The development of group memory therapy. In B.A. Wilson & N. Moffat (eds), *Clinical Management of Memory Problems*, 2nd edn (pp. 243–273). London: Chapman & Hall.

Wilson, B.A. & Watson, P.C. (1996). A practical framework for understanding compensatory behaviour in people with organic memory impairment. *Memory*, **4**, 465–486.

Wilson, B.A., Watson, P.C., Baddeley, A.D. et al. (2000). Improvement or simply practice? The effects of twenty repeated assessments on people with and without brain injury. *Journal of the International Neuropsychological Society*, **6**, 469–479.

Wright, P., Bartram, C., Rogers, N. et al. (2000). Text entry on handheld computers by older users. *Ergonomics*, **43**, 702–716.

Wright, P., Rogers, N., Bartram, C. et al. (in press). Comparison of pocket-computer aids for people with brain injury. *Brain Injury*.

Zangwill, O.L. (1947). Psychological aspects of rehabilitation in cases of brain injury. *British Journal of Psychology*, **37**, 60–69.

Zarkowska, E. (1987). Discrimination and generalisation. In W. Yule & J. Carr (eds), *Behaviour Modification for People with Mental Handicaps* (pp. 79–94). London: Croom Helm.

Zencius, A., Wesolowski, M.D., Krankowski, T. & Burke, W.H. (1991). Memory notebook training with traumatically brain-injured clients. *Brain Injury*, **5**, 321–325.

CHAPTER 31

Assessment and Management of Memory Problems in Children

Judith A. Middleton
Radcliffe Infirmary, Oxford, UK

The assessment of memory and learning in children has changed considerably in the last 15 years or so since more reliable and valid tests of children's memory, which have been well standardized on large numbers of children, have become available. Previous to that, scaled-down versions of adult assessments were often the only available measures, or tests specifically constructed for research purposes, both of which were often unsuitable for use with a clinical population of children. With the advent of new assessment batteries, it is now possible to look at children's memory development and disorders more appropriately. Whether the aim of assessment is to: (a) research into the nature of brain–behaviour links; (b) describe the nature of the impairment; (c) contribute to diagnosis and decisions about treatment; (d) monitor change over time; or (e) plan rehabilitation, it is vital that tests should fulfil the strict standard criteria in order to make them appropriate and meaningful.

ISSUES OF NEUROPSYCHOLOGICAL ASSESSMENT OF MEMORY IN CHILDREN

The basis of a good clinical neuropsychological assessment of memory should be based on six lines of enquiry:

1. Where known, the underlying neuropathology.
2. The child's age, developmental level and cultural background.
3. General level of cognitive functioning and co-morbid difficulties.
4. Functional information gleaned from careful clinical interviewing.
5. Observations of how children complete (or fail) memory and learning tasks, and perform generally.
6. The results of psychometric tests.

The Handbook of Memory Disorders. Edited by A.D. Baddeley, M.D. Kopelman and B.A. Wilson
© 2002 John Wiley & Sons, Ltd.

Major errors can occur when inferences and conclusions are drawn from only the first and last sources of information in isolation. In other words, wrong assumptions can be made about direct brain–behaviour links when the child's age and development, cultural context, clinical history and careful observations of how they go about performing tasks are omitted in forming hypotheses.

A second important point to remember is that young children rarely complain of memory problems themselves if the problem is acquired in infancy, unlike older children (and adults) who have an acquired memory problem, or adults who may know that their memory is not what it used to be. While normal children will be able to discuss memory from a young age (for further discussion, see Joyner & Kurtz-Costes, 1997) their metamemory or understanding that they have memory, that they are able to forget and that they are able to know that they have forgotten what they have known at one time, does not develop until later childhood. Indeed, even older children whose memory may have been poor for a number of years may not know that they have a problem, never having been consciously aware that they did not have a fully functioning memory.

Generally it is parents or teachers who first raise concerns about problems of memory in children. Here again, it may be that it is not a child's poor memory that is described, but that they are failing to learn and make progress that is the presenting problem. This is again a major difference with adults, who will have had the experience of a normal memory for many years. Even if they have lost insight into their problem, their family and associates will notice a loss or difference in them which gives rise to concern. With young children there may be little against which to compare their present memory capacity or processing, so there may not be a sense of loss of memory function, but rather a failure to make progress as expected over time. In older children the loss of memory may be a presenting problem, depending on the aetiology.

CAUSES OF MEMORY PROBLEMS

Neuropathology

Elsewhere in this book (see Chapter 2), the neuropathological underpinnings of memory and memory disorders will have been discussed in detail. Consequently, it is sufficient to say here that damage to the temporal lobes, hippocampus, amygdala, mammillary bodies, thalamus and frontal lobes, those parts of the brain mostly commonly associated with memory problems, may broadly arise from necrosis, injury, inflammation (meningitis and encephalitis), atrophy (following febrile convulsions in childhood), oedema, cerebral haemorrhage, tumours (whether malignant or benign), calcification [e.g after radiotherapy for central nervous system (CNS) involvement in leukaemia], other treatment (surgery or medication), disease (epilepsy) or displacement (i.e. following tumours, bleeds or infection elsewhere in the brain causing midline shift). In addition, there may be developmental disorders where the brain is malformed and consequently memory and learning are compromised. However, a number of case histories highlight that children may present with specific memory problems in the absence of any definite neuropathology. (Casalini et al., 1999; Temple, 1997).

Psychological

There are also some instances where there may be no documented neuropathology, but children still have reported problems in learning and memory in general, but with less specificity than in the above cases. As part of a good clinical assessment, it is important to consider whether there may be psychological causes. Children who are anxious and depressed may be preoccupied with their own concerns and present with complaints about their distractedness, failure to learn and frequent forgetting, both at home and in school. Careful clinical interviews of the child and family are needed to exclude such issues. Lack of motivation and cooperation in the assessment may also be the cause of test failure. There is also evidence that children with posttraumatic stress disorder (PTSD) may also present with memory problems (Canterbury & Yule, 1997), and it is therefore crucial, when a child has had a head injury, that both psychological and neuropathological causes are considered.

AGE, DEVELOPMENTAL LEVEL AND AGE AT LOSS

Irrespective of whether we are assessing memory and learning in children for clinical or research purposes, it is important that there is an appreciation that the model most commonly assumed for adults may be inappropriate when applying it to children, or at least to very young children. As the chapter on the development of memory will have illustrated (Chapter 24, this volume), infants are not born with a fully developed memory system or memory capacity, and will not have the same complexity for encoding, storing and retrieving information at birth that is present in adults. In addition, the means that we have to assess memory in preverbal children and in children with developing but immature language systems is consequently compromised and different paradigms need to be employed. Importantly, children are maturing very rapidly, so assessments at any one age have to be specific to the child's developmental level. Comparisons between assessments at different ages may give unexpected results if their memory capacity, speed of processing and age-appropriate strategies are not understood.

In addition, the age of acquisition of memory loss is crucial in understanding children's memory problems. Younger children are more vulnerable than older children, however the injury is acquired (e.g. head injuries, Levin et al., 1995; or central nervous system radiation, Said et al., 1989).

Fletcher & Taylor (1984) propose a developmental model of assessment whereby the starting point is exploration of the presenting or manifest behaviour, rather than the neuropathology. They argue that brain–behaviour links based on adult models can be misleading, as children are rapidly developing and may use different strategies to adults to carry out tasks. They support a model in which assessment of the specific processing difficulties is based on the manifest problems within a wider assessment of ability. This precedes making a possible link to the known or suspected neuropathology.

CO-MORBID PROBLEMS

It is particularly important in children to ensure that an apparent memory problem is not the result of other physical and/or cognitive problems about which the child may not be able to articulate. Visual and hearing problems are obvious areas to exclude. Delayed language development will mean that test instructions and test content may not be understood, even in nonverbal memory tests. Failure to focus attention on test materials, distractibility and short attention span may also result in deviant memory test scores. As Lezak (1995) points out (p. 429), problems that appear to be related to poor memory may be more to do with difficulties in attention or mental tracking. Perceptual organization problems may be the root difficulty for children with a poor visuospatial memory. If children are only able to process information slowly, then failure on some memory tests where information is presented rapidly, or where there is a set time for them to respond, may be related to this rather than to a memory problem *per se*, although functionally the problem emerges as a difficulty with learning.

Children's general level of cognitive functioning will also impact on their performance in memory tasks. This is especially so in younger children, where memory is more closely correlated to intelligence than in older children (Cohen, 1997). It is not unknown clinically for children with memory problems to be referred for assessment, who, when tested comprehensively, are found to be functioning at the bottom of the normal range on standard assessments of cognitive development and academic achievement, although teachers have reported that the child is functioning reasonably in school. Consequently, any assessment of memory problems needs to start with a formal assessment of general cognitive functioning.

ETHNIC AND CULTURAL CONTEXT

Mistry (1998) has discussed the issue that the development of remembering will be influenced by children's cultural environment. For a start, many assessments have been standardized on USA populations, matching the census data for ethnicity. However, it is worthwhile remembering that when used in the UK there are different minority ethnic groups compared to the USA populations, which may make the assessment batteries less relevant for these children, with the content and process being less familiar to some groups than others. More importantly, Mistry (1998) points out that different cultural backgrounds will place different emphasis on the practice of remembering (p. 364). Children who have been to schools where memory and organizational strategies have been integrated into normal classroom instruction may be at an advantage in assessments compared to those who have not (see Bjorklund & Douglas, 1998). Finally, in some cultures, rote learning of special texts (e.g. the Koran in Muslim cultures) may mean that children from these backgrounds have a specific strength in those tasks where rote learning is crucial. Of course, poor rote learning in these children may have profound cultural implications.

CLINICAL INTERVIEW

A great deal can be learnt from the clinical interview in forming initial hypotheses about the cause and nature of memory problems. A clinical finding has been that some referrals may speak of children losing skills, in other words failing to retain information that they had learnt and been able to retrieve before. If there is known neuropathology (such as localized damage from a cerebral haemorrhage, focal head injury or tumour) this can occur, but in some conditions (such as generalized seizures or diffuse closed head injury) it is often that parents and schools are concerned that the gap between their child and his/her peers is widening, either from a slower or uneven acquisition of knowledge or of a failure to learn at all. Of course, virtually every child will develop to some degree, and those with memory problems still learn to carry out many activities of everyday life and form relationships with their families, all based on implicit procedural learning, frequent repetition and multisensory input. Sometimes their difficulties seem to be related to, or at least may first emerge as, problems relating to explicit memory and learning. In other words they may have difficulties in acquiring skills and knowledge that need to be specifically taught, such as reading, writing and mathematics. Studies by Vargha-Khadem et al. (1997) and Broman et al. (1997) have also described cases of children with specific and profound episodic memory problems arising from bilateral hippocampal pathology, where children attended mainstream school and attained low to low-average levels of functioning in speech and language, literacy and factual knowledge, suggesting that episodic and semantic memory are partly dissociable.

It is critical in all neuropsychological assessments of children to carry out a full clinical and developmental interview with parents, even when there is documented evidence of neuropathology, which could directly explain problems in learning and memory. In acquired problems, premorbid cognitive functioning and behaviour may indicate cognitive style and earlier difficulties which could interact with, and directly affect how to manage, the presenting memory and learning problems. In addition, information about the family history may show that there are specific or general learning difficulties implicating slow learning in other family members, which can give a fuller picture of the child's problem. More specifically, clinical assessment of the problem should include the child's perspective to the extent that he/she can explain what he/she feels is wrong, as well as the perspective of both parents if at all possible. However, younger children tend to overestimate their memory skills and may not see that there is a problem. Older children with frontal damage may lack insight and accurate monitoring of their difficulties. There may be occasions when parents have very differing views as to the aetiology of any difficulties, or when one parent does not acknowledge that there is a problem. While this may not directly affect the assessment procedure and the analysis of the problem, parental disagreement can have major implications for management and rehabilitation.

Areas to consider include: (a) capacity (how much can be remembered); (b) content (verbal/visual: concrete/abstract): (c) type (declarative/procedural, episodic/semantic); (d) speed of acquisition; (e) rate of loss of information after a delay; and (f) process (storage, encoding or retrieval). Useful clinical questions should consider whether children can:

- Remember requests to carry out activities in the future.
- Remember and execute a number of instructions at any one time.
- Be sent shopping, with or without a shopping list (at an appropriate age).
- Remember if they have homework and, if so, what it consists of.
- Remember to take their homework back to school once completed.
- Find their clothes and possessions around the house
- Keep track of their equipment, coat, etc. at school.
- Know the way to school.
- Know their way round the block to neighbours.
- Remember rules in games.

- Remember which team they are on when they play team games.
- Remember arrangements to meet friends after school.
- Remember to pass on information between home and school in connection with meetings, school outings, etc.
- Remember secrets and that secrets are secret.
- Get into trouble at school or home for telling fanciful stories, where fiction is embroidered onto a semblance of the truth.
- Relate what has been happening at school, or to talk with peers or teachers about specific home activities after the weekend or holidays.
- Improve their memory if information is given more slowly, in a simplified form, or if it is repeated.
- Remember something they have been told for an hour, a day, a week.

These questions are not exclusive but serve to illustrate the scope of what needs to be covered in relation to general everyday activities (for further examples, see Ylvisaker & Gioia, 1998, pp. 165–167).

Beyond this, information gathering should become more specific about school performance on different subjects and about a range of functional school activities. Consequently, it is important to include the opinion of teachers within the assessment. Questions that can be illuminating relate to the subjects or areas where there are particular problems, whether there have been any previous attempts to help a child through organizing work, prompting, or cuing a child who has been slow to learn or cannot remember from one day to the next what has been taught. Parents and teachers may complain that, for instance, specific spellings can be repeatedly taught and retained for a week but will be forgotten by the end of the following week, when new material has been learnt. In addition, it is possible that some teaching styles may include organizational strategies or a study skill component which may have been helpful to children (Bjorklund & Douglas, 1998), so classroom observations can be illuminating.

ASSESSMENT VARIABLES

The assessment of memory in children crucially needs to take into account three major sets of variables:

1. *Test variables*, including test selection, standardization, suitability of the test for the population and suitability of the test to answer a specific question for the child.
2. *Testing variables*, i.e. rate of presentation, mode of presentation, mode of response, response elicitation (i.e. cued, prompted or free recall or recognition). These include stimulus properties and characteristics, meaningfulness and familiarity to the child (see Figure 31.1).
3. *Situational and presentation variables*, such as distractions, quietnes and the structure of the assessment session.

Before going on to consider assessment of young children and adults, it is important to consider the assessment of infant memory.

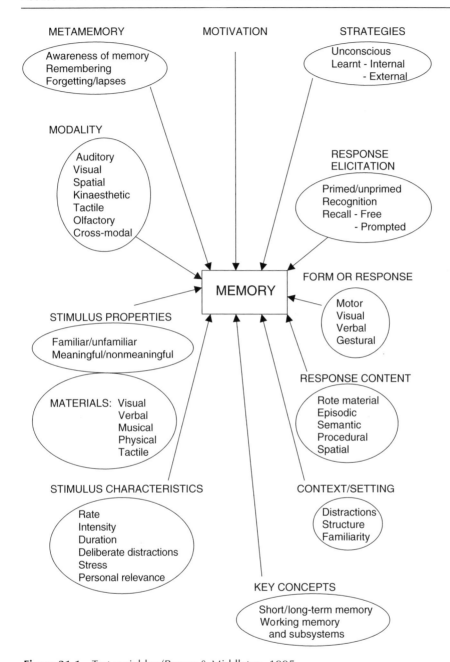

Figure 31.1   Test variables (Berger & Middleton, 1995

ASSESSMENT OF INFANT MEMORY AND LEARNING

Memory and learning are innate capacities of the human brain. From the moment of birth, and before, infants are learning from and about the external world. It is, therefore possible to observe and assess memory and learning from the very earliest periods of an infant's life. Early in life, recognition is context-dependent because of infants' lack of speech. It is necessary to create a similar setting to allow an infant to recognize what he/she has experienced before. As infants grow older, the importance of language as a primary mediator in memory and learning will grow, and with this the development of a verbal memory system which begins to correspond to that of adults and which allows them to begin to hold semantic and abstract information in memory (Rovee-Collier & Gerhardstein, 1997; Temple, 1997).

Infant memory can be assessed through a number of different paradigms, such as paired-comparison, habituation, and classical and operant conditioning (for detailed discussion, see Rovee-Collier & Gerhardstein, 1997). For instance, Walton, Bower & Bower (1992) indicate that infants may show a visual preference for their mother within 12 h of birth and certainly within a day (Bushnell, et al., 1983, in Blass, 1999). This implies very early recognition and learning. By 20 days they can learn to blink at an auditory signal to prevent a puff of air on their cornea (Little et al., 1984, in Rovee-Collier & Gerhardstein, 1997, p. 17). Within the first few weeks of life, infants will recognize the smell of their mother's breast milk and the sound of novel sounds. Using an operant kicking paradigm, they can be taught to operate a mobile at 3 months (Rovee-Collier et al., 1980). The development of casting and searching play indicates that children are beginning to obtain object permanency; and failure to achieve this and apparently miss their primary caregivers when they are absent at age-appropriate levels may be explored to see whether there is a failure to learn and retain information.

Clinical assessment using formal developmental measures can be used judiciously, e.g. one or two items in the Bayley Scales of Infant Development (Bayley, 1993), such as comparing checkerboard patterns or hiding a small toy under one of two cups with the infant having to search for the toy after a set time limit can begin to be used to look at memory and learning formally. However, interpreting failure in these tasks as being indicative of problems with memory and learning needs to be done with caution.

ASSESSMENT OF OLDER CHILDREN AND ADOLESCENTS

Qualitative Assessment

Although observations cannot be standardized and should, therefore, be treated with some caution, watching how children go about completing memory and learning tasks and assessment in general, provides extremely important information about the kinds of problems they may have, and how weaknesses can be managed. In addition, it is by combining this information with test results and the picture gathered from the clinical interview, that will make most sense of the data and inform how problems may be best managed.

As at all times, it is important to remember the child's age and developmental level when observing them complete tasks. Work by Hulme & Mackenzie (1992) has shown that the speed of presentation of verbal material in tasks like word recall is linearly related to age, with more words being recalled with increased speech rate in 7-year-olds compared to 4-year-olds and 10-year-olds compared to 7-year-olds. Thus, children whose speed of processing is slow, both from observations during assessment and on speed of information processing tasks in the Wechsler Intelligence Scale for Children, 3rd edn (WISC-III; Wechsler, 1991) or British Ability Scales, 2nd edn (BAS-II; Elliott et al., 1983)., are likely to do badly in memory tasks where information is presented quickly (see below for a discussion of the various specific demands on a range of tasks purportedly assessing similar abilities). Frequent requests for questions or instructions to be repeated (e.g. in Arithmetic in the WISC-III), or the need for children to check with the model every few seconds (e.g. in Coding, WISC-III) may, but not necessarily, mean that they cannot hold the image or words in their short-term memory for long.

Close clinical observations of children as they complete assessments, and asking them about how they have gone about tackling items, may also indicate whether they are automatically using strategies, whether the strategies are developmentally appropriate and how helpful they are to the child. Bjorklund et al. (1997) have discussed the utilization deficiencies in memory-training studies in normal children. The effectiveness of strategy use is not an all-or-nothing affair and strategy use is dependent on age, other (e.g. frontal) problems, level of general cognitive functioning, motivation, insight and self-monitoring the efficacy of the strategy. Not only is the complexity of the material a factor in what and how much children of different ages can recall, but also the strategies that they could use to help them remember emerge at different stages in their development (Bjorklund et al., 1997). This is important for management of memory problems and will be discussed below in more detail.

Test Selection

Issues of reliability and validity generally will not be discussed in detail here, but it is crucial to consider the psychometric properties of each test carefully. It is important that the assessments are sensitive to strengths and weaknesses in memory, as well as being sufficiently stable over time to pick up subtle changes. As with testing in general, but particularly with memory, repeated assessments will give rise to specific problems relating to practice effects. None of the major batteries (except the Rivermead Behavioural Memory Test) have more than one version, although there are shortened forms for younger children and some have different stories at different ages. With children in particular, it is crucial to bear in mind that they are rapidly developing in a way that adults are not. There should be improvement with time, so failure to develop better memory skills is an extremely important marker that there may be serious problems.

Assessments of General Cognitive Functioning

Hypotheses about a memory problem can be formed not only during clinical interview, but when completing a full assessment of general cognitive functioning. Using Kaufman's (1994) information-processing model in analysing the Wechsler Intelligence Scale for Children, 3rd edn (WISC-III), comparatively lower scores in Arithmetic and Digit Span may suggest short-term verbal memory problems, while lower Information and Vocabulary subtests may be indicative of poor semantic or long term verbal memory. Picture Completion in the performance Scale could be indicative of problems with long-term visual memory. Qualitative observations of both Coding and Symbol Search may indicate short-term visual memory difficulties if children are seen to refer to the test material repeatedly and do not seem to remember the codes/symbols easily. These can only be tentative hypotheses, as weaknesses in these subtests and in the strategies that children use may be due to factors other than memory problems. The corollary is that if children do well in these subtests, it does not mean they do not have real memory problems. Similar analyses can be made of specific subtests in the Wechsler Pre-school and Primary Scales of Intelligence, Revised (WPPSI-R; Wechsler, 1993) or the British Ability Scales, 2nd edn (BAS-2), where there are three short term visual memory tasks, which will be discussed later. The McCarthy Scales (McCarthy, 1972) have a memory index, which can be a useful starter in making hypotheses.

Specific Memory Batteries

There are a number of major test batteries for assessing memory, each with its own relative strengths and weaknesses. The selection of which assessment battery to use may be academic in many departments where there has been the purchase of a single memory battery only. It is, however, essential to look carefully at whatever assessments are used to ensure that they assess what they purport to assess, e.g. so-called visual learning subtests in the Wide Range Assessment of Memory and Learning (WRAML; Sheslow & Adams, 1990) and in the Test of Memory and Learning (TOMAL; Reynolds & Bigler, 1994) are, in fact, spatial learning tasks. Children do not have to remember whether or not a pattern is present, but rather where it is placed on a matrix. Some tests are more explicit in describing the response modality, e.g. the BAS-2 has verbal and spatial recall of pictures of objects on a matrix.

What follows is, first, a description of some of the most frequently used assessment batteries in terms of their breadth and standardization, and a discussion of what their advantages or disadvantages may be. Second, there is an analysis of some of the major components of these batteries, showing that there may be very real differences in factors influencing performance by a child in tests that apparently assess the same function.

Children's Memory Scale (CMS) (Cohen, 1997)

This is becoming one of the most popular assessments to evaluate memory and learning in children aged 5–16 years in the UK. It was standardized on a stratified sample of 1000 children in the USA divided into 10 age bands. Of these 1000 children, 300 were also administered the WISC-III or WPPSI-R. Correlation's between the various CMS and WISC-III indices indicated that: (a) generally, memory and the WISC-III were strongly correlated; and (b) that intelligence has a "small-to-moderate impact" (p.117). on children's memory. The correlations between the WPPSI-R and CMS differed from these. Although the sample size was smaller and the stratification was different, the results did suggest that in younger children memory may be more closely linked to verbal abilities than in older children.

The CMS was also correlated with other ability scales, such as the Differential Ability Scales (DAS; Elliott, 1990); and with various achievement tests, including the Wechsler

Individual Achievement Test (WIAT; Wechsler, 1995). In addition correlations with a number of executive functioning tests were made, such as the Wisconsin Card Sorting Task (WCST; Heaton et al., 1993) and the Children's Category Test (CCT; Boll, 1993); with language assessments, e.g. the Clinical Evaluation of Language Fundamentals, 3rd edn (CELF-3; Semmel et al., 1995); and with other memory assessments, such as the WRAML, Wechsler Memory Scale, 3rd edn (WMS-III; Wechsler, 1997) and the California Verbal Learning Test—Children's Version (CVLT-C; Dean et al., 1994).

The general memory index of the CMS includes measures of verbal and visual memory (immediate and delayed). In addition, there are measures of attention and concentration, learning, and delayed verbal recognition. A disappointment is the use of word pairs as part of the core memory index rather than the word list, also included but as a supplementary subtest. However, generally this test is colourful and child-friendly, with good conversion tables so that actual memory scores can be compared with those predicted from the WISC-III and WPPSI-R.

Test of Memory and Learning (TOMAL)

The TOMAL was designed and standardized on a stratified sample of 1342 children and adolescents, and had extensive piloting based on the 1990/1992 US census demographic characteristics. There are a number of studies quoted in the manual, where it has been correlated with tests such as the Kaufman Assessment Battery for Children (K-ABC; Kaufman & Kaufman, 1984); the Wide Range Achievement Test—Revised (WRAT-R; Jastak & Wilkinson, 1993); the Californian Achievement Test (CAT) and the Wechsler Intelligence Scale for Children—Revised (WISC-R; Wechsler, 1974). It essentially consists of two scales each (verbal and nonverbal memory), with five subtests leading to a composite memory scale. Both a selective reminding word list and word pairs are included in the verbal scale. There is also a composite delayed memory index (made up of four subtests). Supplementary subtests include letters forward and backwards, digits backwards, and manual imitation. As well as the core indices, supplementary indices include sequential recall, free recall, associative recall, learning and attention/concentration. Although of relatively weak validity, they are useful in leading to more specific hypotheses.

This test battery is in the range 5–19.11 years, giving it the advantage over all other memory batteries of having the longest age span. However, because of its US standardization, some of the stories contain words that are less common to UK populations, and need small adaptations. This, of course, interferes to a mild extent with the standardization. Generally it is not a particularly child-friendly battery, with all visual material only being in black and white, which means that younger children in particular are less engaged by it.

Wide-range Assessment of Memory and Learning (WRAML) (Sheslow & Adams, 1990)

The WRAML was one of the earlier batteries to be developed to look comprehensively at children's memory and learning. It was standardized on a stratified sample of 2363 children and young people in the USA and covers an age range of 5–16 years. Reliability in terms of internal consistency and stability appears good. It has been correlated against other measures of memory. These are the memory index from the McCarthy Scales of Children's Ability (MCSCA); the Wechsler Memory Scale—Revised (WMS-R; Wechsler, 1987) and the memory scale of the Stanford–Binet test 4th edn. In addition correlations with the WISC-R and the WRAT-R are also included, and, as predicted, the correlations are moderate.

The battery comprises three indices (verbal, visual and learning). Issues for the UK relate to the American English in two of the three stories, with Story C requiring quite extensive adaptations for English children. Strengths include the sound/symbol learning test, which clinical experience suggests is useful in looking at phoneme–grapheme problems in children with poor reading skills. Another is the "visual" learning subtest already discussed, which is a test of spatial rather than visual learning. However, its simple, bright designs and general format are extremely child-friendly and it is almost always enjoyed by children—a strength in any test. Sentence repetition and a visual span (finger location) are also included.

The WRAML's main failure, however, is its lack of a good measure of delayed memory, and it is best thought of as a battery of immediate memory and learning. The delayed scores are merely calculated by taking a delayed score from the immediate or the last of the learning trial scores. Scores are then compared to broad bands rather than more specific standardized scores. The major problem is that, for example, an immediate score of 10 in stories with a delayed score of 8 (resulting in a score of 2) would be seen as indicating a poorer delayed memory score compared to someone with an immediate and delayed memory score of 3 (score of 0). It is perhaps an indication of forgetting, but still a poor measure.

Rivermead Behavioural Memory Test for Children (5–10 Years) (RBMT-C) (Wilson et al., 1991)

The RBMT-C was developed out of the Rivermead Behavioural Memory Test (RBMT) (Wilson et al., 1985), which in itself can be used with children above the age of 11 years (Wilson et al., 1990). The standardization for the RBMT-C was undertaken in the UK, using a total of 335 children within the normal range of intelligence, and roughly split equally between boys and girls, from three urban, three suburban and three rural schools in the south of England. Scores are converted to standard profile scores, and fall within the normal, borderline or impaired ranges. The battery was correlated with subtests from the BAS and WISC-R. Intelligence and the RBMT-C only correlated in younger but not in older children.

The RBMT-C is made up of a number tasks, including story recall, recognition of faces and pictures, remembering someone's name, a route around a room, instructions to do something on hearing a cue and some orientation questions. Children who fail the RBMT-C will have substantial difficulties in memory in everyday life situations, but falling within the normal range does not exclude memory and learning problems in academic work.

A specific advantage of the RBMT-C (and RBMT) is that there are four parallel versions, which makes it the only one of the tests of children's memory to have this feature. Thus there is an opportunity to use this test serially to monitor early memory recovery in hospital after a head injury etc., or to assess a child at close and regular intervals. This is also one of the rare memory tests that has been standardized in the UK.

NEPSY: A Developmental Neuropsychological Assessment (NEPSY) (Korkman et al., 1998)

The NEPSY is a comprehensive neuropsychological assessment for children aged 3–12 years, and consists of core and expanded assessments, which includes a memory and learning domain. The battery was standardized in the USA using a stratified sample of 1000 cases in 10 age groups. As with the CMS, TOMAL and WRAML, the sample was matched to the US population census, taking into account sex, race/ethnicity, geographical region and parent education.

The test was correlated with the WPPSI-R, WISC-III and WIAT. In addition, correlations were carried out with the Benton Neuropsychological Tests (BNT), the Multilingual Aphasia Examination (MAE; Benton & Hamsher, 1989) and the CMS, with moderate to high correlations with the last of these.

The benefit of this memory and learning index is that it can be compared to the other domains or indices of the NEPSY, namely attention and executive functioning, language, sensorimotor functions and visuospatial processing. This is a distinct advantage compared to the other batteries, as such comparisons cannot be made on a similar sample. For children aged 3–4 years, only two core subtests are used in the memory domain, narrative recall and sentence repetition, with supplementary tests comparing free and cued recall. For the older group (5–12 years), subtests include memory for faces, and for names, narrative memory and sentence repetition. There are supplementary subtests for delayed scores for memory for faces and names, as well as list learning.

The pictures in facial memory subtests are printed in black and white, and pen and ink drawings are used for the memory of names, which can be less attractive to children. However, a major disadvantage in the NEPSY is that there is no delayed recall of the story.

Other Tests of Memory and Learning

Recall of Designs

- *Rey–Osterreith complex figure* (Osterreith, 1944; Rey, 1941). This can be used with children and the Meyers & Meyers (1995) version has good norms for children from the age of 4–16 years. With immediate recall, delayed recall and delayed recognition, it is an extremely useful test to look at children's ability to recall complex abstract visual material. Observations of the way children copy the figure can give clues as to why they may find recall difficult. Those that draw it piecemeal or first draw the outline, thus distorting the general figure, tend to have greater difficulty in recall than those who draw the main component parts. This may suggest that poor performance is due to weak organizational and planning skills as much as recall *per se*.
- *Benton Visual Retention Test* (Benton & Sivan, 1995). There are norms for children in this immediate recall test, which is simpler than the Rey and gives both error and accuracy scores.
- *BAS-2*. There are three explicit memory tests in the BAS-2. These are Visual Recognition, Recall of Designs and Recall of Pictures, and, unlike the above two tests, they have obviously been standardized on a stratified sample of British children. The Visual

Recognition test has black and white drawings of real objects in a single category (e.g. vehicles, chairs/stools or shells, etc.) which are exposed for 5 s. Children then have to identify them from a larger array. The advantage of this subtest is that the age range is wide (2.6–17.11 years) and it is relatively nonthreatening to younger or nervous children, as they merely have to respond by pointing. Recall of Designs is, in many ways, similar to the Benton. The extended age range is 5–17.11 years. Recall of pictures comprises a sheet with 20 coloured pictures of objects (e.g. hat, bird, clock, etc.), which is exposed for 40 s. Children then have 60 s to name as many pictures as they can recall. After this the sheet is exposed on two further occasions, but this time for only 20 s, and they have only 40 s in which to recall the pictures. The immediate score is the total number of pictures recalled on all three trials. After these three trials, children are given a grid and asked to place 20 cards with the pictures (in a specific order) on the grid in the same layout as the stimulus. There is a delay of 10–30 min when they are again asked to recall the pictures and then place the cards on the grid, as before. The advantage with these tests is that they are part of a general ability assessment against which to compare problems, but the failure to include story recall in the battery is a real weakness in terms of assessing memory. In addition, despite the learning trials in Picture Recall, there has been no standardization of the learning curve, which is a disappointment.

Test Variables—The Difficulty of Comparisons

A comprehensive assessment of memory in children should always include, at least, story recall and recall of designs, but most core batteries include facial recognition, spatial memory and word lists in some form or another. Where it is possible to make a choice, it is worthwhile considering the different specific test variables that could influence results. This is especially so when different tests have been used over time with a particular child, as what appears to be a change in memory functioning may in fact relate to specific test variables with regard to the stimulus, the timing, and to the way in which a response is elicited. Such differences are, of course, over and above differences in the standardization of the various assessment batteries. What follows is a breakdown of the five assessment batteries described, looking at these four components to highlight differences.

Story Recall

Each of the five assessment batteries includes story or narrative recall. The Oxford stories (Bearsdworth and Bishop, 1994) are also included as one of the early tests to be standardized on English children, and, like the RBMT-C, they have multiple versions. However, as a quick view of Table 31.1 will show, there is some variation between what is demanded of children in each of the six story tests. The amount children are required to recall varies from one to three stories. In the NEPSY there is no delayed recall, but in the CMS, WRAML and TOMAL there is a 30 min interval before delay. RBMT-C has an interval of 15–20 min and the Oxford stories 45 min.

It is often the qualitative way by which children recall stories that gives important clues as to how their memory deficit may affect them functionally, and which may, in some cases, hint at the underlying neuropathology. For instance, stories may be recalled generally, with

Table 31.1 Story recall

Test	Stories to recall (n)	Versions (Nos)	Versions (years)	Age range (years)	Delay to recall (min)	Prompts	Delayed version	Detail/ theme	Recognition
TOMAL	3	1–3	(5–8)	5–19	30	Name Story	Yes	D	No
		2–4	(9–11)						
		3–5	(12–19)						
CMS	2	1–2	(5–8)	5–16	30	Name Story	Yes	D/T	Yes
		3–4	(9–12)						
		5–6	(12–16)						
WRAML	2	1 & 2	(6–8)	6–16	30	Name Story	Yes	D	Yes
		2 & 3	(9–16)						
RBMT-C	1	4		4–10	15–20	Picture	Yes	D	Yes
NEPSY	1	1		3–12	N/A	Cues IM	No	D	Yes (IM)
Oxford	2	3		8–12	45	Name Story	No	D	Yes

TOMAL, Test of Memory and Learning; CMS, Children's Memory Scale; WRAML, Wide Range Assessment of Memory and Learning; RBMT-C, Rivermead Behavioural Memory Test—Children; NEPSY, A Developmental Neuropsychological Assessment: Oxford, Beardsworth and Bishop (1994).

children remembering the theme quite well but being unable to recollect exact details. Other children will recall the beginning and/or the end word-for-word, but will have failed to understand the story because they have been unable recall the middle section at all. This may lead to poor delayed recall. Furthermore, others will repeat small sections, or just say a few of the key words but in no specific order, in a way that does not hang together semantically. Only the CMS has a standardized measure of both the detailed and thematic recall. Depending on the age of the child, it can be reasonable to hypothesize that, if the impairment in recall is disorganized, it is affected by inefficient storage or retrieval strategies and thus may be affected by frontal pathology.

Aldrich & Wilson (1991) found that prompts with younger children (i.e. 5–7 year-old) affected recall considerably. Beardsworth & Bishop (1994) also reported that, although children may have difficulties in recalling stories, cues (the name of the story) enhanced recall, suggesting that this is often a retrieval rather than a storage problem. Beardsworth & Bishop (1994) go on to argue that cued recall is a better measure of delayed memory than free recall, and point out that failure to recall after a prompt may indicate a serious problem with memory.

The TOMAL does not have a recognition trial at all, but in the CMS and WRAML stories there is a recognition trial which is scored separately from delayed recall. The RBMT-C uniquely provides a picture while the story is being read, and this is used as a prompt in recall, while the others only name the story. In addition, there are differences in how delayed recall and recognition trials are scored. In the NEPSY, the immediate recall and recognition scores are combined in the core battery (although separated as supplementary scores) and in the RBMT-C the immediate and delayed recall combines free recall with the prompted scores. The way in which recognition questions are posed also differs, e.g. in the CMS children are asked whether or not a statement about the story is true, in the WRAML they are given a forced choice, and in the NEPSY and RBMT-C Stories they are asked more open questions (e.g. "What was the name of the dog ?"). Beardsworth & Bishop (1994) raised the issue of how different types of retrieval cues might affect recall, and the question still seems to be unanswered. Temple (1997, p. 98) suggests that the position of questions in a question series may affect performance, which could be because there is either a better initial organization of the story structure or because there is more rapid decay of information.

Word Lists, Paired Words and Verbal Selective Reminding

List learning, etc., is the other major verbal component of most memory batteries. The advantage of word lists and selective reminding tasks compared to word pairs is that it is possible to see whether children begin to impose their own structure or strategy in recalling words. In the case of the Californian Verbal Learning Test—Children's Version (CVLT-C; Dean et al., 1994), it is also possible to see whether they make spontaneous use of given categories once these have been suggested to them in a learning trial. Failure to structure and use a strategy to help recall, and instead randomly recall words in any order over trials, may suggest a frontal component contributing to a memory problem. The CVLT-C allows for comparison both serial-order and semantic strategies, but this can be considered in any list-learning task.

It is interesting to see how each of the five measures listed in Table 31.2 show that no two have exactly the same parameters. The RBMT-C does not have a list-learning component. The WRAML has word lists with a recognition trial, the CMS and CVLT-C have interference tasks in the form of a List B but the WRAML and TOMAL do not. Word pairs in the CMS and TOMAL have three or four trials respectively, but in the former lists are longer for both the younger and older children, and the latter does not have a recognition trial. On the other hand, TOMAL and CMS use a verbal selective reminding subtest with a recognition trial, but there is no formal way of comparing long-term retrieval, long term store and consistent long-term retrieval, as in the original Buschke & Fuld (1974) selective reminding task. One of the disappointments of the CMS are that word-pairs are included in the core battery making up the general memory index, but list learning is only a supplementary test. The number of learning trials for list-learning differs in each of the four batteries, ranging from three to six.

Facial Recognition

Four of the assessment batteries, but not the WRAML, include a facial recognition task, but it is in this task above all others where there are major differences in both presentation and response variables. Table 31.3 illustrates this very clearly.

The number of faces for recognition ranges from five to 16. The CMS has large coloured faces of people (12 for younger children and 16 for the older group), presented one at a time at a fast rate of one every 2 s. In the other three batteries, there are black and white photographs of faces, either small, (NEPSY and TOMAL) or large (RBMT-C). In the NEPSY and the RBMT-C they are presented one at a time. In the TOMAL there is an increase from 1 to 12 over subsequent trials, but a response is elicited after each trial, rather than at the end of the total exposure. Exposure in the NEPSY is 5 s for each picture, in the RBMT-C for 5 s, during which time the child is asked to identify the sex and whether it is an old or young face, and in the TOMAL 5–20 s, depending on the number of faces exposed at any one time.

It will be seen that the speed of presentation and number of faces to be remembered differs quite considerably across batteries. Consequently, memory capacity and speed of

Table 31.2 Word lists/paired words/selective reminding

Test	Type	Words/pairs n (years)	Learning trials	Interference list	Time to delay (min)	Delayed recall			Recognition trial
						Free	Verbal cue	Visual cue	
CMS	Word pairs	10 (5–8) 14 (9+)	3	No	30	yes	No	No	Yes
	Word lists	10 (5–8) 14 (9+)	4	Yes	30	yes	No	No	Yes
NEPSY	Word lists	15 (9+)	5	Yes	30	yes	No	No	No
TOMAL	Word pairs	6 (5–8) 8 (9+)	4	No	N/A	No	No	No	No
	Selective reminding	8 (5–8) 12 (9+)	8	yes	30	Yes	Yes	Yes	Yes
WRAML	Word lists	(6–8) (9+)	3	No	30	Yes	No	No	No
RBMT-C	Not available								
CVLT-C	Word lists	15 (5–16)	5	Yes	Short and 20	Yes	Category	No	Yes

CMS, Children's Memory Scale; NEPSY, A Developmental Neuropsychological Assessment; TOMAL, Test of Memory and Learning; WRAML, Wide Range Assessment of Memory and Learning; RBMT-C, Rivermead Behavioural Memory Test—Children; CVLT-C, Californian Verbal Learning Test—Child Version.

Table 31.3 Facial recognition

Test	Presentation					Response			
	B/W or colour	Size	Type	Exposure(s)	Single/multiple	Learning trials	Y/N Ind.	Mult. Choice	Delayed
CMS	Colour	Large	Photo	2	One at a time	No	Yes		After 30 mins
NEPSY	B/W	Small	Drawing	5	One of three	3	No	One of three	After 30 mins
TOMAL	B/W	Small	Photo	Varies	1–12 rising	No	No	One 3–30	After 30 mins
RBMT-C	B/W	Large	Photo	5 s while child identifies sex/age	One at a time	No	Yes		Not available
WRAML	Not available								

CMS, Children's Memory Scale; NEPSY, A Developmental Neuropsychological Assessment; TOMAL, Test of Memory and Learning; RBMT-C; Rivermead Behavioural Memory Test—Children; WRAML, Wide Range Assessment of Memory and Learning.

information processing are crucial variables, with some children failing the CMS subtest if they take in the information slowly or if they become distracted once presentation begins. In the TOMAL children may use the strategy of trying to remember just a few faces each time when a larger number are exposed simultaneously, rather than scan them all quickly. Thus, they control the amount of time they may take on looking at individual faces, a strategy that cannot be used in other tests.

Second, the recognition trials are all quite different. Both the CMS and RBMT-C require children to make a decision as to whether they have seen a single face before (or whether they were asked to remember it; CMS), but in the NEPSY they are asked to decide which of three faces they have seen before. In all three they wait until all the faces have been exposed before being asked to recall any. The TOMAL, however, requires children to recall which of a number of faces they have seen immediately after exposure, but in the last immediate recall trial, this amounts to 12 faces to find in an array of 30. All but the RBMT-C (which has a short delay between presentation and test) have delayed trials (30 min later).

Spatial Recall

Finally in this analysis of different forms of purportedly similar tests, it is worth looking at spatial recall. As has already been mentioned in this chapter, both the TOMAL and the WRAML have subtests called "visual recall" that are really spatial memory tests. Again, each assessment battery varies in terms of how spatial memory is measured. The NEPSY has no spatial memory task. In the RBMT-C, children are asked to watch as the examiner walks round the room describing the route, and they then have to follow the route as well as remember to pick up a message and leave it in a specific place. There is a delayed trial after about 15–20 min. This task is unique in terms of its face validity, but in fact there are usually not many different options where a child may make an error, and clinically it would seem that errors tend to be in relation to the sequence of the route.

Table 31.4 shows that in CMS, TOMAL and WRAML tasks differ in a number of subtle ways. "Dot location" makes up part of the core battery in the CMS, with children having to place dots (6–8) on a grid after an exposure of 5 s. There are three learning trials and a delayed trial after 30 min. Clinical experience suggests that it is an easy test to administer and, coming at the beginning of the battery, apparently not very challenging to children, who often seem unaware how poorly they do if they find this difficult. There is a supplementary test (Picture Location) without learning trials, where children look at coloured pictures placed on a page for 2 s and they have to point to where they were on a grid. Location memory is also included in a Family Pictures test where, after exposure, children have to locate members of a family in a quadrant of a picture as well as identify who they were and what they were doing.

TOMAL has a selective nonverbal reminding task (to parallel the verbal selective reminding task), where children watch the examiner point to one of five dots in each of 6–8 grids, which they then have to repeat. Errors are corrected and there are seven more learning trials as well as a delayed trial after 30 min. Of all they spatial memory tasks, this subtest would clinically seem to be the one most likely to lead to examiner error, particularly if children respond very quickly. Children can also become dispirited if they find it difficult, and may give up quickly. A separate Memory for Location test is also part of the nonverbal

Table 31.4 Spatial recall

Test	Task	Versions	No. of stimuli n (years)	Exposure time (s)	No. of Trials	B/W or colour	Time to delay (min)
CMS	Dot location (all dots on grid)	1	6 (5–8) 8 (9+)	5	3	Blue	30 min
	Picture location (grid)	1	1–5 (5–8) 1–8 (9+)	2	1	Col	N/A
TOMAL	"Visual" selective reminding (1 of 5 dots in small grid)	1	6 (5–8) 8 (9+)	6 8	8	B/W	30 min
	Memory for location	1	1–9 (5–8)	5	1	B/W	N/A
WRAML	"Visual" learning (covered) grid with each pattern exposed separately	1	12 (5–8) 14 (9+)	2 each	3	Col.	30 min
RBMT-C	Route round room (child observes examiner walk round room)	4	5	20–30	1	N/A	15–20 s
NEPSY	Not available						

CMS, Children's Memory Scale; TOMAL, Test of Memory and Learning; WRAML, Wide Range Assessment of Memory and Learning; RBMT-C, Rivermead Behavioural Memory Test—Children; NEPSY, A Developmental Neuropsychological Assessment.

memory index, with children having to point to a grid after a short exposure of up to nine dots on a 4 × 4 grid.

In the WRAML "visual" selective learning task, 12–14 brightly coloured abstract patterns on a 4 × 4 grid are exposed one at a time before being covered. Children then have to recall the position of an individual pattern. After their response, the target pattern is shown. There are three learning and one delayed trial. Even when children are doing poorly on this task, they seem to enjoy it and can be motivated to continue, even if they make multiple errors. As with the other delayed trials in the WRAML, the delayed scoring strategy is weak.

Summary

It will be obvious from the above discussions that comparisons of a child's performance on different occasions, using the same or another test or test battery, can cause major problems in interpretation in terms of both stability and sensitivity to change over time. If the same test is used, where there is no alternative version, it is likely that there will be practice effects, which will enhance performance and hide continuing weaknesses or failure to develop as expected. Using another battery gives rise to three problems. First, there is the issue of the *different standardization procedures* and the *different populations* upon which the standardization was carried out. Second, despite superficially appearing similar, the *composition of the core index* in different batteries may differ enormously. Third, the above analysis of four core subtests of the major memory batteries for children (narrative recall, word lists, facial recognition and spatial recall) has indicated that making comparisons between test performance on different batteries is, if not virtually impossible, extremely difficult, due to the *multiple differences in subtest variables*. Where there is no alternative, interpretation should be qualified and the problems in interpretation should be made explicit.

These issues also underline the importance of including a wide range of nontest data in understanding an individual child's assessment, e.g. poor performance on facial memory is not always consistent with parents' or teacher's evidence. This may be because of differences in the ability to recognize familiar and unfamiliar faces. Neither do some children seem to be aware they have a problem, although they may have learnt ways to compensate for problems with facial recognition of which they are unaware. It may also be that facial memory is not a problem but there are difficulties with a lower level of processing. Thus, failure in e.g. the CMS, where faces are only exposed for 2 s, may be related to slow speed of processing rather than in a problem with facial memory *per se*. Consequently, the final question to ask in all assessments of memory is related to the ecological validity of the assessment and results in the light of what is else is known about the child.

ISSUES IN THE MANAGEMENT OF MEMORY AND LEARNING PROBLEMS IN CHILDREN

In devising interventions for memory problems in children, the need for generalization of skills beyond the specific training task, and the continuation of improvements after the intervention stops, are crucial outcomes. Ylvisaker & Gioia (1998) have argued that in managing memory and other problems following traumatic brain injury, assessment and management needs to be theory-based, ongoing, contextualized, collaborative and on a hypothesis-testing basis. This approach is not exclusive to head injury and should apply to all children with neurological damage. Consequently, following on from comprehensive interviews, observations and psychometric assessment, a crucial question to ask is how the findings functionally relate to the child's problem. Some of this information will have already been gleaned from clinical interviews and reports, but further hypotheses based on formal assessments can be tested out when reporting back to parents and schools.

In the space allowed here, it is not possible to do more than briefly describe in outline of the kind of interventions that are possible. A number of programmes included in the rehabilitation and management of adults are likely to be appropriate in working with children, particularly older children and adolescents, provided that interventions are suitably adapted to the child's age and level of development.

One major difference compared to adults is the long-term impact of memory problems on children's education and their failure to gain knowledge that will enable them to live independently. There is evidence, however, that children with bilateral hippocampal but no other cortical damage have intact semantic memory and can attain reasonable knowledge in school (Vargha-Khadem et al., 1997), although they still have major problems with episodic memory. Wider CNS involvement leading to both semantic and episodic memory problems can have a profound effect. Adults with an acquired memory loss *may* be able to access the basic information and skills needed for everyday life, which they had acquired and used premorbidly. For children with acquired loss of both episodic and semantic memory, particularly younger children, the effect of problems with memory, and particularly learning and integrating new information into what they know already, may be very debilitating in attempts to add to their knowledge base. This may mean that the effects of memory problems only emerge slowly as children "grow into a deficit" (Mateer et al., 1997). Because they may be able to access premorbid skills and knowledge, initially they may appear to perform well enough for the problem to be thought negligible in school. However, their failure to learn becomes apparent as they slowly slip increasingly behind. These difficulties will be in addition to the daily effects of any episodic memory problems.

Ylvisaker et al. (1998) propose eight intervention premises as the foundation for rehabilitation of memory in children and adolescents following head injury (pp. 182–183):

- Problems with organization and memory are common after traumatic brain injury and have long-term effects.
- Different types of injury can effect organization and memory differentially.
- Organization and memory are intimately related.
- Normal development of organization and memory give insight into how intervention strategies may be effective.
- There are many approaches, all of which are appropriate at some time for some individuals in relation to specific goals.
- Everyday functional activities are the preferred context for intervention.
- Cognitive rehabilitation is collaborative.
- Problems with organization and memory are often misdiagnosed, resulting in inappropriate interventions.

This approach is relevant however memory problems are acquired.

Interventions

Children with memory and learning problems may be helped through a variety of interventions, ranging from specific individual strategies to more general management approaches. These are: (a) informing parents, teachers and, where appropriate, the child of what the problem is; (b) arranging that clinical reports go forward to the Local Educational Authority to get extra help in school and special conditions in examinations; (c) external memory aids and environmental adaptations; (d) direct instruction; and (e) internal memory strategies.

1. *Information and explanation.* A major component in the assessment of memory and learning in children is in informing and advising parents and teachers of the functional implications of having specific memory and learning difficulties, how they affect a child now, and how they can best be managed in the future. Although it might be expected that most parents and children do not understand brain–behaviour links, teachers would also appear to have little in their training that prepares them for working with children with such difficulties, and this may mean that basic information about the neuroanatomical underpinnings of memory and memory problems needs to be explained. Consequently, initial interventions with schools and families, may be in explaining the neuropsychological basis of a child's specific problem, and dispelling any possible misconceptions, e.g.:

   > *Case*: A teacher complained that, 2 years after he had undergone a left temporal lobectomy for intractable epilepsy, J was still forgetting what he was told, despite the resolution of his epilepsy and being off all medication. It was necessary to explain that the surgery, which had very successfully resolved the epilepsy, had removed that part of J's brain involved in verbal memory, and that her difficulties and awkward behaviour arising from this were directly related to the neuropathology.

   Although such simple information may appear a low-level intervention, helping to explain the aetiology and reframing a problem may in itself make a considerable difference to teaching approaches and attitudes, and thus to children with these difficulties. If they are old enough to be part of the explanation, this knowledge may also enhance children's self-esteem, as they may realise that they are not "stupid" as they may have felt, but have a specific difficulty for which they can receive some help. This information may lead them to become more involved and adhere to rehabilitation interventions, particularly when they are older. More particularly, teachers and schools can begin to appreciate that if a child can remember some things but not others, this may not be due to laziness, lack of motivation or oppositional behaviour, and consequently the need for external adaptations and adapted teaching methods, etc., can be accepted and subsequently planned and implemented. Parents, too, benefit from careful explanation, understanding that their child is not necessarily being naughty or careless when he/she loses clothes and equipment at school, or repeatedly forgets what he/she has been told to do.

2. *Contribution to statements of special educational need and special concessions in examinations.* A second way in which a child can benefit from a careful neuropsychological assessment is if the report becomes part of the contribution to a child's Statement of Special Educational Needs. Not only can the above explanations of the aetiology and functional implications be used in drawing up a child's Individual Educational Plan in

school, but children may be able to get extra help in the form of one-to-one support in the classroom to help cope with specific problems. Second, this kind of information may be used to request extra time in examinations, so that children can reread the questions more than once if they begin to forget what they have read, as well as track back through their own written answers a number of times if they have forgotten what they have put down already.

3. *External Adaptations and Memory Aids.* As the rate of information technology develops, there are an increasing number of everyday devices that older children and adolescents can be trained to use to help them compensate for poor memory. Diaries, schedules and notebooks in which to write down anything that has to be remembered are simple compensatory methods, but some older children feel it is unacceptable to use them, and there is always the need for a bag in which to carry them, which may also be felt to be inappropriate.

Electronic organizers, however, have more kudos with older children and adolescents, and they are now easily available in the high street stores. They can act as a diary and note pad, and be programmed to act as an alerting system with a bleep. Bleeper watches with message dials are also available, which can be programmed via a link-up with personal computers. In addition, there are small electronic memo recorders, which can store up to 60–100 messages. These are probably more appropriate for older children and adolescents to record brief messages about something they have to do in the future, or information to pass on later.

If problems relate to episodic rather than procedural memory, then children can learn how to programme these devices themselves, but training is needed in using external memory aids whatever these may be (Sohlberg and Mateer, 1989). However, instruction may need to be over extensive periods. With electronic devices, the programming is more likely to be carried out by parents or teachers for younger compared with older children and adolescents, so instruction in this should include everyone who is involved. If children are to use any of these devices effectively, then teachers and parents need to be committed to, and consistent in, supporting the children and ensure that they have the device, whether it is a bleeper watch or memory book, with them at all times. This is why it is so important to assess parents' and teachers' understanding of the problem, and to inform and advise them of rehabilitation strategies, for without their support any intervention is likely to fail. Physical attachment of the device to a child, either by a chain or string to clothing, or carried in a shoulder bag, or pouch, or attached round the waist, may prevent the external device being mislaid, which is not an uncommon problem.

In severe cases of memory problems, less complex support may be extremely helpful. Children may need to have drawers or cupboards labelled, daily schedules and notices to remind them of the order of carrying out basic tasks, such as the morning routine, etc. More frequently, however, they may need adaptations, such as written homework instructions, questions and worksheets and a home–school diary, maps around the school and clear timetables. Families and teachers may need to ensure that routines are set up to help in relearning old and learning new tasks, although this can be particularly difficult in school, where there are many demands on teaching staff in large classes.

4. *Direct Instruction and Compensatory Strategies.* Errorless learning, first developed by Terrace (1963, 1966) and then used by Sidman & Stoddard (1967) for children with developmental learning disabilities, as well as fading behavioural cues, have both

been strategies used effectively in teaching children with learning difficulties for many years. Glisky et al. (1986) used a similar method called "the Method of Vanishing Cues". These methods have been more recently adapted for rehabilitation, e.g. by Wilson et al. (1994; see Chapter 30, this volume). This method ensures that children do not guess at solutions, as if wrong they can find it very difficult to unlearn the error. Using behavioural methods, skills can be taught by example, guiding, verbal instruction and, finally prompts. In addition, teaching and giving instructions and feedback in a simple, positive and unambiguous manner can be helpful, as well as emphasizing what is important. Asking children to repeat what has been said will enhance learning. Mateer et al. (1997) list task analysis, modelling, shaping and positive reinforcement of success consistently over long periods as adjuncts to the rehabilitation process. For further detailed suggestions for a full range of compensatory strategies, see Ylvisaker et al. (1998).

5. *Training Internal Memory Strategies.* There is little evidence that drilling or practice can restore memory, but some strategy training has been tried. Bjorklund et al. (1997) have carried out an extensive review on how and why children fail to benefit from training in strategies devised to improve their memory, or at best only experience minimal benefit, termed as utilization deficiencies. Although the children in these studies did not have memory problems *per se*, the review is pertinent in considering how children's ability to access different strategies successfully develops with age and suggests why training children in using strategies may fail. Thus, the importance of careful observations of how a child goes about completing memory tests, in order to see whether or not they are using a strategy spontaneously, is critical. As these authors point out, many children carry out a task but achieve it via different route to the one in which they were trained.

   Mateer et al. (1997) point out that there is considerable evidence to suggest that learning internal strategies to enhance memory has limited success, whatever the strategy used. Harris (1996) has looked at "thinking aloud" or verbal rehearsal to help list-learning in children with head injuries. Her results suggested that strategies differ between those children with closed head injury and those without. The severely injured (but not the mildly injured or the control group) showed not only impaired verbal recall but also inefficient rehearsal strategies, poor self-monitoring and a weaker judgement in deciding which strategy might be more effective (metamemory). Bjorklund et al. (1997) propose that memory strategy training in normal children was more effective if children were given a single rather than multiple strategies with task variables, including sorting, clustering and rehearsal, and training variables covering verbal instruction, demonstration and rationale. Their review indicated that a number of child variables also needed to be considered when considering training strategies, such as level of intelligence, age, insight, temperament, motivation and underlying pathology. In addition, children may have difficulties in integrating strategies, shifting from one strategy to another, or inhibiting the use of a previously ineffective strategy, which relate to a lack of insight and consequently poor adherence to strategy use. Such difficulties may be related to frontal lobe pathology, which is frequently present following head injury and which is closely linked to memory problems. In general, however, the lack of support for training internal strategies is likely to be due to many factors, including the fact that the stratetgies are often taught in abstract or at a very specific level and not within context, so that generalization does not take place and any benefit quickly fades after training ends. It should be remembered that internal strategies lead to faster learning for specific pieces of information. Most people with memory problems do not use them spontaneously and maybe we should expect this. For certain things, however, and with help from parents/teachers/therapists, internal strategies can be helpful in teaching some useful everyday information.

SUMMARY AND CONCLUSIONS

Management and rehabilitation of memory can be effective if appropriate and individualized programmes are set up which take into account the many variables discussed above. As in all rehabilitation, specific goals need to be set, put into operation and monitored, with clear steps from the introduction of a programme to its final achievement. As Ylvisaker et al. (1998) recommend, devising programmes and managing their implementations should be within everyday contexts, and be a collaborative venture if they are to be effective. Consequently, careful assessment, not just of the memory problems but of the child generally, as well as his/her environment, is crucial. In addition, the resources and the restrictions of those who are most likely to carry out the management of programmes, in other words families and teachers, should be assessed and understood to achieve the best possible outcome.

REFERENCES

Aldrich, F. & Wilson, B.A. (1991). Rivermead Behavioural Memory Test for Children: a preliminary evaluation. *British Journal of Clinical Psychology*, **30**, 161–168.

Bayley, N. (1993). *Bayley Scales of Infant Development*, 2nd edn. San Antonio, TX: Psychological Corporation/Harcourt Brace & Co.

Beardsworth, E. & Bishop, D. (1994). Assessment of long-term verbal memory in children. *Memory*, **2**, 129–148.

Benton, A.L. & Hamsher, K. de S. (1989). *Multilingual Aphasia Examination*. Iowa City, IO: AJA Associates.

Benton, A.L. & Sivan, A. (1995). *Benton Visual Retention Test*, 5th edn. San Antonio, TX: Psychological Corporation/Harcourt Brace & Co.

Berger, M. & Middleton, J.A. (1995). Figure presented at talk on Assessment of Memory, Charney Manor, Oxford, November.

Bjorklund, D.G. & Douglas, R.N. (1997). The development of memory strategies. In N. Cowan (ed.), *The Development of Memory in Childhood* (pp. 201–246). Hove: Psychology Press.

Bjorklund, D.F., Miller, P.H., Coyle, T.R. & Slawinski, J.L. (1997). Instructing children to use memory strategies: Evidence of utilization deficiencies in memory training studies. *Developmental Review*, **17**, 411–441.

Blass, E.M. (1999). The ontogeny of human infant face recognition: orugustatory, visual and social influences. In P. Rochat (ed.), *Early Social Cognition. Understanding Others in the First Months of Life* (pp. 35–66). London: Erlbaum.

Boll, T. (1993). *Children's Category Test*. San Antonio, TX: Psychological Corporation/Harcourt Brace & Co.

Broman, M., Rose, A.L., Hotson, G. & Casey, C.M. (1997). Severe anterograde amnesia with onset in childhood as a result of anoxic encephalopathy. *Brain*, **120**, 417–433.

Buschke, H. & Fuld, P.A. (1974). Evaluating storage, retention and retrieval in disordered memory and learning. *Neurology*, **11**, 1019–1025.

Canterbury, R. & Yule, W. (1997). The effects on children of road accidents. In M. Mitchell (ed.), *The Aftermath of Road Accidents* (pp. 59–69). London: Routledge.

Casalini, C., Brizzolara, D., Cavallaro, M.C. & Cipriani, P. (1999). Developmental dysmnesia: a case report. *Cortex*, **35**, 713–727.

CCTB Macmillan/McGraw Hill (1988). *Californian Achievement Test*. Monterey, C.A: Macmillan/ McGraw Hill.

Cohen, M. (1997). *Children's Memory Scale*. San Antonio, TX: Psychological Corporation/Harcourt Brace & Co.

Cowan, N. (ed.) (1997). *The Development of Memory in Childhood*. Hove: Psychology Press.

Dean, C.D., Kramer, J.H., Kaplan, E. & Ober, B.A. (1994). *California Verbal Learning Test— Children's Version*. San Antonio, TX: Psychological Corporation Harcourt Brace & Co.

Elliot, C. (1990). *Differential Ability Scales*. San Antonio, TX: The Psychological Corporation/Harcourt Brace & Co.

Elliot, C.D., Murray, D.J. & Pearson, L.S. (1993). *British Ability Scales*. Windsor: NFER Nelson.

Fletcher, J.M. & Taylor, H.G. (1984). Neuropsychological approaches to children: Towards a developmental neuropsychology. *Journal of Clinical Neuropsychology*, **6**, 39–56.

Glisky, E.L., Schacter, D.L. & Tulving, E. (1986). Computer learning by memory impaired patients: Acquisition and retention of complex knowledge. *Neuropsychologia*, **24**, 313–328.

Harris, J.R. (1996). Verbal rehearsal and memory in children with closed head injury: a quantitative and qualitative analysis. *Journal of Communication Disorders*, **29**, 79–93.

Heaton, R.K., Chelune, G.J., Talley, J.L. et al. (1993). *Wisconsin Card Sorting Test*. Odessa, FL: Psychological Assessment Resources.

Hulme, C. & MacKenzie, S. (1992). *Working Memory and Severe Learning Difficulties*. Hove: Erlbaum.

Jastak, J.F. & Wilkinson, G.S. (1993). *Wide Range Achievement Test*, 3rd edn. Wilmington: Jastak Associates.

Joyner, M.H. & Kurtz-Costes, B. (1997). Metamemory development. In N. Cowan (ed.), *The Development of Memory in Childhood* (pp. 275–301). Hove: Psychology Press.

Kaufman, A.S. (1994). *Intelligent Testing with the WISC-III*. New York: Wiley.

Kaufman, A.S. & Kaufman, R.W. (1984). *Kaufman Assessment Battery for Children*. Circle Pines, MN: American Guidance Service.

Korkman, M., Kirk, U. & Kemp, S. (1998). *NEPSY : A Developmental Neuropsychological Assessment*. San Antonio, TX: Psychological Corporation/Harcourt Brace & Co.

Levin, H.S., Ewing-Cobbs, L. & Eisenberg, H.M. (1995). Neurobehavioral outcome of pediatric closed head injury. In S.H. Broman & M.E. Michel (eds), *Traumatic Brain Injury in Children* (pp. 70–94). Oxford: Oxford University Press.

Lezak, M.D. (1995). Neuropsychological Assessment, 3rd edn. New York: Oxford University Press.

Little, A.H., Lipsitt, L.P. & Rovee-Collier, C.K. (1984). Classical conditioning and rentention of the infant's Evelid response: effects of age and interstimulus interval. *Journal of Experimental Child Psychology*, **37**(3), 512–524.

Mateer, C.A., Kerns, K.A. & Eso, K.L. (1997). Management of attention and memory disorders following traumatic brain injury. In E.D. Bigler, E. Clarke & J.E. Farmer (eds), *Childhood Traumatic Brain Injury: Diagnosis, Assessment and Intervention*. Austin, TX: Pro-Ed.

McCarthy, D. (1972). *McCarthy Scales of Children's Abilities*. San Antonio, TX: Psychological Corporation/Harcourt Brace & Co.

Meyers, J.E. & Meyers, K.R. (1995). *Rey Complex Figure Test and Recognition Trial: Professional Manual*. Odessa, FL: Psychological Assessment Resources Inc.

Mistry, J. (1998). The development of remembering in cultural context. In N. Cowan (ed.), *The Development of Memory in Childhood*. Hove: Psychology Press.

Osterreith, P.A. (1944). Le test de copie d'une figure complexe. *Archives de Psychologie*, **30**, 206–356.

Rey, A. (1941). L'examen psychologique dans le cas d'encephalopathie traumatique. *Archives de Psychologie*, **28**, 286–340.

Reynolds, C.R. & Bigler, E.D. (1994). *Test of Memory and Learning*. Austin, TX: Pro-Ed.

Rovee-Collier, C. & Gerhardstein, P. (1997). The development of infant memory. In N. Cowan (ed.), *The Development of Memory in Childhood* (pp. 5–40). Hove: Psychology Press.

Rovee-Collier, C., Sullivan, M.W., Enright, M.K. et al. (1980). Reactivation of infant memory. *Science*, **208**, 1159–1161.

Said, J.A., Waters, B.G.H., Cousens, P. & Stevens, M.M. (1989). Neuropsychological sequelae of central nervous system prophylaxis in survivors of childhood acute lymphoblastic leukaemia. *Journal of Consulting and Clinical Psychology*, **57**, 251–256.

Semmel, E., Wiig, E. & Secord, W. (1995). *Clinical Evaluation of Language Fundamentals*, 3rd edn. San Antonio, TX: Psychological Corporation/Harcourt Brace & Co.

Sheslow, D. & Adams, W. (1990). *Wide Range Assessment of Memory and Learning*. Delaware: Jastak Associates, Inc.

Sidman, M. & Stoddard, L.T. (1967). The effectiveness of fading in programming simultaneous form discrimination for retarded children. *Journal of Experimental Analysis of Behavior*, **10**, 3–15.

Sohlberg, M.M. & Mateer, C.A. (1989). Training use of compensatory memory books: a three stage behavioral approach. *Journal of Clinical and Experimental Neuropsychology*, **11**, 871–891.

Temple, C. (1997). *Developmental Cognitive Neuropsychology*. Hove: Psychology Press.

Terrace, H.S. (1963). Discrimination learning with and without "errors". *Journal of Experimental Analysis of Behavior*, **6**, 1–27.

Terrace, H.S. (1966). Stimulus Control. In W.K. Honig (ed.), *Operant Behavior; Areas of Reserach and Application*. New York: Appleton-Century-Crofts.

Vargha-Khadem, F., Gadian, D.G., Watkins, K.E. et al. (1997). Differential effects of early hippocampal pathology on episodic and semantic memory. *Science*, **277**, 376–380.

Walton, G.E., Bower, N.J.A. & Bower, T.G.R. (1992). Recognition of familiar faces by newborns. *Infant Behavior and Development*, **15**, 265–269.

Wechsler, D. (1974). *Wechsler Intelligence Scale for Children—Revised*. San Antonio, TX: Psychological Corporation/Harcourt Brace & Co.

Wechsler, D. (1987). *Wechsler Memory Scale—Revised*. San Antonio, TX: Psychological Corporation/Harcourt Brace & Co.

Wechsler, D. (1991). *Wechsler Intelligence Scale for Children*, 3rd edn. San Antonio, TX: Psychological Corporation/Harcourt Brace & Co.

Wechsler, D. (1993). *Wechsler Pre-School and Primary Scale of Intelligence—Revised*. San Antonio, TX: Psychological Corporation/Harcourt Brace & Co.

Wechsler, D. (1995). *Wechsler Individual Achievement Test*. San Antonio, TX: Psychological Corporation Harcourt Brace & Co.

Wechsler, D. (1997). *Wechsler Memory Scale*, 3rd edn. San Antonio, TX: Psychological Corporation/Harcourt Brace & Co.

Wilson, B.A., Baddeley, A., Evans, J. & Shiel, A. (1994). Errorless learning in the rehabilitation of memory impaired people. *Neuropsychological Rehabilitation*, **4**, 307–326.

Wilson, B.A. Cockburn, J. & Baddeley, A.D. (1985). *The Rivermead Behavioural Memory Test*. Bury St. Edmunds: Thames Valley Test Company.

Wilson, B.A., Forester, S., Bryant, T. & Cockburn, J. (1990). Performance of 11–14 year-olds on the Rivermead Behavioural Memory Test. *Clinical Psychology Forum*, **December** (30), 8–10.

Wilson, B.A., Ivani-Chalian, R. & Aldrich, B. (1991). *Rivermead Behaviour Memory Test for Children*. Bury St. Edmunds: Thames Valley Test Company.

Ylivsaker, M. & Gioia, G.A. (1998). Cognitive assessment. In M. Ylvisaker (ed.), *Traumatic Brain Injury Rehabilitation*, 2nd edn. Boston, MA: Butterworth-Heinemann.

Ylvisaker, M., Szekeres, S.F. & Haarbauer-Krupa (1998). Cognitive rehabilitation: organisation, memory and language. In M. Ylvisaker (ed.), *Traumatic Brain Injury Rehabilitation*, 2nd edn. Boston, MA: Butterworth-Heinemann.

CHAPTER 32

Assessment and Intervention in Dementia of Alzheimer Type

Linda Clare

Sub-department of Clinical Health Psychology, University College London, UK

Dementia is a major cause of disability and accounts for a considerable proportion of health care expenditure in developed countries (Whitehouse et al., 1993). Prevalence estimates vary, but dementia is thought to affect about 5% of all people over 65 and to increase in prevalence with advancing years, so that over 20% of people over 80 are affected (Woods, 1996a). Dementia with onset before the age of 65 is also a matter of concern (Cox & Keady, 1999; Harvey, 1998). Although "dementia" is a Western diagnostic category, the phenomenon it describes is thought to be universal (Pollitt, 1996). Within the broad disease spectrum of dementia, dementia of the Alzheimer type (DAT) is the most frequently diagnosed subcategory and is said to account for 75% of all dementia diagnoses confirmed at post mortem examination (J.C. Morris, 1996), although estimates of prevalence and incidence vary considerably (Brayne, 1994; Kay, 1991). Behind these figures, striking in themselves, lie the profound personal costs arising from what has been described as "one of the cruellest diseases to assail the human spirit" (Heston & White, 1991).

DEMENTIA OF ALZHEIMER TYPE: A BRIEF OVERVIEW

Consensus diagnostic criteria for DAT are provided by DSM-IV (American Psychiatric Association, 1995), ICD-10 (World Health Organization, 1992) and NINCDS–ADRDA (McKhann et al., 1984). The NINCDS–ADRDA criteria for probable DAT occurring in persons aged 40–90 specify that dementia should be established by clinical examination, documented by Mini-Mental State Examination (MMSE; Folstein et al., 1975) or equivalent screening measure, and confirmed by neuropsychological tests. There should be deficits in at least two areas of cognitive functioning, with progressive deterioration. There should be no disturbance of consciousness, and the possibility of the problems being due to any other disorder should be ruled out. Where there is a second systemic or brain disorder sufficient

The Handbook of Memory Disorders. Edited by A.D. Baddeley, M.D. Kopelman and B.A. Wilson
© 2002 John Wiley & Sons, Ltd.

to produce dementia but not considered to be the cause of dementia, or where there are variations in onset, presentation, or course, a diagnosis of possible AD is made. A diagnosis of definite AD can only be made where the clinical criteria for probable AD are met and there is additional histopathological evidence obtained from biopsy or autopsy.

Use of criteria such as these is said to have improved the reliability of diagnosis when tested against post mortem findings, and estimates of accuracy range from 80% to 95% (J.C. Morris, 1996; Burns & Förstl, 1994; Hodges, 1994; Reifler & Larson, 1990). Burns & Förstl (1994) comment, however, that the improvement in accuracy gained by adhering to these criteria is relatively slight, and Henderson & Sartorius (1994) point out that even with a clearly agreed set of criteria there is still variability in the way in which the criteria are applied by different assessors. It should also be noted that the interpretation of histological changes in the brain observed at post mortem, held up as the "gold standard" by which accuracy of clinical diagnosis is assessed, is "by no means uncontroversial", since the process is not entirely free of subjective judgment (Burns & Förstl, 1994).

A defining element in all diagnostic criteria for DAT is the observation of progressive changes in memory and cognitive function. Memory is usually the first cognitive function to be affected by the onset of DAT, although impairments are initially evident only in certain memory systems, particularly episodic memory (Fox et al., 1998; Greene et al., 1996). Attention (Perry & Hodges, 1999), executive function (Greene et al., 1995; Miller, 1996; R.G. Morris, 1996) and word finding (Hamilton, 1994; Miller, 1996; R.G. Morris, 1996) may also be compromised. As the disorder progresses, deficits in these areas become more extensive, psychomotor function is affected and a decline in global cognitive functioning becomes evident (Morris & McKiernan, 1994; Miller, 1996). Visuospatial perception is usually affected only in the later stages, although in atypical cases it may be observed as one of the earliest symptoms (Morris & McKiernan, 1994). Considerable heterogeneity of presentation has been observed in DAT (Wild & Kaye, 1998; Storandt et al., 1992; Neary et al., 1986).

Heterogeneity is evident, not only in initial presentation, but also in the course and progression of DAT. Consequently, models that emphasize clear stages in the progression of DAT have been criticized for implying a degree of temporal order that is belied by the heterogeneity of individual experience (Gubrium, 1987). However, three broad stages are commonly distinguished (Schneck et al., 1982; J.C. Morris, 1996). These are an early or mild stage, a middle or moderate stage, and an advanced end stage. In research studies, stage or degree of severity is commonly defined either in terms of scores on cognitive screening tests, such as the Mini-Mental State Examination (MMSE; Folstein et al., 1975), although this approach has important limitations (Clarke et al., 1999; Little & Doherty, 1996), or with reference to scores on a global rating of functional level, such as the Clinical Dementia Rating (CDR; Hughes et al., 1982).

Conceptualizing DAT

Situating the concept of dementia within an historical and anthropological context serves as a reminder that both dementia in general and dementia of Alzheimer type (DAT) should be viewed as constructed phenomena (Pollitt, 1996; Berrios, 1994a). The concept of dementia in the sense currently accepted in Western societies was constructed during the nineteenth century (Berrios, 1994a, 1994b), while the so-called "Alzheimerization" of dementia was developed and encouraged during the 1970s (Kitwood, 1997). At present, a disease model of dementia predominates in Western thought and practice, that views DAT as a discrete disease category (Roth, 1994). There is, however, a continuing debate about whether the pathological changes in DAT are qualitatively different to those seen in normal ageing, or form a continuum with normal ageing (Huppert, 1994).

While the disease model has produced valuable advances in understanding and treatment, it has been criticized for a number of reasons (Kitwood, 1997). The key forms of neuropathology in DAT appear in the brains of some healthy older people, while some people may show all the symptoms of DAT but lack any observable pathology at post mortem (see e.g. Sevush & Leve, 1993). Kitwood (1997) argues that this calls into question the notion of DAT as a "disease", since it is not clear that there is any consistent association between symptoms and biological markers. Furthermore, there are considerable difficulties associated with diagnosis and classification (see e.g. Christensen et al., 1997; Small et al., 1997; Kitwood, 1997; Cohen, 1996; J.C. Morris, 1996; O'Connor, 1994; Burns & Förstl, 1994) and DAT has been described as a "diagnostic category of uncertain boundaries" (Pollitt, 1996). DAT is essentially a diagnosis of exclusion, and there may be frequent failures to distinguish different subtypes of dementia (Woods, 1996a). Differential diagnosis of dementia and depression is also problematic (Small et al., 1997) and recent research on white matter lesions in depression calls into question the traditional distinction between organic and functional disorder (O'Brien et al., 1996, 1998). Most importantly, the disease model fails to account for "excess disability", whereby functioning is worse than the degree of impairment would predict (Reifler & Larson, 1990) for periods of "rementing", where functioning improves or stabilizes (Kitwood, 1996; Sixsmith et al., 1993), or for the rapid deterioration that often follows adverse events, such as temporary hospitalization (Kitwood, 1996). Psychosocial factors are likely to be relevant in these situations, and it is therefore necessary to address issues of coping and adjustment and to consider DAT from the perspective of the person with dementia (R.G. Morris, 1996; Cottrell & Schulz, 1993).

For these reasons, it is suggested that a broader model, which incorporates the role of psychological and social variables, is required (Kitwood, 1997). An "alternative paradigm" has been most clearly articulated by Kitwood (1996, 1997), although related ideas have been presented in social constructionist accounts (Sabat, 1994, 1995; Sabat & Harré, 1992; Sabat et al., 1984). Kitwood (1996, 1997) proposes a dialectical model of dementia. The term "dialectical" reflects the emphasis on interactions between variables operating at the biological and psychosocial levels. The aim of this "alternative paradigm" is to present an account of the process of dementia that bridges these two levels (Kitwood, 1996, 1997). It is suggested that the manifestation and progression of DAT in any one individual is influenced by the interplay of neurological impairment, physical health and sensory acuity, personality, biographical experience and social psychology, in terms of environment, communication and interaction. Where the social psychology is "malignant", the result is an involutional spiral of deterioration. Social interactions and care processes that are undermining and discouraging, and fail to take account of personality and life history, lead to a reduction in self-efficacy which in turn attracts further damaging interactions (Sabat, 1994). It is suggested that a pervasive malignant social psychology might contribute to structural changes in the brain, while a benign social psychology coupled with an enriched environment might facilitate some regeneration (Arendt & Jones, 1992), and some evidence is available to support this view (Bråne et al., 1989; Karlsson et al., 1988).

The dialectical model has clear implications for assessment, intervention and care. It indicates that the primary aim should be to maximize well-being and optimize functioning for the person with dementia and to support and foster positive elements in the surrounding social system. To be effective, care should be person-centred, based on an individualized formulation that takes into account all the relevant biological, psychological and social factors, and delivered in a way that promotes a benign rather than malignant social psychology.

ASSESSMENT IN DAT

In keeping with this broad perspective, assessment of memory and other aspects of cognitive functioning aimed at detecting the presence of DAT should form part of a comprehensive, multidisciplinary assessment alongside information on physical health status and current medication, results of medical tests and neuroimaging data. Other information required to complete the picture includes a full history, an assessment of mood and well-being, an evaluation of functional ability, and a consideration of the social and environmental context, including the needs of close family members. Information should be obtained not only from the individual but also, wherever possible, from someone who knows the person well, such as a partner or relative, and from any other professionals involved in the person's care.

While neuropsychological tests form an essential component of the assessment, the results should be interpreted with caution, bearing in mind the range of factors that may affect performance. These may be related to the individual, e.g. sensory loss, pain, restricted mobility or anxiety about the testing situation; to the testing environment, e.g. distracting noise or uncomfortable seating; or to the tests themselves, e.g. requirements for unrealistic levels of mobility or dexterity, or lack of sensitivity to cultural difference. Neuropsychological assessment can often be an aversive experience for the older person, and care should be taken to create a situation that provides a positive and worthwhile experience. The amount of testing should be limited to the minimum necessary to answer the relevant questions satisfactorily, and practical, constructive feedback should be offered to the individual and family.

Assessment Measures

It is necessary to distinguish screening tests (sometimes described as "cognitive" tests) from neuropsychological tests. Screening tests are often used to provide an indication of whether there is cognitive impairment, and can be valuable provided their limitations are clearly understood. They are not, however, a substitute for full neuropsychological assessment.

Screening Measures

The most widely-used cognitive screening measure is the MMSE, which is brief and simple to administer, but which does not properly sample the cognitive functions known to be affected in early-stage DAT. Administration procedures can vary considerably, although a standardized version is available (Molloy et al., 1991). Varying cut-offs are used for presence and degree of impairment and the constraints of test–retest reliability, which indicate that a change of least four points in a given direction is required before one can state confidently that there has been an improvement or a decline, are frequently ignored. Additionally, where the MMSE is administered repeatedly at fairly short intervals, practice effects result in artificial inflation of scores, and it has been suggested that the MMSE should only be administered at intervals of 3 years or more (Clarke et al., 1999). MMSE scores are heavily influenced by education, so that highly educated people may score highly despite severe problems in episodic memory; similarly, results are influenced by ethnicity. Therefore, although a low score (24/30 or below) strongly suggests the presence of impairment, results should always be treated with caution. Furthermore, the MMSE can be seen as rather patronizing and perhaps demeaning in its approach to the older person, so that professionals may feel embarrassed to use it (van Hout et al., 2000) and patients may feel affronted.

Some of the limitations of the MMSE are addressed by the CAMCOG, which is a component of the CAMDEX system for diagnosis of dementia in older people (Roth et al., 1999). The CAMCOG incorporates the MMSE items into a more extensive cognitive screening assessment that does attempt to sample all the relevant cognitive functions. However, none of the relevant functions is assessed in depth. Other widely-used screening measures include the Middlesex Elderly Assessment of Mental State (MEAMS; Golding, 1989) and the Kendrick Scales (Kendrick & Watts, 1999).

Neuropsychological Tests

Where neuropsychological assessment is indicated, the following domains of cognitive functioning should be considered:

- *General cognitive functioning*—both current and estimated prior IQ.
- *Long-term memory*—episodic, semantic, autobiographical and prospective. It is useful to consider memory functions (learning, forgetting), modalities (visual, verbal, sensory), time periods (recent, remote), relation to onset of problems (anterograde, retrograde) and testing methods (recall vs. recognition, immediate vs. delayed recall).
- *Working memory, attention and executive function.*
- *Perception*—object perception, spatial perception.
- *Language*—expressive and receptive.

Table 32.1 provides examples of tests that may be used, in whole or in part, to assess various cognitive functions in older people presenting with possible DAT. As well as tests suitable for use in general neuropsychological assessment, the list includes some tests that can be used to explore further and more specific hypotheses within a cognitive neuropsychological framework. For reviews of specific neuropsychological tests and information on the availability of additional age-specific norms, see Spreen & Strauss (1998) and Lezak (1995). The assessment of memory functioning is discussed in detail by Wilson (Chapter 28, this volume).

Non-cognitive Measures

It is useful to consider including some non-cognitive measures in the assessment; for example mood might be assessed using the Geriatric Depression Scale (Yesavage et al., 1983) or Hospital Anxiety and Depression Scale (Snaith & Zigmond, 1994). Measures of functional ability are reviewed by Carswell & Spiegel (1999) and Little & Doherty (1996). When

Table 32.1 Neuropsychological assessment in DAT

Previous IQ	National Adult Reading Test or Cambridge Contextual Reading Test
Reading ability	Schonell Graded Word Reading Test
Current IQ	WAIS short form Verbal or Full-scale IQ Ravens Coloured or Standard Progressive Matrices
Attention	Test of Everyday Attention Behavioural Inattention Test
Working memory	Digit Span from WAIS or Wechsler Memory Scale WMS Visual Span
Executive function	Trail-making Test Controlled Oral Word Association Test—letter fluency (FAS) Category fluency Modified Wisconsin Card Sorting Test Stroop Test Weigl sorting task Behavioural Assessment of the Dysexecutive Syndrome
Visuospatial perception	Visual Object and Space Perception Battery Benton Judgment of Line Orientation Benton Unfamiliar Face Matching Birmingham Object Recognition Battery
Semantic memory	Pyramids and Palm Trees Graded Naming Test Birmingham Object Recognition Battery Famous faces and names
Long-term memory *Recall, immediate and delayed*	WMS Logical Memory and Visual Reproduction
Recognition	Camden Memory Tests; Recognition Memory Test; Doors and People Test
Everyday memory	Rivermead Behavioural Memory Test; Rivermead Behavioural Memory Test—Extended Version
Autobiographical	Autobiographical Memory Interview
Learning and forgetting	WMS Paired Associate Learning; California Verbal Learning Test; Rey Auditory–Verbal Learning Test; Doors and People Test
Language comprehension	Naming from description Token Test Test for the Reception of Grammar PALPA
Language expression	Graded Naming Test COWA and category fluency Boston Diagnostic Aphasia Examination PALPA
Calculation	WAIS Arithmetic
Praxis	WAIS Block Design
Functioning in moderate or severe dementia	Rivermead Behavioural Memory Test Severe Impairment Battery

gathering information from an informant who is in the role of caregiver, it is useful to assess whether the informant is experiencing high levels of caregiver burden (Gilliard & Rabins, 1999); a number of appropriate measures are reviewed by Vitaliano et al. (1991).

Detecting Dementia

Making the diagnosis of dementia is reasonably straightforward in the moderate and severe stages, but it can be problematic to distinguish the early stages of DAT from "normal" ageing or depression, although recent work has helped to clarify which neuropsychological tests discriminate most effectively (Welsh et al., 1991, 1992; Christensen et al., 1997). Most people who present with concerns about memory problems do not in fact have dementia, and it is also important to note that in specialist clinical practice professionals see an atypical group of patients. O'Connor (1994) found that only 3% of people identified in a community survey as having mild dementia had been referred to specialist services, along with 18% of those with moderate dementia and 33% of those with severe dementia.

Early Detection

Interest in the early detection of DAT has increased with the recent licensing of anti-cholinesterase inhibiting medication as a treatment for the cognitive impairment of early-stage DAT (Rogers et al., 1998a, 1998b; Rogers & Friedhoff, 1998; Corey-Bloom et al., 1998). The detection of early-stage DAT is increasingly undertaken in the context of multidisciplinary memory clinics (Wilcock et al., 1999; Thompson et al., 1997; Wright & Lindesay, 1995; van der Cammen et al., 1987), where neuropsychological assessment plays a critical role in establishing a diagnosis. Early detection of DAT offers the possibility of introducing psychosocial and pharmacological interventions at an early stage. It has been demonstrated that memory clinics can provide an effective focus for early intervention and for the development of integrated psychosocial approaches (Moniz-Cook & Woods, 1997; Moniz-Cook et al., 1998). Early detection of DAT remains a challenge, however, and there are a number of barriers to early detection. People with dementia, and their families, may interpret memory difficulties as part of normal ageing (O'Connor, 1994) or deny that there have been any changes (Cohen & Eisdorfer, 1986), and rates of detection by general medical practitioners are low (O'Connor, 1994; Iliffe, 1997; Rait et al., 1999; van Hout et al., 2000).

Distinguishing Dementia from "Normal" Ageing

The boundaries between dementia and normal forgetfulness appear somewhat fluid, and it remains unclear how the difference between dementia and normal ageing should be conceptualized. Although many older people and their families expect to observe a decline in memory functioning, there is a great deal of variation in the general population as regards the kinds of memory changes seen as part of "normal" ageing, and the issue is compounded by cohort effects. A broad overview suggests that, although memory functioning becomes less efficient from about 67 years onwards, there is no general decline in memory ability and no uniform decline across the range of different memory tasks. Memory functioning is relatively more affected in the very old, so that diagnostic criteria do not allow for a dementia diagnosis made after the age of 90. The following general observations can be made with regard to memory changes in healthy older people (Cohen, 1996):

- Working memory may be affected.
- Episodic memory is affected to a much greater degree than semantic or procedural memory.
- Immediate recall is affected more than delayed recall, while recognition memory is unaffected.
- Retrieval is slower and less efficient, with more rapid and extensive forgetting.
- Prospective memory remains as good as that of younger people if external aids and reminders can be used, but is poorer if no such aids are available.
- Autobiographical memory does *not* show the stereotypical discrepancy between vivid memories of the distant past and hazy memories of more recent events; instead, memories across the lifespan show loss of detail and become more vague.
- Alterations in memory functioning can be offset by intelligence, expertise and use of compensatory strategies, enabling the person to cope well despite any changes.

The Boundaries between Dementia and "Normal" Ageing

As a general rule, the lower the score on cognitive tests, the more likely it is that the person has dementia. However, Storandt & Hill (1989) found that scores of patients with very mild Alzheimer's overlapped considerably with those of both normal older people and people with mild Alzheimer's. Furthermore, even where people do show some degree of memory impairment, progression to dementia is not inevitable (Bowen et al., 1997; Reisberg et al., 1982).

The area of uncertainty between "normal" ageing and dementia has attracted a number of attempts to define diagnostic categories. Among the diagnostic labels suggested are age-associated memory impairment (AAMI), mild cognitive impairment, benign senescent forgetfulness, and minimal or questionable dementia. These concepts remain controversial, and practice varies regarding their use. The category of AAMI, for example, would include large numbers of older people, and it is questionable whether changes that are essentially normative should be labelled in this way (Woods, 1996a).

Which Tests Are Useful in Discriminating between Dementia and Normal Ageing?

The CERAD studies (Welsh et al., 1991, 1992) suggest that the best discriminator is performance on delayed recall tasks. A 10-word list presented in three learning trials and tested after a 5–8 min delay correctly classified 94% of controls and 86% of patients with mild dementia, using a cutting score of 2 SDs below the control group mean. Performance on naming tests was found to be useful as an adjunctive measure. If patients have impairment in delayed recall and problems in naming or verbal fluency, this is a very strong indicator for dementia. Other studies have also emphasized the value of delayed recall. Tierney et al. (1996) found that problems in delayed recall and attention were the best predictors of whether people with mild memory problems would go on to develop Alzheimer's disease.

Distinguishing between Dementia and Depression

Depression in older people often presents somewhat differently to depression in younger adults. Somatic and sleep-related symptoms are less helpful as indicators of depression in older people, since such changes are more widespread in this age group. Factors such as retirement, bereavement, health problems, pain, poor housing, financial hardship and limited social support all contribute to depression, and these form part of the lives of many older people; however, rates of depression are not thought to increase significantly with age. Depression is still an important problem nevertheless, as a substantial number of older people do not recover, and many others relapse. Unfortunately, while depression may affect cognitive functioning, treatments for depression may also have adverse effects in this respect.

The effects of depression on cognitive functioning appear very variable. Some older people with depression show no cognitive impairment, while others perform poorly on cognitive tests. In general, the effects of depression on cognitive test performance are relatively small (e.g. Feehan et al., 1993); the term "depressive pseudodementia" can therefore be misleading, as this represents the extreme case of severe depression. Effects of depression on test performance appear to result more from a conservative response bias and a reluctance to guess for fear of being wrong than from inability to respond. Thus, response to the process of assessment may be a key factor in alerting the clinician to the likelihood of depression. A further important difference is that people with depression are more likely to report subjective concerns about cognitive dysfunction, especially problems with memory and concentration, whereas in the case of people with dementia, it is much more likely to be family members who are worried and who initiate the referral.

The Overlap between Dementia and Depression

The distinction between dementia and depression is not clear-cut. People with depression appear to have a slightly increased risk of getting dementia. Older people with depression, while not having dementia, may show cognitive impairments that prove not to be fully reversible once the depression is treated; these may be accompanied by some structural changes in the brain. People who have dementia frequently display at least some depressive symptoms, and depression is a significant source of excess disability in dementia (Ross et al., 1998); it is also possible that depressive symptoms could represent a prodrome of dementia.

Which Tests Can Help to Discriminate between Depression and Dementia?

Christensen et al. (1997) present a meta-analysis of studies assessing differences in performance between older people with depression and older people with dementia. These can be summarized as follows:

- Depression gave rise to moderate deficits on almost every type of test (with scores on average 0.64 of a SD below control performance) but the extent of the deficits varied according to type of task. People with dementia showed much larger deficits than people with depression, especially on memory tasks.

- Depression led to greater deficits on timed and speeded tasks than on untimed or non-speeded tasks. People with dementia did much worse on nonspeeded tasks than people with depression.
- For people with depression, performance tests were affected more than verbal tests, and there were difficulties in problem-solving.
- People with dementia were more likely to make false-positive errors on recognition memory tasks.
- People with depression did better on memory tasks with depressive content (where the information to be remembered was mood-congruent) than on memory tasks with neutral or pleasant content, whereas people with dementia did not show this differential effect.
- As regards specific tests, the best discriminators were paired associate learning, naming, block design and anomalous sentence repetititon.

Distinguishing Different Types of Dementia

Where it is evident that dementia is present, it is important to determine the specific type of dementia, as this has implications for intervention and care.

Alzheimer's, Vascular Dementia and Dementia with Lewy Bodies

DAT is not easily distinguished from vascular dementia or dementia with Lewy bodies on the basis of neuropsychology, and attempts to differentiate are made with reference to the history, presentation and results of medical investigations. People with vascular dementia have a history of stepwise progression, which contrasts with the gradual onset of DAT, and risk factors for vascular illness are usually present; it is important to note, though, that vascular dementia and DAT may coexist. People who have dementia with Lewy bodies show fluctuating levels of cognitive functioning and typically report characteristic types of visual hallucination which are not seen in DAT.

Alzheimer's and Frontotemporal Dementia

Neuropsychological assessment is helpful, however, in distinguishing between DAT and the frontal and temporal variants of frontotemporal dementia. The key neuropsychological and behavioural features that are observed in the early stages of each of these three forms of dementia are summarized by Hodges et al. (1999). Whereas people with early-stage DAT show severe impairments in episodic memory, mild impairments in semantic memory, verbal letter fluency, attention, executive function and working memory, and may also have subtle impairments in visuospatial perception, the profile of impairments differs markedly in the early stages of frontotemporal dementia. In the frontal variant, impairments are observed in some aspects of executive function, with mild impairments in episodic memory and verbal letter fluency, and there are progressive changes in behaviour and personality, but semantic memory and visuospatial perception are intact. In the temporal variant (often termed "semantic dementia"), there are severe impairments in semantic memory, accompanied by anomia, surface dyslexia and progressive loss of vocabulary, and these may interfere with performance on tests of other cognitive functions, but episodic memory, working memory, visuospatial perception and nonverbal problem-solving are intact, along with behaviour and personality.

Blacker et al. (1994) note, however, that the distinction is made more complex by the observation of "atypical" cases of DAT, where the first symptoms may be in word-finding, perception or praxis, with memory being much less affected than one would normally expect. Early prominent behavioural changes, however, strongly suggest that the problem is *not* DAT, but is much more likely to be frontal dementia. Where the first symptoms observed are language difficulties, the question arises as to whether this is atypical DAT or frontotemporal dementia. Blacker et al. (1994) suggest that these people should be given a diagnosis of Alzheimer's disease if the presentation is otherwise typical, but not if there are behavioural changes or other atypical features.

Components of an Assessment Battery

A good neuropsychological assessment battery aimed at distinguishing between normal ageing, depression and dementia and between different types of dementia might therefore encompass the following components, with an emphasis on nonspeeded tasks:

- Delayed recall—preferably where the information to be remembered is depressive, rather than neutral or pleasant, in content.
- Paired associate learning.
- Recognition memory.
- Semantic memory.
- Naming.
- Constructional praxis.
- Anomalous sentence repetition.
- Verbal letter fluency and category fluency.
- Executive function (abstraction, planning/organizing, set shifting, problem-solving).
- Attention (sustained, selective, divided).

Distinguishing Moderate from Severe Dementia

Understanding the severity of dementia for a given individual plays an important part in planning intervention and care. The CERAD studies (Welsh et al., 1991, 1992) demonstrated that performance on delayed recall tasks was not very useful in establishing the severity of dementia, since performance on delayed recall already showed floor effects in the early stages. For distinguishing between moderate and severe dementia, the best discriminators were verbal category fluency and constructional praxis. People with severe dementia can be assessed on the Severe Impairment Battery (Saxton et al., 1990), which permits identification of preserved areas of ability even in the very severe stages (Wild & Kaye, 1998). Similarly, Cockburn & Keene (in press) were able to identify elements of preserved memory ability in people with severe dementia using the Rivermead Behavioural Memory Test (Wilson et al., 1985).

Giving a Diagnosis

It is now fairly standard practice for carers to be told their relative's diagnosis, but the extent to which people with DAT are told of their own diagnosis remains very variable (Downs, 1999; Heal & Husband, 1998). The burden often falls on carers to decide whether to disclose. Carers may feel that they should disclose the diagnosis because the person has a right to know, or has asked for an explanation, or they may do so because the person asks an explicit question; alternatively, they may feel that disclosure would cause too much distress, or that the person is too cognitively impaired to understand, or that the news might result in a suicide attempt. In fact, although there is a risk of suicide, people with DAT do not attempt suicide at higher rates than those observed in the general population (Cohen & Eisdorfer, 1986). Professionals, too, may find it very difficult to speak honestly about the diagnosis, and may argue that it is not in the person's best interests to be told. However, as there is an increasing expectation of dialogue on an equal footing with professionals, it is likely that there will be an increasing trend for people to want to know (Goldsmith, 1996).

Certainly it is possible that disclosure could cause distress, and it is understandable that some carers may feel that witholding information is more compassionate. Failing to disclose, however, carries the implication that the person is unable to cope or to deal with difficult emotions. There are costs and risks attached to failing to disclose, including emotional distress, misunderstandings and marital discord. Furthermore, there are also possible benefits to disclosure, particularly in the earlier stages of DAT, since it may allow the person and the family to face the future in order to make decisions, settle financial and legal affairs and receive spiritual support (Cohen & Eisdorfer, 1986). Of course, the diagnostic process is characterized by uncertainty, and this does have to be taken into account. Both for this reason and for reasons connected with the psychological and social implications of attaching a label to the problem, practitioners may prefer to discuss the person's difficulties in terms of observable strengths and needs, e.g. referring to memory problems. In any case, if the intention is to give a diagnosis, then it is essential to do this in a sensitive manner (Downs, 1999) and to provide the appropriate back-up in terms of information, practical assistance, links with self-help and voluntary agencies, counselling and, where appropriate, psychological intervention for the person and family.

One issue often raised at the time of assessment is that of driving. Many people with early-stage dementia are able to continue to drive safely. The decision to give up driving when the appropriate time comes, however, can be very difficult for all concerned. McKenna (1998) provides a very clear account of the way in which neuropsychological assessment may contribute to an evaluation of fitness to drive, and the constraints on drawing firm conclusions. In cases of doubt, referral to a specialist driving assessment centre that offers driving assessments incorporating cognitive tasks, off-road vehicle handling and road tests may be helpful.

INTERVENTION IN DAT

The overall aims of intervention in DAT include optimizing functioning and well-being, slowing the progression of impairment, minimizing excess disability, enhancing self-efficacy and coping skills, combating threats to self-esteem, and preventing the development of a malignant social psychology in the person's support network or caregiving system. The concept of rehabilitation, implying as it does a focus on maximizing functioning across a whole range of areas, including physical health, psychological well-being, living skills and social relationships, therefore provides a unifying core concept around which to organize thinking about intervention in DAT (Cohen & Eisdorfer, 1986; Clare, 2000).

In order to begin to understand the particular psychological needs of the person with DAT, it is necessary to consider the role of cognition and emotion, personality and behaviour, life experience and preferred coping styles. There is a great deal of evidence to indicate that psychological distress is common in early-stage DAT, with high levels of anxiety and depression reported in many studies (Ross et al., 1998; Ballard et al., 1993; Burns, 1991; Wands et al., 1990). While subtle changes in behaviour and personality may result from an interaction of neurological and psychological factors (Hagberg, 1997; Hope, 1994; Teri et al., 1992; Petry et al., 1989), behavioural changes in many cases represent a manifestation of excess disability (Bleathman & Morton, 1994). Lack of social contact and environmental stimulation, perhaps resulting from loss of confidence, may contribute to lowered well-being (Woods & Britton, 1985).

Consideration of how the individual copes with the changes resulting from DAT is integral to a psychological understanding of DAT (Droes, 1997; Hagberg, 1997; Cottrell & Schulz, 1993; Woods & Britton, 1985). The development of adaptive coping strategies is important in maximizing well-being and minimizing excess disability, but the onset of DAT places major demands on coping resources. Furthermore, DAT most commonly arises at a time when the individual is negotiating development into later life, and is superimposed on the normative developmental tasks faced by the individual and family in relation to growing older, which may include reviewing one's life, achieving resolution of important themes or issues, accepting losses, and coming to terms with approaching death (Coleman, 1993, 1996). Recent studies of the phenomenological experience and coping strategies of people with early-stage DAT (Clare, 2000; Pearce, 2000) have demonstrated two key dimensions— the attempt to protect or maintain an existing or prior sense of identity, and the attempt to acknowledge and integrate the changes experienced in order to facilitate the development of a modified sense of identity. Understanding the current needs of each individual with respect to these tasks, and the way in which the individual perceives his/her situation, is invaluable in helping to determine what kinds of interventions may be appropriate at any given stage.

The range of psychosocial interventions that may be offered to individuals with DAT and their caregivers is considerable (for a review, see Kasl-Godley & Gatz, 2000). Approaches described in the literature include, for example, life review (Woods et al., 1992), reality orientation (Spector et al., 1998), reminiscence (Bender et al., 1998), self-maintenance therapy (Romero, 1999; Romero & Wenz, 2001), psychotherapy (Cheston, 1998; Sutton & Cheston, 1997; Knight, 1996; Hausman, 1992; Sinason, 1992), family therapy (Huckle, 1994), cognitive-behavioural therapy (Husband, 1999; Koder, 1998; Teri & Gallagher-Thompson, 1991), behavioural approaches (Bird, 2000), psychoeducational and support groups (Yale, 1995; 1999; Bourgeois et al., 1996; Brodaty & Gresham, 1989; Brodaty & Peters, 1991) and environmental modifications (Woods & Britton, 1985), as well as approaches that specifically target memory functioning. The emphasis here will be on the latter category; other approaches are discussed in detail by Bob Woods in Chapter 33, this volume. Before proceeding to a discussion of cognitive rehabilitation, however, the status of pharmacological treatments will be briefly considered.

Pharmacological treatments for DAT are now generally available, but as yet there is no agent that can either prevent the onset of DAT or provide a cure. The aim of the pharmacological treatments presently offered is to mitigate the symptoms of DAT, albeit for a limited period (Richards, 1996). Dysfunction in the cholinergic system provides the strongest association between DAT and neuronal loss, and acetylcholinesterase inhibitors have been the main focus of research (R.G. Morris, 1996). These may offer modest improvements in verbal learning and memory, psychomotor functioning and attention (Richards, 1996; Rogers et al., 1998a, 1998b; Rogers & Friedhoff, 1998; Corey-Bloom et al., 1998); such improvements might be reflected, for example, in a change of 2–3 points on a cognitive screening test such as the MMSE. It is suggested that this might represent at the most a saving of perhaps 6 months of deterioration (Bryson & Benfield, 1997). However, where improvements of one or two points on a cognitive test are evident, it is unclear to what extent this translates into meaningful differences in everyday life. If there is no improvement but performance remains stable, it is impossible to determine whether this is due to the drug or whether the same pattern would have been observed without the drug. Furthermore, there is a possibility that people who take the drug and later stop may show a precipitous decline in functioning once the drug is withdrawn, bringing them very rapidly back onto the trajectory of the untreated disorder. While the use of acetylcholinesterase inhibitors may provide modest benefits in controlled trials, the precise extent and nature of their effectiveness in any individual case is therefore difficult to determine, and side-effects remain a concern (Lovestone et al., 1997; Royal College of Psychiatrists, 1997).

In practice, it is evident that drug treatments are very limited in what they can offer at present. While rapid progress in the further development of approaches targeting the biological changes in DAT is to be expected, and more effective treatments are eagerly awaited, it is likely that psychosocial factors will remain an essential focus of intervention.

Cognitive Rehabilitation: Concept and Application

The goals of rehabilitation in DAT differ according to the needs of the individual and the severity of dementia. In the early stages, when impairments are predominantly in the cognitive domain, cognitive rehabilitation is particularly relevant, especially with regard to memory functioning. Since memory impairments are a defining feature of early-stage DAT and impact extensively on daily life and well-being (Bieliauskas, 1996), interventions targeting coping with memory difficulties are likely to have particular importance. Cognitive rehabilitation has been defined by Wilson (1997) as:

> ... any intervention strategy or technique which intends to enable clients or patients, and their families, to live with, manage, by-pass, reduce or come to terms with deficits precipitated by injury to the brain (p. 488).

The practice of cognitive rehabilitation incorporates a number of elements. Theoretical models in cognitive neuropsychology enable the identification of specific patterns of impaired and preserved functions, while experimental and clinical evidence derived from learning theory provides a basis for developing appropriate training methods. The resulting approach is often largely behavioural and goal-directed. Prigatano (1997) argues, however, that a behavioural approach is inadequate on its own, as it fails to take account of the patient's experiential world and emotional response to injury. Instead, he advocates an holistic approach, in which cognitive, emotional and motivational aspects of functioning are addressed together in an integrated manner, in acknowledgement of the complex interactions between them (Prigatano, 1997, 1999). This philosophy can be applied to cognitive rehabilitation in DAT. However, its expression in practical treatment approaches will need to differ somewhat from that seen in programmes for younger people with nonprogressive brain injury. Cognitive rehabilitation in DAT will require an understanding of the person's current level of awareness in order to work in a way that encourages development of effective strategies and fosters personal adjustment and well-being for the person with DAT and his/her family carers, but is likely to be less confrontational and to place less emphasis on developing realistic awareness of impairments where this is limited or absent. Involving caregivers in the intervention process is essential, and this will require sensitivity to issues in family and marital relationships that may impact on the work (Quayhagen & Quayhagen, 1989, in press).

Theoretical Basis for Cognitive Rehabilitation of Memory in Early DAT

Theoretical justification for the use of cognitive rehabilitation in DAT derives from evidence regarding, first, the neuropsychology and neuroanatomy of memory impairments in DAT, which is presented by Becker & Overman (Chapter 26, this volume) and will be covered only briefly here, and second, the capacity of the person with DAT for new learning.

Consideration of memory systems in early-stage DAT shows that some subsystems are relatively preserved while others are severely impaired. In relation to long-term memory functions, episodic memory is usually severely impaired, while semantic and procedural memory may be relatively spared. This suggests, first, that there is scope for interventions aimed at improving memory functioning to build on those subsystems found to be intact, such as procedural memory. Second, compensatory methods and environmental adaptations may reduce the demands on explicit memory and substitute for impaired aspects of memory.

With regard to memory processes, Glisky (1998) points out that encoding, storage and retrieval are closely interrelated and difficult to separate. In general, however, the evidence suggests that the major difficulty in DAT lies in encoding, and that rates of forgetting are not significantly elevated (Christensen et al., 1998). This suggests that if appropriate help with learning designed to ensure adequate encoding can assist with getting information into the memory store, there is a reasonable likelihood of retention. Acknowledging the impairments in explicit memory, it is probable that such an approach would be most beneficial if reserved for small amounts of important information.

A review of the brain pathology observed in early-stage DAT suggests that while there are likely to be particular difficulties in linking new information with existing stored knowledge, it is possible that other brain areas may be able to take over this function if the right kind of assistance is provided at encoding (Glisky, 1998). This again suggests that the design of interventions should pay careful attention to providing strategies to ensure successful encoding. Additionally, since frontal lobe pathology affects strategic aspects of remembering and retrieval of stored information, it follows that people with DAT can be expected to have particular difficulty implementing strategies to help themselves remember (Bäckman, 1992). Interventions should therefore also incorporate ways of helping people with DAT to compensate for this difficulty and enhance the possibility of successful retrieval.

There is substantial experimental evidence to suggest that learning is possible in people with DAT (Woods, 1996b). Both classical and operant conditioning of responses has been demonstrated (Camp et al., 1993; Burgess et al., 1992) and people with DAT are capable of learning and retaining verbal information (Little et al., 1986). This suggests that people with DAT do have the potential to benefit from interventions targeting memory function.

Despite these positive findings, early studies in which a variety of training approaches were used produced few benefits or were interpreted negatively (see e.g. Yesavage, 1982; Zarit et al., 1982). Although in some cases the results could be regarded as indicating the possible value of cognitive rehabilitation as a component of early intervention, and as providing a challenge to researchers to find ways of enhancing the practical impact for those with mild DAT, some investigators concluded that there was little, if any, potential for memory improvement in DAT (Bäckman & Herlitz, 1996). Given that people with DAT appear to have the potential to learn and retain information, the question arises as to why many early experimental studies were unable to demonstrate effective facilitation of memory performance. This question has been addressed in the context of attempts to enhance performance by facilitating residual explicit memory functioning. Bäckman (1992) argues that DAT affects not only episodic memory but also the ability to make use of cognitive support for remembering. People with DAT, in contrast to healthy older adults, are impaired in their ability to use the kinds of methods that aid encoding and act as cues to facilitate retrieval. Bäckman (1992) notes that those studies that suggested that gains from memory training in DAT were small or nonexistent had generally required participants to use internal memory strategies, such as imagery or the organization of material, which in themselves require a considerable degree of cognitive effort and which are particularly difficult for the person with DAT to adopt.

The results obtained by Bäckman and colleagues indicate that when substantial support is provided both at encoding and at retrieval, termed "dual cognitive support", people with DAT can show improvements in episodic memory at all stages of severity (Bäckman, 1992). Studies attempting to enhance performance by encouraging organization of material and providing category cues indicated that people with DAT need more support than healthy older adults to enhance memory, and that the level of support required to produce an improvement increased as a function of increasing severity (Bäckman, 1996, 1992). That is, the person may need more guidance in encoding the material, and more learning trials, as well as extra prompts and cues for retrieval, compared to healthy older adults, and the amount of help required will increase as the severity of dementia increases. Previous studies failed to show benefits because they failed to provide support at both encoding and retrieval, and because they concentrated on patients with severe impairments rather than patients at earlier stages (Lipinska & Bäckman, 1997). In support of this view, a number of studies show beneficial effects of different types of cognitive support, and a number of guiding principles can be delineated (Herlitz et al., 1992), e.g. memory performance is facilitated when multiple sensory modalities are involved at encoding (Karlsson et al., 1989) or where participants enact the target task (Bird & Kinsella, 1996), while, in accordance with the encoding-specificity principle, provision of retrieval cues that are compatible with conditions at encoding assists recall (R.G. Morris, 1996; Herlitz & Viitanen, 1991).

Bäckman & Herlitz (1996) argue that the ability to benefit from cognitive support in memory interventions relates to the way in which the person's knowledge structures are able to aid encoding and retrieval of episodic information. People with DAT show deficits in using semantic knowledge as an aid for episodic memory (Herlitz & Viitanen, 1991; Bäckman &

Herlitz, 1990). However, people with early-stage DAT can benefit from semantic support when this is provided both at encoding and at retrieval, e.g. performance is facilitated when a semantic orientating task is used at encoding, followed by provision of category cues at retrieval (Lipinska & Bäckman, 1997; Bird & Luszcz, 1991, 1993). Results presented by Lipinska et al., (1994) indicate that participants performed better with self-generated than with experimenter-provided cues. Perlmuter & Monty (1989) emphasize that personalizing a task by allowing the participant to make choices about it increases perceived control and motivation, and consequently is likely to benefit performance.

A number of studies, then, demonstrate that elaboration and effortful processing can improve memory performance. It is essential, however, to consider the extent to which these effects might be harnessed to enhance functioning in real-life situations (Bird & Luszcz, 1991, 1993).

Clinical Interventions for Memory Problems in DAT

Reports of clinical interventions for memory problems in DAT provide valuable information about the suitability and effectiveness of specific rehabilitative techniques. Cognitive rehabilitation interventions are usually patient-driven and individually-designed. It is important to acknowledge that some investigators have reported positive results from general cognitive stimulation and cognitive training programmes for people with dementia (Quayhagen & Quayhagen, in press, 1989; de Rotrou et al., 1999; Breuil et al., 1994; Moore et al., in press; Sandman, 1993). Despite the negative conclusions reached in the brain injury literature about the effectiveness of computerized cognitive remediation (Bird, 2000; Wilson, 1990; Ben-Yishay & Prigatano, 1990; Leng & Copello, 1990), there has also been a recent growth of interest in the use of computerized cognitive stimulation programmes for people with dementia (Butti et al., 1998; Hofmann et al., 1996). General cognitive stimulation programmes may, however, have more in common with the tradition of reality orientation (Spector et al., in press) than with cognitive rehabilitation. General stimulation and reality orientation programmes have been criticized on the grounds that it is not clear whether the observed small improvements in cognitive test scores translate into real-life clinical benefits (Bird, 2000). In addition, it is difficult to determine which elements of any such programme are responsible for observed improvements in particular domains. For these reasons, the present discussion will focus on individually-targeted interventions, where outcome has been assessed in relation to performance on targeted tasks rather than scores on cognitive tests, in an attempt to highlight specific techniques shown to be effective for at least some people with DAT.

Individually-targeted interventions for memory problems in DAT reported in the literature, as in the case of brain injury rehabilitation, can be grouped into three main categories: encouraging compensation through the use of external memory aids, provision of skills training to build on preserved memory ability, and facilitation of residual explicit memory functioning (Franzen & Haut, 1991). Each of these categories will be considered in turn.

Compensation using external memory aids.   Providing external support for remembering in the form of compensatory memory aids can help to reduce the demands on memory. The selection and introduction of external memory aids requires careful consideration. Aids should be targeted as specifically as possible, rather than simply providing a generalized reminder, the reason for which may be unclear to the person with DAT (Woods, 1996a). People with memory impairments are unlikely to start to use new memory aids spontaneously, and usually need training in their use, e.g. by means of prompting and fading of cues.

A number of studies with DAT patients have demonstrated improvements resulting from the use of various external memory aids or equivalent environmental support. In some cases these improvements have been maintained after the support has been withdrawn, while in other cases ongoing support has been required. Hanley (1986) trained in-patients with moderately advanced DAT to use a diary, reality-orientation board or personal notebook to find out personal information, although it is unclear to what extent the improvement was maintained. Bourgeois (1990, 1991, 1992) evaluated the effectiveness of memory wallets in enhancing conversational ability in a small sample of people with moderately advanced DAT, and reported significant improvements, with evidence of generalization to novel utterances. Benefits were maintained at 6 week follow-up, and for three individuals benefits were retained after 30 months. Clare et al. (2000) demonstrated that introduction of a memory aid could reduce repetitive questioning, with benefits maintained up to 6 months following the end of the intervention.

Developing technology offers increasing opportunities for identification of ingenious aids to remembering. An early example is provided by Kurlychek (1983), who used a digital watch set to beep every hour as a cue. Use of technology is now being extended beyond the realm of specific memory aids by developing computer and video equipment to monitor and control the environment of the person with dementia in order to support independent functioning (Marshall, 1999).

There is some evidence, therefore, that the use of compensatory aids may be beneficial. In view of the likely benefits of providing external support for remembering, and the potential for the development of new and more sophisticated forms of memory aid, this is clearly an area in which further research is indicated.

Skills training to optimize procedural memory functioning. The ability to perform everyday skills is particularly important in maintaining independence. Zanetti et al. (1994, 1997, 2001) used a training programme based on preserved procedural memory for rehabilitation of ADL skills in people with mild-to-moderate DAT. Training methods involved comprehensive prompting, with subsequent fading out of prompts. Preliminary results suggested this approach could be effective and produced some generalization of improvements to untrained tasks. Further evidence is provided by Josephsson et al. (1993), who used individualized training programmes for activities of daily living and showed improvements in three out of four participants, although only one maintained the gains 2 months later. An important feature of this study was the selection of tasks which were part of the patient's usual routine and which the patient was motivated to carry out. These studies show that rehabilitation strategies aimed at facilitating procedural memory offer promise in enabling people with early-stage DAT to maintain their skills and level of independence. Again, this is an area that warrants further research.

Facilitating residual long-term memory performance. Strategies for facilitating residual long-term memory performance are generally referred to as internal strategies. These have been categorized as implicit-internal or explicit-internal, depending on the extent to which they are thought to depend on implicit or explicit memory processes (Camp et al., 1993).

One important strategy for people with DAT, generally classified as implicit-internal, is expanding rehearsal. The expanding rehearsal method, termed "spaced retrieval" in the US literature, has been extensively used with people who have DAT. The act of retrieving an item of information is a powerful aid to subsequent retention under any conditions. In addition, the temporal sequencing of retrieval attempts affects the extent to which benefits are observed as a result of retrieval practice, with maximum benefit occurring when test trials are spaced at gradually expanding intervals (Landauer & Bjork, 1978). The expanding rehearsal pattern may be viewed as a shaping procedure for successively approximating the goal of unaided recall after a long delay (Camp & Stevens, 1990). An important aspect of this strategy is that it requires little cognitive effort, unlike many more elaborate mnemonic strategies. Experimental studies have demonstrated that expanding rehearsal can aid new learning in people with memory disorders following brain injury (Schacter et al., 1985). The method has been adapted for use in DAT (Camp et al., 2000; Camp, 1989), and a series of studies have demonstrated clear benefits in teaching face–name associations, object naming (Abrahams & Camp, 1993; Moffat, 1989), memory for object location, prospective memory assignments and use of memory aids (Camp, 1989). The approach has also been used to teach patients with advanced dementia living in residential settings to associate a cue with an adaptive behaviour as a means of reducing severe problem behaviours (Bird, 2000; Camp et al., 2000). A related method involves using instructional audiotapes containing biographical details to prompt rehearsal of information (Arkin,1992, 1998).

Explicit-internal strategies may be most applicable in real-life situations where support for remembering is not readily available. Strategies such as visual imagery mnemonics, chunking of information, the method of loci, the story method and initial letter cueing have been described in relation to the cognitive rehabilitation of memory disorders following brain injury, although some of these strategies may prove too difficult or demanding for many brain-injured patients (Wilson, 1995; Moffat, 1992). There is limited evidence for the success of strategies of this kind in DAT. People with DAT are likely to have difficulty both in learning an explicit mnemonic strategy of this kind and in remembering to use it appropriately (Woods, 1996a; Bäckman, 1992). It is, however, important to distinguish between the use of mnemonic strategies as a way of facilitating learning in specific tasks and the aim of developing spontaneous and independent use of the strategy in a wider sphere. The former is often a more appropriate goal in memory rehabilitation.

Successful use of a mnemonic strategy is reported by Hill et al. (1987). They describe a single case experiment in which a 66-year-old man with DAT was taught to use visual imagery to extend his retention interval for names associated with photographs of faces. When Bäckman et al. (1991) attempted to replicate the findings in a series of eight single-case studies, which included seven DAT patients, only one of the DAT patients showed training gains similar to those demonstrated by Hill et al. (1987). The authors concluded that the generalizability of the approach appears limited, but commented that there might be a subgroup of DAT patients who respond well to this form of memory training. Clare et al. (1999, 2000, 2001) demonstrated significant gains resulting from training with mnemonic strategies and expanding rehearsal in an errorless learning paradigm in a series of single-case designs, and reported long-term maintenance of treatment effects.

The evidence indicates that some approaches offer promise in facilitating residual long-term memory functioning, although gains may be circumscribed and not all patients may benefit. There is clearly scope for further development of appropriate methods that may provide assistance for people with early-stage DAT.

Effectiveness of Memory Rehabilitation

The above review highlights a number of specific methods that offer promise in facilitating memory functioning or development of compensatory behaviour. These include prompting and fading, expanding rehearsal, mnemonic or elaborative strategies, and ensuring effort-ful processing. The limitations on memory rehabilitation, even in early-stage DAT, must, however, be acknowledged (Bäckman, 1992). It is evident that the level of improvement achieved is generally modest. Individual variability is considerable; some people show no benefit from intervention, even in the early stages of the disorder, while others with ap-parently greater difficulties may improve considerably. Koltai et al. (2001) observed that, among the factors influencing outcome of cognitive rehabilitation, awareness of memory difficulties appeared to be important, and a relationship between higher levels of awareness and better outcome has been demonstrated in a prospective study (Clare, 2000). Once again, this highlights the need to understand the phenomenological experience of the individual and target interventions accordingly.

There is at present no evidence to indicate whether memory rehabilitation has any long-term benefits in terms of reversing or arresting the progression of DAT; at best, there may be some slowing in the progression of the disease. Nonetheless, in the context of a progressive condition such as DAT, this is a highly desirable goal. A recent review of empirically validated treatments for older people (Gatz et al., 1998) identified memory therapy as a "probably efficacious treatment", a conclusion also supported by De Vreese et al. (2001). This indicates that further research is warranted to extend the evidence base, clarify outstanding questions, evaluate new methods, and develop clinically-relevant procedures.

SUMMARY AND CONCLUSIONS

Recent conceptual developments have emphasized the need to think broadly about DAT in terms of the interplay of biological and psychosocial variables, and this has important impli-cations for both assessment and intervention. Although detection and differentiation of DAT is complex, and the status of diagnostic classifications remains somewhat controversial, a neuropsychological assessment conducted within the context of a comprehensive multidis-ciplinary assessment can assist in identifying the presence of DAT and, more importantly, can contribute to developing the profile of the individual's strengths and needs that forms the basis for planning intervention and care. A review of the range of interventions available for people with DAT and their families and carers demonstrates that it is no longer possible to argue that nothing can be done. On the contrary, at any stage of DAT, appropriately-targeted interventions can provide some benefit, and cognitive rehabilitation approaches provide one important example of this. Interventions for DAT constitute a rapidly developing area, and future research can be expected to bring new hope for all those living with, and affected by, Alzheimer's disease.

REFERENCES

Abrahams, J.P. & Camp, C.J. (1993). Maintenance and generalisation of object naming training in anomia associated with degenerative dementia. *Clinical Gerontologist*, **12**, 57–72.

American Psychiatric Association. (1995). *Diagnostic and Statistical Manual of Mental Disorders*, 4th edn. Washington, DC: American Psychiatric Association.

Arendt, T. & Jones, G. (1992). Clinicopathologic correlations and the brain–behaviour relationship in Alzheimer's disease. In G.M.M. Jones & B.M.L. Miesen (eds), *Care-giving in Dementia: Research and Applications*. London: Tavistock/Routledge.

Arkin, S.M. (1992). Audio-assisted memory training with early Alzheimer's patients: two single subject experiments. *Clinical Gerontologist*, **12**, 77–96.

Arkin, S.M. (1998). Alzheimer memory training: positive results replicated. *American Journal of Alzheimer's Disease*, **13** (*March/April*), 102–104.

Bäckman, L. (1992). Memory training and memory improvement in Alzheimer's disease: rules and exceptions. *Acta Neurologica Scandinavica* (*suppl*), **139**, 84–89.

Bäckman, L. (1996). Utilizing compensatory task conditions for episodic memory in Alzheimer's disease. *Acta Neurologica Scandinavica* (*suppl*), **165**, 109–113.

Bäckman, L. & Herlitz, A. (1990). The relationship between prior knowledge and face recognition memory in normal aging and Alzheimer's disease. *Journal of Gerontology, Psychological Sciences*, **45**, P94–100.

Bäckman, L. & Herlitz, A. (1996). Knowledge and memory in Alzheimer's disease: a relationship that exists. In R.G. Morris (ed.), *The Cognitive Neuropsychology of Alzheimer-type Dementia*. Oxford: Oxford University Press.

Bäckman, L., Josephsson, S., Herlitz, A. et al. (1991). The generalisability of training gains in dementia: effects of an imagery-based mnemonic on face-name retention duration. *Psychology and Aging*, **6**, 489–492.

Ballard, C.G., Cassidy, G., Bannister, C. & Mohan, R.N.C. (1993). Prevalence, symptom profile, and aetiology of depression in dementia sufferers. *Journal of Affective Disorders*, **29**, 1–6.

Bender, M., Bauckham, P. & Norris, A. (1998). *The Therapeutic Purposes of Reminiscence*. London: Sage.

Ben-Yishay, Y. & Prigatano, G.P. (1990). Cognitive remediation. In M. Rosenthal, E.R. Griffith, M.R. Bond & J.D. Miller (eds), *Rehabilitation of the Adult and Child with Traumatic Brain Injury*. Philadelphia, PA: F.A. Davis.

Berrios, G.E. (1994a). Dementia and aging since the nineteenth century. In F.A. Huppert, C. Brayne & D.W. O'Connor (eds), *Dementia and Normal Aging*. Cambridge: Cambridge University Press.

Berrios, G.E. (1994b). Dementia: historical overview. In A. Burns & R. Levy (eds), *Dementia*. London: Chapman & Hall.

Bieliauskas, L.A. (1996). Practical approaches to ecological validity of neuropsychological measures in the elderly. In R.J. Sbordone & C.J. Long (eds), *Ecological Validity of Neuropsychological Testing*. Delray Beach, FL: GR Press/St Lucie Press.

Bird, M. (2000). Psychosocial rehabilitation for problems arising from cognitive deficits in dementia. In R.D. Hill, L. Bäckman & A.S. Neely (eds), *Cognitive Rehabilitation in Old Age*. Oxford: Oxford University Press.

Bird, M. (2001). Behavioural difficulties and cued recall of adaptive behaviour in dementia: experimental and clinical evidence. *Neuropsychological Rehabilitation*, **11**, 357–375.

Bird, M. & Kinsella, G. (1996). Long-term cued recall of tasks in senile dementia. *Psychology and Aging*, **11**, 45–56.

Bird, M. & Luszcz, M. (1991). Encoding specificity, depth of processing, and cued recall in Alzheimer's disease. *Journal of Clinical and Experimental Neuropsychology*, **13**, 508–520.

Bird, M. & Luszcz, M. (1993). Enhancing memory performance in Alzheimer's disease: acquisition assistance and cue effectiveness. *Journal of Clinical and Experimental Neuropsychology*, **15**, 921–932.

Blacker, D., Albert, M.S., Bassett, S.S. et al. (1994). Reliability and validity of NINCDS–ADRDA criteria for Alzheimer's disease. *Archives of Neurology*, **51**, 1198–1204.

Bleathman, C. & Morton, I. (1994). Psychological treatments. In A. Burns & R. Levy (eds), *Dementia*. London: Chapman & Hall.

Bourgeois, M.S. (1990). Enhancing conversation skills in patients with Alzheimer's disease using a prosthetic memory aid. *Journal of Applied Behavior Analysis*, **23**, 29–42.

Bourgeois, M.S. (1991). Communication treatment for adults with dementia. *Journal of Speech and Hearing Research*, **34**, 831–844.

Bourgeois, M.S. (1992). Evaluating memory wallets in conversations with persons with dementia. *Journal of Speech and Hearing Research*, **35** (*December*), 1344–1357.

Bourgeois, M.S., Schulz, R. & Burgio, L. (1996). Interventions for caregivers of patients with Alzheimer's disease: a review and analysis of content, process, and outcomes. *International Journal of Aging and Human Development*, **43**, 35–92.

Bowen, J., Teri, L., Kukull, W. et al. (1997). Progression to dementia in patients with isolated memory loss. *Lancet*, **349**, 763–765.

Bråne, G., Karlsson, I., Kihlgren, M. & Norberg, A. (1989). Integrity-promoting care of demented nursing home patients: psychological and biochemical changes. *International Journal of Geriatric Psychiatry*, **4**, 165–172.

Brayne, C. (1994). How common are cognitive impairment and dementia? An epidemiological viewpoint. In F.A. Huppert, C. Brayne & D.W. O'Connor (eds), *Dementia and Normal Aging*. Cambridge: Cambridge University Press.

Breuil, V., de Rotrou, J., Forette, F. et al. (1994). Cognitive stimulation of patients with dementia: preliminary results. *International Journal of Geriatric Psychiatry*, **9**, 211–217.

Brodaty, H. & Gresham, M. (1989). Effect of a training programme to reduce stress in carers of patients with dementia. *British Medical Journal*, **299**, 1375–1379.

Brodaty, H. & Peters, K. E. (1991). Cost-effectiveness of a training programme for dementia carers. *International Psychogeriatrics*, **3**, 11–22.

Bryson, H.M. & Benfield, P. (1997). Donepezil. *Drugs and Aging*, **10**, 234–239.

Burgess, I.S., Wearden, J.H., Cox, T. & Rae, M. (1992). Operant conditioning with subjects suffering from dementia. *Behavioural Psychotherapy*, **20**, 219–237.

Burns, A. (1991). Affective symptoms in Alzheimer's disease. *International Journal of Geriatric Psychiatry*, **6**, 371–376.

Burns, A. & Förstl, H. (1994). The clinical diagnosis of Alzheimer's disease. In A. Burns & R. Levy (eds), *Dementia*. London: Chapman & Hall.

Butti, G., Buzzelli, S., Fiori, M. & Giaquinto, S. (1998). Observations on mentally impaired elderly patients treated with THINKable, a computerized cognitive remediation. *Archives of Gerontology and Geriatrics (suppl)*, **6**, 49–56.

Camp, C.J. (1989). Facilitation of new learning in Alzheimer's disease. In G. Gilmore, P. Whitehouse & M. Wykle (eds), *Memory and Aging: Theory, Research and Practice*. New York: Springer.

Camp, C.J., Bird, M.J. & Cherry, K.E. (2000). Retrieval strategies as a rehabilitation aid for cognitive loss in pathological aging. In R.D. Hill, L. Backman & A.S. Neely (eds), *Cognitive Rehabilitation in Old Age*. Oxford: Oxford University Press.

Camp, C.J., Foss, J.W., Stevens, A.B. et al. (1993). Memory training in normal and demented elderly populations: the E–I–E–I–O model. *Experimental Aging Research*, **19**, 277–290.

Camp, C.J. & Stevens, A.B. (1990). Spaced retrieval: a memory intervention for dementia of the Alzheimer's type (DAT). *Clinical Gerontologist*, **10**, 58–61.

Carswell, A. & Spiegel, R. (1999). Functional assessment. In G.K. Wilcock, R.S. Bucks & K. Rockwood (eds), *Diagnosis and Management of Dementia: a Manual for Memory Disorders Teams*. Oxford: Oxford University Press.

Cheston, R. (1998). Psychotherapeutic work with people with dementia: a review of the literature. *British Journal of Medical Psychology*, **71**, 211–231.

Christensen, H., Griffiths, K., MacKinnon, A. & Jacomb, P. (1997). A quantitative review of cognitive deficits in depression and Alzheimer-type dementia. *Journal of the International Neuropsychological Society*, **3**, 631–651.

Christensen, H., Kopelman, M.D., Stanhope, N. et al. (1998). Rates of forgetting in Alzheimer dementia. *Neuropsychologia*, **36**, 547–557.

Clare, L. (2000). Cognitive Rehabilitation in Early-stage Alzheimer's Disease: Learning and the Impact of Awareness. Unpublished PhD Thesis, The Open University, Milton Keynes.

Clare, L. (2002). We'll fight it as long as we can: coping with the onset of Alzheimer's disease. *Aging and Mental Health*, **6**, 139–148.

Clare, L., Wilson, B.A., Breen, K. & Hodges, J.R. (1999). Errorless learning of face-name associations in early Alzheimer's disease. *Neurocase*, **5**, 37–46.

Clare, L., Wilson, B.A., Carter, G. et al. (2000). Intervening with everyday memory problems in early Alzheimer's disease: an errorless learning approach. *Journal of Clinical and Experimental Neuropsychology*, **22**, 132–146.

Clare, L., Wilson, B.A., Carter, G. et al. (2001). Long-term maintenance of treatment gains following a cognitive rehabilitation intervention in early dementia of Alzheimer type: a single case study. *Neuropsychological Rehabilitation*, **11**, 477–494.

Clarke, C., Sheppard, L., Fillenbaum, G. et al. & the CERAD Investigators. (1999). Variability in annual Mini-Mental State Examination score in patients with probable Alzheimer disease. *Archives of Neurology*, **56**, 857–862.

Cockburn, J. & Keene, J. (2001). Are changes in everyday memory over time in autopsy confirmed Alzheimer's disease related to changes in reported behaviour? *Neuropsychological Rehabilitation*, **11**, 201–217.

Cohen, D. & Eisdorfer, C. (1986). *The Loss of Self: a Family Resource for the Care of Alzheimer's Disease and Related Disorders*. New York: W.W. Norton.

Cohen, G. (1996). Memory and learning in normal ageing. In R.T. Woods (ed.), *Handbook of the Clinical Psychology of Ageing*. Chichester: Wiley.

Coleman, P.G. (1993). Adjustment in later life. In J. Bond, P.G. Coleman, & S. Peace (eds), *Ageing in Society: Introduction to Social Gerontology* (2nd edn). London: Sage.

Coleman, P.G. (1996). Identity management in later life. In R.T. Woods (ed.), *Handbook of the Clinical Psychology of Ageing*. Chichester: Wiley.

Corey-Bloom, J., Anand, R. & Veatch, J. for the ENA713 B352 Study Group. (1998). A randomised trial evaluating the efficacy and safety of ENA713 (rivastigmine tartrate), a new acetylcholinesterase inhibitor, in patients with mild to moderately severe Alzheimer's disease. *International Journal of Geriatric Psychopharmacology*, **1**, 55–65.

Cottrell, V. & Schulz, R. (1993). The perspective of the patient with Alzheimer's disease: a neglected dimension of dementia research. *Gerontologist*, **33**, 205–211.

Cox, S. & Keady, J. (eds) (1999). *Younger People with Dementia: Planning, Practice and Development*. London: Jessica Kingsley.

de Rotrou, J., Frambourt, A., de Susbielle, D. et al. (1999). La stimulation cognitive. In Fondation Nationale de Gérontologie (ed.), *La Maladie d'Alzheimer: Prédiction, Prévention, Prise en Charge. 10ème Congrès de la Fondation Nationale de Gérontologie*. Paris: Fondation Nationale de Gérontologie.

De Vreese, L.P., Neri, H., Fioravanti, M., Belloi, L. & Zanetti, O. (2001). Memory rehabilitation in Alzheimer's disease: a review of progress. *International Journal of Genatric Psychiatry*, **16**, 794–809.

Downs, M. (1999). How to tell? Disclosing a diagnosis of dementia. *Generations*, **23**(3), 30–34.

Droes, R.M. (1997). Psychosocial treatment for demented patients: overview of methods and effects. In B.M.L. Miesen & G.M.M. Jones (eds), *Care-giving in Dementia: Research and Applications*, Vol. 2. London: Routledge.

Feehan, M., Knight, R.G. & Partridge, F.M. (1993). Cognitive complaint and test performance in elderly patients suffering from depression or dementia. *International Journal of Geriatric Psychiatry*, **6**, 287–293.

Folstein, M.F., Folstein, S.E. & McHugh, P.R. (1975). "Mini-Mental State": a practical method for grading the cognitive state of patients for the clinician. *Journal of Psychiatric Research*, **12**, 189–198.

Fox, N.C., Warrington, E.K., Seiffer, A.L. et al. (1998). Presymptomatic cognitive deficits in individuals at risk of familial Alzheimer's disease: a longitudinal prospective study. *Brain*, **121**, 1631–1639.

Franzen, M.D. & Haut, M.W. (1991). The psychological treatment of memory impairment: a review of empirical studies. *Neuropsychology Review*, **2**, 29–63.

Gatz, M., Fiske, A., Fox, L. et al. (1998). Empirically validated psychological treatments for older adults. *Journal of Mental Health and Aging*, **4**, 9–45.

Gilliard, J. & Rabins, P.V. (1999). Carer support. In G.K. Wilcock, R.S. Bucks & K. Rockwood (eds), *Diagnosis and Management of Dementia: a Manual for Memory Disorders Teams*. Oxford: Oxford University Press.

Glisky, E.L. (1998). Differential contribution of frontal and medial temporal lobes to memory: evidence from focal lesions and normal aging. In N. Raz (ed.), *The Other Side of the Error Term*. Amsterdam: Elsevier North Holland.

Golding, E. (1989). *The Middlesex Elderly Assessment of Mental State*. Bury St Edmunds: Thames Valley Test Company.

Goldsmith, M. (1996). *Hearing the Voice of People with Dementia: Opportunities and Obstacles*. London: Jessica Kingsley.

Greene, J.D.W., Baddeley, A. & Hodges, J.R. (1996). Analysis of the episodic memory deficit in early Alzheimer's disease: evidence from the Doors and People Test. *Neuropsychologia*, **34**, 537–551.

Greene, J.D.W., Hodges, J.R. & Baddeley, A.D. (1995). Autobiographical memory and executive function in early dementia of Alzheimer type. *Neuropsychologia*, **33**, 1647–1670.

Gubrium, J.F. (1987). Structuring and destructuring the course of illness: the Alzheimer's disease experience. *Sociology of Health and Illness*, **9**, 1–24.

Hagberg, B. (1997). The dementias in a psychodynamic perspective. In B.M.L. Miesen & G.M.M. Jones (eds), *Care-giving in Dementia: Research and Applications*, Vol. 2. London: Routledge.

Hamilton, H.E. (1994). *Conversations with an Alzheimer's Patient: an Interactional Sociolinguistic Study*. Cambridge: Cambridge University Press.

Hanley, I. (1986). Reality orientation in the care of the elderly patient with dementia—three case studies. In I. Hanley & M. Gilhooly (eds), *Psychological Therapies for the Elderly*. Beckenham: Croom Helm.

Harvey, R.J. (1998). *Young Onset Dementia: Epidemiology, Clinical Symptoms, Family Burden, Support and Outcome*. London: Imperial College of Science and Technology & NHS Executive North Thames.

Hausman, C. (1992). Dynamic psychotherapy with elderly demented patients. In G.M.M. Jones & B.M.L. Miesen (eds), *Care-giving in Dementia: Research and Applications*, Vol. 1. London: Tavistock/Routledge.

Heal, H.C., & Husband, H.J. (1998). Disclosing a diagnosis of dementia: is age a factor? *Aging and Mental Health*, **2**, 144–150.

Henderson, A.S. & Sartorius, N. (1994). International criteria and differential diagnosis. In F. Huppert, C. Brayne & D.W. O'Connor (eds), *Dementia and Normal Aging*. Cambridge: Cambridge University Press.

Herlitz, A., Lipinska, B. & Bäckman, L. (1992). Utilization of cognitive support for episodic remembering in Alzheimer's disease. In L. Bäckman (ed.), *Memory Functioning in Dementia*. Amsterdam: Elsevier.

Herlitz, A. & Viitanen, M. (1991). Semantic organisation and verbal episodic memory in patients with mild and moderate Alzheimer's disease. *Journal of Clinical and Experimental Neuropsychology*, **13**, 559–574.

Heston, L.L., & White, J.A. (1991). *The Vanishing Mind: a Practical Guide to Alzheimer's Disease and Other Dementias*. New York: W.H. Freeman.

Hill, R.D., Evankovich, K.D., Sheikh, J.I. & Yesavage, J.A. (1987). Imagery mnemonic training in a patient with primary degenerative dementia. *Psychology and Aging*, **2**, 204–205.

Hodges, J.R. (1994). *Cognitive Assessment for Clinicians*. Oxford: Oxford University Press.

Hodges, J.R., Patterson, K., Ward, R. et al. (1999). The differentiation of semantic dementia and frontal lobe dementia (temporal and frontal variants of frontotemporal dementia) from early Alzheimer's disease: a comparative neuropsychological study. *Neuropsychology*, **13**, 31–40.

Hofmann, M., Hock, C., Kuhler, A. & Muller-Spahn, F. (1996). Interactive computer-based cognitive training in patients with Alzheimer's disease. *Journal of Psychiatric Research*, **30**, 493–501.

Hope, T. (1994). Personality and behaviour in dementia and normal aging. In F. Huppert, C. Brayne & D.W. O'Connor (eds), *Dementia and Normal Aging*. Cambridge: Cambridge University Press.

Huckle, P.L. (1994). Families and dementia. *International Journal of Geriatric Psychiatry*, **9**, 735–741.

Hughes, C., Berg, L., Danziger, W. et al. (1982). A new clinical scale for the staging of dementia. *British Journal of Psychiatry*, **140**, 566–572.

Huppert, F.A. (1994). Memory function in dementia and normal aging—dimension or dichotomy? In F.A. Huppert, C. Brayne & D.W. O'Connor (eds), *Dementia and Normal Aging*. Cambridge: Cambridge University Press.

Husband, H.J. (1999). The psychological consequences of learning a diagnosis of dementia: three case examples. *Aging and Mental Health*, **3**, 179–183.

Iliffe, S. (1997). Can delays in the recognition of dementia in primary care be avoided? *Aging and Mental Health*, **1**, 7–10.

Josephsson, S., Bäckman, L., Borell, L. et al. (1993). Supporting everyday activities in dementia: an intervention study. *International Journal of Geriatric Psychiatry*, **8**, 395–400.

Karlsson, I., Bråne, G., Melin, E. et al. (1988). Effects of environmental stimulation on biochemical and psychological variables in dementia. *Acta Psychiatrica Scandinavica*, **77**, 207–213.

Karlsson, T., Bäckman, L., Herlitz, A., Nilsson, L.-G., Winblad, B. & Osterlind, P.-O. (1989). Memory improvement at different stages of Alzheimer's disease. *Neuropsychologia*, **27**, 737–742.

Kasl-Godley, J. & Gatz, M. (2000). Psychosocial interventions for individuals with dementia: an integration of theory, therapy, and a clinical understanding of dementia. *Clinical Psychology Review*, **20**, 755–782.

Kay, D.W.K. (1991). The epidemiology of dementia: a review of recent work. *Reviews in Clinical Gerontology*, **1**, 55–66.

Kendrick, D. & Watts, G. (1999). *The Kendrick Assessment Scales of Cognitive Ageing*, 2nd edn. Windsor: NFER-Nelson.

Kitwood, T. (1996). A dialectical framework for dementia. In R.T. Woods (ed.), *Handbook of the Clinical Psychology of Ageing*. Chichester: Wiley.

Kitwood, T. (1997). *Dementia Reconsidered: the Person Comes First*. Buckingham: Open University Press.

Knight, B. (1996). *Psychotherapy with Older Adults*, 2nd edn. Beverly Hills, CA: Sage.

Koder, D.-A. (1998). Treatment of anxiety in the cognitively impaired elderly: can cognitive-behavior therapy help? *International Psychogeriatrics*, **10**, 173–182.

Koltai, D.C., Welsh-Bohmer, K.A. & Schmechel, D.E. (2001). Influence of anosognosia on treatment outcome among dementia patients. *Neuropsychological Rehabilitation*, **11**, 455–475.

Kurlychek, R.T. (1983). Use of a digital alarm chronograph as a memory aid in early dementia. *Clinical Gerontologist*, **1**, 93–94.

Landauer, T.K. & Bjork, R.A. (1978). Optimum rehearsal patterns and name learning. In K.M. Gruneberg, P.E. Morris & R.N. Sykes (eds), *Practical Aspects of Memory*. New York: Academic Press.

Leng, N.R.C. & Copello, A.G. (1990). Rehabilitation of memory after brain injury: is there an effective technique? *Clinical Rehabilitation*, **4**, 63–69.

Lezak, M.D. (1995). *Neuropsychological Assessment*, 3rd edn. New York: Oxford University Press.

Lipinska, B. & Bäckman, L. (1997). Encoding-retrieval interactions in mild Alzheimer's disease: the role of access to categorical information. *Brain and Cognition*, **34**, 274–286.

Lipinska, B., Bäckman, L., Mantyla, T. & Viitanen, M. (1994). Effectiveness of self-generated cues in early Alzheimer's disease. *Journal of Clinical and Experimental Neuropsychology*, **16**, 809–819.

Little, A. & Doherty, B. (1996). Going beyond cognitive assessment: assessment of adjustment, behaviour and the environment. In R.T. Woods (ed.), *Handbook of the Clinical Psychology of Ageing*. Chichester: Wiley.

Little, A.G., Volans, P.J., Hemsley, D.R. & Levy, R. (1986). The retention of new information in senile dementia. *British Journal of Clinical Psychology*, **25**, 71–72.

Lovestone, S., Graham, N. & Howard, R. (1997). Guidelines on drug treatments for Alzheimer's disease. *Lancet*, **350**, 232–233.

Marshall, M. (1999). Person centred technology? *Signpost*, **3**(4), 4–5.

McKenna, P. (1998). Fitness to drive: a neuropsychological perspective. *Journal of Mental Health*, **7**, 9–18.

McKhann, G., Drachman, D., Folstein, M. et al. (1984). Clinical diagnosis of Alzheimer's disease: report of the NINCDS–ADRDA Work Group under the auspices of Department of Health and Human Services task force on Alzheimer's disease. *Neurology*, **34**, 939–944.

Miller, E. (1996). The assessment of dementia. In R. Morris (ed.), *The Cognitive Neuropsychology of Alzheimer-type Dementia*. Oxford: Oxford University Press.

Moffat, N. (1989). Home-based cognitive rehabilitation with the elderly. In L.W. Poon, D.C. Rubin & B.A. Wilson (eds), *Everyday Cognition in Adulthood and Late Life*. Cambridge: Cambridge University Press.

Moffat, N. (1992). Strategies of memory therapy. In B.A. Wilson & N. Moffat (eds), *Clinical Management of Memory Problems*, 2nd edn. London: Chapman & Hall.

Molloy, D.W., Alemayehu, E. & Roberts, R. (1991). Reliability of a standardized Mini-Mental State Examination compared with the traditional Mini-Mental State Examination. *American Journal of Psychiatry*, **148**, 102–105.

Moniz-Cook, E., Agar, S., Gibson, G. et al. (1998). A preliminary study of the effects of early intervention with people with dementia and their families in a memory clinic. *Aging and Mental Health*, **2**, 199–211.

Moniz-Cook, E. & Woods, R.T. (1997). The role of memory clinics and psychosocial intervention in the early stages of dementia. *International Journal of Geriatric Psychiatry*, **12**, 1143–1145.

Moore, S., Sandman, C., McGrady, K. & Kesslak, P. (2001). Memory training improves cognitive ability in patients with dementia. *Neuropsychological Rehabilitation*, **11**, 245–261.

Morris, J.C. (1996). Classification of dementia and Alzheimer's disease. *Acta Neurologica Scandinavica (Suppl)*, **165**, 41–50.

Morris, R.G. (1996). The neuropsychology of Alzheimer's disease and related dementias. In R.T. Woods (ed.), *Handbook of the Clinical Psychology of Ageing*. Chichester: Wiley.

Morris, R.G. & McKiernan, F. (1994). Neuropsychological investigations of dementia. In A. Burns & R. Levy (eds), *Dementia*. London: Chapman & Hall.

Neary, D., Snowden, J.S., Bowen, D.M. et al. (1986). Neuropsychological syndromes in presenile dementia due to cerebral atrophy. *Journal of Neurology, Neurosurgery, and Psychiatry*, **49**, 163–174.

O'Brien, J., Ames, D., Chiu, E. et al. (1998). Severe deep white matter lesions and outcome in elderly patients with major depressive disorder: follow-up study. *British Medical Journal*, **317**, 982–984.

O'Brien, J., Desmond, P., Ames, D. et al. (1996). A magnetic resonance imaging study of white matter lesions in depression and Alzheimer's disease. *British Journal of Psychiatry*, **168**, 477–485.

O'Connor, D.W. (1994). Mild dementia: a clinical perspective. In F. Huppert, C. Brayne & D.W. O'Connor (eds), *Dementia and Normal Aging*. Cambridge: Cambridge University Press.

Pearce, A., Clare, L. & Pistrang, N. (in press). Managing sense of self: coping in the early stages of Alzheimer's disease. *Dementia*.

Perlmuter, L.C. & Monty, R.A. (1989). Motivation and aging. In L.W. Poon, D.C. Rubin & B.A. Wilson (eds), *Everyday Cognition in Adulthood and Late Life*. Cambridge: Cambridge University Press.

Perry, R.J. & Hodges, J.R. (1999). Attention and executive deficits in Alzheimer's disease: a critical review. *Brain*, **122**, 383–404.

Petry, S., Cummings, J.L., Hill, M.A. & Shapira, J. (1989). Personality alterations in dementia of the Alzheimer type: a three-year follow-up study. *Journal of Geriatric Psychiatry and Neurology*, **2**, 203–207.

Pollitt, P.A. (1996). Dementia in old age: an anthropological perspective. *Psychological Medicine*, **26**, 1061–1074.

Prigatano, G.P. (1997). Learning from our successes and failures: reflections and comments on "Cognitive rehabilitation: how it is and how it might be". *Journal of the International Neuropsychological Society*, **3**, 497–499.

Prigatano, G.P. (1999). *Principles of Neuropsychological Rehabilitation*. New York: Oxford University Press.

Quayhagen, M.P. & Quayhagen, M. (1989). Differential effects of family-based strategies on Alzheimer's disease. *Gerontologist*, **29**, 150–155.

Quayhagen, M.P. & Quayhagen, M. (2001). Testing of a cognitive stimulation intervention for dementia caregiving dyads. *Neuropsychological Rehabilitation*, **11**, 319–332.

Rait, G., Walters, K. & Iliffe, S. (1999). The diagnosis and management of dementia in primary care: issues in education, service development, and research. *Generations*, **23** (3), 17–23.

Reifler, B.V. & Larson, E. (1990). Excess disability in dementia of the Alzheimer's type. In E. Light & B.D. Lebowitz (eds), *Alzheimer's Disease Treatment and Family Stress*. New York: Hemisphere.

Reisberg, B., Ferris, S.H., Leon, M.J. de & Crook, T. (1982). The global deterioration scale for assessment of primary degenerative dementia. *American Journal of Psychiatry*, **139**, 1136–1139.

Richards, M. (1996). Neurobiological treatment of Alzheimer's disease. In R. Morris (ed.), *The Cognitive Neuropsychology of Alzheimer-type Dementia*. Oxford: Oxford University Press.

Rogers, S.L. et al. & the Donepezil Study Group. (1998a). Donepezil improves cognition and global function in Alzheimer disease: a 15-week, double-blind, placebo-controlled study. *Archives of Internal Medicine*, **158**, 1021–1034.

Rogers, S.L. et al. & the Donepezil Study Group (1998b). A 24-week, double-blind, placebo-controlled trial of donepezil in patients with Alzheimer's disease. *Neurology*, **50**, 136–145.

Rogers, S.L. & Friedhoff, L.T. (1998). Long-term efficacy and safety of donepezil in the treatment of Alzheimer's disease: an interim analysis of the results of a US multicentre open label extension study. *European Neuropsychopharmacology*, **8**, 67–75.

Romero, B. (1999). Rehabilitative Ansätze bei Alzheimer-Krankheit: die Selbsterhaltungstherapie. In P. Frommelt & H. Grötzbach (eds), *Neurorehabilitation: Grundlagen, Praxis, Dokumentation*. Berlin: Blackwell Wissenschafts-Verlag.

Romero, B. & Wenz, M. (2001). Self-maintenance therapy in Alzheimer's disease. *Neuropsychological Rehabilitation*, **11**, 333–355.

Ross, L.K., Arnsberger, P. & Fox, P.J. (1998). The relationship between cognitive functioning and disease severity with depression in dementia of the Alzheimer's type. *Aging and Mental Health*, **2**, 319–327.

Roth, M., Huppert, F.A., Mountjoy, C.Q. & Tym, E. (1999). *The Revised Cambridge Examination for Mental Disorders of the Elderly*, 2nd edn. Cambridge: Cambridge University Press.

Roth, M. (1994). The relationship between dementia and normal aging of the brain. In F.A. Huppert, C. Brayne & D.W. O'Connor (eds), *Dementia and Normal Aging*. Cambridge: Cambridge University Press.

Royal College of Psychiatrists (1997). Interim statement on anti-dementia drugs: implications, concerns and policy proposals. *Psychiatric Bulletin*, **21**, 586–587.

Sabat, S.R. (1994). Excess disability and malignant social psychology: a case study of Alzheimer's disease. *Journal of Community and Applied Social Psychology*, **4**, 157–166.

Sabat, S.R. (1995). The Alzheimer's disease sufferer as a semiotic subject. *Philosophy, Psychiatry, and Psychology*, **1**, 145–160.

Sabat, S.R. & Harré, R. (1992). The construction and deconstruction of self in Alzheimer's disease. *Ageing and Society*, **12**, 443–461.

Sabat, S.R., Wiggs, C. & Pinizzotto, A. (1984). Alzheimer's disease: clinical vs. observational studies of cognitive ability. *Journal of Clinical and Experimental Gerontology*, **6**, 337–359.

Sandman, C.A. (1993). Memory rehabilitation in Alzheimer's disease: preliminary findings. *Clinical Gerontologist*, **13**, 19–33.

Saxton, J., Swihart, A., McGonigle-Gibson, K. et al. (1990). Assessment of the severely impaired patient: description and validation of a new neuropsychological test battery. *Psychological Assessment*, **2**, 298–303.

Schacter, D.L., Rich, S.A. & Stampp, M.S. (1985). Remediation of memory disorders: experimental evaluation of the spaced-retrieval technique. *Journal of Clinical and Experimental Neuropsychology*, **7**, 79–96.

Schneck, M.K., Reisberg, B. & Ferris, S.H. (1982). An overview of current concepts of Alzheimer's disease. *American Journal of Psychiatry*, **139**, 165–173.

Sevush, S. & Leve, N. (1993). Denial of memory deficit in Alzheimer's disease. *American Journal of Psychiatry*, **150**, 748–751.

Sinason, V. (1992). *Mental Handicap and the Human Condition: New Approaches from the Tavistock*. London: Free Association Books.

Sixsmith, A., Stilwell, J. & Copeland, J. (1993). "Rementia": challenging the limits of dementia care. *International Journal of Geriatric Psychiatry*, **8**, 993–1000.

Small, G.W., Rabins, P.V., Barry, P.P. et al. (1997). Diagnosis and treatment of Alzheimer disease and related disorders: consensus statement of the American Association for Geriatric Psychiatry, the Alzheimer's Association and the American Geriatric Society. *Journal of the American Medical Association*, **278**, 1363–1371.

Snaith, R.P. & Zigmond, A.S. (1994). *The Hospital Anxiety and Depression Scale*. Windsor: NFER-Nelson.

Spector, A., Orrell, M., Davies, S. & Woods, B. (2001). Can reality orientation be rehabilitated? Development and piloting of an evidence-based programme of cognition-based therapies for people with dementia. *Neuropsychological Rehabilitation*, **11**, 377–397.

Spector, A., Orrell, M., Davies, S. & Woods, R.T. (1998). *Reality Orientation for Dementia: a Review of the Evidence for Its Effectiveness* (Issue 4). Oxford: Update Software.

Spreen, O. & Strauss, E. (1998). *A Compendium of Neuropsychological Tests: Administration, Norms and Commentary*, 2nd edn. Oxford: Oxford University Press.

Storandt, M. & Hill, R.D. (1989). Very mild senile dementia of the Alzheimer type. II. Psychometric test performance. *Archives of Neurology*, **46**, 383–386.

Storandt, M., Morris, J.C., Rubin, E.H. et al. (1992). Progression of senile dementia of the Alzheimer type on a battery of psychometric tests. In L. Bäckman (ed.), *Memory Functioning in Dementia*. Amsterdam: Elsevier.

Sutton, L.J. & Cheston, R. (1997). Rewriting the story of dementia: a narrative approach to psychotherapy with people with dementia. In M. Marshall (ed.), *State of the Art in Dementia Care*. London: Centre for Policy on Ageing.

Teri, L. & Gallagher-Thompson, D. (1991). Cognitive-behavioral interventions for treatment of depression in Alzheimer's patients. *Gerontologist*, **31**, 413–416.

Teri, L., Truax, P., Logsdon, R. et al. (1992). Assessment of behavioral problems in dementia: the revised memory and behavior problems checklist. *Psychology and Aging*, **7**, 622–631.

Thompson, P., Inglis, F., Findlay, D. et al. (1997). Memory clinic attenders: a review of 150 consecutive patients. *Aging and Mental Health*, **1**, 181–183.

Tierney, M.C., Szalai, J.P., Snow, W.G. & Fisher, R.H. (1996). The prediction of Alzheimer disease. *Archives of Neurology*, **53**, 423–427.

Trenerry, M.R., Crosson, B., DeBoe, J. & Leber, W.R. (1989). Stroop Neuropsychological Screening Test. Odessa, FL: Psychological Assessment Resources.

van der Cammen, T.J.M., Simpson, J.M., Fraser, R.M. et al. (1987). The memory clinic: a new approach to the detection of dementia. *British Journal of Psychiatry*, **150**, 359–364.

van Hout, H., Vernooij-Dassen, M., Bakker, K. et al. (2000). General practitioners on dementia: tasks, practices and obstacles. *Patient Education and Counselling*, **39**, 219–225.

Vitaliano, P.P., Young, H.M. & Russo, J. (1991). Burden: a review of measures used among caregivers of individuals with dementia. *Gerontologist*, **31**, 67–75.

Wands, K., Merskey, H., Hachinski, V. et al. (1990). A questionnaire investigation of anxiety and depression in early dementia. *Journal of the American Geriatrics Society*, **38**, 535–538.

Welsh, K., Butters, N., Hughes, J. & Mohs, R. (1992). Detection and staging of dementia in Alzheimer's disease: use of the neuropsychological measures developed for the Consortium to Establish a Registry for Alzheimer's Disease. *Archives of Neurology*, **49**, 448–452.

Welsh, K., Butters, N., Hughes, J. et al. (1991). Detection of abnormal memory decline in mild cases of Alzheimer's disease using CERAD neuropsychological measures. *Archives of Neurology*, **48**, 278–281.

Whitehouse, P.J., Lerner, A. & Hedera, P. (1993). Dementia. In K.M. Heilman & E. Valenstein (eds), *Clinical Neuropsychology*. Oxford: Oxford University Press.

Wilcock, G.K., Bucks, R.S. & Rockwood, K. (1999). *Diagnosis and Management of Dementia: a Manual for Memory Disorders Teams*. Oxford: Oxford University Press.

Wild, K.V. & Kaye, J.A. (1998). The rate of progression of Alzheimer's disease in the later stages: evidence from the Severe Impairment Battery. *Journal of the International Neuropsychological Society*, **4**, 512–516.

Wilson, B.A. (1990). Cognitive rehabilitation for brain injured adults. In B.G. Deelman, R.J. Saan & A.H. van Zomeren (eds), *Traumatic Brain Injury: Clinical, Social and Rehabilitational Aspects*. Amsterdam: Swets & Zeitlinger.

Wilson, B.A. (1995). Management and remediation of memory problems in brain-injured adults. In A.D. Baddeley, B.A. Wilson & F.N. Watts (eds), *Handbook of Memory Disorders*, 1st edn. Chichester: Wiley.

Wilson, B.A. (1997). Cognitive rehabilitation: how it is and how it might be. *Journal of the International Neuropsychological Society*, **3**, 487–496.

Wilson, B.A., Cockburn, J. & Baddeley, A.D. (1985). *The Rivermead Behavioural Memory Test*. Bury St Edmunds: Thames Valley Test Company.

Woods, B., Portnoy, S., Head, D. & Jones, G. (1992). Reminiscence and life review with persons with dementia: which way forward? In G.M.M. Jones & B.M.L. Miesen (eds), *Care-giving in Dementia: Research and Applications*, Vol. 1. London: Tavistock/Routledge.

Woods, R.T. (1996a). Mental health problems in late life. In R.T. Woods (ed.), *Handbook of the Clinical Psychology of Ageing*. Chichester: Wiley.

Woods, R.T. (1996b). Psychological "therapies" in dementia. In R.T. Woods (ed.), *Handbook of the Clinical Psychology of Ageing*. Chichester: Wiley.

Woods, R.T. & Britton, P.G. (1985). *Clinical Psychology with the Elderly*. London: Croom Helm.

World Health Organization. (1992). *The ICD-10 Classification of Mental and Behavioural disorders: Clinical Descriptions and Diagnostic Guidelines*. Geneva: World Health Organization, Division of Mental Health.

Wright, N. & Lindesay, J. (1995). A survey of memory clinics in the British Isles. *International Journal of Geriatric Psychiatry*, **10**, 379–385.

Yale, R. (1995). *Developing Support Groups for Individuals with Early Stage Alzheimer's Disease: Planning, Implementation and Evaluation*. Baltimore, MD: Health Professions Press.

Yale, R. (1999). Support groups and other services for individuals with early-stage Alzheimer's disease. *Generations*, **23**(3), 57–61.

Yesavage, J.A. (1982). Degree of dementia and improvement with memory training. *Clinical Gerontology*, **1**, 77–81.

Yesavage, J.A., Brink, T.L., Rose, T.L. et al. (1983). Development and validation of a geriatric depression screening scale: a preliminary report. *Journal of Psychiatric Research*, **17**, 37–49.

Zanetti, O., Binetti, G., Magni, E. et al. (1997). Procedural memory stimulation in Alzheimer's disease: impact of a training programme. *Acta Neurologica Scandinavica*, **95**, 152–157.

Zanetti, O., Magni, E., Binetti, G. et al. (1994). Is procedural memory stimulation effective in Alzheimer's disease? *International Journal of Geriatric Psychiatry*, **9**, 1006–1007.

Zanetti, O., Zanieri, G., de Giovanni, G. et al. (2001). Effectiveness of procedural memory stimulation in mild Alzheimer's disease patients: a controlled study. *Neuropsychological Rehabilitation*, **11**, 263–272.

Zarit, S.H., Zarit, J.M. & Reever, K.E. (1982). Memory training for severe memory loss: effects on senile dementia patients and their families. *Gerontologist*, **22**, 373–377.

CHAPTER 33

Reducing the Impact of Cognitive Impairment in Dementia

Bob Woods

Dementia Services Development Centre, University of Wales Bangor, UK

Whilst in their early stages the dementias may be thought of as primarily "memory disorders", diagnostic definitions of a dementia in fact require "global" impairment of cognitive functions. In practice, this may mean memory plus one or two other areas of difficulty (American Psychiatric Association, 1994). The impact of a dementing disorder extends far beyond memory, and indeed many accounts now emphasize the importance of noncognitive features, such as depression, psychotic phenomena, behaviour problems and personality changes in contributing to the strain experienced by family caregivers and in reducing quality of life for the person with dementia. Interventions with people with dementia and their caregivers must, accordingly, have a broad focus if they are to be widely applicable.

Generally, dementing disorders are progressive, although the rate and pattern of change may vary greatly between individuals. This poses a particular difficulty for rehabilitation efforts, which need to be flexible enough to assist the person and caregivers in coping with and adjusting to both day-to-day fluctuations and longer-term deterioration. Maintaining function may be a valid target, rather than necessarily seeking improvements. Careful selection of targets for intervention that will make a real difference to the person's quality of life is also important, in order to maximize the usefulness of therapeutic input.

This chapter aims to outline broad psychosocial strategies for maximizing function in people with dementia, and to examine the evidence for their effectiveness and utility. The first section describes how the care environment might be adapted to support the person's cognitive abilities. Subsequent sections examine the two major cognitive approaches that have seen widespread use in the dementia care field—Reality orientation (RO) and reminiscence. Finally, the interplay between cognitive approaches and noncognitive features, specifically affect and behaviour problems, will be considered. Individually-tailored memory training programmes, using procedures such as spaced retrieval and errorless learning, which constitute a major and welcome development in this field, are considered by Clare in Chapter 32 (this volume).

The Handbook of Memory Disorders. Edited by A.D. Baddeley, M.D. Kopelman and B.A. Wilson
© 2002 John Wiley & Sons, Ltd.

THE CARE ENVIRONMENT

Environmental Design and Dementia

Lawton's "environmental docility" model (Parmelee & Lawton, 1990) suggests that persons with dementia are more likely than average persons to be shaped by and vulnerable to environmental contingencies, because of their lowered competence and function. Those with intact cognitive function are thought to be more able to shape the environment to suit their individual needs; those with dementia are much more vulnerable to the impact of their physical, social and interpersonal surroundings.

How can the care environment be designed to be more dementia-friendly? There has been great interest in this topic in recent years (Carr & Marshall, 1993). Potential environmental adaptations include simplifying the locating of important rooms and places through careful and clear signposting, reducing the number of irrelevant and distracting sources of stimuli, and making use of familiar, well-learned associations wherever possible. A small homely unit, with a few, consistent staff and many familiar items and possessions in the person's own room, should be much less inherently cognitively demanding than a large institution, with long corridors, many other residents and a frequently changing staff group. However, as Parmelee & Lawton (1990) indicate, there is little empirical research specifically evaluating design features, perhaps because of the methodological difficulties which would have to be overcome. It is not even established, for example, that reducing the size of the unit has beneficial effects; smaller units almost inevitably necessitate a higher staff:resident ratio, and this may be the crucial factor. Providing "wandering paths" which safely return the person to his/her starting point, and using colour, architectural and other features to distinguish areas within the unit have also not been adequately evaluated. Netten (1989, 1993) has examined the relationship between architectural complexity of residential homes and the ability of persons with dementia to find their way around; different factors were shown to operate in large, communal homes compared with those homes where residents lived together in small groups. Small group homes tended to assist orientation, with the presence of meaningful decision points acting as helpful landmarks.

There have been developments of specialized, small group-living environments for people with dementia internationally. In France, these are described as "cantou", a word meaning "hearth", reflecting that home is around the fireside (Ritchie et al., 1992). Typically there is one large communal room, with the residents' bedrooms and bathrooms and so on opening off the main room, avoiding confusing corridors and reducing the load on spatial memory. The kitchen area might typically be in a corner of the communal room, with food preparation a central interest and activity (in certain other countries this feature would be unacceptable to regulatory authorities). Ritchie et al. (1992) report that residents in the cantou units were more mobile and less dependent in daily activities, had better language skills and interacted more with other residents than residents in long-term hospital care. However, there were indications that these apparent benefits arose from differences in the patients admitted to the two types of care. Although there was considerable overlap in degree of dementia between the two settings, it appeared that the positive impact of the cantou became less evident at more severe levels of dementia.

In the UK, the "domus" units have been particularly influential. Lindesay et al. (1991) describe "the domus philosophy", which is aimed at tackling staff attitudes and fears which lead to poor quality of life in institutional settings for people with dementia. Emphasis is given to seeking to maintain the independence and preserved abilities of persons with dementia, through having an active role in the life of the domus, where the intention is to apply domestic rather than hospital standards of safety and hygiene. Dean et al. (1993) report a prospective evaluation of a domus unit for people with dementia. Patients were assessed in a longstay hospital ward prior to moving to the purpose-built domus (12 beds) and were then monitored at intervals during their first year of residence. Improvements were identified in cognitive function, self-care and communication skills; increased levels of activities and interactions were also observed. Some dramatic changes were observed: one patient spoke for the first time in 5 years within a week of moving to the domus. Skea & Lindesay (1996) report a further evaluation, involving a domus-type home and a community hospital ward offering enhanced care. Again, there are positive results favouring the domus unit, with an increase in both quantity and quality of interactions, and increases in residents' rated communication skills. Some less marked improvements were also noted on the enhanced-care hospital ward, compared with a traditional hospital unit. The improvements in quality of life in domus units do have a cost: staff–resident ratios are higher than in the hospital wards, and the costs are accordingly higher (Beecham et al., 1993) in contrast to the cantou units in France, which were established in part to lower the costs of care.

In Sweden, "group living homes" have been developed. These typically consist of a group of four flats in an ordinary housing block, in which eight people with dementia live, each having his/her own room and possessions, with 24 h staff cover for the unit as a whole (Wimo et al., 1991). A detailed evaluation of the Swedish group-living units by Annerstedt et al. (1993) compared a group of people with dementia moved from institutional care to such units with a control group who remained. Cognitive and mood changes favoured the group-living group over a 6 month period; although both groups declined over a full year, there were indications of this being less marked in the group-living residents.

The special care units described above involve a change in the pattern of care as well as changes to the physical structure and layout of the unit. Another study that has looked specifically at the impact of changing the care regime, and which included cognitive outcomes as well as outcomes relating to activity, mood and function, is reported from Sweden by Brane et al. (1989), evaluating "integrity-promoting care". This involved staff in a nursing home being trained and supported in implementing individualized care, with patients encouraged to participate more in decisions and activities. Staff were trained to allow more time to residents so that they could go at their own pace and not be rushed. Changes to the physical environment aimed at achieving a more home-like atmosphere, with domestic-style furnishing and personalized clothing and possessions, were also encouraged. Changes over the 3 month intervention period and at a follow-up 6 months later were compared with those of a control group in a second nursing home. Patients in the integrity-promoting care group were reported to have become less confused, anxious and distractible; there were also improvements in mood and motor performance. Many of the benefits remained at the follow-up evaluation.

Reducing Cognitive Load

If cognitive demands can be reduced on the person, their retained abilities may be used more effectively. Alberoni et al. (1992) have suggested that working with people with dementia individually, rather than in groups, would reduce the cognitive demands upon them and thus perhaps improve function. These researchers demonstrated that in group conversations, people with dementia have difficulty in remembering who said what, particularly when the group size was larger. They tended to use spatial location as a cue, with performance being particularly disrupted when group members changed places. It should be noted that these difficulties were elicited in relation to patients watching a videotape of a group conversation, rather than participating themselves. In an actual conversation with familiar people, the problems might not be so marked. Morris (1994) suggests that, because of these deficits, group therapies "can degenerate into a monologue between individual staff members and patients". This contention finds support from the finding of Woods et al. (1992), that in reminiscence sessions the majority of interactions taking place were between staff and patients; as would be predicted, they occurred more often between patients in a smaller group. Gibson (1994) similarly recommends small groups for people with dementia. In choosing whether to work with individuals or a small group, the advantages of working in groups—peer support, a social atmosphere, shared experiences—need to be weighed against their undoubted cognitive demands. Where groups are used they should be as small as possible, with members retaining the same seating position from session to session; background noise and distractions should be kept to a minimum, and care taken to ensure that only one person speaks at a time.

External Memory Aids

External memory aids reduce the level of demand on effortful, self-initiated cognitive processes and provide support for the person in cuing and prompting retrieval of information—key features of effective cognitive training approaches (Bäckman, 1992). Retrieval cues in dementia generally require a high degree of specificity in order to be effective; they also need to be salient and placed so that the person will encounter the cue at the relevant time. Nonspecific external aids, such as an alarm clock or a kitchen timer, serve only to remind the person that something is to be remembered, leaving him/her with the frustration of not recalling what it was that had to be done; a note of an appointment in a diary that is not consulted will not influence the person's behaviour. The effects of more specific aids have mainly been demonstrated through single-case studies, e.g. a 68-year-old patient with a severe memory impairment successfully used a diary to prompt continuing awareness of personal information taught to her in daily individual sessions (Woods, 1983). Hanley & Lusty (1984) report a single-case study where an 84-year-old patient with dementia was able to achieve a higher level of orientation, using a watch and a diary as retrieval cues. Specific training was required in the use of the cues; without this, the patient did not spontaneously make use of them. During the training phase, the patient kept a far greater proportion of her "appointments" than previously, demonstrating an impact on everyday behaviour as well as on testing.

In a series of studies, Bourgeois (1990, 1992) has evaluated the effects of a prosthetic memory aid on conversational skills in people with dementia. The aid consisted of photographs and pictures of past and more recent events, important people in the person's life and so on, in a convenient, robust wallet or book format. The person's spouse and other visitors were encouraged to use the aid when talking with the person. The results suggest that its use was associated with less ambiguous utterances and more statements of fact. The quality of conversation was assessed by independent raters as being significantly improved with the use of the aid as a focus for conversation. The aid is also reported to have proved useful in improving the quality of interaction between pairs of people with dementia. Although the aid is described as a prosthesis, it appears to be effective in prompting a number of memories related to each item, rather than simply acting as a replacement memory store for the specific information contained therein.

External memory aids have been explicitly used by Josephsson et al. (1993) to reduce the load on the person's own memory and to support retrieval in daily living tasks. The performance of four patients with dementia was evaluated on tasks such as preparing and consuming a drink or snack. Signs on drawers and cupboards indicated the location of required items. Physical demonstrations of task components were provided for the patient to repeat. Verbal prompts and cues were also given. Improvements in task performance were shown by three patients; for two of these, continued environmental support and guidance were needed to maintain these gains. The remaining patient's lack of improvement was attributed to a high level of anxiety interfering with the learning process.

The need for staff input, at least initially, in reinforcing the use of the external aids is demonstrated by the RO literature on the effects of signposting on spatial orientation. In several studies where people with dementia have been trained to find locations in a hospital ward or nursing home, signposting alone had less impact than training to use the signposts and other landmarks in the environment (Hanley, 1981; Gilleard et al., 1981; Lam & Woods, 1986). Such signposts may be viewed as retrieval cues; certainly some people with dementia are capable of benefiting from them, with practice in their use, even though not using them spontaneously. Such a use of cues fits well with the conclusion of Bäckman (1992), that people with dementia require support at both the time of learning and at the time of retrieval for optimal performance.

REALITY ORIENTATION (RO)

This long-established psychosocial approach has been used with older people with dementia since the late 1950s, and an extensive literature, both evaluative and descriptive, is available (see e.g. Holden & Woods, 1995). Two major components of reality orientation (RO) are usually described. Twenty-four hour RO (or informal RO) involves a number of changes to the environment, with clear signposting of locations around the ward or home, extensive use of notices and other memory aids, and a consistent approach by all staff in interacting with the person with dementia. In its original form, staff undertaking 24-h RO were intended to offer orientating information in each and every interaction; more recently, a modification has been described where staff are trained to take a more reactive stance, orientating the person only in response to his/her requests (Reeve & Ivison, 1985; Williams et al., 1987). RO sessions (or RO classes) are structured group sessions, involving a small number of patients and staff, meeting regularly, often several times a week for half an hour or so. A wide variety of activities and materials are used to engage the patients with their surroundings, to maintain contact with the wider world and to provide cognitive stimulation. A typical session would go over basic information (such as names of those in the group, day, date, time and place), discuss a current relevant theme of interest, perhaps play a number or naming game, and finish with refreshments. Throughout there would be a tangible focus: a white-board for the current information; pictures or objects appropriate to the theme; personal diaries and notebooks for those able to record information for later use.

Although Holden & Woods (1995) identified over 20 studies meeting the criterion of reporting an evaluation of the effects of RO, in comparison with either no treatment or an alternative intervention, methodological weaknesses meant that only six could be included in a meta-analysis, which focused on randomized controlled trials (RCTs) of RO sessions (Spector et al., 1999a, 2000). This systematic review included studies where patients attended groups for at least 3 weeks, the minimum number of sessions being 10. From the six included RCTs there was a total of 125 patients, of whom 67 received RO and 58 were in control groups. All six studies utilized measures of cognitive function; the results overall were significantly in favour of an effect of RO on cognitive function (estimated effect size 0.59). Measures of behavioural function could be analysed from three studies, having a total of 48 patients (28 experimental, 20 control). In the individual studies the results on behavioural measures were insignificant, but the joint analysis indicated a significant effect of RO sessions in this domain also (estimated effect size 0.66).

Control groups used in the analysed studies included some form of "social therapy", to control for the effects of increased attention in half the studies and "no treatment" in the other half. There was no obvious difference in the results obtained depending on the nature of the control group, and it would appear that the effects observed are not simply attributable to an increase in staff attention and input to those in the experimental groups. The number and duration of RO sessions did not appear to influence the results; however, the severity of dementia of the patients included in each study could not be directly compared, and the amount of RO required for a therapeutic effect could potentially co-vary with severity. The effects reported are those immediately following the intervention. Longer-term follow-up has been attempted in a few studies, with conflicting results. Maintenance of any benefits is generally regarded as an important issue in RO studies, with the expectation that further input, perhaps less intensively, or as "booster" sessions, would almost certainly be required; this has yet to be thoroughly researched; 24 h RO may also have a part to play in the maintenance of improvements following RO sessions (Reeve & Ivison, 1985).

The exact nature of the cognitive improvements associated with RO remains unclear. Whilst it is clear that RO sessions are usually associated with increased scores on measures of verbal orientation, suggestions that more general cognitive improvements may occur are more controversial. Some studies suggest that only those orientation items specifically taught are learned; others that from a battery of cognitive tests, only the orientation items show improvement. More recent reports (e.g. Breuil et al., 1994; Zanetti et al., 1995) have tended to support the notion that more wide-ranging improvements in cognition may follow cognitive stimulation of this type.

Changes in function and behaviour have proved much more elusive than cognitive changes in individual studies; in general they have been the exception rather than the rule. This may reflect the small sample sizes in many studies, with the behaviour rating scales being used often appearing less sensitive to the small changes envisaged. In addition, an environment encouraging dependence (as many have been shown to do) may counteract any benefits from group sessions. It is also doubtful whether verbal orientation has any influence on many of the areas of function, such as feeding and dressing, which comprise much of the content of the behaviour rating scales typically used. It could be argued that direct training of a particular skill will be required to maximize the probability of behavioural change; several workers have shown this in relation to ward orientation—the person finding his/her way around the ward or home. Improvements in this domain have been shown in relation to specific training by Hanley et al. (1981) and associated with 24 h RO by Reeve & Ivison (1985) and

Williams et al. (1987). These studies have in common a demonstrable intervention in the person's living environment, the former through direct training, the latter two through the monitored evaluation of 24 h RO. The greatest range of behavioural improvement reported was evident in these studies. Holden & Woods (1995) conclude that behavioural changes appear to be more likely in studies where the implementation of the 24 h RO has been monitored to ensure that it has actually been carried out as planned. It cannot be assumed that training staff in the approach ensures its implementation (Hanley, 1984). Where the aim is for the patient to be better orientated around the ward or home, direct training for the patient, which can be simply monitored and evaluated, has much to commend it. Evidence of the effectiveness of simple training sessions in finding relevant locations on the ward or in the home is provided by a number of studies, including a small group study (five in each group), involving a comparison with no treatment (Hanley et al., 1981) and several single-case studies: Hanley (1981), reporting a series of eight single-cases; Gilleard et al. (1981), a series of six single-cases; and Lam & Woods (1986), one case. All the single-case studies utilized experimental designs allowing the effect of intervention to be clearly demonstrated. There is some evidence that clear signposting may add to the effectiveness of the training.

Twenty-four hour RO does not lend itself so readily to evaluation through RCTs, in view of the change of environment and regime it requires. However, there have been several comparison group studies (e.g. Zepelin et al., 1981; Williams et al., 1987) where the intervention takes place only in one of two units thought to be similar at baseline. Early studies tended to be disappointing, at least in terms of behavioural change. Indeed, Zepelin's study found a number of changes in behavioural function favouring an untreated control group over a 12 month period. However, this study also encountered a number of problems in relation to the reliability and comparability of the behavioural rating measures used. The modified 24 h RO approach adopted by Williams et al. in Australia appears more successful, being associated with cognitive and behavioural change. Interestingly, in Williams et al.'s (1987) study, cognitive changes were achieved with 24 h RO alone, without RO sessions.

Gatz et al. (1998), reviewing a range of psychological approaches in dementia, conclude that "reality orientation is probably efficacious in slowing cognitive decline". They point out, as do Holden & Woods (1995), the danger of RO being implemented without sufficient sensitivity, leading to possible frustration and distress in the patient (Dietch et al., 1989). This consideration has led the American Psychiatric Association in their 1997 Practice Guideline to suggest that the small gains associated with approaches such as RO do not justify the risk of negative effects. Certainly RO, as a general therapeutic programme, is now rarely encountered in practice, largely because of concerns that it was over-confrontational, tended to emphasize the patient's deficits rather than strengths, and did not focus sufficiently on clinically relevant treatment goals. What is the clinical significance of a change in a few points on a test of verbal orientation? Holden & Woods (1995) argue that there is much to be learned from the research on RO that could be applied in the framework of person-centred care. They suggest there is a need to identify individual goals specific to each patient, to recognize the possibility of learning and change, and to work with the patient on the areas of concern in a collaborative and empathic, rather than a controlling or confrontational, manner. They view an RO-type approach as having some role for selected patients in the context of their individual care plan.

The recent development of drugs which act on the cholinergic system by maintaining levels of acetylcholine (known to be depleted in Alzheimer's disease) has stimulated further interest in whether the impact of psychosocial approaches on cognition might be of a similar order to that of the pharmacological approach (Orrell & Woods, 1996). A major difficulty in making this comparison has been the relative lack of rigour of the research evaluating psychosocial interventions. Whilst double-blind RCTs of drug vs. placebo are standard in drug research, with sample sizes allowing adequate statistical power, and standardized assessment measures used, evaluations of RO, for example, have rarely incorporated assessors blind to treatment group, have had small samples and idiosyncratic outcome measures, and have not generally been adequately randomized or used a credible "placebo" control group. Some of these differences reflect the greater intrinsic complexity of evaluating psychosocial research, where the intervention simply cannot be as neatly packaged as a pill; others reflect the lack of priority and funding given to this area. Orrell & Woods determined to carry out a study of sufficient extent and quality to make a comparison with drug trials feasible. The development of this study is described by Spector et al. (2001). The intervention used has been developed primarily from a consideration of the evidence base reviewed for the systematic review described above, together with some features of reminiscence therapy (see below). It is designed to offer a group programme of 15 sessions, with an extensive cognitive input embedded in activities offering interest and enjoyment. Pilot groups led to the further development of the intervention programme and refinement of measures. The results from the pilot study were encouraging, with improvements in cognition and mood emerging. At the time of writing, the major RCT comparing the intervention package with no treatment continues and is two-thirds complete; a variety of residential homes and day-centres are participating; assessments are made by raters blind to group membership. A preliminary analysis of 142 people with dementia who have completed the trial (80 treatment; 62 control), indicates that significant cognitive changes (on the widely used ADAS–COG instrument) favouring the intervention group are evident. The effect size appears to be almost identical to that obtained using the same measure in trials of the new "antidementia" drugs, although over a shorter time period, of 8 weeks rather than 6 months. Importantly, people with dementia in the intervention group also show significant improvements in quality of life, suggesting that the implementation of this package is, so far, avoiding the negative features associated with the misuse of RO.

REMINISCENCE THERAPY

The use of past memories to establish a point of interest and contact has been often used in RO sessions, and has attracted much interest as an approach in its own right (Woods & McKiernan, 1995; Gibson, 1994). Reminiscence work with older people more generally developed from psychotherapeutic considerations, emphasizing the place of life-review in adaptation (Coleman, 1986; Bornat, 1994). Reminiscence has been used extensively with patients who are depressed as well as those with dementia; it should be recognized that the aims and techniques may need to be different in each case. Norris (1986) provides an excellent description of the practical application of a variety of reminiscence techniques.

Reminiscence work with people with dementia may have a variety of goals, including increasing communication and socialization, and providing pleasure and entertainment. It may take a variety of forms, and use a range of techniques. The use of memory triggers, such as photographs, objects, music and archive recordings, is a common feature of reminiscence work with people with dementia. In evaluating the impact of reminiscence therapy it is vital to specify the approach and procedures used.

Reminiscence work may be given a cognitive rationale. People with dementia often appear able to recall events from their childhood but not from earlier the same day. Accordingly, it may be sensible to tap into the apparently preserved store of remote memories. In fact, studies of remote memory suggest that recall for specific events is not relatively preserved—performance across the lifespan is depressed compared with age-matched controls. People with dementia, like all older people, recall more memories from earlier life (Morris, 1994). Some of the "memories" represent well-rehearsed, much-practised items or anecdotes or have particular personal and/or emotional significance for the person concerned. Morris points out there is an almost complete absence of autobiographical memories from the person's middle years; conceivably the resulting disconnection of past and present might contribute to the person's difficulty in retaining a clear sense of personal identity.

Outcome literature on reminiscence therapy in dementia is sparse, especially in relation to its impact on cognition. The Cochrane systematic review on reminiscence therapy for dementia (Spector et al., 1999b) identified only one suitable RCT, a comparison with RO and no treatment reported by Baines et al. (1987) in a residential home setting. Groups of residents having a moderate to severe degree of cognitive impairment met for 30 min a day, 5 days a week for 4 weeks, and a range of reminiscence aids were used. A variety of measures were used; cognitive (verbal orientation) and behavioural changes were analysed in the Cochrane review, both of which were not significant, although the behavioural scale slightly favoured treatment. However, it should be noted that the sample size was very small, with just five residents in each of the conditions compared. The study used a cross-over design, and it appeared that residents who took part in reminiscence following a period of RO did better than those participating in the interventions in the reverse order, compared with untreated controls. Staff involved in a reminiscence group acquired much more individual knowledge of the residents in the group than they did of residents in a control group who received no additional treatment. Residents were rated as deriving a great deal of enjoyment from the groups, both by staff taking part in the groups and by staff who saw the residents only outside the groups. Attendance at the reminiscence groups was consistently high.

At least one other RCT is available in the literature (Goldwasser et al., 1987). Twenty-seven nursing home residents with a diagnosis of dementia were randomly assigned to a reminiscence group, supportive group therapy or to a no-treatment control. The groups met for 30 min, twice a week for 5 weeks. No changes were evident on a cognitive measure (the Mini-Mental State Examination) or a measure of activities of daily living. There was a significant improvement on a depression scale for the reminiscence group compared with the other two conditions. However, Knight (1996) suggests that this may be largely due to their higher initial level of depression.

The evaluative literature on reminiscence is then inconclusive with regard to cognitive and behavioural change, perhaps because this has not been a major aim of work in this area. There has been perhaps more interest in whether reminiscence encourages communication and engagement in meaningful activity (see Woods & McKiernan, 1995) and, more recently, whether it has an impact on the person's observed well-being, e.g. Brooker & Duce (2000) evaluated well-being in 25 people with dementia attending three different day-hospitals, using an observational method, dementia care mapping, developed by Kitwood & Bredin (1992). They showed that participation in reminiscence groups was associated with higher levels of well-being than other group activities or unstructured time. This study does not claim to show an enduring effect of reminiscence, but does show a clear benefit during the group session.

From a theoretical perspective, if autobiographical memory is, as seems likely, an important contributor to the person's sense of identity, which in turn contributes to the person's mood and well-being, then reminiscence work which aims to enhance the person's autobiographical memory may also have an effect on the person's affective state. In a recently completed study (Woods & Morgan, 2001), the impact of life-review work on people with dementia who had recently been admitted to residential care was evaluated. As the emphasis was on autobiographical memory, individual sessions were conducted, working chronologically through the person's life (approximately 10 sessions were held with each person). A life-story book was compiled for each person in the intervention group, with the assistance of relatives providing relevant photographs and information. The person with dementia exercised editorial control over the contents of the book, and he/she was encouraged to evaluate his/her memories and experiences and to place them in perspective and in the context of his/her life-course. Seventeen people with dementia participated, eight randomly allocated to the intervention group and nine to a no-treatment control group. Outcome measures included the Autobiographical Memory Interview (Kopelman et al., 1990) and the Geriatric Depression Scale (15 item version: Sheikh & Yesavage, 1986); a number of assessments were carried out by an assessor blind to group membership. The results showed a significant increase in autobiographical memory in the life-review group at the end of the treatment phase, compared with the control group. This improvement was maintained at a 6 week follow-up assessment. The intervention group also reported fewer symptoms of depression post-treatment, with continued improvement at follow-up. The average score of the life-review group fell outside the depressed range on this scale at follow-up, whilst that of the control group remained above the cut-off point for depression. Anecdotally, the impact of the life-story books was considerable, with participants proudly showing them to care staff and family, and apparently gaining a stronger sense of identity from the autobiographical memory prompts it provided.

The success of this small-scale study, which appears to be the first RCT to examine the effects of reminiscence work on autobiographical memory, emphasizes the need for careful distinctions to be made between different types of reminiscence work. Whilst the terms "reminiscence" and "life-review" have often been used interchangeably, Haight & Burnside (1993) suggest that life-review be used solely to describe an intervention where the therapist is seeking to assist the person in achieving a sense of integrity. This involves the person recalling and evaluating events and experiences throughout his/her life, usually in a one-to-one setting with the therapist, who acts as a therapeutic listener. Life-review therapy is much more likely to involve working through difficult and painful memories and experiences; it should be undertaken, like any other personal therapy, with the person's consent, with a clear aim, by properly trained and supervised workers.

Reminiscence, on the other hand, may be individual or group-based and may be structured or free-flowing. It may include general memories, rather than recall of specific events or experiences; themes and prompts are frequently used; evaluation of memories is not specifically encouraged; and the focus is on a relaxed, positive atmosphere. Sad memories may emerge, but support is available from the group leader and other members, or from the worker in individual work, to contain any distress or pain associated with such memories. Some caution is still required, taking into account Coleman's (1986) report of large individual differences in attitudes to reminiscence amongst older people and the need to avoid an intrusive approach that invades individuals' privacy. Particularly in a group setting, awareness of participants' life histories is important, to ensure that appropriate support can be given if events that have traumatic connotations for certain individuals are being raised by other members.

COGNITION, EMOTION AND BEHAVIOUR

There are then several procedures and techniques which may be used to enhance and maximize cognitive function in people with dementia. How helpful are these techniques in practice? Given that the person's cognitive abilities would be expected to continue to decline, are these approaches encouraging dementia care workers to make heroic, but ultimately hopeless, efforts to swim against the tide? There can be little question that efforts to generally reduce the cognitive load, to target the person's resources on areas of importance to him/her, to provide an environment where intact memory function is less important, will be of benefit to most people with dementia.

The social psychologist Tom Kitwood made a major contribution to the development of dementia care (Kitwood, 1997) in developing a person-centred model of dementia care, where the person's social environment is seen as central to the clinical picture observed. Environmental manipulations and adaptations may assist in reducing excess disability (disability beyond that necessitated by neuropathological changes). Excess disability may also be related to the person's emotional response to his/her predicament. Estimated rates of anxiety and depression in people with dementia are much higher than in the general population, with perhaps as many as 40% having symptoms of anxiety and/or depression (Cheston & Bender, 1999; Woods, 2001). Some success has been reported in reducing anxiety using progressive muscle relaxation (Suhr et al., 1999) and in depression through increasing participation in pleasurable activities (Teri et al., 1997).

Anxiety and depression may reduce cognitive performance, e.g. the failure of one of the four people with dementia in the study reported by Josephsson et al. (1993) to show learning was attributed to high levels of anxiety. It is important that the effects of interventions on affective state as well as on cognition are monitored. In some situations having an impact on both may be possible, as in the life review study described previously.

There have been some suggestions that behavioural change is possible through the interventions described here, but there are clearly limitations to what may be achieved without individualized, tailored interventions (Woods & Bird, 1999). General programmes may help enrich an environment, so that there is more encouragement for the person to be independent, with more stimulation and generally a more positive approach. This may help reduce the probability of behaviour problems occurring, but when they do occur an individualized approach is essential.

CONCLUSION

Some issues seem to arise in relation to the approaches described in this chapter:

1. *How can family caregivers best be involved?* Much of the work reported here is based in hospitals and residential and nursing homes, yet most people with dementia live at home. Training family caregivers to implement these approaches has not yet been given much attention (for review, see Brodaty, 1992). Some examples exist in the behavioural

literature (e.g. Green et al., 1986) and in the use of a prosthetic memory aid (Bourgeois, 1990) to enhance conversation. It is noteworthy that in the latter study, whilst independent raters confirmed improvements in conversational quality, the relatives involved did not perceive these changes. More attention needs to be given to developing approaches that family caregivers can make use of, without adding to their sense of strain, and which will target areas of value to both caregiver and care recipient. Families have the advantage of knowing the person for many years, and can often assist in holding and supporting the person's autobiographical memory (Cheston, 1998). A life-story book provides a tangible reminder of some important aspects of the person's life, and offers an opportunity for others to communicate to the person with dementia that he/she remains valued and worthy of attention and interest. The added dimension of the existing pattern of relationship may well complicate the application of approaches such as RO and reminiscence, and a good deal of creative work is needed to find ways of implementing useful techniques in the family home.

2. *What are the appropriate goals of intervention?*   For example, is the emphasis placed on improved cognitive function justified, or should well-being and/or quality of life be the ultimate yardstick? If so, how should they be measured? The recent development of a number of quality-of-life scales is welcome in this respect (e.g. Brod et al., 1999). Measuring quality of life and related mood states, such as anxiety and depression, is progressing—largely driven by the requirements of pharmacological research. Bond (1999) suggests that there are, however, a number of radically different meanings of the concept "quality of life" emerging in the field, and some caution is required in taking at face value new assessment measures. The goals that are set in order to evaluate approaches to dementia care must be realistic but based on changes of importance and relevance to the individual with dementia:

> We need to break away from our preoccupation with treatment in the sense of cure and recovery, and be aware of the different types of goal that are feasible, and the value of some of the more limited goals in improving the patient's quality of life (Woods & Britton, 1985, p. 217).

3. *Are there negative effects associated with a particular approach?*   Often, it seems that only positive results are published. RO has been most associated with misuse, but there may potentially be difficulties with other approaches if not used sensitively. Informed consent for people with more advanced dementia is often impossible. How can their wishes and preferences be properly taken into account? Can family members act as satisfactory proxies for the person with dementia?

4. *What works for whom?*   No approach will be universally beneficial, of course. How can we identify what approach is most likely to be useful for a particular individual? Individual differences in response need to be studied in more detail. The weakness of group studies is that there is the danger of missing these individual differences in treatment response which are vitally important at the clinical level. A narrow focus on the person with dementia may mean that beneficial effects elsewhere in the system are not identified. Effects on caregivers—family or staff—may be important and worthwhile, and ultimately result in improved quality of care for the person with dementia.

There are no simple answers to the problems of providing good quality care for people with dementia; however, there are now a number of indications of approaches that can be incorporated sensitively and creatively within a framework of individualized care, that aims to meet the whole range of needs—social, physical and psychological—of the person with dementia.

Kitwood (1997) described how "personhood" might be recognized in people with dementia. This involved identifying indications that the person continued to function as a person, relating, interacting, feeling, choosing, acting in a purposeful manner. Psychological approaches need to be applied in a way that values and respects the individual as a person, taking account of the person's life-story, if they are to serve the best interests of the person with dementia and those who care for him/her.

REFERENCES

Alberoni, M., Baddeley, A., Della-Sala, S. et al. (1992). Keeping track of a conversation: impairments in Alzheimer's disease. *International Journal of Geriatric Psychiatry*, **7**, 639–646.

American Psychiatric Association (1994). *Diagnostic and Statistical Manual of Mental Disorders* (4th edn). Washington, DC: American Psychiatric Association.

American Psychiatric Association (1997). Practice guideline for the treatment of patients with Alzheimer's disease and other dementias of late life. *American Journal of Psychiatry*, **154**(5) (suppl), 1–39.

Annerstedt, L., Gustafson, L. & Nilsson, K. (1993). Medical outcome of psychosocial intervention in demented patients: one-year clinical follow-up after relocation into group living units. *International Journal of Geriatric Psychiatry*, **8**, 833–841.

Bäckman, L. (1992). Memory training and memory improvement in Alzheimer's disease: rules and exceptions. *Acta Neurologia Scandinavica* (suppl), **139**, 84–89.

Baines, S., Saxby, P. & Ehlert, K. (1987). Reality orientation and reminiscence therapy: a controlled cross-over study of elderly confused people. *British Journal of Psychiatry*, **151**, 222–231.

Beecham, J., Cambridge, P., Hallam, A. & Knapp, M. (1993). The costs of domus care. *International Journal of Geriatric Psychiatry*, **8**, 827–831.

Bond, J. (1999). Quality of life for people with dementia: approaches to the challenge of measurement. *Ageing & Society*, **19**, 561–579.

Bornat, J. (ed.) (1994). *Reminiscence Reviewed: Perspectives, Evaluations, Achievements*. Buckingham: Open University Press.

Bourgeois, M.S. (1990). Enhancing conversation skills in patients with Alzheimer's disease using a prosthetic memory aid. *Journal of Applied Behavior Analysis*, **23**, 29–42.

Bourgeois, M.S. (1992). *Conversing with Memory-impaired Individuals Using Memory Aids: a Memory Aid Workbook*. Bicester: Winslow.

Brane, G., Karlsson, I., Kihlgren, M. & Norberg, A. (1989). Integrity-promoting care of demented nursing home patients: psychological and biochemical changes. *International Journal of Geriatric Psychiatry*, **4**, 165–172.

Breuil, V., de Rotrou, J., Forette, F. et al. (1994). Cognitive stimulation of patients with dementia: preliminary results. *International Journal of Geriatric Psychiatry*, **9**, 211–217.

Brod, M., Stewart, A.L., Sands, L. & Walton, P. (1999). Conceptualization and measurement of quality of life in dementia: the dementia quality of life instrument (DQoL). *Gerontologist*, **39**, 25–35.

Brodaty, H. (1992). Carers: training informal carers. In T. Arie (ed.), *Recent advances in psychogeriatrics*, Vol. 2 (pp. 163–171). Edinburgh: Churchill Livingstone.

Brooker, D. & Duce, L. (2000). Wellbeing and activity in dementia: a comparison of group reminiscence therapy, structured goal-directed group activity and unstructured time. *Aging & Mental Health*, **4**(4), 354–358.

Carr, J.S. & Marshall, M. (1993). Innovations in long-stay care for people with dementia. *Reviews in Clinical Gerontology*, **3**, 157–167.

Cheston, R. (1998). Psychotherapeutic work with people with dementia: a review of the literature. *British Journal of Medical Psychology*, **71**, 211–231.

Cheston, R. & Bender, M. (1999). Brains, minds and selves: changing conceptions of the losses involved in dementia. *Ageing & Society*, **72**, 203–216.

Coleman, P.G. (1986). *Ageing and Reminiscence Processes: Social and Clinical Implications*. Chichester: Wiley.

Dean, R., Briggs, K. & Lindesay, J. (1993). The domus philosophy: a prospective evaluation of two residential units for the elderly mentally ill. *International Journal of Geriatric Psychiatry*, **8**, 807–817.

Dietch, J.T., Hewett, L.J. & Jones, S. (1989). Adverse effects of reality orientation. *Journal of American Geriatrics Society*, **37**, 974–976.

Gatz, M., Fiske, A., Fox, L.S. et al. (1998). Empirically validated psychological treatments for older adults. *Journal of Mental Health & Aging*, **4**(1), 9–46.

Gibson, F. (1994). What can reminiscence contribute to people with dementia? In J. Bornat (ed.), *Reminiscence Reviewed: Evaluations, Achievements, Perspectives* (pp. 46–60). Buckingham: Open University Press.

Gilleard, C., Mitchell, R.G. & Riordan, J. (1981). Ward orientation training with psychogeriatric patients. *Journal of Advanced Nursing*, **6**, 95–98.

Goldwasser, A.N., Auerbach, S.M. & Harkins, S.W. (1987). Cognitive, affective and behavioral effects of reminiscence group therapy on demented elderly. *International Journal of Aging & Human Development*, **25**, 209–222.

Green, G.R., Linsk, N.L. & Pinkston, E.M. (1986). Modification of verbal behavior of the mentally impaired elderly by their spouses. *Journal of Applied Behavior Analysis*, **19**, 329–336.

Haight, B.K. & Burnside, I. (1993). Reminiscence and life review: explaining the differences. *Archives of Psychiatric Nursing*, **7**, 91–98.

Hanley, I.G. (1981). The use of signposts and active training to modify ward disorientation in elderly patients. *Journal of Behaviour Therapy & Experimental Psychiatry*, **12**, 241–247.

Hanley, I.G. & Lusty, K. (1984). Memory aids in reality orientation: a single-case study. *Behaviour Research & Therapy*, **22**, 709–712.

Hanley, I.G., McGuire, R.J. & Boyd, W.D. (1981). Reality orientation and dementia: a controlled trial of two approaches. *British Journal of Psychiatry*, **138**, 10–14.

Holden, U.P. & Woods, R.T. (1995). *Positive Approaches to Dementia Care*, 3rd edn. Edinburgh: Churchill Livingstone.

Josephsson, S., Bäckman, L., Borell, L. et al. (1993). Supporting everyday activities in dementia: an intervention study. *International Journal of Geriatric Psychiatry*, **8**, 395–400.

Kitwood, T. (1997). *Dementia Reconsidered: the Person Comes First*. Buckingham: Open University Press.

Kitwood, T. & Bredin, K. (1992). A new approach to the evaluation of dementia care. *Journal of Advances in Health & Nursing Care*, **1**, 41–60.

Knight, B.G. (1996). Psychodynamic therapy with older adults: lessons from scientific gerontology. In R.T. Woods (ed.), *Handbook of the Clinical Psychology of Ageing* (pp. 545–560). Chichester: Wiley.

Kopelman, M., Wilson, B.A. & Baddeley, A. (1990). *The Autobiographical Memory Interview*. Bury St. Edmunds: Thames Valley Test Company.

Lam, D.H. & Woods, R.T. (1986). Ward orientation training in dementia: a single-case study. *International Journal of Geriatric Psychiatry*, **1**, 145–147.

Lindesay, J., Briggs, K., Lawes, M. et al. (1991). The domus philosophy: a comparative evaluation of a new approach to residential care for the demented elderly. *International Journal of Geriatric Psychiatry*, **6**, 727–736.

Morris, R.G. (1994). Recent developments in the neuropsychology of dementia. *International Review of Psychiatry*, **6**, 85–107.

Netten, A. (1989). Environment, orientation and behaviour: the effect of the design of residential homes in creating dependency among confused elderly residents. *International Journal of Geriatric Psychiatry*, **4**, 143–152.

Netten, A. (1993). *A Positive Environment? Physical and Social Influences on People with Senile Dementia in Residential Care*. Aldershot: Ashgate.

Norris, A. (1986). *Reminiscence*. London: Winslow Press.

Orrell, M. & Woods, R.T. (1996). Tacrine and psychological therapies in dementia—no contest? *International Journal of Geriatric Psychiatry*, **11**, 189–192.

Parmelee, P.A. & Lawton, M.P. (1990). The design of special environments for the aged. In J.E. Birren & K.W. Schaie (eds), *Handbook of the Psychology of Aging*, 3rd edn (pp. 464–488). San Diego, CA: Academic Press.

Reeve, W. & Ivison, D. (1985). Use of environmental manipulation and classroom and modified informal reality orientation with institutionalized, confused elderly patients. *Age & Ageing*, **14**, 119–121.

Ritchie, K., Colvez, A., Ankri, J. et al. (1992). The evaluation of long-term care for the dementing elderly: a comparative study of hospital and collective non-medical care in France. *International Journal of Geriatric Psychiatry*, **7**, 549–557.

Sheikh, J.I. & Yesavage, J.A. (1986). Geriatric Depression Scale (GDS): recent evidence and development of a shorter version. In T.L. Brink (ed.), *Clinical Gerontology: a Guide to Assessment and Intervention* (pp. 165–173). New York: Haworth.

Skea, D. & Lindesay, J. (1996). An evaluation of two models of long-term residential care for elderly people with dementia. *International Journal of Geriatric Psychiatry*, **11**, 233–241.

Spector, A., Orrell, M., Davies, S. & Woods, R.T. (1999a). Reality orientation for dementia (Cochrane Review). In *The Cochrane Library*, Issue 4. Oxford: Update Software.

Spector, A., Orrell, M., Davies, S. & Woods, R.T. (1999b). Reminiscence therapy for dementia (Cochrane Review). In The Cochrane Library, Issue 4. Oxford: Update Software.

Spector, A., Davies, S., Woods, B. & Orrell, M. (2000). Reality orientation for dementia: a systematic review of the evidence for its effectiveness. *Gerontologist*, **40**(2), 206–212.

Spector, A., Orrell, M., Davies, S. & Woods, B. (2001). Can reality orientation be rehabilitated? Development and piloting of an evidence-based programme of cognition-based therapies for people with dementia. *Neuropsychological Rehabilitation*, **11**, 377–397.

Suhr, J., Anderson, S. & Tranel, D. (1999). Progressive muscle relaxation in the management of behavioural disturbance in Alzheimer's disease. *Neuropsychological Rehabilitation*, **9**, 31–44.

Teri, L., Logsdon, R.G., Uomoto, J. & McCurry, S.M. (1997). Behavioral treatment of depression in dementia patients: a controlled clinical trial. *Journal of Gerontology*, **52B**, P159–P166.

Williams, R., Reeve, W., Ivison, D. & Kavanagh, D. (1987). Use of environmental manipulation and modified informal reality orientation with institutionalized confused elderly subjects: a replication. *Age & Ageing*, **16**, 315–318.

Wimo, A., Wallin, J.O., Lundgren, K. et al. (1991). Group living, an alternative for dementia patients: a cost analysis. *International Journal of Geriatric Psychiatry*, **6**, 21–29.

Woods, R.T. (1983). Specificity of learning in reality orientation sessions: a single-case study. *Behaviour Research & Therapy*, **21**, 173–175.

Woods, R.T. (2001). Discovering the person with Alzheimer's disease: cognitive, emotional and behavioural aspects. *Aging & Mental Health*, **5**(suppl 1), S7–S16.

Woods, R.T. & Bird, M. (1999). Non-pharmacological approaches to treatment. In G. Wilcock, K. Rockwood & R. Bucks (eds), *Diagnosis and Management of Dementia: a Manual for Memory Disorders Teams* (pp. 311–331). Oxford: Oxford University Press.

Woods, R.T. & Britton, P.G. (1985). *Clinical Psychology with the Elderly*. London: Croom Helm/Chapman Hall.

Woods, R.T. & McKiernan, F. (1995). Evaluating the impact of reminiscence on older people with dementia. In B.K. Haight & J. Webster (eds), *The Art and Science of Reminiscing: Theory, Research, Methods and Applications* (pp. 233–242). Washington, DC: Taylor & Francis.

Woods, R.T. & Morgan, S. (2001). Randomised-controlled trial of life review with people with dementia on entry to residential care. Paper presented at International Congress of Gerontology, Vancouver.

Woods, R.T., Portnoy, S., Head, D. & Jones, G. (1992). Reminiscence and life-review with persons with dementia: which way forward? In G. Jones & B. Miesen (eds), *Care-giving in Dementia* (pp. 137–161). London: Routledge.

Zanetti, O., Frisoni, G.B., DeLeo, D. et al. (1995). Reality orientation therapy in Alzheimer's disease: useful or not? a controlled study. *Alzheimer Disease and Associated Disorders*, **9**, 132–138.

Zepelin, H., Wolfe, C.S. & Kleinplatz, F. (1981). Evaluation of a year-long reality orientation program. *Journal of Gerontology*, **36**, 70–77.

CHAPTER 34

External Memory Aids and Computers in Memory Rehabilitation

Narinder Kapur
Southampton General Hospital and University of Southampton, UK
Elizabeth L. Glisky
University of Arizona, Tuscon, AZ, USA
and
Barbara A. Wilson
MRC Cognition and Brain Sciences Unit, Cambridge, and Oliver Zangwill Centre for Cognitive Rehabilitation, Ely, UK

> Feats can be performed with mnemonic devices that are marvellous and prodigious, but nevertheless it is a barren thing for human uses. It is not well contrived for providing assistance to memory in serious and business affairs (Sir Francis Bacon).

This chapter reviews external memory aids and computer-based resources in the management of patients with memory difficulties following brain disease or brain injury. We are concerned primarily with treatment interventions for memory-disordered people. Although various forms of memory aids and computer-based resources may be useful in the initial neuropsychological assessment and diagnosis of such people, these applications are outside the scope of this chapter. We focus mainly on adults who have suffered a brain insult, although we recognize that children with brain damage and those with memory loss related to psychiatric conditions might also benefit from external aids and computers.

Apart from drugs or other "physical" treatments for psychological management, there are several ways in which memory difficulties associated with neurological disease may be managed: general advice and counselling to provide information to patients and their carers about coping with memory difficulties; advice on the avoidance of exacerbating factors, such as alcohol, fatigue, stress, etc.; advice on simple changes to daily routines or to the environment; instruction in the use of specific cognitive strategies for encoding, rehearsing and retrieving information; and the use of external memory aids, computers, etc., to help improve everyday memory functioning. A number of self-help booklets and guides are

The Handbook of Memory Disorders. Edited by A.D. Baddeley, M.D. Kopelman and B.A. Wilson
© 2002 John Wiley & Sons, Ltd.

available which summarize such advice (Clare & Wilson, 1997; Kapur, 2001; Martyn & Gale, 1999)

Techniques to try to improve memory date back thousands of years (Herrmann & Chaffin, 1988). Memory *strategies* for improving memory have been well documented (Glisky, 1997; Gruneberg, 1992; McGlynn, 1990; Patten, 1990) but rather less attention has been paid to *external memory aids*. These act as a form of "prosthesis" for everyday memory functioning. Unlike the effects of novel cognitive strategies, they are rarely intended to change learning ability as such, although they may sometimes be as valuable or more valuable than conventional techniques for improving memory. Although cognitive-based memory strategies have a role to play in some aspects of memory rehabilitation, many memory-disordered patients may lack the motivation or prerequisite concentration/learning skills to acquire some of the strategies advocated, certainly those that are put forward in popular books on memory improvement. In a study by Park et al. (1990), psychologists involved in memory research indicated that simple external memory aids, such as writing things down on a note-pad, were among the techniques they themselves used most often for improving their memory. A survey of individuals of varying ages found that external memory aids were used more frequently than cognitive strategies to enhance prospective memory functioning (Long et al., 1999).

This chapter reviews the main types of external memory aids currently available, and assesses their suitability for use in clinical settings. More general reviews of memory rehabilitation, which include some discussion of memory aids, are available elsewhere (Glisky & Glisky, 2002; Harrell et al., 1992; Herrmann et al., 1992; Intons-Peterson & Fournier, 1986; Parente & Herrmann, 1996; Wilson, 1999a; Wilson & Evans, 2000; Wilson & Moffat, 1992).

At present, there is no detailed and widely accepted conceptual framework for considering the role of memory aids in neurological rehabilitation. The general importance of concepts in memory research has been emphasized by Tulving (2000). While there have been some promising attempts to develop conceptual frameworks to view aspects of memory rehabilitation (Bäckman & Dixon, 1992; Wilson & Watson, 1996), there is a need to develop new frameworks that take into account the range of cognitive strategies and of agents that can enhance memory functioning, and that also incorporate research findings from clinical and cognate sciences that influence memory functioning.

In this chapter, we shall deal with the following aids: environmental, stationery, mechanical, and electronic, together with computer-based resources. Some of the beneficial effects of memory aids can be considered in terms of the long-established distinction between experiential and knowledge memory (Nielsen, 1958), the subsequent distinctions between episodic and semantic memory (Tulving, 1972), and between memory for events and memory for facts (Warrington, 1986). Thus, aids may be used mainly to enhance event memory, or they may be more useful in knowledge acquisition and utilization. Often a specific memory aid can serve both purposes, and one function may merge into another.

In view of the relative paucity of research in the area of memory aids, we will add some general statements about their use and efficacy, based in part on our own clinical experience. We will review both novel memory aids and also the more obvious ways in which external memory aids may be useful in clinical settings. This allows us to provide a comprehensive overview of devices that can enhance memory functioning in neurological patients, and enables us to bring the wide range of memory aids within some form of coherent conceptual framework.

ENVIRONMENTAL MEMORY AIDS

Features of our environment shape our behaviour, both consciously and unconsciously. We respond (often automatically) to cues in our environment for many of our daily activities. Contextual support from environmental cues may be more critical for those with failing memory (Craik & Jennings, 1992). It makes sense to consider how our environment may be better designed and organized to enhance memory functioning. As in the case of visuospatial functions, where a distinction has been made between personal, peripersonal and extrapersonal space (Robertson & Halligan, 1999), it may be useful to divide environmental memory aids into two categories—proximal environmental and distal environmental memory aids. Memory aids that alter the personal make-up of the individual, such as wearable memory aids, are perhaps better considered along with other portable memory aids and are covered later.

Proximal Environmental Memory Aids

By proximal environment, we include such features as the design and contents of a room or vehicle and the design of equipment the individual uses in everyday domestic or work settings. Specific items that make up the proximal environment but which are not specific to a particular environment, such as clocks, are considered under "portable memory aids". Aspects of the proximal environment form a somewhat neglected area of scientific inquiry in relation to memory aids. Norman's (1988) excellent book remains a useful resource for considering some of the practical manifestations of poor ergonomic design in our everyday environment, and includes instances where poor design may result in memory lapses.

Changes to a work-place or home environment can be engineered to minimize a common memory lapse—forgetting to do something. Examples include leaving something beside the front door, attaching a message to a mirror in the hallway, and leaving around an empty carton of something that needs to be replaced. Simple changes to the design of an environment may act as a catalyst to such memory aids, e.g. items one has to take when leaving home or leaving the office could be located on an appropriate shelf near the exit itself. The shelf should be clearly labelled and within the horizontal and vertical limits of the person's visual field. Putting together two items may act as a visual reminder to carry out a particular action, e.g. a pill-bottle next to a toothbrush may remind a patient to take his medicine before cleaning his teeth. White boards, wall charts, etc. that allow messages to be displayed serve as useful memory aids. They can remind individuals to carry out an activity, and also act as a "knowledge board" to display important information, such as emergency telephone numbers. Moffat (1989) described the use of a simple flow chart of likely places to search to help a man who frequently lost items around the home. Sharps & Price-Sharps (1996) found that brightly coloured plates with internal dividers placed on a dining/kitchen table reduced memory lapses of elderly participants, who used the plates for items that might get lost, or for "things to do" messages. Thus, the plates served as message boards to improve event memory, or as semi-permanent storage devices to help remember where items were located.

Cars, mobile phones and other items may have alarm systems to remind the user to do something. In-built alarms or cut-off devices, as are found in some domestic appliances, help prevent event-memory lapses such as forgetting to carry out a certain activity. Voice-based messages to accompany or replace the actual alarm signal are sometimes helpful in order to tell the individual what the alarm means when it is activated.

A proximal environment, well-structured and organized, is less likely to result in memory lapses such as forgetting where something has been put (cf. Fulton & Hatch, 1991). As a basic principle, the items to be stored for later retrieval should be categorized, and separate shelves or storage units allocated to each category. Categories should be meaningful to the individual in question, and may have a number of subcategories, possibly reflected in the structure of the storage unit. Distinctive storage units should differ in features such as size, shape, colour and/or spatial position. They should be clearly labelled, and containers within the storage units should also be labelled. Labels should be in large print and may be of different colours, although black against white is often best for elderly or neurologically disabled people. If the storage units have to be retrieved according to sequence, then some form of alpha-numeric labelling will be of value. The prominence of a storage unit in a room will depend on how frequently the stored items are used, how important they are, and how often they tend to be forgotten. If possible, there should be some relationship between the contents and the visual features of the unit, e.g. a brown container for storing coffee, a white one for storing sugar, etc. Transparent storage boxes are preferable, as one can see at a glance what is inside and whether the contents need replenishing.

Orientation for time, place and current events will be helped by the presence of items such as clocks that display the day of the week and date, orientation boards, large windows at ground level to allow individuals to see the trees and therefore cues to indicate the time of year, etc. Regularity of routine activities may help improve knowledge such as orientation for time, e.g. if the tea trolley always comes at 11 am, this provides an anchor point for "confused" patients whose internal "clock memory" mechanisms are impaired.

In some circumstances, tactile memory aids may be useful in providing knowledge about the location of an item, e.g. when driving a car it is often impossible to look at the location of various switches. As Norman (1988) pointed out, the layout of such switches often pays little heed to their use in driving behaviour. If, as is often the case, switches of a similar design are in close proximity, or are particularly important to locate, it may be useful to attach a distinctive tactile cue, such as a Velcro pad, onto one of the switches. Similar applications may arise in other settings, such as finding switches in a room in the dark. There are electronic location devices to help locate objects. Thus if one cannot find one's car in the car park, pressing the alarm button an such a device will activate lights on the car.

Distal Environmental Memory Aids

By distal environment, we mean settings such as the layout of a building, shopping centres, the design of streets and towns, the design of transportation networks, and the people with whom we interact.

Wilson & Evans (2000) and Gibbs (2000) noted the emergence of "smart houses", where appliances are centrally controlled and include reminder functions that help prevent memory lapses, e.g. ensuring equipment is turned on or off. Future domestic and work environments may include electronic reminder and knowledge systems as an integral part of the environment. Refrigerators, one of the most commonly visited sites in a typical household, are already on the market with inbuilt reminder and internet facilities on the door! For memory-impaired people, family members and carers may act as reminders to carry out activities, such as taking medication. Dogu & Erkip (2000) point to some design features to be kept in mind if spatial orientation in a shopping complex is to be maximized. For similar observations relating to more general navigational activities, such as route finding, see Canter (1996), and for those relating to the specific needs of patients with dementia, see Passini et al. (1998, 2000).

Name badges and distinctive uniforms are obvious, but sometimes neglected, forms of memory aid to help memory-impaired people identify other residents and care staff. Simple labels help people know what to do in certain settings—as Norman (1988) has pointed out, we are all aware of doors where there is no indication whether to PULL or to PUSH. The carefully planned use of such signs can be of benefit as preventative measures, e.g. warning signs near stairs in homes for elderly people, road traffic warning signs, and so forth. Other forms of visual cues may also help, such as cues on steps to alert someone who is visually impaired of the steps' existence.

In residential homes or hospitals for memory-impaired people, wall or floor markers indicating the direction to somewhere, together with clearly labelled rooms, may help residents to find their way about (cf. Elmstahl et al., 1997; Olsen et al., 1999). Alarms fitted to doors that activate when the door is opened help provide information to care workers on patients who are likely to wander out of the premises. It is useful for the therapist to carry out a "site visit" to a patient's residence to obtain a first-hand perspective of environmental features and how best to modify the environment so as to enhance everyday memory functioning.

PORTABLE EXTERNAL MEMORY AIDS

Stationery, Mechanical and Related Memory Aids

Stationery memory aids are the most commonly used and probably the most widely acceptable form of memory prostheses, for both the general population and for memory-impaired people. Such aids include self-adhesive POST-IT notes, notebooks, diaries, filofaxes, calendars/wall-charts (Gabriel et al., 1977) and address tags that enable lost items to be returned. Effectiveness may be improved by changing their distinctiveness and location. They should be readily visible and accessible, and also in close proximity to the to-be-remembered activity—thus, a note pad with a list of people to phone should be near the telephone, one that deals with groceries to buy could be on the refrigerator door, and a checklist for operating a piece of equipment should be kept near that equipment. Pencils/pens should form an integral part of the stationery memory aid. Diaries and filofaxes vary in the extent to which they incorporate "reminder" sections, and in some cases it may be appropriate to create distinctive sections dealing with separate categories, such as things to buy, people to meet, phone calls to make, etc.

POST-IT notes and similar items can be used as both general reminders and message-reminders. Thus, a blank POST-IT note placed near an item such as a telephone or television can be used as a cue to remind one to make a call or watch a programme. A POST-IT note that has a list of items to buy and is placed on the fridge door serves as a message-reminder. Memory aids such as dry-wipe boards may have a similar purpose. Diaries, filofaxes with TO DO lists, etc., may all serve as event memory aids.

Stationery items can also be used as permanent or temporary stores of knowledge. Thus, address books represent permanent stores of verbal knowledge, maps provide spatial/navigational knowledge, clocks convey knowledge of time and calendars contain temporal information. For "confused" patients, it may be useful to make up a bracelet that indicates essential orientation information, answers to questions repeatedly asked, and information (name, telephone number of current residence) for someone to use in case the patient becomes lost. Photographs of family members by the bedside may help those with severe memory impairment to retrieve both knowledge and event information relating to their loved ones.

Notebooks, diaries, organizers and similar items have been available for some time. Although they seem fairly straightforward to use with patients, their successful use, especially with the more severely impaired, requires some thought. One of the first systematic attempts to develop a coherent teaching method was described by Sohlberg & Mateer (1989b). They made up purpose-built notebooks with different sections and emphasized that these can be reduced or increased in number according to the patient. Their list of possible sections included Orientation, Memory Log, Diary, Things to Do, Transportation, Feeling Log, Names, and Today at Work.

A head-injured patient reported by Sohlberg & Mateer used a Memory Notebook with five sections—Orientation, Memory Log, Calendar, Things to Do and Transportation. Where note-books are especially designed for patients, page lay-out features such as colour coding, size of print, etc., should be carefully considered. In addition, because notebooks may need to be individualized, patients should be involved in their design early on (cf. Donaghy & Williams, 1998). Care-staff or family members also need to be made familiar with the memory aid.

Sohlberg & Mateer (1989b) divided their training into Acquisition, Application and Adaptation. We recommend combining these into two stages: (a) learning about the item and understanding its features; and (b) using it in everyday situations. Learning about the item involves going through the various sections, understanding what they are for and when they should be used, how to make and change entries, etc. One can test the subject's retention by usual question-and-answer techniques. Role rehearsal, involving practice of real-life examples, may be helpful. Use of direct feedback in such role rehearsal, perhaps also with video feedback, is important. Sohlberg & Mateer suggested that before patients can go on to the use of the notebook in real-life settings, they should have explicit knowledge of the book's features. In our experience, however, as long as there is accurate and successful use of the various notebook features, it does not really matter if the patient can provide explicit recall of particular features. Zencius et al. (1990) compared four memory improvement strategies in a group of six head-injured patients with memory difficulties—written rehearsal, oral rehearsal, acronym formation and memory notebook logging. Only the last technique was successful in increasing recall of target material. In a second study from the same centre (Zencius et al., 1991), four brain-injured patients were found, as a result of training in the use of memory notebooks, to show a more general improvement in memory that included both homework assignments and keeping appointments. Schmitter-Edgecombe et al. (1995) compared a 9-week period of notebook training with supportive therapy in the case of a group of memory-impaired patients who had suffered a severe head injury more than 2 years earlier. Their outcome measure included an index of everyday memory failures, and these were documented before treatment, immediately after treatment, and 6 months later. The authors found that, shortly after treatment, there was a significant benefit in favour of the notebook training group. At 6 months, this benefit was still present, but it no longer reached statistical significance. Some researchers (e.g. Burke et al., 1994; Fluharty & Priddy, 1993) have emphasized the importance of making the notebook acceptable to the patient, e.g. by individualizing it to particular patients. Other researchers have made important observations on how notebooks may best be introduced in the context of other changes to the patient's prosthetic environment (e.g. Schwartz, 1995; Wilson, 1999b) and on how they may be of more general benefit in tackling problems such as lack of insight and planning (Finset & Andresen, 1994).

A few mechanical memory aids, such as countdown kitchen timers, are available, although they have been largely overtaken by electronic equivalents. In addition, various types of pill-boxes and containers can be bought which are designed around the days of the week. Several studies have looked at the effectiveness of different medication reminders on patient compliance (Park & Kidder, 1996). Most studies have found that adherence to a medication schedule improves with the introduction of mechanical organizers—the design of the device should be simple and clear, ideally with separate compartments for different days of the week and for different times of the day; in addition, there should be some form of feedback to the patient, perhaps by use of a stationery memory aid, which provides information that the medication in question has actually been taken (McKenney et al., 1992; Nides et al., 1993; Park et al., 1991, 1992; Rehder et al., 1980; Szeto & Giles, 1997).

Electronic Organizers and Related Electronic Reminders

The most common form of commercially available electronic memory aids are electronic organizers. In recent years, these have become more compact, more sophisticated and more diverse in their functions, and also less expensive. In general, such devices can be useful as memory aids in five main ways:

1. An electronic diary to keep a record of appointments.
2. An alarm which provides auditory cues, with or without text information, at preset, regular or irregular times.
3. A temporary store for items such as shopping lists, messages, etc.
4. A more permanent store for information such as addresses, telephone numbers, etc.
5. In more expensive models, a communication device that can receive and send information, such as reminders and factual knowledge.

Electronic organizers range in size from pocket-sized to the size of a wallet/filofax—palmtop devices. Alarms can be set to sound at the same time as a stored message is displayed, and for some models multiple daily, weekly or monthly alarms can be set. Many electronic organizers can be interfaced to enable them to transfer data to computers, and for certain models add-on cards can be bought to store information and allow for specialized applications. Most models have back-up devices to safeguard against loss of stored information. Electronic organizers vary greatly in features which may or may not be applicable to the needs of neurological patients with memory impairment. The following features may be helpful to consider when selecting an electronic organizer for use with memory-impaired people.

General Features

The electronic organizer should be compact enough to fit into a shirt pocket or other handy place. Some of the more expensive electronic organizers may be too bulky to be carried around all of the time, although they could still be kept in a coat pocket or a briefcase.

Databank watches are available which have many of the functions of electronic organizers. While more compact and easier to carry around, they are more limited because of the fine motor control and visual acuity needed to operate them, limited storage capacity, and so forth.

Although batteries may need to be changed only once every few years, one needs to consider the motor dexterity involved in changing the battery and the simplicity of the instructions, in addition to the usual life of the battery and whether there is a back-up battery. Back-up batteries are useful especially where there is a large amount of stored data to be retained in the device's memory. Around 32K memory will usually suffice for most uses. More sophisticated organizers come with removable memory cards.

Patients should not have to consult the manual, but it helps if it is clear and not too intimidating in its length. Summarized forms of information, such as "Help Cards", are useful in that they provide a quick reference to turn to without having to refer to the manual. Those using the organizer as a data-gathering device in settings remote from their work-place will find it useful to be able to link up to a personal computer. In terms of cost, electronic memory aids are not routinely available in publicly-funded healthcare systems, but it is usually possible to buy a model with extensive alarm and text storage facilities for under £50/$75. The length and number of lines that can be displayed on screen is important. Obviously, the larger the screen the better, although the cost will rise with larger screens. At least 10 characters are usually needed on a single line for the minimum sorts of cue words required as reminders. In some cases, especially if there is limited screen space, it is important to train the patient to use key words or abbreviations in order to remember what to do.

The clarity of screen display is also important—some of the less expensive organizers have poor displays despite being useful in other ways. Clarity is a critical item for many neurological patients, especially older people who may have reduced visual acuity.

Since electronic organizers are designed for professionals or executives rather than for people with disability, there are usually keys which are superfluous when the device is used as a memory aid. These may serve as a distraction, especially if the patient has visual search problems, in which case redundant keys should be masked. The keys themselves should be clearly labelled and well laid out, and, if possible, operations should be executed by a single key press rather than by a sequence of keys. Keyboards that provide tone feedback when a key is pressed are desirable.

Voice organizers are available for those who find keyboard entry difficult because of tremor or other movement disorder. These have the same text storage and alarm features as most conventional electronic organizers, but rely on voice input. The device is "trained" to recognize the voice of the user, but even then occasional errors may occur. While current devices are compact, the input keys require a degree of motor control that may be outside the capacity of many neurological patients.

Entering, Storing and Retrieving Information

There are three basic operations that memory-impaired people need to learn: *entering* information; *reviewing* stored information; and *deleting* information from storage. It is useful to check whether these basic operations are simple or complicated for patients. Consider whether word-processing features are useful, e.g. if a phrase is entered frequently, can a code rather than the full phrase be entered?

In addition to a prospective memory feature giving an alarm (with or without an associated message), it is useful to have a general MEMO facility so that items can be stored which need to be done at some time, but not necessarily on a particular day or at a particular time. In less expensive organizers without such a MEMO facility, the telephone storage facility can be used instead.

While all electronic organizers have basic text storage devices that allow for both temporary and permanent stores of knowledge, some now come with the facility to offer advanced storage features, e.g. navigational information, the ability to store pictorial material such as photographs, and the ability to link to information resources on the Internet.

Alarm Features

Electronic organizers may be particularly useful as reminders in the following settings:

1. Instances where events may occur between thinking about doing something and re-membering to do it, e.g. deciding in the morning to buy something later in the day. This is particularly important when intervening activities preoccupy the individual.
2. Situations where a long interval separates thinking about doing something and having to do it—if one makes an appointment for several months in the future.
3. When there is a high premium on very accurate, precise recall and where internal memory aids may be fallible, e.g. remembering to take a cake from an oven at a specific time.
4. Where multiple alarm reminders are required, e.g. having to take tablets several times a day.

There are essentially two types of alarm reminders, those with and those without a text message. The major virtue of electronic organizers is their ability to display text when an alarm goes off. Therefore, having an alarm with a simultaneous message display is a critical feature. This facility can be used for two main purposes—situations where something has to be done on a particular day and at a specific time, and those situations where it is important that certain things are done but which are not necessarily tied to a particular time. Some organizers emit a warning several minutes before the alarm sounds. For certain activities requiring initial preparation, such as having to go to a meeting, this can be useful. Alarms that can be set to occur at regular intervals, such as daily, weekly or monthly, may be helpful in contexts where activities need to be carried out repeatedly and at specific times.

Turning to research findings with electronic organizers, Azrin & Powell (1969) found that a pill container which sounded a tone at the time medication was to be taken, and which dispensed a tablet at the same time the tone was turned off, was better at inducing patient compliance than a simple alarm timer or a container that made no sound. Fowler et al. (1972) used a timer combined with a schedule card to help their patient stick to a daily routine in his rehabilitation programme. Naugle et al. (1988) worked with a man who consistently forgot to use stationery memory aids such as diaries and log books. They found an "alarm display" watch helped him remember rehabilitation activities. Although of benefit, the patient sometimes ignored the alarm, and sometimes turned it off without reading the message first. Further training in the use of the aid was then given. Giles & Shore (1989) used a PSION organizer to help their patient remember to do weekend domestic chores. This was more beneficial than a pocket diary. However, sometimes the alarm was not loud enough to be heard. Kapur (1995) described preliminary data on the use of an electronic organizer to help patients with head injury, multiple sclerosis and epilepsy. In general, an organizer proved to be useful both as a reminder and as a text storage device, but for one patient who was densely amnesic and was living at home, the electronic aid proved to be of little benefit. Van den Broek et al. (2000) found that for five memory-impaired patients who were provided with a voice-organizer, message-alarm reminder functions were effective in reducing memory lapses in two task settings—passing on a message they had been told 9 h earlier, and remembering to carry out specified domestic chores. Kim et al. (2000) reported that most brain-injured patients who had been trained to use a palm-top computer during their period of rehabilitation continued to use the device in everyday memory settings several years later. In a single-case study (Kim et al., 1999), one head-injured patient who used this device as an inpatient was better at remembering to attend therapy sessions and to take medication.

Wright et al. (2001) noted that, in a group of brain-injured patients, high-frequency users of organizers tended to prefer a standard keyboard organizer, whereas less frequent users preferred a more novel, penpad input system. In an earlier study involving elderly and younger participants from the general population, Wright et al. (2000) found that most participants preferred keyboard data entry to touch-screen data entry, and generally made fewer errors using the keyboard modality.

Speech Storage Devices

As memory aids, speech recording devices are useful when long messages need to be stored. They are also helpful for memory-disordered patients who have difficulty using an electronic organizer, possibly due to motor or visual impairment. As well as conventional tape recorders, digital "solid-state" recording devices have recently been introduced that can store up to several hours of speech. The attractive feature of these devices is the ability to store speech in discrete, labelled files that can be rapidly retrieved. Thus, different categories of messages or things to do can be readily stored and accessed.

Some memory-impaired people complain of difficulty in remembering telephone messages, and a few devices are available which automatically tape telephone conversations. Users of such devices should be aware that they need to inform the caller that the conversation is being taped! A few digital voice recorders have alarm features that can be tagged to stored messages, thus enabling the device to be used as an event memory aid.

The main function of these devices is to act as temporary or permanent stores of knowledge. They are of benefit in educational settings, such as listening to lectures, and are used for this purpose by many young patients with brain injury. Although at present they are not used as knowledge resources to the same extent as printed or visual electronic media, it is possible that in the future this may change with the enhanced storage and other features of recording devices.

There appear to be few formal research studies that have explored the use of conventional or newer recording devices as memory aids for brain-injured patients, apart from the study by Van den Broek et al. (2000) noted above, which successfully used a voice organizer for improving memory functioning in a group of memory-impaired patients.

Electronic Communication Devices

Electronic communication devices can be classified into fixed devices, such as standard corded telephones, or free-standing devices, such as cordless telephones, mobile phones and pagers. Laptop and palmtop computers that can access the Internet can also be classified as communication devices, and a number of mobile phones have additional functions similar to those found in electronic organizers, and so can be used to send text messages or pictures. We will mainly deal here with phone and paging systems for conveying verbal messages.

Telephones are available that allow storage and easy retrieval of frequently used numbers. Useful features can be found in most phones, e.g. visual display of a number while it is being dialled and the ability to identify the caller. Fixed phones are currently available in some countries with a "photophone" feature—the face of the person to be called can be represented on a button that is programmed with the person's number. Mobile phones and pagers are available with vibration cues instead of a ringing tone. These are useful for people with auditory impairments. Pagers have similar call-signalling facilities, and some pagers are available with inbuilt alarm features.

Fixed telephones, mobile phones and pagers have a variety of reminder systems associated with them. These range from inbuilt alarms/message-alarms, which may be preset or can be set to signal at specified intervals or on a fixed date, through to alarm systems dependent on some other resource. Telephone-based reminding systems have in the past been shown to be useful in improving patient compliance with taking medication (Leirer et al., 1988, 1991) or keeping appointments (Morrow et al., 1999). In recent years, pagers have been employed to serve as more general reminder memory aids. Commercial paging companies in a number of countries offer reminder services, and a dedicated system for brain-injured patients has also been developed (Hersh & Treadgold, 1994; Wilson et al., 1997, 2001). Phones can also be used to activate devices elsewhere, and thus may help in settings where the individual has to remember to turn on equipment such as domestic appliances.

Most phones have enough storage capacity to store a large number of names and telephone numbers. Those that double-up as organizers have the usual text storage and retrieval facilities of organizers that were outlined above. The ability of both fixed and mobile phones to link up to the Internet has opened up a cornucopia of information resources that may act as knowledge memory aids.

Pagers can be useful as external memory aids, especially as reminders. Milch et al. (1996) found that a paging system used in a hospice environment was useful in improving compliance amongst residents in taking medication. In a single-case study, Aldrich (1998) used a dedicated paging system, NeuroPage, to help a head-injured patient remember to carry out a range of activities, such as getting up and dressing, making lunch, watching the news headlines, feeding the cat, and taking his medication. The pager led to a significant improvement in performance of these activities. After NeuroPage was withdrawn, some improvement was maintained, but this was task-dependent. Similar observations in a further single-case study with NeuroPage were made by Wilson et al. (1999). Wilson et al. (2001) carried out a large-scale study of 143 brain-damaged patients' use of NeuroPage. More than 80% of those who completed the 16 week trial were significantly more successful in carrying out everyday activities, such as self-care, taking medication and keeping appointments. For most patients, this improvement was maintained 7 weeks after returning the pager.

COMPUTER-BASED TECHNOLOGIES FOR ENHANCING MEMORY FUNCTION

While the distinction between desktop computers, laptop computers, palmtop computers and personal organizers is becoming increasingly blurred as a result of advances in technology, in the following sections we mainly deal with those applications where desktop computers have been used in memory rehabilitation. We also consider attempts to use virtual-reality devices to enhance memory functioning, since these invariably use computer-based technologies for their operation.

Exercises and Drills

Although evidence for restoration of function using exercises and drills has not been positive, advances in computer technology and the ready availability of relatively inexpensive hardware have revived interest in such methods (Bradley et al., 1993). The computer represents an ideal medium for presentation of repetitive exercises, and therapists have been attracted by the time-saving features of computer-delivered services. Proponents of the restoration approach to rehabilitation have eagerly adopted computers as "the ultimate drillmasters" (Gianutsos, 1992, p. 34) and have urged others to continue their use "... whatever the outcome" (Gianutsos, 1992, p. 29). However, evidence of beneficial effects of memory exercises has not been forthcoming, whether they are delivered by computer or in the more traditional pencil-and-paper format (Skilbeck & Robertson, 1992). For example, a study by Middleton et al. (1991) found no specific effects of 32 h of drill-orientated computer training of cognitive skills, including memory. Chen et al. (1997) found no major differences across a range of neuropsychological measures between two groups of head-injured patients, one that received computer-assisted cognitive rehabilitation and another that received more traditional rehabilitation. Skilbeck & Robertson (1992), in their review of computer techniques for the management of memory impairment, concluded that when appropriate controls are included in empirical studies, there is little evidence of positive outcome following computer drills.

Some investigators (e.g. Sohlberg & Mateer, 1989a) have suggested that attention may be more amenable to computer training than memory and that improvements in attentional processing might secondarily benefit memory performance. Although the evidence for restoration of function in the attentional domain is more promising than in the memory domain (Matthews et al., 1991; Robertson, 1990), it is, as yet, far from persuasive. For example, Sohlberg & Mateer (1987), in four single-case studies with brain-injured patients, demonstrated improved performance on the Paced Auditory Serial Addition Task (Gronwall, 1977) following computerized practice on other attention-demanding tasks. They also reported improved performance on the Randt Memory Test. Ben-Yishay et al. (1987) found that improved performance on computer training tasks (for attentional deficits) was associated with small gains on relevant neuropsychological tests. Gray et al. (1992) have reported long-term improvements in untrained attentional tasks as a result of computerized training (see also Sturm & Willmes, 1991). On the other hand, Wood & Fussey (1987) found no generalized improvements in attention after 20 h of computer practice, although performance on the specific training tasks did improve; Ponsford & Kinsella (1988) also reported negative results. No benefits for real-life functioning were indicated in any of these studies. Given the paucity and inconsistency of findings with respect to attention, no firm conclusions concerning computerized training of attentional deficits, or of its possible impact on memory, seem warranted (see Wood, 1992).

Exercises and drills have not proved useful for restoring general memory ability. Nevertheless, repetitive practice is probably essential for memory-impaired patients to improve on any specific task or to learn any specific information, and computers may be a useful medium for the repeated presentation of such materials. Because learning does not appear to generalize beyond the training task, it is important that practice is directed towards something relevant or useful in everyday life. Repetitive practice of meaningless lists of numbers, letters, shapes, or locations plays no beneficial role in memory rehabilitation (Glisky & Glisky, in press; Glisky & Schacter, 1989b; Wilson, 1991)

Mnemonic Strategies

There have been few reported attempts to test the effectiveness of computers with respect to the teaching of mnemonic strategies. In one study, Skilbeck (1984) used a microcomputer to teach a head-injured patient the pegword technique for learning short lists of items, such as shopping lists. The patient, who had sustained primarily left-hemisphere damage, learned the 10 pegs (i.e. one is a bun, two is a shoe, etc.) and was then provided with computer instructions concerning the interactive images that were to be formed for each to-be-remembered item and the pegword. The patient was able to use the visual imagery strategy to improve her verbal recall performance, relative to a straightforward repetition condition. However, there was no indication that she employed the strategy on her own. The technique thus enabled her to learn specific information relevant to her everyday functioning but did not improve her memory ability in any general sense.

A somewhat different use of a microcomputer for teaching mnemonic strategies was employed by Johnson (1990). In this study, a relatively high-functioning patient with a mild verbal memory impairment was allowed to experiment on the computer with different strategies for learning word lists. Although he did not adopt any of the presented strategies, he subsequently generated his own techniques after coming to realize the benefits of strategy use for his memory. This study implies that some form of generalized benefits of strategy learning may be possible, at least with mildly impaired patients.

The finding that mnemonic strategies are most useful for patients with relatively mild memory deficits (Benedict, 1989; Wilson, 1987) is consistent with the notion that the strategies rely on the use of residual memory processes. To the extent that memory is damaged rather than lost, residual skills may be tapped to facilitate the acquisition of new information. Such strategies, however, may not be as advantageous for patients with severe memory disorders, who lack the residual memory processes needed for their efficient use.

Evidence on the teaching and use of mnemonic strategies in rehabilitation suggests that the strategies may be beneficially employed by patients with mild-to-moderate disorders for the purposes of learning specific information important in their everyday lives. There is little indication, however, that strategy use generalizes beyond the training situation or that general improvements in memory functioning can be obtained. Repetitive use of strategies with meaningless laboratory materials therefore appears to be of little value (Wilson, 1991).

External Aids

The microcomputer has perhaps the greatest potential of any external aid for beneficial use by memory-impaired patients, although its capabilities have not been fully exploited (Ager, 1985; Harris, 1992). As an external aid, the computer has the power to act as a memory prosthesis, storing and producing on demand all kinds of information relevant to an individual's functioning in everyday life. It may also assist directly in the performance of tasks of daily living (see Cole & Dehdashti, 1990), acting as reminders for activities such as taking medication or meals (Flannery et al., 1997).

Progress in this area, however, has been slow for at least two reasons:

1. Early attempts to teach memory-impaired patients how to use even simple computing devices were not successful. Patients simply could not remember the commands needed to operate them (Wilson et al., 1989; Wilson & Moffat, 1984).
2. Until recently, computers have been too cumbersome to carry around and so their utility in everyday life has been somewhat limited (Harris, 1992; Vanderheiden, 1982).

Both of these problems, however, have been largely solved in the past few years and, although there are as yet few demonstrations of effective use of computers as external aids, there is reason for some optimism concerning the future use of computers by memory-impaired patients.

A series of successful studies employing microcomputers to assist memory-impaired people with tasks of daily living has been conducted by Kirsch et al. (1987, 1992). These investigators used the computer as an "interactive task guidance system", providing a series of cues to guide patients through the sequential steps of real-world tasks, such as cookie-baking and janitorial activities. In these studies, the computer acts solely as a compensatory device, providing the patient with step-by-step instructions for the performance of a task. Little knowledge of computer operation is required on the part of the subject, who merely responds with a single key-press to indicate that the instructions have been followed.

Another promising line of research was conducted by Cole and colleagues (Cole & Dehdashti, 1990; Cole et al., 1993). They designed highly customized computer interventions for brain-injured patients with a variety of cognitive deficits (see also Cole et al., 1988). Each intervention tried to help patients perform an activity of daily living they were able to accomplish prior to trauma but were now unable to perform without assistance, e.g. a patient with severe memory and attentional deficits was able to use a customized text editor and software to construct things-to-do lists, take notes during telephone conversations, and carry out home financial transactions (cheque writing, deposits, withdrawals, mailings, etc.), activities that had become impossible since her injury. In this case, the computer was modified to simplify these tasks and to bypass the particular cognitive deficits that were problematic for the patient.

Memory-impaired patients have been able to learn how to use computers as word-processors, e.g. Batt & Lounsbury (1990) constructed a simple flowchart with coloured symbols and simple wording that enabled a memory-impaired patient to use a word-processing package. The bypassing of confusing menus and the reduction of memory load enabled the patient to carry out the appropriate word-processing steps without difficulty and to operate the computer by himself (see also Glisky, 1995; Hunkin & Parkin, 1995; Van der Linden & Coyette, 1995).

In all of these studies, memory-impaired people used the computer to support some important activity of daily life. Hardware and software were modified so that problems were eliminated or reduced and only a few simple responses needed to be learned. The computer essentially served a prosthetic function, allowing brain-injured patients to perform activities that were otherwise impossible. These kinds of intervention require no assumptions concerning adaptation of the neural or cognitive mechanisms involved in memory, and in general they make no claims concerning restoration or changes in underlying mnemonic ability. Frequently, however, increases in self-confidence and self-esteem are observed in patients following successful computer experience (Batt & Lounsbury, 1990; Cole et al., 1993; Glisky & Schacter, 1987; Johnson, 1990). Whether these psychosocial changes are specifically attributable to computer use, as opposed to other non-specific features of training, has not been empirically documented.

The one negative feature of these interventions, from a clinical perspective, is their high cost and limited applicability. Design of customized systems requires time, money and expertise and each design may be useful only for a single patient. With continued development in this area, however, prototypical systems may become available that might serve a broader range of patients and be easily administered in the clinic.

Acquisition of Domain-specific Knowledge

In an effort to capitalize on the preserved memory abilities of amnesic patients, Glisky et al. (1986b) devised a fading-of-cues technique, called the "method of vanishing cues", which was designed to take advantage of patients' normal responses to partial cues to teach them complex knowledge and skills that might be used in everyday life. The training technique provides as much cue information as patients need to make a correct response and then gradually withdraws it across learning trials. The microcomputer serves essentially the role of teacher, presenting information and feedback in a consistent fashion, controlling the amount of cue information in accordance with patients' needs and prior responses, and allowing people to work independently at their own pace. Unlike interventions in which the computer is provided as a continuing prosthetic support, the goal of these interventions is to teach people the information that they need in order to function without external support (see Glisky, 1992b).

Using the method of vanishing cues, Glisky and colleagues successfully taught memory-impaired patients information associated with the operation of a microcomputer (Glisky et al., 1986a, 1986b; Glisky & Schacter, 1988b), the names of various business-related documents (Butters et al., 1993) and a number of vocational tasks, including computer data-entry

(Glisky, 1992a; Glisky & Schacter, 1987, 1989a), microfilming (Glisky & Schacter, 1988a), database management (Glisky, 1993) and word-processing (Glisky, 1995). Other researchers have demonstrated successful learning of a daily schedule (Heinrichs et al., 1992), basic items of orientation (Moffat, 1992), information pertaining to treatment goals, sections of a college course in sociology, and instructions for behaviour modification (Cotgageorge, personal communication).

There are, however, some caveats concerning the domain-specific learning approach. Although memory-impaired patients are able to learn considerable amounts of complex information, their learning may be exceedingly slow and may result in knowledge representations that are different from those of the general population. In particular, patients cannot always access newly acquired knowledge on demand or use it flexibly in novel situations. In other words, transfer beyond the training context cannot be assumed (Wilson, 1992), although it has been demonstrated under some conditions (Glisky, 1995; Glisky & Schacter, 1989a). It is therefore essential that all information relevant to the performance of a particular functional task be taught directly, so that the need for generalization is minimal (Glisky et al., 1994).

The problems of transfer and generalization are well known to rehabilitation specialists, and seem to plague all rehabilitation methodologies to some degree. The domain-specific learning approach assumes that transfer to new contexts is not automatic, and so the focus of the approach is on teaching information that is useful to memory-impaired people in their everyday lives. Other approaches, which are directed towards the restoration of general memory ability, assume that generalization does occur and that exercising memory is the key to that outcome. The material to be practised is viewed as irrelevant and consists generally of useless information, such as random digits, locations, words and so forth. Evidence suggests, however, that exercising memory does not improve basic memory ability, and so the procedure provides no benefits to patients whatsoever. The method of vanishing cues similarly requires extensive practice and repetition, but the purpose of practice is the acquisition of new meaningful and useful information. The technique has been found to be significantly more effective than simple repetition (Glisky et al., 1986b; Leng et al., 1991) and has enabled the learning of more complex knowledge than was previously thought possible.

The vanishing cues methodology was designed to capitalize on preserved abilities of amnesic patients in order to teach them knowledge and skills relevant in everyday life. Use of intact memory processes to compensate for those that have been disrupted or lost has often been suggested as an appropriate strategy for rehabilitation (Baddeley, 1992; Salmon & Butters, 1987); yet, as Baddeley has pointed out, few interventions of this type, other than the one used by Glisky and colleagues, have been attempted. It is likely that we still lack sufficient knowledge concerning the nature of the processes preserved in amnesia to take optimal advantage of them in rehabilitation. Nevertheless, this approach seems to be a promising one that may gain momentum as basic research provides additional information concerning processes and structures involved in normal memory.

Vocational Tasks

One area in which computers might serve a potentially important function is the workplace. Glisky (1992a, 1992b) has suggested that some vocational tasks requiring the use of a computer may present good opportunities for employment for memory-impaired patients for a number of reasons. First, patients are capable of procedural learning; they can acquire a fixed set of procedures, such as those required for data-entry or word-processing, and apply them in a consistent fashion over time. Second, computers in general require rather rigid adherence to a set of rules and can be counted on to be highly consistent, unlike their human counterparts. Once patients have learned the rules and their applications, they are less likely to be called upon to make online decisions or respond to novel circumstances. Third, many computer tasks lend themselves rather well to laboratory simulations, so that job training can be accomplished before patients enter the workplace. Glisky and colleagues have found that careful step-by-step training in the laboratory of all components of a task facilitates transfer to the real-world environment and allows the patient to enter the workplace with a high degree of confidence and skill (Glisky & Schacter, 1989a).

In general, computer jobs have been overlooked by rehabilitation and vocational specialists, perhaps because they seem too high-tech and complex and, therefore, beyond the capabilities of brain-injured patients. Yet even patients with quite severe memory impairments have been able to acquire the knowledge and skills needed to perform computer data-entry and word-processing tasks (Glisky, 1992a, 1995). It is worth keeping in mind, however, that all aspects of a task need to be taught explicitly and directly in order to minimize problems in generalization. Although transfer of work skills across changes in materials (Glisky, 1992a) and from a training to a work or home environment has been demonstrated (Glisky, 1995; Glisky & Schacter, 1989a), changes in the actual procedures may present serious difficulties.

Virtual Reality Technology

"Virtual reality" (VR) uses similar technology to that found in interactive computer games and simulators. VR provides a means of creating an artificial, computer-generated environment that the individual can explore, such as the inside of a building or an area within a neighbourhood. There are two types of VR, nonimmersive and immersive. Nonimmersive VR generally consists of conventional computer displays with control devices such as joysticks. Immersive VR is technically much more sophisticated and also much more expensive. The individual receives auditory, visual and tactile components of the computer-generated virtual environment through head-mounted displays and also through head and pressure emitting devices in clothing worn by the participant. Movements made by the subject are relayed back to computer systems that are part of the VR system, and these can amend the pattern of sensory stimulation accordingly, so that immersive VR is very much a two-way interaction between the individual and the system. This opens up a range of applications, including using items in the kitchen or similar everyday tasks (Gourlay et al., 2000).

More general reviews of VR in neuropsychological rehabilitation are provided elsewhere (e.g., Riva, 1997; Rose et al., 1996). For present purposes, we consider the relatively few studies that have so far attempted to apply VR to enhance memory functioning in neurological patients. Brooks et al. (1999) used nonimmersive VR to train an amnesic patient to find her way around a rehabilitation unit. This involved practice on a "virtual" route that had been programmed into a computer—the improvement on the VR task appeared to transfer to performance in the real-life environment of the rehabilitation unit. In a study of a group of patients with unilateral cerebrovascular lesions, Rose et al. (1999) used nonimmersive VR to study memory for spatial and object recognition. Participants either actively or passively explored the VR environment, in one case controlling movement through the environment by using a joystick, and in the other case simply passively viewing the journey through the virtual environment. Memory for spatial features of the VR environment was better in active compared to passive participants. However, memory for objects in the environment was better in passive compared to active control participants, but was the same in passive compared to active neurological patients.

THE APPLICATION OF MEMORY AIDS IN REHABILITATION SETTINGS

Factors to be considered in the use of memory aids in rehabilitation include general ones applicable to most forms of neuropsychological intervention and memory rehabilitation, and specific ones relating to the particular use of aids to overcome memory difficulties—a form of "compensatory memory training". In a critical review covering a number of areas of cognitive rehabilitation, Cicerone et al. (2000) offered useful guidelines that are relevant for the use of memory aids. They

> ...found evidence for the effectiveness of compensatory memory training for subjects with mild memory impairments compelling enough to recommend it as a Practice Standard. The evidence also suggests that memory remediation is most effective when subjects are fairly independent in daily function, are actively involved in identifying the memory problems to be treated, and are capable and motivated to continue active, independent strategy use (Cicerone et al., 2000, p. 1605).

General Factors

For any intervention to be effective and to be seen to be effective, some criteria need to be satisfied. These include:

1. The intervention needs to bring about meaningful changes in the patient's everyday memory functioning. How one defines "meaningful change" may vary from patient to patient, but the patient should be able to carry out more memory-related activities, with greater ease and success, and with less distress, than before the intervention.
2. The improvement in memory functioning should be permanent.
3. The improvement should have minimal side-effects.
4. The intervention should be cost-effective in terms of both money and time.
5. The intervention should be easy to administer by a third party.
6. The intervention should be applicable to a large number of patients, ideally across disease categories and severity of memory loss.
7. The intervention should be beneficial over and above any general "placebo" or incidental effects resulting from the treatment.

In individual patients, variables worth considering are:

1. Age, educational level, and premorbid knowledge and skills.
2. Any physical disability, such as sensory or motor loss.

3. The intactness or otherwise of nonmemory cognitive functions.
4. Supportive and possible negative influences that the family/carer may bring to bear on the therapeutic programme.
5. Current daily routine and the demands which this places on memory. Many memory functions, and in particular prospective memory, are better earlier than later in the day (Wilkins & Baddeley, 1978).
6. Any behavioural, attentional or motivational problems. On the one hand, memory aids may act as motivational cues to help with problems such as apathy, but the use of memory aids often requires some involvement of executive functions, such as initiation of behaviour, planning/organizational skills, problem-solving ability, focused attention, etc.

The severity and pattern of memory loss is a major factor, and it is important to pay particular attention to a number of areas:

1. Everyday memory symptoms as reported by the patient and by an informed observer, noting the patient's insight and concern about his/her memory difficulties.
2. Severity and pattern of anterograde memory loss.
3. Severity and pattern of retrograde memory loss, in particular the extent to which past knowledge and skills have been lost.
4. The extent to which new skill learning and implicit memory are preserved.

Specific Factors

There are a number of specific factors to be borne in mind when considering whether to encourage and train patients in the use of memory aids to help everyday memory:

1. How often and which type of memory aid has been used in the past? For example, many elderly people are accustomed to using simple diaries and are reluctant to change to electronic devices, no matter how much more effective they may be. Some patients need to be reassured that using memory aids will not lead to their becoming lazy or their brain wasting away through lack of use. They need to be reassured that using memory aids with other people around is nothing to be ashamed of, perhaps pointing out that such aids are increasingly used by the general population. Memory aids can be seen as status symbols and may enhance the self-esteem of memory-impaired people.
2. Although it is the principal duty of the clinician to find a memory aid simple to use and suitable for a particular patient, the patient should, if possible, be given a choice and be involved in any decisions.
3. A carer/relative needs to be closely involved in the process from the beginning, so as to encourage the use of the aid in domestic settings. In particular, if the aid is complicated to use, this person also needs to be taught to use it so that there is someone to turn to if problems arise in operating the aid.
4. Memory aids are often given to patients to use with little further or no intervention from the therapist. If only life were this simple. As Intons-Peterson & Newsome (1992) have pointed out, there are a number of cognitive processes involved in the use of even simple external memory aids. Thus, memory-impaired people need to be trained in the

"metamemory" skill of being able to identify situations where a memory aid will be useful, they must motivate themselves to use a memory aid, choose an aid that will be useful for the particular circumstances, and remember how to operate and use the memory aid effectively.

5. Memory-impaired people should be motivated to both learn to use the aid and to adapt daily routines and habits so as to incorporate the memory aid into such activities. Ideally, they themselves should formulate some of the reminders so that they are seen as self-cues rather than "nagging" from some external source.

For more complex aids such as electronic organizers, a specific training programme should be designed in which stages of learning a particular procedure are broken down into steps. Principles such as spaced rehearsal, graded reduction of support/vanishing cues and error-free learning, feedback and encouragement, and help-cards may be required in the teaching process. The training programme in the clinic should, as closely as feasible, mimic everyday uses of the memory aid, with concrete examples being drawn from the patient's daily routine. Training in the use of electronic organizers usually requires 4–6 sessions, and if these are provided weekly, homework can be set for the patient. The beginning of a therapy session can test long-term retention of what was learned in an earlier session. Finally, many effective interventions involve a particular combination of environmental, stationery, mechanical and electronic memory aids, as in the case described by Wilson (1999b). The challenge lies with the clinician to use his/her knowledge and experience to suggest and draw up a particular combination of treatment strategies.

CONCLUSIONS AND FUTURE DEVELOPMENTS

External memory aids are effective in improving everyday memory functioning, and this benefit is particularly evident in the area of prospective memory. Computer-related memory rehabilitation strategies remain largely task-specific in their benefit, but may be useful to the extent that they perform similar functions to external memory aids. The use of environmental cues, either to help navigational memory or to enhance man–machine interaction, is another area that is potentially beneficial to people with memory deficits.

While technological innovations may drive many of the developments in memory reha-bilitation, advances in conceptual and clinical spheres are equally important. We do not yet have a comprehensive conceptual framework to consider the various strategies used to en-hance memory functioning. If conceptual and empirical links could be made with other at-tempts to improve memory functioning, such as pharmacological agents and neural implants, rehabilitation might move forwards, especially if these attempts could be integrated into a theoretical framework that accounts for neural plasticity and recovery of memory function following neurological disease or injury (Robertson & Murre, 1999). In the clinical sphere, there may be a greater refinement in our understanding of which patients will benefit most from memory aids. Ideally, a patient's clinical and neuropsychological profile, together with factors such as specific memory needs, should be matched to the features of potential mem-ory aids to inform the clinician of the particular memory aids, or combination of treatments, that will be of maximum benefit to the individual. Careful evaluation of the effectiveness of memory aids will require further advances in memory assessment procedures, in particular those that can reliably assess everyday memory functioning (see Glisky & Glisky, 2002).

The cost-effectiveness of memory aids needs to be considered, especially where computer-based aids or expensive electronic devices may perform functions that can be carried out by stationery memory aids or by less expensive electronic memory aids. Advances in technology may allow for the introduction of more sophisticated, cheaper and more user-friendly aids, and some memory aids may emerge that have been purpose-built for memory-impaired individuals. Future developments in external memory aids include:

1. The integration of multiple memory-related functions within a single electronic unit, which will carry out tasks currently performed by devices such as a personal organizer, mobile phone, e-mail/Internet facility, reminder/pager, etc.
2. Devices such as electronic organizers that more readily accept hand-written input via an adjacent note-pad, which permits infrared transfer of impressions made on paper.
3. Memory pens, which keep a record of what has been written and which allow this information to be transferred to another storage medium.
4. Reminders that have context-sensitive features, such that a message-alarm will activate when the individual engages in a related activity, or when other critical people are in the vicinity (Lamming et al., 1994).
5. Reminders that include a "task enactment–alarm" link, such that the alarm only turns off when the target activity has been carried out (cf. Azrin & Powell, 1969).
6. Wearable memory aids that integrate more naturally with the dress, habits and routines of patients (cf. Hoisko, 2000).
7. Devices that use wireless technology (such as the new "bluetooth" system) to convey information about the location of items.

It is too early to say which, if any, of these developments will have a major impact on the application of memory aids in clinical settings. If conceptual, empirical, biological and technological advances across disciplines are harnessed and harmonized in meaningful ways, and if clinicians and researchers focus their attention and resources on the application of resultant devices in clinical settings, there will be undoubted benefits for memory-impaired neurological patients in the years to come.

ACKNOWLEDGEMENT

N.K. is grateful to Pat Abbott for her help in preparing this chapter.

REFERENCES

Ager, A. (1985). Recent developments in the use of microcomputers in the field of mental handicap: implications for psychological practice. *Bulletin of the British Psychological Society*, **38**, 142–145.

Aldrich, F.K. (1998). Pager messages as self reminders: a case study of their use in memory impairment. *Personal Technologies*, **2**, 1–10.

Azrin, N. & Powell, J. (1969). Behavioral engineering: the use of response priming to improve prescribed medication. *Journal of Applied Behaviour Analysis*, **2**, 39–42.

Bäckman, L. & Dixon, R. (1992). Psychological compensation: a theoretical framework. *Psychological Bulletin*, **12**, 259–283.

Baddeley, A.D. (1992). Implicit memory and errorless learning: a link between cognitive theory and neuropsychological rehabilitation? In L. R. Squire & N. Butters (eds), *Neuropsychology of Memory*, 2nd edn (pp. 309–314). New York: Guilford.

Batt, R.C. & Lounsbury, P.A. (1990). Teaching the patient with cognitive deficits to use a computer. *American Journal of Occupational Therapy*, **44**, 364–367.

Benedict, R.B.H. (1989). The effectiveness of cognitive remediation strategies for victims of traumatic head injury: a review of the literature. *Clinical Psychology Review*, **9**, 605–626.

Ben-Yishay, Y., Piasetsky, E.B. & Rattok, J. (1987). A systematic method for ameliorating disorders in basic attention. In M. J. Meier, A. L. Benton & L. Diller (eds), *Neuropsychological Rehabilitation* (pp. 165–181). New York: Guilford.

Bradley, V.A., Welch, J.L. & Skilbeck, C.E. (1993). *Cognitive Retraining Using Microcomputers*. Hove: Erlbaum.

Brooks, B., McNeil, J., Rose, F. et al. (1999). Route learning in a case of amnesia: a preliminary investigation into the efficacy of training in a virtual environment. *Neuropsychological Rehabilitation*, **9**, 63–76.

Burke, J., Danick, J., Bemis, B. & Durgin, C. (1994). A process approach to memory book training for neurological patients. *Brain Injury*, **8**, 71–81.

Butters, M.A., Glisky, E.L. & Schacter, D.L. (1993). Transfer of learning in memory-impaired patients. *Journal of Clinical and Experimental Neuropsychology*, **15**, 219–230.

Canter, D. (1996). Wayfinding and signposting: penance or prosthesis? In D. Canter (ed.), *Psychology in Action* (pp. 139–155). San Diego, CA: Academic Press.

Chen, S., Thomas, J., Glueckauf, R. & Bracy, O. (1997). The effectiveness of computer-assisted cognitive rehabilitation for persons with traumatic brain injury. *Brain Injury*, **11**, 197–209.

Cicerone, K., Dalhberg, C., Kalmar, K. et al. (2000). Evidence-based cognitive rehabilitation: recommendations for clinical practice. *Archives of Physical Medicine and Rehabilitation*, **81**, 1596–1615.

Clare, L. & Wilson, B. A (1997). *Coping with Memory Problems*. Bury St Edmunds: Thames Valley Test Company.

Cole, E., Dehdashti, P., Petti, L. & Angert, M. (1988). Prosthesis ware: a new class of software supports the activities of daily living. *Neuropsychology*, **2**, 41–57.

Cole, E. & Dehdashti, P. (1990). Interface design as a prosthesis for an individual with a brain injury. *SIGCHI Bulletin*, **22**, 28–32.

Cole, E., Dehdashti, P., Petti, L. & Angert, M. (1993). Design parameters and outcomes for cognitive prosthetic software with brain injury patients. *Proceedings of the RESNA International '93 Conference*, **13**.

Craik, F.I.M. & Jennings, J.M. (1992). Human memory. In F.I.M. Craik & T.A. Salthouse (eds), *Handbook of Aging and Cognition* (pp. 51–110). Mahwah, NJ: Erlbaum.

Dogu, U. & Erkip, F. (2000). Spatial factors affecting wayfinding and orientation. A case study in a shopping mall. *Environment and Behaviour*, **32**, 731–755.

Donaghy, S. & Williams, W. (1998). A new protocol for training severely impaired patients in the usage of memory journals. *Brain Injury*, **12**, 1061–1076.

Elmstahl, S., Annerstedt, L. & Ahlund, O. (1997). How should a group living unit for demented elderly be designed to decrease psychiatric symptoms? *Alzheimer's Disease and Associated Disorders*, **11**, 47–52.

Finset, A. & Andresen, S. (1994). The process diary concept: an approach in training orientation, memory and behavioural control. In R. Wood & I. Fussey (eds), *Cognitive Rehabilitation in Perspective* (pp. 99–116). Hove: Erlbaum.

Flannery, M., Butterbaugh, G., Rice, D. & Rice, J. (1997). Reminding technology for prospective memory disability: a case study. *Pediatric Rehabilitation*, **1**, 239–244.

Fluharty, F. & Priddy, D. (1993). Methods of increasing client acceptance of a memory book. *Brain Injury*, **7**, 85–88.

Fowler, R.S., Hart, J. & Sheehan, M. (1972). A prosthetic memory: an application of the prosthetic environment concept. *Rehabilitation Counselling Bulletin*, **16**, 80–85.

Fulton, A. & Hatch, P. (1991). *It's Here ... Somewhere*. Cincinnati, OH: Writers Digest Books.

Gabriel, M., Gagnon, J. & Bryan, C. (1977). Improved patient compliance through use of a daily drug reminder chart. *American Journal of Public Health*, **67**, 968–969.

Gianutsos, R. (1992). The computer in cognitive rehabilitation: it's not just a tool any more. *Journal of Head Trauma Rehabilitation*, **7**, 26–35.

Gibbs, W. (2000). As we may live. *Scientific American*, **283**, 26–28.

Giles, G.M. & Shore, M. (1989). The effectiveness of an electronic memory aid for a memory-impaired adult of normal intelligence. *American Journal of Occupational Therapy*, **43**, 409–411.

Glisky, E.L. (1992a). Acquisition and transfer of declarative and procedural knowledge by memory-impaired patients: a computer data-entry task. *Neuropsychologia*, **30**, 899–910.

Glisky, E.L. (1992b). Computer-assisted instruction for patients with traumatic brain injury: teaching of domain-specific knowledge. *Journal of Head Trauma Rehabilitation*, **7**, 1–12.

Glisky, E.L. (1993). Training persons with traumatic brain injury for complex computer jobs: the domain-specific learning approach. In D.F. Thomas, F.E. Menz & D.C. McAlees (eds), *Community-based Employment Following Traumatic Brain Injury* (pp. 3–27). Menomonie, WI: University of Wisconsin.

Glisky, E.L. (1995). Acquisition and transfer of word processing skill by an amnesic patient *Neuropsychological Rehabilitation*, **5**, 299–318.

Glisky, E.L. (1997). Rehabilitation of memory dysfunction. In T.E. Feinberg & M.J. Farah (eds), *Behavioral Neurology and Neuropsychology* (pp. 491–495). New York: McGraw-Hill.

Glisky, E.L. & Glisky, M.L. (1999). Memory rehabilitation in the elderly. In D. Stuss, G. Winocur & I. Robertson (eds), *Cognitive Neurorehabilitation* (pp. 347–361). Cambridge: Cambridge University Press.

Glisky, E.L. & Glisky, M.L. (2002). Learning and memory impairments. In P.J. Eslinger (ed.), *Neuropsychological Interventions*, (pp. 137–162). New York: Guilford.

Glisky, E.L. & Schacter, D.L. (1987). Acquisition of domain-specific knowledge in organic amnesia: training for computer-related work. *Neuropsychologia*, **25**, 893–906.

Glisky, E. L. & Schacter, D. L. (1988a). Acquisition of domain-specific knowledge in patients with organic memory disorders. *Journal of Learning Disabilities*, **21**, 333–339.

Glisky, E.L. & Schacter, D.L. (1988b). Long-term retention of computer learning by patients with memory disorders. *Neuropsychologia*, **26**, 173–178.

Glisky, E.L. & Schacter, D.L. (1989a). Extending the limits of complex learning in organic amnesia: computer training in a vocational domain. *Neuropsychologia*, **27**, 107–120.

Glisky, E.L. & Schacter, D.L. (1989b). Models and methods of memory rehabilitation. In F. Boller & J. Grafman (eds), *Handbook of Neuropsychology* (pp. 233–246). Amsterdam: Elsevier.

Glisky, E.L., Schacter, D.L. & Butters, M.A. (1994). Domain-specific learning and memory remediation. In M.J. Riddoch & G.W. Humphreys (eds), *Cognitive Neuropsychology and Cognitive Rehabilitation* (pp. 527–548). London: Erlbaum.

Glisky, E.L., Schacter, D.L. & Tulving, E. (1986a). Computer learning by memory-impaired patients: acquisition and retention of complex knowledge. *Neuropsychologia*, **24**, 313–328.

Glisky, E.L., Schacter, D.L. & Tulving, E. (1986b). Learning and retention of computer-related vocabulary in amnesic patients: method of vanishing cues. *Journal of Clinical and Experimental Neuropsychology*, **8**, 292–312.

Gourlay, D., Lun, K. & Liya, G. (2000). Telemedicinal virtual reality for cognitive rehabilitation. *Studies in Health Technology Informatics*, **77**, 1181–1186.

Gray, J.M., Robertson, I., Pentland, B. & Anderson, S. (1992). Microcomputer-based attentional retraining after brain damage: a randomised group controlled trial. *Neuropsychological Rehabilitation*, **2**, 97–115.

Gronwall, D. (1977). Paced auditory serial addition task: a measure of recovery from concussion. *Perceptual and Motor Skills*, **44**, 367–373.

Gruneberg, M.M. (1992). The practical application of memory aids. In M.M. Gruneberg & P. Morris (eds), *Aspects of Memory, vol. 1: Practical Aspects*, 2nd edn (pp. 168–195). Florence, KY: Taylor & Francis/Routledge.

Harrell, M. Parenté, F., Bellingrath, E.G. & Lisicia K.A. (1992). *Cognitive Rehabilitation of Memory*. Gaithersburg, MD: Aspen.

Harris, J.E. (1992). Ways of improving memory. In B.A. Wilson & N. Moffat (eds), *Clinical Management of Memory Problems*, 2nd edn (pp. 59–85). London: Chapman and Hall.

Heinrichs, R.W., Levitt, H., Arthurs, A. et al. (1992). Learning and retention of a daily activity schedule in a patient with alcoholic Korsakoff's syndrome. *Neuropsychological Rehabilitation*, **2**, 43–58.

Herrmann, D., Brubaker, B., Yoder, C. et al. (1999). Devices that remind. In F. Durso, R. Nickerson, R. Schvaneveldt et al. (eds), *Handbook of Applied Cognition* (pp. 377–407). Chichester: Wiley.

Herrmann, D.J. & Chaffin, R. (1988). *Memory in Historical Perspective*. New York: Springer-Verlag.

Herrmann, D.J., Weingartner, H., Searleman, A. & McEvoy, C. (1992). *Memory Improvement: Implications for Memory Theory*. New York: Springer-Verlag.

Hersh, N. & Treadgold, L. (1994). NeuroPage: the rehabilitation of memory dysfunction by prosthetic memory and cueing. *Neurorehabilitation*, **4**, 187–197.

Hoisko, J. (2000). Context-triggered visual episodic memory prosthesis. In *Proceedings of the Fourth International Symposium on Wearable Computers* (pp. 185–186). Atlanta, GA: IEEE Computer Society.

Hunkin, N.M. & Parkin, A.J. (1995). The method of vanishing cues: an evaluation of its effectiveness in teaching memory-impaired individuals. *Neuropsychologia*, **33**, 1255–1279.

Intons-Peterson, M.J. & Fournier, J. (1986). External and internal memory aids: when and how often do we use them, *Journal of Experimental Psychology: General*, **115**, 267–280.

Intons-Peterson, M.J. & Newsome, G.L. III (1992). External memory aids: effects and effectiveness. In D. J. Herrmann, H. Weingartner, A. Searleman & C. McEvoy (eds), *Memory Improvement: Implications for Memory Theory* (pp. 101–121). New York: Springer-Verlag.

Johnson, R. (1990). Modifying memory function: use of a computer to train mnemonic skill. *British Journal of Clinical Psychology*, **29**, 437–438.

Kapur, N. (1995). Memory aids in the rehabilitation of memory disordered patients. In A.D. Baddeley, B.A. Wilson & F.N. Watts (eds), *Handbook of Memory Disorders*, Ist edn (pp. 535–557). Chichester: Wiley.

Kapur, N. (2001). *Managing your Memory*, 2nd edn. Southampton: Wessex Neurological Centre, Southampton General Hospital.

Kim, H.J., Burke, D.T., Dowds, M.M. & George, J. (1999). Utility of a microcomputer as an external memory aid for memory-impaired head injury patient during inpatient rehabilitation. *Brain Injury*, **13**, 147–150.

Kim, H.J., Burke, D.T., Dowds, M.M. et al. (2000). Electronic memory aids for outpatient brain injury: follow-up findings. *Brain Injury*, **14**, 187–196.

Kirsch, N.L., Levine, S.P., Fallon-Krueger, M. & Jaros, L.A. (1987). The microcomputer as an "orthotic" device for patients with cognitive deficits. *Journal of Head Trauma Rehabilitation*, **2**, 77–86.

Kirsch, N.L., Levine, S.P., Lajiness-O'Neill & Schnyder, M. (1992). Computer-assisted interactive task guidance: facilitating the performance of a simulated vocational task. *Journal of Head Trauma Rehabilitation*, **7**, 13–25.

Lamming, M., Brown, P., Carter, K. et al. (1994). The design of a human memory prosthesis. *Computer Journal*, **37**, 153–163.

Leirer, V., Morrow. D., Pariante, G. & Doksum, T. (1988). Increasing influenza vaccination adherence through voice mail. *Journal of the American Geriatric Society*, **37**, 1147–1150.

Leirer, V., Morrow, D., Tanke, E. & Pariante, G., (1991). Elders' nonadherence: its assessment and medication reminding by voice mail. *Gerontologist*, **31**, 514–520.

Leng, N.R.C., Copello, A.G. & Sayegh, A. (1991). Learning after brain injury by the method of vanishing cues: a case study. *Behavioural Psychotherapy*, **19**, 173–181.

Long, T.E., Cameron, K.A., Harju, B.L. et al. (1999). Women and middle-aged individuals report using more prospective memory aids. *Psychological Reports*, **85**, 1139–1153.

Martyn, C. & Gale, C. (1999). *Forgetfulness and Dementia*. London: Dorling Kindersley.

Matthews, C.G., Harley, J.P. & Malec, J.F. (1991). Guidelines for computer-assisted neuropsychological rehabilitation and cognitive remediation. *Clinical Neuropsychologist*, **5**, 3–19.

McGlynn, S.M. (1990). Behavioural approaches to neuropsychological rehabilitation. *Psychological Bulletin*, **108**, 420–441.

McKenney, J., Munroe, W. & Wright, J. (1992). Impact of an electronic medication compliance aid on long-term blood pressure control. *Journal of Clinical Pharmacology*, **32**, 277–283.

Middleton, D.K., Lambert, M.J. & Seggar, L.B. (1991). Neuropsychological rehabilitation: microcomputer-assisted treatment of brain-injured adults. *Perceptual and Motor Skills*, **72**, 527–530.

Milch, R., Ziv, L., Evans, V. & Hillebrand, M. (1996). The effect of an alphanumeric paging system on patient compliance with medicinal regimens. *American Journal of Hospital and Palliative Care*, **13**, 46–48.

Moffat, N. (1992). Strategies of memory therapy. In B.A. Wilson & N. Moffat (eds), *Clinical Management of Memory Problems* (pp. 86–119). London: Chapman and Hall.

Moffat, N.J. (1989). Home-based cognitive rehabilitation with the elderly. In L.W. Poon, D.C. Rubin & B.A. Wilson (eds), *Everyday Cognition in Adulthood and Late Life* (pp. 659–680). Cambridge: Cambridge University Press.

Morrow, D., Leirer, V., Carver, L. et al. (1999). Repetition improves older and younger adult memory for automated appointment messages. *Human Factors*, **41**, 194–204.

Naugle, R., Naugle, C., Prevey, M. & Delaney, R. (1988). New digital watch as a compensatory device for memory dysfunction. *Cognitive Rehabilitation*, **6**, 22–23.

Nides, M., Tashkin, D., Simmons, M. et al. (1993). Improving inhaler adherence in a clinical trial through the use of the nebulizer chronolog. Chest, **104**, 501–507.

Nielsen, J. (1958). *Memory and Amnesia*. Los Angeles, CA: San Lucas Press.

Norman, D.A. (1988). *The Psychology of Everyday Things*. New York: Basic Books.

Olsen, R., Hutchings, B. & Ehrenkrantz, E. (1999). The physical design of the home as a caregiving support: an environment for persons with dementia. *Care Management Journals*, **1**, 125–131.

Parente, R. & Herrmann, D. (1996). *Retraining Cognition. Techniques and Applications*. Gaithersburg, MD: Aspen.

Park, D., Morrell, R., Frieske, D. et al. (1991). Cognitive factors and the use of over-the-counter medication organizers by arthritic patients. *Human Factors*, **33**, 57–67.

Park, D., Morrell, R., Frieske, D. & Kinkaid, D. (1992). Medication adherence behaviours in older adults: effects of external cognitive supports. *Psychology and Aging*, **7**, 252–256.

Park, D.C. & Kidder, D.P. (1996). Prospective memory and medication adherence. In M. Brandimonte, G. Einstein & M. McDaniel (eds), *Prospective Memory. Theory and Applications* (pp. 369–390). Mahwah, NJ: Erlbaum.

Park, D.C. Smith, A.D. & Cavanaugh, J.C. (1990). Metamemories of memory researchers. *Memory and Cognition*, **18**, 321–327.

Passini, R., Pigot, H., Rainville, C. & Tetreault, M.-H. (2000). Wayfinding in a nursing home for advanced dementia of the Alzheimer-type. *Environment and Behaviour*, **32**, 684–710.

Passini, R., Rainville, C., Marchand, N. & Joanette, Y. (1998). Wayfinding and dementia: some research findings and a new look at design. *Journal of Architecture and Planning Research*, **15**, 133–151.

Patten, B.M. (1990). The history of memory arts. *Neurology*, **40**, 346–352.

Ponsford, J.L. & Kinsella, G. (1988). Evaluation of a remedial programme for attentional deficits following closed head injury. *Journal of Clinical and Experimental Neuropsychology*, **10**, 693–708.

Rehder, T., McCoy, L., Blackwell, B., Whitehead, W. & Robinson, A. (1980). Improving medication compliance by counseling and special prescription container. *American Journal of Hospital Pharmacy*, **37**, 379–384.

Riva, G. (ed.) (1997). *Virtual Reality in Neuropsychophysiology: Cognitive, Clinical and Methodological Issues in Assessment and Rehabilitation*. Amsterdam: IOS Press.

Robertson, I. (1990). Does computerized cognitive rehabilitation work? A review. *Aphasiology*, **4**, 381–405.

Robertson, I. & Halligan, P. (1999). *Spatial Neglect: A Handbook for Diagnosis and Treatment*. Hove: Psychology Press.

Robertson, I.H. & Murre J (1999). Rehabilitation of brain damage: brain plasticity and principles of guided recovery. *Psychological Bulletin*, **125**, 544–575.

Rose, F., Brooks, B., Attree, E. et al. (1999). A preliminary investigation into the use of virtual environments in memory retraining after vascular brain injury: indications for future strategy? *Disability and Rehabilitation*, **21**, 548–554.

Rose, F., Johnson, D., Attree, E. (1996). Virtual reality in neurological rehabilitation. *British Journal of Therapy and Rehabilitation*, **3**, 223–228.

Salmon, D.P. & Butters, N. (1987). Recent developments in learning and memory: implications for the rehabilitation of the amnesic patient. In M.J. Meier, A.L. Benton & L. Diller (eds), *Neuropsychological Rehabilitation* (pp. 280–293). New York: Guilford.

Schmitter-Edgecombe, M., Fahy, J., Whelan, J. & Long, C. (1995). Memory remediation after severe closed head injury: notebook training vs. supportive therapy. *Journal of Consulting and Clinical Psychology*, **63**, 484–489.

Schwartz, S. (1995). Adults with traumatic brain injury: three case studies of cognitive rehabilitation in the home setting. *American Journal of Occupational Therapy*, **49**, 655–667.

Sharps, M. & Price-Sharps, J. (1996). Visual memory support: an effective mnemonic device for older adults. *Gerontologist*, **36**, 706–708.

Skilbeck, C. (1984). Computer assistance in the management of memory and cognitive impairment. In B.A. Wilson & N. Moffat (eds), *Clinical Management of Memory Problems* (pp. 112–133). London: Croom Helm.

Skilbeck, C. & Robertson, I. (1992). Computer assistance in the management of memory and cognitive impairment. In B. A. Wilson & N. Moffat (eds), *Clinical Management of Memory Problems*, 2nd edn (pp. 154–188). London: Chapman and Hall.

Sohlberg, M.M. & Mateer, C.A. (1987). Effectiveness of an attention training program. *Journal of Clinical and Experimental Neuropsychology*, **9**, 117–130.

Sohlberg, M.M. & Mateer, C.A. (1989a). *Introduction to Cognitive Rehabilitation*. New York: Guilford.

Sohlberg, M.M. & Mateer, C.A. (1989b). Training use of compensatory memory books: a three-stage behavioral approach. *Journal of Clinical and Experimental Neuropsychology*, **11**, 871–891.

Sturm, W. & Willmes, K. (1991). Efficacy of a reaction training on various attentional and cognitive functions in stroke patients. *Neuropsychological Rehabilitation*, **1**, 259–280.

Szeto, A. & Giles, J. (1997). Improving oral medication compliance with an electronic aid. *IEEE Engineering and Biology*, **16**, 48–54.

Tulving, E. (1972). Episodic and semantic memory. In E. Tulving & W. Donaldson (eds), *Organization of Memory* (pp. 381–403). New York: Academic Press.

Tulving, E. (2000). Concepts of memory. In E. Tulving & F. Craik (eds), *The Oxford Handbook of Memory* (pp. 33–43). New York: Oxford University Press.

Van den Broek, M.D., Downes, J., Johnson, Z. et al. (2000). Evaluation of an electronic memory aid in the neuropsychological rehabilitation of prospective memory deficits. *Brain Injury*, **14**, 455–462.

Van der Linden, M. & Coyette, F. (1995). Acquisition of word processing knowledge in an amnesiac patient: implications for theory and rehabilitation. In R. Campbell & M. Conway (eds), *Broken Memories*, (pp. 54–76). Oxford: Blackwell.

Vanderheiden, G.C. (1982). The practical use of microcomputers in rehabilitation. *Bulletin of Prosthetic Research*, **19**, 1–5.

Warrington, E.K. (1986). Memory for facts and memory for events. *British Journal of Clinical Psychology*, **25**, 1–12.

Wilkins, A.J. & Baddeley, A.D. (1978). Remembering to recall in everyday life: an approach to absentmindedess. In M. M. Gruneberg, P.E. Morris & R.N. Sykes (eds), *Practical Aspects of Memory* (pp. 27–34). London: Academic Press.

Wilson, B.A. (1987). *Rehabilitation of Memory*. New York: Guilford.

Wilson, B.A. (1991). Theory, assessment, and treatment in neuropsychological rehabilitation. *Neuropsychology*, **5**, 281–291.

Wilson, B.A. (1992). Memory therapy in practice. In B.A. Wilson & N. Moffat (eds), *Clinical Management of Memory Problems*, 2nd edn (pp. 120–153). London: Chapman and Hall.

Wilson, B.A. (1999a). Memory rehabilitation in brain-injured people. In D. Stuss, G. Winocur & I. Robertson (eds), *Cognitive Neurorehabilitation* (pp. 333–346). Cambridge: Cambridge University Press.

Wilson, B.A. (1999b). *Case Studies in Neuropsychological Rehabilitation* (Chapter 4). Oxford: Oxford University Press.

Wilson, B.A., Baddeley, A.D. & Cockburn, J.M. (1989). How do old dogs learn new tricks? Teaching a technological skill to brain injured people. *Cortex*, **25**, 115–119.

Wilson, B.A., Emslie, H.C., Quirk, K. & Evans, J. (2001). Reducing everyday memory and planning problems by means of a paging system: a randomised control crossover study. *Journal of Neurology, Neurosurgery, and Psychiatry*, **70**, 477–482.

Wilson, B.A., Emslie, H., Quirk, K. & Evans J. (1999). George: Learning to live independently with NeuroPage. *Rehabilitation Psychology*, **44**, 284–296.

Wilson, B.A., Evans, J., Emslie, H. & Malinek, V. (1997). Evaluation of NeuroPage: a new memory aid. *Journal of Neurology, Neurosurgery, and Psychiatry*, **63**, 113–115.

Wilson, B.A. & Evans, J. (2000). Practical management of memory problems. In G. Berrios & J. Hodges (eds), *Memory Disorders in Psychiatric Practice* (pp. 291–310). Cambridge: Cambridge University Press.

Wilson, B.A. & Moffat, N. (1984). Rehabilitation of memory for everyday life. In J.E. Harris & P.E. Morris (eds), *Everyday Memory: Actions and Absentmindedness* (pp. 207–233). London: Academic Press.

Wilson, B.A. & Moffat, N. (Eds.) (1992). *Clinical Management of Memory Problems*, 2nd edn. London: Croom Helm.

Wilson, B.A. & Watson, P. (1996). A practical framework for understanding compensatory behaviour in people with organic memory impairment. *Memory*, **4**, 465–486.

Wood, R.L. (1992). Disorders of attention: their effect on behaviour, cognition and rehabilitation. In B.A. Wilson & N. Moffat (eds), *Clinical Management of Memory Problems*, 2nd edn (pp. 216–242). London: Chapman and Hall.

Wood, R.L. & Fussey, I. (1987). Computer-based cognitive retraining: a controlled study. *International Disability Studies*, **9**, 149–153.

Wright, P., Bartram, C., Rogers, N. et al. (2000). Text entry on handheld computers by older users. *Ergonomics*, **43**, 702–716.

Wright, P., Rogers, N., Hall, C. et al. (2001). Comparison of pocket-computer memory aids for people with brain injury. *Brain Injury*, **15**, 787–800.

Zencius, A., Wesolowski, M. & Burke, W. (1990). A comparison of four memory strategies with traumatically brain-injured clients. *Brain Injury*, **4**, 33–38.

Zencius, A., Wesolowski, M., Krankowski, T. & Burke, W. (1991). Memory notebook training with traumatically brain-injured clients. *Brain Injury*, **5**, 321–325.

CHAPTER 35

Emotional and Social Consequences of Memory Disorders

Robyn L. Tate

Rehabilitation Studies Unit, University of Sydney, Australia

> If memory, which makes up the very bones of thought, could be so isolated, and so selectively amputated from a man's mind, what was there to give his mind any human shape at all?... There would be for him nothing upon which he could build a past, or a future. And still more disturbing, he would be unable to form any human relationships. (Philip Hilts, 1995, p. 16, referring to H.M).

SETTING THE SCENE

In her book, *Case Studies in Neuropsychological Rehabilitation,* Wilson (1999) includes seven chapters describing patients with acquired memory disorders. The impact of the memory disorders on the lives of the seven individuals and their families is profound, and in all cases their lifestyles are changed irrevocably. Yet the emotional consequences of the memory disablement show considerable variability, even in the three individuals who suffer a pure amnesic syndrome, uncomplicated by the presence of additional cognitive impairments. The personal accounts of Jack, Alex and Jay provide rich insights into living with amnesia.

Jack comments: "Being continually made aware of mistakes, especially mistakes that I can't help but make, and being forced to challenge my own inability can result in personal humiliation... the feeling of indignation, frustration and fear from that incident has stayed with me" (Wilson, 1999, p. 41). Consequently, he avoids what he terms "high-risk" situations. An almost inevitable consequence of living with amnesia is the necessity for life to be simplified and routinized in order to minimize failures (Elliott, 1990). Alex ultimately made considerable achievements: employment, marriage, and becoming a father. These gains were not without cost, and his biggest problem was his low confidence: "Before I was more confident and sociable... This has changed... My confidence is down and that affects everything... Because I've got a bad memory it doesn't mean I'm intellectually

The Handbook of Memory Disorders. Edited by A.D. Baddeley, M.D. Kopelman and B.A. Wilson
© 2002 John Wiley & Sons, Ltd.

impaired. People talk down to me, they see the handicap, not the person" (pp. 64–66). For some people, the cognitive and physical effort involved in maintaining a lifestyle that approaches their premorbid expectations can strike at the very core of the person's identity and self-esteem (Meltzer, 1983). Jay assiduously refined compensatory strategies, elevating them into something of an art form. Yet in spite of his positive outlook and successful psychosocial reintegration, he has periods of feeling "very low and sad about his life. He was expecting to be a lawyer with a good income and has instead become a craftsman with just enough to live on" (p. 52). The mourning for personal losses, dashed hopes and expectations is a painful but necessary process to enable the person to rebuild his/her life in a different direction (Henderson, 1993).

In the original paper describing Jay (Wilson et al., 1997), the authors sought to understand why he should be so outstandingly successful in his use of compensatory strategies when his amnesia was so severe (screening score of 1/12 on the Rivermead Behavioural Memory Test) (Wilson et al., 1985). They point to "the combination of youth, intelligence, organized behaviour, determination, lack of additional cognitive deficits, and of course a fully supportive and imaginative family who worked with him at every stage of his problems" (p. 54). There is an increasing awareness that emotional and social factors are pivotal to rehabilitation success and, as in this case, override the severity of the initial impairments.

The first edition of this *Handbook* included a chapter by Prigatano (1995), entitled "Personality and Social Aspects of Memory Rehabilitation". He made the observation that memory rehabilitation does not occur in a vacuum, noting that half a century earlier such doyens of neuropsychology as Luria, Goldstein and Zangwill drew attention to the importance of personality factors, not only in shaping the symptom picture, but also potentially influencing the patient's adaptation to the permanent effects of such brain damage. Prigatano contrasted this perspective with "modern methods of memory rehabilitation (which) often emphasize cognitive strategies or mnemonic devices to aid the patient with only passing recognition of how emotional or motivational variables may influence treatment strategies and outcome" (p. 603). He concluded the chapter by calling for a more systematic consideration of social and personality factors in order to understand "how these variables interact and influence efforts . . . (regarding) various memory therapies" (p. 612). In the 7 years since the first edition of this *Handbook*, there is not a lot of evidence to suggest that either current clinical practice has changed or the detailed analytical work has been conducted. This chapter provides a detailed and comparative analysis of the social and emotional functioning of a selective group of individuals with circumscribed memory disorders in order to better understand this aspect of amnesia as a basis upon which to implement therapy programmes.

A CONCEPTUAL FRAMEWORK FOR STUDYING EMOTIONAL AND SOCIAL CONSEQUENCES OF MEMORY DISORDERS

Emotional and social consequences of acquired neuropsychological disorders in general, and memory disorders in particular, fall within the domain of psychosocial functioning. Emotional responses occur within the context of an individual's personality structure and their environment. Most authors make a distinction between underlying stable *traits*, which form the structure of the individual's personality, and transient fluctuations in emotional, affective and mood *states*, which occur in response to day-to-day events (Prigatano, 1992).

In the present chapter, "social" is conceptualized largely in World Health Organization (WHO) (1980, 2000) terms, referring to the person's everyday activities and participation in social roles.

One of the foci of this chapter is to examine emotional and social consequences of amnesia as outcomes, albeit outcomes that are not static and are determined by many intervening factors. Some of these are addressed by the WHO model (1980, 2000) of the consequences of illness or disease. It makes a tripartite distinction among impairments (abnormality or loss), disabilities (labelled "activity limitation" in the revised model), which refers to the restricting effects of impairments in functional performance and activities, and handicaps (labelled "participation restriction" in the revised model), referring to disadvantage arising from impairments and/or disabilities in the individual's performance of roles. The revised model includes a fourth component, contextual factors, involving both external (environmental) and internal (personal) influences on functioning.

This framework is helpful in understanding emotional and social consequences of memory disorders. For the present purposes, the nature and severity of the impairment (i.e. memory disorder) may result in a disability, in that the person is no longer able to engage in everyday activities previously taken for granted. Moreover, the impairments and/or disabilities may cause handicap if the person is no longer able to, or has difficulty in, resuming social roles, such as parent, employee, friend. Whereas a person might be able to minimize the effects of disability in one area of function (e.g. doing household chores) by the use of appropriate strategies (e.g. written lists for the housework schedule), he/she may be less able to compensate for aspects of memory impairment in other areas (such as raising a young child) and hence is significantly handicapped in the parenting area. The revised WHO model also recognizes that impairments, activity limitation (disabilities) and participation restriction (handicaps) are only some of the factors influencing outcome. Personal character (internal influences), together with the degree of emotional and practical support provided by family, friends and other people (external influences), play a crucial role in determining outcome. It is the sum total of all these factors and their interactions that contribute to social functioning, impact upon how a person feels about him/herself, his/her emotional responses to the situation, and thence the psychological adjustment to the amnesia.

It has long been recognized that nonmedical factors (in WHO terms, internal and external influences) affect outcomes. Within the neurological domain, specifically with reference to traumatic brain injury, Lishman (1973) made a distinction between "direct" and "indirect" factors. Direct factors were those directly related to the injury, such as locus and severity of lesion; indirect factors comprised a diverse range, including premorbid variables, environmental influences and emotional repercussions of the injury. It is important to recognize that emotional factors may play not only an "indirect" role but a "direct" role as well, when organic lesions are strategically placed, e.g. the limbic system is of central importance not only as the neural substrate for establishing new memories, but also in regulating emotions, mood and behaviour (Macchi, 1989). Additionally, the effects of orbital prefrontal lesions upon emotions, mood and behaviour can be so profound that the fundamental personality structure is altered (cf. Phineas Gage, described in MacMillan, 1996).

The component functions of the limbic system, as well as the interconnections between the limbic system and the frontal lobes, reinforce the intimate connection between the neural substrates of memory and emotions (see Chapter 20, this volume). Talland (1968) was among the first to recognize that amnesia was not restricted to memory processes alone, but was "regularly accompanied by abnormally reduced spontaneity, and usually

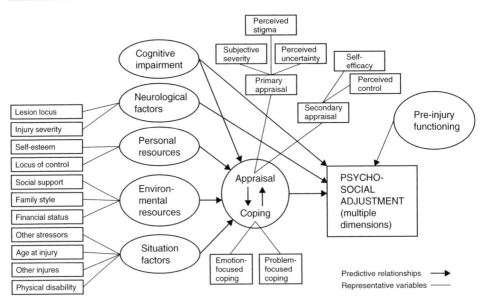

Figure 35.1   Model of psychosocial adjustment after closed head injury. Reproduced by permission of Psychology Press Ltd., Hove, UK, from Kendall & Terry (1996)

also by some anomalies of affect" (p. 22), including lack of initiative. This was observed not only in patients with Korsakoff's syndrome but also in postencephalitic patients and those with ruptured aneurysms of the anterior communicating artery. Similarly, Schacter (1991; Schacter et al., 1990) has written extensively of the problems of unawareness of memory deficit in patients with amnesia. In many of these cases it can be difficult to disentangle the relative contribution of "direct" and "indirect" emotional factors in the resulting symptom picture. Hence, when considering emotional factors from the "indirect" perspective in people with acquired memory disorders, it is important to acknowledge the possibility of a "direct" contribution as well.

Lishman's (1973) conceptualization has received support from other authorities, including Gainotti (1993), Prigatano (1987) and, in its most developed form, by Kendall & Terry (1996). Their model (see Figure 35.1), also with specific reference to traumatic brain injury, is based on the theory of Lazarus & Folkman (1984) as this applies to stress and coping. This model forcefully asserts the central role played by psychosocial factors in influencing outcome or adjustment. A variety of factors are conceptualized as antecedent variables, comprising, in Lishman's (1973) terms, both direct (medical, neurological and neuropsychological) and indirect (demographic, personal and environmental) factors. The model is interactive and recursive in that a second group of factors is posited to intervene and thence mediate the influence of the antecedent variables upon adjustment. These mediating variables are cognitive appraisals and ensuing coping responses of the individual.

Kendall & Terry's (1996) model brings a refreshing perspective to the study of psychosocial consequences in that by including "person" factors, such as premorbid personality, coping style and postmorbid cognitive appraisals, it goes beyond the well-trodden path of focusing exclusively upon emotional well-being and social functioning. With some notable exceptions (e.g. Moore et al., 1989, 1991; Moore & Stambrook, 1995), research into the effects of cognitive appraisals has not featured strongly in the neurological rehabilitation literature to date. Yet their importance is underscored by the striking observation of a number of empirical studies regarding the apparent mismatch between the objective reality of patients' level of disability and their own appraisals of their degree of disability, e.g. Tate & Broe (1999) found that 27% of their traumatic brain injury group with moderate or severe disability as assessed by the Glasgow Outcome Scale (Jennett & Bond, 1975; Jennett et al., 1981) reported having "no" disability or handicap, whereas 14% of those who had made a good recovery reported experiencing "a lot" of disability/handicap. Consideration and understanding of the multitude of diverse factors enumerated in Kendall & Terry's model may also help to explain why Jay (Wilson, 1999; Wilson et al., 1997), described earlier in this chapter, has made such an outstandingly successful adjustment to his memory disorder, whereas other individuals with far less severe impairments experience continued failures and set-backs in their adaptation.

PSYCHOSOCIAL CONSEQUENCES OF MEMORY DISORDERS

There is a dearth of literature regarding the emotional and social consequences of amnesic conditions, and a number of authors have called for more specific and detailed study of this aspect of amnesia (Bachna et al., 1998; Prigatano, 1995; Schacter et al., 1990). There are good reasons to suspect that the broader literature that does exist, regarding the emotional and social functioning of people with *a range* of neuropsychological disorders, is not entirely applicable to the more selective group of individuals with pure memory disorders. First, it has been generally accepted that people with circumscribed memory disorders have their other neuropsychological functions intact, although, as will be argued later, this position is not so clear-cut. Nevertheless, those with fairly circumscribed memory disorders are well placed to harness their intelligence and other neuropsychological strengths and implement compensatory strategies to circumvent the memory disorders. This enables them to access a range of life options that otherwise would be unavailable or difficult to achieve—productive work, independent lifestyles and a regular social life. Second, the presence of other neuropsychological impairments in addition to memory disorder makes it difficult to attribute any emotional or social disturbance to the memory disorder itself, as opposed to some concomitant neuropsychological problem that the person may experience, such as aphasia, executive impairment, attention deficit and so forth. Despite these issues, the literature regarding emotional and social consequences for people with a range of neuropsychological problems is relevant and important, given that, as Wilson (1991) observes, the majority of adults who experience acquired memory disorder also have additional neuropsychological impairments.

Yet some common and, indeed, intriguing themes are evident among the few single case reports that are available regarding the emotional and social functioning of adults whose neuropsychological impairments are reported as being restricted to acquired disorders of memory. These include the well-known cases H.M., N.A. and S.S., whose salient psychosocial and medical features are presented in Table 35.1. The most famous case, H.M., was originally reported in Scoville & Milner (1957). He underwent bilateral resection of the hippocampus for the relief of intractable epilepsy and as a consequence was left with severe anterograde amnesia. He was evaluated psychiatrically in 1982 and 1992 and described briefly in Corkin (1984) and Corkin et al. (1997). Case N.A. sustained damage to the region

Table 35.1 Psychosocial consequences of memory disorders in selected single cases

	H.M. (Corkin, 1984; Corkin et al., 1997; Ogden, 1996)	N.A. (Kaushall et al., 1981)	S.S. (O'Connor et al., 1995)
Background			
Year of onset	1953	1960	1971
Age at onset	27	22	44
Cause of disorder	Neurosurgical resection of medial temporal lobe bilaterally for treatment of intractable epilepsy	Fencing foil penetrating dorsomedial nucleus of thalamus	Herpes simplex encephalitis
Premorbid work	Unemployed at time of operation, but previously process-type work	Radar technician in air force	President of optical physics firm
Presentation	Socially interactive, agreeable, cooperative	Relaxed, amiable, appropriate social graces	Pleasant and outgoing manner, conducts intelligent discourse
Initial cognitive test results (Wechsler Scales)			
Intelligence Quotient	112	99	136
Memory Quotient	67	64	<50 (WMS-R delay)
Social functioning			
Accommodation	Initially with parents, since age 54 in a nursing home	Lives with mother	Lives with wife and family
Use of transport	Unable to go anywhere unaccompanied	Drives to selected venues	No information
Instrumental activities of daily living	Limited information; requires prompt and assistance for showering routines	Appears to rely upon mother	No information
Work	When living at home assisted with domestic activities; attended rehabilitation workshop	Tidies house; small woodwork projects; attends outpatient day treatment centre weekly	Routine household chores under supervision of wife
Leisure activities	Cross word puzzles, reading newspapers and television	Collects memorabilia, goes for walks, assembles models	No information
Relationships with family	Angry outbursts when provoked, otherwise placid	Some conflict with mother	No information
Relationships with friends	No information, but no interest in sexual relationships	No close friends and no sexual relationships	No information

of the left dorsomedial thalamus as a result of an accidental injury with a miniature fencing foil (Teuber et al., 1968). This resulted in a severe memory disorder, particularly for verbal material. His social functioning has been carefully documented, both in the original report and in Kaushall et al. (1981). The case of S.S., who contracted herpes simplex encephalitis, was originally reported by Cermack (1976; Cermack & O'Connor, 1983). His residual impairment was an amnesic syndrome. The emotional functioning and personality structure of S.S. has been studied in detail by O'Connor et al. (1995).

Social Functioning

In the 20 years since his injury, case N.A., aged 42 at the time of the follow-up report, is described as having "a devastated life and isolated mental world" (Kaushall et al., 1981, p. 384). With reference to occupational activities, he has not returned to his previous work as a radar technician and spends most of his time tidying around the house, doing small woodworking projects and attending a hospital outpatient day treatment programme on a weekly basis. Although he takes a keen interest in his collections of memorabilia and goes for walks, his leisure activities are limited by his memory disorder. Television, for instance, is unsatisfying because he forgets the narrative during commercial breaks. In terms of interpersonal relationships, NA remains unmarried and has had virtually no sexual contact since the injury, or, it appears, intimate relationships outside family. He has no close friends and lives with his mother, with whom there is some degree of conflict. His communication and socializing skills are moderately handicapped given that, because of his memory impairment, he is unable to maintain a topic of conversation. Living skills, for the most part, show major restriction. NA does not appear to be able to travel independently around the community, having taken 4 years to learn to drive from his home to the hospital day treatment programme. He relies upon his mother to prepare the meals, and it seems that he would be unable to live in the community without such live-in support and supervision. On the positive side, however, his social skills are well preserved.

The other cases, H.M. and S.S., have similarly impoverished lifestyles dating from the time of their illnesses. Neither of these men engages in any type of productive work. Yet in spite of the large amount of spare time, there is little evidence of a well-developed avocational programme in lieu of work. They are isolated individuals, without the benefits of a social network. Even though, following hospital discharge, they live in the community, they are dependent upon such emotional and practical supports as are provided by family. When these are no longer available, as in the case of H.M., institutional care appears to be the only alternative.

Although it is difficult to compare individual cases with group studies, there is a suggestion in group studies examining other neurological conditions of sudden onset, such as stroke and traumatic brain injury, that many of these people may in fact have less disruption of their social roles than those with pure amnesia, in terms of occupational activity, interpersonal relationships and independent living skills (e.g. Anderson et al., 1995; Fleming et al., 1999; Flick, 1999; Ponsford et al., 1995; Raaymakers et al., 2000; Tate et al., 1989). This is in spite of the additional multiple neuropsychological and motor-sensory disabilities frequently experienced by the stroke and traumatic brain injury groups. It is counter-intuitive that people with fairly circumscribed memory disorders should experience lifestyles that are so extremely disrupted. It appears that case N.A., at least, does not use compensatory memory strategies to enhance his lifestyle. "NA has not developed, or taken an interest in, notekeeping or other mnemonic techniques. He stoutly maintains that note-taking and diary keeping are crutches that would prevent him from improving" (Kaushall et al., 1981, p. 385). Considering the model of Kendall & Terry (1996) presented earlier, however, the severity and nature of the impairment was only one factor contributing to outcome and psychosocial adjustment. A consideration of "person" factors (including the personality structure of the individual and the emotional responses to the situation) is necessary to understand the psychosocial effects of acquired memory disorders.

Personality Structure

In the context of conducting a psychometric study of the Minnesota Multiphasic Personality Inventory (MMPI) and its revised version, MMPI-2 (Butcher et al., 1989), Bachna et al. (1998) examined 10 individuals with circumscribed memory disorders. Two of the MMPI scales, Depression and Schizophrenia, showed significant elevations for the group as a whole, with more than 50% showing elevations on these scales. A literal interpretation of the elevated scales can be misleading, however, because of the preponderance of items that would likely be endorsed by persons with neurological conditions (see also Alfano et al., 1990). Items such as, "There is something wrong with my mind", rather than being indicative of psychiatric abnormality, represent an accurate interpretation of the effects of the impairments these individuals experience. Similar observations have been made about other instruments, such as the Symptom Checklist (Woessner & Caplan, 1995) and the Eysenck Personality Questionnaire (Tate, submitted).

One of the participants in the Bachna et al. (1998) study was case S.S. His MMPI results indicated significant emotional distress, with elevations on clinical scales indicative of depression and anxiety. The Rorschach test was also administered to explore "latent aspects of S.S.'s personality" (O'Connor et al., 1995, p. 49). The quantity of responses was low and additionally qualitative analysis indicated obsessional tendencies, as well as themes of deterioration and decay. The authors suggested that, whereas the latter may reflect a damaged sense of self as a result of his illness, the former may represent either "a lifelong personality pattern . . . [or] his attempt to organize and understand his unpredictable environment" (p. 50). The aberrant results of the MMPI and Rorschach may be explained on the basis of the effects of S.S.'s neurological damage. Hence, if the data are to be interpreted as showing pathology of his personality structure, this is secondary to the amnesic syndrome.

To these standardized results can be added the clinical observations made about H.M., whose personality is described as "placid, happy and uncomplaining" (Ogden, 1996, p. 54). It is also noted that his adjustment to all changes in relationships and circumstances has been smooth (Corkin, 1984), although whether this reflects maturity or is a function of his adynamia is a moot point. H.M. is described as being very compliant, to the extent that, "if he is asked to sit in a particular place, he will do so indefinitely" (Corkin, 1984, p. 251). The personality of N.A. is not described in any detail, although Kaushall et al. (1985) suggest that he has a stable personality structure, given his adjustment to life events, such as his mother's new partner, together with his intact social skills and "signs of continuing personality development" (p. 388). The earlier report (Teuber et al., 1968), however, commenting upon changes in NA's personality at assessments 6–7 years postinjury, also described some inertia-type behaviours, in that NA leads "a rather indolent life, mowing his lawn and performing other chores around the house and garden if, and only if, he is instructed to do so ('driven to it' according to his mother)" (p. 270). The later account (Kaushall et al., 1981) does not describe these types of behaviour or make reference to the comments of Teuber and colleagues. By contrast, they draw a distinction between N.A. and the personality changes in Korsakoff's syndrome patients who, as previously noted by Talland (1968), do exhibit signs of apathy, passivity and lack of initiative, and conclude that "there is no necessary association between amnesia and passivity" (p. 387). One possibility to account for the discrepancy in descriptions of N.A.'s personality profile pertains to the long-term process of adaptation of personality in living with amnesia.

These clinical observations, together with the test data from case S.S., raise many questions about the personality structure of amnesic individuals that warrant further investigation. To date, personality change from the premorbid state has not been examined in people with amnesia. Although the traumatic brain-injured group is one for which changes in personality are commonly reported, very few studies with that group have used standardized measures of personality, including ratings taken of the premorbid state soon after onset of injury. The few reports that are available have shown different patterns of results. Using the NEO Personality Inventory (Costa & McCrae, 1992), Kurtz et al. (1998) found a significant change (decrease) on only one scale, Extraversion, between premorbid and 6 month posttrauma ratings. Employing the Eysenck Personality Questionnaire—Revised (Eysenck & Eysenck, 1991), Tate (submitted) found more extensive changes between premorbid and 6 month posttrauma ratings: significant decrease in Extraversion and increases in Neuroticism and Criminality, as well as Psychoticism at 12 months posttrauma. These data are interpreted as being changes in personality structure that are a direct consequence of the injury.

Other issues have been explored by the Boston group (Bachna et al., 1998; O'Connor et al., 1995). One of these pertains to the effect of the memory disorder on the development of personality over time. What is the effect of an individual being unable to incorporate and integrate new information and life experiences into the existing personality structure? Although Kaushall et al. (1981) gained the impression that N.A.'s personality was developing over time, this was not a finding for the more densely amnesic person, case S.S., when a standardized instrument, Measures of Personality Development (Hawley, 1980), was used. O'Connor and colleagues found that his emotional development was arrested at the time of onset of his illness, in that he had resolved conflicts appropriate to his maturational age at the time of onset of his illness (young adulthood), but not those thereafter (middle and older adulthood).

Bachna et al. (1998) also considered the role of memory processes in relation to the sense of self. They hypothesized that, if individuals with amnesia predominantly draw upon immediate memory as a reference point for their personality structure, then they will likely experience fluctuations in emotional states in response to changes in everyday events. By contrast, if they draw upon remote memories, then a much more stable profile will likely emerge. Their own data point to the latter alternative, but clearly this depends upon the nature of the memory disorder. What happens when the long-term store is difficult to access, as in case C.W. (Wilson et al., 1995; Wilson & Wearing, 1995)?

In 1985, at age 46, C.W., a famous and gifted musical scholar, contracted herpes encephalitis. This left him with the most severe episodic memory impairment reported to date, such that he is described as living in "a *moment* with no past to anchor it and no future to look ahead to" (Wearing, 1988, cited in Wilson & Wearing, 1995, p. 15). In addition, C.W. also has semantic memory impairments for both verbal and visual material, as well as a retrograde amnesia that extends back most of his life. With such devastating losses of personal knowledge, in addition to the inability to retain and build upon new memories, one can only speculate that his memory disorder must cut across his very sense of self. Articulate individuals, such as the psychologist Malcolm Meltzer (1983), who writes about the effect of his own (albeit comparatively less severe) memory disorder on his psyche, had such an experience:

> I felt to some extent that I had lost some of my identity. This was not total or extreme, but there were some questions in my mind about beliefs, values and purposes in life. In addition, I felt I had lost some of my cultural background when I had difficulty remembering some of the customs, traditions and beliefs of the groups to which I belonged. This produces a feeling of being somewhat alone" (p. 3).

Emotional Status

There is a substantial literature on the emotional distress encountered in other groups with acquired neurological conditions, such as stroke and traumatic brain injury, with anxiety and depression, in particular, commonly reported (e.g. Dennis et al., 2000; Gordon & Hibbard, 1997; Gordon et al., 2000; Hanks et al., 1999; Nelson et al., 1994; Satz et al., 1998; Wilson et al., 2000). The data are generally given a straightforward interpretation as being indirect consequences of the neurological event. The situation is much more complex with respect to the cases H.M., N.A. and S.S. in terms of both clinical presentation and aetiology.

Case S.S. did not resume his work as president of an optical physics firm developing laser technology following his illness, but lived at home with his family, doing household chores under the supervision of his wife. The authors contrast the demeanour of S.S., who presents as a well-adjusted individual, with his "dire circumstances", and they raise the question as to whether he has, in fact, a normal capacity for emotional experience: "Although he occasionally expresses concern about memory problems, he does so in an unemotional manner, and his mood varies little over time. In fact, his insight regarding his situation seems entirely superficial" (O'Connor et al., 1995, p. 48). As the authors expected, given his demeanour, S.S. did not endorse symptoms consistent with depression on scales such as the Beck Depression Inventory (BDI) (Beck et al., 1961), scoring 3.

These results suggest that S.S. is not depressed, at least not in an overt manner as assessed by instruments such as the BDI, and this is consistent with other anecdotal accounts. Case N.A. (Kaushall et al., 1981) does not manifest any of the responses indicative of emotional distress that one could reasonably expect, given his dramatically altered lifestyle: sadness, grief, depression, despair, frustration, irritability, poor self-esteem, loss of confidence, hopelessness. Rather, he "maintains a steadfastly optimistic, and sometimes unrealistic, view of his own life and progress" (p. 385). Similarly, the emotional functions of H.M. are described as "typically blunted, but he is capable of displaying the full range of emotions . . . There is no evidence of anxiety, major depression or psychosis" (Corkin et al., 1997, p. 3970). After his mother's death, the staff of the nursing home observed that his grief was mild, again suggesting that his emotional responses may be blunted. Ogden (1996, p. 54) further notes that, "it is surprising that H.M. does not react with some degree of confusion, frustration, or anger from continually facing the situation of not knowing where he is, what year it is, what new type of technology or development he is looking at, or who the people are who speak to him".

The common thread among these three cases of circumscribed amnesia is that the individuals do not admit to emotional distress, and their emotional responses appear to be attenuated. Yet the results of the O'Connor et al. (1995) study, using standardized instruments to evaluate the emotional functioning of case S.S., are inconclusive, in that on some scales (e.g. BDI) he does not endorse responses indicative of depressive symptomatology, but with other tests (e.g. MMPI) his profile indicates significant emotional distress, and specifically depression. The authors suggest three hypotheses to account for the test scores: first, that S.S. may have impaired insight, resulting in his failure to overtly endorse depressive symptomatology with face-valid instruments such as the BDI. A second hypothesis pertains to the presence of psychological denial as a protective mechanism to shield himself from the full knowledge of his situation. Goldstein (1939) had spoken of the catastrophic reaction that can occur in brain-injured people manifest as, in Gainotti's (1972, p. 42) memorable words, "the anxious, desperate reaction of the organism, confronted with a task it could not face". Finally, with respect to the MMPI results, O'Connor and colleagues point to situational factors (viz. item content of assessment instruments) that are related to the medical condition of S.S., rather than his psychological state, an issue noted in the previous section. To these possibilities needs to be added the method by which data are gathered, namely self-report instruments. Hermann (1982, cited in Schacter, 1991) observed that completing a self-report instrument is itself a memory task, and this could be a reason why memory-disordered individuals fail to reliably endorse items on checklists such as the Everyday Memory Questionnaire (Sunderland et al., 1983).

The aforementioned insight hypothesis of O'Connor et al. (1995) pertains to an organic explanation of these individuals' failure to endorse depressive symptomatology, when (in the opinions of researchers) they have every reason to be depressed given their altered life circumstances. The hypothesis is not only of theoretical importance but is also clinically relevant because it impacts upon management. A number of eminent rehabilitation clinicians (e.g. Ben-Yishay, 2000; Prigatano, 2000) maintain that awareness and insight are requisites for successful rehabilitation. Schacter et al. (1990) qualify the insight hypothesis when they observe that only certain groups of people with amnesia have impaired insight—viz. those with concomitant frontal dysfunction (e.g. patients with Korsakoff's syndrome, ruptured aneurysms of the anterior communicating artery, and closed head injury). Those with the so-called "pure amnesias" from circumscribed temporal and diencephalic lesions do not have problems with insight. In this latter category they give, as examples, cases H.M. and N.A., and also include encephalitic patients (cf. case S.S.). Yet, as Kopelman et al. (1998) observe, patient groups with impaired insight do not give "entirely random" responses on self-report measures of their memory competency. Although their temporal lobe group rated their memory performances worst of any group, nonetheless the frontal and diencephalic (mostly Korsakoff) groups endorsed significantly more severe responses than the normal control group.

These observations beg the question: what is meant by "insight"? Presumably it is more than mere awareness that a problem exists. As noted earlier, O'Connor et al. (1995) regarded case S.S.'s acknowledgement that he experienced memory problems as "entirely superficial". Schacter and colleagues (1990) made similar comments about case B.Z., a patient with a ruptured anterior communicating artery aneurysm, at the end of his "awareness training". Alternatively, perhaps it is not a *lack of insight* (i.e. anosognosia) that underlies the blunted emotional responses of these cases, but rather a *lack of concern* about their situation (i.e. anosodiaphoria), a distinction drawn by Babinski (1914, cited in McGlynn & Schacter,

1989). This would imply that these people have shallow and superficial emotional responses to many situations, not just to their own altered life circumstances, but also that their close relationships may be lacking in warmth, sensitivity and spontaneity. In none of the three cases, H.M., N.A. or S.S., are their interpersonal relationships described in sufficient detail to make informed comment, but the number of tantalizing comments peppered throughout the case descriptions suggests that this hypothesis is worthy of closer examination.

A Psychosocial Study of a Person with Amnesia—the Whole Picture

Background

The foregoing cases provide incomplete data from one or other psychosocial perspective: social functioning is well described in case N.A., but scarcely any details are available regarding his personality and emotional functioning; by contrast, the personality structure of case S.S. is documented in a detailed and standardized manner, but social functioning is described only in vague generalities. The following case of a person (who has requested that she be identified as Michelle), reported by Tate et al. (2001), focuses on the consequences of a relatively pure amnesia on each of social, personality and emotional functioning. The data are particularly instructive in that ratings on standardized personality instruments regarding her *premorbid* status were obtained from her father soon after the injury, and then compared with postinjury ratings at 6 and 12 months postinjury. Michelle and her family were recently interviewed at 6 years postinjury.

In 1994, at the age of 23, Michelle was allegedly assaulted during a robbery when an intruder broke into her home. She was stabbed in the region of her left eye with a long, narrow instrument and sustained a penetrating brain injury. The extent of the injury was well documented on magnetic resonance imaging some months later: "The path of the injury passes through the left frontal lobe, head of the left caudate nucleus inferiorly, genu of the internal capsule adjacent to the fornix anteriorly, third ventricle and right thalamus. There may also be a shorter second path a little more superiorly in the left frontal lobe".

On admission to the Lidcombe Hospital Brain Injury Rehabilitation Unit in Sydney, Australia, at 6 weeks postinjury, Michelle was confused, amnesic, tearful and agitated. Over subsequent weeks it became clear that her amnesic syndrome was not showing signs of substantial recovery. The initial neuropsychological examination was conducted between 2 and 3 months postinjury. From the outset, Michelle showed a relatively stable pattern of performances, with Table 35.2 providing the results of neuropsychological examinations. Her severe memory disorder, more pronounced for verbal material, was in the context of preserved IQ levels in the Average range, intact cognitive processing speed and, with the exception of generativity, good performances on tests of executive abilities. Her summary scores on the Wechsler Memory Scale at 4 years posttrauma may imply recovery of some aspects of memory, but in functional terms it is clear that Michelle continues to experience major difficulty in learning and retaining new information, as her scores on the Delayed Index (< 50) and relatively demanding learning tests, both verbal (Rey Auditory Verbal Learning Test) and visuospatial (Austin Maze), indicate. Behavioural evidence of frontal impairment came from early entries in the medical notes that documented her "lack of initative and poor insight", and need for prompting on self-care tasks. Neurological examination was essentially unremarkable, and she showed no motor-sensory impairments, apart from

Table 35.2 Test scores from serial neuropsychological examinations of Michelle

		2–3 Months postinjury	6 Months postinjury	1 Year postinjury	4 Years postinjury
NART		FSIQ 110	103	NA	NA
WAIS-R	Verbal IQ	92	85	93	NA
	Performance IQ	86	81	96	
	Full Scale IQ	88	82	94	
WMS-R	Attention/ Concentration	104	101	92	113
	Verbal Memory	51	68	75	94
	Visual Memory	72	88	91	106
	General Memory	<50	66	74	97
	Delayed Memory	<50	<50	<50	<50
WCST	Number of categories	6	6	6	NA
	Perseverative errors	9	4	8	
TMT	Part A (time, s)	45	42	36	42
	Part B	84	60	80	38
COWAT	Total correct	15	23	29	28
	Number of errors: (repeats/rule breaks)	5/2	9	3/7	3/1
Word fluency	Number correct	NA	18	33	NA
	Number of errors		3	2	
Design fluency	Number correct	NA	11	16	NA
	Number of errors		1	1	
SDMT	Written	NA	50	58	NA
	Oral		58	64	

Supplementary memory tests

RAVLT	
Trials 1–5	7^{+1}, 8, 8, 9, 6^{+2}
List B	5
Recall A	1^{+1}
Delay	3^{+1}
Recognition	12^{+9}
AM*	
Errors for trials 1–30 (Test abandoned at trial 30)	15, 12, 12, 9, 9, 9, 6, 6, 7, 5, 6, 6, 4, 5, 5, 4, 2, 5, 3, 2, 3, 2, 2, 2, 3, 2 ,4, 2, 2, 3

NART, National Adult Reading Test; FSIQ, Full Scale IQ; NA, not administered; WMS-R, Wechsler Memory Scale—Revised; WCST, Wisconsin Card Sorting Test; TMT, Trail Making Test; COWAT, Controlled Word Association Test; SDMT, Symbol-Digit Modality Test. RAVLT, Rey Auditory Verbal Learning Test; AM, Austin Maze.
* AM administered at 6 years posttrauma.

some cranial nerve abnormalities: a dilated left pupil, left IIIrd nerve palsy with ptosis, and partial IVth nerve palsy.

Social Outcome

At the time of her injury, Michelle had just completed a diploma in hotel management and was enrolled in a business administration course. She had previously done well at school, having completed her Higher School Certificate (12 years of education) at a selective high school. She was a single parent with a 5 year-old son and they lived with her parents.

At the 6 year follow-up, the nature and extent of changes in Michelle's social functioning (i.e. handicap or participation limitation) was assessed with the Sydney Psychosocial Reintegration Scale (SPRS) (Tate et al., 1999). This 12-item questionnaire, rated on a seven-point Likert-type scale, assesses functioning in three domains (occupational activities, interpersonal relationships and independent living skills). Total scores are in the range 0–72, with higher scores indicating better levels of reintegration. Her father's responses indicated major handicap (total score 31), particularly in the area of occupational activities (see Table 35.3). Michelle's self-report suggested a more favourable picture in all domains (total score 58).

Michelle has not had gainful employment since her injury, and is presently occupied in caring for her 11 year-old son, although she needs considerable support in her parenting role. She and her family are keen for her to pursue employment compatible with her memory disorder, but over the past 6 years this has been restricted to intermittent periods of work with voluntary community organizations. There has been a reduction in her leisure activities and she has not had a partner since the injury, neither does she have friends outside of the family whom she sees regularly. In terms of living skills, she requires prompts and reminders from other people about personal habits, such as dressing, and she is disorganized with respect to her personal effects and household duties. The severe difficulty she has in managing her finances (e.g. buys impulsively, orders goods which she cannot afford and then forgets she has purchased them) has been of major concern to her family, such that her sister now manages the finances for her. On the positive side, Michelle can drive independently anywhere and does not get lost, and socially she presents well, although she is over-familiar and will strike up conversations with strangers in the street, divulging intimacies, and hence is very vulnerable.

Issues of Insight

Michelle's level of insight was assessed by comparing her report of her memory functioning in everyday life with that of her father. Instruments comprised the Everyday Memory Questionnaire (EMQ) (Sunderland et al., 1983, 1984), Use of Memory Aids Questionnaire (Wilson, 1991) and the Effects of Neuropsychological Deficits Scale (ENDS) (Tate & Perdices, unpublished). The ENDS consists of 30 items rated on a five-point Likert-type scale from "extreme effect" to "no effect at all", examining both self-efficacy and the impact of neuropsychological disorder on 10 domains of everyday living. Scores are in the range 0–120, with higher scores indicating greater effect of neuropsychological impairments on everyday living. The results of these questionnaires are presented in Table 35.3.

Table 35.3 Scores on memory questionnaires regarding Michelle at 6 years postinjury

Instrument	Subscale	Informant ratings	Self-ratings
Sydney Psychosocial Reintegration Scale	Total score (range, 0–72)	31	58
	Occupational Activities (0–24)	5	15
	Interpersonal Relationships (0–24)	13	21
	Independent Living Skills (0–24)	13	22
Everyday Memory Questionnaire	Total score (Michelle) (range, 0–140)	38	31
	Total score (head-injured group)[1]	22	27
	Total score (control group)[1]	15	23
	Specific domains (Michelle):		
	Speech	13	10
	Reading and writing	7	2
	Faces and places	4	3
	Actions	2	7
	Learning new things	12	9
Use of Memory Aids Questionnaire	Total number of strategies used	13	13
Effects of Neuropsychological Deficits Scale	Total score (range, 0–120)	63	52
	Severity, now	Moderate	Moderate
	Severity, future	Moderate	Moderate
	Mean scores[2] on items for:		
	Impact on everyday activities	1.8	0.8
	Impact on the person	2.3	2.7
	Effort to avoid failures	3.0	2.5
	Help from others	3.5	3.0
	Reliance on aids	4.0	3.0
	Self-efficacy[3]	1.7	1.8

[1] Data from Sunderland et al. (1984).
[2] Mean scores: range 0–4 (0, "not at all" to 4, "extreme").
[3] Items for self-efficacy are reverse scored: 0, "extremely confident" to 4, "not at all confident".

On the EMQ, there was fairly good agreement between the ratings of Michelle and her father, although her father rated more memory failures. Her total scores indicated that she experiences more difficulty with memory than do the head-injured and control groups reported by Sunderland et al. (1984), their data also being included in Table 35.3. There was perfect agreement between Michelle and her father regarding the types of strategies she uses in everyday living to circumvent her memory difficulties. She uses 13 separate strategies, which is considerably more than the number reported in Wilson's (1991) survey of individuals with memory disorders (mean = 7.39, SD = 3.12). Some strategies are used more consistently and frequently than others, especially writing on her hand, use of a white board, wall calendar, and asking other people to remind her of things. Notably, in spite of intensive and specific rehabilitation efforts, Michelle does not use a memory notebook or other kind of permanent record. Her rehabilitation doctor, who continues to see her regularly, says that he has never seen her refer to any notes. There was some variability between responses from Michelle and her father on the ENDS, in terms of the effect upon

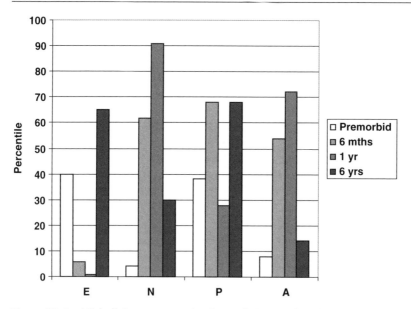

Figure 35.2 Michelle's scores on the Eysenck Personality Questionnaire—Revised. E, extraversion; N, neuroticism; P, psychoticism; A, addiction

everyday living for work, relationships and living skills, which her father considered was moderate, whereas Michelle's ratings suggested the impact was minor. Otherwise agreement was very good. She is concerned about her difficulties and frustrated by them, but they do not affect her emotionally in the sense of "getting her down". She has a lot of support from other people in dealing with her difficulties and relies heavily upon memory aids. Although it is unlikely that the severity of her memory problems will improve in the future, she is very confident about dealing with her difficulties.

Effect upon Personality, Self-concept and Self-esteem

Michelle's *premorbid* personality structure, as assessed by her father's endorsement of the Eysenck Personality Questionnaire—Revised (EPQ-R) (Eysenck & Eysenck, 1991) soon after Michelle's injury, showed a well-adjusted profile (see Figure 35.2). Scores on the E (Extraversion) and P (Psychoticism) scales were at the lower limits of the Average range, suggesting she was somewhat less sociable than her peers and more of a loner, as well as being a more sensitive and well-adjusted person. She had low addictive tendencies and was stable and even-tempered, experiencing low levels of emotionality on the N (Neuroticism) scale. No normative data are available for females for the C scale (Criminality). Following the injury, significant changes occurred on all scales, with data analysed using single-case methodology described in Ley (1972).[1] The changes were not, however, abnormal in a

---

[1] Using the stability coefficients reported in the EPQ-R manual, Michelle's scores between the premorbid and postinjury ratings were examined to determine whether any changes reflected a reliable change or were due to measurement error. The minimum difference (MD) required for the change in score between the two test occasions to be reliable was calculated using the following formula: $MD = z_{MD} \sqrt{(2 \times \sigma^2 (1 - r_{xx}))}$, where z_{MD} is the z score associated with a change in raw test scores of magnitude

Table 35.4 Test scores on personality examinations regarding Michelle at 6 years postinjury

Test	Subscale	Informant ratings	Self-ratings
Eysenck Personality	Extraversion	65	32
Questionnaire—	Neuroticism	30	9
Revised	Psychoticism	68	21
(percentiles)	Addiction	14	2
Tennessee Self-	Validity scales:	Not administered	
concept Scale	Inconsistency		50
(percentiles)	Self-criticism		2.5
	Faking Good		61
	Response Distribution		50
	Summary Scores:		
	Total Self-concept		50
	Conflict		8
	Self-concept Scales		
	Physical		61
	Moral		65
	Personal		46
	Family		9
	Social		75
	Academic/Work		34
	Supplementary Scores:		
	Identity		65
	Satisfaction		57
	Behaviour		65
Self-esteem	(Score range[1] 0–100)	Not administered	65
Inventory			
(raw score)			
Profile of Mood	Tension	3	2
States	Depression	8	18
(percentiles)	Anger	61	38
	Vigour	50	88
	Fatigue	34	72
	Confusion	13	21
Depression, Anxiety	Depression	Not administered	0
and Stress Scale	Anxiety		0
(raw score)	Stress		0

[1] High scores indicate high self-esteem.

clinical sense, with the exception of the E scale at 12 months postinjury (less than 1st percentile) and the N scale was also elevated (91st percentile). When recently reviewed at 6 years postinjury, an unexpected and most encouraging trend was evident in Michelle's EPQ-R ratings by her father, which were now indistinguishable from the premorbid level for all scales, except N, which was borderline. Her own evaluation differed (nonsignificantly) from her father's, with lower scores on all scales (see Table 35.4).

MD between test occasions, σ is the standard deviation of the normative sample, and r_{xx} is the test–retest correlation coefficient provided in the test manual. Given that scores could either increase or decrease over time, two-tailed tests of significance were used, and thus $z_{MD} = 1.96$.

At 6 years postinjury, Michelle completed a number of measures designed to examine her sense of identity and self-esteem, including the Tennessee Self-concept Scale (TSCS) (Fitts & Warren, 1996) and the Self-esteem Inventory (Coopersmith, 1981) (see Table 35.4). Scores on both instruments were mostly unremarkable, being within normal limits, although some interesting findings emerged from the TSCS. A very low score was obtained on one validity scale, Self-criticism (2.5 percentile). Michelle also showed a low Conflict score (8th percentile). Normally this, together with the low Self-criticism score, indicates defensiveness, but other interpretations may be hypothesized in the case of an individual with severe memory disorder. Limited awareness is an obvious contender, but Michelle's tendency to minimize emotional impact, or alternatively to simplify events to reduce the load on memory, are also possible explanations. The other relatively low score on the TSCS was that for Family (9th percentile). This was an unexpected result, given the extensive family support Michelle receives in terms of managing her memory disorder, which she herself also acknowledges. It may suggest she feels some degree of alienation from her family, given that the Family scale "reflects the individual's feelings of adequacy, worth and value as a family member" (Fitts & Warren, 1996, p. 23).

Effect upon Mood and Emotions

With respect to Michelle's emotional status, no premorbid ratings were undertaken because retrospective ratings of mood state are of questionable reliability. Postinjury ratings were made by her father, using the Profile of Mood States (POMS) (McNair et al., 1992). These were essentially unremarkable, as shown in Figure 35.3. Indeed, it is interesting to speculate that at 6 months postinjury the elevations on Fatigue and Confusion (88th and 84th

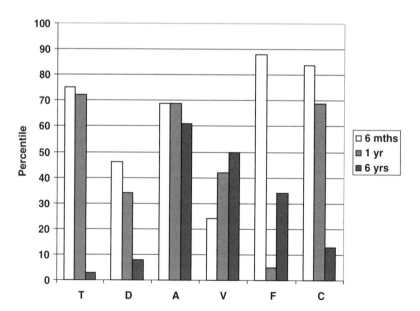

Figure 35.3 Michelle's scores on the Profile of Mood States. T, tension; D, depression; A, anger; V, vigour; F, fatigue; C, confusion

percentiles, respectively) and low score for Vigor (24th percentile) reflect organic-type aspects of the recovery process, whereas by 6 years postinjury, these had resolved (Fatigue, Confusion and Vigor at 34th, 13th and 50th percentiles, respectively). At this point, the (indirect) emotional sequelae (or lack thereof, in keeping with case S.S.) came to the fore, Tension and Depression being the 3rd and 8th percentiles, respectively (previously 75th and 46th percentiles at the 6 month postinjury assessment). It is noted, however, that no significant variation among the three assessments had occurred for Anxiety, ranging between the 61st and 69th percentiles. At the most recent interview (Table 35.4) Michelle's self-ratings on the POMS were in general agreement with those of her father, although her ratings on Vigor and Fatigue were somewhat higher.

Michelle's recent self-ratings on the Depression, Stress and Anxiety Scale (Lovibond & Lovibond, 1995) revealed no emotional distress. Her father says that her memory disorder does not make her unhappy, and he added that he would be unable bear it if Michelle were constantly emotionally distressed about her situation. Occasionally, there is the flicker of an emotional wound, but the effect dissipates quickly. Michelle's sister commented that Michelle has been unable to deal emotionally with some events. If the subject of her mother's death (which occurred 5 years previously, at 14 months postinjury) is brought up, "it is like it only just happened . . . her mood comes in blocks. Yesterday she was so distraught (about her finances) and an hour later she was fine. Ninety percent of the time she is very optimistic". Although Michelle's interpersonal interactions are entirely normal and appropriate in most situations, her family has noticed marked changes in her capacity to respond to another person's distress, such as when her young son falls and injures himself. She does not appear to know how to respond any more, is lost for words and actions, and does not show, in demonstrable terms, the empathy that typified her premorbid character.

CONCLUDING COMMENTS AND FUTURE DIRECTIONS

In the current chapter, a conceptual framework has been described within which emotional and social consequences of memory disorders have been examined. The essential component of that model was a distinction between direct and indirect effects of the causative neurological event. Available psychosocial data from four cases with fairly circumscribed memory disorders were discussed within the framework of the model. Michelle's psychosocial profile is a virtual composite of the famous cases, H.M., N.A. and S.S., and thus provides a good basis upon which to integrate the social and emotional consequences of memory disorders.

Like the other cases, the effects of Michelle's fairly circumscribed memory disorder have caused major disruption to her social functioning at virtually all levels, including instrumental activities of daily living, and without the support of her family she would be an isolated person, unable to live in the community. It is not possible to attribute this impoverished social functioning entirely to the amnesia, however, because these cases have additional neuropsychological, behavioural and/or emotional impairments. For example, H.M.'s other impairments include slight anomia, "clearly impaired" semantic and symbolic verbal fluency, as well as abnormal perception of internal states for pain and hunger (Corkin, 1984; Hebben et al., 1985). Additionally, he has behavioural abnormalities that are suggestive of a disorder of drive or, in Blumer & Benson's (1975) terminology, "pseudodepression": H.M. lacks initiative, rarely complains, and usually does not initiate conversations. The original report of N.A. (Teuber et al., 1968) documented similar inertia-type behaviours.

The most striking feature of these cases pertained to their emotional functioning, where a complex clinical picture emerged, predominantly characterized by an absence of emotional distress and diminished concern about their circumstances. It could reasonably be expected that, given their neuropsychological and social disabilities, these individuals would experience significant emotional distress at their losses. The accounts are noteworthy for the apparent absence of such distress. Although all individuals presented with a genial manner and had stable, even-tempered mood, cases H.M. and S.S. are described as having blunted affect, whereas case N.A. is described as "steadfastly optimistic". There is little additional qualitative comment about cases N.A. and S.S., but H.M. is further described as capable of showing the "full range" of emotions; occasionally, when stressed, he can be roused to anger "but as soon as he was distracted, his anger would dissipate immediately" (Corkin, 1984, p. 251). Michelle incorporates all these features—she presents with a pleasant, friendly and cooperative manner, her mood is characterized as being mostly happy and optimistic, and although she can become emotionally distressed, it is not sustained.

As was also observed in the other cases, Michelle appears to have insight into her memory disorder and its severity, but she tends to minimize its impact, which suggests that the issue here might be an interaction between diminished concern and impaired awareness rather than impaired awareness *per se*. Moreover, she does not display behaviours indicative of depression, loss of confidence, low self-esteem and so forth. Like case S.S., Michelle does not admit to any emotional distress in general when examined with standardized instruments. As the data from case S.S. indicates, however, the situation is ambiguous, in that emotional disturbance is revealed depending upon the standardized instrument used.

In the four cases reviewed here, there was a strong possibility of an organic (i.e. direct) component to the emotional dysfunction, given that the area of damage responsible for the memory disorder (i.e. limbic system) is likely to disrupt their emotional functioning also. O'Connor et al. (1995) suggest that limbic damage could interfere with the ability to derive meaning from emotional events and/or diminish the ability to express feelings. It is clear that a model such as that implied by many studies of other neurological groups, whereby emotional disturbance is conceptualized exclusively as a reaction to (i.e. indirect consequence of) the neurological event, is overly simplistic. In the context of amnesia, the direct factors are of two sorts: first, the emotional responses themselves, which showed some variety, including blunted affect, unconcern and unsustained emotional response; second, the memory variables are an important direct factor: if an individual is always living in "a moment", then there can be no context for an emotional response because the incident that caused emotional distress will not be remembered.

The foregoing does not imply that there is no functional (i.e. indirect) element to the emotional disturbance, such as presence of depression, but rather that the direct factors probably override indirect factors, making it difficult to identify their nature, severity and impact. In a recent interview with Michelle, when completing the Self-esteem Inventory, she omitted a response to one item: "I'm popular with persons my own age". When this was pointed out to her, she replied, "But I don't have friends my own age any more", whereupon her eyes welled up with tears. Her obvious and strong emotional distress was immediately extinguished when her attention was refocused on another matter. Clearly, more empirical study is required in order to understand better the behavioural and emotional responses in cases of fairly circumscribed memory disorders. The report of O'Connor et al. (1995) regarding case S.S. provides an excellent example of the type of specific, hypothesis-driven research that needs to be conducted, and results of such studies will directly inform clinical practice.

ACKNOWLEDGEMENTS

I am grateful to Michelle and her family, who have given permission to report on her experiences. I also thank Ms Kim Ferry, Clinical Neuropsychologist from the Brain Injury Rehabilitation Unit at Liverpool Hospital, Sydney, for data from Michelle's most recent neuropsychological assessment. Discussions with Dr Michael Perdices and his comments on an earlier version of this work were of great benefit, and the support of the Rehabilitation Studies Unit has enabled me to prepare this chapter in a most conducive environment.

REFERENCES

Alfano, D.P., Finlayson, M.A.J., Stearns, G.M. & Neilson, P.M. (1990). The MMPI and neurologic dysfunction: profile configuration and analysis. *Clinical Neuropsychologist*, **4**, 69–79.

Anderson, C.S., Linto, J. & Stewart-Wynne, E.G. (1995). A population-based assessment of the impact and burden of caregiving for long-term stroke survivors. *Stroke*, **26**, 843–849.

Bachna, K., Sieggreen, M.A., Cermack, L. et al. (1998). MMPI/MMPI-2: comparisons of amnesic patients. *Archives of Clinical Neuropsychology*, **13**, 535–542.

Beck, A.T., Ward, C.H., Mendelson, M. et al. (1961). An inventory for measuring depression. *Archives of General Psychiatry*, **4**, 53–62.

Blumer, D. & Benson, D.F. (1975). Personality changes with frontal and temporal lobe lesions. In D.F. Benson & D. Blumer (eds), *Psychiatric Aspects of Neurologic Disease* (pp. 151–170). New York: Grune and Stratton.

Ben-Yishay, Y. (2000). Postacute neuropsychological rehabilitation: a holistic perspective. In A.-L. Christensen & B.P. Uzzell (eds), *International Handbook of Neuropsychological Rehabilitation* (pp. 127–135). New York: Kluwer.

Butcher, J.N., Dahlstrom, W.G., Graham, J.R. et al. (1989). *Manual for the Restandardized Minnesota Multiphasic Personality Inventory: MMPI-2: an Interpretive and Administrative Guide*. Minneapolis, MN: University of Minnesota Press.

Cermack, L.S. (1976). The encoding capacity of a patient with amnesia due to encephalitis. *Neuropsychologia*, **14**, 311–326.

Cermack, L.S. & O'Connor, M. (1983). The anterograde and retrograde retrieval ability of a patient with amnesia due to encephalitis. *Neuropsychologia*, **21**, 213–234.

Coopersmith, S. (1981). *SEI: Self-Esteem Inventories*. Palo Alto, CA: Consulting Psychologists Press.

Corkin, S. (1984). Lasting consequences of bilateral medial temporal lobectomy: clinical course and experimental findings in H.M. *Seminars in Neurology*, 4(2), 249–259.

Corkin, S., Amaral, D.G., Gonzalez, G. et al. (1997). H.M.'s medial temporal lobe lesion: findings from magnetic resonance imaging. *Journal of Neuroscience*, **17**(10), 3964–3979.

Costa, P.T. & McCrae, R.R. (1992). *NEO PI-R. Professional Manual. Revised NEO Personality Inventory (NEO PI-R) and NEO Five-factor Inventory (NEO-FFI)*. Odessa, FL: Psychological Assessment Resources.

Dennis, M., O'Rourke, S., Lewis, S. & Warlow, C. (2000). Emotional outcomes after stroke: factors associated with poor outcome. *Journal of Neurology, Neurosurgery, and Psychiatry*, **68**, 47–52.

Elliott M. (1990). Coping with a memory loss—a personal perspective. *Cognitive Rehabilitation*, **8**, 8–10.

Eysenck, H.J. & Eysenck, S.B.G. (1991). *Manual of the Eysenck Personality Scales (EPS Adult)*. London: Hodder & Stoughton.

Fitts, W.H. & Warren, W.L. (1996). *Tennessee Self-Concept Scale, TSCS:2*. Los Angeles, CA: Western Psychological Services.

Fleming, J., Tooth, L., Hassell, M. & Chan, W. (1999). Prediction of community integration and vocational outcome 2–5 years after traumatic brain injury in Australia. *Brain Injury*, **13**, 417–431.

Flick, C.L. (1999). Stroke outcome and psychosocial consequences. *Archives of Physical Medicine and Rehabilitation*, **80**, S21–S26.

Gainotti, G. (1972). Emotional behaviour and hemispheric side of lesion. *Cortex*, **8**, 41–55.

Gainotti, G. (1993). Emotional and psychosocial problems after brain injury. *Neuropsychological Rehabilitation*, **3**, 259–277.

Goldstein, K. (1939). *The Organism. A Holistic Approach to Biology, Derived from Pathological Data in Man*. New York: American Books.

Gordon, W.A., Haddad, L., Brown, M. et al. (2000). The sensitivity and specificity of self-reported symptoms in individuals with traumatic brain injury. *Brain Injury*, **14**, 21–33.

Gordon, W.A. & Hibbard, M.R. (1997). Poststroke depression: an examination of the literature. *Archives of Physical Medicine and Rehabilitation*, **78**, 658–663.

Hanks, R.A., Temkin, N., Machamer, J. & Dikmen, S.S. (1999). Emotional and behavioral adjustment after traumatic brain injury. *Archives of Physical Medicine and Rehabilitation*, **80**, 991–997.

Hawley, G. (1980). *Measures of Personality Development*. Odessa, FL: Psychological Assessment Resources.

Hebben, N., Corkin, S., Eichenbaum, H. & Shedlack, K. (1985). Diminished ability to interpret and report internal states after bilateral medial temporal resection: case HM. *Behavioural Neurosciences*, **99**, 1031–1039.

Henderson, P. (1993). My life a routine. *Journal of Cognitive Rehabilitation*, **11**, 32–34.

Hilts, P.J. (1995). *Memory's Ghost. The Strange Tale of Mr M and the Nature of Memory*. New York: Simon and Schuster.

Jennett, B. & Bond, M.R. (1975). Assessment of outcome after severe brain damage. A practical scale. *Lancet*, i, 480–484.

Jennett, B., Snoek, J., Bond, M.R. & Brooks, N. (1981). Disability after severe head injury: observations on the use of the Glasgow Outcome Scale. *Journal of Neurology, Neurosurgery, and Psychiatry*, **44**, 285–293.

Kaushall, P.I., Zetin, M. & Squire, L.R. (1981). A psychosocial study of chronic circumscribed amnesia. *Journal of Nervous and Mental Disease*, **169**, 383–389.

Kendall, E. & Terry, D.J. (1996). Psychosocial adjustment following closed head injury. *Neuropsychological Rehabilitation*, **6**, 101–132.

Kopelman, M.D., Stanhope, N. & Guinan, E. (1998). Subjective memory evaluations in patients with focal frontal, diencephalic, and temporal lobe lesion. *Cortex*, **34**, 191–207.

Kurtz, J.E., Putman, S.H. & Stone, C. (1998). Stability of normal personality traits after traumatic brain injury. *Journal of Head Trauma Rehabilitation*, **13**(3), 1–14.

Lazarus, R.D. & Folkman, S. (1984). *Stress, Appraisal and Coping*. New York: Springer.

Lishman, W.A. (1973). The psychiatric sequelae of head injury: a review. *Psychological Medicine*, **3**, 304–318.

Ley, P. (1972). *Quantitative Aspects of Psychological Assessment. An Introduction*. London: Duckworth.

Lovibond, S.H. & Lovibond, P.F. (1995). *Mannual for the Depression, Anxiety and Stress Scale*, 2nd edn. Sydney: Psychology Foundation.

Macchi, G. (1989). Anatomical substrate of emotional reactions. In F. Boller & J. Grafman (eds), *Handbook of Neuropsychology, vol 3, section 6: Emotional Behavior and Its Disorders* (pp. 283–303). Amsterdam: Elsevier.

MacMillan, M. (1996). Phineas Gage: a case for all reasons. In C. Code, C.-W. Eallesch, Y. Joanette & A.R. Lecours (eds), *Classic Cases in Neuropsychology* (pp. 243–262). Hove: Psychology Press.

McNair, D.M., Lorr, M. & Droppleman, L.F. (1992). *POMS Manual: Profile of Mood States*. San Diego, CA: Educational and Industrial Testing Service.

McGlynn, S. & Schacter, D.L. (1989). Unawareness of deficits in neuropsychological syndromes. *Journal of Clinical and Experimental Neuropsychology*, **11**, 143–205.

Meltzer, M. (1983). Poor memory: a case report. *Journal of Clinical Psychology*, **39**(1), 3–10.

Moore, A.D. & Stambrook, M. (1995). Cognitive moderators of outcome following traumatic brain injury: a conceptual model and implications for rehabilitation. *Brain Injury*, **9**, 109–130.

Moore, A.D., Stambrook, M. & Peters, L.C. (1989). Coping strategies and adjustment after closed head injury: a cluster analytic approach. *Brain Injury*, **3**, 171–175.

Moore, A.D., Stambrook, M. & Wilson, K.G. (1991). Cognitive moderators in adjustment to chronic illness: locus of control beliefs following traumatic brain injury. *Neuropsychological Rehabilitation*, **1**, 185–198.

Nelson, L.D., Cicchetti, D., Satz, P. et al. (1994). Emotional sequelae of stroke: a longitudinal perspective. *Journal of Clinical and Experimental Neuropsychology*, **16**, 796–806.

O'Connor, M.G., Cermack, L.S. & Seidman, L.J. (1995). Social and emotional characteristics of a profoundly amnesic postencephalitic patient. In R. Campbell & M.A. Conway (eds), *Broken Memories: Case Studies in Memory Impairment* (pp. 45–53). Oxford: Blackwell.

Odgen, J.A. (1996). *Fractured Minds. A Case-study Approach to Clinical Neuropsychology.* New York: Oxford University Press.

Ponsford, J.L., Olver, J.H. & Curran, C. (1995). A profile of outcome: 2 years after traumatic brain injury. *Brain Injury*, **9**, 1–10.

Prigatano, G.P. (1987). Psychiatric aspects of head injury: problem areas and suggested guidelines for research. In H.S. Levin, J. Grafman & H.M. Eisenberg (eds), *Neurobehavioral Recovery from Head Injury* (pp. 215–231). New York: Oxford University Press.

Prigatano, G.P. (1992). Personality disturbances associated with traumatic brain injury. *Journal of Consulting and Clinical Psychology*, **60**(3), 360–368.

Prigatano, G.P. (1995). Personality and social aspects of memory rehabilitation. In A.D. Baddeley, B.A. Wilson & F.N. Watts (eds), *Handbook of Memory Disorders*, Ist edn (pp. 603–614). Chichester: Wiley.

Prigatano, G.P. (2000). A brief overview of four principles of neuropsychological rehabilitation. In A.-L. Christensen & B.P. Uzzell (eds), *International Handbook of Neuropsychological Rehabilitation* (pp. 115–125). New York: Kluwer.

Raaymakers, T.W.M. on behalf of the MARS Study Group (2000). Functional outcome and quality of life after angiography and operation for unruptured intracranial aneurysms. *Journal of Neurology, Neurosurgery, and Psychiatry*, **68**, 571–576.

Satz, P., Forney, D.L., Zaucha, K. et al. (1998). Depression, cognition and functional correlates of recovery outcome after traumatic brain injury. *Brain Injury*, **12**, 537–553.

Schacter, D.L. (1991). Unawareness of deficit and unawareness of knowledge in patients with memory disorders. In G.P. Prigatano & D.L. Schacter (eds), *Awareness of Deficit after Brain Injury. Clinical and Theoretical Issues* (pp. 127–151). New York: Oxford University Press.

Schacter, D.L., Glisky, E. & McGlynn, S. (1990). Impact of memory disorders on everyday life. Awareness of deficits and return to work. In D.E. Tupper & K.D. Cicerone (eds), *The Neuropsychology of Everyday Life* (pp. 231–257). Norwell, MA: Kluwer.

Scoville, W.B. & Milner, B. (1957). Loss of recent memory after bilateral hippocampal lesions. *Journal of Neurology, Neurosurgery, and Psychiatry*, **20**, 11–21.

Sunderland, A., Harris, J.E. & Baddeley, A.D. (1983). Do laboratory tests predict everyday memory? A neuropsychological study. *Journal of Verbal Learning and Verbal Behavior*, **22**, 341–357.

Sunderland, A., Harris, J.E. & Baddeley, A.D. (1984). Assessing everyday memory after severe head injury. In J.E. Harris & P.E. Morris (eds), *Everyday Memory, Actions and Absent-mindedness* (pp. 191–206). London: Academic Press.

Talland, G.A. (1968). Some observations on the psychological mechanisms impaired in the amnesic syndrome. *International Journal of Neurology*, **7**, 21–30.

Tate, R.L. (submitted). Impact of pre-injury factors on outcome after severe traumatic brain injury: does posttraumatic personality change represent an exacerbation of premorbid traits?

Tate, R.L. & Broe, G.A. (1999). Psychosocial adjustment after traumatic brain injury: what are the important variables? *Psychological Medicine*, **29**, 713–725.

Tate, R., Hodgkinson, A., Veerabangsa, A. & Maggiotto, S. (1999). Measuring psychosocial recovery after traumatic brain injury: psychometric properties of a new scale. *Journal of Head Trauma Rehabilitation*, **14**(6), 543–557.

Tate, R.L., Lulham, J.M., Broe, G.A. et al. (1989). Psychosocial outcome for the survivors of severe blunt head injury: the results of a consecutive series of 100 patients. *Journal of Neurology, Neurosurgery, and Psychiatry*, **52**, 1128–1134.

Tate, R.L., Veerabangsa, A., & Hodgkinson, A. (2001). Where there's a will, there's a way. The functional consequences of amnesia. *Brain Impairment* (abstr), **2**(1), 59–60.

Teuber, H.-L., Milner, B. & Vaughn, H.G. (1968). Persistent anterograde amnesia after stab wound of the basal brain. *Neuropsychologia*, **6**, 267–282.

Wilson, B.A. (1991). Long-term prognosis of patients with severe memory disorders. *Neuropsychological Rehabilitation*, **1**, 117–134.

Wilson, B.A. (1999). *Case Studies in Neuropsychological Rehabilitation*. New York: Oxford University Press.

Wilson, B.A., Baddeley, A.D. & Kapur, N. (1995). Dense amnesia in a professional musician following herpes simplex virus encephalitis. *Journal of Clinical and Experimental Neuropsychology*, **17**, 668–681.

Wilson, B.A., Cockburn, J. & Baddeley, A.D. (1985). *The Rivermead Behavioural Memory Test*. Bury St Edmunds: Thames Valley Test Company.

Wilson, B.A., J.C. & Hughes, E. (1997). Coping with amnesia: the natural history of a compensatory memory system. *Neuropsychological Rehabilitation*, **7**, 43–56.

Wilson, B.A. & Wearing, D. (1995). Prisoner of consciousness: a state of just awakening following herpes simplex encephalitis. In R. Campbell & M.A. Conway (eds), *Broken Memories: Case Studies in Memory Impairment* (pp. 14–30). Oxford: Blackwell.

Wilson, J.T.L., Pettigrew, L.E.L. & Teasdale, G.M. (2000). Emotional and cognitive consequences of head injury in relation to the Glasgow outcome scale. *Journal of Neurology, Neurosurgery, and Psychiatry*, **68**, 204–209.

Woessner, R. & Caplan, B. (1995). Affective disorders following mild to moderate brain injury: interpretive hazards of the SCL-90-R. *Journal of Head Trauma Rehabilitation*, **10**(2), 78–89.

World Health Organization (1980). *International Classification of Impairments, Disabilities and Handicaps. A Manual of Classification Relating to the Consequences of Disease*. Geneva: World Health Organization.

World Health Organization (2000). *ICIDH-2. International Classification of Functioning, Disability and Health. Prefinal Draft*. Geneva: World Health Organization.

Author Index

Index compiled by Judith Reading

Subject Index

Page numbers in **bold** refer to complete chapters
Page numbers in *italics* refer to figures and tables

Index compiled by Judith Reading